The Python Library Reference

Release 3.6.4

Book 1 of 2
Chapters 1-18

Guido van Rossum
and the Python development team

February 03, 2018

Python Software Foundation
Email: docs@python.org

CONTENTS

While reference-index describes the exact syntax and semantics of the Python language, this library reference manual describes the standard library that is distributed with Python. It also describes some of the optional components that are commonly included in Python distributions.

Python's standard library is very extensive, offering a wide range of facilities as indicated by the long table of contents listed below. The library contains built-in modules (written in C) that provide access to system functionality such as file I/O that would otherwise be inaccessible to Python programmers, as well as modules written in Python that provide standardized solutions for many problems that occur in everyday programming. Some of these modules are explicitly designed to encourage and enhance the portability of Python programs by abstracting away platform-specifics into platform-neutral APIs.

The Python installers for the Windows platform usually include the entire standard library and often also include many additional components. For Unix-like operating systems Python is normally provided as a collection of packages, so it may be necessary to use the packaging tools provided with the operating system to obtain some or all of the optional components.

In addition to the standard library, there is a growing collection of several thousand components (from individual programs and modules to packages and entire application development frameworks), available from the Python Package Index.

CHAPTER ONE

INTRODUCTION

The "Python library" contains several different kinds of components.

It contains data types that would normally be considered part of the "core" of a language, such as numbers and lists. For these types, the Python language core defines the form of literals and places some constraints on their semantics, but does not fully define the semantics. (On the other hand, the language core does define syntactic properties like the spelling and priorities of operators.)

The library also contains built-in functions and exceptions — objects that can be used by all Python code without the need of an `import` statement. Some of these are defined by the core language, but many are not essential for the core semantics and are only described here.

The bulk of the library, however, consists of a collection of modules. There are many ways to dissect this collection. Some modules are written in C and built in to the Python interpreter; others are written in Python and imported in source form. Some modules provide interfaces that are highly specific to Python, like printing a stack trace; some provide interfaces that are specific to particular operating systems, such as access to specific hardware; others provide interfaces that are specific to a particular application domain, like the World Wide Web. Some modules are available in all versions and ports of Python; others are only available when the underlying system supports or requires them; yet others are available only when a particular configuration option was chosen at the time when Python was compiled and installed.

This manual is organized "from the inside out:" it first describes the built-in functions, data types and exceptions, and finally the modules, grouped in chapters of related modules.

This means that if you start reading this manual from the start, and skip to the next chapter when you get bored, you will get a reasonable overview of the available modules and application areas that are supported by the Python library. Of course, you don't *have* to read it like a novel — you can also browse the table of contents (in front of the manual), or look for a specific function, module or term in the index (in the back). And finally, if you enjoy learning about random subjects, you choose a random page number (see module *random*) and read a section or two. Regardless of the order in which you read the sections of this manual, it helps to start with chapter *Built-in Functions*, as the remainder of the manual assumes familiarity with this material.

Let the show begin!

CHAPTER TWO

BUILT-IN FUNCTIONS

The Python interpreter has a number of functions and types built into it that are always available. They are listed here in alphabetical order.

		Built-in Functions		
abs()	*dict()*	*help()*	*min()*	*setattr()*
all()	*dir()*	*hex()*	*next()*	*slice()*
any()	*divmod()*	*id()*	*object()*	*sorted()*
ascii()	*enumerate()*	*input()*	*oct()*	*staticmethod()*
bin()	*eval()*	*int()*	*open()*	*str()*
bool()	*exec()*	*isinstance()*	*ord()*	*sum()*
bytearray()	*filter()*	*issubclass()*	*pow()*	*super()*
bytes()	*float()*	*iter()*	*print()*	*tuple()*
callable()	*format()*	*len()*	*property()*	*type()*
chr()	*frozenset()*	*list()*	*range()*	*vars()*
classmethod()	*getattr()*	*locals()*	*repr()*	*zip()*
compile()	*globals()*	*map()*	*reversed()*	*__import__()*
complex()	*hasattr()*	*max()*	*round()*	
delattr()	*hash()*	*memoryview()*	*set()*	

abs(*x*)

Return the absolute value of a number. The argument may be an integer or a floating point number. If the argument is a complex number, its magnitude is returned.

all(*iterable*)

Return `True` if all elements of the *iterable* are true (or if the iterable is empty). Equivalent to:

```
def all(iterable):
    for element in iterable:
        if not element:
            return False
    return True
```

any(*iterable*)

Return `True` if any element of the *iterable* is true. If the iterable is empty, return `False`. Equivalent to:

```
def any(iterable):
    for element in iterable:
        if element:
            return True
    return False
```

ascii(*object*)

As *repr()*, return a string containing a printable representation of an object, but escape the non-ASCII characters in the string returned by *repr()* using `\x`, `\u` or `\U` escapes. This generates a string similar to that returned by *repr()* in Python 2.

bin(*x*)

Convert an integer number to a binary string prefixed with "0b". The result is a valid Python expression. If *x* is not a Python *int* object, it has to define an `__index__()` method that returns an integer. Some examples:

```
>>> bin(3)
'0b11'
>>> bin(-10)
'-0b1010'
```

If prefix "0b" is desired or not, you can use either of the following ways.

```
>>> format(14, '#b'), format(14, 'b')
('0b1110', '1110')
>>> f'{14:#b}', f'{14:b}'
('0b1110', '1110')
```

See also *format()* for more information.

class bool([*x*])

Return a Boolean value, i.e. one of `True` or `False`. *x* is converted using the standard *truth testing procedure*. If *x* is false or omitted, this returns `False`; otherwise it returns `True`. The *bool* class is a subclass of *int* (see *Numeric Types — int, float, complex*). It cannot be subclassed further. Its only instances are `False` and `True` (see *Boolean Values*).

class bytearray([*source*[, *encoding*[, *errors*]]])

Return a new array of bytes. The *bytearray* class is a mutable sequence of integers in the range 0 <= x < 256. It has most of the usual methods of mutable sequences, described in *Mutable Sequence Types*, as well as most methods that the *bytes* type has, see *Bytes and Bytearray Operations*.

The optional *source* parameter can be used to initialize the array in a few different ways:

- If it is a *string*, you must also give the *encoding* (and optionally, *errors*) parameters; *bytearray()* then converts the string to bytes using *str.encode()*.
- If it is an *integer*, the array will have that size and will be initialized with null bytes.
- If it is an object conforming to the *buffer* interface, a read-only buffer of the object will be used to initialize the bytes array.
- If it is an *iterable*, it must be an iterable of integers in the range `0 <= x < 256`, which are used as the initial contents of the array.

Without an argument, an array of size 0 is created.

See also *Binary Sequence Types — bytes, bytearray, memoryview* and *Bytearray Objects*.

class bytes([*source*[, *encoding*[, *errors*]]])

Return a new "bytes" object, which is an immutable sequence of integers in the range `0 <= x < 256`. *bytes* is an immutable version of *bytearray* – it has the same non-mutating methods and the same indexing and slicing behavior.

Accordingly, constructor arguments are interpreted as for *bytearray()*.

Bytes objects can also be created with literals, see strings.

See also *Binary Sequence Types — bytes, bytearray, memoryview*, *Bytes Objects*, and *Bytes and Bytearray Operations*.

callable(*object*)

Return `True` if the *object* argument appears callable, `False` if not. If this returns true, it is still possible that a call fails, but if it is false, calling *object* will never succeed. Note that classes are callable (calling a class returns a new instance); instances are callable if their class has a `__call__()` method.

New in version 3.2: This function was first removed in Python 3.0 and then brought back in Python 3.2.

chr(*i*)

Return the string representing a character whose Unicode code point is the integer *i*. For example, `chr(97)` returns the string `'a'`, while `chr(8364)` returns the string `'€'`. This is the inverse of `ord()`.

The valid range for the argument is from 0 through 1,114,111 (0x10FFFF in base 16). `ValueError` will be raised if *i* is outside that range.

@classmethod

Transform a method into a class method.

A class method receives the class as implicit first argument, just like an instance method receives the instance. To declare a class method, use this idiom:

```
class C:
    @classmethod
    def f(cls, arg1, arg2, ...): ...
```

The `@classmethod` form is a function *decorator* – see the description of function definitions in function for details.

It can be called either on the class (such as `C.f()`) or on an instance (such as `C().f()`). The instance is ignored except for its class. If a class method is called for a derived class, the derived class object is passed as the implied first argument.

Class methods are different than C++ or Java static methods. If you want those, see `staticmethod()` in this section.

For more information on class methods, consult the documentation on the standard type hierarchy in types.

compile(*source, filename, mode, flags=0, dont_inherit=False, optimize=-1*)

Compile the *source* into a code or AST object. Code objects can be executed by `exec()` or `eval()`. *source* can either be a normal string, a byte string, or an AST object. Refer to the `ast` module documentation for information on how to work with AST objects.

The *filename* argument should give the file from which the code was read; pass some recognizable value if it wasn't read from a file (`'<string>'` is commonly used).

The *mode* argument specifies what kind of code must be compiled; it can be `'exec'` if *source* consists of a sequence of statements, `'eval'` if it consists of a single expression, or `'single'` if it consists of a single interactive statement (in the latter case, expression statements that evaluate to something other than `None` will be printed).

The optional arguments *flags* and *dont_inherit* control which future statements (see PEP 236) affect the compilation of *source*. If neither is present (or both are zero) the code is compiled with those future statements that are in effect in the code that is calling `compile()`. If the *flags* argument is given and *dont_inherit* is not (or is zero) then the future statements specified by the *flags* argument are used in addition to those that would be used anyway. If *dont_inherit* is a non-zero integer then the *flags* argument is it – the future statements in effect around the call to compile are ignored.

Future statements are specified by bits which can be bitwise ORed together to specify multiple statements. The bitfield required to specify a given feature can be found as the `compiler_flag` attribute on the `_Feature` instance in the `__future__` module.

The argument *optimize* specifies the optimization level of the compiler; the default value of `-1` selects the optimization level of the interpreter as given by `-O` options. Explicit levels are `0` (no optimization; `__debug__` is true), `1` (asserts are removed, `__debug__` is false) or `2` (docstrings are removed too).

This function raises `SyntaxError` if the compiled source is invalid, and `ValueError` if the source contains null bytes.

If you want to parse Python code into its AST representation, see `ast.parse()`.

Note: When compiling a string with multi-line code in `'single'` or `'eval'` mode, input must be terminated by at least one newline character. This is to facilitate detection of incomplete and complete statements in the `code` module.

Changed in version 3.2: Allowed use of Windows and Mac newlines. Also input in `'exec'` mode does not have to end in a newline anymore. Added the *optimize* parameter.

Changed in version 3.5: Previously, `TypeError` was raised when null bytes were encountered in *source*.

class complex([*real*[, *imag*]])

Return a complex number with the value *real* + *imag**1j or convert a string or number to a complex number. If the first parameter is a string, it will be interpreted as a complex number and the function must be called without a second parameter. The second parameter can never be a string. Each argument may be any numeric type (including complex). If *imag* is omitted, it defaults to zero and the constructor serves as a numeric conversion like `int` and `float`. If both arguments are omitted, returns `0j`.

Note: When converting from a string, the string must not contain whitespace around the central `+` or `-` operator. For example, `complex('1+2j')` is fine, but `complex('1 + 2j')` raises `ValueError`.

The complex type is described in *Numeric Types — int, float, complex*.

Changed in version 3.6: Grouping digits with underscores as in code literals is allowed.

delattr(*object, name*)

This is a relative of `setattr()`. The arguments are an object and a string. The string must be the name of one of the object's attributes. The function deletes the named attribute, provided the object allows it. For example, `delattr(x, 'foobar')` is equivalent to `del x.foobar`.

class dict(***kwarg*)
class dict(*mapping, **kwarg*)
class dict(*iterable, **kwarg*)

Create a new dictionary. The `dict` object is the dictionary class. See `dict` and *Mapping Types — dict* for documentation about this class.

For other containers see the built-in `list`, `set`, and `tuple` classes, as well as the `collections` module.

dir([*object*])

Without arguments, return the list of names in the current local scope. With an argument, attempt to return a list of valid attributes for that object.

If the object has a method named `__dir__()`, this method will be called and must return the list of attributes. This allows objects that implement a custom `__getattr__()` or `__getattribute__()` function to customize the way `dir()` reports their attributes.

If the object does not provide `__dir__()`, the function tries its best to gather information from the object's *__dict__* attribute, if defined, and from its type object. The resulting list is not necessarily complete, and may be inaccurate when the object has a custom `__getattr__()`.

The default *dir()* mechanism behaves differently with different types of objects, as it attempts to produce the most relevant, rather than complete, information:

- If the object is a module object, the list contains the names of the module's attributes.
- If the object is a type or class object, the list contains the names of its attributes, and recursively of the attributes of its bases.
- Otherwise, the list contains the object's attributes' names, the names of its class's attributes, and recursively of the attributes of its class's base classes.

The resulting list is sorted alphabetically. For example:

```
>>> import struct
>>> dir()   # show the names in the module namespace
['__builtins__', '__name__', 'struct']
>>> dir(struct)   # show the names in the struct module
['Struct', '__all__', '__builtins__', '__cached__', '__doc__', '__file__',
 '__initializing__', '__loader__', '__name__', '__package__',
 '_clearcache', 'calcsize', 'error', 'pack', 'pack_into',
 'unpack', 'unpack_from']
>>> class Shape:
...     def __dir__(self):
...         return ['area', 'perimeter', 'location']
>>> s = Shape()
>>> dir(s)
['area', 'location', 'perimeter']
```

Note: Because *dir()* is supplied primarily as a convenience for use at an interactive prompt, it tries to supply an interesting set of names more than it tries to supply a rigorously or consistently defined set of names, and its detailed behavior may change across releases. For example, metaclass attributes are not in the result list when the argument is a class.

divmod(*a*, *b*)

Take two (non complex) numbers as arguments and return a pair of numbers consisting of their quotient and remainder when using integer division. With mixed operand types, the rules for binary arithmetic operators apply. For integers, the result is the same as `(a // b, a % b)`. For floating point numbers the result is `(q, a % b)`, where *q* is usually `math.floor(a / b)` but may be 1 less than that. In any case `q * b + a % b` is very close to *a*, if `a % b` is non-zero it has the same sign as *b*, and `0 <= abs(a % b) < abs(b)`.

enumerate(*iterable*, *start=0*)

Return an enumerate object. *iterable* must be a sequence, an *iterator*, or some other object which supports iteration. The *__next__()* method of the iterator returned by *enumerate()* returns a tuple containing a count (from *start* which defaults to 0) and the values obtained from iterating over *iterable*.

```
>>> seasons = ['Spring', 'Summer', 'Fall', 'Winter']
>>> list(enumerate(seasons))
[(0, 'Spring'), (1, 'Summer'), (2, 'Fall'), (3, 'Winter')]
>>> list(enumerate(seasons, start=1))
[(1, 'Spring'), (2, 'Summer'), (3, 'Fall'), (4, 'Winter')]
```

Equivalent to:

```
def enumerate(sequence, start=0):
    n = start
    for elem in sequence:
        yield n, elem
        n += 1
```

eval(*expression, globals=None, locals=None*)

The arguments are a string and optional globals and locals. If provided, *globals* must be a dictionary. If provided, *locals* can be any mapping object.

The *expression* argument is parsed and evaluated as a Python expression (technically speaking, a condition list) using the *globals* and *locals* dictionaries as global and local namespace. If the *globals* dictionary is present and lacks '__builtins__', the current globals are copied into *globals* before *expression* is parsed. This means that *expression* normally has full access to the standard *builtins* module and restricted environments are propagated. If the *locals* dictionary is omitted it defaults to the *globals* dictionary. If both dictionaries are omitted, the expression is executed in the environment where *eval()* is called. The return value is the result of the evaluated expression. Syntax errors are reported as exceptions. Example:

```
>>> x = 1
>>> eval('x+1')
2
```

This function can also be used to execute arbitrary code objects (such as those created by *compile()*). In this case pass a code object instead of a string. If the code object has been compiled with `'exec'` as the *mode* argument, *eval()*'s return value will be `None`.

Hints: dynamic execution of statements is supported by the *exec()* function. The *globals()* and *locals()* functions returns the current global and local dictionary, respectively, which may be useful to pass around for use by *eval()* or *exec()*.

See *ast.literal_eval()* for a function that can safely evaluate strings with expressions containing only literals.

exec(*object*[, *globals*[, *locals*]])

This function supports dynamic execution of Python code. *object* must be either a string or a code object. If it is a string, the string is parsed as a suite of Python statements which is then executed (unless a syntax error occurs).[1] If it is a code object, it is simply executed. In all cases, the code that's executed is expected to be valid as file input (see the section "File input" in the Reference Manual). Be aware that the `return` and `yield` statements may not be used outside of function definitions even within the context of code passed to the *exec()* function. The return value is `None`.

In all cases, if the optional parts are omitted, the code is executed in the current scope. If only *globals* is provided, it must be a dictionary, which will be used for both the global and the local variables. If *globals* and *locals* are given, they are used for the global and local variables, respectively. If provided, *locals* can be any mapping object. Remember that at module level, globals and locals are the same dictionary. If exec gets two separate objects as *globals* and *locals*, the code will be executed as if it were embedded in a class definition.

If the *globals* dictionary does not contain a value for the key `__builtins__`, a reference to the dictionary of the built-in module *builtins* is inserted under that key. That way you can control what builtins are available to the executed code by inserting your own `__builtins__` dictionary into *globals* before passing it to *exec()*.

Note: The built-in functions *globals()* and *locals()* return the current global and local dictionary,

[1] Note that the parser only accepts the Unix-style end of line convention. If you are reading the code from a file, make sure to use newline conversion mode to convert Windows or Mac-style newlines.

respectively, which may be useful to pass around for use as the second and third argument to *exec()*.

Note: The default *locals* act as described for function *locals()* below: modifications to the default *locals* dictionary should not be attempted. Pass an explicit *locals* dictionary if you need to see effects of the code on *locals* after function *exec()* returns.

---

filter(*function*, *iterable*)

Construct an iterator from those elements of *iterable* for which *function* returns true. *iterable* may be either a sequence, a container which supports iteration, or an iterator. If *function* is `None`, the identity function is assumed, that is, all elements of *iterable* that are false are removed.

Note that `filter(function, iterable)` is equivalent to the generator expression `(item for item in iterable if function(item))` if function is not `None` and `(item for item in iterable if item)` if function is `None`.

See *itertools.filterfalse()* for the complementary function that returns elements of *iterable* for which *function* returns false.

class float([*x*])

Return a floating point number constructed from a number or string *x*.

If the argument is a string, it should contain a decimal number, optionally preceded by a sign, and optionally embedded in whitespace. The optional sign may be `'+'` or `'-'`; a `'+'` sign has no effect on the value produced. The argument may also be a string representing a NaN (not-a-number), or a positive or negative infinity. More precisely, the input must conform to the following grammar after leading and trailing whitespace characters are removed:

```
sign           ::=  "+" | "-"
infinity       ::=  "Infinity" | "inf"
nan            ::=  "nan"
numeric_value  ::=  floatnumber | infinity | nan
numeric_string ::=  [sign] numeric_value
```

Here `floatnumber` is the form of a Python floating-point literal, described in floating. Case is not significant, so, for example, "inf", "Inf", "INFINITY" and "iNfINity" are all acceptable spellings for positive infinity.

Otherwise, if the argument is an integer or a floating point number, a floating point number with the same value (within Python's floating point precision) is returned. If the argument is outside the range of a Python float, an *OverflowError* will be raised.

For a general Python object `x`, `float(x)` delegates to `x.__float__()`.

If no argument is given, `0.0` is returned.

Examples:

```
>>> float('+1.23')
1.23
>>> float('   -12345\n')
-12345.0
>>> float('1e-003')
0.001
>>> float('+1E6')
1000000.0
>>> float('-Infinity')
-inf
```

The float type is described in *Numeric Types — int, float, complex*.

Changed in version 3.6: Grouping digits with underscores as in code literals is allowed.

`format(`*value*[, *format_spec*]`)`

Convert a *value* to a "formatted" representation, as controlled by *format_spec*. The interpretation of *format_spec* will depend on the type of the *value* argument, however there is a standard formatting syntax that is used by most built-in types: *Format Specification Mini-Language*.

The default *format_spec* is an empty string which usually gives the same effect as calling `str(value)`.

A call to `format(value, format_spec)` is translated to `type(value).__format__(value, format_spec)` which bypasses the instance dictionary when searching for the value's `__format__()` method. A `TypeError` exception is raised if the method search reaches `object` and the *format_spec* is non-empty, or if either the *format_spec* or the return value are not strings.

Changed in version 3.4: `object().__format__(format_spec)` raises `TypeError` if *format_spec* is not an empty string.

`class frozenset(`[*iterable*]`)`

Return a new `frozenset` object, optionally with elements taken from *iterable*. `frozenset` is a built-in class. See `frozenset` and *Set Types — set, frozenset* for documentation about this class.

For other containers see the built-in `set`, `list`, `tuple`, and `dict` classes, as well as the `collections` module.

`getattr(`*object*, *name*[, *default*]`)`

Return the value of the named attribute of *object*. *name* must be a string. If the string is the name of one of the object's attributes, the result is the value of that attribute. For example, `getattr(x, 'foobar')` is equivalent to `x.foobar`. If the named attribute does not exist, *default* is returned if provided, otherwise `AttributeError` is raised.

`globals()`

Return a dictionary representing the current global symbol table. This is always the dictionary of the current module (inside a function or method, this is the module where it is defined, not the module from which it is called).

`hasattr(`*object*, *name*`)`

The arguments are an object and a string. The result is `True` if the string is the name of one of the object's attributes, `False` if not. (This is implemented by calling `getattr(object, name)` and seeing whether it raises an `AttributeError` or not.)

`hash(`*object*`)`

Return the hash value of the object (if it has one). Hash values are integers. They are used to quickly compare dictionary keys during a dictionary lookup. Numeric values that compare equal have the same hash value (even if they are of different types, as is the case for 1 and 1.0).

Note: For objects with custom `__hash__()` methods, note that `hash()` truncates the return value based on the bit width of the host machine. See `__hash__()` for details.

`help(`[*object*]`)`

Invoke the built-in help system. (This function is intended for interactive use.) If no argument is given, the interactive help system starts on the interpreter console. If the argument is a string, then the string is looked up as the name of a module, function, class, method, keyword, or documentation topic, and a help page is printed on the console. If the argument is any other kind of object, a help page on the object is generated.

This function is added to the built-in namespace by the *site* module.

Changed in version 3.4: Changes to *pydoc* and *inspect* mean that the reported signatures for callables are now more comprehensive and consistent.

hex(*x*)

Convert an integer number to a lowercase hexadecimal string prefixed with "0x". If x is not a Python *int* object, it has to define an __index__() method that returns an integer. Some examples:

```
>>> hex(255)
'0xff'
>>> hex(-42)
'-0x2a'
```

If you want to convert an integer number to an uppercase or lower hexadecimal string with prefix or not, you can use either of the following ways:

```
>>> '%#x' % 255, '%x' % 255, '%X' % 255
('0xff', 'ff', 'FF')
>>> format(255, '#x'), format(255, 'x'), format(255, 'X')
('0xff', 'ff', 'FF')
>>> f'{255:#x}', f'{255:x}', f'{255:X}'
('0xff', 'ff', 'FF')
```

See also *format()* for more information.

See also *int()* for converting a hexadecimal string to an integer using a base of 16.

Note: To obtain a hexadecimal string representation for a float, use the *float.hex()* method.

---

id(*object*)

Return the "identity" of an object. This is an integer which is guaranteed to be unique and constant for this object during its lifetime. Two objects with non-overlapping lifetimes may have the same *id()* value.

CPython implementation detail: This is the address of the object in memory.

input([*prompt*])

If the *prompt* argument is present, it is written to standard output without a trailing newline. The function then reads a line from input, converts it to a string (stripping a trailing newline), and returns that. When EOF is read, *EOFError* is raised. Example:

```
>>> s = input('--> ')
--> Monty Python's Flying Circus
>>> s
"Monty Python's Flying Circus"
```

If the *readline* module was loaded, then *input()* will use it to provide elaborate line editing and history features.

class int(*x=0*)
class int(*x*, *base=10*)

Return an integer object constructed from a number or string *x*, or return `0` if no arguments are given. If *x* is a number, return `x.__int__()`. For floating point numbers, this truncates towards zero.

If *x* is not a number or if *base* is given, then *x* must be a string, *bytes*, or *bytearray* instance representing an integer literal in radix *base*. Optionally, the literal can be preceded by `+` or `-` (with no space in between) and surrounded by whitespace. A base-n literal consists of the digits 0 to n-1, with `a` to `z` (or `A` to `Z`) having values 10 to 35. The default *base* is 10. The allowed values are 0 and 2–36.

Base-2, -8, and -16 literals can be optionally prefixed with `0b`/`0B`, `0o`/`0O`, or `0x`/`0X`, as with integer literals in code. Base 0 means to interpret exactly as a code literal, so that the actual base is 2, 8, 10, or 16, and so that `int('010', 0)` is not legal, while `int('010')` is, as well as `int('010', 8)`.

The integer type is described in *Numeric Types — int, float, complex*.

Changed in version 3.4: If *base* is not an instance of `int` and the *base* object has a `base.__index__` method, that method is called to obtain an integer for the base. Previous versions used `base.__int__` instead of `base.__index__`.

Changed in version 3.6: Grouping digits with underscores as in code literals is allowed.

isinstance(*object*, *classinfo*)
Return true if the *object* argument is an instance of the *classinfo* argument, or of a (direct, indirect or *virtual*) subclass thereof. If *object* is not an object of the given type, the function always returns false. If *classinfo* is a tuple of type objects (or recursively, other such tuples), return true if *object* is an instance of any of the types. If *classinfo* is not a type or tuple of types and such tuples, a `TypeError` exception is raised.

issubclass(*class*, *classinfo*)
Return true if *class* is a subclass (direct, indirect or *virtual*) of *classinfo*. A class is considered a subclass of itself. *classinfo* may be a tuple of class objects, in which case every entry in *classinfo* will be checked. In any other case, a `TypeError` exception is raised.

iter(*object*[, *sentinel*])
Return an *iterator* object. The first argument is interpreted very differently depending on the presence of the second argument. Without a second argument, *object* must be a collection object which supports the iteration protocol (the `__iter__()` method), or it must support the sequence protocol (the `__getitem__()` method with integer arguments starting at `0`). If it does not support either of those protocols, `TypeError` is raised. If the second argument, *sentinel*, is given, then *object* must be a callable object. The iterator created in this case will call *object* with no arguments for each call to its `__next__()` method; if the value returned is equal to *sentinel*, `StopIteration` will be raised, otherwise the value will be returned.

See also *Iterator Types*.

One useful application of the second form of `iter()` is to read lines of a file until a certain line is reached. The following example reads a file until the `readline()` method returns an empty string:

```
with open('mydata.txt') as fp:
    for line in iter(fp.readline, ''):
        process_line(line)
```

len(*s*)
Return the length (the number of items) of an object. The argument may be a sequence (such as a string, bytes, tuple, list, or range) or a collection (such as a dictionary, set, or frozen set).

class **list**([*iterable*])
Rather than being a function, `list` is actually a mutable sequence type, as documented in *Lists* and *Sequence Types — list, tuple, range*.

locals()
Update and return a dictionary representing the current local symbol table. Free variables are returned by `locals()` when it is called in function blocks, but not in class blocks.

Note: The contents of this dictionary should not be modified; changes may not affect the values of local and free variables used by the interpreter.

map(*function*, *iterable*, ...)
Return an iterator that applies *function* to every item of *iterable*, yielding the results. If additional *iterable* arguments are passed, *function* must take that many arguments and is applied to the items from all iterables in parallel. With multiple iterables, the iterator stops when the shortest iterable is exhausted. For cases where the function inputs are already arranged into argument tuples, see `itertools.starmap()`.

max(*iterable*, *[, *key*, *default*])
max(*arg1*, *arg2*, **args*[, *key*])
Return the largest item in an iterable or the largest of two or more arguments.

If one positional argument is provided, it should be an *iterable*. The largest item in the iterable is returned. If two or more positional arguments are provided, the largest of the positional arguments is returned.

There are two optional keyword-only arguments. The *key* argument specifies a one-argument ordering function like that used for `list.sort()`. The *default* argument specifies an object to return if the provided iterable is empty. If the iterable is empty and *default* is not provided, a `ValueError` is raised.

If multiple items are maximal, the function returns the first one encountered. This is consistent with other sort-stability preserving tools such as `sorted(iterable, key=keyfunc, reverse=True)[0]` and `heapq.nlargest(1, iterable, key=keyfunc)`.

New in version 3.4: The *default* keyword-only argument.

memoryview(*obj*)
Return a "memory view" object created from the given argument. See *Memory Views* for more information.

min(*iterable*, *[, *key*, *default*])
min(*arg1*, *arg2*, **args*[, *key*])
Return the smallest item in an iterable or the smallest of two or more arguments.

If one positional argument is provided, it should be an *iterable*. The smallest item in the iterable is returned. If two or more positional arguments are provided, the smallest of the positional arguments is returned.

There are two optional keyword-only arguments. The *key* argument specifies a one-argument ordering function like that used for `list.sort()`. The *default* argument specifies an object to return if the provided iterable is empty. If the iterable is empty and *default* is not provided, a `ValueError` is raised.

If multiple items are minimal, the function returns the first one encountered. This is consistent with other sort-stability preserving tools such as `sorted(iterable, key=keyfunc)[0]` and `heapq.nsmallest(1, iterable, key=keyfunc)`.

New in version 3.4: The *default* keyword-only argument.

next(*iterator*[, *default*])
Retrieve the next item from the *iterator* by calling its `__next__()` method. If *default* is given, it is returned if the iterator is exhausted, otherwise `StopIteration` is raised.

class object
Return a new featureless object. `object` is a base for all classes. It has the methods that are common to all instances of Python classes. This function does not accept any arguments.

Note: `object` does *not* have a `__dict__`, so you can't assign arbitrary attributes to an instance of the `object` class.

oct(*x*)
Convert an integer number to an octal string prefixed with "0o". The result is a valid Python expression.

If x is not a Python *int* object, it has to define an `__index__()` method that returns an integer. For example:

```
>>> oct(8)
'0o10'
>>> oct(-56)
'-0o70'
```

If you want to convert an integer number to octal string either with prefix "0o" or not, you can use either of the following ways.

```
>>> '%#o' % 10, '%o' % 10
('0o12', '12')
>>> format(10, '#o'), format(10, 'o')
('0o12', '12')
>>> f'{10:#o}', f'{10:o}'
('0o12', '12')
```

See also *format()* for more information.

open(*file, mode='r', buffering=-1, encoding=None, errors=None, newline=None, closefd=True, opener=None*)

Open *file* and return a corresponding *file object*. If the file cannot be opened, an *OSError* is raised.

file is a *path-like object* giving the pathname (absolute or relative to the current working directory) of the file to be opened or an integer file descriptor of the file to be wrapped. (If a file descriptor is given, it is closed when the returned I/O object is closed, unless *closefd* is set to `False`.)

mode is an optional string that specifies the mode in which the file is opened. It defaults to `'r'` which means open for reading in text mode. Other common values are `'w'` for writing (truncating the file if it already exists), `'x'` for exclusive creation and `'a'` for appending (which on *some* Unix systems, means that *all* writes append to the end of the file regardless of the current seek position). In text mode, if *encoding* is not specified the encoding used is platform dependent: `locale.getpreferredencoding(False)` is called to get the current locale encoding. (For reading and writing raw bytes use binary mode and leave *encoding* unspecified.) The available modes are:

Character	Meaning
'r'	open for reading (default)
'w'	open for writing, truncating the file first
'x'	open for exclusive creation, failing if the file already exists
'a'	open for writing, appending to the end of the file if it exists
'b'	binary mode
't'	text mode (default)
'+'	open a disk file for updating (reading and writing)
'U'	*universal newlines* mode (deprecated)

The default mode is `'r'` (open for reading text, synonym of `'rt'`). For binary read-write access, the mode `'w+b'` opens and truncates the file to 0 bytes. `'r+b'` opens the file without truncation.

As mentioned in the *Overview*, Python distinguishes between binary and text I/O. Files opened in binary mode (including `'b'` in the *mode* argument) return contents as *bytes* objects without any decoding. In text mode (the default, or when `'t'` is included in the *mode* argument), the contents of the file are returned as *str*, the bytes having been first decoded using a platform-dependent encoding or using the specified *encoding* if given.

Note: Python doesn't depend on the underlying operating system's notion of text files; all the processing is done by Python itself, and is therefore platform-independent.

buffering is an optional integer used to set the buffering policy. Pass 0 to switch buffering off (only allowed in binary mode), 1 to select line buffering (only usable in text mode), and an integer > 1 to indicate the size in bytes of a fixed-size chunk buffer. When no *buffering* argument is given, the default buffering policy works as follows:

- Binary files are buffered in fixed-size chunks; the size of the buffer is chosen using a heuristic trying to determine the underlying device's "block size" and falling back on `io.DEFAULT_BUFFER_SIZE`. On many systems, the buffer will typically be 4096 or 8192 bytes long.
- "Interactive" text files (files for which `isatty()` returns `True`) use line buffering. Other text files use the policy described above for binary files.

encoding is the name of the encoding used to decode or encode the file. This should only be used in text mode. The default encoding is platform dependent (whatever `locale.getpreferredencoding()` returns), but any *text encoding* supported by Python can be used. See the `codecs` module for the list of supported encodings.

errors is an optional string that specifies how encoding and decoding errors are to be handled—this cannot be used in binary mode. A variety of standard error handlers are available (listed under *Error Handlers*), though any error handling name that has been registered with `codecs.register_error()` is also valid. The standard names include:

- `'strict'` to raise a `ValueError` exception if there is an encoding error. The default value of `None` has the same effect.
- `'ignore'` ignores errors. Note that ignoring encoding errors can lead to data loss.
- `'replace'` causes a replacement marker (such as `'?'`) to be inserted where there is malformed data.
- `'surrogateescape'` will represent any incorrect bytes as code points in the Unicode Private Use Area ranging from U+DC80 to U+DCFF. These private code points will then be turned back into the same bytes when the `surrogateescape` error handler is used when writing data. This is useful for processing files in an unknown encoding.
- `'xmlcharrefreplace'` is only supported when writing to a file. Characters not supported by the encoding are replaced with the appropriate XML character reference `&#nnn;`.
- `'backslashreplace'` replaces malformed data by Python's backslashed escape sequences.
- `'namereplace'` (also only supported when writing) replaces unsupported characters with `\N{...}` escape sequences.

newline controls how *universal newlines* mode works (it only applies to text mode). It can be `None`, `''`, `'\n'`, `'\r'`, and `'\r\n'`. It works as follows:

- When reading input from the stream, if *newline* is `None`, universal newlines mode is enabled. Lines in the input can end in `'\n'`, `'\r'`, or `'\r\n'`, and these are translated into `'\n'` before being returned to the caller. If it is `''`, universal newlines mode is enabled, but line endings are returned to the caller untranslated. If it has any of the other legal values, input lines are only terminated by the given string, and the line ending is returned to the caller untranslated.
- When writing output to the stream, if *newline* is `None`, any `'\n'` characters written are translated to the system default line separator, `os.linesep`. If *newline* is `''` or `'\n'`, no translation takes place. If *newline* is any of the other legal values, any `'\n'` characters written are translated to the given string.

If *closefd* is `False` and a file descriptor rather than a filename was given, the underlying file descriptor will be kept open when the file is closed. If a filename is given *closefd* must be `True` (the default) otherwise an error will be raised.

A custom opener can be used by passing a callable as *opener*. The underlying file descriptor for the file object is then obtained by calling *opener* with (*file*, *flags*). *opener* must return an open file descriptor (passing `os.open` as *opener* results in functionality similar to passing `None`).

The newly created file is *non-inheritable*.

The following example uses the *dir_fd* parameter of the `os.open()` function to open a file relative to a given directory:

```
>>> import os
>>> dir_fd = os.open('somedir', os.O_RDONLY)
>>> def opener(path, flags):
...     return os.open(path, flags, dir_fd=dir_fd)
...
>>> with open('spamspam.txt', 'w', opener=opener) as f:
...     print('This will be written to somedir/spamspam.txt', file=f)
...
>>> os.close(dir_fd)  # don't leak a file descriptor
```

The type of *file object* returned by the `open()` function depends on the mode. When `open()` is used to open a file in a text mode (`'w'`, `'r'`, `'wt'`, `'rt'`, etc.), it returns a subclass of `io.TextIOBase` (specifically `io.TextIOWrapper`). When used to open a file in a binary mode with buffering, the returned class is a subclass of `io.BufferedIOBase`. The exact class varies: in read binary mode, it returns an `io.BufferedReader`; in write binary and append binary modes, it returns an `io.BufferedWriter`, and in read/write mode, it returns an `io.BufferedRandom`. When buffering is disabled, the raw stream, a subclass of `io.RawIOBase`, `io.FileIO`, is returned.

See also the file handling modules, such as, `fileinput`, `io` (where `open()` is declared), `os`, `os.path`, `tempfile`, and `shutil`.

Changed in version 3.3:

- The *opener* parameter was added.
- The `'x'` mode was added.
- `IOError` used to be raised, it is now an alias of `OSError`.
- `FileExistsError` is now raised if the file opened in exclusive creation mode (`'x'`) already exists.

Changed in version 3.4:

- The file is now non-inheritable.

Deprecated since version 3.4, will be removed in version 4.0: The `'U'` mode.

Changed in version 3.5:

- If the system call is interrupted and the signal handler does not raise an exception, the function now retries the system call instead of raising an `InterruptedError` exception (see PEP 475 for the rationale).
- The `'namereplace'` error handler was added.

Changed in version 3.6:

- Support added to accept objects implementing `os.PathLike`.

- On Windows, opening a console buffer may return a subclass of *io.RawIOBase* other than *io.FileIO*.

ord(*c*)

Given a string representing one Unicode character, return an integer representing the Unicode code point of that character. For example, `ord('a')` returns the integer 97 and `ord('€')` (Euro sign) returns 8364. This is the inverse of *chr()*.

pow(*x*, *y*[, *z*])

Return *x* to the power *y*; if *z* is present, return *x* to the power *y*, modulo *z* (computed more efficiently than `pow(x, y) % z`). The two-argument form `pow(x, y)` is equivalent to using the power operator: `x**y`.

The arguments must have numeric types. With mixed operand types, the coercion rules for binary arithmetic operators apply. For *int* operands, the result has the same type as the operands (after coercion) unless the second argument is negative; in that case, all arguments are converted to float and a float result is delivered. For example, `10**2` returns `100`, but `10**-2` returns `0.01`. If the second argument is negative, the third argument must be omitted. If *z* is present, *x* and *y* must be of integer types, and *y* must be non-negative.

print(**objects*, *sep=' '*, *end='\n'*, *file=sys.stdout*, *flush=False*)

Print *objects* to the text stream *file*, separated by *sep* and followed by *end*. *sep*, *end*, *file* and *flush*, if present, must be given as keyword arguments.

All non-keyword arguments are converted to strings like *str()* does and written to the stream, separated by *sep* and followed by *end*. Both *sep* and *end* must be strings; they can also be `None`, which means to use the default values. If no *objects* are given, *print()* will just write *end*.

The *file* argument must be an object with a `write(string)` method; if it is not present or `None`, *sys.stdout* will be used. Since printed arguments are converted to text strings, *print()* cannot be used with binary mode file objects. For these, use `file.write(...)` instead.

Whether output is buffered is usually determined by *file*, but if the *flush* keyword argument is true, the stream is forcibly flushed.

Changed in version 3.3: Added the *flush* keyword argument.

class property(*fget=None*, *fset=None*, *fdel=None*, *doc=None*)

Return a property attribute.

fget is a function for getting an attribute value. *fset* is a function for setting an attribute value. *fdel* is a function for deleting an attribute value. And *doc* creates a docstring for the attribute.

A typical use is to define a managed attribute `x`:

```
class C:
    def __init__(self):
        self._x = None

    def getx(self):
        return self._x

    def setx(self, value):
        self._x = value

    def delx(self):
        del self._x

    x = property(getx, setx, delx, "I'm the 'x' property.")
```

If *c* is an instance of *C*, `c.x` will invoke the getter, `c.x = value` will invoke the setter and `del c.x` the deleter.

If given, *doc* will be the docstring of the property attribute. Otherwise, the property will copy *fget*'s docstring (if it exists). This makes it possible to create read-only properties easily using `property()` as a *decorator*:

```
class Parrot:
    def __init__(self):
        self._voltage = 100000

    @property
    def voltage(self):
        """Get the current voltage."""
        return self._voltage
```

The `@property` decorator turns the `voltage()` method into a "getter" for a read-only attribute with the same name, and it sets the docstring for *voltage* to "Get the current voltage."

A property object has `getter`, `setter`, and `deleter` methods usable as decorators that create a copy of the property with the corresponding accessor function set to the decorated function. This is best explained with an example:

```
class C:
    def __init__(self):
        self._x = None

    @property
    def x(self):
        """I'm the 'x' property."""
        return self._x

    @x.setter
    def x(self, value):
        self._x = value

    @x.deleter
    def x(self):
        del self._x
```

This code is exactly equivalent to the first example. Be sure to give the additional functions the same name as the original property (`x` in this case.)

The returned property object also has the attributes `fget`, `fset`, and `fdel` corresponding to the constructor arguments.

Changed in version 3.5: The docstrings of property objects are now writeable.

range(*stop*)

range(*start*, *stop*[, *step*])

Rather than being a function, `range` is actually an immutable sequence type, as documented in *Ranges* and *Sequence Types — list, tuple, range*.

repr(*object*)

Return a string containing a printable representation of an object. For many types, this function makes an attempt to return a string that would yield an object with the same value when passed to `eval()`, otherwise the representation is a string enclosed in angle brackets that contains the name of the type of the object together with additional information often including the name and address of the object. A class can control what this function returns for its instances by defining a `__repr__()` method.

reversed(*seq*)
Return a reverse *iterator*. *seq* must be an object which has a `__reversed__()` method or supports the sequence protocol (the `__len__()` method and the `__getitem__()` method with integer arguments starting at `0`).

round(*number*[, *ndigits*])
Return *number* rounded to *ndigits* precision after the decimal point. If *ndigits* is omitted or is `None`, it returns the nearest integer to its input.

For the built-in types supporting `round()`, values are rounded to the closest multiple of 10 to the power minus *ndigits*; if two multiples are equally close, rounding is done toward the even choice (so, for example, both `round(0.5)` and `round(-0.5)` are `0`, and `round(1.5)` is `2`). Any integer value is valid for *ndigits* (positive, zero, or negative). The return value is an integer if called with one argument, otherwise of the same type as *number*.

For a general Python object `number`, `round(number, ndigits)` delegates to `number.__round__(ndigits)`.

Note: The behavior of `round()` for floats can be surprising: for example, `round(2.675, 2)` gives `2.67` instead of the expected `2.68`. This is not a bug: it's a result of the fact that most decimal fractions can't be represented exactly as a float. See tut-fp-issues for more information.

class **set**([*iterable*])
Return a new `set` object, optionally with elements taken from *iterable*. `set` is a built-in class. See `set` and *Set Types — set, frozenset* for documentation about this class.

For other containers see the built-in `frozenset`, `list`, `tuple`, and `dict` classes, as well as the `collections` module.

setattr(*object*, *name*, *value*)
This is the counterpart of `getattr()`. The arguments are an object, a string and an arbitrary value. The string may name an existing attribute or a new attribute. The function assigns the value to the attribute, provided the object allows it. For example, `setattr(x, 'foobar', 123)` is equivalent to `x.foobar = 123`.

class **slice**(*stop*)
class **slice**(*start*, *stop*[, *step*])
Return a *slice* object representing the set of indices specified by `range(start, stop, step)`. The *start* and *step* arguments default to `None`. Slice objects have read-only data attributes `start`, `stop` and `step` which merely return the argument values (or their default). They have no other explicit functionality; however they are used by Numerical Python and other third party extensions. Slice objects are also generated when extended indexing syntax is used. For example: `a[start:stop:step]` or `a[start:stop, i]`. See `itertools.islice()` for an alternate version that returns an iterator.

sorted(*iterable*, *, *key=None*, *reverse=False*)
Return a new sorted list from the items in *iterable*.

Has two optional arguments which must be specified as keyword arguments.

key specifies a function of one argument that is used to extract a comparison key from each list element: `key=str.lower`. The default value is `None` (compare the elements directly).

reverse is a boolean value. If set to `True`, then the list elements are sorted as if each comparison were reversed.

Use `functools.cmp_to_key()` to convert an old-style *cmp* function to a *key* function.

The built-in `sorted()` function is guaranteed to be stable. A sort is stable if it guarantees not to change the relative order of elements that compare equal — this is helpful for sorting in multiple passes (for example, sort by department, then by salary grade).

For sorting examples and a brief sorting tutorial, see sortinghowto.

@staticmethod
Transform a method into a static method.

A static method does not receive an implicit first argument. To declare a static method, use this idiom:

```
class C:
    @staticmethod
    def f(arg1, arg2, ...): ...
```

The `@staticmethod` form is a function *decorator* – see the description of function definitions in function for details.

It can be called either on the class (such as `C.f()`) or on an instance (such as `C().f()`). The instance is ignored except for its class.

Static methods in Python are similar to those found in Java or C++. Also see `classmethod()` for a variant that is useful for creating alternate class constructors.

Like all decorators, it is also possible to call `staticmethod` as a regular function and do something with its result. This is needed in some cases where you need a reference to a function from a class body and you want to avoid the automatic transformation to instance method. For these cases, use this idiom:

```
class C:
    builtin_open = staticmethod(open)
```

For more information on static methods, consult the documentation on the standard type hierarchy in types.

class str(*object=''*)
class str(*object=b'', encoding='utf-8', errors='strict'*)
Return a `str` version of *object*. See `str()` for details.

`str` is the built-in string *class*. For general information about strings, see *Text Sequence Type — str*.

sum(*iterable*[, *start*])
Sums *start* and the items of an *iterable* from left to right and returns the total. *start* defaults to `0`. The *iterable*'s items are normally numbers, and the start value is not allowed to be a string.

For some use cases, there are good alternatives to `sum()`. The preferred, fast way to concatenate a sequence of strings is by calling `''.join(sequence)`. To add floating point values with extended precision, see `math.fsum()`. To concatenate a series of iterables, consider using `itertools.chain()`.

super([*type*[, *object-or-type*]])
Return a proxy object that delegates method calls to a parent or sibling class of *type*. This is useful for accessing inherited methods that have been overridden in a class. The search order is same as that used by `getattr()` except that the *type* itself is skipped.

The `__mro__` attribute of the *type* lists the method resolution search order used by both `getattr()` and `super()`. The attribute is dynamic and can change whenever the inheritance hierarchy is updated.

If the second argument is omitted, the super object returned is unbound. If the second argument is an object, `isinstance(obj, type)` must be true. If the second argument is a type, `issubclass(type2, type)` must be true (this is useful for classmethods).

There are two typical use cases for *super*. In a class hierarchy with single inheritance, *super* can be used to refer to parent classes without naming them explicitly, thus making the code more maintainable. This use closely parallels the use of *super* in other programming languages.

The second use case is to support cooperative multiple inheritance in a dynamic execution environment. This use case is unique to Python and is not found in statically compiled languages or languages that only support single inheritance. This makes it possible to implement "diamond diagrams" where multiple base classes implement the same method. Good design dictates that this method have the same calling signature in every case (because the order of calls is determined at runtime, because that order adapts to changes in the class hierarchy, and because that order can include sibling classes that are unknown prior to runtime).

For both use cases, a typical superclass call looks like this:

```
class C(B):
    def method(self, arg):
        super().method(arg)    # This does the same thing as:
                               # super(C, self).method(arg)
```

Note that *super()* is implemented as part of the binding process for explicit dotted attribute lookups such as `super().__getitem__(name)`. It does so by implementing its own `__getattribute__()` method for searching classes in a predictable order that supports cooperative multiple inheritance. Accordingly, *super()* is undefined for implicit lookups using statements or operators such as `super()[name]`.

Also note that, aside from the zero argument form, *super()* is not limited to use inside methods. The two argument form specifies the arguments exactly and makes the appropriate references. The zero argument form only works inside a class definition, as the compiler fills in the necessary details to correctly retrieve the class being defined, as well as accessing the current instance for ordinary methods.

For practical suggestions on how to design cooperative classes using *super()*, see guide to using super().

tuple([*iterable*])
Rather than being a function, *tuple* is actually an immutable sequence type, as documented in *Tuples* and *Sequence Types — list, tuple, range*.

class type(*object*)
class type(*name, bases, dict*)
With one argument, return the type of an *object*. The return value is a type object and generally the same object as returned by *object.__class__*.

The *isinstance()* built-in function is recommended for testing the type of an object, because it takes subclasses into account.

With three arguments, return a new type object. This is essentially a dynamic form of the **class** statement. The *name* string is the class name and becomes the *__name__* attribute; the *bases* tuple itemizes the base classes and becomes the *__bases__* attribute; and the *dict* dictionary is the namespace containing definitions for class body and is copied to a standard dictionary to become the *__dict__* attribute. For example, the following two statements create identical *type* objects:

```
>>> class X:
...     a = 1
...
>>> X = type('X', (object,), dict(a=1))
```

See also *Type Objects*.

Changed in version 3.6: Subclasses of *type* which don't override `type.__new__` may no longer use the one-argument form to get the type of an object.

vars([*object*])
Return the *__dict__* attribute for a module, class, instance, or any other object with a *__dict__* attribute.

Objects such as modules and instances have an updateable *__dict__* attribute; however, other objects may have write restrictions on their *__dict__* attributes (for example, classes use a *types.MappingProxyType* to prevent direct dictionary updates).

Without an argument, *vars()* acts like *locals()*. Note, the locals dictionary is only useful for reads since updates to the locals dictionary are ignored.

zip(**iterables*)

Make an iterator that aggregates elements from each of the iterables.

Returns an iterator of tuples, where the *i*-th tuple contains the *i*-th element from each of the argument sequences or iterables. The iterator stops when the shortest input iterable is exhausted. With a single iterable argument, it returns an iterator of 1-tuples. With no arguments, it returns an empty iterator. Equivalent to:

```
def zip(*iterables):
    # zip('ABCD', 'xy') --> Ax By
    sentinel = object()
    iterators = [iter(it) for it in iterables]
    while iterators:
        result = []
        for it in iterators:
            elem = next(it, sentinel)
            if elem is sentinel:
                return
            result.append(elem)
        yield tuple(result)
```

The left-to-right evaluation order of the iterables is guaranteed. This makes possible an idiom for clustering a data series into n-length groups using `zip(*[iter(s)]*n)`. This repeats the *same* iterator `n` times so that each output tuple has the result of `n` calls to the iterator. This has the effect of dividing the input into n-length chunks.

zip() should only be used with unequal length inputs when you don't care about trailing, unmatched values from the longer iterables. If those values are important, use *itertools.zip_longest()* instead.

zip() in conjunction with the `*` operator can be used to unzip a list:

```
>>> x = [1, 2, 3]
>>> y = [4, 5, 6]
>>> zipped = zip(x, y)
>>> list(zipped)
[(1, 4), (2, 5), (3, 6)]
>>> x2, y2 = zip(*zip(x, y))
>>> x == list(x2) and y == list(y2)
True
```

__import__(*name, globals=None, locals=None, fromlist=(), level=0*)

Note: This is an advanced function that is not needed in everyday Python programming, unlike *importlib.import_module()*.

This function is invoked by the `import` statement. It can be replaced (by importing the *builtins* module and assigning to `builtins.__import__`) in order to change semantics of the `import` statement, but doing so is **strongly** discouraged as it is usually simpler to use import hooks (see PEP 302) to attain the same goals and does not cause issues with code which assumes the default import implementation is in use. Direct use of *__import__()* is also discouraged in favor of *importlib.import_module()*.

The function imports the module *name*, potentially using the given *globals* and *locals* to determine how to interpret the name in a package context. The *fromlist* gives the names of objects or submodules that should be imported from the module given by *name*. The standard implementation does not use its *locals* argument at all, and uses its *globals* only to determine the package context of the `import` statement.

level specifies whether to use absolute or relative imports. `0` (the default) means only perform absolute imports. Positive values for *level* indicate the number of parent directories to search relative to the directory of the module calling `__import__()` (see PEP 328 for the details).

When the *name* variable is of the form `package.module`, normally, the top-level package (the name up till the first dot) is returned, *not* the module named by *name*. However, when a non-empty *fromlist* argument is given, the module named by *name* is returned.

For example, the statement `import spam` results in bytecode resembling the following code:

```
spam = __import__('spam', globals(), locals(), [], 0)
```

The statement `import spam.ham` results in this call:

```
spam = __import__('spam.ham', globals(), locals(), [], 0)
```

Note how `__import__()` returns the toplevel module here because this is the object that is bound to a name by the `import` statement.

On the other hand, the statement `from spam.ham import eggs, sausage as saus` results in

```
_temp = __import__('spam.ham', globals(), locals(), ['eggs', 'sausage'], 0)
eggs = _temp.eggs
saus = _temp.sausage
```

Here, the `spam.ham` module is returned from `__import__()`. From this object, the names to import are retrieved and assigned to their respective names.

If you simply want to import a module (potentially within a package) by name, use `importlib.import_module()`.

Changed in version 3.3: Negative values for *level* are no longer supported (which also changes the default value to 0).

CHAPTER

THREE

BUILT-IN CONSTANTS

A small number of constants live in the built-in namespace. They are:

False
: The false value of the *bool* type. Assignments to False are illegal and raise a *SyntaxError*.

True
: The true value of the *bool* type. Assignments to True are illegal and raise a *SyntaxError*.

None
: The sole value of the type NoneType. None is frequently used to represent the absence of a value, as when default arguments are not passed to a function. Assignments to None are illegal and raise a *SyntaxError*.

NotImplemented
: Special value which should be returned by the binary special methods (e.g. `__eq__()`, `__lt__()`, `__add__()`, `__rsub__()`, etc.) to indicate that the operation is not implemented with respect to the other type; may be returned by the in-place binary special methods (e.g. `__imul__()`, `__iand__()`, etc.) for the same purpose. Its truth value is true.

Note: When a binary (or in-place) method returns NotImplemented the interpreter will try the reflected operation on the other type (or some other fallback, depending on the operator). If all attempts return NotImplemented, the interpreter will raise an appropriate exception. Incorrectly returning NotImplemented will result in a misleading error message or the NotImplemented value being returned to Python code.

See *Implementing the arithmetic operations* for examples.

Note: NotImplementedError and NotImplemented are not interchangeable, even though they have similar names and purposes. See *NotImplementedError* for details on when to use it.

Ellipsis
: The same as .... Special value used mostly in conjunction with extended slicing syntax for user-defined container data types.

__debug__
: This constant is true if Python was not started with an -O option. See also the assert statement.

Note: The names *None*, *False*, *True* and *__debug__* cannot be reassigned (assignments to them, even as an attribute name, raise *SyntaxError*), so they can be considered "true" constants.

3.1 Constants added by the site module

The *site* module (which is imported automatically during startup, except if the -S command-line option is given) adds several constants to the built-in namespace. They are useful for the interactive interpreter shell and should not be used in programs.

quit(*code=None*)
exit(*code=None*)
Objects that when printed, print a message like "Use quit() or Ctrl-D (i.e. EOF) to exit", and when called, raise *SystemExit* with the specified exit code.

copyright
license
credits
Objects that when printed, print a message like "Type license() to see the full license text", and when called, display the corresponding text in a pager-like fashion (one screen at a time).

CHAPTER

FOUR

BUILT-IN TYPES

The following sections describe the standard types that are built into the interpreter.

The principal built-in types are numerics, sequences, mappings, classes, instances and exceptions.

Some collection classes are mutable. The methods that add, subtract, or rearrange their members in place, and don't return a specific item, never return the collection instance itself but `None`.

Some operations are supported by several object types; in particular, practically all objects can be compared, tested for truth value, and converted to a string (with the *repr()* function or the slightly different *str()* function). The latter function is implicitly used when an object is written by the *print()* function.

4.1 Truth Value Testing

Any object can be tested for truth value, for use in an `if` or `while` condition or as operand of the Boolean operations below.

By default, an object is considered true unless its class defines either a `__bool__()` method that returns `False` or a `__len__()` method that returns zero, when called with the object.[1] Here are most of the built-in objects considered false:

- constants defined to be false: `None` and `False`.
- zero of any numeric type: `0`, `0.0`, `0j`, `Decimal(0)`, `Fraction(0, 1)`
- empty sequences and collections: `''`, `()`, `[]`, `{}`, `set()`, `range(0)`

Operations and built-in functions that have a Boolean result always return `0` or `False` for false and `1` or `True` for true, unless otherwise stated. (Important exception: the Boolean operations `or` and `and` always return one of their operands.)

4.2 Boolean Operations — `and`, `or`, `not`

These are the Boolean operations, ordered by ascending priority:

Operation	Result	Notes
`x or y`	if x is false, then y, else x	(1)
`x and y`	if x is false, then x, else y	(2)
`not x`	if x is false, then `True`, else `False`	(3)

Notes:

[1] Additional information on these special methods may be found in the Python Reference Manual (customization).

1. This is a short-circuit operator, so it only evaluates the second argument if the first one is false.
2. This is a short-circuit operator, so it only evaluates the second argument if the first one is true.
3. `not` has a lower priority than non-Boolean operators, so `not a == b` is interpreted as `not (a == b)`, and `a == not b` is a syntax error.

4.3 Comparisons

There are eight comparison operations in Python. They all have the same priority (which is higher than that of the Boolean operations). Comparisons can be chained arbitrarily; for example, `x < y <= z` is equivalent to `x < y and y <= z`, except that *y* is evaluated only once (but in both cases *z* is not evaluated at all when `x < y` is found to be false).

This table summarizes the comparison operations:

Operation	Meaning
`<`	strictly less than
`<=`	less than or equal
`>`	strictly greater than
`>=`	greater than or equal
`==`	equal
`!=`	not equal
`is`	object identity
`is not`	negated object identity

Objects of different types, except different numeric types, never compare equal. Furthermore, some types (for example, function objects) support only a degenerate notion of comparison where any two objects of that type are unequal. The `<`, `<=`, `>` and `>=` operators will raise a *TypeError* exception when comparing a complex number with another built-in numeric type, when the objects are of different types that cannot be compared, or in other cases where there is no defined ordering.

Non-identical instances of a class normally compare as non-equal unless the class defines the `__eq__()` method.

Instances of a class cannot be ordered with respect to other instances of the same class, or other types of object, unless the class defines enough of the methods `__lt__()`, `__le__()`, `__gt__()`, and `__ge__()` (in general, `__lt__()` and `__eq__()` are sufficient, if you want the conventional meanings of the comparison operators).

The behavior of the `is` and `is not` operators cannot be customized; also they can be applied to any two objects and never raise an exception.

Two more operations with the same syntactic priority, `in` and `not in`, are supported only by sequence types (below).

4.4 Numeric Types — `int`, `float`, `complex`

There are three distinct numeric types: *integers*, *floating point numbers*, and *complex numbers*. In addition, Booleans are a subtype of integers. Integers have unlimited precision. Floating point numbers are usually implemented using `double` in C; information about the precision and internal representation of floating point numbers for the machine on which your program is running is available in *sys.float_info*. Complex numbers have a real and imaginary part, which are each a floating point number. To extract these parts from a complex number *z*, use `z.real` and `z.imag`. (The standard library includes additional numeric types, *fractions* that hold rationals, and *decimal* that hold floating-point numbers with user-definable precision.)

Numbers are created by numeric literals or as the result of built-in functions and operators. Unadorned integer literals (including hex, octal and binary numbers) yield integers. Numeric literals containing a decimal point or an exponent sign yield floating point numbers. Appending `'j'` or `'J'` to a numeric literal yields an imaginary number (a complex number with a zero real part) which you can add to an integer or float to get a complex number with real and imaginary parts.

Python fully supports mixed arithmetic: when a binary arithmetic operator has operands of different numeric types, the operand with the "narrower" type is widened to that of the other, where integer is narrower than floating point, which is narrower than complex. Comparisons between numbers of mixed type use the same rule.[2] The constructors *int()*, *float()*, and *complex()* can be used to produce numbers of a specific type.

All numeric types (except complex) support the following operations, sorted by ascending priority (all numeric operations have a higher priority than comparison operations):

Operation	Result	Notes	Full documentation
`x + y`	sum of *x* and *y*		
`x - y`	difference of *x* and *y*		
`x * y`	product of *x* and *y*		
`x / y`	quotient of *x* and *y*		
`x // y`	floored quotient of *x* and *y*	(1)	
`x % y`	remainder of `x / y`	(2)	
`-x`	*x* negated		
`+x`	*x* unchanged		
`abs(x)`	absolute value or magnitude of *x*		*abs()*
`int(x)`	*x* converted to integer	(3)(6)	*int()*
`float(x)`	*x* converted to floating point	(4)(6)	*float()*
`complex(re, im)`	a complex number with real part *re*, imaginary part *im*. *im* defaults to zero.	(6)	*complex()*
`c.conjugate()`	conjugate of the complex number *c*		
`divmod(x, y)`	the pair `(x // y, x % y)`	(2)	*divmod()*
`pow(x, y)`	*x* to the power *y*	(5)	*pow()*
`x ** y`	*x* to the power *y*	(5)	

Notes:

1. Also referred to as integer division. The resultant value is a whole integer, though the result's type is not necessarily int. The result is always rounded towards minus infinity: `1//2` is `0`, `(-1)//2` is `-1`, `1//(-2)` is `-1`, and `(-1)//(-2)` is `0`.
2. Not for complex numbers. Instead convert to floats using *abs()* if appropriate.
3. Conversion from floating point to integer may round or truncate as in C; see functions *math.floor()* and *math.ceil()* for well-defined conversions.
4. float also accepts the strings "nan" and "inf" with an optional prefix "+" or "-" for Not a Number (NaN) and positive or negative infinity.
5. Python defines `pow(0, 0)` and `0 ** 0` to be `1`, as is common for programming languages.
6. The numeric literals accepted include the digits `0` to `9` or any Unicode equivalent (code points with the `Nd` property).

[2] As a consequence, the list `[1, 2]` is considered equal to `[1.0, 2.0]`, and similarly for tuples.

See http://www.unicode.org/Public/9.0.0/ucd/extracted/DerivedNumericType.txt for a complete list of code points with the Nd property.

All *numbers.Real* types (*int* and *float*) also include the following operations:

Operation	Result
math.trunc(x)	x truncated to *Integral*
round(x[, n])	x rounded to n digits, rounding half to even. If n is omitted, it defaults to 0.
math.floor(x)	the greatest *Integral* <= x
math.ceil(x)	the least *Integral* >= x

For additional numeric operations see the *math* and *cmath* modules.

4.4.1 Bitwise Operations on Integer Types

Bitwise operations only make sense for integers. Negative numbers are treated as their 2's complement value (this assumes that there are enough bits so that no overflow occurs during the operation).

The priorities of the binary bitwise operations are all lower than the numeric operations and higher than the comparisons; the unary operation ~ has the same priority as the other unary numeric operations (+ and -).

This table lists the bitwise operations sorted in ascending priority:

Operation	Result	Notes
x | y	bitwise *or* of x and y	
x ^ y	bitwise *exclusive or* of x and y	
x & y	bitwise *and* of x and y	
x << n	x shifted left by n bits	(1)(2)
x >> n	x shifted right by n bits	(1)(3)
~x	the bits of x inverted	

Notes:

1. Negative shift counts are illegal and cause a *ValueError* to be raised.
2. A left shift by n bits is equivalent to multiplication by pow(2, n) without overflow check.
3. A right shift by n bits is equivalent to division by pow(2, n) without overflow check.

4.4.2 Additional Methods on Integer Types

The int type implements the *numbers.Integral abstract base class*. In addition, it provides a few more methods:

int.bit_length()

Return the number of bits necessary to represent an integer in binary, excluding the sign and leading zeros:

```
>>> n = -37
>>> bin(n)
'-0b100101'
>>> n.bit_length()
6
```

More precisely, if `x` is nonzero, then `x.bit_length()` is the unique positive integer `k` such that `2**(k-1) <= abs(x) < 2**k`. Equivalently, when `abs(x)` is small enough to have a correctly rounded logarithm, then `k = 1 + int(log(abs(x), 2))`. If `x` is zero, then `x.bit_length()` returns `0`.

Equivalent to:

```
def bit_length(self):
    s = bin(self)       # binary representation:  bin(-37) --> '-0b100101'
    s = s.lstrip('-0b') # remove leading zeros and minus sign
    return len(s)       # len('100101') --> 6
```

New in version 3.1.

int.to_bytes(*length, byteorder, *, signed=False*)

Return an array of bytes representing an integer.

```
>>> (1024).to_bytes(2, byteorder='big')
b'\x04\x00'
>>> (1024).to_bytes(10, byteorder='big')
b'\x00\x00\x00\x00\x00\x00\x00\x00\x04\x00'
>>> (-1024).to_bytes(10, byteorder='big', signed=True)
b'\xff\xff\xff\xff\xff\xff\xff\xff\xfc\x00'
>>> x = 1000
>>> x.to_bytes((x.bit_length() + 7) // 8, byteorder='little')
b'\xe8\x03'
```

The integer is represented using *length* bytes. An `OverflowError` is raised if the integer is not representable with the given number of bytes.

The *byteorder* argument determines the byte order used to represent the integer. If *byteorder* is `"big"`, the most significant byte is at the beginning of the byte array. If *byteorder* is `"little"`, the most significant byte is at the end of the byte array. To request the native byte order of the host system, use `sys.byteorder` as the byte order value.

The *signed* argument determines whether two's complement is used to represent the integer. If *signed* is `False` and a negative integer is given, an `OverflowError` is raised. The default value for *signed* is `False`.

New in version 3.2.

classmethod int.from_bytes(*bytes, byteorder, *, signed=False*)

Return the integer represented by the given array of bytes.

```
>>> int.from_bytes(b'\x00\x10', byteorder='big')
16
>>> int.from_bytes(b'\x00\x10', byteorder='little')
4096
>>> int.from_bytes(b'\xfc\x00', byteorder='big', signed=True)
-1024
>>> int.from_bytes(b'\xfc\x00', byteorder='big', signed=False)
64512
>>> int.from_bytes([255, 0, 0], byteorder='big')
16711680
```

The argument *bytes* must either be a *bytes-like object* or an iterable producing bytes.

The *byteorder* argument determines the byte order used to represent the integer. If *byteorder* is `"big"`, the most significant byte is at the beginning of the byte array. If *byteorder* is `"little"`, the most significant byte is at the end of the byte array. To request the native byte order of the host system, use `sys.byteorder` as the byte order value.

The *signed* argument indicates whether two's complement is used to represent the integer.

New in version 3.2.

4.4.3 Additional Methods on Float

The float type implements the *numbers.Real abstract base class*. float also has the following additional methods.

float.as_integer_ratio()
Return a pair of integers whose ratio is exactly equal to the original float and with a positive denominator. Raises *OverflowError* on infinities and a *ValueError* on NaNs.

float.is_integer()
Return `True` if the float instance is finite with integral value, and `False` otherwise:

```
>>> (-2.0).is_integer()
True
>>> (3.2).is_integer()
False
```

Two methods support conversion to and from hexadecimal strings. Since Python's floats are stored internally as binary numbers, converting a float to or from a *decimal* string usually involves a small rounding error. In contrast, hexadecimal strings allow exact representation and specification of floating-point numbers. This can be useful when debugging, and in numerical work.

float.hex()
Return a representation of a floating-point number as a hexadecimal string. For finite floating-point numbers, this representation will always include a leading `0x` and a trailing `p` and exponent.

classmethod float.fromhex(*s*)
Class method to return the float represented by a hexadecimal string *s*. The string *s* may have leading and trailing whitespace.

Note that *float.hex()* is an instance method, while *float.fromhex()* is a class method.

A hexadecimal string takes the form:

```
[sign] ['0x'] integer ['.' fraction] ['p' exponent]
```

where the optional `sign` may by either `+` or `-`, `integer` and `fraction` are strings of hexadecimal digits, and `exponent` is a decimal integer with an optional leading sign. Case is not significant, and there must be at least one hexadecimal digit in either the integer or the fraction. This syntax is similar to the syntax specified in section 6.4.4.2 of the C99 standard, and also to the syntax used in Java 1.5 onwards. In particular, the output of *float.hex()* is usable as a hexadecimal floating-point literal in C or Java code, and hexadecimal strings produced by C's `%a` format character or Java's `Double.toHexString` are accepted by *float.fromhex()*.

Note that the exponent is written in decimal rather than hexadecimal, and that it gives the power of 2 by which to multiply the coefficient. For example, the hexadecimal string `0x3.a7p10` represents the floating-point number `(3 + 10./16 + 7./16**2) * 2.0**10`, or `3740.0`:

```
>>> float.fromhex('0x3.a7p10')
3740.0
```

Applying the reverse conversion to `3740.0` gives a different hexadecimal string representing the same number:

```
>>> float.hex(3740.0)
'0x1.d380000000000p+11'
```

4.4.4 Hashing of numeric types

For numbers `x` and `y`, possibly of different types, it's a requirement that `hash(x) == hash(y)` whenever `x == y` (see the `__hash__()` method documentation for more details). For ease of implementation and efficiency across a variety of numeric types (including *int*, *float*, *decimal.Decimal* and *fractions.Fraction*) Python's hash for numeric types is based on a single mathematical function that's defined for any rational number, and hence applies to all instances of *int* and *fractions.Fraction*, and all finite instances of *float* and *decimal.Decimal*. Essentially, this function is given by reduction modulo `P` for a fixed prime `P`. The value of `P` is made available to Python as the `modulus` attribute of *sys.hash_info*.

CPython implementation detail: Currently, the prime used is `P = 2**31 - 1` on machines with 32-bit C longs and `P = 2**61 - 1` on machines with 64-bit C longs.

Here are the rules in detail:

- If `x = m / n` is a nonnegative rational number and `n` is not divisible by `P`, define `hash(x)` as `m * invmod(n, P) % P`, where `invmod(n, P)` gives the inverse of `n` modulo `P`.
- If `x = m / n` is a nonnegative rational number and `n` is divisible by `P` (but `m` is not) then `n` has no inverse modulo `P` and the rule above doesn't apply; in this case define `hash(x)` to be the constant value `sys.hash_info.inf`.
- If `x = m / n` is a negative rational number define `hash(x)` as `-hash(-x)`. If the resulting hash is `-1`, replace it with `-2`.
- The particular values `sys.hash_info.inf`, `-sys.hash_info.inf` and `sys.hash_info.nan` are used as hash values for positive infinity, negative infinity, or nans (respectively). (All hashable nans have the same hash value.)
- For a *complex* number `z`, the hash values of the real and imaginary parts are combined by computing `hash(z.real) + sys.hash_info.imag * hash(z.imag)`, reduced modulo `2**sys.hash_info.width` so that it lies in `range(-2**(sys.hash_info.width - 1), 2**(sys.hash_info.width - 1))`. Again, if the result is `-1`, it's replaced with `-2`.

To clarify the above rules, here's some example Python code, equivalent to the built-in hash, for computing the hash of a rational number, *float*, or *complex*:

```
import sys, math

def hash_fraction(m, n):
    """Compute the hash of a rational number m / n.

    Assumes m and n are integers, with n positive.
    Equivalent to hash(fractions.Fraction(m, n)).

    """
    P = sys.hash_info.modulus
    # Remove common factors of P.  (Unnecessary if m and n already coprime.)
    while m % P == n % P == 0:
        m, n = m // P, n // P

    if n % P == 0:
        hash_value = sys.hash_info.inf
    else:
        # Fermat's Little Theorem: pow(n, P-1, P) is 1, so
        # pow(n, P-2, P) gives the inverse of n modulo P.
        hash_value = (abs(m) % P) * pow(n, P - 2, P) % P
    if m < 0:
        hash_value = -hash_value
    if hash_value == -1:
        hash_value = -2
```

```
    return hash_value

def hash_float(x):
    """Compute the hash of a float x."""

    if math.isnan(x):
        return sys.hash_info.nan
    elif math.isinf(x):
        return sys.hash_info.inf if x > 0 else -sys.hash_info.inf
    else:
        return hash_fraction(*x.as_integer_ratio())

def hash_complex(z):
    """Compute the hash of a complex number z."""

    hash_value = hash_float(z.real) + sys.hash_info.imag * hash_float(z.imag)
    # do a signed reduction modulo 2**sys.hash_info.width
    M = 2**(sys.hash_info.width - 1)
    hash_value = (hash_value & (M - 1)) - (hash_value & M)
    if hash_value == -1:
        hash_value = -2
    return hash_value
```

4.5 Iterator Types

Python supports a concept of iteration over containers. This is implemented using two distinct methods; these are used to allow user-defined classes to support iteration. Sequences, described below in more detail, always support the iteration methods.

One method needs to be defined for container objects to provide iteration support:

`container.__iter__()`
: Return an iterator object. The object is required to support the iterator protocol described below. If a container supports different types of iteration, additional methods can be provided to specifically request iterators for those iteration types. (An example of an object supporting multiple forms of iteration would be a tree structure which supports both breadth-first and depth-first traversal.) This method corresponds to the `tp_iter` slot of the type structure for Python objects in the Python/C API.

The iterator objects themselves are required to support the following two methods, which together form the *iterator protocol*:

`iterator.__iter__()`
: Return the iterator object itself. This is required to allow both containers and iterators to be used with the `for` and `in` statements. This method corresponds to the `tp_iter` slot of the type structure for Python objects in the Python/C API.

`iterator.__next__()`
: Return the next item from the container. If there are no further items, raise the *StopIteration* exception. This method corresponds to the `tp_iternext` slot of the type structure for Python objects in the Python/C API.

Python defines several iterator objects to support iteration over general and specific sequence types, dictionaries, and other more specialized forms. The specific types are not important beyond their implementation of the iterator protocol.

Once an iterator's *__next__()* method raises *StopIteration*, it must continue to do so on subsequent calls. Implementations that do not obey this property are deemed broken.

4.5.1 Generator Types

Python's *generators* provide a convenient way to implement the iterator protocol. If a container object's `__iter__()` method is implemented as a generator, it will automatically return an iterator object (technically, a generator object) supplying the `__iter__()` and `__next__()` methods. More information about generators can be found in the documentation for the yield expression.

4.6 Sequence Types — list, tuple, range

There are three basic sequence types: lists, tuples, and range objects. Additional sequence types tailored for processing of *binary data* and *text strings* are described in dedicated sections.

4.6.1 Common Sequence Operations

The operations in the following table are supported by most sequence types, both mutable and immutable. The *collections.abc.Sequence* ABC is provided to make it easier to correctly implement these operations on custom sequence types.

This table lists the sequence operations sorted in ascending priority. In the table, s and t are sequences of the same type, n, i, j and k are integers and x is an arbitrary object that meets any type and value restrictions imposed by s.

The `in` and `not in` operations have the same priorities as the comparison operations. The `+` (concatenation) and `*` (repetition) operations have the same priority as the corresponding numeric operations.[3]

Operation	Result	Notes
`x in s`	`True` if an item of s is equal to x, else `False`	(1)
`x not in s`	`False` if an item of s is equal to x, else `True`	(1)
`s + t`	the concatenation of s and t	(6)(7)
`s * n` or `n * s`	equivalent to adding s to itself n times	(2)(7)
`s[i]`	ith item of s, origin 0	(3)
`s[i:j]`	slice of s from i to j	(3)(4)
`s[i:j:k]`	slice of s from i to j with step k	(3)(5)
`len(s)`	length of s	
`min(s)`	smallest item of s	
`max(s)`	largest item of s	
`s.index(x[, i[, j]])`	index of the first occurrence of x in s (at or after index i and before index j)	(8)
`s.count(x)`	total number of occurrences of x in s	

Sequences of the same type also support comparisons. In particular, tuples and lists are compared lexicographically by comparing corresponding elements. This means that to compare equal, every element must compare equal and the two sequences must be of the same type and have the same length. (For full details see comparisons in the language reference.)

Notes:

[3] They must have since the parser can't tell the type of the operands.

1. While the `in` and `not in` operations are used only for simple containment testing in the general case, some specialised sequences (such as *str*, *bytes* and *bytearray*) also use them for subsequence testing:

```
>>> "gg" in "eggs"
True
```

2. Values of *n* less than `0` are treated as `0` (which yields an empty sequence of the same type as *s*). Note that items in the sequence *s* are not copied; they are referenced multiple times. This often haunts new Python programmers; consider:

```
>>> lists = [[]] * 3
>>> lists
[[], [], []]
>>> lists[0].append(3)
>>> lists
[[3], [3], [3]]
```

   What has happened is that `[[]]` is a one-element list containing an empty list, so all three elements of `[[]] * 3` are references to this single empty list. Modifying any of the elements of `lists` modifies this single list. You can create a list of different lists this way:

```
>>> lists = [[] for i in range(3)]
>>> lists[0].append(3)
>>> lists[1].append(5)
>>> lists[2].append(7)
>>> lists
[[3], [5], [7]]
```

   Further explanation is available in the FAQ entry faq-multidimensional-list.

3. If *i* or *j* is negative, the index is relative to the end of sequence *s*: `len(s) + i` or `len(s) + j` is substituted. But note that `-0` is still `0`.

4. The slice of *s* from *i* to *j* is defined as the sequence of items with index *k* such that `i <= k < j`. If *i* or *j* is greater than `len(s)`, use `len(s)`. If *i* is omitted or `None`, use `0`. If *j* is omitted or `None`, use `len(s)`. If *i* is greater than or equal to *j*, the slice is empty.

5. The slice of *s* from *i* to *j* with step *k* is defined as the sequence of items with index `x = i + n*k` such that `0 <= n < (j-i)/k`. In other words, the indices are `i`, `i+k`, `i+2*k`, `i+3*k` and so on, stopping when *j* is reached (but never including *j*). When *k* is positive, *i* and *j* are reduced to `len(s)` if they are greater. When *k* is negative, *i* and *j* are reduced to `len(s) - 1` if they are greater. If *i* or *j* are omitted or `None`, they become "end" values (which end depends on the sign of *k*). Note, *k* cannot be zero. If *k* is `None`, it is treated like `1`.

6. Concatenating immutable sequences always results in a new object. This means that building up a sequence by repeated concatenation will have a quadratic runtime cost in the total sequence length. To get a linear runtime cost, you must switch to one of the alternatives below:

   - if concatenating *str* objects, you can build a list and use *str.join()* at the end or else write to an *io.StringIO* instance and retrieve its value when complete
   - if concatenating *bytes* objects, you can similarly use *bytes.join()* or *io.BytesIO*, or you can do in-place concatenation with a *bytearray* object. *bytearray* objects are mutable and have an efficient overallocation mechanism
   - if concatenating *tuple* objects, extend a *list* instead
   - for other types, investigate the relevant class documentation

7. Some sequence types (such as *range*) only support item sequences that follow specific patterns, and hence don't support sequence concatenation or repetition.

8. `index` raises *ValueError* when x is not found in s. Not all implementations support passing the additional arguments i and j. These arguments allow efficient searching of subsections of the sequence. Passing the extra arguments is roughly equivalent to using `s[i:j].index(x)`, only without copying any data and with the returned index being relative to the start of the sequence rather than the start of the slice.

4.6.2 Immutable Sequence Types

The only operation that immutable sequence types generally implement that is not also implemented by mutable sequence types is support for the *hash()* built-in.

This support allows immutable sequences, such as *tuple* instances, to be used as *dict* keys and stored in *set* and *frozenset* instances.

Attempting to hash an immutable sequence that contains unhashable values will result in *TypeError*.

4.6.3 Mutable Sequence Types

The operations in the following table are defined on mutable sequence types. The *collections.abc.MutableSequence* ABC is provided to make it easier to correctly implement these operations on custom sequence types.

In the table s is an instance of a mutable sequence type, t is any iterable object and x is an arbitrary object that meets any type and value restrictions imposed by s (for example, *bytearray* only accepts integers that meet the value restriction `0 <= x <= 255`).

Operation	Result	Notes
`s[i] = x`	item i of s is replaced by x	
`s[i:j] = t`	slice of s from i to j is replaced by the contents of the iterable t	
`del s[i:j]`	same as `s[i:j] = []`	
`s[i:j:k] = t`	the elements of `s[i:j:k]` are replaced by those of t	(1)
`del s[i:j:k]`	removes the elements of `s[i:j:k]` from the list	
`s.append(x)`	appends x to the end of the sequence (same as `s[len(s):len(s)] = [x]`)	
`s.clear()`	removes all items from `s` (same as `del s[:]`)	(5)
`s.copy()`	creates a shallow copy of `s` (same as `s[:]`)	(5)
`s.extend(t)` or `s += t`	extends s with the contents of t (for the most part the same as `s[len(s):len(s)] = t`)	
`s *= n`	updates s with its contents repeated n times	(6)
`s.insert(i, x)`	inserts x into s at the index given by i (same as `s[i:i] = [x]`)	
`s.pop([i])`	retrieves the item at i and also removes it from s	(2)
`s.remove(x)`	remove the first item from s where `s[i] == x`	(3)
`s.reverse()`	reverses the items of s in place	(4)

Notes:

1. t must have the same length as the slice it is replacing.
2. The optional argument i defaults to `-1`, so that by default the last item is removed and returned.
3. `remove` raises *ValueError* when x is not found in s.
4. The `reverse()` method modifies the sequence in place for economy of space when reversing a large sequence. To remind users that it operates by side effect, it does not return the reversed sequence.
5. `clear()` and `copy()` are included for consistency with the interfaces of mutable containers that don't support slicing operations (such as *dict* and *set*)

New in version 3.3: `clear()` and `copy()` methods.

6. The value *n* is an integer, or an object implementing `__index__()`. Zero and negative values of *n* clear the sequence. Items in the sequence are not copied; they are referenced multiple times, as explained for `s * n` under *Common Sequence Operations*.

4.6.4 Lists

Lists are mutable sequences, typically used to store collections of homogeneous items (where the precise degree of similarity will vary by application).

class list([*iterable*])

Lists may be constructed in several ways:

- Using a pair of square brackets to denote the empty list: `[]`
- Using square brackets, separating items with commas: `[a]`, `[a, b, c]`
- Using a list comprehension: `[x for x in iterable]`
- Using the type constructor: `list()` or `list(iterable)`

The constructor builds a list whose items are the same and in the same order as *iterable*'s items. *iterable* may be either a sequence, a container that supports iteration, or an iterator object. If *iterable* is already a list, a copy is made and returned, similar to `iterable[:]`. For example, `list('abc')` returns `['a', 'b', 'c']` and `list( (1, 2, 3) )` returns `[1, 2, 3]`. If no argument is given, the constructor creates a new empty list, `[]`.

Many other operations also produce lists, including the `sorted()` built-in.

Lists implement all of the *common* and *mutable* sequence operations. Lists also provide the following additional method:

sort(*, *key=None*, *reverse=False*)

This method sorts the list in place, using only `<` comparisons between items. Exceptions are not suppressed - if any comparison operations fail, the entire sort operation will fail (and the list will likely be left in a partially modified state).

`sort()` accepts two arguments that can only be passed by keyword (*keyword-only arguments*):

key specifies a function of one argument that is used to extract a comparison key from each list element (for example, `key=str.lower`). The key corresponding to each item in the list is calculated once and then used for the entire sorting process. The default value of `None` means that list items are sorted directly without calculating a separate key value.

The `functools.cmp_to_key()` utility is available to convert a 2.x style *cmp* function to a *key* function.

reverse is a boolean value. If set to `True`, then the list elements are sorted as if each comparison were reversed.

This method modifies the sequence in place for economy of space when sorting a large sequence. To remind users that it operates by side effect, it does not return the sorted sequence (use `sorted()` to explicitly request a new sorted list instance).

The `sort()` method is guaranteed to be stable. A sort is stable if it guarantees not to change the relative order of elements that compare equal — this is helpful for sorting in multiple passes (for example, sort by department, then by salary grade).

CPython implementation detail: While a list is being sorted, the effect of attempting to mutate, or even inspect, the list is undefined. The C implementation of Python makes the list appear empty for the duration, and raises `ValueError` if it can detect that the list has been mutated during a sort.

4.6.5 Tuples

Tuples are immutable sequences, typically used to store collections of heterogeneous data (such as the 2-tuples produced by the *enumerate()* built-in). Tuples are also used for cases where an immutable sequence of homogeneous data is needed (such as allowing storage in a *set* or *dict* instance).

class tuple([*iterable*])

Tuples may be constructed in a number of ways:

- Using a pair of parentheses to denote the empty tuple: `()`
- Using a trailing comma for a singleton tuple: `a,` or `(a,)`
- Separating items with commas: `a, b, c` or `(a, b, c)`
- Using the *tuple()* built-in: `tuple()` or `tuple(iterable)`

The constructor builds a tuple whose items are the same and in the same order as *iterable*'s items. *iterable* may be either a sequence, a container that supports iteration, or an iterator object. If *iterable* is already a tuple, it is returned unchanged. For example, `tuple('abc')` returns `('a', 'b', 'c')` and `tuple( [1, 2, 3] )` returns `(1, 2, 3)`. If no argument is given, the constructor creates a new empty tuple, `()`.

Note that it is actually the comma which makes a tuple, not the parentheses. The parentheses are optional, except in the empty tuple case, or when they are needed to avoid syntactic ambiguity. For example, `f(a, b, c)` is a function call with three arguments, while `f((a, b, c))` is a function call with a 3-tuple as the sole argument.

Tuples implement all of the *common* sequence operations.

For heterogeneous collections of data where access by name is clearer than access by index, *collections.namedtuple()* may be a more appropriate choice than a simple tuple object.

4.6.6 Ranges

The *range* type represents an immutable sequence of numbers and is commonly used for looping a specific number of times in `for` loops.

class range(*stop*)

class range(*start*, *stop*[, *step*])

The arguments to the range constructor must be integers (either built-in *int* or any object that implements the `__index__` special method). If the *step* argument is omitted, it defaults to `1`. If the *start* argument is omitted, it defaults to `0`. If *step* is zero, *ValueError* is raised.

For a positive *step*, the contents of a range `r` are determined by the formula `r[i] = start + step*i` where `i >= 0` and `r[i] < stop`.

For a negative *step*, the contents of the range are still determined by the formula `r[i] = start + step*i`, but the constraints are `i >= 0` and `r[i] > stop`.

A range object will be empty if `r[0]` does not meet the value constraint. Ranges do support negative indices, but these are interpreted as indexing from the end of the sequence determined by the positive indices.

Ranges containing absolute values larger than *sys.maxsize* are permitted but some features (such as *len()*) may raise *OverflowError*.

Range examples:

```
>>> list(range(10))
[0, 1, 2, 3, 4, 5, 6, 7, 8, 9]
>>> list(range(1, 11))
```

```
[1, 2, 3, 4, 5, 6, 7, 8, 9, 10]
>>> list(range(0, 30, 5))
[0, 5, 10, 15, 20, 25]
>>> list(range(0, 10, 3))
[0, 3, 6, 9]
>>> list(range(0, -10, -1))
[0, -1, -2, -3, -4, -5, -6, -7, -8, -9]
>>> list(range(0))
[]
>>> list(range(1, 0))
[]
```

Ranges implement all of the *common* sequence operations except concatenation and repetition (due to the fact that range objects can only represent sequences that follow a strict pattern and repetition and concatenation will usually violate that pattern).

start
The value of the *start* parameter (or `0` if the parameter was not supplied)

stop
The value of the *stop* parameter

step
The value of the *step* parameter (or `1` if the parameter was not supplied)

The advantage of the `range` type over a regular `list` or `tuple` is that a `range` object will always take the same (small) amount of memory, no matter the size of the range it represents (as it only stores the `start`, `stop` and `step` values, calculating individual items and subranges as needed).

Range objects implement the `collections.abc.Sequence` ABC, and provide features such as containment tests, element index lookup, slicing and support for negative indices (see *Sequence Types — list, tuple, range*):

```
>>> r = range(0, 20, 2)
>>> r
range(0, 20, 2)
>>> 11 in r
False
>>> 10 in r
True
>>> r.index(10)
5
>>> r[5]
10
>>> r[:5]
range(0, 10, 2)
>>> r[-1]
18
```

Testing range objects for equality with `==` and `!=` compares them as sequences. That is, two range objects are considered equal if they represent the same sequence of values. (Note that two range objects that compare equal might have different `start`, `stop` and `step` attributes, for example `range(0) == range(2, 1, 3)` or `range(0, 3, 2) == range(0, 4, 2)`.)

Changed in version 3.2: Implement the Sequence ABC. Support slicing and negative indices. Test `int` objects for membership in constant time instead of iterating through all items.

Changed in version 3.3: Define '==' and '!=' to compare range objects based on the sequence of values they define (instead of comparing based on object identity).

New in version 3.3: The `start`, `stop` and `step` attributes.

See also:

- The linspace recipe shows how to implement a lazy version of range that suitable for floating point applications.

4.7 Text Sequence Type — `str`

Textual data in Python is handled with `str` objects, or *strings*. Strings are immutable *sequences* of Unicode code points. String literals are written in a variety of ways:

- Single quotes: `'allows embedded "double" quotes'`
- Double quotes: `"allows embedded 'single' quotes"`.
- Triple quoted: `'''Three single quotes'''`, `"""Three double quotes"""`

Triple quoted strings may span multiple lines - all associated whitespace will be included in the string literal.

String literals that are part of a single expression and have only whitespace between them will be implicitly converted to a single string literal. That is, `("spam " "eggs") == "spam eggs"`.

See strings for more about the various forms of string literal, including supported escape sequences, and the `r` ("raw") prefix that disables most escape sequence processing.

Strings may also be created from other objects using the `str` constructor.

Since there is no separate "character" type, indexing a string produces strings of length 1. That is, for a non-empty string *s*, `s[0] == s[0:1]`.

There is also no mutable string type, but `str.join()` or `io.StringIO` can be used to efficiently construct strings from multiple fragments.

Changed in version 3.3: For backwards compatibility with the Python 2 series, the `u` prefix is once again permitted on string literals. It has no effect on the meaning of string literals and cannot be combined with the `r` prefix.

class str(*object=''*)
class str(*object=b'', encoding='utf-8', errors='strict'*)

Return a *string* version of *object*. If *object* is not provided, returns the empty string. Otherwise, the behavior of `str()` depends on whether *encoding* or *errors* is given, as follows.

If neither *encoding* nor *errors* is given, `str(object)` returns `object.__str__()`, which is the "informal" or nicely printable string representation of *object*. For string objects, this is the string itself. If *object* does not have a `__str__()` method, then `str()` falls back to returning `repr(object)`.

If at least one of *encoding* or *errors* is given, *object* should be a *bytes-like object* (e.g. `bytes` or `bytearray`). In this case, if *object* is a `bytes` (or `bytearray`) object, then `str(bytes, encoding, errors)` is equivalent to `bytes.decode(encoding, errors)`. Otherwise, the bytes object underlying the buffer object is obtained before calling `bytes.decode()`. See *Binary Sequence Types — bytes, bytearray, memoryview* and bufferobjects for information on buffer objects.

Passing a `bytes` object to `str()` without the *encoding* or *errors* arguments falls under the first case of returning the informal string representation (see also the `-b` command-line option to Python). For example:

```
>>> str(b'Zoot!')
"b'Zoot!'"
```

For more information on the `str` class and its methods, see *Text Sequence Type — str* and the *String Methods* section below. To output formatted strings, see the f-strings and *Format String Syntax* sections. In addition, see the *Text Processing Services* section.

4.7.1 String Methods

Strings implement all of the *common* sequence operations, along with the additional methods described below.

Strings also support two styles of string formatting, one providing a large degree of flexibility and customization (see `str.format()`, *Format String Syntax* and *Custom String Formatting*) and the other based on C **printf** style formatting that handles a narrower range of types and is slightly harder to use correctly, but is often faster for the cases it can handle (*printf-style String Formatting*).

The *Text Processing Services* section of the standard library covers a number of other modules that provide various text related utilities (including regular expression support in the *re* module).

str.capitalize()
Return a copy of the string with its first character capitalized and the rest lowercased.

str.casefold()
Return a casefolded copy of the string. Casefolded strings may be used for caseless matching.

Casefolding is similar to lowercasing but more aggressive because it is intended to remove all case distinctions in a string. For example, the German lowercase letter `'ß'` is equivalent to `"ss"`. Since it is already lowercase, `lower()` would do nothing to `'ß'`; `casefold()` converts it to `"ss"`.

The casefolding algorithm is described in section 3.13 of the Unicode Standard.

New in version 3.3.

str.center(*width*[, *fillchar*])
Return centered in a string of length *width*. Padding is done using the specified *fillchar* (default is an ASCII space). The original string is returned if *width* is less than or equal to `len(s)`.

str.count(*sub*[, *start*[, *end*]])
Return the number of non-overlapping occurrences of substring *sub* in the range [*start*, *end*]. Optional arguments *start* and *end* are interpreted as in slice notation.

str.encode(*encoding="utf-8", errors="strict"*)
Return an encoded version of the string as a bytes object. Default encoding is `'utf-8'`. *errors* may be given to set a different error handling scheme. The default for *errors* is `'strict'`, meaning that encoding errors raise a `UnicodeError`. Other possible values are `'ignore'`, `'replace'`, `'xmlcharrefreplace'`, `'backslashreplace'` and any other name registered via `codecs.register_error()`, see section *Error Handlers*. For a list of possible encodings, see section *Standard Encodings*.

Changed in version 3.1: Support for keyword arguments added.

str.endswith(*suffix*[, *start*[, *end*]])
Return `True` if the string ends with the specified *suffix*, otherwise return `False`. *suffix* can also be a tuple of suffixes to look for. With optional *start*, test beginning at that position. With optional *end*, stop comparing at that position.

str.expandtabs(*tabsize=8*)
Return a copy of the string where all tab characters are replaced by one or more spaces, depending on the current column and the given tab size. Tab positions occur every *tabsize* characters (default is 8, giving tab positions at columns 0, 8, 16 and so on). To expand the string, the current column is set to zero and the string is examined character by character. If the character is a tab (`\t`), one or more space characters are inserted in the result until the current column is equal to the next tab position. (The tab character itself is not copied.) If the character is a newline (`\n`) or return (`\r`), it is copied and the current column is reset to zero. Any other character is copied unchanged and the current column is incremented by one regardless of how the character is represented when printed.

```
>>> '01\t012\t0123\t01234'.expandtabs()
'01      012     0123    01234'
>>> '01\t012\t0123\t01234'.expandtabs(4)
'01  012 0123    01234'
```

`str.find(sub[, start[, end]])`

Return the lowest index in the string where substring *sub* is found within the slice `s[start:end]`. Optional arguments *start* and *end* are interpreted as in slice notation. Return `-1` if *sub* is not found.

Note: The *find()* method should be used only if you need to know the position of *sub*. To check if *sub* is a substring or not, use the `in` operator:

```
>>> 'Py' in 'Python'
True
```

`str.format(*args, **kwargs)`

Perform a string formatting operation. The string on which this method is called can contain literal text or replacement fields delimited by braces `{}`. Each replacement field contains either the numeric index of a positional argument, or the name of a keyword argument. Returns a copy of the string where each replacement field is replaced with the string value of the corresponding argument.

```
>>> "The sum of 1 + 2 is {0}".format(1+2)
'The sum of 1 + 2 is 3'
```

See *Format String Syntax* for a description of the various formatting options that can be specified in format strings.

Note: When formatting a number (*int*, *float*, *float* and subclasses) with the `n` type (ex: `'{:n}'.format(1234)`), the function sets temporarily the `LC_CTYPE` locale to the `LC_NUMERIC` locale to decode `decimal_point` and `thousands_sep` fields of `localeconv()` if they are non-ASCII or longer than 1 byte, and the `LC_NUMERIC` locale is different than the `LC_CTYPE` locale. This temporary change affects other threads.

Changed in version 3.6.5: When formatting a number with the `n` type, the function sets temporarily the `LC_CTYPE` locale to the `LC_NUMERIC` locale in some cases.

`str.format_map(mapping)`

Similar to `str.format(**mapping)`, except that `mapping` is used directly and not copied to a *dict*. This is useful if for example `mapping` is a dict subclass:

```
>>> class Default(dict):
...     def __missing__(self, key):
...         return key
...
>>> '{name} was born in {country}'.format_map(Default(name='Guido'))
'Guido was born in country'
```

New in version 3.2.

`str.index(sub[, start[, end]])`

Like *find()*, but raise *ValueError* when the substring is not found.

`str.isalnum()`

Return true if all characters in the string are alphanumeric and there is at least one character, false otherwise. A character `c` is alphanumeric if one of the following returns `True`: `c.isalpha()`, `c.isdecimal()`, `c.isdigit()`, or `c.isnumeric()`.

`str.isalpha()`
Return true if all characters in the string are alphabetic and there is at least one character, false otherwise. Alphabetic characters are those characters defined in the Unicode character database as "Letter", i.e., those with general category property being one of "Lm", "Lt", "Lu", "Ll", or "Lo". Note that this is different from the "Alphabetic" property defined in the Unicode Standard.

`str.isdecimal()`
Return true if all characters in the string are decimal characters and there is at least one character, false otherwise. Decimal characters are those that can be used to form numbers in base 10, e.g. U+0660, ARABIC-INDIC DIGIT ZERO. Formally a decimal character is a character in the Unicode General Category "Nd".

`str.isdigit()`
Return true if all characters in the string are digits and there is at least one character, false otherwise. Digits include decimal characters and digits that need special handling, such as the compatibility superscript digits. This covers digits which cannot be used to form numbers in base 10, like the Kharosthi numbers. Formally, a digit is a character that has the property value Numeric_Type=Digit or Numeric_Type=Decimal.

`str.isidentifier()`
Return true if the string is a valid identifier according to the language definition, section identifiers.

Use *keyword.iskeyword()* to test for reserved identifiers such as `def` and `class`.

`str.islower()`
Return true if all cased characters[4] in the string are lowercase and there is at least one cased character, false otherwise.

`str.isnumeric()`
Return true if all characters in the string are numeric characters, and there is at least one character, false otherwise. Numeric characters include digit characters, and all characters that have the Unicode numeric value property, e.g. U+2155, VULGAR FRACTION ONE FIFTH. Formally, numeric characters are those with the property value Numeric_Type=Digit, Numeric_Type=Decimal or Numeric_Type=Numeric.

`str.isprintable()`
Return true if all characters in the string are printable or the string is empty, false otherwise. Non-printable characters are those characters defined in the Unicode character database as "Other" or "Separator", excepting the ASCII space (0x20) which is considered printable. (Note that printable characters in this context are those which should not be escaped when *repr()* is invoked on a string. It has no bearing on the handling of strings written to *sys.stdout* or *sys.stderr*.)

`str.isspace()`
Return true if there are only whitespace characters in the string and there is at least one character, false otherwise. Whitespace characters are those characters defined in the Unicode character database as "Other" or "Separator" and those with bidirectional property being one of "WS", "B", or "S".

`str.istitle()`
Return true if the string is a titlecased string and there is at least one character, for example uppercase characters may only follow uncased characters and lowercase characters only cased ones. Return false otherwise.

`str.isupper()`
Return true if all cased characters[4] in the string are uppercase and there is at least one cased character, false otherwise.

[4] Cased characters are those with general category property being one of "Lu" (Letter, uppercase), "Ll" (Letter, lowercase), or "Lt" (Letter, titlecase).

str.join(*iterable*)
Return a string which is the concatenation of the strings in *iterable*. A `TypeError` will be raised if there are any non-string values in *iterable*, including `bytes` objects. The separator between elements is the string providing this method.

str.ljust(*width*[, *fillchar*])
Return the string left justified in a string of length *width*. Padding is done using the specified *fillchar* (default is an ASCII space). The original string is returned if *width* is less than or equal to `len(s)`.

str.lower()
Return a copy of the string with all the cased characters[4] converted to lowercase.

The lowercasing algorithm used is described in section 3.13 of the Unicode Standard.

str.lstrip([*chars*])
Return a copy of the string with leading characters removed. The *chars* argument is a string specifying the set of characters to be removed. If omitted or `None`, the *chars* argument defaults to removing whitespace. The *chars* argument is not a prefix; rather, all combinations of its values are stripped:

```
>>> '   spacious   '.lstrip()
'spacious   '
>>> 'www.example.com'.lstrip('cmowz.')
'example.com'
```

static **str.maketrans**(*x*[, *y*[, *z*]])
This static method returns a translation table usable for `str.translate()`.

If there is only one argument, it must be a dictionary mapping Unicode ordinals (integers) or characters (strings of length 1) to Unicode ordinals, strings (of arbitrary lengths) or `None`. Character keys will then be converted to ordinals.

If there are two arguments, they must be strings of equal length, and in the resulting dictionary, each character in x will be mapped to the character at the same position in y. If there is a third argument, it must be a string, whose characters will be mapped to `None` in the result.

str.partition(*sep*)
Split the string at the first occurrence of *sep*, and return a 3-tuple containing the part before the separator, the separator itself, and the part after the separator. If the separator is not found, return a 3-tuple containing the string itself, followed by two empty strings.

str.replace(*old*, *new*[, *count*])
Return a copy of the string with all occurrences of substring *old* replaced by *new*. If the optional argument *count* is given, only the first *count* occurrences are replaced.

str.rfind(*sub*[, *start*[, *end*]])
Return the highest index in the string where substring *sub* is found, such that *sub* is contained within `s[start:end]`. Optional arguments *start* and *end* are interpreted as in slice notation. Return `-1` on failure.

str.rindex(*sub*[, *start*[, *end*]])
Like `rfind()` but raises `ValueError` when the substring *sub* is not found.

str.rjust(*width*[, *fillchar*])
Return the string right justified in a string of length *width*. Padding is done using the specified *fillchar* (default is an ASCII space). The original string is returned if *width* is less than or equal to `len(s)`.

str.rpartition(*sep*)
Split the string at the last occurrence of *sep*, and return a 3-tuple containing the part before the separator, the separator itself, and the part after the separator. If the separator is not found, return a 3-tuple containing two empty strings, followed by the string itself.

str.rsplit(*sep=None*, *maxsplit=-1*)

Return a list of the words in the string, using *sep* as the delimiter string. If *maxsplit* is given, at most *maxsplit* splits are done, the *rightmost* ones. If *sep* is not specified or `None`, any whitespace string is a separator. Except for splitting from the right, `rsplit()` behaves like `split()` which is described in detail below.

str.rstrip([*chars*])

Return a copy of the string with trailing characters removed. The *chars* argument is a string specifying the set of characters to be removed. If omitted or `None`, the *chars* argument defaults to removing whitespace. The *chars* argument is not a suffix; rather, all combinations of its values are stripped:

```
>>> '   spacious   '.rstrip()
'   spacious'
>>> 'mississippi'.rstrip('ipz')
'mississ'
```

str.split(*sep=None*, *maxsplit=-1*)

Return a list of the words in the string, using *sep* as the delimiter string. If *maxsplit* is given, at most *maxsplit* splits are done (thus, the list will have at most `maxsplit+1` elements). If *maxsplit* is not specified or `-1`, then there is no limit on the number of splits (all possible splits are made).

If *sep* is given, consecutive delimiters are not grouped together and are deemed to delimit empty strings (for example, `'1,,2'.split(',')` returns `['1', '', '2']`). The *sep* argument may consist of multiple characters (for example, `'1<>2<>3'.split('<>')` returns `['1', '2', '3']`). Splitting an empty string with a specified separator returns `['']`.

For example:

```
>>> '1,2,3'.split(',')
['1', '2', '3']
>>> '1,2,3'.split(',', maxsplit=1)
['1', '2,3']
>>> '1,2,,3,'.split(',')
['1', '2', '', '3', '']
```

If *sep* is not specified or is `None`, a different splitting algorithm is applied: runs of consecutive whitespace are regarded as a single separator, and the result will contain no empty strings at the start or end if the string has leading or trailing whitespace. Consequently, splitting an empty string or a string consisting of just whitespace with a `None` separator returns `[]`.

For example:

```
>>> '1 2 3'.split()
['1', '2', '3']
>>> '1 2 3'.split(maxsplit=1)
['1', '2 3']
>>> '   1   2   3   '.split()
['1', '2', '3']
```

str.splitlines([*keepends*])

Return a list of the lines in the string, breaking at line boundaries. Line breaks are not included in the resulting list unless *keepends* is given and true.

This method splits on the following line boundaries. In particular, the boundaries are a superset of *universal newlines*.

Representation	Description
\n	Line Feed
\r	Carriage Return
\r\n	Carriage Return + Line Feed
\v or \x0b	Line Tabulation
\f or \x0c	Form Feed
\x1c	File Separator
\x1d	Group Separator
\x1e	Record Separator
\x85	Next Line (C1 Control Code)
\u2028	Line Separator
\u2029	Paragraph Separator

Changed in version 3.2: `\v` and `\f` added to list of line boundaries.

For example:

```
>>> 'ab c\n\nde fg\rkl\r\n'.splitlines()
['ab c', '', 'de fg', 'kl']
>>> 'ab c\n\nde fg\rkl\r\n'.splitlines(keepends=True)
['ab c\n', '\n', 'de fg\r', 'kl\r\n']
```

Unlike *split()* when a delimiter string *sep* is given, this method returns an empty list for the empty string, and a terminal line break does not result in an extra line:

```
>>> "".splitlines()
[]
>>> "One line\n".splitlines()
['One line']
```

For comparison, `split('\n')` gives:

```
>>> ''.split('\n')
['']
>>> 'Two lines\n'.split('\n')
['Two lines', '']
```

`str.startswith`(*prefix*[, *start*[, *end*]])

Return `True` if string starts with the *prefix*, otherwise return `False`. *prefix* can also be a tuple of prefixes to look for. With optional *start*, test string beginning at that position. With optional *end*, stop comparing string at that position.

`str.strip`([*chars*])

Return a copy of the string with the leading and trailing characters removed. The *chars* argument is a string specifying the set of characters to be removed. If omitted or `None`, the *chars* argument defaults to removing whitespace. The *chars* argument is not a prefix or suffix; rather, all combinations of its values are stripped:

```
>>> '   spacious   '.strip()
'spacious'
>>> 'www.example.com'.strip('cmowz.')
'example'
```

The outermost leading and trailing *chars* argument values are stripped from the string. Characters are removed from the leading end until reaching a string character that is not contained in the set of characters in *chars*. A similar action takes place on the trailing end. For example:

```
>>> comment_string = '#....... Section 3.2.1 Issue #32 .......'
>>> comment_string.strip('.#! ')
'Section 3.2.1 Issue #32'
```

`str.swapcase()`
Return a copy of the string with uppercase characters converted to lowercase and vice versa. Note that it is not necessarily true that `s.swapcase().swapcase() == s`.

`str.title()`
Return a titlecased version of the string where words start with an uppercase character and the remaining characters are lowercase.

For example:

```
>>> 'Hello world'.title()
'Hello World'
```

The algorithm uses a simple language-independent definition of a word as groups of consecutive letters. The definition works in many contexts but it means that apostrophes in contractions and possessives form word boundaries, which may not be the desired result:

```
>>> "they're bill's friends from the UK".title()
"They'Re Bill'S Friends From The Uk"
```

A workaround for apostrophes can be constructed using regular expressions:

```
>>> import re
>>> def titlecase(s):
...     return re.sub(r"[A-Za-z]+('[A-Za-z]+)?",
...                   lambda mo: mo.group(0)[0].upper() +
...                              mo.group(0)[1:].lower(),
...                   s)
...
>>> titlecase("they're bill's friends.")
"They're Bill's Friends."
```

`str.translate(`*table*`)`
Return a copy of the string in which each character has been mapped through the given translation table. The table must be an object that implements indexing via `__getitem__()`, typically a *mapping* or *sequence*. When indexed by a Unicode ordinal (an integer), the table object can do any of the following: return a Unicode ordinal or a string, to map the character to one or more other characters; return `None`, to delete the character from the return string; or raise a *LookupError* exception, to map the character to itself.

You can use `str.maketrans()` to create a translation map from character-to-character mappings in different formats.

See also the `codecs` module for a more flexible approach to custom character mappings.

`str.upper()`
Return a copy of the string with all the cased characters[4] converted to uppercase. Note that `str.upper().isupper()` might be `False` if `s` contains uncased characters or if the Unicode category of the resulting character(s) is not "Lu" (Letter, uppercase), but e.g. "Lt" (Letter, titlecase).

The uppercasing algorithm used is described in section 3.13 of the Unicode Standard.

`str.zfill(`*width*`)`
Return a copy of the string left filled with ASCII `'0'` digits to make a string of length *width*. A leading sign prefix (`'+'`/`'-'`) is handled by inserting the padding *after* the sign character rather than before. The original string is returned if *width* is less than or equal to `len(s)`.

For example:

```
>>> "42".zfill(5)
'00042'
>>> "-42".zfill(5)
'-0042'
```

4.7.2 printf-style String Formatting

Note: The formatting operations described here exhibit a variety of quirks that lead to a number of common errors (such as failing to display tuples and dictionaries correctly). Using the newer formatted string literals or the *str.format()* interface helps avoid these errors. These alternatives also provide more powerful, flexible and extensible approaches to formatting text.

String objects have one unique built-in operation: the `%` operator (modulo). This is also known as the string *formatting* or *interpolation* operator. Given `format % values` (where *format* is a string), `%` conversion specifications in *format* are replaced with zero or more elements of *values*. The effect is similar to using the `sprintf()` in the C language.

If *format* requires a single argument, *values* may be a single non-tuple object.[5] Otherwise, *values* must be a tuple with exactly the number of items specified by the format string, or a single mapping object (for example, a dictionary).

A conversion specifier contains two or more characters and has the following components, which must occur in this order:

1. The `'%'` character, which marks the start of the specifier.
2. Mapping key (optional), consisting of a parenthesised sequence of characters (for example, `(somename)`).
3. Conversion flags (optional), which affect the result of some conversion types.
4. Minimum field width (optional). If specified as an `'*'` (asterisk), the actual width is read from the next element of the tuple in *values*, and the object to convert comes after the minimum field width and optional precision.
5. Precision (optional), given as a `'.'` (dot) followed by the precision. If specified as `'*'` (an asterisk), the actual precision is read from the next element of the tuple in *values*, and the value to convert comes after the precision.
6. Length modifier (optional).
7. Conversion type.

When the right argument is a dictionary (or other mapping type), then the formats in the string *must* include a parenthesised mapping key into that dictionary inserted immediately after the `'%'` character. The mapping key selects the value to be formatted from the mapping. For example:

```
>>> print('%(language)s has %(number)03d quote types.' %
...       {'language': "Python", "number": 2})
Python has 002 quote types.
```

In this case no `*` specifiers may occur in a format (since they require a sequential parameter list).

The conversion flag characters are:

[5] To format only a tuple you should therefore provide a singleton tuple whose only element is the tuple to be formatted.

Flag	Meaning
'#'	The value conversion will use the "alternate form" (where defined below).
'0'	The conversion will be zero padded for numeric values.
'-'	The converted value is left adjusted (overrides the '0' conversion if both are given).
' '	(a space) A blank should be left before a positive number (or empty string) produced by a signed conversion.
'+'	A sign character ('+' or '-') will precede the conversion (overrides a "space" flag).

A length modifier (h, l, or L) may be present, but is ignored as it is not necessary for Python – so e.g. %ld is identical to %d.

The conversion types are:

Conversion	Meaning	Notes
'd'	Signed integer decimal.	
'i'	Signed integer decimal.	
'o'	Signed octal value.	(1)
'u'	Obsolete type – it is identical to 'd'.	(6)
'x'	Signed hexadecimal (lowercase).	(2)
'X'	Signed hexadecimal (uppercase).	(2)
'e'	Floating point exponential format (lowercase).	(3)
'E'	Floating point exponential format (uppercase).	(3)
'f'	Floating point decimal format.	(3)
'F'	Floating point decimal format.	(3)
'g'	Floating point format. Uses lowercase exponential format if exponent is less than -4 or not less than precision, decimal format otherwise.	(4)
'G'	Floating point format. Uses uppercase exponential format if exponent is less than -4 or not less than precision, decimal format otherwise.	(4)
'c'	Single character (accepts integer or single character string).	
'r'	String (converts any Python object using *repr()*).	(5)
's'	String (converts any Python object using *str()*).	(5)
'a'	String (converts any Python object using *ascii()*).	(5)
'%'	No argument is converted, results in a '%' character in the result.	

Notes:

1. The alternate form causes a leading octal specifier ('0o') to be inserted before the first digit.
2. The alternate form causes a leading '0x' or '0X' (depending on whether the 'x' or 'X' format was used) to be inserted before the first digit.
3. The alternate form causes the result to always contain a decimal point, even if no digits follow it.

   The precision determines the number of digits after the decimal point and defaults to 6.
4. The alternate form causes the result to always contain a decimal point, and trailing zeroes are not removed as they would otherwise be.

   The precision determines the number of significant digits before and after the decimal point and defaults to 6.
5. If precision is N, the output is truncated to N characters.
6. See PEP 237.

Since Python strings have an explicit length, %s conversions do not assume that '\0' is the end of the string.

Changed in version 3.1: `%f` conversions for numbers whose absolute value is over 1e50 are no longer replaced by `%g` conversions.

4.8 Binary Sequence Types — bytes, bytearray, memoryview

The core built-in types for manipulating binary data are *bytes* and *bytearray*. They are supported by *memoryview* which uses the buffer protocol to access the memory of other binary objects without needing to make a copy.

The *array* module supports efficient storage of basic data types like 32-bit integers and IEEE754 double-precision floating values.

4.8.1 Bytes Objects

Bytes objects are immutable sequences of single bytes. Since many major binary protocols are based on the ASCII text encoding, bytes objects offer several methods that are only valid when working with ASCII compatible data and are closely related to string objects in a variety of other ways.

class bytes([*source*[, *encoding*[, *errors*]]])

Firstly, the syntax for bytes literals is largely the same as that for string literals, except that a `b` prefix is added:

- Single quotes: `b'still allows embedded "double" quotes'`
- Double quotes: `b"still allows embedded 'single' quotes"`.
- Triple quoted: `b'''3 single quotes'''`, `b"""3 double quotes"""`

Only ASCII characters are permitted in bytes literals (regardless of the declared source code encoding). Any binary values over 127 must be entered into bytes literals using the appropriate escape sequence.

As with string literals, bytes literals may also use a `r` prefix to disable processing of escape sequences. See strings for more about the various forms of bytes literal, including supported escape sequences.

While bytes literals and representations are based on ASCII text, bytes objects actually behave like immutable sequences of integers, with each value in the sequence restricted such that `0 <= x < 256` (attempts to violate this restriction will trigger *ValueError*. This is done deliberately to emphasise that while many binary formats include ASCII based elements and can be usefully manipulated with some text-oriented algorithms, this is not generally the case for arbitrary binary data (blindly applying text processing algorithms to binary data formats that are not ASCII compatible will usually lead to data corruption).

In addition to the literal forms, bytes objects can be created in a number of other ways:

- A zero-filled bytes object of a specified length: `bytes(10)`
- From an iterable of integers: `bytes(range(20))`
- Copying existing binary data via the buffer protocol: `bytes(obj)`

Also see the *bytes* built-in.

Since 2 hexadecimal digits correspond precisely to a single byte, hexadecimal numbers are a commonly used format for describing binary data. Accordingly, the bytes type has an additional class method to read data in that format:

classmethod fromhex(*string*)

This *bytes* class method returns a bytes object, decoding the given string object. The string must contain two hexadecimal digits per byte, with ASCII whitespace being ignored.

```
>>> bytes.fromhex('2Ef0 F1f2  ')
b'.\xf0\xf1\xf2'
```

A reverse conversion function exists to transform a bytes object into its hexadecimal representation.

hex()

Return a string object containing two hexadecimal digits for each byte in the instance.

```
>>> b'\xf0\xf1\xf2'.hex()
'f0f1f2'
```

New in version 3.5.

Since bytes objects are sequences of integers (akin to a tuple), for a bytes object *b*, `b[0]` will be an integer, while `b[0:1]` will be a bytes object of length 1. (This contrasts with text strings, where both indexing and slicing will produce a string of length 1)

The representation of bytes objects uses the literal format (`b'...'`) since it is often more useful than e.g. `bytes([46, 46, 46])`. You can always convert a bytes object into a list of integers using `list(b)`.

Note: For Python 2.x users: In the Python 2.x series, a variety of implicit conversions between 8-bit strings (the closest thing 2.x offers to a built-in binary data type) and Unicode strings were permitted. This was a backwards compatibility workaround to account for the fact that Python originally only supported 8-bit text, and Unicode text was a later addition. In Python 3.x, those implicit conversions are gone - conversions between 8-bit binary data and Unicode text must be explicit, and bytes and string objects will always compare unequal.

4.8.2 Bytearray Objects

bytearray objects are a mutable counterpart to *bytes* objects.

class bytearray([*source*[, *encoding*[, *errors*]]])

There is no dedicated literal syntax for bytearray objects, instead they are always created by calling the constructor:

- Creating an empty instance: `bytearray()`
- Creating a zero-filled instance with a given length: `bytearray(10)`
- From an iterable of integers: `bytearray(range(20))`
- Copying existing binary data via the buffer protocol: `bytearray(b'Hi!')`

As bytearray objects are mutable, they support the *mutable* sequence operations in addition to the common bytes and bytearray operations described in *Bytes and Bytearray Operations*.

Also see the *bytearray* built-in.

Since 2 hexadecimal digits correspond precisely to a single byte, hexadecimal numbers are a commonly used format for describing binary data. Accordingly, the bytearray type has an additional class method to read data in that format:

classmethod fromhex(*string*)

This *bytearray* class method returns bytearray object, decoding the given string object. The string must contain two hexadecimal digits per byte, with ASCII whitespace being ignored.

```
>>> bytearray.fromhex('2Ef0 F1f2  ')
bytearray(b'.\xf0\xf1\xf2')
```

A reverse conversion function exists to transform a bytearray object into its hexadecimal representation.

hex()
Return a string object containing two hexadecimal digits for each byte in the instance.

```
>>> bytearray(b'\xf0\xf1\xf2').hex()
'f0f1f2'
```

New in version 3.5.

Since bytearray objects are sequences of integers (akin to a list), for a bytearray object *b*, `b[0]` will be an integer, while `b[0:1]` will be a bytearray object of length 1. (This contrasts with text strings, where both indexing and slicing will produce a string of length 1)

The representation of bytearray objects uses the bytes literal format (`bytearray(b'...')`) since it is often more useful than e.g. `bytearray([46, 46, 46])`. You can always convert a bytearray object into a list of integers using `list(b)`.

4.8.3 Bytes and Bytearray Operations

Both bytes and bytearray objects support the *common* sequence operations. They interoperate not just with operands of the same type, but with any *bytes-like object*. Due to this flexibility, they can be freely mixed in operations without causing errors. However, the return type of the result may depend on the order of operands.

Note: The methods on bytes and bytearray objects don't accept strings as their arguments, just as the methods on strings don't accept bytes as their arguments. For example, you have to write:

```
a = "abc"
b = a.replace("a", "f")
```

and:

```
a = b"abc"
b = a.replace(b"a", b"f")
```

Some bytes and bytearray operations assume the use of ASCII compatible binary formats, and hence should be avoided when working with arbitrary binary data. These restrictions are covered below.

Note: Using these ASCII based operations to manipulate binary data that is not stored in an ASCII based format may lead to data corruption.

The following methods on bytes and bytearray objects can be used with arbitrary binary data.

bytes.**count**(*sub*[, *start*[, *end*]])
bytearray.**count**(*sub*[, *start*[, *end*]])
Return the number of non-overlapping occurrences of subsequence *sub* in the range [*start*, *end*]. Optional arguments *start* and *end* are interpreted as in slice notation.

The subsequence to search for may be any *bytes-like object* or an integer in the range 0 to 255.

Changed in version 3.3: Also accept an integer in the range 0 to 255 as the subsequence.

bytes.**decode**(*encoding="utf-8"*, *errors="strict"*)

`bytearray.decode`(*encoding="utf-8", errors="strict"*)

Return a string decoded from the given bytes. Default encoding is `'utf-8'`. *errors* may be given to set a different error handling scheme. The default for *errors* is `'strict'`, meaning that encoding errors raise a *UnicodeError*. Other possible values are `'ignore'`, `'replace'` and any other name registered via *codecs.register_error()*, see section *Error Handlers*. For a list of possible encodings, see section *Standard Encodings*.

Note: Passing the *encoding* argument to *str* allows decoding any *bytes-like object* directly, without needing to make a temporary bytes or bytearray object.

Changed in version 3.1: Added support for keyword arguments.

`bytes.endswith`(*suffix*[, *start*[, *end*]])

`bytearray.endswith`(*suffix*[, *start*[, *end*]])

Return `True` if the binary data ends with the specified *suffix*, otherwise return `False`. *suffix* can also be a tuple of suffixes to look for. With optional *start*, test beginning at that position. With optional *end*, stop comparing at that position.

The suffix(es) to search for may be any *bytes-like object*.

`bytes.find`(*sub*[, *start*[, *end*]])

`bytearray.find`(*sub*[, *start*[, *end*]])

Return the lowest index in the data where the subsequence *sub* is found, such that *sub* is contained in the slice `s[start:end]`. Optional arguments *start* and *end* are interpreted as in slice notation. Return `-1` if *sub* is not found.

The subsequence to search for may be any *bytes-like object* or an integer in the range 0 to 255.

Note: The *find()* method should be used only if you need to know the position of *sub*. To check if *sub* is a substring or not, use the `in` operator:

```
>>> b'Py' in b'Python'
True
```

Changed in version 3.3: Also accept an integer in the range 0 to 255 as the subsequence.

`bytes.index`(*sub*[, *start*[, *end*]])

`bytearray.index`(*sub*[, *start*[, *end*]])

Like *find()*, but raise *ValueError* when the subsequence is not found.

The subsequence to search for may be any *bytes-like object* or an integer in the range 0 to 255.

Changed in version 3.3: Also accept an integer in the range 0 to 255 as the subsequence.

`bytes.join`(*iterable*)

`bytearray.join`(*iterable*)

Return a bytes or bytearray object which is the concatenation of the binary data sequences in *iterable*. A *TypeError* will be raised if there are any values in *iterable* that are not *bytes-like objects*, including *str* objects. The separator between elements is the contents of the bytes or bytearray object providing this method.

static `bytes.maketrans`(*from, to*)

static `bytearray.maketrans`(*from, to*)

This static method returns a translation table usable for *bytes.translate()* that will map each character in *from* into the character at the same position in *to*; *from* and *to* must both be *bytes-like objects* and have the same length.

New in version 3.1.

`bytes.partition(sep)`
`bytearray.partition(sep)`

Split the sequence at the first occurrence of *sep*, and return a 3-tuple containing the part before the separator, the separator itself or its bytearray copy, and the part after the separator. If the separator is not found, return a 3-tuple containing a copy of the original sequence, followed by two empty bytes or bytearray objects.

The separator to search for may be any *bytes-like object*.

`bytes.replace(old, new[, count])`
`bytearray.replace(old, new[, count])`

Return a copy of the sequence with all occurrences of subsequence *old* replaced by *new*. If the optional argument *count* is given, only the first *count* occurrences are replaced.

The subsequence to search for and its replacement may be any *bytes-like object*.

Note: The bytearray version of this method does *not* operate in place - it always produces a new object, even if no changes were made.

`bytes.rfind(sub[, start[, end]])`
`bytearray.rfind(sub[, start[, end]])`

Return the highest index in the sequence where the subsequence *sub* is found, such that *sub* is contained within `s[start:end]`. Optional arguments *start* and *end* are interpreted as in slice notation. Return `-1` on failure.

The subsequence to search for may be any *bytes-like object* or an integer in the range 0 to 255.

Changed in version 3.3: Also accept an integer in the range 0 to 255 as the subsequence.

`bytes.rindex(sub[, start[, end]])`
`bytearray.rindex(sub[, start[, end]])`

Like `rfind()` but raises `ValueError` when the subsequence *sub* is not found.

The subsequence to search for may be any *bytes-like object* or an integer in the range 0 to 255.

Changed in version 3.3: Also accept an integer in the range 0 to 255 as the subsequence.

`bytes.rpartition(sep)`
`bytearray.rpartition(sep)`

Split the sequence at the last occurrence of *sep*, and return a 3-tuple containing the part before the separator, the separator itself or its bytearray copy, and the part after the separator. If the separator is not found, return a 3-tuple containing a copy of the original sequence, followed by two empty bytes or bytearray objects.

The separator to search for may be any *bytes-like object*.

`bytes.startswith(prefix[, start[, end]])`
`bytearray.startswith(prefix[, start[, end]])`

Return `True` if the binary data starts with the specified *prefix*, otherwise return `False`. *prefix* can also be a tuple of prefixes to look for. With optional *start*, test beginning at that position. With optional *end*, stop comparing at that position.

The prefix(es) to search for may be any *bytes-like object*.

`bytes.translate(table, delete=b'')`
`bytearray.translate(table, delete=b'')`

Return a copy of the bytes or bytearray object where all bytes occurring in the optional argument *delete* are removed, and the remaining bytes have been mapped through the given translation table, which must be a bytes object of length 256.

You can use the `bytes.maketrans()` method to create a translation table.

Set the *table* argument to `None` for translations that only delete characters:

```
>>> b'read this short text'.translate(None, b'aeiou')
b'rd ths shrt txt'
```

Changed in version 3.6: *delete* is now supported as a keyword argument.

The following methods on bytes and bytearray objects have default behaviours that assume the use of ASCII compatible binary formats, but can still be used with arbitrary binary data by passing appropriate arguments. Note that all of the bytearray methods in this section do *not* operate in place, and instead produce new objects.

`bytes.center(`*width*[, *fillbyte*]`)`

`bytearray.center(`*width*[, *fillbyte*]`)`

Return a copy of the object centered in a sequence of length *width*. Padding is done using the specified *fillbyte* (default is an ASCII space). For `bytes` objects, the original sequence is returned if *width* is less than or equal to `len(s)`.

Note: The bytearray version of this method does *not* operate in place - it always produces a new object, even if no changes were made.

`bytes.ljust(`*width*[, *fillbyte*]`)`

`bytearray.ljust(`*width*[, *fillbyte*]`)`

Return a copy of the object left justified in a sequence of length *width*. Padding is done using the specified *fillbyte* (default is an ASCII space). For `bytes` objects, the original sequence is returned if *width* is less than or equal to `len(s)`.

Note: The bytearray version of this method does *not* operate in place - it always produces a new object, even if no changes were made.

`bytes.lstrip(`[*chars*]`)`

`bytearray.lstrip(`[*chars*]`)`

Return a copy of the sequence with specified leading bytes removed. The *chars* argument is a binary sequence specifying the set of byte values to be removed - the name refers to the fact this method is usually used with ASCII characters. If omitted or `None`, the *chars* argument defaults to removing ASCII whitespace. The *chars* argument is not a prefix; rather, all combinations of its values are stripped:

```
>>> b'   spacious   '.lstrip()
b'spacious   '
>>> b'www.example.com'.lstrip(b'cmowz.')
b'example.com'
```

The binary sequence of byte values to remove may be any *bytes-like object*.

Note: The bytearray version of this method does *not* operate in place - it always produces a new object, even if no changes were made.

`bytes.rjust(`*width*[, *fillbyte*]`)`

bytearray.**rjust**(*width*[, *fillbyte*])

Return a copy of the object right justified in a sequence of length *width*. Padding is done using the specified *fillbyte* (default is an ASCII space). For *bytes* objects, the original sequence is returned if *width* is less than or equal to `len(s)`.

Note: The bytearray version of this method does *not* operate in place - it always produces a new object, even if no changes were made.

bytes.**rsplit**(*sep=None*, *maxsplit=-1*)
bytearray.**rsplit**(*sep=None*, *maxsplit=-1*)

Split the binary sequence into subsequences of the same type, using *sep* as the delimiter string. If *maxsplit* is given, at most *maxsplit* splits are done, the *rightmost* ones. If *sep* is not specified or `None`, any subsequence consisting solely of ASCII whitespace is a separator. Except for splitting from the right, *rsplit()* behaves like *split()* which is described in detail below.

bytes.**rstrip**([*chars*])
bytearray.**rstrip**([*chars*])

Return a copy of the sequence with specified trailing bytes removed. The *chars* argument is a binary sequence specifying the set of byte values to be removed - the name refers to the fact this method is usually used with ASCII characters. If omitted or `None`, the *chars* argument defaults to removing ASCII whitespace. The *chars* argument is not a suffix; rather, all combinations of its values are stripped:

```
>>> b'   spacious   '.rstrip()
b'   spacious'
>>> b'mississippi'.rstrip(b'ipz')
b'mississ'
```

The binary sequence of byte values to remove may be any *bytes-like object*.

Note: The bytearray version of this method does *not* operate in place - it always produces a new object, even if no changes were made.

bytes.**split**(*sep=None*, *maxsplit=-1*)
bytearray.**split**(*sep=None*, *maxsplit=-1*)

Split the binary sequence into subsequences of the same type, using *sep* as the delimiter string. If *maxsplit* is given and non-negative, at most *maxsplit* splits are done (thus, the list will have at most `maxsplit+1` elements). If *maxsplit* is not specified or is `-1`, then there is no limit on the number of splits (all possible splits are made).

If *sep* is given, consecutive delimiters are not grouped together and are deemed to delimit empty subsequences (for example, `b'1,,2'.split(b',')` returns `[b'1', b'', b'2']`). The *sep* argument may consist of a multibyte sequence (for example, `b'1<>2<>3'.split(b'<>')` returns `[b'1', b'2', b'3']`). Splitting an empty sequence with a specified separator returns `[b'']` or `[bytearray(b'')]` depending on the type of object being split. The *sep* argument may be any *bytes-like object*.

For example:

```
>>> b'1,2,3'.split(b',')
[b'1', b'2', b'3']
>>> b'1,2,3'.split(b',', maxsplit=1)
[b'1', b'2,3']
>>> b'1,2,,3,'.split(b',')
[b'1', b'2', b'', b'3', b'']
```

If *sep* is not specified or is `None`, a different splitting algorithm is applied: runs of consecutive ASCII whitespace are regarded as a single separator, and the result will contain no empty strings at the start or end if the sequence has leading or trailing whitespace. Consequently, splitting an empty sequence or a sequence consisting solely of ASCII whitespace without a specified separator returns `[]`.

For example:

```
>>> b'1 2 3'.split()
[b'1', b'2', b'3']
>>> b'1 2 3'.split(maxsplit=1)
[b'1', b'2 3']
>>> b'   1   2   3   '.split()
[b'1', b'2', b'3']
```

bytes.strip([*chars*])
bytearray.strip([*chars*])

Return a copy of the sequence with specified leading and trailing bytes removed. The *chars* argument is a binary sequence specifying the set of byte values to be removed - the name refers to the fact this method is usually used with ASCII characters. If omitted or `None`, the *chars* argument defaults to removing ASCII whitespace. The *chars* argument is not a prefix or suffix; rather, all combinations of its values are stripped:

```
>>> b'   spacious   '.strip()
b'spacious'
>>> b'www.example.com'.strip(b'cmowz.')
b'example'
```

The binary sequence of byte values to remove may be any *bytes-like object*.

Note: The bytearray version of this method does *not* operate in place - it always produces a new object, even if no changes were made.

The following methods on bytes and bytearray objects assume the use of ASCII compatible binary formats and should not be applied to arbitrary binary data. Note that all of the bytearray methods in this section do *not* operate in place, and instead produce new objects.

bytes.capitalize()
bytearray.capitalize()

Return a copy of the sequence with each byte interpreted as an ASCII character, and the first byte capitalized and the rest lowercased. Non-ASCII byte values are passed through unchanged.

Note: The bytearray version of this method does *not* operate in place - it always produces a new object, even if no changes were made.

bytes.expandtabs(*tabsize=8*)
bytearray.expandtabs(*tabsize=8*)

Return a copy of the sequence where all ASCII tab characters are replaced by one or more ASCII spaces, depending on the current column and the given tab size. Tab positions occur every *tabsize* bytes (default is 8, giving tab positions at columns 0, 8, 16 and so on). To expand the sequence, the current column is set to zero and the sequence is examined byte by byte. If the byte is an ASCII tab character (`b'\t'`), one or more space characters are inserted in the result until the current column is equal to the next tab position. (The tab character itself is not copied.) If the current byte is an ASCII newline (`b'\n'`) or carriage return (`b'\r'`), it is copied and the current column is reset to zero. Any other byte value is copied unchanged and the current column is incremented by one regardless of how the byte value is represented when printed:

```
>>> b'01\t012\t0123\t01234'.expandtabs()
b'01      012     0123    01234'
>>> b'01\t012\t0123\t01234'.expandtabs(4)
b'01  012 0123    01234'
```

Note: The bytearray version of this method does *not* operate in place - it always produces a new object, even if no changes were made.

`bytes.isalnum()`
`bytearray.isalnum()`

Return true if all bytes in the sequence are alphabetical ASCII characters or ASCII decimal digits and the sequence is not empty, false otherwise. Alphabetic ASCII characters are those byte values in the sequence `b'abcdefghijklmnopqrstuvwxyzABCDEFGHIJKLMNOPQRSTUVWXYZ'`. ASCII decimal digits are those byte values in the sequence `b'0123456789'`.

For example:

```
>>> b'ABCabc1'.isalnum()
True
>>> b'ABC abc1'.isalnum()
False
```

`bytes.isalpha()`
`bytearray.isalpha()`

Return true if all bytes in the sequence are alphabetic ASCII characters and the sequence is not empty, false otherwise. Alphabetic ASCII characters are those byte values in the sequence `b'abcdefghijklmnopqrstuvwxyzABCDEFGHIJKLMNOPQRSTUVWXYZ'`.

For example:

```
>>> b'ABCabc'.isalpha()
True
>>> b'ABCabc1'.isalpha()
False
```

`bytes.isdigit()`
`bytearray.isdigit()`

Return true if all bytes in the sequence are ASCII decimal digits and the sequence is not empty, false otherwise. ASCII decimal digits are those byte values in the sequence `b'0123456789'`.

For example:

```
>>> b'1234'.isdigit()
True
>>> b'1.23'.isdigit()
False
```

`bytes.islower()`
`bytearray.islower()`

Return true if there is at least one lowercase ASCII character in the sequence and no uppercase ASCII characters, false otherwise.

For example:

```
>>> b'hello world'.islower()
True
```

```
>>> b'Hello world'.islower()
False
```

Lowercase ASCII characters are those byte values in the sequence `b'abcdefghijklmnopqrstuvwxyz'`. Uppercase ASCII characters are those byte values in the sequence `b'ABCDEFGHIJKLMNOPQRSTUVWXYZ'`.

`bytes.isspace()`
`bytearray.isspace()`

Return true if all bytes in the sequence are ASCII whitespace and the sequence is not empty, false otherwise. ASCII whitespace characters are those byte values in the sequence `b' \t\n\r\x0b\f'` (space, tab, newline, carriage return, vertical tab, form feed).

`bytes.istitle()`
`bytearray.istitle()`

Return true if the sequence is ASCII titlecase and the sequence is not empty, false otherwise. See *bytes.title()* for more details on the definition of "titlecase".

For example:

```
>>> b'Hello World'.istitle()
True
>>> b'Hello world'.istitle()
False
```

`bytes.isupper()`
`bytearray.isupper()`

Return true if there is at least one uppercase alphabetic ASCII character in the sequence and no lowercase ASCII characters, false otherwise.

For example:

```
>>> b'HELLO WORLD'.isupper()
True
>>> b'Hello world'.isupper()
False
```

Lowercase ASCII characters are those byte values in the sequence `b'abcdefghijklmnopqrstuvwxyz'`. Uppercase ASCII characters are those byte values in the sequence `b'ABCDEFGHIJKLMNOPQRSTUVWXYZ'`.

`bytes.lower()`
`bytearray.lower()`

Return a copy of the sequence with all the uppercase ASCII characters converted to their corresponding lowercase counterpart.

For example:

```
>>> b'Hello World'.lower()
b'hello world'
```

Lowercase ASCII characters are those byte values in the sequence `b'abcdefghijklmnopqrstuvwxyz'`. Uppercase ASCII characters are those byte values in the sequence `b'ABCDEFGHIJKLMNOPQRSTUVWXYZ'`.

Note: The bytearray version of this method does *not* operate in place - it always produces a new object, even if no changes were made.

`bytes.splitlines(`*keepends=False*`)`
`bytearray.splitlines(`*keepends=False*`)`

Return a list of the lines in the binary sequence, breaking at ASCII line boundaries. This method uses the *universal newlines* approach to splitting lines. Line breaks are not included in the resulting list unless *keepends* is given and true.

For example:

```
>>> b'ab c\n\nde fg\rkl\r\n'.splitlines()
[b'ab c', b'', b'de fg', b'kl']
>>> b'ab c\n\nde fg\rkl\r\n'.splitlines(keepends=True)
[b'ab c\n', b'\n', b'de fg\r', b'kl\r\n']
```

Unlike `split()` when a delimiter string *sep* is given, this method returns an empty list for the empty string, and a terminal line break does not result in an extra line:

```
>>> b"".split(b'\n'), b"Two lines\n".split(b'\n')
([b''], [b'Two lines', b''])
>>> b"".splitlines(), b"One line\n".splitlines()
([], [b'One line'])
```

bytes.swapcase()
bytearray.swapcase()

Return a copy of the sequence with all the lowercase ASCII characters converted to their corresponding uppercase counterpart and vice-versa.

For example:

```
>>> b'Hello World'.swapcase()
b'hELLO wORLD'
```

Lowercase ASCII characters are those byte values in the sequence `b'abcdefghijklmnopqrstuvwxyz'`. Uppercase ASCII characters are those byte values in the sequence `b'ABCDEFGHIJKLMNOPQRSTUVWXYZ'`.

Unlike `str.swapcase()`, it is always the case that `bin.swapcase().swapcase() == bin` for the binary versions. Case conversions are symmetrical in ASCII, even though that is not generally true for arbitrary Unicode code points.

Note: The bytearray version of this method does *not* operate in place - it always produces a new object, even if no changes were made.

bytes.title()
bytearray.title()

Return a titlecased version of the binary sequence where words start with an uppercase ASCII character and the remaining characters are lowercase. Uncased byte values are left unmodified.

For example:

```
>>> b'Hello world'.title()
b'Hello World'
```

Lowercase ASCII characters are those byte values in the sequence `b'abcdefghijklmnopqrstuvwxyz'`. Uppercase ASCII characters are those byte values in the sequence `b'ABCDEFGHIJKLMNOPQRSTUVWXYZ'`. All other byte values are uncased.

The algorithm uses a simple language-independent definition of a word as groups of consecutive letters. The definition works in many contexts but it means that apostrophes in contractions and possessives form word boundaries, which may not be the desired result:

```
>>> b"they're bill's friends from the UK".title()
b"They'Re Bill'S Friends From The Uk"
```

A workaround for apostrophes can be constructed using regular expressions:

```
>>> import re
>>> def titlecase(s):
...     return re.sub(rb"[A-Za-z]+('[A-Za-z]+)?",
...                   lambda mo: mo.group(0)[0:1].upper() +
...                              mo.group(0)[1:].lower(),
...                   s)
...
>>> titlecase(b"they're bill's friends.")
b"They're Bill's Friends."
```

Note: The bytearray version of this method does *not* operate in place - it always produces a new object, even if no changes were made.

`bytes.upper()`
`bytearray.upper()`

Return a copy of the sequence with all the lowercase ASCII characters converted to their corresponding uppercase counterpart.

For example:

```
>>> b'Hello World'.upper()
b'HELLO WORLD'
```

Lowercase ASCII characters are those byte values in the sequence `b'abcdefghijklmnopqrstuvwxyz'`. Uppercase ASCII characters are those byte values in the sequence `b'ABCDEFGHIJKLMNOPQRSTUVWXYZ'`.

Note: The bytearray version of this method does *not* operate in place - it always produces a new object, even if no changes were made.

`bytes.zfill(width)`
`bytearray.zfill(width)`

Return a copy of the sequence left filled with ASCII `b'0'` digits to make a sequence of length *width*. A leading sign prefix (`b'+'`/ `b'-'` is handled by inserting the padding *after* the sign character rather than before. For `bytes` objects, the original sequence is returned if *width* is less than or equal to `len(seq)`.

For example:

```
>>> b"42".zfill(5)
b'00042'
>>> b"-42".zfill(5)
b'-0042'
```

Note: The bytearray version of this method does *not* operate in place - it always produces a new object, even if no changes were made.

4.8.4 printf-style Bytes Formatting

Note: The formatting operations described here exhibit a variety of quirks that lead to a number of common errors (such as failing to display tuples and dictionaries correctly). If the value being printed may be a tuple or dictionary, wrap it in a tuple.

Bytes objects (`bytes`/`bytearray`) have one unique built-in operation: the `%` operator (modulo). This is also known as the bytes *formatting* or *interpolation* operator. Given `format % values` (where *format* is a bytes object), `%` conversion specifications in *format* are replaced with zero or more elements of *values*. The effect is similar to using the `sprintf()` in the C language.

If *format* requires a single argument, *values* may be a single non-tuple object.[5] Otherwise, *values* must be a tuple with exactly the number of items specified by the format bytes object, or a single mapping object (for example, a dictionary).

A conversion specifier contains two or more characters and has the following components, which must occur in this order:

1. The `'%'` character, which marks the start of the specifier.
2. Mapping key (optional), consisting of a parenthesised sequence of characters (for example, `(somename)`).
3. Conversion flags (optional), which affect the result of some conversion types.
4. Minimum field width (optional). If specified as an `'*'` (asterisk), the actual width is read from the next element of the tuple in *values*, and the object to convert comes after the minimum field width and optional precision.
5. Precision (optional), given as a `'.'` (dot) followed by the precision. If specified as `'*'` (an asterisk), the actual precision is read from the next element of the tuple in *values*, and the value to convert comes after the precision.
6. Length modifier (optional).
7. Conversion type.

When the right argument is a dictionary (or other mapping type), then the formats in the bytes object *must* include a parenthesised mapping key into that dictionary inserted immediately after the `'%'` character. The mapping key selects the value to be formatted from the mapping. For example:

```
>>> print(b'%(language)s has %(number)03d quote types.' %
...       {b'language': b"Python", b"number": 2})
b'Python has 002 quote types.'
```

In this case no `*` specifiers may occur in a format (since they require a sequential parameter list).

The conversion flag characters are:

Flag	Meaning
`'#'`	The value conversion will use the "alternate form" (where defined below).
`'0'`	The conversion will be zero padded for numeric values.
`'-'`	The converted value is left adjusted (overrides the `'0'` conversion if both are given).
`' '`	(a space) A blank should be left before a positive number (or empty string) produced by a signed conversion.
`'+'`	A sign character (`'+'` or `'-'`) will precede the conversion (overrides a "space" flag).

A length modifier (`h`, `l`, or `L`) may be present, but is ignored as it is not necessary for Python – so e.g. `%ld` is identical to `%d`.

The conversion types are:

Conversion	Meaning	Notes
'd'	Signed integer decimal.	
'i'	Signed integer decimal.	
'o'	Signed octal value.	(1)
'u'	Obsolete type – it is identical to 'd'.	(8)
'x'	Signed hexadecimal (lowercase).	(2)
'X'	Signed hexadecimal (uppercase).	(2)
'e'	Floating point exponential format (lowercase).	(3)
'E'	Floating point exponential format (uppercase).	(3)
'f'	Floating point decimal format.	(3)
'F'	Floating point decimal format.	(3)
'g'	Floating point format. Uses lowercase exponential format if exponent is less than -4 or not less than precision, decimal format otherwise.	(4)
'G'	Floating point format. Uses uppercase exponential format if exponent is less than -4 or not less than precision, decimal format otherwise.	(4)
'c'	Single byte (accepts integer or single byte objects).	
'b'	Bytes (any object that follows the buffer protocol or has `__bytes__()`).	(5)
's'	's' is an alias for 'b' and should only be used for Python2/3 code bases.	(6)
'a'	Bytes (converts any Python object using `repr(obj).encode('ascii', 'backslashreplace')`).	(5)
'r'	'r' is an alias for 'a' and should only be used for Python2/3 code bases.	(7)
'%'	No argument is converted, results in a '%' character in the result.	

Notes:

1. The alternate form causes a leading octal specifier ('0o') to be inserted before the first digit.
2. The alternate form causes a leading '0x' or '0X' (depending on whether the 'x' or 'X' format was used) to be inserted before the first digit.
3. The alternate form causes the result to always contain a decimal point, even if no digits follow it.

   The precision determines the number of digits after the decimal point and defaults to 6.
4. The alternate form causes the result to always contain a decimal point, and trailing zeroes are not removed as they would otherwise be.

   The precision determines the number of significant digits before and after the decimal point and defaults to 6.
5. If precision is N, the output is truncated to N characters.
6. b'%s' is deprecated, but will not be removed during the 3.x series.
7. b'%r' is deprecated, but will not be removed during the 3.x series.
8. See PEP 237.

Note: The bytearray version of this method does *not* operate in place - it always produces a new object, even if no changes were made.

See also:

PEP 461.

New in version 3.5.

4.8.5 Memory Views

memoryview objects allow Python code to access the internal data of an object that supports the buffer protocol without copying.

class memoryview(*obj*)

Create a *memoryview* that references *obj*. *obj* must support the buffer protocol. Built-in objects that support the buffer protocol include *bytes* and *bytearray*.

A *memoryview* has the notion of an *element*, which is the atomic memory unit handled by the originating object *obj*. For many simple types such as *bytes* and *bytearray*, an element is a single byte, but other types such as *array.array* may have bigger elements.

`len(view)` is equal to the length of *tolist*. If `view.ndim = 0`, the length is 1. If `view.ndim = 1`, the length is equal to the number of elements in the view. For higher dimensions, the length is equal to the length of the nested list representation of the view. The *itemsize* attribute will give you the number of bytes in a single element.

A *memoryview* supports slicing and indexing to expose its data. One-dimensional slicing will result in a subview:

```
>>> v = memoryview(b'abcefg')
>>> v[1]
98
>>> v[-1]
103
>>> v[1:4]
<memory at 0x7f3ddc9f4350>
>>> bytes(v[1:4])
b'bce'
```

If *format* is one of the native format specifiers from the *struct* module, indexing with an integer or a tuple of integers is also supported and returns a single *element* with the correct type. One-dimensional memoryviews can be indexed with an integer or a one-integer tuple. Multi-dimensional memoryviews can be indexed with tuples of exactly *ndim* integers where *ndim* is the number of dimensions. Zero-dimensional memoryviews can be indexed with the empty tuple.

Here is an example with a non-byte format:

```
>>> import array
>>> a = array.array('l', [-11111111, 22222222, -33333333, 44444444])
>>> m = memoryview(a)
>>> m[0]
-11111111
>>> m[-1]
44444444
>>> m[::2].tolist()
[-11111111, -33333333]
```

If the underlying object is writable, the memoryview supports one-dimensional slice assignment. Resizing is not allowed:

```
>>> data = bytearray(b'abcefg')
>>> v = memoryview(data)
>>> v.readonly
False
>>> v[0] = ord(b'z')
>>> data
bytearray(b'zbcefg')
>>> v[1:4] = b'123'
```

```
>>> data
bytearray(b'z123fg')
>>> v[2:3] = b'spam'
Traceback (most recent call last):
  File "<stdin>", line 1, in <module>
ValueError: memoryview assignment: lvalue and rvalue have different structures
>>> v[2:6] = b'spam'
>>> data
bytearray(b'z1spam')
```

One-dimensional memoryviews of hashable (read-only) types with formats 'B', 'b' or 'c' are also hashable. The hash is defined as `hash(m) == hash(m.tobytes())`:

```
>>> v = memoryview(b'abcefg')
>>> hash(v) == hash(b'abcefg')
True
>>> hash(v[2:4]) == hash(b'ce')
True
>>> hash(v[::-2]) == hash(b'abcefg'[::-2])
True
```

Changed in version 3.3: One-dimensional memoryviews can now be sliced. One-dimensional memoryviews with formats 'B', 'b' or 'c' are now hashable.

Changed in version 3.4: memoryview is now registered automatically with *collections.abc.Sequence*

Changed in version 3.5: memoryviews can now be indexed with tuple of integers.

memoryview has several methods:

__eq__(*exporter*)
A memoryview and a PEP 3118 exporter are equal if their shapes are equivalent and if all corresponding values are equal when the operands' respective format codes are interpreted using *struct* syntax.

For the subset of *struct* format strings currently supported by *tolist()*, `v` and `w` are equal if `v.tolist() == w.tolist()`:

```
>>> import array
>>> a = array.array('I', [1, 2, 3, 4, 5])
>>> b = array.array('d', [1.0, 2.0, 3.0, 4.0, 5.0])
>>> c = array.array('b', [5, 3, 1])
>>> x = memoryview(a)
>>> y = memoryview(b)
>>> x == a == y == b
True
>>> x.tolist() == a.tolist() == y.tolist() == b.tolist()
True
>>> z = y[::-2]
>>> z == c
True
>>> z.tolist() == c.tolist()
True
```

If either format string is not supported by the *struct* module, then the objects will always compare as unequal (even if the format strings and buffer contents are identical):

```
>>> from ctypes import BigEndianStructure, c_long
>>> class BEPoint(BigEndianStructure):
...     _fields_ = [("x", c_long), ("y", c_long)]
```

```
...
>>> point = BEPoint(100, 200)
>>> a = memoryview(point)
>>> b = memoryview(point)
>>> a == point
False
>>> a == b
False
```

Note that, as with floating point numbers, `v is w` does *not* imply `v == w` for memoryview objects.

Changed in version 3.3: Previous versions compared the raw memory disregarding the item format and the logical array structure.

tobytes()
Return the data in the buffer as a bytestring. This is equivalent to calling the *bytes* constructor on the memoryview.

```
>>> m = memoryview(b"abc")
>>> m.tobytes()
b'abc'
>>> bytes(m)
b'abc'
```

For non-contiguous arrays the result is equal to the flattened list representation with all elements converted to bytes. *tobytes()* supports all format strings, including those that are not in *struct* module syntax.

hex()
Return a string object containing two hexadecimal digits for each byte in the buffer.

```
>>> m = memoryview(b"abc")
>>> m.hex()
'616263'
```

New in version 3.5.

tolist()
Return the data in the buffer as a list of elements.

```
>>> memoryview(b'abc').tolist()
[97, 98, 99]
>>> import array
>>> a = array.array('d', [1.1, 2.2, 3.3])
>>> m = memoryview(a)
>>> m.tolist()
[1.1, 2.2, 3.3]
```

Changed in version 3.3: *tolist()* now supports all single character native formats in *struct* module syntax as well as multi-dimensional representations.

release()
Release the underlying buffer exposed by the memoryview object. Many objects take special actions when a view is held on them (for example, a *bytearray* would temporarily forbid resizing); therefore, calling release() is handy to remove these restrictions (and free any dangling resources) as soon as possible.

After this method has been called, any further operation on the view raises a *ValueError* (except *release()* itself which can be called multiple times):

```
>>> m = memoryview(b'abc')
>>> m.release()
>>> m[0]
Traceback (most recent call last):
  File "<stdin>", line 1, in <module>
ValueError: operation forbidden on released memoryview object
```

The context management protocol can be used for a similar effect, using the `with` statement:

```
>>> with memoryview(b'abc') as m:
...     m[0]
...
97
>>> m[0]
Traceback (most recent call last):
  File "<stdin>", line 1, in <module>
ValueError: operation forbidden on released memoryview object
```

New in version 3.2.

`cast`(*format*[, *shape*])
Cast a memoryview to a new format or shape. *shape* defaults to `[byte_length//new_itemsize]`, which means that the result view will be one-dimensional. The return value is a new memoryview, but the buffer itself is not copied. Supported casts are 1D -> C-*contiguous* and C-contiguous -> 1D.

The destination format is restricted to a single element native format in `struct` syntax. One of the formats must be a byte format ('B', 'b' or 'c'). The byte length of the result must be the same as the original length.

Cast 1D/long to 1D/unsigned bytes:

```
>>> import array
>>> a = array.array('l', [1,2,3])
>>> x = memoryview(a)
>>> x.format
'l'
>>> x.itemsize
8
>>> len(x)
3
>>> x.nbytes
24
>>> y = x.cast('B')
>>> y.format
'B'
>>> y.itemsize
1
>>> len(y)
24
>>> y.nbytes
24
```

Cast 1D/unsigned bytes to 1D/char:

```
>>> b = bytearray(b'zyz')
>>> x = memoryview(b)
>>> x[0] = b'a'
Traceback (most recent call last):
```

```
  File "<stdin>", line 1, in <module>
ValueError: memoryview: invalid value for format "B"
>>> y = x.cast('c')
>>> y[0] = b'a'
>>> b
bytearray(b'ayz')
```

Cast 1D/bytes to 3D/ints to 1D/signed char:

```
>>> import struct
>>> buf = struct.pack("i"*12, *list(range(12)))
>>> x = memoryview(buf)
>>> y = x.cast('i', shape=[2,2,3])
>>> y.tolist()
[[[0, 1, 2], [3, 4, 5]], [[6, 7, 8], [9, 10, 11]]]
>>> y.format
'i'
>>> y.itemsize
4
>>> len(y)
2
>>> y.nbytes
48
>>> z = y.cast('b')
>>> z.format
'b'
>>> z.itemsize
1
>>> len(z)
48
>>> z.nbytes
48
```

Cast 1D/unsigned char to 2D/unsigned long:

```
>>> buf = struct.pack("L"*6, *list(range(6)))
>>> x = memoryview(buf)
>>> y = x.cast('L', shape=[2,3])
>>> len(y)
2
>>> y.nbytes
48
>>> y.tolist()
[[0, 1, 2], [3, 4, 5]]
```

New in version 3.3.

Changed in version 3.5: The source format is no longer restricted when casting to a byte view.

There are also several readonly attributes available:

obj

The underlying object of the memoryview:

```
>>> b  = bytearray(b'xyz')
>>> m = memoryview(b)
>>> m.obj is b
True
```

New in version 3.3.

nbytes

`nbytes == product(shape) * itemsize == len(m.tobytes())`. This is the amount of space in bytes that the array would use in a contiguous representation. It is not necessarily equal to len(m):

```
>>> import array
>>> a = array.array('i', [1,2,3,4,5])
>>> m = memoryview(a)
>>> len(m)
5
>>> m.nbytes
20
>>> y = m[::2]
>>> len(y)
3
>>> y.nbytes
12
>>> len(y.tobytes())
12
```

Multi-dimensional arrays:

```
>>> import struct
>>> buf = struct.pack("d"*12, *[1.5*x for x in range(12)])
>>> x = memoryview(buf)
>>> y = x.cast('d', shape=[3,4])
>>> y.tolist()
[[0.0, 1.5, 3.0, 4.5], [6.0, 7.5, 9.0, 10.5], [12.0, 13.5, 15.0, 16.5]]
>>> len(y)
3
>>> y.nbytes
96
```

New in version 3.3.

readonly

A bool indicating whether the memory is read only.

format

A string containing the format (in *struct* module style) for each element in the view. A memoryview can be created from exporters with arbitrary format strings, but some methods (e.g. *tolist()*) are restricted to native single element formats.

Changed in version 3.3: format `'B'` is now handled according to the struct module syntax. This means that `memoryview(b'abc')[0] == b'abc'[0] == 97`.

itemsize

The size in bytes of each element of the memoryview:

```
>>> import array, struct
>>> m = memoryview(array.array('H', [32000, 32001, 32002]))
>>> m.itemsize
2
>>> m[0]
32000
>>> struct.calcsize('H') == m.itemsize
True
```

ndim

An integer indicating how many dimensions of a multi-dimensional array the memory represents.

shape
A tuple of integers the length of *ndim* giving the shape of the memory as an N-dimensional array.

Changed in version 3.3: An empty tuple instead of `None` when ndim = 0.

strides
A tuple of integers the length of *ndim* giving the size in bytes to access each element for each dimension of the array.

Changed in version 3.3: An empty tuple instead of `None` when ndim = 0.

suboffsets
Used internally for PIL-style arrays. The value is informational only.

c_contiguous
A bool indicating whether the memory is C-*contiguous*.

New in version 3.3.

f_contiguous
A bool indicating whether the memory is Fortran *contiguous*.

New in version 3.3.

contiguous
A bool indicating whether the memory is *contiguous*.

New in version 3.3.

4.9 Set Types — set, frozenset

A *set* object is an unordered collection of distinct *hashable* objects. Common uses include membership testing, removing duplicates from a sequence, and computing mathematical operations such as intersection, union, difference, and symmetric difference. (For other containers see the built-in `dict`, `list`, and `tuple` classes, and the `collections` module.)

Like other collections, sets support `x in set`, `len(set)`, and `for x in set`. Being an unordered collection, sets do not record element position or order of insertion. Accordingly, sets do not support indexing, slicing, or other sequence-like behavior.

There are currently two built-in set types, `set` and `frozenset`. The `set` type is mutable — the contents can be changed using methods like `add()` and `remove()`. Since it is mutable, it has no hash value and cannot be used as either a dictionary key or as an element of another set. The `frozenset` type is immutable and *hashable* — its contents cannot be altered after it is created; it can therefore be used as a dictionary key or as an element of another set.

Non-empty sets (not frozensets) can be created by placing a comma-separated list of elements within braces, for example: `{'jack', 'sjoerd'}`, in addition to the `set` constructor.

The constructors for both classes work the same:

class set([*iterable*])

class frozenset([*iterable*])
Return a new set or frozenset object whose elements are taken from *iterable*. The elements of a set must be *hashable*. To represent sets of sets, the inner sets must be `frozenset` objects. If *iterable* is not specified, a new empty set is returned.

Instances of `set` and `frozenset` provide the following operations:

len(s)
Return the number of elements in set *s* (cardinality of *s*).

x in s
Test x for membership in *s*.

x not in s
Test x for non-membership in *s*.

isdisjoint(*other*)
Return **True** if the set has no elements in common with *other*. Sets are disjoint if and only if their intersection is the empty set.

issubset(*other*)
set <= other
Test whether every element in the set is in *other*.

set < other
Test whether the set is a proper subset of *other*, that is, `set <= other and set != other`.

issuperset(*other*)
set >= other
Test whether every element in *other* is in the set.

set > other
Test whether the set is a proper superset of *other*, that is, `set >= other and set != other`.

union(**others*)
set | other | ...
Return a new set with elements from the set and all others.

intersection(**others*)
set & other & ...
Return a new set with elements common to the set and all others.

difference(**others*)
set - other - ...
Return a new set with elements in the set that are not in the others.

symmetric_difference(*other*)
set ^ other
Return a new set with elements in either the set or *other* but not both.

copy()
Return a new set with a shallow copy of *s*.

Note, the non-operator versions of *union()*, *intersection()*, *difference()*, and *symmetric_difference()*, *issubset()*, and *issuperset()* methods will accept any iterable as an argument. In contrast, their operator based counterparts require their arguments to be sets. This precludes error-prone constructions like `set('abc') & 'cbs'` in favor of the more readable `set('abc').intersection('cbs')`.

Both *set* and *frozenset* support set to set comparisons. Two sets are equal if and only if every element of each set is contained in the other (each is a subset of the other). A set is less than another set if and only if the first set is a proper subset of the second set (is a subset, but is not equal). A set is greater than another set if and only if the first set is a proper superset of the second set (is a superset, but is not equal).

Instances of *set* are compared to instances of *frozenset* based on their members. For example, `set('abc') == frozenset('abc')` returns `True` and so does `set('abc') in set([frozenset('abc')])`.

The subset and equality comparisons do not generalize to a total ordering function. For example, any two nonempty disjoint sets are not equal and are not subsets of each other, so *all* of the following return `False`: `a<b`, `a==b`, or `a>b`.

Since sets only define partial ordering (subset relationships), the output of the *list.sort()* method is undefined for lists of sets.

Set elements, like dictionary keys, must be *hashable*.

Binary operations that mix *set* instances with *frozenset* return the type of the first operand. For example: `frozenset('ab') | set('bc')` returns an instance of *frozenset*.

The following table lists operations available for *set* that do not apply to immutable instances of *frozenset*:

update(**others*)
set |= other | ...
    Update the set, adding elements from all others.

intersection_update(**others*)
set &= other & ...
    Update the set, keeping only elements found in it and all others.

difference_update(**others*)
set -= other | ...
    Update the set, removing elements found in others.

symmetric_difference_update(*other*)
set ^= other
    Update the set, keeping only elements found in either set, but not in both.

add(*elem*)
    Add element *elem* to the set.

remove(*elem*)
    Remove element *elem* from the set. Raises *KeyError* if *elem* is not contained in the set.

discard(*elem*)
    Remove element *elem* from the set if it is present.

pop()
    Remove and return an arbitrary element from the set. Raises *KeyError* if the set is empty.

clear()
    Remove all elements from the set.

Note, the non-operator versions of the *update()*, *intersection_update()*, *difference_update()*, and *symmetric_difference_update()* methods will accept any iterable as an argument.

Note, the *elem* argument to the `__contains__()`, *remove()*, and *discard()* methods may be a set. To support searching for an equivalent frozenset, a temporary one is created from *elem*.

4.10 Mapping Types — dict

A *mapping* object maps *hashable* values to arbitrary objects. Mappings are mutable objects. There is currently only one standard mapping type, the *dictionary*. (For other containers see the built-in *list*, *set*, and *tuple* classes, and the *collections* module.)

A dictionary's keys are *almost* arbitrary values. Values that are not *hashable*, that is, values containing lists, dictionaries or other mutable types (that are compared by value rather than by object identity) may not be used as keys. Numeric types used for keys obey the normal rules for numeric comparison: if two numbers compare equal (such as `1` and `1.0`) then they can be used interchangeably to index the same dictionary entry. (Note however, that since computers store floating-point numbers as approximations it is usually unwise to use them as dictionary keys.)

Dictionaries can be created by placing a comma-separated list of `key: value` pairs within braces, for example: `{'jack': 4098, 'sjoerd': 4127}` or `{4098: 'jack', 4127: 'sjoerd'}`, or by the `dict` constructor.

class dict(***kwarg*)
class dict(*mapping, **kwarg*)
class dict(*iterable, **kwarg*)

Return a new dictionary initialized from an optional positional argument and a possibly empty set of keyword arguments.

If no positional argument is given, an empty dictionary is created. If a positional argument is given and it is a mapping object, a dictionary is created with the same key-value pairs as the mapping object. Otherwise, the positional argument must be an *iterable* object. Each item in the iterable must itself be an iterable with exactly two objects. The first object of each item becomes a key in the new dictionary, and the second object the corresponding value. If a key occurs more than once, the last value for that key becomes the corresponding value in the new dictionary.

If keyword arguments are given, the keyword arguments and their values are added to the dictionary created from the positional argument. If a key being added is already present, the value from the keyword argument replaces the value from the positional argument.

To illustrate, the following examples all return a dictionary equal to `{"one": 1, "two": 2, "three": 3}`:

```
>>> a = dict(one=1, two=2, three=3)
>>> b = {'one': 1, 'two': 2, 'three': 3}
>>> c = dict(zip(['one', 'two', 'three'], [1, 2, 3]))
>>> d = dict([('two', 2), ('one', 1), ('three', 3)])
>>> e = dict({'three': 3, 'one': 1, 'two': 2})
>>> a == b == c == d == e
True
```

Providing keyword arguments as in the first example only works for keys that are valid Python identifiers. Otherwise, any valid keys can be used.

These are the operations that dictionaries support (and therefore, custom mapping types should support too):

len(d)

Return the number of items in the dictionary *d*.

d[key]

Return the item of *d* with key *key*. Raises a *KeyError* if *key* is not in the map.

If a subclass of dict defines a method `__missing__()` and *key* is not present, the `d[key]` operation calls that method with the key *key* as argument. The `d[key]` operation then returns or raises whatever is returned or raised by the `__missing__(key)` call. No other operations or methods invoke `__missing__()`. If `__missing__()` is not defined, *KeyError* is raised. `__missing__()` must be a method; it cannot be an instance variable:

```
>>> class Counter(dict):
...     def __missing__(self, key):
...         return 0
>>> c = Counter()
>>> c['red']
0
>>> c['red'] += 1
>>> c['red']
1
```

The example above shows part of the implementation of *collections.Counter*. A different `__missing__` method is used by *collections.defaultdict*.

d[key] = value
Set `d[key]` to *value*.

del d[key]
Remove `d[key]` from *d*. Raises a *KeyError* if *key* is not in the map.

key in d
Return `True` if *d* has a key *key*, else `False`.

key not in d
Equivalent to `not key in d`.

iter(d)
Return an iterator over the keys of the dictionary. This is a shortcut for `iter(d.keys())`.

clear()
Remove all items from the dictionary.

copy()
Return a shallow copy of the dictionary.

classmethod fromkeys(*seq*[, *value*])
Create a new dictionary with keys from *seq* and values set to *value*.

fromkeys() is a class method that returns a new dictionary. *value* defaults to `None`.

get(*key*[, *default*])
Return the value for *key* if *key* is in the dictionary, else *default*. If *default* is not given, it defaults to `None`, so that this method never raises a *KeyError*.

items()
Return a new view of the dictionary's items (`(key, value)` pairs). See the *documentation of view objects*.

keys()
Return a new view of the dictionary's keys. See the *documentation of view objects*.

pop(*key*[, *default*])
If *key* is in the dictionary, remove it and return its value, else return *default*. If *default* is not given and *key* is not in the dictionary, a *KeyError* is raised.

popitem()
Remove and return an arbitrary `(key, value)` pair from the dictionary.

popitem() is useful to destructively iterate over a dictionary, as often used in set algorithms. If the dictionary is empty, calling *popitem()* raises a *KeyError*.

setdefault(*key*[, *default*])
If *key* is in the dictionary, return its value. If not, insert *key* with a value of *default* and return *default*. *default* defaults to `None`.

update([*other*])
Update the dictionary with the key/value pairs from *other*, overwriting existing keys. Return `None`.

update() accepts either another dictionary object or an iterable of key/value pairs (as tuples or other iterables of length two). If keyword arguments are specified, the dictionary is then updated with those key/value pairs: `d.update(red=1, blue=2)`.

values()
Return a new view of the dictionary's values. See the *documentation of view objects*.

Dictionaries compare equal if and only if they have the same `(key, value)` pairs. Order comparisons ('<', '<=', '>=', '>') raise *TypeError*.

See also:

types.MappingProxyType can be used to create a read-only view of a *dict*.

4.10.1 Dictionary view objects

The objects returned by *dict.keys()*, *dict.values()* and *dict.items()* are *view objects*. They provide a dynamic view on the dictionary's entries, which means that when the dictionary changes, the view reflects these changes.

Dictionary views can be iterated over to yield their respective data, and support membership tests:

len(dictview)
Return the number of entries in the dictionary.

iter(dictview)
Return an iterator over the keys, values or items (represented as tuples of `(key, value)`) in the dictionary.

Keys and values are iterated over in an arbitrary order which is non-random, varies across Python implementations, and depends on the dictionary's history of insertions and deletions. If keys, values and items views are iterated over with no intervening modifications to the dictionary, the order of items will directly correspond. This allows the creation of `(value, key)` pairs using *zip()*: `pairs = zip(d.values(), d.keys())`. Another way to create the same list is `pairs = [(v, k) for (k, v) in d.items()]`.

Iterating views while adding or deleting entries in the dictionary may raise a *RuntimeError* or fail to iterate over all entries.

x in dictview
Return `True` if x is in the underlying dictionary's keys, values or items (in the latter case, x should be a `(key, value)` tuple).

Keys views are set-like since their entries are unique and hashable. If all values are hashable, so that `(key, value)` pairs are unique and hashable, then the items view is also set-like. (Values views are not treated as set-like since the entries are generally not unique.) For set-like views, all of the operations defined for the abstract base class *collections.abc.Set* are available (for example, `==`, `<`, or `^`).

An example of dictionary view usage:

```
>>> dishes = {'eggs': 2, 'sausage': 1, 'bacon': 1, 'spam': 500}
>>> keys = dishes.keys()
>>> values = dishes.values()

>>> # iteration
>>> n = 0
>>> for val in values:
...     n += val
>>> print(n)
504

>>> # keys and values are iterated over in the same order
>>> list(keys)
['eggs', 'bacon', 'sausage', 'spam']
>>> list(values)
[2, 1, 1, 500]
```

```
>>> # view objects are dynamic and reflect dict changes
>>> del dishes['eggs']
>>> del dishes['sausage']
>>> list(keys)
['spam', 'bacon']

>>> # set operations
>>> keys & {'eggs', 'bacon', 'salad'}
{'bacon'}
>>> keys ^ {'sausage', 'juice'}
{'juice', 'sausage', 'bacon', 'spam'}
```

4.11 Context Manager Types

Python's `with` statement supports the concept of a runtime context defined by a context manager. This is implemented using a pair of methods that allow user-defined classes to define a runtime context that is entered before the statement body is executed and exited when the statement ends:

`contextmanager.__enter__()`

Enter the runtime context and return either this object or another object related to the runtime context. The value returned by this method is bound to the identifier in the `as` clause of `with` statements using this context manager.

An example of a context manager that returns itself is a *file object*. File objects return themselves from __enter__() to allow `open()` to be used as the context expression in a `with` statement.

An example of a context manager that returns a related object is the one returned by `decimal.localcontext()`. These managers set the active decimal context to a copy of the original decimal context and then return the copy. This allows changes to be made to the current decimal context in the body of the `with` statement without affecting code outside the `with` statement.

`contextmanager.__exit__(exc_type, exc_val, exc_tb)`

Exit the runtime context and return a Boolean flag indicating if any exception that occurred should be suppressed. If an exception occurred while executing the body of the `with` statement, the arguments contain the exception type, value and traceback information. Otherwise, all three arguments are `None`.

Returning a true value from this method will cause the `with` statement to suppress the exception and continue execution with the statement immediately following the `with` statement. Otherwise the exception continues propagating after this method has finished executing. Exceptions that occur during execution of this method will replace any exception that occurred in the body of the `with` statement.

The exception passed in should never be reraised explicitly - instead, this method should return a false value to indicate that the method completed successfully and does not want to suppress the raised exception. This allows context management code to easily detect whether or not an `__exit__()` method has actually failed.

Python defines several context managers to support easy thread synchronisation, prompt closure of files or other objects, and simpler manipulation of the active decimal arithmetic context. The specific types are not treated specially beyond their implementation of the context management protocol. See the `contextlib` module for some examples.

Python's *generators* and the `contextlib.contextmanager` decorator provide a convenient way to implement these protocols. If a generator function is decorated with the `contextlib.contextmanager` decorator, it will return a context manager implementing the necessary `__enter__()` and `__exit__()` methods, rather than the iterator produced by an undecorated generator function.

Note that there is no specific slot for any of these methods in the type structure for Python objects in the Python/C API. Extension types wanting to define these methods must provide them as a normal Python accessible method. Compared to the overhead of setting up the runtime context, the overhead of a single class dictionary lookup is negligible.

4.12 Other Built-in Types

The interpreter supports several other kinds of objects. Most of these support only one or two operations.

4.12.1 Modules

The only special operation on a module is attribute access: `m.name`, where *m* is a module and *name* accesses a name defined in *m*'s symbol table. Module attributes can be assigned to. (Note that the `import` statement is not, strictly speaking, an operation on a module object; `import foo` does not require a module object named *foo* to exist, rather it requires an (external) *definition* for a module named *foo* somewhere.)

A special attribute of every module is *__dict__*. This is the dictionary containing the module's symbol table. Modifying this dictionary will actually change the module's symbol table, but direct assignment to the *__dict__* attribute is not possible (you can write `m.__dict__['a'] = 1`, which defines `m.a` to be `1`, but you can't write `m.__dict__ = {}`). Modifying *__dict__* directly is not recommended.

Modules built into the interpreter are written like this: `<module 'sys' (built-in)>`. If loaded from a file, they are written as `<module 'os' from '/usr/local/lib/pythonX.Y/os.pyc'>`.

4.12.2 Classes and Class Instances

See objects and class for these.

4.12.3 Functions

Function objects are created by function definitions. The only operation on a function object is to call it: `func(argument-list)`.

There are really two flavors of function objects: built-in functions and user-defined functions. Both support the same operation (to call the function), but the implementation is different, hence the different object types.

See function for more information.

4.12.4 Methods

Methods are functions that are called using the attribute notation. There are two flavors: built-in methods (such as `append()` on lists) and class instance methods. Built-in methods are described with the types that support them.

If you access a method (a function defined in a class namespace) through an instance, you get a special object: a *bound method* (also called *instance method*) object. When called, it will add the `self` argument to the argument list. Bound methods have two special read-only attributes: `m.__self__` is the object on which the method operates, and `m.__func__` is the function implementing the method. Calling `m(arg-1, arg-2, ..., arg-n)` is completely equivalent to calling `m.__func__(m.__self__, arg-1, arg-2, ..., arg-n)`.

Like function objects, bound method objects support getting arbitrary attributes. However, since method attributes are actually stored on the underlying function object (`meth.__func__`), setting method attributes on bound methods is disallowed. Attempting to set an attribute on a method results in an *AttributeError* being raised. In order to set a method attribute, you need to explicitly set it on the underlying function object:

```
>>> class C:
...     def method(self):
...         pass
...
>>> c = C()
>>> c.method.whoami = 'my name is method'  # can't set on the method
Traceback (most recent call last):
  File "<stdin>", line 1, in <module>
AttributeError: 'method' object has no attribute 'whoami'
>>> c.method.__func__.whoami = 'my name is method'
>>> c.method.whoami
'my name is method'
```

See types for more information.

4.12.5 Code Objects

Code objects are used by the implementation to represent "pseudo-compiled" executable Python code such as a function body. They differ from function objects because they don't contain a reference to their global execution environment. Code objects are returned by the built-in *compile()* function and can be extracted from function objects through their `__code__` attribute. See also the *code* module.

A code object can be executed or evaluated by passing it (instead of a source string) to the *exec()* or *eval()* built-in functions.

See types for more information.

4.12.6 Type Objects

Type objects represent the various object types. An object's type is accessed by the built-in function *type()*. There are no special operations on types. The standard module *types* defines names for all standard built-in types.

Types are written like this: `<class 'int'>`.

4.12.7 The Null Object

This object is returned by functions that don't explicitly return a value. It supports no special operations. There is exactly one null object, named `None` (a built-in name). `type(None)()` produces the same singleton.

It is written as `None`.

4.12.8 The Ellipsis Object

This object is commonly used by slicing (see slicings). It supports no special operations. There is exactly one ellipsis object, named *Ellipsis* (a built-in name). `type(Ellipsis)()` produces the *Ellipsis* singleton.

It is written as `Ellipsis` or `...`.

4.12.9 The NotImplemented Object

This object is returned from comparisons and binary operations when they are asked to operate on types they don't support. See comparisons for more information. There is exactly one `NotImplemented` object. `type(NotImplemented)()` produces the singleton instance.

It is written as `NotImplemented`.

4.12.10 Boolean Values

Boolean values are the two constant objects `False` and `True`. They are used to represent truth values (although other values can also be considered false or true). In numeric contexts (for example when used as the argument to an arithmetic operator), they behave like the integers 0 and 1, respectively. The built-in function *bool()* can be used to convert any value to a Boolean, if the value can be interpreted as a truth value (see section *Truth Value Testing* above).

They are written as `False` and `True`, respectively.

4.12.11 Internal Objects

See types for this information. It describes stack frame objects, traceback objects, and slice objects.

4.13 Special Attributes

The implementation adds a few special read-only attributes to several object types, where they are relevant. Some of these are not reported by the *dir()* built-in function.

`object.__dict__`
: A dictionary or other mapping object used to store an object's (writable) attributes.

`instance.__class__`
: The class to which a class instance belongs.

`class.__bases__`
: The tuple of base classes of a class object.

`definition.__name__`
: The name of the class, function, method, descriptor, or generator instance.

`definition.__qualname__`
: The *qualified name* of the class, function, method, descriptor, or generator instance.

  New in version 3.3.

`class.__mro__`
: This attribute is a tuple of classes that are considered when looking for base classes during method resolution.

`class.mro()`
: This method can be overridden by a metaclass to customize the method resolution order for its instances. It is called at class instantiation, and its result is stored in *__mro__*.

`class.__subclasses__()`
: Each class keeps a list of weak references to its immediate subclasses. This method returns a list of all those references still alive. Example:

```
>>> int.__subclasses__()
[<class 'bool'>]
```

CHAPTER

FIVE

BUILT-IN EXCEPTIONS

In Python, all exceptions must be instances of a class that derives from *BaseException*. In a **try** statement with an **except** clause that mentions a particular class, that clause also handles any exception classes derived from that class (but not exception classes from which *it* is derived). Two exception classes that are not related via subclassing are never equivalent, even if they have the same name.

The built-in exceptions listed below can be generated by the interpreter or built-in functions. Except where mentioned, they have an "associated value" indicating the detailed cause of the error. This may be a string or a tuple of several items of information (e.g., an error code and a string explaining the code). The associated value is usually passed as arguments to the exception class's constructor.

User code can raise built-in exceptions. This can be used to test an exception handler or to report an error condition "just like" the situation in which the interpreter raises the same exception; but beware that there is nothing to prevent user code from raising an inappropriate error.

The built-in exception classes can be subclassed to define new exceptions; programmers are encouraged to derive new exceptions from the *Exception* class or one of its subclasses, and not from *BaseException*. More information on defining exceptions is available in the Python Tutorial under tut-userexceptions.

When raising (or re-raising) an exception in an **except** or **finally** clause `__context__` is automatically set to the last exception caught; if the new exception is not handled the traceback that is eventually displayed will include the originating exception(s) and the final exception.

When raising a new exception (rather than using a bare **raise** to re-raise the exception currently being handled), the implicit exception context can be supplemented with an explicit cause by using **from** with **raise**:

```
raise new_exc from original_exc
```

The expression following **from** must be an exception or `None`. It will be set as `__cause__` on the raised exception. Setting `__cause__` also implicitly sets the `__suppress_context__` attribute to `True`, so that using `raise new_exc from None` effectively replaces the old exception with the new one for display purposes (e.g. converting *KeyError* to *AttributeError*, while leaving the old exception available in `__context__` for introspection when debugging.

The default traceback display code shows these chained exceptions in addition to the traceback for the exception itself. An explicitly chained exception in `__cause__` is always shown when present. An implicitly chained exception in `__context__` is shown only if `__cause__` is *None* and `__suppress_context__` is false.

In either case, the exception itself is always shown after any chained exceptions so that the final line of the traceback always shows the last exception that was raised.

5.1 Base classes

The following exceptions are used mostly as base classes for other exceptions.

exception BaseException

The base class for all built-in exceptions. It is not meant to be directly inherited by user-defined classes (for that, use *Exception*). If *str()* is called on an instance of this class, the representation of the argument(s) to the instance are returned, or the empty string when there were no arguments.

args

The tuple of arguments given to the exception constructor. Some built-in exceptions (like *OSError*) expect a certain number of arguments and assign a special meaning to the elements of this tuple, while others are usually called only with a single string giving an error message.

with_traceback(*tb*)

This method sets *tb* as the new traceback for the exception and returns the exception object. It is usually used in exception handling code like this:

```
try:
    ...
except SomeException:
    tb = sys.exc_info()[2]
    raise OtherException(...).with_traceback(tb)
```

exception Exception

All built-in, non-system-exiting exceptions are derived from this class. All user-defined exceptions should also be derived from this class.

exception ArithmeticError

The base class for those built-in exceptions that are raised for various arithmetic errors: *OverflowError*, *ZeroDivisionError*, *FloatingPointError*.

exception BufferError

Raised when a buffer related operation cannot be performed.

exception LookupError

The base class for the exceptions that are raised when a key or index used on a mapping or sequence is invalid: *IndexError*, *KeyError*. This can be raised directly by *codecs.lookup()*.

5.2 Concrete exceptions

The following exceptions are the exceptions that are usually raised.

exception AssertionError

Raised when an **assert** statement fails.

exception AttributeError

Raised when an attribute reference (see attribute-references) or assignment fails. (When an object does not support attribute references or attribute assignments at all, *TypeError* is raised.)

exception EOFError

Raised when the *input()* function hits an end-of-file condition (EOF) without reading any data. (N.B.: the `io.IOBase.read()` and *io.IOBase.readline()* methods return an empty string when they hit EOF.)

exception FloatingPointError

Raised when a floating point operation fails. This exception is always defined, but can only be raised when Python is configured with the **--with-fpectl** option, or the `WANT_SIGFPE_HANDLER` symbol is defined in the `pyconfig.h` file.

exception GeneratorExit

Raised when a *generator* or *coroutine* is closed; see `generator.close()` and `coroutine.close()`. It directly inherits from *BaseException* instead of *Exception* since it is technically not an error.

exception ImportError

Raised when the `import` statement has troubles trying to load a module. Also raised when the "from list" in `from ... import` has a name that cannot be found.

The `name` and `path` attributes can be set using keyword-only arguments to the constructor. When set they represent the name of the module that was attempted to be imported and the path to any file which triggered the exception, respectively.

Changed in version 3.3: Added the `name` and `path` attributes.

exception ModuleNotFoundError

A subclass of *ImportError* which is raised by `import` when a module could not be located. It is also raised when `None` is found in *sys.modules*.

New in version 3.6.

exception IndexError

Raised when a sequence subscript is out of range. (Slice indices are silently truncated to fall in the allowed range; if an index is not an integer, *TypeError* is raised.)

exception KeyError

Raised when a mapping (dictionary) key is not found in the set of existing keys.

exception KeyboardInterrupt

Raised when the user hits the interrupt key (normally `Control-C` or `Delete`). During execution, a check for interrupts is made regularly. The exception inherits from *BaseException* so as to not be accidentally caught by code that catches *Exception* and thus prevent the interpreter from exiting.

exception MemoryError

Raised when an operation runs out of memory but the situation may still be rescued (by deleting some objects). The associated value is a string indicating what kind of (internal) operation ran out of memory. Note that because of the underlying memory management architecture (C's `malloc()` function), the interpreter may not always be able to completely recover from this situation; it nevertheless raises an exception so that a stack traceback can be printed, in case a run-away program was the cause.

exception NameError

Raised when a local or global name is not found. This applies only to unqualified names. The associated value is an error message that includes the name that could not be found.

exception NotImplementedError

This exception is derived from *RuntimeError*. In user defined base classes, abstract methods should raise this exception when they require derived classes to override the method, or while the class is being developed to indicate that the real implementation still needs to be added.

Note: It should not be used to indicate that an operator or method is not meant to be supported at all – in that case either leave the operator / method undefined or, if a subclass, set it to *None*.

Note: `NotImplementedError` and `NotImplemented` are not interchangeable, even though they have similar names and purposes. See *NotImplemented* for details on when to use it.

---

exception OSError([*arg*])

exception OSError(*errno*, *strerror*[, *filename*[, *winerror*[, *filename2*]]])

This exception is raised when a system function returns a system-related error, including I/O failures such as "file not found" or "disk full" (not for illegal argument types or other incidental errors).

The second form of the constructor sets the corresponding attributes, described below. The attributes default to *None* if not specified. For backwards compatibility, if three arguments are passed, the *args* attribute contains only a 2-tuple of the first two constructor arguments.

The constructor often actually returns a subclass of *OSError*, as described in *OS exceptions* below. The particular subclass depends on the final *errno* value. This behaviour only occurs when constructing *OSError* directly or via an alias, and is not inherited when subclassing.

errno
A numeric error code from the C variable `errno`.

winerror
Under Windows, this gives you the native Windows error code. The *errno* attribute is then an approximate translation, in POSIX terms, of that native error code.

Under Windows, if the *winerror* constructor argument is an integer, the *errno* attribute is determined from the Windows error code, and the *errno* argument is ignored. On other platforms, the *winerror* argument is ignored, and the *winerror* attribute does not exist.

strerror
The corresponding error message, as provided by the operating system. It is formatted by the C functions `perror()` under POSIX, and `FormatMessage()` under Windows.

filename
filename2
For exceptions that involve a file system path (such as *open()* or *os.unlink()*), *filename* is the file name passed to the function. For functions that involve two file system paths (such as *os.rename()*), *filename2* corresponds to the second file name passed to the function.

Changed in version 3.3: *EnvironmentError*, *IOError*, *WindowsError*, *socket.error*, *select.error* and `mmap.error` have been merged into *OSError*, and the constructor may return a subclass.

Changed in version 3.4: The *filename* attribute is now the original file name passed to the function, instead of the name encoded to or decoded from the filesystem encoding. Also, the *filename2* constructor argument and attribute was added.

exception OverflowError
Raised when the result of an arithmetic operation is too large to be represented. This cannot occur for integers (which would rather raise *MemoryError* than give up). However, for historical reasons, OverflowError is sometimes raised for integers that are outside a required range. Because of the lack of standardization of floating point exception handling in C, most floating point operations are not checked.

exception RecursionError
This exception is derived from *RuntimeError*. It is raised when the interpreter detects that the maximum recursion depth (see *sys.getrecursionlimit()*) is exceeded.

New in version 3.5: Previously, a plain *RuntimeError* was raised.

exception ReferenceError
This exception is raised when a weak reference proxy, created by the *weakref.proxy()* function, is used to access an attribute of the referent after it has been garbage collected. For more information on weak references, see the *weakref* module.

exception RuntimeError
Raised when an error is detected that doesn't fall in any of the other categories. The associated value is a string indicating what precisely went wrong.

exception StopIteration
Raised by built-in function *next()* and an *iterator*'s *__next__()* method to signal that there are no further items produced by the iterator.

The exception object has a single attribute `value`, which is given as an argument when constructing the exception, and defaults to *None*.

When a *generator* or *coroutine* function returns, a new *StopIteration* instance is raised, and the value returned by the function is used as the `value` parameter to the constructor of the exception.

If a generator function defined in the presence of a `from __future__ import generator_stop` directive raises *StopIteration*, it will be converted into a *RuntimeError* (retaining the *StopIteration* as the new exception's cause).

Changed in version 3.3: Added `value` attribute and the ability for generator functions to use it to return a value.

Changed in version 3.5: Introduced the RuntimeError transformation.

exception StopAsyncIteration
Must be raised by `__anext__()` method of an *asynchronous iterator* object to stop the iteration.

New in version 3.5.

exception SyntaxError
Raised when the parser encounters a syntax error. This may occur in an `import` statement, in a call to the built-in functions *exec()* or *eval()*, or when reading the initial script or standard input (also interactively).

Instances of this class have attributes `filename`, `lineno`, `offset` and `text` for easier access to the details. *str()* of the exception instance returns only the message.

exception IndentationError
Base class for syntax errors related to incorrect indentation. This is a subclass of *SyntaxError*.

exception TabError
Raised when indentation contains an inconsistent use of tabs and spaces. This is a subclass of *IndentationError*.

exception SystemError
Raised when the interpreter finds an internal error, but the situation does not look so serious to cause it to abandon all hope. The associated value is a string indicating what went wrong (in low-level terms).

You should report this to the author or maintainer of your Python interpreter. Be sure to report the version of the Python interpreter (`sys.version`; it is also printed at the start of an interactive Python session), the exact error message (the exception's associated value) and if possible the source of the program that triggered the error.

exception SystemExit
This exception is raised by the *sys.exit()* function. It inherits from *BaseException* instead of *Exception* so that it is not accidentally caught by code that catches *Exception*. This allows the exception to properly propagate up and cause the interpreter to exit. When it is not handled, the Python interpreter exits; no stack traceback is printed. The constructor accepts the same optional argument passed to *sys.exit()*. If the value is an integer, it specifies the system exit status (passed to C's `exit()` function); if it is `None`, the exit status is zero; if it has another type (such as a string), the object's value is printed and the exit status is one.

A call to *sys.exit()* is translated into an exception so that clean-up handlers (`finally` clauses of `try` statements) can be executed, and so that a debugger can execute a script without running the risk of losing control. The *os._exit()* function can be used if it is absolutely positively necessary to exit immediately (for example, in the child process after a call to *os.fork()*).

code
The exit status or error message that is passed to the constructor. (Defaults to `None`.)

exception TypeError
Raised when an operation or function is applied to an object of inappropriate type. The associated value is a string giving details about the type mismatch.

This exception may be raised by user code to indicate that an attempted operation on an object is not supported, and is not meant to be. If an object is meant to support a given operation but has not yet provided an implementation, *NotImplementedError* is the proper exception to raise.

Passing arguments of the wrong type (e.g. passing a *list* when an *int* is expected) should result in a *TypeError*, but passing arguments with the wrong value (e.g. a number outside expected boundaries) should result in a *ValueError*.

exception UnboundLocalError
Raised when a reference is made to a local variable in a function or method, but no value has been bound to that variable. This is a subclass of *NameError*.

exception UnicodeError
Raised when a Unicode-related encoding or decoding error occurs. It is a subclass of *ValueError*.

UnicodeError has attributes that describe the encoding or decoding error. For example, `err.object[err.start:err.end]` gives the particular invalid input that the codec failed on.

encoding
The name of the encoding that raised the error.

reason
A string describing the specific codec error.

object
The object the codec was attempting to encode or decode.

start
The first index of invalid data in *object*.

end
The index after the last invalid data in *object*.

exception UnicodeEncodeError
Raised when a Unicode-related error occurs during encoding. It is a subclass of *UnicodeError*.

exception UnicodeDecodeError
Raised when a Unicode-related error occurs during decoding. It is a subclass of *UnicodeError*.

exception UnicodeTranslateError
Raised when a Unicode-related error occurs during translating. It is a subclass of *UnicodeError*.

exception ValueError
Raised when a built-in operation or function receives an argument that has the right type but an inappropriate value, and the situation is not described by a more precise exception such as *IndexError*.

exception ZeroDivisionError
Raised when the second argument of a division or modulo operation is zero. The associated value is a string indicating the type of the operands and the operation.

The following exceptions are kept for compatibility with previous versions; starting from Python 3.3, they are aliases of *OSError*.

exception EnvironmentError

exception IOError

exception WindowsError
Only available on Windows.

5.2.1 OS exceptions

The following exceptions are subclasses of *OSError*, they get raised depending on the system error code.

exception BlockingIOError
Raised when an operation would block on an object (e.g. socket) set for non-blocking operation. Corresponds to `errno` `EAGAIN`, `EALREADY`, `EWOULDBLOCK` and `EINPROGRESS`.

In addition to those of *OSError*, *BlockingIOError* can have one more attribute:

characters_written
An integer containing the number of characters written to the stream before it blocked. This attribute is available when using the buffered I/O classes from the *io* module.

exception ChildProcessError
Raised when an operation on a child process failed. Corresponds to errno ECHILD.

exception ConnectionError
A base class for connection-related issues.

Subclasses are *BrokenPipeError*, *ConnectionAbortedError*, *ConnectionRefusedError* and *ConnectionResetError*.

exception BrokenPipeError
A subclass of *ConnectionError*, raised when trying to write on a pipe while the other end has been closed, or trying to write on a socket which has been shutdown for writing. Corresponds to errno EPIPE and ESHUTDOWN.

exception ConnectionAbortedError
A subclass of *ConnectionError*, raised when a connection attempt is aborted by the peer. Corresponds to errno ECONNABORTED.

exception ConnectionRefusedError
A subclass of *ConnectionError*, raised when a connection attempt is refused by the peer. Corresponds to errno ECONNREFUSED.

exception ConnectionResetError
A subclass of *ConnectionError*, raised when a connection is reset by the peer. Corresponds to errno ECONNRESET.

exception FileExistsError
Raised when trying to create a file or directory which already exists. Corresponds to errno EEXIST.

exception FileNotFoundError
Raised when a file or directory is requested but doesn't exist. Corresponds to errno ENOENT.

exception InterruptedError
Raised when a system call is interrupted by an incoming signal. Corresponds to errno *EINTR*.

Changed in version 3.5: Python now retries system calls when a syscall is interrupted by a signal, except if the signal handler raises an exception (see PEP 475 for the rationale), instead of raising *InterruptedError*.

exception IsADirectoryError
Raised when a file operation (such as *os.remove()*) is requested on a directory. Corresponds to errno EISDIR.

exception NotADirectoryError
Raised when a directory operation (such as *os.listdir()*) is requested on something which is not a directory. Corresponds to errno ENOTDIR.

exception PermissionError
Raised when trying to run an operation without the adequate access rights - for example filesystem permissions. Corresponds to errno EACCES and EPERM.

exception ProcessLookupError
Raised when a given process doesn't exist. Corresponds to errno ESRCH.

exception TimeoutError
Raised when a system function timed out at the system level. Corresponds to errno ETIMEDOUT.

New in version 3.3: All the above *OSError* subclasses were added.

See also:

PEP 3151 - Reworking the OS and IO exception hierarchy

5.3 Warnings

The following exceptions are used as warning categories; see the *warnings* module for more information.

exception Warning
Base class for warning categories.

exception UserWarning
Base class for warnings generated by user code.

exception DeprecationWarning
Base class for warnings about deprecated features.

exception PendingDeprecationWarning
Base class for warnings about features which will be deprecated in the future.

exception SyntaxWarning
Base class for warnings about dubious syntax.

exception RuntimeWarning
Base class for warnings about dubious runtime behavior.

exception FutureWarning
Base class for warnings about constructs that will change semantically in the future.

exception ImportWarning
Base class for warnings about probable mistakes in module imports.

exception UnicodeWarning
Base class for warnings related to Unicode.

exception BytesWarning
Base class for warnings related to *bytes* and *bytearray*.

exception ResourceWarning
Base class for warnings related to resource usage.

New in version 3.2.

5.4 Exception hierarchy

The class hierarchy for built-in exceptions is:

```
BaseException
 +-- SystemExit
 +-- KeyboardInterrupt
 +-- GeneratorExit
 +-- Exception
      +-- StopIteration
      +-- StopAsyncIteration
      +-- ArithmeticError
      |    +-- FloatingPointError
      |    +-- OverflowError
      |    +-- ZeroDivisionError
```

```
+-- AssertionError
+-- AttributeError
+-- BufferError
+-- EOFError
+-- ImportError
|    +-- ModuleNotFoundError
+-- LookupError
|    +-- IndexError
|    +-- KeyError
+-- MemoryError
+-- NameError
|    +-- UnboundLocalError
+-- OSError
|    +-- BlockingIOError
|    +-- ChildProcessError
|    +-- ConnectionError
|    |    +-- BrokenPipeError
|    |    +-- ConnectionAbortedError
|    |    +-- ConnectionRefusedError
|    |    +-- ConnectionResetError
|    +-- FileExistsError
|    +-- FileNotFoundError
|    +-- InterruptedError
|    +-- IsADirectoryError
|    +-- NotADirectoryError
|    +-- PermissionError
|    +-- ProcessLookupError
|    +-- TimeoutError
+-- ReferenceError
+-- RuntimeError
|    +-- NotImplementedError
|    +-- RecursionError
+-- SyntaxError
|    +-- IndentationError
|         +-- TabError
+-- SystemError
+-- TypeError
+-- ValueError
|    +-- UnicodeError
|         +-- UnicodeDecodeError
|         +-- UnicodeEncodeError
|         +-- UnicodeTranslateError
+-- Warning
     +-- DeprecationWarning
     +-- PendingDeprecationWarning
     +-- RuntimeWarning
     +-- SyntaxWarning
     +-- UserWarning
     +-- FutureWarning
     +-- ImportWarning
     +-- UnicodeWarning
     +-- BytesWarning
     +-- ResourceWarning
```

CHAPTER

SIX

TEXT PROCESSING SERVICES

The modules described in this chapter provide a wide range of string manipulation operations and other text processing services.

The *codecs* module described under *Binary Data Services* is also highly relevant to text processing. In addition, see the documentation for Python's built-in string type in *Text Sequence Type — str*.

6.1 string — Common string operations

Source code: Lib/string.py

See also:

Text Sequence Type — str

String Methods

6.1.1 String constants

The constants defined in this module are:

string.ascii_letters
The concatenation of the *ascii_lowercase* and *ascii_uppercase* constants described below. This value is not locale-dependent.

string.ascii_lowercase
The lowercase letters `'abcdefghijklmnopqrstuvwxyz'`. This value is not locale-dependent and will not change.

string.ascii_uppercase
The uppercase letters `'ABCDEFGHIJKLMNOPQRSTUVWXYZ'`. This value is not locale-dependent and will not change.

string.digits
The string `'0123456789'`.

string.hexdigits
The string `'0123456789abcdefABCDEF'`.

string.octdigits
The string `'01234567'`.

string.punctuation
String of ASCII characters which are considered punctuation characters in the `C` locale.

string.printable
String of ASCII characters which are considered printable. This is a combination of *digits*, *ascii_letters*, *punctuation*, and *whitespace*.

string.whitespace
A string containing all ASCII characters that are considered whitespace. This includes the characters space, tab, linefeed, return, formfeed, and vertical tab.

6.1.2 Custom String Formatting

The built-in string class provides the ability to do complex variable substitutions and value formatting via the *format()* method described in PEP 3101. The *Formatter* class in the *string* module allows you to create and customize your own string formatting behaviors using the same implementation as the built-in *format()* method.

class string.Formatter
The *Formatter* class has the following public methods:

format(*format_string*, **args*, ***kwargs*)
The primary API method. It takes a format string and an arbitrary set of positional and keyword arguments. It is just a wrapper that calls *vformat()*.

Deprecated since version 3.5: Passing a format string as keyword argument *format_string* has been deprecated.

vformat(*format_string*, *args*, *kwargs*)
This function does the actual work of formatting. It is exposed as a separate function for cases where you want to pass in a predefined dictionary of arguments, rather than unpacking and repacking the dictionary as individual arguments using the `*args` and `**kwargs` syntax. *vformat()* does the work of breaking up the format string into character data and replacement fields. It calls the various methods described below.

In addition, the *Formatter* defines a number of methods that are intended to be replaced by subclasses:

parse(*format_string*)
Loop over the format_string and return an iterable of tuples (*literal_text*, *field_name*, *format_spec*, *conversion*). This is used by *vformat()* to break the string into either literal text, or replacement fields.

The values in the tuple conceptually represent a span of literal text followed by a single replacement field. If there is no literal text (which can happen if two replacement fields occur consecutively), then *literal_text* will be a zero-length string. If there is no replacement field, then the values of *field_name*, *format_spec* and *conversion* will be `None`.

get_field(*field_name*, *args*, *kwargs*)
Given *field_name* as returned by *parse()* (see above), convert it to an object to be formatted. Returns a tuple (obj, used_key). The default version takes strings of the form defined in PEP 3101, such as "0[name]" or "label.title". *args* and *kwargs* are as passed in to *vformat()*. The return value *used_key* has the same meaning as the *key* parameter to *get_value()*.

get_value(*key*, *args*, *kwargs*)
Retrieve a given field value. The *key* argument will be either an integer or a string. If it is an integer, it represents the index of the positional argument in *args*; if it is a string, then it represents a named argument in *kwargs*.

The *args* parameter is set to the list of positional arguments to *vformat()*, and the *kwargs* parameter is set to the dictionary of keyword arguments.

For compound field names, these functions are only called for the first component of the field name; Subsequent components are handled through normal attribute and indexing operations.

So for example, the field expression '0.name' would cause `get_value()` to be called with a *key* argument of 0. The **name** attribute will be looked up after `get_value()` returns by calling the built-in `getattr()` function.

If the index or keyword refers to an item that does not exist, then an *IndexError* or *KeyError* should be raised.

check_unused_args(*used_args*, *args*, *kwargs*)
Implement checking for unused arguments if desired. The arguments to this function is the set of all argument keys that were actually referred to in the format string (integers for positional arguments, and strings for named arguments), and a reference to the *args* and *kwargs* that was passed to vformat. The set of unused args can be calculated from these parameters. `check_unused_args()` is assumed to raise an exception if the check fails.

format_field(*value*, *format_spec*)
`format_field()` simply calls the global `format()` built-in. The method is provided so that subclasses can override it.

convert_field(*value*, *conversion*)
Converts the value (returned by `get_field()`) given a conversion type (as in the tuple returned by the `parse()` method). The default version understands 's' (str), 'r' (repr) and 'a' (ascii) conversion types.

6.1.3 Format String Syntax

The `str.format()` method and the `Formatter` class share the same syntax for format strings (although in the case of `Formatter`, subclasses can define their own format string syntax). The syntax is related to that of formatted string literals, but there are differences.

Format strings contain "replacement fields" surrounded by curly braces `{}`. Anything that is not contained in braces is considered literal text, which is copied unchanged to the output. If you need to include a brace character in the literal text, it can be escaped by doubling: `{{` and `}}`.

The grammar for a replacement field is as follows:

```
replacement_field ::=  "{" [field_name] ["!" conversion] [":" format_spec] "}"
field_name        ::=  arg_name ("." attribute_name | "[" element_index "]")*
arg_name          ::=  [identifier | integer]
attribute_name    ::=  identifier
element_index     ::=  integer | index_string
index_string      ::=  <any source character except "]"> +
conversion        ::=  "r" | "s" | "a"
format_spec       ::=  <described in the next section>
```

In less formal terms, the replacement field can start with a *field_name* that specifies the object whose value is to be formatted and inserted into the output instead of the replacement field. The *field_name* is optionally followed by a *conversion* field, which is preceded by an exclamation point `'!'`, and a *format_spec*, which is preceded by a colon `':'`. These specify a non-default format for the replacement value.

See also the *Format Specification Mini-Language* section.

The *field_name* itself begins with an *arg_name* that is either a number or a keyword. If it's a number, it refers to a positional argument, and if it's a keyword, it refers to a named keyword argument. If the numerical arg_names in a format string are 0, 1, 2, ... in sequence, they can all be omitted (not just some) and the numbers 0, 1, 2, ... will be automatically inserted in that order. Because *arg_name* is not quote-delimited, it is not possible to specify arbitrary dictionary keys (e.g., the strings '10' or ':-]') within a format string. The *arg_name* can be followed by any number of index or attribute expressions. An expression of the form '.name' selects the named attribute using getattr(), while an expression of the form '[index]' does an index lookup using `__getitem__()`.

Changed in version 3.1: The positional argument specifiers can be omitted, so '{} {}' is equivalent to '{0} {1}'.

Some simple format string examples:

```
"First, thou shalt count to {0}"  # References first positional argument
"Bring me a {}"                   # Implicitly references the first positional argument
"From {} to {}"                   # Same as "From {0} to {1}"
"My quest is {name}"              # References keyword argument 'name'
"Weight in tons {0.weight}"       # 'weight' attribute of first positional arg
"Units destroyed: {players[0]}"   # First element of keyword argument 'players'.
```

The *conversion* field causes a type coercion before formatting. Normally, the job of formatting a value is done by the `__format__()` method of the value itself. However, in some cases it is desirable to force a type to be formatted as a string, overriding its own definition of formatting. By converting the value to a string before calling `__format__()`, the normal formatting logic is bypassed.

Three conversion flags are currently supported: '!s' which calls *str()* on the value, '!r' which calls *repr()* and '!a' which calls *ascii()*.

Some examples:

```
"Harold's a clever {0!s}"        # Calls str() on the argument first
"Bring out the holy {name!r}"    # Calls repr() on the argument first
"More {!a}"                      # Calls ascii() on the argument first
```

The *format_spec* field contains a specification of how the value should be presented, including such details as field width, alignment, padding, decimal precision and so on. Each value type can define its own "formatting mini-language" or interpretation of the *format_spec*.

Most built-in types support a common formatting mini-language, which is described in the next section.

A *format_spec* field can also include nested replacement fields within it. These nested replacement fields may contain a field name, conversion flag and format specification, but deeper nesting is not allowed. The replacement fields within the format_spec are substituted before the *format_spec* string is interpreted. This allows the formatting of a value to be dynamically specified.

See the *Format examples* section for some examples.

Format Specification Mini-Language

"Format specifications" are used within replacement fields contained within a format string to define how individual values are presented (see *Format String Syntax* and f-strings). They can also be passed directly to the built-in *format()* function. Each formattable type may define how the format specification is to be interpreted.

Most built-in types implement the following options for format specifications, although some of the formatting options are only supported by the numeric types.

A general convention is that an empty format string ("") produces the same result as if you had called *str()* on the value. A non-empty format string typically modifies the result.

The general form of a *standard format specifier* is:

```
format_spec      ::=  [[fill]align][sign][#][0][width][grouping_option][.precision][type]
fill             ::=  <any character>
align            ::=  "<" | ">" | "=" | "^"
sign             ::=  "+" | "-" | " "
width            ::=  integer
grouping_option  ::=  "_" | ","
precision        ::=  integer
type             ::=  "b" | "c" | "d" | "e" | "E" | "f" | "F" | "g" | "G" | "n" | "o" | "s" |
```

If a valid *align* value is specified, it can be preceded by a *fill* character that can be any character and defaults to a space if omitted. It is not possible to use a literal curly brace ("{" or "}") as the *fill* character in a formatted string literal or when using the `str.format()` method. However, it is possible to insert a curly brace with a nested replacement field. This limitation doesn't affect the `format()` function.

The meaning of the various alignment options is as follows:

Option	Meaning
'<'	Forces the field to be left-aligned within the available space (this is the default for most objects).
'>'	Forces the field to be right-aligned within the available space (this is the default for numbers).
'='	Forces the padding to be placed after the sign (if any) but before the digits. This is used for printing fields in the form '+000000120'. This alignment option is only valid for numeric types. It becomes the default when '0' immediately precedes the field width.
'^'	Forces the field to be centered within the available space.

Note that unless a minimum field width is defined, the field width will always be the same size as the data to fill it, so that the alignment option has no meaning in this case.

The *sign* option is only valid for number types, and can be one of the following:

Option	Meaning
'+'	indicates that a sign should be used for both positive as well as negative numbers.
'-'	indicates that a sign should be used only for negative numbers (this is the default behavior).
space	indicates that a leading space should be used on positive numbers, and a minus sign on negative numbers.

The '#' option causes the "alternate form" to be used for the conversion. The alternate form is defined differently for different types. This option is only valid for integer, float, complex and Decimal types. For integers, when binary, octal, or hexadecimal output is used, this option adds the prefix respective '0b', '0o', or '0x' to the output value. For floats, complex and Decimal the alternate form causes the result of the conversion to always contain a decimal-point character, even if no digits follow it. Normally, a decimal-point character appears in the result of these conversions only if a digit follows it. In addition, for 'g' and 'G' conversions, trailing zeros are not removed from the result.

The ',' option signals the use of a comma for a thousands separator. For a locale aware separator, use the 'n' integer presentation type instead.

Changed in version 3.1: Added the ',' option (see also PEP 378).

The '_' option signals the use of an underscore for a thousands separator for floating point presentation types and for integer presentation type 'd'. For integer presentation types 'b', 'o', 'x', and 'X', underscores will be inserted every 4 digits. For other presentation types, specifying this option is an error.

Changed in version 3.6: Added the '_' option (see also PEP 515).

width is a decimal integer defining the minimum field width. If not specified, then the field width will be determined by the content.

When no explicit alignment is given, preceding the *width* field by a zero ('0') character enables sign-aware zero-padding for numeric types. This is equivalent to a *fill* character of '0' with an *alignment* type of '='.

The *precision* is a decimal number indicating how many digits should be displayed after the decimal point for a floating point value formatted with 'f' and 'F', or before and after the decimal point for a floating point value formatted with 'g' or 'G'. For non-number types the field indicates the maximum field size - in other words, how many characters will be used from the field content. The *precision* is not allowed for integer values.

Finally, the *type* determines how the data should be presented.

The available string presentation types are:

Type	Meaning
's'	String format. This is the default type for strings and may be omitted.
None	The same as 's'.

The available integer presentation types are:

Type	Meaning
'b'	Binary format. Outputs the number in base 2.
'c'	Character. Converts the integer to the corresponding unicode character before printing.
'd'	Decimal Integer. Outputs the number in base 10.
'o'	Octal format. Outputs the number in base 8.
'x'	Hex format. Outputs the number in base 16, using lower- case letters for the digits above 9.
'X'	Hex format. Outputs the number in base 16, using upper- case letters for the digits above 9.
'n'	Number. This is the same as 'd', except that it uses the current locale setting to insert the appropriate number separator characters.
None	The same as 'd'.

In addition to the above presentation types, integers can be formatted with the floating point presentation types listed below (except 'n' and None). When doing so, *float()* is used to convert the integer to a floating point number before formatting.

The available presentation types for floating point and decimal values are:

Type	Meaning
'e'	Exponent notation. Prints the number in scientific notation using the letter 'e' to indicate the exponent. The default precision is 6.
'E'	Exponent notation. Same as 'e' except it uses an upper case 'E' as the separator character.
'f'	Fixed point. Displays the number as a fixed-point number. The default precision is 6.
'F'	Fixed point. Same as 'f', but converts nan to NAN and inf to INF.
'g'	General format. For a given precision p >= 1, this rounds the number to p significant digits and then formats the result in either fixed-point format or in scientific notation, depending on its magnitude. The precise rules are as follows: suppose that the result formatted with presentation type 'e' and precision p-1 would have exponent exp. Then if -4 <= exp < p, the number is formatted with presentation type 'f' and precision p-1-exp. Otherwise, the number is formatted with presentation type 'e' and precision p-1. In both cases insignificant trailing zeros are removed from the significand, and the decimal point is also removed if there are no remaining digits following it. Positive and negative infinity, positive and negative zero, and nans, are formatted as inf, -inf, 0, -0 and nan respectively, regardless of the precision. A precision of 0 is treated as equivalent to a precision of 1. The default precision is 6.
'G'	General format. Same as 'g' except switches to 'E' if the number gets too large. The representations of infinity and NaN are uppercased, too.
'n'	Number. This is the same as 'g', except that it uses the current locale setting to insert the appropriate number separator characters.
'%'	Percentage. Multiplies the number by 100 and displays in fixed ('f') format, followed by a percent sign.
None	Similar to 'g', except that fixed-point notation, when used, has at least one digit past the decimal point. The default precision is as high as needed to represent the particular value. The overall effect is to match the output of *str()* as altered by the other format modifiers.

Format examples

This section contains examples of the *str.format()* syntax and comparison with the old %-formatting.

In most of the cases the syntax is similar to the old %-formatting, with the addition of the {} and with : used instead of %. For example, '%03.2f' can be translated to '{:03.2f}'.

The new format syntax also supports new and different options, shown in the follow examples.

Accessing arguments by position:

```
>>> '{0}, {1}, {2}'.format('a', 'b', 'c')
'a, b, c'
>>> '{}, {}, {}'.format('a', 'b', 'c')  # 3.1+ only
'a, b, c'
>>> '{2}, {1}, {0}'.format('a', 'b', 'c')
'c, b, a'
>>> '{2}, {1}, {0}'.format(*'abc')      # unpacking argument sequence
'c, b, a'
>>> '{0}{1}{0}'.format('abra', 'cad')   # arguments' indices can be repeated
'abracadabra'
```

Accessing arguments by name:

```
>>> 'Coordinates: {latitude}, {longitude}'.format(latitude='37.24N', longitude='-115.81W')
'Coordinates: 37.24N, -115.81W'
>>> coord = {'latitude': '37.24N', 'longitude': '-115.81W'}
>>> 'Coordinates: {latitude}, {longitude}'.format(**coord)
'Coordinates: 37.24N, -115.81W'
```

Accessing arguments' attributes:

```
>>> c = 3-5j
>>> ('The complex number {0} is formed from the real part {0.real} '
...  'and the imaginary part {0.imag}.').format(c)
'The complex number (3-5j) is formed from the real part 3.0 and the imaginary part -5.0.'
>>> class Point:
...     def __init__(self, x, y):
...         self.x, self.y = x, y
...     def __str__(self):
...         return 'Point({self.x}, {self.y})'.format(self=self)
...
>>> str(Point(4, 2))
'Point(4, 2)'
```

Accessing arguments' items:

```
>>> coord = (3, 5)
>>> 'X: {0[0]};  Y: {0[1]}'.format(coord)
'X: 3;  Y: 5'
```

Replacing %s and %r:

```
>>> "repr() shows quotes: {!r}; str() doesn't: {!s}".format('test1', 'test2')
"repr() shows quotes: 'test1'; str() doesn't: test2"
```

Aligning the text and specifying a width:

```
>>> '{:<30}'.format('left aligned')
'left aligned                  '
>>> '{:>30}'.format('right aligned')
'                 right aligned'
>>> '{:^30}'.format('centered')
'           centered           '
>>> '{:*^30}'.format('centered')  # use '*' as a fill char
'***********centered***********'
```

Replacing %+f, %-f, and % f and specifying a sign:

```
>>> '{:+f}; {:+f}'.format(3.14, -3.14)  # show it always
'+3.140000; -3.140000'
>>> '{: f}; {: f}'.format(3.14, -3.14)  # show a space for positive numbers
' 3.140000; -3.140000'
>>> '{:-f}; {:-f}'.format(3.14, -3.14)  # show only the minus -- same as '{:f}; {:f}'
'3.140000; -3.140000'
```

Replacing %x and %o and converting the value to different bases:

```
>>> # format also supports binary numbers
>>> "int: {0:d};  hex: {0:x};  oct: {0:o};  bin: {0:b}".format(42)
'int: 42;  hex: 2a;  oct: 52;  bin: 101010'
>>> # with 0x, 0o, or 0b as prefix:
```

```
>>> "int: {0:d};  hex: {0:#x};  oct: {0:#o};  bin: {0:#b}".format(42)
'int: 42;  hex: 0x2a;  oct: 0o52;  bin: 0b101010'
```

Using the comma as a thousands separator:

```
>>> '{:,}'.format(1234567890)
'1,234,567,890'
```

Expressing a percentage:

```
>>> points = 19
>>> total = 22
>>> 'Correct answers: {:.2%}'.format(points/total)
'Correct answers: 86.36%'
```

Using type-specific formatting:

```
>>> import datetime
>>> d = datetime.datetime(2010, 7, 4, 12, 15, 58)
>>> '{:%Y-%m-%d %H:%M:%S}'.format(d)
'2010-07-04 12:15:58'
```

Nesting arguments and more complex examples:

```
>>> for align, text in zip('<^>', ['left', 'center', 'right']):
...     '{0:{fill}{align}16}'.format(text, fill=align, align=align)
...
'left<<<<<<<<<<<<'
'^^^^^center^^^^^'
'>>>>>>>>>>>right'
>>>
>>> octets = [192, 168, 0, 1]
>>> '{:02X}{:02X}{:02X}{:02X}'.format(*octets)
'C0A80001'
>>> int(_, 16)
3232235521
>>>
>>> width = 5
>>> for num in range(5,12):
...     for base in 'dXob':
...         print('{0:{width}{base}}'.format(num, base=base, width=width), end=' ')
...     print()
...
    5     5     5   101
    6     6     6   110
    7     7     7   111
    8     8    10  1000
    9     9    11  1001
   10     A    12  1010
   11     B    13  1011
```

6.1.4 Template strings

Templates provide simpler string substitutions as described in PEP 292. Instead of the normal %-based substitutions, Templates support $-based substitutions, using the following rules:

- $$ is an escape; it is replaced with a single $.

- `$identifier` names a substitution placeholder matching a mapping key of `"identifier"`. By default, `"identifier"` is restricted to any case-insensitive ASCII alphanumeric string (including underscores) that starts with an underscore or ASCII letter. The first non-identifier character after the `$` character terminates this placeholder specification.
- `${identifier}` is equivalent to `$identifier`. It is required when valid identifier characters follow the placeholder but are not part of the placeholder, such as `"${noun}ification"`.

Any other appearance of `$` in the string will result in a *ValueError* being raised.

The *string* module provides a *Template* class that implements these rules. The methods of *Template* are:

class string.Template(*template*)

The constructor takes a single argument which is the template string.

substitute(*mapping*, ***kwds*)

Performs the template substitution, returning a new string. *mapping* is any dictionary-like object with keys that match the placeholders in the template. Alternatively, you can provide keyword arguments, where the keywords are the placeholders. When both *mapping* and *kwds* are given and there are duplicates, the placeholders from *kwds* take precedence.

safe_substitute(*mapping*, ***kwds*)

Like *substitute()*, except that if placeholders are missing from *mapping* and *kwds*, instead of raising a *KeyError* exception, the original placeholder will appear in the resulting string intact. Also, unlike with *substitute()*, any other appearances of the `$` will simply return `$` instead of raising *ValueError*.

While other exceptions may still occur, this method is called "safe" because substitutions always tries to return a usable string instead of raising an exception. In another sense, *safe_substitute()* may be anything other than safe, since it will silently ignore malformed templates containing dangling delimiters, unmatched braces, or placeholders that are not valid Python identifiers.

Template instances also provide one public data attribute:

template

This is the object passed to the constructor's *template* argument. In general, you shouldn't change it, but read-only access is not enforced.

Here is an example of how to use a Template:

```
>>> from string import Template
>>> s = Template('$who likes $what')
>>> s.substitute(who='tim', what='kung pao')
'tim likes kung pao'
>>> d = dict(who='tim')
>>> Template('Give $who $100').substitute(d)
Traceback (most recent call last):
...
ValueError: Invalid placeholder in string: line 1, col 11
>>> Template('$who likes $what').substitute(d)
Traceback (most recent call last):
...
KeyError: 'what'
>>> Template('$who likes $what').safe_substitute(d)
'tim likes $what'
```

Advanced usage: you can derive subclasses of *Template* to customize the placeholder syntax, delimiter character, or the entire regular expression used to parse template strings. To do this, you can override these class attributes:

- *delimiter* – This is the literal string describing a placeholder introducing delimiter. The default value is `$`. Note that this should *not* be a regular expression, as the implementation will call `re.escape()` on this string as needed.
- *idpattern* – This is the regular expression describing the pattern for non-braced placeholders (the braces will be added automatically as appropriate). The default value is the regular expression `(?-i:[_a-zA-Z][_a-zA-Z0-9]*)`.

Note: Since default *flags* is `re.IGNORECASE`, pattern `[a-z]` can match with some non-ASCII characters. That's why we use local `-i` flag here.

While *flags* is kept to `re.IGNORECASE` for backward compatibility, you can override it to `0` or `re.IGNORECASE | re.ASCII` when subclassing.

- *flags* – The regular expression flags that will be applied when compiling the regular expression used for recognizing substitutions. The default value is `re.IGNORECASE`. Note that `re.VERBOSE` will always be added to the flags, so custom *idpatterns* must follow conventions for verbose regular expressions.

  New in version 3.2.

Alternatively, you can provide the entire regular expression pattern by overriding the class attribute *pattern*. If you do this, the value must be a regular expression object with four named capturing groups. The capturing groups correspond to the rules given above, along with the invalid placeholder rule:

- *escaped* – This group matches the escape sequence, e.g. `$$`, in the default pattern.
- *named* – This group matches the unbraced placeholder name; it should not include the delimiter in capturing group.
- *braced* – This group matches the brace enclosed placeholder name; it should not include either the delimiter or braces in the capturing group.
- *invalid* – This group matches any other delimiter pattern (usually a single delimiter), and it should appear last in the regular expression.

6.1.5 Helper functions

string.capwords(*s*, *sep=None*)

Split the argument into words using `str.split()`, capitalize each word using `str.capitalize()`, and join the capitalized words using `str.join()`. If the optional second argument *sep* is absent or `None`, runs of whitespace characters are replaced by a single space and leading and trailing whitespace are removed, otherwise *sep* is used to split and join the words.

6.2 re — Regular expression operations

Source code: Lib/re.py

This module provides regular expression matching operations similar to those found in Perl.

Both patterns and strings to be searched can be Unicode strings (`str`) as well as 8-bit strings (`bytes`). However, Unicode strings and 8-bit strings cannot be mixed: that is, you cannot match a Unicode string with a byte pattern or vice-versa; similarly, when asking for a substitution, the replacement string must be of the same type as both the pattern and the search string.

Regular expressions use the backslash character (`'\'`) to indicate special forms or to allow special characters to be used without invoking their special meaning. This collides with Python's usage of the same character for the same purpose in string literals; for example, to match a literal backslash, one might have to write `'\\\\'` as the pattern string, because the regular expression must be `\\`, and each backslash must be expressed as `\\` inside a regular Python string literal.

The solution is to use Python's raw string notation for regular expression patterns; backslashes are not handled in any special way in a string literal prefixed with `'r'`. So `r"\n"` is a two-character string containing `'\'` and `'n'`, while `"\n"` is a one-character string containing a newline. Usually patterns will be expressed in Python code using this raw string notation.

It is important to note that most regular expression operations are available as module-level functions and methods on *compiled regular expressions*. The functions are shortcuts that don't require you to compile a regex object first, but miss some fine-tuning parameters.

See also:

The third-party regex module, which has an API compatible with the standard library *re* module, but offers additional functionality and a more thorough Unicode support.

6.2.1 Regular Expression Syntax

A regular expression (or RE) specifies a set of strings that matches it; the functions in this module let you check if a particular string matches a given regular expression (or if a given regular expression matches a particular string, which comes down to the same thing).

Regular expressions can be concatenated to form new regular expressions; if *A* and *B* are both regular expressions, then *AB* is also a regular expression. In general, if a string *p* matches *A* and another string *q* matches *B*, the string *pq* will match AB. This holds unless *A* or *B* contain low precedence operations; boundary conditions between *A* and *B*; or have numbered group references. Thus, complex expressions can easily be constructed from simpler primitive expressions like the ones described here. For details of the theory and implementation of regular expressions, consult the Friedl book referenced above, or almost any textbook about compiler construction.

A brief explanation of the format of regular expressions follows. For further information and a gentler presentation, consult the regex-howto.

Regular expressions can contain both special and ordinary characters. Most ordinary characters, like `'A'`, `'a'`, or `'0'`, are the simplest regular expressions; they simply match themselves. You can concatenate ordinary characters, so `last` matches the string `'last'`. (In the rest of this section, we'll write RE's in `this special style`, usually without quotes, and strings to be matched `'in single quotes'`.)

Some characters, like `'|'` or `'('`, are special. Special characters either stand for classes of ordinary characters, or affect how the regular expressions around them are interpreted.

Repetition qualifiers (`*`, `+`, `?`, `{m,n}`, etc) cannot be directly nested. This avoids ambiguity with the non-greedy modifier suffix `?`, and with other modifiers in other implementations. To apply a second repetition to an inner repetition, parentheses may be used. For example, the expression `(?:a{6})*` matches any multiple of six `'a'` characters.

The special characters are:

`.` (Dot.) In the default mode, this matches any character except a newline. If the *DOTALL* flag has been specified, this matches any character including a newline.

`^` (Caret.) Matches the start of the string, and in *MULTILINE* mode also matches immediately after each newline.

`$` Matches the end of the string or just before the newline at the end of the string, and in *MULTILINE* mode also matches before a newline. `foo` matches both 'foo' and 'foobar', while the regular expression `foo$` matches only 'foo'. More interestingly, searching for `foo.$` in `'foo1\nfoo2\n'` matches 'foo2' normally, but 'foo1' in *MULTILINE* mode; searching for a single `$` in `'foo\n'` will find two (empty) matches: one just before the newline, and one at the end of the string.

* Causes the resulting RE to match 0 or more repetitions of the preceding RE, as many repetitions as are possible. ab* will match 'a', 'ab', or 'a' followed by any number of 'b's.

+ Causes the resulting RE to match 1 or more repetitions of the preceding RE. ab+ will match 'a' followed by any non-zero number of 'b's; it will not match just 'a'.

? Causes the resulting RE to match 0 or 1 repetitions of the preceding RE. ab? will match either 'a' or 'ab'.

?, +?, ?? The '', '+', and '?' qualifiers are all *greedy*; they match as much text as possible. Sometimes this behaviour isn't desired; if the RE <.*> is matched against '<a> b <c>', it will match the entire string, and not just '<a>'. Adding ? after the qualifier makes it perform the match in *non-greedy* or *minimal* fashion; as *few* characters as possible will be matched. Using the RE <.*?> will match only '<a>'.

{m} Specifies that exactly *m* copies of the previous RE should be matched; fewer matches cause the entire RE not to match. For example, a{6} will match exactly six 'a' characters, but not five.

{m,n} Causes the resulting RE to match from *m* to *n* repetitions of the preceding RE, attempting to match as many repetitions as possible. For example, a{3,5} will match from 3 to 5 'a' characters. Omitting *m* specifies a lower bound of zero, and omitting *n* specifies an infinite upper bound. As an example, a{4,}b will match 'aaaab' or a thousand 'a' characters followed by a 'b', but not 'aaab'. The comma may not be omitted or the modifier would be confused with the previously described form.

{m,n}? Causes the resulting RE to match from *m* to *n* repetitions of the preceding RE, attempting to match as *few* repetitions as possible. This is the non-greedy version of the previous qualifier. For example, on the 6-character string 'aaaaaa', a{3,5} will match 5 'a' characters, while a{3,5}? will only match 3 characters.

\ Either escapes special characters (permitting you to match characters like '*', '?', and so forth), or signals a special sequence; special sequences are discussed below.

If you're not using a raw string to express the pattern, remember that Python also uses the backslash as an escape sequence in string literals; if the escape sequence isn't recognized by Python's parser, the backslash and subsequent character are included in the resulting string. However, if Python would recognize the resulting sequence, the backslash should be repeated twice. This is complicated and hard to understand, so it's highly recommended that you use raw strings for all but the simplest expressions.

[] Used to indicate a set of characters. In a set:

- Characters can be listed individually, e.g. [amk] will match 'a', 'm', or 'k'.
- Ranges of characters can be indicated by giving two characters and separating them by a '-', for example [a-z] will match any lowercase ASCII letter, [0-5][0-9] will match all the two-digits numbers from 00 to 59, and [0-9A-Fa-f] will match any hexadecimal digit. If - is escaped (e.g. [a\-z]) or if it's placed as the first or last character (e.g. [-a] or [a-]), it will match a literal '-'.
- Special characters lose their special meaning inside sets. For example, [(+*)] will match any of the literal characters '(', '+', '*', or ')'.
- Character classes such as \w or \S (defined below) are also accepted inside a set, although the characters they match depends on whether *ASCII* or *LOCALE* mode is in force.
- Characters that are not within a range can be matched by *complementing* the set. If the first character of the set is '^', all the characters that are *not* in the set will be matched. For example, [^5] will match any character except '5', and [^^] will match any character except '^'. ^ has no special meaning if it's not the first character in the set.
- To match a literal ']' inside a set, precede it with a backslash, or place it at the beginning of the set. For example, both [()[\]{}] and []()[{}] will both match a parenthesis.

| A|B, where *A* and *B* can be arbitrary REs, creates a regular expression that will match either *A* or *B*. An arbitrary number of REs can be separated by the '|' in this way. This can be used inside groups

(see below) as well. As the target string is scanned, REs separated by '|' are tried from left to right. When one pattern completely matches, that branch is accepted. This means that once *A* matches, *B* will not be tested further, even if it would produce a longer overall match. In other words, the '|' operator is never greedy. To match a literal '|', use \|, or enclose it inside a character class, as in [|].

(...) Matches whatever regular expression is inside the parentheses, and indicates the start and end of a group; the contents of a group can be retrieved after a match has been performed, and can be matched later in the string with the `\number` special sequence, described below. To match the literals '(' or ')', use \(or \), or enclose them inside a character class: [(], [)].

(?...) This is an extension notation (a '?' following a '(' is not meaningful otherwise). The first character after the '?' determines what the meaning and further syntax of the construct is. Extensions usually do not create a new group; (?P<name>...) is the only exception to this rule. Following are the currently supported extensions.

(?aiLmsux) (One or more letters from the set 'a', 'i', 'L', 'm', 's', 'u', 'x'.) The group matches the empty string; the letters set the corresponding flags: *re.A* (ASCII-only matching), *re.I* (ignore case), *re.L* (locale dependent), *re.M* (multi-line), *re.S* (dot matches all), **re.U** (Unicode matching), and *re.X* (verbose), for the entire regular expression. (The flags are described in *Module Contents*.) This is useful if you wish to include the flags as part of the regular expression, instead of passing a *flag* argument to the *re.compile()* function. Flags should be used first in the expression string.

(?:...) A non-capturing version of regular parentheses. Matches whatever regular expression is inside the parentheses, but the substring matched by the group *cannot* be retrieved after performing a match or referenced later in the pattern.

(?imsx-imsx:...) (Zero or more letters from the set 'i', 'm', 's', 'x', optionally followed by '-' followed by one or more letters from the same set.) The letters set or removes the corresponding flags: *re.I* (ignore case), *re.M* (multi-line), *re.S* (dot matches all), and *re.X* (verbose), for the part of the expression. (The flags are described in *Module Contents*.)

New in version 3.6.

(?P<name>...) Similar to regular parentheses, but the substring matched by the group is accessible via the symbolic group name *name*. Group names must be valid Python identifiers, and each group name must be defined only once within a regular expression. A symbolic group is also a numbered group, just as if the group were not named.

Named groups can be referenced in three contexts. If the pattern is `(?P<quote>['"]).*?(?P=quote)` (i.e. matching a string quoted with either single or double quotes):

Context of reference to group "quote"	Ways to reference it
in the same pattern itself	• (?P=quote) (as shown) • \1
when processing match object *m*	• m.group('quote') • m.end('quote') (etc.)
in a string passed to the *repl* argument of re.sub()	• \g<quote> • \g<1> • \1

(?P=name) A backreference to a named group; it matches whatever text was matched by the earlier group named *name*.

(?#...) A comment; the contents of the parentheses are simply ignored.

(?=...) Matches if ... matches next, but doesn't consume any of the string. This is called a *lookahead assertion*. For example, Isaac (?=Asimov) will match 'Isaac ' only if it's followed by 'Asimov'.

(?!...) Matches if ... doesn't match next. This is a *negative lookahead assertion*. For example, Isaac (?!Asimov) will match 'Isaac ' only if it's *not* followed by 'Asimov'.

(?<=...) Matches if the current position in the string is preceded by a match for ... that ends at the current position. This is called a *positive lookbehind assertion*. (?<=abc)def will find a match in 'abcdef', since the lookbehind will back up 3 characters and check if the contained pattern matches. The contained pattern must only match strings of some fixed length, meaning that abc or a|b are allowed, but a* and a{3,4} are not. Note that patterns which start with positive lookbehind assertions will not match at the beginning of the string being searched; you will most likely want to use the *search()* function rather than the *match()* function:

```
>>> import re
>>> m = re.search('(?<=abc)def', 'abcdef')
>>> m.group(0)
'def'
```

This example looks for a word following a hyphen:

```
>>> m = re.search(r'(?<=-)\w+', 'spam-egg')
>>> m.group(0)
'egg'
```

Changed in version 3.5: Added support for group references of fixed length.

(?<!...) Matches if the current position in the string is not preceded by a match for .... This is called a *negative lookbehind assertion*. Similar to positive lookbehind assertions, the contained pattern must only match strings of some fixed length. Patterns which start with negative lookbehind assertions may match at the beginning of the string being searched.

(?(id/name)yes-pattern|no-pattern) Will try to match with yes-pattern if the group with given *id* or *name* exists, and with no-pattern if it doesn't. no-pattern is optional and can be omitted. For example, (<)?(\w+@\w+(?:\.\w+)+)(?(1)>|$) is a poor email matching pattern, which will match with '<user@host.com>' as well as 'user@host.com', but not with '<user@host.com' nor 'user@host.com>'.

The special sequences consist of '\' and a character from the list below. If the ordinary character is not an ASCII digit or an ASCII letter, then the resulting RE will match the second character. For example, \$ matches the character '$'.

\number Matches the contents of the group of the same number. Groups are numbered starting from 1. For example, (.+) \1 matches 'the the' or '55 55', but not 'thethe' (note the space after the group). This special sequence can only be used to match one of the first 99 groups. If the first digit of *number* is 0, or *number* is 3 octal digits long, it will not be interpreted as a group match, but as the character with octal value *number*. Inside the '[' and ']' of a character class, all numeric escapes are treated as characters.

\A Matches only at the start of the string.

\b Matches the empty string, but only at the beginning or end of a word. A word is defined as a sequence of word characters. Note that formally, \b is defined as the boundary between a \w and a \W character (or vice versa), or between \w and the beginning/end of the string. This means that r'\bfoo\b' matches 'foo', 'foo.', '(foo)', 'bar foo baz' but not 'foobar' or 'foo3'.

By default Unicode alphanumerics are the ones used in Unicode patterns, but this can be changed by using the *ASCII* flag. Word boundaries are determined by the current locale if the *LOCALE* flag is used.

Inside a character range, \b represents the backspace character, for compatibility with Python's string literals.

\B Matches the empty string, but only when it is *not* at the beginning or end of a word. This means that r'py\B' matches 'python', 'py3', 'py2', but not 'py', 'py.', or 'py!'. \B is just the opposite of \b, so word characters in Unicode patterns are Unicode alphanumerics or the underscore, although this can be changed by using the *ASCII* flag. Word boundaries are determined by the current locale if the *LOCALE* flag is used.

\d

For Unicode (str) patterns: Matches any Unicode decimal digit (that is, any character in Unicode character category [Nd]). This includes [0-9], and also many other digit characters. If the *ASCII* flag is used only [0-9] is matched (but the flag affects the entire regular expression, so in such cases using an explicit [0-9] may be a better choice).

For 8-bit (bytes) patterns: Matches any decimal digit; this is equivalent to [0-9].

\D Matches any character which is not a decimal digit. This is the opposite of \d. If the *ASCII* flag is used this becomes the equivalent of [^0-9] (but the flag affects the entire regular expression, so in such cases using an explicit [^0-9] may be a better choice).

\s

For Unicode (str) patterns: Matches Unicode whitespace characters (which includes [\t\n\r\f\v], and also many other characters, for example the non-breaking spaces mandated by typography rules in many languages). If the *ASCII* flag is used, only [\t\n\r\f\v] is matched (but the flag affects the entire regular expression, so in such cases using an explicit [\t\n\r\f\v] may be a better choice).

For 8-bit (bytes) patterns: Matches characters considered whitespace in the ASCII character set; this is equivalent to [\t\n\r\f\v].

\S Matches any character which is not a whitespace character. This is the opposite of \s. If the *ASCII* flag is used this becomes the equivalent of [^ \t\n\r\f\v] (but the flag affects the entire regular expression, so in such cases using an explicit [^ \t\n\r\f\v] may be a better choice).

\w

For Unicode (str) patterns: Matches Unicode word characters; this includes most characters that can be part of a word in any language, as well as numbers and the underscore. If the *ASCII* flag is used, only [a-zA-Z0-9_] is matched (but the flag affects the entire regular expression, so in such cases using an explicit [a-zA-Z0-9_] may be a better choice).

For 8-bit (bytes) patterns: Matches characters considered alphanumeric in the ASCII character set; this is equivalent to [a-zA-Z0-9_]. If the *LOCALE* flag is used, matches characters considered alphanumeric in the current locale and the underscore.

\W Matches any character which is not a word character. This is the opposite of \w. If the *ASCII* flag is used this becomes the equivalent of [^a-zA-Z0-9_] (but the flag affects the entire regular expression, so in such cases using an explicit [^a-zA-Z0-9_] may be a better choice). If the *LOCALE* flag is used, matches characters considered alphanumeric in the current locale and the underscore.

\Z Matches only at the end of the string.

Most of the standard escapes supported by Python string literals are also accepted by the regular expression parser:

```
\a      \b      \f      \n
\r      \t      \u      \U
\v      \x      \\
```

(Note that \b is used to represent word boundaries, and means "backspace" only inside character classes.)

'\u' and '\U' escape sequences are only recognized in Unicode patterns. In bytes patterns they are errors.

Octal escapes are included in a limited form. If the first digit is a 0, or if there are three octal digits, it is considered an octal escape. Otherwise, it is a group reference. As for string literals, octal escapes are always at most three digits in length.

Changed in version 3.3: The '\u' and '\U' escape sequences have been added.

Changed in version 3.6: Unknown escapes consisting of '\' and an ASCII letter now are errors.

See also:

Mastering Regular Expressions Book on regular expressions by Jeffrey Friedl, published by O'Reilly. The second edition of the book no longer covers Python at all, but the first edition covered writing good regular expression patterns in great detail.

6.2.2 Module Contents

The module defines several functions, constants, and an exception. Some of the functions are simplified versions of the full featured methods for compiled regular expressions. Most non-trivial applications always use the compiled form.

Changed in version 3.6: Flag constants are now instances of `RegexFlag`, which is a subclass of *enum.IntFlag*.

`re.compile`(*pattern*, *flags=0*)

Compile a regular expression pattern into a *regular expression object*, which can be used for matching using its *match()*, *search()* and other methods, described below.

The expression's behaviour can be modified by specifying a *flags* value. Values can be any of the following variables, combined using bitwise OR (the | operator).

The sequence

```
prog = re.compile(pattern)
result = prog.match(string)
```

is equivalent to

```
result = re.match(pattern, string)
```

but using *re.compile()* and saving the resulting regular expression object for reuse is more efficient when the expression will be used several times in a single program.

Note: The compiled versions of the most recent patterns passed to *re.compile()* and the module-level matching functions are cached, so programs that use only a few regular expressions at a time needn't worry about compiling regular expressions.

`re.A`
`re.ASCII`

Make \w, \W, \b, \B, \d, \D, \s and \S perform ASCII-only matching instead of full Unicode matching. This is only meaningful for Unicode patterns, and is ignored for byte patterns. Corresponds to the inline flag (?a).

Note that for backward compatibility, the `re.U` flag still exists (as well as its synonym `re.UNICODE` and its embedded counterpart (?u)), but these are redundant in Python 3 since matches are Unicode by default for strings (and Unicode matching isn't allowed for bytes).

re.DEBUG

Display debug information about compiled expression. No corresponding inline flag.

re.I
re.IGNORECASE

Perform case-insensitive matching; expressions like [A-Z] will also match lowercase letters. Full Unicode matching (such as Ü matching ü) also works unless the *re.ASCII* flag is used to disable non-ASCII matches. The current locale does not change the effect of this flag unless the *re.LOCALE* flag is also used. Corresponds to the inline flag (?i).

Note that when the Unicode patterns [a-z] or [A-Z] are used in combination with the *IGNORECASE* flag, they will match the 52 ASCII letters and 4 additional non-ASCII letters: 'İ' (U+0130, Latin capital letter I with dot above), 'ı' (U+0131, Latin small letter dotless i), 'ſ' (U+017F, Latin small letter long s) and 'K' (U+212A, Kelvin sign). If the *ASCII* flag is used, only letters 'a' to 'z' and 'A' to 'Z' are matched (but the flag affects the entire regular expression, so in such cases using an explicit (?-i:[a-zA-Z]) may be a better choice).

re.L
re.LOCALE

Make \w, \W, \b, \B and case-insensitive matching dependent on the current locale. This flag can be used only with bytes patterns. The use of this flag is discouraged as the locale mechanism is very unreliable, it only handles one "culture" at a time, and it only works with 8-bit locales. Unicode matching is already enabled by default in Python 3 for Unicode (str) patterns, and it is able to handle different locales/languages. Corresponds to the inline flag (?L).

Changed in version 3.6: *re.LOCALE* can be used only with bytes patterns and is not compatible with *re.ASCII*.

re.M
re.MULTILINE

When specified, the pattern character '^' matches at the beginning of the string and at the beginning of each line (immediately following each newline); and the pattern character '$' matches at the end of the string and at the end of each line (immediately preceding each newline). By default, '^' matches only at the beginning of the string, and '$' only at the end of the string and immediately before the newline (if any) at the end of the string. Corresponds to the inline flag (?m).

re.S
re.DOTALL

Make the '.' special character match any character at all, including a newline; without this flag, '.' will match anything *except* a newline. Corresponds to the inline flag (?s).

re.X
re.VERBOSE

This flag allows you to write regular expressions that look nicer and are more readable by allowing you to visually separate logical sections of the pattern and add comments. Whitespace within the pattern is ignored, except when in a character class, or when preceded by an unescaped backslash, or within tokens like *?, (?: or (?P<...>. When a line contains a # that is not in a character class and is not preceded by an unescaped backslash, all characters from the leftmost such # through the end of the line are ignored.

This means that the two following regular expression objects that match a decimal number are functionally equal:

```
a = re.compile(r"""\d +  # the integral part
                   \.    # the decimal point
                   \d *  # some fractional digits""", re.X)
b = re.compile(r"\d+\.\d*")
```

Corresponds to the inline flag (?x).

re.**search**(*pattern*, *string*, *flags=0*)
Scan through *string* looking for the first location where the regular expression *pattern* produces a match, and return a corresponding *match object*. Return `None` if no position in the string matches the pattern; note that this is different from finding a zero-length match at some point in the string.

re.**match**(*pattern*, *string*, *flags=0*)
If zero or more characters at the beginning of *string* match the regular expression *pattern*, return a corresponding *match object*. Return `None` if the string does not match the pattern; note that this is different from a zero-length match.

Note that even in *MULTILINE* mode, *re.match()* will only match at the beginning of the string and not at the beginning of each line.

If you want to locate a match anywhere in *string*, use *search()* instead (see also *search() vs. match()*).

re.**fullmatch**(*pattern*, *string*, *flags=0*)
If the whole *string* matches the regular expression *pattern*, return a corresponding *match object*. Return `None` if the string does not match the pattern; note that this is different from a zero-length match.

New in version 3.4.

re.**split**(*pattern*, *string*, *maxsplit=0*, *flags=0*)
Split *string* by the occurrences of *pattern*. If capturing parentheses are used in *pattern*, then the text of all groups in the pattern are also returned as part of the resulting list. If *maxsplit* is nonzero, at most *maxsplit* splits occur, and the remainder of the string is returned as the final element of the list.

```
>>> re.split(r'\W+', 'Words, words, words.')
['Words', 'words', 'words', '']
>>> re.split(r'(\W+)', 'Words, words, words.')
['Words', ', ', 'words', ', ', 'words', '.', '']
>>> re.split(r'\W+', 'Words, words, words.', 1)
['Words', 'words, words.']
>>> re.split('[a-f]+', '0a3B9', flags=re.IGNORECASE)
['0', '3', '9']
```

If there are capturing groups in the separator and it matches at the start of the string, the result will start with an empty string. The same holds for the end of the string:

```
>>> re.split(r'(\W+)', '...words, words...')
['', '...', 'words', ', ', 'words', '...', '']
```

That way, separator components are always found at the same relative indices within the result list.

Note: *split()* doesn't currently split a string on an empty pattern match. For example:

```
>>> re.split('x*', 'axbc')
['a', 'bc']
```

Even though `'x*'` also matches 0 'x' before 'a', between 'b' and 'c', and after 'c', currently these matches are ignored. The correct behavior (i.e. splitting on empty matches too and returning `['', 'a', 'b', 'c', '']`) will be implemented in future versions of Python, but since this is a backward incompatible change, a *FutureWarning* will be raised in the meanwhile.

Patterns that can only match empty strings currently never split the string. Since this doesn't match the expected behavior, a *ValueError* will be raised starting from Python 3.5:

```
>>> re.split("^$", "foo\n\nbar\n", flags=re.M)
Traceback (most recent call last):
  File "<stdin>", line 1, in <module>
```

```
...
ValueError: split() requires a non-empty pattern match.
```

Changed in version 3.1: Added the optional flags argument.

Changed in version 3.5: Splitting on a pattern that could match an empty string now raises a warning. Patterns that can only match empty strings are now rejected.

re.**findall**(*pattern, string, flags=0*)
Return all non-overlapping matches of *pattern* in *string*, as a list of strings. The *string* is scanned left-to-right, and matches are returned in the order found. If one or more groups are present in the pattern, return a list of groups; this will be a list of tuples if the pattern has more than one group. Empty matches are included in the result.

Note: Due to the limitation of the current implementation the character following an empty match is not included in a next match, so `findall(r'^|\w+', 'two words')` returns `['', 'wo', 'words']` (note missed "t"). This is changed in Python 3.7.

re.**finditer**(*pattern, string, flags=0*)
Return an *iterator* yielding *match objects* over all non-overlapping matches for the RE *pattern* in *string*. The *string* is scanned left-to-right, and matches are returned in the order found. Empty matches are included in the result. See also the note about *findall()*.

re.**sub**(*pattern, repl, string, count=0, flags=0*)
Return the string obtained by replacing the leftmost non-overlapping occurrences of *pattern* in *string* by the replacement *repl*. If the pattern isn't found, *string* is returned unchanged. *repl* can be a string or a function; if it is a string, any backslash escapes in it are processed. That is, `\n` is converted to a single newline character, `\r` is converted to a carriage return, and so forth. Unknown escapes such as `\&` are left alone. Backreferences, such as `\6`, are replaced with the substring matched by group 6 in the pattern. For example:

```
>>> re.sub(r'def\s+([a-zA-Z_][a-zA-Z_0-9]*)\s*\(\s*\):',
...        r'static PyObject*\npy_\1(void)\n{',
...        'def myfunc():')
'static PyObject*\npy_myfunc(void)\n{'
```

If *repl* is a function, it is called for every non-overlapping occurrence of *pattern*. The function takes a single *match object* argument, and returns the replacement string. For example:

```
>>> def dashrepl(matchobj):
...     if matchobj.group(0) == '-': return ' '
...     else: return '-'
>>> re.sub('-{1,2}', dashrepl, 'pro----gram-files')
'pro--gram files'
>>> re.sub(r'\sAND\s', ' & ', 'Baked Beans And Spam', flags=re.IGNORECASE)
'Baked Beans & Spam'
```

The pattern may be a string or a *pattern object*.

The optional argument *count* is the maximum number of pattern occurrences to be replaced; *count* must be a non-negative integer. If omitted or zero, all occurrences will be replaced. Empty matches for the pattern are replaced only when not adjacent to a previous match, so `sub('x*', '-', 'abc')` returns `'-a-b-c-'`.

In string-type *repl* arguments, in addition to the character escapes and backreferences described above, `\g<name>` will use the substring matched by the group named `name`, as defined by the `(?P<name>...)`

syntax. \g<number> uses the corresponding group number; \g<2> is therefore equivalent to \2, but isn't ambiguous in a replacement such as \g<2>0. \20 would be interpreted as a reference to group 20, not a reference to group 2 followed by the literal character '0'. The backreference \g<0> substitutes in the entire substring matched by the RE.

Changed in version 3.1: Added the optional flags argument.

Changed in version 3.5: Unmatched groups are replaced with an empty string.

Changed in version 3.6: Unknown escapes in *pattern* consisting of '\' and an ASCII letter now are errors.

Deprecated since version 3.5, will be removed in version 3.7: Unknown escapes in *repl* consisting of '\' and an ASCII letter now raise a deprecation warning and will be forbidden in Python 3.7.

re.subn(*pattern*, *repl*, *string*, *count=0*, *flags=0*)

Perform the same operation as *sub()*, but return a tuple (new_string, number_of_subs_made).

Changed in version 3.1: Added the optional flags argument.

Changed in version 3.5: Unmatched groups are replaced with an empty string.

re.escape(*pattern*)

Escape all the characters in *pattern* except ASCII letters, numbers and '_'. This is useful if you want to match an arbitrary literal string that may have regular expression metacharacters in it. For example:

```
>>> print(re.escape('python.exe'))
python\.exe

>>> legal_chars = string.ascii_lowercase + string.digits + "!#$%&'*+-.^_`|~:"
>>> print('[%s]+' % re.escape(legal_chars))
[abcdefghijklmnopqrstuvwxyz0123456789\!\#\$\%\&\'\*\+\-\.\^\_\`\|\~\:]+

>>> operators = ['+', '-', '*', '/', '**']
>>> print('|'.join(map(re.escape, sorted(operators, reverse=True))))
\/|\-|\+|\*\*|\*
```

This functions must not be used for the replacement string in *sub()* and *subn()*, only backslashes should be escaped. For example:

```
>>> digits_re = r'\d+'
>>> sample = '/usr/sbin/sendmail - 0 errors, 12 warnings'
>>> print(re.sub(digits_re, digits_re.replace('\\', r'\\'), sample))
/usr/sbin/sendmail - \d+ errors, \d+ warnings
```

Changed in version 3.3: The '_' character is no longer escaped.

re.purge()

Clear the regular expression cache.

exception re.error(*msg*, *pattern=None*, *pos=None*)

Exception raised when a string passed to one of the functions here is not a valid regular expression (for example, it might contain unmatched parentheses) or when some other error occurs during compilation or matching. It is never an error if a string contains no match for a pattern. The error instance has the following additional attributes:

msg

The unformatted error message.

pattern

The regular expression pattern.

pos
The index in *pattern* where compilation failed (may be `None`).

lineno
The line corresponding to *pos* (may be `None`).

colno
The column corresponding to *pos* (may be `None`).

Changed in version 3.5: Added additional attributes.

6.2.3 Regular Expression Objects

Compiled regular expression objects support the following methods and attributes:

`regex.search(string[, pos[, endpos]])`
Scan through *string* looking for the first location where this regular expression produces a match, and return a corresponding *match object*. Return `None` if no position in the string matches the pattern; note that this is different from finding a zero-length match at some point in the string.

The optional second parameter *pos* gives an index in the string where the search is to start; it defaults to `0`. This is not completely equivalent to slicing the string; the `'^'` pattern character matches at the real beginning of the string and at positions just after a newline, but not necessarily at the index where the search is to start.

The optional parameter *endpos* limits how far the string will be searched; it will be as if the string is *endpos* characters long, so only the characters from *pos* to `endpos - 1` will be searched for a match. If *endpos* is less than *pos*, no match will be found; otherwise, if *rx* is a compiled regular expression object, `rx.search(string, 0, 50)` is equivalent to `rx.search(string[:50], 0)`.

```
>>> pattern = re.compile("d")
>>> pattern.search("dog")     # Match at index 0
<_sre.SRE_Match object; span=(0, 1), match='d'>
>>> pattern.search("dog", 1)  # No match; search doesn't include the "d"
```

`regex.match(string[, pos[, endpos]])`
If zero or more characters at the *beginning* of *string* match this regular expression, return a corresponding *match object*. Return `None` if the string does not match the pattern; note that this is different from a zero-length match.

The optional *pos* and *endpos* parameters have the same meaning as for the *search()* method.

```
>>> pattern = re.compile("o")
>>> pattern.match("dog")      # No match as "o" is not at the start of "dog".
>>> pattern.match("dog", 1)   # Match as "o" is the 2nd character of "dog".
<_sre.SRE_Match object; span=(1, 2), match='o'>
```

If you want to locate a match anywhere in *string*, use *search()* instead (see also *search() vs. match()*).

`regex.fullmatch(string[, pos[, endpos]])`
If the whole *string* matches this regular expression, return a corresponding *match object*. Return `None` if the string does not match the pattern; note that this is different from a zero-length match.

The optional *pos* and *endpos* parameters have the same meaning as for the *search()* method.

```
>>> pattern = re.compile("o[gh]")
>>> pattern.fullmatch("dog")      # No match as "o" is not at the start of "dog".
>>> pattern.fullmatch("ogre")     # No match as not the full string matches.
>>> pattern.fullmatch("doggie", 1, 3)   # Matches within given limits.
<_sre.SRE_Match object; span=(1, 3), match='og'>
```

New in version 3.4.

regex.split(*string*, *maxsplit=0*)
Identical to the *split()* function, using the compiled pattern.

regex.findall(*string*[, *pos*[, *endpos*]])
Similar to the *findall()* function, using the compiled pattern, but also accepts optional *pos* and *endpos* parameters that limit the search region like for *search()*.

regex.finditer(*string*[, *pos*[, *endpos*]])
Similar to the *finditer()* function, using the compiled pattern, but also accepts optional *pos* and *endpos* parameters that limit the search region like for *search()*.

regex.sub(*repl*, *string*, *count=0*)
Identical to the *sub()* function, using the compiled pattern.

regex.subn(*repl*, *string*, *count=0*)
Identical to the *subn()* function, using the compiled pattern.

regex.flags
The regex matching flags. This is a combination of the flags given to *compile()*, any `(?...)` inline flags in the pattern, and implicit flags such as `UNICODE` if the pattern is a Unicode string.

regex.groups
The number of capturing groups in the pattern.

regex.groupindex
A dictionary mapping any symbolic group names defined by `(?P<id>)` to group numbers. The dictionary is empty if no symbolic groups were used in the pattern.

regex.pattern
The pattern string from which the RE object was compiled.

6.2.4 Match Objects

Match objects always have a boolean value of `True`. Since *match()* and *search()* return `None` when there is no match, you can test whether there was a match with a simple `if` statement:

```
match = re.search(pattern, string)
if match:
    process(match)
```

Match objects support the following methods and attributes:

match.expand(*template*)
Return the string obtained by doing backslash substitution on the template string *template*, as done by the *sub()* method. Escapes such as `\n` are converted to the appropriate characters, and numeric backreferences (`\1`, `\2`) and named backreferences (`\g<1>`, `\g<name>`) are replaced by the contents of the corresponding group.

Changed in version 3.5: Unmatched groups are replaced with an empty string.

match.group([*group1*, ...])
Returns one or more subgroups of the match. If there is a single argument, the result is a single string; if there are multiple arguments, the result is a tuple with one item per argument. Without arguments, *group1* defaults to zero (the whole match is returned). If a *groupN* argument is zero, the corresponding return value is the entire matching string; if it is in the inclusive range [1..99], it is the string matching the corresponding parenthesized group. If a group number is negative or larger than the number of groups defined in the pattern, an *IndexError* exception is raised. If a group is contained in a part of

the pattern that did not match, the corresponding result is `None`. If a group is contained in a part of the pattern that matched multiple times, the last match is returned.

```
>>> m = re.match(r"(\w+) (\w+)", "Isaac Newton, physicist")
>>> m.group(0)       # The entire match
'Isaac Newton'
>>> m.group(1)       # The first parenthesized subgroup.
'Isaac'
>>> m.group(2)       # The second parenthesized subgroup.
'Newton'
>>> m.group(1, 2)    # Multiple arguments give us a tuple.
('Isaac', 'Newton')
```

If the regular expression uses the `(?P<name>...)` syntax, the *groupN* arguments may also be strings identifying groups by their group name. If a string argument is not used as a group name in the pattern, an *IndexError* exception is raised.

A moderately complicated example:

```
>>> m = re.match(r"(?P<first_name>\w+) (?P<last_name>\w+)", "Malcolm Reynolds")
>>> m.group('first_name')
'Malcolm'
>>> m.group('last_name')
'Reynolds'
```

Named groups can also be referred to by their index:

```
>>> m.group(1)
'Malcolm'
>>> m.group(2)
'Reynolds'
```

If a group matches multiple times, only the last match is accessible:

```
>>> m = re.match(r"(..)+", "a1b2c3")  # Matches 3 times.
>>> m.group(1)                        # Returns only the last match.
'c3'
```

`match.__getitem__(g)`
This is identical to `m.group(g)`. This allows easier access to an individual group from a match:

```
>>> m = re.match(r"(\w+) (\w+)", "Isaac Newton, physicist")
>>> m[0]       # The entire match
'Isaac Newton'
>>> m[1]       # The first parenthesized subgroup.
'Isaac'
>>> m[2]       # The second parenthesized subgroup.
'Newton'
```

New in version 3.6.

`match.groups(default=None)`
Return a tuple containing all the subgroups of the match, from 1 up to however many groups are in the pattern. The *default* argument is used for groups that did not participate in the match; it defaults to `None`.

For example:

```
>>> m = re.match(r"(\d+)\.(\d+)", "24.1632")
>>> m.groups()
('24', '1632')
```

If we make the decimal place and everything after it optional, not all groups might participate in the match. These groups will default to `None` unless the *default* argument is given:

```
>>> m = re.match(r"(\d+)\.?(\d+)?", "24")
>>> m.groups()      # Second group defaults to None.
('24', None)
>>> m.groups('0')   # Now, the second group defaults to '0'.
('24', '0')
```

`match.groupdict(default=None)`
Return a dictionary containing all the *named* subgroups of the match, keyed by the subgroup name. The *default* argument is used for groups that did not participate in the match; it defaults to `None`. For example:

```
>>> m = re.match(r"(?P<first_name>\w+) (?P<last_name>\w+)", "Malcolm Reynolds")
>>> m.groupdict()
{'first_name': 'Malcolm', 'last_name': 'Reynolds'}
```

`match.start([group])`
`match.end([group])`
Return the indices of the start and end of the substring matched by *group*; *group* defaults to zero (meaning the whole matched substring). Return `-1` if *group* exists but did not contribute to the match. For a match object *m*, and a group *g* that did contribute to the match, the substring matched by group *g* (equivalent to `m.group(g)`) is

```
m.string[m.start(g):m.end(g)]
```

Note that `m.start(group)` will equal `m.end(group)` if *group* matched a null string. For example, after `m = re.search('b(c?)', 'cba')`, `m.start(0)` is 1, `m.end(0)` is 2, `m.start(1)` and `m.end(1)` are both 2, and `m.start(2)` raises an *IndexError* exception.

An example that will remove *remove_this* from email addresses:

```
>>> email = "tony@tiremove_thisger.net"
>>> m = re.search("remove_this", email)
>>> email[:m.start()] + email[m.end():]
'tony@tiger.net'
```

`match.span([group])`
For a match *m*, return the 2-tuple `(m.start(group), m.end(group))`. Note that if *group* did not contribute to the match, this is `(-1, -1)`. *group* defaults to zero, the entire match.

`match.pos`
The value of *pos* which was passed to the *search()* or *match()* method of a *regex object*. This is the index into the string at which the RE engine started looking for a match.

`match.endpos`
The value of *endpos* which was passed to the *search()* or *match()* method of a *regex object*. This is the index into the string beyond which the RE engine will not go.

`match.lastindex`
The integer index of the last matched capturing group, or `None` if no group was matched at all. For example, the expressions `(a)b`, `((a)(b))`, and `((ab))` will have `lastindex == 1` if applied to the string `'ab'`, while the expression `(a)(b)` will have `lastindex == 2`, if applied to the same string.

match.lastgroup
The name of the last matched capturing group, or None if the group didn't have a name, or if no group was matched at all.

match.re
The *regular expression object* whose *match()* or *search()* method produced this match instance.

match.string
The string passed to *match()* or *search()*.

6.2.5 Regular Expression Examples

Checking for a Pair

In this example, we'll use the following helper function to display match objects a little more gracefully:

```
def displaymatch(match):
    if match is None:
        return None
    return '<Match: %r, groups=%r>' % (match.group(), match.groups())
```

Suppose you are writing a poker program where a player's hand is represented as a 5-character string with each character representing a card, "a" for ace, "k" for king, "q" for queen, "j" for jack, "t" for 10, and "2" through "9" representing the card with that value.

To see if a given string is a valid hand, one could do the following:

```
>>> valid = re.compile(r"^[a2-9tjqk]{5}$")
>>> displaymatch(valid.match("akt5q"))  # Valid.
"<Match: 'akt5q', groups=()>"
>>> displaymatch(valid.match("akt5e"))  # Invalid.
>>> displaymatch(valid.match("akt"))    # Invalid.
>>> displaymatch(valid.match("727ak"))  # Valid.
"<Match: '727ak', groups=()>"
```

That last hand, "727ak", contained a pair, or two of the same valued cards. To match this with a regular expression, one could use backreferences as such:

```
>>> pair = re.compile(r".*(.).*\1")
>>> displaymatch(pair.match("717ak"))     # Pair of 7s.
"<Match: '717', groups=('7',)>"
>>> displaymatch(pair.match("718ak"))     # No pairs.
>>> displaymatch(pair.match("354aa"))     # Pair of aces.
"<Match: '354aa', groups=('a',)>"
```

To find out what card the pair consists of, one could use the *group()* method of the match object in the following manner:

```
>>> pair.match("717ak").group(1)
'7'

# Error because re.match() returns None, which doesn't have a group() method:
>>> pair.match("718ak").group(1)
Traceback (most recent call last):
  File "<pyshell#23>", line 1, in <module>
    re.match(r".*(.).*\1", "718ak").group(1)
AttributeError: 'NoneType' object has no attribute 'group'
```

```
>>> pair.match("354aa").group(1)
'a'
```

Simulating scanf()

Python does not currently have an equivalent to `scanf()`. Regular expressions are generally more powerful, though also more verbose, than `scanf()` format strings. The table below offers some more-or-less equivalent mappings between `scanf()` format tokens and regular expressions.

scanf() Token	Regular Expression
%c	.
%5c	.{5}
%d	[-+]?\d+
%e, %E, %f, %g	[-+]?(\d+(\.\d*)?|\.\d+)([eE][-+]?\d+)?
%i	[-+]?(0[xX][\dA-Fa-f]+|0[0-7]*|\d+)
%o	[-+]?[0-7]+
%s	\S+
%u	\d+
%x, %X	[-+]?(0[xX])?[\dA-Fa-f]+

To extract the filename and numbers from a string like

```
/usr/sbin/sendmail - 0 errors, 4 warnings
```

you would use a `scanf()` format like

```
%s - %d errors, %d warnings
```

The equivalent regular expression would be

```
(\S+) - (\d+) errors, (\d+) warnings
```

search() vs. match()

Python offers two different primitive operations based on regular expressions: *re.match()* checks for a match only at the beginning of the string, while *re.search()* checks for a match anywhere in the string (this is what Perl does by default).

For example:

```
>>> re.match("c", "abcdef")    # No match
>>> re.search("c", "abcdef")   # Match
<_sre.SRE_Match object; span=(2, 3), match='c'>
```

Regular expressions beginning with `'^'` can be used with *search()* to restrict the match at the beginning of the string:

```
>>> re.match("c", "abcdef")    # No match
>>> re.search("^c", "abcdef")  # No match
>>> re.search("^a", "abcdef")  # Match
<_sre.SRE_Match object; span=(0, 1), match='a'>
```

Note however that in *MULTILINE* mode *match()* only matches at the beginning of the string, whereas using *search()* with a regular expression beginning with `'^'` will match at the beginning of each line.

```
>>> re.match('X', 'A\nB\nX', re.MULTILINE)  # No match
>>> re.search('^X', 'A\nB\nX', re.MULTILINE)  # Match
<_sre.SRE_Match object; span=(4, 5), match='X'>
```

Making a Phonebook

split() splits a string into a list delimited by the passed pattern. The method is invaluable for converting textual data into data structures that can be easily read and modified by Python as demonstrated in the following example that creates a phonebook.

First, here is the input. Normally it may come from a file, here we are using triple-quoted string syntax:

```
>>> text = """Ross McFluff: 834.345.1254 155 Elm Street
...
... Ronald Heathmore: 892.345.3428 436 Finley Avenue
... Frank Burger: 925.541.7625 662 South Dogwood Way
...
...
... Heather Albrecht: 548.326.4584 919 Park Place"""
```

The entries are separated by one or more newlines. Now we convert the string into a list with each nonempty line having its own entry:

```
>>> entries = re.split("\n+", text)
>>> entries
['Ross McFluff: 834.345.1254 155 Elm Street',
'Ronald Heathmore: 892.345.3428 436 Finley Avenue',
'Frank Burger: 925.541.7625 662 South Dogwood Way',
'Heather Albrecht: 548.326.4584 919 Park Place']
```

Finally, split each entry into a list with first name, last name, telephone number, and address. We use the `maxsplit` parameter of *split()* because the address has spaces, our splitting pattern, in it:

```
>>> [re.split(":? ", entry, 3) for entry in entries]
[['Ross', 'McFluff', '834.345.1254', '155 Elm Street'],
['Ronald', 'Heathmore', '892.345.3428', '436 Finley Avenue'],
['Frank', 'Burger', '925.541.7625', '662 South Dogwood Way'],
['Heather', 'Albrecht', '548.326.4584', '919 Park Place']]
```

The `:?` pattern matches the colon after the last name, so that it does not occur in the result list. With a `maxsplit` of 4, we could separate the house number from the street name:

```
>>> [re.split(":? ", entry, 4) for entry in entries]
[['Ross', 'McFluff', '834.345.1254', '155', 'Elm Street'],
['Ronald', 'Heathmore', '892.345.3428', '436', 'Finley Avenue'],
['Frank', 'Burger', '925.541.7625', '662', 'South Dogwood Way'],
['Heather', 'Albrecht', '548.326.4584', '919', 'Park Place']]
```

Text Munging

sub() replaces every occurrence of a pattern with a string or the result of a function. This example demonstrates using *sub()* with a function to "munge" text, or randomize the order of all the characters in each word of a sentence except for the first and last characters:

```
>>> def repl(m):
...     inner_word = list(m.group(2))
...     random.shuffle(inner_word)
...     return m.group(1) + "".join(inner_word) + m.group(3)
>>> text = "Professor Abdolmalek, please report your absences promptly."
>>> re.sub(r"(\w)(\w+)(\w)", repl, text)
'Poefsrosr Aealmlobdk, pslaee reorpt your abnseces plmrptoy.'
>>> re.sub(r"(\w)(\w+)(\w)", repl, text)
'Pofsroser Aodlambelk, plasee reoprt yuor asnebces potlmrpy.'
```

Finding all Adverbs

findall() matches *all* occurrences of a pattern, not just the first one as *search()* does. For example, if one was a writer and wanted to find all of the adverbs in some text, he or she might use *findall()* in the following manner:

```
>>> text = "He was carefully disguised but captured quickly by police."
>>> re.findall(r"\w+ly", text)
['carefully', 'quickly']
```

Finding all Adverbs and their Positions

If one wants more information about all matches of a pattern than the matched text, *finditer()* is useful as it provides *match objects* instead of strings. Continuing with the previous example, if one was a writer who wanted to find all of the adverbs *and their positions* in some text, he or she would use *finditer()* in the following manner:

```
>>> text = "He was carefully disguised but captured quickly by police."
>>> for m in re.finditer(r"\w+ly", text):
...     print('%02d-%02d: %s' % (m.start(), m.end(), m.group(0)))
07-16: carefully
40-47: quickly
```

Raw String Notation

Raw string notation (`r"text"`) keeps regular expressions sane. Without it, every backslash (`'\'`) in a regular expression would have to be prefixed with another one to escape it. For example, the two following lines of code are functionally identical:

```
>>> re.match(r"\W(.)\1\W", " ff ")
<_sre.SRE_Match object; span=(0, 4), match=' ff '>
>>> re.match("\\W(.)\\1\\W", " ff ")
<_sre.SRE_Match object; span=(0, 4), match=' ff '>
```

When one wants to match a literal backslash, it must be escaped in the regular expression. With raw string notation, this means `r"\\"`. Without raw string notation, one must use `"\\\\"`, making the following lines of code functionally identical:

```
>>> re.match(r"\\", r"\\")
<_sre.SRE_Match object; span=(0, 1), match='\\'>
>>> re.match("\\\\", r"\\")
<_sre.SRE_Match object; span=(0, 1), match='\\'>
```

Writing a Tokenizer

A tokenizer or scanner analyzes a string to categorize groups of characters. This is a useful first step in writing a compiler or interpreter.

The text categories are specified with regular expressions. The technique is to combine those into a single master regular expression and to loop over successive matches:

```
import collections
import re

Token = collections.namedtuple('Token', ['typ', 'value', 'line', 'column'])

def tokenize(code):
    keywords = {'IF', 'THEN', 'ENDIF', 'FOR', 'NEXT', 'GOSUB', 'RETURN'}
    token_specification = [
        ('NUMBER',  r'\d+(\.\d*)?'),  # Integer or decimal number
        ('ASSIGN',  r':='),           # Assignment operator
        ('END',     r';'),            # Statement terminator
        ('ID',      r'[A-Za-z]+'),    # Identifiers
        ('OP',      r'[+\-*/]'),      # Arithmetic operators
        ('NEWLINE', r'\n'),           # Line endings
        ('SKIP',    r'[ \t]+'),       # Skip over spaces and tabs
        ('MISMATCH',r'.'),            # Any other character
    ]
    tok_regex = '|'.join('(?P<%s>%s)' % pair for pair in token_specification)
    line_num = 1
    line_start = 0
    for mo in re.finditer(tok_regex, code):
        kind = mo.lastgroup
        value = mo.group(kind)
        if kind == 'NEWLINE':
            line_start = mo.end()
            line_num += 1
        elif kind == 'SKIP':
            pass
        elif kind == 'MISMATCH':
            raise RuntimeError(f'{value!r} unexpected on line {line_num}')
        else:
            if kind == 'ID' and value in keywords:
                kind = value
            column = mo.start() - line_start
            yield Token(kind, value, line_num, column)

statements = '''
    IF quantity THEN
        total := total + price * quantity;
        tax := price * 0.05;
    ENDIF;
'''

for token in tokenize(statements):
    print(token)
```

The tokenizer produces the following output:

```
Token(typ='IF', value='IF', line=2, column=4)
Token(typ='ID', value='quantity', line=2, column=7)
Token(typ='THEN', value='THEN', line=2, column=16)
```

```
Token(typ='ID', value='total', line=3, column=8)
Token(typ='ASSIGN', value=':=', line=3, column=14)
Token(typ='ID', value='total', line=3, column=17)
Token(typ='OP', value='+', line=3, column=23)
Token(typ='ID', value='price', line=3, column=25)
Token(typ='OP', value='*', line=3, column=31)
Token(typ='ID', value='quantity', line=3, column=33)
Token(typ='END', value=';', line=3, column=41)
Token(typ='ID', value='tax', line=4, column=8)
Token(typ='ASSIGN', value=':=', line=4, column=12)
Token(typ='ID', value='price', line=4, column=15)
Token(typ='OP', value='*', line=4, column=21)
Token(typ='NUMBER', value='0.05', line=4, column=23)
Token(typ='END', value=';', line=4, column=27)
Token(typ='ENDIF', value='ENDIF', line=5, column=4)
Token(typ='END', value=';', line=5, column=9)
```

6.3 `difflib` — Helpers for computing deltas

Source code: Lib/difflib.py

This module provides classes and functions for comparing sequences. It can be used for example, for comparing files, and can produce difference information in various formats, including HTML and context and unified diffs. For comparing directories and files, see also, the `filecmp` module.

class difflib.SequenceMatcher

This is a flexible class for comparing pairs of sequences of any type, so long as the sequence elements are *hashable*. The basic algorithm predates, and is a little fancier than, an algorithm published in the late 1980's by Ratcliff and Obershelp under the hyperbolic name "gestalt pattern matching." The idea is to find the longest contiguous matching subsequence that contains no "junk" elements; these "junk" elements are ones that are uninteresting in some sense, such as blank lines or whitespace. (Handling junk is an extension to the Ratcliff and Obershelp algorithm.) The same idea is then applied recursively to the pieces of the sequences to the left and to the right of the matching subsequence. This does not yield minimal edit sequences, but does tend to yield matches that "look right" to people.

Timing: The basic Ratcliff-Obershelp algorithm is cubic time in the worst case and quadratic time in the expected case. `SequenceMatcher` is quadratic time for the worst case and has expected-case behavior dependent in a complicated way on how many elements the sequences have in common; best case time is linear.

Automatic junk heuristic: `SequenceMatcher` supports a heuristic that automatically treats certain sequence items as junk. The heuristic counts how many times each individual item appears in the sequence. If an item's duplicates (after the first one) account for more than 1% of the sequence and the sequence is at least 200 items long, this item is marked as "popular" and is treated as junk for the purpose of sequence matching. This heuristic can be turned off by setting the `autojunk` argument to `False` when creating the `SequenceMatcher`.

New in version 3.2: The *autojunk* parameter.

class difflib.Differ

This is a class for comparing sequences of lines of text, and producing human-readable differences or deltas. Differ uses `SequenceMatcher` both to compare sequences of lines, and to compare sequences of characters within similar (near-matching) lines.

Each line of a `Differ` delta begins with a two-letter code:

Code	Meaning
'- '	line unique to sequence 1
'+ '	line unique to sequence 2
' '	line common to both sequences
'? '	line not present in either input sequence

Lines beginning with '?' attempt to guide the eye to intraline differences, and were not present in either input sequence. These lines can be confusing if the sequences contain tab characters.

class difflib.HtmlDiff

This class can be used to create an HTML table (or a complete HTML file containing the table) showing a side by side, line by line comparison of text with inter-line and intra-line change highlights. The table can be generated in either full or contextual difference mode.

The constructor for this class is:

__init__(*tabsize=8, wrapcolumn=None, linejunk=None, charjunk=IS_CHARACTER_JUNK*)

Initializes instance of *HtmlDiff*.

tabsize is an optional keyword argument to specify tab stop spacing and defaults to `8`.

wrapcolumn is an optional keyword to specify column number where lines are broken and wrapped, defaults to `None` where lines are not wrapped.

linejunk and *charjunk* are optional keyword arguments passed into *ndiff()* (used by *HtmlDiff* to generate the side by side HTML differences). See *ndiff()* documentation for argument default values and descriptions.

The following methods are public:

make_file(*fromlines, tolines, fromdesc='', todesc='', context=False, numlines=5, *, charset='utf-8'*)

Compares *fromlines* and *tolines* (lists of strings) and returns a string which is a complete HTML file containing a table showing line by line differences with inter-line and intra-line changes highlighted.

fromdesc and *todesc* are optional keyword arguments to specify from/to file column header strings (both default to an empty string).

context and *numlines* are both optional keyword arguments. Set *context* to `True` when contextual differences are to be shown, else the default is `False` to show the full files. *numlines* defaults to `5`. When *context* is `True` *numlines* controls the number of context lines which surround the difference highlights. When *context* is `False` *numlines* controls the number of lines which are shown before a difference highlight when using the "next" hyperlinks (setting to zero would cause the "next" hyperlinks to place the next difference highlight at the top of the browser without any leading context).

Changed in version 3.5: *charset* keyword-only argument was added. The default charset of HTML document changed from `'ISO-8859-1'` to `'utf-8'`.

make_table(*fromlines, tolines, fromdesc='', todesc='', context=False, numlines=5*)

Compares *fromlines* and *tolines* (lists of strings) and returns a string which is a complete HTML table showing line by line differences with inter-line and intra-line changes highlighted.

The arguments for this method are the same as those for the *make_file()* method.

`Tools/scripts/diff.py` is a command-line front-end to this class and contains a good example of its use.

difflib.context_diff(*a, b, fromfile='', tofile='', fromfiledate='', tofiledate='', n=3, lineterm='\n'*)

Compare *a* and *b* (lists of strings); return a delta (a *generator* generating the delta lines) in context diff format.

Context diffs are a compact way of showing just the lines that have changed plus a few lines of context. The changes are shown in a before/after style. The number of context lines is set by *n* which defaults to three.

By default, the diff control lines (those with `***` or `---`) are created with a trailing newline. This is helpful so that inputs created from `io.IOBase.readlines()` result in diffs that are suitable for use with `io.IOBase.writelines()` since both the inputs and outputs have trailing newlines.

For inputs that do not have trailing newlines, set the *lineterm* argument to `""` so that the output will be uniformly newline free.

The context diff format normally has a header for filenames and modification times. Any or all of these may be specified using strings for *fromfile*, *tofile*, *fromfiledate*, and *tofiledate*. The modification times are normally expressed in the ISO 8601 format. If not specified, the strings default to blanks.

```
>>> s1 = ['bacon\n', 'eggs\n', 'ham\n', 'guido\n']
>>> s2 = ['python\n', 'eggy\n', 'hamster\n', 'guido\n']
>>> sys.stdout.writelines(context_diff(s1, s2, fromfile='before.py', tofile='after.py'))
*** before.py
--- after.py
***************
*** 1,4 ****
! bacon
! eggs
! ham
  guido
--- 1,4 ----
! python
! eggy
! hamster
  guido
```

See *A command-line interface to difflib* for a more detailed example.

difflib.get_close_matches(*word*, *possibilities*, *n=3*, *cutoff=0.6*)

Return a list of the best "good enough" matches. *word* is a sequence for which close matches are desired (typically a string), and *possibilities* is a list of sequences against which to match *word* (typically a list of strings).

Optional argument *n* (default `3`) is the maximum number of close matches to return; *n* must be greater than `0`.

Optional argument *cutoff* (default `0.6`) is a float in the range [0, 1]. Possibilities that don't score at least that similar to *word* are ignored.

The best (no more than *n*) matches among the possibilities are returned in a list, sorted by similarity score, most similar first.

```
>>> get_close_matches('appel', ['ape', 'apple', 'peach', 'puppy'])
['apple', 'ape']
>>> import keyword
>>> get_close_matches('wheel', keyword.kwlist)
['while']
>>> get_close_matches('pineapple', keyword.kwlist)
[]
>>> get_close_matches('accept', keyword.kwlist)
['except']
```

difflib.ndiff(*a*, *b*, *linejunk=None*, *charjunk=IS_CHARACTER_JUNK*)

Compare *a* and *b* (lists of strings); return a `Differ`-style delta (a *generator* generating the delta lines).

Optional keyword parameters *linejunk* and *charjunk* are filtering functions (or `None`):

linejunk: A function that accepts a single string argument, and returns true if the string is junk, or false if not. The default is `None`. There is also a module-level function *IS_LINE_JUNK()*, which filters out lines without visible characters, except for at most one pound character (`'#'`) – however the underlying *SequenceMatcher* class does a dynamic analysis of which lines are so frequent as to constitute noise, and this usually works better than using this function.

charjunk: A function that accepts a character (a string of length 1), and returns if the character is junk, or false if not. The default is module-level function *IS_CHARACTER_JUNK()*, which filters out whitespace characters (a blank or tab; it's a bad idea to include newline in this!).

`Tools/scripts/ndiff.py` is a command-line front-end to this function.

```
>>> diff = ndiff('one\ntwo\nthree\n'.splitlines(keepends=True),
...              'ore\ntree\nemu\n'.splitlines(keepends=True))
>>> print(''.join(diff), end="")
- one
?  ^
+ ore
?  ^
- two
- three
?  -
+ tree
+ emu
```

`difflib.restore`(*sequence*, *which*)

Return one of the two sequences that generated a delta.

Given a *sequence* produced by *Differ.compare()* or *ndiff()*, extract lines originating from file 1 or 2 (parameter *which*), stripping off line prefixes.

Example:

```
>>> diff = ndiff('one\ntwo\nthree\n'.splitlines(keepends=True),
...              'ore\ntree\nemu\n'.splitlines(keepends=True))
>>> diff = list(diff) # materialize the generated delta into a list
>>> print(''.join(restore(diff, 1)), end="")
one
two
three
>>> print(''.join(restore(diff, 2)), end="")
ore
tree
emu
```

`difflib.unified_diff`(*a*, *b*, *fromfile=''*, *tofile=''*, *fromfiledate=''*, *tofiledate=''*, *n=3*, *lineterm='\n'*)

Compare *a* and *b* (lists of strings); return a delta (a *generator* generating the delta lines) in unified diff format.

Unified diffs are a compact way of showing just the lines that have changed plus a few lines of context. The changes are shown in an inline style (instead of separate before/after blocks). The number of context lines is set by *n* which defaults to three.

By default, the diff control lines (those with `---`, `+++`, or `@@`) are created with a trailing newline. This is helpful so that inputs created from *io.IOBase.readlines()* result in diffs that are suitable for use with *io.IOBase.writelines()* since both the inputs and outputs have trailing newlines.

For inputs that do not have trailing newlines, set the *lineterm* argument to `""` so that the output will be uniformly newline free.

The context diff format normally has a header for filenames and modification times. Any or all of these may be specified using strings for *fromfile*, *tofile*, *fromfiledate*, and *tofiledate*. The modification times are normally expressed in the ISO 8601 format. If not specified, the strings default to blanks.

```
>>> s1 = ['bacon\n', 'eggs\n', 'ham\n', 'guido\n']
>>> s2 = ['python\n', 'eggy\n', 'hamster\n', 'guido\n']
>>> sys.stdout.writelines(unified_diff(s1, s2, fromfile='before.py', tofile='after.py'))
--- before.py
+++ after.py
@@ -1,4 +1,4 @@
-bacon
-eggs
-ham
+python
+eggy
+hamster
 guido
```

See *A command-line interface to difflib* for a more detailed example.

difflib.diff_bytes(*dfunc*, *a*, *b*, *fromfile=b"*, *tofile=b"*, *fromfiledate=b"*, *tofiledate=b"*, *n=3*, *lineterm=b'\n'*)

Compare *a* and *b* (lists of bytes objects) using *dfunc*; yield a sequence of delta lines (also bytes) in the format returned by *dfunc*. *dfunc* must be a callable, typically either `unified_diff()` or `context_diff()`.

Allows you to compare data with unknown or inconsistent encoding. All inputs except *n* must be bytes objects, not str. Works by losslessly converting all inputs (except *n*) to str, and calling `dfunc(a, b, fromfile, tofile, fromfiledate, tofiledate, n, lineterm)`. The output of *dfunc* is then converted back to bytes, so the delta lines that you receive have the same unknown/inconsistent encodings as *a* and *b*.

New in version 3.5.

difflib.IS_LINE_JUNK(*line*)

Return true for ignorable lines. The line *line* is ignorable if *line* is blank or contains a single `'#'`, otherwise it is not ignorable. Used as a default for parameter *linejunk* in `ndiff()` in older versions.

difflib.IS_CHARACTER_JUNK(*ch*)

Return true for ignorable characters. The character *ch* is ignorable if *ch* is a space or tab, otherwise it is not ignorable. Used as a default for parameter *charjunk* in `ndiff()`.

See also:

Pattern Matching: The Gestalt Approach Discussion of a similar algorithm by John W. Ratcliff and D. E. Metzener. This was published in Dr. Dobb's Journal in July, 1988.

6.3.1 SequenceMatcher Objects

The `SequenceMatcher` class has this constructor:

class difflib.SequenceMatcher(*isjunk=None*, *a="*, *b="*, *autojunk=True*)

Optional argument *isjunk* must be `None` (the default) or a one-argument function that takes a sequence element and returns true if and only if the element is "junk" and should be ignored. Passing `None` for *isjunk* is equivalent to passing `lambda x: 0`; in other words, no elements are ignored. For example, pass:

```
lambda x: x in " \t"
```

if you're comparing lines as sequences of characters, and don't want to synch up on blanks or hard tabs.

The optional arguments *a* and *b* are sequences to be compared; both default to empty strings. The elements of both sequences must be *hashable*.

The optional argument *autojunk* can be used to disable the automatic junk heuristic.

New in version 3.2: The *autojunk* parameter.

SequenceMatcher objects get three data attributes: *bjunk* is the set of elements of *b* for which *isjunk* is `True`; *bpopular* is the set of non-junk elements considered popular by the heuristic (if it is not disabled); *b2j* is a dict mapping the remaining elements of *b* to a list of positions where they occur. All three are reset whenever *b* is reset with `set_seqs()` or `set_seq2()`.

New in version 3.2: The *bjunk* and *bpopular* attributes.

`SequenceMatcher` objects have the following methods:

set_seqs(*a*, *b*)
Set the two sequences to be compared.

`SequenceMatcher` computes and caches detailed information about the second sequence, so if you want to compare one sequence against many sequences, use `set_seq2()` to set the commonly used sequence once and call `set_seq1()` repeatedly, once for each of the other sequences.

set_seq1(*a*)
Set the first sequence to be compared. The second sequence to be compared is not changed.

set_seq2(*b*)
Set the second sequence to be compared. The first sequence to be compared is not changed.

find_longest_match(*alo*, *ahi*, *blo*, *bhi*)
Find longest matching block in `a[alo:ahi]` and `b[blo:bhi]`.

If *isjunk* was omitted or `None`, `find_longest_match()` returns `(i, j, k)` such that `a[i:i+k]` is equal to `b[j:j+k]`, where `alo <= i <= i+k <= ahi` and `blo <= j <= j+k <= bhi`. For all `(i', j', k')` meeting those conditions, the additional conditions `k >= k'`, `i <= i'`, and if `i == i'`, `j <= j'` are also met. In other words, of all maximal matching blocks, return one that starts earliest in *a*, and of all those maximal matching blocks that start earliest in *a*, return the one that starts earliest in *b*.

```
>>> s = SequenceMatcher(None, " abcd", "abcd abcd")
>>> s.find_longest_match(0, 5, 0, 9)
Match(a=0, b=4, size=5)
```

If *isjunk* was provided, first the longest matching block is determined as above, but with the additional restriction that no junk element appears in the block. Then that block is extended as far as possible by matching (only) junk elements on both sides. So the resulting block never matches on junk except as identical junk happens to be adjacent to an interesting match.

Here's the same example as before, but considering blanks to be junk. That prevents `' abcd'` from matching the `' abcd'` at the tail end of the second sequence directly. Instead only the `'abcd'` can match, and matches the leftmost `'abcd'` in the second sequence:

```
>>> s = SequenceMatcher(lambda x: x==" ", " abcd", "abcd abcd")
>>> s.find_longest_match(0, 5, 0, 9)
Match(a=1, b=0, size=4)
```

If no blocks match, this returns `(alo, blo, 0)`.

This method returns a *named tuple* `Match(a, b, size)`.

get_matching_blocks()
Return list of triples describing matching subsequences. Each triple is of the form `(i, j, n)`, and means that `a[i:i+n] == b[j:j+n]`. The triples are monotonically increasing in *i* and *j*.

The last triple is a dummy, and has the value `(len(a), len(b), 0)`. It is the only triple with `n == 0`. If `(i, j, n)` and `(i', j', n')` are adjacent triples in the list, and the second is not the last triple in the list, then `i+n != i'` or `j+n != j'`; in other words, adjacent triples always describe non-adjacent equal blocks.

```
>>> s = SequenceMatcher(None, "abxcd", "abcd")
>>> s.get_matching_blocks()
[Match(a=0, b=0, size=2), Match(a=3, b=2, size=2), Match(a=5, b=4, size=0)]
```

get_opcodes()

Return list of 5-tuples describing how to turn *a* into *b*. Each tuple is of the form `(tag, i1, i2, j1, j2)`. The first tuple has `i1 == j1 == 0`, and remaining tuples have *i1* equal to the *i2* from the preceding tuple, and, likewise, *j1* equal to the previous *j2*.

The *tag* values are strings, with these meanings:

Value	Meaning
`'replace'`	`a[i1:i2]` should be replaced by `b[j1:j2]`.
`'delete'`	`a[i1:i2]` should be deleted. Note that `j1 == j2` in this case.
`'insert'`	`b[j1:j2]` should be inserted at `a[i1:i1]`. Note that `i1 == i2` in this case.
`'equal'`	`a[i1:i2] == b[j1:j2]` (the sub-sequences are equal).

For example:

```
>>> a = "qabxcd"
>>> b = "abycdf"
>>> s = SequenceMatcher(None, a, b)
>>> for tag, i1, i2, j1, j2 in s.get_opcodes():
...     print('{:7}   a[{}:{}] --> b[{}:{}] {!r:>8} --> {!r}'.format(
...         tag, i1, i2, j1, j2, a[i1:i2], b[j1:j2]))
delete    a[0:1] --> b[0:0]      'q' --> ''
equal     a[1:3] --> b[0:2]     'ab' --> 'ab'
replace   a[3:4] --> b[2:3]      'x' --> 'y'
equal     a[4:6] --> b[3:5]     'cd' --> 'cd'
insert    a[6:6] --> b[5:6]       '' --> 'f'
```

get_grouped_opcodes(*n=3*)

Return a *generator* of groups with up to *n* lines of context.

Starting with the groups returned by *get_opcodes()*, this method splits out smaller change clusters and eliminates intervening ranges which have no changes.

The groups are returned in the same format as *get_opcodes()*.

ratio()

Return a measure of the sequences' similarity as a float in the range [0, 1].

Where T is the total number of elements in both sequences, and M is the number of matches, this is 2.0*M / T. Note that this is `1.0` if the sequences are identical, and `0.0` if they have nothing in common.

This is expensive to compute if *get_matching_blocks()* or *get_opcodes()* hasn't already been called, in which case you may want to try *quick_ratio()* or *real_quick_ratio()* first to get an upper bound.

quick_ratio()

Return an upper bound on *ratio()* relatively quickly.

real_quick_ratio()

Return an upper bound on *ratio()* very quickly.

The three methods that return the ratio of matching to total characters can give different results due to differing levels of approximation, although `quick_ratio()` and `real_quick_ratio()` are always at least as large as `ratio()`:

```
>>> s = SequenceMatcher(None, "abcd", "bcde")
>>> s.ratio()
0.75
>>> s.quick_ratio()
0.75
>>> s.real_quick_ratio()
1.0
```

6.3.2 SequenceMatcher Examples

This example compares two strings, considering blanks to be "junk":

```
>>> s = SequenceMatcher(lambda x: x == " ",
...                     "private Thread currentThread;",
...                     "private volatile Thread currentThread;")
```

`ratio()` returns a float in [0, 1], measuring the similarity of the sequences. As a rule of thumb, a `ratio()` value over 0.6 means the sequences are close matches:

```
>>> print(round(s.ratio(), 3))
0.866
```

If you're only interested in where the sequences match, `get_matching_blocks()` is handy:

```
>>> for block in s.get_matching_blocks():
...     print("a[%d] and b[%d] match for %d elements" % block)
a[0] and b[0] match for 8 elements
a[8] and b[17] match for 21 elements
a[29] and b[38] match for 0 elements
```

Note that the last tuple returned by `get_matching_blocks()` is always a dummy, `(len(a), len(b), 0)`, and this is the only case in which the last tuple element (number of elements matched) is `0`.

If you want to know how to change the first sequence into the second, use `get_opcodes()`:

```
>>> for opcode in s.get_opcodes():
...     print("%6s a[%d:%d] b[%d:%d]" % opcode)
 equal a[0:8] b[0:8]
insert a[8:8] b[8:17]
 equal a[8:29] b[17:38]
```

See also:

- The *get_close_matches()* function in this module which shows how simple code building on *SequenceMatcher* can be used to do useful work.
- Simple version control recipe for a small application built with *SequenceMatcher*.

6.3.3 Differ Objects

Note that *Differ*-generated deltas make no claim to be **minimal** diffs. To the contrary, minimal diffs are often counter-intuitive, because they synch up anywhere possible, sometimes accidental matches 100 pages apart. Restricting synch points to contiguous matches preserves some notion of locality, at the occasional cost of producing a longer diff.

The *Differ* class has this constructor:

class difflib.Differ(*linejunk=None, charjunk=None*)

Optional keyword parameters *linejunk* and *charjunk* are for filter functions (or `None`):

linejunk: A function that accepts a single string argument, and returns true if the string is junk. The default is `None`, meaning that no line is considered junk.

charjunk: A function that accepts a single character argument (a string of length 1), and returns true if the character is junk. The default is `None`, meaning that no character is considered junk.

These junk-filtering functions speed up matching to find differences and do not cause any differing lines or characters to be ignored. Read the description of the *find_longest_match()* method's *isjunk* parameter for an explanation.

Differ objects are used (deltas generated) via a single method:

compare(*a, b*)

Compare two sequences of lines, and generate the delta (a sequence of lines).

Each sequence must contain individual single-line strings ending with newlines. Such sequences can be obtained from the *readlines()* method of file-like objects. The delta generated also consists of newline-terminated strings, ready to be printed as-is via the *writelines()* method of a file-like object.

6.3.4 Differ Example

This example compares two texts. First we set up the texts, sequences of individual single-line strings ending with newlines (such sequences can also be obtained from the `readlines()` method of file-like objects):

```
>>> text1 = '''  1. Beautiful is better than ugly.
...   2. Explicit is better than implicit.
...   3. Simple is better than complex.
...   4. Complex is better than complicated.
... '''.splitlines(keepends=True)
>>> len(text1)
4
>>> text1[0][-1]
'\n'
>>> text2 = '''  1. Beautiful is better than ugly.
...   3.   Simple is better than complex.
...   4. Complicated is better than complex.
...   5. Flat is better than nested.
... '''.splitlines(keepends=True)
```

Next we instantiate a Differ object:

```
>>> d = Differ()
```

Note that when instantiating a *Differ* object we may pass functions to filter out line and character "junk." See the *Differ()* constructor for details.

Finally, we compare the two:

```
>>> result = list(d.compare(text1, text2))
```

`result` is a list of strings, so let's pretty-print it:

```
>>> from pprint import pprint
>>> pprint(result)
['    1. Beautiful is better than ugly.\n',
 '-   2. Explicit is better than implicit.\n',
 '-   3. Simple is better than complex.\n',
 '+   3.   Simple is better than complex.\n',
 '?     ++\n',
 '-   4. Complex is better than complicated.\n',
 '?            ^                     ---- ^\n',
 '+   4. Complicated is better than complex.\n',
 '?           ++++ ^                      ^\n',
 '+   5. Flat is better than nested.\n']
```

As a single multi-line string it looks like this:

```
>>> import sys
>>> sys.stdout.writelines(result)
    1. Beautiful is better than ugly.
-   2. Explicit is better than implicit.
-   3. Simple is better than complex.
+   3.   Simple is better than complex.
?     ++
-   4. Complex is better than complicated.
?            ^                     ---- ^
+   4. Complicated is better than complex.
?           ++++ ^                      ^
+   5. Flat is better than nested.
```

6.3.5 A command-line interface to difflib

This example shows how to use difflib to create a `diff`-like utility. It is also contained in the Python source distribution, as `Tools/scripts/diff.py`.

```
#!/usr/bin/env python3
""" Command line interface to difflib.py providing diffs in four formats:

* ndiff:    lists every line and highlights interline changes.
* context:  highlights clusters of changes in a before/after format.
* unified:  highlights clusters of changes in an inline format.
* html:     generates side by side comparison with change highlights.

"""

import sys, os, difflib, argparse
from datetime import datetime, timezone

def file_mtime(path):
    t = datetime.fromtimestamp(os.stat(path).st_mtime,
                               timezone.utc)
    return t.astimezone().isoformat()

def main():

    parser = argparse.ArgumentParser()
    parser.add_argument('-c', action='store_true', default=False,
                        help='Produce a context format diff (default)')
```

```
    parser.add_argument('-u', action='store_true', default=False,
                        help='Produce a unified format diff')
    parser.add_argument('-m', action='store_true', default=False,
                        help='Produce HTML side by side diff '
                             '(can use -c and -l in conjunction)')
    parser.add_argument('-n', action='store_true', default=False,
                        help='Produce a ndiff format diff')
    parser.add_argument('-l', '--lines', type=int, default=3,
                        help='Set number of context lines (default 3)')
    parser.add_argument('fromfile')
    parser.add_argument('tofile')
    options = parser.parse_args()

    n = options.lines
    fromfile = options.fromfile
    tofile = options.tofile

    fromdate = file_mtime(fromfile)
    todate = file_mtime(tofile)
    with open(fromfile) as ff:
        fromlines = ff.readlines()
    with open(tofile) as tf:
        tolines = tf.readlines()

    if options.u:
        diff = difflib.unified_diff(fromlines, tolines, fromfile, tofile, fromdate, todate, n=n)
    elif options.n:
        diff = difflib.ndiff(fromlines, tolines)
    elif options.m:
        diff = difflib.HtmlDiff().make_file(fromlines,tolines,fromfile,tofile,context=options.c,
→numlines=n)
    else:
        diff = difflib.context_diff(fromlines, tolines, fromfile, tofile, fromdate, todate, n=n)

    sys.stdout.writelines(diff)

if __name__ == '__main__':
    main()
```

6.4 textwrap — Text wrapping and filling

Source code: Lib/textwrap.py

The *textwrap* module provides some convenience functions, as well as *TextWrapper*, the class that does all the work. If you're just wrapping or filling one or two text strings, the convenience functions should be good enough; otherwise, you should use an instance of *TextWrapper* for efficiency.

`textwrap.wrap(`*text*, *width=70*, ***kwargs*`)`

Wraps the single paragraph in *text* (a string) so every line is at most *width* characters long. Returns a list of output lines, without final newlines.

Optional keyword arguments correspond to the instance attributes of *TextWrapper*, documented below. *width* defaults to 70.

See the *TextWrapper.wrap()* method for additional details on how *wrap()* behaves.

`textwrap.fill(text, width=70, **kwargs)`

Wraps the single paragraph in *text*, and returns a single string containing the wrapped paragraph. `fill()` is shorthand for

```
"\n".join(wrap(text, ...))
```

In particular, `fill()` accepts exactly the same keyword arguments as `wrap()`.

`textwrap.shorten(text, width, **kwargs)`

Collapse and truncate the given *text* to fit in the given *width*.

First the whitespace in *text* is collapsed (all whitespace is replaced by single spaces). If the result fits in the *width*, it is returned. Otherwise, enough words are dropped from the end so that the remaining words plus the `placeholder` fit within `width`:

```
>>> textwrap.shorten("Hello  world!", width=12)
'Hello world!'
>>> textwrap.shorten("Hello  world!", width=11)
'Hello [...]'
>>> textwrap.shorten("Hello world", width=10, placeholder="...")
'Hello...'
```

Optional keyword arguments correspond to the instance attributes of `TextWrapper`, documented below. Note that the whitespace is collapsed before the text is passed to the `TextWrapper fill()` function, so changing the value of `tabsize`, `expand_tabs`, `drop_whitespace`, and `replace_whitespace` will have no effect.

New in version 3.4.

`textwrap.dedent(text)`

Remove any common leading whitespace from every line in *text*.

This can be used to make triple-quoted strings line up with the left edge of the display, while still presenting them in the source code in indented form.

Note that tabs and spaces are both treated as whitespace, but they are not equal: the lines `"  hello"` and `"\thello"` are considered to have no common leading whitespace.

For example:

```
def test():
    # end first line with \ to avoid the empty line!
    s = '''\
    hello
      world
    '''
    print(repr(s))          # prints '    hello\n      world\n    '
    print(repr(dedent(s)))  # prints 'hello\n  world\n'
```

`textwrap.indent(text, prefix, predicate=None)`

Add *prefix* to the beginning of selected lines in *text*.

Lines are separated by calling `text.splitlines(True)`.

By default, *prefix* is added to all lines that do not consist solely of whitespace (including any line endings).

For example:

```
>>> s = 'hello\n\n \nworld'
>>> indent(s, '  ')
'  hello\n\n \n  world'
```

The optional *predicate* argument can be used to control which lines are indented. For example, it is easy to add *prefix* to even empty and whitespace-only lines:

```
>>> print(indent(s, '+ ', lambda line: True))
+ hello
+
+
+ world
```

New in version 3.3.

wrap(), *fill()* and *shorten()* work by creating a *TextWrapper* instance and calling a single method on it. That instance is not reused, so for applications that process many text strings using *wrap()* and/or *fill()*, it may be more efficient to create your own *TextWrapper* object.

Text is preferably wrapped on whitespaces and right after the hyphens in hyphenated words; only then will long words be broken if necessary, unless *TextWrapper.break_long_words* is set to false.

class textwrap.TextWrapper(*****kwargs*** **)**

The *TextWrapper* constructor accepts a number of optional keyword arguments. Each keyword argument corresponds to an instance attribute, so for example

```
wrapper = TextWrapper(initial_indent="* ")
```

is the same as

```
wrapper = TextWrapper()
wrapper.initial_indent = "* "
```

You can re-use the same *TextWrapper* object many times, and you can change any of its options through direct assignment to instance attributes between uses.

The *TextWrapper* instance attributes (and keyword arguments to the constructor) are as follows:

width

(default: `70`) The maximum length of wrapped lines. As long as there are no individual words in the input text longer than *width*, *TextWrapper* guarantees that no output line will be longer than *width* characters.

expand_tabs

(default: `True`) If true, then all tab characters in *text* will be expanded to spaces using the `expandtabs()` method of *text*.

tabsize

(default: `8`) If *expand_tabs* is true, then all tab characters in *text* will be expanded to zero or more spaces, depending on the current column and the given tab size.

New in version 3.3.

replace_whitespace

(default: `True`) If true, after tab expansion but before wrapping, the *wrap()* method will replace each whitespace character with a single space. The whitespace characters replaced are as follows: tab, newline, vertical tab, formfeed, and carriage return (`'\t\n\v\f\r'`).

Note: If *expand_tabs* is false and *replace_whitespace* is true, each tab character will be replaced by a single space, which is *not* the same as tab expansion.

Note: If *replace_whitespace* is false, newlines may appear in the middle of a line and cause strange output. For this reason, text should be split into paragraphs (using *str.splitlines()*

or similar) which are wrapped separately.

drop_whitespace
(default: True) If true, whitespace at the beginning and ending of every line (after wrapping but before indenting) is dropped. Whitespace at the beginning of the paragraph, however, is not dropped if non-whitespace follows it. If whitespace being dropped takes up an entire line, the whole line is dropped.

initial_indent
(default: '') String that will be prepended to the first line of wrapped output. Counts towards the length of the first line. The empty string is not indented.

subsequent_indent
(default: '') String that will be prepended to all lines of wrapped output except the first. Counts towards the length of each line except the first.

fix_sentence_endings
(default: False) If true, *TextWrapper* attempts to detect sentence endings and ensure that sentences are always separated by exactly two spaces. This is generally desired for text in a monospaced font. However, the sentence detection algorithm is imperfect: it assumes that a sentence ending consists of a lowercase letter followed by one of '.', '!', or '?', possibly followed by one of '"' or "'", followed by a space. One problem with this is algorithm is that it is unable to detect the difference between "Dr." in

```
[...] Dr. Frankenstein's monster [...]
```

and "Spot." in

```
[...] See Spot. See Spot run [...]
```

fix_sentence_endings is false by default.

Since the sentence detection algorithm relies on string.lowercase for the definition of "lowercase letter," and a convention of using two spaces after a period to separate sentences on the same line, it is specific to English-language texts.

break_long_words
(default: True) If true, then words longer than *width* will be broken in order to ensure that no lines are longer than *width*. If it is false, long words will not be broken, and some lines may be longer than *width*. (Long words will be put on a line by themselves, in order to minimize the amount by which *width* is exceeded.)

break_on_hyphens
(default: True) If true, wrapping will occur preferably on whitespaces and right after hyphens in compound words, as it is customary in English. If false, only whitespaces will be considered as potentially good places for line breaks, but you need to set *break_long_words* to false if you want truly insecable words. Default behaviour in previous versions was to always allow breaking hyphenated words.

max_lines
(default: None) If not None, then the output will contain at most *max_lines* lines, with *placeholder* appearing at the end of the output.

New in version 3.4.

placeholder
(default: ' [...]') String that will appear at the end of the output text if it has been truncated.

New in version 3.4.

TextWrapper also provides some public methods, analogous to the module-level convenience functions:

wrap(*text*)
Wraps the single paragraph in *text* (a string) so every line is at most *width* characters long. All wrapping options are taken from instance attributes of the *TextWrapper* instance. Returns a list of output lines, without final newlines. If the wrapped output has no content, the returned list is empty.

fill(*text*)
Wraps the single paragraph in *text*, and returns a single string containing the wrapped paragraph.

6.5 unicodedata — Unicode Database

This module provides access to the Unicode Character Database (UCD) which defines character properties for all Unicode characters. The data contained in this database is compiled from the UCD version 9.0.0.

The module uses the same names and symbols as defined by Unicode Standard Annex #44, "Unicode Character Database". It defines the following functions:

unicodedata.**lookup**(*name*)
Look up character by name. If a character with the given name is found, return the corresponding character. If not found, *KeyError* is raised.

Changed in version 3.3: Support for name aliases[1] and named sequences[2] has been added.

unicodedata.**name**(*chr*[, *default*])
Returns the name assigned to the character *chr* as a string. If no name is defined, *default* is returned, or, if not given, *ValueError* is raised.

unicodedata.**decimal**(*chr*[, *default*])
Returns the decimal value assigned to the character *chr* as integer. If no such value is defined, *default* is returned, or, if not given, *ValueError* is raised.

unicodedata.**digit**(*chr*[, *default*])
Returns the digit value assigned to the character *chr* as integer. If no such value is defined, *default* is returned, or, if not given, *ValueError* is raised.

unicodedata.**numeric**(*chr*[, *default*])
Returns the numeric value assigned to the character *chr* as float. If no such value is defined, *default* is returned, or, if not given, *ValueError* is raised.

unicodedata.**category**(*chr*)
Returns the general category assigned to the character *chr* as string.

unicodedata.**bidirectional**(*chr*)
Returns the bidirectional class assigned to the character *chr* as string. If no such value is defined, an empty string is returned.

unicodedata.**combining**(*chr*)
Returns the canonical combining class assigned to the character *chr* as integer. Returns 0 if no combining class is defined.

unicodedata.**east_asian_width**(*chr*)
Returns the east asian width assigned to the character *chr* as string.

[1] http://www.unicode.org/Public/9.0.0/ucd/NameAliases.txt
[2] http://www.unicode.org/Public/9.0.0/ucd/NamedSequences.txt

`unicodedata.mirrored(chr)`
Returns the mirrored property assigned to the character *chr* as integer. Returns `1` if the character has been identified as a "mirrored" character in bidirectional text, `0` otherwise.

`unicodedata.decomposition(chr)`
Returns the character decomposition mapping assigned to the character *chr* as string. An empty string is returned in case no such mapping is defined.

`unicodedata.normalize(form, unistr)`
Return the normal form *form* for the Unicode string *unistr*. Valid values for *form* are 'NFC', 'NFKC', 'NFD', and 'NFKD'.

The Unicode standard defines various normalization forms of a Unicode string, based on the definition of canonical equivalence and compatibility equivalence. In Unicode, several characters can be expressed in various way. For example, the character U+00C7 (LATIN CAPITAL LETTER C WITH CEDILLA) can also be expressed as the sequence U+0043 (LATIN CAPITAL LETTER C) U+0327 (COMBINING CEDILLA).

For each character, there are two normal forms: normal form C and normal form D. Normal form D (NFD) is also known as canonical decomposition, and translates each character into its decomposed form. Normal form C (NFC) first applies a canonical decomposition, then composes pre-combined characters again.

In addition to these two forms, there are two additional normal forms based on compatibility equivalence. In Unicode, certain characters are supported which normally would be unified with other characters. For example, U+2160 (ROMAN NUMERAL ONE) is really the same thing as U+0049 (LATIN CAPITAL LETTER I). However, it is supported in Unicode for compatibility with existing character sets (e.g. gb2312).

The normal form KD (NFKD) will apply the compatibility decomposition, i.e. replace all compatibility characters with their equivalents. The normal form KC (NFKC) first applies the compatibility decomposition, followed by the canonical composition.

Even if two unicode strings are normalized and look the same to a human reader, if one has combining characters and the other doesn't, they may not compare equal.

In addition, the module exposes the following constant:

`unicodedata.unidata_version`
The version of the Unicode database used in this module.

`unicodedata.ucd_3_2_0`
This is an object that has the same methods as the entire module, but uses the Unicode database version 3.2 instead, for applications that require this specific version of the Unicode database (such as IDNA).

Examples:

```
>>> import unicodedata
>>> unicodedata.lookup('LEFT CURLY BRACKET')
'{'
>>> unicodedata.name('/')
'SOLIDUS'
>>> unicodedata.decimal('9')
9
>>> unicodedata.decimal('a')
Traceback (most recent call last):
  File "<stdin>", line 1, in <module>
ValueError: not a decimal
>>> unicodedata.category('A')  # 'L'etter, 'u'ppercase
'Lu'
```

```
>>> unicodedata.bidirectional('\u0660') # 'A'rabic, 'N'umber
'AN'
```

6.6 stringprep — Internet String Preparation

Source code: Lib/stringprep.py

When identifying things (such as host names) in the internet, it is often necessary to compare such identifications for "equality". Exactly how this comparison is executed may depend on the application domain, e.g. whether it should be case-insensitive or not. It may be also necessary to restrict the possible identifications, to allow only identifications consisting of "printable" characters.

RFC 3454 defines a procedure for "preparing" Unicode strings in internet protocols. Before passing strings onto the wire, they are processed with the preparation procedure, after which they have a certain normalized form. The RFC defines a set of tables, which can be combined into profiles. Each profile must define which tables it uses, and what other optional parts of the **stringprep** procedure are part of the profile. One example of a **stringprep** profile is **nameprep**, which is used for internationalized domain names.

The module *stringprep* only exposes the tables from RFC 3454. As these tables would be very large to represent them as dictionaries or lists, the module uses the Unicode character database internally. The module source code itself was generated using the **mkstringprep.py** utility.

As a result, these tables are exposed as functions, not as data structures. There are two kinds of tables in the RFC: sets and mappings. For a set, *stringprep* provides the "characteristic function", i.e. a function that returns true if the parameter is part of the set. For mappings, it provides the mapping function: given the key, it returns the associated value. Below is a list of all functions available in the module.

stringprep.in_table_a1(*code*)
Determine whether *code* is in tableA.1 (Unassigned code points in Unicode 3.2).

stringprep.in_table_b1(*code*)
Determine whether *code* is in tableB.1 (Commonly mapped to nothing).

stringprep.map_table_b2(*code*)
Return the mapped value for *code* according to tableB.2 (Mapping for case-folding used with NFKC).

stringprep.map_table_b3(*code*)
Return the mapped value for *code* according to tableB.3 (Mapping for case-folding used with no normalization).

stringprep.in_table_c11(*code*)
Determine whether *code* is in tableC.1.1 (ASCII space characters).

stringprep.in_table_c12(*code*)
Determine whether *code* is in tableC.1.2 (Non-ASCII space characters).

stringprep.in_table_c11_c12(*code*)
Determine whether *code* is in tableC.1 (Space characters, union of C.1.1 and C.1.2).

stringprep.in_table_c21(*code*)
Determine whether *code* is in tableC.2.1 (ASCII control characters).

stringprep.in_table_c22(*code*)
Determine whether *code* is in tableC.2.2 (Non-ASCII control characters).

stringprep.in_table_c21_c22(*code*)
Determine whether *code* is in tableC.2 (Control characters, union of C.2.1 and C.2.2).

`stringprep.in_table_c3(code)`
: Determine whether *code* is in tableC.3 (Private use).

`stringprep.in_table_c4(code)`
: Determine whether *code* is in tableC.4 (Non-character code points).

`stringprep.in_table_c5(code)`
: Determine whether *code* is in tableC.5 (Surrogate codes).

`stringprep.in_table_c6(code)`
: Determine whether *code* is in tableC.6 (Inappropriate for plain text).

`stringprep.in_table_c7(code)`
: Determine whether *code* is in tableC.7 (Inappropriate for canonical representation).

`stringprep.in_table_c8(code)`
: Determine whether *code* is in tableC.8 (Change display properties or are deprecated).

`stringprep.in_table_c9(code)`
: Determine whether *code* is in tableC.9 (Tagging characters).

`stringprep.in_table_d1(code)`
: Determine whether *code* is in tableD.1 (Characters with bidirectional property "R" or "AL").

`stringprep.in_table_d2(code)`
: Determine whether *code* is in tableD.2 (Characters with bidirectional property "L").

6.7 `readline` — GNU readline interface

The `readline` module defines a number of functions to facilitate completion and reading/writing of history files from the Python interpreter. This module can be used directly, or via the `rlcompleter` module, which supports completion of Python identifiers at the interactive prompt. Settings made using this module affect the behaviour of both the interpreter's interactive prompt and the prompts offered by the built-in `input()` function.

Note: The underlying Readline library API may be implemented by the `libedit` library instead of GNU readline. On MacOS X the `readline` module detects which library is being used at run time.

The configuration file for `libedit` is different from that of GNU readline. If you programmatically load configuration strings you can check for the text "libedit" in `readline.__doc__` to differentiate between GNU readline and libedit.

Readline keybindings may be configured via an initialization file, typically `.inputrc` in your home directory. See Readline Init File in the GNU Readline manual for information about the format and allowable constructs of that file, and the capabilities of the Readline library in general.

6.7.1 Init file

The following functions relate to the init file and user configuration:

`readline.parse_and_bind(string)`
: Execute the init line provided in the *string* argument. This calls `rl_parse_and_bind()` in the underlying library.

readline.read_init_file([*filename*])
Execute a readline initialization file. The default filename is the last filename used. This calls `rl_read_init_file()` in the underlying library.

6.7.2 Line buffer

The following functions operate on the line buffer:

readline.get_line_buffer()
Return the current contents of the line buffer (`rl_line_buffer` in the underlying library).

readline.insert_text(*string*)
Insert text into the line buffer at the cursor position. This calls `rl_insert_text()` in the underlying library, but ignores the return value.

readline.redisplay()
Change what's displayed on the screen to reflect the current contents of the line buffer. This calls `rl_redisplay()` in the underlying library.

6.7.3 History file

The following functions operate on a history file:

readline.read_history_file([*filename*])
Load a readline history file, and append it to the history list. The default filename is `~/.history`. This calls `read_history()` in the underlying library.

readline.write_history_file([*filename*])
Save the history list to a readline history file, overwriting any existing file. The default filename is `~/.history`. This calls `write_history()` in the underlying library.

readline.append_history_file(*nelements*[, *filename*])
Append the last *nelements* items of history to a file. The default filename is `~/.history`. The file must already exist. This calls `append_history()` in the underlying library. This function only exists if Python was compiled for a version of the library that supports it.

New in version 3.5.

readline.get_history_length()
readline.set_history_length(*length*)
Set or return the desired number of lines to save in the history file. The *write_history_file()* function uses this value to truncate the history file, by calling `history_truncate_file()` in the underlying library. Negative values imply unlimited history file size.

6.7.4 History list

The following functions operate on a global history list:

readline.clear_history()
Clear the current history. This calls `clear_history()` in the underlying library. The Python function only exists if Python was compiled for a version of the library that supports it.

readline.get_current_history_length()
Return the number of items currently in the history. (This is different from *get_history_length()*, which returns the maximum number of lines that will be written to a history file.)

`readline.get_history_item(index)`
Return the current contents of history item at *index*. The item index is one-based. This calls `history_get()` in the underlying library.

`readline.remove_history_item(pos)`
Remove history item specified by its position from the history. The position is zero-based. This calls `remove_history()` in the underlying library.

`readline.replace_history_item(pos, line)`
Replace history item specified by its position with *line*. The position is zero-based. This calls `replace_history_entry()` in the underlying library.

`readline.add_history(line)`
Append *line* to the history buffer, as if it was the last line typed. This calls `add_history()` in the underlying library.

`readline.set_auto_history(enabled)`
Enable or disable automatic calls to `add_history()` when reading input via readline. The *enabled* argument should be a Boolean value that when true, enables auto history, and that when false, disables auto history.

New in version 3.6.

CPython implementation detail: Auto history is enabled by default, and changes to this do not persist across multiple sessions.

6.7.5 Startup hooks

`readline.set_startup_hook([function])`
Set or remove the function invoked by the `rl_startup_hook` callback of the underlying library. If *function* is specified, it will be used as the new hook function; if omitted or `None`, any function already installed is removed. The hook is called with no arguments just before readline prints the first prompt.

`readline.set_pre_input_hook([function])`
Set or remove the function invoked by the `rl_pre_input_hook` callback of the underlying library. If *function* is specified, it will be used as the new hook function; if omitted or `None`, any function already installed is removed. The hook is called with no arguments after the first prompt has been printed and just before readline starts reading input characters. This function only exists if Python was compiled for a version of the library that supports it.

6.7.6 Completion

The following functions relate to implementing a custom word completion function. This is typically operated by the Tab key, and can suggest and automatically complete a word being typed. By default, Readline is set up to be used by `rlcompleter` to complete Python identifiers for the interactive interpreter. If the `readline` module is to be used with a custom completer, a different set of word delimiters should be set.

`readline.set_completer([function])`
Set or remove the completer function. If *function* is specified, it will be used as the new completer function; if omitted or `None`, any completer function already installed is removed. The completer function is called as `function(text, state)`, for *state* in `0`, `1`, `2`, ..., until it returns a non-string value. It should return the next possible completion starting with *text*.

The installed completer function is invoked by the *entry_func* callback passed to `rl_completion_matches()` in the underlying library. The *text* string comes from the first parameter to the `rl_attempted_completion_function` callback of the underlying library.

readline.get_completer()
Get the completer function, or `None` if no completer function has been set.

readline.get_completion_type()
Get the type of completion being attempted. This returns the `rl_completion_type` variable in the underlying library as an integer.

readline.get_begidx()
readline.get_endidx()
Get the beginning or ending index of the completion scope. These indexes are the *start* and *end* arguments passed to the `rl_attempted_completion_function` callback of the underlying library.

readline.set_completer_delims(*string*)
readline.get_completer_delims()
Set or get the word delimiters for completion. These determine the start of the word to be considered for completion (the completion scope). These functions access the `rl_completer_word_break_characters` variable in the underlying library.

readline.set_completion_display_matches_hook([*function*])
Set or remove the completion display function. If *function* is specified, it will be used as the new completion display function; if omitted or `None`, any completion display function already installed is removed. This sets or clears the `rl_completion_display_matches_hook` callback in the underlying library. The completion display function is called as `function(substitution, [matches], longest_match_length)` once each time matches need to be displayed.

6.7.7 Example

The following example demonstrates how to use the *readline* module's history reading and writing functions to automatically load and save a history file named `.python_history` from the user's home directory. The code below would normally be executed automatically during interactive sessions from the user's `PYTHONSTARTUP` file.

```
import atexit
import os
import readline

histfile = os.path.join(os.path.expanduser("~"), ".python_history")
try:
    readline.read_history_file(histfile)
    # default history len is -1 (infinite), which may grow unruly
    readline.set_history_length(1000)
except FileNotFoundError:
    pass

atexit.register(readline.write_history_file, histfile)
```

This code is actually automatically run when Python is run in interactive mode (see *Readline configuration*).

The following example achieves the same goal but supports concurrent interactive sessions, by only appending the new history.

```
import atexit
import os
import readline
histfile = os.path.join(os.path.expanduser("~"), ".python_history")

try:
    readline.read_history_file(histfile)
```

```
    h_len = readline.get_current_history_length()
except FileNotFoundError:
    open(histfile, 'wb').close()
    h_len = 0

def save(prev_h_len, histfile):
    new_h_len = readline.get_current_history_length()
    readline.set_history_length(1000)
    readline.append_history_file(new_h_len - prev_h_len, histfile)
atexit.register(save, h_len, histfile)
```

The following example extends the *code.InteractiveConsole* class to support history save/restore.

```
import atexit
import code
import os
import readline

class HistoryConsole(code.InteractiveConsole):
    def __init__(self, locals=None, filename="<console>",
                 histfile=os.path.expanduser("~/.console-history")):
        code.InteractiveConsole.__init__(self, locals, filename)
        self.init_history(histfile)

    def init_history(self, histfile):
        readline.parse_and_bind("tab: complete")
        if hasattr(readline, "read_history_file"):
            try:
                readline.read_history_file(histfile)
            except FileNotFoundError:
                pass
            atexit.register(self.save_history, histfile)

    def save_history(self, histfile):
        readline.set_history_length(1000)
        readline.write_history_file(histfile)
```

6.8 rlcompleter — Completion function for GNU readline

Source code: Lib/rlcompleter.py

The *rlcompleter* module defines a completion function suitable for the *readline* module by completing valid Python identifiers and keywords.

When this module is imported on a Unix platform with the *readline* module available, an instance of the `Completer` class is automatically created and its `complete()` method is set as the *readline* completer.

Example:

```
>>> import rlcompleter
>>> import readline
>>> readline.parse_and_bind("tab: complete")
>>> readline. <TAB PRESSED>
readline.__doc__          readline.get_line_buffer(  readline.read_init_file(
readline.__file__         readline.insert_text(      readline.set_completer(
```

```
readline.__name__          readline.parse_and_bind(
>>> readline.
```

The *rlcompleter* module is designed for use with Python's interactive mode. Unless Python is run with the `-S` option, the module is automatically imported and configured (see *Readline configuration*).

On platforms without *readline*, the `Completer` class defined by this module can still be used for custom purposes.

6.8.1 Completer Objects

Completer objects have the following method:

`Completer.complete(`*text*, *state*`)`

Return the *state*th completion for *text*.

If called for *text* that doesn't include a period character (`'.'`), it will complete from names currently defined in *__main__*, *builtins* and keywords (as defined by the *keyword* module).

If called for a dotted name, it will try to evaluate anything without obvious side-effects (functions will not be evaluated, but it can generate calls to `__getattr__()`) up to the last part, and find matches for the rest via the *dir()* function. Any exception raised during the evaluation of the expression is caught, silenced and *None* is returned.

CHAPTER

SEVEN

BINARY DATA SERVICES

The modules described in this chapter provide some basic services operations for manipulation of binary data. Other operations on binary data, specifically in relation to file formats and network protocols, are described in the relevant sections.

Some libraries described under *Text Processing Services* also work with either ASCII-compatible binary formats (for example, `re`) or all binary data (for example, `difflib`).

In addition, see the documentation for Python's built-in binary data types in *Binary Sequence Types — bytes, bytearray, memoryview*.

7.1 struct — Interpret bytes as packed binary data

Source code: Lib/struct.py

This module performs conversions between Python values and C structs represented as Python `bytes` objects. This can be used in handling binary data stored in files or from network connections, among other sources. It uses *Format Strings* as compact descriptions of the layout of the C structs and the intended conversion to/from Python values.

Note: By default, the result of packing a given C struct includes pad bytes in order to maintain proper alignment for the C types involved; similarly, alignment is taken into account when unpacking. This behavior is chosen so that the bytes of a packed struct correspond exactly to the layout in memory of the corresponding C struct. To handle platform-independent data formats or omit implicit pad bytes, use `standard` size and alignment instead of `native` size and alignment: see *Byte Order, Size, and Alignment* for details.

Several `struct` functions (and methods of `Struct`) take a *buffer* argument. This refers to objects that implement the bufferobjects and provide either a readable or read-writable buffer. The most common types used for that purpose are `bytes` and `bytearray`, but many other types that can be viewed as an array of bytes implement the buffer protocol, so that they can be read/filled without additional copying from a `bytes` object.

7.1.1 Functions and Exceptions

The module defines the following exception and functions:

exception struct.error

Exception raised on various occasions; argument is a string describing what is wrong.

`struct.pack`(*fmt*, *v1*, *v2*, ...)
Return a bytes object containing the values *v1*, *v2*, ... packed according to the format string *fmt*. The arguments must match the values required by the format exactly.

`struct.pack_into`(*fmt*, *buffer*, *offset*, *v1*, *v2*, ...)
Pack the values *v1*, *v2*, ... according to the format string *fmt* and write the packed bytes into the writable buffer *buffer* starting at position *offset*. Note that *offset* is a required argument.

`struct.unpack`(*fmt*, *buffer*)
Unpack from the buffer *buffer* (presumably packed by `pack(fmt, ...)`) according to the format string *fmt*. The result is a tuple even if it contains exactly one item. The buffer's size in bytes must match the size required by the format, as reflected by `calcsize()`.

`struct.unpack_from`(*fmt*, *buffer*, *offset=0*)
Unpack from *buffer* starting at position *offset*, according to the format string *fmt*. The result is a tuple even if it contains exactly one item. The buffer's size in bytes, minus *offset*, must be at least the size required by the format, as reflected by `calcsize()`.

`struct.iter_unpack`(*fmt*, *buffer*)
Iteratively unpack from the buffer *buffer* according to the format string *fmt*. This function returns an iterator which will read equally-sized chunks from the buffer until all its contents have been consumed. The buffer's size in bytes must be a multiple of the size required by the format, as reflected by `calcsize()`.

Each iteration yields a tuple as specified by the format string.

New in version 3.4.

`struct.calcsize`(*fmt*)
Return the size of the struct (and hence of the bytes object produced by `pack(fmt, ...)`) corresponding to the format string *fmt*.

7.1.2 Format Strings

Format strings are the mechanism used to specify the expected layout when packing and unpacking data. They are built up from *Format Characters*, which specify the type of data being packed/unpacked. In addition, there are special characters for controlling the *Byte Order, Size, and Alignment*.

Byte Order, Size, and Alignment

By default, C types are represented in the machine's native format and byte order, and properly aligned by skipping pad bytes if necessary (according to the rules used by the C compiler).

Alternatively, the first character of the format string can be used to indicate the byte order, size and alignment of the packed data, according to the following table:

Character	Byte order	Size	Alignment
@	native	native	native
=	native	standard	none
<	little-endian	standard	none
>	big-endian	standard	none
!	network (= big-endian)	standard	none

If the first character is not one of these, `'@'` is assumed.

Native byte order is big-endian or little-endian, depending on the host system. For example, Intel x86 and AMD64 (x86-64) are little-endian; Motorola 68000 and PowerPC G5 are big-endian; ARM and Intel Itanium feature switchable endianness (bi-endian). Use `sys.byteorder` to check the endianness of your system.

Native size and alignment are determined using the C compiler's `sizeof` expression. This is always combined with native byte order.

Standard size depends only on the format character; see the table in the *Format Characters* section.

Note the difference between `'@'` and `'='`: both use native byte order, but the size and alignment of the latter is standardized.

The form `'!'` is available for those poor souls who claim they can't remember whether network byte order is big-endian or little-endian.

There is no way to indicate non-native byte order (force byte-swapping); use the appropriate choice of `'<'` or `'>'`.

Notes:

1. Padding is only automatically added between successive structure members. No padding is added at the beginning or the end of the encoded struct.
2. No padding is added when using non-native size and alignment, e.g. with '<', '>', '=', and '!'.
3. To align the end of a structure to the alignment requirement of a particular type, end the format with the code for that type with a repeat count of zero. See *Examples*.

Format Characters

Format characters have the following meaning; the conversion between C and Python values should be obvious given their types. The 'Standard size' column refers to the size of the packed value in bytes when using standard size; that is, when the format string starts with one of `'<'`, `'>'`, `'!'` or `'='`. When using native size, the size of the packed value is platform-dependent.

Format	C Type	Python type	Standard size	Notes
`x`	pad byte	no value		
`c`	`char`	bytes of length 1	1	
`b`	`signed char`	integer	1	(1),(3)
`B`	`unsigned char`	integer	1	(3)
`?`	`_Bool`	bool	1	(1)
`h`	`short`	integer	2	(3)
`H`	`unsigned short`	integer	2	(3)
`i`	`int`	integer	4	(3)
`I`	`unsigned int`	integer	4	(3)
`l`	`long`	integer	4	(3)
`L`	`unsigned long`	integer	4	(3)
`q`	`long long`	integer	8	(2), (3)
`Q`	`unsigned long long`	integer	8	(2), (3)
`n`	`ssize_t`	integer		(4)
`N`	`size_t`	integer		(4)
`e`	(7)	float	2	(5)
`f`	`float`	float	4	(5)
`d`	`double`	float	8	(5)
`s`	`char[]`	bytes		
`p`	`char[]`	bytes		
`P`	`void *`	integer		(6)

Changed in version 3.3: Added support for the `'n'` and `'N'` formats.

Changed in version 3.6: Added support for the `'e'` format.

Notes:

1. The `'?'` conversion code corresponds to the `_Bool` type defined by C99. If this type is not available, it is simulated using a `char`. In standard mode, it is always represented by one byte.
2. The `'q'` and `'Q'` conversion codes are available in native mode only if the platform C compiler supports C `long long`, or, on Windows, `__int64`. They are always available in standard modes.
3. When attempting to pack a non-integer using any of the integer conversion codes, if the non-integer has a `__index__()` method then that method is called to convert the argument to an integer before packing.

   Changed in version 3.2: Use of the `__index__()` method for non-integers is new in 3.2.
4. The `'n'` and `'N'` conversion codes are only available for the native size (selected as the default or with the `'@'` byte order character). For the standard size, you can use whichever of the other integer formats fits your application.
5. For the `'f'`, `'d'` and `'e'` conversion codes, the packed representation uses the IEEE 754 binary32, binary64 or binary16 format (for `'f'`, `'d'` or `'e'` respectively), regardless of the floating-point format used by the platform.
6. The `'P'` format character is only available for the native byte ordering (selected as the default or with the `'@'` byte order character). The byte order character `'='` chooses to use little- or big-endian ordering based on the host system. The struct module does not interpret this as native ordering, so the `'P'` format is not available.
7. The IEEE 754 binary16 "half precision" type was introduced in the 2008 revision of the IEEE 754 standard. It has a sign bit, a 5-bit exponent and 11-bit precision (with 10 bits explicitly stored), and can represent numbers between approximately `6.1e-05` and `6.5e+04` at full precision. This type is not widely supported by C compilers: on a typical machine, an unsigned short can be used for storage, but not for math operations. See the Wikipedia page on the half-precision floating-point format for more information.

A format character may be preceded by an integral repeat count. For example, the format string `'4h'` means exactly the same as `'hhhh'`.

Whitespace characters between formats are ignored; a count and its format must not contain whitespace though.

For the `'s'` format character, the count is interpreted as the length of the bytes, not a repeat count like for the other format characters; for example, `'10s'` means a single 10-byte string, while `'10c'` means 10 characters. If a count is not given, it defaults to 1. For packing, the string is truncated or padded with null bytes as appropriate to make it fit. For unpacking, the resulting bytes object always has exactly the specified number of bytes. As a special case, `'0s'` means a single, empty string (while `'0c'` means 0 characters).

When packing a value `x` using one of the integer formats (`'b'`, `'B'`, `'h'`, `'H'`, `'i'`, `'I'`, `'l'`, `'L'`, `'q'`, `'Q'`), if `x` is outside the valid range for that format then *struct.error* is raised.

Changed in version 3.1: In 3.0, some of the integer formats wrapped out-of-range values and raised *DeprecationWarning* instead of *struct.error*.

The `'p'` format character encodes a "Pascal string", meaning a short variable-length string stored in a *fixed number of bytes*, given by the count. The first byte stored is the length of the string, or 255, whichever is smaller. The bytes of the string follow. If the string passed in to *pack()* is too long (longer than the count minus 1), only the leading `count-1` bytes of the string are stored. If the string is shorter than `count-1`, it is padded with null bytes so that exactly count bytes in all are used. Note that for *unpack()*, the `'p'` format character consumes `count` bytes, but that the string returned can never contain more than 255 bytes.

For the `'?'` format character, the return value is either *True* or *False*. When packing, the truth value of the argument object is used. Either 0 or 1 in the native or standard bool representation will be packed, and any non-zero value will be `True` when unpacking.

Examples

Note: All examples assume a native byte order, size, and alignment with a big-endian machine.

A basic example of packing/unpacking three integers:

```
>>> from struct import *
>>> pack('hhl', 1, 2, 3)
b'\x00\x01\x00\x02\x00\x00\x00\x03'
>>> unpack('hhl', b'\x00\x01\x00\x02\x00\x00\x00\x03')
(1, 2, 3)
>>> calcsize('hhl')
8
```

Unpacked fields can be named by assigning them to variables or by wrapping the result in a named tuple:

```
>>> record = b'raymond   \x32\x12\x08\x01\x08'
>>> name, serialnum, school, gradelevel = unpack('<10sHHb', record)

>>> from collections import namedtuple
>>> Student = namedtuple('Student', 'name serialnum school gradelevel')
>>> Student._make(unpack('<10sHHb', record))
Student(name=b'raymond   ', serialnum=4658, school=264, gradelevel=8)
```

The ordering of format characters may have an impact on size since the padding needed to satisfy alignment requirements is different:

```
>>> pack('ci', b'*', 0x12131415)
b'*\x00\x00\x00\x12\x13\x14\x15'
>>> pack('ic', 0x12131415, b'*')
b'\x12\x13\x14\x15*'
>>> calcsize('ci')
8
>>> calcsize('ic')
5
```

The following format `'llh0l'` specifies two pad bytes at the end, assuming longs are aligned on 4-byte boundaries:

```
>>> pack('llh0l', 1, 2, 3)
b'\x00\x00\x00\x01\x00\x00\x00\x02\x00\x03\x00\x00'
```

This only works when native size and alignment are in effect; standard size and alignment does not enforce any alignment.

See also:

Module *array* Packed binary storage of homogeneous data.

Module *xdrlib* Packing and unpacking of XDR data.

7.1.3 Classes

The *struct* module also defines the following type:

`class struct.Struct(format)`

Return a new Struct object which writes and reads binary data according to the format string *format*.

Creating a Struct object once and calling its methods is more efficient than calling the `struct` functions with the same format since the format string only needs to be compiled once.

Compiled Struct objects support the following methods and attributes:

pack(*v1, v2, ...*)
Identical to the `pack()` function, using the compiled format. (`len(result)` will equal `size`.)

pack_into(*buffer, offset, v1, v2, ...*)
Identical to the `pack_into()` function, using the compiled format.

unpack(*buffer*)
Identical to the `unpack()` function, using the compiled format. The buffer's size in bytes must equal `size`.

unpack_from(*buffer, offset=0*)
Identical to the `unpack_from()` function, using the compiled format. The buffer's size in bytes, minus *offset*, must be at least `size`.

iter_unpack(*buffer*)
Identical to the `iter_unpack()` function, using the compiled format. The buffer's size in bytes must be a multiple of `size`.

New in version 3.4.

format
The format string used to construct this Struct object.

size
The calculated size of the struct (and hence of the bytes object produced by the `pack()` method) corresponding to `format`.

7.2 codecs — Codec registry and base classes

Source code: Lib/codecs.py

This module defines base classes for standard Python codecs (encoders and decoders) and provides access to the internal Python codec registry, which manages the codec and error handling lookup process. Most standard codecs are *text encodings*, which encode text to bytes, but there are also codecs provided that encode text to text, and bytes to bytes. Custom codecs may encode and decode between arbitrary types, but some module features are restricted to use specifically with *text encodings*, or with codecs that encode to `bytes`.

The module defines the following functions for encoding and decoding with any codec:

codecs.**encode**(*obj, encoding='utf-8', errors='strict'*)
Encodes *obj* using the codec registered for *encoding*.

Errors may be given to set the desired error handling scheme. The default error handler is `'strict'` meaning that encoding errors raise `ValueError` (or a more codec specific subclass, such as `UnicodeEncodeError`). Refer to *Codec Base Classes* for more information on codec error handling.

codecs.**decode**(*obj, encoding='utf-8', errors='strict'*)
Decodes *obj* using the codec registered for *encoding*.

Errors may be given to set the desired error handling scheme. The default error handler is `'strict'` meaning that decoding errors raise `ValueError` (or a more codec specific subclass, such as `UnicodeDecodeError`). Refer to *Codec Base Classes* for more information on codec error handling.

The full details for each codec can also be looked up directly:

`codecs.lookup(encoding)`
Looks up the codec info in the Python codec registry and returns a *CodecInfo* object as defined below.

Encodings are first looked up in the registry's cache. If not found, the list of registered search functions is scanned. If no *CodecInfo* object is found, a *LookupError* is raised. Otherwise, the *CodecInfo* object is stored in the cache and returned to the caller.

`class codecs.CodecInfo(encode, decode, streamreader=None, streamwriter=None, incrementalencoder=None, incrementaldecoder=None, name=None)`
Codec details when looking up the codec registry. The constructor arguments are stored in attributes of the same name:

name
The name of the encoding.

encode
decode
The stateless encoding and decoding functions. These must be functions or methods which have the same interface as the *encode()* and *decode()* methods of Codec instances (see *Codec Interface*). The functions or methods are expected to work in a stateless mode.

incrementalencoder
incrementaldecoder
Incremental encoder and decoder classes or factory functions. These have to provide the interface defined by the base classes *IncrementalEncoder* and *IncrementalDecoder*, respectively. Incremental codecs can maintain state.

streamwriter
streamreader
Stream writer and reader classes or factory functions. These have to provide the interface defined by the base classes *StreamWriter* and *StreamReader*, respectively. Stream codecs can maintain state.

To simplify access to the various codec components, the module provides these additional functions which use *lookup()* for the codec lookup:

`codecs.getencoder(encoding)`
Look up the codec for the given encoding and return its encoder function.

Raises a *LookupError* in case the encoding cannot be found.

`codecs.getdecoder(encoding)`
Look up the codec for the given encoding and return its decoder function.

Raises a *LookupError* in case the encoding cannot be found.

`codecs.getincrementalencoder(encoding)`
Look up the codec for the given encoding and return its incremental encoder class or factory function.

Raises a *LookupError* in case the encoding cannot be found or the codec doesn't support an incremental encoder.

`codecs.getincrementaldecoder(encoding)`
Look up the codec for the given encoding and return its incremental decoder class or factory function.

Raises a *LookupError* in case the encoding cannot be found or the codec doesn't support an incremental decoder.

`codecs.getreader(encoding)`
Look up the codec for the given encoding and return its *StreamReader* class or factory function.

Raises a *LookupError* in case the encoding cannot be found.

`codecs.getwriter(encoding)`
Look up the codec for the given encoding and return its *StreamWriter* class or factory function.

Raises a *LookupError* in case the encoding cannot be found.

Custom codecs are made available by registering a suitable codec search function:

`codecs.`**`register`**`(`*search_function*`)`

Register a codec search function. Search functions are expected to take one argument, being the encoding name in all lower case letters, and return a *CodecInfo* object. In case a search function cannot find a given encoding, it should return `None`.

Note: Search function registration is not currently reversible, which may cause problems in some cases, such as unit testing or module reloading.

While the builtin *open()* and the associated *io* module are the recommended approach for working with encoded text files, this module provides additional utility functions and classes that allow the use of a wider range of codecs when working with binary files:

`codecs.`**`open`**`(`*filename, mode='r', encoding=None, errors='strict', buffering=1*`)`

Open an encoded file using the given *mode* and return an instance of *StreamReaderWriter*, providing transparent encoding/decoding. The default file mode is `'r'`, meaning to open the file in read mode.

Note: Underlying encoded files are always opened in binary mode. No automatic conversion of `'\n'` is done on reading and writing. The *mode* argument may be any binary mode acceptable to the built-in *open()* function; the `'b'` is automatically added.

encoding specifies the encoding which is to be used for the file. Any encoding that encodes to and decodes from bytes is allowed, and the data types supported by the file methods depend on the codec used.

errors may be given to define the error handling. It defaults to `'strict'` which causes a *ValueError* to be raised in case an encoding error occurs.

buffering has the same meaning as for the built-in *open()* function. It defaults to line buffered.

`codecs.`**`EncodedFile`**`(`*file, data_encoding, file_encoding=None, errors='strict'*`)`

Return a *StreamRecoder* instance, a wrapped version of *file* which provides transparent transcoding. The original file is closed when the wrapped version is closed.

Data written to the wrapped file is decoded according to the given *data_encoding* and then written to the original file as bytes using *file_encoding*. Bytes read from the original file are decoded according to *file_encoding*, and the result is encoded using *data_encoding*.

If *file_encoding* is not given, it defaults to *data_encoding*.

errors may be given to define the error handling. It defaults to `'strict'`, which causes *ValueError* to be raised in case an encoding error occurs.

`codecs.`**`iterencode`**`(`*iterator, encoding, errors='strict', **kwargs*`)`

Uses an incremental encoder to iteratively encode the input provided by *iterator*. This function is a *generator*. The *errors* argument (as well as any other keyword argument) is passed through to the incremental encoder.

This function requires that the codec accept text *str* objects to encode. Therefore it does not support bytes-to-bytes encoders such as `base64_codec`.

`codecs.`**`iterdecode`**`(`*iterator, encoding, errors='strict', **kwargs*`)`

Uses an incremental decoder to iteratively decode the input provided by *iterator*. This function is a *generator*. The *errors* argument (as well as any other keyword argument) is passed through to the incremental decoder.

This function requires that the codec accept *bytes* objects to decode. Therefore it does not support text-to-text encoders such as `rot_13`, although `rot_13` may be used equivalently with *iterencode()*.

The module also provides the following constants which are useful for reading and writing to platform dependent files:

codecs.**BOM**
codecs.**BOM_BE**
codecs.**BOM_LE**
codecs.**BOM_UTF8**
codecs.**BOM_UTF16**
codecs.**BOM_UTF16_BE**
codecs.**BOM_UTF16_LE**
codecs.**BOM_UTF32**
codecs.**BOM_UTF32_BE**
codecs.**BOM_UTF32_LE**

These constants define various byte sequences, being Unicode byte order marks (BOMs) for several encodings. They are used in UTF-16 and UTF-32 data streams to indicate the byte order used, and in UTF-8 as a Unicode signature. *BOM_UTF16* is either *BOM_UTF16_BE* or *BOM_UTF16_LE* depending on the platform's native byte order, *BOM* is an alias for *BOM_UTF16*, *BOM_LE* for *BOM_UTF16_LE* and *BOM_BE* for *BOM_UTF16_BE*. The others represent the BOM in UTF-8 and UTF-32 encodings.

7.2.1 Codec Base Classes

The *codecs* module defines a set of base classes which define the interfaces for working with codec objects, and can also be used as the basis for custom codec implementations.

Each codec has to define four interfaces to make it usable as codec in Python: stateless encoder, stateless decoder, stream reader and stream writer. The stream reader and writers typically reuse the stateless encoder/decoder to implement the file protocols. Codec authors also need to define how the codec will handle encoding and decoding errors.

Error Handlers

To simplify and standardize error handling, codecs may implement different error handling schemes by accepting the *errors* string argument. The following string values are defined and implemented by all standard Python codecs:

Value	Meaning
`'strict'`	Raise *UnicodeError* (or a subclass); this is the default. Implemented in *strict_errors()*.
`'ignore'`	Ignore the malformed data and continue without further notice. Implemented in *ignore_errors()*.

The following error handlers are only applicable to *text encodings*:

Value	Meaning
'replace'	Replace with a suitable replacement marker; Python will use the official U+FFFD REPLACEMENT CHARACTER for the built-in codecs on decoding, and '?' on encoding. Implemented in *replace_errors()*.
'xmlcharrefreplace'	Replace with the appropriate XML character reference (only for encoding). Implemented in *xmlcharrefreplace_errors()*.
'backslashreplace'	Replace with backslashed escape sequences. Implemented in *backslashreplace_errors()*.
'namereplace'	Replace with \N{...} escape sequences (only for encoding). Implemented in *namereplace_errors()*.
'surrogateescape'	On decoding, replace byte with individual surrogate code ranging from U+DC80 to U+DCFF. This code will then be turned back into the same byte when the 'surrogateescape' error handler is used when encoding the data. (See PEP 383 for more.)

In addition, the following error handler is specific to the given codecs:

Value	Codecs	Meaning
'surrogatepass'	utf-8, utf-16, utf-32, utf-16-be, utf-16-le, utf-32-be, utf-32-le	Allow encoding and decoding of surrogate codes. These codecs normally treat the presence of surrogates as an error.

New in version 3.1: The 'surrogateescape' and 'surrogatepass' error handlers.

Changed in version 3.4: The 'surrogatepass' error handlers now works with utf-16* and utf-32* codecs.

New in version 3.5: The 'namereplace' error handler.

Changed in version 3.5: The 'backslashreplace' error handlers now works with decoding and translating.

The set of allowed values can be extended by registering a new named error handler:

codecs.**register_error**(*name*, *error_handler*)

Register the error handling function *error_handler* under the name *name*. The *error_handler* argument will be called during encoding and decoding in case of an error, when *name* is specified as the errors parameter.

For encoding, *error_handler* will be called with a *UnicodeEncodeError* instance, which contains information about the location of the error. The error handler must either raise this or a different exception, or return a tuple with a replacement for the unencodable part of the input and a position where encoding should continue. The replacement may be either *str* or *bytes*. If the replacement is bytes, the encoder will simply copy them into the output buffer. If the replacement is a string, the encoder will encode the replacement. Encoding continues on original input at the specified position. Negative position values will be treated as being relative to the end of the input string. If the resulting position is out of bound an *IndexError* will be raised.

Decoding and translating works similarly, except *UnicodeDecodeError* or *UnicodeTranslateError* will be passed to the handler and that the replacement from the error handler will be put into the output directly.

Previously registered error handlers (including the standard error handlers) can be looked up by name:

codecs.**lookup_error**(*name*)

Return the error handler previously registered under the name *name*.

Raises a *LookupError* in case the handler cannot be found.

The following standard error handlers are also made available as module level functions:

codecs.**strict_errors**(*exception*)

Implements the 'strict' error handling: each encoding or decoding error raises a *UnicodeError*.

codecs.**replace_errors**(*exception*)
Implements the 'replace' error handling (for *text encodings* only): substitutes '?' for encoding errors (to be encoded by the codec), and '\ufffd' (the Unicode replacement character) for decoding errors.

codecs.**ignore_errors**(*exception*)
Implements the 'ignore' error handling: malformed data is ignored and encoding or decoding is continued without further notice.

codecs.**xmlcharrefreplace_errors**(*exception*)
Implements the 'xmlcharrefreplace' error handling (for encoding with *text encodings* only): the unencodable character is replaced by an appropriate XML character reference.

codecs.**backslashreplace_errors**(*exception*)
Implements the 'backslashreplace' error handling (for *text encodings* only): malformed data is replaced by a backslashed escape sequence.

codecs.**namereplace_errors**(*exception*)
Implements the 'namereplace' error handling (for encoding with *text encodings* only): the unencodable character is replaced by a \N{...} escape sequence.

New in version 3.5.

Stateless Encoding and Decoding

The base Codec class defines these methods which also define the function interfaces of the stateless encoder and decoder:

Codec.**encode**(*input*[, *errors*])
Encodes the object *input* and returns a tuple (output object, length consumed). For instance, *text encoding* converts a string object to a bytes object using a particular character set encoding (e.g., cp1252 or iso-8859-1).

The *errors* argument defines the error handling to apply. It defaults to 'strict' handling.

The method may not store state in the Codec instance. Use *StreamWriter* for codecs which have to keep state in order to make encoding efficient.

The encoder must be able to handle zero length input and return an empty object of the output object type in this situation.

Codec.**decode**(*input*[, *errors*])
Decodes the object *input* and returns a tuple (output object, length consumed). For instance, for a *text encoding*, decoding converts a bytes object encoded using a particular character set encoding to a string object.

For text encodings and bytes-to-bytes codecs, *input* must be a bytes object or one which provides the read-only buffer interface – for example, buffer objects and memory mapped files.

The *errors* argument defines the error handling to apply. It defaults to 'strict' handling.

The method may not store state in the Codec instance. Use *StreamReader* for codecs which have to keep state in order to make decoding efficient.

The decoder must be able to handle zero length input and return an empty object of the output object type in this situation.

Incremental Encoding and Decoding

The *IncrementalEncoder* and *IncrementalDecoder* classes provide the basic interface for incremental encoding and decoding. Encoding/decoding the input isn't done with one call to the stateless encoder/decoder function, but with multiple calls to the *encode()/decode()* method of the incremental encoder/decoder. The incremental encoder/decoder keeps track of the encoding/decoding process during method calls.

The joined output of calls to the *encode()/decode()* method is the same as if all the single inputs were joined into one, and this input was encoded/decoded with the stateless encoder/decoder.

IncrementalEncoder Objects

The *IncrementalEncoder* class is used for encoding an input in multiple steps. It defines the following methods which every incremental encoder must define in order to be compatible with the Python codec registry.

class codecs.IncrementalEncoder(*errors='strict'*)

Constructor for an *IncrementalEncoder* instance.

All incremental encoders must provide this constructor interface. They are free to add additional keyword arguments, but only the ones defined here are used by the Python codec registry.

The *IncrementalEncoder* may implement different error handling schemes by providing the *errors* keyword argument. See *Error Handlers* for possible values.

The *errors* argument will be assigned to an attribute of the same name. Assigning to this attribute makes it possible to switch between different error handling strategies during the lifetime of the *IncrementalEncoder* object.

encode(*object*[, *final*])

Encodes *object* (taking the current state of the encoder into account) and returns the resulting encoded object. If this is the last call to *encode()* *final* must be true (the default is false).

reset()

Reset the encoder to the initial state. The output is discarded: call `.encode(object, final=True)`, passing an empty byte or text string if necessary, to reset the encoder and to get the output.

getstate()

Return the current state of the encoder which must be an integer. The implementation should make sure that `0` is the most common state. (States that are more complicated than integers can be converted into an integer by marshaling/pickling the state and encoding the bytes of the resulting string into an integer).

setstate(*state*)

Set the state of the encoder to *state*. *state* must be an encoder state returned by *getstate()*.

IncrementalDecoder Objects

The *IncrementalDecoder* class is used for decoding an input in multiple steps. It defines the following methods which every incremental decoder must define in order to be compatible with the Python codec registry.

class codecs.IncrementalDecoder(*errors='strict'*)

Constructor for an *IncrementalDecoder* instance.

All incremental decoders must provide this constructor interface. They are free to add additional keyword arguments, but only the ones defined here are used by the Python codec registry.

The *IncrementalDecoder* may implement different error handling schemes by providing the *errors* keyword argument. See *Error Handlers* for possible values.

The *errors* argument will be assigned to an attribute of the same name. Assigning to this attribute makes it possible to switch between different error handling strategies during the lifetime of the `IncrementalDecoder` object.

decode(*object*[, *final*])
Decodes *object* (taking the current state of the decoder into account) and returns the resulting decoded object. If this is the last call to `decode()` *final* must be true (the default is false). If *final* is true the decoder must decode the input completely and must flush all buffers. If this isn't possible (e.g. because of incomplete byte sequences at the end of the input) it must initiate error handling just like in the stateless case (which might raise an exception).

reset()
Reset the decoder to the initial state.

getstate()
Return the current state of the decoder. This must be a tuple with two items, the first must be the buffer containing the still undecoded input. The second must be an integer and can be additional state info. (The implementation should make sure that `0` is the most common additional state info.) If this additional state info is `0` it must be possible to set the decoder to the state which has no input buffered and `0` as the additional state info, so that feeding the previously buffered input to the decoder returns it to the previous state without producing any output. (Additional state info that is more complicated than integers can be converted into an integer by marshaling/pickling the info and encoding the bytes of the resulting string into an integer.)

setstate(*state*)
Set the state of the encoder to *state*. *state* must be a decoder state returned by `getstate()`.

Stream Encoding and Decoding

The `StreamWriter` and `StreamReader` classes provide generic working interfaces which can be used to implement new encoding submodules very easily. See `encodings.utf_8` for an example of how this is done.

StreamWriter Objects

The `StreamWriter` class is a subclass of `Codec` and defines the following methods which every stream writer must define in order to be compatible with the Python codec registry.

class codecs.StreamWriter(*stream*, *errors='strict'*)
Constructor for a `StreamWriter` instance.

All stream writers must provide this constructor interface. They are free to add additional keyword arguments, but only the ones defined here are used by the Python codec registry.

The *stream* argument must be a file-like object open for writing text or binary data, as appropriate for the specific codec.

The `StreamWriter` may implement different error handling schemes by providing the *errors* keyword argument. See *Error Handlers* for the standard error handlers the underlying stream codec may support.

The *errors* argument will be assigned to an attribute of the same name. Assigning to this attribute makes it possible to switch between different error handling strategies during the lifetime of the `StreamWriter` object.

write(*object*)
Writes the object's contents encoded to the stream.

writelines(*list*)
Writes the concatenated list of strings to the stream (possibly by reusing the `write()` method). The standard bytes-to-bytes codecs do not support this method.

reset()
Flushes and resets the codec buffers used for keeping state.

Calling this method should ensure that the data on the output is put into a clean state that allows appending of new fresh data without having to rescan the whole stream to recover state.

In addition to the above methods, the `StreamWriter` must also inherit all other methods and attributes from the underlying stream.

StreamReader Objects

The `StreamReader` class is a subclass of `Codec` and defines the following methods which every stream reader must define in order to be compatible with the Python codec registry.

class codecs.StreamReader(*stream*, *errors='strict'*)
Constructor for a `StreamReader` instance.

All stream readers must provide this constructor interface. They are free to add additional keyword arguments, but only the ones defined here are used by the Python codec registry.

The *stream* argument must be a file-like object open for reading text or binary data, as appropriate for the specific codec.

The `StreamReader` may implement different error handling schemes by providing the *errors* keyword argument. See *Error Handlers* for the standard error handlers the underlying stream codec may support.

The *errors* argument will be assigned to an attribute of the same name. Assigning to this attribute makes it possible to switch between different error handling strategies during the lifetime of the `StreamReader` object.

The set of allowed values for the *errors* argument can be extended with `register_error()`.

read([*size*[, *chars*[, *firstline*]]])
Decodes data from the stream and returns the resulting object.

The *chars* argument indicates the number of decoded code points or bytes to return. The `read()` method will never return more data than requested, but it might return less, if there is not enough available.

The *size* argument indicates the approximate maximum number of encoded bytes or code points to read for decoding. The decoder can modify this setting as appropriate. The default value -1 indicates to read and decode as much as possible. This parameter is intended to prevent having to decode huge files in one step.

The *firstline* flag indicates that it would be sufficient to only return the first line, if there are decoding errors on later lines.

The method should use a greedy read strategy meaning that it should read as much data as is allowed within the definition of the encoding and the given size, e.g. if optional encoding endings or state markers are available on the stream, these should be read too.

readline([*size*[, *keepends*]])
Read one line from the input stream and return the decoded data.

size, if given, is passed as size argument to the stream's `read()` method.

If *keepends* is false line-endings will be stripped from the lines returned.

readlines([*sizehint*[, *keepends*]])

Read all lines available on the input stream and return them as a list of lines.

Line-endings are implemented using the codec's decoder method and are included in the list entries if *keepends* is true.

sizehint, if given, is passed as the *size* argument to the stream's `read()` method.

reset()

Resets the codec buffers used for keeping state.

Note that no stream repositioning should take place. This method is primarily intended to be able to recover from decoding errors.

In addition to the above methods, the `StreamReader` must also inherit all other methods and attributes from the underlying stream.

StreamReaderWriter Objects

The `StreamReaderWriter` is a convenience class that allows wrapping streams which work in both read and write modes.

The design is such that one can use the factory functions returned by the `lookup()` function to construct the instance.

class codecs.**StreamReaderWriter**(*stream*, *Reader*, *Writer*, *errors='strict'*)

Creates a `StreamReaderWriter` instance. *stream* must be a file-like object. *Reader* and *Writer* must be factory functions or classes providing the `StreamReader` and `StreamWriter` interface resp. Error handling is done in the same way as defined for the stream readers and writers.

`StreamReaderWriter` instances define the combined interfaces of `StreamReader` and `StreamWriter` classes. They inherit all other methods and attributes from the underlying stream.

StreamRecoder Objects

The `StreamRecoder` translates data from one encoding to another, which is sometimes useful when dealing with different encoding environments.

The design is such that one can use the factory functions returned by the `lookup()` function to construct the instance.

class codecs.**StreamRecoder**(*stream*, *encode*, *decode*, *Reader*, *Writer*, *errors='strict'*)

Creates a `StreamRecoder` instance which implements a two-way conversion: *encode* and *decode* work on the frontend — the data visible to code calling `read()` and `write()`, while *Reader* and *Writer* work on the backend — the data in *stream*.

You can use these objects to do transparent transcodings from e.g. Latin-1 to UTF-8 and back.

The *stream* argument must be a file-like object.

The *encode* and *decode* arguments must adhere to the `Codec` interface. *Reader* and *Writer* must be factory functions or classes providing objects of the `StreamReader` and `StreamWriter` interface respectively.

Error handling is done in the same way as defined for the stream readers and writers.

`StreamRecoder` instances define the combined interfaces of `StreamReader` and `StreamWriter` classes. They inherit all other methods and attributes from the underlying stream.

7.2.2 Encodings and Unicode

Strings are stored internally as sequences of code points in range `0x0–0x10FFFF`. (See PEP 393 for more details about the implementation.) Once a string object is used outside of CPU and memory, endianness and how these arrays are stored as bytes become an issue. As with other codecs, serialising a string into a sequence of bytes is known as *encoding*, and recreating the string from the sequence of bytes is known as *decoding*. There are a variety of different text serialisation codecs, which are collectivity referred to as *text encodings*.

The simplest text encoding (called `'latin-1'` or `'iso-8859-1'`) maps the code points 0–255 to the bytes `0x0–0xff`, which means that a string object that contains code points above `U+00FF` can't be encoded with this codec. Doing so will raise a *UnicodeEncodeError* that looks like the following (although the details of the error message may differ): `UnicodeEncodeError: 'latin-1' codec can't encode character '\u1234' in position 3: ordinal not in range(256)`.

There's another group of encodings (the so called charmap encodings) that choose a different subset of all Unicode code points and how these code points are mapped to the bytes `0x0–0xff`. To see how this is done simply open e.g. `encodings/cp1252.py` (which is an encoding that is used primarily on Windows). There's a string constant with 256 characters that shows you which character is mapped to which byte value.

All of these encodings can only encode 256 of the 1114112 code points defined in Unicode. A simple and straightforward way that can store each Unicode code point, is to store each code point as four consecutive bytes. There are two possibilities: store the bytes in big endian or in little endian order. These two encodings are called `UTF-32-BE` and `UTF-32-LE` respectively. Their disadvantage is that if e.g. you use `UTF-32-BE` on a little endian machine you will always have to swap bytes on encoding and decoding. `UTF-32` avoids this problem: bytes will always be in natural endianness. When these bytes are read by a CPU with a different endianness, then bytes have to be swapped though. To be able to detect the endianness of a `UTF-16` or `UTF-32` byte sequence, there's the so called BOM ("Byte Order Mark"). This is the Unicode character `U+FEFF`. This character can be prepended to every `UTF-16` or `UTF-32` byte sequence. The byte swapped version of this character (`0xFFFE`) is an illegal character that may not appear in a Unicode text. So when the first character in an `UTF-16` or `UTF-32` byte sequence appears to be a `U+FFFE` the bytes have to be swapped on decoding. Unfortunately the character `U+FEFF` had a second purpose as a `ZERO WIDTH NO-BREAK SPACE`: a character that has no width and doesn't allow a word to be split. It can e.g. be used to give hints to a ligature algorithm. With Unicode 4.0 using `U+FEFF` as a `ZERO WIDTH NO-BREAK SPACE` has been deprecated (with `U+2060` (`WORD JOINER`) assuming this role). Nevertheless Unicode software still must be able to handle `U+FEFF` in both roles: as a BOM it's a device to determine the storage layout of the encoded bytes, and vanishes once the byte sequence has been decoded into a string; as a `ZERO WIDTH NO-BREAK SPACE` it's a normal character that will be decoded like any other.

There's another encoding that is able to encoding the full range of Unicode characters: UTF-8. UTF-8 is an 8-bit encoding, which means there are no issues with byte order in UTF-8. Each byte in a UTF-8 byte sequence consists of two parts: marker bits (the most significant bits) and payload bits. The marker bits are a sequence of zero to four `1` bits followed by a `0` bit. Unicode characters are encoded like this (with x being payload bits, which when concatenated give the Unicode character):

Range	Encoding
`U-00000000 ... U-0000007F`	0xxxxxxx
`U-00000080 ... U-000007FF`	110xxxxx 10xxxxxx
`U-00000800 ... U-0000FFFF`	1110xxxx 10xxxxxx 10xxxxxx
`U-00010000 ... U-0010FFFF`	11110xxx 10xxxxxx 10xxxxxx 10xxxxxx

The least significant bit of the Unicode character is the rightmost x bit.

As UTF-8 is an 8-bit encoding no BOM is required and any `U+FEFF` character in the decoded string (even if it's the first character) is treated as a `ZERO WIDTH NO-BREAK SPACE`.

Without external information it's impossible to reliably determine which encoding was used for encoding a string. Each charmap encoding can decode any random byte sequence. However that's not possible with UTF-8, as UTF-8 byte sequences have a structure that doesn't allow arbitrary byte sequences. To increase the reliability with which a UTF-8 encoding can be detected, Microsoft invented a variant of UTF-8 (that Python 2.5 calls `"utf-8-sig"`) for its Notepad program: Before any of the Unicode characters is written to the file, a UTF-8 encoded BOM (which looks like this as a byte sequence: `0xef`, `0xbb`, `0xbf`) is written. As it's rather improbable that any charmap encoded file starts with these byte values (which would e.g. map to

LATIN SMALL LETTER I WITH DIAERESIS
RIGHT-POINTING DOUBLE ANGLE QUOTATION MARK
INVERTED QUESTION MARK

in iso-8859-1), this increases the probability that a `utf-8-sig` encoding can be correctly guessed from the byte sequence. So here the BOM is not used to be able to determine the byte order used for generating the byte sequence, but as a signature that helps in guessing the encoding. On encoding the utf-8-sig codec will write `0xef`, `0xbb`, `0xbf` as the first three bytes to the file. On decoding `utf-8-sig` will skip those three bytes if they appear as the first three bytes in the file. In UTF-8, the use of the BOM is discouraged and should generally be avoided.

7.2.3 Standard Encodings

Python comes with a number of codecs built-in, either implemented as C functions or with dictionaries as mapping tables. The following table lists the codecs by name, together with a few common aliases, and the languages for which the encoding is likely used. Neither the list of aliases nor the list of languages is meant to be exhaustive. Notice that spelling alternatives that only differ in case or use a hyphen instead of an underscore are also valid aliases; therefore, e.g. `'utf-8'` is a valid alias for the `'utf_8'` codec.

CPython implementation detail: Some common encodings can bypass the codecs lookup machinery to improve performance. These optimization opportunities are only recognized by CPython for a limited set of (case insensitive) aliases: utf-8, utf8, latin-1, latin1, iso-8859-1, iso8859-1, mbcs (Windows only), ascii, us-ascii, utf-16, utf16, utf-32, utf32, and the same using underscores instead of dashes. Using alternative aliases for these encodings may result in slower execution.

Changed in version 3.6: Optimization opportunity recognized for us-ascii.

Many of the character sets support the same languages. They vary in individual characters (e.g. whether the EURO SIGN is supported or not), and in the assignment of characters to code positions. For the European languages in particular, the following variants typically exist:

- an ISO 8859 codeset
- a Microsoft Windows code page, which is typically derived from an 8859 codeset, but replaces control characters with additional graphic characters
- an IBM EBCDIC code page
- an IBM PC code page, which is ASCII compatible

Codec	Aliases	Languages
ascii	646, us-ascii	English
big5	big5-tw, csbig5	Traditional Chinese
big5hkscs	big5-hkscs, hkscs	Traditional Chinese
cp037	IBM037, IBM039	English
cp273	273, IBM273, csIBM273	German New in version 3.4.
cp424	EBCDIC-CP-HE, IBM424	Hebrew
cp437	437, IBM437	English

Continued on next page

Table 7.1 – continued from previous page

Codec	Aliases	Languages
cp500	EBCDIC-CP-BE, EBCDIC-CP-CH, IBM500	Western Europe
cp720		Arabic
cp737		Greek
cp775	IBM775	Baltic languages
cp850	850, IBM850	Western Europe
cp852	852, IBM852	Central and Eastern Europe
cp855	855, IBM855	Bulgarian, Byelorussian, Macedonian, Russian, Serbian
cp856		Hebrew
cp857	857, IBM857	Turkish
cp858	858, IBM858	Western Europe
cp860	860, IBM860	Portuguese
cp861	861, CP-IS, IBM861	Icelandic
cp862	862, IBM862	Hebrew
cp863	863, IBM863	Canadian
cp864	IBM864	Arabic
cp865	865, IBM865	Danish, Norwegian
cp866	866, IBM866	Russian
cp869	869, CP-GR, IBM869	Greek
cp874		Thai
cp875		Greek
cp932	932, ms932, mskanji, ms-kanji	Japanese
cp949	949, ms949, uhc	Korean
cp950	950, ms950	Traditional Chinese
cp1006		Urdu
cp1026	ibm1026	Turkish
cp1125	1125, ibm1125, cp866u, ruscii	Ukrainian New in version 3.4.
cp1140	ibm1140	Western Europe
cp1250	windows-1250	Central and Eastern Europe
cp1251	windows-1251	Bulgarian, Byelorussian, Macedonian, Russian, Serbian
cp1252	windows-1252	Western Europe
cp1253	windows-1253	Greek
cp1254	windows-1254	Turkish
cp1255	windows-1255	Hebrew
cp1256	windows-1256	Arabic
cp1257	windows-1257	Baltic languages
cp1258	windows-1258	Vietnamese
cp65001		Windows only: Windows UTF-8 (`CP_UTF8`) New in version 3.3.
euc_jp	eucjp, ujis, u-jis	Japanese
euc_jis_2004	jisx0213, eucjis2004	Japanese
euc_jisx0213	eucjisx0213	Japanese
euc_kr	euckr, korean, ksc5601, ks_c-5601, ks_c-5601-1987, ksx1001, ks_x-1001	Korean

Continued on next page

Table 7.1 – continued from previous page

Codec	Aliases	Languages
gb2312	chinese, csiso58gb231280, euc- cn, euccn, eucgb2312-cn, gb2312-1980, gb2312-80, iso-ir-58	Simplified Chinese
gbk	936, cp936, ms936	Unified Chinese
gb18030	gb18030-2000	Unified Chinese
hz	hzgb, hz-gb, hz-gb-2312	Simplified Chinese
iso2022_jp	csiso2022jp, iso2022jp, iso-2022-jp	Japanese
iso2022_jp_1	iso2022jp-1, iso-2022-jp-1	Japanese
iso2022_jp_2	iso2022jp-2, iso-2022-jp-2	Japanese, Korean, Simplified Chinese, Western Europe, Greek
iso2022_jp_2004	iso2022jp-2004, iso-2022-jp-2004	Japanese
iso2022_jp_3	iso2022jp-3, iso-2022-jp-3	Japanese
iso2022_jp_ext	iso2022jp-ext, iso-2022-jp-ext	Japanese
iso2022_kr	csiso2022kr, iso2022kr, iso-2022-kr	Korean
latin_1	iso-8859-1, iso8859-1, 8859, cp819, latin, latin1, L1	West Europe
iso8859_2	iso-8859-2, latin2, L2	Central and Eastern Europe
iso8859_3	iso-8859-3, latin3, L3	Esperanto, Maltese
iso8859_4	iso-8859-4, latin4, L4	Baltic languages
iso8859_5	iso-8859-5, cyrillic	Bulgarian, Byelorussian, Macedonian, Russian, Serbian
iso8859_6	iso-8859-6, arabic	Arabic
iso8859_7	iso-8859-7, greek, greek8	Greek
iso8859_8	iso-8859-8, hebrew	Hebrew
iso8859_9	iso-8859-9, latin5, L5	Turkish
iso8859_10	iso-8859-10, latin6, L6	Nordic languages
iso8859_11	iso-8859-11, thai	Thai languages
iso8859_13	iso-8859-13, latin7, L7	Baltic languages
iso8859_14	iso-8859-14, latin8, L8	Celtic languages
iso8859_15	iso-8859-15, latin9, L9	Western Europe
iso8859_16	iso-8859-16, latin10, L10	South-Eastern Europe
johab	cp1361, ms1361	Korean
koi8_r		Russian
koi8_t		Tajik New in version 3.5.
koi8_u		Ukrainian
kz1048	kz_1048, strk1048_2002, rk1048	Kazakh New in version 3.5.
mac_cyrillic	maccyrillic	Bulgarian, Byelorussian, Macedonian, Russian, Serbian
mac_greek	macgreek	Greek
mac_iceland	maciceland	Icelandic
mac_latin2	maclatin2, maccentraleurope	Central and Eastern Europe
mac_roman	macroman, macintosh	Western Europe
mac_turkish	macturkish	Turkish
ptcp154	csptcp154, pt154, cp154, cyrillic-asian	Kazakh

Continued on next page

Table 7.1 – continued from previous page

Codec	Aliases	Languages
shift_jis	csshiftjis, shiftjis, sjis, s_jis	Japanese
shift_jis_2004	shiftjis2004, sjis_2004, sjis2004	Japanese
shift_jisx0213	shiftjisx0213, sjisx0213, s_jisx0213	Japanese
utf_32	U32, utf32	all languages
utf_32_be	UTF-32BE	all languages
utf_32_le	UTF-32LE	all languages
utf_16	U16, utf16	all languages
utf_16_be	UTF-16BE	all languages
utf_16_le	UTF-16LE	all languages
utf_7	U7, unicode-1-1-utf-7	all languages
utf_8	U8, UTF, utf8	all languages
utf_8_sig		all languages

Changed in version 3.4: The utf-16* and utf-32* encoders no longer allow surrogate code points (`U+D800`–`U+DFFF`) to be encoded. The utf-32* decoders no longer decode byte sequences that correspond to surrogate code points.

7.2.4 Python Specific Encodings

A number of predefined codecs are specific to Python, so their codec names have no meaning outside Python. These are listed in the tables below based on the expected input and output types (note that while text encodings are the most common use case for codecs, the underlying codec infrastructure supports arbitrary data transforms rather than just text encodings). For asymmetric codecs, the stated purpose describes the encoding direction.

Text Encodings

The following codecs provide `str` to `bytes` encoding and *bytes-like object* to `str` decoding, similar to the Unicode text encodings.

Codec	Aliases	Purpose
idna		Implements RFC 3490, see also *encodings.idna*. Only `errors='strict'` is supported.
mbcs	ansi, dbcs	Windows only: Encode operand according to the ANSI codepage (CP_ACP)
oem		Windows only: Encode operand according to the OEM codepage (CP_OEMCP) New in version 3.6.
palmos		Encoding of PalmOS 3.5
punycode		Implements RFC 3492. Stateful codecs are not supported.
raw_unicode_escape		Latin-1 encoding with `\uXXXX` and `\UXXXXXXXX` for other code points. Existing backslashes are not escaped in any way. It is used in the Python pickle protocol.
undefined		Raise an exception for all conversions, even empty strings. The error handler is ignored.
unicode_escape		Encoding suitable as the contents of a Unicode literal in ASCII-encoded Python source code, except that quotes are not escaped. Decodes from Latin-1 source code. Beware that Python source code actually uses UTF-8 by default.
unicode_internal		Return the internal representation of the operand. Stateful codecs are not supported. Deprecated since version 3.3: This representation is obsoleted by PEP 393.

Binary Transforms

The following codecs provide binary transforms: *bytes-like object* to *bytes* mappings. They are not supported by *bytes.decode()* (which only produces *str* output).

Codec	Aliases	Purpose	Encoder / decoder
base64_codec[1]	base64, base_64	Convert operand to multiline MIME base64 (the result always includes a trailing '\n') Changed in version 3.4: accepts any *bytes-like object* as input for encoding and decoding	*base64.encodebytes()* / *base64.decodebytes()*
bz2_codec	bz2	Compress the operand using bz2	*bz2.compress()* / *bz2.decompress()*
hex_codec	hex	Convert operand to hexadecimal representation, with two digits per byte	*binascii.b2a_hex()* / *binascii.a2b_hex()*
quopri_codec	quopri, quoted-printable, quoted_printable	Convert operand to MIME quoted printable	*quopri.encode()* with `quotetabs=True` / *quopri.decode()*
uu_codec	uu	Convert the operand using uuencode	*uu.encode()* / *uu.decode()*
zlib_codec	zip, zlib	Compress the operand using gzip	*zlib.compress()* / *zlib.decompress()*

New in version 3.2: Restoration of the binary transforms.

Changed in version 3.4: Restoration of the aliases for the binary transforms.

Text Transforms

The following codec provides a text transform: a *str* to *str* mapping. It is not supported by *str.encode()* (which only produces *bytes* output).

Codec	Aliases	Purpose
rot_13	rot13	Returns the Caesar-cypher encryption of the operand

New in version 3.2: Restoration of the `rot_13` text transform.

Changed in version 3.4: Restoration of the `rot13` alias.

7.2.5 `encodings.idna` — Internationalized Domain Names in Applications

This module implements RFC 3490 (Internationalized Domain Names in Applications) and RFC 3492 (Nameprep: A Stringprep Profile for Internationalized Domain Names (IDN)). It builds upon the `punycode` encoding and *stringprep*.

These RFCs together define a protocol to support non-ASCII characters in domain names. A domain name containing non-ASCII characters (such as `www.Alliancefrançaise.nu`) is converted into an ASCII-compatible encoding (ACE, such as `www.xn--alliancefranaise-npb.nu`). The ACE form of the domain name is then used in all places where arbitrary characters are not allowed by the protocol, such as DNS queries, HTTP ***Host*** fields, and so on. This conversion is carried out in the application; if possible invisible

[1] In addition to *bytes-like objects*, `'base64_codec'` also accepts ASCII-only instances of *str* for decoding

to the user: The application should transparently convert Unicode domain labels to IDNA on the wire, and convert back ACE labels to Unicode before presenting them to the user.

Python supports this conversion in several ways: the `idna` codec performs conversion between Unicode and ACE, separating an input string into labels based on the separator characters defined in section 3.1 (1) of RFC 3490 and converting each label to ACE as required, and conversely separating an input byte string into labels based on the `.` separator and converting any ACE labels found into unicode. Furthermore, the `socket` module transparently converts Unicode host names to ACE, so that applications need not be concerned about converting host names themselves when they pass them to the socket module. On top of that, modules that have host names as function parameters, such as `http.client` and `ftplib`, accept Unicode host names (`http.client` then also transparently sends an IDNA hostname in the **Host** field if it sends that field at all).

When receiving host names from the wire (such as in reverse name lookup), no automatic conversion to Unicode is performed: Applications wishing to present such host names to the user should decode them to Unicode.

The module `encodings.idna` also implements the nameprep procedure, which performs certain normalizations on host names, to achieve case-insensitivity of international domain names, and to unify similar characters. The nameprep functions can be used directly if desired.

`encodings.idna.nameprep(label)`
: Return the nameprepped version of *label*. The implementation currently assumes query strings, so `AllowUnassigned` is true.

`encodings.idna.ToASCII(label)`
: Convert a label to ASCII, as specified in RFC 3490. `UseSTD3ASCIIRules` is assumed to be false.

`encodings.idna.ToUnicode(label)`
: Convert a label to Unicode, as specified in RFC 3490.

7.2.6 `encodings.mbcs` — Windows ANSI codepage

Encode operand according to the ANSI codepage (CP_ACP).

Availability: Windows only.

Changed in version 3.3: Support any error handler.

Changed in version 3.2: Before 3.2, the *errors* argument was ignored; `'replace'` was always used to encode, and `'ignore'` to decode.

7.2.7 `encodings.utf_8_sig` — UTF-8 codec with BOM signature

This module implements a variant of the UTF-8 codec: On encoding a UTF-8 encoded BOM will be prepended to the UTF-8 encoded bytes. For the stateful encoder this is only done once (on the first write to the byte stream). For decoding an optional UTF-8 encoded BOM at the start of the data will be skipped.

CHAPTER

EIGHT

DATA TYPES

The modules described in this chapter provide a variety of specialized data types such as dates and times, fixed-type arrays, heap queues, synchronized queues, and sets.

Python also provides some built-in data types, in particular, *dict*, *list*, *set* and *frozenset*, and *tuple*. The *str* class is used to hold Unicode strings, and the *bytes* class is used to hold binary data.

The following modules are documented in this chapter:

8.1 datetime — Basic date and time types

Source code: Lib/datetime.py

The *datetime* module supplies classes for manipulating dates and times in both simple and complex ways. While date and time arithmetic is supported, the focus of the implementation is on efficient attribute extraction for output formatting and manipulation. For related functionality, see also the *time* and *calendar* modules.

There are two kinds of date and time objects: "naive" and "aware".

An aware object has sufficient knowledge of applicable algorithmic and political time adjustments, such as time zone and daylight saving time information, to locate itself relative to other aware objects. An aware object is used to represent a specific moment in time that is not open to interpretation[1].

A naive object does not contain enough information to unambiguously locate itself relative to other date/time objects. Whether a naive object represents Coordinated Universal Time (UTC), local time, or time in some other timezone is purely up to the program, just like it is up to the program whether a particular number represents metres, miles, or mass. Naive objects are easy to understand and to work with, at the cost of ignoring some aspects of reality.

For applications requiring aware objects, *datetime* and *time* objects have an optional time zone information attribute, `tzinfo`, that can be set to an instance of a subclass of the abstract *tzinfo* class. These *tzinfo* objects capture information about the offset from UTC time, the time zone name, and whether Daylight Saving Time is in effect. Note that only one concrete *tzinfo* class, the *timezone* class, is supplied by the *datetime* module. The *timezone* class can represent simple timezones with fixed offset from UTC, such as UTC itself or North American EST and EDT timezones. Supporting timezones at deeper levels of detail is up to the application. The rules for time adjustment across the world are more political than rational, change frequently, and there is no standard suitable for every application aside from UTC.

The *datetime* module exports the following constants:

datetime.MINYEAR

The smallest year number allowed in a *date* or *datetime* object. *MINYEAR* is `1`.

[1] If, that is, we ignore the effects of Relativity

`datetime.MAXYEAR`
The largest year number allowed in a *date* or *datetime* object. *MAXYEAR* is 9999.

See also:

Module *calendar* General calendar related functions.

Module *time* Time access and conversions.

8.1.1 Available Types

class datetime.date
An idealized naive date, assuming the current Gregorian calendar always was, and always will be, in effect. Attributes: *year*, *month*, and *day*.

class datetime.time
An idealized time, independent of any particular day, assuming that every day has exactly 24*60*60 seconds (there is no notion of "leap seconds" here). Attributes: *hour*, *minute*, *second*, *microsecond*, and *tzinfo*.

class datetime.datetime
A combination of a date and a time. Attributes: *year*, *month*, *day*, *hour*, *minute*, *second*, *microsecond*, and *tzinfo*.

class datetime.timedelta
A duration expressing the difference between two *date*, *time*, or *datetime* instances to microsecond resolution.

class datetime.tzinfo
An abstract base class for time zone information objects. These are used by the *datetime* and *time* classes to provide a customizable notion of time adjustment (for example, to account for time zone and/or daylight saving time).

class datetime.timezone
A class that implements the *tzinfo* abstract base class as a fixed offset from the UTC.

New in version 3.2.

Objects of these types are immutable.

Objects of the *date* type are always naive.

An object of type *time* or *datetime* may be naive or aware. A *datetime* object *d* is aware if `d.tzinfo` is not `None` and `d.tzinfo.utcoffset(d)` does not return `None`. If `d.tzinfo` is `None`, or if `d.tzinfo` is not `None` but `d.tzinfo.utcoffset(d)` returns `None`, *d* is naive. A *time* object *t* is aware if `t.tzinfo` is not `None` and `t.tzinfo.utcoffset(None)` does not return `None`. Otherwise, *t* is naive.

The distinction between naive and aware doesn't apply to *timedelta* objects.

Subclass relationships:

```
object
    timedelta
    tzinfo
        timezone
    time
    date
        datetime
```

8.1.2 timedelta Objects

A *timedelta* object represents a duration, the difference between two dates or times.

class datetime.timedelta(*days=0, seconds=0, microseconds=0, milliseconds=0, minutes=0, hours=0, weeks=0*)

All arguments are optional and default to `0`. Arguments may be integers or floats, and may be positive or negative.

Only *days*, *seconds* and *microseconds* are stored internally. Arguments are converted to those units:

- A millisecond is converted to 1000 microseconds.
- A minute is converted to 60 seconds.
- An hour is converted to 3600 seconds.
- A week is converted to 7 days.

and days, seconds and microseconds are then normalized so that the representation is unique, with

- `0 <= microseconds < 1000000`
- `0 <= seconds < 3600*24` (the number of seconds in one day)
- `-999999999 <= days <= 999999999`

If any argument is a float and there are fractional microseconds, the fractional microseconds left over from all arguments are combined and their sum is rounded to the nearest microsecond using round-half-to-even tiebreaker. If no argument is a float, the conversion and normalization processes are exact (no information is lost).

If the normalized value of days lies outside the indicated range, *OverflowError* is raised.

Note that normalization of negative values may be surprising at first. For example,

```
>>> from datetime import timedelta
>>> d = timedelta(microseconds=-1)
>>> (d.days, d.seconds, d.microseconds)
(-1, 86399, 999999)
```

Class attributes are:

timedelta.min

The most negative *timedelta* object, `timedelta(-999999999)`.

timedelta.max

The most positive *timedelta* object, `timedelta(days=999999999, hours=23, minutes=59, seconds=59, microseconds=999999)`.

timedelta.resolution

The smallest possible difference between non-equal *timedelta* objects, `timedelta(microseconds=1)`.

Note that, because of normalization, `timedelta.max` > `-timedelta.min`. `-timedelta.max` is not representable as a *timedelta* object.

Instance attributes (read-only):

Attribute	Value
`days`	Between -999999999 and 999999999 inclusive
`seconds`	Between 0 and 86399 inclusive
`microseconds`	Between 0 and 999999 inclusive

Supported operations:

Operation	Result
`t1 = t2 + t3`	Sum of *t2* and *t3*. Afterwards *t1*-*t2* == *t3* and *t1*-*t3* == *t2* are true. (1)
`t1 = t2 - t3`	Difference of *t2* and *t3*. Afterwards *t1* == *t2* - *t3* and *t2* == *t1* + *t3* are true. (1)
`t1 = t2 * i or t1 = i * t2`	Delta multiplied by an integer. Afterwards *t1* // i == *t2* is true, provided `i != 0`.
	In general, *t1* * i == *t1* * (i-1) + *t1* is true. (1)
`t1 = t2 * f or t1 = f * t2`	Delta multiplied by a float. The result is rounded to the nearest multiple of timedelta.resolution using round-half-to-even.
`f = t2 / t3`	Division (3) of *t2* by *t3*. Returns a *float* object.
`t1 = t2 / f or t1 = t2 / i`	Delta divided by a float or an int. The result is rounded to the nearest multiple of timedelta.resolution using round-half-to-even.
`t1 = t2 // i` or `t1 = t2 // t3`	The floor is computed and the remainder (if any) is thrown away. In the second case, an integer is returned. (3)
`t1 = t2 % t3`	The remainder is computed as a *timedelta* object. (3)
`q, r = divmod(t1, t2)`	Computes the quotient and the remainder: `q = t1 // t2` (3) and `r = t1 % t2`. q is an integer and r is a *timedelta* object.
`+t1`	Returns a *timedelta* object with the same value. (2)
`-t1`	equivalent to *timedelta*(*-t1.days*, *-t1.seconds*, *-t1.microseconds*), and to *t1** -1. (1)(4)
`abs(t)`	equivalent to +*t* when `t.days >= 0`, and to -*t* when `t.days < 0`. (2)
`str(t)`	Returns a string in the form `[D day[s], ][H]H:MM:SS[.UUUUUU]`, where D is negative for negative `t`. (5)
`repr(t)`	Returns a string in the form `datetime.timedelta(D[, S[, U]])`, where D is negative for negative `t`. (5)

Notes:

1. This is exact, but may overflow.
2. This is exact, and cannot overflow.
3. Division by 0 raises *ZeroDivisionError*.
4. *-timedelta.max* is not representable as a *timedelta* object.
5. String representations of *timedelta* objects are normalized similarly to their internal representation. This leads to somewhat unusual results for negative timedeltas. For example:

```
>>> timedelta(hours=-5)
datetime.timedelta(-1, 68400)
>>> print(_)
-1 day, 19:00:00
```

In addition to the operations listed above *timedelta* objects support certain additions and subtractions with *date* and *datetime* objects (see below).

Changed in version 3.2: Floor division and true division of a *timedelta* object by another *timedelta* object are now supported, as are remainder operations and the *divmod()* function. True division and multiplication of a *timedelta* object by a *float* object are now supported.

Comparisons of *timedelta* objects are supported with the *timedelta* object representing the smaller duration considered to be the smaller timedelta. In order to stop mixed-type comparisons from falling back to the default comparison by object address, when a *timedelta* object is compared to an object of a different type, *TypeError* is raised unless the comparison is `==` or `!=`. The latter cases return *False* or *True*, respectively.

timedelta objects are *hashable* (usable as dictionary keys), support efficient pickling, and in Boolean contexts, a *timedelta* object is considered to be true if and only if it isn't equal to `timedelta(0)`.

Instance methods:

`timedelta.total_seconds()`
Return the total number of seconds contained in the duration. Equivalent to `td / timedelta(seconds=1)`.

Note that for very large time intervals (greater than 270 years on most platforms) this method will lose microsecond accuracy.

New in version 3.2.

Example usage:

```
>>> from datetime import timedelta
>>> year = timedelta(days=365)
>>> another_year = timedelta(weeks=40, days=84, hours=23,
...                          minutes=50, seconds=600)  # adds up to 365 days
>>> year.total_seconds()
31536000.0
>>> year == another_year
True
>>> ten_years = 10 * year
>>> ten_years, ten_years.days // 365
(datetime.timedelta(3650), 10)
>>> nine_years = ten_years - year
>>> nine_years, nine_years.days // 365
(datetime.timedelta(3285), 9)
>>> three_years = nine_years // 3;
>>> three_years, three_years.days // 365
(datetime.timedelta(1095), 3)
>>> abs(three_years - ten_years) == 2 * three_years + year
True
```

8.1.3 date Objects

A *date* object represents a date (year, month and day) in an idealized calendar, the current Gregorian calendar indefinitely extended in both directions. January 1 of year 1 is called day number 1, January 2 of year 1 is called day number 2, and so on. This matches the definition of the "proleptic Gregorian" calendar in Dershowitz and Reingold's book Calendrical Calculations, where it's the base calendar for all computations. See the book for algorithms for converting between proleptic Gregorian ordinals and many other calendar systems.

class datetime.date(*year*, *month*, *day*)
All arguments are required. Arguments may be integers, in the following ranges:

- `MINYEAR <= year <= MAXYEAR`
- `1 <= month <= 12`
- `1 <= day <= number of days in the given month and year`

If an argument outside those ranges is given, *ValueError* is raised.

Other constructors, all class methods:

classmethod date.today()
Return the current local date. This is equivalent to `date.fromtimestamp(time.time())`.

classmethod date.fromtimestamp(*timestamp*)
Return the local date corresponding to the POSIX timestamp, such as is returned by *time.time()*. This may raise *OverflowError*, if the timestamp is out of the range of values supported by the platform

C `localtime()` function, and *OSError* on `localtime()` failure. It's common for this to be restricted to years from 1970 through 2038. Note that on non-POSIX systems that include leap seconds in their notion of a timestamp, leap seconds are ignored by *fromtimestamp()*.

Changed in version 3.3: Raise *OverflowError* instead of *ValueError* if the timestamp is out of the range of values supported by the platform C `localtime()` function. Raise *OSError* instead of *ValueError* on `localtime()` failure.

classmethod date.fromordinal(*ordinal*)
Return the date corresponding to the proleptic Gregorian ordinal, where January 1 of year 1 has ordinal 1. *ValueError* is raised unless `1 <= ordinal <= date.max.toordinal()`. For any date *d*, `date.fromordinal(d.toordinal()) == d`.

Class attributes:

date.min
The earliest representable date, `date(MINYEAR, 1, 1)`.

date.max
The latest representable date, `date(MAXYEAR, 12, 31)`.

date.resolution
The smallest possible difference between non-equal date objects, `timedelta(days=1)`.

Instance attributes (read-only):

date.year
Between *MINYEAR* and *MAXYEAR* inclusive.

date.month
Between 1 and 12 inclusive.

date.day
Between 1 and the number of days in the given month of the given year.

Supported operations:

Operation	Result
`date2 = date1 + timedelta`	*date2* is `timedelta.days` days removed from *date1*. (1)
`date2 = date1 - timedelta`	Computes *date2* such that `date2 + timedelta == date1`. (2)
`timedelta = date1 - date2`	(3)
`date1 < date2`	*date1* is considered less than *date2* when *date1* precedes *date2* in time. (4)

Notes:

1. *date2* is moved forward in time if `timedelta.days > 0`, or backward if `timedelta.days < 0`. Afterward `date2 - date1 == timedelta.days`. `timedelta.seconds` and `timedelta.microseconds` are ignored. *OverflowError* is raised if `date2.year` would be smaller than *MINYEAR* or larger than *MAXYEAR*.
2. This isn't quite equivalent to date1 + (-timedelta), because -timedelta in isolation can overflow in cases where date1 - timedelta does not. `timedelta.seconds` and `timedelta.microseconds` are ignored.
3. This is exact, and cannot overflow. timedelta.seconds and timedelta.microseconds are 0, and date2 + timedelta == date1 after.
4. In other words, `date1 < date2` if and only if `date1.toordinal() < date2.toordinal()`. In order to stop comparison from falling back to the default scheme of comparing object addresses, date comparison normally raises *TypeError* if the other comparand isn't also a *date* object. However, `NotImplemented` is returned instead if the other comparand has a `timetuple()` attribute. This hook gives other kinds of date objects a chance at implementing mixed-type comparison. If not, when a *date* object is compared

to an object of a different type, *TypeError* is raised unless the comparison is `==` or `!=`. The latter cases return *False* or *True*, respectively.

Dates can be used as dictionary keys. In Boolean contexts, all *date* objects are considered to be true.

Instance methods:

`date.replace`(*year=self.year, month=self.month, day=self.day*)
Return a date with the same value, except for those parameters given new values by whichever keyword arguments are specified. For example, if `d == date(2002, 12, 31)`, then `d.replace(day=26) == date(2002, 12, 26)`.

`date.timetuple()`
Return a *time.struct_time* such as returned by *time.localtime()*. The hours, minutes and seconds are 0, and the DST flag is -1. `d.timetuple()` is equivalent to `time.struct_time((d.year, d.month, d.day, 0, 0, 0, d.weekday(), yday, -1))`, where `yday = d.toordinal() - date(d.year, 1, 1).toordinal() + 1` is the day number within the current year starting with `1` for January 1st.

`date.toordinal()`
Return the proleptic Gregorian ordinal of the date, where January 1 of year 1 has ordinal 1. For any *date* object *d*, `date.fromordinal(d.toordinal()) == d`.

`date.weekday()`
Return the day of the week as an integer, where Monday is 0 and Sunday is 6. For example, `date(2002, 12, 4).weekday() == 2`, a Wednesday. See also *isoweekday()*.

`date.isoweekday()`
Return the day of the week as an integer, where Monday is 1 and Sunday is 7. For example, `date(2002, 12, 4).isoweekday() == 3`, a Wednesday. See also *weekday()*, *isocalendar()*.

`date.isocalendar()`
Return a 3-tuple, (ISO year, ISO week number, ISO weekday).

The ISO calendar is a widely used variant of the Gregorian calendar. See https://www.staff.science.uu.nl/~gent0113/calendar/isocalendar.htm for a good explanation.

The ISO year consists of 52 or 53 full weeks, and where a week starts on a Monday and ends on a Sunday. The first week of an ISO year is the first (Gregorian) calendar week of a year containing a Thursday. This is called week number 1, and the ISO year of that Thursday is the same as its Gregorian year.

For example, 2004 begins on a Thursday, so the first week of ISO year 2004 begins on Monday, 29 Dec 2003 and ends on Sunday, 4 Jan 2004, so that `date(2003, 12, 29).isocalendar() == (2004, 1, 1)` and `date(2004, 1, 4).isocalendar() == (2004, 1, 7)`.

`date.isoformat()`
Return a string representing the date in ISO 8601 format, 'YYYY-MM-DD'. For example, `date(2002, 12, 4).isoformat() == '2002-12-04'`.

`date.__str__()`
For a date *d*, `str(d)` is equivalent to `d.isoformat()`.

`date.ctime()`
Return a string representing the date, for example `date(2002, 12, 4).ctime() == 'Wed Dec 4 00:00:00 2002'`. `d.ctime()` is equivalent to `time.ctime(time.mktime(d.timetuple()))` on platforms where the native C `ctime()` function (which *time.ctime()* invokes, but which *date.ctime()* does not invoke) conforms to the C standard.

`date.strftime`(*format*)
Return a string representing the date, controlled by an explicit format string. Format codes referring to hours, minutes or seconds will see 0 values. For a complete list of formatting directives, see *strftime() and strptime() Behavior*.

`date.__format__`(*format*)

Same as *date.strftime()*. This makes it possible to specify a format string for a *date* object in formatted string literals and when using *str.format()*. For a complete list of formatting directives, see *strftime() and strptime() Behavior*.

Example of counting days to an event:

```
>>> import time
>>> from datetime import date
>>> today = date.today()
>>> today
datetime.date(2007, 12, 5)
>>> today == date.fromtimestamp(time.time())
True
>>> my_birthday = date(today.year, 6, 24)
>>> if my_birthday < today:
...     my_birthday = my_birthday.replace(year=today.year + 1)
>>> my_birthday
datetime.date(2008, 6, 24)
>>> time_to_birthday = abs(my_birthday - today)
>>> time_to_birthday.days
202
```

Example of working with *date*:

```
>>> from datetime import date
>>> d = date.fromordinal(730920) # 730920th day after 1. 1. 0001
>>> d
datetime.date(2002, 3, 11)
>>> t = d.timetuple()
>>> for i in t:
...     print(i)
2002                # year
3                   # month
11                  # day
0
0
0
0                   # weekday (0 = Monday)
70                  # 70th day in the year
-1
>>> ic = d.isocalendar()
>>> for i in ic:
...     print(i)
2002                # ISO year
11                  # ISO week number
1                   # ISO day number ( 1 = Monday )
>>> d.isoformat()
'2002-03-11'
>>> d.strftime("%d/%m/%y")
'11/03/02'
>>> d.strftime("%A %d. %B %Y")
'Monday 11. March 2002'
>>> 'The {1} is {0:%d}, the {2} is {0:%B}.'.format(d, "day", "month")
'The day is 11, the month is March.'
```

8.1.4 datetime Objects

A *datetime* object is a single object containing all the information from a *date* object and a *time* object. Like a *date* object, *datetime* assumes the current Gregorian calendar extended in both directions; like a time object, *datetime* assumes there are exactly 3600*24 seconds in every day.

Constructor:

class datetime.datetime(*year, month, day, hour=0, minute=0, second=0, microsecond=0, tzinfo=None, *, fold=0*)

The year, month and day arguments are required. *tzinfo* may be `None`, or an instance of a *tzinfo* subclass. The remaining arguments may be integers, in the following ranges:

- `MINYEAR <= year <= MAXYEAR`,
- `1 <= month <= 12`,
- `1 <= day <= number of days in the given month and year`,
- `0 <= hour < 24`,
- `0 <= minute < 60`,
- `0 <= second < 60`,
- `0 <= microsecond < 1000000`,
- `fold in [0, 1]`.

If an argument outside those ranges is given, *ValueError* is raised.

New in version 3.6: Added the `fold` argument.

Other constructors, all class methods:

classmethod datetime.today()

Return the current local datetime, with *tzinfo* `None`. This is equivalent to `datetime.fromtimestamp(time.time())`. See also *now()*, *fromtimestamp()*.

classmethod datetime.now(*tz=None*)

Return the current local date and time. If optional argument *tz* is `None` or not specified, this is like *today()*, but, if possible, supplies more precision than can be gotten from going through a *time.time()* timestamp (for example, this may be possible on platforms supplying the C `gettimeofday()` function).

If *tz* is not `None`, it must be an instance of a *tzinfo* subclass, and the current date and time are converted to *tz*'s time zone. In this case the result is equivalent to `tz.fromutc(datetime.utcnow().replace(tzinfo=tz))`. See also *today()*, *utcnow()*.

classmethod datetime.utcnow()

Return the current UTC date and time, with *tzinfo* `None`. This is like *now()*, but returns the current UTC date and time, as a naive *datetime* object. An aware current UTC datetime can be obtained by calling `datetime.now(timezone.utc)`. See also *now()*.

classmethod datetime.fromtimestamp(*timestamp, tz=None*)

Return the local date and time corresponding to the POSIX timestamp, such as is returned by *time.time()*. If optional argument *tz* is `None` or not specified, the timestamp is converted to the platform's local date and time, and the returned *datetime* object is naive.

If *tz* is not `None`, it must be an instance of a *tzinfo* subclass, and the timestamp is converted to *tz*'s time zone. In this case the result is equivalent to `tz.fromutc(datetime.utcfromtimestamp(timestamp).replace(tzinfo=tz))`.

fromtimestamp() may raise *OverflowError*, if the timestamp is out of the range of values supported by the platform C `localtime()` or `gmtime()` functions, and *OSError* on `localtime()` or `gmtime()`

failure. It's common for this to be restricted to years in 1970 through 2038. Note that on non-POSIX systems that include leap seconds in their notion of a timestamp, leap seconds are ignored by *fromtimestamp()*, and then it's possible to have two timestamps differing by a second that yield identical *datetime* objects. See also *utcfromtimestamp()*.

Changed in version 3.3: Raise *OverflowError* instead of *ValueError* if the timestamp is out of the range of values supported by the platform C `localtime()` or `gmtime()` functions. Raise *OSError* instead of *ValueError* on `localtime()` or `gmtime()` failure.

Changed in version 3.6: *fromtimestamp()* may return instances with *fold* set to 1.

classmethod datetime.utcfromtimestamp(*timestamp*)

Return the UTC *datetime* corresponding to the POSIX timestamp, with *tzinfo* `None`. This may raise *OverflowError*, if the timestamp is out of the range of values supported by the platform C `gmtime()` function, and *OSError* on `gmtime()` failure. It's common for this to be restricted to years in 1970 through 2038.

To get an aware *datetime* object, call *fromtimestamp()*:

```
datetime.fromtimestamp(timestamp, timezone.utc)
```

On the POSIX compliant platforms, it is equivalent to the following expression:

```
datetime(1970, 1, 1, tzinfo=timezone.utc) + timedelta(seconds=timestamp)
```

except the latter formula always supports the full years range: between *MINYEAR* and *MAXYEAR* inclusive.

Changed in version 3.3: Raise *OverflowError* instead of *ValueError* if the timestamp is out of the range of values supported by the platform C `gmtime()` function. Raise *OSError* instead of *ValueError* on `gmtime()` failure.

classmethod datetime.fromordinal(*ordinal*)

Return the *datetime* corresponding to the proleptic Gregorian ordinal, where January 1 of year 1 has ordinal 1. *ValueError* is raised unless `1 <= ordinal <= datetime.max.toordinal()`. The hour, minute, second and microsecond of the result are all 0, and *tzinfo* is `None`.

classmethod datetime.combine(*date, time, tzinfo=self.tzinfo*)

Return a new *datetime* object whose date components are equal to the given *date* object's, and whose time components are equal to the given *time* object's. If the *tzinfo* argument is provided, its value is used to set the *tzinfo* attribute of the result, otherwise the *tzinfo* attribute of the *time* argument is used.

For any *datetime* object *d*, `d == datetime.combine(d.date(), d.time(), d.tzinfo)`. If date is a *datetime* object, its time components and *tzinfo* attributes are ignored.

Changed in version 3.6: Added the *tzinfo* argument.

classmethod datetime.strptime(*date_string, format*)

Return a *datetime* corresponding to *date_string*, parsed according to *format*. This is equivalent to `datetime(*(time.strptime(date_string, format)[0:6]))`. *ValueError* is raised if the date_string and format can't be parsed by *time.strptime()* or if it returns a value which isn't a time tuple. For a complete list of formatting directives, see *strftime() and strptime() Behavior*.

Class attributes:

datetime.min

The earliest representable *datetime*, `datetime(MINYEAR, 1, 1, tzinfo=None)`.

datetime.max

The latest representable *datetime*, `datetime(MAXYEAR, 12, 31, 23, 59, 59, 999999, tzinfo=None)`.

datetime.resolution
: The smallest possible difference between non-equal *datetime* objects, `timedelta(microseconds=1)`.

Instance attributes (read-only):

datetime.year
: Between *MINYEAR* and *MAXYEAR* inclusive.

datetime.month
: Between 1 and 12 inclusive.

datetime.day
: Between 1 and the number of days in the given month of the given year.

datetime.hour
: In `range(24)`.

datetime.minute
: In `range(60)`.

datetime.second
: In `range(60)`.

datetime.microsecond
: In `range(1000000)`.

datetime.tzinfo
: The object passed as the *tzinfo* argument to the *datetime* constructor, or `None` if none was passed.

datetime.fold
: In `[0, 1]`. Used to disambiguate wall times during a repeated interval. (A repeated interval occurs when clocks are rolled back at the end of daylight saving time or when the UTC offset for the current zone is decreased for political reasons.) The value 0 (1) represents the earlier (later) of the two moments with the same wall time representation.

  New in version 3.6.

Supported operations:

Operation	Result
`datetime2 = datetime1 + timedelta`	(1)
`datetime2 = datetime1 - timedelta`	(2)
`timedelta = datetime1 - datetime2`	(3)
`datetime1 < datetime2`	Compares *datetime* to *datetime*. (4)

1. datetime2 is a duration of timedelta removed from datetime1, moving forward in time if `timedelta.days` > 0, or backward if `timedelta.days` < 0. The result has the same *tzinfo* attribute as the input datetime, and datetime2 - datetime1 == timedelta after. *OverflowError* is raised if datetime2.year would be smaller than *MINYEAR* or larger than *MAXYEAR*. Note that no time zone adjustments are done even if the input is an aware object.
2. Computes the datetime2 such that datetime2 + timedelta == datetime1. As for addition, the result has the same *tzinfo* attribute as the input datetime, and no time zone adjustments are done even if the input is aware. This isn't quite equivalent to datetime1 + (-timedelta), because -timedelta in isolation can overflow in cases where datetime1 - timedelta does not.
3. Subtraction of a *datetime* from a *datetime* is defined only if both operands are naive, or if both are aware. If one is aware and the other is naive, *TypeError* is raised.

   If both are naive, or both are aware and have the same *tzinfo* attribute, the *tzinfo* attributes are ignored, and the result is a *timedelta* object *t* such that `datetime2 + t == datetime1`. No time zone adjustments are done in this case.

If both are aware and have different *tzinfo* attributes, `a-b` acts as if *a* and *b* were first converted to naive UTC datetimes first. The result is `(a.replace(tzinfo=None) - a.utcoffset()) - (b.replace(tzinfo=None) - b.utcoffset())` except that the implementation never overflows.

4. *datetime1* is considered less than *datetime2* when *datetime1* precedes *datetime2* in time.

   If one comparand is naive and the other is aware, *TypeError* is raised if an order comparison is attempted. For equality comparisons, naive instances are never equal to aware instances.

   If both comparands are aware, and have the same *tzinfo* attribute, the common *tzinfo* attribute is ignored and the base datetimes are compared. If both comparands are aware and have different *tzinfo* attributes, the comparands are first adjusted by subtracting their UTC offsets (obtained from `self.utcoffset()`).

   Changed in version 3.3: Equality comparisons between naive and aware *datetime* instances don't raise *TypeError*.

Note: In order to stop comparison from falling back to the default scheme of comparing object addresses, datetime comparison normally raises *TypeError* if the other comparand isn't also a *datetime* object. However, `NotImplemented` is returned instead if the other comparand has a `timetuple()` attribute. This hook gives other kinds of date objects a chance at implementing mixed-type comparison. If not, when a *datetime* object is compared to an object of a different type, *TypeError* is raised unless the comparison is `==` or `!=`. The latter cases return *False* or *True*, respectively.

---

datetime objects can be used as dictionary keys. In Boolean contexts, all *datetime* objects are considered to be true.

Instance methods:

`datetime.date()`
Return *date* object with same year, month and day.

`datetime.time()`
Return *time* object with same hour, minute, second, microsecond and fold. *tzinfo* is `None`. See also method *timetz()*.

Changed in version 3.6: The fold value is copied to the returned *time* object.

`datetime.timetz()`
Return *time* object with same hour, minute, second, microsecond, fold, and tzinfo attributes. See also method *time()*.

Changed in version 3.6: The fold value is copied to the returned *time* object.

`datetime.replace(`*year=self.year, month=self.month, day=self.day, hour=self.hour, minute=self.minute, second=self.second, microsecond=self.microsecond, tzinfo=self.tzinfo, * fold=0*`)`
Return a datetime with the same attributes, except for those attributes given new values by whichever keyword arguments are specified. Note that `tzinfo=None` can be specified to create a naive datetime from an aware datetime with no conversion of date and time data.

New in version 3.6: Added the `fold` argument.

`datetime.astimezone(`*tz=None*`)`
Return a *datetime* object with new *tzinfo* attribute *tz*, adjusting the date and time data so the result is the same UTC time as *self*, but in *tz*'s local time.

If provided, *tz* must be an instance of a *tzinfo* subclass, and its *utcoffset()* and *dst()* methods must not return `None`. If *self* is naive (`self.tzinfo is None`), it is presumed to represent time in the system timezone.

If called without arguments (or with `tz=None`) the system local timezone is assumed for the target timezone. The `.tzinfo` attribute of the converted datetime instance will be set to an instance of *timezone* with the zone name and offset obtained from the OS.

If `self.tzinfo` is *tz*, `self.astimezone(tz)` is equal to *self*: no adjustment of date or time data is performed. Else the result is local time in the timezone *tz*, representing the same UTC time as *self*: after `astz = dt.astimezone(tz)`, `astz - astz.utcoffset()` will have the same date and time data as `dt - dt.utcoffset()`.

If you merely want to attach a time zone object *tz* to a datetime *dt* without adjustment of date and time data, use `dt.replace(tzinfo=tz)`. If you merely want to remove the time zone object from an aware datetime *dt* without conversion of date and time data, use `dt.replace(tzinfo=None)`.

Note that the default *tzinfo.fromutc()* method can be overridden in a *tzinfo* subclass to affect the result returned by *astimezone()*. Ignoring error cases, *astimezone()* acts like:

```
def astimezone(self, tz):
    if self.tzinfo is tz:
        return self
    # Convert self to UTC, and attach the new time zone object.
    utc = (self - self.utcoffset()).replace(tzinfo=tz)
    # Convert from UTC to tz's local time.
    return tz.fromutc(utc)
```

Changed in version 3.3: *tz* now can be omitted.

Changed in version 3.6: The *astimezone()* method can now be called on naive instances that are presumed to represent system local time.

datetime.utcoffset()

If *tzinfo* is `None`, returns `None`, else returns `self.tzinfo.utcoffset(self)`, and raises an exception if the latter doesn't return `None`, or a *timedelta* object representing a whole number of minutes with magnitude less than one day.

datetime.dst()

If *tzinfo* is `None`, returns `None`, else returns `self.tzinfo.dst(self)`, and raises an exception if the latter doesn't return `None`, or a *timedelta* object representing a whole number of minutes with magnitude less than one day.

datetime.tzname()

If *tzinfo* is `None`, returns `None`, else returns `self.tzinfo.tzname(self)`, raises an exception if the latter doesn't return `None` or a string object,

datetime.timetuple()

Return a *time.struct_time* such as returned by *time.localtime()*. `d.timetuple()` is equivalent to `time.struct_time((d.year, d.month, d.day, d.hour, d.minute, d.second, d.weekday(), yday, dst))`, where `yday = d.toordinal() - date(d.year, 1, 1).toordinal() + 1` is the day number within the current year starting with `1` for January 1st. The `tm_isdst` flag of the result is set according to the *dst()* method: *tzinfo* is `None` or *dst()* returns `None`, `tm_isdst` is set to `-1`; else if *dst()* returns a non-zero value, `tm_isdst` is set to `1`; else `tm_isdst` is set to `0`.

datetime.utctimetuple()

If *datetime* instance *d* is naive, this is the same as `d.timetuple()` except that `tm_isdst` is forced to 0 regardless of what `d.dst()` returns. DST is never in effect for a UTC time.

If *d* is aware, *d* is normalized to UTC time, by subtracting `d.utcoffset()`, and a *time.struct_time* for the normalized time is returned. `tm_isdst` is forced to 0. Note that an *OverflowError* may be raised if *d*.year was `MINYEAR` or `MAXYEAR` and UTC adjustment spills over a year boundary.

datetime.toordinal()

Return the proleptic Gregorian ordinal of the date. The same as `self.date().toordinal()`.

`datetime.timestamp()`

Return POSIX timestamp corresponding to the *datetime* instance. The return value is a *float* similar to that returned by *time.time()*.

Naive *datetime* instances are assumed to represent local time and this method relies on the platform C `mktime()` function to perform the conversion. Since *datetime* supports wider range of values than `mktime()` on many platforms, this method may raise *OverflowError* for times far in the past or far in the future.

For aware *datetime* instances, the return value is computed as:

```
(dt - datetime(1970, 1, 1, tzinfo=timezone.utc)).total_seconds()
```

New in version 3.3.

Changed in version 3.6: The *timestamp()* method uses the *fold* attribute to disambiguate the times during a repeated interval.

Note: There is no method to obtain the POSIX timestamp directly from a naive *datetime* instance representing UTC time. If your application uses this convention and your system timezone is not set to UTC, you can obtain the POSIX timestamp by supplying `tzinfo=timezone.utc`:

```
timestamp = dt.replace(tzinfo=timezone.utc).timestamp()
```

or by calculating the timestamp directly:

```
timestamp = (dt - datetime(1970, 1, 1)) / timedelta(seconds=1)
```

`datetime.weekday()`

Return the day of the week as an integer, where Monday is 0 and Sunday is 6. The same as `self.date().weekday()`. See also *isoweekday()*.

`datetime.isoweekday()`

Return the day of the week as an integer, where Monday is 1 and Sunday is 7. The same as `self.date().isoweekday()`. See also *weekday()*, *isocalendar()*.

`datetime.isocalendar()`

Return a 3-tuple, (ISO year, ISO week number, ISO weekday). The same as `self.date().isocalendar()`.

`datetime.isoformat(sep='T', timespec='auto')`

Return a string representing the date and time in ISO 8601 format, YYYY-MM-DDTHH:MM:SS.mmmmmm or, if *microsecond* is 0, YYYY-MM-DDTHH:MM:SS

If *utcoffset()* does not return `None`, a 6-character string is appended, giving the UTC offset in (signed) hours and minutes: YYYY-MM-DDTHH:MM:SS.mmmmmm+HH:MM or, if *microsecond* is 0 YYYY-MM-DDTHH:MM:SS+HH:MM

The optional argument *sep* (default `'T'`) is a one-character separator, placed between the date and time portions of the result. For example,

```
>>> from datetime import tzinfo, timedelta, datetime
>>> class TZ(tzinfo):
...     def utcoffset(self, dt): return timedelta(minutes=-399)
...
>>> datetime(2002, 12, 25, tzinfo=TZ()).isoformat(' ')
'2002-12-25 00:00:00-06:39'
```

The optional argument *timespec* specifies the number of additional components of the time to include (the default is `'auto'`). It can be one of the following:

- `'auto'`: Same as `'seconds'` if *microsecond* is 0, same as `'microseconds'` otherwise.
- `'hours'`: Include the *hour* in the two-digit HH format.
- `'minutes'`: Include *hour* and *minute* in HH:MM format.
- `'seconds'`: Include *hour*, *minute*, and *second* in HH:MM:SS format.
- `'milliseconds'`: Include full time, but truncate fractional second part to milliseconds. HH:MM:SS.sss format.
- `'microseconds'`: Include full time in HH:MM:SS.mmmmmm format.

Note: Excluded time components are truncated, not rounded.

ValueError will be raised on an invalid *timespec* argument.

```
>>> from datetime import datetime
>>> datetime.now().isoformat(timespec='minutes')
'2002-12-25T00:00'
>>> dt = datetime(2015, 1, 1, 12, 30, 59, 0)
>>> dt.isoformat(timespec='microseconds')
'2015-01-01T12:30:59.000000'
```

New in version 3.6: Added the *timespec* argument.

`datetime.__str__()`
For a *datetime* instance *d*, `str(d)` is equivalent to `d.isoformat(' ')`.

`datetime.ctime()`
Return a string representing the date and time, for example `datetime(2002, 12, 4, 20, 30, 40).ctime() == 'Wed Dec 4 20:30:40 2002'`. `d.ctime()` is equivalent to `time.ctime(time.mktime(d.timetuple()))` on platforms where the native C `ctime()` function (which *time.ctime()* invokes, but which *datetime.ctime()* does not invoke) conforms to the C standard.

`datetime.strftime(`*format*`)`
Return a string representing the date and time, controlled by an explicit format string. For a complete list of formatting directives, see *strftime() and strptime() Behavior*.

`datetime.__format__(`*format*`)`
Same as *datetime.strftime()*. This makes it possible to specify a format string for a *datetime* object in formatted string literals and when using *str.format()*. For a complete list of formatting directives, see *strftime() and strptime() Behavior*.

Examples of working with datetime objects:

```
>>> from datetime import datetime, date, time
>>> # Using datetime.combine()
>>> d = date(2005, 7, 14)
>>> t = time(12, 30)
>>> datetime.combine(d, t)
datetime.datetime(2005, 7, 14, 12, 30)
>>> # Using datetime.now() or datetime.utcnow()
>>> datetime.now()
datetime.datetime(2007, 12, 6, 16, 29, 43, 79043)   # GMT +1
>>> datetime.utcnow()
datetime.datetime(2007, 12, 6, 15, 29, 43, 79060)
>>> # Using datetime.strptime()
```

```
>>> dt = datetime.strptime("21/11/06 16:30", "%d/%m/%y %H:%M")
>>> dt
datetime.datetime(2006, 11, 21, 16, 30)
>>> # Using datetime.timetuple() to get tuple of all attributes
>>> tt = dt.timetuple()
>>> for it in tt:
...     print(it)
...
2006    # year
11      # month
21      # day
16      # hour
30      # minute
0       # second
1       # weekday (0 = Monday)
325     # number of days since 1st January
-1      # dst - method tzinfo.dst() returned None
>>> # Date in ISO format
>>> ic = dt.isocalendar()
>>> for it in ic:
...     print(it)
...
2006    # ISO year
47      # ISO week
2       # ISO weekday
>>> # Formatting datetime
>>> dt.strftime("%A, %d. %B %Y %I:%M%p")
'Tuesday, 21. November 2006 04:30PM'
>>> 'The {1} is {0:%d}, the {2} is {0:%B}, the {3} is {0:%I:%M%p}.'.format(dt, "day", "month",
↪"time")
'The day is 21, the month is November, the time is 04:30PM.'
```

Using datetime with tzinfo:

```
>>> from datetime import timedelta, datetime, tzinfo
>>> class GMT1(tzinfo):
...     def utcoffset(self, dt):
...         return timedelta(hours=1) + self.dst(dt)
...     def dst(self, dt):
...         # DST starts last Sunday in March
...         d = datetime(dt.year, 4, 1)   # ends last Sunday in October
...         self.dston = d - timedelta(days=d.weekday() + 1)
...         d = datetime(dt.year, 11, 1)
...         self.dstoff = d - timedelta(days=d.weekday() + 1)
...         if self.dston <=  dt.replace(tzinfo=None) < self.dstoff:
...             return timedelta(hours=1)
...         else:
...             return timedelta(0)
...     def tzname(self,dt):
...          return "GMT +1"
...
>>> class GMT2(tzinfo):
...     def utcoffset(self, dt):
...         return timedelta(hours=2) + self.dst(dt)
...     def dst(self, dt):
...         d = datetime(dt.year, 4, 1)
...         self.dston = d - timedelta(days=d.weekday() + 1)
...         d = datetime(dt.year, 11, 1)
```

```
...         self.dstoff = d - timedelta(days=d.weekday() + 1)
...         if self.dston <=  dt.replace(tzinfo=None) < self.dstoff:
...             return timedelta(hours=1)
...         else:
...             return timedelta(0)
...     def tzname(self,dt):
...         return "GMT +2"
...
>>> gmt1 = GMT1()
>>> # Daylight Saving Time
>>> dt1 = datetime(2006, 11, 21, 16, 30, tzinfo=gmt1)
>>> dt1.dst()
datetime.timedelta(0)
>>> dt1.utcoffset()
datetime.timedelta(0, 3600)
>>> dt2 = datetime(2006, 6, 14, 13, 0, tzinfo=gmt1)
>>> dt2.dst()
datetime.timedelta(0, 3600)
>>> dt2.utcoffset()
datetime.timedelta(0, 7200)
>>> # Convert datetime to another time zone
>>> dt3 = dt2.astimezone(GMT2())
>>> dt3
datetime.datetime(2006, 6, 14, 14, 0, tzinfo=<GMT2 object at 0x...>)
>>> dt2
datetime.datetime(2006, 6, 14, 13, 0, tzinfo=<GMT1 object at 0x...>)
>>> dt2.utctimetuple() == dt3.utctimetuple()
True
```

8.1.5 `time` Objects

A time object represents a (local) time of day, independent of any particular day, and subject to adjustment via a *tzinfo* object.

class `datetime.time`(*hour=0, minute=0, second=0, microsecond=0, tzinfo=None, *, fold=0*)

All arguments are optional. *tzinfo* may be `None`, or an instance of a *tzinfo* subclass. The remaining arguments may be integers, in the following ranges:

- `0 <= hour < 24`,
- `0 <= minute < 60`,
- `0 <= second < 60`,
- `0 <= microsecond < 1000000`,
- `fold in [0, 1]`.

If an argument outside those ranges is given, *ValueError* is raised. All default to `0` except *tzinfo*, which defaults to *None*.

Class attributes:

`time.min`

The earliest representable *time*, `time(0, 0, 0, 0)`.

`time.max`

The latest representable *time*, `time(23, 59, 59, 999999)`.

time.resolution
The smallest possible difference between non-equal *time* objects, `timedelta(microseconds=1)`, although note that arithmetic on *time* objects is not supported.

Instance attributes (read-only):

time.hour
In `range(24)`.

time.minute
In `range(60)`.

time.second
In `range(60)`.

time.microsecond
In `range(1000000)`.

time.tzinfo
The object passed as the tzinfo argument to the *time* constructor, or `None` if none was passed.

time.fold
In `[0, 1]`. Used to disambiguate wall times during a repeated interval. (A repeated interval occurs when clocks are rolled back at the end of daylight saving time or when the UTC offset for the current zone is decreased for political reasons.) The value 0 (1) represents the earlier (later) of the two moments with the same wall time representation.

New in version 3.6.

Supported operations:

- comparison of *time* to *time*, where *a* is considered less than *b* when *a* precedes *b* in time. If one comparand is naive and the other is aware, *TypeError* is raised if an order comparison is attempted. For equality comparisons, naive instances are never equal to aware instances.

  If both comparands are aware, and have the same *tzinfo* attribute, the common *tzinfo* attribute is ignored and the base times are compared. If both comparands are aware and have different *tzinfo* attributes, the comparands are first adjusted by subtracting their UTC offsets (obtained from `self.utcoffset()`). In order to stop mixed-type comparisons from falling back to the default comparison by object address, when a *time* object is compared to an object of a different type, *TypeError* is raised unless the comparison is `==` or `!=`. The latter cases return *False* or *True*, respectively.

  Changed in version 3.3: Equality comparisons between naive and aware *time* instances don't raise *TypeError*.

- hash, use as dict key
- efficient pickling

In boolean contexts, a *time* object is always considered to be true.

Changed in version 3.5: Before Python 3.5, a *time* object was considered to be false if it represented midnight in UTC. This behavior was considered obscure and error-prone and has been removed in Python 3.5. See bpo-13936 for full details.

Instance methods:

time.replace(*hour=self.hour, minute=self.minute, second=self.second, microsecond=self.microsecond, tzinfo=self.tzinfo, * fold=0*)
Return a *time* with the same value, except for those attributes given new values by whichever keyword arguments are specified. Note that `tzinfo=None` can be specified to create a naive *time* from an aware *time*, without conversion of the time data.

New in version 3.6: Added the `fold` argument.

`time.isoformat(timespec='auto')`
Return a string representing the time in ISO 8601 format, HH:MM:SS.mmmmmm or, if *microsecond* is 0, HH:MM:SS If *utcoffset()* does not return None, a 6-character string is appended, giving the UTC offset in (signed) hours and minutes: HH:MM:SS.mmmmmm+HH:MM or, if self.microsecond is 0, HH:MM:SS+HH:MM

The optional argument *timespec* specifies the number of additional components of the time to include (the default is `'auto'`). It can be one of the following:

- `'auto'`: Same as `'seconds'` if *microsecond* is 0, same as `'microseconds'` otherwise.
- `'hours'`: Include the *hour* in the two-digit HH format.
- `'minutes'`: Include *hour* and *minute* in HH:MM format.
- `'seconds'`: Include *hour*, *minute*, and *second* in HH:MM:SS format.
- `'milliseconds'`: Include full time, but truncate fractional second part to milliseconds. HH:MM:SS.sss format.
- `'microseconds'`: Include full time in HH:MM:SS.mmmmmm format.

Note: Excluded time components are truncated, not rounded.

ValueError will be raised on an invalid *timespec* argument.

```
>>> from datetime import time
>>> time(hour=12, minute=34, second=56, microsecond=123456).isoformat(timespec='minutes')
'12:34'
>>> dt = time(hour=12, minute=34, second=56, microsecond=0)
>>> dt.isoformat(timespec='microseconds')
'12:34:56.000000'
>>> dt.isoformat(timespec='auto')
'12:34:56'
```

New in version 3.6: Added the *timespec* argument.

`time.__str__()`
For a time *t*, `str(t)` is equivalent to `t.isoformat()`.

`time.strftime(format)`
Return a string representing the time, controlled by an explicit format string. For a complete list of formatting directives, see *strftime() and strptime() Behavior*.

`time.__format__(format)`
Same as *time.strftime()*. This makes it possible to specify a format string for a *time* object in formatted string literals and when using *str.format()*. For a complete list of formatting directives, see *strftime() and strptime() Behavior*.

`time.utcoffset()`
If *tzinfo* is None, returns None, else returns `self.tzinfo.utcoffset(None)`, and raises an exception if the latter doesn't return None or a *timedelta* object representing a whole number of minutes with magnitude less than one day.

`time.dst()`
If *tzinfo* is None, returns None, else returns `self.tzinfo.dst(None)`, and raises an exception if the latter doesn't return None, or a *timedelta* object representing a whole number of minutes with magnitude less than one day.

`time.tzname()`
If *tzinfo* is None, returns None, else returns `self.tzinfo.tzname(None)`, or raises an exception if the latter doesn't return None or a string object.

Example:

```
>>> from datetime import time, tzinfo, timedelta
>>> class GMT1(tzinfo):
...     def utcoffset(self, dt):
...         return timedelta(hours=1)
...     def dst(self, dt):
...         return timedelta(0)
...     def tzname(self,dt):
...         return "Europe/Prague"
...
>>> t = time(12, 10, 30, tzinfo=GMT1())
>>> t
datetime.time(12, 10, 30, tzinfo=<GMT1 object at 0x...>)
>>> gmt = GMT1()
>>> t.isoformat()
'12:10:30+01:00'
>>> t.dst()
datetime.timedelta(0)
>>> t.tzname()
'Europe/Prague'
>>> t.strftime("%H:%M:%S %Z")
'12:10:30 Europe/Prague'
>>> 'The {} is {:%H:%M}.'.format("time", t)
'The time is 12:10.'
```

8.1.6 `tzinfo` Objects

class datetime.tzinfo

This is an abstract base class, meaning that this class should not be instantiated directly. You need to derive a concrete subclass, and (at least) supply implementations of the standard *tzinfo* methods needed by the *datetime* methods you use. The *datetime* module supplies a simple concrete subclass of *tzinfo*, *timezone*, which can represent timezones with fixed offset from UTC such as UTC itself or North American EST and EDT.

An instance of (a concrete subclass of) *tzinfo* can be passed to the constructors for *datetime* and *time* objects. The latter objects view their attributes as being in local time, and the *tzinfo* object supports methods revealing offset of local time from UTC, the name of the time zone, and DST offset, all relative to a date or time object passed to them.

Special requirement for pickling: A *tzinfo* subclass must have an `__init__()` method that can be called with no arguments, else it can be pickled but possibly not unpickled again. This is a technical requirement that may be relaxed in the future.

A concrete subclass of *tzinfo* may need to implement the following methods. Exactly which methods are needed depends on the uses made of aware *datetime* objects. If in doubt, simply implement all of them.

tzinfo.utcoffset(*dt*)

Return offset of local time from UTC, in minutes east of UTC. If local time is west of UTC, this should be negative. Note that this is intended to be the total offset from UTC; for example, if a *tzinfo* object represents both time zone and DST adjustments, *utcoffset()* should return their sum. If the UTC offset isn't known, return `None`. Else the value returned must be a *timedelta* object specifying a whole number of minutes in the range -1439 to 1439 inclusive (1440 = 24*60; the magnitude of the offset must be less than one day). Most implementations of *utcoffset()* will probably look like one of these two:

```
return CONSTANT                 # fixed-offset class
return CONSTANT + self.dst(dt)  # daylight-aware class
```

If `utcoffset()` does not return `None`, `dst()` should not return `None` either.

The default implementation of `utcoffset()` raises `NotImplementedError`.

tzinfo.dst(*dt*)

Return the daylight saving time (DST) adjustment, in minutes east of UTC, or `None` if DST information isn't known. Return `timedelta(0)` if DST is not in effect. If DST is in effect, return the offset as a `timedelta` object (see `utcoffset()` for details). Note that DST offset, if applicable, has already been added to the UTC offset returned by `utcoffset()`, so there's no need to consult `dst()` unless you're interested in obtaining DST info separately. For example, `datetime.timetuple()` calls its `tzinfo` attribute's `dst()` method to determine how the `tm_isdst` flag should be set, and `tzinfo.fromutc()` calls `dst()` to account for DST changes when crossing time zones.

An instance *tz* of a `tzinfo` subclass that models both standard and daylight times must be consistent in this sense:

`tz.utcoffset(dt) - tz.dst(dt)`

must return the same result for every `datetime` *dt* with `dt.tzinfo == tz` For sane `tzinfo` subclasses, this expression yields the time zone's "standard offset", which should not depend on the date or the time, but only on geographic location. The implementation of `datetime.astimezone()` relies on this, but cannot detect violations; it's the programmer's responsibility to ensure it. If a `tzinfo` subclass cannot guarantee this, it may be able to override the default implementation of `tzinfo.fromutc()` to work correctly with `astimezone()` regardless.

Most implementations of `dst()` will probably look like one of these two:

```
def dst(self, dt):
    # a fixed-offset class:  doesn't account for DST
    return timedelta(0)
```

or

```
def dst(self, dt):
    # Code to set dston and dstoff to the time zone's DST
    # transition times based on the input dt.year, and expressed
    # in standard local time.  Then

    if dston <= dt.replace(tzinfo=None) < dstoff:
        return timedelta(hours=1)
    else:
        return timedelta(0)
```

The default implementation of `dst()` raises `NotImplementedError`.

tzinfo.tzname(*dt*)

Return the time zone name corresponding to the `datetime` object *dt*, as a string. Nothing about string names is defined by the `datetime` module, and there's no requirement that it mean anything in particular. For example, "GMT", "UTC", "-500", "-5:00", "EDT", "US/Eastern", "America/New York" are all valid replies. Return `None` if a string name isn't known. Note that this is a method rather than a fixed string primarily because some `tzinfo` subclasses will wish to return different names depending on the specific value of *dt* passed, especially if the `tzinfo` class is accounting for daylight time.

The default implementation of `tzname()` raises `NotImplementedError`.

These methods are called by a *datetime* or *time* object, in response to their methods of the same names. A *datetime* object passes itself as the argument, and a *time* object passes `None` as the argument. A *tzinfo* subclass's methods should therefore be prepared to accept a *dt* argument of `None`, or of class *datetime*.

When `None` is passed, it's up to the class designer to decide the best response. For example, returning `None` is appropriate if the class wishes to say that time objects don't participate in the *tzinfo* protocols. It may be more useful for `utcoffset(None)` to return the standard UTC offset, as there is no other convention for discovering the standard offset.

When a *datetime* object is passed in response to a *datetime* method, `dt.tzinfo` is the same object as *self*. *tzinfo* methods can rely on this, unless user code calls *tzinfo* methods directly. The intent is that the *tzinfo* methods interpret *dt* as being in local time, and not need worry about objects in other timezones.

There is one more *tzinfo* method that a subclass may wish to override:

tzinfo.fromutc(*dt*)

This is called from the default *datetime.astimezone()* implementation. When called from that, `dt.tzinfo` is *self*, and *dt*'s date and time data are to be viewed as expressing a UTC time. The purpose of *fromutc()* is to adjust the date and time data, returning an equivalent datetime in *self*'s local time.

Most *tzinfo* subclasses should be able to inherit the default *fromutc()* implementation without problems. It's strong enough to handle fixed-offset time zones, and time zones accounting for both standard and daylight time, and the latter even if the DST transition times differ in different years. An example of a time zone the default *fromutc()* implementation may not handle correctly in all cases is one where the standard offset (from UTC) depends on the specific date and time passed, which can happen for political reasons. The default implementations of `astimezone()` and *fromutc()* may not produce the result you want if the result is one of the hours straddling the moment the standard offset changes.

Skipping code for error cases, the default *fromutc()* implementation acts like:

```
def fromutc(self, dt):
    # raise ValueError error if dt.tzinfo is not self
    dtoff = dt.utcoffset()
    dtdst = dt.dst()
    # raise ValueError if dtoff is None or dtdst is None
    delta = dtoff - dtdst  # this is self's standard offset
    if delta:
        dt += delta   # convert to standard local time
        dtdst = dt.dst()
        # raise ValueError if dtdst is None
    if dtdst:
        return dt + dtdst
    else:
        return dt
```

Example *tzinfo* classes:

```
from datetime import tzinfo, timedelta, datetime, timezone

ZERO = timedelta(0)
HOUR = timedelta(hours=1)
SECOND = timedelta(seconds=1)

# A class capturing the platform's idea of local time.
# (May result in wrong values on historical times in
#  timezones where UTC offset and/or the DST rules had
#  changed in the past.)
import time as _time
```

```
STDOFFSET = timedelta(seconds = -_time.timezone)
if _time.daylight:
    DSTOFFSET = timedelta(seconds = -_time.altzone)
else:
    DSTOFFSET = STDOFFSET

DSTDIFF = DSTOFFSET - STDOFFSET

class LocalTimezone(tzinfo):

    def fromutc(self, dt):
        assert dt.tzinfo is self
        stamp = (dt - datetime(1970, 1, 1, tzinfo=self)) // SECOND
        args = _time.localtime(stamp)[:6]
        dst_diff = DSTDIFF // SECOND
        # Detect fold
        fold = (args == _time.localtime(stamp - dst_diff))
        return datetime(*args, microsecond=dt.microsecond,
                        tzinfo=self, fold=fold)

    def utcoffset(self, dt):
        if self._isdst(dt):
            return DSTOFFSET
        else:
            return STDOFFSET

    def dst(self, dt):
        if self._isdst(dt):
            return DSTDIFF
        else:
            return ZERO

    def tzname(self, dt):
        return _time.tzname[self._isdst(dt)]

    def _isdst(self, dt):
        tt = (dt.year, dt.month, dt.day,
              dt.hour, dt.minute, dt.second,
              dt.weekday(), 0, 0)
        stamp = _time.mktime(tt)
        tt = _time.localtime(stamp)
        return tt.tm_isdst > 0

Local = LocalTimezone()


# A complete implementation of current DST rules for major US time zones.

def first_sunday_on_or_after(dt):
    days_to_go = 6 - dt.weekday()
    if days_to_go:
        dt += timedelta(days_to_go)
    return dt


# US DST Rules
#
# This is a simplified (i.e., wrong for a few cases) set of rules for US
```

```
# DST start and end times. For a complete and up-to-date set of DST rules
# and timezone definitions, visit the Olson Database (or try pytz):
# http://www.twinsun.com/tz/tz-link.htm
# http://sourceforge.net/projects/pytz/ (might not be up-to-date)
#
# In the US, since 2007, DST starts at 2am (standard time) on the second
# Sunday in March, which is the first Sunday on or after Mar 8.
DSTSTART_2007 = datetime(1, 3, 8, 2)
# and ends at 2am (DST time) on the first Sunday of Nov.
DSTEND_2007 = datetime(1, 11, 1, 2)
# From 1987 to 2006, DST used to start at 2am (standard time) on the first
# Sunday in April and to end at 2am (DST time) on the last
# Sunday of October, which is the first Sunday on or after Oct 25.
DSTSTART_1987_2006 = datetime(1, 4, 1, 2)
DSTEND_1987_2006 = datetime(1, 10, 25, 2)
# From 1967 to 1986, DST used to start at 2am (standard time) on the last
# Sunday in April (the one on or after April 24) and to end at 2am (DST time)
# on the last Sunday of October, which is the first Sunday
# on or after Oct 25.
DSTSTART_1967_1986 = datetime(1, 4, 24, 2)
DSTEND_1967_1986 = DSTEND_1987_2006

def us_dst_range(year):
    # Find start and end times for US DST. For years before 1967, return
    # start = end for no DST.
    if 2006 < year:
        dststart, dstend = DSTSTART_2007, DSTEND_2007
    elif 1986 < year < 2007:
        dststart, dstend = DSTSTART_1987_2006, DSTEND_1987_2006
    elif 1966 < year < 1987:
        dststart, dstend = DSTSTART_1967_1986, DSTEND_1967_1986
    else:
        return (datetime(year, 1, 1), ) * 2

    start = first_sunday_on_or_after(dststart.replace(year=year))
    end = first_sunday_on_or_after(dstend.replace(year=year))
    return start, end


class USTimeZone(tzinfo):

    def __init__(self, hours, reprname, stdname, dstname):
        self.stdoffset = timedelta(hours=hours)
        self.reprname = reprname
        self.stdname = stdname
        self.dstname = dstname

    def __repr__(self):
        return self.reprname

    def tzname(self, dt):
        if self.dst(dt):
            return self.dstname
        else:
            return self.stdname

    def utcoffset(self, dt):
        return self.stdoffset + self.dst(dt)
```

```
    def dst(self, dt):
        if dt is None or dt.tzinfo is None:
            # An exception may be sensible here, in one or both cases.
            # It depends on how you want to treat them.  The default
            # fromutc() implementation (called by the default astimezone()
            # implementation) passes a datetime with dt.tzinfo is self.
            return ZERO
        assert dt.tzinfo is self
        start, end = us_dst_range(dt.year)
        # Can't compare naive to aware objects, so strip the timezone from
        # dt first.
        dt = dt.replace(tzinfo=None)
        if start + HOUR <= dt < end - HOUR:
            # DST is in effect.
            return HOUR
        if end - HOUR <= dt < end:
            # Fold (an ambiguous hour): use dt.fold to disambiguate.
            return ZERO if dt.fold else HOUR
        if start <= dt < start + HOUR:
            # Gap (a non-existent hour): reverse the fold rule.
            return HOUR if dt.fold else ZERO
        # DST is off.
        return ZERO

    def fromutc(self, dt):
        assert dt.tzinfo is self
        start, end = us_dst_range(dt.year)
        start = start.replace(tzinfo=self)
        end = end.replace(tzinfo=self)
        std_time = dt + self.stdoffset
        dst_time = std_time + HOUR
        if end <= dst_time < end + HOUR:
            # Repeated hour
            return std_time.replace(fold=1)
        if std_time < start or dst_time >= end:
            # Standard time
            return std_time
        if start <= std_time < end - HOUR:
            # Daylight saving time
            return dst_time


Eastern  = USTimeZone(-5, "Eastern",  "EST", "EDT")
Central  = USTimeZone(-6, "Central",  "CST", "CDT")
Mountain = USTimeZone(-7, "Mountain", "MST", "MDT")
Pacific  = USTimeZone(-8, "Pacific",  "PST", "PDT")
```

Note that there are unavoidable subtleties twice per year in a *tzinfo* subclass accounting for both standard and daylight time, at the DST transition points. For concreteness, consider US Eastern (UTC -0500), where EDT begins the minute after 1:59 (EST) on the second Sunday in March, and ends the minute after 1:59 (EDT) on the first Sunday in November:

```
  UTC   3:MM  4:MM  5:MM  6:MM  7:MM  8:MM
  EST  22:MM 23:MM  0:MM  1:MM  2:MM  3:MM
  EDT  23:MM  0:MM  1:MM  2:MM  3:MM  4:MM

start  22:MM 23:MM  0:MM  1:MM  3:MM  4:MM
```

```
end  23:MM  0:MM  1:MM  1:MM  2:MM  3:MM
```

When DST starts (the "start" line), the local wall clock leaps from 1:59 to 3:00. A wall time of the form 2:MM doesn't really make sense on that day, so `astimezone(Eastern)` won't deliver a result with `hour == 2` on the day DST begins. For example, at the Spring forward transition of 2016, we get

```
>>> u0 = datetime(2016, 3, 13, 5, tzinfo=timezone.utc)
>>> for i in range(4):
...     u = u0 + i*HOUR
...     t = u.astimezone(Eastern)
...     print(u.time(), 'UTC =', t.time(), t.tzname())
...
05:00:00 UTC = 00:00:00 EST
06:00:00 UTC = 01:00:00 EST
07:00:00 UTC = 03:00:00 EDT
08:00:00 UTC = 04:00:00 EDT
```

When DST ends (the "end" line), there's a potentially worse problem: there's an hour that can't be spelled unambiguously in local wall time: the last hour of daylight time. In Eastern, that's times of the form 5:MM UTC on the day daylight time ends. The local wall clock leaps from 1:59 (daylight time) back to 1:00 (standard time) again. Local times of the form 1:MM are ambiguous. `astimezone()` mimics the local clock's behavior by mapping two adjacent UTC hours into the same local hour then. In the Eastern example, UTC times of the form 5:MM and 6:MM both map to 1:MM when converted to Eastern, but earlier times have the *fold* attribute set to 0 and the later times have it set to 1. For example, at the Fall back transition of 2016, we get

```
>>> u0 = datetime(2016, 11, 6, 4, tzinfo=timezone.utc)
>>> for i in range(4):
...     u = u0 + i*HOUR
...     t = u.astimezone(Eastern)
...     print(u.time(), 'UTC =', t.time(), t.tzname(), t.fold)
...
04:00:00 UTC = 00:00:00 EDT 0
05:00:00 UTC = 01:00:00 EDT 0
06:00:00 UTC = 01:00:00 EST 1
07:00:00 UTC = 02:00:00 EST 0
```

Note that the *datetime* instances that differ only by the value of the *fold* attribute are considered equal in comparisons.

Applications that can't bear wall-time ambiguities should explicitly check the value of the *fold* attribute or avoid using hybrid *tzinfo* subclasses; there are no ambiguities when using *timezone*, or any other fixed-offset *tzinfo* subclass (such as a class representing only EST (fixed offset -5 hours), or only EDT (fixed offset -4 hours)).

See also:

dateutil.tz The standard library has *timezone* class for handling arbitrary fixed offsets from UTC and *timezone.utc* as UTC timezone instance.

dateutil.tz library brings the *IANA timezone database* (also known as the Olson database) to Python and its usage is recommended.

IANA timezone database The Time Zone Database (often called tz, tzdata or zoneinfo) contains code and data that represent the history of local time for many representative locations around the globe. It is updated periodically to reflect changes made by political bodies to time zone boundaries, UTC offsets, and daylight-saving rules.

8.1.7 timezone Objects

The *timezone* class is a subclass of *tzinfo*, each instance of which represents a timezone defined by a fixed offset from UTC. Note that objects of this class cannot be used to represent timezone information in the locations where different offsets are used in different days of the year or where historical changes have been made to civil time.

class datetime.timezone(*offset*, *name=None*)

The *offset* argument must be specified as a *timedelta* object representing the difference between the local time and UTC. It must be strictly between `-timedelta(hours=24)` and `timedelta(hours=24)` and represent a whole number of minutes, otherwise *ValueError* is raised.

The *name* argument is optional. If specified it must be a string that will be used as the value returned by the *datetime.tzname()* method.

New in version 3.2.

timezone.utcoffset(*dt*)

Return the fixed value specified when the *timezone* instance is constructed. The *dt* argument is ignored. The return value is a *timedelta* instance equal to the difference between the local time and UTC.

timezone.tzname(*dt*)

Return the fixed value specified when the *timezone* instance is constructed. If *name* is not provided in the constructor, the name returned by `tzname(dt)` is generated from the value of the `offset` as follows. If *offset* is `timedelta(0)`, the name is "UTC", otherwise it is a string 'UTC±HH:MM', where ± is the sign of `offset`, HH and MM are two digits of `offset.hours` and `offset.minutes` respectively.

Changed in version 3.6: Name generated from `offset=timedelta(0)` is now plain 'UTC', not 'UTC+00:00'.

timezone.dst(*dt*)

Always returns `None`.

timezone.fromutc(*dt*)

Return `dt + offset`. The *dt* argument must be an aware *datetime* instance, with `tzinfo` set to `self`.

Class attributes:

timezone.utc

The UTC timezone, `timezone(timedelta(0))`.

8.1.8 strftime() and strptime() Behavior

date, *datetime*, and *time* objects all support a `strftime(format)` method, to create a string representing the time under the control of an explicit format string. Broadly speaking, `d.strftime(fmt)` acts like the *time* module's `time.strftime(fmt, d.timetuple())` although not all objects support a `timetuple()` method.

Conversely, the *datetime.strptime()* class method creates a *datetime* object from a string representing a date and time and a corresponding format string. `datetime.strptime(date_string, format)` is equivalent to `datetime(*(time.strptime(date_string, format)[0:6]))`.

For *time* objects, the format codes for year, month, and day should not be used, as time objects have no such values. If they're used anyway, `1900` is substituted for the year, and `1` for the month and day.

For *date* objects, the format codes for hours, minutes, seconds, and microseconds should not be used, as *date* objects have no such values. If they're used anyway, `0` is substituted for them.

The full set of format codes supported varies across platforms, because Python calls the platform C library's `strftime()` function, and platform variations are common. To see the full set of format codes supported on your platform, consult the *strftime(3)* documentation.

The following is a list of all the format codes that the C standard (1989 version) requires, and these work on all platforms with a standard C implementation. Note that the 1999 version of the C standard added additional format codes.

Directive	Meaning	Example	Notes
%a	Weekday as locale's abbreviated name.	Sun, Mon, ..., Sat (en_US); So, Mo, ..., Sa (de_DE)	(1)
%A	Weekday as locale's full name.	Sunday, Monday, ..., Saturday (en_US); Sonntag, Montag, ..., Samstag (de_DE)	(1)
%w	Weekday as a decimal number, where 0 is Sunday and 6 is Saturday.	0, 1, ..., 6	
%d	Day of the month as a zero-padded decimal number.	01, 02, ..., 31	
%b	Month as locale's abbreviated name.	Jan, Feb, ..., Dec (en_US); Jan, Feb, ..., Dez (de_DE)	(1)
%B	Month as locale's full name.	January, February, ..., December (en_US); Januar, Februar, ..., Dezember (de_DE)	(1)
%m	Month as a zero-padded decimal number.	01, 02, ..., 12	
%y	Year without century as a zero-padded decimal number.	00, 01, ..., 99	
%Y	Year with century as a decimal number.	0001, 0002, ..., 2013, 2014, ..., 9998, 9999	(2)
%H	Hour (24-hour clock) as a zero-padded decimal number.	00, 01, ..., 23	
%I	Hour (12-hour clock) as a zero-padded decimal number.	01, 02, ..., 12	
%p	Locale's equivalent of either AM or PM.	AM, PM (en_US); am, pm (de_DE)	(1), (3)
%M	Minute as a zero-padded decimal number.	00, 01, ..., 59	
%S	Second as a zero-padded decimal number.	00, 01, ..., 59	(4)
%f	Microsecond as a decimal number, zero-padded on the left.	000000, 000001, ..., 999999	(5)

Several additional directives not required by the C89 standard are included for convenience. These parameters all correspond to ISO 8601 date values. These may not be available on all platforms when used with the `strftime()` method. The ISO 8601 year and ISO 8601 week directives are not interchangeable with the year and week number directives above. Calling `strptime()` with incomplete or ambiguous ISO 8601 directives will raise a *ValueError*.

Directive	Meaning	Example	Notes
`%G`	ISO 8601 year with century representing the year that contains the greater part of the ISO week (`%V`).	0001, 0002, ..., 2013, 2014, ..., 9998, 9999	(8)
`%u`	ISO 8601 weekday as a decimal number where 1 is Monday.	1, 2, ..., 7	
`%V`	ISO 8601 week as a decimal number with Monday as the first day of the week. Week 01 is the week containing Jan 4.	01, 02, ..., 53	(8)

New in version 3.6: `%G`, `%u` and `%V` were added.

Notes:

1. Because the format depends on the current locale, care should be taken when making assumptions about the output value. Field orderings will vary (for example, "month/day/year" versus "day/month/year"), and the output may contain Unicode characters encoded using the locale's default encoding (for example, if the current locale is `ja_JP`, the default encoding could be any one of `eucJP`, `SJIS`, or `utf-8`; use *locale.getlocale()* to determine the current locale's encoding).

2. The `strptime()` method can parse years in the full [1, 9999] range, but years < 1000 must be zero-filled to 4-digit width.

   Changed in version 3.2: In previous versions, `strftime()` method was restricted to years >= 1900.

   Changed in version 3.3: In version 3.2, `strftime()` method was restricted to years >= 1000.

3. When used with the `strptime()` method, the `%p` directive only affects the output hour field if the `%I` directive is used to parse the hour.

4. Unlike the *time* module, the *datetime* module does not support leap seconds.

5. When used with the `strptime()` method, the `%f` directive accepts from one to six digits and zero pads on the right. `%f` is an extension to the set of format characters in the C standard (but implemented separately in datetime objects, and therefore always available).

6. For a naive object, the `%z` and `%Z` format codes are replaced by empty strings.

   For an aware object:

   `%z` `utcoffset()` is transformed into a 5-character string of the form +HHMM or -HHMM, where HH is a 2-digit string giving the number of UTC offset hours, and MM is a 2-digit string giving the number of UTC offset minutes. For example, if `utcoffset()` returns `timedelta(hours=-3, minutes=-30)`, `%z` is replaced with the string `'-0330'`.

   `%Z` If `tzname()` returns `None`, `%Z` is replaced by an empty string. Otherwise `%Z` is replaced by the returned value, which must be a string.

   Changed in version 3.2: When the `%z` directive is provided to the `strptime()` method, an aware *datetime* object will be produced. The `tzinfo` of the result will be set to a *timezone* instance.

7. When used with the `strptime()` method, `%U` and `%W` are only used in calculations when the day of the week and the calendar year (`%Y`) are specified.

8. Similar to `%U` and `%W`, `%V` is only used in calculations when the day of the week and the ISO year (`%G`) are specified in a `strptime()` format string. Also note that `%G` and `%Y` are not interchangeable.

8.2 `calendar` — General calendar-related functions

Source code: Lib/calendar.py

This module allows you to output calendars like the Unix **`cal`** program, and provides additional useful functions related to the calendar. By default, these calendars have Monday as the first day of the week, and Sunday as the last (the European convention). Use `setfirstweekday()` to set the first day of the week to Sunday (6) or to any other weekday. Parameters that specify dates are given as integers. For related functionality, see also the `datetime` and `time` modules.

Most of these functions and classes rely on the `datetime` module which uses an idealized calendar, the current Gregorian calendar extended in both directions. This matches the definition of the "proleptic Gregorian" calendar in Dershowitz and Reingold's book "Calendrical Calculations", where it's the base calendar for all computations.

class calendar.Calendar(*firstweekday=0*)

Creates a `Calendar` object. *firstweekday* is an integer specifying the first day of the week. `0` is Monday (the default), `6` is Sunday.

A `Calendar` object provides several methods that can be used for preparing the calendar data for formatting. This class doesn't do any formatting itself. This is the job of subclasses.

`Calendar` instances have the following methods:

iterweekdays()

Return an iterator for the week day numbers that will be used for one week. The first value from the iterator will be the same as the value of the `firstweekday` property.

itermonthdates(*year, month*)

Return an iterator for the month *month* (1–12) in the year *year*. This iterator will return all days (as `datetime.date` objects) for the month and all days before the start of the month or after the end of the month that are required to get a complete week.

itermonthdays2(*year, month*)

Return an iterator for the month *month* in the year *year* similar to `itermonthdates()`. Days returned will be tuples consisting of a day number and a week day number.

itermonthdays(*year, month*)

Return an iterator for the month *month* in the year *year* similar to `itermonthdates()`. Days returned will simply be day numbers.

monthdatescalendar(*year, month*)

Return a list of the weeks in the month *month* of the *year* as full weeks. Weeks are lists of seven `datetime.date` objects.

monthdays2calendar(*year, month*)

Return a list of the weeks in the month *month* of the *year* as full weeks. Weeks are lists of seven tuples of day numbers and weekday numbers.

monthdayscalendar(*year, month*)

Return a list of the weeks in the month *month* of the *year* as full weeks. Weeks are lists of seven day numbers.

yeardatescalendar(*year, width=3*)

Return the data for the specified year ready for formatting. The return value is a list of month rows. Each month row contains up to *width* months (defaulting to 3). Each month contains between 4 and 6 weeks and each week contains 1–7 days. Days are `datetime.date` objects.

yeardays2calendar(*year*, *width=3*)
Return the data for the specified year ready for formatting (similar to *yeardatescalendar()*). Entries in the week lists are tuples of day numbers and weekday numbers. Day numbers outside this month are zero.

yeardayscalendar(*year*, *width=3*)
Return the data for the specified year ready for formatting (similar to *yeardatescalendar()*). Entries in the week lists are day numbers. Day numbers outside this month are zero.

class calendar.**TextCalendar**(*firstweekday=0*)
This class can be used to generate plain text calendars.

TextCalendar instances have the following methods:

formatmonth(*theyear*, *themonth*, *w=0*, *l=0*)
Return a month's calendar in a multi-line string. If *w* is provided, it specifies the width of the date columns, which are centered. If *l* is given, it specifies the number of lines that each week will use. Depends on the first weekday as specified in the constructor or set by the *setfirstweekday()* method.

prmonth(*theyear*, *themonth*, *w=0*, *l=0*)
Print a month's calendar as returned by *formatmonth()*.

formatyear(*theyear*, *w=2*, *l=1*, *c=6*, *m=3*)
Return a *m*-column calendar for an entire year as a multi-line string. Optional parameters *w*, *l*, and *c* are for date column width, lines per week, and number of spaces between month columns, respectively. Depends on the first weekday as specified in the constructor or set by the *setfirstweekday()* method. The earliest year for which a calendar can be generated is platform-dependent.

pryear(*theyear*, *w=2*, *l=1*, *c=6*, *m=3*)
Print the calendar for an entire year as returned by *formatyear()*.

class calendar.**HTMLCalendar**(*firstweekday=0*)
This class can be used to generate HTML calendars.

HTMLCalendar instances have the following methods:

formatmonth(*theyear*, *themonth*, *withyear=True*)
Return a month's calendar as an HTML table. If *withyear* is true the year will be included in the header, otherwise just the month name will be used.

formatyear(*theyear*, *width=3*)
Return a year's calendar as an HTML table. *width* (defaulting to 3) specifies the number of months per row.

formatyearpage(*theyear*, *width=3*, *css='calendar.css'*, *encoding=None*)
Return a year's calendar as a complete HTML page. *width* (defaulting to 3) specifies the number of months per row. *css* is the name for the cascading style sheet to be used. *None* can be passed if no style sheet should be used. *encoding* specifies the encoding to be used for the output (defaulting to the system default encoding).

class calendar.**LocaleTextCalendar**(*firstweekday=0*, *locale=None*)
This subclass of *TextCalendar* can be passed a locale name in the constructor and will return month and weekday names in the specified locale. If this locale includes an encoding all strings containing month and weekday names will be returned as unicode.

class calendar.**LocaleHTMLCalendar**(*firstweekday=0*, *locale=None*)
This subclass of *HTMLCalendar* can be passed a locale name in the constructor and will return month and weekday names in the specified locale. If this locale includes an encoding all strings containing month and weekday names will be returned as unicode.

Note: The `formatweekday()` and `formatmonthname()` methods of these two classes temporarily change the current locale to the given *locale*. Because the current locale is a process-wide setting, they are not thread-safe.

For simple text calendars this module provides the following functions.

`calendar.setfirstweekday(weekday)`
Sets the weekday (0 is Monday, 6 is Sunday) to start each week. The values MONDAY, TUESDAY, WEDNESDAY, THURSDAY, FRIDAY, SATURDAY, and SUNDAY are provided for convenience. For example, to set the first weekday to Sunday:

```
import calendar
calendar.setfirstweekday(calendar.SUNDAY)
```

`calendar.firstweekday()`
Returns the current setting for the weekday to start each week.

`calendar.isleap(year)`
Returns *True* if *year* is a leap year, otherwise *False*.

`calendar.leapdays(y1, y2)`
Returns the number of leap years in the range from *y1* to *y2* (exclusive), where *y1* and *y2* are years.

This function works for ranges spanning a century change.

`calendar.weekday(year, month, day)`
Returns the day of the week (0 is Monday) for *year* (1970–...), *month* (1–12), *day* (1–31).

`calendar.weekheader(n)`
Return a header containing abbreviated weekday names. *n* specifies the width in characters for one weekday.

`calendar.monthrange(year, month)`
Returns weekday of first day of the month and number of days in month, for the specified *year* and *month*.

`calendar.monthcalendar(year, month)`
Returns a matrix representing a month's calendar. Each row represents a week; days outside of the month a represented by zeros. Each week begins with Monday unless set by *setfirstweekday()*.

`calendar.prmonth(theyear, themonth, w=0, l=0)`
Prints a month's calendar as returned by *month()*.

`calendar.month(theyear, themonth, w=0, l=0)`
Returns a month's calendar in a multi-line string using the `formatmonth()` of the *TextCalendar* class.

`calendar.prcal(year, w=0, l=0, c=6, m=3)`
Prints the calendar for an entire year as returned by *calendar()*.

`calendar.calendar(year, w=2, l=1, c=6, m=3)`
Returns a 3-column calendar for an entire year as a multi-line string using the `formatyear()` of the *TextCalendar* class.

`calendar.timegm(tuple)`
An unrelated but handy function that takes a time tuple such as returned by the *gmtime()* function in the *time* module, and returns the corresponding Unix timestamp value, assuming an epoch of 1970, and the POSIX encoding. In fact, *time.gmtime()* and *timegm()* are each others' inverse.

The *calendar* module exports the following data attributes:

`calendar.day_name`
An array that represents the days of the week in the current locale.

`calendar.day_abbr`
An array that represents the abbreviated days of the week in the current locale.

`calendar.month_name`
An array that represents the months of the year in the current locale. This follows normal convention of January being month number 1, so it has a length of 13 and `month_name[0]` is the empty string.

`calendar.month_abbr`
An array that represents the abbreviated months of the year in the current locale. This follows normal convention of January being month number 1, so it has a length of 13 and `month_abbr[0]` is the empty string.

See also:

Module *datetime* Object-oriented interface to dates and times with similar functionality to the *time* module.

Module *time* Low-level time related functions.

8.3 `collections` — Container datatypes

Source code: Lib/collections/__init__.py

This module implements specialized container datatypes providing alternatives to Python's general purpose built-in containers, *dict*, *list*, *set*, and *tuple*.

namedtuple()	factory function for creating tuple subclasses with named fields
deque	list-like container with fast appends and pops on either end
ChainMap	dict-like class for creating a single view of multiple mappings
Counter	dict subclass for counting hashable objects
OrderedDict	dict subclass that remembers the order entries were added
defaultdict	dict subclass that calls a factory function to supply missing values
UserDict	wrapper around dictionary objects for easier dict subclassing
UserList	wrapper around list objects for easier list subclassing
UserString	wrapper around string objects for easier string subclassing

Changed in version 3.3: Moved *Collections Abstract Base Classes* to the *collections.abc* module. For backwards compatibility, they continue to be visible in this module as well.

8.3.1 `ChainMap` objects

New in version 3.3.

A *ChainMap* class is provided for quickly linking a number of mappings so they can be treated as a single unit. It is often much faster than creating a new dictionary and running multiple *update()* calls.

The class can be used to simulate nested scopes and is useful in templating.

`class collections.ChainMap(*maps)`
A *ChainMap* groups multiple dicts or other mappings together to create a single, updateable view. If no *maps* are specified, a single empty dictionary is provided so that a new chain always has at least one mapping.

The underlying mappings are stored in a list. That list is public and can be accessed or updated using the *maps* attribute. There is no other state.

Lookups search the underlying mappings successively until a key is found. In contrast, writes, updates, and deletions only operate on the first mapping.

A *ChainMap* incorporates the underlying mappings by reference. So, if one of the underlying mappings gets updated, those changes will be reflected in *ChainMap*.

All of the usual dictionary methods are supported. In addition, there is a *maps* attribute, a method for creating new subcontexts, and a property for accessing all but the first mapping:

maps
A user updateable list of mappings. The list is ordered from first-searched to last-searched. It is the only stored state and can be modified to change which mappings are searched. The list should always contain at least one mapping.

new_child(*m=None*)
Returns a new *ChainMap* containing a new map followed by all of the maps in the current instance. If `m` is specified, it becomes the new map at the front of the list of mappings; if not specified, an empty dict is used, so that a call to `d.new_child()` is equivalent to: `ChainMap({}, *d.maps)`. This method is used for creating subcontexts that can be updated without altering values in any of the parent mappings.

Changed in version 3.4: The optional `m` parameter was added.

parents
Property returning a new *ChainMap* containing all of the maps in the current instance except the first one. This is useful for skipping the first map in the search. Use cases are similar to those for the `nonlocal` keyword used in *nested scopes*. The use cases also parallel those for the built-in *super()* function. A reference to `d.parents` is equivalent to: `ChainMap(*d.maps[1:])`.

See also:

- The MultiContext class in the Enthought CodeTools package has options to support writing to any mapping in the chain.
- Django's Context class for templating is a read-only chain of mappings. It also features pushing and popping of contexts similar to the *new_child()* method and the *parents()* property.
- The Nested Contexts recipe has options to control whether writes and other mutations apply only to the first mapping or to any mapping in the chain.
- A greatly simplified read-only version of Chainmap.

ChainMap Examples and Recipes

This section shows various approaches to working with chained maps.

Example of simulating Python's internal lookup chain:

```
import builtins
pylookup = ChainMap(locals(), globals(), vars(builtins))
```

Example of letting user specified command-line arguments take precedence over environment variables which in turn take precedence over default values:

```
import os, argparse

defaults = {'color': 'red', 'user': 'guest'}

parser = argparse.ArgumentParser()
parser.add_argument('-u', '--user')
parser.add_argument('-c', '--color')
```

```
namespace = parser.parse_args()
command_line_args = {k:v for k, v in vars(namespace).items() if v}

combined = ChainMap(command_line_args, os.environ, defaults)
print(combined['color'])
print(combined['user'])
```

Example patterns for using the *ChainMap* class to simulate nested contexts:

```
c = ChainMap()          # Create root context
d = c.new_child()       # Create nested child context
e = c.new_child()       # Child of c, independent from d
e.maps[0]               # Current context dictionary -- like Python's locals()
e.maps[-1]              # Root context -- like Python's globals()
e.parents               # Enclosing context chain -- like Python's nonlocals

d['x']                  # Get first key in the chain of contexts
d['x'] = 1              # Set value in current context
del d['x']              # Delete from current context
list(d)                 # All nested values
k in d                  # Check all nested values
len(d)                  # Number of nested values
d.items()               # All nested items
dict(d)                 # Flatten into a regular dictionary
```

The *ChainMap* class only makes updates (writes and deletions) to the first mapping in the chain while lookups will search the full chain. However, if deep writes and deletions are desired, it is easy to make a subclass that updates keys found deeper in the chain:

```
class DeepChainMap(ChainMap):
    'Variant of ChainMap that allows direct updates to inner scopes'

    def __setitem__(self, key, value):
        for mapping in self.maps:
            if key in mapping:
                mapping[key] = value
                return
        self.maps[0][key] = value

    def __delitem__(self, key):
        for mapping in self.maps:
            if key in mapping:
                del mapping[key]
                return
        raise KeyError(key)

>>> d = DeepChainMap({'zebra': 'black'}, {'elephant': 'blue'}, {'lion': 'yellow'})
>>> d['lion'] = 'orange'         # update an existing key two levels down
>>> d['snake'] = 'red'           # new keys get added to the topmost dict
>>> del d['elephant']            # remove an existing key one level down
DeepChainMap({'zebra': 'black', 'snake': 'red'}, {}, {'lion': 'orange'})
```

8.3.2 Counter objects

A counter tool is provided to support convenient and rapid tallies. For example:

```
>>> # Tally occurrences of words in a list
>>> cnt = Counter()
>>> for word in ['red', 'blue', 'red', 'green', 'blue', 'blue']:
...     cnt[word] += 1
>>> cnt
Counter({'blue': 3, 'red': 2, 'green': 1})

>>> # Find the ten most common words in Hamlet
>>> import re
>>> words = re.findall(r'\w+', open('hamlet.txt').read().lower())
>>> Counter(words).most_common(10)
[('the', 1143), ('and', 966), ('to', 762), ('of', 669), ('i', 631),
 ('you', 554),  ('a', 546), ('my', 514), ('hamlet', 471), ('in', 451)]
```

class collections.Counter([*iterable-or-mapping*]**)**

A *Counter* is a *dict* subclass for counting hashable objects. It is an unordered collection where elements are stored as dictionary keys and their counts are stored as dictionary values. Counts are allowed to be any integer value including zero or negative counts. The *Counter* class is similar to bags or multisets in other languages.

Elements are counted from an *iterable* or initialized from another *mapping* (or counter):

```
>>> c = Counter()                           # a new, empty counter
>>> c = Counter('gallahad')                 # a new counter from an iterable
>>> c = Counter({'red': 4, 'blue': 2})      # a new counter from a mapping
>>> c = Counter(cats=4, dogs=8)             # a new counter from keyword args
```

Counter objects have a dictionary interface except that they return a zero count for missing items instead of raising a *KeyError*:

```
>>> c = Counter(['eggs', 'ham'])
>>> c['bacon']                              # count of a missing element is zero
0
```

Setting a count to zero does not remove an element from a counter. Use `del` to remove it entirely:

```
>>> c['sausage'] = 0                        # counter entry with a zero count
>>> del c['sausage']                        # del actually removes the entry
```

New in version 3.1.

Counter objects support three methods beyond those available for all dictionaries:

elements()

Return an iterator over elements repeating each as many times as its count. Elements are returned in arbitrary order. If an element's count is less than one, *elements()* will ignore it.

```
>>> c = Counter(a=4, b=2, c=0, d=-2)
>>> sorted(c.elements())
['a', 'a', 'a', 'a', 'b', 'b']
```

most_common([*n*]**)**

Return a list of the *n* most common elements and their counts from the most common to the least. If *n* is omitted or `None`, *most_common()* returns *all* elements in the counter. Elements with equal counts are ordered arbitrarily:

```
>>> Counter('abracadabra').most_common(3)
[('a', 5), ('r', 2), ('b', 2)]
```

subtract([*iterable-or-mapping*])

Elements are subtracted from an *iterable* or from another *mapping* (or counter). Like *dict.update()* but subtracts counts instead of replacing them. Both inputs and outputs may be zero or negative.

```
>>> c = Counter(a=4, b=2, c=0, d=-2)
>>> d = Counter(a=1, b=2, c=3, d=4)
>>> c.subtract(d)
>>> c
Counter({'a': 3, 'b': 0, 'c': -3, 'd': -6})
```

New in version 3.2.

The usual dictionary methods are available for *Counter* objects except for two which work differently for counters.

fromkeys(*iterable*)

This class method is not implemented for *Counter* objects.

update([*iterable-or-mapping*])

Elements are counted from an *iterable* or added-in from another *mapping* (or counter). Like *dict.update()* but adds counts instead of replacing them. Also, the *iterable* is expected to be a sequence of elements, not a sequence of `(key, value)` pairs.

Common patterns for working with *Counter* objects:

```
sum(c.values())                 # total of all counts
c.clear()                       # reset all counts
list(c)                         # list unique elements
set(c)                          # convert to a set
dict(c)                         # convert to a regular dictionary
c.items()                       # convert to a list of (elem, cnt) pairs
Counter(dict(list_of_pairs))    # convert from a list of (elem, cnt) pairs
c.most_common()[:-n-1:-1]       # n least common elements
+c                              # remove zero and negative counts
```

Several mathematical operations are provided for combining *Counter* objects to produce multisets (counters that have counts greater than zero). Addition and subtraction combine counters by adding or subtracting the counts of corresponding elements. Intersection and union return the minimum and maximum of corresponding counts. Each operation can accept inputs with signed counts, but the output will exclude results with counts of zero or less.

```
>>> c = Counter(a=3, b=1)
>>> d = Counter(a=1, b=2)
>>> c + d                       # add two counters together:  c[x] + d[x]
Counter({'a': 4, 'b': 3})
>>> c - d                       # subtract (keeping only positive counts)
Counter({'a': 2})
>>> c & d                       # intersection:  min(c[x], d[x])
Counter({'a': 1, 'b': 1})
>>> c | d                       # union:  max(c[x], d[x])
Counter({'a': 3, 'b': 2})
```

Unary addition and subtraction are shortcuts for adding an empty counter or subtracting from an empty counter.

```
>>> c = Counter(a=2, b=-4)
>>> +c
Counter({'a': 2})
```

```
>>> -c
Counter({'b': 4})
```

New in version 3.3: Added support for unary plus, unary minus, and in-place multiset operations.

Note: Counters were primarily designed to work with positive integers to represent running counts; however, care was taken to not unnecessarily preclude use cases needing other types or negative values. To help with those use cases, this section documents the minimum range and type restrictions.

- The `Counter` class itself is a dictionary subclass with no restrictions on its keys and values. The values are intended to be numbers representing counts, but you *could* store anything in the value field.
- The `most_common()` method requires only that the values be orderable.
- For in-place operations such as `c[key] += 1`, the value type need only support addition and subtraction. So fractions, floats, and decimals would work and negative values are supported. The same is also true for `update()` and `subtract()` which allow negative and zero values for both inputs and outputs.
- The multiset methods are designed only for use cases with positive values. The inputs may be negative or zero, but only outputs with positive values are created. There are no type restrictions, but the value type needs to support addition, subtraction, and comparison.
- The `elements()` method requires integer counts. It ignores zero and negative counts.

See also:

- Bag class in Smalltalk.
- Wikipedia entry for Multisets.
- C++ multisets tutorial with examples.
- For mathematical operations on multisets and their use cases, see *Knuth, Donald. The Art of Computer Programming Volume II, Section 4.6.3, Exercise 19.*
- To enumerate all distinct multisets of a given size over a given set of elements, see `itertools.combinations_with_replacement()`:

  map(Counter, combinations_with_replacement('ABC', 2)) -> AA AB AC BB BC CC

8.3.3 deque objects

class collections.deque([*iterable*[, *maxlen*]])

Returns a new deque object initialized left-to-right (using `append()`) with data from *iterable*. If *iterable* is not specified, the new deque is empty.

Deques are a generalization of stacks and queues (the name is pronounced "deck" and is short for "double-ended queue"). Deques support thread-safe, memory efficient appends and pops from either side of the deque with approximately the same O(1) performance in either direction.

Though `list` objects support similar operations, they are optimized for fast fixed-length operations and incur O(n) memory movement costs for `pop(0)` and `insert(0, v)` operations which change both the size and position of the underlying data representation.

If *maxlen* is not specified or is `None`, deques may grow to an arbitrary length. Otherwise, the deque is bounded to the specified maximum length. Once a bounded length deque is full, when new items are added, a corresponding number of items are discarded from the opposite end. Bounded length deques provide functionality similar to the `tail` filter in Unix. They are also useful for tracking transactions and other pools of data where only the most recent activity is of interest.

Deque objects support the following methods:

append(*x*)
Add *x* to the right side of the deque.

appendleft(*x*)
Add *x* to the left side of the deque.

clear()
Remove all elements from the deque leaving it with length 0.

copy()
Create a shallow copy of the deque.

New in version 3.5.

count(*x*)
Count the number of deque elements equal to *x*.

New in version 3.2.

extend(*iterable*)
Extend the right side of the deque by appending elements from the iterable argument.

extendleft(*iterable*)
Extend the left side of the deque by appending elements from *iterable*. Note, the series of left appends results in reversing the order of elements in the iterable argument.

index(*x*[, *start*[, *stop*]])
Return the position of *x* in the deque (at or after index *start* and before index *stop*). Returns the first match or raises *ValueError* if not found.

New in version 3.5.

insert(*i*, *x*)
Insert *x* into the deque at position *i*.

If the insertion would cause a bounded deque to grow beyond *maxlen*, an *IndexError* is raised.

New in version 3.5.

pop()
Remove and return an element from the right side of the deque. If no elements are present, raises an *IndexError*.

popleft()
Remove and return an element from the left side of the deque. If no elements are present, raises an *IndexError*.

remove(*value*)
Remove the first occurrence of *value*. If not found, raises a *ValueError*.

reverse()
Reverse the elements of the deque in-place and then return `None`.

New in version 3.2.

rotate(*n*)
Rotate the deque *n* steps to the right. If *n* is negative, rotate to the left. Rotating one step to the right is equivalent to: `d.appendleft(d.pop())`.

Deque objects also provide one read-only attribute:

maxlen
Maximum size of a deque or `None` if unbounded.

New in version 3.1.

In addition to the above, deques support iteration, pickling, `len(d)`, `reversed(d)`, `copy.copy(d)`, `copy.deepcopy(d)`, membership testing with the `in` operator, and subscript references such as `d[-1]`. Indexed access is O(1) at both ends but slows to O(n) in the middle. For fast random access, use lists instead.

Starting in version 3.5, deques support `__add__()`, `__mul__()`, and `__imul__()`.

Example:

```
>>> from collections import deque
>>> d = deque('ghi')                 # make a new deque with three items
>>> for elem in d:                   # iterate over the deque's elements
...     print(elem.upper())
G
H
I

>>> d.append('j')                    # add a new entry to the right side
>>> d.appendleft('f')                # add a new entry to the left side
>>> d                                # show the representation of the deque
deque(['f', 'g', 'h', 'i', 'j'])

>>> d.pop()                          # return and remove the rightmost item
'j'
>>> d.popleft()                      # return and remove the leftmost item
'f'
>>> list(d)                          # list the contents of the deque
['g', 'h', 'i']
>>> d[0]                             # peek at leftmost item
'g'
>>> d[-1]                            # peek at rightmost item
'i'

>>> list(reversed(d))                # list the contents of a deque in reverse
['i', 'h', 'g']
>>> 'h' in d                         # search the deque
True
>>> d.extend('jkl')                  # add multiple elements at once
>>> d
deque(['g', 'h', 'i', 'j', 'k', 'l'])
>>> d.rotate(1)                      # right rotation
>>> d
deque(['l', 'g', 'h', 'i', 'j', 'k'])
>>> d.rotate(-1)                     # left rotation
>>> d
deque(['g', 'h', 'i', 'j', 'k', 'l'])

>>> deque(reversed(d))               # make a new deque in reverse order
deque(['l', 'k', 'j', 'i', 'h', 'g'])
>>> d.clear()                        # empty the deque
>>> d.pop()                          # cannot pop from an empty deque
Traceback (most recent call last):
    File "<pyshell#6>", line 1, in -toplevel-
        d.pop()
IndexError: pop from an empty deque

>>> d.extendleft('abc')              # extendleft() reverses the input order
>>> d
deque(['c', 'b', 'a'])
```

deque Recipes

This section shows various approaches to working with deques.

Bounded length deques provide functionality similar to the `tail` filter in Unix:

```
def tail(filename, n=10):
    'Return the last n lines of a file'
    with open(filename) as f:
        return deque(f, n)
```

Another approach to using deques is to maintain a sequence of recently added elements by appending to the right and popping to the left:

```
def moving_average(iterable, n=3):
    # moving_average([40, 30, 50, 46, 39, 44]) --> 40.0 42.0 45.0 43.0
    # http://en.wikipedia.org/wiki/Moving_average
    it = iter(iterable)
    d = deque(itertools.islice(it, n-1))
    d.appendleft(0)
    s = sum(d)
    for elem in it:
        s += elem - d.popleft()
        d.append(elem)
        yield s / n
```

The `rotate()` method provides a way to implement *deque* slicing and deletion. For example, a pure Python implementation of `del d[n]` relies on the `rotate()` method to position elements to be popped:

```
def delete_nth(d, n):
    d.rotate(-n)
    d.popleft()
    d.rotate(n)
```

To implement *deque* slicing, use a similar approach applying `rotate()` to bring a target element to the left side of the deque. Remove old entries with `popleft()`, add new entries with `extend()`, and then reverse the rotation. With minor variations on that approach, it is easy to implement Forth style stack manipulations such as `dup`, `drop`, `swap`, `over`, `pick`, `rot`, and `roll`.

8.3.4 defaultdict objects

class collections.defaultdict([*default_factory*[, ...]])

Returns a new dictionary-like object. *defaultdict* is a subclass of the built-in *dict* class. It overrides one method and adds one writable instance variable. The remaining functionality is the same as for the *dict* class and is not documented here.

The first argument provides the initial value for the *default_factory* attribute; it defaults to `None`. All remaining arguments are treated the same as if they were passed to the *dict* constructor, including keyword arguments.

defaultdict objects support the following method in addition to the standard *dict* operations:

__missing__(*key*)

If the *default_factory* attribute is `None`, this raises a *KeyError* exception with the *key* as argument.

If *default_factory* is not `None`, it is called without arguments to provide a default value for the given *key*, this value is inserted in the dictionary for the *key*, and returned.

If calling *default_factory* raises an exception this exception is propagated unchanged.

This method is called by the `__getitem__()` method of the *dict* class when the requested key is not found; whatever it returns or raises is then returned or raised by `__getitem__()`.

Note that *__missing__()* is *not* called for any operations besides `__getitem__()`. This means that `get()` will, like normal dictionaries, return `None` as a default rather than using *default_factory*.

defaultdict objects support the following instance variable:

default_factory
This attribute is used by the *__missing__()* method; it is initialized from the first argument to the constructor, if present, or to `None`, if absent.

defaultdict Examples

Using *list* as the `default_factory`, it is easy to group a sequence of key-value pairs into a dictionary of lists:

```
>>> s = [('yellow', 1), ('blue', 2), ('yellow', 3), ('blue', 4), ('red', 1)]
>>> d = defaultdict(list)
>>> for k, v in s:
...     d[k].append(v)
...
>>> sorted(d.items())
[('blue', [2, 4]), ('red', [1]), ('yellow', [1, 3])]
```

When each key is encountered for the first time, it is not already in the mapping; so an entry is automatically created using the `default_factory` function which returns an empty *list*. The `list.append()` operation then attaches the value to the new list. When keys are encountered again, the look-up proceeds normally (returning the list for that key) and the `list.append()` operation adds another value to the list. This technique is simpler and faster than an equivalent technique using *dict.setdefault()*:

```
>>> d = {}
>>> for k, v in s:
...     d.setdefault(k, []).append(v)
...
>>> sorted(d.items())
[('blue', [2, 4]), ('red', [1]), ('yellow', [1, 3])]
```

Setting the `default_factory` to *int* makes the *defaultdict* useful for counting (like a bag or multiset in other languages):

```
>>> s = 'mississippi'
>>> d = defaultdict(int)
>>> for k in s:
...     d[k] += 1
...
>>> sorted(d.items())
[('i', 4), ('m', 1), ('p', 2), ('s', 4)]
```

When a letter is first encountered, it is missing from the mapping, so the `default_factory` function calls *int()* to supply a default count of zero. The increment operation then builds up the count for each letter.

The function *int()* which always returns zero is just a special case of constant functions. A faster and more flexible way to create constant functions is to use a lambda function which can supply any constant value (not just zero):

```
>>> def constant_factory(value):
...     return lambda: value
>>> d = defaultdict(constant_factory('<missing>'))
>>> d.update(name='John', action='ran')
>>> '%(name)s %(action)s to %(object)s' % d
'John ran to <missing>'
```

Setting the `default_factory` to *set* makes the *defaultdict* useful for building a dictionary of sets:

```
>>> s = [('red', 1), ('blue', 2), ('red', 3), ('blue', 4), ('red', 1), ('blue', 4)]
>>> d = defaultdict(set)
>>> for k, v in s:
...     d[k].add(v)
...
>>> sorted(d.items())
[('blue', {2, 4}), ('red', {1, 3})]
```

8.3.5 `namedtuple()` Factory Function for Tuples with Named Fields

Named tuples assign meaning to each position in a tuple and allow for more readable, self-documenting code. They can be used wherever regular tuples are used, and they add the ability to access fields by name instead of position index.

`collections.namedtuple`(*typename*, *field_names*, *, *verbose=False*, *rename=False*, *module=None*)

Returns a new tuple subclass named *typename*. The new subclass is used to create tuple-like objects that have fields accessible by attribute lookup as well as being indexable and iterable. Instances of the subclass also have a helpful docstring (with typename and field_names) and a helpful `__repr__()` method which lists the tuple contents in a `name=value` format.

The *field_names* are a sequence of strings such as `['x', 'y']`. Alternatively, *field_names* can be a single string with each fieldname separated by whitespace and/or commas, for example `'x y'` or `'x, y'`.

Any valid Python identifier may be used for a fieldname except for names starting with an underscore. Valid identifiers consist of letters, digits, and underscores but do not start with a digit or underscore and cannot be a *keyword* such as *class*, *for*, *return*, *global*, *pass*, or *raise*.

If *rename* is true, invalid fieldnames are automatically replaced with positional names. For example, `['abc', 'def', 'ghi', 'abc']` is converted to `['abc', '_1', 'ghi', '_3']`, eliminating the keyword `def` and the duplicate fieldname `abc`.

If *verbose* is true, the class definition is printed after it is built. This option is outdated; instead, it is simpler to print the `_source` attribute.

If *module* is defined, the `__module__` attribute of the named tuple is set to that value.

Named tuple instances do not have per-instance dictionaries, so they are lightweight and require no more memory than regular tuples.

Changed in version 3.1: Added support for *rename*.

Changed in version 3.6: The *verbose* and *rename* parameters became *keyword-only arguments*.

Changed in version 3.6: Added the *module* parameter.

```
>>> # Basic example
>>> Point = namedtuple('Point', ['x', 'y'])
>>> p = Point(11, y=22)     # instantiate with positional or keyword arguments
>>> p[0] + p[1]             # indexable like the plain tuple (11, 22)
33
```

```
>>> x, y = p                # unpack like a regular tuple
>>> x, y
(11, 22)
>>> p.x + p.y               # fields also accessible by name
33
>>> p                       # readable __repr__ with a name=value style
Point(x=11, y=22)
```

Named tuples are especially useful for assigning field names to result tuples returned by the *csv* or *sqlite3* modules:

```
EmployeeRecord = namedtuple('EmployeeRecord', 'name, age, title, department, paygrade')

import csv
for emp in map(EmployeeRecord._make, csv.reader(open("employees.csv", "rb"))):
    print(emp.name, emp.title)

import sqlite3
conn = sqlite3.connect('/companydata')
cursor = conn.cursor()
cursor.execute('SELECT name, age, title, department, paygrade FROM employees')
for emp in map(EmployeeRecord._make, cursor.fetchall()):
    print(emp.name, emp.title)
```

In addition to the methods inherited from tuples, named tuples support three additional methods and two attributes. To prevent conflicts with field names, the method and attribute names start with an underscore.

classmethod somenamedtuple._make(*iterable*)
Class method that makes a new instance from an existing sequence or iterable.

```
>>> t = [11, 22]
>>> Point._make(t)
Point(x=11, y=22)
```

somenamedtuple._asdict()
Return a new *OrderedDict* which maps field names to their corresponding values:

```
>>> p = Point(x=11, y=22)
>>> p._asdict()
OrderedDict([('x', 11), ('y', 22)])
```

Changed in version 3.1: Returns an *OrderedDict* instead of a regular *dict*.

somenamedtuple._replace(***kwargs*)
Return a new instance of the named tuple replacing specified fields with new values:

```
>>> p = Point(x=11, y=22)
>>> p._replace(x=33)
Point(x=33, y=22)

>>> for partnum, record in inventory.items():
...     inventory[partnum] = record._replace(price=newprices[partnum], timestamp=time.now())
```

somenamedtuple._source
A string with the pure Python source code used to create the named tuple class. The source makes the named tuple self-documenting. It can be printed, executed using *exec()*, or saved to a file and imported.

New in version 3.3.

somenamedtuple._fields

Tuple of strings listing the field names. Useful for introspection and for creating new named tuple types from existing named tuples.

```
>>> p._fields            # view the field names
('x', 'y')

>>> Color = namedtuple('Color', 'red green blue')
>>> Pixel = namedtuple('Pixel', Point._fields + Color._fields)
>>> Pixel(11, 22, 128, 255, 0)
Pixel(x=11, y=22, red=128, green=255, blue=0)
```

To retrieve a field whose name is stored in a string, use the *getattr()* function:

```
>>> getattr(p, 'x')
11
```

To convert a dictionary to a named tuple, use the double-star-operator (as described in tut-unpacking-arguments):

```
>>> d = {'x': 11, 'y': 22}
>>> Point(**d)
Point(x=11, y=22)
```

Since a named tuple is a regular Python class, it is easy to add or change functionality with a subclass. Here is how to add a calculated field and a fixed-width print format:

```
>>> class Point(namedtuple('Point', ['x', 'y'])):
...     __slots__ = ()
...     @property
...     def hypot(self):
...         return (self.x ** 2 + self.y ** 2) ** 0.5
...     def __str__(self):
...         return 'Point: x=%6.3f  y=%6.3f  hypot=%6.3f' % (self.x, self.y, self.hypot)

>>> for p in Point(3, 4), Point(14, 5/7):
...     print(p)
Point: x= 3.000  y= 4.000  hypot= 5.000
Point: x=14.000  y= 0.714  hypot=14.018
```

The subclass shown above sets `__slots__` to an empty tuple. This helps keep memory requirements low by preventing the creation of instance dictionaries.

Subclassing is not useful for adding new, stored fields. Instead, simply create a new named tuple type from the `_fields` attribute:

```
>>> Point3D = namedtuple('Point3D', Point._fields + ('z',))
```

Docstrings can be customized by making direct assignments to the `__doc__` fields:

```
>>> Book = namedtuple('Book', ['id', 'title', 'authors'])
>>> Book.__doc__ += ': Hardcover book in active collection'
>>> Book.id.__doc__ = '13-digit ISBN'
>>> Book.title.__doc__ = 'Title of first printing'
>>> Book.authors.__doc__ = 'List of authors sorted by last name'
```

Changed in version 3.5: Property docstrings became writeable.

Default values can be implemented by using `_replace()` to customize a prototype instance:

```
>>> Account = namedtuple('Account', 'owner balance transaction_count')
>>> default_account = Account('<owner name>', 0.0, 0)
>>> johns_account = default_account._replace(owner='John')
>>> janes_account = default_account._replace(owner='Jane')
```

See also:

- Recipe for named tuple abstract base class with a metaclass mix-in by Jan Kaliszewski. Besides providing an *abstract base class* for named tuples, it also supports an alternate *metaclass*-based constructor that is convenient for use cases where named tuples are being subclassed.
- See *types.SimpleNamespace()* for a mutable namespace based on an underlying dictionary instead of a tuple.
- See *typing.NamedTuple()* for a way to add type hints for named tuples.

8.3.6 `OrderedDict` objects

Ordered dictionaries are just like regular dictionaries but they remember the order that items were inserted. When iterating over an ordered dictionary, the items are returned in the order their keys were first added.

class collections.**OrderedDict**([*items*])

Return an instance of a dict subclass, supporting the usual *dict* methods. An *OrderedDict* is a dict that remembers the order that keys were first inserted. If a new entry overwrites an existing entry, the original insertion position is left unchanged. Deleting an entry and reinserting it will move it to the end.

New in version 3.1.

popitem(*last=True*)

The *popitem()* method for ordered dictionaries returns and removes a (key, value) pair. The pairs are returned in LIFO (last-in, first-out) order if *last* is true or FIFO (first-in, first-out) order if false.

move_to_end(*key*, *last=True*)

Move an existing *key* to either end of an ordered dictionary. The item is moved to the right end if *last* is true (the default) or to the beginning if *last* is false. Raises *KeyError* if the *key* does not exist:

```
>>> d = OrderedDict.fromkeys('abcde')
>>> d.move_to_end('b')
>>> ''.join(d.keys())
'acdeb'
>>> d.move_to_end('b', last=False)
>>> ''.join(d.keys())
'bacde'
```

New in version 3.2.

In addition to the usual mapping methods, ordered dictionaries also support reverse iteration using *reversed()*.

Equality tests between *OrderedDict* objects are order-sensitive and are implemented as `list(od1.items())==list(od2.items())`. Equality tests between *OrderedDict* objects and other *Mapping* objects are order-insensitive like regular dictionaries. This allows *OrderedDict* objects to be substituted anywhere a regular dictionary is used.

Changed in version 3.5: The items, keys, and values *views* of *OrderedDict* now support reverse iteration using *reversed()*.

Changed in version 3.6: With the acceptance of PEP 468, order is retained for keyword arguments passed to the *OrderedDict* constructor and its `update()` method.

OrderedDict Examples and Recipes

Since an ordered dictionary remembers its insertion order, it can be used in conjunction with sorting to make a sorted dictionary:

```
>>> # regular unsorted dictionary
>>> d = {'banana': 3, 'apple': 4, 'pear': 1, 'orange': 2}

>>> # dictionary sorted by key
>>> OrderedDict(sorted(d.items(), key=lambda t: t[0]))
OrderedDict([('apple', 4), ('banana', 3), ('orange', 2), ('pear', 1)])

>>> # dictionary sorted by value
>>> OrderedDict(sorted(d.items(), key=lambda t: t[1]))
OrderedDict([('pear', 1), ('orange', 2), ('banana', 3), ('apple', 4)])

>>> # dictionary sorted by length of the key string
>>> OrderedDict(sorted(d.items(), key=lambda t: len(t[0])))
OrderedDict([('pear', 1), ('apple', 4), ('orange', 2), ('banana', 3)])
```

The new sorted dictionaries maintain their sort order when entries are deleted. But when new keys are added, the keys are appended to the end and the sort is not maintained.

It is also straight-forward to create an ordered dictionary variant that remembers the order the keys were *last* inserted. If a new entry overwrites an existing entry, the original insertion position is changed and moved to the end:

```
class LastUpdatedOrderedDict(OrderedDict):
    'Store items in the order the keys were last added'

    def __setitem__(self, key, value):
        if key in self:
            del self[key]
        OrderedDict.__setitem__(self, key, value)
```

An ordered dictionary can be combined with the *Counter* class so that the counter remembers the order elements are first encountered:

```
class OrderedCounter(Counter, OrderedDict):
    'Counter that remembers the order elements are first encountered'

    def __repr__(self):
        return '%s(%r)' % (self.__class__.__name__, OrderedDict(self))

    def __reduce__(self):
        return self.__class__, (OrderedDict(self),)
```

8.3.7 UserDict objects

The class, *UserDict* acts as a wrapper around dictionary objects. The need for this class has been partially supplanted by the ability to subclass directly from *dict*; however, this class can be easier to work with because the underlying dictionary is accessible as an attribute.

class collections.UserDict([*initialdata*])

Class that simulates a dictionary. The instance's contents are kept in a regular dictionary, which is accessible via the `data` attribute of `UserDict` instances. If *initialdata* is provided, `data` is initialized with its contents; note that a reference to *initialdata* will not be kept, allowing it be used for other purposes.

In addition to supporting the methods and operations of mappings, `UserDict` instances provide the following attribute:

data

A real dictionary used to store the contents of the `UserDict` class.

8.3.8 UserList objects

This class acts as a wrapper around list objects. It is a useful base class for your own list-like classes which can inherit from them and override existing methods or add new ones. In this way, one can add new behaviors to lists.

The need for this class has been partially supplanted by the ability to subclass directly from `list`; however, this class can be easier to work with because the underlying list is accessible as an attribute.

class collections.UserList([*list*])

Class that simulates a list. The instance's contents are kept in a regular list, which is accessible via the `data` attribute of `UserList` instances. The instance's contents are initially set to a copy of *list*, defaulting to the empty list `[]`. *list* can be any iterable, for example a real Python list or a `UserList` object.

In addition to supporting the methods and operations of mutable sequences, `UserList` instances provide the following attribute:

data

A real `list` object used to store the contents of the `UserList` class.

Subclassing requirements: Subclasses of `UserList` are expected to offer a constructor which can be called with either no arguments or one argument. List operations which return a new sequence attempt to create an instance of the actual implementation class. To do so, it assumes that the constructor can be called with a single parameter, which is a sequence object used as a data source.

If a derived class does not wish to comply with this requirement, all of the special methods supported by this class will need to be overridden; please consult the sources for information about the methods which need to be provided in that case.

8.3.9 UserString objects

The class, `UserString` acts as a wrapper around string objects. The need for this class has been partially supplanted by the ability to subclass directly from `str`; however, this class can be easier to work with because the underlying string is accessible as an attribute.

class collections.UserString([*sequence*])

Class that simulates a string or a Unicode string object. The instance's content is kept in a regular string object, which is accessible via the `data` attribute of `UserString` instances. The instance's contents are initially set to a copy of *sequence*. The *sequence* can be an instance of `bytes`, `str`, `UserString` (or a subclass) or an arbitrary sequence which can be converted into a string using the built-in `str()` function.

Changed in version 3.5: New methods `__getnewargs__`, `__rmod__`, `casefold`, `format_map`, `isprintable`, and `maketrans`.

8.4 `collections.abc` — Abstract Base Classes for Containers

New in version 3.3: Formerly, this module was part of the *collections* module.

Source code: Lib/_collections_abc.py

This module provides *abstract base classes* that can be used to test whether a class provides a particular interface; for example, whether it is hashable or whether it is a mapping.

8.4.1 Collections Abstract Base Classes

The collections module offers the following *ABCs*:

ABC	Inherits from	Abstract Methods	Mixin Methods
Container		`__contains__`	
Hashable		`__hash__`	
Iterable		`__iter__`	
Iterator	*Iterable*	`__next__`	`__iter__`
Reversible	*Iterable*	`__reversed__`	
Generator	*Iterator*	`send`, `throw`	`close`, `__iter__`, `__next__`
Sized		`__len__`	
Callable		`__call__`	
Collection	*Sized*, *Iterable*, *Container*	`__contains__`, `__iter__`, `__len__`	
Sequence	*Reversible*, *Collection*	`__getitem__`, `__len__`	`__contains__`, `__iter__`, `__reversed__`, `index`, and `count`
MutableSequence	*Sequence*	`__getitem__`, `__setitem__`, `__delitem__`, `__len__`, `insert`	Inherited *Sequence* methods and `append`, `reverse`, `extend`, `pop`, `remove`, and `__iadd__`
ByteString	*Sequence*	`__getitem__`, `__len__`	Inherited *Sequence* methods
Set	*Collection*	`__contains__`, `__iter__`, `__len__`	`__le__`, `__lt__`, `__eq__`, `__ne__`, `__gt__`, `__ge__`, `__and__`, `__or__`, `__sub__`, `__xor__`, and `isdisjoint`
MutableSet	*Set*	`__contains__`, `__iter__`, `__len__`, `add`, `discard`	Inherited *Set* methods and `clear`, `pop`, `remove`, `__ior__`, `__iand__`, `__ixor__`, and `__isub__`
Mapping	*Collection*	`__getitem__`, `__iter__`, `__len__`	`__contains__`, `keys`, `items`, `values`, `get`, `__eq__`, and `__ne__`
MutableMapping	*Mapping*	`__getitem__`, `__setitem__`, `__delitem__`, `__iter__`, `__len__`	Inherited *Mapping* methods and `pop`, `popitem`, `clear`, `update`, and `setdefault`
MappingView	*Sized*		`__len__`
ItemsView	*MappingView*, *Set*		`__contains__`, `__iter__`
KeysView	*MappingView*, *Set*		`__contains__`, `__iter__`
ValuesView	*MappingView*		`__contains__`, `__iter__`
Awaitable		`__await__`	
Coroutine	*Awaitable*	`send`, `throw`	`close`
AsyncIterable		`__aiter__`	
AsyncIterator	*AsyncIterable*	`__anext__`	`__aiter__`
AsyncGenerator	*AsyncIterator*	`asend`, `athrow`	`aclose`, `__aiter__`, `__anext__`

class collections.abc.**Container**
class collections.abc.**Hashable**
class collections.abc.**Sized**
class collections.abc.**Callable**

ABCs for classes that provide respectively the methods `__contains__()`, `__hash__()`, `__len__()`, and `__call__()`.

class collections.abc.**Iterable**

ABC for classes that provide the `__iter__()` method.

Checking `isinstance(obj, Iterable)` detects classes that are registered as *Iterable* or that have an `__iter__()` method, but it does not detect classes that iterate with the `__getitem__()` method. The only reliable way to determine whether an object is *iterable* is to call `iter(obj)`.

class collections.abc.Collection
ABC for sized iterable container classes.

New in version 3.6.

class collections.abc.Iterator
ABC for classes that provide the *__iter__()* and *__next__()* methods. See also the definition of *iterator*.

class collections.abc.Reversible
ABC for iterable classes that also provide the `__reversed__()` method.

New in version 3.6.

class collections.abc.Generator
ABC for generator classes that implement the protocol defined in PEP 342 that extends iterators with the `send()`, `throw()` and `close()` methods. See also the definition of *generator*.

New in version 3.5.

class collections.abc.Sequence
class collections.abc.MutableSequence
class collections.abc.ByteString
ABCs for read-only and mutable *sequences*.

Implementation note: Some of the mixin methods, such as `__iter__()`, `__reversed__()` and `index()`, make repeated calls to the underlying `__getitem__()` method. Consequently, if `__getitem__()` is implemented with constant access speed, the mixin methods will have linear performance; however, if the underlying method is linear (as it would be with a linked list), the mixins will have quadratic performance and will likely need to be overridden.

Changed in version 3.5: The index() method added support for *stop* and *start* arguments.

class collections.abc.Set
class collections.abc.MutableSet
ABCs for read-only and mutable sets.

class collections.abc.Mapping
class collections.abc.MutableMapping
ABCs for read-only and mutable *mappings*.

class collections.abc.MappingView
class collections.abc.ItemsView
class collections.abc.KeysView
class collections.abc.ValuesView
ABCs for mapping, items, keys, and values *views*.

class collections.abc.Awaitable
ABC for *awaitable* objects, which can be used in `await` expressions. Custom implementations must provide the `__await__()` method.

Coroutine objects and instances of the *Coroutine* ABC are all instances of this ABC.

Note: In CPython, generator-based coroutines (generators decorated with *types.coroutine()* or *asyncio.coroutine()*) are *awaitables*, even though they do not have an `__await__()` method. Using `isinstance(gencoro, Awaitable)` for them will return `False`. Use *inspect.isawaitable()* to detect them.

New in version 3.5.

class collections.abc.Coroutine

ABC for coroutine compatible classes. These implement the following methods, defined in coroutine-objects: `send()`, `throw()`, and `close()`. Custom implementations must also implement `__await__()`. All *Coroutine* instances are also instances of *Awaitable*. See also the definition of *coroutine*.

Note: In CPython, generator-based coroutines (generators decorated with *types.coroutine()* or *asyncio.coroutine()*) are *awaitables*, even though they do not have an `__await__()` method. Using `isinstance(gencoro, Coroutine)` for them will return `False`. Use *inspect.isawaitable()* to detect them.

New in version 3.5.

class collections.abc.AsyncIterable

ABC for classes that provide `__aiter__` method. See also the definition of *asynchronous iterable*.

New in version 3.5.

class collections.abc.AsyncIterator

ABC for classes that provide `__aiter__` and `__anext__` methods. See also the definition of *asynchronous iterator*.

New in version 3.5.

class collections.abc.AsyncGenerator

ABC for asynchronous generator classes that implement the protocol defined in PEP 525 and PEP 492.

New in version 3.6.

These ABCs allow us to ask classes or instances if they provide particular functionality, for example:

```
size = None
if isinstance(myvar, collections.abc.Sized):
    size = len(myvar)
```

Several of the ABCs are also useful as mixins that make it easier to develop classes supporting container APIs. For example, to write a class supporting the full *Set* API, it is only necessary to supply the three underlying abstract methods: `__contains__()`, `__iter__()`, and `__len__()`. The ABC supplies the remaining methods such as `__and__()` and `isdisjoint()`:

```
class ListBasedSet(collections.abc.Set):
    ''' Alternate set implementation favoring space over speed
        and not requiring the set elements to be hashable. '''
    def __init__(self, iterable):
        self.elements = lst = []
        for value in iterable:
            if value not in lst:
                lst.append(value)

    def __iter__(self):
        return iter(self.elements)

    def __contains__(self, value):
        return value in self.elements

    def __len__(self):
        return len(self.elements)
```

```
s1 = ListBasedSet('abcdef')
s2 = ListBasedSet('defghi')
overlap = s1 & s2            # The __and__() method is supported automatically
```

Notes on using *Set* and *MutableSet* as a mixin:

1. Since some set operations create new sets, the default mixin methods need a way to create new instances from an iterable. The class constructor is assumed to have a signature in the form `ClassName(iterable)`. That assumption is factored-out to an internal classmethod called `_from_iterable()` which calls `cls(iterable)` to produce a new set. If the *Set* mixin is being used in a class with a different constructor signature, you will need to override `_from_iterable()` with a classmethod that can construct new instances from an iterable argument.
2. To override the comparisons (presumably for speed, as the semantics are fixed), redefine `__le__()` and `__ge__()`, then the other operations will automatically follow suit.
3. The *Set* mixin provides a `_hash()` method to compute a hash value for the set; however, `__hash__()` is not defined because not all sets are hashable or immutable. To add set hashability using mixins, inherit from both *Set()* and *Hashable()*, then define `__hash__ = Set._hash`.

See also:

- OrderedSet recipe for an example built on *MutableSet*.
- For more about ABCs, see the *abc* module and PEP 3119.

8.5 heapq — Heap queue algorithm

Source code: Lib/heapq.py

This module provides an implementation of the heap queue algorithm, also known as the priority queue algorithm.

Heaps are binary trees for which every parent node has a value less than or equal to any of its children. This implementation uses arrays for which `heap[k] <= heap[2*k+1]` and `heap[k] <= heap[2*k+2]` for all *k*, counting elements from zero. For the sake of comparison, non-existing elements are considered to be infinite. The interesting property of a heap is that its smallest element is always the root, `heap[0]`.

The API below differs from textbook heap algorithms in two aspects: (a) We use zero-based indexing. This makes the relationship between the index for a node and the indexes for its children slightly less obvious, but is more suitable since Python uses zero-based indexing. (b) Our pop method returns the smallest item, not the largest (called a "min heap" in textbooks; a "max heap" is more common in texts because of its suitability for in-place sorting).

These two make it possible to view the heap as a regular Python list without surprises: `heap[0]` is the smallest item, and `heap.sort()` maintains the heap invariant!

To create a heap, use a list initialized to `[]`, or you can transform a populated list into a heap via function *heapify()*.

The following functions are provided:

`heapq.heappush(heap, item)`
: Push the value *item* onto the *heap*, maintaining the heap invariant.

`heapq.heappop(heap)`
: Pop and return the smallest item from the *heap*, maintaining the heap invariant. If the heap is empty, *IndexError* is raised. To access the smallest item without popping it, use `heap[0]`.

`heapq.heappushpop(heap, item)`
Push *item* on the heap, then pop and return the smallest item from the *heap*. The combined action runs more efficiently than *heappush()* followed by a separate call to *heappop()*.

`heapq.heapify(x)`
Transform list *x* into a heap, in-place, in linear time.

`heapq.heapreplace(heap, item)`
Pop and return the smallest item from the *heap*, and also push the new *item*. The heap size doesn't change. If the heap is empty, *IndexError* is raised.

This one step operation is more efficient than a *heappop()* followed by *heappush()* and can be more appropriate when using a fixed-size heap. The pop/push combination always returns an element from the heap and replaces it with *item*.

The value returned may be larger than the *item* added. If that isn't desired, consider using *heappushpop()* instead. Its push/pop combination returns the smaller of the two values, leaving the larger value on the heap.

The module also offers three general purpose functions based on heaps.

`heapq.merge(*iterables, key=None, reverse=False)`
Merge multiple sorted inputs into a single sorted output (for example, merge timestamped entries from multiple log files). Returns an *iterator* over the sorted values.

Similar to `sorted(itertools.chain(*iterables))` but returns an iterable, does not pull the data into memory all at once, and assumes that each of the input streams is already sorted (smallest to largest).

Has two optional arguments which must be specified as keyword arguments.

key specifies a *key function* of one argument that is used to extract a comparison key from each input element. The default value is `None` (compare the elements directly).

reverse is a boolean value. If set to `True`, then the input elements are merged as if each comparison were reversed.

Changed in version 3.5: Added the optional *key* and *reverse* parameters.

`heapq.nlargest(n, iterable, key=None)`
Return a list with the *n* largest elements from the dataset defined by *iterable*. *key*, if provided, specifies a function of one argument that is used to extract a comparison key from each element in the iterable: `key=str.lower` Equivalent to: `sorted(iterable, key=key, reverse=True)[:n]`

`heapq.nsmallest(n, iterable, key=None)`
Return a list with the *n* smallest elements from the dataset defined by *iterable*. *key*, if provided, specifies a function of one argument that is used to extract a comparison key from each element in the iterable: `key=str.lower` Equivalent to: `sorted(iterable, key=key)[:n]`

The latter two functions perform best for smaller values of *n*. For larger values, it is more efficient to use the *sorted()* function. Also, when `n==1`, it is more efficient to use the built-in *min()* and *max()* functions. If repeated usage of these functions is required, consider turning the iterable into an actual heap.

8.5.1 Basic Examples

A heapsort can be implemented by pushing all values onto a heap and then popping off the smallest values one at a time:

```
>>> def heapsort(iterable):
...     h = []
...     for value in iterable:
...         heappush(h, value)
```

```
...     return [heappop(h) for i in range(len(h))]
...
>>> heapsort([1, 3, 5, 7, 9, 2, 4, 6, 8, 0])
[0, 1, 2, 3, 4, 5, 6, 7, 8, 9]
```

This is similar to `sorted(iterable)`, but unlike *sorted()*, this implementation is not stable.

Heap elements can be tuples. This is useful for assigning comparison values (such as task priorities) alongside the main record being tracked:

```
>>> h = []
>>> heappush(h, (5, 'write code'))
>>> heappush(h, (7, 'release product'))
>>> heappush(h, (1, 'write spec'))
>>> heappush(h, (3, 'create tests'))
>>> heappop(h)
(1, 'write spec')
```

8.5.2 Priority Queue Implementation Notes

A priority queue is common use for a heap, and it presents several implementation challenges:

- Sort stability: how do you get two tasks with equal priorities to be returned in the order they were originally added?
- Tuple comparison breaks for (priority, task) pairs if the priorities are equal and the tasks do not have a default comparison order.
- If the priority of a task changes, how do you move it to a new position in the heap?
- Or if a pending task needs to be deleted, how do you find it and remove it from the queue?

A solution to the first two challenges is to store entries as 3-element list including the priority, an entry count, and the task. The entry count serves as a tie-breaker so that two tasks with the same priority are returned in the order they were added. And since no two entry counts are the same, the tuple comparison will never attempt to directly compare two tasks.

The remaining challenges revolve around finding a pending task and making changes to its priority or removing it entirely. Finding a task can be done with a dictionary pointing to an entry in the queue.

Removing the entry or changing its priority is more difficult because it would break the heap structure invariants. So, a possible solution is to mark the entry as removed and add a new entry with the revised priority:

```
pq = []                         # list of entries arranged in a heap
entry_finder = {}               # mapping of tasks to entries
REMOVED = '<removed-task>'      # placeholder for a removed task
counter = itertools.count()     # unique sequence count

def add_task(task, priority=0):
    'Add a new task or update the priority of an existing task'
    if task in entry_finder:
        remove_task(task)
    count = next(counter)
    entry = [priority, count, task]
    entry_finder[task] = entry
    heappush(pq, entry)

def remove_task(task):
```

```
    'Mark an existing task as REMOVED.  Raise KeyError if not found.'
    entry = entry_finder.pop(task)
    entry[-1] = REMOVED

def pop_task():
    'Remove and return the lowest priority task. Raise KeyError if empty.'
    while pq:
        priority, count, task = heappop(pq)
        if task is not REMOVED:
            del entry_finder[task]
            return task
    raise KeyError('pop from an empty priority queue')
```

8.5.3 Theory

Heaps are arrays for which `a[k] <= a[2*k+1]` and `a[k] <= a[2*k+2]` for all *k*, counting elements from 0. For the sake of comparison, non-existing elements are considered to be infinite. The interesting property of a heap is that `a[0]` is always its smallest element.

The strange invariant above is meant to be an efficient memory representation for a tournament. The numbers below are *k*, not `a[k]`:

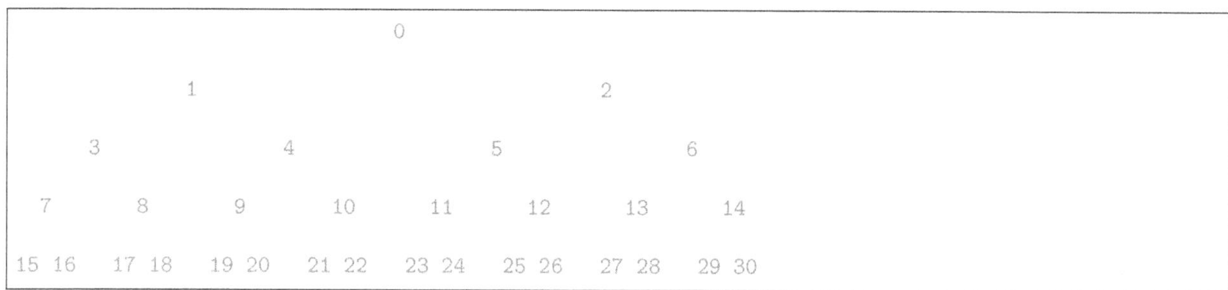

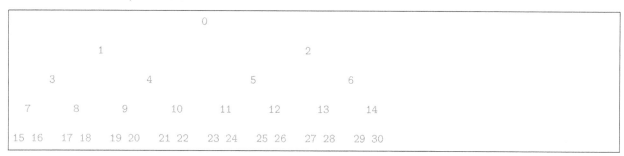

In the tree above, each cell *k* is topping `2*k+1` and `2*k+2`. In a usual binary tournament we see in sports, each cell is the winner over the two cells it tops, and we can trace the winner down the tree to see all opponents s/he had. However, in many computer applications of such tournaments, we do not need to trace the history of a winner. To be more memory efficient, when a winner is promoted, we try to replace it by something else at a lower level, and the rule becomes that a cell and the two cells it tops contain three different items, but the top cell "wins" over the two topped cells.

If this heap invariant is protected at all time, index 0 is clearly the overall winner. The simplest algorithmic way to remove it and find the "next" winner is to move some loser (let's say cell 30 in the diagram above) into the 0 position, and then percolate this new 0 down the tree, exchanging values, until the invariant is re-established. This is clearly logarithmic on the total number of items in the tree. By iterating over all items, you get an O(n log n) sort.

A nice feature of this sort is that you can efficiently insert new items while the sort is going on, provided that the inserted items are not "better" than the last 0'th element you extracted. This is especially useful in simulation contexts, where the tree holds all incoming events, and the "win" condition means the smallest scheduled time. When an event schedules other events for execution, they are scheduled into the future, so they can easily go into the heap. So, a heap is a good structure for implementing schedulers (this is what I used for my MIDI sequencer :-).

Various structures for implementing schedulers have been extensively studied, and heaps are good for this, as they are reasonably speedy, the speed is almost constant, and the worst case is not much different than the average case. However, there are other representations which are more efficient overall, yet the worst cases might be terrible.

Heaps are also very useful in big disk sorts. You most probably all know that a big sort implies producing "runs" (which are pre-sorted sequences, whose size is usually related to the amount of CPU memory), followed by a merging passes for these runs, which merging is often very cleverly organised[1]. It is very important that the initial sort produces the longest runs possible. Tournaments are a good way to achieve that. If, using all the memory available to hold a tournament, you replace and percolate items that happen to fit the current run, you'll produce runs which are twice the size of the memory for random input, and much better for input fuzzily ordered.

Moreover, if you output the 0'th item on disk and get an input which may not fit in the current tournament (because the value "wins" over the last output value), it cannot fit in the heap, so the size of the heap decreases. The freed memory could be cleverly reused immediately for progressively building a second heap, which grows at exactly the same rate the first heap is melting. When the first heap completely vanishes, you switch heaps and start a new run. Clever and quite effective!

In a word, heaps are useful memory structures to know. I use them in a few applications, and I think it is good to keep a 'heap' module around. :-)

8.6 `bisect` — Array bisection algorithm

Source code: Lib/bisect.py

This module provides support for maintaining a list in sorted order without having to sort the list after each insertion. For long lists of items with expensive comparison operations, this can be an improvement over the more common approach. The module is called `bisect` because it uses a basic bisection algorithm to do its work. The source code may be most useful as a working example of the algorithm (the boundary conditions are already right!).

The following functions are provided:

`bisect.bisect_left`(*a*, *x*, *lo=0*, *hi=len(a)*)

Locate the insertion point for *x* in *a* to maintain sorted order. The parameters *lo* and *hi* may be used to specify a subset of the list which should be considered; by default the entire list is used. If *x* is already present in *a*, the insertion point will be before (to the left of) any existing entries. The return value is suitable for use as the first parameter to `list.insert()` assuming that *a* is already sorted.

The returned insertion point *i* partitions the array *a* into two halves so that `all(val < x for val in a[lo:i])` for the left side and `all(val >= x for val in a[i:hi])` for the right side.

`bisect.bisect_right`(*a*, *x*, *lo=0*, *hi=len(a)*)
`bisect.bisect`(*a*, *x*, *lo=0*, *hi=len(a)*)

Similar to `bisect_left()`, but returns an insertion point which comes after (to the right of) any existing entries of *x* in *a*.

The returned insertion point *i* partitions the array *a* into two halves so that `all(val <= x for val in a[lo:i])` for the left side and `all(val > x for val in a[i:hi])` for the right side.

`bisect.insort_left`(*a*, *x*, *lo=0*, *hi=len(a)*)

Insert *x* in *a* in sorted order. This is equivalent to `a.insert(bisect.bisect_left(a, x, lo, hi), x)` assuming that *a* is already sorted. Keep in mind that the O(log n) search is dominated by the slow O(n) insertion step.

---

[1] The disk balancing algorithms which are current, nowadays, are more annoying than clever, and this is a consequence of the seeking capabilities of the disks. On devices which cannot seek, like big tape drives, the story was quite different, and one had to be very clever to ensure (far in advance) that each tape movement will be the most effective possible (that is, will best participate at "progressing" the merge). Some tapes were even able to read backwards, and this was also used to avoid the rewinding time. Believe me, real good tape sorts were quite spectacular to watch! From all times, sorting has always been a Great Art! :-)

bisect.insort_right(*a, x, lo=0, hi=len(a)*)
bisect.insort(*a, x, lo=0, hi=len(a)*)
Similar to `insort_left()`, but inserting x in a after any existing entries of x.

See also:

SortedCollection recipe that uses bisect to build a full-featured collection class with straight-forward search methods and support for a key-function. The keys are precomputed to save unnecessary calls to the key function during searches.

8.6.1 Searching Sorted Lists

The above `bisect()` functions are useful for finding insertion points but can be tricky or awkward to use for common searching tasks. The following five functions show how to transform them into the standard lookups for sorted lists:

```
def index(a, x):
    'Locate the leftmost value exactly equal to x'
    i = bisect_left(a, x)
    if i != len(a) and a[i] == x:
        return i
    raise ValueError

def find_lt(a, x):
    'Find rightmost value less than x'
    i = bisect_left(a, x)
    if i:
        return a[i-1]
    raise ValueError

def find_le(a, x):
    'Find rightmost value less than or equal to x'
    i = bisect_right(a, x)
    if i:
        return a[i-1]
    raise ValueError

def find_gt(a, x):
    'Find leftmost value greater than x'
    i = bisect_right(a, x)
    if i != len(a):
        return a[i]
    raise ValueError

def find_ge(a, x):
    'Find leftmost item greater than or equal to x'
    i = bisect_left(a, x)
    if i != len(a):
        return a[i]
    raise ValueError
```

8.6.2 Other Examples

The `bisect()` function can be useful for numeric table lookups. This example uses `bisect()` to look up a letter grade for an exam score (say) based on a set of ordered numeric breakpoints: 90 and up is an 'A', 80 to 89 is a 'B', and so on:

```
>>> def grade(score, breakpoints=[60, 70, 80, 90], grades='FDCBA'):
...     i = bisect(breakpoints, score)
...     return grades[i]
...
>>> [grade(score) for score in [33, 99, 77, 70, 89, 90, 100]]
['F', 'A', 'C', 'C', 'B', 'A', 'A']
```

Unlike the `sorted()` function, it does not make sense for the `bisect()` functions to have *key* or *reversed* arguments because that would lead to an inefficient design (successive calls to bisect functions would not "remember" all of the previous key lookups).

Instead, it is better to search a list of precomputed keys to find the index of the record in question:

```
>>> data = [('red', 5), ('blue', 1), ('yellow', 8), ('black', 0)]
>>> data.sort(key=lambda r: r[1])
>>> keys = [r[1] for r in data]         # precomputed list of keys
>>> data[bisect_left(keys, 0)]
('black', 0)
>>> data[bisect_left(keys, 1)]
('blue', 1)
>>> data[bisect_left(keys, 5)]
('red', 5)
>>> data[bisect_left(keys, 8)]
('yellow', 8)
```

8.7 `array` — Efficient arrays of numeric values

This module defines an object type which can compactly represent an array of basic values: characters, integers, floating point numbers. Arrays are sequence types and behave very much like lists, except that the type of objects stored in them is constrained. The type is specified at object creation time by using a *type code*, which is a single character. The following type codes are defined:

Type code	C Type	Python Type	Minimum size in bytes	Notes
'b'	signed char	int	1	
'B'	unsigned char	int	1	
'u'	Py_UNICODE	Unicode character	2	(1)
'h'	signed short	int	2	
'H'	unsigned short	int	2	
'i'	signed int	int	2	
'I'	unsigned int	int	2	
'l'	signed long	int	4	
'L'	unsigned long	int	4	
'q'	signed long long	int	8	(2)
'Q'	unsigned long long	int	8	(2)
'f'	float	float	4	
'd'	double	float	8	

Notes:

1. The `'u'` type code corresponds to Python's obsolete unicode character (`Py_UNICODE` which is `wchar_t`). Depending on the platform, it can be 16 bits or 32 bits.

'u' will be removed together with the rest of the Py_UNICODE API.

Deprecated since version 3.3, will be removed in version 4.0.

2. The 'q' and 'Q' type codes are available only if the platform C compiler used to build Python supports C `long long`, or, on Windows, `__int64`.

   New in version 3.3.

The actual representation of values is determined by the machine architecture (strictly speaking, by the C implementation). The actual size can be accessed through the `itemsize` attribute.

The module defines the following type:

`class array.array(`*typecode*[, *initializer*]`)`
A new array whose items are restricted by *typecode*, and initialized from the optional *initializer* value, which must be a list, a *bytes-like object*, or iterable over elements of the appropriate type.

If given a list or string, the initializer is passed to the new array's *fromlist()*, *frombytes()*, or *fromunicode()* method (see below) to add initial items to the array. Otherwise, the iterable initializer is passed to the *extend()* method.

`array.typecodes`
A string with all available type codes.

Array objects support the ordinary sequence operations of indexing, slicing, concatenation, and multiplication. When using slice assignment, the assigned value must be an array object with the same type code; in all other cases, *TypeError* is raised. Array objects also implement the buffer interface, and may be used wherever *bytes-like objects* are supported.

The following data items and methods are also supported:

`array.typecode`
The typecode character used to create the array.

`array.itemsize`
The length in bytes of one array item in the internal representation.

`array.append(`*x*`)`
Append a new item with value *x* to the end of the array.

`array.buffer_info()`
Return a tuple `(address, length)` giving the current memory address and the length in elements of the buffer used to hold array's contents. The size of the memory buffer in bytes can be computed as `array.buffer_info()[1] * array.itemsize`. This is occasionally useful when working with low-level (and inherently unsafe) I/O interfaces that require memory addresses, such as certain `ioctl()` operations. The returned numbers are valid as long as the array exists and no length-changing operations are applied to it.

Note: When using array objects from code written in C or C++ (the only way to effectively make use of this information), it makes more sense to use the buffer interface supported by array objects. This method is maintained for backward compatibility and should be avoided in new code. The buffer interface is documented in bufferobjects.

`array.byteswap()`
"Byteswap" all items of the array. This is only supported for values which are 1, 2, 4, or 8 bytes in size; for other types of values, *RuntimeError* is raised. It is useful when reading data from a file written on a machine with a different byte order.

`array.count(`*x*`)`
Return the number of occurrences of *x* in the array.

array.extend(*iterable*)
Append items from *iterable* to the end of the array. If *iterable* is another array, it must have *exactly* the same type code; if not, *TypeError* will be raised. If *iterable* is not an array, it must be iterable and its elements must be the right type to be appended to the array.

array.frombytes(*s*)
Appends items from the string, interpreting the string as an array of machine values (as if it had been read from a file using the *fromfile()* method).

New in version 3.2: *fromstring()* is renamed to *frombytes()* for clarity.

array.fromfile(*f*, *n*)
Read *n* items (as machine values) from the *file object* *f* and append them to the end of the array. If less than *n* items are available, *EOFError* is raised, but the items that were available are still inserted into the array. *f* must be a real built-in file object; something else with a `read()` method won't do.

array.fromlist(*list*)
Append items from the list. This is equivalent to `for x in list: a.append(x)` except that if there is a type error, the array is unchanged.

array.fromstring()
Deprecated alias for *frombytes()*.

array.fromunicode(*s*)
Extends this array with data from the given unicode string. The array must be a type `'u'` array; otherwise a *ValueError* is raised. Use `array.frombytes(unicodestring.encode(enc))` to append Unicode data to an array of some other type.

array.index(*x*)
Return the smallest *i* such that *i* is the index of the first occurrence of *x* in the array.

array.insert(*i*, *x*)
Insert a new item with value *x* in the array before position *i*. Negative values are treated as being relative to the end of the array.

array.pop([*i*])
Removes the item with the index *i* from the array and returns it. The optional argument defaults to `-1`, so that by default the last item is removed and returned.

array.remove(*x*)
Remove the first occurrence of *x* from the array.

array.reverse()
Reverse the order of the items in the array.

array.tobytes()
Convert the array to an array of machine values and return the bytes representation (the same sequence of bytes that would be written to a file by the *tofile()* method.)

New in version 3.2: *tostring()* is renamed to *tobytes()* for clarity.

array.tofile(*f*)
Write all items (as machine values) to the *file object* *f*.

array.tolist()
Convert the array to an ordinary list with the same items.

array.tostring()
Deprecated alias for *tobytes()*.

array.tounicode()
Convert the array to a unicode string. The array must be a type `'u'` array; otherwise a *ValueError* is raised. Use `array.tobytes().decode(enc)` to obtain a unicode string from an array of some other type.

When an array object is printed or converted to a string, it is represented as `array(typecode, initializer)`. The *initializer* is omitted if the array is empty, otherwise it is a string if the *typecode* is `'u'`, otherwise it is a list of numbers. The string is guaranteed to be able to be converted back to an array with the same type and value using `eval()`, so long as the `array` class has been imported using `from array import array`. Examples:

```
array('l')
array('u', 'hello \u2641')
array('l', [1, 2, 3, 4, 5])
array('d', [1.0, 2.0, 3.14])
```

See also:

Module `struct` Packing and unpacking of heterogeneous binary data.

Module `xdrlib` Packing and unpacking of External Data Representation (XDR) data as used in some remote procedure call systems.

The Numerical Python Documentation The Numeric Python extension (NumPy) defines another array type; see http://www.numpy.org/ for further information about Numerical Python.

8.8 weakref — Weak references

Source code: Lib/weakref.py

The `weakref` module allows the Python programmer to create *weak references* to objects.

In the following, the term *referent* means the object which is referred to by a weak reference.

A weak reference to an object is not enough to keep the object alive: when the only remaining references to a referent are weak references, *garbage collection* is free to destroy the referent and reuse its memory for something else. However, until the object is actually destroyed the weak reference may return the object even if there are no strong references to it.

A primary use for weak references is to implement caches or mappings holding large objects, where it's desired that a large object not be kept alive solely because it appears in a cache or mapping.

For example, if you have a number of large binary image objects, you may wish to associate a name with each. If you used a Python dictionary to map names to images, or images to names, the image objects would remain alive just because they appeared as values or keys in the dictionaries. The `WeakKeyDictionary` and `WeakValueDictionary` classes supplied by the `weakref` module are an alternative, using weak references to construct mappings that don't keep objects alive solely because they appear in the mapping objects. If, for example, an image object is a value in a `WeakValueDictionary`, then when the last remaining references to that image object are the weak references held by weak mappings, garbage collection can reclaim the object, and its corresponding entries in weak mappings are simply deleted.

`WeakKeyDictionary` and `WeakValueDictionary` use weak references in their implementation, setting up callback functions on the weak references that notify the weak dictionaries when a key or value has been reclaimed by garbage collection. `WeakSet` implements the `set` interface, but keeps weak references to its elements, just like a `WeakKeyDictionary` does.

`finalize` provides a straight forward way to register a cleanup function to be called when an object is garbage collected. This is simpler to use than setting up a callback function on a raw weak reference, since the module automatically ensures that the finalizer remains alive until the object is collected.

Most programs should find that using one of these weak container types or `finalize` is all they need – it's not usually necessary to create your own weak references directly. The low-level machinery is exposed by the `weakref` module for the benefit of advanced uses.

Not all objects can be weakly referenced; those objects which can include class instances, functions written in Python (but not in C), instance methods, sets, frozensets, some *file objects*, *generators*, type objects, sockets, arrays, deques, regular expression pattern objects, and code objects.

Changed in version 3.2: Added support for thread.lock, threading.Lock, and code objects.

Several built-in types such as `list` and `dict` do not directly support weak references but can add support through subclassing:

```
class Dict(dict):
    pass

obj = Dict(red=1, green=2, blue=3)   # this object is weak referenceable
```

Other built-in types such as `tuple` and `int` do not support weak references even when subclassed (This is an implementation detail and may be different across various Python implementations.).

Extension types can easily be made to support weak references; see weakref-support.

class weakref.ref(*object*[, *callback*])

Return a weak reference to *object*. The original object can be retrieved by calling the reference object if the referent is still alive; if the referent is no longer alive, calling the reference object will cause `None` to be returned. If *callback* is provided and not `None`, and the returned weakref object is still alive, the callback will be called when the object is about to be finalized; the weak reference object will be passed as the only parameter to the callback; the referent will no longer be available.

It is allowable for many weak references to be constructed for the same object. Callbacks registered for each weak reference will be called from the most recently registered callback to the oldest registered callback.

Exceptions raised by the callback will be noted on the standard error output, but cannot be propagated; they are handled in exactly the same way as exceptions raised from an object's `__del__()` method.

Weak references are *hashable* if the *object* is hashable. They will maintain their hash value even after the *object* was deleted. If `hash()` is called the first time only after the *object* was deleted, the call will raise `TypeError`.

Weak references support tests for equality, but not ordering. If the referents are still alive, two references have the same equality relationship as their referents (regardless of the *callback*). If either referent has been deleted, the references are equal only if the reference objects are the same object.

This is a subclassable type rather than a factory function.

__callback__

This read-only attribute returns the callback currently associated to the weakref. If there is no callback or if the referent of the weakref is no longer alive then this attribute will have value `None`.

Changed in version 3.4: Added the `__callback__` attribute.

weakref.proxy(*object*[, *callback*])

Return a proxy to *object* which uses a weak reference. This supports use of the proxy in most contexts instead of requiring the explicit dereferencing used with weak reference objects. The returned object will have a type of either `ProxyType` or `CallableProxyType`, depending on whether *object* is callable. Proxy objects are not *hashable* regardless of the referent; this avoids a number of problems related to their fundamentally mutable nature, and prevent their use as dictionary keys. *callback* is the same as the parameter of the same name to the `ref()` function.

weakref.getweakrefcount(*object*)

Return the number of weak references and proxies which refer to *object*.

weakref.getweakrefs(*object*)

Return a list of all weak reference and proxy objects which refer to *object*.

class weakref.WeakKeyDictionary([*dict*]**)**

Mapping class that references keys weakly. Entries in the dictionary will be discarded when there is no longer a strong reference to the key. This can be used to associate additional data with an object owned by other parts of an application without adding attributes to those objects. This can be especially useful with objects that override attribute accesses.

Note: Caution: Because a *WeakKeyDictionary* is built on top of a Python dictionary, it must not change size when iterating over it. This can be difficult to ensure for a *WeakKeyDictionary* because actions performed by the program during iteration may cause items in the dictionary to vanish "by magic" (as a side effect of garbage collection).

WeakKeyDictionary objects have an additional method that exposes the internal references directly. The references are not guaranteed to be "live" at the time they are used, so the result of calling the references needs to be checked before being used. This can be used to avoid creating references that will cause the garbage collector to keep the keys around longer than needed.

WeakKeyDictionary.keyrefs()

Return an iterable of the weak references to the keys.

class weakref.WeakValueDictionary([*dict*]**)**

Mapping class that references values weakly. Entries in the dictionary will be discarded when no strong reference to the value exists any more.

Note: Caution: Because a *WeakValueDictionary* is built on top of a Python dictionary, it must not change size when iterating over it. This can be difficult to ensure for a *WeakValueDictionary* because actions performed by the program during iteration may cause items in the dictionary to vanish "by magic" (as a side effect of garbage collection).

WeakValueDictionary objects have an additional method that has the same issues as the `keyrefs()` method of *WeakKeyDictionary* objects.

WeakValueDictionary.valuerefs()

Return an iterable of the weak references to the values.

class weakref.WeakSet([*elements*]**)**

Set class that keeps weak references to its elements. An element will be discarded when no strong reference to it exists any more.

class weakref.WeakMethod(*method***)**

A custom *ref* subclass which simulates a weak reference to a bound method (i.e., a method defined on a class and looked up on an instance). Since a bound method is ephemeral, a standard weak reference cannot keep hold of it. *WeakMethod* has special code to recreate the bound method until either the object or the original function dies:

```
>>> class C:
...     def method(self):
...         print("method called!")
...
>>> c = C()
>>> r = weakref.ref(c.method)
>>> r()
>>> r = weakref.WeakMethod(c.method)
>>> r()
<bound method C.method of <__main__.C object at 0x7fc859830220>>
>>> r()()
method called!
```

```
>>> del c
>>> gc.collect()
0
>>> r()
>>>
```

New in version 3.4.

class weakref.finalize(*obj*, *func*, **args*, ***kwargs*)

Return a callable finalizer object which will be called when *obj* is garbage collected. Unlike an ordinary weak reference, a finalizer will always survive until the reference object is collected, greatly simplifying lifecycle management.

A finalizer is considered *alive* until it is called (either explicitly or at garbage collection), and after that it is *dead*. Calling a live finalizer returns the result of evaluating `func(*arg, **kwargs)`, whereas calling a dead finalizer returns *None*.

Exceptions raised by finalizer callbacks during garbage collection will be shown on the standard error output, but cannot be propagated. They are handled in the same way as exceptions raised from an object's `__del__()` method or a weak reference's callback.

When the program exits, each remaining live finalizer is called unless its *atexit* attribute has been set to false. They are called in reverse order of creation.

A finalizer will never invoke its callback during the later part of the *interpreter shutdown* when module globals are liable to have been replaced by *None*.

__call__()

If *self* is alive then mark it as dead and return the result of calling `func(*args, **kwargs)`. If *self* is dead then return *None*.

detach()

If *self* is alive then mark it as dead and return the tuple `(obj, func, args, kwargs)`. If *self* is dead then return *None*.

peek()

If *self* is alive then return the tuple `(obj, func, args, kwargs)`. If *self* is dead then return *None*.

alive

Property which is true if the finalizer is alive, false otherwise.

atexit

A writable boolean property which by default is true. When the program exits, it calls all remaining live finalizers for which *atexit* is true. They are called in reverse order of creation.

Note: It is important to ensure that *func*, *args* and *kwargs* do not own any references to *obj*, either directly or indirectly, since otherwise *obj* will never be garbage collected. In particular, *func* should not be a bound method of *obj*.

New in version 3.4.

weakref.ReferenceType

The type object for weak references objects.

weakref.ProxyType

The type object for proxies of objects which are not callable.

weakref.CallableProxyType

The type object for proxies of callable objects.

`weakref.ProxyTypes`
Sequence containing all the type objects for proxies. This can make it simpler to test if an object is a proxy without being dependent on naming both proxy types.

`exception weakref.ReferenceError`
Exception raised when a proxy object is used but the underlying object has been collected. This is the same as the standard *ReferenceError* exception.

See also:

PEP 205 - **Weak References** The proposal and rationale for this feature, including links to earlier implementations and information about similar features in other languages.

8.8.1 Weak Reference Objects

Weak reference objects have no methods and no attributes besides *ref.__callback__*. A weak reference object allows the referent to be obtained, if it still exists, by calling it:

```
>>> import weakref
>>> class Object:
...     pass
...
>>> o = Object()
>>> r = weakref.ref(o)
>>> o2 = r()
>>> o is o2
True
```

If the referent no longer exists, calling the reference object returns *None*:

```
>>> del o, o2
>>> print(r())
None
```

Testing that a weak reference object is still live should be done using the expression `ref() is not None`. Normally, application code that needs to use a reference object should follow this pattern:

```
# r is a weak reference object
o = r()
if o is None:
    # referent has been garbage collected
    print("Object has been deallocated; can't frobnicate.")
else:
    print("Object is still live!")
    o.do_something_useful()
```

Using a separate test for "liveness" creates race conditions in threaded applications; another thread can cause a weak reference to become invalidated before the weak reference is called; the idiom shown above is safe in threaded applications as well as single-threaded applications.

Specialized versions of *ref* objects can be created through subclassing. This is used in the implementation of the *WeakValueDictionary* to reduce the memory overhead for each entry in the mapping. This may be most useful to associate additional information with a reference, but could also be used to insert additional processing on calls to retrieve the referent.

This example shows how a subclass of *ref* can be used to store additional information about an object and affect the value that's returned when the referent is accessed:

```
import weakref

class ExtendedRef(weakref.ref):
    def __init__(self, ob, callback=None, **annotations):
        super(ExtendedRef, self).__init__(ob, callback)
        self.__counter = 0
        for k, v in annotations.items():
            setattr(self, k, v)

    def __call__(self):
        """Return a pair containing the referent and the number of
        times the reference has been called.
        """
        ob = super(ExtendedRef, self).__call__()
        if ob is not None:
            self.__counter += 1
            ob = (ob, self.__counter)
        return ob
```

8.8.2 Example

This simple example shows how an application can use object IDs to retrieve objects that it has seen before. The IDs of the objects can then be used in other data structures without forcing the objects to remain alive, but the objects can still be retrieved by ID if they do.

```
import weakref

_id2obj_dict = weakref.WeakValueDictionary()

def remember(obj):
    oid = id(obj)
    _id2obj_dict[oid] = obj
    return oid

def id2obj(oid):
    return _id2obj_dict[oid]
```

8.8.3 Finalizer Objects

The main benefit of using *finalize* is that it makes it simple to register a callback without needing to preserve the returned finalizer object. For instance

```
>>> import weakref
>>> class Object:
...     pass
...
>>> kenny = Object()
>>> weakref.finalize(kenny, print, "You killed Kenny!")
<finalize object at ...; for 'Object' at ...>
>>> del kenny
You killed Kenny!
```

The finalizer can be called directly as well. However the finalizer will invoke the callback at most once.

```
>>> def callback(x, y, z):
...     print("CALLBACK")
...     return x + y + z
...
>>> obj = Object()
>>> f = weakref.finalize(obj, callback, 1, 2, z=3)
>>> assert f.alive
>>> assert f() == 6
CALLBACK
>>> assert not f.alive
>>> f()                     # callback not called because finalizer dead
>>> del obj                 # callback not called because finalizer dead
```

You can unregister a finalizer using its *detach()* method. This kills the finalizer and returns the arguments passed to the constructor when it was created.

```
>>> obj = Object()
>>> f = weakref.finalize(obj, callback, 1, 2, z=3)
>>> f.detach()
(<__main__.Object object ...>, <function callback ...>, (1, 2), {'z': 3})
>>> newobj, func, args, kwargs = _
>>> assert not f.alive
>>> assert newobj is obj
>>> assert func(*args, **kwargs) == 6
CALLBACK
```

Unless you set the *atexit* attribute to *False*, a finalizer will be called when the program exits if it is still alive. For instance

```
>>> obj = Object()
>>> weakref.finalize(obj, print, "obj dead or exiting")
<finalize object at ...; for 'Object' at ...>
>>> exit()
obj dead or exiting
```

8.8.4 Comparing finalizers with `__del__()` methods

Suppose we want to create a class whose instances represent temporary directories. The directories should be deleted with their contents when the first of the following events occurs:

- the object is garbage collected,
- the object's `remove()` method is called, or
- the program exits.

We might try to implement the class using a `__del__()` method as follows:

```
class TempDir:
    def __init__(self):
        self.name = tempfile.mkdtemp()

    def remove(self):
        if self.name is not None:
            shutil.rmtree(self.name)
            self.name = None

    @property
```

```
    def removed(self):
        return self.name is None

    def __del__(self):
        self.remove()
```

Starting with Python 3.4, `__del__()` methods no longer prevent reference cycles from being garbage collected, and module globals are no longer forced to *None* during *interpreter shutdown*. So this code should work without any issues on CPython.

However, handling of `__del__()` methods is notoriously implementation specific, since it depends on internal details of the interpreter's garbage collector implementation.

A more robust alternative can be to define a finalizer which only references the specific functions and objects that it needs, rather than having access to the full state of the object:

```
class TempDir:
    def __init__(self):
        self.name = tempfile.mkdtemp()
        self._finalizer = weakref.finalize(self, shutil.rmtree, self.name)

    def remove(self):
        self._finalizer()

    @property
    def removed(self):
        return not self._finalizer.alive
```

Defined like this, our finalizer only receives a reference to the details it needs to clean up the directory appropriately. If the object never gets garbage collected the finalizer will still be called at exit.

The other advantage of weakref based finalizers is that they can be used to register finalizers for classes where the definition is controlled by a third party, such as running code when a module is unloaded:

```
import weakref, sys
def unloading_module():
    # implicit reference to the module globals from the function body
weakref.finalize(sys.modules[__name__], unloading_module)
```

Note: If you create a finalizer object in a daemonic thread just as the program exits then there is the possibility that the finalizer does not get called at exit. However, in a daemonic thread *atexit.register()*, `try: ... finally: ...` and `with: ...` do not guarantee that cleanup occurs either.

8.9 types — Dynamic type creation and names for built-in types

Source code: Lib/types.py

This module defines utility function to assist in dynamic creation of new types.

It also defines names for some object types that are used by the standard Python interpreter, but not exposed as builtins like *int* or *str* are.

Finally, it provides some additional type-related utility classes and functions that are not fundamental enough to be builtins.

8.9.1 Dynamic Type Creation

types.**new_class**(*name, bases=(), kwds=None, exec_body=None*)

Creates a class object dynamically using the appropriate metaclass.

The first three arguments are the components that make up a class definition header: the class name, the base classes (in order), the keyword arguments (such as `metaclass`).

The *exec_body* argument is a callback that is used to populate the freshly created class namespace. It should accept the class namespace as its sole argument and update the namespace directly with the class contents. If no callback is provided, it has the same effect as passing in `lambda ns: ns`.

New in version 3.3.

types.**prepare_class**(*name, bases=(), kwds=None*)

Calculates the appropriate metaclass and creates the class namespace.

The arguments are the components that make up a class definition header: the class name, the base classes (in order) and the keyword arguments (such as `metaclass`).

The return value is a 3-tuple: `metaclass, namespace, kwds`

metaclass is the appropriate metaclass, *namespace* is the prepared class namespace and *kwds* is an updated copy of the passed in *kwds* argument with any `'metaclass'` entry removed. If no *kwds* argument is passed in, this will be an empty dict.

New in version 3.3.

Changed in version 3.6: The default value for the `namespace` element of the returned tuple has changed. Now an insertion-order-preserving mapping is used when the metaclass does not have a `__prepare__` method,

See also:

metaclasses Full details of the class creation process supported by these functions

PEP 3115 - **Metaclasses in Python 3000** Introduced the `__prepare__` namespace hook

8.9.2 Standard Interpreter Types

This module provides names for many of the types that are required to implement a Python interpreter. It deliberately avoids including some of the types that arise only incidentally during processing such as the `listiterator` type.

Typical use of these names is for *isinstance()* or *issubclass()* checks.

Standard names are defined for the following types:

types.**FunctionType**
types.**LambdaType**

The type of user-defined functions and functions created by `lambda` expressions.

types.**GeneratorType**

The type of *generator*-iterator objects, created by generator functions.

types.**CoroutineType**

The type of *coroutine* objects, created by `async def` functions.

New in version 3.5.

types.**AsyncGeneratorType**

The type of *asynchronous generator*-iterator objects, created by asynchronous generator functions.

New in version 3.6.

types.CodeType
The type for code objects such as returned by *compile()*.

types.MethodType
The type of methods of user-defined class instances.

types.BuiltinFunctionType
types.BuiltinMethodType
The type of built-in functions like *len()* or *sys.exit()*, and methods of built-in classes. (Here, the term "built-in" means "written in C".)

class **types.ModuleType**(*name, doc=None*)
The type of *modules*. Constructor takes the name of the module to be created and optionally its *docstring*.

Note: Use *importlib.util.module_from_spec()* to create a new module if you wish to set the various import-controlled attributes.

__doc__
The *docstring* of the module. Defaults to None.

__loader__
The *loader* which loaded the module. Defaults to None.

Changed in version 3.4: Defaults to None. Previously the attribute was optional.

__name__
The name of the module.

__package__
Which *package* a module belongs to. If the module is top-level (i.e. not a part of any specific package) then the attribute should be set to '', else it should be set to the name of the package (which can be __name__ if the module is a package itself). Defaults to None.

Changed in version 3.4: Defaults to None. Previously the attribute was optional.

types.TracebackType
The type of traceback objects such as found in sys.exc_info()[2].

types.FrameType
The type of frame objects such as found in tb.tb_frame if tb is a traceback object.

types.GetSetDescriptorType
The type of objects defined in extension modules with PyGetSetDef, such as FrameType.f_locals or array.array.typecode. This type is used as descriptor for object attributes; it has the same purpose as the *property* type, but for classes defined in extension modules.

types.MemberDescriptorType
The type of objects defined in extension modules with PyMemberDef, such as datetime.timedelta.days. This type is used as descriptor for simple C data members which use standard conversion functions; it has the same purpose as the *property* type, but for classes defined in extension modules.

CPython implementation detail: In other implementations of Python, this type may be identical to GetSetDescriptorType.

class **types.MappingProxyType**(*mapping*)
Read-only proxy of a mapping. It provides a dynamic view on the mapping's entries, which means that when the mapping changes, the view reflects these changes.

New in version 3.3.

key in proxy
Return True if the underlying mapping has a key *key*, else False.

proxy[key]
Return the item of the underlying mapping with key *key*. Raises a *KeyError* if *key* is not in the underlying mapping.

iter(proxy)
Return an iterator over the keys of the underlying mapping. This is a shortcut for iter(proxy.keys()).

len(proxy)
Return the number of items in the underlying mapping.

copy()
Return a shallow copy of the underlying mapping.

get(*key*[, *default*])
Return the value for *key* if *key* is in the underlying mapping, else *default*. If *default* is not given, it defaults to None, so that this method never raises a *KeyError*.

items()
Return a new view of the underlying mapping's items ((key, value) pairs).

keys()
Return a new view of the underlying mapping's keys.

values()
Return a new view of the underlying mapping's values.

8.9.3 Additional Utility Classes and Functions

class types.SimpleNamespace
A simple *object* subclass that provides attribute access to its namespace, as well as a meaningful repr.

Unlike *object*, with SimpleNamespace you can add and remove attributes. If a SimpleNamespace object is initialized with keyword arguments, those are directly added to the underlying namespace.

The type is roughly equivalent to the following code:

```
class SimpleNamespace:
    def __init__(self, **kwargs):
        self.__dict__.update(kwargs)

    def __repr__(self):
        keys = sorted(self.__dict__)
        items = ("{}={!r}".format(k, self.__dict__[k]) for k in keys)
        return "{}({})".format(type(self).__name__, ", ".join(items))

    def __eq__(self, other):
        return self.__dict__ == other.__dict__
```

SimpleNamespace may be useful as a replacement for class NS: pass. However, for a structured record type use *namedtuple()* instead.

New in version 3.3.

types.DynamicClassAttribute(*fget=None*, *fset=None*, *fdel=None*, *doc=None*)
Route attribute access on a class to `__getattr__`.

This is a descriptor, used to define attributes that act differently when accessed through an instance and through a class. Instance access remains normal, but access to an attribute through a class will be routed to the class's __getattr__ method; this is done by raising AttributeError.

This allows one to have properties active on an instance, and have virtual attributes on the class with the same name (see Enum for an example).

New in version 3.4.

8.9.4 Coroutine Utility Functions

`types.coroutine(gen_func)`

This function transforms a *generator* function into a *coroutine function* which returns a generator-based coroutine. The generator-based coroutine is still a *generator iterator*, but is also considered to be a *coroutine* object and is *awaitable*. However, it may not necessarily implement the `__await__()` method.

If *gen_func* is a generator function, it will be modified in-place.

If *gen_func* is not a generator function, it will be wrapped. If it returns an instance of `collections.abc.Generator`, the instance will be wrapped in an *awaitable* proxy object. All other types of objects will be returned as is.

New in version 3.5.

8.10 copy — Shallow and deep copy operations

Source code: Lib/copy.py

Assignment statements in Python do not copy objects, they create bindings between a target and an object. For collections that are mutable or contain mutable items, a copy is sometimes needed so one can change one copy without changing the other. This module provides generic shallow and deep copy operations (explained below).

Interface summary:

`copy.copy(x)`

Return a shallow copy of *x*.

`copy.deepcopy(x)`

Return a deep copy of *x*.

`exception copy.error`

Raised for module specific errors.

The difference between shallow and deep copying is only relevant for compound objects (objects that contain other objects, like lists or class instances):

- A *shallow copy* constructs a new compound object and then (to the extent possible) inserts *references* into it to the objects found in the original.
- A *deep copy* constructs a new compound object and then, recursively, inserts *copies* into it of the objects found in the original.

Two problems often exist with deep copy operations that don't exist with shallow copy operations:

- Recursive objects (compound objects that, directly or indirectly, contain a reference to themselves) may cause a recursive loop.

- Because deep copy copies everything it may copy too much, such as data which is intended to be shared between copies.

The *deepcopy()* function avoids these problems by:

- keeping a "memo" dictionary of objects already copied during the current copying pass; and
- letting user-defined classes override the copying operation or the set of components copied.

This module does not copy types like module, method, stack trace, stack frame, file, socket, window, array, or any similar types. It does "copy" functions and classes (shallow and deeply), by returning the original object unchanged; this is compatible with the way these are treated by the *pickle* module.

Shallow copies of dictionaries can be made using *dict.copy()*, and of lists by assigning a slice of the entire list, for example, `copied_list = original_list[:]`.

Classes can use the same interfaces to control copying that they use to control pickling. See the description of module *pickle* for information on these methods. In fact, the *copy* module uses the registered pickle functions from the *copyreg* module.

In order for a class to define its own copy implementation, it can define special methods `__copy__()` and `__deepcopy__()`. The former is called to implement the shallow copy operation; no additional arguments are passed. The latter is called to implement the deep copy operation; it is passed one argument, the memo dictionary. If the `__deepcopy__()` implementation needs to make a deep copy of a component, it should call the *deepcopy()* function with the component as first argument and the memo dictionary as second argument.

See also:

Module *pickle* Discussion of the special methods used to support object state retrieval and restoration.

8.11 pprint — Data pretty printer

Source code: Lib/pprint.py

The *pprint* module provides a capability to "pretty-print" arbitrary Python data structures in a form which can be used as input to the interpreter. If the formatted structures include objects which are not fundamental Python types, the representation may not be loadable. This may be the case if objects such as files, sockets or classes are included, as well as many other objects which are not representable as Python literals.

The formatted representation keeps objects on a single line if it can, and breaks them onto multiple lines if they don't fit within the allowed width. Construct *PrettyPrinter* objects explicitly if you need to adjust the width constraint.

Dictionaries are sorted by key before the display is computed.

The *pprint* module defines one class:

class pprint.PrettyPrinter(*indent=1, width=80, depth=None, stream=None, *, compact=False*)

Construct a *PrettyPrinter* instance. This constructor understands several keyword parameters. An output stream may be set using the *stream* keyword; the only method used on the stream object is the file protocol's `write()` method. If not specified, the *PrettyPrinter* adopts `sys.stdout`. The amount of indentation added for each recursive level is specified by *indent*; the default is one. Other values can cause output to look a little odd, but can make nesting easier to spot. The number of levels which may be printed is controlled by *depth*; if the data structure being printed is too deep, the next contained level is replaced by `...`. By default, there is no constraint on the depth of the objects being formatted. The desired output width is constrained using the *width* parameter; the default is 80 characters. If a structure cannot be formatted within the constrained width, a best effort will be made. If *compact* is false (the default) each item of a long sequence will be formatted on a separate line. If *compact* is true, as many items as will fit within the *width* will be formatted on each output line.

Changed in version 3.4: Added the *compact* parameter.

```
>>> import pprint
>>> stuff = ['spam', 'eggs', 'lumberjack', 'knights', 'ni']
>>> stuff.insert(0, stuff[:])
>>> pp = pprint.PrettyPrinter(indent=4)
>>> pp.pprint(stuff)
[   ['spam', 'eggs', 'lumberjack', 'knights', 'ni'],
    'spam',
    'eggs',
    'lumberjack',
    'knights',
    'ni']
>>> pp = pprint.PrettyPrinter(width=41, compact=True)
>>> pp.pprint(stuff)
[['spam', 'eggs', 'lumberjack',
  'knights', 'ni'],
 'spam', 'eggs', 'lumberjack', 'knights',
 'ni']
>>> tup = ('spam', ('eggs', ('lumberjack', ('knights', ('ni', ('dead',
... ('parrot', ('fresh fruit',))))))))
>>> pp = pprint.PrettyPrinter(depth=6)
>>> pp.pprint(tup)
('spam', ('eggs', ('lumberjack', ('knights', ('ni', ('dead', (...)))))))
```

The *pprint* module also provides several shortcut functions:

`pprint.pformat`(*object*, *indent=1*, *width=80*, *depth=None*, *, *compact=False*)
Return the formatted representation of *object* as a string. *indent*, *width*, *depth* and *compact* will be passed to the *PrettyPrinter* constructor as formatting parameters.

Changed in version 3.4: Added the *compact* parameter.

`pprint.pprint`(*object*, *stream=None*, *indent=1*, *width=80*, *depth=None*, *, *compact=False*)
Prints the formatted representation of *object* on *stream*, followed by a newline. If *stream* is `None`, `sys.stdout` is used. This may be used in the interactive interpreter instead of the *print()* function for inspecting values (you can even reassign `print = pprint.pprint` for use within a scope). *indent*, *width*, *depth* and *compact* will be passed to the *PrettyPrinter* constructor as formatting parameters.

Changed in version 3.4: Added the *compact* parameter.

```
>>> import pprint
>>> stuff = ['spam', 'eggs', 'lumberjack', 'knights', 'ni']
>>> stuff.insert(0, stuff)
>>> pprint.pprint(stuff)
[<Recursion on list with id=...>,
 'spam',
 'eggs',
 'lumberjack',
 'knights',
 'ni']
```

`pprint.isreadable`(*object*)
Determine if the formatted representation of *object* is "readable," or can be used to reconstruct the value using *eval()*. This always returns `False` for recursive objects.

```
>>> pprint.isreadable(stuff)
False
```

pprint.isrecursive(*object*)
Determine if *object* requires a recursive representation.

One more support function is also defined:

pprint.saferepr(*object*)
Return a string representation of *object*, protected against recursive data structures. If the representation of *object* exposes a recursive entry, the recursive reference will be represented as `<Recursion on typename with id=number>`. The representation is not otherwise formatted.

```
>>> pprint.saferepr(stuff)
"[<Recursion on list with id=...>, 'spam', 'eggs', 'lumberjack', 'knights', 'ni']"
```

8.11.1 PrettyPrinter Objects

PrettyPrinter instances have the following methods:

PrettyPrinter.pformat(*object*)
Return the formatted representation of *object*. This takes into account the options passed to the *PrettyPrinter* constructor.

PrettyPrinter.pprint(*object*)
Print the formatted representation of *object* on the configured stream, followed by a newline.

The following methods provide the implementations for the corresponding functions of the same names. Using these methods on an instance is slightly more efficient since new *PrettyPrinter* objects don't need to be created.

PrettyPrinter.isreadable(*object*)
Determine if the formatted representation of the object is "readable," or can be used to reconstruct the value using *eval()*. Note that this returns `False` for recursive objects. If the *depth* parameter of the *PrettyPrinter* is set and the object is deeper than allowed, this returns `False`.

PrettyPrinter.isrecursive(*object*)
Determine if the object requires a recursive representation.

This method is provided as a hook to allow subclasses to modify the way objects are converted to strings. The default implementation uses the internals of the *saferepr()* implementation.

PrettyPrinter.format(*object, context, maxlevels, level*)
Returns three values: the formatted version of *object* as a string, a flag indicating whether the result is readable, and a flag indicating whether recursion was detected. The first argument is the object to be presented. The second is a dictionary which contains the *id()* of objects that are part of the current presentation context (direct and indirect containers for *object* that are affecting the presentation) as the keys; if an object needs to be presented which is already represented in *context*, the third return value should be `True`. Recursive calls to the *format()* method should add additional entries for containers to this dictionary. The third argument, *maxlevels*, gives the requested limit to recursion; this will be `0` if there is no requested limit. This argument should be passed unmodified to recursive calls. The fourth argument, *level*, gives the current level; recursive calls should be passed a value less than that of the current call.

8.11.2 Example

To demonstrate several uses of the *pprint()* function and its parameters, let's fetch information about a project from PyPI:

```
>>> import json
>>> import pprint
>>> from urllib.request import urlopen
>>> with urlopen('http://pypi.python.org/pypi/Twisted/json') as url:
...     http_info = url.info()
...     raw_data = url.read().decode(http_info.get_content_charset())
>>> project_info = json.loads(raw_data)
```

In its basic form, *pprint()* shows the whole object:

```
>>> pprint.pprint(project_info)
{'info': {'_pypi_hidden': False,
          '_pypi_ordering': 125,
          'author': 'Glyph Lefkowitz',
          'author_email': 'glyph@twistedmatrix.com',
          'bugtrack_url': '',
          'cheesecake_code_kwalitee_id': None,
          'cheesecake_documentation_id': None,
          'cheesecake_installability_id': None,
          'classifiers': ['Programming Language :: Python :: 2.6',
                          'Programming Language :: Python :: 2.7',
                          'Programming Language :: Python :: 2 :: Only'],
          'description': 'An extensible framework for Python programming, with '
                         'special focus\r\n'
                         'on event-based network programming and multiprotocol '
                         'integration.',
          'docs_url': '',
          'download_url': 'UNKNOWN',
          'home_page': 'http://twistedmatrix.com/',
          'keywords': '',
          'license': 'MIT',
          'maintainer': '',
          'maintainer_email': '',
          'name': 'Twisted',
          'package_url': 'http://pypi.python.org/pypi/Twisted',
          'platform': 'UNKNOWN',
          'release_url': 'http://pypi.python.org/pypi/Twisted/12.3.0',
          'requires_python': None,
          'stable_version': None,
          'summary': 'An asynchronous networking framework written in Python',
          'version': '12.3.0'},
 'urls': [{'comment_text': '',
           'downloads': 71844,
           'filename': 'Twisted-12.3.0.tar.bz2',
           'has_sig': False,
           'md5_digest': '6e289825f3bf5591cfd670874cc0862d',
           'packagetype': 'sdist',
           'python_version': 'source',
           'size': 2615733,
           'upload_time': '2012-12-26T12:47:03',
           'url': 'https://pypi.python.org/packages/source/T/Twisted/Twisted-12.3.0.tar.bz2'},
          {'comment_text': '',
           'downloads': 5224,
           'filename': 'Twisted-12.3.0.win32-py2.7.msi',
```

```
            'has_sig': False,
            'md5_digest': '6b778f5201b622a5519a2aca1a2fe512',
            'packagetype': 'bdist_msi',
            'python_version': '2.7',
            'size': 2916352,
            'upload_time': '2012-12-26T12:48:15',
            'url': 'https://pypi.python.org/packages/2.7/T/Twisted/Twisted-12.3.0.win32-py2.7.msi'}
↪]}
```

The result can be limited to a certain *depth* (ellipsis is used for deeper contents):

```
>>> pprint.pprint(project_info, depth=2)
{'info': {'_pypi_hidden': False,
          '_pypi_ordering': 125,
          'author': 'Glyph Lefkowitz',
          'author_email': 'glyph@twistedmatrix.com',
          'bugtrack_url': '',
          'cheesecake_code_kwalitee_id': None,
          'cheesecake_documentation_id': None,
          'cheesecake_installability_id': None,
          'classifiers': [...],
          'description': 'An extensible framework for Python programming, with '
                         'special focus\r\n'
                         'on event-based network programming and multiprotocol '
                         'integration.',
          'docs_url': '',
          'download_url': 'UNKNOWN',
          'home_page': 'http://twistedmatrix.com/',
          'keywords': '',
          'license': 'MIT',
          'maintainer': '',
          'maintainer_email': '',
          'name': 'Twisted',
          'package_url': 'http://pypi.python.org/pypi/Twisted',
          'platform': 'UNKNOWN',
          'release_url': 'http://pypi.python.org/pypi/Twisted/12.3.0',
          'requires_python': None,
          'stable_version': None,
          'summary': 'An asynchronous networking framework written in Python',
          'version': '12.3.0'},
 'urls': [{...}, {...}]}
```

Additionally, maximum character *width* can be suggested. If a long object cannot be split, the specified width will be exceeded:

```
>>> pprint.pprint(project_info, depth=2, width=50)
{'info': {'_pypi_hidden': False,
          '_pypi_ordering': 125,
          'author': 'Glyph Lefkowitz',
          'author_email': 'glyph@twistedmatrix.com',
          'bugtrack_url': '',
          'cheesecake_code_kwalitee_id': None,
          'cheesecake_documentation_id': None,
          'cheesecake_installability_id': None,
          'classifiers': [...],
          'description': 'An extensible '
                         'framework for Python '
                         'programming, with '
```

```
                         'special focus\r\n'
                         'on event-based network '
                         'programming and '
                         'multiprotocol '
                         'integration.',
            'docs_url': '',
            'download_url': 'UNKNOWN',
            'home_page': 'http://twistedmatrix.com/',
            'keywords': '',
            'license': 'MIT',
            'maintainer': '',
            'maintainer_email': '',
            'name': 'Twisted',
            'package_url': 'http://pypi.python.org/pypi/Twisted',
            'platform': 'UNKNOWN',
            'release_url': 'http://pypi.python.org/pypi/Twisted/12.3.0',
            'requires_python': None,
            'stable_version': None,
            'summary': 'An asynchronous networking '
                       'framework written in '
                       'Python',
            'version': '12.3.0'},
 'urls': [{...}, {...}]}
```

8.12 reprlib — Alternate repr() implementation

Source code: Lib/reprlib.py

The *reprlib* module provides a means for producing object representations with limits on the size of the resulting strings. This is used in the Python debugger and may be useful in other contexts as well.

This module provides a class, an instance, and a function:

class reprlib.Repr
  Class which provides formatting services useful in implementing functions similar to the built-in *repr()*; size limits for different object types are added to avoid the generation of representations which are excessively long.

reprlib.aRepr
  This is an instance of *Repr* which is used to provide the *repr()* function described below. Changing the attributes of this object will affect the size limits used by *repr()* and the Python debugger.

reprlib.repr(*obj*)
  This is the *repr()* method of **aRepr**. It returns a string similar to that returned by the built-in function of the same name, but with limits on most sizes.

In addition to size-limiting tools, the module also provides a decorator for detecting recursive calls to `__repr__()` and substituting a placeholder string instead.

@reprlib.recursive_repr(*fillvalue="..."*)
  Decorator for `__repr__()` methods to detect recursive calls within the same thread. If a recursive call is made, the *fillvalue* is returned, otherwise, the usual `__repr__()` call is made. For example:

```
>>> class MyList(list):
...     @recursive_repr()
...     def __repr__(self):
```

```
...         return '<' + '|'.join(map(repr, self)) + '>'
...
>>> m = MyList('abc')
>>> m.append(m)
>>> m.append('x')
>>> print(m)
<'a'|'b'|'c'|...|'x'>
```

New in version 3.2.

8.12.1 Repr Objects

Repr instances provide several attributes which can be used to provide size limits for the representations of different object types, and methods which format specific object types.

`Repr.maxlevel`
    Depth limit on the creation of recursive representations. The default is `6`.

`Repr.maxdict`
`Repr.maxlist`
`Repr.maxtuple`
`Repr.maxset`
`Repr.maxfrozenset`
`Repr.maxdeque`
`Repr.maxarray`
    Limits on the number of entries represented for the named object type. The default is `4` for *maxdict*, `5` for *maxarray*, and `6` for the others.

`Repr.maxlong`
    Maximum number of characters in the representation for an integer. Digits are dropped from the middle. The default is `40`.

`Repr.maxstring`
    Limit on the number of characters in the representation of the string. Note that the "normal" representation of the string is used as the character source: if escape sequences are needed in the representation, these may be mangled when the representation is shortened. The default is `30`.

`Repr.maxother`
    This limit is used to control the size of object types for which no specific formatting method is available on the *Repr* object. It is applied in a similar manner as *maxstring*. The default is `20`.

`Repr.repr(obj)`
    The equivalent to the built-in *repr()* that uses the formatting imposed by the instance.

`Repr.repr1(obj, level)`
    Recursive implementation used by *repr()*. This uses the type of *obj* to determine which formatting method to call, passing it *obj* and *level*. The type-specific methods should call *repr1()* to perform recursive formatting, with `level - 1` for the value of *level* in the recursive call.

`Repr.repr_TYPE(obj, level)`
    Formatting methods for specific types are implemented as methods with a name based on the type name. In the method name, **TYPE** is replaced by `'_'.join(type(obj).__name__.split())`. Dispatch to these methods is handled by *repr1()*. Type-specific methods which need to recursively format a value should call `self.repr1(subobj, level - 1)`.

8.12.2 Subclassing Repr Objects

The use of dynamic dispatching by *Repr.repr1()* allows subclasses of *Repr* to add support for additional built-in object types or to modify the handling of types already supported. This example shows how special support for file objects could be added:

```
import reprlib
import sys

class MyRepr(reprlib.Repr):

    def repr_TextIOWrapper(self, obj, level):
        if obj.name in {'<stdin>', '<stdout>', '<stderr>'}:
            return obj.name
        return repr(obj)

aRepr = MyRepr()
print(aRepr.repr(sys.stdin))          # prints '<stdin>'
```

8.13 enum — Support for enumerations

New in version 3.4.

Source code: Lib/enum.py

An enumeration is a set of symbolic names (members) bound to unique, constant values. Within an enumeration, the members can be compared by identity, and the enumeration itself can be iterated over.

8.13.1 Module Contents

This module defines four enumeration classes that can be used to define unique sets of names and values: *Enum*, *IntEnum*, *Flag*, and *IntFlag*. It also defines one decorator, *unique()*, and one helper, *auto*.

class enum.Enum
Base class for creating enumerated constants. See section *Functional API* for an alternate construction syntax.

class enum.IntEnum
Base class for creating enumerated constants that are also subclasses of *int*.

class enum.IntFlag
Base class for creating enumerated constants that can be combined using the bitwise operators without losing their *IntFlag* membership. *IntFlag* members are also subclasses of *int*.

class enum.Flag
Base class for creating enumerated constants that can be combined using the bitwise operations without losing their *Flag* membership.

enum.unique()
Enum class decorator that ensures only one name is bound to any one value.

class enum.auto
Instances are replaced with an appropriate value for Enum members.

New in version 3.6: `Flag`, `IntFlag`, `auto`

8.13.2 Creating an Enum

Enumerations are created using the `class` syntax, which makes them easy to read and write. An alternative creation method is described in *Functional API*. To define an enumeration, subclass *Enum* as follows:

```
>>> from enum import Enum
>>> class Color(Enum):
...     RED = 1
...     GREEN = 2
...     BLUE = 3
...
```

Note: Enum member values

Member values can be anything: `int`, `str`, etc.. If the exact value is unimportant you may use `auto` instances and an appropriate value will be chosen for you. Care must be taken if you mix `auto` with other values.

Note: Nomenclature

- The class `Color` is an *enumeration* (or *enum*)
- The attributes `Color.RED`, `Color.GREEN`, etc., are *enumeration members* (or *enum members*) and are functionally constants.
- The enum members have *names* and *values* (the name of `Color.RED` is `RED`, the value of `Color.BLUE` is `3`, etc.)

Note: Even though we use the `class` syntax to create Enums, Enums are not normal Python classes. See *How are Enums different?* for more details.

Enumeration members have human readable string representations:

```
>>> print(Color.RED)
Color.RED
```

...while their `repr` has more information:

```
>>> print(repr(Color.RED))
<Color.RED: 1>
```

The *type* of an enumeration member is the enumeration it belongs to:

```
>>> type(Color.RED)
<enum 'Color'>
>>> isinstance(Color.GREEN, Color)
True
>>>
```

Enum members also have a property that contains just their item name:

```
>>> print(Color.RED.name)
RED
```

Enumerations support iteration, in definition order:

```
>>> class Shake(Enum):
...     VANILLA = 7
...     CHOCOLATE = 4
...     COOKIES = 9
...     MINT = 3
...
>>> for shake in Shake:
...     print(shake)
...
Shake.VANILLA
Shake.CHOCOLATE
Shake.COOKIES
Shake.MINT
```

Enumeration members are hashable, so they can be used in dictionaries and sets:

```
>>> apples = {}
>>> apples[Color.RED] = 'red delicious'
>>> apples[Color.GREEN] = 'granny smith'
>>> apples == {Color.RED: 'red delicious', Color.GREEN: 'granny smith'}
True
```

8.13.3 Programmatic access to enumeration members and their attributes

Sometimes it's useful to access members in enumerations programmatically (i.e. situations where `Color.RED` won't do because the exact color is not known at program-writing time). `Enum` allows such access:

```
>>> Color(1)
<Color.RED: 1>
>>> Color(3)
<Color.BLUE: 3>
```

If you want to access enum members by *name*, use item access:

```
>>> Color['RED']
<Color.RED: 1>
>>> Color['GREEN']
<Color.GREEN: 2>
```

If you have an enum member and need its `name` or `value`:

```
>>> member = Color.RED
>>> member.name
'RED'
>>> member.value
1
```

8.13.4 Duplicating enum members and values

Having two enum members with the same name is invalid:

```
>>> class Shape(Enum):
...     SQUARE = 2
...     SQUARE = 3
...
```

```
Traceback (most recent call last):
...
TypeError: Attempted to reuse key: 'SQUARE'
```

However, two enum members are allowed to have the same value. Given two members A and B with the same value (and A defined first), B is an alias to A. By-value lookup of the value of A and B will return A. By-name lookup of B will also return A:

```
>>> class Shape(Enum):
...     SQUARE = 2
...     DIAMOND = 1
...     CIRCLE = 3
...     ALIAS_FOR_SQUARE = 2
...
>>> Shape.SQUARE
<Shape.SQUARE: 2>
>>> Shape.ALIAS_FOR_SQUARE
<Shape.SQUARE: 2>
>>> Shape(2)
<Shape.SQUARE: 2>
```

Note: Attempting to create a member with the same name as an already defined attribute (another member, a method, etc.) or attempting to create an attribute with the same name as a member is not allowed.

8.13.5 Ensuring unique enumeration values

By default, enumerations allow multiple names as aliases for the same value. When this behavior isn't desired, the following decorator can be used to ensure each value is used only once in the enumeration:

@enum.unique

A `class` decorator specifically for enumerations. It searches an enumeration's `__members__` gathering any aliases it finds; if any are found *ValueError* is raised with the details:

```
>>> from enum import Enum, unique
>>> @unique
... class Mistake(Enum):
...     ONE = 1
...     TWO = 2
...     THREE = 3
...     FOUR = 3
...
Traceback (most recent call last):
...
ValueError: duplicate values found in <enum 'Mistake'>: FOUR -> THREE
```

8.13.6 Using automatic values

If the exact value is unimportant you can use *auto*:

```
>>> from enum import Enum, auto
>>> class Color(Enum):
...     RED = auto()
```

```
...     BLUE = auto()
...     GREEN = auto()
...
>>> list(Color)
[<Color.RED: 1>, <Color.BLUE: 2>, <Color.GREEN: 3>]
```

The values are chosen by `_generate_next_value_()`, which can be overridden:

```
>>> class AutoName(Enum):
...     def _generate_next_value_(name, start, count, last_values):
...         return name
...
>>> class Ordinal(AutoName):
...     NORTH = auto()
...     SOUTH = auto()
...     EAST = auto()
...     WEST = auto()
...
>>> list(Ordinal)
[<Ordinal.NORTH: 'NORTH'>, <Ordinal.SOUTH: 'SOUTH'>, <Ordinal.EAST: 'EAST'>, <Ordinal.WEST: 'WEST'>
↪]
```

Note: The goal of the default `_generate_next_value_()` methods is to provide the next *int* in sequence with the last *int* provided, but the way it does this is an implementation detail and may change.

8.13.7 Iteration

Iterating over the members of an enum does not provide the aliases:

```
>>> list(Shape)
[<Shape.SQUARE: 2>, <Shape.DIAMOND: 1>, <Shape.CIRCLE: 3>]
```

The special attribute `__members__` is an ordered dictionary mapping names to members. It includes all names defined in the enumeration, including the aliases:

```
>>> for name, member in Shape.__members__.items():
...     name, member
...
('SQUARE', <Shape.SQUARE: 2>)
('DIAMOND', <Shape.DIAMOND: 1>)
('CIRCLE', <Shape.CIRCLE: 3>)
('ALIAS_FOR_SQUARE', <Shape.SQUARE: 2>)
```

The `__members__` attribute can be used for detailed programmatic access to the enumeration members. For example, finding all the aliases:

```
>>> [name for name, member in Shape.__members__.items() if member.name != name]
['ALIAS_FOR_SQUARE']
```

8.13.8 Comparisons

Enumeration members are compared by identity:

```
>>> Color.RED is Color.RED
True
>>> Color.RED is Color.BLUE
False
>>> Color.RED is not Color.BLUE
True
```

Ordered comparisons between enumeration values are *not* supported. Enum members are not integers (but see *IntEnum* below):

```
>>> Color.RED < Color.BLUE
Traceback (most recent call last):
  File "<stdin>", line 1, in <module>
TypeError: '<' not supported between instances of 'Color' and 'Color'
```

Equality comparisons are defined though:

```
>>> Color.BLUE == Color.RED
False
>>> Color.BLUE != Color.RED
True
>>> Color.BLUE == Color.BLUE
True
```

Comparisons against non-enumeration values will always compare not equal (again, *IntEnum* was explicitly designed to behave differently, see below):

```
>>> Color.BLUE == 2
False
```

8.13.9 Allowed members and attributes of enumerations

The examples above use integers for enumeration values. Using integers is short and handy (and provided by default by the *Functional API*), but not strictly enforced. In the vast majority of use-cases, one doesn't care what the actual value of an enumeration is. But if the value *is* important, enumerations can have arbitrary values.

Enumerations are Python classes, and can have methods and special methods as usual. If we have this enumeration:

```
>>> class Mood(Enum):
...     FUNKY = 1
...     HAPPY = 3
...
...     def describe(self):
...         # self is the member here
...         return self.name, self.value
...
...     def __str__(self):
...         return 'my custom str! {0}'.format(self.value)
...
...     @classmethod
...     def favorite_mood(cls):
...         # cls here is the enumeration
...         return cls.HAPPY
...
```

Then:

```
>>> Mood.favorite_mood()
<Mood.HAPPY: 3>
>>> Mood.HAPPY.describe()
('HAPPY', 3)
>>> str(Mood.FUNKY)
'my custom str! 1'
```

The rules for what is allowed are as follows: names that start and end with a single underscore are reserved by enum and cannot be used; all other attributes defined within an enumeration will become members of this enumeration, with the exception of special methods (`__str__()`, `__add__()`, etc.) and descriptors (methods are also descriptors).

Note: if your enumeration defines `__new__()` and/or `__init__()` then whatever value(s) were given to the enum member will be passed into those methods. See *Planet* for an example.

8.13.10 Restricted subclassing of enumerations

Subclassing an enumeration is allowed only if the enumeration does not define any members. So this is forbidden:

```
>>> class MoreColor(Color):
...     PINK = 17
...
Traceback (most recent call last):
...
TypeError: Cannot extend enumerations
```

But this is allowed:

```
>>> class Foo(Enum):
...     def some_behavior(self):
...         pass
...
>>> class Bar(Foo):
...     HAPPY = 1
...     SAD = 2
...
```

Allowing subclassing of enums that define members would lead to a violation of some important invariants of types and instances. On the other hand, it makes sense to allow sharing some common behavior between a group of enumerations. (See *OrderedEnum* for an example.)

8.13.11 Pickling

Enumerations can be pickled and unpickled:

```
>>> from test.test_enum import Fruit
>>> from pickle import dumps, loads
>>> Fruit.TOMATO is loads(dumps(Fruit.TOMATO))
True
```

The usual restrictions for pickling apply: picklable enums must be defined in the top level of a module, since unpickling requires them to be importable from that module.

Note: With pickle protocol version 4 it is possible to easily pickle enums nested in other classes.

It is possible to modify how Enum members are pickled/unpickled by defining *__reduce_ex__()* in the enumeration class.

8.13.12 Functional API

The *Enum* class is callable, providing the following functional API:

```
>>> Animal = Enum('Animal', 'ANT BEE CAT DOG')
>>> Animal
<enum 'Animal'>
>>> Animal.ANT
<Animal.ANT: 1>
>>> Animal.ANT.value
1
>>> list(Animal)
[<Animal.ANT: 1>, <Animal.BEE: 2>, <Animal.CAT: 3>, <Animal.DOG: 4>]
```

The semantics of this API resemble *namedtuple*. The first argument of the call to *Enum* is the name of the enumeration.

The second argument is the *source* of enumeration member names. It can be a whitespace-separated string of names, a sequence of names, a sequence of 2-tuples with key/value pairs, or a mapping (e.g. dictionary) of names to values. The last two options enable assigning arbitrary values to enumerations; the others auto-assign increasing integers starting with 1 (use the `start` parameter to specify a different starting value). A new class derived from *Enum* is returned. In other words, the above assignment to `Animal` is equivalent to:

```
>>> class Animal(Enum):
...     ANT = 1
...     BEE = 2
...     CAT = 3
...     DOG = 4
...
```

The reason for defaulting to `1` as the starting number and not `0` is that `0` is `False` in a boolean sense, but enum members all evaluate to `True`.

Pickling enums created with the functional API can be tricky as frame stack implementation details are used to try and figure out which module the enumeration is being created in (e.g. it will fail if you use a utility function in separate module, and also may not work on IronPython or Jython). The solution is to specify the module name explicitly as follows:

```
>>> Animal = Enum('Animal', 'ANT BEE CAT DOG', module=__name__)
```

Warning: If `module` is not supplied, and Enum cannot determine what it is, the new Enum members will not be unpicklable; to keep errors closer to the source, pickling will be disabled.

The new pickle protocol 4 also, in some circumstances, relies on *__qualname__* being set to the location where pickle will be able to find the class. For example, if the class was made available in class SomeData in the global scope:

```
>>> Animal = Enum('Animal', 'ANT BEE CAT DOG', qualname='SomeData.Animal')
```

The complete signature is:

```
Enum(value='NewEnumName', names=<...>, *, module='...', qualname='...', type=<mixed-in class>,␣
↪start=1)
```

value What the new Enum class will record as its name.

names The Enum members. This can be a whitespace or comma separated string (values will start at 1 unless otherwise specified):

```
'RED GREEN BLUE' | 'RED,GREEN,BLUE' | 'RED, GREEN, BLUE'
```

or an iterator of names:

```
['RED', 'GREEN', 'BLUE']
```

or an iterator of (name, value) pairs:

```
[('CYAN', 4), ('MAGENTA', 5), ('YELLOW', 6)]
```

or a mapping:

```
{'CHARTREUSE': 7, 'SEA_GREEN': 11, 'ROSEMARY': 42}
```

module name of module where new Enum class can be found.

qualname where in module new Enum class can be found.

type type to mix in to new Enum class.

start number to start counting at if only names are passed in.

Changed in version 3.5: The *start* parameter was added.

8.13.13 Derived Enumerations

IntEnum

The first variation of *Enum* that is provided is also a subclass of *int*. Members of an *IntEnum* can be compared to integers; by extension, integer enumerations of different types can also be compared to each other:

```
>>> from enum import IntEnum
>>> class Shape(IntEnum):
...     CIRCLE = 1
...     SQUARE = 2
...
>>> class Request(IntEnum):
...     POST = 1
...     GET = 2
...
>>> Shape == 1
False
>>> Shape.CIRCLE == 1
True
>>> Shape.CIRCLE == Request.POST
True
```

However, they still can't be compared to standard *Enum* enumerations:

```
>>> class Shape(IntEnum):
...     CIRCLE = 1
...     SQUARE = 2
...
>>> class Color(Enum):
...     RED = 1
...     GREEN = 2
...
>>> Shape.CIRCLE == Color.RED
False
```

IntEnum values behave like integers in other ways you'd expect:

```
>>> int(Shape.CIRCLE)
1
>>> ['a', 'b', 'c'][Shape.CIRCLE]
'b'
>>> [i for i in range(Shape.SQUARE)]
[0, 1]
```

IntFlag

The next variation of *Enum* provided, *IntFlag*, is also based on *int*. The difference being *IntFlag* members can be combined using the bitwise operators (&, |, ^, ~) and the result is still an *IntFlag* member. However, as the name implies, *IntFlag* members also subclass *int* and can be used wherever an *int* is used. Any operation on an *IntFlag* member besides the bit-wise operations will lose the *IntFlag* membership.

New in version 3.6.

Sample *IntFlag* class:

```
>>> from enum import IntFlag
>>> class Perm(IntFlag):
...     R = 4
...     W = 2
...     X = 1
...
>>> Perm.R | Perm.W
<Perm.R|W: 6>
>>> Perm.R + Perm.W
6
>>> RW = Perm.R | Perm.W
>>> Perm.R in RW
True
```

It is also possible to name the combinations:

```
>>> class Perm(IntFlag):
...     R = 4
...     W = 2
...     X = 1
...     RWX = 7
>>> Perm.RWX
<Perm.RWX: 7>
>>> ~Perm.RWX
<Perm.-8: -8>
```

Another important difference between *IntFlag* and *Enum* is that if no flags are set (the value is 0), its boolean evaluation is *False*:

```
>>> Perm.R & Perm.X
<Perm.0: 0>
>>> bool(Perm.R & Perm.X)
False
```

Because *IntFlag* members are also subclasses of *int* they can be combined with them:

```
>>> Perm.X | 8
<Perm.8|X: 9>
```

Flag

The last variation is *Flag*. Like *IntFlag*, *Flag* members can be combined using the bitwise operators (&, |, ^, ~). Unlike *IntFlag*, they cannot be combined with, nor compared against, any other *Flag* enumeration, nor *int*. While it is possible to specify the values directly it is recommended to use *auto* as the value and let *Flag* select an appropriate value.

New in version 3.6.

Like *IntFlag*, if a combination of *Flag* members results in no flags being set, the boolean evaluation is *False*:

```
>>> from enum import Flag, auto
>>> class Color(Flag):
...     RED = auto()
...     BLUE = auto()
...     GREEN = auto()
...
>>> Color.RED & Color.GREEN
<Color.0: 0>
>>> bool(Color.RED & Color.GREEN)
False
```

Individual flags should have values that are powers of two (1, 2, 4, 8, ...), while combinations of flags won't:

```
>>> class Color(Flag):
...     RED = auto()
...     BLUE = auto()
...     GREEN = auto()
...     WHITE = RED | BLUE | GREEN
...
>>> Color.WHITE
<Color.WHITE: 7>
```

Giving a name to the "no flags set" condition does not change its boolean value:

```
>>> class Color(Flag):
...     BLACK = 0
...     RED = auto()
...     BLUE = auto()
...     GREEN = auto()
...
>>> Color.BLACK
<Color.BLACK: 0>
```

```
>>> bool(Color.BLACK)
False
```

Note: For the majority of new code, *Enum* and *Flag* are strongly recommended, since *IntEnum* and *IntFlag* break some semantic promises of an enumeration (by being comparable to integers, and thus by transitivity to other unrelated enumerations). *IntEnum* and *IntFlag* should be used only in cases where *Enum* and *Flag* will not do; for example, when integer constants are replaced with enumerations, or for interoperability with other systems.

Others

While *IntEnum* is part of the *enum* module, it would be very simple to implement independently:

```
class IntEnum(int, Enum):
    pass
```

This demonstrates how similar derived enumerations can be defined; for example a `StrEnum` that mixes in *str* instead of *int*.

Some rules:

1. When subclassing *Enum*, mix-in types must appear before *Enum* itself in the sequence of bases, as in the *IntEnum* example above.
2. While *Enum* can have members of any type, once you mix in an additional type, all the members must have values of that type, e.g. *int* above. This restriction does not apply to mix-ins which only add methods and don't specify another data type such as *int* or *str*.
3. When another data type is mixed in, the `value` attribute is *not the same* as the enum member itself, although it is equivalent and will compare equal.
4. %-style formatting: *%s* and *%r* call the *Enum* class's `__str__()` and `__repr__()` respectively; other codes (such as *%i* or *%h* for IntEnum) treat the enum member as its mixed-in type.
5. Formatted string literals, *str.format()*, and *format()* will use the mixed-in type's `__format__()`. If the *Enum* class's *str()* or *repr()* is desired, use the *!s* or *!r* format codes.

8.13.14 Interesting examples

While *Enum*, *IntEnum*, *IntFlag*, and *Flag* are expected to cover the majority of use-cases, they cannot cover them all. Here are recipes for some different types of enumerations that can be used directly, or as examples for creating one's own.

Omitting values

In many use-cases one doesn't care what the actual value of an enumeration is. There are several ways to define this type of simple enumeration:

- use instances of *auto* for the value
- use instances of *object* as the value
- use a descriptive string as the value
- use a tuple as the value and a custom `__new__()` to replace the tuple with an *int* value

Using any of these methods signifies to the user that these values are not important, and also enables one to add, remove, or reorder members without having to renumber the remaining members.

Whichever method you choose, you should provide a *repr()* that also hides the (unimportant) value:

```
>>> class NoValue(Enum):
...     def __repr__(self):
...         return '<%s.%s>' % (self.__class__.__name__, self.name)
...
```

Using auto

Using *auto* would look like:

```
>>> class Color(NoValue):
...     RED = auto()
...     BLUE = auto()
...     GREEN = auto()
...
>>> Color.GREEN
<Color.GREEN>
```

Using object

Using *object* would look like:

```
>>> class Color(NoValue):
...     RED = object()
...     GREEN = object()
...     BLUE = object()
...
>>> Color.GREEN
<Color.GREEN>
```

Using a descriptive string

Using a string as the value would look like:

```
>>> class Color(NoValue):
...     RED = 'stop'
...     GREEN = 'go'
...     BLUE = 'too fast!'
...
>>> Color.GREEN
<Color.GREEN>
>>> Color.GREEN.value
'go'
```

Using a custom __new__()

Using an auto-numbering `__new__()` would look like:

```
>>> class AutoNumber(NoValue):
...     def __new__(cls):
...         value = len(cls.__members__) + 1
...         obj = object.__new__(cls)
...         obj._value_ = value
...         return obj
...
>>> class Color(AutoNumber):
...     RED = ()
...     GREEN = ()
...     BLUE = ()
...
>>> Color.GREEN
<Color.GREEN>
>>> Color.GREEN.value
2
```

Note: The `__new__()` method, if defined, is used during creation of the Enum members; it is then replaced by Enum's `__new__()` which is used after class creation for lookup of existing members.

OrderedEnum

An ordered enumeration that is not based on *IntEnum* and so maintains the normal *Enum* invariants (such as not being comparable to other enumerations):

```
>>> class OrderedEnum(Enum):
...     def __ge__(self, other):
...         if self.__class__ is other.__class__:
...             return self.value >= other.value
...         return NotImplemented
...     def __gt__(self, other):
...         if self.__class__ is other.__class__:
...             return self.value > other.value
...         return NotImplemented
...     def __le__(self, other):
...         if self.__class__ is other.__class__:
...             return self.value <= other.value
...         return NotImplemented
...     def __lt__(self, other):
...         if self.__class__ is other.__class__:
...             return self.value < other.value
...         return NotImplemented
...
>>> class Grade(OrderedEnum):
...     A = 5
...     B = 4
...     C = 3
...     D = 2
...     F = 1
...
>>> Grade.C < Grade.A
True
```

DuplicateFreeEnum

Raises an error if a duplicate member name is found instead of creating an alias:

```
>>> class DuplicateFreeEnum(Enum):
...     def __init__(self, *args):
...         cls = self.__class__
...         if any(self.value == e.value for e in cls):
...             a = self.name
...             e = cls(self.value).name
...             raise ValueError(
...                 "aliases not allowed in DuplicateFreeEnum:  %r --> %r"
...                 % (a, e))
...
>>> class Color(DuplicateFreeEnum):
...     RED = 1
...     GREEN = 2
...     BLUE = 3
...     GRENE = 2
...
Traceback (most recent call last):
...
ValueError: aliases not allowed in DuplicateFreeEnum:  'GRENE' --> 'GREEN'
```

Note: This is a useful example for subclassing Enum to add or change other behaviors as well as disallowing aliases. If the only desired change is disallowing aliases, the *unique()* decorator can be used instead.

Planet

If `__new__()` or `__init__()` is defined the value of the enum member will be passed to those methods:

```
>>> class Planet(Enum):
...     MERCURY = (3.303e+23, 2.4397e6)
...     VENUS   = (4.869e+24, 6.0518e6)
...     EARTH   = (5.976e+24, 6.37814e6)
...     MARS    = (6.421e+23, 3.3972e6)
...     JUPITER = (1.9e+27,   7.1492e7)
...     SATURN  = (5.688e+26, 6.0268e7)
...     URANUS  = (8.686e+25, 2.5559e7)
...     NEPTUNE = (1.024e+26, 2.4746e7)
...     def __init__(self, mass, radius):
...         self.mass = mass       # in kilograms
...         self.radius = radius   # in meters
...     @property
...     def surface_gravity(self):
...         # universal gravitational constant  (m3 kg-1 s-2)
...         G = 6.67300E-11
...         return G * self.mass / (self.radius * self.radius)
...
>>> Planet.EARTH.value
(5.976e+24, 6378140.0)
>>> Planet.EARTH.surface_gravity
9.802652743337129
```

8.13.15 How are Enums different?

Enums have a custom metaclass that affects many aspects of both derived Enum classes and their instances (members).

Enum Classes

The `EnumMeta` metaclass is responsible for providing the `__contains__()`, `__dir__()`, `__iter__()` and other methods that allow one to do things with an *Enum* class that fail on a typical class, such as *list(Color)* or *some_var in Color*. `EnumMeta` is responsible for ensuring that various other methods on the final *Enum* class are correct (such as `__new__()`, *`__getnewargs__()`*, `__str__()` and `__repr__()`).

Enum Members (aka instances)

The most interesting thing about Enum members is that they are singletons. `EnumMeta` creates them all while it is creating the *Enum* class itself, and then puts a custom `__new__()` in place to ensure that no new ones are ever instantiated by returning only the existing member instances.

Finer Points

Supported `__dunder__` names

`__members__` is an `OrderedDict` of `member_name:member` items. It is only available on the class.

`__new__()`, if specified, must create and return the enum members; it is also a very good idea to set the member's `_value_` appropriately. Once all the members are created it is no longer used.

Supported `_sunder_` names

- `_name_` – name of the member
- `_value_` – value of the member; can be set / modified in `__new__`
- `_missing_` – a lookup function used when a value is not found; may be overridden
- `_order_` – used in Python 2/3 code to ensure member order is consistent (class attribute, removed during class creation)
- `_generate_next_value_` – used by the *Functional API* and by *`auto`* to get an appropriate value for an enum member; may be overridden

New in version 3.6: `_missing_`, `_order_`, `_generate_next_value_`

To help keep Python 2 / Python 3 code in sync an `_order_` attribute can be provided. It will be checked against the actual order of the enumeration and raise an error if the two do not match:

```
>>> class Color(Enum):
...     _order_ = 'RED GREEN BLUE'
...     RED = 1
...     BLUE = 3
...     GREEN = 2
...
Traceback (most recent call last):
...
TypeError: member order does not match _order_
```

Note: In Python 2 code the `_order_` attribute is necessary as definition order is lost before it can be recorded.

Enum member type

Enum members are instances of their *Enum* class, and are normally accessed as `EnumClass.member`. Under certain circumstances they can also be accessed as `EnumClass.member.member`, but you should never do this as that lookup may fail or, worse, return something besides the *Enum* member you are looking for (this is another good reason to use all-uppercase names for members):

```
>>> class FieldTypes(Enum):
...     name = 0
...     value = 1
...     size = 2
...
>>> FieldTypes.value.size
<FieldTypes.size: 2>
>>> FieldTypes.size.value
2
```

Changed in version 3.5.

Boolean value of Enum classes and members

Enum members that are mixed with non-*Enum* types (such as *int*, *str*, etc.) are evaluated according to the mixed-in type's rules; otherwise, all members evaluate as *True*. To make your own Enum's boolean evaluation depend on the member's value add the following to your class:

```
def __bool__(self):
    return bool(self.value)
```

Enum classes always evaluate as *True*.

Enum classes with methods

If you give your *Enum* subclass extra methods, like the *Planet* class above, those methods will show up in a *dir()* of the member, but not of the class:

```
>>> dir(Planet)
['EARTH', 'JUPITER', 'MARS', 'MERCURY', 'NEPTUNE', 'SATURN', 'URANUS', 'VENUS', '__class__', '__
↪doc__', '__members__', '__module__']
>>> dir(Planet.EARTH)
['__class__', '__doc__', '__module__', 'name', 'surface_gravity', 'value']
```

Combining members of Flag

If a combination of Flag members is not named, the *repr()* will include all named flags and all named combinations of flags that are in the value:

```
>>> class Color(Flag):
...     RED = auto()
...     GREEN = auto()
...     BLUE = auto()
...     MAGENTA = RED | BLUE
...     YELLOW = RED | GREEN
...     CYAN = GREEN | BLUE
...
>>> Color(3)  # named combination
<Color.YELLOW: 3>
>>> Color(7)      # not named combination
<Color.CYAN|MAGENTA|BLUE|YELLOW|GREEN|RED: 7>
```

CHAPTER

NINE

NUMERIC AND MATHEMATICAL MODULES

The modules described in this chapter provide numeric and math-related functions and data types. The *numbers* module defines an abstract hierarchy of numeric types. The *math* and *cmath* modules contain various mathematical functions for floating-point and complex numbers. The *decimal* module supports exact representations of decimal numbers, using arbitrary precision arithmetic.

The following modules are documented in this chapter:

9.1 numbers — Numeric abstract base classes

Source code: Lib/numbers.py

The *numbers* module (PEP 3141) defines a hierarchy of numeric *abstract base classes* which progressively define more operations. None of the types defined in this module can be instantiated.

class numbers.Number

The root of the numeric hierarchy. If you just want to check if an argument *x* is a number, without caring what kind, use `isinstance(x, Number)`.

9.1.1 The numeric tower

class numbers.Complex

Subclasses of this type describe complex numbers and include the operations that work on the built-in *complex* type. These are: conversions to *complex* and *bool*, *real*, *imag*, +, -, *, /, *abs()*, *conjugate()*, ==, and !=. All except - and != are abstract.

real

Abstract. Retrieves the real component of this number.

imag

Abstract. Retrieves the imaginary component of this number.

abstractmethod conjugate()

Abstract. Returns the complex conjugate. For example, `(1+3j).conjugate() == (1-3j)`.

class numbers.Real

To *Complex*, *Real* adds the operations that work on real numbers.

In short, those are: a conversion to *float*, *math.trunc()*, *round()*, *math.floor()*, *math.ceil()*, *divmod()*, //, %, <, <=, >, and >=.

Real also provides defaults for *complex()*, *real*, *imag*, and *conjugate()*.

class numbers.Rational

Subtypes *Real* and adds *numerator* and *denominator* properties, which should be in lowest terms. With these, it provides a default for *float()*.

numerator

Abstract.

denominator

Abstract.

class numbers.Integral

Subtypes *Rational* and adds a conversion to *int*. Provides defaults for *float()*, *numerator*, and *denominator*. Adds abstract methods for ** and bit-string operations: <<, >>, &, ^, |, ~.

9.1.2 Notes for type implementors

Implementors should be careful to make equal numbers equal and hash them to the same values. This may be subtle if there are two different extensions of the real numbers. For example, *fractions.Fraction* implements *hash()* as follows:

```
def __hash__(self):
    if self.denominator == 1:
        # Get integers right.
        return hash(self.numerator)
    # Expensive check, but definitely correct.
    if self == float(self):
        return hash(float(self))
    else:
        # Use tuple's hash to avoid a high collision rate on
        # simple fractions.
        return hash((self.numerator, self.denominator))
```

Adding More Numeric ABCs

There are, of course, more possible ABCs for numbers, and this would be a poor hierarchy if it precluded the possibility of adding those. You can add MyFoo between *Complex* and *Real* with:

```
class MyFoo(Complex): ...
MyFoo.register(Real)
```

Implementing the arithmetic operations

We want to implement the arithmetic operations so that mixed-mode operations either call an implementation whose author knew about the types of both arguments, or convert both to the nearest built in type and do the operation there. For subtypes of *Integral*, this means that `__add__()` and `__radd__()` should be defined as:

```
class MyIntegral(Integral):

    def __add__(self, other):
        if isinstance(other, MyIntegral):
            return do_my_adding_stuff(self, other)
        elif isinstance(other, OtherTypeIKnowAbout):
            return do_my_other_adding_stuff(self, other)
        else:
```

```
            return NotImplemented

    def __radd__(self, other):
        if isinstance(other, MyIntegral):
            return do_my_adding_stuff(other, self)
        elif isinstance(other, OtherTypeIKnowAbout):
            return do_my_other_adding_stuff(other, self)
        elif isinstance(other, Integral):
            return int(other) + int(self)
        elif isinstance(other, Real):
            return float(other) + float(self)
        elif isinstance(other, Complex):
            return complex(other) + complex(self)
        else:
            return NotImplemented
```

There are 5 different cases for a mixed-type operation on subclasses of *Complex*. I'll refer to all of the above code that doesn't refer to `MyIntegral` and `OtherTypeIKnowAbout` as "boilerplate". `a` will be an instance of `A`, which is a subtype of *Complex* (`a : A <: Complex`), and `b : B <: Complex`. I'll consider `a + b`:

1. If `A` defines an `__add__()` which accepts `b`, all is well.
2. If `A` falls back to the boilerplate code, and it were to return a value from `__add__()`, we'd miss the possibility that `B` defines a more intelligent `__radd__()`, so the boilerplate should return *NotImplemented* from `__add__()`. (Or `A` may not implement `__add__()` at all.)
3. Then `B`'s `__radd__()` gets a chance. If it accepts `a`, all is well.
4. If it falls back to the boilerplate, there are no more possible methods to try, so this is where the default implementation should live.
5. If `B <: A`, Python tries `B.__radd__` before `A.__add__`. This is ok, because it was implemented with knowledge of `A`, so it can handle those instances before delegating to *Complex*.

If `A <: Complex` and `B <: Real` without sharing any other knowledge, then the appropriate shared operation is the one involving the built in *complex*, and both `__radd__()` s land there, so `a+b == b+a`.

Because most of the operations on any given type will be very similar, it can be useful to define a helper function which generates the forward and reverse instances of any given operator. For example, *fractions.Fraction* uses:

```
def _operator_fallbacks(monomorphic_operator, fallback_operator):
    def forward(a, b):
        if isinstance(b, (int, Fraction)):
            return monomorphic_operator(a, b)
        elif isinstance(b, float):
            return fallback_operator(float(a), b)
        elif isinstance(b, complex):
            return fallback_operator(complex(a), b)
        else:
            return NotImplemented
    forward.__name__ = '__' + fallback_operator.__name__ + '__'
    forward.__doc__ = monomorphic_operator.__doc__

    def reverse(b, a):
        if isinstance(a, Rational):
            # Includes ints.
            return monomorphic_operator(a, b)
        elif isinstance(a, numbers.Real):
            return fallback_operator(float(a), float(b))
```

```
        elif isinstance(a, numbers.Complex):
            return fallback_operator(complex(a), complex(b))
        else:
            return NotImplemented
    reverse.__name__ = '__r' + fallback_operator.__name__ + '__'
    reverse.__doc__ = monomorphic_operator.__doc__

    return forward, reverse

def _add(a, b):
    """a + b"""
    return Fraction(a.numerator * b.denominator +
                    b.numerator * a.denominator,
                    a.denominator * b.denominator)

__add__, __radd__ = _operator_fallbacks(_add, operator.add)

# ...
```

9.2 math — Mathematical functions

This module is always available. It provides access to the mathematical functions defined by the C standard.

These functions cannot be used with complex numbers; use the functions of the same name from the *cmath* module if you require support for complex numbers. The distinction between functions which support complex numbers and those which don't is made since most users do not want to learn quite as much mathematics as required to understand complex numbers. Receiving an exception instead of a complex result allows earlier detection of the unexpected complex number used as a parameter, so that the programmer can determine how and why it was generated in the first place.

The following functions are provided by this module. Except when explicitly noted otherwise, all return values are floats.

9.2.1 Number-theoretic and representation functions

math.ceil(*x*)
Return the ceiling of x, the smallest integer greater than or equal to x. If x is not a float, delegates to `x.__ceil__()`, which should return an *Integral* value.

math.copysign(*x*, *y*)
Return a float with the magnitude (absolute value) of x but the sign of y. On platforms that support signed zeros, `copysign(1.0, -0.0)` returns *-1.0*.

math.fabs(*x*)
Return the absolute value of x.

math.factorial(*x*)
Return x factorial. Raises *ValueError* if x is not integral or is negative.

math.floor(*x*)
Return the floor of x, the largest integer less than or equal to x. If x is not a float, delegates to `x.__floor__()`, which should return an *Integral* value.

math.fmod(*x*, *y*)

Return `fmod(x, y)`, as defined by the platform C library. Note that the Python expression `x % y` may not return the same result. The intent of the C standard is that `fmod(x, y)` be exactly (mathematically; to infinite precision) equal to `x - n*y` for some integer *n* such that the result has the same sign as *x* and magnitude less than `abs(y)`. Python's `x % y` returns a result with the sign of *y* instead, and may not be exactly computable for float arguments. For example, `fmod(-1e-100, 1e100)` is `-1e-100`, but the result of Python's `-1e-100 % 1e100` is `1e100-1e-100`, which cannot be represented exactly as a float, and rounds to the surprising `1e100`. For this reason, function *fmod()* is generally preferred when working with floats, while Python's `x % y` is preferred when working with integers.

math.frexp(*x*)

Return the mantissa and exponent of *x* as the pair `(m, e)`. *m* is a float and *e* is an integer such that `x == m * 2**e` exactly. If *x* is zero, returns `(0.0, 0)`, otherwise `0.5 <= abs(m) < 1`. This is used to "pick apart" the internal representation of a float in a portable way.

math.fsum(*iterable*)

Return an accurate floating point sum of values in the iterable. Avoids loss of precision by tracking multiple intermediate partial sums:

```
>>> sum([.1, .1, .1, .1, .1, .1, .1, .1, .1, .1])
0.9999999999999999
>>> fsum([.1, .1, .1, .1, .1, .1, .1, .1, .1, .1])
1.0
```

The algorithm's accuracy depends on IEEE-754 arithmetic guarantees and the typical case where the rounding mode is half-even. On some non-Windows builds, the underlying C library uses extended precision addition and may occasionally double-round an intermediate sum causing it to be off in its least significant bit.

For further discussion and two alternative approaches, see the ASPN cookbook recipes for accurate floating point summation.

math.gcd(*a*, *b*)

Return the greatest common divisor of the integers *a* and *b*. If either *a* or *b* is nonzero, then the value of `gcd(a, b)` is the largest positive integer that divides both *a* and *b*. `gcd(0, 0)` returns `0`.

New in version 3.5.

math.isclose(*a*, *b*, ***, *rel_tol=1e-09*, *abs_tol=0.0*)

Return `True` if the values *a* and *b* are close to each other and `False` otherwise.

Whether or not two values are considered close is determined according to given absolute and relative tolerances.

rel_tol is the relative tolerance – it is the maximum allowed difference between *a* and *b*, relative to the larger absolute value of *a* or *b*. For example, to set a tolerance of 5%, pass `rel_tol=0.05`. The default tolerance is `1e-09`, which assures that the two values are the same within about 9 decimal digits. *rel_tol* must be greater than zero.

abs_tol is the minimum absolute tolerance – useful for comparisons near zero. *abs_tol* must be at least zero.

If no errors occur, the result will be: `abs(a-b) <= max(rel_tol * max(abs(a), abs(b)), abs_tol)`.

The IEEE 754 special values of `NaN`, `inf`, and `-inf` will be handled according to IEEE rules. Specifically, `NaN` is not considered close to any other value, including `NaN`. `inf` and `-inf` are only considered close to themselves.

New in version 3.5.

See also:

PEP 485 – A function for testing approximate equality

math.isfinite(*x*)
Return `True` if *x* is neither an infinity nor a NaN, and `False` otherwise. (Note that `0.0` *is* considered finite.)

New in version 3.2.

math.isinf(*x*)
Return `True` if *x* is a positive or negative infinity, and `False` otherwise.

math.isnan(*x*)
Return `True` if *x* is a NaN (not a number), and `False` otherwise.

math.ldexp(*x*, *i*)
Return `x * (2**i)`. This is essentially the inverse of function *frexp()*.

math.modf(*x*)
Return the fractional and integer parts of *x*. Both results carry the sign of *x* and are floats.

math.trunc(*x*)
Return the *Real* value *x* truncated to an *Integral* (usually an integer). Delegates to `x.__trunc__()`.

Note that *frexp()* and *modf()* have a different call/return pattern than their C equivalents: they take a single argument and return a pair of values, rather than returning their second return value through an 'output parameter' (there is no such thing in Python).

For the *ceil()*, *floor()*, and *modf()* functions, note that *all* floating-point numbers of sufficiently large magnitude are exact integers. Python floats typically carry no more than 53 bits of precision (the same as the platform C double type), in which case any float *x* with `abs(x) >= 2**52` necessarily has no fractional bits.

9.2.2 Power and logarithmic functions

math.exp(*x*)
Return `e**x`.

math.expm1(*x*)
Return `e**x - 1`. For small floats *x*, the subtraction in `exp(x) - 1` can result in a significant loss of precision; the *expm1()* function provides a way to compute this quantity to full precision:

```
>>> from math import exp, expm1
>>> exp(1e-5) - 1  # gives result accurate to 11 places
1.0000050000069649e-05
>>> expm1(1e-5)    # result accurate to full precision
1.0000050000166668e-05
```

New in version 3.2.

math.log(*x*[, *base*])
With one argument, return the natural logarithm of *x* (to base *e*).

With two arguments, return the logarithm of *x* to the given *base*, calculated as `log(x)/log(base)`.

math.log1p(*x*)
Return the natural logarithm of *1+x* (base *e*). The result is calculated in a way which is accurate for *x* near zero.

math.log2(*x*)
Return the base-2 logarithm of *x*. This is usually more accurate than `log(x, 2)`.

New in version 3.3.

See also:

int.bit_length() returns the number of bits necessary to represent an integer in binary, excluding the sign and leading zeros.

`math.log10(x)`
Return the base-10 logarithm of x. This is usually more accurate than `log(x, 10)`.

`math.pow(x, y)`
Return `x` raised to the power `y`. Exceptional cases follow Annex 'F' of the C99 standard as far as possible. In particular, `pow(1.0, x)` and `pow(x, 0.0)` always return `1.0`, even when `x` is a zero or a NaN. If both `x` and `y` are finite, `x` is negative, and `y` is not an integer then `pow(x, y)` is undefined, and raises *ValueError*.

Unlike the built-in `**` operator, *math.pow()* converts both its arguments to type *float*. Use `**` or the built-in *pow()* function for computing exact integer powers.

`math.sqrt(x)`
Return the square root of x.

9.2.3 Trigonometric functions

`math.acos(x)`
Return the arc cosine of x, in radians.

`math.asin(x)`
Return the arc sine of x, in radians.

`math.atan(x)`
Return the arc tangent of x, in radians.

`math.atan2(y, x)`
Return `atan(y / x)`, in radians. The result is between `-pi` and `pi`. The vector in the plane from the origin to point `(x, y)` makes this angle with the positive X axis. The point of *atan2()* is that the signs of both inputs are known to it, so it can compute the correct quadrant for the angle. For example, `atan(1)` and `atan2(1, 1)` are both `pi/4`, but `atan2(-1, -1)` is `-3*pi/4`.

`math.cos(x)`
Return the cosine of x radians.

`math.hypot(x, y)`
Return the Euclidean norm, `sqrt(x*x + y*y)`. This is the length of the vector from the origin to point `(x, y)`.

`math.sin(x)`
Return the sine of x radians.

`math.tan(x)`
Return the tangent of x radians.

9.2.4 Angular conversion

`math.degrees(x)`
Convert angle x from radians to degrees.

`math.radians(x)`
Convert angle x from degrees to radians.

9.2.5 Hyperbolic functions

Hyperbolic functions are analogs of trigonometric functions that are based on hyperbolas instead of circles.

`math.acosh(x)`
Return the inverse hyperbolic cosine of x.

`math.asinh(x)`
Return the inverse hyperbolic sine of x.

`math.atanh(x)`
Return the inverse hyperbolic tangent of x.

`math.cosh(x)`
Return the hyperbolic cosine of x.

`math.sinh(x)`
Return the hyperbolic sine of x.

`math.tanh(x)`
Return the hyperbolic tangent of x.

9.2.6 Special functions

`math.erf(x)`
Return the error function at x.

The *erf()* function can be used to compute traditional statistical functions such as the cumulative standard normal distribution:

```
def phi(x):
    'Cumulative distribution function for the standard normal distribution'
    return (1.0 + erf(x / sqrt(2.0))) / 2.0
```

New in version 3.2.

`math.erfc(x)`
Return the complementary error function at x. The complementary error function is defined as `1.0 - erf(x)`. It is used for large values of x where a subtraction from one would cause a loss of significance.

New in version 3.2.

`math.gamma(x)`
Return the Gamma function at x.

New in version 3.2.

`math.lgamma(x)`
Return the natural logarithm of the absolute value of the Gamma function at x.

New in version 3.2.

9.2.7 Constants

`math.pi`
The mathematical constant $\pi = 3.141592...$, to available precision.

`math.e`
The mathematical constant e = 2.718281..., to available precision.

`math.tau`

The mathematical constant $\tau = 6.283185...$, to available precision. Tau is a circle constant equal to 2π, the ratio of a circle's circumference to its radius. To learn more about Tau, check out Vi Hart's video Pi is (still) Wrong, and start celebrating Tau day by eating twice as much pie!

New in version 3.6.

`math.inf`

A floating-point positive infinity. (For negative infinity, use `-math.inf`.) Equivalent to the output of `float('inf')`.

New in version 3.5.

`math.nan`

A floating-point "not a number" (NaN) value. Equivalent to the output of `float('nan')`.

New in version 3.5.

CPython implementation detail: The *math* module consists mostly of thin wrappers around the platform C math library functions. Behavior in exceptional cases follows Annex F of the C99 standard where appropriate. The current implementation will raise *ValueError* for invalid operations like `sqrt(-1.0)` or `log(0.0)` (where C99 Annex F recommends signaling invalid operation or divide-by-zero), and *OverflowError* for results that overflow (for example, `exp(1000.0)`). A NaN will not be returned from any of the functions above unless one or more of the input arguments was a NaN; in that case, most functions will return a NaN, but (again following C99 Annex F) there are some exceptions to this rule, for example `pow(float('nan'), 0.0)` or `hypot(float('nan'), float('inf'))`.

Note that Python makes no effort to distinguish signaling NaNs from quiet NaNs, and behavior for signaling NaNs remains unspecified. Typical behavior is to treat all NaNs as though they were quiet.

See also:

Module *cmath* Complex number versions of many of these functions.

9.3 `cmath` — Mathematical functions for complex numbers

This module is always available. It provides access to mathematical functions for complex numbers. The functions in this module accept integers, floating-point numbers or complex numbers as arguments. They will also accept any Python object that has either a `__complex__()` or a `__float__()` method: these methods are used to convert the object to a complex or floating-point number, respectively, and the function is then applied to the result of the conversion.

Note: On platforms with hardware and system-level support for signed zeros, functions involving branch cuts are continuous on *both* sides of the branch cut: the sign of the zero distinguishes one side of the branch cut from the other. On platforms that do not support signed zeros the continuity is as specified below.

9.3.1 Conversions to and from polar coordinates

A Python complex number `z` is stored internally using *rectangular* or *Cartesian* coordinates. It is completely determined by its *real part* `z.real` and its *imaginary part* `z.imag`. In other words:

```
z == z.real + z.imag*1j
```

Polar coordinates give an alternative way to represent a complex number. In polar coordinates, a complex number z is defined by the modulus r and the phase angle *phi*. The modulus r is the distance from z to the origin, while the phase *phi* is the counterclockwise angle, measured in radians, from the positive x-axis to the line segment that joins the origin to z.

The following functions can be used to convert from the native rectangular coordinates to polar coordinates and back.

`cmath.phase(x)`
: Return the phase of x (also known as the *argument* of x), as a float. `phase(x)` is equivalent to `math.atan2(x.imag, x.real)`. The result lies in the range $[-\pi, \pi]$, and the branch cut for this operation lies along the negative real axis, continuous from above. On systems with support for signed zeros (which includes most systems in current use), this means that the sign of the result is the same as the sign of `x.imag`, even when `x.imag` is zero:

```
>>> phase(complex(-1.0, 0.0))
3.141592653589793
>>> phase(complex(-1.0, -0.0))
-3.141592653589793
```

Note: The modulus (absolute value) of a complex number x can be computed using the built-in `abs()` function. There is no separate `cmath` module function for this operation.

`cmath.polar(x)`
: Return the representation of x in polar coordinates. Returns a pair `(r, phi)` where r is the modulus of x and phi is the phase of x. `polar(x)` is equivalent to `(abs(x), phase(x))`.

`cmath.rect(r, phi)`
: Return the complex number x with polar coordinates r and *phi*. Equivalent to `r * (math.cos(phi) + math.sin(phi)*1j)`.

9.3.2 Power and logarithmic functions

`cmath.exp(x)`
: Return the exponential value `e**x`.

`cmath.log(x[, base])`
: Returns the logarithm of x to the given *base*. If the *base* is not specified, returns the natural logarithm of x. There is one branch cut, from 0 along the negative real axis to $-\infty$, continuous from above.

`cmath.log10(x)`
: Return the base-10 logarithm of x. This has the same branch cut as `log()`.

`cmath.sqrt(x)`
: Return the square root of x. This has the same branch cut as `log()`.

9.3.3 Trigonometric functions

`cmath.acos(x)`
: Return the arc cosine of x. There are two branch cuts: One extends right from 1 along the real axis to ∞, continuous from below. The other extends left from -1 along the real axis to $-\infty$, continuous from above.

`cmath.asin(x)`
: Return the arc sine of x. This has the same branch cuts as `acos()`.

cmath.atan(*x*)
Return the arc tangent of *x*. There are two branch cuts: One extends from `1j` along the imaginary axis to `∞j`, continuous from the right. The other extends from `-1j` along the imaginary axis to `-∞j`, continuous from the left.

cmath.cos(*x*)
Return the cosine of *x*.

cmath.sin(*x*)
Return the sine of *x*.

cmath.tan(*x*)
Return the tangent of *x*.

9.3.4 Hyperbolic functions

cmath.acosh(*x*)
Return the inverse hyperbolic cosine of *x*. There is one branch cut, extending left from 1 along the real axis to -∞, continuous from above.

cmath.asinh(*x*)
Return the inverse hyperbolic sine of *x*. There are two branch cuts: One extends from `1j` along the imaginary axis to `∞j`, continuous from the right. The other extends from `-1j` along the imaginary axis to `-∞j`, continuous from the left.

cmath.atanh(*x*)
Return the inverse hyperbolic tangent of *x*. There are two branch cuts: One extends from `1` along the real axis to ∞, continuous from below. The other extends from `-1` along the real axis to -∞, continuous from above.

cmath.cosh(*x*)
Return the hyperbolic cosine of *x*.

cmath.sinh(*x*)
Return the hyperbolic sine of *x*.

cmath.tanh(*x*)
Return the hyperbolic tangent of *x*.

9.3.5 Classification functions

cmath.isfinite(*x*)
Return `True` if both the real and imaginary parts of *x* are finite, and `False` otherwise.

New in version 3.2.

cmath.isinf(*x*)
Return `True` if either the real or the imaginary part of *x* is an infinity, and `False` otherwise.

cmath.isnan(*x*)
Return `True` if either the real or the imaginary part of *x* is a NaN, and `False` otherwise.

cmath.isclose(*a, b, *, rel_tol=1e-09, abs_tol=0.0*)
Return `True` if the values *a* and *b* are close to each other and `False` otherwise.

Whether or not two values are considered close is determined according to given absolute and relative tolerances.

rel_tol is the relative tolerance – it is the maximum allowed difference between *a* and *b*, relative to the larger absolute value of *a* or *b*. For example, to set a tolerance of 5%, pass `rel_tol=0.05`. The default tolerance is `1e-09`, which assures that the two values are the same within about 9 decimal digits. *rel_tol* must be greater than zero.

abs_tol is the minimum absolute tolerance – useful for comparisons near zero. *abs_tol* must be at least zero.

If no errors occur, the result will be: `abs(a-b) <= max(rel_tol * max(abs(a), abs(b)), abs_tol)`.

The IEEE 754 special values of `NaN`, `inf`, and `-inf` will be handled according to IEEE rules. Specifically, `NaN` is not considered close to any other value, including `NaN`. `inf` and `-inf` are only considered close to themselves.

New in version 3.5.

See also:

PEP 485 – A function for testing approximate equality

9.3.6 Constants

`cmath.pi`
The mathematical constant π, as a float.

`cmath.e`
The mathematical constant e, as a float.

`cmath.tau`
The mathematical constant τ, as a float.

New in version 3.6.

`cmath.inf`
Floating-point positive infinity. Equivalent to `float('inf')`.

New in version 3.6.

`cmath.infj`
Complex number with zero real part and positive infinity imaginary part. Equivalent to `complex(0.0, float('inf'))`.

New in version 3.6.

`cmath.nan`
A floating-point "not a number" (NaN) value. Equivalent to `float('nan')`.

New in version 3.6.

`cmath.nanj`
Complex number with zero real part and NaN imaginary part. Equivalent to `complex(0.0, float('nan'))`.

New in version 3.6.

Note that the selection of functions is similar, but not identical, to that in module *math*. The reason for having two modules is that some users aren't interested in complex numbers, and perhaps don't even know what they are. They would rather have `math.sqrt(-1)` raise an exception than return a complex number. Also note that the functions defined in *cmath* always return a complex number, even if the answer can be expressed as a real number (in which case the complex number has an imaginary part of zero).

A note on branch cuts: They are curves along which the given function fails to be continuous. They are a necessary feature of many complex functions. It is assumed that if you need to compute with complex functions, you will understand about branch cuts. Consult almost any (not too elementary) book on complex variables for enlightenment. For information of the proper choice of branch cuts for numerical purposes, a good reference should be the following:

See also:

Kahan, W: Branch cuts for complex elementary functions; or, Much ado about nothing's sign bit. In Iserles, A., and Powell, M. (eds.), The state of the art in numerical analysis. Clarendon Press (1987) pp165–211.

9.4 decimal — Decimal fixed point and floating point arithmetic

Source code: Lib/decimal.py

The *decimal* module provides support for fast correctly-rounded decimal floating point arithmetic. It offers several advantages over the *float* datatype:

- Decimal "is based on a floating-point model which was designed with people in mind, and necessarily has a paramount guiding principle – computers must provide an arithmetic that works in the same way as the arithmetic that people learn at school." – excerpt from the decimal arithmetic specification.
- Decimal numbers can be represented exactly. In contrast, numbers like `1.1` and `2.2` do not have exact representations in binary floating point. End users typically would not expect `1.1 + 2.2` to display as `3.3000000000000003` as it does with binary floating point.
- The exactness carries over into arithmetic. In decimal floating point, `0.1 + 0.1 + 0.1 - 0.3` is exactly equal to zero. In binary floating point, the result is `5.5511151231257827e-017`. While near to zero, the differences prevent reliable equality testing and differences can accumulate. For this reason, decimal is preferred in accounting applications which have strict equality invariants.
- The decimal module incorporates a notion of significant places so that `1.30 + 1.20` is `2.50`. The trailing zero is kept to indicate significance. This is the customary presentation for monetary applications. For multiplication, the "schoolbook" approach uses all the figures in the multiplicands. For instance, `1.3 * 1.2` gives `1.56` while `1.30 * 1.20` gives `1.5600`.
- Unlike hardware based binary floating point, the decimal module has a user alterable precision (defaulting to 28 places) which can be as large as needed for a given problem:

```
>>> from decimal import *
>>> getcontext().prec = 6
>>> Decimal(1) / Decimal(7)
Decimal('0.142857')
>>> getcontext().prec = 28
>>> Decimal(1) / Decimal(7)
Decimal('0.1428571428571428571428571429')
```

- Both binary and decimal floating point are implemented in terms of published standards. While the built-in float type exposes only a modest portion of its capabilities, the decimal module exposes all required parts of the standard. When needed, the programmer has full control over rounding and signal handling. This includes an option to enforce exact arithmetic by using exceptions to block any inexact operations.
- The decimal module was designed to support "without prejudice, both exact unrounded decimal arithmetic (sometimes called fixed-point arithmetic) and rounded floating-point arithmetic." – excerpt from the decimal arithmetic specification.

The module design is centered around three concepts: the decimal number, the context for arithmetic, and signals.

A decimal number is immutable. It has a sign, coefficient digits, and an exponent. To preserve significance, the coefficient digits do not truncate trailing zeros. Decimals also include special values such as `Infinity`, `-Infinity`, and `NaN`. The standard also differentiates `-0` from `+0`.

The context for arithmetic is an environment specifying precision, rounding rules, limits on exponents, flags indicating the results of operations, and trap enablers which determine whether signals are treated as exceptions. Rounding options include *ROUND_CEILING*, *ROUND_DOWN*, *ROUND_FLOOR*, *ROUND_HALF_DOWN*, *ROUND_HALF_EVEN*, *ROUND_HALF_UP*, *ROUND_UP*, and *ROUND_05UP*.

Signals are groups of exceptional conditions arising during the course of computation. Depending on the needs of the application, signals may be ignored, considered as informational, or treated as exceptions. The signals in the decimal module are: *Clamped*, *InvalidOperation*, *DivisionByZero*, *Inexact*, *Rounded*, *Subnormal*, *Overflow*, *Underflow* and *FloatOperation*.

For each signal there is a flag and a trap enabler. When a signal is encountered, its flag is set to one, then, if the trap enabler is set to one, an exception is raised. Flags are sticky, so the user needs to reset them before monitoring a calculation.

See also:

- IBM's General Decimal Arithmetic Specification, The General Decimal Arithmetic Specification.

9.4.1 Quick-start Tutorial

The usual start to using decimals is importing the module, viewing the current context with *getcontext()* and, if necessary, setting new values for precision, rounding, or enabled traps:

```
>>> from decimal import *
>>> getcontext()
Context(prec=28, rounding=ROUND_HALF_EVEN, Emin=-999999, Emax=999999,
        capitals=1, clamp=0, flags=[], traps=[Overflow, DivisionByZero,
        InvalidOperation])

>>> getcontext().prec = 7       # Set a new precision
```

Decimal instances can be constructed from integers, strings, floats, or tuples. Construction from an integer or a float performs an exact conversion of the value of that integer or float. Decimal numbers include special values such as `NaN` which stands for "Not a number", positive and negative `Infinity`, and `-0`:

```
>>> getcontext().prec = 28
>>> Decimal(10)
Decimal('10')
>>> Decimal('3.14')
Decimal('3.14')
>>> Decimal(3.14)
Decimal('3.140000000000000124344978758017532527446746826171875')
>>> Decimal((0, (3, 1, 4), -2))
Decimal('3.14')
>>> Decimal(str(2.0 ** 0.5))
Decimal('1.4142135623730951')
>>> Decimal(2) ** Decimal('0.5')
Decimal('1.414213562373095048801688724')
>>> Decimal('NaN')
Decimal('NaN')
>>> Decimal('-Infinity')
Decimal('-Infinity')
```

If the *FloatOperation* signal is trapped, accidental mixing of decimals and floats in constructors or ordering comparisons raises an exception:

```
>>> c = getcontext()
>>> c.traps[FloatOperation] = True
```

```
>>> Decimal(3.14)
Traceback (most recent call last):
  File "<stdin>", line 1, in <module>
decimal.FloatOperation: [<class 'decimal.FloatOperation'>]
>>> Decimal('3.5') < 3.7
Traceback (most recent call last):
  File "<stdin>", line 1, in <module>
decimal.FloatOperation: [<class 'decimal.FloatOperation'>]
>>> Decimal('3.5') == 3.5
True
```

New in version 3.3.

The significance of a new Decimal is determined solely by the number of digits input. Context precision and rounding only come into play during arithmetic operations.

```
>>> getcontext().prec = 6
>>> Decimal('3.0')
Decimal('3.0')
>>> Decimal('3.1415926535')
Decimal('3.1415926535')
>>> Decimal('3.1415926535') + Decimal('2.7182818285')
Decimal('5.85987')
>>> getcontext().rounding = ROUND_UP
>>> Decimal('3.1415926535') + Decimal('2.7182818285')
Decimal('5.85988')
```

If the internal limits of the C version are exceeded, constructing a decimal raises *InvalidOperation*:

```
>>> Decimal("1e9999999999999999999")
Traceback (most recent call last):
  File "<stdin>", line 1, in <module>
decimal.InvalidOperation: [<class 'decimal.InvalidOperation'>]
```

Changed in version 3.3.

Decimals interact well with much of the rest of Python. Here is a small decimal floating point flying circus:

```
>>> data = list(map(Decimal, '1.34 1.87 3.45 2.35 1.00 0.03 9.25'.split()))
>>> max(data)
Decimal('9.25')
>>> min(data)
Decimal('0.03')
>>> sorted(data)
[Decimal('0.03'), Decimal('1.00'), Decimal('1.34'), Decimal('1.87'),
 Decimal('2.35'), Decimal('3.45'), Decimal('9.25')]
>>> sum(data)
Decimal('19.29')
>>> a,b,c = data[:3]
>>> str(a)
'1.34'
>>> float(a)
1.34
>>> round(a, 1)
Decimal('1.3')
>>> int(a)
1
>>> a * 5
Decimal('6.70')
```

```
>>> a * b
Decimal('2.5058')
>>> c % a
Decimal('0.77')
```

And some mathematical functions are also available to Decimal:

```
>>> getcontext().prec = 28
>>> Decimal(2).sqrt()
Decimal('1.414213562373095048801688724')
>>> Decimal(1).exp()
Decimal('2.718281828459045235360287471')
>>> Decimal('10').ln()
Decimal('2.302585092994045684017991455')
>>> Decimal('10').log10()
Decimal('1')
```

The `quantize()` method rounds a number to a fixed exponent. This method is useful for monetary applications that often round results to a fixed number of places:

```
>>> Decimal('7.325').quantize(Decimal('.01'), rounding=ROUND_DOWN)
Decimal('7.32')
>>> Decimal('7.325').quantize(Decimal('1.'), rounding=ROUND_UP)
Decimal('8')
```

As shown above, the *getcontext()* function accesses the current context and allows the settings to be changed. This approach meets the needs of most applications.

For more advanced work, it may be useful to create alternate contexts using the Context() constructor. To make an alternate active, use the *setcontext()* function.

In accordance with the standard, the *decimal* module provides two ready to use standard contexts, *BasicContext* and *ExtendedContext*. The former is especially useful for debugging because many of the traps are enabled:

```
>>> myothercontext = Context(prec=60, rounding=ROUND_HALF_DOWN)
>>> setcontext(myothercontext)
>>> Decimal(1) / Decimal(7)
Decimal('0.142857142857142857142857142857142857142857142857142857142857')

>>> ExtendedContext
Context(prec=9, rounding=ROUND_HALF_EVEN, Emin=-999999, Emax=999999,
        capitals=1, clamp=0, flags=[], traps=[])
>>> setcontext(ExtendedContext)
>>> Decimal(1) / Decimal(7)
Decimal('0.142857143')
>>> Decimal(42) / Decimal(0)
Decimal('Infinity')

>>> setcontext(BasicContext)
>>> Decimal(42) / Decimal(0)
Traceback (most recent call last):
  File "<pyshell#143>", line 1, in -toplevel-
    Decimal(42) / Decimal(0)
DivisionByZero: x / 0
```

Contexts also have signal flags for monitoring exceptional conditions encountered during computations. The flags remain set until explicitly cleared, so it is best to clear the flags before each set of monitored computations by using the `clear_flags()` method.

```
>>> setcontext(ExtendedContext)
>>> getcontext().clear_flags()
>>> Decimal(355) / Decimal(113)
Decimal('3.14159292')
>>> getcontext()
Context(prec=9, rounding=ROUND_HALF_EVEN, Emin=-999999, Emax=999999,
        capitals=1, clamp=0, flags=[Inexact, Rounded], traps=[])
```

The *flags* entry shows that the rational approximation to `Pi` was rounded (digits beyond the context precision were thrown away) and that the result is inexact (some of the discarded digits were non-zero).

Individual traps are set using the dictionary in the `traps` field of a context:

```
>>> setcontext(ExtendedContext)
>>> Decimal(1) / Decimal(0)
Decimal('Infinity')
>>> getcontext().traps[DivisionByZero] = 1
>>> Decimal(1) / Decimal(0)
Traceback (most recent call last):
  File "<pyshell#112>", line 1, in -toplevel-
    Decimal(1) / Decimal(0)
DivisionByZero: x / 0
```

Most programs adjust the current context only once, at the beginning of the program. And, in many applications, data is converted to `Decimal` with a single cast inside a loop. With context set and decimals created, the bulk of the program manipulates the data no differently than with other Python numeric types.

9.4.2 Decimal objects

class decimal.Decimal(*value="0", context=None*)

Construct a new `Decimal` object based from *value*.

value can be an integer, string, tuple, `float`, or another `Decimal` object. If no *value* is given, returns `Decimal('0')`. If *value* is a string, it should conform to the decimal numeric string syntax after leading and trailing whitespace characters, as well as underscores throughout, are removed:

```
sign           ::=  '+' | '-'
digit          ::=  '0' | '1' | '2' | '3' | '4' | '5' | '6' | '7' | '8' | '9'
indicator      ::=  'e' | 'E'
digits         ::=  digit [digit]...
decimal-part   ::=  digits '.' [digits] | ['.'] digits
exponent-part  ::=  indicator [sign] digits
infinity       ::=  'Infinity' | 'Inf'
nan            ::=  'NaN' [digits] | 'sNaN' [digits]
numeric-value  ::=  decimal-part [exponent-part] | infinity
numeric-string ::=  [sign] numeric-value | [sign] nan
```

Other Unicode decimal digits are also permitted where `digit` appears above. These include decimal digits from various other alphabets (for example, Arabic-Indic and Devanāgarī digits) along with the fullwidth digits `'\uff10'` through `'\uff19'`.

If *value* is a `tuple`, it should have three components, a sign (`0` for positive or `1` for negative), a `tuple` of digits, and an integer exponent. For example, `Decimal((0, (1, 4, 1, 4), -3))` returns `Decimal('1.414')`.

If *value* is a `float`, the binary floating point value is losslessly converted to its exact decimal equivalent. This conversion can often require 53 or more digits of precision. For example, `Decimal(float('1.1'))` converts to `Decimal('1.100000000000000088817841970012523233890533447265625')`.

The *context* precision does not affect how many digits are stored. That is determined exclusively by the number of digits in *value*. For example, `Decimal('3.00000')` records all five zeros even if the context precision is only three.

The purpose of the *context* argument is determining what to do if *value* is a malformed string. If the context traps *InvalidOperation*, an exception is raised; otherwise, the constructor returns a new Decimal with the value of `NaN`.

Once constructed, *Decimal* objects are immutable.

Changed in version 3.2: The argument to the constructor is now permitted to be a *float* instance.

Changed in version 3.3: *float* arguments raise an exception if the *FloatOperation* trap is set. By default the trap is off.

Changed in version 3.6: Underscores are allowed for grouping, as with integral and floating-point literals in code.

Decimal floating point objects share many properties with the other built-in numeric types such as *float* and *int*. All of the usual math operations and special methods apply. Likewise, decimal objects can be copied, pickled, printed, used as dictionary keys, used as set elements, compared, sorted, and coerced to another type (such as *float* or *int*).

There are some small differences between arithmetic on Decimal objects and arithmetic on integers and floats. When the remainder operator `%` is applied to Decimal objects, the sign of the result is the sign of the *dividend* rather than the sign of the divisor:

```
>>> (-7) % 4
1
>>> Decimal(-7) % Decimal(4)
Decimal('-3')
```

The integer division operator `//` behaves analogously, returning the integer part of the true quotient (truncating towards zero) rather than its floor, so as to preserve the usual identity `x == (x // y) * y + x % y`:

```
>>> -7 // 4
-2
>>> Decimal(-7) // Decimal(4)
Decimal('-1')
```

The `%` and `//` operators implement the `remainder` and `divide-integer` operations (respectively) as described in the specification.

Decimal objects cannot generally be combined with floats or instances of *fractions.Fraction* in arithmetic operations: an attempt to add a *Decimal* to a *float*, for example, will raise a *TypeError*. However, it is possible to use Python's comparison operators to compare a *Decimal* instance `x` with another number `y`. This avoids confusing results when doing equality comparisons between numbers of different types.

Changed in version 3.2: Mixed-type comparisons between *Decimal* instances and other numeric types are now fully supported.

In addition to the standard numeric properties, decimal floating point objects also have a number of specialized methods:

adjusted()

Return the adjusted exponent after shifting out the coefficient's rightmost digits until only the lead digit remains: `Decimal('321e+5').adjusted()` returns seven. Used for determining the position of the most significant digit with respect to the decimal point.

as_integer_ratio()

Return a pair (n, d) of integers that represent the given *Decimal* instance as a fraction, in lowest terms and with a positive denominator:

```
>>> Decimal('-3.14').as_integer_ratio()
(-157, 50)
```

The conversion is exact. Raise OverflowError on infinities and ValueError on NaNs.

New in version 3.6.

as_tuple()

Return a *named tuple* representation of the number: DecimalTuple(sign, digits, exponent).

canonical()

Return the canonical encoding of the argument. Currently, the encoding of a *Decimal* instance is always canonical, so this operation returns its argument unchanged.

compare(*other*, *context=None*)

Compare the values of two Decimal instances. *compare()* returns a Decimal instance, and if either operand is a NaN then the result is a NaN:

```
a or b is a NaN  ==> Decimal('NaN')
a < b            ==> Decimal('-1')
a == b           ==> Decimal('0')
a > b            ==> Decimal('1')
```

compare_signal(*other*, *context=None*)

This operation is identical to the *compare()* method, except that all NaNs signal. That is, if neither operand is a signaling NaN then any quiet NaN operand is treated as though it were a signaling NaN.

compare_total(*other*, *context=None*)

Compare two operands using their abstract representation rather than their numerical value. Similar to the *compare()* method, but the result gives a total ordering on *Decimal* instances. Two *Decimal* instances with the same numeric value but different representations compare unequal in this ordering:

```
>>> Decimal('12.0').compare_total(Decimal('12'))
Decimal('-1')
```

Quiet and signaling NaNs are also included in the total ordering. The result of this function is Decimal('0') if both operands have the same representation, Decimal('-1') if the first operand is lower in the total order than the second, and Decimal('1') if the first operand is higher in the total order than the second operand. See the specification for details of the total order.

This operation is unaffected by context and is quiet: no flags are changed and no rounding is performed. As an exception, the C version may raise InvalidOperation if the second operand cannot be converted exactly.

compare_total_mag(*other*, *context=None*)

Compare two operands using their abstract representation rather than their value as in *compare_total()*, but ignoring the sign of each operand. x.compare_total_mag(y) is equivalent to x.copy_abs().compare_total(y.copy_abs()).

This operation is unaffected by context and is quiet: no flags are changed and no rounding is performed. As an exception, the C version may raise InvalidOperation if the second operand cannot be converted exactly.

conjugate()

Just returns self, this method is only to comply with the Decimal Specification.

copy_abs()
Return the absolute value of the argument. This operation is unaffected by the context and is quiet: no flags are changed and no rounding is performed.

copy_negate()
Return the negation of the argument. This operation is unaffected by the context and is quiet: no flags are changed and no rounding is performed.

copy_sign(*other*, *context=None*)
Return a copy of the first operand with the sign set to be the same as the sign of the second operand. For example:

```
>>> Decimal('2.3').copy_sign(Decimal('-1.5'))
Decimal('-2.3')
```

This operation is unaffected by context and is quiet: no flags are changed and no rounding is performed. As an exception, the C version may raise InvalidOperation if the second operand cannot be converted exactly.

exp(*context=None*)
Return the value of the (natural) exponential function `e**x` at the given number. The result is correctly rounded using the *ROUND_HALF_EVEN* rounding mode.

```
>>> Decimal(1).exp()
Decimal('2.718281828459045235360287471')
>>> Decimal(321).exp()
Decimal('2.561702493119680037517373933E+139')
```

from_float(*f*)
Classmethod that converts a float to a decimal number, exactly.

Note *Decimal.from_float(0.1)* is not the same as *Decimal('0.1')*. Since 0.1 is not exactly representable in binary floating point, the value is stored as the nearest representable value which is *0x1.999999999999ap-4*. That equivalent value in decimal is *0.1000000000000000055511151231257827021181583404541015625*.

Note: From Python 3.2 onwards, a *Decimal* instance can also be constructed directly from a *float*.

```
>>> Decimal.from_float(0.1)
Decimal('0.1000000000000000055511151231257827021181583404541015625')
>>> Decimal.from_float(float('nan'))
Decimal('NaN')
>>> Decimal.from_float(float('inf'))
Decimal('Infinity')
>>> Decimal.from_float(float('-inf'))
Decimal('-Infinity')
```

New in version 3.1.

fma(*other*, *third*, *context=None*)
Fused multiply-add. Return self*other+third with no rounding of the intermediate product self*other.

```
>>> Decimal(2).fma(3, 5)
Decimal('11')
```

is_canonical()
Return *True* if the argument is canonical and *False* otherwise. Currently, a *Decimal* instance is always canonical, so this operation always returns *True*.

is_finite()
Return *True* if the argument is a finite number, and *False* if the argument is an infinity or a NaN.

is_infinite()
Return *True* if the argument is either positive or negative infinity and *False* otherwise.

is_nan()
Return *True* if the argument is a (quiet or signaling) NaN and *False* otherwise.

is_normal(*context=None*)
Return *True* if the argument is a *normal* finite number. Return *False* if the argument is zero, subnormal, infinite or a NaN.

is_qnan()
Return *True* if the argument is a quiet NaN, and *False* otherwise.

is_signed()
Return *True* if the argument has a negative sign and *False* otherwise. Note that zeros and NaNs can both carry signs.

is_snan()
Return *True* if the argument is a signaling NaN and *False* otherwise.

is_subnormal(*context=None*)
Return *True* if the argument is subnormal, and *False* otherwise.

is_zero()
Return *True* if the argument is a (positive or negative) zero and *False* otherwise.

ln(*context=None*)
Return the natural (base e) logarithm of the operand. The result is correctly rounded using the *ROUND_HALF_EVEN* rounding mode.

log10(*context=None*)
Return the base ten logarithm of the operand. The result is correctly rounded using the *ROUND_HALF_EVEN* rounding mode.

logb(*context=None*)
For a nonzero number, return the adjusted exponent of its operand as a *Decimal* instance. If the operand is a zero then `Decimal('-Infinity')` is returned and the *DivisionByZero* flag is raised. If the operand is an infinity then `Decimal('Infinity')` is returned.

logical_and(*other*, *context=None*)
logical_and() is a logical operation which takes two *logical operands* (see *Logical operands*). The result is the digit-wise `and` of the two operands.

logical_invert(*context=None*)
logical_invert() is a logical operation. The result is the digit-wise inversion of the operand.

logical_or(*other*, *context=None*)
logical_or() is a logical operation which takes two *logical operands* (see *Logical operands*). The result is the digit-wise `or` of the two operands.

logical_xor(*other*, *context=None*)
logical_xor() is a logical operation which takes two *logical operands* (see *Logical operands*). The result is the digit-wise exclusive or of the two operands.

max(*other*, *context=None*)
Like `max(self, other)` except that the context rounding rule is applied before returning and

that NaN values are either signaled or ignored (depending on the context and whether they are signaling or quiet).

max_mag(*other*, *context=None*)
Similar to the *max()* method, but the comparison is done using the absolute values of the operands.

min(*other*, *context=None*)
Like min(self, other) except that the context rounding rule is applied before returning and that NaN values are either signaled or ignored (depending on the context and whether they are signaling or quiet).

min_mag(*other*, *context=None*)
Similar to the *min()* method, but the comparison is done using the absolute values of the operands.

next_minus(*context=None*)
Return the largest number representable in the given context (or in the current thread's context if no context is given) that is smaller than the given operand.

next_plus(*context=None*)
Return the smallest number representable in the given context (or in the current thread's context if no context is given) that is larger than the given operand.

next_toward(*other*, *context=None*)
If the two operands are unequal, return the number closest to the first operand in the direction of the second operand. If both operands are numerically equal, return a copy of the first operand with the sign set to be the same as the sign of the second operand.

normalize(*context=None*)
Normalize the number by stripping the rightmost trailing zeros and converting any result equal to Decimal('0') to Decimal('0e0'). Used for producing canonical values for attributes of an equivalence class. For example, Decimal('32.100') and Decimal('0.321000e+2') both normalize to the equivalent value Decimal('32.1').

number_class(*context=None*)
Return a string describing the *class* of the operand. The returned value is one of the following ten strings.

- "-Infinity", indicating that the operand is negative infinity.
- "-Normal", indicating that the operand is a negative normal number.
- "-Subnormal", indicating that the operand is negative and subnormal.
- "-Zero", indicating that the operand is a negative zero.
- "+Zero", indicating that the operand is a positive zero.
- "+Subnormal", indicating that the operand is positive and subnormal.
- "+Normal", indicating that the operand is a positive normal number.
- "+Infinity", indicating that the operand is positive infinity.
- "NaN", indicating that the operand is a quiet NaN (Not a Number).
- "sNaN", indicating that the operand is a signaling NaN.

quantize(*exp*, *rounding=None*, *context=None*)
Return a value equal to the first operand after rounding and having the exponent of the second operand.

```
>>> Decimal('1.41421356').quantize(Decimal('1.000'))
Decimal('1.414')
```

Unlike other operations, if the length of the coefficient after the quantize operation would be greater than precision, then an *InvalidOperation* is signaled. This guarantees that, unless there is an error condition, the quantized exponent is always equal to that of the right-hand operand.

Also unlike other operations, quantize never signals Underflow, even if the result is subnormal and inexact.

If the exponent of the second operand is larger than that of the first then rounding may be necessary. In this case, the rounding mode is determined by the `rounding` argument if given, else by the given `context` argument; if neither argument is given the rounding mode of the current thread's context is used.

An error is returned whenever the resulting exponent is greater than `Emax` or less than `Etiny`.

radix()
Return `Decimal(10)`, the radix (base) in which the *Decimal* class does all its arithmetic. Included for compatibility with the specification.

remainder_near(*other*, *context=None*)
Return the remainder from dividing *self* by *other*. This differs from `self % other` in that the sign of the remainder is chosen so as to minimize its absolute value. More precisely, the return value is `self - n * other` where `n` is the integer nearest to the exact value of `self / other`, and if two integers are equally near then the even one is chosen.

If the result is zero then its sign will be the sign of *self*.

```
>>> Decimal(18).remainder_near(Decimal(10))
Decimal('-2')
>>> Decimal(25).remainder_near(Decimal(10))
Decimal('5')
>>> Decimal(35).remainder_near(Decimal(10))
Decimal('-5')
```

rotate(*other*, *context=None*)
Return the result of rotating the digits of the first operand by an amount specified by the second operand. The second operand must be an integer in the range -precision through precision. The absolute value of the second operand gives the number of places to rotate. If the second operand is positive then rotation is to the left; otherwise rotation is to the right. The coefficient of the first operand is padded on the left with zeros to length precision if necessary. The sign and exponent of the first operand are unchanged.

same_quantum(*other*, *context=None*)
Test whether self and other have the same exponent or whether both are `NaN`.

This operation is unaffected by context and is quiet: no flags are changed and no rounding is performed. As an exception, the C version may raise InvalidOperation if the second operand cannot be converted exactly.

scaleb(*other*, *context=None*)
Return the first operand with exponent adjusted by the second. Equivalently, return the first operand multiplied by `10**other`. The second operand must be an integer.

shift(*other*, *context=None*)
Return the result of shifting the digits of the first operand by an amount specified by the second operand. The second operand must be an integer in the range -precision through precision. The absolute value of the second operand gives the number of places to shift. If the second operand is positive then the shift is to the left; otherwise the shift is to the right. Digits shifted into the coefficient are zeros. The sign and exponent of the first operand are unchanged.

sqrt(*context=None*)
Return the square root of the argument to full precision.

to_eng_string(*context=None*)
Convert to a string, using engineering notation if an exponent is needed.

Engineering notation has an exponent which is a multiple of 3. This can leave up to 3 digits to the left of the decimal place and may require the addition of either one or two trailing zeros.

For example, this converts `Decimal('123E+1')` to `Decimal('1.23E+3')`.

to_integral(*rounding=None*, *context=None*)
Identical to the *to_integral_value()* method. The **to_integral** name has been kept for compatibility with older versions.

to_integral_exact(*rounding=None*, *context=None*)
Round to the nearest integer, signaling *Inexact* or *Rounded* as appropriate if rounding occurs. The rounding mode is determined by the **rounding** parameter if given, else by the given **context**. If neither parameter is given then the rounding mode of the current context is used.

to_integral_value(*rounding=None*, *context=None*)
Round to the nearest integer without signaling *Inexact* or *Rounded*. If given, applies *rounding*; otherwise, uses the rounding method in either the supplied *context* or the current context.

Logical operands

The `logical_and()`, `logical_invert()`, `logical_or()`, and `logical_xor()` methods expect their arguments to be *logical operands*. A *logical operand* is a *Decimal* instance whose exponent and sign are both zero, and whose digits are all either `0` or `1`.

9.4.3 Context objects

Contexts are environments for arithmetic operations. They govern precision, set rules for rounding, determine which signals are treated as exceptions, and limit the range for exponents.

Each thread has its own current context which is accessed or changed using the *getcontext()* and *setcontext()* functions:

decimal.**getcontext**()
Return the current context for the active thread.

decimal.**setcontext**(*c*)
Set the current context for the active thread to *c*.

You can also use the **with** statement and the *localcontext()* function to temporarily change the active context.

decimal.**localcontext**(*ctx=None*)
Return a context manager that will set the current context for the active thread to a copy of *ctx* on entry to the with-statement and restore the previous context when exiting the with-statement. If no context is specified, a copy of the current context is used.

For example, the following code sets the current decimal precision to 42 places, performs a calculation, and then automatically restores the previous context:

```
from decimal import localcontext

with localcontext() as ctx:
    ctx.prec = 42   # Perform a high precision calculation
    s = calculate_something()
s = +s  # Round the final result back to the default precision
```

New contexts can also be created using the *Context* constructor described below. In addition, the module provides three pre-made contexts:

class decimal.BasicContext

This is a standard context defined by the General Decimal Arithmetic Specification. Precision is set to nine. Rounding is set to *ROUND_HALF_UP*. All flags are cleared. All traps are enabled (treated as exceptions) except *Inexact*, *Rounded*, and *Subnormal*.

Because many of the traps are enabled, this context is useful for debugging.

class decimal.ExtendedContext

This is a standard context defined by the General Decimal Arithmetic Specification. Precision is set to nine. Rounding is set to *ROUND_HALF_EVEN*. All flags are cleared. No traps are enabled (so that exceptions are not raised during computations).

Because the traps are disabled, this context is useful for applications that prefer to have result value of `NaN` or `Infinity` instead of raising exceptions. This allows an application to complete a run in the presence of conditions that would otherwise halt the program.

class decimal.DefaultContext

This context is used by the *Context* constructor as a prototype for new contexts. Changing a field (such a precision) has the effect of changing the default for new contexts created by the *Context* constructor.

This context is most useful in multi-threaded environments. Changing one of the fields before threads are started has the effect of setting system-wide defaults. Changing the fields after threads have started is not recommended as it would require thread synchronization to prevent race conditions.

In single threaded environments, it is preferable to not use this context at all. Instead, simply create contexts explicitly as described below.

The default values are **prec**=28, **rounding**=*ROUND_HALF_EVEN*, and enabled traps for *Overflow*, *InvalidOperation*, and *DivisionByZero*.

In addition to the three supplied contexts, new contexts can be created with the *Context* constructor.

class decimal.Context(*prec=None, rounding=None, Emin=None, Emax=None, capitals=None, clamp=None, flags=None, traps=None*)

Creates a new context. If a field is not specified or is *None*, the default values are copied from the *DefaultContext*. If the *flags* field is not specified or is *None*, all flags are cleared.

prec is an integer in the range [`1`, *MAX_PREC*] that sets the precision for arithmetic operations in the context.

The *rounding* option is one of the constants listed in the section *Rounding Modes*.

The *traps* and *flags* fields list any signals to be set. Generally, new contexts should only set traps and leave the flags clear.

The *Emin* and *Emax* fields are integers specifying the outer limits allowable for exponents. *Emin* must be in the range [*MIN_EMIN*, `0`], *Emax* in the range [`0`, *MAX_EMAX*].

The *capitals* field is either `0` or `1` (the default). If set to `1`, exponents are printed with a capital `E`; otherwise, a lowercase `e` is used: `Decimal('6.02e+23')`.

The *clamp* field is either `0` (the default) or `1`. If set to `1`, the exponent `e` of a *Decimal* instance representable in this context is strictly limited to the range `Emin - prec + 1 <= e <= Emax - prec + 1`. If *clamp* is `0` then a weaker condition holds: the adjusted exponent of the *Decimal* instance is at most `Emax`. When *clamp* is `1`, a large normal number will, where possible, have its exponent reduced and a corresponding number of zeros added to its coefficient, in order to fit the exponent constraints; this preserves the value of the number but loses information about significant trailing zeros. For example:

```
>>> Context(prec=6, Emax=999, clamp=1).create_decimal('1.23e999')
Decimal('1.23000E+999')
```

A *clamp* value of `1` allows compatibility with the fixed-width decimal interchange formats specified in IEEE 754.

The *Context* class defines several general purpose methods as well as a large number of methods for doing arithmetic directly in a given context. In addition, for each of the *Decimal* methods described above (with the exception of the `adjusted()` and `as_tuple()` methods) there is a corresponding *Context* method. For example, for a *Context* instance `C` and *Decimal* instance `x`, `C.exp(x)` is equivalent to `x.exp(context=C)`. Each *Context* method accepts a Python integer (an instance of *int*) anywhere that a Decimal instance is accepted.

clear_flags()
Resets all of the flags to `0`.

clear_traps()
Resets all of the traps to `0`.

New in version 3.3.

copy()
Return a duplicate of the context.

copy_decimal(*num*)
Return a copy of the Decimal instance num.

create_decimal(*num*)
Creates a new Decimal instance from *num* but using *self* as context. Unlike the *Decimal* constructor, the context precision, rounding method, flags, and traps are applied to the conversion.

This is useful because constants are often given to a greater precision than is needed by the application. Another benefit is that rounding immediately eliminates unintended effects from digits beyond the current precision. In the following example, using unrounded inputs means that adding zero to a sum can change the result:

```
>>> getcontext().prec = 3
>>> Decimal('3.4445') + Decimal('1.0023')
Decimal('4.45')
>>> Decimal('3.4445') + Decimal(0) + Decimal('1.0023')
Decimal('4.44')
```

This method implements the to-number operation of the IBM specification. If the argument is a string, no leading or trailing whitespace or underscores are permitted.

create_decimal_from_float(*f*)
Creates a new Decimal instance from a float *f* but rounding using *self* as the context. Unlike the *Decimal.from_float()* class method, the context precision, rounding method, flags, and traps are applied to the conversion.

```
>>> context = Context(prec=5, rounding=ROUND_DOWN)
>>> context.create_decimal_from_float(math.pi)
Decimal('3.1415')
>>> context = Context(prec=5, traps=[Inexact])
>>> context.create_decimal_from_float(math.pi)
Traceback (most recent call last):
    ...
decimal.Inexact: None
```

New in version 3.1.

Etiny()
Returns a value equal to `Emin - prec + 1` which is the minimum exponent value for subnormal results. When underflow occurs, the exponent is set to *Etiny*.

Etop()
Returns a value equal to `Emax - prec + 1`.

The usual approach to working with decimals is to create *Decimal* instances and then apply arithmetic operations which take place within the current context for the active thread. An alternative approach is to use context methods for calculating within a specific context. The methods are similar to those for the *Decimal* class and are only briefly recounted here.

abs(*x*)
Returns the absolute value of *x*.

add(*x*, *y*)
Return the sum of *x* and *y*.

canonical(*x*)
Returns the same Decimal object *x*.

compare(*x*, *y*)
Compares *x* and *y* numerically.

compare_signal(*x*, *y*)
Compares the values of the two operands numerically.

compare_total(*x*, *y*)
Compares two operands using their abstract representation.

compare_total_mag(*x*, *y*)
Compares two operands using their abstract representation, ignoring sign.

copy_abs(*x*)
Returns a copy of *x* with the sign set to 0.

copy_negate(*x*)
Returns a copy of *x* with the sign inverted.

copy_sign(*x*, *y*)
Copies the sign from *y* to *x*.

divide(*x*, *y*)
Return *x* divided by *y*.

divide_int(*x*, *y*)
Return *x* divided by *y*, truncated to an integer.

divmod(*x*, *y*)
Divides two numbers and returns the integer part of the result.

exp(*x*)
Returns *e* ** *x*.

fma(*x*, *y*, *z*)
Returns *x* multiplied by *y*, plus *z*.

is_canonical(*x*)
Returns `True` if *x* is canonical; otherwise returns `False`.

is_finite(*x*)
Returns `True` if *x* is finite; otherwise returns `False`.

is_infinite(*x*)
Returns `True` if *x* is infinite; otherwise returns `False`.

is_nan(*x*)
Returns True if *x* is a qNaN or sNaN; otherwise returns False.

is_normal(*x*)
Returns True if *x* is a normal number; otherwise returns False.

is_qnan(*x*)
Returns True if *x* is a quiet NaN; otherwise returns False.

is_signed(*x*)
Returns True if *x* is negative; otherwise returns False.

is_snan(*x*)
Returns True if *x* is a signaling NaN; otherwise returns False.

is_subnormal(*x*)
Returns True if *x* is subnormal; otherwise returns False.

is_zero(*x*)
Returns True if *x* is a zero; otherwise returns False.

ln(*x*)
Returns the natural (base e) logarithm of *x*.

log10(*x*)
Returns the base 10 logarithm of *x*.

logb(*x*)
Returns the exponent of the magnitude of the operand's MSD.

logical_and(*x*, *y*)
Applies the logical operation *and* between each operand's digits.

logical_invert(*x*)
Invert all the digits in *x*.

logical_or(*x*, *y*)
Applies the logical operation *or* between each operand's digits.

logical_xor(*x*, *y*)
Applies the logical operation *xor* between each operand's digits.

max(*x*, *y*)
Compares two values numerically and returns the maximum.

max_mag(*x*, *y*)
Compares the values numerically with their sign ignored.

min(*x*, *y*)
Compares two values numerically and returns the minimum.

min_mag(*x*, *y*)
Compares the values numerically with their sign ignored.

minus(*x*)
Minus corresponds to the unary prefix minus operator in Python.

multiply(*x*, *y*)
Return the product of *x* and *y*.

next_minus(*x*)
Returns the largest representable number smaller than *x*.

next_plus(*x*)
Returns the smallest representable number larger than *x*.

next_toward(*x*, *y*)
Returns the number closest to *x*, in direction towards *y*.

normalize(*x*)
Reduces *x* to its simplest form.

number_class(*x*)
Returns an indication of the class of *x*.

plus(*x*)
Plus corresponds to the unary prefix plus operator in Python. This operation applies the context precision and rounding, so it is *not* an identity operation.

power(*x*, *y*, *modulo=None*)
Return `x` to the power of `y`, reduced modulo `modulo` if given.

With two arguments, compute `x**y`. If `x` is negative then `y` must be integral. The result will be inexact unless `y` is integral and the result is finite and can be expressed exactly in 'precision' digits. The rounding mode of the context is used. Results are always correctly-rounded in the Python version.

Changed in version 3.3: The C module computes *power()* in terms of the correctly-rounded *exp()* and *ln()* functions. The result is well-defined but only "almost always correctly-rounded".

With three arguments, compute `(x**y) % modulo`. For the three argument form, the following restrictions on the arguments hold:

- all three arguments must be integral
- `y` must be nonnegative
- at least one of `x` or `y` must be nonzero
- `modulo` must be nonzero and have at most 'precision' digits

The value resulting from `Context.power(x, y, modulo)` is equal to the value that would be obtained by computing `(x**y) % modulo` with unbounded precision, but is computed more efficiently. The exponent of the result is zero, regardless of the exponents of `x`, `y` and `modulo`. The result is always exact.

quantize(*x*, *y*)
Returns a value equal to *x* (rounded), having the exponent of *y*.

radix()
Just returns 10, as this is Decimal, :)

remainder(*x*, *y*)
Returns the remainder from integer division.

The sign of the result, if non-zero, is the same as that of the original dividend.

remainder_near(*x*, *y*)
Returns `x - y * n`, where *n* is the integer nearest the exact value of `x / y` (if the result is 0 then its sign will be the sign of *x*).

rotate(*x*, *y*)
Returns a rotated copy of *x*, *y* times.

same_quantum(*x*, *y*)
Returns `True` if the two operands have the same exponent.

scaleb(*x*, *y*)
Returns the first operand after adding the second value its exp.

shift(*x*, *y*)
Returns a shifted copy of *x*, *y* times.

sqrt(x)
Square root of a non-negative number to context precision.

subtract(x, y)
Return the difference between x and y.

to_eng_string(x)
Convert to a string, using engineering notation if an exponent is needed.

Engineering notation has an exponent which is a multiple of 3. This can leave up to 3 digits to the left of the decimal place and may require the addition of either one or two trailing zeros.

to_integral_exact(x)
Rounds to an integer.

to_sci_string(x)
Converts a number to a string using scientific notation.

9.4.4 Constants

The constants in this section are only relevant for the C module. They are also included in the pure Python version for compatibility.

	32-bit	64-bit
decimal.MAX_PREC	425000000	999999999999999999
decimal.MAX_EMAX	425000000	999999999999999999
decimal.MIN_EMIN	-425000000	-999999999999999999
decimal.MIN_ETINY	-849999999	-1999999999999999997

decimal.**HAVE_THREADS**
The default value is `True`. If Python is compiled without threads, the C version automatically disables the expensive thread local context machinery. In this case, the value is `False`.

9.4.5 Rounding modes

decimal.**ROUND_CEILING**
Round towards `Infinity`.

decimal.**ROUND_DOWN**
Round towards zero.

decimal.**ROUND_FLOOR**
Round towards `-Infinity`.

decimal.**ROUND_HALF_DOWN**
Round to nearest with ties going towards zero.

decimal.**ROUND_HALF_EVEN**
Round to nearest with ties going to nearest even integer.

decimal.**ROUND_HALF_UP**
Round to nearest with ties going away from zero.

`decimal.ROUND_UP`
Round away from zero.

`decimal.ROUND_05UP`
Round away from zero if last digit after rounding towards zero would have been 0 or 5; otherwise round towards zero.

9.4.6 Signals

Signals represent conditions that arise during computation. Each corresponds to one context flag and one context trap enabler.

The context flag is set whenever the condition is encountered. After the computation, flags may be checked for informational purposes (for instance, to determine whether a computation was exact). After checking the flags, be sure to clear all flags before starting the next computation.

If the context's trap enabler is set for the signal, then the condition causes a Python exception to be raised. For example, if the *DivisionByZero* trap is set, then a *DivisionByZero* exception is raised upon encountering the condition.

`class decimal.Clamped`
Altered an exponent to fit representation constraints.

Typically, clamping occurs when an exponent falls outside the context's `Emin` and `Emax` limits. If possible, the exponent is reduced to fit by adding zeros to the coefficient.

`class decimal.DecimalException`
Base class for other signals and a subclass of *ArithmeticError*.

`class decimal.DivisionByZero`
Signals the division of a non-infinite number by zero.

Can occur with division, modulo division, or when raising a number to a negative power. If this signal is not trapped, returns `Infinity` or `-Infinity` with the sign determined by the inputs to the calculation.

`class decimal.Inexact`
Indicates that rounding occurred and the result is not exact.

Signals when non-zero digits were discarded during rounding. The rounded result is returned. The signal flag or trap is used to detect when results are inexact.

`class decimal.InvalidOperation`
An invalid operation was performed.

Indicates that an operation was requested that does not make sense. If not trapped, returns `NaN`. Possible causes include:

```
Infinity - Infinity
0 * Infinity
Infinity / Infinity
x % 0
Infinity % x
sqrt(-x) and x > 0
0 ** 0
x ** (non-integer)
x ** Infinity
```

`class decimal.Overflow`
Numerical overflow.

Indicates the exponent is larger than **Emax** after rounding has occurred. If not trapped, the result depends on the rounding mode, either pulling inward to the largest representable finite number or rounding outward to `Infinity`. In either case, *Inexact* and *Rounded* are also signaled.

class decimal.Rounded
Rounding occurred though possibly no information was lost.

Signaled whenever rounding discards digits; even if those digits are zero (such as rounding `5.00` to `5.0`). If not trapped, returns the result unchanged. This signal is used to detect loss of significant digits.

class decimal.Subnormal
Exponent was lower than **Emin** prior to rounding.

Occurs when an operation result is subnormal (the exponent is too small). If not trapped, returns the result unchanged.

class decimal.Underflow
Numerical underflow with result rounded to zero.

Occurs when a subnormal result is pushed to zero by rounding. *Inexact* and *Subnormal* are also signaled.

class decimal.FloatOperation
Enable stricter semantics for mixing floats and Decimals.

If the signal is not trapped (default), mixing floats and Decimals is permitted in the *Decimal* constructor, *create_decimal()* and all comparison operators. Both conversion and comparisons are exact. Any occurrence of a mixed operation is silently recorded by setting *FloatOperation* in the context flags. Explicit conversions with *from_float()* or *create_decimal_from_float()* do not set the flag.

Otherwise (the signal is trapped), only equality comparisons and explicit conversions are silent. All other mixed operations raise *FloatOperation*.

The following table summarizes the hierarchy of signals:

```
exceptions.ArithmeticError(exceptions.Exception)
    DecimalException
        Clamped
        DivisionByZero(DecimalException, exceptions.ZeroDivisionError)
        Inexact
            Overflow(Inexact, Rounded)
            Underflow(Inexact, Rounded, Subnormal)
        InvalidOperation
        Rounded
        Subnormal
        FloatOperation(DecimalException, exceptions.TypeError)
```

9.4.7 Floating Point Notes

Mitigating round-off error with increased precision

The use of decimal floating point eliminates decimal representation error (making it possible to represent `0.1` exactly); however, some operations can still incur round-off error when non-zero digits exceed the fixed precision.

The effects of round-off error can be amplified by the addition or subtraction of nearly offsetting quantities resulting in loss of significance. Knuth provides two instructive examples where rounded floating point arithmetic with insufficient precision causes the breakdown of the associative and distributive properties of addition:

```
# Examples from Seminumerical Algorithms, Section 4.2.2.
>>> from decimal import Decimal, getcontext
>>> getcontext().prec = 8

>>> u, v, w = Decimal(11111113), Decimal(-11111111), Decimal('7.51111111')
>>> (u + v) + w
Decimal('9.5111111')
>>> u + (v + w)
Decimal('10')

>>> u, v, w = Decimal(20000), Decimal(-6), Decimal('6.0000003')
>>> (u*v) + (u*w)
Decimal('0.01')
>>> u * (v+w)
Decimal('0.0060000')
```

The *decimal* module makes it possible to restore the identities by expanding the precision sufficiently to avoid loss of significance:

```
>>> getcontext().prec = 20
>>> u, v, w = Decimal(11111113), Decimal(-11111111), Decimal('7.51111111')
>>> (u + v) + w
Decimal('9.51111111')
>>> u + (v + w)
Decimal('9.51111111')
>>>
>>> u, v, w = Decimal(20000), Decimal(-6), Decimal('6.0000003')
>>> (u*v) + (u*w)
Decimal('0.0060000')
>>> u * (v+w)
Decimal('0.0060000')
```

Special values

The number system for the *decimal* module provides special values including `NaN`, `sNaN`, `-Infinity`, `Infinity`, and two zeros, `+0` and `-0`.

Infinities can be constructed directly with: `Decimal('Infinity')`. Also, they can arise from dividing by zero when the *DivisionByZero* signal is not trapped. Likewise, when the *Overflow* signal is not trapped, infinity can result from rounding beyond the limits of the largest representable number.

The infinities are signed (affine) and can be used in arithmetic operations where they get treated as very large, indeterminate numbers. For instance, adding a constant to infinity gives another infinite result.

Some operations are indeterminate and return `NaN`, or if the *InvalidOperation* signal is trapped, raise an exception. For example, `0/0` returns `NaN` which means "not a number". This variety of `NaN` is quiet and, once created, will flow through other computations always resulting in another `NaN`. This behavior can be useful for a series of computations that occasionally have missing inputs — it allows the calculation to proceed while flagging specific results as invalid.

A variant is `sNaN` which signals rather than remaining quiet after every operation. This is a useful return value when an invalid result needs to interrupt a calculation for special handling.

The behavior of Python's comparison operators can be a little surprising where a `NaN` is involved. A test for equality where one of the operands is a quiet or signaling `NaN` always returns *False* (even when doing `Decimal('NaN')==Decimal('NaN')`), while a test for inequality always returns *True*. An attempt to compare two Decimals using any of the `<`, `<=`, `>` or `>=` operators will raise the *InvalidOperation* signal if either operand is a `NaN`, and return *False* if this signal is not trapped. Note that the General Decimal Arithmetic specification does not specify the behavior of direct comparisons; these rules for comparisons involving a `NaN` were taken from the IEEE 854 standard (see Table 3 in section 5.7). To ensure strict standards-compliance, use the `compare()` and `compare-signal()` methods instead.

The signed zeros can result from calculations that underflow. They keep the sign that would have resulted if the calculation had been carried out to greater precision. Since their magnitude is zero, both positive and negative zeros are treated as equal and their sign is informational.

In addition to the two signed zeros which are distinct yet equal, there are various representations of zero with differing precisions yet equivalent in value. This takes a bit of getting used to. For an eye accustomed to normalized floating point representations, it is not immediately obvious that the following calculation returns a value equal to zero:

```
>>> 1 / Decimal('Infinity')
Decimal('0E-1000026')
```

9.4.8 Working with threads

The *getcontext()* function accesses a different *Context* object for each thread. Having separate thread contexts means that threads may make changes (such as `getcontext().prec=10`) without interfering with other threads.

Likewise, the *setcontext()* function automatically assigns its target to the current thread.

If *setcontext()* has not been called before *getcontext()*, then *getcontext()* will automatically create a new context for use in the current thread.

The new context is copied from a prototype context called *DefaultContext*. To control the defaults so that each thread will use the same values throughout the application, directly modify the *DefaultContext* object. This should be done *before* any threads are started so that there won't be a race condition between threads calling *getcontext()*. For example:

```
# Set applicationwide defaults for all threads about to be launched
DefaultContext.prec = 12
DefaultContext.rounding = ROUND_DOWN
DefaultContext.traps = ExtendedContext.traps.copy()
DefaultContext.traps[InvalidOperation] = 1
setcontext(DefaultContext)

# Afterwards, the threads can be started
t1.start()
t2.start()
t3.start()
 . . .
```

9.4.9 Recipes

Here are a few recipes that serve as utility functions and that demonstrate ways to work with the *Decimal* class:

```
def moneyfmt(value, places=2, curr='', sep=',', dp='.',
             pos='', neg='-', trailneg=''):
    """Convert Decimal to a money formatted string.

    places:  required number of places after the decimal point
    curr:    optional currency symbol before the sign (may be blank)
    sep:     optional grouping separator (comma, period, space, or blank)
```

```
    dp:       decimal point indicator (comma or period)
              only specify as blank when places is zero
    pos:      optional sign for positive numbers: '+', space or blank
    neg:      optional sign for negative numbers: '-', '(', space or blank
    trailneg:optional trailing minus indicator:  '-', ')', space or blank

    >>> d = Decimal('-1234567.8901')
    >>> moneyfmt(d, curr='$')
    '-$1,234,567.89'
    >>> moneyfmt(d, places=0, sep='.', dp='', neg='', trailneg='-')
    '1.234.568-'
    >>> moneyfmt(d, curr='$', neg='(', trailneg=')')
    '($1,234,567.89)'
    >>> moneyfmt(Decimal(123456789), sep=' ')
    '123 456 789.00'
    >>> moneyfmt(Decimal('-0.02'), neg='<', trailneg='>')
    '<0.02>'

    """
    q = Decimal(10) ** -places      # 2 places --> '0.01'
    sign, digits, exp = value.quantize(q).as_tuple()
    result = []
    digits = list(map(str, digits))
    build, next = result.append, digits.pop
    if sign:
        build(trailneg)
    for i in range(places):
        build(next() if digits else '0')
    if places:
        build(dp)
    if not digits:
        build('0')
    i = 0
    while digits:
        build(next())
        i += 1
        if i == 3 and digits:
            i = 0
            build(sep)
    build(curr)
    build(neg if sign else pos)
    return ''.join(reversed(result))

def pi():
    """Compute Pi to the current precision.

    >>> print(pi())
    3.141592653589793238462643383

    """
    getcontext().prec += 2  # extra digits for intermediate steps
    three = Decimal(3)      # substitute "three=3.0" for regular floats
    lasts, t, s, n, na, d, da = 0, three, 3, 1, 0, 0, 24
    while s != lasts:
        lasts = s
        n, na = n+na, na+8
        d, da = d+da, da+32
        t = (t * n) / d
```

```
        s += t
    getcontext().prec -= 2
    return +s               # unary plus applies the new precision

def exp(x):
    """Return e raised to the power of x.  Result type matches input type.

    >>> print(exp(Decimal(1)))
    2.718281828459045235360287471
    >>> print(exp(Decimal(2)))
    7.389056098930650227230427461
    >>> print(exp(2.0))
    7.38905609893
    >>> print(exp(2+0j))
    (7.38905609893+0j)

    """
    getcontext().prec += 2
    i, lasts, s, fact, num = 0, 0, 1, 1, 1
    while s != lasts:
        lasts = s
        i += 1
        fact *= i
        num *= x
        s += num / fact
    getcontext().prec -= 2
    return +s

def cos(x):
    """Return the cosine of x as measured in radians.

    The Taylor series approximation works best for a small value of x.
    For larger values, first compute x = x % (2 * pi).

    >>> print(cos(Decimal('0.5')))
    0.8775825618903727161162815826
    >>> print(cos(0.5))
    0.87758256189
    >>> print(cos(0.5+0j))
    (0.87758256189+0j)

    """
    getcontext().prec += 2
    i, lasts, s, fact, num, sign = 0, 0, 1, 1, 1, 1
    while s != lasts:
        lasts = s
        i += 2
        fact *= i * (i-1)
        num *= x * x
        sign *= -1
        s += num / fact * sign
    getcontext().prec -= 2
    return +s

def sin(x):
    """Return the sine of x as measured in radians.

    The Taylor series approximation works best for a small value of x.
```

```
    For larger values, first compute x = x % (2 * pi).

    >>> print(sin(Decimal('0.5')))
    0.4794255386042030002732879352
    >>> print(sin(0.5))
    0.479425538604
    >>> print(sin(0.5+0j))
    (0.479425538604+0j)

    """
    getcontext().prec += 2
    i, lasts, s, fact, num, sign = 1, 0, x, 1, x, 1
    while s != lasts:
        lasts = s
        i += 2
        fact *= i * (i-1)
        num *= x * x
        sign *= -1
        s += num / fact * sign
    getcontext().prec -= 2
    return +s
```

9.4.10 Decimal FAQ

Q. It is cumbersome to type `decimal.Decimal('1234.5')`. Is there a way to minimize typing when using the interactive interpreter?

A. Some users abbreviate the constructor to just a single letter:

```
>>> D = decimal.Decimal
>>> D('1.23') + D('3.45')
Decimal('4.68')
```

Q. In a fixed-point application with two decimal places, some inputs have many places and need to be rounded. Others are not supposed to have excess digits and need to be validated. What methods should be used?

A. The `quantize()` method rounds to a fixed number of decimal places. If the *Inexact* trap is set, it is also useful for validation:

```
>>> TWOPLACES = Decimal(10) ** -2       # same as Decimal('0.01')
```

```
>>> # Round to two places
>>> Decimal('3.214').quantize(TWOPLACES)
Decimal('3.21')
```

```
>>> # Validate that a number does not exceed two places
>>> Decimal('3.21').quantize(TWOPLACES, context=Context(traps=[Inexact]))
Decimal('3.21')
```

```
>>> Decimal('3.214').quantize(TWOPLACES, context=Context(traps=[Inexact]))
Traceback (most recent call last):
   ...
Inexact: None
```

Q. Once I have valid two place inputs, how do I maintain that invariant throughout an application?

A. Some operations like addition, subtraction, and multiplication by an integer will automatically preserve fixed point. Others operations, like division and non-integer multiplication, will change the number of decimal places and need to be followed-up with a `quantize()` step:

```
>>> a = Decimal('102.72')           # Initial fixed-point values
>>> b = Decimal('3.17')
>>> a + b                           # Addition preserves fixed-point
Decimal('105.89')
>>> a - b
Decimal('99.55')
>>> a * 42                          # So does integer multiplication
Decimal('4314.24')
>>> (a * b).quantize(TWOPLACES)     # Must quantize non-integer multiplication
Decimal('325.62')
>>> (b / a).quantize(TWOPLACES)     # And quantize division
Decimal('0.03')
```

In developing fixed-point applications, it is convenient to define functions to handle the `quantize()` step:

```
>>> def mul(x, y, fp=TWOPLACES):
...     return (x * y).quantize(fp)
>>> def div(x, y, fp=TWOPLACES):
...     return (x / y).quantize(fp)
```

```
>>> mul(a, b)                       # Automatically preserve fixed-point
Decimal('325.62')
>>> div(b, a)
Decimal('0.03')
```

Q. There are many ways to express the same value. The numbers 200, 200.000, 2E2, and 02E+4 all have the same value at various precisions. Is there a way to transform them to a single recognizable canonical value?

A. The `normalize()` method maps all equivalent values to a single representative:

```
>>> values = map(Decimal, '200 200.000 2E2 .02E+4'.split())
>>> [v.normalize() for v in values]
[Decimal('2E+2'), Decimal('2E+2'), Decimal('2E+2'), Decimal('2E+2')]
```

Q. Some decimal values always print with exponential notation. Is there a way to get a non-exponential representation?

A. For some values, exponential notation is the only way to express the number of significant places in the coefficient. For example, expressing 5.0E+3 as 5000 keeps the value constant but cannot show the original's two-place significance.

If an application does not care about tracking significance, it is easy to remove the exponent and trailing zeroes, losing significance, but keeping the value unchanged:

```
>>> def remove_exponent(d):
...     return d.quantize(Decimal(1)) if d == d.to_integral() else d.normalize()
```

```
>>> remove_exponent(Decimal('5E+3'))
Decimal('5000')
```

Q. Is there a way to convert a regular float to a *Decimal*?

A. Yes, any binary floating point number can be exactly expressed as a Decimal though an exact conversion may take more precision than intuition would suggest:

```
>>> Decimal(math.pi)
Decimal('3.141592653589793115997963468544185161590576171875')
```

Q. Within a complex calculation, how can I make sure that I haven't gotten a spurious result because of insufficient precision or rounding anomalies.

A. The decimal module makes it easy to test results. A best practice is to re-run calculations using greater precision and with various rounding modes. Widely differing results indicate insufficient precision, rounding mode issues, ill-conditioned inputs, or a numerically unstable algorithm.

Q. I noticed that context precision is applied to the results of operations but not to the inputs. Is there anything to watch out for when mixing values of different precisions?

A. Yes. The principle is that all values are considered to be exact and so is the arithmetic on those values. Only the results are rounded. The advantage for inputs is that "what you type is what you get". A disadvantage is that the results can look odd if you forget that the inputs haven't been rounded:

```
>>> getcontext().prec = 3
>>> Decimal('3.104') + Decimal('2.104')
Decimal('5.21')
>>> Decimal('3.104') + Decimal('0.000') + Decimal('2.104')
Decimal('5.20')
```

The solution is either to increase precision or to force rounding of inputs using the unary plus operation:

```
>>> getcontext().prec = 3
>>> +Decimal('1.23456789')      # unary plus triggers rounding
Decimal('1.23')
```

Alternatively, inputs can be rounded upon creation using the *Context.create_decimal()* method:

```
>>> Context(prec=5, rounding=ROUND_DOWN).create_decimal('1.2345678')
Decimal('1.2345')
```

9.5 fractions — Rational numbers

Source code: Lib/fractions.py

The *fractions* module provides support for rational number arithmetic.

A Fraction instance can be constructed from a pair of integers, from another rational number, or from a string.

class fractions.Fraction(*numerator=0, denominator=1*)
class fractions.Fraction(*other_fraction*)
class fractions.Fraction(*float*)
class fractions.Fraction(*decimal*)
class fractions.Fraction(*string*)

The first version requires that *numerator* and *denominator* are instances of *numbers.Rational* and returns a new *Fraction* instance with value `numerator/denominator`. If *denominator* is 0, it raises a *ZeroDivisionError*. The second version requires that *other_fraction* is an instance of *numbers.Rational* and returns a *Fraction* instance with the same value. The next two versions accept either a *float* or a *decimal.Decimal* instance, and return a *Fraction* instance with exactly the same value. Note that due to the usual issues with binary floating-point (see tut-fp-issues), the argument to `Fraction(1.1)` is not exactly equal to 11/10, and so `Fraction(1.1)` does *not* return `Fraction(11,`

10) as one might expect. (But see the documentation for the *limit_denominator()* method below.) The last version of the constructor expects a string or unicode instance. The usual form for this instance is:

```
[sign] numerator ['/' denominator]
```

where the optional **sign** may be either '+' or '-' and **numerator** and **denominator** (if present) are strings of decimal digits. In addition, any string that represents a finite value and is accepted by the *float* constructor is also accepted by the *Fraction* constructor. In either form the input string may also have leading and/or trailing whitespace. Here are some examples:

```
>>> from fractions import Fraction
>>> Fraction(16, -10)
Fraction(-8, 5)
>>> Fraction(123)
Fraction(123, 1)
>>> Fraction()
Fraction(0, 1)
>>> Fraction('3/7')
Fraction(3, 7)
>>> Fraction(' -3/7 ')
Fraction(-3, 7)
>>> Fraction('1.414213 \t\n')
Fraction(1414213, 1000000)
>>> Fraction('-.125')
Fraction(-1, 8)
>>> Fraction('7e-6')
Fraction(7, 1000000)
>>> Fraction(2.25)
Fraction(9, 4)
>>> Fraction(1.1)
Fraction(2476979795053773, 2251799813685248)
>>> from decimal import Decimal
>>> Fraction(Decimal('1.1'))
Fraction(11, 10)
```

The *Fraction* class inherits from the abstract base class *numbers.Rational*, and implements all of the methods and operations from that class. *Fraction* instances are hashable, and should be treated as immutable. In addition, *Fraction* has the following properties and methods:

Changed in version 3.2: The *Fraction* constructor now accepts *float* and *decimal.Decimal* instances.

numerator
Numerator of the Fraction in lowest term.

denominator
Denominator of the Fraction in lowest term.

from_float(*flt*)
This class method constructs a *Fraction* representing the exact value of *flt*, which must be a *float*. Beware that `Fraction.from_float(0.3)` is not the same value as `Fraction(3, 10)`.

> **Note:** From Python 3.2 onwards, you can also construct a *Fraction* instance directly from a *float*.

from_decimal(*dec*)
This class method constructs a *Fraction* representing the exact value of *dec*, which must be a

decimal.Decimal instance.

Note: From Python 3.2 onwards, you can also construct a *Fraction* instance directly from a *decimal.Decimal* instance.

---

limit_denominator(*max_denominator=1000000*)
Finds and returns the closest *Fraction* to `self` that has denominator at most max_denominator. This method is useful for finding rational approximations to a given floating-point number:

```
>>> from fractions import Fraction
>>> Fraction('3.1415926535897932').limit_denominator(1000)
Fraction(355, 113)
```

or for recovering a rational number that's represented as a float:

```
>>> from math import pi, cos
>>> Fraction(cos(pi/3))
Fraction(4503599627370497, 9007199254740992)
>>> Fraction(cos(pi/3)).limit_denominator()
Fraction(1, 2)
>>> Fraction(1.1).limit_denominator()
Fraction(11, 10)
```

__floor__()
Returns the greatest *int* `<= self`. This method can also be accessed through the *math.floor()* function:

```
>>> from math import floor
>>> floor(Fraction(355, 113))
3
```

__ceil__()
Returns the least *int* `>= self`. This method can also be accessed through the *math.ceil()* function.

__round__()
__round__(*ndigits*)
The first version returns the nearest *int* to `self`, rounding half to even. The second version rounds `self` to the nearest multiple of `Fraction(1, 10**ndigits)` (logically, if `ndigits` is negative), again rounding half toward even. This method can also be accessed through the *round()* function.

fractions.gcd(*a, b*)
Return the greatest common divisor of the integers *a* and *b*. If either *a* or *b* is nonzero, then the absolute value of `gcd(a, b)` is the largest integer that divides both *a* and *b*. `gcd(a,b)` has the same sign as *b* if *b* is nonzero; otherwise it takes the sign of *a*. `gcd(0, 0)` returns `0`.

Deprecated since version 3.5: Use *math.gcd()* instead.

See also:

Module *numbers* The abstract base classes making up the numeric tower.

9.6 random — Generate pseudo-random numbers

Source code: Lib/random.py

This module implements pseudo-random number generators for various distributions.

For integers, there is uniform selection from a range. For sequences, there is uniform selection of a random element, a function to generate a random permutation of a list in-place, and a function for random sampling without replacement.

On the real line, there are functions to compute uniform, normal (Gaussian), lognormal, negative exponential, gamma, and beta distributions. For generating distributions of angles, the von Mises distribution is available.

Almost all module functions depend on the basic function *random()*, which generates a random float uniformly in the semi-open range [0.0, 1.0). Python uses the Mersenne Twister as the core generator. It produces 53-bit precision floats and has a period of 2**19937-1. The underlying implementation in C is both fast and threadsafe. The Mersenne Twister is one of the most extensively tested random number generators in existence. However, being completely deterministic, it is not suitable for all purposes, and is completely unsuitable for cryptographic purposes.

The functions supplied by this module are actually bound methods of a hidden instance of the `random.Random` class. You can instantiate your own instances of `Random` to get generators that don't share state.

Class `Random` can also be subclassed if you want to use a different basic generator of your own devising: in that case, override the `random()`, `seed()`, `getstate()`, and `setstate()` methods. Optionally, a new generator can supply a `getrandbits()` method — this allows *randrange()* to produce selections over an arbitrarily large range.

The *random* module also provides the *SystemRandom* class which uses the system function *os.urandom()* to generate random numbers from sources provided by the operating system.

> **Warning:** The pseudo-random generators of this module should not be used for security purposes. For security or cryptographic uses, see the *secrets* module.

See also:

M. Matsumoto and T. Nishimura, "Mersenne Twister: A 623-dimensionally equidistributed uniform pseudorandom number generator", ACM Transactions on Modeling and Computer Simulation Vol. 8, No. 1, January pp.3–30 1998.

Complementary-Multiply-with-Carry recipe for a compatible alternative random number generator with a long period and comparatively simple update operations.

9.6.1 Bookkeeping functions

`random.seed(`*a=None*, *version=2*`)`

Initialize the random number generator.

If *a* is omitted or `None`, the current system time is used. If randomness sources are provided by the operating system, they are used instead of the system time (see the *os.urandom()* function for details on availability).

If *a* is an int, it is used directly.

With version 2 (the default), a *str*, *bytes*, or *bytearray* object gets converted to an *int* and all of its bits are used.

With version 1 (provided for reproducing random sequences from older versions of Python), the algorithm for *str* and *bytes* generates a narrower range of seeds.

Changed in version 3.2: Moved to the version 2 scheme which uses all of the bits in a string seed.

random.**getstate**()
Return an object capturing the current internal state of the generator. This object can be passed to *setstate()* to restore the state.

random.**setstate**(*state*)
state should have been obtained from a previous call to *getstate()*, and *setstate()* restores the internal state of the generator to what it was at the time *getstate()* was called.

random.**getrandbits**(*k*)
Returns a Python integer with *k* random bits. This method is supplied with the MersenneTwister generator and some other generators may also provide it as an optional part of the API. When available, *getrandbits()* enables *randrange()* to handle arbitrarily large ranges.

9.6.2 Functions for integers

random.**randrange**(*stop*)
random.**randrange**(*start*, *stop*[, *step*])
Return a randomly selected element from `range(start, stop, step)`. This is equivalent to `choice(range(start, stop, step))`, but doesn't actually build a range object.

The positional argument pattern matches that of *range()*. Keyword arguments should not be used because the function may use them in unexpected ways.

Changed in version 3.2: *randrange()* is more sophisticated about producing equally distributed values. Formerly it used a style like `int(random()*n)` which could produce slightly uneven distributions.

random.**randint**(*a*, *b*)
Return a random integer *N* such that `a <= N <= b`. Alias for `randrange(a, b+1)`.

9.6.3 Functions for sequences

random.**choice**(*seq*)
Return a random element from the non-empty sequence *seq*. If *seq* is empty, raises *IndexError*.

random.**choices**(*population*, *weights=None*, *, *cum_weights=None*, *k=1*)
Return a *k* sized list of elements chosen from the *population* with replacement. If the *population* is empty, raises *IndexError*.

If a *weights* sequence is specified, selections are made according to the relative weights. Alternatively, if a *cum_weights* sequence is given, the selections are made according to the cumulative weights (perhaps computed using *itertools.accumulate()*). For example, the relative weights `[10, 5, 30, 5]` are equivalent to the cumulative weights `[10, 15, 45, 50]`. Internally, the relative weights are converted to cumulative weights before making selections, so supplying the cumulative weights saves work.

If neither *weights* nor *cum_weights* are specified, selections are made with equal probability. If a weights sequence is supplied, it must be the same length as the *population* sequence. It is a *TypeError* to specify both *weights* and *cum_weights*.

The *weights* or *cum_weights* can use any numeric type that interoperates with the *float* values returned by *random()* (that includes integers, floats, and fractions but excludes decimals).

New in version 3.6.

random.**shuffle**(*x*[, *random*])
Shuffle the sequence *x* in place.

The optional argument *random* is a 0-argument function returning a random float in [0.0, 1.0); by default, this is the function *random()*.

To shuffle an immutable sequence and return a new shuffled list, use `sample(x, k=len(x))` instead.

Note that even for small `len(x)`, the total number of permutations of x can quickly grow larger than the period of most random number generators. This implies that most permutations of a long sequence can never be generated. For example, a sequence of length 2080 is the largest that can fit within the period of the Mersenne Twister random number generator.

`random.sample(population, k)`
Return a k length list of unique elements chosen from the population sequence or set. Used for random sampling without replacement.

Returns a new list containing elements from the population while leaving the original population unchanged. The resulting list is in selection order so that all sub-slices will also be valid random samples. This allows raffle winners (the sample) to be partitioned into grand prize and second place winners (the subslices).

Members of the population need not be *hashable* or unique. If the population contains repeats, then each occurrence is a possible selection in the sample.

To choose a sample from a range of integers, use a `range()` object as an argument. This is especially fast and space efficient for sampling from a large population: `sample(range(10000000), k=60)`.

If the sample size is larger than the population size, a `ValueError` is raised.

9.6.4 Real-valued distributions

The following functions generate specific real-valued distributions. Function parameters are named after the corresponding variables in the distribution's equation, as used in common mathematical practice; most of these equations can be found in any statistics text.

`random.random()`
Return the next random floating point number in the range [0.0, 1.0).

`random.uniform(a, b)`
Return a random floating point number N such that `a <= N <= b` for `a <= b` and `b <= N <= a` for `b < a`.

The end-point value `b` may or may not be included in the range depending on floating-point rounding in the equation `a + (b-a) * random()`.

`random.triangular(low, high, mode)`
Return a random floating point number N such that `low <= N <= high` and with the specified *mode* between those bounds. The *low* and *high* bounds default to zero and one. The *mode* argument defaults to the midpoint between the bounds, giving a symmetric distribution.

`random.betavariate(alpha, beta)`
Beta distribution. Conditions on the parameters are `alpha > 0` and `beta > 0`. Returned values range between 0 and 1.

`random.expovariate(lambd)`
Exponential distribution. *lambd* is 1.0 divided by the desired mean. It should be nonzero. (The parameter would be called "lambda", but that is a reserved word in Python.) Returned values range from 0 to positive infinity if *lambd* is positive, and from negative infinity to 0 if *lambd* is negative.

`random.gammavariate(alpha, beta)`
Gamma distribution. (*Not* the gamma function!) Conditions on the parameters are `alpha > 0` and `beta > 0`.

The probability distribution function is:

```
          x ** (alpha - 1) * math.exp(-x / beta)
pdf(x) =  --------------------------------------
            math.gamma(alpha) * beta ** alpha
```

`random.gauss(mu, sigma)`
Gaussian distribution. *mu* is the mean, and *sigma* is the standard deviation. This is slightly faster than the `normalvariate()` function defined below.

`random.lognormvariate(mu, sigma)`
Log normal distribution. If you take the natural logarithm of this distribution, you'll get a normal distribution with mean *mu* and standard deviation *sigma*. *mu* can have any value, and *sigma* must be greater than zero.

`random.normalvariate(mu, sigma)`
Normal distribution. *mu* is the mean, and *sigma* is the standard deviation.

`random.vonmisesvariate(mu, kappa)`
mu is the mean angle, expressed in radians between 0 and 2**pi*, and *kappa* is the concentration parameter, which must be greater than or equal to zero. If *kappa* is equal to zero, this distribution reduces to a uniform random angle over the range 0 to 2**pi*.

`random.paretovariate(alpha)`
Pareto distribution. *alpha* is the shape parameter.

`random.weibullvariate(alpha, beta)`
Weibull distribution. *alpha* is the scale parameter and *beta* is the shape parameter.

9.6.5 Alternative Generator

`class random.SystemRandom([seed])`
Class that uses the `os.urandom()` function for generating random numbers from sources provided by the operating system. Not available on all systems. Does not rely on software state, and sequences are not reproducible. Accordingly, the `seed()` method has no effect and is ignored. The `getstate()` and `setstate()` methods raise `NotImplementedError` if called.

9.6.6 Notes on Reproducibility

Sometimes it is useful to be able to reproduce the sequences given by a pseudo random number generator. By re-using a seed value, the same sequence should be reproducible from run to run as long as multiple threads are not running.

Most of the random module's algorithms and seeding functions are subject to change across Python versions, but two aspects are guaranteed not to change:

- If a new seeding method is added, then a backward compatible seeder will be offered.
- The generator's `random()` method will continue to produce the same sequence when the compatible seeder is given the same seed.

9.6.7 Examples and Recipes

Basic examples:

```
>>> random()                             # Random float:  0.0 <= x < 1.0
0.37444887175646646

>>> uniform(2.5, 10.0)                   # Random float:  2.5 <= x < 10.0
3.1800146073117523

>>> expovariate(1 / 5)                   # Interval between arrivals averaging 5 seconds
5.148957571865031
```

```
>>> randrange(10)                        # Integer from 0 to 9 inclusive
7

>>> randrange(0, 101, 2)                 # Even integer from 0 to 100 inclusive
26

>>> choice(['win', 'lose', 'draw'])      # Single random element from a sequence
'draw'

>>> deck = 'ace two three four'.split()
>>> shuffle(deck)                        # Shuffle a list
>>> deck
['four', 'two', 'ace', 'three']

>>> sample([10, 20, 30, 40, 50], k=4)    # Four samples without replacement
[40, 10, 50, 30]
```

Simulations:

```
>>> # Six roulette wheel spins (weighted sampling with replacement)
>>> choices(['red', 'black', 'green'], [18, 18, 2], k=6)
['red', 'green', 'black', 'black', 'red', 'black']

>>> # Deal 20 cards without replacement from a deck of 52 playing cards
>>> # and determine the proportion of cards with a ten-value
>>> # (a ten, jack, queen, or king).
>>> deck = collections.Counter(tens=16, low_cards=36)
>>> seen = sample(list(deck.elements()), k=20)
>>> seen.count('tens') / 20
0.15

>>> # Estimate the probability of getting 5 or more heads from 7 spins
>>> # of a biased coin that settles on heads 60% of the time.
>>> trial = lambda: choices('HT', cum_weights=(0.60, 1.00), k=7).count('H') >= 5
>>> sum(trial() for i in range(10000)) / 10000
0.4169

>>> # Probability of the median of 5 samples being in middle two quartiles
>>> trial = lambda : 2500 <= sorted(choices(range(10000), k=5))[2]  < 7500
>>> sum(trial() for i in range(10000)) / 10000
0.7958
```

Example of statistical bootstrapping using resampling with replacement to estimate a confidence interval for the mean of a sample of size five:

```
# http://statistics.about.com/od/Applications/a/Example-Of-Bootstrapping.htm
from statistics import mean
from random import choices

data = 1, 2, 4, 4, 10
means = sorted(mean(choices(data, k=5)) for i in range(20))
print(f'The sample mean of {mean(data):.1f} has a 90% confidence '
      f'interval from {means[1]:.1f} to {means[-2]:.1f}')
```

Example of a resampling permutation test to determine the statistical significance or p-value of an observed difference between the effects of a drug versus a placebo:

```
# Example from "Statistics is Easy" by Dennis Shasha and Manda Wilson
from statistics import mean
from random import shuffle

drug = [54, 73, 53, 70, 73, 68, 52, 65, 65]
placebo = [54, 51, 58, 44, 55, 52, 42, 47, 58, 46]
observed_diff = mean(drug) - mean(placebo)

n = 10000
count = 0
combined = drug + placebo
for i in range(n):
    shuffle(combined)
    new_diff = mean(combined[:len(drug)]) - mean(combined[len(drug):])
    count += (new_diff >= observed_diff)

print(f'{n} label reshufflings produced only {count} instances with a difference')
print(f'at least as extreme as the observed difference of {observed_diff:.1f}.')
print(f'The one-sided p-value of {count / n:.4f} leads us to reject the null')
print(f'hypothesis that there is no difference between the drug and the placebo.')
```

Simulation of arrival times and service deliveries in a single server queue:

```
from random import expovariate, gauss
from statistics import mean, median, stdev

average_arrival_interval = 5.6
average_service_time = 5.0
stdev_service_time = 0.5

num_waiting = 0
arrivals = []
starts = []
arrival = service_end = 0.0
for i in range(20000):
    if arrival <= service_end:
        num_waiting += 1
        arrival += expovariate(1.0 / average_arrival_interval)
        arrivals.append(arrival)
    else:
        num_waiting -= 1
        service_start = service_end if num_waiting else arrival
        service_time = gauss(average_service_time, stdev_service_time)
        service_end = service_start + service_time
        starts.append(service_start)

waits = [start - arrival for arrival, start in zip(arrivals, starts)]
print(f'Mean wait: {mean(waits):.1f}.  Stdev wait: {stdev(waits):.1f}.')
print(f'Median wait: {median(waits):.1f}.  Max wait: {max(waits):.1f}.')
```

See also:

Statistics for Hackers a video tutorial by Jake Vanderplas on statistical analysis using just a few fundamental concepts including simulation, sampling, shuffling, and cross-validation.

Economics Simulation a simulation of a marketplace by Peter Norvig that shows effective use of many of the tools and distributions provided by this module (gauss, uniform, sample, betavariate, choice, triangular, and randrange).

A Concrete Introduction to Probability (using Python) a tutorial by Peter Norvig covering the basics of probability theory, how to write simulations, and how to perform data analysis using Python.

9.7 `statistics` — Mathematical statistics functions

New in version 3.4.

Source code: Lib/statistics.py

This module provides functions for calculating mathematical statistics of numeric (`Real`-valued) data.

Note: Unless explicitly noted otherwise, these functions support *int*, *float*, *decimal.Decimal* and *fractions.Fraction*. Behaviour with other types (whether in the numeric tower or not) is currently unsupported. Mixed types are also undefined and implementation-dependent. If your input data consists of mixed types, you may be able to use *map()* to ensure a consistent result, e.g. `map(float, input_data)`.

9.7.1 Averages and measures of central location

These functions calculate an average or typical value from a population or sample.

mean()	Arithmetic mean ("average") of data.
harmonic_mean()	Harmonic mean of data.
median()	Median (middle value) of data.
median_low()	Low median of data.
median_high()	High median of data.
median_grouped()	Median, or 50th percentile, of grouped data.
mode()	Mode (most common value) of discrete data.

9.7.2 Measures of spread

These functions calculate a measure of how much the population or sample tends to deviate from the typical or average values.

pstdev()	Population standard deviation of data.
pvariance()	Population variance of data.
stdev()	Sample standard deviation of data.
variance()	Sample variance of data.

9.7.3 Function details

Note: The functions do not require the data given to them to be sorted. However, for reading convenience, most of the examples show sorted sequences.

`statistics.mean(`*data*`)`

Return the sample arithmetic mean of *data* which can be a sequence or iterator.

The arithmetic mean is the sum of the data divided by the number of data points. It is commonly called "the average", although it is only one of many different mathematical averages. It is a measure of the central location of the data.

If *data* is empty, *StatisticsError* will be raised.

Some examples of use:

```
>>> mean([1, 2, 3, 4, 4])
2.8
>>> mean([-1.0, 2.5, 3.25, 5.75])
2.625

>>> from fractions import Fraction as F
>>> mean([F(3, 7), F(1, 21), F(5, 3), F(1, 3)])
Fraction(13, 21)

>>> from decimal import Decimal as D
>>> mean([D("0.5"), D("0.75"), D("0.625"), D("0.375")])
Decimal('0.5625')
```

Note: The mean is strongly affected by outliers and is not a robust estimator for central location: the mean is not necessarily a typical example of the data points. For more robust, although less efficient, measures of central location, see *median()* and *mode()*. (In this case, "efficient" refers to statistical efficiency rather than computational efficiency.)

The sample mean gives an unbiased estimate of the true population mean, which means that, taken on average over all the possible samples, `mean(sample)` converges on the true mean of the entire population. If *data* represents the entire population rather than a sample, then `mean(data)` is equivalent to calculating the true population mean μ.

`statistics.harmonic_mean(`*data*`)`

Return the harmonic mean of *data*, a sequence or iterator of real-valued numbers.

The harmonic mean, sometimes called the subcontrary mean, is the reciprocal of the arithmetic *mean()* of the reciprocals of the data. For example, the harmonic mean of three values *a*, *b* and *c* will be equivalent to `3/(1/a + 1/b + 1/c)`.

The harmonic mean is a type of average, a measure of the central location of the data. It is often appropriate when averaging quantities which are rates or ratios, for example speeds. For example:

Suppose an investor purchases an equal value of shares in each of three companies, with P/E (price/earning) ratios of 2.5, 3 and 10. What is the average P/E ratio for the investor's portfolio?

```
>>> harmonic_mean([2.5, 3, 10])  # For an equal investment portfolio.
3.6
```

Using the arithmetic mean would give an average of about 5.167, which is too high.

StatisticsError is raised if *data* is empty, or any element is less than zero.

New in version 3.6.

`statistics.median(`*data*`)`

Return the median (middle value) of numeric data, using the common "mean of middle two" method. If *data* is empty, *StatisticsError* is raised. *data* can be a sequence or iterator.

The median is a robust measure of central location, and is less affected by the presence of outliers in your data. When the number of data points is odd, the middle data point is returned:

```
>>> median([1, 3, 5])
3
```

When the number of data points is even, the median is interpolated by taking the average of the two middle values:

```
>>> median([1, 3, 5, 7])
4.0
```

This is suited for when your data is discrete, and you don't mind that the median may not be an actual data point.

See also:

median_low(), *median_high()*, *median_grouped()*

`statistics.median_low(data)`
Return the low median of numeric data. If *data* is empty, *StatisticsError* is raised. *data* can be a sequence or iterator.

The low median is always a member of the data set. When the number of data points is odd, the middle value is returned. When it is even, the smaller of the two middle values is returned.

```
>>> median_low([1, 3, 5])
3
>>> median_low([1, 3, 5, 7])
3
```

Use the low median when your data are discrete and you prefer the median to be an actual data point rather than interpolated.

`statistics.median_high(data)`
Return the high median of data. If *data* is empty, *StatisticsError* is raised. *data* can be a sequence or iterator.

The high median is always a member of the data set. When the number of data points is odd, the middle value is returned. When it is even, the larger of the two middle values is returned.

```
>>> median_high([1, 3, 5])
3
>>> median_high([1, 3, 5, 7])
5
```

Use the high median when your data are discrete and you prefer the median to be an actual data point rather than interpolated.

`statistics.median_grouped(data, interval=1)`
Return the median of grouped continuous data, calculated as the 50th percentile, using interpolation. If *data* is empty, *StatisticsError* is raised. *data* can be a sequence or iterator.

```
>>> median_grouped([52, 52, 53, 54])
52.5
```

In the following example, the data are rounded, so that each value represents the midpoint of data classes, e.g. 1 is the midpoint of the class 0.5–1.5, 2 is the midpoint of 1.5–2.5, 3 is the midpoint of 2.5–3.5, etc. With the data given, the middle value falls somewhere in the class 3.5–4.5, and interpolation is used to estimate it:

```
>>> median_grouped([1, 2, 2, 3, 4, 4, 4, 4, 4, 5])
3.7
```

Optional argument *interval* represents the class interval, and defaults to 1. Changing the class interval naturally will change the interpolation:

```
>>> median_grouped([1, 3, 3, 5, 7], interval=1)
3.25
>>> median_grouped([1, 3, 3, 5, 7], interval=2)
3.5
```

This function does not check whether the data points are at least *interval* apart.

CPython implementation detail: Under some circumstances, `median_grouped()` may coerce data points to floats. This behaviour is likely to change in the future.

See also:

- "Statistics for the Behavioral Sciences", Frederick J Gravetter and Larry B Wallnau (8th Edition).
- Calculating the median.
- The SSMEDIAN function in the Gnome Gnumeric spreadsheet, including this discussion.

`statistics.mode(`*data*`)`

Return the most common data point from discrete or nominal *data*. The mode (when it exists) is the most typical value, and is a robust measure of central location.

If *data* is empty, or if there is not exactly one most common value, `StatisticsError` is raised.

`mode` assumes discrete data, and returns a single value. This is the standard treatment of the mode as commonly taught in schools:

```
>>> mode([1, 1, 2, 3, 3, 3, 3, 4])
3
```

The mode is unique in that it is the only statistic which also applies to nominal (non-numeric) data:

```
>>> mode(["red", "blue", "blue", "red", "green", "red", "red"])
'red'
```

`statistics.pstdev(`*data, mu=None*`)`

Return the population standard deviation (the square root of the population variance). See `pvariance()` for arguments and other details.

```
>>> pstdev([1.5, 2.5, 2.5, 2.75, 3.25, 4.75])
0.986893273527251
```

`statistics.pvariance(`*data, mu=None*`)`

Return the population variance of *data*, a non-empty iterable of real-valued numbers. Variance, or second moment about the mean, is a measure of the variability (spread or dispersion) of data. A large variance indicates that the data is spread out; a small variance indicates it is clustered closely around the mean.

If the optional second argument *mu* is given, it should be the mean of *data*. If it is missing or `None` (the default), the mean is automatically calculated.

Use this function to calculate the variance from the entire population. To estimate the variance from a sample, the `variance()` function is usually a better choice.

Raises `StatisticsError` if *data* is empty.

Examples:

```
>>> data = [0.0, 0.25, 0.25, 1.25, 1.5, 1.75, 2.75, 3.25]
>>> pvariance(data)
1.25
```

If you have already calculated the mean of your data, you can pass it as the optional second argument *mu* to avoid recalculation:

```
>>> mu = mean(data)
>>> pvariance(data, mu)
1.25
```

This function does not attempt to verify that you have passed the actual mean as *mu*. Using arbitrary values for *mu* may lead to invalid or impossible results.

Decimals and Fractions are supported:

```
>>> from decimal import Decimal as D
>>> pvariance([D("27.5"), D("30.25"), D("30.25"), D("34.5"), D("41.75")])
Decimal('24.815')

>>> from fractions import Fraction as F
>>> pvariance([F(1, 4), F(5, 4), F(1, 2)])
Fraction(13, 72)
```

Note: When called with the entire population, this gives the population variance σ^2. When called on a sample instead, this is the biased sample variance s^2, also known as variance with N degrees of freedom.

If you somehow know the true population mean μ, you may use this function to calculate the variance of a sample, giving the known population mean as the second argument. Provided the data points are representative (e.g. independent and identically distributed), the result will be an unbiased estimate of the population variance.

`statistics.stdev(`*data, xbar=None*`)`

Return the sample standard deviation (the square root of the sample variance). See *variance()* for arguments and other details.

```
>>> stdev([1.5, 2.5, 2.5, 2.75, 3.25, 4.75])
1.0810874155219827
```

`statistics.variance(`*data, xbar=None*`)`

Return the sample variance of *data*, an iterable of at least two real-valued numbers. Variance, or second moment about the mean, is a measure of the variability (spread or dispersion) of data. A large variance indicates that the data is spread out; a small variance indicates it is clustered closely around the mean.

If the optional second argument *xbar* is given, it should be the mean of *data*. If it is missing or `None` (the default), the mean is automatically calculated.

Use this function when your data is a sample from a population. To calculate the variance from the entire population, see *pvariance()*.

Raises *StatisticsError* if *data* has fewer than two values.

Examples:

```
>>> data = [2.75, 1.75, 1.25, 0.25, 0.5, 1.25, 3.5]
>>> variance(data)
1.3720238095238095
```

If you have already calculated the mean of your data, you can pass it as the optional second argument *xbar* to avoid recalculation:

```
>>> m = mean(data)
>>> variance(data, m)
1.3720238095238095
```

This function does not attempt to verify that you have passed the actual mean as *xbar*. Using arbitrary values for *xbar* can lead to invalid or impossible results.

Decimal and Fraction values are supported:

```
>>> from decimal import Decimal as D
>>> variance([D("27.5"), D("30.25"), D("30.25"), D("34.5"), D("41.75")])
Decimal('31.01875')

>>> from fractions import Fraction as F
>>> variance([F(1, 6), F(1, 2), F(5, 3)])
Fraction(67, 108)
```

Note: This is the sample variance s^2 with Bessel's correction, also known as variance with N-1 degrees of freedom. Provided that the data points are representative (e.g. independent and identically distributed), the result should be an unbiased estimate of the true population variance.

If you somehow know the actual population mean μ you should pass it to the *pvariance()* function as the *mu* parameter to get the variance of a sample.

9.7.4 Exceptions

A single exception is defined:

exception statistics.StatisticsError
Subclass of *ValueError* for statistics-related exceptions.

CHAPTER

TEN

FUNCTIONAL PROGRAMMING MODULES

The modules described in this chapter provide functions and classes that support a functional programming style, and general operations on callables.

The following modules are documented in this chapter:

10.1 `itertools` — Functions creating iterators for efficient looping

This module implements a number of *iterator* building blocks inspired by constructs from APL, Haskell, and SML. Each has been recast in a form suitable for Python.

The module standardizes a core set of fast, memory efficient tools that are useful by themselves or in combination. Together, they form an "iterator algebra" making it possible to construct specialized tools succinctly and efficiently in pure Python.

For instance, SML provides a tabulation tool: `tabulate(f)` which produces a sequence `f(0), f(1), ...`. The same effect can be achieved in Python by combining *map()* and *count()* to form `map(f, count())`.

These tools and their built-in counterparts also work well with the high-speed functions in the *operator* module. For example, the multiplication operator can be mapped across two vectors to form an efficient dot-product: `sum(map(operator.mul, vector1, vector2))`.

Infinite iterators:

Iterator	Arguments	Results	Example
count()	start, [step]	start, start+step, start+2*step, ...	`count(10) --> 10 11 12 13 14 ...`
cycle()	p	p0, p1, ... plast, p0, p1, ...	`cycle('ABCD') --> A B C D A B C D ...`
repeat()	elem [,n]	elem, elem, elem, ... endlessly or up to n times	`repeat(10, 3) --> 10 10 10`

Iterators terminating on the shortest input sequence:

Iterator	Arguments	Results	Example
accumulate()	p [,func]	p0, p0+p1, p0+p1+p2, ...	`accumulate([1,2,3,4,5]) --> 1 3 6 10 15`
chain()	p, q, ...	p0, p1, ... plast, q0, q1, ...	`chain('ABC', 'DEF') --> A B C D E F`
chain.from_iterable()	iterable	p0, p1, ... plast, q0, q1, ...	`chain.from_iterable(['ABC', 'DEF']) --> A B C D E F`
compress()	data, selectors	(d[0] if s[0]), (d[1] if s[1]), ...	`compress('ABCDEF', [1,0,1,0,1,1]) --> A C E F`
dropwhile()	pred, seq	seq[n], seq[n+1], starting when pred fails	`dropwhile(lambda x: x<5, [1,4,6,4,1]) --> 6 4 1`
filterfalse()	pred, seq	elements of seq where pred(elem) is false	`filterfalse(lambda x: x%2, range(10)) --> 0 2 4 6 8`
groupby()	iterable[, key]	sub-iterators grouped by value of key(v)	
islice()	seq, [start,] stop [, step]	elements from seq[start:stop:step]	`islice('ABCDEFG', 2, None) --> C D E F G`
starmap()	func, seq	func(*seq[0]), func(*seq[1]), ...	`starmap(pow, [(2,5), (3,2), (10, 3)]) --> 32 9 1000`
takewhile()	pred, seq	seq[0], seq[1], until pred fails	`takewhile(lambda x: x<5, [1,4,6,4,1]) --> 1 4`
tee()	it, n	it1, it2, ... itn splits one iterator into n	
zip_longest()	p, q, ...	(p[0], q[0]), (p[1], q[1]), ...	`zip_longest('ABCD', 'xy', fillvalue='-') --> Ax By C- D-`

Combinatoric iterators:

Iterator	Arguments	Results
product()	p, q, ... [repeat=1]	cartesian product, equivalent to a nested for-loop
permutations()	p[, r]	r-length tuples, all possible orderings, no repeated elements
combinations()	p, r	r-length tuples, in sorted order, no repeated elements
combinations_with_replacement()	p, r	r-length tuples, in sorted order, with repeated elements
`product('ABCD', repeat=2)`		`AA AB AC AD BA BB BC BD CA CB CC CD DA DB DC DD`
`permutations('ABCD', 2)`		`AB AC AD BA BC BD CA CB CD DA DB DC`
`combinations('ABCD', 2)`		`AB AC AD BC BD CD`
`combinations_with_replacement('ABCD', 2)`		`AA AB AC AD BB BC BD CC CD DD`

10.1.1 Itertool functions

The following module functions all construct and return iterators. Some provide streams of infinite length, so they should only be accessed by functions or loops that truncate the stream.

`itertools.accumulate`(*iterable*[, *func*])

Make an iterator that returns accumulated sums, or accumulated results of other binary functions (specified via the optional *func* argument). If *func* is supplied, it should be a function of two arguments.

Elements of the input *iterable* may be any type that can be accepted as arguments to *func*. (For example, with the default operation of addition, elements may be any addable type including `Decimal` or `Fraction`.) If the input iterable is empty, the output iterable will also be empty.

Roughly equivalent to:

```
def accumulate(iterable, func=operator.add):
    'Return running totals'
    # accumulate([1,2,3,4,5]) --> 1 3 6 10 15
    # accumulate([1,2,3,4,5], operator.mul) --> 1 2 6 24 120
    it = iter(iterable)
    try:
        total = next(it)
    except StopIteration:
        return
    yield total
    for element in it:
        total = func(total, element)
        yield total
```

There are a number of uses for the *func* argument. It can be set to `min()` for a running minimum, `max()` for a running maximum, or `operator.mul()` for a running product. Amortization tables can be built by accumulating interest and applying payments. First-order recurrence relations can be modeled by supplying the initial value in the iterable and using only the accumulated total in *func* argument:

```
>>> data = [3, 4, 6, 2, 1, 9, 0, 7, 5, 8]
>>> list(accumulate(data, operator.mul))     # running product
[3, 12, 72, 144, 144, 1296, 0, 0, 0, 0]
>>> list(accumulate(data, max))              # running maximum
[3, 4, 6, 6, 6, 9, 9, 9, 9, 9]

# Amortize a 5% loan of 1000 with 4 annual payments of 90
>>> cashflows = [1000, -90, -90, -90, -90]
>>> list(accumulate(cashflows, lambda bal, pmt: bal*1.05 + pmt))
[1000, 960.0, 918.0, 873.9000000000001, 827.5950000000001]

# Chaotic recurrence relation https://en.wikipedia.org/wiki/Logistic_map
>>> logistic_map = lambda x, _:  r * x * (1 - x)
>>> r = 3.8
>>> x0 = 0.4
>>> inputs = repeat(x0, 36)     # only the initial value is used
>>> [format(x, '.2f') for x in accumulate(inputs, logistic_map)]
['0.40', '0.91', '0.30', '0.81', '0.60', '0.92', '0.29', '0.79', '0.63',
 '0.88', '0.39', '0.90', '0.33', '0.84', '0.52', '0.95', '0.18', '0.57',
 '0.93', '0.25', '0.71', '0.79', '0.63', '0.88', '0.39', '0.91', '0.32',
 '0.83', '0.54', '0.95', '0.20', '0.60', '0.91', '0.30', '0.80', '0.60']
```

See `functools.reduce()` for a similar function that returns only the final accumulated value.

New in version 3.2.

Changed in version 3.3: Added the optional *func* parameter.

itertools.chain(**iterables*)

Make an iterator that returns elements from the first iterable until it is exhausted, then proceeds to the next iterable, until all of the iterables are exhausted. Used for treating consecutive sequences as a single sequence. Roughly equivalent to:

```
def chain(*iterables):
    # chain('ABC', 'DEF') --> A B C D E F
```

```
    for it in iterables:
        for element in it:
            yield element
```

classmethod **chain.from_iterable**(*iterable*)

Alternate constructor for *chain()*. Gets chained inputs from a single iterable argument that is evaluated lazily. Roughly equivalent to:

```
def from_iterable(iterables):
    # chain.from_iterable(['ABC', 'DEF']) --> A B C D E F
    for it in iterables:
        for element in it:
            yield element
```

itertools.**combinations**(*iterable*, *r*)

Return *r* length subsequences of elements from the input *iterable*.

Combinations are emitted in lexicographic sort order. So, if the input *iterable* is sorted, the combination tuples will be produced in sorted order.

Elements are treated as unique based on their position, not on their value. So if the input elements are unique, there will be no repeat values in each combination.

Roughly equivalent to:

```
def combinations(iterable, r):
    # combinations('ABCD', 2) --> AB AC AD BC BD CD
    # combinations(range(4), 3) --> 012 013 023 123
    pool = tuple(iterable)
    n = len(pool)
    if r > n:
        return
    indices = list(range(r))
    yield tuple(pool[i] for i in indices)
    while True:
        for i in reversed(range(r)):
            if indices[i] != i + n - r:
                break
        else:
            return
        indices[i] += 1
        for j in range(i+1, r):
            indices[j] = indices[j-1] + 1
        yield tuple(pool[i] for i in indices)
```

The code for *combinations()* can be also expressed as a subsequence of *permutations()* after filtering entries where the elements are not in sorted order (according to their position in the input pool):

```
def combinations(iterable, r):
    pool = tuple(iterable)
    n = len(pool)
    for indices in permutations(range(n), r):
        if sorted(indices) == list(indices):
            yield tuple(pool[i] for i in indices)
```

The number of items returned is `n! / r! / (n-r)!` when `0 <= r <= n` or zero when `r > n`.

itertools.**combinations_with_replacement**(*iterable*, *r*)

Return *r* length subsequences of elements from the input *iterable* allowing individual elements to be repeated more than once.

Combinations are emitted in lexicographic sort order. So, if the input *iterable* is sorted, the combination tuples will be produced in sorted order.

Elements are treated as unique based on their position, not on their value. So if the input elements are unique, the generated combinations will also be unique.

Roughly equivalent to:

```
def combinations_with_replacement(iterable, r):
    # combinations_with_replacement('ABC', 2) --> AA AB AC BB BC CC
    pool = tuple(iterable)
    n = len(pool)
    if not n and r:
        return
    indices = [0] * r
    yield tuple(pool[i] for i in indices)
    while True:
        for i in reversed(range(r)):
            if indices[i] != n - 1:
                break
        else:
            return
        indices[i:] = [indices[i] + 1] * (r - i)
        yield tuple(pool[i] for i in indices)
```

The code for `combinations_with_replacement()` can be also expressed as a subsequence of `product()` after filtering entries where the elements are not in sorted order (according to their position in the input pool):

```
def combinations_with_replacement(iterable, r):
    pool = tuple(iterable)
    n = len(pool)
    for indices in product(range(n), repeat=r):
        if sorted(indices) == list(indices):
            yield tuple(pool[i] for i in indices)
```

The number of items returned is `(n+r-1)! / r! / (n-1)!` when `n > 0`.

New in version 3.1.

`itertools.compress`(*data*, *selectors*)

Make an iterator that filters elements from *data* returning only those that have a corresponding element in *selectors* that evaluates to `True`. Stops when either the *data* or *selectors* iterables has been exhausted. Roughly equivalent to:

```
def compress(data, selectors):
    # compress('ABCDEF', [1,0,1,0,1,1]) --> A C E F
    return (d for d, s in zip(data, selectors) if s)
```

New in version 3.1.

`itertools.count`(*start=0*, *step=1*)

Make an iterator that returns evenly spaced values starting with number *start*. Often used as an argument to `map()` to generate consecutive data points. Also, used with `zip()` to add sequence numbers. Roughly equivalent to:

```
def count(start=0, step=1):
    # count(10) --> 10 11 12 13 14 ...
    # count(2.5, 0.5) -> 2.5 3.0 3.5 ...
    n = start
```

```
    while True:
        yield n
        n += step
```

When counting with floating point numbers, better accuracy can sometimes be achieved by substituting multiplicative code such as: `(start + step * i for i in count())`.

Changed in version 3.1: Added *step* argument and allowed non-integer arguments.

`itertools.cycle`(*iterable*)
Make an iterator returning elements from the iterable and saving a copy of each. When the iterable is exhausted, return elements from the saved copy. Repeats indefinitely. Roughly equivalent to:

```
def cycle(iterable):
    # cycle('ABCD') --> A B C D A B C D A B C D ...
    saved = []
    for element in iterable:
        yield element
        saved.append(element)
    while saved:
        for element in saved:
              yield element
```

Note, this member of the toolkit may require significant auxiliary storage (depending on the length of the iterable).

`itertools.dropwhile`(*predicate*, *iterable*)
Make an iterator that drops elements from the iterable as long as the predicate is true; afterwards, returns every element. Note, the iterator does not produce *any* output until the predicate first becomes false, so it may have a lengthy start-up time. Roughly equivalent to:

```
def dropwhile(predicate, iterable):
    # dropwhile(lambda x: x<5, [1,4,6,4,1]) --> 6 4 1
    iterable = iter(iterable)
    for x in iterable:
        if not predicate(x):
            yield x
            break
    for x in iterable:
        yield x
```

`itertools.filterfalse`(*predicate*, *iterable*)
Make an iterator that filters elements from iterable returning only those for which the predicate is `False`. If *predicate* is `None`, return the items that are false. Roughly equivalent to:

```
def filterfalse(predicate, iterable):
    # filterfalse(lambda x: x%2, range(10)) --> 0 2 4 6 8
    if predicate is None:
        predicate = bool
    for x in iterable:
        if not predicate(x):
            yield x
```

`itertools.groupby`(*iterable*, *key=None*)
Make an iterator that returns consecutive keys and groups from the *iterable*. The *key* is a function computing a key value for each element. If not specified or is `None`, *key* defaults to an identity function and returns the element unchanged. Generally, the iterable needs to already be sorted on the same key function.

The operation of *groupby()* is similar to the `uniq` filter in Unix. It generates a break or new group every time the value of the key function changes (which is why it is usually necessary to have sorted the data using the same key function). That behavior differs from SQL's GROUP BY which aggregates common elements regardless of their input order.

The returned group is itself an iterator that shares the underlying iterable with *groupby()*. Because the source is shared, when the *groupby()* object is advanced, the previous group is no longer visible. So, if that data is needed later, it should be stored as a list:

```
groups = []
uniquekeys = []
data = sorted(data, key=keyfunc)
for k, g in groupby(data, keyfunc):
    groups.append(list(g))      # Store group iterator as a list
    uniquekeys.append(k)
```

groupby() is roughly equivalent to:

```
class groupby:
    # [k for k, g in groupby('AAAABBBCCDAABBB')] --> A B C D A B
    # [list(g) for k, g in groupby('AAAABBBCCD')] --> AAAA BBB CC D
    def __init__(self, iterable, key=None):
        if key is None:
            key = lambda x: x
        self.keyfunc = key
        self.it = iter(iterable)
        self.tgtkey = self.currkey = self.currvalue = object()
    def __iter__(self):
        return self
    def __next__(self):
        while self.currkey == self.tgtkey:
            self.currvalue = next(self.it)    # Exit on StopIteration
            self.currkey = self.keyfunc(self.currvalue)
        self.tgtkey = self.currkey
        return (self.currkey, self._grouper(self.tgtkey))
    def _grouper(self, tgtkey):
        while self.currkey == tgtkey:
            yield self.currvalue
            try:
                self.currvalue = next(self.it)
            except StopIteration:
                return
            self.currkey = self.keyfunc(self.currvalue)
```

`itertools.islice`(*iterable*, *stop*)
`itertools.islice`(*iterable*, *start*, *stop*[, *step*])

Make an iterator that returns selected elements from the iterable. If *start* is non-zero, then elements from the iterable are skipped until start is reached. Afterward, elements are returned consecutively unless *step* is set higher than one which results in items being skipped. If *stop* is `None`, then iteration continues until the iterator is exhausted, if at all; otherwise, it stops at the specified position. Unlike regular slicing, *islice()* does not support negative values for *start*, *stop*, or *step*. Can be used to extract related fields from data where the internal structure has been flattened (for example, a multi-line report may list a name field on every third line). Roughly equivalent to:

```
def islice(iterable, *args):
    # islice('ABCDEFG', 2) --> A B
    # islice('ABCDEFG', 2, 4) --> C D
    # islice('ABCDEFG', 2, None) --> C D E F G
```

```
    # islice('ABCDEFG', 0, None, 2) --> A C E G
    s = slice(*args)
    it = iter(range(s.start or 0, s.stop or sys.maxsize, s.step or 1))
    try:
        nexti = next(it)
    except StopIteration:
        return
    for i, element in enumerate(iterable):
        if i == nexti:
            yield element
            nexti = next(it)
```

If *start* is None, then iteration starts at zero. If *step* is None, then the step defaults to one.

`itertools.permutations(iterable, r=None)`

Return successive *r* length permutations of elements in the *iterable*.

If *r* is not specified or is None, then *r* defaults to the length of the *iterable* and all possible full-length permutations are generated.

Permutations are emitted in lexicographic sort order. So, if the input *iterable* is sorted, the permutation tuples will be produced in sorted order.

Elements are treated as unique based on their position, not on their value. So if the input elements are unique, there will be no repeat values in each permutation.

Roughly equivalent to:

```
def permutations(iterable, r=None):
    # permutations('ABCD', 2) --> AB AC AD BA BC BD CA CB CD DA DB DC
    # permutations(range(3)) --> 012 021 102 120 201 210
    pool = tuple(iterable)
    n = len(pool)
    r = n if r is None else r
    if r > n:
        return
    indices = list(range(n))
    cycles = list(range(n, n-r, -1))
    yield tuple(pool[i] for i in indices[:r])
    while n:
        for i in reversed(range(r)):
            cycles[i] -= 1
            if cycles[i] == 0:
                indices[i:] = indices[i+1:] + indices[i:i+1]
                cycles[i] = n - i
            else:
                j = cycles[i]
                indices[i], indices[-j] = indices[-j], indices[i]
                yield tuple(pool[i] for i in indices[:r])
                break
        else:
            return
```

The code for *permutations()* can be also expressed as a subsequence of *product()*, filtered to exclude entries with repeated elements (those from the same position in the input pool):

```
def permutations(iterable, r=None):
    pool = tuple(iterable)
    n = len(pool)
    r = n if r is None else r
```

```
    for indices in product(range(n), repeat=r):
        if len(set(indices)) == r:
            yield tuple(pool[i] for i in indices)
```

The number of items returned is `n! / (n-r)!` when `0 <= r <= n` or zero when `r > n`.

`itertools.product(*iterables, repeat=1)`
Cartesian product of input iterables.

Roughly equivalent to nested for-loops in a generator expression. For example, `product(A, B)` returns the same as `((x,y) for x in A for y in B)`.

The nested loops cycle like an odometer with the rightmost element advancing on every iteration. This pattern creates a lexicographic ordering so that if the input's iterables are sorted, the product tuples are emitted in sorted order.

To compute the product of an iterable with itself, specify the number of repetitions with the optional *repeat* keyword argument. For example, `product(A, repeat=4)` means the same as `product(A, A, A, A)`.

This function is roughly equivalent to the following code, except that the actual implementation does not build up intermediate results in memory:

```
def product(*args, repeat=1):
    # product('ABCD', 'xy') --> Ax Ay Bx By Cx Cy Dx Dy
    # product(range(2), repeat=3) --> 000 001 010 011 100 101 110 111
    pools = [tuple(pool) for pool in args] * repeat
    result = [[]]
    for pool in pools:
        result = [x+[y] for x in result for y in pool]
    for prod in result:
        yield tuple(prod)
```

`itertools.repeat(object[, times])`
Make an iterator that returns *object* over and over again. Runs indefinitely unless the *times* argument is specified. Used as argument to *map()* for invariant parameters to the called function. Also used with *zip()* to create an invariant part of a tuple record.

Roughly equivalent to:

```
def repeat(object, times=None):
    # repeat(10, 3) --> 10 10 10
    if times is None:
        while True:
            yield object
    else:
        for i in range(times):
            yield object
```

A common use for *repeat* is to supply a stream of constant values to *map* or *zip*:

```
>>> list(map(pow, range(10), repeat(2)))
[0, 1, 4, 9, 16, 25, 36, 49, 64, 81]
```

`itertools.starmap(function, iterable)`
Make an iterator that computes the function using arguments obtained from the iterable. Used instead of *map()* when argument parameters are already grouped in tuples from a single iterable (the data has been "pre-zipped"). The difference between *map()* and *starmap()* parallels the distinction between `function(a,b)` and `function(*c)`. Roughly equivalent to:

```
def starmap(function, iterable):
    # starmap(pow, [(2,5), (3,2), (10,3)]) --> 32 9 1000
    for args in iterable:
        yield function(*args)
```

itertools.**takewhile**(*predicate*, *iterable*)
Make an iterator that returns elements from the iterable as long as the predicate is true. Roughly equivalent to:

```
def takewhile(predicate, iterable):
    # takewhile(lambda x: x<5, [1,4,6,4,1]) --> 1 4
    for x in iterable:
        if predicate(x):
            yield x
        else:
            break
```

itertools.**tee**(*iterable*, *n=2*)
Return *n* independent iterators from a single iterable.

The following Python code helps explain what *tee* does (although the actual implementation is more complex and uses only a single underlying FIFO queue).

Roughly equivalent to:

```
def tee(iterable, n=2):
    it = iter(iterable)
    deques = [collections.deque() for i in range(n)]
    def gen(mydeque):
        while True:
            if not mydeque:             # when the local deque is empty
                try:
                    newval = next(it)   # fetch a new value and
                except StopIteration:
                    return
                for d in deques:        # load it to all the deques
                    d.append(newval)
            yield mydeque.popleft()
    return tuple(gen(d) for d in deques)
```

Once *tee()* has made a split, the original *iterable* should not be used anywhere else; otherwise, the *iterable* could get advanced without the tee objects being informed.

This itertool may require significant auxiliary storage (depending on how much temporary data needs to be stored). In general, if one iterator uses most or all of the data before another iterator starts, it is faster to use *list()* instead of *tee()*.

itertools.**zip_longest**(**iterables*, *fillvalue=None*)
Make an iterator that aggregates elements from each of the iterables. If the iterables are of uneven length, missing values are filled-in with *fillvalue*. Iteration continues until the longest iterable is exhausted. Roughly equivalent to:

```
class ZipExhausted(Exception):
    pass

def zip_longest(*args, **kwds):
    # zip_longest('ABCD', 'xy', fillvalue='-') --> Ax By C- D-
    fillvalue = kwds.get('fillvalue')
    counter = len(args) - 1
```

```
    def sentinel():
        nonlocal counter
        if not counter:
            raise ZipExhausted
        counter -= 1
        yield fillvalue
    fillers = repeat(fillvalue)
    iterators = [chain(it, sentinel(), fillers) for it in args]
    try:
        while iterators:
            yield tuple(map(next, iterators))
    except ZipExhausted:
        pass
```

If one of the iterables is potentially infinite, then the *zip_longest()* function should be wrapped with something that limits the number of calls (for example *islice()* or *takewhile()*). If not specified, *fillvalue* defaults to None.

10.1.2 Itertools Recipes

This section shows recipes for creating an extended toolset using the existing itertools as building blocks.

The extended tools offer the same high performance as the underlying toolset. The superior memory performance is kept by processing elements one at a time rather than bringing the whole iterable into memory all at once. Code volume is kept small by linking the tools together in a functional style which helps eliminate temporary variables. High speed is retained by preferring "vectorized" building blocks over the use of for-loops and *generators* which incur interpreter overhead.

```
def take(n, iterable):
    "Return first n items of the iterable as a list"
    return list(islice(iterable, n))

def tabulate(function, start=0):
    "Return function(0), function(1), ..."
    return map(function, count(start))

def tail(n, iterable):
    "Return an iterator over the last n items"
    # tail(3, 'ABCDEFG') --> E F G
    return iter(collections.deque(iterable, maxlen=n))

def consume(iterator, n):
    "Advance the iterator n-steps ahead. If n is none, consume entirely."
    # Use functions that consume iterators at C speed.
    if n is None:
        # feed the entire iterator into a zero-length deque
        collections.deque(iterator, maxlen=0)
    else:
        # advance to the empty slice starting at position n
        next(islice(iterator, n, n), None)

def nth(iterable, n, default=None):
    "Returns the nth item or a default value"
    return next(islice(iterable, n, None), default)

def all_equal(iterable):
    "Returns True if all the elements are equal to each other"
```

```
    g = groupby(iterable)
    return next(g, True) and not next(g, False)

def quantify(iterable, pred=bool):
    "Count how many times the predicate is true"
    return sum(map(pred, iterable))

def padnone(iterable):
    """Returns the sequence elements and then returns None indefinitely.

    Useful for emulating the behavior of the built-in map() function.
    """
    return chain(iterable, repeat(None))

def ncycles(iterable, n):
    "Returns the sequence elements n times"
    return chain.from_iterable(repeat(tuple(iterable), n))

def dotproduct(vec1, vec2):
    return sum(map(operator.mul, vec1, vec2))

def flatten(listOfLists):
    "Flatten one level of nesting"
    return chain.from_iterable(listOfLists)

def repeatfunc(func, times=None, *args):
    """Repeat calls to func with specified arguments.

    Example:  repeatfunc(random.random)
    """
    if times is None:
        return starmap(func, repeat(args))
    return starmap(func, repeat(args, times))

def pairwise(iterable):
    "s -> (s0,s1), (s1,s2), (s2, s3), ..."
    a, b = tee(iterable)
    next(b, None)
    return zip(a, b)

def grouper(iterable, n, fillvalue=None):
    "Collect data into fixed-length chunks or blocks"
    # grouper('ABCDEFG', 3, 'x') --> ABC DEF Gxx"
    args = [iter(iterable)] * n
    return zip_longest(*args, fillvalue=fillvalue)

def roundrobin(*iterables):
    "roundrobin('ABC', 'D', 'EF') --> A D E B F C"
    # Recipe credited to George Sakkis
    num_active = len(iterables)
    nexts = cycle(iter(it).__next__ for it in iterables)
    while num_active:
        try:
            for next in nexts:
                yield next()
        except StopIteration:
            # Remove the iterator we just exhausted from the cycle.
            num_active -= 1
```

```
            nexts = cycle(islice(nexts, num_active))

def partition(pred, iterable):
    'Use a predicate to partition entries into false entries and true entries'
    # partition(is_odd, range(10)) --> 0 2 4 6 8   and  1 3 5 7 9
    t1, t2 = tee(iterable)
    return filterfalse(pred, t1), filter(pred, t2)

def powerset(iterable):
    "powerset([1,2,3]) --> () (1,) (2,) (3,) (1,2) (1,3) (2,3) (1,2,3)"
    s = list(iterable)
    return chain.from_iterable(combinations(s, r) for r in range(len(s)+1))

def unique_everseen(iterable, key=None):
    "List unique elements, preserving order. Remember all elements ever seen."
    # unique_everseen('AAAABBBCCDAABBB') --> A B C D
    # unique_everseen('ABBCcAD', str.lower) --> A B C D
    seen = set()
    seen_add = seen.add
    if key is None:
        for element in filterfalse(seen.__contains__, iterable):
            seen_add(element)
            yield element
    else:
        for element in iterable:
            k = key(element)
            if k not in seen:
                seen_add(k)
                yield element

def unique_justseen(iterable, key=None):
    "List unique elements, preserving order. Remember only the element just seen."
    # unique_justseen('AAAABBBCCDAABBB') --> A B C D A B
    # unique_justseen('ABBCcAD', str.lower) --> A B C A D
    return map(next, map(itemgetter(1), groupby(iterable, key)))

def iter_except(func, exception, first=None):
    """ Call a function repeatedly until an exception is raised.

    Converts a call-until-exception interface to an iterator interface.
    Like builtins.iter(func, sentinel) but uses an exception instead
    of a sentinel to end the loop.

    Examples:
        iter_except(functools.partial(heappop, h), IndexError)   # priority queue iterator
        iter_except(d.popitem, KeyError)                         # non-blocking dict iterator
        iter_except(d.popleft, IndexError)                       # non-blocking deque iterator
        iter_except(q.get_nowait, Queue.Empty)                   # loop over a producer Queue
        iter_except(s.pop, KeyError)                             # non-blocking set iterator

    """
    try:
        if first is not None:
            yield first()            # For database APIs needing an initial cast to db.first()
        while True:
            yield func()
    except exception:
        pass
```

```
def first_true(iterable, default=False, pred=None):
    """Returns the first true value in the iterable.

    If no true value is found, returns *default*

    If *pred* is not None, returns the first item
    for which pred(item) is true.

    """
    # first_true([a,b,c], x) --> a or b or c or x
    # first_true([a,b], x, f) --> a if f(a) else b if f(b) else x
    return next(filter(pred, iterable), default)

def random_product(*args, repeat=1):
    "Random selection from itertools.product(*args, **kwds)"
    pools = [tuple(pool) for pool in args] * repeat
    return tuple(random.choice(pool) for pool in pools)

def random_permutation(iterable, r=None):
    "Random selection from itertools.permutations(iterable, r)"
    pool = tuple(iterable)
    r = len(pool) if r is None else r
    return tuple(random.sample(pool, r))

def random_combination(iterable, r):
    "Random selection from itertools.combinations(iterable, r)"
    pool = tuple(iterable)
    n = len(pool)
    indices = sorted(random.sample(range(n), r))
    return tuple(pool[i] for i in indices)

def random_combination_with_replacement(iterable, r):
    "Random selection from itertools.combinations_with_replacement(iterable, r)"
    pool = tuple(iterable)
    n = len(pool)
    indices = sorted(random.randrange(n) for i in range(r))
    return tuple(pool[i] for i in indices)

def nth_combination(iterable, r, index):
    'Equivalent to list(combinations(iterable, r))[index]'
    pool = tuple(iterable)
    n = len(pool)
    if r < 0 or r > n:
        raise ValueError
    c = 1
    k = min(r, n-r)
    for i in range(1, k+1):
        c = c * (n - k + i) // i
    if index < 0:
        index += c
    if index < 0 or index >= c:
        raise IndexError
    result = []
    while r:
        c, n, r = c*r//n, n-1, r-1
        while index >= c:
            index -= c
```

```
        c, n = c*(n-r)//n, n-1
        result.append(pool[-1-n])
    return tuple(result)
```

Note, many of the above recipes can be optimized by replacing global lookups with local variables defined as default values. For example, the *dotproduct* recipe can be written as:

```
def dotproduct(vec1, vec2, sum=sum, map=map, mul=operator.mul):
    return sum(map(mul, vec1, vec2))
```

10.2 `functools` — Higher-order functions and operations on callable objects

Source code: Lib/functools.py

The *functools* module is for higher-order functions: functions that act on or return other functions. In general, any callable object can be treated as a function for the purposes of this module.

The *functools* module defines the following functions:

`functools.cmp_to_key(`*func*`)`

Transform an old-style comparison function to a *key function*. Used with tools that accept key functions (such as *sorted()*, *min()*, *max()*, *heapq.nlargest()*, *heapq.nsmallest()*, *itertools.groupby()*). This function is primarily used as a transition tool for programs being converted from Python 2 which supported the use of comparison functions.

A comparison function is any callable that accept two arguments, compares them, and returns a negative number for less-than, zero for equality, or a positive number for greater-than. A key function is a callable that accepts one argument and returns another value to be used as the sort key.

Example:

```
sorted(iterable, key=cmp_to_key(locale.strcoll))  # locale-aware sort order
```

For sorting examples and a brief sorting tutorial, see sortinghowto.

New in version 3.2.

`@functools.lru_cache(`*maxsize=128*, *typed=False*`)`

Decorator to wrap a function with a memoizing callable that saves up to the *maxsize* most recent calls. It can save time when an expensive or I/O bound function is periodically called with the same arguments.

Since a dictionary is used to cache results, the positional and keyword arguments to the function must be hashable.

If *maxsize* is set to `None`, the LRU feature is disabled and the cache can grow without bound. The LRU feature performs best when *maxsize* is a power-of-two.

If *typed* is set to true, function arguments of different types will be cached separately. For example, `f(3)` and `f(3.0)` will be treated as distinct calls with distinct results.

To help measure the effectiveness of the cache and tune the *maxsize* parameter, the wrapped function is instrumented with a `cache_info()` function that returns a *named tuple* showing *hits*, *misses*, *maxsize* and *currsize*. In a multi-threaded environment, the hits and misses are approximate.

The decorator also provides a `cache_clear()` function for clearing or invalidating the cache.

The original underlying function is accessible through the `__wrapped__` attribute. This is useful for introspection, for bypassing the cache, or for rewrapping the function with a different cache.

An LRU (least recently used) cache works best when the most recent calls are the best predictors of upcoming calls (for example, the most popular articles on a news server tend to change each day). The cache's size limit assures that the cache does not grow without bound on long-running processes such as web servers.

Example of an LRU cache for static web content:

```
@lru_cache(maxsize=32)
def get_pep(num):
    'Retrieve text of a Python Enhancement Proposal'
    resource = 'http://www.python.org/dev/peps/pep-%04d/' % num
    try:
        with urllib.request.urlopen(resource) as s:
            return s.read()
    except urllib.error.HTTPError:
        return 'Not Found'

>>> for n in 8, 290, 308, 320, 8, 218, 320, 279, 289, 320, 9991:
...     pep = get_pep(n)
...     print(n, len(pep))

>>> get_pep.cache_info()
CacheInfo(hits=3, misses=8, maxsize=32, currsize=8)
```

Example of efficiently computing Fibonacci numbers using a cache to implement a dynamic programming technique:

```
@lru_cache(maxsize=None)
def fib(n):
    if n < 2:
        return n
    return fib(n-1) + fib(n-2)

>>> [fib(n) for n in range(16)]
[0, 1, 1, 2, 3, 5, 8, 13, 21, 34, 55, 89, 144, 233, 377, 610]

>>> fib.cache_info()
CacheInfo(hits=28, misses=16, maxsize=None, currsize=16)
```

New in version 3.2.

Changed in version 3.3: Added the *typed* option.

@functools.total_ordering

Given a class defining one or more rich comparison ordering methods, this class decorator supplies the rest. This simplifies the effort involved in specifying all of the possible rich comparison operations:

The class must define one of `__lt__()`, `__le__()`, `__gt__()`, or `__ge__()`. In addition, the class should supply an `__eq__()` method.

For example:

```
@total_ordering
class Student:
    def _is_valid_operand(self, other):
        return (hasattr(other, "lastname") and
                hasattr(other, "firstname"))
    def __eq__(self, other):
```

```
        if not self._is_valid_operand(other):
            return NotImplemented
        return ((self.lastname.lower(), self.firstname.lower()) ==
                (other.lastname.lower(), other.firstname.lower()))
    def __lt__(self, other):
        if not self._is_valid_operand(other):
            return NotImplemented
        return ((self.lastname.lower(), self.firstname.lower()) <
                (other.lastname.lower(), other.firstname.lower()))
```

Note: While this decorator makes it easy to create well behaved totally ordered types, it *does* come at the cost of slower execution and more complex stack traces for the derived comparison methods. If performance benchmarking indicates this is a bottleneck for a given application, implementing all six rich comparison methods instead is likely to provide an easy speed boost.

New in version 3.2.

Changed in version 3.4: Returning NotImplemented from the underlying comparison function for unrecognised types is now supported.

`functools.partial`(*func*, **args*, ***keywords*)

Return a new `partial` object which when called will behave like *func* called with the positional arguments *args* and keyword arguments *keywords*. If more arguments are supplied to the call, they are appended to *args*. If additional keyword arguments are supplied, they extend and override *keywords*. Roughly equivalent to:

```
def partial(func, *args, **keywords):
    def newfunc(*fargs, **fkeywords):
        newkeywords = keywords.copy()
        newkeywords.update(fkeywords)
        return func(*args, *fargs, **newkeywords)
    newfunc.func = func
    newfunc.args = args
    newfunc.keywords = keywords
    return newfunc
```

The `partial()` is used for partial function application which "freezes" some portion of a function's arguments and/or keywords resulting in a new object with a simplified signature. For example, `partial()` can be used to create a callable that behaves like the `int()` function where the *base* argument defaults to two:

```
>>> from functools import partial
>>> basetwo = partial(int, base=2)
>>> basetwo.__doc__ = 'Convert base 2 string to an int.'
>>> basetwo('10010')
18
```

`class functools.partialmethod`(*func*, **args*, ***keywords*)

Return a new `partialmethod` descriptor which behaves like `partial` except that it is designed to be used as a method definition rather than being directly callable.

func must be a *descriptor* or a callable (objects which are both, like normal functions, are handled as descriptors).

When *func* is a descriptor (such as a normal Python function, `classmethod()`, `staticmethod()`, `abstractmethod()` or another instance of `partialmethod`), calls to `__get__` are delegated to the underlying descriptor, and an appropriate `partial` object returned as the result.

When *func* is a non-descriptor callable, an appropriate bound method is created dynamically. This behaves like a normal Python function when used as a method: the *self* argument will be inserted as the first positional argument, even before the *args* and *keywords* supplied to the `partialmethod` constructor.

Example:

```
>>> class Cell(object):
...     def __init__(self):
...         self._alive = False
...     @property
...     def alive(self):
...         return self._alive
...     def set_state(self, state):
...         self._alive = bool(state)
...     set_alive = partialmethod(set_state, True)
...     set_dead = partialmethod(set_state, False)
...
>>> c = Cell()
>>> c.alive
False
>>> c.set_alive()
>>> c.alive
True
```

New in version 3.4.

`functools.reduce`(*function*, *iterable*[, *initializer*])

Apply *function* of two arguments cumulatively to the items of *sequence*, from left to right, so as to reduce the sequence to a single value. For example, `reduce(lambda x, y: x+y, [1, 2, 3, 4, 5])` calculates `((((1+2)+3)+4)+5)`. The left argument, *x*, is the accumulated value and the right argument, *y*, is the update value from the *sequence*. If the optional *initializer* is present, it is placed before the items of the sequence in the calculation, and serves as a default when the sequence is empty. If *initializer* is not given and *sequence* contains only one item, the first item is returned.

Roughly equivalent to:

```
def reduce(function, iterable, initializer=None):
    it = iter(iterable)
    if initializer is None:
        value = next(it)
    else:
        value = initializer
    for element in it:
        value = function(value, element)
    return value
```

`@functools.singledispatch`

Transform a function into a *single-dispatch generic function*.

To define a generic function, decorate it with the `@singledispatch` decorator. Note that the dispatch happens on the type of the first argument, create your function accordingly:

```
>>> from functools import singledispatch
>>> @singledispatch
... def fun(arg, verbose=False):
...     if verbose:
...         print("Let me just say,", end=" ")
...     print(arg)
```

To add overloaded implementations to the function, use the `register()` attribute of the generic function. It is a decorator, taking a type parameter and decorating a function implementing the operation for that type:

```
>>> @fun.register(int)
... def _(arg, verbose=False):
...     if verbose:
...         print("Strength in numbers, eh?", end=" ")
...     print(arg)
...
>>> @fun.register(list)
... def _(arg, verbose=False):
...     if verbose:
...         print("Enumerate this:")
...     for i, elem in enumerate(arg):
...         print(i, elem)
```

To enable registering lambdas and pre-existing functions, the `register()` attribute can be used in a functional form:

```
>>> def nothing(arg, verbose=False):
...     print("Nothing.")
...
>>> fun.register(type(None), nothing)
```

The `register()` attribute returns the undecorated function which enables decorator stacking, pickling, as well as creating unit tests for each variant independently:

```
>>> @fun.register(float)
... @fun.register(Decimal)
... def fun_num(arg, verbose=False):
...     if verbose:
...         print("Half of your number:", end=" ")
...     print(arg / 2)
...
>>> fun_num is fun
False
```

When called, the generic function dispatches on the type of the first argument:

```
>>> fun("Hello, world.")
Hello, world.
>>> fun("test.", verbose=True)
Let me just say, test.
>>> fun(42, verbose=True)
Strength in numbers, eh? 42
>>> fun(['spam', 'spam', 'eggs', 'spam'], verbose=True)
Enumerate this:
0 spam
1 spam
2 eggs
3 spam
>>> fun(None)
Nothing.
>>> fun(1.23)
0.615
```

Where there is no registered implementation for a specific type, its method resolution order is used to find a more generic implementation. The original function decorated with `@singledispatch` is registered for the base `object` type, which means it is used if no better implementation is found.

To check which implementation will the generic function choose for a given type, use the `dispatch()` attribute:

```
>>> fun.dispatch(float)
<function fun_num at 0x1035a2840>
>>> fun.dispatch(dict)    # note: default implementation
<function fun at 0x103fe0000>
```

To access all registered implementations, use the read-only `registry` attribute:

```
>>> fun.registry.keys()
dict_keys([<class 'NoneType'>, <class 'int'>, <class 'object'>,
          <class 'decimal.Decimal'>, <class 'list'>,
          <class 'float'>])
>>> fun.registry[float]
<function fun_num at 0x1035a2840>
>>> fun.registry[object]
<function fun at 0x103fe0000>
```

New in version 3.4.

`functools.update_wrapper(`*wrapper*, *wrapped*, *assigned=WRAPPER_ASSIGNMENTS*, *updated=WRAPPER_UPDATES*`)`

Update a *wrapper* function to look like the *wrapped* function. The optional arguments are tuples to specify which attributes of the original function are assigned directly to the matching attributes on the wrapper function and which attributes of the wrapper function are updated with the corresponding attributes from the original function. The default values for these arguments are the module level constants `WRAPPER_ASSIGNMENTS` (which assigns to the wrapper function's `__module__`, `__name__`, `__qualname__`, `__annotations__` and `__doc__`, the documentation string) and `WRAPPER_UPDATES` (which updates the wrapper function's `__dict__`, i.e. the instance dictionary).

To allow access to the original function for introspection and other purposes (e.g. bypassing a caching decorator such as `lru_cache()`), this function automatically adds a `__wrapped__` attribute to the wrapper that refers to the function being wrapped.

The main intended use for this function is in *decorator* functions which wrap the decorated function and return the wrapper. If the wrapper function is not updated, the metadata of the returned function will reflect the wrapper definition rather than the original function definition, which is typically less than helpful.

`update_wrapper()` may be used with callables other than functions. Any attributes named in *assigned* or *updated* that are missing from the object being wrapped are ignored (i.e. this function will not attempt to set them on the wrapper function). `AttributeError` is still raised if the wrapper function itself is missing any attributes named in *updated*.

New in version 3.2: Automatic addition of the `__wrapped__` attribute.

New in version 3.2: Copying of the `__annotations__` attribute by default.

Changed in version 3.2: Missing attributes no longer trigger an `AttributeError`.

Changed in version 3.4: The `__wrapped__` attribute now always refers to the wrapped function, even if that function defined a `__wrapped__` attribute. (see bpo-17482)

`@functools.wraps(`*wrapped*, *assigned=WRAPPER_ASSIGNMENTS*, *updated=WRAPPER_UPDATES*`)`

This is a convenience function for invoking `update_wrapper()` as a function decorator when defining a wrapper function. It is equivalent to `partial(update_wrapper, wrapped=wrapped, assigned=assigned, updated=updated)`. For example:

```
>>> from functools import wraps
>>> def my_decorator(f):
...     @wraps(f)
...     def wrapper(*args, **kwds):
...         print('Calling decorated function')
...         return f(*args, **kwds)
...     return wrapper
...
>>> @my_decorator
... def example():
...     """Docstring"""
...     print('Called example function')
...
>>> example()
Calling decorated function
Called example function
>>> example.__name__
'example'
>>> example.__doc__
'Docstring'
```

Without the use of this decorator factory, the name of the example function would have been `'wrapper'`, and the docstring of the original `example()` would have been lost.

10.2.1 `partial` Objects

partial objects are callable objects created by *partial()*. They have three read-only attributes:

partial.func
A callable object or function. Calls to the *partial* object will be forwarded to *func* with new arguments and keywords.

partial.args
The leftmost positional arguments that will be prepended to the positional arguments provided to a *partial* object call.

partial.keywords
The keyword arguments that will be supplied when the *partial* object is called.

partial objects are like `function` objects in that they are callable, weak referencable, and can have attributes. There are some important differences. For instance, the *__name__* and `__doc__` attributes are not created automatically. Also, *partial* objects defined in classes behave like static methods and do not transform into bound methods during instance attribute look-up.

10.3 `operator` — Standard operators as functions

Source code: Lib/operator.py

The *operator* module exports a set of efficient functions corresponding to the intrinsic operators of Python. For example, `operator.add(x, y)` is equivalent to the expression `x+y`. Many function names are those used for special methods, without the double underscores. For backward compatibility, many of these have a variant with the double underscores kept. The variants without the double underscores are preferred for clarity.

The functions fall into categories that perform object comparisons, logical operations, mathematical operations and sequence operations.

The object comparison functions are useful for all objects, and are named after the rich comparison operators they support:

`operator.lt(a, b)`
`operator.le(a, b)`
`operator.eq(a, b)`
`operator.ne(a, b)`
`operator.ge(a, b)`
`operator.gt(a, b)`
`operator.__lt__(a, b)`
`operator.__le__(a, b)`
`operator.__eq__(a, b)`
`operator.__ne__(a, b)`
`operator.__ge__(a, b)`
`operator.__gt__(a, b)`

Perform "rich comparisons" between *a* and *b*. Specifically, `lt(a, b)` is equivalent to `a < b`, `le(a, b)` is equivalent to `a <= b`, `eq(a, b)` is equivalent to `a == b`, `ne(a, b)` is equivalent to `a != b`, `gt(a, b)` is equivalent to `a > b` and `ge(a, b)` is equivalent to `a >= b`. Note that these functions can return any value, which may or may not be interpretable as a Boolean value. See comparisons for more information about rich comparisons.

The logical operations are also generally applicable to all objects, and support truth tests, identity tests, and boolean operations:

`operator.not_(obj)`
`operator.__not__(obj)`

Return the outcome of `not` *obj*. (Note that there is no `__not__()` method for object instances; only the interpreter core defines this operation. The result is affected by the `__bool__()` and `__len__()` methods.)

`operator.truth(obj)`

Return `True` if *obj* is true, and `False` otherwise. This is equivalent to using the `bool` constructor.

`operator.is_(a, b)`

Return `a is b`. Tests object identity.

`operator.is_not(a, b)`

Return `a is not b`. Tests object identity.

The mathematical and bitwise operations are the most numerous:

`operator.abs(obj)`
`operator.__abs__(obj)`

Return the absolute value of *obj*.

`operator.add(a, b)`
`operator.__add__(a, b)`

Return `a + b`, for *a* and *b* numbers.

`operator.and_(a, b)`
`operator.__and__(a, b)`

Return the bitwise and of *a* and *b*.

`operator.floordiv(a, b)`
`operator.__floordiv__(a, b)`

Return `a // b`.

`operator.index(a)`

operator.**__index__**(*a*)
Return *a* converted to an integer. Equivalent to `a.__index__()`.

operator.**inv**(*obj*)
operator.**invert**(*obj*)
operator.**__inv__**(*obj*)
operator.**__invert__**(*obj*)
Return the bitwise inverse of the number *obj*. This is equivalent to `~obj`.

operator.**lshift**(*a, b*)
operator.**__lshift__**(*a, b*)
Return *a* shifted left by *b*.

operator.**mod**(*a, b*)
operator.**__mod__**(*a, b*)
Return `a % b`.

operator.**mul**(*a, b*)
operator.**__mul__**(*a, b*)
Return `a * b`, for *a* and *b* numbers.

operator.**matmul**(*a, b*)
operator.**__matmul__**(*a, b*)
Return `a @ b`.

New in version 3.5.

operator.**neg**(*obj*)
operator.**__neg__**(*obj*)
Return *obj* negated (`-obj`).

operator.**or_**(*a, b*)
operator.**__or__**(*a, b*)
Return the bitwise or of *a* and *b*.

operator.**pos**(*obj*)
operator.**__pos__**(*obj*)
Return *obj* positive (`+obj`).

operator.**pow**(*a, b*)
operator.**__pow__**(*a, b*)
Return `a ** b`, for *a* and *b* numbers.

operator.**rshift**(*a, b*)
operator.**__rshift__**(*a, b*)
Return *a* shifted right by *b*.

operator.**sub**(*a, b*)
operator.**__sub__**(*a, b*)
Return `a - b`.

operator.**truediv**(*a, b*)
operator.**__truediv__**(*a, b*)
Return `a / b` where 2/3 is .66 rather than 0. This is also known as "true" division.

operator.**xor**(*a, b*)
operator.**__xor__**(*a, b*)
Return the bitwise exclusive or of *a* and *b*.

Operations which work with sequences (some of them with mappings too) include:

operator.**concat**(*a, b*)

operator.**__concat__**(*a*, *b*)
Return `a + b` for *a* and *b* sequences.

operator.**contains**(*a*, *b*)
operator.**__contains__**(*a*, *b*)
Return the outcome of the test `b in a`. Note the reversed operands.

operator.**countOf**(*a*, *b*)
Return the number of occurrences of *b* in *a*.

operator.**delitem**(*a*, *b*)
operator.**__delitem__**(*a*, *b*)
Remove the value of *a* at index *b*.

operator.**getitem**(*a*, *b*)
operator.**__getitem__**(*a*, *b*)
Return the value of *a* at index *b*.

operator.**indexOf**(*a*, *b*)
Return the index of the first of occurrence of *b* in *a*.

operator.**setitem**(*a*, *b*, *c*)
operator.**__setitem__**(*a*, *b*, *c*)
Set the value of *a* at index *b* to *c*.

operator.**length_hint**(*obj*, *default=0*)
Return an estimated length for the object *o*. First try to return its actual length, then an estimate using `object.__length_hint__()`, and finally return the default value.

New in version 3.4.

The *operator* module also defines tools for generalized attribute and item lookups. These are useful for making fast field extractors as arguments for *map()*, *sorted()*, *itertools.groupby()*, or other functions that expect a function argument.

operator.**attrgetter**(*attr*)
operator.**attrgetter**(**attrs*)
Return a callable object that fetches *attr* from its operand. If more than one attribute is requested, returns a tuple of attributes. The attribute names can also contain dots. For example:

- After `f = attrgetter('name')`, the call `f(b)` returns `b.name`.
- After `f = attrgetter('name', 'date')`, the call `f(b)` returns `(b.name, b.date)`.
- After `f = attrgetter('name.first', 'name.last')`, the call `f(b)` returns `(b.name.first, b.name.last)`.

Equivalent to:

```
def attrgetter(*items):
    if any(not isinstance(item, str) for item in items):
        raise TypeError('attribute name must be a string')
    if len(items) == 1:
        attr = items[0]
        def g(obj):
            return resolve_attr(obj, attr)
    else:
        def g(obj):
            return tuple(resolve_attr(obj, attr) for attr in items)
    return g

def resolve_attr(obj, attr):
    for name in attr.split("."):
```

```
        obj = getattr(obj, name)
    return obj
```

operator.**itemgetter**(*item*)
operator.**itemgetter**(**items*)

Return a callable object that fetches *item* from its operand using the operand's *__getitem__()* method. If multiple items are specified, returns a tuple of lookup values. For example:

- After `f = itemgetter(2)`, the call `f(r)` returns `r[2]`.
- After `g = itemgetter(2, 5, 3)`, the call `g(r)` returns `(r[2], r[5], r[3])`.

Equivalent to:

```
def itemgetter(*items):
    if len(items) == 1:
        item = items[0]
        def g(obj):
            return obj[item]
    else:
        def g(obj):
            return tuple(obj[item] for item in items)
    return g
```

The items can be any type accepted by the operand's *__getitem__()* method. Dictionaries accept any hashable value. Lists, tuples, and strings accept an index or a slice:

```
>>> itemgetter(1)('ABCDEFG')
'B'
>>> itemgetter(1,3,5)('ABCDEFG')
('B', 'D', 'F')
>>> itemgetter(slice(2,None))('ABCDEFG')
'CDEFG'
```

Example of using *itemgetter()* to retrieve specific fields from a tuple record:

```
>>> inventory = [('apple', 3), ('banana', 2), ('pear', 5), ('orange', 1)]
>>> getcount = itemgetter(1)
>>> list(map(getcount, inventory))
[3, 2, 5, 1]
>>> sorted(inventory, key=getcount)
[('orange', 1), ('banana', 2), ('apple', 3), ('pear', 5)]
```

operator.**methodcaller**(*name*[, *args...*])

Return a callable object that calls the method *name* on its operand. If additional arguments and/or keyword arguments are given, they will be given to the method as well. For example:

- After `f = methodcaller('name')`, the call `f(b)` returns `b.name()`.
- After `f = methodcaller('name', 'foo', bar=1)`, the call `f(b)` returns `b.name('foo', bar=1)`.

Equivalent to:

```
def methodcaller(name, *args, **kwargs):
    def caller(obj):
        return getattr(obj, name)(*args, **kwargs)
    return caller
```

10.3.1 Mapping Operators to Functions

This table shows how abstract operations correspond to operator symbols in the Python syntax and the functions in the *operator* module.

Operation	Syntax	Function
Addition	`a + b`	`add(a, b)`
Concatenation	`seq1 + seq2`	`concat(seq1, seq2)`
Containment Test	`obj in seq`	`contains(seq, obj)`
Division	`a / b`	`truediv(a, b)`
Division	`a // b`	`floordiv(a, b)`
Bitwise And	`a & b`	`and_(a, b)`
Bitwise Exclusive Or	`a ^ b`	`xor(a, b)`
Bitwise Inversion	`~ a`	`invert(a)`
Bitwise Or	`a | b`	`or_(a, b)`
Exponentiation	`a ** b`	`pow(a, b)`
Identity	`a is b`	`is_(a, b)`
Identity	`a is not b`	`is_not(a, b)`
Indexed Assignment	`obj[k] = v`	`setitem(obj, k, v)`
Indexed Deletion	`del obj[k]`	`delitem(obj, k)`
Indexing	`obj[k]`	`getitem(obj, k)`
Left Shift	`a << b`	`lshift(a, b)`
Modulo	`a % b`	`mod(a, b)`
Multiplication	`a * b`	`mul(a, b)`
Matrix Multiplication	`a @ b`	`matmul(a, b)`
Negation (Arithmetic)	`- a`	`neg(a)`
Negation (Logical)	`not a`	`not_(a)`
Positive	`+ a`	`pos(a)`
Right Shift	`a >> b`	`rshift(a, b)`
Slice Assignment	`seq[i:j] = values`	`setitem(seq, slice(i, j), values)`
Slice Deletion	`del seq[i:j]`	`delitem(seq, slice(i, j))`
Slicing	`seq[i:j]`	`getitem(seq, slice(i, j))`
String Formatting	`s % obj`	`mod(s, obj)`
Subtraction	`a - b`	`sub(a, b)`
Truth Test	`obj`	`truth(obj)`
Ordering	`a < b`	`lt(a, b)`
Ordering	`a <= b`	`le(a, b)`
Equality	`a == b`	`eq(a, b)`
Difference	`a != b`	`ne(a, b)`
Ordering	`a >= b`	`ge(a, b)`
Ordering	`a > b`	`gt(a, b)`

10.3.2 Inplace Operators

Many operations have an "in-place" version. Listed below are functions providing a more primitive access to in-place operators than the usual syntax does; for example, the *statement* `x += y` is equivalent to `x = operator.iadd(x, y)`. Another way to put it is to say that `z = operator.iadd(x, y)` is equivalent to the compound statement `z = x; z += y`.

In those examples, note that when an in-place method is called, the computation and assignment are performed in two separate steps. The in-place functions listed below only do the first step, calling the in-place method. The second step, assignment, is not handled.

For immutable targets such as strings, numbers, and tuples, the updated value is computed, but not assigned back to the input variable:

```
>>> a = 'hello'
>>> iadd(a, ' world')
'hello world'
>>> a
'hello'
```

For mutable targets such as lists and dictionaries, the inplace method will perform the update, so no subsequent assignment is necessary:

```
>>> s = ['h', 'e', 'l', 'l', 'o']
>>> iadd(s, [' ', 'w', 'o', 'r', 'l', 'd'])
['h', 'e', 'l', 'l', 'o', ' ', 'w', 'o', 'r', 'l', 'd']
>>> s
['h', 'e', 'l', 'l', 'o', ' ', 'w', 'o', 'r', 'l', 'd']
```

operator.**iadd**(*a*, *b*)
operator.**__iadd__**(*a*, *b*)
`a = iadd(a, b)` is equivalent to `a += b`.

operator.**iand**(*a*, *b*)
operator.**__iand__**(*a*, *b*)
`a = iand(a, b)` is equivalent to `a &= b`.

operator.**iconcat**(*a*, *b*)
operator.**__iconcat__**(*a*, *b*)
`a = iconcat(a, b)` is equivalent to `a += b` for *a* and *b* sequences.

operator.**ifloordiv**(*a*, *b*)
operator.**__ifloordiv__**(*a*, *b*)
`a = ifloordiv(a, b)` is equivalent to `a //= b`.

operator.**ilshift**(*a*, *b*)
operator.**__ilshift__**(*a*, *b*)
`a = ilshift(a, b)` is equivalent to `a <<= b`.

operator.**imod**(*a*, *b*)
operator.**__imod__**(*a*, *b*)
`a = imod(a, b)` is equivalent to `a %= b`.

operator.**imul**(*a*, *b*)
operator.**__imul__**(*a*, *b*)
`a = imul(a, b)` is equivalent to `a *= b`.

operator.**imatmul**(*a*, *b*)
operator.**__imatmul__**(*a*, *b*)
`a = imatmul(a, b)` is equivalent to `a @= b`.

New in version 3.5.

operator.**ior**(*a*, *b*)
operator.**__ior__**(*a*, *b*)
`a = ior(a, b)` is equivalent to `a |= b`.

operator.**ipow**(*a*, *b*)
operator.**__ipow__**(*a*, *b*)
`a = ipow(a, b)` is equivalent to `a **= b`.

operator.**irshift**(*a*, *b*)

operator.**__irshift__**(*a*, *b*)
    a = irshift(a, b) is equivalent to a >>= b.

operator.**isub**(*a*, *b*)
operator.**__isub__**(*a*, *b*)
    a = isub(a, b) is equivalent to a -= b.

operator.**itruediv**(*a*, *b*)
operator.**__itruediv__**(*a*, *b*)
    a = itruediv(a, b) is equivalent to a /= b.

operator.**ixor**(*a*, *b*)
operator.**__ixor__**(*a*, *b*)
    a = ixor(a, b) is equivalent to a ^= b.

CHAPTER

ELEVEN

FILE AND DIRECTORY ACCESS

The modules described in this chapter deal with disk files and directories. For example, there are modules for reading the properties of files, manipulating paths in a portable way, and creating temporary files. The full list of modules in this chapter is:

11.1 pathlib — Object-oriented filesystem paths

New in version 3.4.

Source code: Lib/pathlib.py

This module offers classes representing filesystem paths with semantics appropriate for different operating systems. Path classes are divided between *pure paths*, which provide purely computational operations without I/O, and *concrete paths*, which inherit from pure paths but also provide I/O operations.

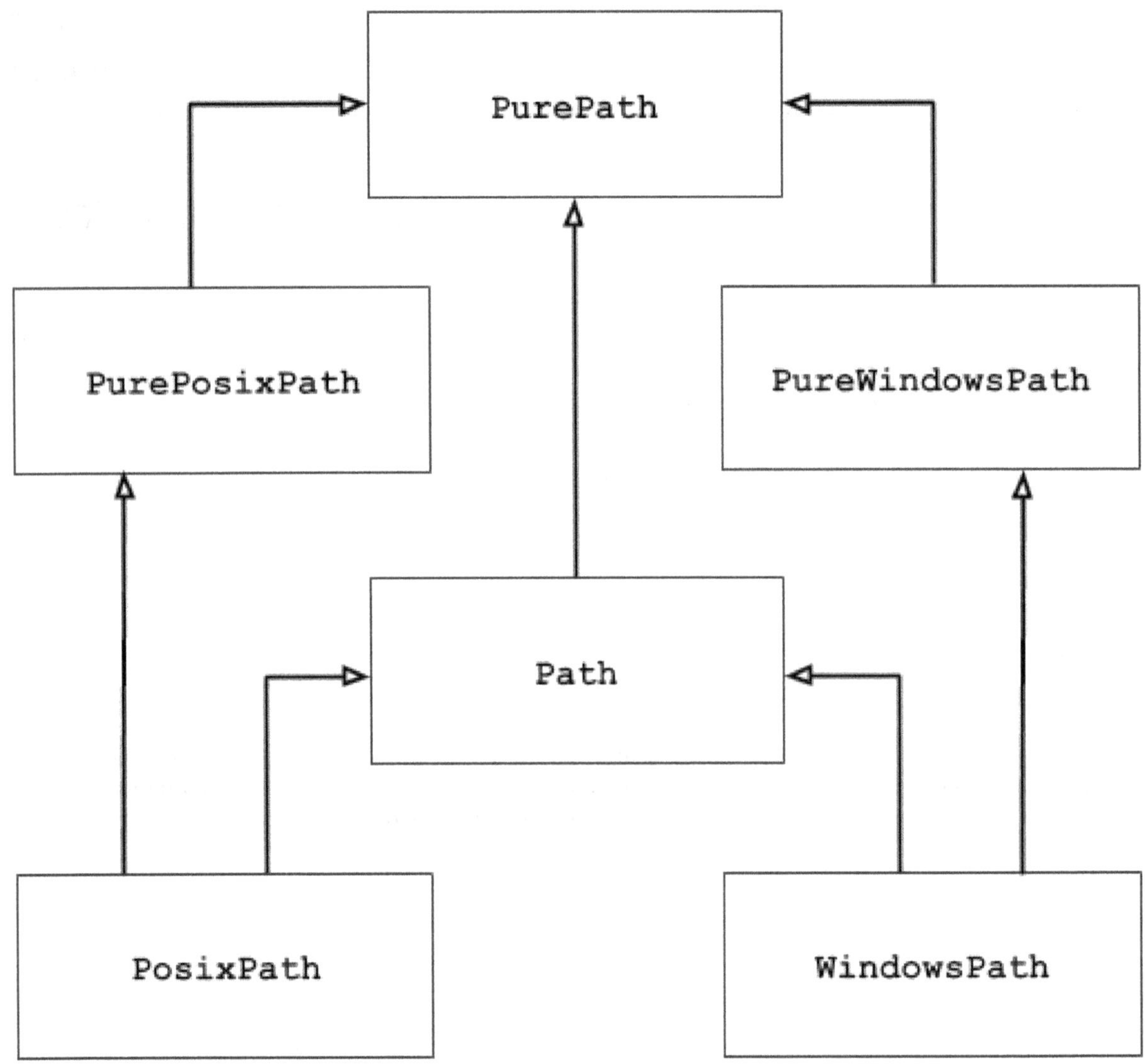

If you've never used this module before or just aren't sure which class is right for your task, *Path* is most likely what you need. It instantiates a *concrete path* for the platform the code is running on.

Pure paths are useful in some special cases; for example:

1. If you want to manipulate Windows paths on a Unix machine (or vice versa). You cannot instantiate a *WindowsPath* when running on Unix, but you can instantiate *PureWindowsPath*.
2. You want to make sure that your code only manipulates paths without actually accessing the OS. In this case, instantiating one of the pure classes may be useful since those simply don't have any OS-accessing operations.

See also:

PEP 428: The pathlib module – object-oriented filesystem paths.

See also:

For low-level path manipulation on strings, you can also use the *os.path* module.

11.1.1 Basic use

Importing the main class:

```
>>> from pathlib import Path
```

Listing subdirectories:

```
>>> p = Path('.')
>>> [x for x in p.iterdir() if x.is_dir()]
[PosixPath('.hg'), PosixPath('docs'), PosixPath('dist'),
 PosixPath('__pycache__'), PosixPath('build')]
```

Listing Python source files in this directory tree:

```
>>> list(p.glob('**/*.py'))
[PosixPath('test_pathlib.py'), PosixPath('setup.py'),
 PosixPath('pathlib.py'), PosixPath('docs/conf.py'),
 PosixPath('build/lib/pathlib.py')]
```

Navigating inside a directory tree:

```
>>> p = Path('/etc')
>>> q = p / 'init.d' / 'reboot'
>>> q
PosixPath('/etc/init.d/reboot')
>>> q.resolve()
PosixPath('/etc/rc.d/init.d/halt')
```

Querying path properties:

```
>>> q.exists()
True
>>> q.is_dir()
False
```

Opening a file:

```
>>> with q.open() as f: f.readline()
...
'#!/bin/bash\n'
```

11.1.2 Pure paths

Pure path objects provide path-handling operations which don't actually access a filesystem. There are three ways to access these classes, which we also call *flavours*:

class pathlib.PurePath(pathsegments*)**

A generic class that represents the system's path flavour (instantiating it creates either a *PurePosixPath* or a *PureWindowsPath*):

```
>>> PurePath('setup.py')      # Running on a Unix machine
PurePosixPath('setup.py')
```

Each element of *pathsegments* can be either a string representing a path segment, an object implementing the *os.PathLike* interface which returns a string, or another path object:

```
>>> PurePath('foo', 'some/path', 'bar')
PurePosixPath('foo/some/path/bar')
>>> PurePath(Path('foo'), Path('bar'))
PurePosixPath('foo/bar')
```

When *pathsegments* is empty, the current directory is assumed:

```
>>> PurePath()
PurePosixPath('.')
```

When several absolute paths are given, the last is taken as an anchor (mimicking *os.path.join()*'s behaviour):

```
>>> PurePath('/etc', '/usr', 'lib64')
PurePosixPath('/usr/lib64')
>>> PureWindowsPath('c:/Windows', 'd:bar')
PureWindowsPath('d:bar')
```

However, in a Windows path, changing the local root doesn't discard the previous drive setting:

```
>>> PureWindowsPath('c:/Windows', '/Program Files')
PureWindowsPath('c:/Program Files')
```

Spurious slashes and single dots are collapsed, but double dots (`'..'`) are not, since this would change the meaning of a path in the face of symbolic links:

```
>>> PurePath('foo//bar')
PurePosixPath('foo/bar')
>>> PurePath('foo/./bar')
PurePosixPath('foo/bar')
>>> PurePath('foo/../bar')
PurePosixPath('foo/../bar')
```

(a naïve approach would make `PurePosixPath('foo/../bar')` equivalent to `PurePosixPath('bar')`, which is wrong if `foo` is a symbolic link to another directory)

Pure path objects implement the *os.PathLike* interface, allowing them to be used anywhere the interface is accepted.

Changed in version 3.6: Added support for the *os.PathLike* interface.

class pathlib.PurePosixPath(*pathsegments)

A subclass of *PurePath*, this path flavour represents non-Windows filesystem paths:

```
>>> PurePosixPath('/etc')
PurePosixPath('/etc')
```

pathsegments is specified similarly to *PurePath*.

class pathlib.PureWindowsPath(*pathsegments)

A subclass of *PurePath*, this path flavour represents Windows filesystem paths:

```
>>> PureWindowsPath('c:/Program Files/')
PureWindowsPath('c:/Program Files')
```

pathsegments is specified similarly to *PurePath*.

Regardless of the system you're running on, you can instantiate all of these classes, since they don't provide any operation that does system calls.

General properties

Paths are immutable and hashable. Paths of a same flavour are comparable and orderable. These properties respect the flavour's case-folding semantics:

```
>>> PurePosixPath('foo') == PurePosixPath('FOO')
False
>>> PureWindowsPath('foo') == PureWindowsPath('FOO')
True
>>> PureWindowsPath('FOO') in { PureWindowsPath('foo') }
True
>>> PureWindowsPath('C:') < PureWindowsPath('d:')
True
```

Paths of a different flavour compare unequal and cannot be ordered:

```
>>> PureWindowsPath('foo') == PurePosixPath('foo')
False
>>> PureWindowsPath('foo') < PurePosixPath('foo')
Traceback (most recent call last):
  File "<stdin>", line 1, in <module>
TypeError: '<' not supported between instances of 'PureWindowsPath' and 'PurePosixPath'
```

Operators

The slash operator helps create child paths, similarly to *os.path.join()*:

```
>>> p = PurePath('/etc')
>>> p
PurePosixPath('/etc')
>>> p / 'init.d' / 'apache2'
PurePosixPath('/etc/init.d/apache2')
>>> q = PurePath('bin')
>>> '/usr' / q
PurePosixPath('/usr/bin')
```

A path object can be used anywhere an object implementing *os.PathLike* is accepted:

```
>>> import os
>>> p = PurePath('/etc')
>>> os.fspath(p)
'/etc'
```

The string representation of a path is the raw filesystem path itself (in native form, e.g. with backslashes under Windows), which you can pass to any function taking a file path as a string:

```
>>> p = PurePath('/etc')
>>> str(p)
'/etc'
>>> p = PureWindowsPath('c:/Program Files')
>>> str(p)
'c:\\Program Files'
```

Similarly, calling *bytes* on a path gives the raw filesystem path as a bytes object, as encoded by *os.fsencode()*:

```
>>> bytes(p)
b'/etc'
```

Note: Calling *bytes* is only recommended under Unix. Under Windows, the unicode form is the canonical representation of filesystem paths.

Accessing individual parts

To access the individual "parts" (components) of a path, use the following property:

PurePath.parts

A tuple giving access to the path's various components:

```
>>> p = PurePath('/usr/bin/python3')
>>> p.parts
('/', 'usr', 'bin', 'python3')

>>> p = PureWindowsPath('c:/Program Files/PSF')
>>> p.parts
('c:\\', 'Program Files', 'PSF')
```

(note how the drive and local root are regrouped in a single part)

Methods and properties

Pure paths provide the following methods and properties:

PurePath.drive

A string representing the drive letter or name, if any:

```
>>> PureWindowsPath('c:/Program Files/').drive
'c:'
>>> PureWindowsPath('/Program Files/').drive
''
>>> PurePosixPath('/etc').drive
''
```

UNC shares are also considered drives:

```
>>> PureWindowsPath('//host/share/foo.txt').drive
'\\\\host\\share'
```

PurePath.root

A string representing the (local or global) root, if any:

```
>>> PureWindowsPath('c:/Program Files/').root
'\\'
>>> PureWindowsPath('c:Program Files/').root
''
>>> PurePosixPath('/etc').root
'/'
```

UNC shares always have a root:

```
>>> PureWindowsPath('//host/share').root
'\\'
```

PurePath.anchor
The concatenation of the drive and root:

```
>>> PureWindowsPath('c:/Program Files/').anchor
'c:\\'
>>> PureWindowsPath('c:Program Files/').anchor
'c:'
>>> PurePosixPath('/etc').anchor
'/'
>>> PureWindowsPath('//host/share').anchor
'\\\\host\\share\\'
```

PurePath.parents
An immutable sequence providing access to the logical ancestors of the path:

```
>>> p = PureWindowsPath('c:/foo/bar/setup.py')
>>> p.parents[0]
PureWindowsPath('c:/foo/bar')
>>> p.parents[1]
PureWindowsPath('c:/foo')
>>> p.parents[2]
PureWindowsPath('c:/')
```

PurePath.parent
The logical parent of the path:

```
>>> p = PurePosixPath('/a/b/c/d')
>>> p.parent
PurePosixPath('/a/b/c')
```

You cannot go past an anchor, or empty path:

```
>>> p = PurePosixPath('/')
>>> p.parent
PurePosixPath('/')
>>> p = PurePosixPath('.')
>>> p.parent
PurePosixPath('.')
```

Note: This is a purely lexical operation, hence the following behaviour:

```
>>> p = PurePosixPath('foo/..')
>>> p.parent
PurePosixPath('foo')
```

If you want to walk an arbitrary filesystem path upwards, it is recommended to first call *Path.resolve()* so as to resolve symlinks and eliminate ".." components.

PurePath.name
A string representing the final path component, excluding the drive and root, if any:

```
>>> PurePosixPath('my/library/setup.py').name
'setup.py'
```

UNC drive names are not considered:

```
>>> PureWindowsPath('//some/share/setup.py').name
'setup.py'
>>> PureWindowsPath('//some/share').name
''
```

PurePath.**suffix**

The file extension of the final component, if any:

```
>>> PurePosixPath('my/library/setup.py').suffix
'.py'
>>> PurePosixPath('my/library.tar.gz').suffix
'.gz'
>>> PurePosixPath('my/library').suffix
''
```

PurePath.**suffixes**

A list of the path's file extensions:

```
>>> PurePosixPath('my/library.tar.gar').suffixes
['.tar', '.gar']
>>> PurePosixPath('my/library.tar.gz').suffixes
['.tar', '.gz']
>>> PurePosixPath('my/library').suffixes
[]
```

PurePath.**stem**

The final path component, without its suffix:

```
>>> PurePosixPath('my/library.tar.gz').stem
'library.tar'
>>> PurePosixPath('my/library.tar').stem
'library'
>>> PurePosixPath('my/library').stem
'library'
```

PurePath.**as_posix**()

Return a string representation of the path with forward slashes (/):

```
>>> p = PureWindowsPath('c:\\windows')
>>> str(p)
'c:\\windows'
>>> p.as_posix()
'c:/windows'
```

PurePath.**as_uri**()

Represent the path as a `file` URI. *ValueError* is raised if the path isn't absolute.

```
>>> p = PurePosixPath('/etc/passwd')
>>> p.as_uri()
'file:///etc/passwd'
>>> p = PureWindowsPath('c:/Windows')
>>> p.as_uri()
'file:///c:/Windows'
```

PurePath.**is_absolute**()

Return whether the path is absolute or not. A path is considered absolute if it has both a root and (if the flavour allows) a drive:

```
>>> PurePosixPath('/a/b').is_absolute()
True
>>> PurePosixPath('a/b').is_absolute()
False

>>> PureWindowsPath('c:/a/b').is_absolute()
True
>>> PureWindowsPath('/a/b').is_absolute()
False
>>> PureWindowsPath('c:').is_absolute()
False
>>> PureWindowsPath('//some/share').is_absolute()
True
```

PurePath.is_reserved()

With *PureWindowsPath*, return `True` if the path is considered reserved under Windows, `False` otherwise. With *PurePosixPath*, `False` is always returned.

```
>>> PureWindowsPath('nul').is_reserved()
True
>>> PurePosixPath('nul').is_reserved()
False
```

File system calls on reserved paths can fail mysteriously or have unintended effects.

PurePath.joinpath(*other)

Calling this method is equivalent to combining the path with each of the *other* arguments in turn:

```
>>> PurePosixPath('/etc').joinpath('passwd')
PurePosixPath('/etc/passwd')
>>> PurePosixPath('/etc').joinpath(PurePosixPath('passwd'))
PurePosixPath('/etc/passwd')
>>> PurePosixPath('/etc').joinpath('init.d', 'apache2')
PurePosixPath('/etc/init.d/apache2')
>>> PureWindowsPath('c:').joinpath('/Program Files')
PureWindowsPath('c:/Program Files')
```

PurePath.match(pattern)

Match this path against the provided glob-style pattern. Return `True` if matching is successful, `False` otherwise.

If *pattern* is relative, the path can be either relative or absolute, and matching is done from the right:

```
>>> PurePath('a/b.py').match('*.py')
True
>>> PurePath('/a/b/c.py').match('b/*.py')
True
>>> PurePath('/a/b/c.py').match('a/*.py')
False
```

If *pattern* is absolute, the path must be absolute, and the whole path must match:

```
>>> PurePath('/a.py').match('/*.py')
True
>>> PurePath('a/b.py').match('/*.py')
False
```

As with other methods, case-sensitivity is observed:

```
>>> PureWindowsPath('b.py').match('*.PY')
True
```

PurePath.**relative_to**(**other*)

Compute a version of this path relative to the path represented by *other*. If it's impossible, ValueError is raised:

```
>>> p = PurePosixPath('/etc/passwd')
>>> p.relative_to('/')
PurePosixPath('etc/passwd')
>>> p.relative_to('/etc')
PurePosixPath('passwd')
>>> p.relative_to('/usr')
Traceback (most recent call last):
  File "<stdin>", line 1, in <module>
  File "pathlib.py", line 694, in relative_to
    .format(str(self), str(formatted)))
ValueError: '/etc/passwd' does not start with '/usr'
```

PurePath.**with_name**(*name*)

Return a new path with the *name* changed. If the original path doesn't have a name, ValueError is raised:

```
>>> p = PureWindowsPath('c:/Downloads/pathlib.tar.gz')
>>> p.with_name('setup.py')
PureWindowsPath('c:/Downloads/setup.py')
>>> p = PureWindowsPath('c:/')
>>> p.with_name('setup.py')
Traceback (most recent call last):
  File "<stdin>", line 1, in <module>
  File "/home/antoine/cpython/default/Lib/pathlib.py", line 751, in with_name
    raise ValueError("%r has an empty name" % (self,))
ValueError: PureWindowsPath('c:/') has an empty name
```

PurePath.**with_suffix**(*suffix*)

Return a new path with the *suffix* changed. If the original path doesn't have a suffix, the new *suffix* is appended instead:

```
>>> p = PureWindowsPath('c:/Downloads/pathlib.tar.gz')
>>> p.with_suffix('.bz2')
PureWindowsPath('c:/Downloads/pathlib.tar.bz2')
>>> p = PureWindowsPath('README')
>>> p.with_suffix('.txt')
PureWindowsPath('README.txt')
```

11.1.3 Concrete paths

Concrete paths are subclasses of the pure path classes. In addition to operations provided by the latter, they also provide methods to do system calls on path objects. There are three ways to instantiate concrete paths:

class pathlib.**Path**(**pathsegments*)

A subclass of *PurePath*, this class represents concrete paths of the system's path flavour (instantiating it creates either a *PosixPath* or a *WindowsPath*):

```
>>> Path('setup.py')
PosixPath('setup.py')
```

pathsegments is specified similarly to *PurePath*.

class pathlib.PosixPath(pathsegments*)**

A subclass of *Path* and *PurePosixPath*, this class represents concrete non-Windows filesystem paths:

```
>>> PosixPath('/etc')
PosixPath('/etc')
```

pathsegments is specified similarly to *PurePath*.

class pathlib.WindowsPath(pathsegments*)**

A subclass of *Path* and *PureWindowsPath*, this class represents concrete Windows filesystem paths:

```
>>> WindowsPath('c:/Program Files/')
WindowsPath('c:/Program Files')
```

pathsegments is specified similarly to *PurePath*.

You can only instantiate the class flavour that corresponds to your system (allowing system calls on non-compatible path flavours could lead to bugs or failures in your application):

```
>>> import os
>>> os.name
'posix'
>>> Path('setup.py')
PosixPath('setup.py')
>>> PosixPath('setup.py')
PosixPath('setup.py')
>>> WindowsPath('setup.py')
Traceback (most recent call last):
  File "<stdin>", line 1, in <module>
  File "pathlib.py", line 798, in __new__
    % (cls.__name__,))
NotImplementedError: cannot instantiate 'WindowsPath' on your system
```

Methods

Concrete paths provide the following methods in addition to pure paths methods. Many of these methods can raise an *OSError* if a system call fails (for example because the path doesn't exist):

classmethod Path.cwd()

Return a new path object representing the current directory (as returned by *os.getcwd()*):

```
>>> Path.cwd()
PosixPath('/home/antoine/pathlib')
```

classmethod Path.home()

Return a new path object representing the user's home directory (as returned by *os.path.expanduser()* with ~ construct):

```
>>> Path.home()
PosixPath('/home/antoine')
```

New in version 3.5.

Path.stat()
Return information about this path (similarly to *os.stat()*). The result is looked up at each call to this method.

```
>>> p = Path('setup.py')
>>> p.stat().st_size
956
>>> p.stat().st_mtime
1327883547.852554
```

Path.chmod(*mode*)
Change the file mode and permissions, like *os.chmod()*:

```
>>> p = Path('setup.py')
>>> p.stat().st_mode
33277
>>> p.chmod(0o444)
>>> p.stat().st_mode
33060
```

Path.exists()
Whether the path points to an existing file or directory:

```
>>> Path('.').exists()
True
>>> Path('setup.py').exists()
True
>>> Path('/etc').exists()
True
>>> Path('nonexistentfile').exists()
False
```

Note: If the path points to a symlink, *exists()* returns whether the symlink *points to* an existing file or directory.

Path.expanduser()
Return a new path with expanded ~ and ~user constructs, as returned by *os.path.expanduser()*:

```
>>> p = PosixPath('~/films/Monty Python')
>>> p.expanduser()
PosixPath('/home/eric/films/Monty Python')
```

New in version 3.5.

Path.glob(*pattern*)
Glob the given *pattern* in the directory represented by this path, yielding all matching files (of any kind):

```
>>> sorted(Path('.').glob('*.py'))
[PosixPath('pathlib.py'), PosixPath('setup.py'), PosixPath('test_pathlib.py')]
>>> sorted(Path('.').glob('*/*.py'))
[PosixPath('docs/conf.py')]
```

The "**" pattern means "this directory and all subdirectories, recursively". In other words, it enables recursive globbing:

```
>>> sorted(Path('.').glob('**/*.py'))
[PosixPath('build/lib/pathlib.py'),
 PosixPath('docs/conf.py'),
 PosixPath('pathlib.py'),
 PosixPath('setup.py'),
 PosixPath('test_pathlib.py')]
```

Note: Using the "`**`" pattern in large directory trees may consume an inordinate amount of time.

`Path.group()`
Return the name of the group owning the file. *KeyError* is raised if the file's gid isn't found in the system database.

`Path.is_dir()`
Return `True` if the path points to a directory (or a symbolic link pointing to a directory), `False` if it points to another kind of file.

`False` is also returned if the path doesn't exist or is a broken symlink; other errors (such as permission errors) are propagated.

`Path.is_file()`
Return `True` if the path points to a regular file (or a symbolic link pointing to a regular file), `False` if it points to another kind of file.

`False` is also returned if the path doesn't exist or is a broken symlink; other errors (such as permission errors) are propagated.

`Path.is_symlink()`
Return `True` if the path points to a symbolic link, `False` otherwise.

`False` is also returned if the path doesn't exist; other errors (such as permission errors) are propagated.

`Path.is_socket()`
Return `True` if the path points to a Unix socket (or a symbolic link pointing to a Unix socket), `False` if it points to another kind of file.

`False` is also returned if the path doesn't exist or is a broken symlink; other errors (such as permission errors) are propagated.

`Path.is_fifo()`
Return `True` if the path points to a FIFO (or a symbolic link pointing to a FIFO), `False` if it points to another kind of file.

`False` is also returned if the path doesn't exist or is a broken symlink; other errors (such as permission errors) are propagated.

`Path.is_block_device()`
Return `True` if the path points to a block device (or a symbolic link pointing to a block device), `False` if it points to another kind of file.

`False` is also returned if the path doesn't exist or is a broken symlink; other errors (such as permission errors) are propagated.

`Path.is_char_device()`
Return `True` if the path points to a character device (or a symbolic link pointing to a character device), `False` if it points to another kind of file.

`False` is also returned if the path doesn't exist or is a broken symlink; other errors (such as permission errors) are propagated.

`Path.iterdir()`
When the path points to a directory, yield path objects of the directory contents:

```
>>> p = Path('docs')
>>> for child in p.iterdir(): child
...
PosixPath('docs/conf.py')
PosixPath('docs/_templates')
PosixPath('docs/make.bat')
PosixPath('docs/index.rst')
PosixPath('docs/_build')
PosixPath('docs/_static')
PosixPath('docs/Makefile')
```

`Path.lchmod(mode)`
Like *Path.chmod()* but, if the path points to a symbolic link, the symbolic link's mode is changed rather than its target's.

`Path.lstat()`
Like *Path.stat()* but, if the path points to a symbolic link, return the symbolic link's information rather than its target's.

`Path.mkdir(mode=0o777, parents=False, exist_ok=False)`
Create a new directory at this given path. If *mode* is given, it is combined with the process' `umask` value to determine the file mode and access flags. If the path already exists, *FileExistsError* is raised.

If *parents* is true, any missing parents of this path are created as needed; they are created with the default permissions without taking *mode* into account (mimicking the POSIX `mkdir -p` command).

If *parents* is false (the default), a missing parent raises *FileNotFoundError*.

If *exist_ok* is false (the default), *FileExistsError* is raised if the target directory already exists.

If *exist_ok* is true, *FileExistsError* exceptions will be ignored (same behavior as the POSIX `mkdir -p` command), but only if the last path component is not an existing non-directory file.

Changed in version 3.5: The *exist_ok* parameter was added.

`Path.open(mode='r', buffering=-1, encoding=None, errors=None, newline=None)`
Open the file pointed to by the path, like the built-in *open()* function does:

```
>>> p = Path('setup.py')
>>> with p.open() as f:
...     f.readline()
...
'#!/usr/bin/env python3\n'
```

`Path.owner()`
Return the name of the user owning the file. *KeyError* is raised if the file's uid isn't found in the system database.

`Path.read_bytes()`
Return the binary contents of the pointed-to file as a bytes object:

```
>>> p = Path('my_binary_file')
>>> p.write_bytes(b'Binary file contents')
20
>>> p.read_bytes()
b'Binary file contents'
```

New in version 3.5.

Path.read_text(*encoding=None, errors=None*)

Return the decoded contents of the pointed-to file as a string:

```
>>> p = Path('my_text_file')
>>> p.write_text('Text file contents')
18
>>> p.read_text()
'Text file contents'
```

The optional parameters have the same meaning as in *open()*.

New in version 3.5.

Path.rename(*target*)

Rename this file or directory to the given *target*. On Unix, if *target* exists and is a file, it will be replaced silently if the user has permission. *target* can be either a string or another path object:

```
>>> p = Path('foo')
>>> p.open('w').write('some text')
9
>>> target = Path('bar')
>>> p.rename(target)
>>> target.open().read()
'some text'
```

Path.replace(*target*)

Rename this file or directory to the given *target*. If *target* points to an existing file or directory, it will be unconditionally replaced.

Path.resolve(*strict=False*)

Make the path absolute, resolving any symlinks. A new path object is returned:

```
>>> p = Path()
>>> p
PosixPath('.')
>>> p.resolve()
PosixPath('/home/antoine/pathlib')
```

"`..`" components are also eliminated (this is the only method to do so):

```
>>> p = Path('docs/../setup.py')
>>> p.resolve()
PosixPath('/home/antoine/pathlib/setup.py')
```

If the path doesn't exist and *strict* is `True`, *FileNotFoundError* is raised. If *strict* is `False`, the path is resolved as far as possible and any remainder is appended without checking whether it exists. If an infinite loop is encountered along the resolution path, *RuntimeError* is raised.

New in version 3.6: The *strict* argument.

Path.rglob(*pattern*)

This is like calling *Path.glob()* with "`**`" added in front of the given *pattern*:

```
>>> sorted(Path().rglob("*.py"))
[PosixPath('build/lib/pathlib.py'),
 PosixPath('docs/conf.py'),
 PosixPath('pathlib.py'),
 PosixPath('setup.py'),
 PosixPath('test_pathlib.py')]
```

Path.rmdir()
Remove this directory. The directory must be empty.

Path.samefile(*other_path*)
Return whether this path points to the same file as *other_path*, which can be either a Path object, or a string. The semantics are similar to `os.path.samefile()` and `os.path.samestat()`.

An `OSError` can be raised if either file cannot be accessed for some reason.

```
>>> p = Path('spam')
>>> q = Path('eggs')
>>> p.samefile(q)
False
>>> p.samefile('spam')
True
```

New in version 3.5.

Path.symlink_to(*target*, *target_is_directory=False*)
Make this path a symbolic link to *target*. Under Windows, *target_is_directory* must be true (default `False`) if the link's target is a directory. Under POSIX, *target_is_directory*'s value is ignored.

```
>>> p = Path('mylink')
>>> p.symlink_to('setup.py')
>>> p.resolve()
PosixPath('/home/antoine/pathlib/setup.py')
>>> p.stat().st_size
956
>>> p.lstat().st_size
8
```

Note: The order of arguments (link, target) is the reverse of `os.symlink()`'s.

Path.touch(*mode=0o666*, *exist_ok=True*)
Create a file at this given path. If *mode* is given, it is combined with the process' `umask` value to determine the file mode and access flags. If the file already exists, the function succeeds if *exist_ok* is true (and its modification time is updated to the current time), otherwise `FileExistsError` is raised.

Path.unlink()
Remove this file or symbolic link. If the path points to a directory, use `Path.rmdir()` instead.

Path.write_bytes(*data*)
Open the file pointed to in bytes mode, write *data* to it, and close the file:

```
>>> p = Path('my_binary_file')
>>> p.write_bytes(b'Binary file contents')
20
>>> p.read_bytes()
b'Binary file contents'
```

An existing file of the same name is overwritten.

New in version 3.5.

Path.write_text(*data*, *encoding=None*, *errors=None*)
Open the file pointed to in text mode, write *data* to it, and close the file:

```
>>> p = Path('my_text_file')
>>> p.write_text('Text file contents')
```

```
18
>>> p.read_text()
'Text file contents'
```

New in version 3.5.

11.2 os.path — Common pathname manipulations

Source code: Lib/posixpath.py (for POSIX), Lib/ntpath.py (for Windows NT), and Lib/macpath.py (for Macintosh)

This module implements some useful functions on pathnames. To read or write files see *open()*, and for accessing the filesystem see the *os* module. The path parameters can be passed as either strings, or bytes. Applications are encouraged to represent file names as (Unicode) character strings. Unfortunately, some file names may not be representable as strings on Unix, so applications that need to support arbitrary file names on Unix should use bytes objects to represent path names. Vice versa, using bytes objects cannot represent all file names on Windows (in the standard `mbcs` encoding), hence Windows applications should use string objects to access all files.

Unlike a unix shell, Python does not do any *automatic* path expansions. Functions such as *expanduser()* and *expandvars()* can be invoked explicitly when an application desires shell-like path expansion. (See also the *glob* module.)

See also:

The *pathlib* module offers high-level path objects.

Note: All of these functions accept either only bytes or only string objects as their parameters. The result is an object of the same type, if a path or file name is returned.

Note: Since different operating systems have different path name conventions, there are several versions of this module in the standard library. The *os.path* module is always the path module suitable for the operating system Python is running on, and therefore usable for local paths. However, you can also import and use the individual modules if you want to manipulate a path that is *always* in one of the different formats. They all have the same interface:

- `posixpath` for UNIX-style paths
- `ntpath` for Windows paths
- *macpath* for old-style MacOS paths

`os.path.abspath(path)`

Return a normalized absolutized version of the pathname *path*. On most platforms, this is equivalent to calling the function *normpath()* as follows: `normpath(join(os.getcwd(), path))`.

Changed in version 3.6: Accepts a *path-like object*.

`os.path.basename(path)`

Return the base name of pathname *path*. This is the second element of the pair returned by passing *path* to the function *split()*. Note that the result of this function is different from the Unix `basename` program; where `basename` for `'/foo/bar/'` returns `'bar'`, the *basename()* function returns an empty string (`''`).

Changed in version 3.6: Accepts a *path-like object*.

`os.path.commonpath(paths)`
Return the longest common sub-path of each pathname in the sequence *paths*. Raise ValueError if *paths* contains both absolute and relative pathnames, or if *paths* is empty. Unlike `commonprefix()`, this returns a valid path.

Availability: Unix, Windows

New in version 3.5.

Changed in version 3.6: Accepts a sequence of *path-like objects*.

`os.path.commonprefix(list)`
Return the longest path prefix (taken character-by-character) that is a prefix of all paths in *list*. If *list* is empty, return the empty string (`''`).

Note: This function may return invalid paths because it works a character at a time. To obtain a valid path, see `commonpath()`.

```
>>> os.path.commonprefix(['/usr/lib', '/usr/local/lib'])
'/usr/l'

>>> os.path.commonpath(['/usr/lib', '/usr/local/lib'])
'/usr'
```

Changed in version 3.6: Accepts a *path-like object*.

`os.path.dirname(path)`
Return the directory name of pathname *path*. This is the first element of the pair returned by passing *path* to the function `split()`.

Changed in version 3.6: Accepts a *path-like object*.

`os.path.exists(path)`
Return `True` if *path* refers to an existing path or an open file descriptor. Returns `False` for broken symbolic links. On some platforms, this function may return `False` if permission is not granted to execute `os.stat()` on the requested file, even if the *path* physically exists.

Changed in version 3.3: *path* can now be an integer: `True` is returned if it is an open file descriptor, `False` otherwise.

Changed in version 3.6: Accepts a *path-like object*.

`os.path.lexists(path)`
Return `True` if *path* refers to an existing path. Returns `True` for broken symbolic links. Equivalent to `exists()` on platforms lacking `os.lstat()`.

Changed in version 3.6: Accepts a *path-like object*.

`os.path.expanduser(path)`
On Unix and Windows, return the argument with an initial component of `~` or `~user` replaced by that *user*'s home directory.

On Unix, an initial `~` is replaced by the environment variable `HOME` if it is set; otherwise the current user's home directory is looked up in the password directory through the built-in module *pwd*. An initial `~user` is looked up directly in the password directory.

On Windows, `HOME` and `USERPROFILE` will be used if set, otherwise a combination of `HOMEPATH` and `HOMEDRIVE` will be used. An initial `~user` is handled by stripping the last directory component from the created user path derived above.

If the expansion fails or if the path does not begin with a tilde, the path is returned unchanged.

Changed in version 3.6: Accepts a *path-like object*.

`os.path.expandvars(path)`
Return the argument with environment variables expanded. Substrings of the form `$name` or `${name}` are replaced by the value of environment variable *name*. Malformed variable names and references to non-existing variables are left unchanged.

On Windows, `%name%` expansions are supported in addition to `$name` and `${name}`.

Changed in version 3.6: Accepts a *path-like object*.

`os.path.getatime(path)`
Return the time of last access of *path*. The return value is a number giving the number of seconds since the epoch (see the `time` module). Raise `OSError` if the file does not exist or is inaccessible.

If `os.stat_float_times()` returns `True`, the result is a floating point number.

`os.path.getmtime(path)`
Return the time of last modification of *path*. The return value is a number giving the number of seconds since the epoch (see the `time` module). Raise `OSError` if the file does not exist or is inaccessible.

If `os.stat_float_times()` returns `True`, the result is a floating point number.

Changed in version 3.6: Accepts a *path-like object*.

`os.path.getctime(path)`
Return the system's ctime which, on some systems (like Unix) is the time of the last metadata change, and, on others (like Windows), is the creation time for *path*. The return value is a number giving the number of seconds since the epoch (see the `time` module). Raise `OSError` if the file does not exist or is inaccessible.

Changed in version 3.6: Accepts a *path-like object*.

`os.path.getsize(path)`
Return the size, in bytes, of *path*. Raise `OSError` if the file does not exist or is inaccessible.

Changed in version 3.6: Accepts a *path-like object*.

`os.path.isabs(path)`
Return `True` if *path* is an absolute pathname. On Unix, that means it begins with a slash, on Windows that it begins with a (back)slash after chopping off a potential drive letter.

Changed in version 3.6: Accepts a *path-like object*.

`os.path.isfile(path)`
Return `True` if *path* is an `existing` regular file. This follows symbolic links, so both `islink()` and `isfile()` can be true for the same path.

Changed in version 3.6: Accepts a *path-like object*.

`os.path.isdir(path)`
Return `True` if *path* is an `existing` directory. This follows symbolic links, so both `islink()` and `isdir()` can be true for the same path.

Changed in version 3.6: Accepts a *path-like object*.

`os.path.islink(path)`
Return `True` if *path* refers to an `existing` directory entry that is a symbolic link. Always `False` if symbolic links are not supported by the Python runtime.

Changed in version 3.6: Accepts a *path-like object*.

`os.path.ismount(path)`
Return `True` if pathname *path* is a *mount point*: a point in a file system where a different file system has been mounted. On POSIX, the function checks whether *path*'s parent, `path/..`, is on a different device than *path*, or whether `path/..` and *path* point to the same i-node on the same device — this

should detect mount points for all Unix and POSIX variants. On Windows, a drive letter root and a share UNC are always mount points, and for any other path `GetVolumePathName` is called to see if it is different from the input path.

New in version 3.4: Support for detecting non-root mount points on Windows.

Changed in version 3.6: Accepts a *path-like object*.

`os.path.join(path, *paths)`
Join one or more path components intelligently. The return value is the concatenation of *path* and any members of **paths* with exactly one directory separator (`os.sep`) following each non-empty part except the last, meaning that the result will only end in a separator if the last part is empty. If a component is an absolute path, all previous components are thrown away and joining continues from the absolute path component.

On Windows, the drive letter is not reset when an absolute path component (e.g., `r'\foo'`) is encountered. If a component contains a drive letter, all previous components are thrown away and the drive letter is reset. Note that since there is a current directory for each drive, `os.path.join("c:", "foo")` represents a path relative to the current directory on drive `C:` (`c:foo`), not `c:\foo`.

Changed in version 3.6: Accepts a *path-like object* for *path* and *paths*.

`os.path.normcase(path)`
Normalize the case of a pathname. On Unix and Mac OS X, this returns the path unchanged; on case-insensitive filesystems, it converts the path to lowercase. On Windows, it also converts forward slashes to backward slashes. Raise a TypeError if the type of *path* is not `str` or `bytes` (directly or indirectly through the `os.PathLike` interface).

Changed in version 3.6: Accepts a *path-like object*.

`os.path.normpath(path)`
Normalize a pathname by collapsing redundant separators and up-level references so that `A//B`, `A/B/`, `A/./B` and `A/foo/../B` all become `A/B`. This string manipulation may change the meaning of a path that contains symbolic links. On Windows, it converts forward slashes to backward slashes. To normalize case, use `normcase()`.

Changed in version 3.6: Accepts a *path-like object*.

`os.path.realpath(path)`
Return the canonical path of the specified filename, eliminating any symbolic links encountered in the path (if they are supported by the operating system).

Changed in version 3.6: Accepts a *path-like object*.

`os.path.relpath(path, start=os.curdir)`
Return a relative filepath to *path* either from the current directory or from an optional *start* directory. This is a path computation: the filesystem is not accessed to confirm the existence or nature of *path* or *start*.

start defaults to `os.curdir`.

Availability: Unix, Windows.

Changed in version 3.6: Accepts a *path-like object*.

`os.path.samefile(path1, path2)`
Return `True` if both pathname arguments refer to the same file or directory. This is determined by the device number and i-node number and raises an exception if an `os.stat()` call on either pathname fails.

Availability: Unix, Windows.

Changed in version 3.2: Added Windows support.

Changed in version 3.4: Windows now uses the same implementation as all other platforms.

Changed in version 3.6: Accepts a *path-like object*.

`os.path.sameopenfile(fp1, fp2)`

Return `True` if the file descriptors *fp1* and *fp2* refer to the same file.

Availability: Unix, Windows.

Changed in version 3.2: Added Windows support.

Changed in version 3.6: Accepts a *path-like object*.

`os.path.samestat(stat1, stat2)`

Return `True` if the stat tuples *stat1* and *stat2* refer to the same file. These structures may have been returned by `os.fstat()`, `os.lstat()`, or `os.stat()`. This function implements the underlying comparison used by `samefile()` and `sameopenfile()`.

Availability: Unix, Windows.

Changed in version 3.4: Added Windows support.

Changed in version 3.6: Accepts a *path-like object*.

`os.path.split(path)`

Split the pathname *path* into a pair, `(head, tail)` where *tail* is the last pathname component and *head* is everything leading up to that. The *tail* part will never contain a slash; if *path* ends in a slash, *tail* will be empty. If there is no slash in *path*, *head* will be empty. If *path* is empty, both *head* and *tail* are empty. Trailing slashes are stripped from *head* unless it is the root (one or more slashes only). In all cases, `join(head, tail)` returns a path to the same location as *path* (but the strings may differ). Also see the functions `dirname()` and `basename()`.

Changed in version 3.6: Accepts a *path-like object*.

`os.path.splitdrive(path)`

Split the pathname *path* into a pair `(drive, tail)` where *drive* is either a mount point or the empty string. On systems which do not use drive specifications, *drive* will always be the empty string. In all cases, `drive + tail` will be the same as *path*.

On Windows, splits a pathname into drive/UNC sharepoint and relative path.

If the path contains a drive letter, drive will contain everything up to and including the colon. e.g. `splitdrive("c:/dir")` returns `("c:", "/dir")`

If the path contains a UNC path, drive will contain the host name and share, up to but not including the fourth separator. e.g. `splitdrive("//host/computer/dir")` returns `("//host/computer", "/dir")`

Changed in version 3.6: Accepts a *path-like object*.

`os.path.splitext(path)`

Split the pathname *path* into a pair `(root, ext)` such that `root + ext == path`, and *ext* is empty or begins with a period and contains at most one period. Leading periods on the basename are ignored; `splitext('.cshrc')` returns `('.cshrc', '')`.

Changed in version 3.6: Accepts a *path-like object*.

`os.path.splitunc(path)`

Deprecated since version 3.1: Use *splitdrive* instead.

Split the pathname *path* into a pair `(unc, rest)` so that *unc* is the UNC mount point (such as `r'\\host\mount'`), if present, and *rest* the rest of the path (such as `r'\path\file.ext'`). For paths containing drive letters, *unc* will always be the empty string.

Availability: Windows.

`os.path.supports_unicode_filenames`
True if arbitrary Unicode strings can be used as file names (within limitations imposed by the file system).

11.3 fileinput — Iterate over lines from multiple input streams

Source code: Lib/fileinput.py

This module implements a helper class and functions to quickly write a loop over standard input or a list of files. If you just want to read or write one file see *open()*.

The typical use is:

```
import fileinput
for line in fileinput.input():
    process(line)
```

This iterates over the lines of all files listed in `sys.argv[1:]`, defaulting to `sys.stdin` if the list is empty. If a filename is `'-'`, it is also replaced by `sys.stdin`. To specify an alternative list of filenames, pass it as the first argument to *input()*. A single file name is also allowed.

All files are opened in text mode by default, but you can override this by specifying the *mode* parameter in the call to *input()* or *FileInput*. If an I/O error occurs during opening or reading a file, *OSError* is raised.

Changed in version 3.3: *IOError* used to be raised; it is now an alias of *OSError*.

If `sys.stdin` is used more than once, the second and further use will return no lines, except perhaps for interactive use, or if it has been explicitly reset (e.g. using `sys.stdin.seek(0)`).

Empty files are opened and immediately closed; the only time their presence in the list of filenames is noticeable at all is when the last file opened is empty.

Lines are returned with any newlines intact, which means that the last line in a file may not have one.

You can control how files are opened by providing an opening hook via the *openhook* parameter to *fileinput.input()* or *FileInput()*. The hook must be a function that takes two arguments, *filename* and *mode*, and returns an accordingly opened file-like object. Two useful hooks are already provided by this module.

The following function is the primary interface of this module:

`fileinput.input`(*files=None*, *inplace=False*, *backup=''*, *bufsize=0*, *mode='r'*, *openhook=None*)
Create an instance of the *FileInput* class. The instance will be used as global state for the functions of this module, and is also returned to use during iteration. The parameters to this function will be passed along to the constructor of the *FileInput* class.

The *FileInput* instance can be used as a context manager in the `with` statement. In this example, *input* is closed after the `with` statement is exited, even if an exception occurs:

```
with fileinput.input(files=('spam.txt', 'eggs.txt')) as f:
    for line in f:
        process(line)
```

Changed in version 3.2: Can be used as a context manager.

Deprecated since version 3.6, will be removed in version 3.8: The *bufsize* parameter.

The following functions use the global state created by *fileinput.input()*; if there is no active state, *RuntimeError* is raised.

fileinput.filename()
Return the name of the file currently being read. Before the first line has been read, returns `None`.

fileinput.fileno()
Return the integer "file descriptor" for the current file. When no file is opened (before the first line and between files), returns `-1`.

fileinput.lineno()
Return the cumulative line number of the line that has just been read. Before the first line has been read, returns `0`. After the last line of the last file has been read, returns the line number of that line.

fileinput.filelineno()
Return the line number in the current file. Before the first line has been read, returns `0`. After the last line of the last file has been read, returns the line number of that line within the file.

fileinput.isfirstline()
Returns true if the line just read is the first line of its file, otherwise returns false.

fileinput.isstdin()
Returns true if the last line was read from `sys.stdin`, otherwise returns false.

fileinput.nextfile()
Close the current file so that the next iteration will read the first line from the next file (if any); lines not read from the file will not count towards the cumulative line count. The filename is not changed until after the first line of the next file has been read. Before the first line has been read, this function has no effect; it cannot be used to skip the first file. After the last line of the last file has been read, this function has no effect.

fileinput.close()
Close the sequence.

The class which implements the sequence behavior provided by the module is available for subclassing as well:

class fileinput.FileInput(*files=None, inplace=False, backup='', bufsize=0, mode='r', openhook=None*)
Class `FileInput` is the implementation; its methods `filename()`, `fileno()`, `lineno()`, `filelineno()`, `isfirstline()`, `isstdin()`, `nextfile()` and `close()` correspond to the functions of the same name in the module. In addition it has a `readline()` method which returns the next input line, and a `__getitem__()` method which implements the sequence behavior. The sequence must be accessed in strictly sequential order; random access and `readline()` cannot be mixed.

With *mode* you can specify which file mode will be passed to `open()`. It must be one of `'r'`, `'rU'`, `'U'` and `'rb'`.

The *openhook*, when given, must be a function that takes two arguments, *filename* and *mode*, and returns an accordingly opened file-like object. You cannot use *inplace* and *openhook* together.

A `FileInput` instance can be used as a context manager in the `with` statement. In this example, *input* is closed after the `with` statement is exited, even if an exception occurs:

```
with FileInput(files=('spam.txt', 'eggs.txt')) as input:
    process(input)
```

Changed in version 3.2: Can be used as a context manager.

Deprecated since version 3.4: The `'rU'` and `'U'` modes.

Deprecated since version 3.6, will be removed in version 3.8: The *bufsize* parameter.

Optional in-place filtering: if the keyword argument `inplace=True` is passed to `fileinput.input()` or to the `FileInput` constructor, the file is moved to a backup file and standard output is directed to the input file (if a file of the same name as the backup file already exists, it will be replaced silently). This makes it possible to write a filter that rewrites its input file in place. If the *backup* parameter is given (typically as `backup='.<some extension>'`), it specifies the extension for the backup file, and the backup file remains around; by default, the extension is `'.bak'` and it is deleted when the output file is closed. In-place filtering is disabled when standard input is read.

The two following opening hooks are provided by this module:

`fileinput.hook_compressed`(*filename*, *mode*)
Transparently opens files compressed with gzip and bzip2 (recognized by the extensions `'.gz'` and `'.bz2'`) using the *gzip* and *bz2* modules. If the filename extension is not `'.gz'` or `'.bz2'`, the file is opened normally (ie, using *open()* without any decompression).

Usage example: `fi = fileinput.FileInput(openhook=fileinput.hook_compressed)`

`fileinput.hook_encoded`(*encoding*, *errors=None*)
Returns a hook which opens each file with *open()*, using the given *encoding* and *errors* to read the file.

Usage example: `fi = fileinput.FileInput(openhook=fileinput.hook_encoded("utf-8", "surrogateescape"))`

Changed in version 3.6: Added the optional *errors* parameter.

11.4 stat — Interpreting stat() results

Source code: Lib/stat.py

The *stat* module defines constants and functions for interpreting the results of *os.stat()*, *os.fstat()* and *os.lstat()* (if they exist). For complete details about the `stat()`, `fstat()` and `lstat()` calls, consult the documentation for your system.

Changed in version 3.4: The stat module is backed by a C implementation.

The *stat* module defines the following functions to test for specific file types:

`stat.S_ISDIR`(*mode*)
Return non-zero if the mode is from a directory.

`stat.S_ISCHR`(*mode*)
Return non-zero if the mode is from a character special device file.

`stat.S_ISBLK`(*mode*)
Return non-zero if the mode is from a block special device file.

`stat.S_ISREG`(*mode*)
Return non-zero if the mode is from a regular file.

`stat.S_ISFIFO`(*mode*)
Return non-zero if the mode is from a FIFO (named pipe).

`stat.S_ISLNK`(*mode*)
Return non-zero if the mode is from a symbolic link.

`stat.S_ISSOCK`(*mode*)
Return non-zero if the mode is from a socket.

`stat.S_ISDOOR`(*mode*)
Return non-zero if the mode is from a door.

New in version 3.4.

stat.**S_ISPORT**(*mode*)
Return non-zero if the mode is from an event port.

New in version 3.4.

stat.**S_ISWHT**(*mode*)
Return non-zero if the mode is from a whiteout.

New in version 3.4.

Two additional functions are defined for more general manipulation of the file's mode:

stat.**S_IMODE**(*mode*)
Return the portion of the file's mode that can be set by *os.chmod()*—that is, the file's permission bits, plus the sticky bit, set-group-id, and set-user-id bits (on systems that support them).

stat.**S_IFMT**(*mode*)
Return the portion of the file's mode that describes the file type (used by the S_IS*() functions above).

Normally, you would use the os.path.is*() functions for testing the type of a file; the functions here are useful when you are doing multiple tests of the same file and wish to avoid the overhead of the stat() system call for each test. These are also useful when checking for information about a file that isn't handled by *os.path*, like the tests for block and character devices.

Example:

```
import os, sys
from stat import *

def walktree(top, callback):
    '''recursively descend the directory tree rooted at top,
       calling the callback function for each regular file'''

    for f in os.listdir(top):
        pathname = os.path.join(top, f)
        mode = os.stat(pathname).st_mode
        if S_ISDIR(mode):
            # It's a directory, recurse into it
            walktree(pathname, callback)
        elif S_ISREG(mode):
            # It's a file, call the callback function
            callback(pathname)
        else:
            # Unknown file type, print a message
            print('Skipping %s' % pathname)

def visitfile(file):
    print('visiting', file)

if __name__ == '__main__':
    walktree(sys.argv[1], visitfile)
```

An additional utility function is provided to convert a file's mode in a human readable string:

stat.**filemode**(*mode*)
Convert a file's mode to a string of the form '-rwxrwxrwx'.

New in version 3.3.

Changed in version 3.4: The function supports *S_IFDOOR*, *S_IFPORT* and *S_IFWHT*.

All the variables below are simply symbolic indexes into the 10-tuple returned by *os.stat()*, *os.fstat()* or *os.lstat()*.

stat.**ST_MODE**
Inode protection mode.

stat.**ST_INO**
Inode number.

stat.**ST_DEV**
Device inode resides on.

stat.**ST_NLINK**
Number of links to the inode.

stat.**ST_UID**
User id of the owner.

stat.**ST_GID**
Group id of the owner.

stat.**ST_SIZE**
Size in bytes of a plain file; amount of data waiting on some special files.

stat.**ST_ATIME**
Time of last access.

stat.**ST_MTIME**
Time of last modification.

stat.**ST_CTIME**
The "ctime" as reported by the operating system. On some systems (like Unix) is the time of the last metadata change, and, on others (like Windows), is the creation time (see platform documentation for details).

The interpretation of "file size" changes according to the file type. For plain files this is the size of the file in bytes. For FIFOs and sockets under most flavors of Unix (including Linux in particular), the "size" is the number of bytes waiting to be read at the time of the call to *os.stat()*, *os.fstat()*, or *os.lstat()*; this can sometimes be useful, especially for polling one of these special files after a non-blocking open. The meaning of the size field for other character and block devices varies more, depending on the implementation of the underlying system call.

The variables below define the flags used in the *ST_MODE* field.

Use of the functions above is more portable than use of the first set of flags:

stat.**S_IFSOCK**
Socket.

stat.**S_IFLNK**
Symbolic link.

stat.**S_IFREG**
Regular file.

stat.**S_IFBLK**
Block device.

stat.**S_IFDIR**
Directory.

stat.**S_IFCHR**
Character device.

stat.**S_IFIFO**
FIFO.

`stat.S_IFDOOR`
Door.

New in version 3.4.

`stat.S_IFPORT`
Event port.

New in version 3.4.

`stat.S_IFWHT`
Whiteout.

New in version 3.4.

Note: *S_IFDOOR*, *S_IFPORT* or *S_IFWHT* are defined as 0 when the platform does not have support for the file types.

The following flags can also be used in the *mode* argument of *os.chmod()*:

`stat.S_ISUID`
Set UID bit.

`stat.S_ISGID`
Set-group-ID bit. This bit has several special uses. For a directory it indicates that BSD semantics is to be used for that directory: files created there inherit their group ID from the directory, not from the effective group ID of the creating process, and directories created there will also get the *S_ISGID* bit set. For a file that does not have the group execution bit (*S_IXGRP*) set, the set-group-ID bit indicates mandatory file/record locking (see also *S_ENFMT*).

`stat.S_ISVTX`
Sticky bit. When this bit is set on a directory it means that a file in that directory can be renamed or deleted only by the owner of the file, by the owner of the directory, or by a privileged process.

`stat.S_IRWXU`
Mask for file owner permissions.

`stat.S_IRUSR`
Owner has read permission.

`stat.S_IWUSR`
Owner has write permission.

`stat.S_IXUSR`
Owner has execute permission.

`stat.S_IRWXG`
Mask for group permissions.

`stat.S_IRGRP`
Group has read permission.

`stat.S_IWGRP`
Group has write permission.

`stat.S_IXGRP`
Group has execute permission.

`stat.S_IRWXO`
Mask for permissions for others (not in group).

`stat.S_IROTH`
Others have read permission.

stat.**S_IWOTH**
Others have write permission.

stat.**S_IXOTH**
Others have execute permission.

stat.**S_ENFMT**
System V file locking enforcement. This flag is shared with *S_ISGID*: file/record locking is enforced on files that do not have the group execution bit (*S_IXGRP*) set.

stat.**S_IREAD**
Unix V7 synonym for *S_IRUSR*.

stat.**S_IWRITE**
Unix V7 synonym for *S_IWUSR*.

stat.**S_IEXEC**
Unix V7 synonym for *S_IXUSR*.

The following flags can be used in the *flags* argument of *os.chflags()*:

stat.**UF_NODUMP**
Do not dump the file.

stat.**UF_IMMUTABLE**
The file may not be changed.

stat.**UF_APPEND**
The file may only be appended to.

stat.**UF_OPAQUE**
The directory is opaque when viewed through a union stack.

stat.**UF_NOUNLINK**
The file may not be renamed or deleted.

stat.**UF_COMPRESSED**
The file is stored compressed (Mac OS X 10.6+).

stat.**UF_HIDDEN**
The file should not be displayed in a GUI (Mac OS X 10.5+).

stat.**SF_ARCHIVED**
The file may be archived.

stat.**SF_IMMUTABLE**
The file may not be changed.

stat.**SF_APPEND**
The file may only be appended to.

stat.**SF_NOUNLINK**
The file may not be renamed or deleted.

stat.**SF_SNAPSHOT**
The file is a snapshot file.

See the *BSD or Mac OS systems man page **chflags(2)** for more information.

On Windows, the following file attribute constants are available for use when testing bits in the `st_file_attributes` member returned by *os.stat()*. See the Windows API documentation for more detail on the meaning of these constants.

stat.**FILE_ATTRIBUTE_ARCHIVE**
stat.**FILE_ATTRIBUTE_COMPRESSED**
stat.**FILE_ATTRIBUTE_DEVICE**

`stat.FILE_ATTRIBUTE_DIRECTORY`
`stat.FILE_ATTRIBUTE_ENCRYPTED`
`stat.FILE_ATTRIBUTE_HIDDEN`
`stat.FILE_ATTRIBUTE_INTEGRITY_STREAM`
`stat.FILE_ATTRIBUTE_NORMAL`
`stat.FILE_ATTRIBUTE_NOT_CONTENT_INDEXED`
`stat.FILE_ATTRIBUTE_NO_SCRUB_DATA`
`stat.FILE_ATTRIBUTE_OFFLINE`
`stat.FILE_ATTRIBUTE_READONLY`
`stat.FILE_ATTRIBUTE_REPARSE_POINT`
`stat.FILE_ATTRIBUTE_SPARSE_FILE`
`stat.FILE_ATTRIBUTE_SYSTEM`
`stat.FILE_ATTRIBUTE_TEMPORARY`
`stat.FILE_ATTRIBUTE_VIRTUAL`

New in version 3.5.

11.5 `filecmp` — File and Directory Comparisons

Source code: Lib/filecmp.py

The `filecmp` module defines functions to compare files and directories, with various optional time/correctness trade-offs. For comparing files, see also the `difflib` module.

The `filecmp` module defines the following functions:

`filecmp.cmp`(*f1*, *f2*, *shallow=True*)

Compare the files named *f1* and *f2*, returning `True` if they seem equal, `False` otherwise.

If *shallow* is true, files with identical `os.stat()` signatures are taken to be equal. Otherwise, the contents of the files are compared.

Note that no external programs are called from this function, giving it portability and efficiency.

This function uses a cache for past comparisons and the results, with cache entries invalidated if the `os.stat()` information for the file changes. The entire cache may be cleared using `clear_cache()`.

`filecmp.cmpfiles`(*dir1*, *dir2*, *common*, *shallow=True*)

Compare the files in the two directories *dir1* and *dir2* whose names are given by *common*.

Returns three lists of file names: *match*, *mismatch*, *errors*. *match* contains the list of files that match, *mismatch* contains the names of those that don't, and *errors* lists the names of files which could not be compared. Files are listed in *errors* if they don't exist in one of the directories, the user lacks permission to read them or if the comparison could not be done for some other reason.

The *shallow* parameter has the same meaning and default value as for `filecmp.cmp()`.

For example, `cmpfiles('a', 'b', ['c', 'd/e'])` will compare `a/c` with `b/c` and `a/d/e` with `b/d/e`. `'c'` and `'d/e'` will each be in one of the three returned lists.

`filecmp.clear_cache`()

Clear the filecmp cache. This may be useful if a file is compared so quickly after it is modified that it is within the mtime resolution of the underlying filesystem.

New in version 3.4.

11.5.1 The dircmp class

class filecmp.dircmp(*a*, *b*, *ignore=None*, *hide=None*)

Construct a new directory comparison object, to compare the directories *a* and *b*. *ignore* is a list of names to ignore, and defaults to *filecmp.DEFAULT_IGNORES*. *hide* is a list of names to hide, and defaults to `[os.curdir, os.pardir]`.

The *dircmp* class compares files by doing *shallow* comparisons as described for *filecmp.cmp()*.

The *dircmp* class provides the following methods:

report()

Print (to *sys.stdout*) a comparison between *a* and *b*.

report_partial_closure()

Print a comparison between *a* and *b* and common immediate subdirectories.

report_full_closure()

Print a comparison between *a* and *b* and common subdirectories (recursively).

The *dircmp* class offers a number of interesting attributes that may be used to get various bits of information about the directory trees being compared.

Note that via `__getattr__()` hooks, all attributes are computed lazily, so there is no speed penalty if only those attributes which are lightweight to compute are used.

left

The directory *a*.

right

The directory *b*.

left_list

Files and subdirectories in *a*, filtered by *hide* and *ignore*.

right_list

Files and subdirectories in *b*, filtered by *hide* and *ignore*.

common

Files and subdirectories in both *a* and *b*.

left_only

Files and subdirectories only in *a*.

right_only

Files and subdirectories only in *b*.

common_dirs

Subdirectories in both *a* and *b*.

common_files

Files in both *a* and *b*.

common_funny

Names in both *a* and *b*, such that the type differs between the directories, or names for which *os.stat()* reports an error.

same_files

Files which are identical in both *a* and *b*, using the class's file comparison operator.

diff_files

Files which are in both *a* and *b*, whose contents differ according to the class's file comparison operator.

funny_files

Files which are in both *a* and *b*, but could not be compared.

subdirs
A dictionary mapping names in *common_dirs* to *dircmp* objects.

filecmp.DEFAULT_IGNORES
New in version 3.4.

List of directories ignored by *dircmp* by default.

Here is a simplified example of using the subdirs attribute to search recursively through two directories to show common different files:

```
>>> from filecmp import dircmp
>>> def print_diff_files(dcmp):
...     for name in dcmp.diff_files:
...         print("diff_file %s found in %s and %s" % (name, dcmp.left,
...               dcmp.right))
...     for sub_dcmp in dcmp.subdirs.values():
...         print_diff_files(sub_dcmp)
...
>>> dcmp = dircmp('dir1', 'dir2')
>>> print_diff_files(dcmp)
```

11.6 tempfile — Generate temporary files and directories

Source code: Lib/tempfile.py

This module creates temporary files and directories. It works on all supported platforms. *TemporaryFile*, *NamedTemporaryFile*, *TemporaryDirectory*, and *SpooledTemporaryFile* are high-level interfaces which provide automatic cleanup and can be used as context managers. *mkstemp()* and *mkdtemp()* are lower-level functions which require manual cleanup.

All the user-callable functions and constructors take additional arguments which allow direct control over the location and name of temporary files and directories. Files names used by this module include a string of random characters which allows those files to be securely created in shared temporary directories. To maintain backward compatibility, the argument order is somewhat odd; it is recommended to use keyword arguments for clarity.

The module defines the following user-callable items:

tempfile.TemporaryFile(*mode='w+b', buffering=None, encoding=None, newline=None, suffix=None, prefix=None, dir=None*)
Return a *file-like object* that can be used as a temporary storage area. The file is created securely, using the same rules as *mkstemp()*. It will be destroyed as soon as it is closed (including an implicit close when the object is garbage collected). Under Unix, the directory entry for the file is either not created at all or is removed immediately after the file is created. Other platforms do not support this; your code should not rely on a temporary file created using this function having or not having a visible name in the file system.

The resulting object can be used as a context manager (see *Examples*). On completion of the context or destruction of the file object the temporary file will be removed from the filesystem.

The *mode* parameter defaults to 'w+b' so that the file created can be read and written without being closed. Binary mode is used so that it behaves consistently on all platforms without regard for the data that is stored. *buffering*, *encoding* and *newline* are interpreted as for *open()*.

The *dir*, *prefix* and *suffix* parameters have the same meaning and defaults as with *mkstemp()*.

The returned object is a true file object on POSIX platforms. On other platforms, it is a file-like object whose `file` attribute is the underlying true file object.

The *os.O_TMPFILE* flag is used if it is available and works (Linux-specific, requires Linux kernel 3.11 or later).

Changed in version 3.5: The *os.O_TMPFILE* flag is now used if available.

`tempfile.NamedTemporaryFile`(*mode='w+b', buffering=None, encoding=None, newline=None, suffix=None, prefix=None, dir=None, delete=True*)

This function operates exactly as *TemporaryFile()* does, except that the file is guaranteed to have a visible name in the file system (on Unix, the directory entry is not unlinked). That name can be retrieved from the `name` attribute of the returned file-like object. Whether the name can be used to open the file a second time, while the named temporary file is still open, varies across platforms (it can be so used on Unix; it cannot on Windows NT or later). If *delete* is true (the default), the file is deleted as soon as it is closed. The returned object is always a file-like object whose `file` attribute is the underlying true file object. This file-like object can be used in a `with` statement, just like a normal file.

`tempfile.SpooledTemporaryFile`(*max_size=0, mode='w+b', buffering=None, encoding=None, newline=None, suffix=None, prefix=None, dir=None*)

This function operates exactly as *TemporaryFile()* does, except that data is spooled in memory until the file size exceeds *max_size*, or until the file's `fileno()` method is called, at which point the contents are written to disk and operation proceeds as with *TemporaryFile()*.

The resulting file has one additional method, `rollover()`, which causes the file to roll over to an on-disk file regardless of its size.

The returned object is a file-like object whose `_file` attribute is either an *io.BytesIO* or *io.StringIO* object (depending on whether binary or text *mode* was specified) or a true file object, depending on whether `rollover()` has been called. This file-like object can be used in a `with` statement, just like a normal file.

Changed in version 3.3: the truncate method now accepts a `size` argument.

`tempfile.TemporaryDirectory`(*suffix=None, prefix=None, dir=None*)

This function securely creates a temporary directory using the same rules as *mkdtemp()*. The resulting object can be used as a context manager (see *Examples*). On completion of the context or destruction of the temporary directory object the newly created temporary directory and all its contents are removed from the filesystem.

The directory name can be retrieved from the `name` attribute of the returned object. When the returned object is used as a context manager, the `name` will be assigned to the target of the `as` clause in the `with` statement, if there is one.

The directory can be explicitly cleaned up by calling the `cleanup()` method.

New in version 3.2.

`tempfile.mkstemp`(*suffix=None, prefix=None, dir=None, text=False*)

Creates a temporary file in the most secure manner possible. There are no race conditions in the file's creation, assuming that the platform properly implements the *os.O_EXCL* flag for *os.open()*. The file is readable and writable only by the creating user ID. If the platform uses permission bits to indicate whether a file is executable, the file is executable by no one. The file descriptor is not inherited by child processes.

Unlike *TemporaryFile()*, the user of *mkstemp()* is responsible for deleting the temporary file when done with it.

If *suffix* is not `None`, the file name will end with that suffix, otherwise there will be no suffix. *mkstemp()* does not put a dot between the file name and the suffix; if you need one, put it at the beginning of *suffix*.

If *prefix* is not `None`, the file name will begin with that prefix; otherwise, a default prefix is used. The default is the return value of *gettempprefix()* or *gettempprefixb()*, as appropriate.

If *dir* is not `None`, the file will be created in that directory; otherwise, a default directory is used. The default directory is chosen from a platform-dependent list, but the user of the application can control the directory location by setting the *TMPDIR*, *TEMP* or *TMP* environment variables. There is thus no guarantee that the generated filename will have any nice properties, such as not requiring quoting when passed to external commands via `os.popen()`.

If any of *suffix*, *prefix*, and *dir* are not `None`, they must be the same type. If they are bytes, the returned name will be bytes instead of str. If you want to force a bytes return value with otherwise default behavior, pass `suffix=b''`.

If *text* is specified, it indicates whether to open the file in binary mode (the default) or text mode. On some platforms, this makes no difference.

mkstemp() returns a tuple containing an OS-level handle to an open file (as would be returned by *os.open()*) and the absolute pathname of that file, in that order.

Changed in version 3.5: *suffix*, *prefix*, and *dir* may now be supplied in bytes in order to obtain a bytes return value. Prior to this, only str was allowed. *suffix* and *prefix* now accept and default to `None` to cause an appropriate default value to be used.

`tempfile.mkdtemp(`*suffix=None, prefix=None, dir=None*`)`

Creates a temporary directory in the most secure manner possible. There are no race conditions in the directory's creation. The directory is readable, writable, and searchable only by the creating user ID.

The user of *mkdtemp()* is responsible for deleting the temporary directory and its contents when done with it.

The *prefix*, *suffix*, and *dir* arguments are the same as for *mkstemp()*.

mkdtemp() returns the absolute pathname of the new directory.

Changed in version 3.5: *suffix*, *prefix*, and *dir* may now be supplied in bytes in order to obtain a bytes return value. Prior to this, only str was allowed. *suffix* and *prefix* now accept and default to `None` to cause an appropriate default value to be used.

`tempfile.gettempdir()`

Return the name of the directory used for temporary files. This defines the default value for the *dir* argument to all functions in this module.

Python searches a standard list of directories to find one which the calling user can create files in. The list is:

1. The directory named by the `TMPDIR` environment variable.
2. The directory named by the `TEMP` environment variable.
3. The directory named by the `TMP` environment variable.
4. A platform-specific location:
   - On Windows, the directories `C:\TEMP`, `C:\TMP`, `\TEMP`, and `\TMP`, in that order.
   - On all other platforms, the directories `/tmp`, `/var/tmp`, and `/usr/tmp`, in that order.
5. As a last resort, the current working directory.

The result of this search is cached, see the description of *tempdir* below.

`tempfile.gettempdirb()`

Same as *gettempdir()* but the return value is in bytes.

New in version 3.5.

`tempfile.gettempprefix()`
Return the filename prefix used to create temporary files. This does not contain the directory component.

`tempfile.gettempprefixb()`
Same as *gettempprefix()* but the return value is in bytes.

New in version 3.5.

The module uses a global variable to store the name of the directory used for temporary files returned by *gettempdir()*. It can be set directly to override the selection process, but this is discouraged. All functions in this module take a *dir* argument which can be used to specify the directory and this is the recommended approach.

`tempfile.tempdir`
When set to a value other than `None`, this variable defines the default value for the *dir* argument to the functions defined in this module.

If `tempdir` is unset or `None` at any call to any of the above functions except *gettempprefix()* it is initialized following the algorithm described in *gettempdir()*.

11.6.1 Examples

Here are some examples of typical usage of the *tempfile* module:

```
>>> import tempfile

# create a temporary file and write some data to it
>>> fp = tempfile.TemporaryFile()
>>> fp.write(b'Hello world!')
# read data from file
>>> fp.seek(0)
>>> fp.read()
b'Hello world!'
# close the file, it will be removed
>>> fp.close()

# create a temporary file using a context manager
>>> with tempfile.TemporaryFile() as fp:
...     fp.write(b'Hello world!')
...     fp.seek(0)
...     fp.read()
b'Hello world!'
>>>
# file is now closed and removed

# create a temporary directory using the context manager
>>> with tempfile.TemporaryDirectory() as tmpdirname:
...     print('created temporary directory', tmpdirname)
>>>
# directory and contents have been removed
```

11.6.2 Deprecated functions and variables

A historical way to create temporary files was to first generate a file name with the *mktemp()* function and then create a file using this name. Unfortunately this is not secure, because a different process may create a file with this name in the time between the call to *mktemp()* and the subsequent attempt to create the file by the first process. The solution is to combine the two steps and create the file immediately. This approach is used by *mkstemp()* and the other functions described above.

`tempfile.mktemp(`*suffix='', prefix='tmp', dir=None*`)`
Deprecated since version 2.3: Use *mkstemp()* instead.

Return an absolute pathname of a file that did not exist at the time the call is made. The *prefix*, *suffix*, and *dir* arguments are similar to those of *mkstemp()*, except that bytes file names, `suffix=None` and `prefix=None` are not supported.

Warning: Use of this function may introduce a security hole in your program. By the time you get around to doing anything with the file name it returns, someone else may have beaten you to the punch. *mktemp()* usage can be replaced easily with *NamedTemporaryFile()*, passing it the `delete=False` parameter:

```
>>> f = NamedTemporaryFile(delete=False)
>>> f.name
'/tmp/tmptjujjt'
>>> f.write(b"Hello World!\n")
13
>>> f.close()
>>> os.unlink(f.name)
>>> os.path.exists(f.name)
False
```

11.7 glob — Unix style pathname pattern expansion

Source code: Lib/glob.py

The *glob* module finds all the pathnames matching a specified pattern according to the rules used by the Unix shell, although results are returned in arbitrary order. No tilde expansion is done, but `*`, `?`, and character ranges expressed with `[]` will be correctly matched. This is done by using the *os.scandir()* and *fnmatch.fnmatch()* functions in concert, and not by actually invoking a subshell. Note that unlike *fnmatch.fnmatch()*, *glob* treats filenames beginning with a dot (`.`) as special cases. (For tilde and shell variable expansion, use *os.path.expanduser()* and *os.path.expandvars()*.)

For a literal match, wrap the meta-characters in brackets. For example, `'[?]'` matches the character `'?'`.

See also:

The *pathlib* module offers high-level path objects.

`glob.glob(`*pathname, *, recursive=False*`)`
Return a possibly-empty list of path names that match *pathname*, which must be a string containing a path specification. *pathname* can be either absolute (like `/usr/src/Python-1.5/Makefile`) or relative (like `../../Tools/*/*.gif`), and can contain shell-style wildcards. Broken symlinks are included in the results (as in the shell).

If *recursive* is true, the pattern "`**`" will match any files and zero or more directories and subdirectories. If the pattern is followed by an `os.sep`, only directories and subdirectories match.

Note: Using the "`**`" pattern in large directory trees may consume an inordinate amount of time.

Changed in version 3.5: Support for recursive globs using "`**`".

glob.**iglob**(*pathname*, *recursive=False*)
Return an *iterator* which yields the same values as `glob()` without actually storing them all simultaneously.

glob.**escape**(*pathname*)
Escape all special characters (`'?'`, `'*'` and `'['`). This is useful if you want to match an arbitrary literal string that may have special characters in it. Special characters in drive/UNC sharepoints are not escaped, e.g. on Windows `escape('//?/c:/Quo vadis?.txt')` returns `'//?/c:/Quo vadis[?].txt'`.

New in version 3.4.

For example, consider a directory containing the following files: `1.gif`, `2.txt`, `card.gif` and a subdirectory `sub` which contains only the file `3.txt`. `glob()` will produce the following results. Notice how any leading components of the path are preserved.

```
>>> import glob
>>> glob.glob('./[0-9].*')
['./1.gif', './2.txt']
>>> glob.glob('*.gif')
['1.gif', 'card.gif']
>>> glob.glob('?.gif')
['1.gif']
>>> glob.glob('**/*.txt', recursive=True)
['2.txt', 'sub/3.txt']
>>> glob.glob('./**/', recursive=True)
['./', './sub/']
```

If the directory contains files starting with `.` they won't be matched by default. For example, consider a directory containing `card.gif` and `.card.gif`:

```
>>> import glob
>>> glob.glob('*.gif')
['card.gif']
>>> glob.glob('.c*')
['.card.gif']
```

See also:

Module `fnmatch` Shell-style filename (not path) expansion

11.8 fnmatch — Unix filename pattern matching

Source code: Lib/fnmatch.py

This module provides support for Unix shell-style wildcards, which are *not* the same as regular expressions (which are documented in the `re` module). The special characters used in shell-style wildcards are:

Pattern	Meaning
*	matches everything
?	matches any single character
[seq]	matches any character in *seq*
[!seq]	matches any character not in *seq*

For a literal match, wrap the meta-characters in brackets. For example, `'[?]'` matches the character `'?'`.

Note that the filename separator ('/' on Unix) is *not* special to this module. See module *glob* for pathname expansion (*glob* uses *fnmatch()* to match pathname segments). Similarly, filenames starting with a period are not special for this module, and are matched by the * and ? patterns.

`fnmatch.fnmatch(filename, pattern)`

Test whether the *filename* string matches the *pattern* string, returning *True* or *False*. Both parameters are case-normalized using *os.path.normcase()*. *fnmatchcase()* can be used to perform a case-sensitive comparison, regardless of whether that's standard for the operating system.

This example will print all file names in the current directory with the extension .txt:

```
import fnmatch
import os

for file in os.listdir('.'):
    if fnmatch.fnmatch(file, '*.txt'):
        print(file)
```

`fnmatch.fnmatchcase(filename, pattern)`

Test whether *filename* matches *pattern*, returning *True* or *False*; the comparison is case-sensitive and does not apply *os.path.normcase()*.

`fnmatch.filter(names, pattern)`

Return the subset of the list of *names* that match *pattern*. It is the same as `[n for n in names if fnmatch(n, pattern)]`, but implemented more efficiently.

`fnmatch.translate(pattern)`

Return the shell-style *pattern* converted to a regular expression for using with *re.match()*.

Example:

```
>>> import fnmatch, re
>>>
>>> regex = fnmatch.translate('*.txt')
>>> regex
'(?s:.*\\.txt)\\Z'
>>> reobj = re.compile(regex)
>>> reobj.match('foobar.txt')
<_sre.SRE_Match object; span=(0, 10), match='foobar.txt'>
```

See also:

Module *glob* Unix shell-style path expansion.

11.9 linecache — Random access to text lines

Source code: Lib/linecache.py

The *linecache* module allows one to get any line from a Python source file, while attempting to optimize internally, using a cache, the common case where many lines are read from a single file. This is used by the *traceback* module to retrieve source lines for inclusion in the formatted traceback.

The *tokenize.open()* function is used to open files. This function uses *tokenize.detect_encoding()* to get the encoding of the file; in the absence of an encoding token, the file encoding defaults to UTF-8.

The *linecache* module defines the following functions:

linecache.**getline**(*filename*, *lineno*, *module_globals=None*)

Get line *lineno* from file named *filename*. This function will never raise an exception — it will return '' on errors (the terminating newline character will be included for lines that are found).

If a file named *filename* is not found, the function will look for it in the module search path, `sys.path`, after first checking for a PEP 302 `__loader__` in *module_globals*, in case the module was imported from a zipfile or other non-filesystem import source.

linecache.**clearcache**()

Clear the cache. Use this function if you no longer need lines from files previously read using *getline()*.

linecache.**checkcache**(*filename=None*)

Check the cache for validity. Use this function if files in the cache may have changed on disk, and you require the updated version. If *filename* is omitted, it will check all the entries in the cache.

linecache.**lazycache**(*filename*, *module_globals*)

Capture enough detail about a non-file-based module to permit getting its lines later via *getline()* even if *module_globals* is `None` in the later call. This avoids doing I/O until a line is actually needed, without having to carry the module globals around indefinitely.

New in version 3.5.

Example:

```
>>> import linecache
>>> linecache.getline(linecache.__file__, 8)
'import sys\n'
```

11.10 shutil — High-level file operations

Source code: Lib/shutil.py

The *shutil* module offers a number of high-level operations on files and collections of files. In particular, functions are provided which support file copying and removal. For operations on individual files, see also the *os* module.

> **Warning:** Even the higher-level file copying functions (*shutil.copy()*, *shutil.copy2()*) cannot copy all file metadata.
>
> On POSIX platforms, this means that file owner and group are lost as well as ACLs. On Mac OS, the resource fork and other metadata are not used. This means that resources will be lost and file type and creator codes will not be correct. On Windows, file owners, ACLs and alternate data streams are not copied.

11.10.1 Directory and files operations

shutil.**copyfileobj**(*fsrc*, *fdst*[, *length*])

Copy the contents of the file-like object *fsrc* to the file-like object *fdst*. The integer *length*, if given, is the buffer size. In particular, a negative *length* value means to copy the data without looping over the source data in chunks; by default the data is read in chunks to avoid uncontrolled memory consumption. Note that if the current file position of the *fsrc* object is not 0, only the contents from the current file position to the end of the file will be copied.

shutil.copyfile(*src, dst, *, follow_symlinks=True*)

Copy the contents (no metadata) of the file named *src* to a file named *dst* and return *dst*. *src* and *dst* are path names given as strings. *dst* must be the complete target file name; look at `shutil.copy()` for a copy that accepts a target directory path. If *src* and *dst* specify the same file, `SameFileError` is raised.

The destination location must be writable; otherwise, an `OSError` exception will be raised. If *dst* already exists, it will be replaced. Special files such as character or block devices and pipes cannot be copied with this function.

If *follow_symlinks* is false and *src* is a symbolic link, a new symbolic link will be created instead of copying the file *src* points to.

Changed in version 3.3: `IOError` used to be raised instead of `OSError`. Added *follow_symlinks* argument. Now returns *dst*.

Changed in version 3.4: Raise `SameFileError` instead of `Error`. Since the former is a subclass of the latter, this change is backward compatible.

exception shutil.SameFileError

This exception is raised if source and destination in `copyfile()` are the same file.

New in version 3.4.

shutil.copymode(*src, dst, *, follow_symlinks=True*)

Copy the permission bits from *src* to *dst*. The file contents, owner, and group are unaffected. *src* and *dst* are path names given as strings. If *follow_symlinks* is false, and both *src* and *dst* are symbolic links, `copymode()` will attempt to modify the mode of *dst* itself (rather than the file it points to). This functionality is not available on every platform; please see `copystat()` for more information. If `copymode()` cannot modify symbolic links on the local platform, and it is asked to do so, it will do nothing and return.

Changed in version 3.3: Added *follow_symlinks* argument.

shutil.copystat(*src, dst, *, follow_symlinks=True*)

Copy the permission bits, last access time, last modification time, and flags from *src* to *dst*. On Linux, `copystat()` also copies the "extended attributes" where possible. The file contents, owner, and group are unaffected. *src* and *dst* are path names given as strings.

If *follow_symlinks* is false, and *src* and *dst* both refer to symbolic links, `copystat()` will operate on the symbolic links themselves rather than the files the symbolic links refer to—reading the information from the *src* symbolic link, and writing the information to the *dst* symbolic link.

Note: Not all platforms provide the ability to examine and modify symbolic links. Python itself can tell you what functionality is locally available.

- If `os.chmod in os.supports_follow_symlinks` is `True`, `copystat()` can modify the permission bits of a symbolic link.
- If `os.utime in os.supports_follow_symlinks` is `True`, `copystat()` can modify the last access and modification times of a symbolic link.
- If `os.chflags in os.supports_follow_symlinks` is `True`, `copystat()` can modify the flags of a symbolic link. (`os.chflags` is not available on all platforms.)

On platforms where some or all of this functionality is unavailable, when asked to modify a symbolic link, `copystat()` will copy everything it can. `copystat()` never returns failure.

Please see `os.supports_follow_symlinks` for more information.

Changed in version 3.3: Added *follow_symlinks* argument and support for Linux extended attributes.

`shutil.copy`(*src*, *dst*, ***, *follow_symlinks=True*)
Copies the file *src* to the file or directory *dst*. *src* and *dst* should be strings. If *dst* specifies a directory, the file will be copied into *dst* using the base filename from *src*. Returns the path to the newly created file.

If *follow_symlinks* is false, and *src* is a symbolic link, *dst* will be created as a symbolic link. If *follow_symlinks* is true and *src* is a symbolic link, *dst* will be a copy of the file *src* refers to.

`copy()` copies the file data and the file's permission mode (see `os.chmod()`). Other metadata, like the file's creation and modification times, is not preserved. To preserve all file metadata from the original, use `copy2()` instead.

Changed in version 3.3: Added *follow_symlinks* argument. Now returns path to the newly created file.

`shutil.copy2`(*src*, *dst*, ***, *follow_symlinks=True*)
Identical to `copy()` except that `copy2()` also attempts to preserve all file metadata.

When *follow_symlinks* is false, and *src* is a symbolic link, `copy2()` attempts to copy all metadata from the *src* symbolic link to the newly-created *dst* symbolic link. However, this functionality is not available on all platforms. On platforms where some or all of this functionality is unavailable, `copy2()` will preserve all the metadata it can; `copy2()` never returns failure.

`copy2()` uses `copystat()` to copy the file metadata. Please see `copystat()` for more information about platform support for modifying symbolic link metadata.

Changed in version 3.3: Added *follow_symlinks* argument, try to copy extended file system attributes too (currently Linux only). Now returns path to the newly created file.

`shutil.ignore_patterns`(**patterns*)
This factory function creates a function that can be used as a callable for `copytree()`'s *ignore* argument, ignoring files and directories that match one of the glob-style *patterns* provided. See the example below.

`shutil.copytree`(*src*, *dst*, *symlinks=False*, *ignore=None*, *copy_function=copy2*, *ignore_dangling_symlinks=False*)
Recursively copy an entire directory tree rooted at *src*, returning the destination directory. The destination directory, named by *dst*, must not already exist; it will be created as well as missing parent directories. Permissions and times of directories are copied with `copystat()`, individual files are copied using `shutil.copy2()`.

If *symlinks* is true, symbolic links in the source tree are represented as symbolic links in the new tree and the metadata of the original links will be copied as far as the platform allows; if false or omitted, the contents and metadata of the linked files are copied to the new tree.

When *symlinks* is false, if the file pointed by the symlink doesn't exist, an exception will be added in the list of errors raised in an `Error` exception at the end of the copy process. You can set the optional *ignore_dangling_symlinks* flag to true if you want to silence this exception. Notice that this option has no effect on platforms that don't support `os.symlink()`.

If *ignore* is given, it must be a callable that will receive as its arguments the directory being visited by `copytree()`, and a list of its contents, as returned by `os.listdir()`. Since `copytree()` is called recursively, the *ignore* callable will be called once for each directory that is copied. The callable must return a sequence of directory and file names relative to the current directory (i.e. a subset of the items in its second argument); these names will then be ignored in the copy process. `ignore_patterns()` can be used to create such a callable that ignores names based on glob-style patterns.

If exception(s) occur, an `Error` is raised with a list of reasons.

If *copy_function* is given, it must be a callable that will be used to copy each file. It will be called with the source path and the destination path as arguments. By default, `shutil.copy2()` is used, but any function that supports the same signature (like `shutil.copy()`) can be used.

Changed in version 3.3: Copy metadata when *symlinks* is false. Now returns *dst*.

Changed in version 3.2: Added the *copy_function* argument to be able to provide a custom copy function. Added the *ignore_dangling_symlinks* argument to silent dangling symlinks errors when *symlinks* is false.

shutil.rmtree(*path*, *ignore_errors=False*, *onerror=None*)

Delete an entire directory tree; *path* must point to a directory (but not a symbolic link to a directory). If *ignore_errors* is true, errors resulting from failed removals will be ignored; if false or omitted, such errors are handled by calling a handler specified by *onerror* or, if that is omitted, they raise an exception.

Note: On platforms that support the necessary fd-based functions a symlink attack resistant version of `rmtree()` is used by default. On other platforms, the `rmtree()` implementation is susceptible to a symlink attack: given proper timing and circumstances, attackers can manipulate symlinks on the filesystem to delete files they wouldn't be able to access otherwise. Applications can use the `rmtree.avoids_symlink_attacks` function attribute to determine which case applies.

If *onerror* is provided, it must be a callable that accepts three parameters: *function*, *path*, and *excinfo*.

The first parameter, *function*, is the function which raised the exception; it depends on the platform and implementation. The second parameter, *path*, will be the path name passed to *function*. The third parameter, *excinfo*, will be the exception information returned by `sys.exc_info()`. Exceptions raised by *onerror* will not be caught.

Changed in version 3.3: Added a symlink attack resistant version that is used automatically if platform supports fd-based functions.

rmtree.avoids_symlink_attacks

Indicates whether the current platform and implementation provides a symlink attack resistant version of `rmtree()`. Currently this is only true for platforms supporting fd-based directory access functions.

New in version 3.3.

shutil.move(*src*, *dst*, *copy_function=copy2*)

Recursively move a file or directory (*src*) to another location (*dst*) and return the destination.

If the destination is an existing directory, then *src* is moved inside that directory. If the destination already exists but is not a directory, it may be overwritten depending on `os.rename()` semantics.

If the destination is on the current filesystem, then `os.rename()` is used. Otherwise, *src* is copied to *dst* using *copy_function* and then removed. In case of symlinks, a new symlink pointing to the target of *src* will be created in or as *dst* and *src* will be removed.

If *copy_function* is given, it must be a callable that takes two arguments *src* and *dst*, and will be used to copy *src* to *dest* if `os.rename()` cannot be used. If the source is a directory, `copytree()` is called, passing it the `copy_function()`. The default *copy_function* is `copy2()`. Using `copy()` as the *copy_function* allows the move to succeed when it is not possible to also copy the metadata, at the expense of not copying any of the metadata.

Changed in version 3.3: Added explicit symlink handling for foreign filesystems, thus adapting it to the behavior of GNU's `mv`. Now returns *dst*.

Changed in version 3.5: Added the *copy_function* keyword argument.

shutil.disk_usage(*path*)

Return disk usage statistics about the given path as a named tuple with the attributes *total*, *used* and *free*, which are the amount of total, used and free space, in bytes. On Windows, *path* must be a directory; on Unix, it can be a file or directory.

New in version 3.3.

Availability: Unix, Windows.

shutil.chown(*path*, *user=None*, *group=None*)

Change owner *user* and/or *group* of the given *path*.

user can be a system user name or a uid; the same applies to *group*. At least one argument is required.

See also *os.chown()*, the underlying function.

Availability: Unix.

New in version 3.3.

shutil.which(*cmd*, *mode=os.F_OK | os.X_OK*, *path=None*)

Return the path to an executable which would be run if the given *cmd* was called. If no *cmd* would be called, return `None`.

mode is a permission mask passed to *os.access()*, by default determining if the file exists and executable.

When no *path* is specified, the results of *os.environ()* are used, returning either the "PATH" value or a fallback of *os.defpath*.

On Windows, the current directory is always prepended to the *path* whether or not you use the default or provide your own, which is the behavior the command shell uses when finding executables. Additionally, when finding the *cmd* in the *path*, the `PATHEXT` environment variable is checked. For example, if you call `shutil.which("python")`, *which()* will search `PATHEXT` to know that it should look for `python.exe` within the *path* directories. For example, on Windows:

```
>>> shutil.which("python")
'C:\\Python33\\python.EXE'
```

New in version 3.3.

exception shutil.Error

This exception collects exceptions that are raised during a multi-file operation. For *copytree()*, the exception argument is a list of 3-tuples (*srcname*, *dstname*, *exception*).

copytree example

This example is the implementation of the *copytree()* function, described above, with the docstring omitted. It demonstrates many of the other functions provided by this module.

```
def copytree(src, dst, symlinks=False):
    names = os.listdir(src)
    os.makedirs(dst)
    errors = []
    for name in names:
        srcname = os.path.join(src, name)
        dstname = os.path.join(dst, name)
        try:
            if symlinks and os.path.islink(srcname):
                linkto = os.readlink(srcname)
                os.symlink(linkto, dstname)
            elif os.path.isdir(srcname):
                copytree(srcname, dstname, symlinks)
            else:
                copy2(srcname, dstname)
            # XXX What about devices, sockets etc.?
        except OSError as why:
            errors.append((srcname, dstname, str(why)))
```

```
        # catch the Error from the recursive copytree so that we can
        # continue with other files
        except Error as err:
            errors.extend(err.args[0])
    try:
        copystat(src, dst)
    except OSError as why:
        # can't copy file access times on Windows
        if why.winerror is None:
            errors.extend((src, dst, str(why)))
    if errors:
        raise Error(errors)
```

Another example that uses the *ignore_patterns()* helper:

```
from shutil import copytree, ignore_patterns

copytree(source, destination, ignore=ignore_patterns('*.pyc', 'tmp*'))
```

This will copy everything except `.pyc` files and files or directories whose name starts with `tmp`.

Another example that uses the *ignore* argument to add a logging call:

```
from shutil import copytree
import logging

def _logpath(path, names):
    logging.info('Working in %s', path)
    return []   # nothing will be ignored

copytree(source, destination, ignore=_logpath)
```

rmtree example

This example shows how to remove a directory tree on Windows where some of the files have their read-only bit set. It uses the onerror callback to clear the readonly bit and reattempt the remove. Any subsequent failure will propagate.

```
import os, stat
import shutil

def remove_readonly(func, path, _):
    "Clear the readonly bit and reattempt the removal"
    os.chmod(path, stat.S_IWRITE)
    func(path)

shutil.rmtree(directory, onerror=remove_readonly)
```

11.10.2 Archiving operations

New in version 3.2.

Changed in version 3.5: Added support for the *xztar* format.

High-level utilities to create and read compressed and archived files are also provided. They rely on the *zipfile* and *tarfile* modules.

shutil.make_archive(*base_name*, *format*[, *root_dir*[, *base_dir*[, *verbose*[, *dry_run*[, *owner*[, *group*[, *logger*]]]]]]])

Create an archive file (such as zip or tar) and return its name.

base_name is the name of the file to create, including the path, minus any format-specific extension. *format* is the archive format: one of "zip" (if the `zlib` module is available), "tar", "gztar" (if the `zlib` module is available), "bztar" (if the `bz2` module is available), or "xztar" (if the `lzma` module is available).

root_dir is a directory that will be the root directory of the archive; for example, we typically chdir into *root_dir* before creating the archive.

base_dir is the directory where we start archiving from; i.e. *base_dir* will be the common prefix of all files and directories in the archive.

root_dir and *base_dir* both default to the current directory.

If *dry_run* is true, no archive is created, but the operations that would be executed are logged to *logger*.

owner and *group* are used when creating a tar archive. By default, uses the current owner and group.

logger must be an object compatible with PEP 282, usually an instance of `logging.Logger`.

The *verbose* argument is unused and deprecated.

shutil.get_archive_formats()

Return a list of supported formats for archiving. Each element of the returned sequence is a tuple `(name, description)`.

By default `shutil` provides these formats:

- *zip*: ZIP file (if the `zlib` module is available).
- *tar*: uncompressed tar file.
- *gztar*: gzip'ed tar-file (if the `zlib` module is available).
- *bztar*: bzip2'ed tar-file (if the `bz2` module is available).
- *xztar*: xz'ed tar-file (if the `lzma` module is available).

You can register new formats or provide your own archiver for any existing formats, by using `register_archive_format()`.

shutil.register_archive_format(*name*, *function*[, *extra_args*[, *description*]])

Register an archiver for the format *name*.

function is the callable that will be used to unpack archives. The callable will receive the *base_name* of the file to create, followed by the *base_dir* (which defaults to `os.curdir`) to start archiving from. Further arguments are passed as keyword arguments: *owner*, *group*, *dry_run* and *logger* (as passed in `make_archive()`).

If given, *extra_args* is a sequence of `(name, value)` pairs that will be used as extra keywords arguments when the archiver callable is used.

description is used by `get_archive_formats()` which returns the list of archivers. Defaults to an empty string.

shutil.unregister_archive_format(*name*)

Remove the archive format *name* from the list of supported formats.

shutil.unpack_archive(*filename*[, *extract_dir*[, *format*]])

Unpack an archive. *filename* is the full path of the archive.

extract_dir is the name of the target directory where the archive is unpacked. If not provided, the current working directory is used.

format is the archive format: one of "zip", "tar", "gztar", "bztar", or "xztar". Or any other format registered with *register_unpack_format()*. If not provided, *unpack_archive()* will use the archive file name extension and see if an unpacker was registered for that extension. In case none is found, a *ValueError* is raised.

shutil.register_unpack_format(*name, extensions, function*[, *extra_args*[, *description*]])
Registers an unpack format. *name* is the name of the format and *extensions* is a list of extensions corresponding to the format, like `.zip` for Zip files.

function is the callable that will be used to unpack archives. The callable will receive the path of the archive, followed by the directory the archive must be extracted to.

When provided, *extra_args* is a sequence of `(name, value)` tuples that will be passed as keywords arguments to the callable.

description can be provided to describe the format, and will be returned by the *get_unpack_formats()* function.

shutil.unregister_unpack_format(*name*)
Unregister an unpack format. *name* is the name of the format.

shutil.get_unpack_formats()
Return a list of all registered formats for unpacking. Each element of the returned sequence is a tuple `(name, extensions, description)`.

By default *shutil* provides these formats:

- *zip*: ZIP file (unpacking compressed files works only if the corresponding module is available).
- *tar*: uncompressed tar file.
- *gztar*: gzip'ed tar-file (if the *zlib* module is available).
- *bztar*: bzip2'ed tar-file (if the *bz2* module is available).
- *xztar*: xz'ed tar-file (if the *lzma* module is available).

You can register new formats or provide your own unpacker for any existing formats, by using *register_unpack_format()*.

Archiving example

In this example, we create a gzip'ed tar-file archive containing all files found in the `.ssh` directory of the user:

```
>>> from shutil import make_archive
>>> import os
>>> archive_name = os.path.expanduser(os.path.join('~', 'myarchive'))
>>> root_dir = os.path.expanduser(os.path.join('~', '.ssh'))
>>> make_archive(archive_name, 'gztar', root_dir)
'/Users/tarek/myarchive.tar.gz'
```

The resulting archive contains:

```
$ tar -tzvf /Users/tarek/myarchive.tar.gz
drwx------ tarek/staff       0 2010-02-01 16:23:40 ./
-rw-r--r-- tarek/staff     609 2008-06-09 13:26:54 ./authorized_keys
-rwxr-xr-x tarek/staff      65 2008-06-09 13:26:54 ./config
-rwx------ tarek/staff     668 2008-06-09 13:26:54 ./id_dsa
-rwxr-xr-x tarek/staff     609 2008-06-09 13:26:54 ./id_dsa.pub
-rw------- tarek/staff    1675 2008-06-09 13:26:54 ./id_rsa
-rw-r--r-- tarek/staff     397 2008-06-09 13:26:54 ./id_rsa.pub
-rw-r--r-- tarek/staff   37192 2010-02-06 18:23:10 ./known_hosts
```

11.10.3 Querying the size of the output terminal

`shutil.get_terminal_size(fallback=(columns, lines))`
Get the size of the terminal window.

For each of the two dimensions, the environment variable, `COLUMNS` and `LINES` respectively, is checked. If the variable is defined and the value is a positive integer, it is used.

When `COLUMNS` or `LINES` is not defined, which is the common case, the terminal connected to *sys.__stdout__* is queried by invoking *os.get_terminal_size()*.

If the terminal size cannot be successfully queried, either because the system doesn't support querying, or because we are not connected to a terminal, the value given in `fallback` parameter is used. `fallback` defaults to `(80, 24)` which is the default size used by many terminal emulators.

The value returned is a named tuple of type *os.terminal_size*.

See also: The Single UNIX Specification, Version 2, Other Environment Variables.

New in version 3.3.

11.11 macpath — Mac OS 9 path manipulation functions

Source code: Lib/macpath.py

This module is the Mac OS 9 (and earlier) implementation of the *os.path* module. It can be used to manipulate old-style Macintosh pathnames on Mac OS X (or any other platform).

The following functions are available in this module: `normcase()`, `normpath()`, `isabs()`, `join()`, `split()`, `isdir()`, `isfile()`, `walk()`, `exists()`. For other functions available in *os.path* dummy counterparts are available.

See also:

Module *os* Operating system interfaces, including functions to work with files at a lower level than Python *file objects*.

Module *io* Python's built-in I/O library, including both abstract classes and some concrete classes such as file I/O.

Built-in function *open()* The standard way to open files for reading and writing with Python.

CHAPTER

TWELVE

DATA PERSISTENCE

The modules described in this chapter support storing Python data in a persistent form on disk. The *pickle* and *marshal* modules can turn many Python data types into a stream of bytes and then recreate the objects from the bytes. The various DBM-related modules support a family of hash-based file formats that store a mapping of strings to other strings.

The list of modules described in this chapter is:

12.1 pickle — Python object serialization

Source code: Lib/pickle.py

The *pickle* module implements binary protocols for serializing and de-serializing a Python object structure. *"Pickling"* is the process whereby a Python object hierarchy is converted into a byte stream, and *"unpickling"* is the inverse operation, whereby a byte stream (from a *binary file* or *bytes-like object*) is converted back into an object hierarchy. Pickling (and unpickling) is alternatively known as "serialization", "marshalling,"[1] or "flattening"; however, to avoid confusion, the terms used here are "pickling" and "unpickling".

> **Warning:** The *pickle* module is not secure against erroneous or maliciously constructed data. Never unpickle data received from an untrusted or unauthenticated source.

12.1.1 Relationship to other Python modules

Comparison with marshal

Python has a more primitive serialization module called *marshal*, but in general *pickle* should always be the preferred way to serialize Python objects. *marshal* exists primarily to support Python's `.pyc` files.

The *pickle* module differs from *marshal* in several significant ways:

- The *pickle* module keeps track of the objects it has already serialized, so that later references to the same object won't be serialized again. *marshal* doesn't do this.

  This has implications both for recursive objects and object sharing. Recursive objects are objects that contain references to themselves. These are not handled by marshal, and in fact, attempting to marshal recursive objects will crash your Python interpreter. Object sharing happens when there are multiple references to the same object in different places in the object hierarchy being serialized. *pickle* stores such objects only once, and ensures that all other references point to the master copy. Shared objects remain shared, which can be very important for mutable objects.

[1] Don't confuse this with the *marshal* module

- *marshal* cannot be used to serialize user-defined classes and their instances. *pickle* can save and restore class instances transparently, however the class definition must be importable and live in the same module as when the object was stored.
- The *marshal* serialization format is not guaranteed to be portable across Python versions. Because its primary job in life is to support `.pyc` files, the Python implementers reserve the right to change the serialization format in non-backwards compatible ways should the need arise. The *pickle* serialization format is guaranteed to be backwards compatible across Python releases.

Comparison with `json`

There are fundamental differences between the pickle protocols and JSON (JavaScript Object Notation):

- JSON is a text serialization format (it outputs unicode text, although most of the time it is then encoded to `utf-8`), while pickle is a binary serialization format;
- JSON is human-readable, while pickle is not;
- JSON is interoperable and widely used outside of the Python ecosystem, while pickle is Python-specific;
- JSON, by default, can only represent a subset of the Python built-in types, and no custom classes; pickle can represent an extremely large number of Python types (many of them automatically, by clever usage of Python's introspection facilities; complex cases can be tackled by implementing *specific object APIs*).

See also:

The *json* module: a standard library module allowing JSON serialization and deserialization.

12.1.2 Data stream format

The data format used by *pickle* is Python-specific. This has the advantage that there are no restrictions imposed by external standards such as JSON or XDR (which can't represent pointer sharing); however it means that non-Python programs may not be able to reconstruct pickled Python objects.

By default, the *pickle* data format uses a relatively compact binary representation. If you need optimal size characteristics, you can efficiently *compress* pickled data.

The module *pickletools* contains tools for analyzing data streams generated by *pickle*. *pickletools* source code has extensive comments about opcodes used by pickle protocols.

There are currently 5 different protocols which can be used for pickling. The higher the protocol used, the more recent the version of Python needed to read the pickle produced.

- Protocol version 0 is the original "human-readable" protocol and is backwards compatible with earlier versions of Python.
- Protocol version 1 is an old binary format which is also compatible with earlier versions of Python.
- Protocol version 2 was introduced in Python 2.3. It provides much more efficient pickling of *new-style classes*. Refer to PEP 307 for information about improvements brought by protocol 2.
- Protocol version 3 was added in Python 3.0. It has explicit support for *bytes* objects and cannot be unpickled by Python 2.x. This is the default protocol, and the recommended protocol when compatibility with other Python 3 versions is required.
- Protocol version 4 was added in Python 3.4. It adds support for very large objects, pickling more kinds of objects, and some data format optimizations. Refer to PEP 3154 for information about improvements brought by protocol 4.

Note: Serialization is a more primitive notion than persistence; although `pickle` reads and writes file objects, it does not handle the issue of naming persistent objects, nor the (even more complicated) issue of concurrent access to persistent objects. The `pickle` module can transform a complex object into a byte stream and it can transform the byte stream into an object with the same internal structure. Perhaps the most obvious thing to do with these byte streams is to write them onto a file, but it is also conceivable to send them across a network or store them in a database. The `shelve` module provides a simple interface to pickle and unpickle objects on DBM-style database files.

12.1.3 Module Interface

To serialize an object hierarchy, you simply call the `dumps()` function. Similarly, to de-serialize a data stream, you call the `loads()` function. However, if you want more control over serialization and de-serialization, you can create a `Pickler` or an `Unpickler` object, respectively.

The `pickle` module provides the following constants:

`pickle.HIGHEST_PROTOCOL`
An integer, the highest *protocol version* available. This value can be passed as a *protocol* value to functions `dump()` and `dumps()` as well as the `Pickler` constructor.

`pickle.DEFAULT_PROTOCOL`
An integer, the default *protocol version* used for pickling. May be less than `HIGHEST_PROTOCOL`. Currently the default protocol is 3, a new protocol designed for Python 3.

The `pickle` module provides the following functions to make the pickling process more convenient:

`pickle.dump(`*obj, file, protocol=None, *, fix_imports=True*`)`
Write a pickled representation of *obj* to the open *file object* *file*. This is equivalent to `Pickler(file, protocol).dump(obj)`.

The optional *protocol* argument, an integer, tells the pickler to use the given protocol; supported protocols are 0 to `HIGHEST_PROTOCOL`. If not specified, the default is `DEFAULT_PROTOCOL`. If a negative number is specified, `HIGHEST_PROTOCOL` is selected.

The *file* argument must have a write() method that accepts a single bytes argument. It can thus be an on-disk file opened for binary writing, an `io.BytesIO` instance, or any other custom object that meets this interface.

If *fix_imports* is true and *protocol* is less than 3, pickle will try to map the new Python 3 names to the old module names used in Python 2, so that the pickle data stream is readable with Python 2.

`pickle.dumps(`*obj, protocol=None, *, fix_imports=True*`)`
Return the pickled representation of the object as a `bytes` object, instead of writing it to a file.

Arguments *protocol* and *fix_imports* have the same meaning as in `dump()`.

`pickle.load(`*file, *, fix_imports=True, encoding="ASCII", errors="strict"*`)`
Read a pickled object representation from the open *file object* *file* and return the reconstituted object hierarchy specified therein. This is equivalent to `Unpickler(file).load()`.

The protocol version of the pickle is detected automatically, so no protocol argument is needed. Bytes past the pickled object's representation are ignored.

The argument *file* must have two methods, a read() method that takes an integer argument, and a readline() method that requires no arguments. Both methods should return bytes. Thus *file* can be an on-disk file opened for binary reading, an `io.BytesIO` object, or any other custom object that meets this interface.

Optional keyword arguments are *fix_imports*, *encoding* and *errors*, which are used to control compatibility support for pickle stream generated by Python 2. If *fix_imports* is true, pickle will try to map the old Python 2 names to the new names used in Python 3. The *encoding* and *errors* tell pickle how to decode 8-bit string instances pickled by Python 2; these default to 'ASCII' and 'strict', respectively. The *encoding* can be 'bytes' to read these 8-bit string instances as bytes objects.

`pickle.loads`(*bytes_object*, ***, *fix_imports=True*, *encoding="ASCII"*, *errors="strict"*)
Read a pickled object hierarchy from a `bytes` object and return the reconstituted object hierarchy specified therein.

The protocol version of the pickle is detected automatically, so no protocol argument is needed. Bytes past the pickled object's representation are ignored.

Optional keyword arguments are *fix_imports*, *encoding* and *errors*, which are used to control compatibility support for pickle stream generated by Python 2. If *fix_imports* is true, pickle will try to map the old Python 2 names to the new names used in Python 3. The *encoding* and *errors* tell pickle how to decode 8-bit string instances pickled by Python 2; these default to 'ASCII' and 'strict', respectively. The *encoding* can be 'bytes' to read these 8-bit string instances as bytes objects.

The `pickle` module defines three exceptions:

exception pickle.PickleError
Common base class for the other pickling exceptions. It inherits `Exception`.

exception pickle.PicklingError
Error raised when an unpicklable object is encountered by `Pickler`. It inherits `PickleError`.

Refer to *What can be pickled and unpickled?* to learn what kinds of objects can be pickled.

exception pickle.UnpicklingError
Error raised when there is a problem unpickling an object, such as a data corruption or a security violation. It inherits `PickleError`.

Note that other exceptions may also be raised during unpickling, including (but not necessarily limited to) AttributeError, EOFError, ImportError, and IndexError.

The `pickle` module exports two classes, `Pickler` and `Unpickler`:

class pickle.Pickler(*file*, *protocol=None*, ***, *fix_imports=True*)
This takes a binary file for writing a pickle data stream.

The optional *protocol* argument, an integer, tells the pickler to use the given protocol; supported protocols are 0 to `HIGHEST_PROTOCOL`. If not specified, the default is `DEFAULT_PROTOCOL`. If a negative number is specified, `HIGHEST_PROTOCOL` is selected.

The *file* argument must have a write() method that accepts a single bytes argument. It can thus be an on-disk file opened for binary writing, an `io.BytesIO` instance, or any other custom object that meets this interface.

If *fix_imports* is true and *protocol* is less than 3, pickle will try to map the new Python 3 names to the old module names used in Python 2, so that the pickle data stream is readable with Python 2.

dump(*obj*)
Write a pickled representation of *obj* to the open file object given in the constructor.

persistent_id(*obj*)
Do nothing by default. This exists so a subclass can override it.

If `persistent_id()` returns `None`, *obj* is pickled as usual. Any other value causes `Pickler` to emit the returned value as a persistent ID for *obj*. The meaning of this persistent ID should be defined by `Unpickler.persistent_load()`. Note that the value returned by `persistent_id()` cannot itself have a persistent ID.

See *Persistence of External Objects* for details and examples of uses.

dispatch_table

A pickler object's dispatch table is a registry of *reduction functions* of the kind which can be declared using `copyreg.pickle()`. It is a mapping whose keys are classes and whose values are reduction functions. A reduction function takes a single argument of the associated class and should conform to the same interface as a `__reduce__()` method.

By default, a pickler object will not have a `dispatch_table` attribute, and it will instead use the global dispatch table managed by the `copyreg` module. However, to customize the pickling for a specific pickler object one can set the `dispatch_table` attribute to a dict-like object. Alternatively, if a subclass of `Pickler` has a `dispatch_table` attribute then this will be used as the default dispatch table for instances of that class.

See *Dispatch Tables* for usage examples.

New in version 3.3.

fast

Deprecated. Enable fast mode if set to a true value. The fast mode disables the usage of memo, therefore speeding the pickling process by not generating superfluous PUT opcodes. It should not be used with self-referential objects, doing otherwise will cause `Pickler` to recurse infinitely.

Use `pickletools.optimize()` if you need more compact pickles.

class pickle.Unpickler(*file*, ***, *fix_imports=True*, *encoding="ASCII"*, *errors="strict"*)

This takes a binary file for reading a pickle data stream.

The protocol version of the pickle is detected automatically, so no protocol argument is needed.

The argument *file* must have two methods, a read() method that takes an integer argument, and a readline() method that requires no arguments. Both methods should return bytes. Thus *file* can be an on-disk file object opened for binary reading, an `io.BytesIO` object, or any other custom object that meets this interface.

Optional keyword arguments are *fix_imports*, *encoding* and *errors*, which are used to control compatibility support for pickle stream generated by Python 2. If *fix_imports* is true, pickle will try to map the old Python 2 names to the new names used in Python 3. The *encoding* and *errors* tell pickle how to decode 8-bit string instances pickled by Python 2; these default to 'ASCII' and 'strict', respectively. The *encoding* can be 'bytes' to read these 8-bit string instances as bytes objects.

load()

Read a pickled object representation from the open file object given in the constructor, and return the reconstituted object hierarchy specified therein. Bytes past the pickled object's representation are ignored.

persistent_load(*pid*)

Raise an `UnpicklingError` by default.

If defined, `persistent_load()` should return the object specified by the persistent ID *pid*. If an invalid persistent ID is encountered, an `UnpicklingError` should be raised.

See *Persistence of External Objects* for details and examples of uses.

find_class(*module*, *name*)

Import *module* if necessary and return the object called *name* from it, where the *module* and *name* arguments are `str` objects. Note, unlike its name suggests, `find_class()` is also used for finding functions.

Subclasses may override this to gain control over what type of objects and how they can be loaded, potentially reducing security risks. Refer to *Restricting Globals* for details.

12.1.4 What can be pickled and unpickled?

The following types can be pickled:

- None, True, and False
- integers, floating point numbers, complex numbers
- strings, bytes, bytearrays
- tuples, lists, sets, and dictionaries containing only picklable objects
- functions defined at the top level of a module (using def, not lambda)
- built-in functions defined at the top level of a module
- classes that are defined at the top level of a module
- instances of such classes whose *__dict__* or the result of calling *__getstate__()* is picklable (see section *Pickling Class Instances* for details).

Attempts to pickle unpicklable objects will raise the *PicklingError* exception; when this happens, an unspecified number of bytes may have already been written to the underlying file. Trying to pickle a highly recursive data structure may exceed the maximum recursion depth, a *RecursionError* will be raised in this case. You can carefully raise this limit with *sys.setrecursionlimit()*.

Note that functions (built-in and user-defined) are pickled by "fully qualified" name reference, not by value.[2] This means that only the function name is pickled, along with the name of the module the function is defined in. Neither the function's code, nor any of its function attributes are pickled. Thus the defining module must be importable in the unpickling environment, and the module must contain the named object, otherwise an exception will be raised.[3]

Similarly, classes are pickled by named reference, so the same restrictions in the unpickling environment apply. Note that none of the class's code or data is pickled, so in the following example the class attribute attr is not restored in the unpickling environment:

```
class Foo:
    attr = 'A class attribute'

picklestring = pickle.dumps(Foo)
```

These restrictions are why picklable functions and classes must be defined in the top level of a module.

Similarly, when class instances are pickled, their class's code and data are not pickled along with them. Only the instance data are pickled. This is done on purpose, so you can fix bugs in a class or add methods to the class and still load objects that were created with an earlier version of the class. If you plan to have long-lived objects that will see many versions of a class, it may be worthwhile to put a version number in the objects so that suitable conversions can be made by the class's *__setstate__()* method.

12.1.5 Pickling Class Instances

In this section, we describe the general mechanisms available to you to define, customize, and control how class instances are pickled and unpickled.

In most cases, no additional code is needed to make instances picklable. By default, pickle will retrieve the class and the attributes of an instance via introspection. When a class instance is unpickled, its __init__() method is usually *not* invoked. The default behaviour first creates an uninitialized instance and then restores the saved attributes. The following code shows an implementation of this behaviour:

[2] This is why lambda functions cannot be pickled: all lambda functions share the same name: <lambda>.

[3] The exception raised will likely be an *ImportError* or an *AttributeError* but it could be something else.

```
def save(obj):
    return (obj.__class__, obj.__dict__)

def load(cls, attributes):
    obj = cls.__new__(cls)
    obj.__dict__.update(attributes)
    return obj
```

Classes can alter the default behaviour by providing one or several special methods:

object.**__getnewargs_ex__**()

In protocols 2 and newer, classes that implements the *__getnewargs_ex__()* method can dictate the values passed to the `__new__()` method upon unpickling. The method must return a pair `(args, kwargs)` where *args* is a tuple of positional arguments and *kwargs* a dictionary of named arguments for constructing the object. Those will be passed to the `__new__()` method upon unpickling.

You should implement this method if the `__new__()` method of your class requires keyword-only arguments. Otherwise, it is recommended for compatibility to implement *__getnewargs__()*.

Changed in version 3.6: *__getnewargs_ex__()* is now used in protocols 2 and 3.

object.**__getnewargs__**()

This method serve a similar purpose as *__getnewargs_ex__()*, but supports only positional arguments. It must return a tuple of arguments `args` which will be passed to the `__new__()` method upon unpickling.

__getnewargs__() will not be called if *__getnewargs_ex__()* is defined.

Changed in version 3.6: Before Python 3.6, *__getnewargs__()* was called instead of *__getnewargs_ex__()* in protocols 2 and 3.

object.**__getstate__**()

Classes can further influence how their instances are pickled; if the class defines the method *__getstate__()*, it is called and the returned object is pickled as the contents for the instance, instead of the contents of the instance's dictionary. If the *__getstate__()* method is absent, the instance's *__dict__* is pickled as usual.

object.**__setstate__**(*state*)

Upon unpickling, if the class defines *__setstate__()*, it is called with the unpickled state. In that case, there is no requirement for the state object to be a dictionary. Otherwise, the pickled state must be a dictionary and its items are assigned to the new instance's dictionary.

Note: If *__getstate__()* returns a false value, the *__setstate__()* method will not be called upon unpickling.

Refer to the section *Handling Stateful Objects* for more information about how to use the methods *__getstate__()* and *__setstate__()*.

Note: At unpickling time, some methods like `__getattr__()`, `__getattribute__()`, or `__setattr__()` may be called upon the instance. In case those methods rely on some internal invariant being true, the type should implement *__getnewargs__()* or *__getnewargs_ex__()* to establish such an invariant; otherwise, neither `__new__()` nor `__init__()` will be called.

As we shall see, pickle does not use directly the methods described above. In fact, these methods are part of the copy protocol which implements the *__reduce__()* special method. The copy protocol provides a unified interface for retrieving the data necessary for pickling and copying objects.[4]

[4] The *copy* module uses this protocol for shallow and deep copying operations.

Although powerful, implementing *__reduce__()* directly in your classes is error prone. For this reason, class designers should use the high-level interface (i.e., *__getnewargs_ex__()*, *__getstate__()* and *__setstate__()*) whenever possible. We will show, however, cases where using *__reduce__()* is the only option or leads to more efficient pickling or both.

`object.__reduce__()`

The interface is currently defined as follows. The *__reduce__()* method takes no argument and shall return either a string or preferably a tuple (the returned object is often referred to as the "reduce value").

If a string is returned, the string should be interpreted as the name of a global variable. It should be the object's local name relative to its module; the pickle module searches the module namespace to determine the object's module. This behaviour is typically useful for singletons.

When a tuple is returned, it must be between two and five items long. Optional items can either be omitted, or `None` can be provided as their value. The semantics of each item are in order:

- A callable object that will be called to create the initial version of the object.
- A tuple of arguments for the callable object. An empty tuple must be given if the callable does not accept any argument.
- Optionally, the object's state, which will be passed to the object's *__setstate__()* method as previously described. If the object has no such method then, the value must be a dictionary and it will be added to the object's *__dict__* attribute.
- Optionally, an iterator (and not a sequence) yielding successive items. These items will be appended to the object either using `obj.append(item)` or, in batch, using `obj.extend(list_of_items)`. This is primarily used for list subclasses, but may be used by other classes as long as they have `append()` and `extend()` methods with the appropriate signature. (Whether `append()` or `extend()` is used depends on which pickle protocol version is used as well as the number of items to append, so both must be supported.)
- Optionally, an iterator (not a sequence) yielding successive key-value pairs. These items will be stored to the object using `obj[key] = value`. This is primarily used for dictionary subclasses, but may be used by other classes as long as they implement `__setitem__()`.

`object.__reduce_ex__(protocol)`

Alternatively, a *__reduce_ex__()* method may be defined. The only difference is this method should take a single integer argument, the protocol version. When defined, pickle will prefer it over the *__reduce__()* method. In addition, *__reduce__()* automatically becomes a synonym for the extended version. The main use for this method is to provide backwards-compatible reduce values for older Python releases.

Persistence of External Objects

For the benefit of object persistence, the *pickle* module supports the notion of a reference to an object outside the pickled data stream. Such objects are referenced by a persistent ID, which should be either a string of alphanumeric characters (for protocol 0)[5] or just an arbitrary object (for any newer protocol).

The resolution of such persistent IDs is not defined by the *pickle* module; it will delegate this resolution to the user defined methods on the pickler and unpickler, *persistent_id()* and *persistent_load()* respectively.

To pickle objects that have an external persistent id, the pickler must have a custom *persistent_id()* method that takes an object as an argument and returns either `None` or the persistent id for that object. When `None` is returned, the pickler simply pickles the object as normal. When a persistent ID string is

[5] The limitation on alphanumeric characters is due to the fact the persistent IDs, in protocol 0, are delimited by the newline character. Therefore if any kind of newline characters occurs in persistent IDs, the resulting pickle will become unreadable.

returned, the pickler will pickle that object, along with a marker so that the unpickler will recognize it as a persistent ID.

To unpickle external objects, the unpickler must have a custom *persistent_load()* method that takes a persistent ID object and returns the referenced object.

Here is a comprehensive example presenting how persistent ID can be used to pickle external objects by reference.

```
# Simple example presenting how persistent ID can be used to pickle
# external objects by reference.

import pickle
import sqlite3
from collections import namedtuple

# Simple class representing a record in our database.
MemoRecord = namedtuple("MemoRecord", "key, task")

class DBPickler(pickle.Pickler):

    def persistent_id(self, obj):
        # Instead of pickling MemoRecord as a regular class instance, we emit a
        # persistent ID.
        if isinstance(obj, MemoRecord):
            # Here, our persistent ID is simply a tuple, containing a tag and a
            # key, which refers to a specific record in the database.
            return ("MemoRecord", obj.key)
        else:
            # If obj does not have a persistent ID, return None. This means obj
            # needs to be pickled as usual.
            return None


class DBUnpickler(pickle.Unpickler):

    def __init__(self, file, connection):
        super().__init__(file)
        self.connection = connection

    def persistent_load(self, pid):
        # This method is invoked whenever a persistent ID is encountered.
        # Here, pid is the tuple returned by DBPickler.
        cursor = self.connection.cursor()
        type_tag, key_id = pid
        if type_tag == "MemoRecord":
            # Fetch the referenced record from the database and return it.
            cursor.execute("SELECT * FROM memos WHERE key=?", (str(key_id),))
            key, task = cursor.fetchone()
            return MemoRecord(key, task)
        else:
            # Always raises an error if you cannot return the correct object.
            # Otherwise, the unpickler will think None is the object referenced
            # by the persistent ID.
            raise pickle.UnpicklingError("unsupported persistent object")


def main():
    import io
```

```
    import pprint

    # Initialize and populate our database.
    conn = sqlite3.connect(":memory:")
    cursor = conn.cursor()
    cursor.execute("CREATE TABLE memos(key INTEGER PRIMARY KEY, task TEXT)")
    tasks = (
        'give food to fish',
        'prepare group meeting',
        'fight with a zebra',
        )
    for task in tasks:
        cursor.execute("INSERT INTO memos VALUES(NULL, ?)", (task,))

    # Fetch the records to be pickled.
    cursor.execute("SELECT * FROM memos")
    memos = [MemoRecord(key, task) for key, task in cursor]
    # Save the records using our custom DBPickler.
    file = io.BytesIO()
    DBPickler(file).dump(memos)

    print("Pickled records:")
    pprint.pprint(memos)

    # Update a record, just for good measure.
    cursor.execute("UPDATE memos SET task='learn italian' WHERE key=1")

    # Load the records from the pickle data stream.
    file.seek(0)
    memos = DBUnpickler(file, conn).load()

    print("Unpickled records:")
    pprint.pprint(memos)


if __name__ == '__main__':
    main()
```

Dispatch Tables

If one wants to customize pickling of some classes without disturbing any other code which depends on pickling, then one can create a pickler with a private dispatch table.

The global dispatch table managed by the *copyreg* module is available as `copyreg.dispatch_table`. Therefore, one may choose to use a modified copy of `copyreg.dispatch_table` as a private dispatch table.

For example

```
f = io.BytesIO()
p = pickle.Pickler(f)
p.dispatch_table = copyreg.dispatch_table.copy()
p.dispatch_table[SomeClass] = reduce_SomeClass
```

creates an instance of *pickle.Pickler* with a private dispatch table which handles the `SomeClass` class specially. Alternatively, the code

```
class MyPickler(pickle.Pickler):
    dispatch_table = copyreg.dispatch_table.copy()
    dispatch_table[SomeClass] = reduce_SomeClass
f = io.BytesIO()
p = MyPickler(f)
```

does the same, but all instances of `MyPickler` will by default share the same dispatch table. The equivalent code using the *copyreg* module is

```
copyreg.pickle(SomeClass, reduce_SomeClass)
f = io.BytesIO()
p = pickle.Pickler(f)
```

Handling Stateful Objects

Here's an example that shows how to modify pickling behavior for a class. The `TextReader` class opens a text file, and returns the line number and line contents each time its `readline()` method is called. If a `TextReader` instance is pickled, all attributes *except* the file object member are saved. When the instance is unpickled, the file is reopened, and reading resumes from the last location. The *__setstate__()* and *__getstate__()* methods are used to implement this behavior.

```
class TextReader:
    """Print and number lines in a text file."""

    def __init__(self, filename):
        self.filename = filename
        self.file = open(filename)
        self.lineno = 0

    def readline(self):
        self.lineno += 1
        line = self.file.readline()
        if not line:
            return None
        if line.endswith('\n'):
            line = line[:-1]
        return "%i: %s" % (self.lineno, line)

    def __getstate__(self):
        # Copy the object's state from self.__dict__ which contains
        # all our instance attributes. Always use the dict.copy()
        # method to avoid modifying the original state.
        state = self.__dict__.copy()
        # Remove the unpicklable entries.
        del state['file']
        return state

    def __setstate__(self, state):
        # Restore instance attributes (i.e., filename and lineno).
        self.__dict__.update(state)
        # Restore the previously opened file's state. To do so, we need to
        # reopen it and read from it until the line count is restored.
        file = open(self.filename)
        for _ in range(self.lineno):
            file.readline()
        # Finally, save the file.
```

```
        self.file = file
```

A sample usage might be something like this:

```
>>> reader = TextReader("hello.txt")
>>> reader.readline()
'1: Hello world!'
>>> reader.readline()
'2: I am line number two.'
>>> new_reader = pickle.loads(pickle.dumps(reader))
>>> new_reader.readline()
'3: Goodbye!'
```

12.1.6 Restricting Globals

By default, unpickling will import any class or function that it finds in the pickle data. For many applications, this behaviour is unacceptable as it permits the unpickler to import and invoke arbitrary code. Just consider what this hand-crafted pickle data stream does when loaded:

```
>>> import pickle
>>> pickle.loads(b"cos\nsystem\n(S'echo hello world'\ntR.")
hello world
0
```

In this example, the unpickler imports the *os.system()* function and then apply the string argument "echo hello world". Although this example is inoffensive, it is not difficult to imagine one that could damage your system.

For this reason, you may want to control what gets unpickled by customizing *Unpickler.find_class()*. Unlike its name suggests, *Unpickler.find_class()* is called whenever a global (i.e., a class or a function) is requested. Thus it is possible to either completely forbid globals or restrict them to a safe subset.

Here is an example of an unpickler allowing only few safe classes from the *builtins* module to be loaded:

```
import builtins
import io
import pickle

safe_builtins = {
    'range',
    'complex',
    'set',
    'frozenset',
    'slice',
}

class RestrictedUnpickler(pickle.Unpickler):

    def find_class(self, module, name):
        # Only allow safe classes from builtins.
        if module == "builtins" and name in safe_builtins:
            return getattr(builtins, name)
        # Forbid everything else.
        raise pickle.UnpicklingError("global '%s.%s' is forbidden" %
                                     (module, name))

def restricted_loads(s):
```

```
    """Helper function analogous to pickle.loads()."""
    return RestrictedUnpickler(io.BytesIO(s)).load()
```

A sample usage of our unpickler working has intended:

```
>>> restricted_loads(pickle.dumps([1, 2, range(15)]))
[1, 2, range(0, 15)]
>>> restricted_loads(b"cos\nsystem\n(S'echo hello world'\ntR.")
Traceback (most recent call last):
  ...
pickle.UnpicklingError: global 'os.system' is forbidden
>>> restricted_loads(b'cbuiltins\neval\n'
...                  b'(S\'getattr(__import__("os"), "system")'
...                  b'("echo hello world")\'\ntR.')
Traceback (most recent call last):
  ...
pickle.UnpicklingError: global 'builtins.eval' is forbidden
```

As our examples shows, you have to be careful with what you allow to be unpickled. Therefore if security is a concern, you may want to consider alternatives such as the marshalling API in *xmlrpc.client* or third-party solutions.

12.1.7 Performance

Recent versions of the pickle protocol (from protocol 2 and upwards) feature efficient binary encodings for several common features and built-in types. Also, the *pickle* module has a transparent optimizer written in C.

12.1.8 Examples

For the simplest code, use the *dump()* and *load()* functions.

```
import pickle

# An arbitrary collection of objects supported by pickle.
data = {
    'a': [1, 2.0, 3, 4+6j],
    'b': ("character string", b"byte string"),
    'c': {None, True, False}
}

with open('data.pickle', 'wb') as f:
    # Pickle the 'data' dictionary using the highest protocol available.
    pickle.dump(data, f, pickle.HIGHEST_PROTOCOL)
```

The following example reads the resulting pickled data.

```
import pickle

with open('data.pickle', 'rb') as f:
    # The protocol version used is detected automatically, so we do not
    # have to specify it.
    data = pickle.load(f)
```

See also:

Module *copyreg* Pickle interface constructor registration for extension types.

Module *pickletools* Tools for working with and analyzing pickled data.

Module *shelve* Indexed databases of objects; uses *pickle*.

Module *copy* Shallow and deep object copying.

Module *marshal* High-performance serialization of built-in types.

12.2 copyreg — Register pickle support functions

Source code: Lib/copyreg.py

The *copyreg* module offers a way to define functions used while pickling specific objects. The *pickle* and *copy* modules use those functions when pickling/copying those objects. The module provides configuration information about object constructors which are not classes. Such constructors may be factory functions or class instances.

copyreg.**constructor**(*object*)
Declares *object* to be a valid constructor. If *object* is not callable (and hence not valid as a constructor), raises *TypeError*.

copyreg.**pickle**(*type*, *function*, *constructor=None*)
Declares that *function* should be used as a "reduction" function for objects of type *type*. *function* should return either a string or a tuple containing two or three elements.

The optional *constructor* parameter, if provided, is a callable object which can be used to reconstruct the object when called with the tuple of arguments returned by *function* at pickling time. *TypeError* will be raised if *object* is a class or *constructor* is not callable.

See the *pickle* module for more details on the interface expected of *function* and *constructor*. Note that the *dispatch_table* attribute of a pickler object or subclass of *pickle.Pickler* can also be used for declaring reduction functions.

12.2.1 Example

The example below would like to show how to register a pickle function and how it will be used:

```
>>> import copyreg, copy, pickle
>>> class C(object):
...     def __init__(self, a):
...         self.a = a
...
>>> def pickle_c(c):
...     print("pickling a C instance...")
...     return C, (c.a,)
...
>>> copyreg.pickle(C, pickle_c)
>>> c = C(1)
>>> d = copy.copy(c)
pickling a C instance...
>>> p = pickle.dumps(c)
pickling a C instance...
```

12.3 shelve — Python object persistence

Source code: Lib/shelve.py

A "shelf" is a persistent, dictionary-like object. The difference with "dbm" databases is that the values (not the keys!) in a shelf can be essentially arbitrary Python objects — anything that the *pickle* module can handle. This includes most class instances, recursive data types, and objects containing lots of shared sub-objects. The keys are ordinary strings.

shelve.open(*filename, flag='c', protocol=None, writeback=False*)

Open a persistent dictionary. The filename specified is the base filename for the underlying database. As a side-effect, an extension may be added to the filename and more than one file may be created. By default, the underlying database file is opened for reading and writing. The optional *flag* parameter has the same interpretation as the *flag* parameter of *dbm.open()*.

By default, version 3 pickles are used to serialize values. The version of the pickle protocol can be specified with the *protocol* parameter.

Because of Python semantics, a shelf cannot know when a mutable persistent-dictionary entry is modified. By default modified objects are written *only* when assigned to the shelf (see *Example*). If the optional *writeback* parameter is set to **True**, all entries accessed are also cached in memory, and written back on *sync()* and *close()*; this can make it handier to mutate mutable entries in the persistent dictionary, but, if many entries are accessed, it can consume vast amounts of memory for the cache, and it can make the close operation very slow since all accessed entries are written back (there is no way to determine which accessed entries are mutable, nor which ones were actually mutated).

Note: Do not rely on the shelf being closed automatically; always call *close()* explicitly when you don't need it any more, or use *shelve.open()* as a context manager:

```
with shelve.open('spam') as db:
    db['eggs'] = 'eggs'
```

Warning: Because the *shelve* module is backed by *pickle*, it is insecure to load a shelf from an untrusted source. Like with pickle, loading a shelf can execute arbitrary code.

Shelf objects support all methods supported by dictionaries. This eases the transition from dictionary based scripts to those requiring persistent storage.

Two additional methods are supported:

Shelf.sync()

Write back all entries in the cache if the shelf was opened with *writeback* set to *True*. Also empty the cache and synchronize the persistent dictionary on disk, if feasible. This is called automatically when the shelf is closed with *close()*.

Shelf.close()

Synchronize and close the persistent *dict* object. Operations on a closed shelf will fail with a *ValueError*.

See also:

Persistent dictionary recipe with widely supported storage formats and having the speed of native dictionaries.

12.3.1 Restrictions

- The choice of which database package will be used (such as *dbm.ndbm* or *dbm.gnu*) depends on which interface is available. Therefore it is not safe to open the database directly using *dbm*. The database is also (unfortunately) subject to the limitations of *dbm*, if it is used — this means that (the pickled representation of) the objects stored in the database should be fairly small, and in rare cases key collisions may cause the database to refuse updates.
- The *shelve* module does not support *concurrent* read/write access to shelved objects. (Multiple simultaneous read accesses are safe.) When a program has a shelf open for writing, no other program should have it open for reading or writing. Unix file locking can be used to solve this, but this differs across Unix versions and requires knowledge about the database implementation used.

class shelve.Shelf(*dict, protocol=None, writeback=False, keyencoding='utf-8'*)

A subclass of *collections.abc.MutableMapping* which stores pickled values in the *dict* object.

By default, version 3 pickles are used to serialize values. The version of the pickle protocol can be specified with the *protocol* parameter. See the *pickle* documentation for a discussion of the pickle protocols.

If the *writeback* parameter is `True`, the object will hold a cache of all entries accessed and write them back to the *dict* at sync and close times. This allows natural operations on mutable entries, but can consume much more memory and make sync and close take a long time.

The *keyencoding* parameter is the encoding used to encode keys before they are used with the underlying dict.

A *Shelf* object can also be used as a context manager, in which case it will be automatically closed when the `with` block ends.

Changed in version 3.2: Added the *keyencoding* parameter; previously, keys were always encoded in UTF-8.

Changed in version 3.4: Added context manager support.

class shelve.BsdDbShelf(*dict, protocol=None, writeback=False, keyencoding='utf-8'*)

A subclass of *Shelf* which exposes `first()`, `next()`, `previous()`, `last()` and `set_location()` which are available in the third-party `bsddb` module from pybsddb but not in other database modules. The *dict* object passed to the constructor must support those methods. This is generally accomplished by calling one of `bsddb.hashopen()`, `bsddb.btopen()` or `bsddb.rnopen()`. The optional *protocol*, *writeback*, and *keyencoding* parameters have the same interpretation as for the *Shelf* class.

class shelve.DbfilenameShelf(*filename, flag='c', protocol=None, writeback=False*)

A subclass of *Shelf* which accepts a *filename* instead of a dict-like object. The underlying file will be opened using *dbm.open()*. By default, the file will be created and opened for both read and write. The optional *flag* parameter has the same interpretation as for the *open()* function. The optional *protocol* and *writeback* parameters have the same interpretation as for the *Shelf* class.

12.3.2 Example

To summarize the interface (`key` is a string, `data` is an arbitrary object):

```
import shelve

d = shelve.open(filename)  # open -- file may get suffix added by low-level
                           # library

d[key] = data              # store data at key (overwrites old data if
```

```
                             # using an existing key)
data = d[key]                # retrieve a COPY of data at key (raise KeyError
                             # if no such key)
del d[key]                   # delete data stored at key (raises KeyError
                             # if no such key)

flag = key in d              # true if the key exists
klist = list(d.keys())       # a list of all existing keys (slow!)

# as d was opened WITHOUT writeback=True, beware:
d['xx'] = [0, 1, 2]          # this works as expected, but...
d['xx'].append(3)            # *this doesn't!* -- d['xx'] is STILL [0, 1, 2]!

# having opened d without writeback=True, you need to code carefully:
temp = d['xx']               # extracts the copy
temp.append(5)               # mutates the copy
d['xx'] = temp               # stores the copy right back, to persist it

# or, d=shelve.open(filename,writeback=True) would let you just code
# d['xx'].append(5) and have it work as expected, BUT it would also
# consume more memory and make the d.close() operation slower.

d.close()                    # close it
```

See also:

Module *dbm* Generic interface to dbm-style databases.

Module *pickle* Object serialization used by *shelve*.

12.4 marshal — Internal Python object serialization

This module contains functions that can read and write Python values in a binary format. The format is specific to Python, but independent of machine architecture issues (e.g., you can write a Python value to a file on a PC, transport the file to a Sun, and read it back there). Details of the format are undocumented on purpose; it may change between Python versions (although it rarely does).[1]

This is not a general "persistence" module. For general persistence and transfer of Python objects through RPC calls, see the modules *pickle* and *shelve*. The *marshal* module exists mainly to support reading and writing the "pseudo-compiled" code for Python modules of .pyc files. Therefore, the Python maintainers reserve the right to modify the marshal format in backward incompatible ways should the need arise. If you're serializing and de-serializing Python objects, use the *pickle* module instead – the performance is comparable, version independence is guaranteed, and pickle supports a substantially wider range of objects than marshal.

Warning: The *marshal* module is not intended to be secure against erroneous or maliciously constructed data. Never unmarshal data received from an untrusted or unauthenticated source.

Not all Python object types are supported; in general, only objects whose value is independent from a particular invocation of Python can be written and read by this module. The following types are supported:

[1] The name of this module stems from a bit of terminology used by the designers of Modula-3 (amongst others), who use the term "marshalling" for shipping of data around in a self-contained form. Strictly speaking, "to marshal" means to convert some data from internal to external form (in an RPC buffer for instance) and "unmarshalling" for the reverse process.

booleans, integers, floating point numbers, complex numbers, strings, bytes, bytearrays, tuples, lists, sets, frozensets, dictionaries, and code objects, where it should be understood that tuples, lists, sets, frozensets and dictionaries are only supported as long as the values contained therein are themselves supported. The singletons *None*, *Ellipsis* and *StopIteration* can also be marshalled and unmarshalled. For format *version* lower than 3, recursive lists, sets and dictionaries cannot be written (see below).

There are functions that read/write files as well as functions operating on bytes-like objects.

The module defines these functions:

`marshal.dump(value, file[, version])`

Write the value on the open file. The value must be a supported type. The file must be a writeable *binary file*.

If the value has (or contains an object that has) an unsupported type, a *ValueError* exception is raised — but garbage data will also be written to the file. The object will not be properly read back by *load()*.

The *version* argument indicates the data format that **dump** should use (see below).

`marshal.load(file)`

Read one value from the open file and return it. If no valid value is read (e.g. because the data has a different Python version's incompatible marshal format), raise *EOFError*, *ValueError* or *TypeError*. The file must be a readable *binary file*.

Note: If an object containing an unsupported type was marshalled with *dump()*, *load()* will substitute `None` for the unmarshallable type.

`marshal.dumps(value[, version])`

Return the bytes object that would be written to a file by `dump(value, file)`. The value must be a supported type. Raise a *ValueError* exception if value has (or contains an object that has) an unsupported type.

The *version* argument indicates the data format that **dumps** should use (see below).

`marshal.loads(bytes)`

Convert the *bytes-like object* to a value. If no valid value is found, raise *EOFError*, *ValueError* or *TypeError*. Extra bytes in the input are ignored.

In addition, the following constants are defined:

`marshal.version`

Indicates the format that the module uses. Version 0 is the historical format, version 1 shares interned strings and version 2 uses a binary format for floating point numbers. Version 3 adds support for object instancing and recursion. The current version is 4.

12.5 dbm — Interfaces to Unix "databases"

Source code: Lib/dbm/__init__.py

dbm is a generic interface to variants of the DBM database — *dbm.gnu* or *dbm.ndbm*. If none of these modules is installed, the slow-but-simple implementation in module *dbm.dumb* will be used. There is a third party interface to the Oracle Berkeley DB.

`exception dbm.error`

A tuple containing the exceptions that can be raised by each of the supported modules, with a unique exception also named *dbm.error* as the first item — the latter is used when *dbm.error* is raised.

dbm.whichdb(*filename*)

This function attempts to guess which of the several simple database modules available — *dbm.gnu*, *dbm.ndbm* or *dbm.dumb* — should be used to open a given file.

Returns one of the following values: `None` if the file can't be opened because it's unreadable or doesn't exist; the empty string (`''`) if the file's format can't be guessed; or a string containing the required module name, such as `'dbm.ndbm'` or `'dbm.gnu'`.

dbm.open(*file*, *flag='r'*, *mode=0o666*)

Open the database file *file* and return a corresponding object.

If the database file already exists, the *whichdb()* function is used to determine its type and the appropriate module is used; if it does not exist, the first module listed above that can be imported is used.

The optional *flag* argument can be:

Value	Meaning
'r'	Open existing database for reading only (default)
'w'	Open existing database for reading and writing
'c'	Open database for reading and writing, creating it if it doesn't exist
'n'	Always create a new, empty database, open for reading and writing

The optional *mode* argument is the Unix mode of the file, used only when the database has to be created. It defaults to octal `0o666` (and will be modified by the prevailing umask).

The object returned by *open()* supports the same basic functionality as dictionaries; keys and their corresponding values can be stored, retrieved, and deleted, and the `in` operator and the `keys()` method are available, as well as `get()` and `setdefault()`.

Changed in version 3.2: `get()` and `setdefault()` are now available in all database modules.

Key and values are always stored as bytes. This means that when strings are used they are implicitly converted to the default encoding before being stored.

These objects also support being used in a `with` statement, which will automatically close them when done.

Changed in version 3.4: Added native support for the context management protocol to the objects returned by *open()*.

The following example records some hostnames and a corresponding title, and then prints out the contents of the database:

```
import dbm

# Open database, creating it if necessary.
with dbm.open('cache', 'c') as db:

    # Record some values
    db[b'hello'] = b'there'
    db['www.python.org'] = 'Python Website'
    db['www.cnn.com'] = 'Cable News Network'

    # Note that the keys are considered bytes now.
    assert db[b'www.python.org'] == b'Python Website'
    # Notice how the value is now in bytes.
    assert db['www.cnn.com'] == b'Cable News Network'

    # Often-used methods of the dict interface work too.
    print(db.get('python.org', b'not present'))
```

```
    # Storing a non-string key or value will raise an exception (most
    # likely a TypeError).
    db['www.yahoo.com'] = 4

# db is automatically closed when leaving the with statement.
```

See also:

Module *shelve* Persistence module which stores non-string data.

The individual submodules are described in the following sections.

12.5.1 dbm.gnu — GNU's reinterpretation of dbm

Source code: Lib/dbm/gnu.py

This module is quite similar to the *dbm* module, but uses the GNU library **gdbm** instead to provide some additional functionality. Please note that the file formats created by *dbm.gnu* and *dbm.ndbm* are incompatible.

The *dbm.gnu* module provides an interface to the GNU DBM library. **dbm.gnu.gdbm** objects behave like mappings (dictionaries), except that keys and values are always converted to bytes before storing. Printing a **gdbm** object doesn't print the keys and values, and the **items()** and **values()** methods are not supported.

exception dbm.gnu.error

Raised on *dbm.gnu*-specific errors, such as I/O errors. *KeyError* is raised for general mapping errors like specifying an incorrect key.

dbm.gnu.open(*filename*[, *flag*[, *mode*]])

Open a **gdbm** database and return a **gdbm** object. The *filename* argument is the name of the database file.

The optional *flag* argument can be:

Value	Meaning
'r'	Open existing database for reading only (default)
'w'	Open existing database for reading and writing
'c'	Open database for reading and writing, creating it if it doesn't exist
'n'	Always create a new, empty database, open for reading and writing

The following additional characters may be appended to the flag to control how the database is opened:

Value	Meaning
'f'	Open the database in fast mode. Writes to the database will not be synchronized.
's'	Synchronized mode. This will cause changes to the database to be immediately written to the file.
'u'	Do not lock database.

Not all flags are valid for all versions of **gdbm**. The module constant **open_flags** is a string of supported flag characters. The exception *error* is raised if an invalid flag is specified.

The optional *mode* argument is the Unix mode of the file, used only when the database has to be created. It defaults to octal 0o666.

In addition to the dictionary-like methods, **gdbm** objects have the following methods:

gdbm.firstkey()
It's possible to loop over every key in the database using this method and the *nextkey()* method. The traversal is ordered by **gdbm**'s internal hash values, and won't be sorted by the key values. This method returns the starting key.

gdbm.nextkey(*key*)
Returns the key that follows *key* in the traversal. The following code prints every key in the database **db**, without having to create a list in memory that contains them all:

```
k = db.firstkey()
while k != None:
    print(k)
    k = db.nextkey(k)
```

gdbm.reorganize()
If you have carried out a lot of deletions and would like to shrink the space used by the **gdbm** file, this routine will reorganize the database. **gdbm** objects will not shorten the length of a database file except by using this reorganization; otherwise, deleted file space will be kept and reused as new (key, value) pairs are added.

gdbm.sync()
When the database has been opened in fast mode, this method forces any unwritten data to be written to the disk.

gdbm.close()
Close the **gdbm** database.

12.5.2 dbm.ndbm — Interface based on ndbm

Source code: Lib/dbm/ndbm.py

The *dbm.ndbm* module provides an interface to the Unix "(n)dbm" library. Dbm objects behave like mappings (dictionaries), except that keys and values are always stored as bytes. Printing a **dbm** object doesn't print the keys and values, and the **items()** and **values()** methods are not supported.

This module can be used with the "classic" ndbm interface or the GNU GDBM compatibility interface. On Unix, the **configure** script will attempt to locate the appropriate header file to simplify building this module.

exception dbm.ndbm.error
Raised on *dbm.ndbm*-specific errors, such as I/O errors. *KeyError* is raised for general mapping errors like specifying an incorrect key.

dbm.ndbm.library
Name of the **ndbm** implementation library used.

dbm.ndbm.open(*filename*[, *flag*[, *mode*]])
Open a dbm database and return a **ndbm** object. The *filename* argument is the name of the database file (without the **.dir** or **.pag** extensions).

The optional *flag* argument must be one of these values:

Value	Meaning
'r'	Open existing database for reading only (default)
'w'	Open existing database for reading and writing
'c'	Open database for reading and writing, creating it if it doesn't exist
'n'	Always create a new, empty database, open for reading and writing

The optional *mode* argument is the Unix mode of the file, used only when the database has to be created. It defaults to octal `0o666` (and will be modified by the prevailing umask).

In addition to the dictionary-like methods, `ndbm` objects provide the following method:

ndbm.close()
Close the `ndbm` database.

12.5.3 dbm.dumb — Portable DBM implementation

Source code: Lib/dbm/dumb.py

Note: The *dbm.dumb* module is intended as a last resort fallback for the *dbm* module when a more robust module is not available. The *dbm.dumb* module is not written for speed and is not nearly as heavily used as the other database modules.

The *dbm.dumb* module provides a persistent dictionary-like interface which is written entirely in Python. Unlike other modules such as *dbm.gnu* no external library is required. As with other persistent mappings, the keys and values are always stored as bytes.

The module defines the following:

exception dbm.dumb.error
Raised on *dbm.dumb*-specific errors, such as I/O errors. *KeyError* is raised for general mapping errors like specifying an incorrect key.

dbm.dumb.open(*filename*[, *flag*[, *mode*]])
Open a `dumbdbm` database and return a dumbdbm object. The *filename* argument is the basename of the database file (without any specific extensions). When a dumbdbm database is created, files with `.dat` and `.dir` extensions are created.

The optional *flag* argument supports only the semantics of `'c'` and `'n'` values. Other values will default to database being always opened for update, and will be created if it does not exist.

The optional *mode* argument is the Unix mode of the file, used only when the database has to be created. It defaults to octal `0o666` (and will be modified by the prevailing umask).

Changed in version 3.5: *open()* always creates a new database when the flag has the value `'n'`.

Deprecated since version 3.6, will be removed in version 3.8: Creating database in `'r'` and `'w'` modes. Modifying database in `'r'` mode.

In addition to the methods provided by the *collections.abc.MutableMapping* class, `dumbdbm` objects provide the following methods:

dumbdbm.sync()
Synchronize the on-disk directory and data files. This method is called by the `Shelve.sync()` method.

dumbdbm.close()
Close the `dumbdbm` database.

12.6 sqlite3 — DB-API 2.0 interface for SQLite databases

Source code: Lib/sqlite3/

SQLite is a C library that provides a lightweight disk-based database that doesn't require a separate server process and allows accessing the database using a nonstandard variant of the SQL query language. Some applications can use SQLite for internal data storage. It's also possible to prototype an application using SQLite and then port the code to a larger database such as PostgreSQL or Oracle.

The sqlite3 module was written by Gerhard Häring. It provides a SQL interface compliant with the DB-API 2.0 specification described by PEP 249.

To use the module, you must first create a *Connection* object that represents the database. Here the data will be stored in the `example.db` file:

```
import sqlite3
conn = sqlite3.connect('example.db')
```

You can also supply the special name `:memory:` to create a database in RAM.

Once you have a *Connection*, you can create a *Cursor* object and call its *execute()* method to perform SQL commands:

```
c = conn.cursor()

# Create table
c.execute('''CREATE TABLE stocks
             (date text, trans text, symbol text, qty real, price real)''')

# Insert a row of data
c.execute("INSERT INTO stocks VALUES ('2006-01-05','BUY','RHAT',100,35.14)")

# Save (commit) the changes
conn.commit()

# We can also close the connection if we are done with it.
# Just be sure any changes have been committed or they will be lost.
conn.close()
```

The data you've saved is persistent and is available in subsequent sessions:

```
import sqlite3
conn = sqlite3.connect('example.db')
c = conn.cursor()
```

Usually your SQL operations will need to use values from Python variables. You shouldn't assemble your query using Python's string operations because doing so is insecure; it makes your program vulnerable to an SQL injection attack (see https://xkcd.com/327/ for humorous example of what can go wrong).

Instead, use the DB-API's parameter substitution. Put `?` as a placeholder wherever you want to use a value, and then provide a tuple of values as the second argument to the cursor's *execute()* method. (Other database modules may use a different placeholder, such as `%s` or `:1`.) For example:

```
# Never do this -- insecure!
symbol = 'RHAT'
c.execute("SELECT * FROM stocks WHERE symbol = '%s'" % symbol)

# Do this instead
t = ('RHAT',)
c.execute('SELECT * FROM stocks WHERE symbol=?', t)
print(c.fetchone())

# Larger example that inserts many records at a time
purchases = [('2006-03-28', 'BUY', 'IBM', 1000, 45.00),
```

```
            ('2006-04-05', 'BUY', 'MSFT', 1000, 72.00),
            ('2006-04-06', 'SELL', 'IBM', 500, 53.00),
           ]
c.executemany('INSERT INTO stocks VALUES (?,?,?,?,?)', purchases)
```

To retrieve data after executing a SELECT statement, you can either treat the cursor as an *iterator*, call the cursor's `fetchone()` method to retrieve a single matching row, or call `fetchall()` to get a list of the matching rows.

This example uses the iterator form:

```
>>> for row in c.execute('SELECT * FROM stocks ORDER BY price'):
        print(row)

('2006-01-05', 'BUY', 'RHAT', 100, 35.14)
('2006-03-28', 'BUY', 'IBM', 1000, 45.0)
('2006-04-06', 'SELL', 'IBM', 500, 53.0)
('2006-04-05', 'BUY', 'MSFT', 1000, 72.0)
```

See also:

https://github.com/ghaering/pysqlite The pysqlite web page – sqlite3 is developed externally under the name "pysqlite".

https://www.sqlite.org The SQLite web page; the documentation describes the syntax and the available data types for the supported SQL dialect.

http://www.w3schools.com/sql/ Tutorial, reference and examples for learning SQL syntax.

PEP 249 - **Database API Specification 2.0** PEP written by Marc-André Lemburg.

12.6.1 Module functions and constants

`sqlite3.version`
The version number of this module, as a string. This is not the version of the SQLite library.

`sqlite3.version_info`
The version number of this module, as a tuple of integers. This is not the version of the SQLite library.

`sqlite3.sqlite_version`
The version number of the run-time SQLite library, as a string.

`sqlite3.sqlite_version_info`
The version number of the run-time SQLite library, as a tuple of integers.

`sqlite3.PARSE_DECLTYPES`
This constant is meant to be used with the *detect_types* parameter of the `connect()` function.

Setting it makes the `sqlite3` module parse the declared type for each column it returns. It will parse out the first word of the declared type, i. e. for "integer primary key", it will parse out "integer", or for "number(10)" it will parse out "number". Then for that column, it will look into the converters dictionary and use the converter function registered for that type there.

`sqlite3.PARSE_COLNAMES`
This constant is meant to be used with the *detect_types* parameter of the `connect()` function.

Setting this makes the SQLite interface parse the column name for each column it returns. It will look for a string formed [mytype] in there, and then decide that 'mytype' is the type of the column. It will try to find an entry of 'mytype' in the converters dictionary and then use the converter function found there to return the value. The column name found in `Cursor.description` is only the first word of the column name, i. e. if you use something like `'as "x [datetime]"'` in your SQL, then we will parse out everything until the first blank for the column name: the column name would simply be "x".

`sqlite3.connect(`*database*[, *timeout*, *detect_types*, *isolation_level*, *check_same_thread*, *factory*, *cached_statements*, *uri*]`)`

Opens a connection to the SQLite database file *database*. You can use `":memory:"` to open a database connection to a database that resides in RAM instead of on disk.

When a database is accessed by multiple connections, and one of the processes modifies the database, the SQLite database is locked until that transaction is committed. The *timeout* parameter specifies how long the connection should wait for the lock to go away until raising an exception. The default for the timeout parameter is 5.0 (five seconds).

For the *isolation_level* parameter, please see the `isolation_level` property of `Connection` objects.

SQLite natively supports only the types TEXT, INTEGER, REAL, BLOB and NULL. If you want to use other types you must add support for them yourself. The *detect_types* parameter and the using custom **converters** registered with the module-level `register_converter()` function allow you to easily do that.

detect_types defaults to 0 (i. e. off, no type detection), you can set it to any combination of `PARSE_DECLTYPES` and `PARSE_COLNAMES` to turn type detection on.

By default, *check_same_thread* is `True` and only the creating thread may use the connection. If set `False`, the returned connection may be shared across multiple threads. When using multiple threads with the same connection writing operations should be serialized by the user to avoid data corruption.

By default, the `sqlite3` module uses its `Connection` class for the connect call. You can, however, subclass the `Connection` class and make `connect()` use your class instead by providing your class for the *factory* parameter.

Consult the section *SQLite and Python types* of this manual for details.

The `sqlite3` module internally uses a statement cache to avoid SQL parsing overhead. If you want to explicitly set the number of statements that are cached for the connection, you can set the *cached_statements* parameter. The currently implemented default is to cache 100 statements.

If *uri* is true, *database* is interpreted as a URI. This allows you to specify options. For example, to open a database in read-only mode you can use:

```
db = sqlite3.connect('file:path/to/database?mode=ro', uri=True)
```

More information about this feature, including a list of recognized options, can be found in the SQLite URI documentation.

Changed in version 3.4: Added the *uri* parameter.

`sqlite3.register_converter(`*typename*, *callable*`)`

Registers a callable to convert a bytestring from the database into a custom Python type. The callable will be invoked for all database values that are of the type *typename*. Confer the parameter *detect_types* of the `connect()` function for how the type detection works. Note that the case of *typename* and the name of the type in your query must match!

`sqlite3.register_adapter(`*type*, *callable*`)`

Registers a callable to convert the custom Python type *type* into one of SQLite's supported types. The callable *callable* accepts as single parameter the Python value, and must return a value of the following types: int, float, str or bytes.

`sqlite3.complete_statement(`*sql*`)`

Returns `True` if the string *sql* contains one or more complete SQL statements terminated by semicolons. It does not verify that the SQL is syntactically correct, only that there are no unclosed string literals and the statement is terminated by a semicolon.

This can be used to build a shell for SQLite, as in the following example:

```
# A minimal SQLite shell for experiments

import sqlite3

con = sqlite3.connect(":memory:")
con.isolation_level = None
cur = con.cursor()

buffer = ""

print("Enter your SQL commands to execute in sqlite3.")
print("Enter a blank line to exit.")

while True:
    line = input()
    if line == "":
        break
    buffer += line
    if sqlite3.complete_statement(buffer):
        try:
            buffer = buffer.strip()
            cur.execute(buffer)

            if buffer.lstrip().upper().startswith("SELECT"):
                print(cur.fetchall())
        except sqlite3.Error as e:
            print("An error occurred:", e.args[0])
        buffer = ""

con.close()
```

sqlite3.**enable_callback_tracebacks**(*flag*)
By default you will not get any tracebacks in user-defined functions, aggregates, converters, authorizer callbacks etc. If you want to debug them, you can call this function with *flag* set to `True`. Afterwards, you will get tracebacks from callbacks on `sys.stderr`. Use *False* to disable the feature again.

12.6.2 Connection Objects

class sqlite3.**Connection**
A SQLite database connection has the following attributes and methods:

isolation_level
Get or set the current isolation level. *None* for autocommit mode or one of "DEFERRED", "IMMEDIATE" or "EXCLUSIVE". See section *Controlling Transactions* for a more detailed explanation.

in_transaction
True if a transaction is active (there are uncommitted changes), *False* otherwise. Read-only attribute.

New in version 3.2.

cursor(*factory=Cursor*)
The cursor method accepts a single optional parameter *factory*. If supplied, this must be a callable returning an instance of *Cursor* or its subclasses.

commit()
This method commits the current transaction. If you don't call this method, anything you did since the last call to `commit()` is not visible from other database connections. If you wonder why you don't see the data you've written to the database, please check you didn't forget to call this method.

rollback()
This method rolls back any changes to the database since the last call to `commit()`.

close()
This closes the database connection. Note that this does not automatically call `commit()`. If you just close your database connection without calling `commit()` first, your changes will be lost!

execute(*sql*[, *parameters*])
This is a nonstandard shortcut that creates a cursor object by calling the `cursor()` method, calls the cursor's `execute()` method with the *parameters* given, and returns the cursor.

executemany(*sql*[, *parameters*])
This is a nonstandard shortcut that creates a cursor object by calling the `cursor()` method, calls the cursor's `executemany()` method with the *parameters* given, and returns the cursor.

executescript(*sql_script*)
This is a nonstandard shortcut that creates a cursor object by calling the `cursor()` method, calls the cursor's `executescript()` method with the given *sql_script*, and returns the cursor.

create_function(*name*, *num_params*, *func*)
Creates a user-defined function that you can later use from within SQL statements under the function name *name*. *num_params* is the number of parameters the function accepts (if *num_params* is -1, the function may take any number of arguments), and *func* is a Python callable that is called as the SQL function.

The function can return any of the types supported by SQLite: bytes, str, int, float and `None`.

Example:

```
import sqlite3
import hashlib

def md5sum(t):
    return hashlib.md5(t).hexdigest()

con = sqlite3.connect(":memory:")
con.create_function("md5", 1, md5sum)
cur = con.cursor()
cur.execute("select md5(?)", (b"foo",))
print(cur.fetchone()[0])
```

create_aggregate(*name*, *num_params*, *aggregate_class*)
Creates a user-defined aggregate function.

The aggregate class must implement a `step` method, which accepts the number of parameters *num_params* (if *num_params* is -1, the function may take any number of arguments), and a `finalize` method which will return the final result of the aggregate.

The `finalize` method can return any of the types supported by SQLite: bytes, str, int, float and `None`.

Example:

```
import sqlite3
```

```
class MySum:
    def __init__(self):
        self.count = 0

    def step(self, value):
        self.count += value

    def finalize(self):
        return self.count

con = sqlite3.connect(":memory:")
con.create_aggregate("mysum", 1, MySum)
cur = con.cursor()
cur.execute("create table test(i)")
cur.execute("insert into test(i) values (1)")
cur.execute("insert into test(i) values (2)")
cur.execute("select mysum(i) from test")
print(cur.fetchone()[0])
```

create_collation(*name, callable*)

Creates a collation with the specified *name* and *callable*. The callable will be passed two string arguments. It should return -1 if the first is ordered lower than the second, 0 if they are ordered equal and 1 if the first is ordered higher than the second. Note that this controls sorting (ORDER BY in SQL) so your comparisons don't affect other SQL operations.

Note that the callable will get its parameters as Python bytestrings, which will normally be encoded in UTF-8.

The following example shows a custom collation that sorts "the wrong way":

```
import sqlite3

def collate_reverse(string1, string2):
    if string1 == string2:
        return 0
    elif string1 < string2:
        return 1
    else:
        return -1

con = sqlite3.connect(":memory:")
con.create_collation("reverse", collate_reverse)

cur = con.cursor()
cur.execute("create table test(x)")
cur.executemany("insert into test(x) values (?)", [("a",), ("b",)])
cur.execute("select x from test order by x collate reverse")
for row in cur:
    print(row)
con.close()
```

To remove a collation, call `create_collation` with `None` as callable:

```
con.create_collation("reverse", None)
```

interrupt()

You can call this method from a different thread to abort any queries that might be executing on the connection. The query will then abort and the caller will get an exception.

set_authorizer(*authorizer_callback*)

This routine registers a callback. The callback is invoked for each attempt to access a column of a table in the database. The callback should return `SQLITE_OK` if access is allowed, `SQLITE_DENY` if the entire SQL statement should be aborted with an error and `SQLITE_IGNORE` if the column should be treated as a NULL value. These constants are available in the `sqlite3` module.

The first argument to the callback signifies what kind of operation is to be authorized. The second and third argument will be arguments or `None` depending on the first argument. The 4th argument is the name of the database ("main", "temp", etc.) if applicable. The 5th argument is the name of the inner-most trigger or view that is responsible for the access attempt or `None` if this access attempt is directly from input SQL code.

Please consult the SQLite documentation about the possible values for the first argument and the meaning of the second and third argument depending on the first one. All necessary constants are available in the `sqlite3` module.

set_progress_handler(*handler, n*)

This routine registers a callback. The callback is invoked for every *n* instructions of the SQLite virtual machine. This is useful if you want to get called from SQLite during long-running operations, for example to update a GUI.

If you want to clear any previously installed progress handler, call the method with `None` for *handler*.

Returning a non-zero value from the handler function will terminate the currently executing query and cause it to raise an `OperationalError` exception.

set_trace_callback(*trace_callback*)

Registers *trace_callback* to be called for each SQL statement that is actually executed by the SQLite backend.

The only argument passed to the callback is the statement (as string) that is being executed. The return value of the callback is ignored. Note that the backend does not only run statements passed to the `Cursor.execute()` methods. Other sources include the transaction management of the Python module and the execution of triggers defined in the current database.

Passing `None` as *trace_callback* will disable the trace callback.

New in version 3.3.

enable_load_extension(*enabled*)

This routine allows/disallows the SQLite engine to load SQLite extensions from shared libraries. SQLite extensions can define new functions, aggregates or whole new virtual table implementations. One well-known extension is the fulltext-search extension distributed with SQLite.

Loadable extensions are disabled by default. See[1].

New in version 3.2.

```
import sqlite3

con = sqlite3.connect(":memory:")

# enable extension loading
con.enable_load_extension(True)

# Load the fulltext search extension
con.execute("select load_extension('./fts3.so')")
```

[1] The sqlite3 module is not built with loadable extension support by default, because some platforms (notably Mac OS X) have SQLite libraries which are compiled without this feature. To get loadable extension support, you must pass –enable-loadable-sqlite-extensions to configure.

```
# alternatively you can load the extension using an API call:
# con.load_extension("./fts3.so")

# disable extension loading again
con.enable_load_extension(False)

# example from SQLite wiki
con.execute("create virtual table recipe using fts3(name, ingredients)")
con.executescript("""
    insert into recipe (name, ingredients) values ('broccoli stew', 'broccoli peppers␣
↪cheese tomatoes');
    insert into recipe (name, ingredients) values ('pumpkin stew', 'pumpkin onions␣
↪garlic celery');
    insert into recipe (name, ingredients) values ('broccoli pie', 'broccoli cheese␣
↪onions flour');
    insert into recipe (name, ingredients) values ('pumpkin pie', 'pumpkin sugar flour␣
↪butter');
    """)
for row in con.execute("select rowid, name, ingredients from recipe where name match 'pie
↪'"):
    print(row)
```

load_extension(*path*)

This routine loads a SQLite extension from a shared library. You have to enable extension loading with *enable_load_extension()* before you can use this routine.

Loadable extensions are disabled by default. See[1].

New in version 3.2.

row_factory

You can change this attribute to a callable that accepts the cursor and the original row as a tuple and will return the real result row. This way, you can implement more advanced ways of returning results, such as returning an object that can also access columns by name.

Example:

```
import sqlite3

def dict_factory(cursor, row):
    d = {}
    for idx, col in enumerate(cursor.description):
        d[col[0]] = row[idx]
    return d

con = sqlite3.connect(":memory:")
con.row_factory = dict_factory
cur = con.cursor()
cur.execute("select 1 as a")
print(cur.fetchone()["a"])
```

If returning a tuple doesn't suffice and you want name-based access to columns, you should consider setting *row_factory* to the highly-optimized *sqlite3.Row* type. *Row* provides both index-based and case-insensitive name-based access to columns with almost no memory overhead. It will probably be better than your own custom dictionary-based approach or even a db_row based solution.

text_factory

Using this attribute you can control what objects are returned for the TEXT data type. By default, this attribute is set to *str* and the *sqlite3* module will return Unicode objects for `TEXT`. If you want to return bytestrings instead, you can set it to *bytes*.

You can also set it to any other callable that accepts a single bytestring parameter and returns the resulting object.

See the following example code for illustration:

```
import sqlite3

con = sqlite3.connect(":memory:")
cur = con.cursor()

AUSTRIA = "\xd6sterreich"

# by default, rows are returned as Unicode
cur.execute("select ?", (AUSTRIA,))
row = cur.fetchone()
assert row[0] == AUSTRIA

# but we can make sqlite3 always return bytestrings ...
con.text_factory = bytes
cur.execute("select ?", (AUSTRIA,))
row = cur.fetchone()
assert type(row[0]) is bytes
# the bytestrings will be encoded in UTF-8, unless you stored garbage in the
# database ...
assert row[0] == AUSTRIA.encode("utf-8")

# we can also implement a custom text_factory ...
# here we implement one that appends "foo" to all strings
con.text_factory = lambda x: x.decode("utf-8") + "foo"
cur.execute("select ?", ("bar",))
row = cur.fetchone()
assert row[0] == "barfoo"
```

total_changes
Returns the total number of database rows that have been modified, inserted, or deleted since the database connection was opened.

iterdump()
Returns an iterator to dump the database in an SQL text format. Useful when saving an in-memory database for later restoration. This function provides the same capabilities as the `.dump` command in the **sqlite3** shell.

Example:

```
# Convert file existing_db.db to SQL dump file dump.sql
import sqlite3

con = sqlite3.connect('existing_db.db')
with open('dump.sql', 'w') as f:
    for line in con.iterdump():
        f.write('%s\n' % line)
```

12.6.3 Cursor Objects

class sqlite3.Cursor
A *Cursor* instance has the following attributes and methods.

execute(*sql*[, *parameters*])
Executes an SQL statement. The SQL statement may be parameterized (i. e. placeholders instead of SQL literals). The *sqlite3* module supports two kinds of placeholders: question marks (qmark style) and named placeholders (named style).

Here's an example of both styles:

```
import sqlite3

con = sqlite3.connect(":memory:")
cur = con.cursor()
cur.execute("create table people (name_last, age)")

who = "Yeltsin"
age = 72

# This is the qmark style:
cur.execute("insert into people values (?, ?)", (who, age))

# And this is the named style:
cur.execute("select * from people where name_last=:who and age=:age", {"who": who, "age
↪": age})

print(cur.fetchone())
```

execute() will only execute a single SQL statement. If you try to execute more than one statement with it, it will raise a *Warning*. Use *executescript()* if you want to execute multiple SQL statements with one call.

executemany(*sql*, *seq_of_parameters*)
Executes an SQL command against all parameter sequences or mappings found in the sequence *seq_of_parameters*. The *sqlite3* module also allows using an *iterator* yielding parameters instead of a sequence.

```
import sqlite3

class IterChars:
    def __init__(self):
        self.count = ord('a')

    def __iter__(self):
        return self

    def __next__(self):
        if self.count > ord('z'):
            raise StopIteration
        self.count += 1
        return (chr(self.count - 1),) # this is a 1-tuple

con = sqlite3.connect(":memory:")
cur = con.cursor()
cur.execute("create table characters(c)")

theIter = IterChars()
cur.executemany("insert into characters(c) values (?)", theIter)

cur.execute("select c from characters")
print(cur.fetchall())
```

Here's a shorter example using a *generator*:

```
import sqlite3
import string

def char_generator():
    for c in string.ascii_lowercase:
        yield (c,)

con = sqlite3.connect(":memory:")
cur = con.cursor()
cur.execute("create table characters(c)")

cur.executemany("insert into characters(c) values (?)", char_generator())

cur.execute("select c from characters")
print(cur.fetchall())
```

executescript(*sql_script*)

This is a nonstandard convenience method for executing multiple SQL statements at once. It issues a `COMMIT` statement first, then executes the SQL script it gets as a parameter.

sql_script can be an instance of `str`.

Example:

```
import sqlite3

con = sqlite3.connect(":memory:")
cur = con.cursor()
cur.executescript("""
    create table person(
        firstname,
        lastname,
        age
    );

    create table book(
        title,
        author,
        published
    );

    insert into book(title, author, published)
    values (
        'Dirk Gently''s Holistic Detective Agency',
        'Douglas Adams',
        1987
    );
    """)
```

fetchone()

Fetches the next row of a query result set, returning a single sequence, or *None* when no more data is available.

fetchmany(*size=cursor.arraysize*)

Fetches the next set of rows of a query result, returning a list. An empty list is returned when no more rows are available.

The number of rows to fetch per call is specified by the *size* parameter. If it is not given, the cursor's arraysize determines the number of rows to be fetched. The method should try to fetch as many rows as indicated by the size parameter. If this is not possible due to the specified number of rows not being available, fewer rows may be returned.

Note there are performance considerations involved with the *size* parameter. For optimal performance, it is usually best to use the arraysize attribute. If the *size* parameter is used, then it is best for it to retain the same value from one `fetchmany()` call to the next.

fetchall()
Fetches all (remaining) rows of a query result, returning a list. Note that the cursor's arraysize attribute can affect the performance of this operation. An empty list is returned when no rows are available.

close()
Close the cursor now (rather than whenever `__del__` is called).

The cursor will be unusable from this point forward; a `ProgrammingError` exception will be raised if any operation is attempted with the cursor.

rowcount
Although the `Cursor` class of the `sqlite3` module implements this attribute, the database engine's own support for the determination of "rows affected"/"rows selected" is quirky.

For `executemany()` statements, the number of modifications are summed up into `rowcount`.

As required by the Python DB API Spec, the `rowcount` attribute "is -1 in case no `executeXX()` has been performed on the cursor or the rowcount of the last operation is not determinable by the interface". This includes `SELECT` statements because we cannot determine the number of rows a query produced until all rows were fetched.

With SQLite versions before 3.6.5, `rowcount` is set to 0 if you make a `DELETE FROM table` without any condition.

lastrowid
This read-only attribute provides the rowid of the last modified row. It is only set if you issued an `INSERT` or a `REPLACE` statement using the `execute()` method. For operations other than `INSERT` or `REPLACE` or when `executemany()` is called, `lastrowid` is set to `None`.

If the `INSERT` or `REPLACE` statement failed to insert the previous successful rowid is returned.

Changed in version 3.6: Added support for the `REPLACE` statement.

arraysize
Read/write attribute that controls the number of rows returned by `fetchmany()`. The default value is 1 which means a single row would be fetched per call.

description
This read-only attribute provides the column names of the last query. To remain compatible with the Python DB API, it returns a 7-tuple for each column where the last six items of each tuple are `None`.

It is set for `SELECT` statements without any matching rows as well.

connection
This read-only attribute provides the SQLite database `Connection` used by the `Cursor` object. A `Cursor` object created by calling `con.cursor()` will have a `connection` attribute that refers to *con*:

```
>>> con = sqlite3.connect(":memory:")
>>> cur = con.cursor()
>>> cur.connection == con
True
```

12.6.4 Row Objects

class sqlite3.Row

A *Row* instance serves as a highly optimized *row_factory* for *Connection* objects. It tries to mimic a tuple in most of its features.

It supports mapping access by column name and index, iteration, representation, equality testing and *len()*.

If two *Row* objects have exactly the same columns and their members are equal, they compare equal.

keys()

This method returns a list of column names. Immediately after a query, it is the first member of each tuple in *Cursor.description*.

Changed in version 3.5: Added support of slicing.

Let's assume we initialize a table as in the example given above:

```
conn = sqlite3.connect(":memory:")
c = conn.cursor()
c.execute('''create table stocks
(date text, trans text, symbol text,
 qty real, price real)''')
c.execute("""insert into stocks
          values ('2006-01-05','BUY','RHAT',100,35.14)""")
conn.commit()
c.close()
```

Now we plug *Row* in:

```
>>> conn.row_factory = sqlite3.Row
>>> c = conn.cursor()
>>> c.execute('select * from stocks')
<sqlite3.Cursor object at 0x7f4e7dd8fa80>
>>> r = c.fetchone()
>>> type(r)
<class 'sqlite3.Row'>
>>> tuple(r)
('2006-01-05', 'BUY', 'RHAT', 100.0, 35.14)
>>> len(r)
5
>>> r[2]
'RHAT'
>>> r.keys()
['date', 'trans', 'symbol', 'qty', 'price']
>>> r['qty']
100.0
>>> for member in r:
...     print(member)
...
2006-01-05
BUY
RHAT
100.0
35.14
```

12.6.5 Exceptions

exception sqlite3.Warning
A subclass of *Exception*.

exception sqlite3.Error
The base class of the other exceptions in this module. It is a subclass of *Exception*.

exception sqlite3.DatabaseError
Exception raised for errors that are related to the database.

exception sqlite3.IntegrityError
Exception raised when the relational integrity of the database is affected, e.g. a foreign key check fails. It is a subclass of *DatabaseError*.

exception sqlite3.ProgrammingError
Exception raised for programming errors, e.g. table not found or already exists, syntax error in the SQL statement, wrong number of parameters specified, etc. It is a subclass of *DatabaseError*.

12.6.6 SQLite and Python types

Introduction

SQLite natively supports the following types: NULL, INTEGER, REAL, TEXT, BLOB.

The following Python types can thus be sent to SQLite without any problem:

Python type	SQLite type
None	NULL
int	INTEGER
float	REAL
str	TEXT
bytes	BLOB

This is how SQLite types are converted to Python types by default:

SQLite type	Python type
NULL	*None*
INTEGER	*int*
REAL	*float*
TEXT	depends on *text_factory*, *str* by default
BLOB	*bytes*

The type system of the *sqlite3* module is extensible in two ways: you can store additional Python types in a SQLite database via object adaptation, and you can let the *sqlite3* module convert SQLite types to different Python types via converters.

Using adapters to store additional Python types in SQLite databases

As described before, SQLite supports only a limited set of types natively. To use other Python types with SQLite, you must **adapt** them to one of the sqlite3 module's supported types for SQLite: one of NoneType, int, float, str, bytes.

There are two ways to enable the *sqlite3* module to adapt a custom Python type to one of the supported ones.

Letting your object adapt itself

This is a good approach if you write the class yourself. Let's suppose you have a class like this:

```
class Point:
    def __init__(self, x, y):
        self.x, self.y = x, y
```

Now you want to store the point in a single SQLite column. First you'll have to choose one of the supported types first to be used for representing the point. Let's just use str and separate the coordinates using a semicolon. Then you need to give your class a method `__conform__(self, protocol)` which must return the converted value. The parameter *protocol* will be `PrepareProtocol`.

```
import sqlite3

class Point:
    def __init__(self, x, y):
        self.x, self.y = x, y

    def __conform__(self, protocol):
        if protocol is sqlite3.PrepareProtocol:
            return "%f;%f" % (self.x, self.y)

con = sqlite3.connect(":memory:")
cur = con.cursor()

p = Point(4.0, -3.2)
cur.execute("select ?", (p,))
print(cur.fetchone()[0])
```

Registering an adapter callable

The other possibility is to create a function that converts the type to the string representation and register the function with *register_adapter()*.

```
import sqlite3

class Point:
    def __init__(self, x, y):
        self.x, self.y = x, y

def adapt_point(point):
    return "%f;%f" % (point.x, point.y)

sqlite3.register_adapter(Point, adapt_point)

con = sqlite3.connect(":memory:")
cur = con.cursor()

p = Point(4.0, -3.2)
cur.execute("select ?", (p,))
print(cur.fetchone()[0])
```

The *sqlite3* module has two default adapters for Python's built-in *datetime.date* and *datetime.datetime* types. Now let's suppose we want to store *datetime.datetime* objects not in ISO representation, but as a Unix timestamp.

```
import sqlite3
import datetime
import time

def adapt_datetime(ts):
    return time.mktime(ts.timetuple())

sqlite3.register_adapter(datetime.datetime, adapt_datetime)

con = sqlite3.connect(":memory:")
cur = con.cursor()

now = datetime.datetime.now()
cur.execute("select ?", (now,))
print(cur.fetchone()[0])
```

Converting SQLite values to custom Python types

Writing an adapter lets you send custom Python types to SQLite. But to make it really useful we need to make the Python to SQLite to Python roundtrip work.

Enter converters.

Let's go back to the `Point` class. We stored the x and y coordinates separated via semicolons as strings in SQLite.

First, we'll define a converter function that accepts the string as a parameter and constructs a `Point` object from it.

Note: Converter functions **always** get called with a *bytes* object, no matter under which data type you sent the value to SQLite.

```
def convert_point(s):
    x, y = map(float, s.split(b";"))
    return Point(x, y)
```

Now you need to make the *sqlite3* module know that what you select from the database is actually a point. There are two ways of doing this:

- Implicitly via the declared type
- Explicitly via the column name

Both ways are described in section *Module functions and constants*, in the entries for the constants *PARSE_DECLTYPES* and *PARSE_COLNAMES*.

The following example illustrates both approaches.

```
import sqlite3

class Point:
    def __init__(self, x, y):
        self.x, self.y = x, y

    def __repr__(self):
        return "(%f;%f)" % (self.x, self.y)

def adapt_point(point):
```

```
    return ("%f;%f" % (point.x, point.y)).encode('ascii')

def convert_point(s):
    x, y = list(map(float, s.split(b";")))
    return Point(x, y)

# Register the adapter
sqlite3.register_adapter(Point, adapt_point)

# Register the converter
sqlite3.register_converter("point", convert_point)

p = Point(4.0, -3.2)

#########################
# 1) Using declared types
con = sqlite3.connect(":memory:", detect_types=sqlite3.PARSE_DECLTYPES)
cur = con.cursor()
cur.execute("create table test(p point)")

cur.execute("insert into test(p) values (?)", (p,))
cur.execute("select p from test")
print("with declared types:", cur.fetchone()[0])
cur.close()
con.close()

#######################
# 1) Using column names
con = sqlite3.connect(":memory:", detect_types=sqlite3.PARSE_COLNAMES)
cur = con.cursor()
cur.execute("create table test(p)")

cur.execute("insert into test(p) values (?)", (p,))
cur.execute('select p as "p [point]" from test')
print("with column names:", cur.fetchone()[0])
cur.close()
con.close()
```

Default adapters and converters

There are default adapters for the date and datetime types in the datetime module. They will be sent as ISO dates/ISO timestamps to SQLite.

The default converters are registered under the name "date" for *datetime.date* and under the name "timestamp" for *datetime.datetime*.

This way, you can use date/timestamps from Python without any additional fiddling in most cases. The format of the adapters is also compatible with the experimental SQLite date/time functions.

The following example demonstrates this.

```
import sqlite3
import datetime

con = sqlite3.connect(":memory:", detect_types=sqlite3.PARSE_DECLTYPES|sqlite3.PARSE_COLNAMES)
cur = con.cursor()
cur.execute("create table test(d date, ts timestamp)")
```

```
today = datetime.date.today()
now = datetime.datetime.now()

cur.execute("insert into test(d, ts) values (?, ?)", (today, now))
cur.execute("select d, ts from test")
row = cur.fetchone()
print(today, "=>", row[0], type(row[0]))
print(now, "=>", row[1], type(row[1]))

cur.execute('select current_date as "d [date]", current_timestamp as "ts [timestamp]"')
row = cur.fetchone()
print("current_date", row[0], type(row[0]))
print("current_timestamp", row[1], type(row[1]))
```

If a timestamp stored in SQLite has a fractional part longer than 6 numbers, its value will be truncated to microsecond precision by the timestamp converter.

12.6.7 Controlling Transactions

By default, the *sqlite3* module opens transactions implicitly before a Data Modification Language (DML) statement (i.e. `INSERT`/`UPDATE`/`DELETE`/`REPLACE`).

You can control which kind of `BEGIN` statements sqlite3 implicitly executes (or none at all) via the *isolation_level* parameter to the *connect()* call, or via the `isolation_level` property of connections.

If you want **autocommit mode**, then set `isolation_level` to `None`.

Otherwise leave it at its default, which will result in a plain "BEGIN" statement, or set it to one of SQLite's supported isolation levels: "DEFERRED", "IMMEDIATE" or "EXCLUSIVE".

The current transaction state is exposed through the *Connection.in_transaction* attribute of the connection object.

Changed in version 3.6: *sqlite3* used to implicitly commit an open transaction before DDL statements. This is no longer the case.

12.6.8 Using `sqlite3` efficiently

Using shortcut methods

Using the nonstandard `execute()`, `executemany()` and `executescript()` methods of the *Connection* object, your code can be written more concisely because you don't have to create the (often superfluous) *Cursor* objects explicitly. Instead, the *Cursor* objects are created implicitly and these shortcut methods return the cursor objects. This way, you can execute a `SELECT` statement and iterate over it directly using only a single call on the *Connection* object.

```
import sqlite3

persons = [
    ("Hugo", "Boss"),
    ("Calvin", "Klein")
    ]

con = sqlite3.connect(":memory:")

# Create the table
con.execute("create table person(firstname, lastname)")
```

```
# Fill the table
con.executemany("insert into person(firstname, lastname) values (?, ?)", persons)

# Print the table contents
for row in con.execute("select firstname, lastname from person"):
    print(row)

print("I just deleted", con.execute("delete from person").rowcount, "rows")
```

Accessing columns by name instead of by index

One useful feature of the *sqlite3* module is the built-in *sqlite3.Row* class designed to be used as a row factory.

Rows wrapped with this class can be accessed both by index (like tuples) and case-insensitively by name:

```
import sqlite3

con = sqlite3.connect(":memory:")
con.row_factory = sqlite3.Row

cur = con.cursor()
cur.execute("select 'John' as name, 42 as age")
for row in cur:
    assert row[0] == row["name"]
    assert row["name"] == row["nAmE"]
    assert row[1] == row["age"]
    assert row[1] == row["AgE"]
```

Using the connection as a context manager

Connection objects can be used as context managers that automatically commit or rollback transactions. In the event of an exception, the transaction is rolled back; otherwise, the transaction is committed:

```
import sqlite3

con = sqlite3.connect(":memory:")
con.execute("create table person (id integer primary key, firstname varchar unique)")

# Successful, con.commit() is called automatically afterwards
with con:
    con.execute("insert into person(firstname) values (?)", ("Joe",))

# con.rollback() is called after the with block finishes with an exception, the
# exception is still raised and must be caught
try:
    with con:
        con.execute("insert into person(firstname) values (?)", ("Joe",))
except sqlite3.IntegrityError:
    print("couldn't add Joe twice")
```

12.6.9 Common issues

Multithreading

Older SQLite versions had issues with sharing connections between threads. That's why the Python module disallows sharing connections and cursors between threads. If you still try to do so, you will get an exception at runtime.

The only exception is calling the *interrupt()* method, which only makes sense to call from a different thread.

CHAPTER

THIRTEEN

DATA COMPRESSION AND ARCHIVING

The modules described in this chapter support data compression with the zlib, gzip, bzip2 and lzma algorithms, and the creation of ZIP- and tar-format archives. See also *Archiving operations* provided by the *shutil* module.

13.1 zlib — Compression compatible with gzip

For applications that require data compression, the functions in this module allow compression and decompression, using the zlib library. The zlib library has its own home page at http://www.zlib.net. There are known incompatibilities between the Python module and versions of the zlib library earlier than 1.1.3; 1.1.3 has a security vulnerability, so we recommend using 1.1.4 or later.

zlib's functions have many options and often need to be used in a particular order. This documentation doesn't attempt to cover all of the permutations; consult the zlib manual at http://www.zlib.net/manual.html for authoritative information.

For reading and writing `.gz` files see the *gzip* module.

The available exception and functions in this module are:

exception zlib.error

Exception raised on compression and decompression errors.

`zlib.`**adler32**(*data*[, *value*])

Computes an Adler-32 checksum of *data*. (An Adler-32 checksum is almost as reliable as a CRC32 but can be computed much more quickly.) The result is an unsigned 32-bit integer. If *value* is present, it is used as the starting value of the checksum; otherwise, a default value of 1 is used. Passing in *value* allows computing a running checksum over the concatenation of several inputs. The algorithm is not cryptographically strong, and should not be used for authentication or digital signatures. Since the algorithm is designed for use as a checksum algorithm, it is not suitable for use as a general hash algorithm.

Changed in version 3.0: Always returns an unsigned value. To generate the same numeric value across all Python versions and platforms, use `adler32(data) & 0xffffffff`.

`zlib.`**compress**(*data*, *level=-1*)

Compresses the bytes in *data*, returning a bytes object containing compressed data. *level* is an integer from `0` to `9` or `-1` controlling the level of compression; `1` is fastest and produces the least compression, `9` is slowest and produces the most. `0` is no compression. The default value is `-1` (Z_DEFAULT_COMPRESSION). Z_DEFAULT_COMPRESSION represents a default compromise between speed and compression (currently equivalent to level 6). Raises the *error* exception if any error occurs.

Changed in version 3.6: *level* can now be used as a keyword parameter.

zlib.**compressobj**(*level=-1, method=DEFLATED, wbits=15, memLevel=8, strategy=Z_DEFAULT_STRATEGY*[, *zdict*])

Returns a compression object, to be used for compressing data streams that won't fit into memory at once.

level is the compression level – an integer from `0` to `9` or `-1`. A value of `1` is fastest and produces the least compression, while a value of `9` is slowest and produces the most. `0` is no compression. The default value is `-1` (Z_DEFAULT_COMPRESSION). Z_DEFAULT_COMPRESSION represents a default compromise between speed and compression (currently equivalent to level 6).

method is the compression algorithm. Currently, the only supported value is `DEFLATED`.

The *wbits* argument controls the size of the history buffer (or the "window size") used when compressing data, and whether a header and trailer is included in the output. It can take several ranges of values:

- +9 to +15: The base-two logarithm of the window size, which therefore ranges between 512 and 32768. Larger values produce better compression at the expense of greater memory usage. The resulting output will include a zlib-specific header and trailer.
- −9 to −15: Uses the absolute value of *wbits* as the window size logarithm, while producing a raw output stream with no header or trailing checksum.
- +25 to +31 = 16 + (9 to 15): Uses the low 4 bits of the value as the window size logarithm, while including a basic **gzip** header and trailing checksum in the output.

The *memLevel* argument controls the amount of memory used for the internal compression state. Valid values range from `1` to `9`. Higher values use more memory, but are faster and produce smaller output.

strategy is used to tune the compression algorithm. Possible values are `Z_DEFAULT_STRATEGY`, `Z_FILTERED`, and `Z_HUFFMAN_ONLY`.

zdict is a predefined compression dictionary. This is a sequence of bytes (such as a `bytes` object) containing subsequences that are expected to occur frequently in the data that is to be compressed. Those subsequences that are expected to be most common should come at the end of the dictionary.

Changed in version 3.3: Added the *zdict* parameter and keyword argument support.

zlib.**crc32**(*data*[, *value*])

Computes a CRC (Cyclic Redundancy Check) checksum of *data*. The result is an unsigned 32-bit integer. If *value* is present, it is used as the starting value of the checksum; otherwise, a default value of 0 is used. Passing in *value* allows computing a running checksum over the concatenation of several inputs. The algorithm is not cryptographically strong, and should not be used for authentication or digital signatures. Since the algorithm is designed for use as a checksum algorithm, it is not suitable for use as a general hash algorithm.

Changed in version 3.0: Always returns an unsigned value. To generate the same numeric value across all Python versions and platforms, use `crc32(data) & 0xffffffff`.

zlib.**decompress**(*data, wbits=MAX_WBITS, bufsize=DEF_BUF_SIZE*)

Decompresses the bytes in *data*, returning a bytes object containing the uncompressed data. The *wbits* parameter depends on the format of *data*, and is discussed further below. If *bufsize* is given, it is used as the initial size of the output buffer. Raises the `error` exception if any error occurs. The *wbits* parameter controls the size of the history buffer (or "window size"), and what header and trailer format is expected. It is similar to the parameter for `compressobj()`, but accepts more ranges of values:

- +8 to +15: The base-two logarithm of the window size. The input must include a zlib header and trailer.
- 0: Automatically determine the window size from the zlib header. Only supported since zlib 1.2.3.5.
- −8 to −15: Uses the absolute value of *wbits* as the window size logarithm. The input must be a raw stream with no header or trailer.

- +24 to +31 = 16 + (8 to 15): Uses the low 4 bits of the value as the window size logarithm. The input must include a gzip header and trailer.
- +40 to +47 = 32 + (8 to 15): Uses the low 4 bits of the value as the window size logarithm, and automatically accepts either the zlib or gzip format.

When decompressing a stream, the window size must not be smaller than the size originally used to compress the stream; using a too-small value may result in an `error` exception. The default *wbits* value corresponds to the largest window size and requires a zlib header and trailer to be included.

bufsize is the initial size of the buffer used to hold decompressed data. If more space is required, the buffer size will be increased as needed, so you don't have to get this value exactly right; tuning it will only save a few calls to `malloc()`.

Changed in version 3.6: *wbits* and *bufsize* can be used as keyword arguments.

`zlib.decompressobj(wbits=15[, zdict])`
Returns a decompression object, to be used for decompressing data streams that won't fit into memory at once.

The *wbits* parameter controls the size of the history buffer (or the "window size"), and what header and trailer format is expected. It has the same meaning as *described for decompress()*.

The *zdict* parameter specifies a predefined compression dictionary. If provided, this must be the same dictionary as was used by the compressor that produced the data that is to be decompressed.

Note: If *zdict* is a mutable object (such as a `bytearray`), you must not modify its contents between the call to `decompressobj()` and the first call to the decompressor's `decompress()` method.

Changed in version 3.3: Added the *zdict* parameter.

Compression objects support the following methods:

`Compress.compress(data)`
Compress *data*, returning a bytes object containing compressed data for at least part of the data in *data*. This data should be concatenated to the output produced by any preceding calls to the `compress()` method. Some input may be kept in internal buffers for later processing.

`Compress.flush([mode])`
All pending input is processed, and a bytes object containing the remaining compressed output is returned. *mode* can be selected from the constants `Z_SYNC_FLUSH`, `Z_FULL_FLUSH`, or `Z_FINISH`, defaulting to `Z_FINISH`. `Z_SYNC_FLUSH` and `Z_FULL_FLUSH` allow compressing further bytestrings of data, while `Z_FINISH` finishes the compressed stream and prevents compressing any more data. After calling `flush()` with *mode* set to `Z_FINISH`, the `compress()` method cannot be called again; the only realistic action is to delete the object.

`Compress.copy()`
Returns a copy of the compression object. This can be used to efficiently compress a set of data that share a common initial prefix.

Decompression objects support the following methods and attributes:

`Decompress.unused_data`
A bytes object which contains any bytes past the end of the compressed data. That is, this remains `b""` until the last byte that contains compression data is available. If the whole bytestring turned out to contain compressed data, this is `b""`, an empty bytes object.

`Decompress.unconsumed_tail`
A bytes object that contains any data that was not consumed by the last `decompress()` call because it exceeded the limit for the uncompressed data buffer. This data has not yet been seen by the zlib

machinery, so you must feed it (possibly with further data concatenated to it) back to a subsequent `decompress()` method call in order to get correct output.

`Decompress.eof`
A boolean indicating whether the end of the compressed data stream has been reached.

This makes it possible to distinguish between a properly-formed compressed stream, and an incomplete or truncated one.

New in version 3.3.

`Decompress.decompress(data, max_length=0)`
Decompress *data*, returning a bytes object containing the uncompressed data corresponding to at least part of the data in *string*. This data should be concatenated to the output produced by any preceding calls to the `decompress()` method. Some of the input data may be preserved in internal buffers for later processing.

If the optional parameter *max_length* is non-zero then the return value will be no longer than *max_length*. This may mean that not all of the compressed input can be processed; and unconsumed data will be stored in the attribute `unconsumed_tail`. This bytestring must be passed to a subsequent call to `decompress()` if decompression is to continue. If *max_length* is zero then the whole input is decompressed, and `unconsumed_tail` is empty.

Changed in version 3.6: *max_length* can be used as a keyword argument.

`Decompress.flush([length])`
All pending input is processed, and a bytes object containing the remaining uncompressed output is returned. After calling `flush()`, the `decompress()` method cannot be called again; the only realistic action is to delete the object.

The optional parameter *length* sets the initial size of the output buffer.

`Decompress.copy()`
Returns a copy of the decompression object. This can be used to save the state of the decompressor midway through the data stream in order to speed up random seeks into the stream at a future point.

Information about the version of the zlib library in use is available through the following constants:

`zlib.ZLIB_VERSION`
The version string of the zlib library that was used for building the module. This may be different from the zlib library actually used at runtime, which is available as `ZLIB_RUNTIME_VERSION`.

`zlib.ZLIB_RUNTIME_VERSION`
The version string of the zlib library actually loaded by the interpreter.

New in version 3.3.

See also:

Module `gzip` Reading and writing **gzip**-format files.

http://www.zlib.net The zlib library home page.

http://www.zlib.net/manual.html The zlib manual explains the semantics and usage of the library's many functions.

13.2 gzip — Support for gzip files

Source code: Lib/gzip.py

This module provides a simple interface to compress and decompress files just like the GNU programs **gzip** and **gunzip** would.

The data compression is provided by the `zlib` module.

The `gzip` module provides the `GzipFile` class, as well as the `open()`, `compress()` and `decompress()` convenience functions. The `GzipFile` class reads and writes **gzip**-format files, automatically compressing or decompressing the data so that it looks like an ordinary *file object*.

Note that additional file formats which can be decompressed by the **gzip** and **gunzip** programs, such as those produced by **compress** and **pack**, are not supported by this module.

The module defines the following items:

`gzip.open`(*filename*, *mode='rb'*, *compresslevel=9*, *encoding=None*, *errors=None*, *newline=None*)
Open a gzip-compressed file in binary or text mode, returning a *file object*.

The *filename* argument can be an actual filename (a `str` or `bytes` object), or an existing file object to read from or write to.

The *mode* argument can be any of `'r'`, `'rb'`, `'a'`, `'ab'`, `'w'`, `'wb'`, `'x'` or `'xb'` for binary mode, or `'rt'`, `'at'`, `'wt'`, or `'xt'` for text mode. The default is `'rb'`.

The *compresslevel* argument is an integer from 0 to 9, as for the `GzipFile` constructor.

For binary mode, this function is equivalent to the `GzipFile` constructor: `GzipFile(filename, mode, compresslevel)`. In this case, the *encoding*, *errors* and *newline* arguments must not be provided.

For text mode, a `GzipFile` object is created, and wrapped in an `io.TextIOWrapper` instance with the specified encoding, error handling behavior, and line ending(s).

Changed in version 3.3: Added support for *filename* being a file object, support for text mode, and the *encoding*, *errors* and *newline* arguments.

Changed in version 3.4: Added support for the `'x'`, `'xb'` and `'xt'` modes.

Changed in version 3.6: Accepts a *path-like object*.

class `gzip.GzipFile`(*filename=None*, *mode=None*, *compresslevel=9*, *fileobj=None*, *mtime=None*)
Constructor for the `GzipFile` class, which simulates most of the methods of a *file object*, with the exception of the `truncate()` method. At least one of *fileobj* and *filename* must be given a non-trivial value.

The new class instance is based on *fileobj*, which can be a regular file, an `io.BytesIO` object, or any other object which simulates a file. It defaults to `None`, in which case *filename* is opened to provide a file object.

When *fileobj* is not `None`, the *filename* argument is only used to be included in the **gzip** file header, which may include the original filename of the uncompressed file. It defaults to the filename of *fileobj*, if discernible; otherwise, it defaults to the empty string, and in this case the original filename is not included in the header.

The *mode* argument can be any of `'r'`, `'rb'`, `'a'`, `'ab'`, `'w'`, `'wb'`, `'x'`, or `'xb'`, depending on whether the file will be read or written. The default is the mode of *fileobj* if discernible; otherwise, the default is `'rb'`.

Note that the file is always opened in binary mode. To open a compressed file in text mode, use `open()` (or wrap your `GzipFile` with an `io.TextIOWrapper`).

The *compresslevel* argument is an integer from `0` to `9` controlling the level of compression; `1` is fastest and produces the least compression, and `9` is slowest and produces the most compression. `0` is no compression. The default is `9`.

The *mtime* argument is an optional numeric timestamp to be written to the last modification time field in the stream when compressing. It should only be provided in compression mode. If omitted or `None`, the current time is used. See the `mtime` attribute for more details.

Calling a *GzipFile* object's `close()` method does not close *fileobj*, since you might wish to append more material after the compressed data. This also allows you to pass an *io.BytesIO* object opened for writing as *fileobj*, and retrieve the resulting memory buffer using the *io.BytesIO* object's *getvalue()* method.

GzipFile supports the *io.BufferedIOBase* interface, including iteration and the **with** statement. Only the `truncate()` method isn't implemented.

GzipFile also provides the following method and attribute:

peek(*n*)
Read *n* uncompressed bytes without advancing the file position. At most one single read on the compressed stream is done to satisfy the call. The number of bytes returned may be more or less than requested.

Note: While calling *peek()* does not change the file position of the *GzipFile*, it may change the position of the underlying file object (e.g. if the *GzipFile* was constructed with the *fileobj* parameter).

New in version 3.2.

mtime
When decompressing, the value of the last modification time field in the most recently read header may be read from this attribute, as an integer. The initial value before reading any headers is `None`.

All **gzip** compressed streams are required to contain this timestamp field. Some programs, such as **gunzip**, make use of the timestamp. The format is the same as the return value of *time.time()* and the *st_mtime* attribute of the object returned by *os.stat()*.

Changed in version 3.1: Support for the **with** statement was added, along with the *mtime* constructor argument and *mtime* attribute.

Changed in version 3.2: Support for zero-padded and unseekable files was added.

Changed in version 3.3: The *io.BufferedIOBase.read1()* method is now implemented.

Changed in version 3.4: Added support for the `'x'` and `'xb'` modes.

Changed in version 3.5: Added support for writing arbitrary *bytes-like objects*. The *read()* method now accepts an argument of `None`.

Changed in version 3.6: Accepts a *path-like object*.

gzip.**compress**(*data*, *compresslevel=9*)
Compress the *data*, returning a *bytes* object containing the compressed data. *compresslevel* has the same meaning as in the *GzipFile* constructor above.

New in version 3.2.

gzip.**decompress**(*data*)
Decompress the *data*, returning a *bytes* object containing the uncompressed data.

New in version 3.2.

13.2.1 Examples of usage

Example of how to read a compressed file:

```
import gzip
with gzip.open('/home/joe/file.txt.gz', 'rb') as f:
    file_content = f.read()
```

Example of how to create a compressed GZIP file:

```
import gzip
content = b"Lots of content here"
with gzip.open('/home/joe/file.txt.gz', 'wb') as f:
    f.write(content)
```

Example of how to GZIP compress an existing file:

```
import gzip
import shutil
with open('/home/joe/file.txt', 'rb') as f_in:
    with gzip.open('/home/joe/file.txt.gz', 'wb') as f_out:
        shutil.copyfileobj(f_in, f_out)
```

Example of how to GZIP compress a binary string:

```
import gzip
s_in = b"Lots of content here"
s_out = gzip.compress(s_in)
```

See also:

Module *zlib* The basic data compression module needed to support the **gzip** file format.

13.3 bz2 — Support for bzip2 compression

Source code: Lib/bz2.py

This module provides a comprehensive interface for compressing and decompressing data using the bzip2 compression algorithm.

The *bz2* module contains:

- The *open()* function and *BZ2File* class for reading and writing compressed files.
- The *BZ2Compressor* and *BZ2Decompressor* classes for incremental (de)compression.
- The *compress()* and *decompress()* functions for one-shot (de)compression.

All of the classes in this module may safely be accessed from multiple threads.

13.3.1 (De)compression of files

`bz2.open`(*filename*, *mode='r'*, *compresslevel=9*, *encoding=None*, *errors=None*, *newline=None*)

Open a bzip2-compressed file in binary or text mode, returning a *file object*.

As with the constructor for *BZ2File*, the *filename* argument can be an actual filename (a *str* or *bytes* object), or an existing file object to read from or write to.

The *mode* argument can be any of `'r'`, `'rb'`, `'w'`, `'wb'`, `'x'`, `'xb'`, `'a'` or `'ab'` for binary mode, or `'rt'`, `'wt'`, `'xt'`, or `'at'` for text mode. The default is `'rb'`.

The *compresslevel* argument is an integer from 1 to 9, as for the *BZ2File* constructor.

For binary mode, this function is equivalent to the *BZ2File* constructor: `BZ2File(filename, mode, compresslevel=compresslevel)`. In this case, the *encoding*, *errors* and *newline* arguments must not be provided.

For text mode, a *BZ2File* object is created, and wrapped in an *io.TextIOWrapper* instance with the specified encoding, error handling behavior, and line ending(s).

New in version 3.3.

Changed in version 3.4: The `'x'` (exclusive creation) mode was added.

Changed in version 3.6: Accepts a *path-like object*.

class bz2.BZ2File(*filename*, *mode='r'*, *buffering=None*, *compresslevel=9*)

Open a bzip2-compressed file in binary mode.

If *filename* is a *str* or *bytes* object, open the named file directly. Otherwise, *filename* should be a *file object*, which will be used to read or write the compressed data.

The *mode* argument can be either `'r'` for reading (default), `'w'` for overwriting, `'x'` for exclusive creation, or `'a'` for appending. These can equivalently be given as `'rb'`, `'wb'`, `'xb'` and `'ab'` respectively.

If *filename* is a file object (rather than an actual file name), a mode of `'w'` does not truncate the file, and is instead equivalent to `'a'`.

The *buffering* argument is ignored. Its use is deprecated.

If *mode* is `'w'` or `'a'`, *compresslevel* can be a number between `1` and `9` specifying the level of compression: `1` produces the least compression, and `9` (default) produces the most compression.

If *mode* is `'r'`, the input file may be the concatenation of multiple compressed streams.

BZ2File provides all of the members specified by the *io.BufferedIOBase*, except for `detach()` and `truncate()`. Iteration and the `with` statement are supported.

BZ2File also provides the following method:

peek([*n*])

Return buffered data without advancing the file position. At least one byte of data will be returned (unless at EOF). The exact number of bytes returned is unspecified.

Note: While calling *peek()* does not change the file position of the *BZ2File*, it may change the position of the underlying file object (e.g. if the *BZ2File* was constructed by passing a file object for *filename*).

New in version 3.3.

Changed in version 3.1: Support for the `with` statement was added.

Changed in version 3.3: The `fileno()`, `readable()`, `seekable()`, `writable()`, `read1()` and `readinto()` methods were added.

Changed in version 3.3: Support was added for *filename* being a *file object* instead of an actual filename.

Changed in version 3.3: The `'a'` (append) mode was added, along with support for reading multi-stream files.

Changed in version 3.4: The `'x'` (exclusive creation) mode was added.

Changed in version 3.5: The *read()* method now accepts an argument of `None`.

Changed in version 3.6: Accepts a *path-like object*.

13.3.2 Incremental (de)compression

class bz2.BZ2Compressor(*compresslevel=9*)

Create a new compressor object. This object may be used to compress data incrementally. For one-shot compression, use the *compress()* function instead.

compresslevel, if given, must be a number between `1` and `9`. The default is `9`.

compress(*data*)

Provide data to the compressor object. Returns a chunk of compressed data if possible, or an empty byte string otherwise.

When you have finished providing data to the compressor, call the *flush()* method to finish the compression process.

flush()

Finish the compression process. Returns the compressed data left in internal buffers.

The compressor object may not be used after this method has been called.

class bz2.BZ2Decompressor

Create a new decompressor object. This object may be used to decompress data incrementally. For one-shot compression, use the *decompress()* function instead.

Note: This class does not transparently handle inputs containing multiple compressed streams, unlike *decompress()* and *BZ2File*. If you need to decompress a multi-stream input with *BZ2Decompressor*, you must use a new decompressor for each stream.

---

decompress(*data*, *max_length=-1*)

Decompress *data* (a *bytes-like object*), returning uncompressed data as bytes. Some of *data* may be buffered internally, for use in later calls to *decompress()*. The returned data should be concatenated with the output of any previous calls to *decompress()*.

If *max_length* is nonnegative, returns at most *max_length* bytes of decompressed data. If this limit is reached and further output can be produced, the *needs_input* attribute will be set to `False`. In this case, the next call to *decompress()* may provide *data* as `b''` to obtain more of the output.

If all of the input data was decompressed and returned (either because this was less than *max_length* bytes, or because *max_length* was negative), the *needs_input* attribute will be set to `True`.

Attempting to decompress data after the end of stream is reached raises an *EOFError*. Any data found after the end of the stream is ignored and saved in the *unused_data* attribute.

Changed in version 3.5: Added the *max_length* parameter.

eof

`True` if the end-of-stream marker has been reached.

New in version 3.3.

unused_data

Data found after the end of the compressed stream.

If this attribute is accessed before the end of the stream has been reached, its value will be `b''`.

needs_input

`False` if the *decompress()* method can provide more decompressed data before requiring new uncompressed input.

New in version 3.5.

13.3.3 One-shot (de)compression

`bz2.compress(data, compresslevel=9)`

Compress *data*.

compresslevel, if given, must be a number between `1` and `9`. The default is `9`.

For incremental compression, use a *BZ2Compressor* instead.

`bz2.decompress(data)`

Decompress *data*.

If *data* is the concatenation of multiple compressed streams, decompress all of the streams.

For incremental decompression, use a *BZ2Decompressor* instead.

Changed in version 3.3: Support for multi-stream inputs was added.

13.4 `lzma` — Compression using the LZMA algorithm

New in version 3.3.

Source code: Lib/lzma.py

This module provides classes and convenience functions for compressing and decompressing data using the LZMA compression algorithm. Also included is a file interface supporting the `.xz` and legacy `.lzma` file formats used by the **xz** utility, as well as raw compressed streams.

The interface provided by this module is very similar to that of the *bz2* module. However, note that *LZMAFile* is *not* thread-safe, unlike *bz2.BZ2File*, so if you need to use a single *LZMAFile* instance from multiple threads, it is necessary to protect it with a lock.

`exception lzma.LZMAError`

This exception is raised when an error occurs during compression or decompression, or while initializing the compressor/decompressor state.

13.4.1 Reading and writing compressed files

`lzma.open(filename, mode="rb", *, format=None, check=-1, preset=None, filters=None, encoding=None, errors=None, newline=None)`

Open an LZMA-compressed file in binary or text mode, returning a *file object*.

The *filename* argument can be either an actual file name (given as a *str*, *bytes* or *path-like* object), in which case the named file is opened, or it can be an existing file object to read from or write to.

The *mode* argument can be any of `"r"`, `"rb"`, `"w"`, `"wb"`, `"x"`, `"xb"`, `"a"` or `"ab"` for binary mode, or `"rt"`, `"wt"`, `"xt"`, or `"at"` for text mode. The default is `"rb"`.

When opening a file for reading, the *format* and *filters* arguments have the same meanings as for *LZMADecompressor*. In this case, the *check* and *preset* arguments should not be used.

When opening a file for writing, the *format*, *check*, *preset* and *filters* arguments have the same meanings as for *LZMACompressor*.

For binary mode, this function is equivalent to the *LZMAFile* constructor: `LZMAFile(filename, mode, ...)`. In this case, the *encoding*, *errors* and *newline* arguments must not be provided.

For text mode, a *LZMAFile* object is created, and wrapped in an *io.TextIOWrapper* instance with the specified encoding, error handling behavior, and line ending(s).

Changed in version 3.4: Added support for the "x", "xb" and "xt" modes.

Changed in version 3.6: Accepts a *path-like object*.

class lzma.LZMAFile(*filename=None, mode="r", *, format=None, check=-1, preset=None, filters=None*)

Open an LZMA-compressed file in binary mode.

An `LZMAFile` can wrap an already-open *file object*, or operate directly on a named file. The *filename* argument specifies either the file object to wrap, or the name of the file to open (as a `str`, `bytes` or *path-like* object). When wrapping an existing file object, the wrapped file will not be closed when the `LZMAFile` is closed.

The *mode* argument can be either "r" for reading (default), "w" for overwriting, "x" for exclusive creation, or "a" for appending. These can equivalently be given as "rb", "wb", "xb" and "ab" respectively.

If *filename* is a file object (rather than an actual file name), a mode of "w" does not truncate the file, and is instead equivalent to "a".

When opening a file for reading, the input file may be the concatenation of multiple separate compressed streams. These are transparently decoded as a single logical stream.

When opening a file for reading, the *format* and *filters* arguments have the same meanings as for `LZMADecompressor`. In this case, the *check* and *preset* arguments should not be used.

When opening a file for writing, the *format*, *check*, *preset* and *filters* arguments have the same meanings as for `LZMACompressor`.

`LZMAFile` supports all the members specified by `io.BufferedIOBase`, except for `detach()` and `truncate()`. Iteration and the `with` statement are supported.

The following method is also provided:

peek(*size=-1*)

Return buffered data without advancing the file position. At least one byte of data will be returned, unless EOF has been reached. The exact number of bytes returned is unspecified (the *size* argument is ignored).

Note: While calling `peek()` does not change the file position of the `LZMAFile`, it may change the position of the underlying file object (e.g. if the `LZMAFile` was constructed by passing a file object for *filename*).

Changed in version 3.4: Added support for the "x" and "xb" modes.

Changed in version 3.5: The `read()` method now accepts an argument of `None`.

Changed in version 3.6: Accepts a *path-like object*.

13.4.2 Compressing and decompressing data in memory

class lzma.LZMACompressor(*format=FORMAT_XZ, check=-1, preset=None, filters=None*)

Create a compressor object, which can be used to compress data incrementally.

For a more convenient way of compressing a single chunk of data, see `compress()`.

The *format* argument specifies what container format should be used. Possible values are:

- **FORMAT_XZ: The .xz container format.** This is the default format.
- **FORMAT_ALONE: The legacy .lzma container format.** This format is more limited than .xz – it does not support integrity checks or multiple filters.

- FORMAT_RAW: **A raw data stream, not using any container format.** This format specifier does not support integrity checks, and requires that you always specify a custom filter chain (for both compression and decompression). Additionally, data compressed in this manner cannot be decompressed using FORMAT_AUTO (see *LZMADecompressor*).

The *check* argument specifies the type of integrity check to include in the compressed data. This check is used when decompressing, to ensure that the data has not been corrupted. Possible values are:

- CHECK_NONE: No integrity check. This is the default (and the only acceptable value) for FORMAT_ALONE and FORMAT_RAW.
- CHECK_CRC32: 32-bit Cyclic Redundancy Check.
- CHECK_CRC64: 64-bit Cyclic Redundancy Check. This is the default for FORMAT_XZ.
- CHECK_SHA256: 256-bit Secure Hash Algorithm.

If the specified check is not supported, an *LZMAError* is raised.

The compression settings can be specified either as a preset compression level (with the *preset* argument), or in detail as a custom filter chain (with the *filters* argument).

The *preset* argument (if provided) should be an integer between 0 and 9 (inclusive), optionally OR-ed with the constant PRESET_EXTREME. If neither *preset* nor *filters* are given, the default behavior is to use PRESET_DEFAULT (preset level 6). Higher presets produce smaller output, but make the compression process slower.

Note: In addition to being more CPU-intensive, compression with higher presets also requires much more memory (and produces output that needs more memory to decompress). With preset 9 for example, the overhead for an *LZMACompressor* object can be as high as 800 MiB. For this reason, it is generally best to stick with the default preset.

The *filters* argument (if provided) should be a filter chain specifier. See *Specifying custom filter chains* for details.

compress(*data*)

Compress *data* (a *bytes* object), returning a *bytes* object containing compressed data for at least part of the input. Some of *data* may be buffered internally, for use in later calls to *compress()* and *flush()*. The returned data should be concatenated with the output of any previous calls to *compress()*.

flush()

Finish the compression process, returning a *bytes* object containing any data stored in the compressor's internal buffers.

The compressor cannot be used after this method has been called.

class lzma.**LZMADecompressor**(*format=FORMAT_AUTO*, *memlimit=None*, *filters=None*)

Create a decompressor object, which can be used to decompress data incrementally.

For a more convenient way of decompressing an entire compressed stream at once, see *decompress()*.

The *format* argument specifies the container format that should be used. The default is FORMAT_AUTO, which can decompress both .xz and .lzma files. Other possible values are FORMAT_XZ, FORMAT_ALONE, and FORMAT_RAW.

The *memlimit* argument specifies a limit (in bytes) on the amount of memory that the decompressor can use. When this argument is used, decompression will fail with an *LZMAError* if it is not possible to decompress the input within the given memory limit.

The *filters* argument specifies the filter chain that was used to create the stream being decompressed. This argument is required if *format* is FORMAT_RAW, but should not be used for other formats. See

Specifying custom filter chains for more information about filter chains.

Note: This class does not transparently handle inputs containing multiple compressed streams, unlike `decompress()` and `LZMAFile`. To decompress a multi-stream input with `LZMADecompressor`, you must create a new decompressor for each stream.

---

decompress(*data, max_length=-1*)

Decompress *data* (a *bytes-like object*), returning uncompressed data as bytes. Some of *data* may be buffered internally, for use in later calls to `decompress()`. The returned data should be concatenated with the output of any previous calls to `decompress()`.

If *max_length* is nonnegative, returns at most *max_length* bytes of decompressed data. If this limit is reached and further output can be produced, the `needs_input` attribute will be set to `False`. In this case, the next call to `decompress()` may provide *data* as `b''` to obtain more of the output.

If all of the input data was decompressed and returned (either because this was less than *max_length* bytes, or because *max_length* was negative), the `needs_input` attribute will be set to `True`.

Attempting to decompress data after the end of stream is reached raises an *EOFError*. Any data found after the end of the stream is ignored and saved in the `unused_data` attribute.

Changed in version 3.5: Added the *max_length* parameter.

check

The ID of the integrity check used by the input stream. This may be `CHECK_UNKNOWN` until enough of the input has been decoded to determine what integrity check it uses.

eof

`True` if the end-of-stream marker has been reached.

unused_data

Data found after the end of the compressed stream.

Before the end of the stream is reached, this will be `b""`.

needs_input

`False` if the `decompress()` method can provide more decompressed data before requiring new uncompressed input.

New in version 3.5.

`lzma.`**compress**(*data, format=FORMAT_XZ, check=-1, preset=None, filters=None*)

Compress *data* (a `bytes` object), returning the compressed data as a `bytes` object.

See `LZMACompressor` above for a description of the *format*, *check*, *preset* and *filters* arguments.

`lzma.`**decompress**(*data, format=FORMAT_AUTO, memlimit=None, filters=None*)

Decompress *data* (a `bytes` object), returning the uncompressed data as a `bytes` object.

If *data* is the concatenation of multiple distinct compressed streams, decompress all of these streams, and return the concatenation of the results.

See `LZMADecompressor` above for a description of the *format*, *memlimit* and *filters* arguments.

13.4.3 Miscellaneous

`lzma.`**is_check_supported**(*check*)

Returns true if the given integrity check is supported on this system.

CHECK_NONE and CHECK_CRC32 are always supported. CHECK_CRC64 and CHECK_SHA256 may be unavailable if you are using a version of **liblzma** that was compiled with a limited feature set.

13.4.4 Specifying custom filter chains

A filter chain specifier is a sequence of dictionaries, where each dictionary contains the ID and options for a single filter. Each dictionary must contain the key "id", and may contain additional keys to specify filter-dependent options. Valid filter IDs are as follows:

- **Compression filters:**
  - FILTER_LZMA1 (for use with FORMAT_ALONE)
  - FILTER_LZMA2 (for use with FORMAT_XZ and FORMAT_RAW)
- **Delta filter:**
  - FILTER_DELTA
- **Branch-Call-Jump (BCJ) filters:**
  - FILTER_X86
  - FILTER_IA64
  - FILTER_ARM
  - FILTER_ARMTHUMB
  - FILTER_POWERPC
  - FILTER_SPARC

A filter chain can consist of up to 4 filters, and cannot be empty. The last filter in the chain must be a compression filter, and any other filters must be delta or BCJ filters.

Compression filters support the following options (specified as additional entries in the dictionary representing the filter):

- preset: A compression preset to use as a source of default values for options that are not specified explicitly.
- dict_size: Dictionary size in bytes. This should be between 4 KiB and 1.5 GiB (inclusive).
- lc: Number of literal context bits.
- lp: Number of literal position bits. The sum lc + lp must be at most 4.
- pb: Number of position bits; must be at most 4.
- mode: MODE_FAST or MODE_NORMAL.
- nice_len: What should be considered a "nice length" for a match. This should be 273 or less.
- mf: What match finder to use – MF_HC3, MF_HC4, MF_BT2, MF_BT3, or MF_BT4.
- depth: Maximum search depth used by match finder. 0 (default) means to select automatically based on other filter options.

The delta filter stores the differences between bytes, producing more repetitive input for the compressor in certain circumstances. It supports one option, dist. This indicates the distance between bytes to be subtracted. The default is 1, i.e. take the differences between adjacent bytes.

The BCJ filters are intended to be applied to machine code. They convert relative branches, calls and jumps in the code to use absolute addressing, with the aim of increasing the redundancy that can be exploited by the compressor. These filters support one option, start_offset. This specifies the address that should be mapped to the beginning of the input data. The default is 0.

13.4.5 Examples

Reading in a compressed file:

```
import lzma
with lzma.open("file.xz") as f:
    file_content = f.read()
```

Creating a compressed file:

```
import lzma
data = b"Insert Data Here"
with lzma.open("file.xz", "w") as f:
    f.write(data)
```

Compressing data in memory:

```
import lzma
data_in = b"Insert Data Here"
data_out = lzma.compress(data_in)
```

Incremental compression:

```
import lzma
lzc = lzma.LZMACompressor()
out1 = lzc.compress(b"Some data\n")
out2 = lzc.compress(b"Another piece of data\n")
out3 = lzc.compress(b"Even more data\n")
out4 = lzc.flush()
# Concatenate all the partial results:
result = b"".join([out1, out2, out3, out4])
```

Writing compressed data to an already-open file:

```
import lzma
with open("file.xz", "wb") as f:
    f.write(b"This data will not be compressed\n")
    with lzma.open(f, "w") as lzf:
        lzf.write(b"This *will* be compressed\n")
    f.write(b"Not compressed\n")
```

Creating a compressed file using a custom filter chain:

```
import lzma
my_filters = [
    {"id": lzma.FILTER_DELTA, "dist": 5},
    {"id": lzma.FILTER_LZMA2, "preset": 7 | lzma.PRESET_EXTREME},
]
with lzma.open("file.xz", "w", filters=my_filters) as f:
    f.write(b"blah blah blah")
```

13.5 zipfile — Work with ZIP archives

Source code: Lib/zipfile.py

The ZIP file format is a common archive and compression standard. This module provides tools to create, read, write, append, and list a ZIP file. Any advanced use of this module will require an understanding of the format, as defined in PKZIP Application Note.

This module does not currently handle multi-disk ZIP files. It can handle ZIP files that use the ZIP64 extensions (that is ZIP files that are more than 4 GiB in size). It supports decryption of encrypted files in ZIP archives, but it currently cannot create an encrypted file. Decryption is extremely slow as it is implemented in native Python rather than C.

The module defines the following items:

exception zipfile.BadZipFile
The error raised for bad ZIP files.

New in version 3.2.

exception zipfile.BadZipfile
Alias of *BadZipFile*, for compatibility with older Python versions.

Deprecated since version 3.2.

exception zipfile.LargeZipFile
The error raised when a ZIP file would require ZIP64 functionality but that has not been enabled.

class zipfile.ZipFile
The class for reading and writing ZIP files. See section *ZipFile Objects* for constructor details.

class zipfile.PyZipFile
Class for creating ZIP archives containing Python libraries.

class zipfile.ZipInfo(*filename='NoName', date_time=(1980, 1, 1, 0, 0, 0)*)
Class used to represent information about a member of an archive. Instances of this class are returned by the `getinfo()` and `infolist()` methods of `ZipFile` objects. Most users of the `zipfile` module will not need to create these, but only use those created by this module. *filename* should be the full name of the archive member, and *date_time* should be a tuple containing six fields which describe the time of the last modification to the file; the fields are described in section *ZipInfo Objects*.

zipfile.is_zipfile(*filename*)
Returns `True` if *filename* is a valid ZIP file based on its magic number, otherwise returns `False`. *filename* may be a file or file-like object too.

Changed in version 3.1: Support for file and file-like objects.

zipfile.ZIP_STORED
The numeric constant for an uncompressed archive member.

zipfile.ZIP_DEFLATED
The numeric constant for the usual ZIP compression method. This requires the `zlib` module.

zipfile.ZIP_BZIP2
The numeric constant for the BZIP2 compression method. This requires the `bz2` module.

New in version 3.3.

zipfile.ZIP_LZMA
The numeric constant for the LZMA compression method. This requires the `lzma` module.

New in version 3.3.

Note: The ZIP file format specification has included support for bzip2 compression since 2001, and for LZMA compression since 2006. However, some tools (including older Python releases) do not support these compression methods, and may either refuse to process the ZIP file altogether, or fail to extract individual files.

See also:

PKZIP Application Note Documentation on the ZIP file format by Phil Katz, the creator of the format and algorithms used.

Info-ZIP Home Page Information about the Info-ZIP project's ZIP archive programs and development libraries.

13.5.1 ZipFile Objects

class zipfile.ZipFile(*file*, *mode='r'*, *compression=ZIP_STORED*, *allowZip64=True*)

Open a ZIP file, where *file* can be a path to a file (a string), a file-like object or a *path-like object*. The *mode* parameter should be `'r'` to read an existing file, `'w'` to truncate and write a new file, `'a'` to append to an existing file, or `'x'` to exclusively create and write a new file. If *mode* is `'x'` and *file* refers to an existing file, a `FileExistsError` will be raised. If *mode* is `'a'` and *file* refers to an existing ZIP file, then additional files are added to it. If *file* does not refer to a ZIP file, then a new ZIP archive is appended to the file. This is meant for adding a ZIP archive to another file (such as `python.exe`). If *mode* is `'a'` and the file does not exist at all, it is created. If *mode* is `'r'` or `'a'`, the file should be seekable. *compression* is the ZIP compression method to use when writing the archive, and should be `ZIP_STORED`, `ZIP_DEFLATED`, `ZIP_BZIP2` or `ZIP_LZMA`; unrecognized values will cause `NotImplementedError` to be raised. If `ZIP_DEFLATED`, `ZIP_BZIP2` or `ZIP_LZMA` is specified but the corresponding module (`zlib`, `bz2` or `lzma`) is not available, `RuntimeError` is raised. The default is `ZIP_STORED`. If *allowZip64* is `True` (the default) zipfile will create ZIP files that use the ZIP64 extensions when the zipfile is larger than 4 GiB. If it is false `zipfile` will raise an exception when the ZIP file would require ZIP64 extensions.

If the file is created with mode `'w'`, `'x'` or `'a'` and then `closed` without adding any files to the archive, the appropriate ZIP structures for an empty archive will be written to the file.

ZipFile is also a context manager and therefore supports the `with` statement. In the example, *myzip* is closed after the `with` statement's suite is finished—even if an exception occurs:

```
with ZipFile('spam.zip', 'w') as myzip:
    myzip.write('eggs.txt')
```

New in version 3.2: Added the ability to use `ZipFile` as a context manager.

Changed in version 3.3: Added support for `bzip2` and `lzma` compression.

Changed in version 3.4: ZIP64 extensions are enabled by default.

Changed in version 3.5: Added support for writing to unseekable streams. Added support for the `'x'` mode.

Changed in version 3.6: Previously, a plain `RuntimeError` was raised for unrecognized compression values.

Changed in version 3.6.2: The *file* parameter accepts a *path-like object*.

ZipFile.close()

Close the archive file. You must call `close()` before exiting your program or essential records will not be written.

ZipFile.getinfo(*name*)

Return a `ZipInfo` object with information about the archive member *name*. Calling `getinfo()` for a name not currently contained in the archive will raise a `KeyError`.

ZipFile.infolist()

Return a list containing a `ZipInfo` object for each member of the archive. The objects are in the same order as their entries in the actual ZIP file on disk if an existing archive was opened.

`ZipFile.namelist()`
Return a list of archive members by name.

`ZipFile.open(`*name, mode='r', pwd=None, *, force_zip64=False*`)`
Access a member of the archive as a binary file-like object. *name* can be either the name of a file within the archive or a *ZipInfo* object. The *mode* parameter, if included, must be `'r'` (the default) or `'w'`. *pwd* is the password used to decrypt encrypted ZIP files.

open() is also a context manager and therefore supports the `with` statement:

```
with ZipFile('spam.zip') as myzip:
    with myzip.open('eggs.txt') as myfile:
        print(myfile.read())
```

With *mode* `'r'` the file-like object (`ZipExtFile`) is read-only and provides the following methods: *read()*, *readline()*, *readlines()*, `__iter__()`, *__next__()*. These objects can operate independently of the ZipFile.

With `mode='w'`, a writable file handle is returned, which supports the *write()* method. While a writable file handle is open, attempting to read or write other files in the ZIP file will raise a *ValueError*.

When writing a file, if the file size is not known in advance but may exceed 2 GiB, pass `force_zip64=True` to ensure that the header format is capable of supporting large files. If the file size is known in advance, construct a *ZipInfo* object with *file_size* set, and use that as the *name* parameter.

Note: The *open()*, *read()* and *extract()* methods can take a filename or a *ZipInfo* object. You will appreciate this when trying to read a ZIP file that contains members with duplicate names.

Changed in version 3.6: Removed support of `mode='U'`. Use *io.TextIOWrapper* for reading compressed text files in *universal newlines* mode.

Changed in version 3.6: *open()* can now be used to write files into the archive with the `mode='w'` option.

Changed in version 3.6: Calling *open()* on a closed ZipFile will raise a *ValueError*. Previously, a *RuntimeError* was raised.

`ZipFile.extract(`*member, path=None, pwd=None*`)`
Extract a member from the archive to the current working directory; *member* must be its full name or a *ZipInfo* object. Its file information is extracted as accurately as possible. *path* specifies a different directory to extract to. *member* can be a filename or a *ZipInfo* object. *pwd* is the password used for encrypted files.

Returns the normalized path created (a directory or new file).

Note: If a member filename is an absolute path, a drive/UNC sharepoint and leading (back)slashes will be stripped, e.g.: `///foo/bar` becomes `foo/bar` on Unix, and `C:\foo\bar` becomes `foo\bar` on Windows. And all `".."` components in a member filename will be removed, e.g.: `../../foo../../ba..r` becomes `foo../ba..r`. On Windows illegal characters (`:`, `<`, `>`, `|`, `"`, `?`, and `*`) replaced by underscore (`_`).

Changed in version 3.6: Calling *extract()* on a closed ZipFile will raise a *ValueError*. Previously, a *RuntimeError* was raised.

Changed in version 3.6.2: The *path* parameter accepts a *path-like object*.

`ZipFile.extractall(path=None, members=None, pwd=None)`

Extract all members from the archive to the current working directory. *path* specifies a different directory to extract to. *members* is optional and must be a subset of the list returned by `namelist()`. *pwd* is the password used for encrypted files.

> **Warning:** Never extract archives from untrusted sources without prior inspection. It is possible that files are created outside of *path*, e.g. members that have absolute filenames starting with `"/"` or filenames with two dots `".."`. This module attempts to prevent that. See `extract()` note.

Changed in version 3.6: Calling `extractall()` on a closed ZipFile will raise a `ValueError`. Previously, a `RuntimeError` was raised.

Changed in version 3.6.2: The *path* parameter accepts a *path-like object*.

`ZipFile.printdir()`

Print a table of contents for the archive to `sys.stdout`.

`ZipFile.setpassword(pwd)`

Set *pwd* as default password to extract encrypted files.

`ZipFile.read(name, pwd=None)`

Return the bytes of the file *name* in the archive. *name* is the name of the file in the archive, or a `ZipInfo` object. The archive must be open for read or append. *pwd* is the password used for encrypted files and, if specified, it will override the default password set with `setpassword()`. Calling `read()` on a ZipFile that uses a compression method other than `ZIP_STORED`, `ZIP_DEFLATED`, `ZIP_BZIP2` or `ZIP_LZMA` will raise a `NotImplementedError`. An error will also be raised if the corresponding compression module is not available.

Changed in version 3.6: Calling `read()` on a closed ZipFile will raise a `ValueError`. Previously, a `RuntimeError` was raised.

`ZipFile.testzip()`

Read all the files in the archive and check their CRC's and file headers. Return the name of the first bad file, or else return `None`.

Changed in version 3.6: Calling `testfile()` on a closed ZipFile will raise a `ValueError`. Previously, a `RuntimeError` was raised.

`ZipFile.write(filename, arcname=None, compress_type=None)`

Write the file named *filename* to the archive, giving it the archive name *arcname* (by default, this will be the same as *filename*, but without a drive letter and with leading path separators removed). If given, *compress_type* overrides the value given for the *compression* parameter to the constructor for the new entry. The archive must be open with mode `'w'`, `'x'` or `'a'`.

> **Note:** There is no official file name encoding for ZIP files. If you have unicode file names, you must convert them to byte strings in your desired encoding before passing them to `write()`. WinZip interprets all file names as encoded in CP437, also known as DOS Latin.

> **Note:** Archive names should be relative to the archive root, that is, they should not start with a path separator.

> **Note:** If `arcname` (or `filename`, if `arcname` is not given) contains a null byte, the name of the file in the archive will be truncated at the null byte.

Changed in version 3.6: Calling *write()* on a ZipFile created with mode 'r' or a closed ZipFile will raise a *ValueError*. Previously, a *RuntimeError* was raised.

ZipFile.writestr(*zinfo_or_arcname*, *data*[, *compress_type*])

Write the string *data* to the archive; *zinfo_or_arcname* is either the file name it will be given in the archive, or a *ZipInfo* instance. If it's an instance, at least the filename, date, and time must be given. If it's a name, the date and time is set to the current date and time. The archive must be opened with mode 'w', 'x' or 'a'.

If given, *compress_type* overrides the value given for the *compression* parameter to the constructor for the new entry, or in the *zinfo_or_arcname* (if that is a *ZipInfo* instance).

Note: When passing a *ZipInfo* instance as the *zinfo_or_arcname* parameter, the compression method used will be that specified in the *compress_type* member of the given *ZipInfo* instance. By default, the *ZipInfo* constructor sets this member to *ZIP_STORED*.

Changed in version 3.2: The *compress_type* argument.

Changed in version 3.6: Calling *writestr()* on a ZipFile created with mode 'r' or a closed ZipFile will raise a *ValueError*. Previously, a *RuntimeError* was raised.

The following data attributes are also available:

ZipFile.filename

Name of the ZIP file.

ZipFile.debug

The level of debug output to use. This may be set from 0 (the default, no output) to 3 (the most output). Debugging information is written to sys.stdout.

ZipFile.comment

The comment text associated with the ZIP file. If assigning a comment to a *ZipFile* instance created with mode 'w', 'x' or 'a', this should be a string no longer than 65535 bytes. Comments longer than this will be truncated in the written archive when *close()* is called.

13.5.2 PyZipFile Objects

The *PyZipFile* constructor takes the same parameters as the *ZipFile* constructor, and one additional parameter, *optimize*.

class zipfile.PyZipFile(*file*, *mode='r'*, *compression=ZIP_STORED*, *allowZip64=True*, *optimize=-1*)

New in version 3.2: The *optimize* parameter.

Changed in version 3.4: ZIP64 extensions are enabled by default.

Instances have one method in addition to those of *ZipFile* objects:

writepy(*pathname*, *basename=''*, *filterfunc=None*)

Search for files *.py and add the corresponding file to the archive.

If the *optimize* parameter to *PyZipFile* was not given or -1, the corresponding file is a *.pyc file, compiling if necessary.

If the *optimize* parameter to *PyZipFile* was 0, 1 or 2, only files with that optimization level (see *compile()*) are added to the archive, compiling if necessary.

If *pathname* is a file, the filename must end with .py, and just the (corresponding *.pyc) file is added at the top level (no path information). If *pathname* is a file that does not end with .py, a *RuntimeError* will be raised. If it is a directory, and the directory is not a package directory, then all the files *.pyc are added at the top level. If the directory is a package directory, then all *.pyc are added under the package name as a file path, and if any subdirectories are package directories, all of these are added recursively.

basename is intended for internal use only.

filterfunc, if given, must be a function taking a single string argument. It will be passed each path (including each individual full file path) before it is added to the archive. If *filterfunc* returns a false value, the path will not be added, and if it is a directory its contents will be ignored. For example, if our test files are all either in test directories or start with the string test_, we can use a *filterfunc* to exclude them:

```
>>> zf = PyZipFile('myprog.zip')
>>> def notests(s):
...     fn = os.path.basename(s)
...     return (not (fn == 'test' or fn.startswith('test_')))
>>> zf.writepy('myprog', filterfunc=notests)
```

The *writepy()* method makes archives with file names like this:

```
string.pyc                  # Top level name
test/__init__.pyc           # Package directory
test/testall.pyc            # Module test.testall
test/bogus/__init__.pyc     # Subpackage directory
test/bogus/myfile.pyc       # Submodule test.bogus.myfile
```

New in version 3.4: The *filterfunc* parameter.

Changed in version 3.6.2: The *pathname* parameter accepts a *path-like object*.

13.5.3 ZipInfo Objects

Instances of the *ZipInfo* class are returned by the *getinfo()* and *infolist()* methods of *ZipFile* objects. Each object stores information about a single member of the ZIP archive.

There is one classmethod to make a *ZipInfo* instance for a filesystem file:

classmethod ZipInfo.from_file(*filename*, *arcname=None*)

Construct a *ZipInfo* instance for a file on the filesystem, in preparation for adding it to a zip file.

filename should be the path to a file or directory on the filesystem.

If *arcname* is specified, it is used as the name within the archive. If *arcname* is not specified, the name will be the same as *filename*, but with any drive letter and leading path separators removed.

New in version 3.6.

Changed in version 3.6.2: The *filename* parameter accepts a *path-like object*.

Instances have the following methods and attributes:

ZipInfo.**is_dir**()

Return True if this archive member is a directory.

This uses the entry's name: directories should always end with /.

New in version 3.6.

ZipInfo.**filename**

Name of the file in the archive.

ZipInfo.**date_time**

The time and date of the last modification to the archive member. This is a tuple of six values:

Index	Value
0	Year (>= 1980)
1	Month (one-based)
2	Day of month (one-based)
3	Hours (zero-based)
4	Minutes (zero-based)
5	Seconds (zero-based)

Note: The ZIP file format does not support timestamps before 1980.

`ZipInfo.compress_type`
Type of compression for the archive member.

`ZipInfo.comment`
Comment for the individual archive member.

`ZipInfo.extra`
Expansion field data. The PKZIP Application Note contains some comments on the internal structure of the data contained in this string.

`ZipInfo.create_system`
System which created ZIP archive.

`ZipInfo.create_version`
PKZIP version which created ZIP archive.

`ZipInfo.extract_version`
PKZIP version needed to extract archive.

`ZipInfo.reserved`
Must be zero.

`ZipInfo.flag_bits`
ZIP flag bits.

`ZipInfo.volume`
Volume number of file header.

`ZipInfo.internal_attr`
Internal attributes.

`ZipInfo.external_attr`
External file attributes.

`ZipInfo.header_offset`
Byte offset to the file header.

`ZipInfo.CRC`
CRC-32 of the uncompressed file.

`ZipInfo.compress_size`
Size of the compressed data.

`ZipInfo.file_size`
Size of the uncompressed file.

13.5.4 Command-Line Interface

The *zipfile* module provides a simple command-line interface to interact with ZIP archives.

If you want to create a new ZIP archive, specify its name after the *-c* option and then list the filename(s) that should be included:

```
$ python -m zipfile -c monty.zip spam.txt eggs.txt
```

Passing a directory is also acceptable:

```
$ python -m zipfile -c monty.zip life-of-brian_1979/
```

If you want to extract a ZIP archive into the specified directory, use the *-e* option:

```
$ python -m zipfile -e monty.zip target-dir/
```

For a list of the files in a ZIP archive, use the *-l* option:

```
$ python -m zipfile -l monty.zip
```

Command-line options

`-l <zipfile>`
List files in a zipfile.

`-c <zipfile> <source1> ... <sourceN>`
Create zipfile from source files.

`-e <zipfile> <output_dir>`
Extract zipfile into target directory.

`-t <zipfile>`
Test whether the zipfile is valid or not.

13.6 `tarfile` — Read and write tar archive files

Source code: Lib/tarfile.py

The `tarfile` module makes it possible to read and write tar archives, including those using gzip, bz2 and lzma compression. Use the `zipfile` module to read or write `.zip` files, or the higher-level functions in *shutil*.

Some facts and figures:

- reads and writes `gzip`, `bz2` and `lzma` compressed archives if the respective modules are available.
- read/write support for the POSIX.1-1988 (ustar) format.
- read/write support for the GNU tar format including *longname* and *longlink* extensions, read-only support for all variants of the *sparse* extension including restoration of sparse files.
- read/write support for the POSIX.1-2001 (pax) format.
- handles directories, regular files, hardlinks, symbolic links, fifos, character devices and block devices and is able to acquire and restore file information like timestamp, access permissions and owner.

Changed in version 3.3: Added support for `lzma` compression.

tarfile.open(*name=None, mode='r', fileobj=None, bufsize=10240, **kwargs*)
Return a `TarFile` object for the pathname *name*. For detailed information on `TarFile` objects and the keyword arguments that are allowed, see *TarFile Objects*.

mode has to be a string of the form 'filemode[:compression]', it defaults to 'r'. Here is a full list of mode combinations:

mode	action
'r' or 'r:*'	Open for reading with transparent compression (recommended).
'r:'	Open for reading exclusively without compression.
'r:gz'	Open for reading with gzip compression.
'r:bz2'	Open for reading with bzip2 compression.
'r:xz'	Open for reading with lzma compression.
'x' or 'x:'	Create a tarfile exclusively without compression. Raise an *FileExistsError* exception if it already exists.
'x:gz'	Create a tarfile with gzip compression. Raise an *FileExistsError* exception if it already exists.
'x:bz2'	Create a tarfile with bzip2 compression. Raise an *FileExistsError* exception if it already exists.
'x:xz'	Create a tarfile with lzma compression. Raise an *FileExistsError* exception if it already exists.
'a' or 'a:'	Open for appending with no compression. The file is created if it does not exist.
'w' or 'w:'	Open for uncompressed writing.
'w:gz'	Open for gzip compressed writing.
'w:bz2'	Open for bzip2 compressed writing.
'w:xz'	Open for lzma compressed writing.

Note that 'a:gz', 'a:bz2' or 'a:xz' is not possible. If *mode* is not suitable to open a certain (compressed) file for reading, *ReadError* is raised. Use *mode* 'r' to avoid this. If a compression method is not supported, *CompressionError* is raised.

If *fileobj* is specified, it is used as an alternative to a *file object* opened in binary mode for *name*. It is supposed to be at position 0.

For modes 'w:gz', 'r:gz', 'w:bz2', 'r:bz2', 'x:gz', 'x:bz2', *tarfile.open()* accepts the keyword argument *compresslevel* (default 9) to specify the compression level of the file.

For special purposes, there is a second format for *mode*: 'filemode|[compression]'. *tarfile.open()* will return a *TarFile* object that processes its data as a stream of blocks. No random seeking will be done on the file. If given, *fileobj* may be any object that has a **read()** or **write()** method (depending on the *mode*). *bufsize* specifies the blocksize and defaults to 20 * 512 bytes. Use this variant in combination with e.g. sys.stdin, a socket *file object* or a tape device. However, such a *TarFile* object is limited in that it does not allow random access, see *Examples*. The currently possible modes:

Mode	Action
'r|*'	Open a *stream* of tar blocks for reading with transparent compression.
'r|'	Open a *stream* of uncompressed tar blocks for reading.
'r|gz'	Open a gzip compressed *stream* for reading.
'r|bz2'	Open a bzip2 compressed *stream* for reading.
'r|xz'	Open an lzma compressed *stream* for reading.
'w|'	Open an uncompressed *stream* for writing.
'w|gz'	Open a gzip compressed *stream* for writing.
'w|bz2'	Open a bzip2 compressed *stream* for writing.
'w|xz'	Open an lzma compressed *stream* for writing.

Changed in version 3.5: The `'x'` (exclusive creation) mode was added.

Changed in version 3.6: The *name* parameter accepts a *path-like object*.

class tarfile.TarFile
Class for reading and writing tar archives. Do not use this class directly: use `tarfile.open()` instead. See *TarFile Objects*.

tarfile.is_tarfile(*name*)
Return `True` if *name* is a tar archive file, that the `tarfile` module can read.

The `tarfile` module defines the following exceptions:

exception tarfile.TarError
Base class for all `tarfile` exceptions.

exception tarfile.ReadError
Is raised when a tar archive is opened, that either cannot be handled by the `tarfile` module or is somehow invalid.

exception tarfile.CompressionError
Is raised when a compression method is not supported or when the data cannot be decoded properly.

exception tarfile.StreamError
Is raised for the limitations that are typical for stream-like `TarFile` objects.

exception tarfile.ExtractError
Is raised for *non-fatal* errors when using `TarFile.extract()`, but only if `TarFile.errorlevel== 2`.

exception tarfile.HeaderError
Is raised by `TarInfo.frombuf()` if the buffer it gets is invalid.

The following constants are available at the module level:

tarfile.ENCODING
The default character encoding: `'utf-8'` on Windows, the value returned by `sys.getfilesystemencoding()` otherwise.

Each of the following constants defines a tar archive format that the `tarfile` module is able to create. See section *Supported tar formats* for details.

tarfile.USTAR_FORMAT
POSIX.1-1988 (ustar) format.

tarfile.GNU_FORMAT
GNU tar format.

tarfile.PAX_FORMAT
POSIX.1-2001 (pax) format.

tarfile.DEFAULT_FORMAT
The default format for creating archives. This is currently `GNU_FORMAT`.

See also:

Module `zipfile` Documentation of the `zipfile` standard module.

Archiving operations Documentation of the higher-level archiving facilities provided by the standard `shutil` module.

GNU tar manual, Basic Tar Format Documentation for tar archive files, including GNU tar extensions.

13.6.1 TarFile Objects

The *TarFile* object provides an interface to a tar archive. A tar archive is a sequence of blocks. An archive member (a stored file) is made up of a header block followed by data blocks. It is possible to store a file in a tar archive several times. Each archive member is represented by a *TarInfo* object, see *TarInfo Objects* for details.

A *TarFile* object can be used as a context manager in a `with` statement. It will automatically be closed when the block is completed. Please note that in the event of an exception an archive opened for writing will not be finalized; only the internally used file object will be closed. See the *Examples* section for a use case.

New in version 3.2: Added support for the context management protocol.

class tarfile.TarFile(*name=None, mode='r', fileobj=None, format=DEFAULT_FORMAT, tarinfo=TarInfo, dereference=False, ignore_zeros=False, encoding=ENCODING, errors='surrogateescape', pax_headers=None, debug=0, errorlevel=0*)

All following arguments are optional and can be accessed as instance attributes as well.

name is the pathname of the archive. *name* may be a *path-like object*. It can be omitted if *fileobj* is given. In this case, the file object's `name` attribute is used if it exists.

mode is either `'r'` to read from an existing archive, `'a'` to append data to an existing file, `'w'` to create a new file overwriting an existing one, or `'x'` to create a new file only if it does not already exist.

If *fileobj* is given, it is used for reading or writing data. If it can be determined, *mode* is overridden by *fileobj*'s mode. *fileobj* will be used from position 0.

Note: *fileobj* is not closed, when *TarFile* is closed.

---

format controls the archive format. It must be one of the constants *USTAR_FORMAT*, *GNU_FORMAT* or *PAX_FORMAT* that are defined at module level.

The *tarinfo* argument can be used to replace the default *TarInfo* class with a different one.

If *dereference* is *False*, add symbolic and hard links to the archive. If it is *True*, add the content of the target files to the archive. This has no effect on systems that do not support symbolic links.

If *ignore_zeros* is *False*, treat an empty block as the end of the archive. If it is *True*, skip empty (and invalid) blocks and try to get as many members as possible. This is only useful for reading concatenated or damaged archives.

debug can be set from `0` (no debug messages) up to `3` (all debug messages). The messages are written to `sys.stderr`.

If *errorlevel* is `0`, all errors are ignored when using *TarFile.extract()*. Nevertheless, they appear as error messages in the debug output, when debugging is enabled. If `1`, all *fatal* errors are raised as *OSError* exceptions. If `2`, all *non-fatal* errors are raised as *TarError* exceptions as well.

The *encoding* and *errors* arguments define the character encoding to be used for reading or writing the archive and how conversion errors are going to be handled. The default settings will work for most users. See section *Unicode issues* for in-depth information.

The *pax_headers* argument is an optional dictionary of strings which will be added as a pax global header if *format* is *PAX_FORMAT*.

Changed in version 3.2: Use `'surrogateescape'` as the default for the *errors* argument.

Changed in version 3.5: The `'x'` (exclusive creation) mode was added.

Changed in version 3.6: The *name* parameter accepts a *path-like object*.

classmethod TarFile.**open**(...)
Alternative constructor. The `tarfile.open()` function is actually a shortcut to this classmethod.

TarFile.**getmember**(*name*)
Return a `TarInfo` object for member *name*. If *name* can not be found in the archive, `KeyError` is raised.

Note: If a member occurs more than once in the archive, its last occurrence is assumed to be the most up-to-date version.

TarFile.**getmembers**()
Return the members of the archive as a list of `TarInfo` objects. The list has the same order as the members in the archive.

TarFile.**getnames**()
Return the members as a list of their names. It has the same order as the list returned by `getmembers()`.

TarFile.**list**(*verbose=True*, ***, *members=None*)
Print a table of contents to `sys.stdout`. If *verbose* is `False`, only the names of the members are printed. If it is `True`, output similar to that of `ls -l` is produced. If optional *members* is given, it must be a subset of the list returned by `getmembers()`.

Changed in version 3.5: Added the *members* parameter.

TarFile.**next**()
Return the next member of the archive as a `TarInfo` object, when `TarFile` is opened for reading. Return `None` if there is no more available.

TarFile.**extractall**(*path="."*, *members=None*, ***, *numeric_owner=False*)
Extract all members from the archive to the current working directory or directory *path*. If optional *members* is given, it must be a subset of the list returned by `getmembers()`. Directory information like owner, modification time and permissions are set after all members have been extracted. This is done to work around two problems: A directory's modification time is reset each time a file is created in it. And, if a directory's permissions do not allow writing, extracting files to it will fail.

If *numeric_owner* is `True`, the uid and gid numbers from the tarfile are used to set the owner/group for the extracted files. Otherwise, the named values from the tarfile are used.

Warning: Never extract archives from untrusted sources without prior inspection. It is possible that files are created outside of *path*, e.g. members that have absolute filenames starting with `"/"` or filenames with two dots `".."`.

Changed in version 3.5: Added the *numeric_owner* parameter.

Changed in version 3.6: The *path* parameter accepts a *path-like object*.

TarFile.**extract**(*member*, *path=""*, *set_attrs=True*, ***, *numeric_owner=False*)
Extract a member from the archive to the current working directory, using its full name. Its file information is extracted as accurately as possible. *member* may be a filename or a `TarInfo` object. You can specify a different directory using *path*. *path* may be a *path-like object*. File attributes (owner, mtime, mode) are set unless *set_attrs* is false.

If *numeric_owner* is `True`, the uid and gid numbers from the tarfile are used to set the owner/group for the extracted files. Otherwise, the named values from the tarfile are used.

Note: The `extract()` method does not take care of several extraction issues. In most cases you should consider using the `extractall()` method.

Warning: See the warning for `extractall()`.

Changed in version 3.2: Added the *set_attrs* parameter.

Changed in version 3.5: Added the *numeric_owner* parameter.

Changed in version 3.6: The *path* parameter accepts a *path-like object*.

`TarFile.extractfile(member)`

Extract a member from the archive as a file object. *member* may be a filename or a `TarInfo` object. If *member* is a regular file or a link, an `io.BufferedReader` object is returned. Otherwise, `None` is returned.

Changed in version 3.3: Return an `io.BufferedReader` object.

`TarFile.add(name, arcname=None, recursive=True, exclude=None, *, filter=None)`

Add the file *name* to the archive. *name* may be any type of file (directory, fifo, symbolic link, etc.). If given, *arcname* specifies an alternative name for the file in the archive. Directories are added recursively by default. This can be avoided by setting *recursive* to `False`. If *exclude* is given, it must be a function that takes one filename argument and returns a boolean value. Depending on this value the respective file is either excluded (`True`) or added (`False`). If *filter* is specified it must be a keyword argument. It should be a function that takes a `TarInfo` object argument and returns the changed `TarInfo` object. If it instead returns `None` the `TarInfo` object will be excluded from the archive. See *Examples* for an example.

Changed in version 3.2: Added the *filter* parameter.

Deprecated since version 3.2: The *exclude* parameter is deprecated, please use the *filter* parameter instead.

`TarFile.addfile(tarinfo, fileobj=None)`

Add the `TarInfo` object *tarinfo* to the archive. If *fileobj* is given, it should be a *binary file*, and **`tarinfo.size`** bytes are read from it and added to the archive. You can create `TarInfo` objects directly, or by using `gettarinfo()`.

`TarFile.gettarinfo(name=None, arcname=None, fileobj=None)`

Create a `TarInfo` object from the result of `os.stat()` or equivalent on an existing file. The file is either named by *name*, or specified as a *file object* *fileobj* with a file descriptor. *name* may be a *path-like object*. If given, *arcname* specifies an alternative name for the file in the archive, otherwise, the name is taken from *fileobj*'s `name` attribute, or the *name* argument. The name should be a text string.

You can modify some of the `TarInfo`'s attributes before you add it using `addfile()`. If the file object is not an ordinary file object positioned at the beginning of the file, attributes such as `size` may need modifying. This is the case for objects such as `GzipFile`. The `name` may also be modified, in which case *arcname* could be a dummy string.

Changed in version 3.6: The *name* parameter accepts a *path-like object*.

`TarFile.close()`

Close the `TarFile`. In write mode, two finishing zero blocks are appended to the archive.

`TarFile.pax_headers`

A dictionary containing key-value pairs of pax global headers.

13.6.2 TarInfo Objects

A *TarInfo* object represents one member in a *TarFile*. Aside from storing all required attributes of a file (like file type, size, time, permissions, owner etc.), it provides some useful methods to determine its type. It does *not* contain the file's data itself.

TarInfo objects are returned by *TarFile*'s methods `getmember()`, `getmembers()` and `gettarinfo()`.

class tarfile.TarInfo(*name=""*)
Create a *TarInfo* object.

classmethod TarInfo.frombuf(*buf, encoding, errors*)
Create and return a *TarInfo* object from string buffer *buf*.

Raises *HeaderError* if the buffer is invalid.

classmethod TarInfo.fromtarfile(*tarfile*)
Read the next member from the *TarFile* object *tarfile* and return it as a *TarInfo* object.

TarInfo.tobuf(*format=DEFAULT_FORMAT, encoding=ENCODING, errors='surrogateescape'*)
Create a string buffer from a *TarInfo* object. For information on the arguments see the constructor of the *TarFile* class.

Changed in version 3.2: Use `'surrogateescape'` as the default for the *errors* argument.

A `TarInfo` object has the following public data attributes:

TarInfo.name
Name of the archive member.

TarInfo.size
Size in bytes.

TarInfo.mtime
Time of last modification.

TarInfo.mode
Permission bits.

TarInfo.type
File type. *type* is usually one of these constants: `REGTYPE`, `AREGTYPE`, `LNKTYPE`, `SYMTYPE`, `DIRTYPE`, `FIFOTYPE`, `CONTTYPE`, `CHRTYPE`, `BLKTYPE`, `GNUTYPE_SPARSE`. To determine the type of a *TarInfo* object more conveniently, use the `is*()` methods below.

TarInfo.linkname
Name of the target file name, which is only present in *TarInfo* objects of type `LNKTYPE` and `SYMTYPE`.

TarInfo.uid
User ID of the user who originally stored this member.

TarInfo.gid
Group ID of the user who originally stored this member.

TarInfo.uname
User name.

TarInfo.gname
Group name.

TarInfo.pax_headers
A dictionary containing key-value pairs of an associated pax extended header.

A *TarInfo* object also provides some convenient query methods:

TarInfo.isfile()
Return *True* if the `Tarinfo` object is a regular file.

`TarInfo.isreg()`
Same as *isfile()*.

`TarInfo.isdir()`
Return *True* if it is a directory.

`TarInfo.issym()`
Return *True* if it is a symbolic link.

`TarInfo.islnk()`
Return *True* if it is a hard link.

`TarInfo.ischr()`
Return *True* if it is a character device.

`TarInfo.isblk()`
Return *True* if it is a block device.

`TarInfo.isfifo()`
Return *True* if it is a FIFO.

`TarInfo.isdev()`
Return *True* if it is one of character device, block device or FIFO.

13.6.3 Command-Line Interface

New in version 3.4.

The *tarfile* module provides a simple command-line interface to interact with tar archives.

If you want to create a new tar archive, specify its name after the *-c* option and then list the filename(s) that should be included:

```
$ python -m tarfile -c monty.tar  spam.txt eggs.txt
```

Passing a directory is also acceptable:

```
$ python -m tarfile -c monty.tar life-of-brian_1979/
```

If you want to extract a tar archive into the current directory, use the *-e* option:

```
$ python -m tarfile -e monty.tar
```

You can also extract a tar archive into a different directory by passing the directory's name:

```
$ python -m tarfile -e monty.tar  other-dir/
```

For a list of the files in a tar archive, use the *-l* option:

```
$ python -m tarfile -l monty.tar
```

Command-line options

`-l <tarfile>`
`--list <tarfile>`
List files in a tarfile.

`-c <tarfile> <source1> ... <sourceN>`
`--create <tarfile> <source1> ... <sourceN>`
Create tarfile from source files.

-e <tarfile> [<output_dir>]
--extract <tarfile> [<output_dir>]
Extract tarfile into the current directory if *output_dir* is not specified.

-t <tarfile>
--test <tarfile>
Test whether the tarfile is valid or not.

-v, --verbose
Verbose output.

13.6.4 Examples

How to extract an entire tar archive to the current working directory:

```
import tarfile
tar = tarfile.open("sample.tar.gz")
tar.extractall()
tar.close()
```

How to extract a subset of a tar archive with *TarFile.extractall()* using a generator function instead of a list:

```
import os
import tarfile

def py_files(members):
    for tarinfo in members:
        if os.path.splitext(tarinfo.name)[1] == ".py":
            yield tarinfo

tar = tarfile.open("sample.tar.gz")
tar.extractall(members=py_files(tar))
tar.close()
```

How to create an uncompressed tar archive from a list of filenames:

```
import tarfile
tar = tarfile.open("sample.tar", "w")
for name in ["foo", "bar", "quux"]:
    tar.add(name)
tar.close()
```

The same example using the `with` statement:

```
import tarfile
with tarfile.open("sample.tar", "w") as tar:
    for name in ["foo", "bar", "quux"]:
        tar.add(name)
```

How to read a gzip compressed tar archive and display some member information:

```
import tarfile
tar = tarfile.open("sample.tar.gz", "r:gz")
for tarinfo in tar:
    print(tarinfo.name, "is", tarinfo.size, "bytes in size and is", end="")
    if tarinfo.isreg():
        print("a regular file.")
```

```
    elif tarinfo.isdir():
        print("a directory.")
    else:
        print("something else.")
tar.close()
```

How to create an archive and reset the user information using the *filter* parameter in `TarFile.add()`:

```
import tarfile
def reset(tarinfo):
    tarinfo.uid = tarinfo.gid = 0
    tarinfo.uname = tarinfo.gname = "root"
    return tarinfo
tar = tarfile.open("sample.tar.gz", "w:gz")
tar.add("foo", filter=reset)
tar.close()
```

13.6.5 Supported tar formats

There are three tar formats that can be created with the `tarfile` module:

- The POSIX.1-1988 ustar format (`USTAR_FORMAT`). It supports filenames up to a length of at best 256 characters and linknames up to 100 characters. The maximum file size is 8 GiB. This is an old and limited but widely supported format.
- The GNU tar format (`GNU_FORMAT`). It supports long filenames and linknames, files bigger than 8 GiB and sparse files. It is the de facto standard on GNU/Linux systems. `tarfile` fully supports the GNU tar extensions for long names, sparse file support is read-only.
- The POSIX.1-2001 pax format (`PAX_FORMAT`). It is the most flexible format with virtually no limits. It supports long filenames and linknames, large files and stores pathnames in a portable way. However, not all tar implementations today are able to handle pax archives properly.

  The *pax* format is an extension to the existing *ustar* format. It uses extra headers for information that cannot be stored otherwise. There are two flavours of pax headers: Extended headers only affect the subsequent file header, global headers are valid for the complete archive and affect all following files. All the data in a pax header is encoded in *UTF-8* for portability reasons.

There are some more variants of the tar format which can be read, but not created:

- The ancient V7 format. This is the first tar format from Unix Seventh Edition, storing only regular files and directories. Names must not be longer than 100 characters, there is no user/group name information. Some archives have miscalculated header checksums in case of fields with non-ASCII characters.
- The SunOS tar extended format. This format is a variant of the POSIX.1-2001 pax format, but is not compatible.

13.6.6 Unicode issues

The tar format was originally conceived to make backups on tape drives with the main focus on preserving file system information. Nowadays tar archives are commonly used for file distribution and exchanging archives over networks. One problem of the original format (which is the basis of all other formats) is that there is no concept of supporting different character encodings. For example, an ordinary tar archive created on a *UTF-8* system cannot be read correctly on a *Latin-1* system if it contains non-*ASCII* characters. Textual metadata (like filenames, linknames, user/group names) will appear damaged. Unfortunately, there is no way to autodetect the encoding of an archive. The pax format was designed to solve this problem. It stores non-ASCII metadata using the universal character encoding *UTF-8*.

The details of character conversion in `tarfile` are controlled by the *encoding* and *errors* keyword arguments of the `TarFile` class.

encoding defines the character encoding to use for the metadata in the archive. The default value is `sys.getfilesystemencoding()` or `'ascii'` as a fallback. Depending on whether the archive is read or written, the metadata must be either decoded or encoded. If *encoding* is not set appropriately, this conversion may fail.

The *errors* argument defines how characters are treated that cannot be converted. Possible values are listed in section *Error Handlers*. The default scheme is `'surrogateescape'` which Python also uses for its file system calls, see *File Names, Command Line Arguments, and Environment Variables*.

In case of `PAX_FORMAT` archives, *encoding* is generally not needed because all the metadata is stored using *UTF-8*. *encoding* is only used in the rare cases when binary pax headers are decoded or when strings with surrogate characters are stored.

CHAPTER

FOURTEEN

FILE FORMATS

The modules described in this chapter parse various miscellaneous file formats that aren't markup languages and are not related to e-mail.

14.1 csv — CSV File Reading and Writing

Source code: Lib/csv.py

The so-called CSV (Comma Separated Values) format is the most common import and export format for spreadsheets and databases. CSV format was used for many years prior to attempts to describe the format in a standardized way in RFC 4180. The lack of a well-defined standard means that subtle differences often exist in the data produced and consumed by different applications. These differences can make it annoying to process CSV files from multiple sources. Still, while the delimiters and quoting characters vary, the overall format is similar enough that it is possible to write a single module which can efficiently manipulate such data, hiding the details of reading and writing the data from the programmer.

The *csv* module implements classes to read and write tabular data in CSV format. It allows programmers to say, "write this data in the format preferred by Excel," or "read data from this file which was generated by Excel," without knowing the precise details of the CSV format used by Excel. Programmers can also describe the CSV formats understood by other applications or define their own special-purpose CSV formats.

The *csv* module's *reader* and *writer* objects read and write sequences. Programmers can also read and write data in dictionary form using the *DictReader* and *DictWriter* classes.

See also:

PEP 305 - **CSV File API** The Python Enhancement Proposal which proposed this addition to Python.

14.1.1 Module Contents

The *csv* module defines the following functions:

csv.**reader**(*csvfile*, *dialect='excel'*, ***fmtparams*)

Return a reader object which will iterate over lines in the given *csvfile*. *csvfile* can be any object which supports the *iterator* protocol and returns a string each time its `__next__()` method is called — *file objects* and list objects are both suitable. If *csvfile* is a file object, it should be opened with `newline=''`.[1] An optional *dialect* parameter can be given which is used to define a set of parameters specific to a particular CSV dialect. It may be an instance of a subclass of the *Dialect* class or one of the strings returned by the *list_dialects()* function. The other optional *fmtparams* keyword

[1] If `newline=''` is not specified, newlines embedded inside quoted fields will not be interpreted correctly, and on platforms that use `\r\n` linendings on write an extra `\r` will be added. It should always be safe to specify `newline=''`, since the csv module does its own (*universal*) newline handling.

arguments can be given to override individual formatting parameters in the current dialect. For full details about the dialect and formatting parameters, see section *Dialects and Formatting Parameters*.

Each row read from the csv file is returned as a list of strings. No automatic data type conversion is performed unless the `QUOTE_NONNUMERIC` format option is specified (in which case unquoted fields are transformed into floats).

A short usage example:

```
>>> import csv
>>> with open('eggs.csv', newline='') as csvfile:
...     spamreader = csv.reader(csvfile, delimiter=' ', quotechar='|')
...     for row in spamreader:
...         print(', '.join(row))
Spam, Spam, Spam, Spam, Spam, Baked Beans
Spam, Lovely Spam, Wonderful Spam
```

`csv.writer(`*csvfile*, *dialect='excel'*, ***fmtparams*`)`

Return a writer object responsible for converting the user's data into delimited strings on the given file-like object. *csvfile* can be any object with a `write()` method. If *csvfile* is a file object, it should be opened with `newline=''`[1]. An optional *dialect* parameter can be given which is used to define a set of parameters specific to a particular CSV dialect. It may be an instance of a subclass of the `Dialect` class or one of the strings returned by the `list_dialects()` function. The other optional *fmtparams* keyword arguments can be given to override individual formatting parameters in the current dialect. For full details about the dialect and formatting parameters, see section *Dialects and Formatting Parameters*. To make it as easy as possible to interface with modules which implement the DB API, the value `None` is written as the empty string. While this isn't a reversible transformation, it makes it easier to dump SQL NULL data values to CSV files without preprocessing the data returned from a `cursor.fetch*` call. All other non-string data are stringified with `str()` before being written.

A short usage example:

```
import csv
with open('eggs.csv', 'w', newline='') as csvfile:
    spamwriter = csv.writer(csvfile, delimiter=' ',
                            quotechar='|', quoting=csv.QUOTE_MINIMAL)
    spamwriter.writerow(['Spam'] * 5 + ['Baked Beans'])
    spamwriter.writerow(['Spam', 'Lovely Spam', 'Wonderful Spam'])
```

`csv.register_dialect(`*name*[, *dialect*[, ***fmtparams*]]`)`

Associate *dialect* with *name*. *name* must be a string. The dialect can be specified either by passing a sub-class of `Dialect`, or by *fmtparams* keyword arguments, or both, with keyword arguments overriding parameters of the dialect. For full details about the dialect and formatting parameters, see section *Dialects and Formatting Parameters*.

`csv.unregister_dialect(`*name*`)`

Delete the dialect associated with *name* from the dialect registry. An `Error` is raised if *name* is not a registered dialect name.

`csv.get_dialect(`*name*`)`

Return the dialect associated with *name*. An `Error` is raised if *name* is not a registered dialect name. This function returns an immutable `Dialect`.

`csv.list_dialects()`

Return the names of all registered dialects.

`csv.field_size_limit(`[*new_limit*]`)`

Returns the current maximum field size allowed by the parser. If *new_limit* is given, this becomes the new limit.

The *csv* module defines the following classes:

class csv.DictReader(*f*, *fieldnames=None*, *restkey=None*, *restval=None*, *dialect='excel'*, **args*, ***kwds*)

Create an object that operates like a regular reader but maps the information in each row to an *OrderedDict* whose keys are given by the optional *fieldnames* parameter.

The *fieldnames* parameter is a *sequence*. If *fieldnames* is omitted, the values in the first row of file *f* will be used as the fieldnames. Regardless of how the fieldnames are determined, the ordered dictionary preserves their original ordering.

If a row has more fields than fieldnames, the remaining data is put in a list and stored with the fieldname specified by *restkey* (which defaults to `None`). If a non-blank row has fewer fields than fieldnames, the missing values are filled-in with `None`.

All other optional or keyword arguments are passed to the underlying *reader* instance.

Changed in version 3.6: Returned rows are now of type `OrderedDict`.

A short usage example:

```
>>> import csv
>>> with open('names.csv', newline='') as csvfile:
...     reader = csv.DictReader(csvfile)
...     for row in reader:
...         print(row['first_name'], row['last_name'])
...
Eric Idle
John Cleese

>>> print(row)
OrderedDict([('first_name', 'John'), ('last_name', 'Cleese')])
```

class csv.DictWriter(*f*, *fieldnames*, *restval=''*, *extrasaction='raise'*, *dialect='excel'*, **args*, ***kwds*)

Create an object which operates like a regular writer but maps dictionaries onto output rows. The *fieldnames* parameter is a *sequence* of keys that identify the order in which values in the dictionary passed to the `writerow()` method are written to file *f*. The optional *restval* parameter specifies the value to be written if the dictionary is missing a key in *fieldnames*. If the dictionary passed to the `writerow()` method contains a key not found in *fieldnames*, the optional *extrasaction* parameter indicates what action to take. If it is set to `'raise'`, the default value, a *ValueError* is raised. If it is set to `'ignore'`, extra values in the dictionary are ignored. Any other optional or keyword arguments are passed to the underlying *writer* instance.

Note that unlike the *DictReader* class, the *fieldnames* parameter of the *DictWriter* is not optional. Since Python's *dict* objects are not ordered, there is not enough information available to deduce the order in which the row should be written to file *f*.

A short usage example:

```
import csv

with open('names.csv', 'w', newline='') as csvfile:
    fieldnames = ['first_name', 'last_name']
    writer = csv.DictWriter(csvfile, fieldnames=fieldnames)

    writer.writeheader()
    writer.writerow({'first_name': 'Baked', 'last_name': 'Beans'})
    writer.writerow({'first_name': 'Lovely', 'last_name': 'Spam'})
    writer.writerow({'first_name': 'Wonderful', 'last_name': 'Spam'})
```

class csv.Dialect
The *Dialect* class is a container class relied on primarily for its attributes, which are used to define the parameters for a specific *reader* or *writer* instance.

class csv.excel
The *excel* class defines the usual properties of an Excel-generated CSV file. It is registered with the dialect name `'excel'`.

class csv.excel_tab
The *excel_tab* class defines the usual properties of an Excel-generated TAB-delimited file. It is registered with the dialect name `'excel-tab'`.

class csv.unix_dialect
The *unix_dialect* class defines the usual properties of a CSV file generated on UNIX systems, i.e. using `'\n'` as line terminator and quoting all fields. It is registered with the dialect name `'unix'`.

New in version 3.2.

class csv.Sniffer
The *Sniffer* class is used to deduce the format of a CSV file.

The *Sniffer* class provides two methods:

sniff(*sample, delimiters=None*)
Analyze the given *sample* and return a *Dialect* subclass reflecting the parameters found. If the optional *delimiters* parameter is given, it is interpreted as a string containing possible valid delimiter characters.

has_header(*sample*)
Analyze the sample text (presumed to be in CSV format) and return *True* if the first row appears to be a series of column headers.

An example for *Sniffer* use:

```
with open('example.csv', newline='') as csvfile:
    dialect = csv.Sniffer().sniff(csvfile.read(1024))
    csvfile.seek(0)
    reader = csv.reader(csvfile, dialect)
    # ... process CSV file contents here ...
```

The *csv* module defines the following constants:

csv.QUOTE_ALL
Instructs *writer* objects to quote all fields.

csv.QUOTE_MINIMAL
Instructs *writer* objects to only quote those fields which contain special characters such as *delimiter*, *quotechar* or any of the characters in *lineterminator*.

csv.QUOTE_NONNUMERIC
Instructs *writer* objects to quote all non-numeric fields.

Instructs the reader to convert all non-quoted fields to type *float*.

csv.QUOTE_NONE
Instructs *writer* objects to never quote fields. When the current *delimiter* occurs in output data it is preceded by the current *escapechar* character. If *escapechar* is not set, the writer will raise *Error* if any characters that require escaping are encountered.

Instructs *reader* to perform no special processing of quote characters.

The *csv* module defines the following exception:

exception csv.Error
Raised by any of the functions when an error is detected.

14.1.2 Dialects and Formatting Parameters

To make it easier to specify the format of input and output records, specific formatting parameters are grouped together into dialects. A dialect is a subclass of the *Dialect* class having a set of specific methods and a single `validate()` method. When creating *reader* or *writer* objects, the programmer can specify a string or a subclass of the *Dialect* class as the dialect parameter. In addition to, or instead of, the *dialect* parameter, the programmer can also specify individual formatting parameters, which have the same names as the attributes defined below for the *Dialect* class.

Dialects support the following attributes:

`Dialect.delimiter`
A one-character string used to separate fields. It defaults to `','`.

`Dialect.doublequote`
Controls how instances of *quotechar* appearing inside a field should themselves be quoted. When *True*, the character is doubled. When *False*, the *escapechar* is used as a prefix to the *quotechar*. It defaults to *True*.

On output, if *doublequote* is *False* and no *escapechar* is set, *Error* is raised if a *quotechar* is found in a field.

`Dialect.escapechar`
A one-character string used by the writer to escape the *delimiter* if *quoting* is set to *QUOTE_NONE* and the *quotechar* if *doublequote* is *False*. On reading, the *escapechar* removes any special meaning from the following character. It defaults to *None*, which disables escaping.

`Dialect.lineterminator`
The string used to terminate lines produced by the *writer*. It defaults to `'\r\n'`.

Note: The *reader* is hard-coded to recognise either `'\r'` or `'\n'` as end-of-line, and ignores *lineterminator*. This behavior may change in the future.

`Dialect.quotechar`
A one-character string used to quote fields containing special characters, such as the *delimiter* or *quotechar*, or which contain new-line characters. It defaults to `'"'`.

`Dialect.quoting`
Controls when quotes should be generated by the writer and recognised by the reader. It can take on any of the `QUOTE_*` constants (see section *Module Contents*) and defaults to *QUOTE_MINIMAL*.

`Dialect.skipinitialspace`
When *True*, whitespace immediately following the *delimiter* is ignored. The default is *False*.

`Dialect.strict`
When `True`, raise exception *Error* on bad CSV input. The default is `False`.

14.1.3 Reader Objects

Reader objects (*DictReader* instances and objects returned by the *reader()* function) have the following public methods:

`csvreader.__next__()`
Return the next row of the reader's iterable object as a list (if the object was returned from *reader()*) or a dict (if it is a *DictReader* instance), parsed according to the current dialect. Usually you should call this as `next(reader)`.

Reader objects have the following public attributes:

csvreader.dialect
A read-only description of the dialect in use by the parser.

csvreader.line_num
The number of lines read from the source iterator. This is not the same as the number of records returned, as records can span multiple lines.

DictReader objects have the following public attribute:

csvreader.fieldnames
If not passed as a parameter when creating the object, this attribute is initialized upon first access or when the first record is read from the file.

14.1.4 Writer Objects

`Writer` objects (*DictWriter* instances and objects returned by the *writer()* function) have the following public methods. A *row* must be an iterable of strings or numbers for `Writer` objects and a dictionary mapping fieldnames to strings or numbers (by passing them through *str()* first) for *DictWriter* objects. Note that complex numbers are written out surrounded by parens. This may cause some problems for other programs which read CSV files (assuming they support complex numbers at all).

csvwriter.writerow(*row*)
Write the *row* parameter to the writer's file object, formatted according to the current dialect.

Changed in version 3.5: Added support of arbitrary iterables.

csvwriter.writerows(*rows*)
Write all the *rows* parameters (a list of *row* objects as described above) to the writer's file object, formatted according to the current dialect.

Writer objects have the following public attribute:

csvwriter.dialect
A read-only description of the dialect in use by the writer.

DictWriter objects have the following public method:

DictWriter.writeheader()
Write a row with the field names (as specified in the constructor).

New in version 3.2.

14.1.5 Examples

The simplest example of reading a CSV file:

```
import csv
with open('some.csv', newline='') as f:
    reader = csv.reader(f)
    for row in reader:
        print(row)
```

Reading a file with an alternate format:

```
import csv
with open('passwd', newline='') as f:
    reader = csv.reader(f, delimiter=':', quoting=csv.QUOTE_NONE)
    for row in reader:
        print(row)
```

The corresponding simplest possible writing example is:

```
import csv
with open('some.csv', 'w', newline='') as f:
    writer = csv.writer(f)
    writer.writerows(someiterable)
```

Since *open()* is used to open a CSV file for reading, the file will by default be decoded into unicode using the system default encoding (see *locale.getpreferredencoding()*). To decode a file using a different encoding, use the `encoding` argument of open:

```
import csv
with open('some.csv', newline='', encoding='utf-8') as f:
    reader = csv.reader(f)
    for row in reader:
        print(row)
```

The same applies to writing in something other than the system default encoding: specify the encoding argument when opening the output file.

Registering a new dialect:

```
import csv
csv.register_dialect('unixpwd', delimiter=':', quoting=csv.QUOTE_NONE)
with open('passwd', newline='') as f:
    reader = csv.reader(f, 'unixpwd')
```

A slightly more advanced use of the reader — catching and reporting errors:

```
import csv, sys
filename = 'some.csv'
with open(filename, newline='') as f:
    reader = csv.reader(f)
    try:
        for row in reader:
            print(row)
    except csv.Error as e:
        sys.exit('file {}, line {}: {}'.format(filename, reader.line_num, e))
```

And while the module doesn't directly support parsing strings, it can easily be done:

```
import csv
for row in csv.reader(['one,two,three']):
    print(row)
```

14.2 `configparser` — Configuration file parser

Source code: Lib/configparser.py

This module provides the *ConfigParser* class which implements a basic configuration language which provides a structure similar to what's found in Microsoft Windows INI files. You can use this to write Python programs which can be customized by end users easily.

Note: This library does *not* interpret or write the value-type prefixes used in the Windows Registry extended version of INI syntax.

See also:

Module *shlex* Support for creating Unix shell-like mini-languages which can be used as an alternate format for application configuration files.

Module *json* The json module implements a subset of JavaScript syntax which can also be used for this purpose.

14.2.1 Quick Start

Let's take a very basic configuration file that looks like this:

```
[DEFAULT]
ServerAliveInterval = 45
Compression = yes
CompressionLevel = 9
ForwardX11 = yes

[bitbucket.org]
User = hg

[topsecret.server.com]
Port = 50022
ForwardX11 = no
```

The structure of INI files is described *in the following section*. Essentially, the file consists of sections, each of which contains keys with values. *configparser* classes can read and write such files. Let's start by creating the above configuration file programmatically.

```
>>> import configparser
>>> config = configparser.ConfigParser()
>>> config['DEFAULT'] = {'ServerAliveInterval': '45',
...                      'Compression': 'yes',
...                      'CompressionLevel': '9'}
>>> config['bitbucket.org'] = {}
>>> config['bitbucket.org']['User'] = 'hg'
>>> config['topsecret.server.com'] = {}
>>> topsecret = config['topsecret.server.com']
>>> topsecret['Port'] = '50022'     # mutates the parser
>>> topsecret['ForwardX11'] = 'no'  # same here
>>> config['DEFAULT']['ForwardX11'] = 'yes'
>>> with open('example.ini', 'w') as configfile:
...   config.write(configfile)
...
```

As you can see, we can treat a config parser much like a dictionary. There are differences, *outlined later*, but the behavior is very close to what you would expect from a dictionary.

Now that we have created and saved a configuration file, let's read it back and explore the data it holds.

```
>>> import configparser
>>> config = configparser.ConfigParser()
>>> config.sections()
[]
```

```
>>> config.read('example.ini')
['example.ini']
>>> config.sections()
['bitbucket.org', 'topsecret.server.com']
>>> 'bitbucket.org' in config
True
>>> 'bytebong.com' in config
False
>>> config['bitbucket.org']['User']
'hg'
>>> config['DEFAULT']['Compression']
'yes'
>>> topsecret = config['topsecret.server.com']
>>> topsecret['ForwardX11']
'no'
>>> topsecret['Port']
'50022'
>>> for key in config['bitbucket.org']: print(key)
...
user
compressionlevel
serveraliveinterval
compression
forwardx11
>>> config['bitbucket.org']['ForwardX11']
'yes'
```

As we can see above, the API is pretty straightforward. The only bit of magic involves the `DEFAULT` section which provides default values for all other sections[1]. Note also that keys in sections are case-insensitive and stored in lowercase[1].

14.2.2 Supported Datatypes

Config parsers do not guess datatypes of values in configuration files, always storing them internally as strings. This means that if you need other datatypes, you should convert on your own:

```
>>> int(topsecret['Port'])
50022
>>> float(topsecret['CompressionLevel'])
9.0
```

Since this task is so common, config parsers provide a range of handy getter methods to handle integers, floats and booleans. The last one is the most interesting because simply passing the value to `bool()` would do no good since `bool('False')` is still `True`. This is why config parsers also provide *getboolean()*. This method is case-insensitive and recognizes Boolean values from `'yes'`/`'no'`, `'on'`/`'off'`, `'true'`/`'false'` and `'1'`/`'0'`[1]. For example:

```
>>> topsecret.getboolean('ForwardX11')
False
>>> config['bitbucket.org'].getboolean('ForwardX11')
True
>>> config.getboolean('bitbucket.org', 'Compression')
True
```

[1] Config parsers allow for heavy customization. If you are interested in changing the behaviour outlined by the footnote reference, consult the *Customizing Parser Behaviour* section.

Apart from *getboolean()*, config parsers also provide equivalent *getint()* and *getfloat()* methods. You can register your own converters and customize the provided ones.[1]

14.2.3 Fallback Values

As with a dictionary, you can use a section's `get()` method to provide fallback values:

```
>>> topsecret.get('Port')
'50022'
>>> topsecret.get('CompressionLevel')
'9'
>>> topsecret.get('Cipher')
>>> topsecret.get('Cipher', '3des-cbc')
'3des-cbc'
```

Please note that default values have precedence over fallback values. For instance, in our example the `'CompressionLevel'` key was specified only in the `'DEFAULT'` section. If we try to get it from the section `'topsecret.server.com'`, we will always get the default, even if we specify a fallback:

```
>>> topsecret.get('CompressionLevel', '3')
'9'
```

One more thing to be aware of is that the parser-level `get()` method provides a custom, more complex interface, maintained for backwards compatibility. When using this method, a fallback value can be provided via the `fallback` keyword-only argument:

```
>>> config.get('bitbucket.org', 'monster',
...            fallback='No such things as monsters')
'No such things as monsters'
```

The same `fallback` argument can be used with the *getint()*, *getfloat()* and *getboolean()* methods, for example:

```
>>> 'BatchMode' in topsecret
False
>>> topsecret.getboolean('BatchMode', fallback=True)
True
>>> config['DEFAULT']['BatchMode'] = 'no'
>>> topsecret.getboolean('BatchMode', fallback=True)
False
```

14.2.4 Supported INI File Structure

A configuration file consists of sections, each led by a `[section]` header, followed by key/value entries separated by a specific string (`=` or `:` by default[1]). By default, section names are case sensitive but keys are not[1]. Leading and trailing whitespace is removed from keys and values. Values can be omitted, in which case the key/value delimiter may also be left out. Values can also span multiple lines, as long as they are indented deeper than the first line of the value. Depending on the parser's mode, blank lines may be treated as parts of multiline values or ignored.

Configuration files may include comments, prefixed by specific characters (`#` and `;` by default[1]). Comments may appear on their own on an otherwise empty line, possibly indented.[1]

For example:

```
[Simple Values]
key=value
spaces in keys=allowed
spaces in values=allowed as well
spaces around the delimiter = obviously
you can also use : to delimit keys from values

[All Values Are Strings]
values like this: 1000000
or this: 3.14159265359
are they treated as numbers? : no
integers, floats and booleans are held as: strings
can use the API to get converted values directly: true

[Multiline Values]
chorus: I'm a lumberjack, and I'm okay
    I sleep all night and I work all day

[No Values]
key_without_value
empty string value here =

[You can use comments]
# like this
; or this

# By default only in an empty line.
# Inline comments can be harmful because they prevent users
# from using the delimiting characters as parts of values.
# That being said, this can be customized.

    [Sections Can Be Indented]
        can_values_be_as_well = True
        does_that_mean_anything_special = False
        purpose = formatting for readability
        multiline_values = are
            handled just fine as
            long as they are indented
            deeper than the first line
            of a value
        # Did I mention we can indent comments, too?
```

14.2.5 Interpolation of values

On top of the core functionality, *ConfigParser* supports interpolation. This means values can be preprocessed before returning them from `get()` calls.

class configparser.BasicInterpolation

The default implementation used by *ConfigParser*. It enables values to contain format strings which refer to other values in the same section, or values in the special default section[1]. Additional default values can be provided on initialization.

For example:

```
[Paths]
home_dir: /Users
```

```
my_dir: %(home_dir)s/lumberjack
my_pictures: %(my_dir)s/Pictures
```

In the example above, *ConfigParser* with *interpolation* set to `BasicInterpolation()` would resolve `%(home_dir)s` to the value of `home_dir` (`/Users` in this case). `%(my_dir)s` in effect would resolve to `/Users/lumberjack`. All interpolations are done on demand so keys used in the chain of references do not have to be specified in any specific order in the configuration file.

With `interpolation` set to `None`, the parser would simply return `%(my_dir)s/Pictures` as the value of `my_pictures` and `%(home_dir)s/lumberjack` as the value of `my_dir`.

class configparser.ExtendedInterpolation

An alternative handler for interpolation which implements a more advanced syntax, used for instance in `zc.buildout`. Extended interpolation is using `${section:option}` to denote a value from a foreign section. Interpolation can span multiple levels. For convenience, if the `section:` part is omitted, interpolation defaults to the current section (and possibly the default values from the special section).

For example, the configuration specified above with basic interpolation, would look like this with extended interpolation:

```
[Paths]
home_dir: /Users
my_dir: ${home_dir}/lumberjack
my_pictures: ${my_dir}/Pictures
```

Values from other sections can be fetched as well:

```
[Common]
home_dir: /Users
library_dir: /Library
system_dir: /System
macports_dir: /opt/local

[Frameworks]
Python: 3.2
path: ${Common:system_dir}/Library/Frameworks/

[Arthur]
nickname: Two Sheds
last_name: Jackson
my_dir: ${Common:home_dir}/twosheds
my_pictures: ${my_dir}/Pictures
python_dir: ${Frameworks:path}/Python/Versions/${Frameworks:Python}
```

14.2.6 Mapping Protocol Access

New in version 3.2.

Mapping protocol access is a generic name for functionality that enables using custom objects as if they were dictionaries. In case of *configparser*, the mapping interface implementation is using the `parser['section']['option']` notation.

`parser['section']` in particular returns a proxy for the section's data in the parser. This means that the values are not copied but they are taken from the original parser on demand. What's even more important is that when values are changed on a section proxy, they are actually mutated in the original parser.

configparser objects behave as close to actual dictionaries as possible. The mapping interface is complete and adheres to the *MutableMapping* ABC. However, there are a few differences that should be taken into account:

- By default, all keys in sections are accessible in a case-insensitive manner[1]. E.g. `for option in parser["section"]` yields only `optionxform`'ed option key names. This means lowercased keys by default. At the same time, for a section that holds the key `'a'`, both expressions return `True`:

```
"a" in parser["section"]
"A" in parser["section"]
```

- All sections include `DEFAULTSECT` values as well which means that `.clear()` on a section may not leave the section visibly empty. This is because default values cannot be deleted from the section (because technically they are not there). If they are overridden in the section, deleting causes the default value to be visible again. Trying to delete a default value causes a `KeyError`.
- `DEFAULTSECT` cannot be removed from the parser:
  - trying to delete it raises `ValueError`,
  - `parser.clear()` leaves it intact,
  - `parser.popitem()` never returns it.
- `parser.get(section, option, **kwargs)` - the second argument is **not** a fallback value. Note however that the section-level `get()` methods are compatible both with the mapping protocol and the classic configparser API.
- `parser.items()` is compatible with the mapping protocol (returns a list of *section_name*, *section_proxy* pairs including the DEFAULTSECT). However, this method can also be invoked with arguments: `parser.items(section, raw, vars)`. The latter call returns a list of *option*, *value* pairs for a specified `section`, with all interpolations expanded (unless `raw=True` is provided).

The mapping protocol is implemented on top of the existing legacy API so that subclasses overriding the original interface still should have mappings working as expected.

14.2.7 Customizing Parser Behaviour

There are nearly as many INI format variants as there are applications using it. *configparser* goes a long way to provide support for the largest sensible set of INI styles available. The default functionality is mainly dictated by historical background and it's very likely that you will want to customize some of the features.

The most common way to change the way a specific config parser works is to use the `__init__()` options:

- *defaults*, default value: `None`

  This option accepts a dictionary of key-value pairs which will be initially put in the `DEFAULT` section. This makes for an elegant way to support concise configuration files that don't specify values which are the same as the documented default.

  Hint: if you want to specify default values for a specific section, use `read_dict()` before you read the actual file.

- *dict_type*, default value: *collections.OrderedDict*

  This option has a major impact on how the mapping protocol will behave and how the written configuration files look. With the default ordered dictionary, every section is stored in the order they were added to the parser. Same goes for options within sections.

  An alternative dictionary type can be used for example to sort sections and options on write-back. You can also use a regular dictionary for performance reasons.

  Please note: there are ways to add a set of key-value pairs in a single operation. When you use a regular dictionary in those operations, the order of the keys may be random. For example:

```
>>> parser = configparser.ConfigParser()
>>> parser.read_dict({'section1': {'key1': 'value1',
...                                'key2': 'value2',
...                                'key3': 'value3'},
...                   'section2': {'keyA': 'valueA',
...                                'keyB': 'valueB',
...                                'keyC': 'valueC'},
...                   'section3': {'foo': 'x',
...                                'bar': 'y',
...                                'baz': 'z'}
... })
>>> parser.sections()
['section3', 'section2', 'section1']
>>> [option for option in parser['section3']]
['baz', 'foo', 'bar']
```

In these operations you need to use an ordered dictionary as well:

```
>>> from collections import OrderedDict
>>> parser = configparser.ConfigParser()
>>> parser.read_dict(
...   OrderedDict((
...     ('s1',
...      OrderedDict((
...        ('1', '2'),
...        ('3', '4'),
...        ('5', '6'),
...      ))
...     ),
...     ('s2',
...      OrderedDict((
...        ('a', 'b'),
...        ('c', 'd'),
...        ('e', 'f'),
...      ))
...     ),
...   ))
... )
>>> parser.sections()
['s1', 's2']
>>> [option for option in parser['s1']]
['1', '3', '5']
>>> [option for option in parser['s2'].values()]
['b', 'd', 'f']
```

- *allow_no_value*, default value: `False`

  Some configuration files are known to include settings without values, but which otherwise conform to the syntax supported by *configparser*. The *allow_no_value* parameter to the constructor can be used to indicate that such values should be accepted:

```
>>> import configparser

>>> sample_config = """
... [mysqld]
...   user = mysql
...   pid-file = /var/run/mysqld/mysqld.pid
...   skip-external-locking
```

```
...     old_passwords = 1
...     skip-bdb
...     # we don't need ACID today
...     skip-innodb
... """
>>> config = configparser.ConfigParser(allow_no_value=True)
>>> config.read_string(sample_config)

>>> # Settings with values are treated as before:
>>> config["mysqld"]["user"]
'mysql'

>>> # Settings without values provide None:
>>> config["mysqld"]["skip-bdb"]

>>> # Settings which aren't specified still raise an error:
>>> config["mysqld"]["does-not-exist"]
Traceback (most recent call last):
  ...
KeyError: 'does-not-exist'
```

- *delimiters*, default value: `('=', ':')`

  Delimiters are substrings that delimit keys from values within a section. The first occurrence of a delimiting substring on a line is considered a delimiter. This means values (but not keys) can contain the delimiters.

  See also the *space_around_delimiters* argument to `ConfigParser.write()`.

- *comment_prefixes*, default value: `('#', ';')`
- *inline_comment_prefixes*, default value: `None`

  Comment prefixes are strings that indicate the start of a valid comment within a config file. *comment_prefixes* are used only on otherwise empty lines (optionally indented) whereas *inline_comment_prefixes* can be used after every valid value (e.g. section names, options and empty lines as well). By default inline comments are disabled and `'#'` and `';'` are used as prefixes for whole line comments.

  Changed in version 3.2: In previous versions of `configparser` behaviour matched `comment_prefixes=('#',';')` and `inline_comment_prefixes=(';',)`.

  Please note that config parsers don't support escaping of comment prefixes so using *inline_comment_prefixes* may prevent users from specifying option values with characters used as comment prefixes. When in doubt, avoid setting *inline_comment_prefixes*. In any circumstances, the only way of storing comment prefix characters at the beginning of a line in multiline values is to interpolate the prefix, for example:

```
>>> from configparser import ConfigParser, ExtendedInterpolation
>>> parser = ConfigParser(interpolation=ExtendedInterpolation())
>>> # the default BasicInterpolation could be used as well
>>> parser.read_string("""
... [DEFAULT]
... hash = #
...
... [hashes]
... shebang =
...   ${hash}!/usr/bin/env python
...   ${hash} -*- coding: utf-8 -*-
...
```

```
... extensions =
...   enabled_extension
...   another_extension
...   #disabled_by_comment
...   yet_another_extension
...
... interpolation not necessary = if # is not at line start
... even in multiline values = line #1
...   line #2
...   line #3
... """)
>>> print(parser['hashes']['shebang'])

#!/usr/bin/env python
# -*- coding: utf-8 -*-
>>> print(parser['hashes']['extensions'])

enabled_extension
another_extension
yet_another_extension
>>> print(parser['hashes']['interpolation not necessary'])
if # is not at line start
>>> print(parser['hashes']['even in multiline values'])
line #1
line #2
line #3
```

- *strict*, default value: `True`

  When set to `True`, the parser will not allow for any section or option duplicates while reading from a single source (using `read_file()`, `read_string()` or `read_dict()`). It is recommended to use strict parsers in new applications.

  Changed in version 3.2: In previous versions of *configparser* behaviour matched `strict=False`.

- *empty_lines_in_values*, default value: `True`

  In config parsers, values can span multiple lines as long as they are indented more than the key that holds them. By default parsers also let empty lines to be parts of values. At the same time, keys can be arbitrarily indented themselves to improve readability. In consequence, when configuration files get big and complex, it is easy for the user to lose track of the file structure. Take for instance:

```
[Section]
key = multiline
  value with a gotcha

 this = is still a part of the multiline value of 'key'
```

  This can be especially problematic for the user to see if she's using a proportional font to edit the file. That is why when your application does not need values with empty lines, you should consider disallowing them. This will make empty lines split keys every time. In the example above, it would produce two keys, `key` and `this`.

- *default_section*, default value: `configparser.DEFAULTSECT` (that is: `"DEFAULT"`)

  The convention of allowing a special section of default values for other sections or interpolation purposes is a powerful concept of this library, letting users create complex declarative configurations. This section is normally called `"DEFAULT"` but this can be customized to point to any other valid section name. Some typical values include: `"general"` or `"common"`. The name provided is used for recognizing default sections when reading from any source and is used when writing configuration back to a file.

Its current value can be retrieved using the `parser_instance.default_section` attribute and may be modified at runtime (i.e. to convert files from one format to another).

- *interpolation*, default value: `configparser.BasicInterpolation`

  Interpolation behaviour may be customized by providing a custom handler through the *interpolation* argument. `None` can be used to turn off interpolation completely, `ExtendedInterpolation()` provides a more advanced variant inspired by `zc.buildout`. More on the subject in the *dedicated documentation section*. *RawConfigParser* has a default value of `None`.

- *converters*, default value: not set

  Config parsers provide option value getters that perform type conversion. By default *getint()*, *getfloat()*, and *getboolean()* are implemented. Should other getters be desirable, users may define them in a subclass or pass a dictionary where each key is a name of the converter and each value is a callable implementing said conversion. For instance, passing `{'decimal': decimal.Decimal}` would add `getdecimal()` on both the parser object and all section proxies. In other words, it will be possible to write both `parser_instance.getdecimal('section', 'key', fallback=0)` and `parser_instance['section'].getdecimal('key', 0)`.

  If the converter needs to access the state of the parser, it can be implemented as a method on a config parser subclass. If the name of this method starts with `get`, it will be available on all section proxies, in the dict-compatible form (see the `getdecimal()` example above).

More advanced customization may be achieved by overriding default values of these parser attributes. The defaults are defined on the classes, so they may be overridden by subclasses or by attribute assignment.

`configparser.BOOLEAN_STATES`

By default when using *getboolean()*, config parsers consider the following values `True`: `'1'`, `'yes'`, `'true'`, `'on'` and the following values `False`: `'0'`, `'no'`, `'false'`, `'off'`. You can override this by specifying a custom dictionary of strings and their Boolean outcomes. For example:

```
>>> custom = configparser.ConfigParser()
>>> custom['section1'] = {'funky': 'nope'}
>>> custom['section1'].getboolean('funky')
Traceback (most recent call last):
...
ValueError: Not a boolean: nope
>>> custom.BOOLEAN_STATES = {'sure': True, 'nope': False}
>>> custom['section1'].getboolean('funky')
False
```

Other typical Boolean pairs include `accept`/`reject` or `enabled`/`disabled`.

`configparser.optionxform(`*option*`)`

This method transforms option names on every read, get, or set operation. The default converts the name to lowercase. This also means that when a configuration file gets written, all keys will be lowercase. Override this method if that's unsuitable. For example:

```
>>> config = """
... [Section1]
... Key = Value
...
... [Section2]
... AnotherKey = Value
... """
>>> typical = configparser.ConfigParser()
>>> typical.read_string(config)
>>> list(typical['Section1'].keys())
['key']
>>> list(typical['Section2'].keys())
```

```
['anotherkey']
>>> custom = configparser.RawConfigParser()
>>> custom.optionxform = lambda option: option
>>> custom.read_string(config)
>>> list(custom['Section1'].keys())
['Key']
>>> list(custom['Section2'].keys())
['AnotherKey']
```

configparser.SECTCRE

A compiled regular expression used to parse section headers. The default matches `[section]` to the name `"section"`. Whitespace is considered part of the section name, thus `[  larch  ]` will be read as a section of name `"  larch  "`. Override this attribute if that's unsuitable. For example:

```
>>> config = """
... [Section 1]
... option = value
...
... [  Section 2  ]
... another = val
... """
>>> typical = ConfigParser()
>>> typical.read_string(config)
>>> typical.sections()
['Section 1', '  Section 2  ']
>>> custom = ConfigParser()
>>> custom.SECTCRE = re.compile(r"\[ *(?P<header>[^]]+?) *\]")
>>> custom.read_string(config)
>>> custom.sections()
['Section 1', 'Section 2']
```

Note: While ConfigParser objects also use an `OPTCRE` attribute for recognizing option lines, it's not recommended to override it because that would interfere with constructor options *allow_no_value* and *delimiters*.

14.2.8 Legacy API Examples

Mainly because of backwards compatibility concerns, `configparser` provides also a legacy API with explicit `get/set` methods. While there are valid use cases for the methods outlined below, mapping protocol access is preferred for new projects. The legacy API is at times more advanced, low-level and downright counterintuitive.

An example of writing to a configuration file:

```
import configparser

config = configparser.RawConfigParser()

# Please note that using RawConfigParser's set functions, you can assign
# non-string values to keys internally, but will receive an error when
# attempting to write to a file or when you get it in non-raw mode. Setting
# values using the mapping protocol or ConfigParser's set() does not allow
# such assignments to take place.
config.add_section('Section1')
config.set('Section1', 'an_int', '15')
```

```
config.set('Section1', 'a_bool', 'true')
config.set('Section1', 'a_float', '3.1415')
config.set('Section1', 'baz', 'fun')
config.set('Section1', 'bar', 'Python')
config.set('Section1', 'foo', '%(bar)s is %(baz)s!')

# Writing our configuration file to 'example.cfg'
with open('example.cfg', 'w') as configfile:
    config.write(configfile)
```

An example of reading the configuration file again:

```
import configparser

config = configparser.RawConfigParser()
config.read('example.cfg')

# getfloat() raises an exception if the value is not a float
# getint() and getboolean() also do this for their respective types
a_float = config.getfloat('Section1', 'a_float')
an_int = config.getint('Section1', 'an_int')
print(a_float + an_int)

# Notice that the next output does not interpolate '%(bar)s' or '%(baz)s'.
# This is because we are using a RawConfigParser().
if config.getboolean('Section1', 'a_bool'):
    print(config.get('Section1', 'foo'))
```

To get interpolation, use *ConfigParser*:

```
import configparser

cfg = configparser.ConfigParser()
cfg.read('example.cfg')

# Set the optional *raw* argument of get() to True if you wish to disable
# interpolation in a single get operation.
print(cfg.get('Section1', 'foo', raw=False)) # -> "Python is fun!"
print(cfg.get('Section1', 'foo', raw=True))  # -> "%(bar)s is %(baz)s!"

# The optional *vars* argument is a dict with members that will take
# precedence in interpolation.
print(cfg.get('Section1', 'foo', vars={'bar': 'Documentation',
                                       'baz': 'evil'}))

# The optional *fallback* argument can be used to provide a fallback value
print(cfg.get('Section1', 'foo'))
      # -> "Python is fun!"

print(cfg.get('Section1', 'foo', fallback='Monty is not.'))
      # -> "Python is fun!"

print(cfg.get('Section1', 'monster', fallback='No such things as monsters.'))
      # -> "No such things as monsters."

# A bare print(cfg.get('Section1', 'monster')) would raise NoOptionError
# but we can also use:
```

```
print(cfg.get('Section1', 'monster', fallback=None))
      # -> None
```

Default values are available in both types of ConfigParsers. They are used in interpolation if an option used is not defined elsewhere.

```
import configparser

# New instance with 'bar' and 'baz' defaulting to 'Life' and 'hard' each
config = configparser.ConfigParser({'bar': 'Life', 'baz': 'hard'})
config.read('example.cfg')

print(config.get('Section1', 'foo'))     # -> "Python is fun!"
config.remove_option('Section1', 'bar')
config.remove_option('Section1', 'baz')
print(config.get('Section1', 'foo'))     # -> "Life is hard!"
```

14.2.9 ConfigParser Objects

class configparser.ConfigParser(*defaults=None, dict_type=collections.OrderedDict, allow_no_value=False, delimiters=('=', ':'), comment_prefixes=('#', ';'), inline_comment_prefixes=None, strict=True, empty_lines_in_values=True, default_section=configparser.DEFAULTSECT, interpolation=BasicInterpolation(), converters={}*)

The main configuration parser. When *defaults* is given, it is initialized into the dictionary of intrinsic defaults. When *dict_type* is given, it will be used to create the dictionary objects for the list of sections, for the options within a section, and for the default values.

When *delimiters* is given, it is used as the set of substrings that divide keys from values. When *comment_prefixes* is given, it will be used as the set of substrings that prefix comments in otherwise empty lines. Comments can be indented. When *inline_comment_prefixes* is given, it will be used as the set of substrings that prefix comments in non-empty lines.

When *strict* is `True` (the default), the parser won't allow for any section or option duplicates while reading from a single source (file, string or dictionary), raising *DuplicateSectionError* or *DuplicateOptionError*. When *empty_lines_in_values* is `False` (default: `True`), each empty line marks the end of an option. Otherwise, internal empty lines of a multiline option are kept as part of the value. When *allow_no_value* is `True` (default: `False`), options without values are accepted; the value held for these is `None` and they are serialized without the trailing delimiter.

When *default_section* is given, it specifies the name for the special section holding default values for other sections and interpolation purposes (normally named `"DEFAULT"`). This value can be retrieved and changed on runtime using the `default_section` instance attribute.

Interpolation behaviour may be customized by providing a custom handler through the *interpolation* argument. `None` can be used to turn off interpolation completely, `ExtendedInterpolation()` provides a more advanced variant inspired by `zc.buildout`. More on the subject in the *dedicated documentation section*.

All option names used in interpolation will be passed through the *optionxform()* method just like any other option name reference. For example, using the default implementation of *optionxform()* (which converts option names to lower case), the values `foo %(bar)s` and `foo %(BAR)s` are equivalent.

When *converters* is given, it should be a dictionary where each key represents the name of a type converter and each value is a callable implementing the conversion from string to the desired datatype. Every converter gets its own corresponding `get*()` method on the parser object and section proxies.

Changed in version 3.1: The default *dict_type* is `collections.OrderedDict`.

Changed in version 3.2: *allow_no_value*, *delimiters*, *comment_prefixes*, *strict*, *empty_lines_in_values*, *default_section* and *interpolation* were added.

Changed in version 3.5: The *converters* argument was added.

defaults()
Return a dictionary containing the instance-wide defaults.

sections()
Return a list of the sections available; the *default section* is not included in the list.

add_section(*section***)**
Add a section named *section* to the instance. If a section by the given name already exists, `DuplicateSectionError` is raised. If the *default section* name is passed, `ValueError` is raised. The name of the section must be a string; if not, `TypeError` is raised.

Changed in version 3.2: Non-string section names raise `TypeError`.

has_section(*section***)**
Indicates whether the named *section* is present in the configuration. The *default section* is not acknowledged.

options(*section***)**
Return a list of options available in the specified *section*.

has_option(*section, option***)**
If the given *section* exists, and contains the given *option*, return `True`; otherwise return `False`. If the specified *section* is `None` or an empty string, DEFAULT is assumed.

read(*filenames, encoding=None***)**
Attempt to read and parse a list of filenames, returning a list of filenames which were successfully parsed.

If *filenames* is a string or *path-like object*, it is treated as a single filename. If a file named in *filenames* cannot be opened, that file will be ignored. This is designed so that you can specify a list of potential configuration file locations (for example, the current directory, the user's home directory, and some system-wide directory), and all existing configuration files in the list will be read.

If none of the named files exist, the `ConfigParser` instance will contain an empty dataset. An application which requires initial values to be loaded from a file should load the required file or files using `read_file()` before calling `read()` for any optional files:

```
import configparser, os

config = configparser.ConfigParser()
config.read_file(open('defaults.cfg'))
config.read(['site.cfg', os.path.expanduser('~/.myapp.cfg')],
            encoding='cp1250')
```

New in version 3.2: The *encoding* parameter. Previously, all files were read using the default encoding for `open()`.

New in version 3.6.1: The *filenames* parameter accepts a *path-like object*.

read_file(*f, source=None***)**
Read and parse configuration data from *f* which must be an iterable yielding Unicode strings (for example files opened in text mode).

Optional argument *source* specifies the name of the file being read. If not given and *f* has a `name` attribute, that is used for *source*; the default is `'<???>'`.

New in version 3.2: Replaces *readfp()*.

read_string(*string*, *source='<string>'*)
Parse configuration data from a string.

Optional argument *source* specifies a context-specific name of the string passed. If not given, `'<string>'` is used. This should commonly be a filesystem path or a URL.

New in version 3.2.

read_dict(*dictionary*, *source='<dict>'*)
Load configuration from any object that provides a dict-like `items()` method. Keys are section names, values are dictionaries with keys and values that should be present in the section. If the used dictionary type preserves order, sections and their keys will be added in order. Values are automatically converted to strings.

Optional argument *source* specifies a context-specific name of the dictionary passed. If not given, `<dict>` is used.

This method can be used to copy state between parsers.

New in version 3.2.

get(*section*, *option*, ***, *raw=False*, *vars=None*[, *fallback*])
Get an *option* value for the named *section*. If *vars* is provided, it must be a dictionary. The *option* is looked up in *vars* (if provided), *section*, and in *DEFAULTSECT* in that order. If the key is not found and *fallback* is provided, it is used as a fallback value. `None` can be provided as a *fallback* value.

All the `'%'` interpolations are expanded in the return values, unless the *raw* argument is true. Values for interpolation keys are looked up in the same manner as the option.

Changed in version 3.2: Arguments *raw*, *vars* and *fallback* are keyword only to protect users from trying to use the third argument as the *fallback* fallback (especially when using the mapping protocol).

getint(*section*, *option*, ***, *raw=False*, *vars=None*[, *fallback*])
A convenience method which coerces the *option* in the specified *section* to an integer. See *get()* for explanation of *raw*, *vars* and *fallback*.

getfloat(*section*, *option*, ***, *raw=False*, *vars=None*[, *fallback*])
A convenience method which coerces the *option* in the specified *section* to a floating point number. See *get()* for explanation of *raw*, *vars* and *fallback*.

getboolean(*section*, *option*, ***, *raw=False*, *vars=None*[, *fallback*])
A convenience method which coerces the *option* in the specified *section* to a Boolean value. Note that the accepted values for the option are `'1'`, `'yes'`, `'true'`, and `'on'`, which cause this method to return `True`, and `'0'`, `'no'`, `'false'`, and `'off'`, which cause it to return `False`. These string values are checked in a case-insensitive manner. Any other value will cause it to raise *ValueError*. See *get()* for explanation of *raw*, *vars* and *fallback*.

items(*raw=False*, *vars=None*)
items(*section*, *raw=False*, *vars=None*)
When *section* is not given, return a list of *section_name*, *section_proxy* pairs, including DEFAULTSECT.

Otherwise, return a list of *name*, *value* pairs for the options in the given *section*. Optional arguments have the same meaning as for the *get()* method.

Changed in version 3.2: Items present in *vars* no longer appear in the result. The previous behaviour mixed actual parser options with variables provided for interpolation.

set(*section, option, value*)
If the given section exists, set the given option to the specified value; otherwise raise *NoSectionError*. *option* and *value* must be strings; if not, *TypeError* is raised.

write(*fileobject, space_around_delimiters=True*)
Write a representation of the configuration to the specified *file object*, which must be opened in text mode (accepting strings). This representation can be parsed by a future *read()* call. If *space_around_delimiters* is true, delimiters between keys and values are surrounded by spaces.

remove_option(*section, option*)
Remove the specified *option* from the specified *section*. If the section does not exist, raise *NoSectionError*. If the option existed to be removed, return *True*; otherwise return *False*.

remove_section(*section*)
Remove the specified *section* from the configuration. If the section in fact existed, return `True`. Otherwise return `False`.

optionxform(*option*)
Transforms the option name *option* as found in an input file or as passed in by client code to the form that should be used in the internal structures. The default implementation returns a lower-case version of *option*; subclasses may override this or client code can set an attribute of this name on instances to affect this behavior.

You don't need to subclass the parser to use this method, you can also set it on an instance, to a function that takes a string argument and returns a string. Setting it to `str`, for example, would make option names case sensitive:

```
cfgparser = ConfigParser()
cfgparser.optionxform = str
```

Note that when reading configuration files, whitespace around the option names is stripped before *optionxform()* is called.

readfp(*fp, filename=None*)
Deprecated since version 3.2: Use *read_file()* instead.

Changed in version 3.2: *readfp()* now iterates on *fp* instead of calling `fp.readline()`.

For existing code calling *readfp()* with arguments which don't support iteration, the following generator may be used as a wrapper around the file-like object:

```
def readline_generator(fp):
    line = fp.readline()
    while line:
        yield line
        line = fp.readline()
```

Instead of `parser.readfp(fp)` use `parser.read_file(readline_generator(fp))`.

configparser.**MAX_INTERPOLATION_DEPTH**
The maximum depth for recursive interpolation for `get()` when the *raw* parameter is false. This is relevant only when the default *interpolation* is used.

14.2.10 RawConfigParser Objects

class configparser.**RawConfigParser**(*defaults=None, dict_type=collections.OrderedDict, allow_no_value=False, *, delimiters=('=', ':'), comment_prefixes=('#', ';'), inline_comment_prefixes=None, strict=True, empty_lines_in_values=True, default_section=configparser.DEFAULTSECT*[, *interpolation*])

Legacy variant of the *ConfigParser* with interpolation disabled by default and unsafe `add_section` and `set` methods.

Note: Consider using *ConfigParser* instead which checks types of the values to be stored internally. If you don't want interpolation, you can use `ConfigParser(interpolation=None)`.

---

add_section(*section*)
Add a section named *section* to the instance. If a section by the given name already exists, *DuplicateSectionError* is raised. If the *default section* name is passed, *ValueError* is raised.

Type of *section* is not checked which lets users create non-string named sections. This behaviour is unsupported and may cause internal errors.

set(*section, option, value*)
If the given section exists, set the given option to the specified value; otherwise raise *NoSectionError*. While it is possible to use *RawConfigParser* (or *ConfigParser* with *raw* parameters set to true) for *internal* storage of non-string values, full functionality (including interpolation and output to files) can only be achieved using string values.

This method lets users assign non-string values to keys internally. This behaviour is unsupported and will cause errors when attempting to write to a file or get it in non-raw mode. **Use the mapping protocol API** which does not allow such assignments to take place.

14.2.11 Exceptions

exception configparser.**Error**
Base class for all other *configparser* exceptions.

exception configparser.**NoSectionError**
Exception raised when a specified section is not found.

exception configparser.**DuplicateSectionError**
Exception raised if `add_section()` is called with the name of a section that is already present or in strict parsers when a section if found more than once in a single input file, string or dictionary.

New in version 3.2: Optional `source` and `lineno` attributes and arguments to `__init__()` were added.

exception configparser.**DuplicateOptionError**
Exception raised by strict parsers if a single option appears twice during reading from a single file, string or dictionary. This catches misspellings and case sensitivity-related errors, e.g. a dictionary may have two keys representing the same case-insensitive configuration key.

exception configparser.**NoOptionError**
Exception raised when a specified option is not found in the specified section.

exception configparser.**InterpolationError**
Base class for exceptions raised when problems occur performing string interpolation.

exception configparser.InterpolationDepthError
Exception raised when string interpolation cannot be completed because the number of iterations exceeds *MAX_INTERPOLATION_DEPTH*. Subclass of *InterpolationError*.

exception configparser.InterpolationMissingOptionError
Exception raised when an option referenced from a value does not exist. Subclass of *InterpolationError*.

exception configparser.InterpolationSyntaxError
Exception raised when the source text into which substitutions are made does not conform to the required syntax. Subclass of *InterpolationError*.

exception configparser.MissingSectionHeaderError
Exception raised when attempting to parse a file which has no section headers.

exception configparser.ParsingError
Exception raised when errors occur attempting to parse a file.

Changed in version 3.2: The `filename` attribute and `__init__()` argument were renamed to `source` for consistency.

14.3 netrc — netrc file processing

Source code: Lib/netrc.py

The *netrc* class parses and encapsulates the netrc file format used by the Unix **ftp** program and other FTP clients.

class netrc.netrc([*file*])
A *netrc* instance or subclass instance encapsulates data from a netrc file. The initialization argument, if present, specifies the file to parse. If no argument is given, the file `.netrc` in the user's home directory will be read. Parse errors will raise *NetrcParseError* with diagnostic information including the file name, line number, and terminating token. If no argument is specified on a POSIX system, the presence of passwords in the `.netrc` file will raise a *NetrcParseError* if the file ownership or permissions are insecure (owned by a user other than the user running the process, or accessible for read or write by any other user). This implements security behavior equivalent to that of ftp and other programs that use `.netrc`.

Changed in version 3.4: Added the POSIX permission check.

exception netrc.NetrcParseError
Exception raised by the *netrc* class when syntactical errors are encountered in source text. Instances of this exception provide three interesting attributes: `msg` is a textual explanation of the error, `filename` is the name of the source file, and `lineno` gives the line number on which the error was found.

14.3.1 netrc Objects

A *netrc* instance has the following methods:

netrc.authenticators(*host*)
Return a 3-tuple `(login, account, password)` of authenticators for *host*. If the netrc file did not contain an entry for the given host, return the tuple associated with the 'default' entry. If neither matching host nor default entry is available, return `None`.

netrc.__repr__()
Dump the class data as a string in the format of a netrc file. (This discards comments and may reorder the entries.)

Instances of *netrc* have public instance variables:

`netrc.hosts`
: Dictionary mapping host names to `(login, account, password)` tuples. The 'default' entry, if any, is represented as a pseudo-host by that name.

`netrc.macros`
: Dictionary mapping macro names to string lists.

Note: Passwords are limited to a subset of the ASCII character set. All ASCII punctuation is allowed in passwords, however, note that whitespace and non-printable characters are not allowed in passwords. This is a limitation of the way the .netrc file is parsed and may be removed in the future.

14.4 `xdrlib` — Encode and decode XDR data

Source code: Lib/xdrlib.py

The *xdrlib* module supports the External Data Representation Standard as described in RFC 1014, written by Sun Microsystems, Inc. June 1987. It supports most of the data types described in the RFC.

The *xdrlib* module defines two classes, one for packing variables into XDR representation, and another for unpacking from XDR representation. There are also two exception classes.

`class xdrlib.Packer`
: *Packer* is the class for packing data into XDR representation. The *Packer* class is instantiated with no arguments.

`class xdrlib.Unpacker(`*data*`)`
: `Unpacker` is the complementary class which unpacks XDR data values from a string buffer. The input buffer is given as *data*.

See also:

RFC 1014 - **XDR: External Data Representation Standard** This RFC defined the encoding of data which was XDR at the time this module was originally written. It has apparently been obsoleted by RFC 1832.

RFC 1832 - **XDR: External Data Representation Standard** Newer RFC that provides a revised definition of XDR.

14.4.1 Packer Objects

Packer instances have the following methods:

`Packer.get_buffer()`
: Returns the current pack buffer as a string.

`Packer.reset()`
: Resets the pack buffer to the empty string.

In general, you can pack any of the most common XDR data types by calling the appropriate `pack_type()` method. Each method takes a single argument, the value to pack. The following simple data type packing methods are supported: `pack_uint()`, `pack_int()`, `pack_enum()`, `pack_bool()`, `pack_uhyper()`, and `pack_hyper()`.

`Packer.pack_float(value)`
Packs the single-precision floating point number *value*.

`Packer.pack_double(value)`
Packs the double-precision floating point number *value*.

The following methods support packing strings, bytes, and opaque data:

`Packer.pack_fstring(n, s)`
Packs a fixed length string, *s*. *n* is the length of the string but it is *not* packed into the data buffer. The string is padded with null bytes if necessary to guaranteed 4 byte alignment.

`Packer.pack_fopaque(n, data)`
Packs a fixed length opaque data stream, similarly to `pack_fstring()`.

`Packer.pack_string(s)`
Packs a variable length string, *s*. The length of the string is first packed as an unsigned integer, then the string data is packed with `pack_fstring()`.

`Packer.pack_opaque(data)`
Packs a variable length opaque data string, similarly to `pack_string()`.

`Packer.pack_bytes(bytes)`
Packs a variable length byte stream, similarly to `pack_string()`.

The following methods support packing arrays and lists:

`Packer.pack_list(list, pack_item)`
Packs a *list* of homogeneous items. This method is useful for lists with an indeterminate size; i.e. the size is not available until the entire list has been walked. For each item in the list, an unsigned integer `1` is packed first, followed by the data value from the list. *pack_item* is the function that is called to pack the individual item. At the end of the list, an unsigned integer `0` is packed.

For example, to pack a list of integers, the code might appear like this:

```
import xdrlib
p = xdrlib.Packer()
p.pack_list([1, 2, 3], p.pack_int)
```

`Packer.pack_farray(n, array, pack_item)`
Packs a fixed length list (*array*) of homogeneous items. *n* is the length of the list; it is *not* packed into the buffer, but a `ValueError` exception is raised if `len(array)` is not equal to *n*. As above, *pack_item* is the function used to pack each element.

`Packer.pack_array(list, pack_item)`
Packs a variable length *list* of homogeneous items. First, the length of the list is packed as an unsigned integer, then each element is packed as in `pack_farray()` above.

14.4.2 Unpacker Objects

The `Unpacker` class offers the following methods:

`Unpacker.reset(data)`
Resets the string buffer with the given *data*.

`Unpacker.get_position()`
Returns the current unpack position in the data buffer.

`Unpacker.set_position(position)`
Sets the data buffer unpack position to *position*. You should be careful about using `get_position()` and `set_position()`.

`Unpacker.get_buffer()`
Returns the current unpack data buffer as a string.

`Unpacker.done()`
Indicates unpack completion. Raises an *Error* exception if all of the data has not been unpacked.

In addition, every data type that can be packed with a *Packer*, can be unpacked with an *Unpacker*. Unpacking methods are of the form `unpack_type()`, and take no arguments. They return the unpacked object.

`Unpacker.unpack_float()`
Unpacks a single-precision floating point number.

`Unpacker.unpack_double()`
Unpacks a double-precision floating point number, similarly to *unpack_float()*.

In addition, the following methods unpack strings, bytes, and opaque data:

`Unpacker.unpack_fstring(n)`
Unpacks and returns a fixed length string. *n* is the number of characters expected. Padding with null bytes to guaranteed 4 byte alignment is assumed.

`Unpacker.unpack_fopaque(n)`
Unpacks and returns a fixed length opaque data stream, similarly to *unpack_fstring()*.

`Unpacker.unpack_string()`
Unpacks and returns a variable length string. The length of the string is first unpacked as an unsigned integer, then the string data is unpacked with *unpack_fstring()*.

`Unpacker.unpack_opaque()`
Unpacks and returns a variable length opaque data string, similarly to *unpack_string()*.

`Unpacker.unpack_bytes()`
Unpacks and returns a variable length byte stream, similarly to *unpack_string()*.

The following methods support unpacking arrays and lists:

`Unpacker.unpack_list(unpack_item)`
Unpacks and returns a list of homogeneous items. The list is unpacked one element at a time by first unpacking an unsigned integer flag. If the flag is `1`, then the item is unpacked and appended to the list. A flag of `0` indicates the end of the list. *unpack_item* is the function that is called to unpack the items.

`Unpacker.unpack_farray(n, unpack_item)`
Unpacks and returns (as a list) a fixed length array of homogeneous items. *n* is number of list elements to expect in the buffer. As above, *unpack_item* is the function used to unpack each element.

`Unpacker.unpack_array(unpack_item)`
Unpacks and returns a variable length *list* of homogeneous items. First, the length of the list is unpacked as an unsigned integer, then each element is unpacked as in *unpack_farray()* above.

14.4.3 Exceptions

Exceptions in this module are coded as class instances:

`exception xdrlib.Error`
The base exception class. *Error* has a single public attribute `msg` containing the description of the error.

`exception xdrlib.ConversionError`
Class derived from *Error*. Contains no additional instance variables.

Here is an example of how you would catch one of these exceptions:

```
import xdrlib
p = xdrlib.Packer()
try:
    p.pack_double(8.01)
except xdrlib.ConversionError as instance:
    print('packing the double failed:', instance.msg)
```

14.5 plistlib — Generate and parse Mac OS X .plist files

Source code: Lib/plistlib.py

This module provides an interface for reading and writing the "property list" files used mainly by Mac OS X and supports both binary and XML plist files.

The property list (`.plist`) file format is a simple serialization supporting basic object types, like dictionaries, lists, numbers and strings. Usually the top level object is a dictionary.

To write out and to parse a plist file, use the `dump()` and `load()` functions.

To work with plist data in bytes objects, use `dumps()` and `loads()`.

Values can be strings, integers, floats, booleans, tuples, lists, dictionaries (but only with string keys), `Data`, `bytes`, `bytesarray` or `datetime.datetime` objects.

Changed in version 3.4: New API, old API deprecated. Support for binary format plists added.

See also:

PList manual page Apple's documentation of the file format.

This module defines the following functions:

`plistlib.load`(*fp*, *, *fmt=None*, *use_builtin_types=True*, *dict_type=dict*)
Read a plist file. *fp* should be a readable and binary file object. Return the unpacked root object (which usually is a dictionary).

The *fmt* is the format of the file and the following values are valid:

- `None`: Autodetect the file format
- `FMT_XML`: XML file format
- `FMT_BINARY`: Binary plist format

If *use_builtin_types* is true (the default) binary data will be returned as instances of `bytes`, otherwise it is returned as instances of `Data`.

The *dict_type* is the type used for dictionaries that are read from the plist file. The exact structure of the plist can be recovered by using `collections.OrderedDict` (although the order of keys shouldn't be important in plist files).

XML data for the `FMT_XML` format is parsed using the Expat parser from `xml.parsers.expat` – see its documentation for possible exceptions on ill-formed XML. Unknown elements will simply be ignored by the plist parser.

The parser for the binary format raises `InvalidFileException` when the file cannot be parsed.

New in version 3.4.

`plistlib.loads`(*data*, *, *fmt=None*, *use_builtin_types=True*, *dict_type=dict*)
Load a plist from a bytes object. See `load()` for an explanation of the keyword arguments.

New in version 3.4.

plistlib.**dump**(*value, fp, *, fmt=FMT_XML, sort_keys=True, skipkeys=False*)

Write *value* to a plist file. *Fp* should be a writable, binary file object.

The *fmt* argument specifies the format of the plist file and can be one of the following values:

- *FMT_XML*: XML formatted plist file
- *FMT_BINARY*: Binary formatted plist file

When *sort_keys* is true (the default) the keys for dictionaries will be written to the plist in sorted order, otherwise they will be written in the iteration order of the dictionary.

When *skipkeys* is false (the default) the function raises *TypeError* when a key of a dictionary is not a string, otherwise such keys are skipped.

A *TypeError* will be raised if the object is of an unsupported type or a container that contains objects of unsupported types.

An *OverflowError* will be raised for integer values that cannot be represented in (binary) plist files.

New in version 3.4.

plistlib.**dumps**(*value, *, fmt=FMT_XML, sort_keys=True, skipkeys=False*)

Return *value* as a plist-formatted bytes object. See the documentation for *dump()* for an explanation of the keyword arguments of this function.

New in version 3.4.

The following functions are deprecated:

plistlib.**readPlist**(*pathOrFile*)

Read a plist file. *pathOrFile* may be either a file name or a (readable and binary) file object. Returns the unpacked root object (which usually is a dictionary).

This function calls *load()* to do the actual work, see the documentation of *that function* for an explanation of the keyword arguments.

Note: Dict values in the result have a `__getattr__` method that defers to `__getitem_`. This means that you can use attribute access to access items of these dictionaries.

Deprecated since version 3.4: Use *load()* instead.

plistlib.**writePlist**(*rootObject, pathOrFile*)

Write *rootObject* to an XML plist file. *pathOrFile* may be either a file name or a (writable and binary) file object

Deprecated since version 3.4: Use *dump()* instead.

plistlib.**readPlistFromBytes**(*data*)

Read a plist data from a bytes object. Return the root object.

See *load()* for a description of the keyword arguments.

Note: Dict values in the result have a `__getattr__` method that defers to `__getitem_`. This means that you can use attribute access to access items of these dictionaries.

Deprecated since version 3.4: Use *loads()* instead.

plistlib.**writePlistToBytes**(*rootObject*)

Return *rootObject* as an XML plist-formatted bytes object.

Deprecated since version 3.4: Use *dumps()* instead.

The following classes are available:

`Dict([dict]):`

Return an extended mapping object with the same value as dictionary *dict*.

This class is a subclass of *dict* where attribute access can be used to access items. That is, `aDict.key` is the same as `aDict['key']` for getting, setting and deleting items in the mapping.

Deprecated since version 3.0.

`class plistlib.Data(`*data*`)`

Return a "data" wrapper object around the bytes object *data*. This is used in functions converting from/to plists to represent the `<data>` type available in plists.

It has one attribute, `data`, that can be used to retrieve the Python bytes object stored in it.

Deprecated since version 3.4: Use a *bytes* object instead.

The following constants are available:

`plistlib.FMT_XML`

The XML format for plist files.

New in version 3.4.

`plistlib.FMT_BINARY`

The binary format for plist files

New in version 3.4.

14.5.1 Examples

Generating a plist:

```
pl = dict(
    aString = "Doodah",
    aList = ["A", "B", 12, 32.1, [1, 2, 3]],
    aFloat = 0.1,
    anInt = 728,
    aDict = dict(
        anotherString = "<hello & hi there!>",
        aThirdString = "M\xe4ssig, Ma\xdf",
        aTrueValue = True,
        aFalseValue = False,
    ),
    someData = b"<binary gunk>",
    someMoreData = b"<lots of binary gunk>" * 10,
    aDate = datetime.datetime.fromtimestamp(time.mktime(time.gmtime())),
)
with open(fileName, 'wb') as fp:
    dump(pl, fp)
```

Parsing a plist:

```
with open(fileName, 'rb') as fp:
    pl = load(fp)
print(pl["aKey"])
```

CHAPTER

FIFTEEN

CRYPTOGRAPHIC SERVICES

The modules described in this chapter implement various algorithms of a cryptographic nature. They are available at the discretion of the installation. On Unix systems, the *crypt* module may also be available. Here's an overview:

15.1 hashlib — Secure hashes and message digests

Source code: Lib/hashlib.py

This module implements a common interface to many different secure hash and message digest algorithms. Included are the FIPS secure hash algorithms SHA1, SHA224, SHA256, SHA384, and SHA512 (defined in FIPS 180-2) as well as RSA's MD5 algorithm (defined in Internet RFC 1321). The terms "secure hash" and "message digest" are interchangeable. Older algorithms were called message digests. The modern term is secure hash.

Note: If you want the adler32 or crc32 hash functions, they are available in the *zlib* module.

Warning: Some algorithms have known hash collision weaknesses, refer to the "See also" section at the end.

15.1.1 Hash algorithms

There is one constructor method named for each type of *hash*. All return a hash object with the same simple interface. For example: use `sha256()` to create a SHA-256 hash object. You can now feed this object with *bytes-like objects* (normally `bytes`) using the `update()` method. At any point you can ask it for the *digest* of the concatenation of the data fed to it so far using the `digest()` or `hexdigest()` methods.

Note: For better multithreading performance, the Python *GIL* is released for data larger than 2047 bytes at object creation or on update.

Note: Feeding string objects into `update()` is not supported, as hashes work on bytes, not on characters.

Constructors for hash algorithms that are always present in this module are `sha1()`, `sha224()`, `sha256()`, `sha384()`, `sha512()`, *blake2b()*, and *blake2s()*. `md5()` is normally available as well, though it may be missing if you are using a rare "FIPS compliant" build of Python. Additional algorithms may also be available depending upon the OpenSSL library that Python uses on your platform. On most platforms the `sha3_224()`, `sha3_256()`, `sha3_384()`, `sha3_512()`, `shake_128()`, `shake_256()` are also available.

New in version 3.6: SHA3 (Keccak) and SHAKE constructors `sha3_224()`, `sha3_256()`, `sha3_384()`, `sha3_512()`, `shake_128()`, `shake_256()`.

New in version 3.6: *blake2b()* and *blake2s()* were added.

For example, to obtain the digest of the byte string `b'Nobody inspects the spammish repetition'`:

```
>>> import hashlib
>>> m = hashlib.sha256()
>>> m.update(b"Nobody inspects")
>>> m.update(b" the spammish repetition")
>>> m.digest()
b'\x03\x1e\xdd}Ae\x15\x93\xc5\xfe\\\x00o\xa5u+7\xfd\xdf\xf7\xbcN\x84:\xa6\xaf\x0c\x95\x0fK\x94\x06'
>>> m.digest_size
32
>>> m.block_size
64
```

More condensed:

```
>>> hashlib.sha224(b"Nobody inspects the spammish repetition").hexdigest()
'a4337bc45a8fc544c03f52dc550cd6e1e87021bc896588bd79e901e2'
```

`hashlib.new(`*name*[, *data*]`)`
: Is a generic constructor that takes the string name of the desired algorithm as its first parameter. It also exists to allow access to the above listed hashes as well as any other algorithms that your OpenSSL library may offer. The named constructors are much faster than *new()* and should be preferred.

Using *new()* with an algorithm provided by OpenSSL:

```
>>> h = hashlib.new('ripemd160')
>>> h.update(b"Nobody inspects the spammish repetition")
>>> h.hexdigest()
'cc4a5ce1b3df48aec5d22d1f16b894a0b894eccc'
```

Hashlib provides the following constant attributes:

`hashlib.algorithms_guaranteed`
: A set containing the names of the hash algorithms guaranteed to be supported by this module on all platforms. Note that 'md5' is in this list despite some upstream vendors offering an odd "FIPS compliant" Python build that excludes it.

  New in version 3.2.

`hashlib.algorithms_available`
: A set containing the names of the hash algorithms that are available in the running Python interpreter. These names will be recognized when passed to *new()*. *algorithms_guaranteed* will always be a subset. The same algorithm may appear multiple times in this set under different names (thanks to OpenSSL).

  New in version 3.2.

The following values are provided as constant attributes of the hash objects returned by the constructors:

`hash.digest_size`
: The size of the resulting hash in bytes.

`hash.block_size`
: The internal block size of the hash algorithm in bytes.

A hash object has the following attributes:

`hash.name`
The canonical name of this hash, always lowercase and always suitable as a parameter to `new()` to create another hash of this type.

Changed in version 3.4: The name attribute has been present in CPython since its inception, but until Python 3.4 was not formally specified, so may not exist on some platforms.

A hash object has the following methods:

`hash.update(`*arg*`)`
Update the hash object with the object *arg*, which must be interpretable as a buffer of bytes. Repeated calls are equivalent to a single call with the concatenation of all the arguments: `m.update(a); m.update(b)` is equivalent to `m.update(a+b)`.

Changed in version 3.1: The Python GIL is released to allow other threads to run while hash updates on data larger than 2047 bytes is taking place when using hash algorithms supplied by OpenSSL.

`hash.digest()`
Return the digest of the data passed to the `update()` method so far. This is a bytes object of size `digest_size` which may contain bytes in the whole range from 0 to 255.

`hash.hexdigest()`
Like `digest()` except the digest is returned as a string object of double length, containing only hexadecimal digits. This may be used to exchange the value safely in email or other non-binary environments.

`hash.copy()`
Return a copy ("clone") of the hash object. This can be used to efficiently compute the digests of data sharing a common initial substring.

15.1.2 SHAKE variable length digests

The `shake_128()` and `shake_256()` algorithms provide variable length digests with length_in_bits//2 up to 128 or 256 bits of security. As such, their digest methods require a length. Maximum length is not limited by the SHAKE algorithm.

`shake.digest(`*length*`)`
Return the digest of the data passed to the `update()` method so far. This is a bytes object of size `length` which may contain bytes in the whole range from 0 to 255.

`shake.hexdigest(`*length*`)`
Like `digest()` except the digest is returned as a string object of double length, containing only hexadecimal digits. This may be used to exchange the value safely in email or other non-binary environments.

15.1.3 Key derivation

Key derivation and key stretching algorithms are designed for secure password hashing. Naive algorithms such as `sha1(password)` are not resistant against brute-force attacks. A good password hashing function must be tunable, slow, and include a salt.

`hashlib.pbkdf2_hmac(`*hash_name, password, salt, iterations, dklen=None*`)`
The function provides PKCS#5 password-based key derivation function 2. It uses HMAC as pseudorandom function.

The string *hash_name* is the desired name of the hash digest algorithm for HMAC, e.g. 'sha1' or 'sha256'. *password* and *salt* are interpreted as buffers of bytes. Applications and libraries should limit *password* to a sensible length (e.g. 1024). *salt* should be about 16 or more bytes from a proper source, e.g. `os.urandom()`.

The number of *iterations* should be chosen based on the hash algorithm and computing power. As of 2013, at least 100,000 iterations of SHA-256 are suggested.

dklen is the length of the derived key. If *dklen* is `None` then the digest size of the hash algorithm *hash_name* is used, e.g. 64 for SHA-512.

```
>>> import hashlib, binascii
>>> dk = hashlib.pbkdf2_hmac('sha256', b'password', b'salt', 100000)
>>> binascii.hexlify(dk)
b'0394a2ede332c9a13eb82e9b24631604c31df978b4e2f0fbd2c549944f9d79a5'
```

New in version 3.4.

Note: A fast implementation of *pbkdf2_hmac* is available with OpenSSL. The Python implementation uses an inline version of *hmac*. It is about three times slower and doesn't release the GIL.

`hashlib.scrypt`(*password*, **, *salt*, *n*, *r*, *p*, *maxmem=0*, *dklen=64*)
The function provides scrypt password-based key derivation function as defined in RFC 7914.

password and *salt* must be bytes-like objects. Applications and libraries should limit *password* to a sensible length (e.g. 1024). *salt* should be about 16 or more bytes from a proper source, e.g. *os.urandom()*.

n is the CPU/Memory cost factor, *r* the block size, *p* parallelization factor and *maxmem* limits memory (OpenSSL 1.1.0 defaults to 32 MB). *dklen* is the length of the derived key.

Availability: OpenSSL 1.1+

New in version 3.6.

15.1.4 BLAKE2

BLAKE2 is a cryptographic hash function defined in RFC-7693 that comes in two flavors:

- **BLAKE2b**, optimized for 64-bit platforms and produces digests of any size between 1 and 64 bytes,
- **BLAKE2s**, optimized for 8- to 32-bit platforms and produces digests of any size between 1 and 32 bytes.

BLAKE2 supports **keyed mode** (a faster and simpler replacement for HMAC), **salted hashing**, **personalization**, and **tree hashing**.

Hash objects from this module follow the API of standard library's *hashlib* objects.

Creating hash objects

New hash objects are created by calling constructor functions:

`hashlib.blake2b`(*data=b", digest_size=64, key=b", salt=b", person=b", fanout=1, depth=1, leaf_size=0, node_offset=0, node_depth=0, inner_size=0, last_node=False*)

`hashlib.blake2s`(*data=b", digest_size=32, key=b", salt=b", person=b", fanout=1, depth=1, leaf_size=0, node_offset=0, node_depth=0, inner_size=0, last_node=False*)

These functions return the corresponding hash objects for calculating BLAKE2b or BLAKE2s. They optionally take these general parameters:

- *data*: initial chunk of data to hash, which must be interpretable as buffer of bytes.
- *digest_size*: size of output digest in bytes.
- *key*: key for keyed hashing (up to 64 bytes for BLAKE2b, up to 32 bytes for BLAKE2s).

- *salt*: salt for randomized hashing (up to 16 bytes for BLAKE2b, up to 8 bytes for BLAKE2s).
- *person*: personalization string (up to 16 bytes for BLAKE2b, up to 8 bytes for BLAKE2s).

The following table shows limits for general parameters (in bytes):

Hash	digest_size	len(key)	len(salt)	len(person)
BLAKE2b	64	64	16	16
BLAKE2s	32	32	8	8

Note: BLAKE2 specification defines constant lengths for salt and personalization parameters, however, for convenience, this implementation accepts byte strings of any size up to the specified length. If the length of the parameter is less than specified, it is padded with zeros, thus, for example, `b'salt'` and `b'salt\x00'` is the same value. (This is not the case for *key*.)

These sizes are available as module *constants* described below.

Constructor functions also accept the following tree hashing parameters:

- *fanout*: fanout (0 to 255, 0 if unlimited, 1 in sequential mode).
- *depth*: maximal depth of tree (1 to 255, 255 if unlimited, 1 in sequential mode).
- *leaf_size*: maximal byte length of leaf (0 to 2**32-1, 0 if unlimited or in sequential mode).
- *node_offset*: node offset (0 to 2**64-1 for BLAKE2b, 0 to 2**48-1 for BLAKE2s, 0 for the first, leftmost, leaf, or in sequential mode).
- *node_depth*: node depth (0 to 255, 0 for leaves, or in sequential mode).
- *inner_size*: inner digest size (0 to 64 for BLAKE2b, 0 to 32 for BLAKE2s, 0 in sequential mode).
- *last_node*: boolean indicating whether the processed node is the last one (*False* for sequential mode).

See section 2.10 in BLAKE2 specification for comprehensive review of tree hashing.

Constants

`blake2b.SALT_SIZE`

`blake2s.SALT_SIZE`

Salt length (maximum length accepted by constructors).

`blake2b.PERSON_SIZE`

`blake2s.PERSON_SIZE`

Personalization string length (maximum length accepted by constructors).

`blake2b.MAX_KEY_SIZE`

`blake2s.MAX_KEY_SIZE`

Maximum key size.

`blake2b.MAX_DIGEST_SIZE`

`blake2s.MAX_DIGEST_SIZE`

Maximum digest size that the hash function can output.

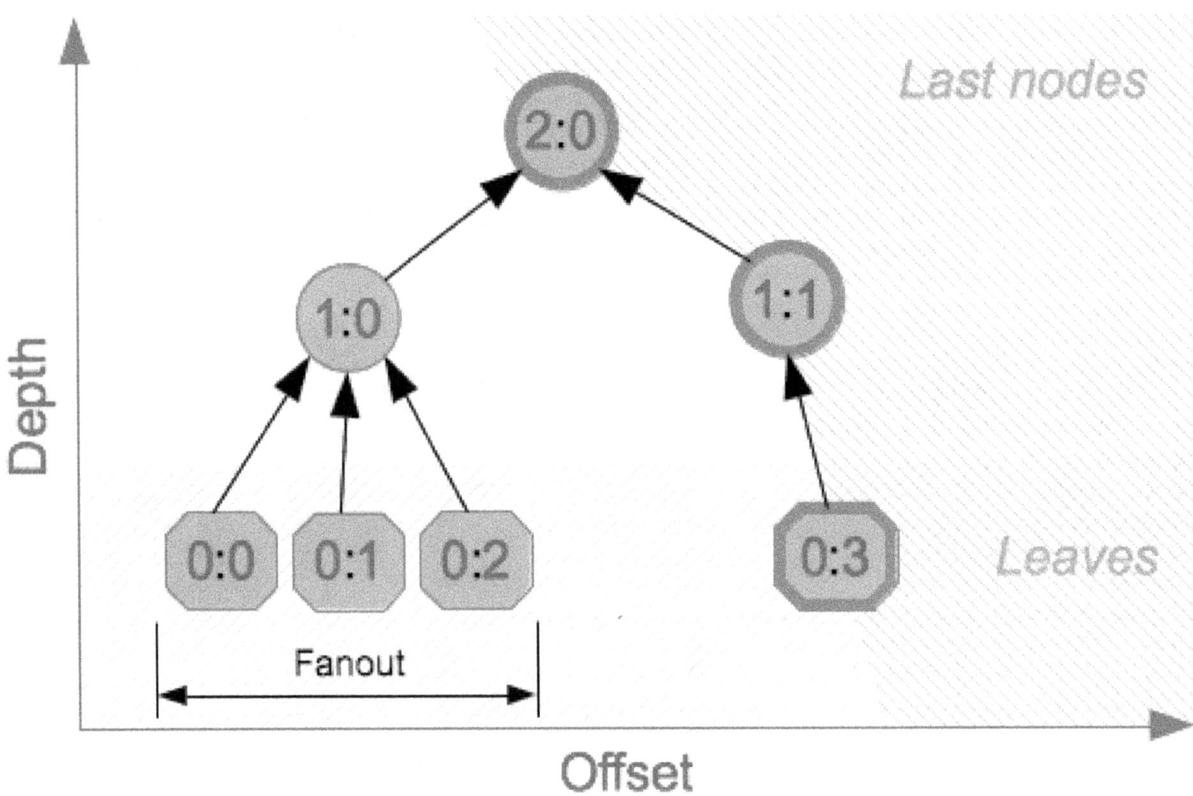

Examples

Simple hashing

To calculate hash of some data, you should first construct a hash object by calling the appropriate constructor function (*blake2b()* or *blake2s()*), then update it with the data by calling `update()` on the object, and, finally, get the digest out of the object by calling `digest()` (or `hexdigest()` for hex-encoded string).

```
>>> from hashlib import blake2b
>>> h = blake2b()
>>> h.update(b'Hello world')
>>> h.hexdigest()
'6ff843ba685842aa82031d3f53c48b66326df7639a63d128974c5c14f31a0f33343a8c65551134ed1ae0f2b0dd2bb495dc81039e3eeb0a
'
```

As a shortcut, you can pass the first chunk of data to update directly to the constructor as the first argument (or as *data* keyword argument):

```
>>> from hashlib import blake2b
>>> blake2b(b'Hello world').hexdigest()
'6ff843ba685842aa82031d3f53c48b66326df7639a63d128974c5c14f31a0f33343a8c65551134ed1ae0f2b0dd2bb495dc81039e3eeb0a
'
```

You can call *hash.update()* as many times as you need to iteratively update the hash:

```
>>> from hashlib import blake2b
>>> items = [b'Hello', b' ', b'world']
```

```
>>> h = blake2b()
>>> for item in items:
...     h.update(item)
>>> h.hexdigest()

'6ff843ba685842aa82031d3f53c48b66326df7639a63d128974c5c14f31a0f33343a8c65551134ed1ae0f2b0dd2bb495dc81039e
'
```

Using different digest sizes

BLAKE2 has configurable size of digests up to 64 bytes for BLAKE2b and up to 32 bytes for BLAKE2s. For example, to replace SHA-1 with BLAKE2b without changing the size of output, we can tell BLAKE2b to produce 20-byte digests:

```
>>> from hashlib import blake2b
>>> h = blake2b(digest_size=20)
>>> h.update(b'Replacing SHA1 with the more secure function')
>>> h.hexdigest()
'd24f26cf8de66472d58d4e1b1774b4c9158b1f4c'
>>> h.digest_size
20
>>> len(h.digest())
20
```

Hash objects with different digest sizes have completely different outputs (shorter hashes are *not* prefixes of longer hashes); BLAKE2b and BLAKE2s produce different outputs even if the output length is the same:

```
>>> from hashlib import blake2b, blake2s
>>> blake2b(digest_size=10).hexdigest()
'6fa1d8fcfd719046d762'
>>> blake2b(digest_size=11).hexdigest()
'eb6ec15daf9546254f0809'
>>> blake2s(digest_size=10).hexdigest()
'1bf21a98c78a1c376ae9'
>>> blake2s(digest_size=11).hexdigest()
'567004bf96e4a25773ebf4'
```

Keyed hashing

Keyed hashing can be used for authentication as a faster and simpler replacement for Hash-based message authentication code (HMAC). BLAKE2 can be securely used in prefix-MAC mode thanks to the indifferentiability property inherited from BLAKE.

This example shows how to get a (hex-encoded) 128-bit authentication code for message `b'message data'` with key `b'pseudorandom key'`:

```
>>> from hashlib import blake2b
>>> h = blake2b(key=b'pseudorandom key', digest_size=16)
>>> h.update(b'message data')
>>> h.hexdigest()
'3d363ff7401e02026f4a4687d4863ced'
```

As a practical example, a web application can symmetrically sign cookies sent to users and later verify them to make sure they weren't tampered with:

```
>>> from hashlib import blake2b
>>> from hmac import compare_digest
>>>
>>> SECRET_KEY = b'pseudorandomly generated server secret key'
>>> AUTH_SIZE = 16
>>>
>>> def sign(cookie):
...     h = blake2b(digest_size=AUTH_SIZE, key=SECRET_KEY)
...     h.update(cookie)
...     return h.hexdigest().encode('utf-8')
>>>
>>> def verify(cookie, sig):
...     good_sig = sign(cookie)
...     return compare_digest(good_sig, sig)
>>>
>>> cookie = b'user-alice'
>>> sig = sign(cookie)
>>> print("{0},{1}".format(cookie.decode('utf-8'), sig))
user-alice,b'43b3c982cf697e0c5ab22172d1ca7421'
>>> verify(cookie, sig)
True
>>> verify(b'user-bob', sig)
False
>>> verify(cookie, b'0102030405060708090a0b0c0d0e0f00')
False
```

Even though there's a native keyed hashing mode, BLAKE2 can, of course, be used in HMAC construction with *hmac* module:

```
>>> import hmac, hashlib
>>> m = hmac.new(b'secret key', digestmod=hashlib.blake2s)
>>> m.update(b'message')
>>> m.hexdigest()
'e3c8102868d28b5ff85fc35dda07329970d1a01e273c37481326fe0c861c8142'
```

Randomized hashing

By setting *salt* parameter users can introduce randomization to the hash function. Randomized hashing is useful for protecting against collision attacks on the hash function used in digital signatures.

> Randomized hashing is designed for situations where one party, the message preparer, generates all or part of a message to be signed by a second party, the message signer. If the message preparer is able to find cryptographic hash function collisions (i.e., two messages producing the same hash value), then she might prepare meaningful versions of the message that would produce the same hash value and digital signature, but with different results (e.g., transferring $1,000,000 to an account, rather than $10). Cryptographic hash functions have been designed with collision resistance as a major goal, but the current concentration on attacking cryptographic hash functions may result in a given cryptographic hash function providing less collision resistance than expected. Randomized hashing offers the signer additional protection by reducing the likelihood that a preparer can generate two or more messages that ultimately yield the same hash value during the digital signature generation process — even if it is practical to find collisions for the hash function. However, the use of randomized hashing may reduce the amount of security provided by a digital signature when all portions of the message are prepared by the signer.
>
> (NIST SP-800-106 "Randomized Hashing for Digital Signatures")

In BLAKE2 the salt is processed as a one-time input to the hash function during initialization, rather than as an input to each compression function.

> **Warning:** *Salted hashing* (or just hashing) with BLAKE2 or any other general-purpose cryptographic hash function, such as SHA-256, is not suitable for hashing passwords. See BLAKE2 FAQ for more information.

```
>>> import os
>>> from hashlib import blake2b
>>> msg = b'some message'
>>> # Calculate the first hash with a random salt.
>>> salt1 = os.urandom(blake2b.SALT_SIZE)
>>> h1 = blake2b(salt=salt1)
>>> h1.update(msg)
>>> # Calculate the second hash with a different random salt.
>>> salt2 = os.urandom(blake2b.SALT_SIZE)
>>> h2 = blake2b(salt=salt2)
>>> h2.update(msg)
>>> # The digests are different.
>>> h1.digest() != h2.digest()
True
```

Personalization

Sometimes it is useful to force hash function to produce different digests for the same input for different purposes. Quoting the authors of the Skein hash function:

> We recommend that all application designers seriously consider doing this; we have seen many protocols where a hash that is computed in one part of the protocol can be used in an entirely different part because two hash computations were done on similar or related data, and the attacker can force the application to make the hash inputs the same. Personalizing each hash function used in the protocol summarily stops this type of attack.
>
> (The Skein Hash Function Family, p. 21)

BLAKE2 can be personalized by passing bytes to the *person* argument:

```
>>> from hashlib import blake2b
>>> FILES_HASH_PERSON = b'MyApp Files Hash'
>>> BLOCK_HASH_PERSON = b'MyApp Block Hash'
>>> h = blake2b(digest_size=32, person=FILES_HASH_PERSON)
>>> h.update(b'the same content')
>>> h.hexdigest()
'20d9cd024d4fb086aae819a1432dd2466de12947831b75c5a30cf2676095d3b4'
>>> h = blake2b(digest_size=32, person=BLOCK_HASH_PERSON)
>>> h.update(b'the same content')
>>> h.hexdigest()
'cf68fb5761b9c44e7878bfb2c4c9aea52264a80b75005e65619778de59f383a3'
```

Personalization together with the keyed mode can also be used to derive different keys from a single one.

```
>>> from hashlib import blake2s
>>> from base64 import b64decode, b64encode
>>> orig_key = b64decode(b'Rm5EPJai72qcK3RGBpW3vPNfZy5OZothY+kHY6h21KM=')
>>> enc_key = blake2s(key=orig_key, person=b'kEncrypt').digest()
>>> mac_key = blake2s(key=orig_key, person=b'kMAC').digest()
```

```
>>> print(b64encode(enc_key).decode('utf-8'))
rbPb15S/Z9t+agffno5wuhB77VbRi6F9Iv2qIxU7WHw=
>>> print(b64encode(mac_key).decode('utf-8'))
G9GtHFE1YluXY1zWPlYk1e/nWfu0WSEb0KRcjhDeP/o=
```

Tree mode

Here's an example of hashing a minimal tree with two leaf nodes:

```
  10
 /  \
00  01
```

This example uses 64-byte internal digests, and returns the 32-byte final digest:

```
>>> from hashlib import blake2b
>>>
>>> FANOUT = 2
>>> DEPTH = 2
>>> LEAF_SIZE = 4096
>>> INNER_SIZE = 64
>>>
>>> buf = bytearray(6000)
>>>
>>> # Left leaf
... h00 = blake2b(buf[0:LEAF_SIZE], fanout=FANOUT, depth=DEPTH,
...               leaf_size=LEAF_SIZE, inner_size=INNER_SIZE,
...               node_offset=0, node_depth=0, last_node=False)
>>> # Right leaf
... h01 = blake2b(buf[LEAF_SIZE:], fanout=FANOUT, depth=DEPTH,
...               leaf_size=LEAF_SIZE, inner_size=INNER_SIZE,
...               node_offset=1, node_depth=0, last_node=True)
>>> # Root node
... h10 = blake2b(digest_size=32, fanout=FANOUT, depth=DEPTH,
...               leaf_size=LEAF_SIZE, inner_size=INNER_SIZE,
...               node_offset=0, node_depth=1, last_node=True)
>>> h10.update(h00.digest())
>>> h10.update(h01.digest())
>>> h10.hexdigest()
'3ad2a9b37c6070e374c7a8c508fe20ca86b6ed54e286e93a0318e95e881db5aa'
```

Credits

BLAKE2 was designed by *Jean-Philippe Aumasson*, *Samuel Neves*, *Zooko Wilcox-O'Hearn*, and *Christian Winnerlein* based on SHA-3 finalist BLAKE created by *Jean-Philippe Aumasson*, *Luca Henzen*, *Willi Meier*, and *Raphael C.-W. Phan*.

It uses core algorithm from ChaCha cipher designed by *Daniel J. Bernstein*.

The stdlib implementation is based on pyblake2 module. It was written by *Dmitry Chestnykh* based on C implementation written by *Samuel Neves*. The documentation was copied from pyblake2 and written by *Dmitry Chestnykh*.

The C code was partly rewritten for Python by *Christian Heimes*.

The following public domain dedication applies for both C hash function implementation, extension code, and this documentation:

To the extent possible under law, the author(s) have dedicated all copyright and related and neighboring rights to this software to the public domain worldwide. This software is distributed without any warranty.

You should have received a copy of the CC0 Public Domain Dedication along with this software. If not, see http://creativecommons.org/publicdomain/zero/1.0/.

The following people have helped with development or contributed their changes to the project and the public domain according to the Creative Commons Public Domain Dedication 1.0 Universal:

- *Alexandr Sokolovskiy*

See also:

Module *hmac* A module to generate message authentication codes using hashes.

Module *base64* Another way to encode binary hashes for non-binary environments.

https://blake2.net Official BLAKE2 website.

http://csrc.nist.gov/publications/fips/fips180-2/fips180-2.pdf The FIPS 180-2 publication on Secure Hash Algorithms.

https://en.wikipedia.org/wiki/Cryptographic_hash_function#Cryptographic_hash_algorithms Wikipedia article with information on which algorithms have known issues and what that means regarding their use.

https://www.ietf.org/rfc/rfc2898.txt PKCS #5: Password-Based Cryptography Specification Version 2.0

15.2 `hmac` — Keyed-Hashing for Message Authentication

Source code: Lib/hmac.py

This module implements the HMAC algorithm as described by RFC 2104.

`hmac.new`(*key*, *msg=None*, *digestmod=None*)

Return a new hmac object. *key* is a bytes or bytearray object giving the secret key. If *msg* is present, the method call `update(msg)` is made. *digestmod* is the digest name, digest constructor or module for the HMAC object to use. It supports any name suitable to *hashlib.new()* and defaults to the `hashlib.md5` constructor.

Changed in version 3.4: Parameter *key* can be a bytes or bytearray object. Parameter *msg* can be of any type supported by *hashlib*. Parameter *digestmod* can be the name of a hash algorithm.

Deprecated since version 3.4: MD5 as implicit default digest for *digestmod* is deprecated.

An HMAC object has the following methods:

`HMAC.update`(*msg*)

Update the hmac object with *msg*. Repeated calls are equivalent to a single call with the concatenation of all the arguments: `m.update(a); m.update(b)` is equivalent to `m.update(a + b)`.

Changed in version 3.4: Parameter *msg* can be of any type supported by *hashlib*.

`HMAC.digest`()

Return the digest of the bytes passed to the *update()* method so far. This bytes object will be the same length as the *digest_size* of the digest given to the constructor. It may contain non-ASCII bytes, including NUL bytes.

> **Warning:** When comparing the output of *digest()* to an externally-supplied digest during a verification routine, it is recommended to use the *compare_digest()* function instead of the == operator to reduce the vulnerability to timing attacks.

HMAC.**hexdigest**()
Like *digest()* except the digest is returned as a string twice the length containing only hexadecimal digits. This may be used to exchange the value safely in email or other non-binary environments.

> **Warning:** When comparing the output of *hexdigest()* to an externally-supplied digest during a verification routine, it is recommended to use the *compare_digest()* function instead of the == operator to reduce the vulnerability to timing attacks.

HMAC.**copy**()
Return a copy ("clone") of the hmac object. This can be used to efficiently compute the digests of strings that share a common initial substring.

A hash object has the following attributes:

HMAC.**digest_size**
The size of the resulting HMAC digest in bytes.

HMAC.**block_size**
The internal block size of the hash algorithm in bytes.

New in version 3.4.

HMAC.**name**
The canonical name of this HMAC, always lowercase, e.g. `hmac-md5`.

New in version 3.4.

This module also provides the following helper function:

hmac.**compare_digest**(*a*, *b*)
Return `a == b`. This function uses an approach designed to prevent timing analysis by avoiding content-based short circuiting behaviour, making it appropriate for cryptography. *a* and *b* must both be of the same type: either *str* (ASCII only, as e.g. returned by *HMAC.hexdigest()*), or a *bytes-like object*.

> **Note:** If *a* and *b* are of different lengths, or if an error occurs, a timing attack could theoretically reveal information about the types and lengths of *a* and *b*—but not their values.

New in version 3.3.

See also:

Module *hashlib* The Python module providing secure hash functions.

15.3 secrets — Generate secure random numbers for managing secrets

New in version 3.6.

Source code: Lib/secrets.py

The *secrets* module is used for generating cryptographically strong random numbers suitable for managing data such as passwords, account authentication, security tokens, and related secrets.

In particularly, *secrets* should be used in preference to the default pseudo-random number generator in the *random* module, which is designed for modelling and simulation, not security or cryptography.

See also:

PEP 506

15.3.1 Random numbers

The *secrets* module provides access to the most secure source of randomness that your operating system provides.

class secrets.SystemRandom
A class for generating random numbers using the highest-quality sources provided by the operating system. See *random.SystemRandom* for additional details.

secrets.choice(*sequence*)
Return a randomly-chosen element from a non-empty sequence.

secrets.randbelow(*n*)
Return a random int in the range [0, *n*).

secrets.randbits(*k*)
Return an int with *k* random bits.

15.3.2 Generating tokens

The *secrets* module provides functions for generating secure tokens, suitable for applications such as password resets, hard-to-guess URLs, and similar.

secrets.token_bytes([*nbytes=None*])
Return a random byte string containing *nbytes* number of bytes. If *nbytes* is None or not supplied, a reasonable default is used.

```
>>> token_bytes(16)
b'\xebr\x17D*t\xae\xd4\xe3S\xb6\xe2\xebP1\x8b'
```

secrets.token_hex([*nbytes=None*])
Return a random text string, in hexadecimal. The string has *nbytes* random bytes, each byte converted to two hex digits. If *nbytes* is None or not supplied, a reasonable default is used.

```
>>> token_hex(16)
'f9bf78b9a18ce6d46a0cd2b0b86df9da'
```

secrets.token_urlsafe([*nbytes=None*])
Return a random URL-safe text string, containing *nbytes* random bytes. The text is Base64 encoded, so on average each byte results in approximately 1.3 characters. If *nbytes* is None or not supplied, a reasonable default is used.

```
>>> token_urlsafe(16)
'Drmhze6EPcv0fN_81Bj-nA'
```

How many bytes should tokens use?

To be secure against brute-force attacks, tokens need to have sufficient randomness. Unfortunately, what is considered sufficient will necessarily increase as computers get more powerful and able to make more guesses in a shorter period. As of 2015, it is believed that 32 bytes (256 bits) of randomness is sufficient for the typical use-case expected for the *secrets* module.

For those who want to manage their own token length, you can explicitly specify how much randomness is used for tokens by giving an *int* argument to the various `token_*` functions. That argument is taken as the number of bytes of randomness to use.

Otherwise, if no argument is provided, or if the argument is `None`, the `token_*` functions will use a reasonable default instead.

Note: That default is subject to change at any time, including during maintenance releases.

15.3.3 Other functions

`secrets.compare_digest(a, b)`
Return `True` if strings *a* and *b* are equal, otherwise `False`, in such a way as to reduce the risk of timing attacks. See *hmac.compare_digest()* for additional details.

15.3.4 Recipes and best practices

This section shows recipes and best practices for using *secrets* to manage a basic level of security.

Generate an eight-character alphanumeric password:

```
import string
alphabet = string.ascii_letters + string.digits
password = ''.join(choice(alphabet) for i in range(8))
```

Note: Applications should not store passwords in a recoverable format, whether plain text or encrypted. They should be salted and hashed using a cryptographically-strong one-way (irreversible) hash function.

Generate a ten-character alphanumeric password with at least one lowercase character, at least one uppercase character, and at least three digits:

```
import string
alphabet = string.ascii_letters + string.digits
while True:
    password = ''.join(choice(alphabet) for i in range(10))
    if (any(c.islower() for c in password)
            and any(c.isupper() for c in password)
            and sum(c.isdigit() for c in password) >= 3):
        break
```

Generate an XKCD-style passphrase:

```
# On standard Linux systems, use a convenient dictionary file.
# Other platforms may need to provide their own word-list.
with open('/usr/share/dict/words') as f:
    words = [word.strip() for word in f]
    password = ' '.join(choice(words) for i in range(4))
```

Generate a hard-to-guess temporary URL containing a security token suitable for password recovery applications:

```
url = 'https://mydomain.com/reset=' + token_urlsafe()
```

CHAPTER

SIXTEEN

GENERIC OPERATING SYSTEM SERVICES

The modules described in this chapter provide interfaces to operating system features that are available on (almost) all operating systems, such as files and a clock. The interfaces are generally modeled after the Unix or C interfaces, but they are available on most other systems as well. Here's an overview:

16.1 os — Miscellaneous operating system interfaces

Source code: Lib/os.py

This module provides a portable way of using operating system dependent functionality. If you just want to read or write a file see *open()*, if you want to manipulate paths, see the *os.path* module, and if you want to read all the lines in all the files on the command line see the *fileinput* module. For creating temporary files and directories see the *tempfile* module, and for high-level file and directory handling see the *shutil* module.

Notes on the availability of these functions:

- The design of all built-in operating system dependent modules of Python is such that as long as the same functionality is available, it uses the same interface; for example, the function `os.stat(path)` returns stat information about *path* in the same format (which happens to have originated with the POSIX interface).
- Extensions peculiar to a particular operating system are also available through the *os* module, but using them is of course a threat to portability.
- All functions accepting path or file names accept both bytes and string objects, and result in an object of the same type, if a path or file name is returned.
- An "Availability: Unix" note means that this function is commonly found on Unix systems. It does not make any claims about its existence on a specific operating system.
- If not separately noted, all functions that claim "Availability: Unix" are supported on Mac OS X, which builds on a Unix core.

Note: All functions in this module raise *OSError* in the case of invalid or inaccessible file names and paths, or other arguments that have the correct type, but are not accepted by the operating system.

---

exception os.error
An alias for the built-in *OSError* exception.

os.name
The name of the operating system dependent module imported. The following names have currently been registered: `'posix'`, `'nt'`, `'java'`.

See also:

sys.platform has a finer granularity. *os.uname()* gives system-dependent version information.

The *platform* module provides detailed checks for the system's identity.

16.1.1 File Names, Command Line Arguments, and Environment Variables

In Python, file names, command line arguments, and environment variables are represented using the string type. On some systems, decoding these strings to and from bytes is necessary before passing them to the operating system. Python uses the file system encoding to perform this conversion (see *sys.getfilesystemencoding()*).

Changed in version 3.1: On some systems, conversion using the file system encoding may fail. In this case, Python uses the *surrogateescape encoding error handler*, which means that undecodable bytes are replaced by a Unicode character U+DCxx on decoding, and these are again translated to the original byte on encoding.

The file system encoding must guarantee to successfully decode all bytes below 128. If the file system encoding fails to provide this guarantee, API functions may raise UnicodeErrors.

16.1.2 Process Parameters

These functions and data items provide information and operate on the current process and user.

`os.ctermid()`

Return the filename corresponding to the controlling terminal of the process.

Availability: Unix.

`os.environ`

A *mapping* object representing the string environment. For example, `environ['HOME']` is the pathname of your home directory (on some platforms), and is equivalent to `getenv("HOME")` in C.

This mapping is captured the first time the *os* module is imported, typically during Python startup as part of processing `site.py`. Changes to the environment made after this time are not reflected in `os.environ`, except for changes made by modifying `os.environ` directly.

If the platform supports the *putenv()* function, this mapping may be used to modify the environment as well as query the environment. *putenv()* will be called automatically when the mapping is modified.

On Unix, keys and values use *sys.getfilesystemencoding()* and `'surrogateescape'` error handler. Use *environb* if you would like to use a different encoding.

Note: Calling *putenv()* directly does not change `os.environ`, so it's better to modify `os.environ`.

Note: On some platforms, including FreeBSD and Mac OS X, setting `environ` may cause memory leaks. Refer to the system documentation for `putenv()`.

If *putenv()* is not provided, a modified copy of this mapping may be passed to the appropriate process-creation functions to cause child processes to use a modified environment.

If the platform supports the *unsetenv()* function, you can delete items in this mapping to unset environment variables. *unsetenv()* will be called automatically when an item is deleted from `os.environ`, and when one of the `pop()` or `clear()` methods is called.

os.environb

Bytes version of *environ*: a *mapping* object representing the environment as byte strings. *environ* and *environb* are synchronized (modify *environb* updates *environ*, and vice versa).

environb is only available if *supports_bytes_environ* is True.

New in version 3.2.

os.chdir(*path*)
os.fchdir(*fd*)
os.getcwd()

These functions are described in *Files and Directories*.

os.fsencode(*filename*)

Encode *path-like filename* to the filesystem encoding with `'surrogateescape'` error handler, or `'strict'` on Windows; return *bytes* unchanged.

fsdecode() is the reverse function.

New in version 3.2.

Changed in version 3.6: Support added to accept objects implementing the *os.PathLike* interface.

os.fsdecode(*filename*)

Decode the *path-like filename* from the filesystem encoding with `'surrogateescape'` error handler, or `'strict'` on Windows; return *str* unchanged.

fsencode() is the reverse function.

New in version 3.2.

Changed in version 3.6: Support added to accept objects implementing the *os.PathLike* interface.

os.fspath(*path*)

Return the file system representation of the path.

If *str* or *bytes* is passed in, it is returned unchanged. Otherwise *__fspath__()* is called and its value is returned as long as it is a *str* or *bytes* object. In all other cases, *TypeError* is raised.

New in version 3.6.

class os.PathLike

An *abstract base class* for objects representing a file system path, e.g. *pathlib.PurePath*.

New in version 3.6.

abstractmethod __fspath__()

Return the file system path representation of the object.

The method should only return a *str* or *bytes* object, with the preference being for *str*.

os.getenv(*key*, *default=None*)

Return the value of the environment variable *key* if it exists, or *default* if it doesn't. *key*, *default* and the result are str.

On Unix, keys and values are decoded with *sys.getfilesystemencoding()* and `'surrogateescape'` error handler. Use *os.getenvb()* if you would like to use a different encoding.

Availability: most flavors of Unix, Windows.

os.getenvb(*key*, *default=None*)

Return the value of the environment variable *key* if it exists, or *default* if it doesn't. *key*, *default* and the result are bytes.

getenvb() is only available if *supports_bytes_environ* is True.

Availability: most flavors of Unix.

New in version 3.2.

os.**get_exec_path**(*env=None*)
Returns the list of directories that will be searched for a named executable, similar to a shell, when launching a process. *env*, when specified, should be an environment variable dictionary to lookup the PATH in. By default, when *env* is `None`, *environ* is used.

New in version 3.2.

os.**getegid**()
Return the effective group id of the current process. This corresponds to the "set id" bit on the file being executed in the current process.

Availability: Unix.

os.**geteuid**()
Return the current process's effective user id.

Availability: Unix.

os.**getgid**()
Return the real group id of the current process.

Availability: Unix.

os.**getgrouplist**(*user*, *group*)
Return list of group ids that *user* belongs to. If *group* is not in the list, it is included; typically, *group* is specified as the group ID field from the password record for *user*.

Availability: Unix.

New in version 3.3.

os.**getgroups**()
Return list of supplemental group ids associated with the current process.

Availability: Unix.

Note: On Mac OS X, *getgroups()* behavior differs somewhat from other Unix platforms. If the Python interpreter was built with a deployment target of `10.5` or earlier, *getgroups()* returns the list of effective group ids associated with the current user process; this list is limited to a system-defined number of entries, typically 16, and may be modified by calls to *setgroups()* if suitably privileged. If built with a deployment target greater than `10.5`, *getgroups()* returns the current group access list for the user associated with the effective user id of the process; the group access list may change over the lifetime of the process, it is not affected by calls to *setgroups()*, and its length is not limited to 16. The deployment target value, `MACOSX_DEPLOYMENT_TARGET`, can be obtained with *sysconfig.get_config_var()*.

---

os.**getlogin**()
Return the name of the user logged in on the controlling terminal of the process. For most purposes, it is more useful to use *getpass.getuser()* since the latter checks the environment variables `LOGNAME` or `USERNAME` to find out who the user is, and falls back to `pwd.getpwuid(os.getuid())[0]` to get the login name of the current real user id.

Availability: Unix, Windows.

os.**getpgid**(*pid*)
Return the process group id of the process with process id *pid*. If *pid* is 0, the process group id of the current process is returned.

Availability: Unix.

os.**getpgrp**()

Return the id of the current process group.

Availability: Unix.

os.**getpid**()

Return the current process id.

os.**getppid**()

Return the parent's process id. When the parent process has exited, on Unix the id returned is the one of the init process (1), on Windows it is still the same id, which may be already reused by another process.

Availability: Unix, Windows.

Changed in version 3.2: Added support for Windows.

os.**getpriority**(*which, who*)

Get program scheduling priority. The value *which* is one of *PRIO_PROCESS*, *PRIO_PGRP*, or *PRIO_USER*, and *who* is interpreted relative to *which* (a process identifier for *PRIO_PROCESS*, process group identifier for *PRIO_PGRP*, and a user ID for *PRIO_USER*). A zero value for *who* denotes (respectively) the calling process, the process group of the calling process, or the real user ID of the calling process.

Availability: Unix.

New in version 3.3.

os.**PRIO_PROCESS**
os.**PRIO_PGRP**
os.**PRIO_USER**

Parameters for the *getpriority()* and *setpriority()* functions.

Availability: Unix.

New in version 3.3.

os.**getresuid**()

Return a tuple (ruid, euid, suid) denoting the current process's real, effective, and saved user ids.

Availability: Unix.

New in version 3.2.

os.**getresgid**()

Return a tuple (rgid, egid, sgid) denoting the current process's real, effective, and saved group ids.

Availability: Unix.

New in version 3.2.

os.**getuid**()

Return the current process's real user id.

Availability: Unix.

os.**initgroups**(*username, gid*)

Call the system initgroups() to initialize the group access list with all of the groups of which the specified username is a member, plus the specified group id.

Availability: Unix.

New in version 3.2.

os.**putenv**(*key, value*)

Set the environment variable named *key* to the string *value*. Such changes to the environment affect subprocesses started with *os.system()*, *popen()* or *fork()* and *execv()*.

Availability: most flavors of Unix, Windows.

Note: On some platforms, including FreeBSD and Mac OS X, setting `environ` may cause memory leaks. Refer to the system documentation for putenv.

When *putenv()* is supported, assignments to items in `os.environ` are automatically translated into corresponding calls to *putenv()*; however, calls to *putenv()* don't update `os.environ`, so it is actually preferable to assign to items of `os.environ`.

`os.setegid(egid)`
Set the current process's effective group id.

Availability: Unix.

`os.seteuid(euid)`
Set the current process's effective user id.

Availability: Unix.

`os.setgid(gid)`
Set the current process' group id.

Availability: Unix.

`os.setgroups(groups)`
Set the list of supplemental group ids associated with the current process to *groups*. *groups* must be a sequence, and each element must be an integer identifying a group. This operation is typically available only to the superuser.

Availability: Unix.

Note: On Mac OS X, the length of *groups* may not exceed the system-defined maximum number of effective group ids, typically 16. See the documentation for *getgroups()* for cases where it may not return the same group list set by calling setgroups().

`os.setpgrp()`
Call the system call `setpgrp()` or `setpgrp(0, 0)` depending on which version is implemented (if any). See the Unix manual for the semantics.

Availability: Unix.

`os.setpgid(pid, pgrp)`
Call the system call `setpgid()` to set the process group id of the process with id *pid* to the process group with id *pgrp*. See the Unix manual for the semantics.

Availability: Unix.

`os.setpriority(which, who, priority)`
Set program scheduling priority. The value *which* is one of *PRIO_PROCESS*, *PRIO_PGRP*, or *PRIO_USER*, and *who* is interpreted relative to *which* (a process identifier for *PRIO_PROCESS*, process group identifier for *PRIO_PGRP*, and a user ID for *PRIO_USER*). A zero value for *who* denotes (respectively) the calling process, the process group of the calling process, or the real user ID of the calling process. *priority* is a value in the range -20 to 19. The default priority is 0; lower priorities cause more favorable scheduling.

Availability: Unix

New in version 3.3.

`os.setregid(rgid, egid)`
Set the current process's real and effective group ids.

Availability: Unix.

os.**setresgid**(*rgid, egid, sgid*)
Set the current process's real, effective, and saved group ids.

Availability: Unix.

New in version 3.2.

os.**setresuid**(*ruid, euid, suid*)
Set the current process's real, effective, and saved user ids.

Availability: Unix.

New in version 3.2.

os.**setreuid**(*ruid, euid*)
Set the current process's real and effective user ids.

Availability: Unix.

os.**getsid**(*pid*)
Call the system call `getsid()`. See the Unix manual for the semantics.

Availability: Unix.

os.**setsid**()
Call the system call `setsid()`. See the Unix manual for the semantics.

Availability: Unix.

os.**setuid**(*uid*)
Set the current process's user id.

Availability: Unix.

os.**strerror**(*code*)
Return the error message corresponding to the error code in *code*. On platforms where `strerror()` returns `NULL` when given an unknown error number, *ValueError* is raised.

os.**supports_bytes_environ**
`True` if the native OS type of the environment is bytes (eg. `False` on Windows).

New in version 3.2.

os.**umask**(*mask*)
Set the current numeric umask and return the previous umask.

os.**uname**()
Returns information identifying the current operating system. The return value is an object with five attributes:

- `sysname` - operating system name
- `nodename` - name of machine on network (implementation-defined)
- `release` - operating system release
- `version` - operating system version
- `machine` - hardware identifier

For backwards compatibility, this object is also iterable, behaving like a five-tuple containing `sysname`, `nodename`, `release`, `version`, and `machine` in that order.

Some systems truncate `nodename` to 8 characters or to the leading component; a better way to get the hostname is *socket.gethostname()* or even `socket.gethostbyaddr(socket.gethostname())`.

Availability: recent flavors of Unix.

Changed in version 3.3: Return type changed from a tuple to a tuple-like object with named attributes.

os.**unsetenv**(*key*)
Unset (delete) the environment variable named *key*. Such changes to the environment affect subprocesses started with *os.system()*, *popen()* or *fork()* and *execv()*.

When *unsetenv()* is supported, deletion of items in `os.environ` is automatically translated into a corresponding call to *unsetenv()*; however, calls to *unsetenv()* don't update `os.environ`, so it is actually preferable to delete items of `os.environ`.

Availability: most flavors of Unix, Windows.

16.1.3 File Object Creation

This function creates new *file objects*. (See also *open()* for opening file descriptors.)

os.**fdopen**(*fd*, **args*, ***kwargs*)
Return an open file object connected to the file descriptor *fd*. This is an alias of the *open()* built-in function and accepts the same arguments. The only difference is that the first argument of *fdopen()* must always be an integer.

16.1.4 File Descriptor Operations

These functions operate on I/O streams referenced using file descriptors.

File descriptors are small integers corresponding to a file that has been opened by the current process. For example, standard input is usually file descriptor 0, standard output is 1, and standard error is 2. Further files opened by a process will then be assigned 3, 4, 5, and so forth. The name "file descriptor" is slightly deceptive; on Unix platforms, sockets and pipes are also referenced by file descriptors.

The *fileno()* method can be used to obtain the file descriptor associated with a *file object* when required. Note that using the file descriptor directly will bypass the file object methods, ignoring aspects such as internal buffering of data.

os.**close**(*fd*)
Close file descriptor *fd*.

Note: This function is intended for low-level I/O and must be applied to a file descriptor as returned by *os.open()* or *pipe()*. To close a "file object" returned by the built-in function *open()* or by *popen()* or *fdopen()*, use its *close()* method.

os.**closerange**(*fd_low*, *fd_high*)
Close all file descriptors from *fd_low* (inclusive) to *fd_high* (exclusive), ignoring errors. Equivalent to (but much faster than):

```
for fd in range(fd_low, fd_high):
    try:
        os.close(fd)
    except OSError:
        pass
```

os.**device_encoding**(*fd*)
Return a string describing the encoding of the device associated with *fd* if it is connected to a terminal; else return *None*.

os.**dup**(*fd*)
Return a duplicate of file descriptor *fd*. The new file descriptor is *non-inheritable*.

On Windows, when duplicating a standard stream (0: stdin, 1: stdout, 2: stderr), the new file descriptor is *inheritable*.

Changed in version 3.4: The new file descriptor is now non-inheritable.

os.**dup2**(*fd*, *fd2*, *inheritable=True*)
Duplicate file descriptor *fd* to *fd2*, closing the latter first if necessary. The file descriptor *fd2* is *inheritable* by default, or non-inheritable if *inheritable* is `False`.

Changed in version 3.4: Add the optional *inheritable* parameter.

os.**fchmod**(*fd*, *mode*)
Change the mode of the file given by *fd* to the numeric *mode*. See the docs for `chmod()` for possible values of *mode*. As of Python 3.3, this is equivalent to `os.chmod(fd, mode)`.

Availability: Unix.

os.**fchown**(*fd*, *uid*, *gid*)
Change the owner and group id of the file given by *fd* to the numeric *uid* and *gid*. To leave one of the ids unchanged, set it to -1. See `chown()`. As of Python 3.3, this is equivalent to `os.chown(fd, uid, gid)`.

Availability: Unix.

os.**fdatasync**(*fd*)
Force write of file with filedescriptor *fd* to disk. Does not force update of metadata.

Availability: Unix.

Note: This function is not available on MacOS.

os.**fpathconf**(*fd*, *name*)
Return system configuration information relevant to an open file. *name* specifies the configuration value to retrieve; it may be a string which is the name of a defined system value; these names are specified in a number of standards (POSIX.1, Unix 95, Unix 98, and others). Some platforms define additional names as well. The names known to the host operating system are given in the `pathconf_names` dictionary. For configuration variables not included in that mapping, passing an integer for *name* is also accepted.

If *name* is a string and is not known, `ValueError` is raised. If a specific value for *name* is not supported by the host system, even if it is included in `pathconf_names`, an `OSError` is raised with `errno.EINVAL` for the error number.

As of Python 3.3, this is equivalent to `os.pathconf(fd, name)`.

Availability: Unix.

os.**fstat**(*fd*)
Get the status of the file descriptor *fd*. Return a `stat_result` object.

As of Python 3.3, this is equivalent to `os.stat(fd)`.

See also:

The `stat()` function.

os.**fstatvfs**(*fd*)
Return information about the filesystem containing the file associated with file descriptor *fd*, like `statvfs()`. As of Python 3.3, this is equivalent to `os.statvfs(fd)`.

Availability: Unix.

`os.fsync(fd)`
Force write of file with filedescriptor *fd* to disk. On Unix, this calls the native `fsync()` function; on Windows, the MS `_commit()` function.

If you're starting with a buffered Python *file object* *f*, first do `f.flush()`, and then do `os.fsync(f.fileno())`, to ensure that all internal buffers associated with *f* are written to disk.

Availability: Unix, Windows.

`os.ftruncate(fd, length)`
Truncate the file corresponding to file descriptor *fd*, so that it is at most *length* bytes in size. As of Python 3.3, this is equivalent to `os.truncate(fd, length)`.

Availability: Unix, Windows.

Changed in version 3.5: Added support for Windows

`os.get_blocking(fd)`
Get the blocking mode of the file descriptor: `False` if the `O_NONBLOCK` flag is set, `True` if the flag is cleared.

See also `set_blocking()` and `socket.socket.setblocking()`.

Availability: Unix.

New in version 3.5.

`os.isatty(fd)`
Return `True` if the file descriptor *fd* is open and connected to a tty(-like) device, else `False`.

`os.lockf(fd, cmd, len)`
Apply, test or remove a POSIX lock on an open file descriptor. *fd* is an open file descriptor. *cmd* specifies the command to use - one of `F_LOCK`, `F_TLOCK`, `F_ULOCK` or `F_TEST`. *len* specifies the section of the file to lock.

Availability: Unix.

New in version 3.3.

`os.F_LOCK`
`os.F_TLOCK`
`os.F_ULOCK`
`os.F_TEST`
Flags that specify what action `lockf()` will take.

Availability: Unix.

New in version 3.3.

`os.lseek(fd, pos, how)`
Set the current position of file descriptor *fd* to position *pos*, modified by *how*: `SEEK_SET` or `0` to set the position relative to the beginning of the file; `SEEK_CUR` or `1` to set it relative to the current position; `SEEK_END` or `2` to set it relative to the end of the file. Return the new cursor position in bytes, starting from the beginning.

`os.SEEK_SET`
`os.SEEK_CUR`
`os.SEEK_END`
Parameters to the `lseek()` function. Their values are 0, 1, and 2, respectively.

New in version 3.3: Some operating systems could support additional values, like `os.SEEK_HOLE` or `os.SEEK_DATA`.

`os.open(path, flags, mode=0o777, *, dir_fd=None)`
Open the file *path* and set various flags according to *flags* and possibly its mode according to *mode*.

When computing *mode*, the current umask value is first masked out. Return the file descriptor for the newly opened file. The new file descriptor is *non-inheritable*.

For a description of the flag and mode values, see the C run-time documentation; flag constants (like `O_RDONLY` and `O_WRONLY`) are defined in the `os` module. In particular, on Windows adding `O_BINARY` is needed to open files in binary mode.

This function can support *paths relative to directory descriptors* with the *dir_fd* parameter.

Changed in version 3.4: The new file descriptor is now non-inheritable.

Note: This function is intended for low-level I/O. For normal usage, use the built-in function `open()`, which returns a *file object* with `read()` and `write()` methods (and many more). To wrap a file descriptor in a file object, use `fdopen()`.

New in version 3.3: The *dir_fd* argument.

Changed in version 3.5: If the system call is interrupted and the signal handler does not raise an exception, the function now retries the system call instead of raising an `InterruptedError` exception (see PEP 475 for the rationale).

Changed in version 3.6: Accepts a *path-like object*.

The following constants are options for the *flags* parameter to the `open()` function. They can be combined using the bitwise OR operator `|`. Some of them are not available on all platforms. For descriptions of their availability and use, consult the ***open(2)*** manual page on Unix or the MSDN on Windows.

`os.O_RDONLY`
`os.O_WRONLY`
`os.O_RDWR`
`os.O_APPEND`
`os.O_CREAT`
`os.O_EXCL`
`os.O_TRUNC`

The above constants are available on Unix and Windows.

`os.O_DSYNC`
`os.O_RSYNC`
`os.O_SYNC`
`os.O_NDELAY`
`os.O_NONBLOCK`
`os.O_NOCTTY`
`os.O_CLOEXEC`

The above constants are only available on Unix.

Changed in version 3.3: Add `O_CLOEXEC` constant.

`os.O_BINARY`
`os.O_NOINHERIT`
`os.O_SHORT_LIVED`
`os.O_TEMPORARY`
`os.O_RANDOM`
`os.O_SEQUENTIAL`
`os.O_TEXT`

The above constants are only available on Windows.

`os.O_ASYNC`
`os.O_DIRECT`
`os.O_DIRECTORY`

os.O_NOFOLLOW
os.O_NOATIME
os.O_PATH
os.O_TMPFILE
os.O_SHLOCK
os.O_EXLOCK

The above constants are extensions and not present if they are not defined by the C library.

Changed in version 3.4: Add *O_PATH* on systems that support it. Add *O_TMPFILE*, only available on Linux Kernel 3.11 or newer.

os.openpty()

Open a new pseudo-terminal pair. Return a pair of file descriptors `(master, slave)` for the pty and the tty, respectively. The new file descriptors are *non-inheritable*. For a (slightly) more portable approach, use the *pty* module.

Availability: some flavors of Unix.

Changed in version 3.4: The new file descriptors are now non-inheritable.

os.pipe()

Create a pipe. Return a pair of file descriptors `(r, w)` usable for reading and writing, respectively. The new file descriptor is *non-inheritable*.

Availability: Unix, Windows.

Changed in version 3.4: The new file descriptors are now non-inheritable.

os.pipe2(*flags*)

Create a pipe with *flags* set atomically. *flags* can be constructed by ORing together one or more of these values: *O_NONBLOCK*, *O_CLOEXEC*. Return a pair of file descriptors `(r, w)` usable for reading and writing, respectively.

Availability: some flavors of Unix.

New in version 3.3.

os.posix_fallocate(*fd*, *offset*, *len*)

Ensures that enough disk space is allocated for the file specified by *fd* starting from *offset* and continuing for *len* bytes.

Availability: Unix.

New in version 3.3.

os.posix_fadvise(*fd*, *offset*, *len*, *advice*)

Announces an intention to access data in a specific pattern thus allowing the kernel to make optimizations. The advice applies to the region of the file specified by *fd* starting at *offset* and continuing for *len* bytes. *advice* is one of *POSIX_FADV_NORMAL*, *POSIX_FADV_SEQUENTIAL*, *POSIX_FADV_RANDOM*, *POSIX_FADV_NOREUSE*, *POSIX_FADV_WILLNEED* or *POSIX_FADV_DONTNEED*.

Availability: Unix.

New in version 3.3.

os.POSIX_FADV_NORMAL
os.POSIX_FADV_SEQUENTIAL
os.POSIX_FADV_RANDOM
os.POSIX_FADV_NOREUSE
os.POSIX_FADV_WILLNEED
os.POSIX_FADV_DONTNEED

Flags that can be used in *advice* in *posix_fadvise()* that specify the access pattern that is likely to be used.

Availability: Unix.

New in version 3.3.

`os.pread(fd, buffersize, offset)`

Read from a file descriptor, *fd*, at a position of *offset*. It will read up to *buffersize* number of bytes. The file offset remains unchanged.

Availability: Unix.

New in version 3.3.

`os.pwrite(fd, str, offset)`

Write *bytestring* to a file descriptor, *fd*, from *offset*, leaving the file offset unchanged.

Availability: Unix.

New in version 3.3.

`os.read(fd, n)`

Read at most *n* bytes from file descriptor *fd*. Return a bytestring containing the bytes read. If the end of the file referred to by *fd* has been reached, an empty bytes object is returned.

Note: This function is intended for low-level I/O and must be applied to a file descriptor as returned by `os.open()` or `pipe()`. To read a "file object" returned by the built-in function `open()` or by `popen()` or `fdopen()`, or `sys.stdin`, use its `read()` or `readline()` methods.

Changed in version 3.5: If the system call is interrupted and the signal handler does not raise an exception, the function now retries the system call instead of raising an `InterruptedError` exception (see PEP 475 for the rationale).

`os.sendfile(out, in, offset, count)`

`os.sendfile(out, in, offset, count[, headers][, trailers], flags=0)`

Copy *count* bytes from file descriptor *in* to file descriptor *out* starting at *offset*. Return the number of bytes sent. When EOF is reached return 0.

The first function notation is supported by all platforms that define `sendfile()`.

On Linux, if *offset* is given as `None`, the bytes are read from the current position of *in* and the position of *in* is updated.

The second case may be used on Mac OS X and FreeBSD where *headers* and *trailers* are arbitrary sequences of buffers that are written before and after the data from *in* is written. It returns the same as the first case.

On Mac OS X and FreeBSD, a value of 0 for *count* specifies to send until the end of *in* is reached.

All platforms support sockets as *out* file descriptor, and some platforms allow other types (e.g. regular file, pipe) as well.

Cross-platform applications should not use *headers*, *trailers* and *flags* arguments.

Availability: Unix.

Note: For a higher-level wrapper of `sendfile()`, see `socket.socket.sendfile()`.

New in version 3.3.

`os.set_blocking(fd, blocking)`

Set the blocking mode of the specified file descriptor. Set the `O_NONBLOCK` flag if blocking is `False`, clear the flag otherwise.

See also `get_blocking()` and `socket.socket.setblocking()`.

Availability: Unix.

New in version 3.5.

os.**SF_NODISKIO**
os.**SF_MNOWAIT**
os.**SF_SYNC**

Parameters to the `sendfile()` function, if the implementation supports them.

Availability: Unix.

New in version 3.3.

os.**readv**(*fd*, *buffers*)

Read from a file descriptor *fd* into a number of mutable bytes-like objects *buffers*. `readv()` will transfer data into each buffer until it is full and then move on to the next buffer in the sequence to hold the rest of the data. `readv()` returns the total number of bytes read (which may be less than the total capacity of all the objects).

Availability: Unix.

New in version 3.3.

os.**tcgetpgrp**(*fd*)

Return the process group associated with the terminal given by *fd* (an open file descriptor as returned by `os.open()`).

Availability: Unix.

os.**tcsetpgrp**(*fd*, *pg*)

Set the process group associated with the terminal given by *fd* (an open file descriptor as returned by `os.open()`) to *pg*.

Availability: Unix.

os.**ttyname**(*fd*)

Return a string which specifies the terminal device associated with file descriptor *fd*. If *fd* is not associated with a terminal device, an exception is raised.

Availability: Unix.

os.**write**(*fd*, *str*)

Write the bytestring in *str* to file descriptor *fd*. Return the number of bytes actually written.

Note: This function is intended for low-level I/O and must be applied to a file descriptor as returned by `os.open()` or `pipe()`. To write a "file object" returned by the built-in function `open()` or by `popen()` or `fdopen()`, or `sys.stdout` or `sys.stderr`, use its `write()` method.

Changed in version 3.5: If the system call is interrupted and the signal handler does not raise an exception, the function now retries the system call instead of raising an `InterruptedError` exception (see PEP 475 for the rationale).

os.**writev**(*fd*, *buffers*)

Write the contents of *buffers* to file descriptor *fd*. *buffers* must be a sequence of bytes-like objects. Buffers are processed in array order. Entire contents of first buffer is written before proceeding to second, and so on. The operating system may set a limit (sysconf() value SC_IOV_MAX) on the number of buffers that can be used.

`writev()` writes the contents of each object to the file descriptor and returns the total number of bytes written.

Availability: Unix.

New in version 3.3.

Querying the size of a terminal

New in version 3.3.

`os.get_terminal_size(fd=STDOUT_FILENO)`
Return the size of the terminal window as `(columns, lines)`, tuple of type *terminal_size*.

The optional argument `fd` (default `STDOUT_FILENO`, or standard output) specifies which file descriptor should be queried.

If the file descriptor is not connected to a terminal, an *OSError* is raised.

shutil.get_terminal_size() is the high-level function which should normally be used, `os.get_terminal_size` is the low-level implementation.

Availability: Unix, Windows.

`class os.terminal_size`
A subclass of tuple, holding `(columns, lines)` of the terminal window size.

`columns`
Width of the terminal window in characters.

`lines`
Height of the terminal window in characters.

Inheritance of File Descriptors

New in version 3.4.

A file descriptor has an "inheritable" flag which indicates if the file descriptor can be inherited by child processes. Since Python 3.4, file descriptors created by Python are non-inheritable by default.

On UNIX, non-inheritable file descriptors are closed in child processes at the execution of a new program, other file descriptors are inherited.

On Windows, non-inheritable handles and file descriptors are closed in child processes, except for standard streams (file descriptors 0, 1 and 2: stdin, stdout and stderr), which are always inherited. Using *spawn** functions, all inheritable handles and all inheritable file descriptors are inherited. Using the *subprocess* module, all file descriptors except standard streams are closed, and inheritable handles are only inherited if the *close_fds* parameter is `False`.

`os.get_inheritable(fd)`
Get the "inheritable" flag of the specified file descriptor (a boolean).

`os.set_inheritable(fd, inheritable)`
Set the "inheritable" flag of the specified file descriptor.

`os.get_handle_inheritable(handle)`
Get the "inheritable" flag of the specified handle (a boolean).

Availability: Windows.

`os.set_handle_inheritable(handle, inheritable)`
Set the "inheritable" flag of the specified handle.

Availability: Windows.

16.1.5 Files and Directories

On some Unix platforms, many of these functions support one or more of these features:

- **specifying a file descriptor:** For some functions, the *path* argument can be not only a string giving a path name, but also a file descriptor. The function will then operate on the file referred to by the descriptor. (For POSIX systems, Python will call the `f...` version of the function.)

  You can check whether or not *path* can be specified as a file descriptor on your platform using `os.supports_fd`. If it is unavailable, using it will raise a `NotImplementedError`.

  If the function also supports *dir_fd* or *follow_symlinks* arguments, it is an error to specify one of those when supplying *path* as a file descriptor.

- **paths relative to directory descriptors:** If *dir_fd* is not `None`, it should be a file descriptor referring to a directory, and the path to operate on should be relative; path will then be relative to that directory. If the path is absolute, *dir_fd* is ignored. (For POSIX systems, Python will call the `...at` or `f...at` version of the function.)

  You can check whether or not *dir_fd* is supported on your platform using `os.supports_dir_fd`. If it is unavailable, using it will raise a `NotImplementedError`.

- **not following symlinks:** If *follow_symlinks* is `False`, and the last element of the path to operate on is a symbolic link, the function will operate on the symbolic link itself instead of the file the link points to. (For POSIX systems, Python will call the `l...` version of the function.)

  You can check whether or not *follow_symlinks* is supported on your platform using `os.supports_follow_symlinks`. If it is unavailable, using it will raise a `NotImplementedError`.

`os.access`(*path, mode, *, dir_fd=None, effective_ids=False, follow_symlinks=True*)

Use the real uid/gid to test for access to *path*. Note that most operations will use the effective uid/gid, therefore this routine can be used in a suid/sgid environment to test if the invoking user has the specified access to *path*. *mode* should be `F_OK` to test the existence of *path*, or it can be the inclusive OR of one or more of `R_OK`, `W_OK`, and `X_OK` to test permissions. Return `True` if access is allowed, `False` if not. See the Unix man page **access(2)** for more information.

This function can support specifying *paths relative to directory descriptors* and *not following symlinks*.

If *effective_ids* is `True`, `access()` will perform its access checks using the effective uid/gid instead of the real uid/gid. *effective_ids* may not be supported on your platform; you can check whether or not it is available using `os.supports_effective_ids`. If it is unavailable, using it will raise a `NotImplementedError`.

Note: Using `access()` to check if a user is authorized to e.g. open a file before actually doing so using `open()` creates a security hole, because the user might exploit the short time interval between checking and opening the file to manipulate it. It's preferable to use *EAFP* techniques. For example:

```
if os.access("myfile", os.R_OK):
    with open("myfile") as fp:
        return fp.read()
return "some default data"
```

is better written as:

```
try:
    fp = open("myfile")
except PermissionError:
    return "some default data"
else:
    with fp:
        return fp.read()
```

Note: I/O operations may fail even when *access()* indicates that they would succeed, particularly for operations on network filesystems which may have permissions semantics beyond the usual POSIX permission-bit model.

Changed in version 3.3: Added the *dir_fd*, *effective_ids*, and *follow_symlinks* parameters.

Changed in version 3.6: Accepts a *path-like object*.

`os.F_OK`
`os.R_OK`
`os.W_OK`
`os.X_OK`
Values to pass as the *mode* parameter of *access()* to test the existence, readability, writability and executability of *path*, respectively.

`os.chdir(path)`
Change the current working directory to *path*.

This function can support *specifying a file descriptor*. The descriptor must refer to an opened directory, not an open file.

New in version 3.3: Added support for specifying *path* as a file descriptor on some platforms.

Changed in version 3.6: Accepts a *path-like object*.

`os.chflags(path, flags, *, follow_symlinks=True)`
Set the flags of *path* to the numeric *flags*. *flags* may take a combination (bitwise OR) of the following values (as defined in the *stat* module):

- *stat.UF_NODUMP*
- *stat.UF_IMMUTABLE*
- *stat.UF_APPEND*
- *stat.UF_OPAQUE*
- *stat.UF_NOUNLINK*
- *stat.UF_COMPRESSED*
- *stat.UF_HIDDEN*
- *stat.SF_ARCHIVED*
- *stat.SF_IMMUTABLE*
- *stat.SF_APPEND*
- *stat.SF_NOUNLINK*
- *stat.SF_SNAPSHOT*

This function can support *not following symlinks*.

Availability: Unix.

New in version 3.3: The *follow_symlinks* argument.

Changed in version 3.6: Accepts a *path-like object*.

`os.chmod(path, mode, *, dir_fd=None, follow_symlinks=True)`
Change the mode of *path* to the numeric *mode*. *mode* may take one of the following values (as defined in the *stat* module) or bitwise ORed combinations of them:

- *stat.S_ISUID*
- *stat.S_ISGID*

- *stat.S_ENFMT*
- *stat.S_ISVTX*
- *stat.S_IREAD*
- *stat.S_IWRITE*
- *stat.S_IEXEC*
- *stat.S_IRWXU*
- *stat.S_IRUSR*
- *stat.S_IWUSR*
- *stat.S_IXUSR*
- *stat.S_IRWXG*
- *stat.S_IRGRP*
- *stat.S_IWGRP*
- *stat.S_IXGRP*
- *stat.S_IRWXO*
- *stat.S_IROTH*
- *stat.S_IWOTH*
- *stat.S_IXOTH*

This function can support *specifying a file descriptor*, *paths relative to directory descriptors* and *not following symlinks*.

Note: Although Windows supports *chmod()*, you can only set the file's read-only flag with it (via the `stat.S_IWRITE` and `stat.S_IREAD` constants or a corresponding integer value). All other bits are ignored.

New in version 3.3: Added support for specifying *path* as an open file descriptor, and the *dir_fd* and *follow_symlinks* arguments.

Changed in version 3.6: Accepts a *path-like object*.

os.**chown**(*path*, *uid*, *gid*, *, *dir_fd=None*, *follow_symlinks=True*)

Change the owner and group id of *path* to the numeric *uid* and *gid*. To leave one of the ids unchanged, set it to -1.

This function can support *specifying a file descriptor*, *paths relative to directory descriptors* and *not following symlinks*.

See *shutil.chown()* for a higher-level function that accepts names in addition to numeric ids.

Availability: Unix.

New in version 3.3: Added support for specifying an open file descriptor for *path*, and the *dir_fd* and *follow_symlinks* arguments.

Changed in version 3.6: Supports a *path-like object*.

os.**chroot**(*path*)

Change the root directory of the current process to *path*.

Availability: Unix.

Changed in version 3.6: Accepts a *path-like object*.

os.**fchdir**(*fd*)

Change the current working directory to the directory represented by the file descriptor *fd*. The descriptor must refer to an opened directory, not an open file. As of Python 3.3, this is equivalent to `os.chdir(fd)`.

Availability: Unix.

os.**getcwd**()

Return a string representing the current working directory.

os.**getcwdb**()

Return a bytestring representing the current working directory.

os.**lchflags**(*path*, *flags*)

Set the flags of *path* to the numeric *flags*, like *chflags()*, but do not follow symbolic links. As of Python 3.3, this is equivalent to `os.chflags(path, flags, follow_symlinks=False)`.

Availability: Unix.

Changed in version 3.6: Accepts a *path-like object*.

os.**lchmod**(*path*, *mode*)

Change the mode of *path* to the numeric *mode*. If path is a symlink, this affects the symlink rather than the target. See the docs for *chmod()* for possible values of *mode*. As of Python 3.3, this is equivalent to `os.chmod(path, mode, follow_symlinks=False)`.

Availability: Unix.

Changed in version 3.6: Accepts a *path-like object*.

os.**lchown**(*path*, *uid*, *gid*)

Change the owner and group id of *path* to the numeric *uid* and *gid*. This function will not follow symbolic links. As of Python 3.3, this is equivalent to `os.chown(path, uid, gid, follow_symlinks=False)`.

Availability: Unix.

Changed in version 3.6: Accepts a *path-like object*.

os.**link**(*src*, *dst*, *, *src_dir_fd=None*, *dst_dir_fd=None*, *follow_symlinks=True*)

Create a hard link pointing to *src* named *dst*.

This function can support specifying *src_dir_fd* and/or *dst_dir_fd* to supply *paths relative to directory descriptors*, and *not following symlinks*.

Availability: Unix, Windows.

Changed in version 3.2: Added Windows support.

New in version 3.3: Added the *src_dir_fd*, *dst_dir_fd*, and *follow_symlinks* arguments.

Changed in version 3.6: Accepts a *path-like object* for *src* and *dst*.

os.**listdir**(*path='.'*)

Return a list containing the names of the entries in the directory given by *path*. The list is in arbitrary order, and does not include the special entries `'.'` and `'..'` even if they are present in the directory.

path may be a *path-like object*. If *path* is of type `bytes` (directly or indirectly through the *PathLike* interface), the filenames returned will also be of type `bytes`; in all other circumstances, they will be of type `str`.

This function can also support *specifying a file descriptor*; the file descriptor must refer to a directory.

Note: To encode `str` filenames to `bytes`, use *fsencode()*.

See also:

The *scandir()* function returns directory entries along with file attribute information, giving better performance for many common use cases.

Changed in version 3.2: The *path* parameter became optional.

New in version 3.3: Added support for specifying an open file descriptor for *path*.

Changed in version 3.6: Accepts a *path-like object*.

`os.lstat(path, *, dir_fd=None)`

Perform the equivalent of an `lstat()` system call on the given path. Similar to *stat()*, but does not follow symbolic links. Return a *stat_result* object.

On platforms that do not support symbolic links, this is an alias for *stat()*.

As of Python 3.3, this is equivalent to `os.stat(path, dir_fd=dir_fd, follow_symlinks=False)`.

This function can also support *paths relative to directory descriptors*.

See also:

The *stat()* function.

Changed in version 3.2: Added support for Windows 6.0 (Vista) symbolic links.

Changed in version 3.3: Added the *dir_fd* parameter.

Changed in version 3.6: Accepts a *path-like object* for *src* and *dst*.

`os.mkdir(path, mode=0o777, *, dir_fd=None)`

Create a directory named *path* with numeric mode *mode*.

If the directory already exists, *FileExistsError* is raised. On some systems, *mode* is ignored. Where it is used, the current umask value is first masked out. If bits other than the last 9 (i.e. the last 3 digits of the octal representation of the *mode*) are set, their meaning is platform-dependent. On some platforms, they are ignored and you should call *chmod()* explicitly to set them.

This function can also support *paths relative to directory descriptors*.

It is also possible to create temporary directories; see the *tempfile* module's *tempfile.mkdtemp()* function.

New in version 3.3: The *dir_fd* argument.

Changed in version 3.6: Accepts a *path-like object*.

`os.makedirs(name, mode=0o777, exist_ok=False)`

Recursive directory creation function. Like *mkdir()*, but makes all intermediate-level directories needed to contain the leaf directory.

The *mode* parameter is passed to *mkdir()*; see *the mkdir() description* for how it is interpreted.

If *exist_ok* is `False` (the default), an *OSError* is raised if the target directory already exists.

Note: *makedirs()* will become confused if the path elements to create include *pardir* (eg. ".." on UNIX systems).

This function handles UNC paths correctly.

New in version 3.2: The *exist_ok* parameter.

Changed in version 3.4.1: Before Python 3.4.1, if *exist_ok* was `True` and the directory existed, *makedirs()* would still raise an error if *mode* did not match the mode of the existing directory. Since this behavior was impossible to implement safely, it was removed in Python 3.4.1. See bpo-21082.

Changed in version 3.6: Accepts a *path-like object*.

os.**mkfifo**(*path*, *mode=0o666*, ***, *dir_fd=None*)
Create a FIFO (a named pipe) named *path* with numeric mode *mode*. The current umask value is first masked out from the mode.

This function can also support *paths relative to directory descriptors*.

FIFOs are pipes that can be accessed like regular files. FIFOs exist until they are deleted (for example with `os.unlink()`). Generally, FIFOs are used as rendezvous between "client" and "server" type processes: the server opens the FIFO for reading, and the client opens it for writing. Note that `mkfifo()` doesn't open the FIFO — it just creates the rendezvous point.

Availability: Unix.

New in version 3.3: The *dir_fd* argument.

Changed in version 3.6: Accepts a *path-like object*.

os.**mknod**(*path*, *mode=0o600*, *device=0*, ***, *dir_fd=None*)
Create a filesystem node (file, device special file or named pipe) named *path*. *mode* specifies both the permissions to use and the type of node to be created, being combined (bitwise OR) with one of `stat.S_IFREG`, `stat.S_IFCHR`, `stat.S_IFBLK`, and `stat.S_IFIFO` (those constants are available in `stat`). For `stat.S_IFCHR` and `stat.S_IFBLK`, *device* defines the newly created device special file (probably using `os.makedev()`), otherwise it is ignored.

This function can also support *paths relative to directory descriptors*.

Availability: Unix.

New in version 3.3: The *dir_fd* argument.

Changed in version 3.6: Accepts a *path-like object*.

os.**major**(*device*)
Extract the device major number from a raw device number (usually the `st_dev` or `st_rdev` field from `stat`).

os.**minor**(*device*)
Extract the device minor number from a raw device number (usually the `st_dev` or `st_rdev` field from `stat`).

os.**makedev**(*major*, *minor*)
Compose a raw device number from the major and minor device numbers.

os.**pathconf**(*path*, *name*)
Return system configuration information relevant to a named file. *name* specifies the configuration value to retrieve; it may be a string which is the name of a defined system value; these names are specified in a number of standards (POSIX.1, Unix 95, Unix 98, and others). Some platforms define additional names as well. The names known to the host operating system are given in the `pathconf_names` dictionary. For configuration variables not included in that mapping, passing an integer for *name* is also accepted.

If *name* is a string and is not known, `ValueError` is raised. If a specific value for *name* is not supported by the host system, even if it is included in `pathconf_names`, an `OSError` is raised with `errno.EINVAL` for the error number.

This function can support *specifying a file descriptor*.

Availability: Unix.

Changed in version 3.6: Accepts a *path-like object*.

os.**pathconf_names**
Dictionary mapping names accepted by `pathconf()` and `fpathconf()` to the integer values defined for those names by the host operating system. This can be used to determine the set of names known to the system.

Availability: Unix.

os.**readlink**(*path*, *, *dir_fd=None*)

Return a string representing the path to which the symbolic link points. The result may be either an absolute or relative pathname; if it is relative, it may be converted to an absolute pathname using `os.path.join(os.path.dirname(path), result)`.

If the *path* is a string object (directly or indirectly through a *PathLike* interface), the result will also be a string object, and the call may raise a UnicodeDecodeError. If the *path* is a bytes object (direct or indirectly), the result will be a bytes object.

This function can also support *paths relative to directory descriptors*.

Availability: Unix, Windows

Changed in version 3.2: Added support for Windows 6.0 (Vista) symbolic links.

New in version 3.3: The *dir_fd* argument.

Changed in version 3.6: Accepts a *path-like object*.

os.**remove**(*path*, *, *dir_fd=None*)

Remove (delete) the file *path*. If *path* is a directory, *OSError* is raised. Use *rmdir()* to remove directories.

This function can support *paths relative to directory descriptors*.

On Windows, attempting to remove a file that is in use causes an exception to be raised; on Unix, the directory entry is removed but the storage allocated to the file is not made available until the original file is no longer in use.

This function is semantically identical to *unlink()*.

New in version 3.3: The *dir_fd* argument.

Changed in version 3.6: Accepts a *path-like object*.

os.**removedirs**(*name*)

Remove directories recursively. Works like *rmdir()* except that, if the leaf directory is successfully removed, *removedirs()* tries to successively remove every parent directory mentioned in *path* until an error is raised (which is ignored, because it generally means that a parent directory is not empty). For example, `os.removedirs('foo/bar/baz')` will first remove the directory `'foo/bar/baz'`, and then remove `'foo/bar'` and `'foo'` if they are empty. Raises *OSError* if the leaf directory could not be successfully removed.

Changed in version 3.6: Accepts a *path-like object*.

os.**rename**(*src*, *dst*, *, *src_dir_fd=None*, *dst_dir_fd=None*)

Rename the file or directory *src* to *dst*. If *dst* is a directory, *OSError* will be raised. On Unix, if *dst* exists and is a file, it will be replaced silently if the user has permission. The operation may fail on some Unix flavors if *src* and *dst* are on different filesystems. If successful, the renaming will be an atomic operation (this is a POSIX requirement). On Windows, if *dst* already exists, *OSError* will be raised even if it is a file.

This function can support specifying *src_dir_fd* and/or *dst_dir_fd* to supply *paths relative to directory descriptors*.

If you want cross-platform overwriting of the destination, use *replace()*.

New in version 3.3: The *src_dir_fd* and *dst_dir_fd* arguments.

Changed in version 3.6: Accepts a *path-like object* for *src* and *dst*.

os.**renames**(*old*, *new*)

Recursive directory or file renaming function. Works like *rename()*, except creation of any intermediate directories needed to make the new pathname good is attempted first. After the rename, directories corresponding to rightmost path segments of the old name will be pruned away using *removedirs()*.

Note: This function can fail with the new directory structure made if you lack permissions needed to remove the leaf directory or file.

Changed in version 3.6: Accepts a *path-like object* for *old* and *new*.

`os.replace(src, dst, *, src_dir_fd=None, dst_dir_fd=None)`

Rename the file or directory *src* to *dst*. If *dst* is a directory, *OSError* will be raised. If *dst* exists and is a file, it will be replaced silently if the user has permission. The operation may fail if *src* and *dst* are on different filesystems. If successful, the renaming will be an atomic operation (this is a POSIX requirement).

This function can support specifying *src_dir_fd* and/or *dst_dir_fd* to supply *paths relative to directory descriptors*.

New in version 3.3.

Changed in version 3.6: Accepts a *path-like object* for *src* and *dst*.

`os.rmdir(path, *, dir_fd=None)`

Remove (delete) the directory *path*. Only works when the directory is empty, otherwise, *OSError* is raised. In order to remove whole directory trees, *shutil.rmtree()* can be used.

This function can support *paths relative to directory descriptors*.

New in version 3.3: The *dir_fd* parameter.

Changed in version 3.6: Accepts a *path-like object*.

`os.scandir(path='.')`

Return an iterator of *os.DirEntry* objects corresponding to the entries in the directory given by *path*. The entries are yielded in arbitrary order, and the special entries `'.'` and `'..'` are not included.

Using *scandir()* instead of *listdir()* can significantly increase the performance of code that also needs file type or file attribute information, because *os.DirEntry* objects expose this information if the operating system provides it when scanning a directory. All *os.DirEntry* methods may perform a system call, but *is_dir()* and *is_file()* usually only require a system call for symbolic links; *os.DirEntry.stat()* always requires a system call on Unix but only requires one for symbolic links on Windows.

path may be a *path-like object*. If *path* is of type `bytes` (directly or indirectly through the *PathLike* interface), the type of the *name* and *path* attributes of each *os.DirEntry* will be `bytes`; in all other circumstances, they will be of type `str`.

The *scandir()* iterator supports the *context manager* protocol and has the following method:

`scandir.close()`

Close the iterator and free acquired resources.

This is called automatically when the iterator is exhausted or garbage collected, or when an error happens during iterating. However it is advisable to call it explicitly or use the `with` statement.

New in version 3.6.

The following example shows a simple use of *scandir()* to display all the files (excluding directories) in the given *path* that don't start with `'.'`. The `entry.is_file()` call will generally not make an additional system call:

```
with os.scandir(path) as it:
    for entry in it:
```

```
        if not entry.name.startswith('.') and entry.is_file():
            print(entry.name)
```

Note: On Unix-based systems, *scandir()* uses the system's opendir() and readdir() functions. On Windows, it uses the Win32 FindFirstFileW and FindNextFileW functions.

New in version 3.5.

New in version 3.6: Added support for the *context manager* protocol and the *close()* method. If a *scandir()* iterator is neither exhausted nor explicitly closed a *ResourceWarning* will be emitted in its destructor.

The function accepts a *path-like object*.

class os.DirEntry

Object yielded by *scandir()* to expose the file path and other file attributes of a directory entry.

scandir() will provide as much of this information as possible without making additional system calls. When a `stat()` or `lstat()` system call is made, the `os.DirEntry` object will cache the result.

`os.DirEntry` instances are not intended to be stored in long-lived data structures; if you know the file metadata has changed or if a long time has elapsed since calling *scandir()*, call `os.stat(entry.path)` to fetch up-to-date information.

Because the `os.DirEntry` methods can make operating system calls, they may also raise *OSError*. If you need very fine-grained control over errors, you can catch *OSError* when calling one of the `os.DirEntry` methods and handle as appropriate.

To be directly usable as a *path-like object*, `os.DirEntry` implements the *PathLike* interface.

Attributes and methods on a `os.DirEntry` instance are as follows:

name

The entry's base filename, relative to the *scandir()* *path* argument.

The *name* attribute will be `bytes` if the *scandir()* *path* argument is of type `bytes` and `str` otherwise. Use *fsdecode()* to decode byte filenames.

path

The entry's full path name: equivalent to `os.path.join(scandir_path, entry.name)` where *scandir_path* is the *scandir()* *path* argument. The path is only absolute if the *scandir()* *path* argument was absolute.

The *path* attribute will be `bytes` if the *scandir()* *path* argument is of type `bytes` and `str` otherwise. Use *fsdecode()* to decode byte filenames.

inode()

Return the inode number of the entry.

The result is cached on the `os.DirEntry` object. Use `os.stat(entry.path, follow_symlinks=False).st_ino` to fetch up-to-date information.

On the first, uncached call, a system call is required on Windows but not on Unix.

is_dir(**, follow_symlinks=True*)

Return `True` if this entry is a directory or a symbolic link pointing to a directory; return `False` if the entry is or points to any other kind of file, or if it doesn't exist anymore.

If *follow_symlinks* is `False`, return `True` only if this entry is a directory (without following symlinks); return `False` if the entry is any other kind of file or if it doesn't exist anymore.

The result is cached on the `os.DirEntry` object, with a separate cache for *follow_symlinks* `True` and `False`. Call *os.stat()* along with *stat.S_ISDIR()* to fetch up-to-date information.

On the first, uncached call, no system call is required in most cases. Specifically, for non-symlinks, neither Windows or Unix require a system call, except on certain Unix file systems, such as network file systems, that return `dirent.d_type == DT_UNKNOWN`. If the entry is a symlink, a system call will be required to follow the symlink unless *follow_symlinks* is `False`.

This method can raise *OSError*, such as *PermissionError*, but *FileNotFoundError* is caught and not raised.

is_file(*, *follow_symlinks=True*)

Return `True` if this entry is a file or a symbolic link pointing to a file; return `False` if the entry is or points to a directory or other non-file entry, or if it doesn't exist anymore.

If *follow_symlinks* is `False`, return `True` only if this entry is a file (without following symlinks); return `False` if the entry is a directory or other non-file entry, or if it doesn't exist anymore.

The result is cached on the `os.DirEntry` object. Caching, system calls made, and exceptions raised are as per *is_dir()*.

is_symlink()

Return `True` if this entry is a symbolic link (even if broken); return `False` if the entry points to a directory or any kind of file, or if it doesn't exist anymore.

The result is cached on the `os.DirEntry` object. Call *os.path.islink()* to fetch up-to-date information.

On the first, uncached call, no system call is required in most cases. Specifically, neither Windows or Unix require a system call, except on certain Unix file systems, such as network file systems, that return `dirent.d_type == DT_UNKNOWN`.

This method can raise *OSError*, such as *PermissionError*, but *FileNotFoundError* is caught and not raised.

stat(*, *follow_symlinks=True*)

Return a *stat_result* object for this entry. This method follows symbolic links by default; to stat a symbolic link add the `follow_symlinks=False` argument.

On Unix, this method always requires a system call. On Windows, it only requires a system call if *follow_symlinks* is `True` and the entry is a symbolic link.

On Windows, the `st_ino`, `st_dev` and `st_nlink` attributes of the *stat_result* are always set to zero. Call *os.stat()* to get these attributes.

The result is cached on the `os.DirEntry` object, with a separate cache for *follow_symlinks* `True` and `False`. Call *os.stat()* to fetch up-to-date information.

Note that there is a nice correspondence between several attributes and methods of `os.DirEntry` and of *pathlib.Path*. In particular, the `name` attribute has the same meaning, as do the `is_dir()`, `is_file()`, `is_symlink()` and `stat()` methods.

New in version 3.5.

Changed in version 3.6: Added support for the *PathLike* interface. Added support for *bytes* paths on Windows.

os.**stat**(*path*, *, *dir_fd=None*, *follow_symlinks=True*)

Get the status of a file or a file descriptor. Perform the equivalent of a `stat()` system call on the given path. *path* may be specified as either a string or bytes – directly or indirectly through the *PathLike* interface – or as an open file descriptor. Return a *stat_result* object.

This function normally follows symlinks; to stat a symlink add the argument `follow_symlinks=False`, or use *lstat()*.

This function can support *specifying a file descriptor* and *not following symlinks*.

Example:

```
>>> import os
>>> statinfo = os.stat('somefile.txt')
>>> statinfo
os.stat_result(st_mode=33188, st_ino=7876932, st_dev=234881026,
st_nlink=1, st_uid=501, st_gid=501, st_size=264, st_atime=1297230295,
st_mtime=1297230027, st_ctime=1297230027)
>>> statinfo.st_size
264
```

See also:

fstat() and *lstat()* functions.

New in version 3.3: Added the *dir_fd* and *follow_symlinks* arguments, specifying a file descriptor instead of a path.

Changed in version 3.6: Accepts a *path-like object*.

class os.stat_result

Object whose attributes correspond roughly to the members of the **stat** structure. It is used for the result of *os.stat()*, *os.fstat()* and *os.lstat()*.

Attributes:

st_mode
File mode: file type and file mode bits (permissions).

st_ino
Inode number.

st_dev
Identifier of the device on which this file resides.

st_nlink
Number of hard links.

st_uid
User identifier of the file owner.

st_gid
Group identifier of the file owner.

st_size
Size of the file in bytes, if it is a regular file or a symbolic link. The size of a symbolic link is the length of the pathname it contains, without a terminating null byte.

Timestamps:

st_atime
Time of most recent access expressed in seconds.

st_mtime
Time of most recent content modification expressed in seconds.

st_ctime
Platform dependent:

- the time of most recent metadata change on Unix,
- the time of creation on Windows, expressed in seconds.

st_atime_ns
Time of most recent access expressed in nanoseconds as an integer.

st_mtime_ns
Time of most recent content modification expressed in nanoseconds as an integer.

st_ctime_ns
Platform dependent:

- the time of most recent metadata change on Unix,
- the time of creation on Windows, expressed in nanoseconds as an integer.

See also the *stat_float_times()* function.

Note: The exact meaning and resolution of the *st_atime*, *st_mtime*, and *st_ctime* attributes depend on the operating system and the file system. For example, on Windows systems using the FAT or FAT32 file systems, *st_mtime* has 2-second resolution, and *st_atime* has only 1-day resolution. See your operating system documentation for details.

Similarly, although *st_atime_ns*, *st_mtime_ns*, and *st_ctime_ns* are always expressed in nanoseconds, many systems do not provide nanosecond precision. On systems that do provide nanosecond precision, the floating-point object used to store *st_atime*, *st_mtime*, and *st_ctime* cannot preserve all of it, and as such will be slightly inexact. If you need the exact timestamps you should always use *st_atime_ns*, *st_mtime_ns*, and *st_ctime_ns*.

On some Unix systems (such as Linux), the following attributes may also be available:

st_blocks
Number of 512-byte blocks allocated for file. This may be smaller than *st_size*/512 when the file has holes.

st_blksize
"Preferred" blocksize for efficient file system I/O. Writing to a file in smaller chunks may cause an inefficient read-modify-rewrite.

st_rdev
Type of device if an inode device.

st_flags
User defined flags for file.

On other Unix systems (such as FreeBSD), the following attributes may be available (but may be only filled out if root tries to use them):

st_gen
File generation number.

st_birthtime
Time of file creation.

On Mac OS systems, the following attributes may also be available:

st_rsize
Real size of the file.

st_creator
Creator of the file.

st_type
File type.

On Windows systems, the following attribute is also available:

st_file_attributes
Windows file attributes: `dwFileAttributes` member of the `BY_HANDLE_FILE_INFORMATION` structure returned by `GetFileInformationByHandle()`. See the `FILE_ATTRIBUTE_*` constants in the *stat* module.

The standard module *stat* defines functions and constants that are useful for extracting information from a stat structure. (On Windows, some items are filled with dummy values.)

For backward compatibility, a *stat_result* instance is also accessible as a tuple of at least 10 integers giving the most important (and portable) members of the stat structure, in the order *st_mode*, *st_ino*, *st_dev*, *st_nlink*, *st_uid*, *st_gid*, *st_size*, *st_atime*, *st_mtime*, *st_ctime*. More items may be added at the end by some implementations. For compatibility with older Python versions, accessing *stat_result* as a tuple always returns integers.

New in version 3.3: Added the *st_atime_ns*, *st_mtime_ns*, and *st_ctime_ns* members.

New in version 3.5: Added the *st_file_attributes* member on Windows.

os.stat_float_times([*newvalue*])

Determine whether *stat_result* represents time stamps as float objects. If *newvalue* is True, future calls to *stat()* return floats, if it is False, future calls return ints. If *newvalue* is omitted, return the current setting.

For compatibility with older Python versions, accessing *stat_result* as a tuple always returns integers.

Python now returns float values by default. Applications which do not work correctly with floating point time stamps can use this function to restore the old behaviour.

The resolution of the timestamps (that is the smallest possible fraction) depends on the system. Some systems only support second resolution; on these systems, the fraction will always be zero.

It is recommended that this setting is only changed at program startup time in the *__main__* module; libraries should never change this setting. If an application uses a library that works incorrectly if floating point time stamps are processed, this application should turn the feature off until the library has been corrected.

Deprecated since version 3.3.

os.statvfs(*path*)

Perform a statvfs() system call on the given path. The return value is an object whose attributes describe the filesystem on the given path, and correspond to the members of the statvfs structure, namely: f_bsize, f_frsize, f_blocks, f_bfree, f_bavail, f_files, f_ffree, f_favail, f_flag, f_namemax.

Two module-level constants are defined for the f_flag attribute's bit-flags: if ST_RDONLY is set, the filesystem is mounted read-only, and if ST_NOSUID is set, the semantics of setuid/setgid bits are disabled or not supported.

Additional module-level constants are defined for GNU/glibc based systems. These are ST_NODEV (disallow access to device special files), ST_NOEXEC (disallow program execution), ST_SYNCHRONOUS (writes are synced at once), ST_MANDLOCK (allow mandatory locks on an FS), ST_WRITE (write on file/directory/symlink), ST_APPEND (append-only file), ST_IMMUTABLE (immutable file), ST_NOATIME (do not update access times), ST_NODIRATIME (do not update directory access times), ST_RELATIME (update atime relative to mtime/ctime).

This function can support *specifying a file descriptor*.

Availability: Unix.

Changed in version 3.2: The ST_RDONLY and ST_NOSUID constants were added.

New in version 3.3: Added support for specifying an open file descriptor for *path*.

Changed in version 3.4: The ST_NODEV, ST_NOEXEC, ST_SYNCHRONOUS, ST_MANDLOCK, ST_WRITE, ST_APPEND, ST_IMMUTABLE, ST_NOATIME, ST_NODIRATIME, and ST_RELATIME constants were added.

Changed in version 3.6: Accepts a *path-like object*.

os.supports_dir_fd

A *Set* object indicating which functions in the *os* module permit use of their *dir_fd* parameter.

Different platforms provide different functionality, and an option that might work on one might be unsupported on another. For consistency's sakes, functions that support *dir_fd* always allow specifying the parameter, but will raise an exception if the functionality is not actually available.

To check whether a particular function permits use of its *dir_fd* parameter, use the `in` operator on `supports_dir_fd`. As an example, this expression determines whether the *dir_fd* parameter of `os.stat()` is locally available:

```
os.stat in os.supports_dir_fd
```

Currently *dir_fd* parameters only work on Unix platforms; none of them work on Windows.

New in version 3.3.

os.supports_effective_ids

A `Set` object indicating which functions in the `os` module permit use of the *effective_ids* parameter for `os.access()`. If the local platform supports it, the collection will contain `os.access()`, otherwise it will be empty.

To check whether you can use the *effective_ids* parameter for `os.access()`, use the `in` operator on `supports_effective_ids`, like so:

```
os.access in os.supports_effective_ids
```

Currently *effective_ids* only works on Unix platforms; it does not work on Windows.

New in version 3.3.

os.supports_fd

A `Set` object indicating which functions in the `os` module permit specifying their *path* parameter as an open file descriptor. Different platforms provide different functionality, and an option that might work on one might be unsupported on another. For consistency's sakes, functions that support *fd* always allow specifying the parameter, but will raise an exception if the functionality is not actually available.

To check whether a particular function permits specifying an open file descriptor for its *path* parameter, use the `in` operator on `supports_fd`. As an example, this expression determines whether `os.chdir()` accepts open file descriptors when called on your local platform:

```
os.chdir in os.supports_fd
```

New in version 3.3.

os.supports_follow_symlinks

A `Set` object indicating which functions in the `os` module permit use of their *follow_symlinks* parameter. Different platforms provide different functionality, and an option that might work on one might be unsupported on another. For consistency's sakes, functions that support *follow_symlinks* always allow specifying the parameter, but will raise an exception if the functionality is not actually available.

To check whether a particular function permits use of its *follow_symlinks* parameter, use the `in` operator on `supports_follow_symlinks`. As an example, this expression determines whether the *follow_symlinks* parameter of `os.stat()` is locally available:

```
os.stat in os.supports_follow_symlinks
```

New in version 3.3.

os.symlink(*src, dst, target_is_directory=False, *, dir_fd=None*)

Create a symbolic link pointing to *src* named *dst*.

On Windows, a symlink represents either a file or a directory, and does not morph to the target dynamically. If the target is present, the type of the symlink will be created to match. Otherwise, the symlink will be created as a directory if *target_is_directory* is `True` or a file symlink (the default) otherwise. On non-Window platforms, *target_is_directory* is ignored.

Symbolic link support was introduced in Windows 6.0 (Vista). `symlink()` will raise a `NotImplementedError` on Windows versions earlier than 6.0.

This function can support *paths relative to directory descriptors*.

Note: On Windows, the *SeCreateSymbolicLinkPrivilege* is required in order to successfully create symlinks. This privilege is not typically granted to regular users but is available to accounts which can escalate privileges to the administrator level. Either obtaining the privilege or running your application as an administrator are ways to successfully create symlinks.

`OSError` is raised when the function is called by an unprivileged user.

Availability: Unix, Windows.

Changed in version 3.2: Added support for Windows 6.0 (Vista) symbolic links.

New in version 3.3: Added the *dir_fd* argument, and now allow *target_is_directory* on non-Windows platforms.

Changed in version 3.6: Accepts a *path-like object* for *src* and *dst*.

`os.sync()`
Force write of everything to disk.

Availability: Unix.

New in version 3.3.

`os.truncate(`*path*, *length*`)`
Truncate the file corresponding to *path*, so that it is at most *length* bytes in size.

This function can support *specifying a file descriptor*.

Availability: Unix, Windows.

New in version 3.3.

Changed in version 3.5: Added support for Windows

Changed in version 3.6: Accepts a *path-like object*.

`os.unlink(`*path*, *, *dir_fd=None*`)`
Remove (delete) the file *path*. This function is semantically identical to `remove()`; the `unlink` name is its traditional Unix name. Please see the documentation for `remove()` for further information.

New in version 3.3: The *dir_fd* parameter.

Changed in version 3.6: Accepts a *path-like object*.

`os.utime(`*path*, *times=None*, *[, *ns*], *dir_fd=None*, *follow_symlinks=True*`)`
Set the access and modified times of the file specified by *path*.

`utime()` takes two optional parameters, *times* and *ns*. These specify the times set on *path* and are used as follows:

- If *ns* is specified, it must be a 2-tuple of the form `(atime_ns, mtime_ns)` where each member is an int expressing nanoseconds.
- If *times* is not `None`, it must be a 2-tuple of the form `(atime, mtime)` where each member is an int or float expressing seconds.
- If *times* is `None` and *ns* is unspecified, this is equivalent to specifying `ns=(atime_ns, mtime_ns)` where both times are the current time.

It is an error to specify tuples for both *times* and *ns*.

Whether a directory can be given for *path* depends on whether the operating system implements directories as files (for example, Windows does not). Note that the exact times you set here may not be returned by a subsequent `stat()` call, depending on the resolution with which your operating system records access and modification times; see `stat()`. The best way to preserve exact times is to use the *st_atime_ns* and *st_mtime_ns* fields from the `os.stat()` result object with the *ns* parameter to *utime*.

This function can support *specifying a file descriptor*, *paths relative to directory descriptors* and *not following symlinks*.

New in version 3.3: Added support for specifying an open file descriptor for *path*, and the *dir_fd*, *follow_symlinks*, and *ns* parameters.

Changed in version 3.6: Accepts a *path-like object*.

os.**walk**(*top*, *topdown=True*, *onerror=None*, *followlinks=False*)

Generate the file names in a directory tree by walking the tree either top-down or bottom-up. For each directory in the tree rooted at directory *top* (including *top* itself), it yields a 3-tuple `(dirpath, dirnames, filenames)`.

dirpath is a string, the path to the directory. *dirnames* is a list of the names of the subdirectories in *dirpath* (excluding `'.'` and `'..'`). *filenames* is a list of the names of the non-directory files in *dirpath*. Note that the names in the lists contain no path components. To get a full path (which begins with *top*) to a file or directory in *dirpath*, do `os.path.join(dirpath, name)`.

If optional argument *topdown* is `True` or not specified, the triple for a directory is generated before the triples for any of its subdirectories (directories are generated top-down). If *topdown* is `False`, the triple for a directory is generated after the triples for all of its subdirectories (directories are generated bottom-up). No matter the value of *topdown*, the list of subdirectories is retrieved before the tuples for the directory and its subdirectories are generated.

When *topdown* is `True`, the caller can modify the *dirnames* list in-place (perhaps using `del` or slice assignment), and `walk()` will only recurse into the subdirectories whose names remain in *dirnames*; this can be used to prune the search, impose a specific order of visiting, or even to inform `walk()` about directories the caller creates or renames before it resumes `walk()` again. Modifying *dirnames* when *topdown* is `False` has no effect on the behavior of the walk, because in bottom-up mode the directories in *dirnames* are generated before *dirpath* itself is generated.

By default, errors from the `listdir()` call are ignored. If optional argument *onerror* is specified, it should be a function; it will be called with one argument, an `OSError` instance. It can report the error to continue with the walk, or raise the exception to abort the walk. Note that the filename is available as the `filename` attribute of the exception object.

By default, `walk()` will not walk down into symbolic links that resolve to directories. Set *followlinks* to `True` to visit directories pointed to by symlinks, on systems that support them.

Note: Be aware that setting *followlinks* to `True` can lead to infinite recursion if a link points to a parent directory of itself. `walk()` does not keep track of the directories it visited already.

Note: If you pass a relative pathname, don't change the current working directory between resumptions of `walk()`. `walk()` never changes the current directory, and assumes that its caller doesn't either.

This example displays the number of bytes taken by non-directory files in each directory under the starting directory, except that it doesn't look under any CVS subdirectory:

```
import os
from os.path import join, getsize
for root, dirs, files in os.walk('python/Lib/email'):
    print(root, "consumes", end=" ")
    print(sum(getsize(join(root, name)) for name in files), end=" ")
    print("bytes in", len(files), "non-directory files")
    if 'CVS' in dirs:
        dirs.remove('CVS')  # don't visit CVS directories
```

In the next example (simple implementation of *shutil.rmtree()*), walking the tree bottom-up is essential, *rmdir()* doesn't allow deleting a directory before the directory is empty:

```
# Delete everything reachable from the directory named in "top",
# assuming there are no symbolic links.
# CAUTION:  This is dangerous!  For example, if top == '/', it
# could delete all your disk files.
import os
for root, dirs, files in os.walk(top, topdown=False):
    for name in files:
        os.remove(os.path.join(root, name))
    for name in dirs:
        os.rmdir(os.path.join(root, name))
```

Changed in version 3.5: This function now calls *os.scandir()* instead of *os.listdir()*, making it faster by reducing the number of calls to *os.stat()*.

Changed in version 3.6: Accepts a *path-like object*.

os.fwalk(*top='.', topdown=True, onerror=None, *, follow_symlinks=False, dir_fd=None*)

This behaves exactly like *walk()*, except that it yields a 4-tuple `(dirpath, dirnames, filenames, dirfd)`, and it supports `dir_fd`.

dirpath, *dirnames* and *filenames* are identical to *walk()* output, and *dirfd* is a file descriptor referring to the directory *dirpath*.

This function always supports *paths relative to directory descriptors* and *not following symlinks*. Note however that, unlike other functions, the *fwalk()* default value for *follow_symlinks* is `False`.

Note: Since *fwalk()* yields file descriptors, those are only valid until the next iteration step, so you should duplicate them (e.g. with *dup()*) if you want to keep them longer.

This example displays the number of bytes taken by non-directory files in each directory under the starting directory, except that it doesn't look under any CVS subdirectory:

```
import os
for root, dirs, files, rootfd in os.fwalk('python/Lib/email'):
    print(root, "consumes", end="")
    print(sum([os.stat(name, dir_fd=rootfd).st_size for name in files]),
          end="")
    print("bytes in", len(files), "non-directory files")
    if 'CVS' in dirs:
        dirs.remove('CVS')  # don't visit CVS directories
```

In the next example, walking the tree bottom-up is essential: *rmdir()* doesn't allow deleting a directory before the directory is empty:

```
# Delete everything reachable from the directory named in "top",
# assuming there are no symbolic links.
```

```
# CAUTION:  This is dangerous!  For example, if top == '/', it
# could delete all your disk files.
import os
for root, dirs, files, rootfd in os.fwalk(top, topdown=False):
    for name in files:
        os.unlink(name, dir_fd=rootfd)
    for name in dirs:
        os.rmdir(name, dir_fd=rootfd)
```

Availability: Unix.

New in version 3.3.

Changed in version 3.6: Accepts a *path-like object*.

Linux extended attributes

New in version 3.3.

These functions are all available on Linux only.

`os.getxattr`(*path*, *attribute*, *, *follow_symlinks=True*)
Return the value of the extended filesystem attribute *attribute* for *path*. *attribute* can be bytes or str (directly or indirectly through the `PathLike` interface). If it is str, it is encoded with the filesystem encoding.

This function can support *specifying a file descriptor* and *not following symlinks*.

Changed in version 3.6: Accepts a *path-like object* for *path* and *attribute*.

`os.listxattr`(*path=None*, *, *follow_symlinks=True*)
Return a list of the extended filesystem attributes on *path*. The attributes in the list are represented as strings decoded with the filesystem encoding. If *path* is `None`, `listxattr()` will examine the current directory.

This function can support *specifying a file descriptor* and *not following symlinks*.

Changed in version 3.6: Accepts a *path-like object*.

`os.removexattr`(*path*, *attribute*, *, *follow_symlinks=True*)
Removes the extended filesystem attribute *attribute* from *path*. *attribute* should be bytes or str (directly or indirectly through the `PathLike` interface). If it is a string, it is encoded with the filesystem encoding.

This function can support *specifying a file descriptor* and *not following symlinks*.

Changed in version 3.6: Accepts a *path-like object* for *path* and *attribute*.

`os.setxattr`(*path*, *attribute*, *value*, *flags=0*, *, *follow_symlinks=True*)
Set the extended filesystem attribute *attribute* on *path* to *value*. *attribute* must be a bytes or str with no embedded NULs (directly or indirectly through the `PathLike` interface). If it is a str, it is encoded with the filesystem encoding. *flags* may be `XATTR_REPLACE` or `XATTR_CREATE`. If `XATTR_REPLACE` is given and the attribute does not exist, `EEXISTS` will be raised. If `XATTR_CREATE` is given and the attribute already exists, the attribute will not be created and `ENODATA` will be raised.

This function can support *specifying a file descriptor* and *not following symlinks*.

Note: A bug in Linux kernel versions less than 2.6.39 caused the flags argument to be ignored on some filesystems.

Changed in version 3.6: Accepts a *path-like object* for *path* and *attribute*.

os.**XATTR_SIZE_MAX**
The maximum size the value of an extended attribute can be. Currently, this is 64 KiB on Linux.

os.**XATTR_CREATE**
This is a possible value for the flags argument in *setxattr()*. It indicates the operation must create an attribute.

os.**XATTR_REPLACE**
This is a possible value for the flags argument in *setxattr()*. It indicates the operation must replace an existing attribute.

16.1.6 Process Management

These functions may be used to create and manage processes.

The various *exec** functions take a list of arguments for the new program loaded into the process. In each case, the first of these arguments is passed to the new program as its own name rather than as an argument a user may have typed on a command line. For the C programmer, this is the `argv[0]` passed to a program's `main()`. For example, `os.execv('/bin/echo', ['foo', 'bar'])` will only print `bar` on standard output; `foo` will seem to be ignored.

os.**abort**()
Generate a `SIGABRT` signal to the current process. On Unix, the default behavior is to produce a core dump; on Windows, the process immediately returns an exit code of 3. Be aware that calling this function will not call the Python signal handler registered for `SIGABRT` with *signal.signal()*.

os.**execl**(*path, arg0, arg1, ...*)
os.**execle**(*path, arg0, arg1, ..., env*)
os.**execlp**(*file, arg0, arg1, ...*)
os.**execlpe**(*file, arg0, arg1, ..., env*)
os.**execv**(*path, args*)
os.**execve**(*path, args, env*)
os.**execvp**(*file, args*)
os.**execvpe**(*file, args, env*)
These functions all execute a new program, replacing the current process; they do not return. On Unix, the new executable is loaded into the current process, and will have the same process id as the caller. Errors will be reported as *OSError* exceptions.

The current process is replaced immediately. Open file objects and descriptors are not flushed, so if there may be data buffered on these open files, you should flush them using `sys.stdout.flush()` or *os.fsync()* before calling an *exec** function.

The "l" and "v" variants of the *exec** functions differ in how command-line arguments are passed. The "l" variants are perhaps the easiest to work with if the number of parameters is fixed when the code is written; the individual parameters simply become additional parameters to the `execl*()` functions. The "v" variants are good when the number of parameters is variable, with the arguments being passed in a list or tuple as the *args* parameter. In either case, the arguments to the child process should start with the name of the command being run, but this is not enforced.

The variants which include a "p" near the end (*execlp()*, *execlpe()*, *execvp()*, and *execvpe()*) will use the `PATH` environment variable to locate the program *file*. When the environment is being replaced (using one of the *exec*e* variants, discussed in the next paragraph), the new environment is used as the source of the `PATH` variable. The other variants, *execl()*, *execle()*, *execv()*, and *execve()*, will not use the `PATH` variable to locate the executable; *path* must contain an appropriate absolute or relative path.

For *execle()*, *execlpe()*, *execve()*, and *execvpe()* (note that these all end in "e"), the *env* parameter must be a mapping which is used to define the environment variables for the new process (these are used instead of the current process' environment); the functions *execl()*, *execlp()*, *execv()*, and *execvp()* all cause the new process to inherit the environment of the current process.

For *execve()* on some platforms, *path* may also be specified as an open file descriptor. This functionality may not be supported on your platform; you can check whether or not it is available using *os.supports_fd*. If it is unavailable, using it will raise a *NotImplementedError*.

Availability: Unix, Windows.

New in version 3.3: Added support for specifying an open file descriptor for *path* for *execve()*.

Changed in version 3.6: Accepts a *path-like object*.

os.**_exit**(*n*)
Exit the process with status *n*, without calling cleanup handlers, flushing stdio buffers, etc.

Note: The standard way to exit is `sys.exit(n)`. *_exit()* should normally only be used in the child process after a *fork()*.

The following exit codes are defined and can be used with *_exit()*, although they are not required. These are typically used for system programs written in Python, such as a mail server's external command delivery program.

Note: Some of these may not be available on all Unix platforms, since there is some variation. These constants are defined where they are defined by the underlying platform.

os.**EX_OK**
Exit code that means no error occurred.

Availability: Unix.

os.**EX_USAGE**
Exit code that means the command was used incorrectly, such as when the wrong number of arguments are given.

Availability: Unix.

os.**EX_DATAERR**
Exit code that means the input data was incorrect.

Availability: Unix.

os.**EX_NOINPUT**
Exit code that means an input file did not exist or was not readable.

Availability: Unix.

os.**EX_NOUSER**
Exit code that means a specified user did not exist.

Availability: Unix.

os.**EX_NOHOST**
Exit code that means a specified host did not exist.

Availability: Unix.

os.**EX_UNAVAILABLE**
Exit code that means that a required service is unavailable.

Availability: Unix.

os.**EX_SOFTWARE**
Exit code that means an internal software error was detected.

Availability: Unix.

os.**EX_OSERR**
Exit code that means an operating system error was detected, such as the inability to fork or create a pipe.

Availability: Unix.

os.**EX_OSFILE**
Exit code that means some system file did not exist, could not be opened, or had some other kind of error.

Availability: Unix.

os.**EX_CANTCREAT**
Exit code that means a user specified output file could not be created.

Availability: Unix.

os.**EX_IOERR**
Exit code that means that an error occurred while doing I/O on some file.

Availability: Unix.

os.**EX_TEMPFAIL**
Exit code that means a temporary failure occurred. This indicates something that may not really be an error, such as a network connection that couldn't be made during a retryable operation.

Availability: Unix.

os.**EX_PROTOCOL**
Exit code that means that a protocol exchange was illegal, invalid, or not understood.

Availability: Unix.

os.**EX_NOPERM**
Exit code that means that there were insufficient permissions to perform the operation (but not intended for file system problems).

Availability: Unix.

os.**EX_CONFIG**
Exit code that means that some kind of configuration error occurred.

Availability: Unix.

os.**EX_NOTFOUND**
Exit code that means something like "an entry was not found".

Availability: Unix.

os.**fork()**
Fork a child process. Return `0` in the child and the child's process id in the parent. If an error occurs *OSError* is raised.

Note that some platforms including FreeBSD <= 6.3 and Cygwin have known issues when using fork() from a thread.

> **Warning:** See *ssl* for applications that use the SSL module with fork().

Availability: Unix.

`os.forkpty()`
Fork a child process, using a new pseudo-terminal as the child's controlling terminal. Return a pair of `(pid, fd)`, where *pid* is `0` in the child, the new child's process id in the parent, and *fd* is the file descriptor of the master end of the pseudo-terminal. For a more portable approach, use the `pty` module. If an error occurs `OSError` is raised.

Availability: some flavors of Unix.

`os.kill(pid, sig)`
Send signal *sig* to the process *pid*. Constants for the specific signals available on the host platform are defined in the `signal` module.

Windows: The `signal.CTRL_C_EVENT` and `signal.CTRL_BREAK_EVENT` signals are special signals which can only be sent to console processes which share a common console window, e.g., some subprocesses. Any other value for *sig* will cause the process to be unconditionally killed by the TerminateProcess API, and the exit code will be set to *sig*. The Windows version of `kill()` additionally takes process handles to be killed.

See also `signal.pthread_kill()`.

New in version 3.2: Windows support.

`os.killpg(pgid, sig)`
Send the signal *sig* to the process group *pgid*.

Availability: Unix.

`os.nice(increment)`
Add *increment* to the process's "niceness". Return the new niceness.

Availability: Unix.

`os.plock(op)`
Lock program segments into memory. The value of *op* (defined in `<sys/lock.h>`) determines which segments are locked.

Availability: Unix.

`os.popen(cmd, mode='r', buffering=-1)`
Open a pipe to or from command *cmd*. The return value is an open file object connected to the pipe, which can be read or written depending on whether *mode* is `'r'` (default) or `'w'`. The *buffering* argument has the same meaning as the corresponding argument to the built-in `open()` function. The returned file object reads or writes text strings rather than bytes.

The `close` method returns `None` if the subprocess exited successfully, or the subprocess's return code if there was an error. On POSIX systems, if the return code is positive it represents the return value of the process left-shifted by one byte. If the return code is negative, the process was terminated by the signal given by the negated value of the return code. (For example, the return value might be `-signal.SIGKILL` if the subprocess was killed.) On Windows systems, the return value contains the signed integer return code from the child process.

This is implemented using `subprocess.Popen`; see that class's documentation for more powerful ways to manage and communicate with subprocesses.

`os.spawnl(mode, path, ...)`
`os.spawnle(mode, path, ..., env)`
`os.spawnlp(mode, file, ...)`
`os.spawnlpe(mode, file, ..., env)`
`os.spawnv(mode, path, args)`
`os.spawnve(mode, path, args, env)`
`os.spawnvp(mode, file, args)`
`os.spawnvpe(mode, file, args, env)`
Execute the program *path* in a new process.

(Note that the *subprocess* module provides more powerful facilities for spawning new processes and retrieving their results; using that module is preferable to using these functions. Check especially the *Replacing Older Functions with the subprocess Module* section.)

If *mode* is *P_NOWAIT*, this function returns the process id of the new process; if *mode* is *P_WAIT*, returns the process's exit code if it exits normally, or `-signal`, where *signal* is the signal that killed the process. On Windows, the process id will actually be the process handle, so can be used with the *waitpid()* function.

The "l" and "v" variants of the *spawn** functions differ in how command-line arguments are passed. The "l" variants are perhaps the easiest to work with if the number of parameters is fixed when the code is written; the individual parameters simply become additional parameters to the `spawnl*()` functions. The "v" variants are good when the number of parameters is variable, with the arguments being passed in a list or tuple as the *args* parameter. In either case, the arguments to the child process must start with the name of the command being run.

The variants which include a second "p" near the end (*spawnlp()*, *spawnlpe()*, *spawnvp()*, and *spawnvpe()*) will use the `PATH` environment variable to locate the program *file*. When the environment is being replaced (using one of the *spawn*e* variants, discussed in the next paragraph), the new environment is used as the source of the `PATH` variable. The other variants, *spawnl()*, *spawnle()*, *spawnv()*, and *spawnve()*, will not use the `PATH` variable to locate the executable; *path* must contain an appropriate absolute or relative path.

For *spawnle()*, *spawnlpe()*, *spawnve()*, and *spawnvpe()* (note that these all end in "e"), the *env* parameter must be a mapping which is used to define the environment variables for the new process (they are used instead of the current process' environment); the functions *spawnl()*, *spawnlp()*, *spawnv()*, and *spawnvp()* all cause the new process to inherit the environment of the current process. Note that keys and values in the *env* dictionary must be strings; invalid keys or values will cause the function to fail, with a return value of `127`.

As an example, the following calls to *spawnlp()* and *spawnvpe()* are equivalent:

```
import os
os.spawnlp(os.P_WAIT, 'cp', 'cp', 'index.html', '/dev/null')

L = ['cp', 'index.html', '/dev/null']
os.spawnvpe(os.P_WAIT, 'cp', L, os.environ)
```

Availability: Unix, Windows. *spawnlp()*, *spawnlpe()*, *spawnvp()* and *spawnvpe()* are not available on Windows. *spawnle()* and *spawnve()* are not thread-safe on Windows; we advise you to use the *subprocess* module instead.

Changed in version 3.6: Accepts a *path-like object*.

`os.P_NOWAIT`
`os.P_NOWAITO`

Possible values for the *mode* parameter to the *spawn** family of functions. If either of these values is given, the `spawn*()` functions will return as soon as the new process has been created, with the process id as the return value.

Availability: Unix, Windows.

`os.P_WAIT`

Possible value for the *mode* parameter to the *spawn** family of functions. If this is given as *mode*, the `spawn*()` functions will not return until the new process has run to completion and will return the exit code of the process the run is successful, or `-signal` if a signal kills the process.

Availability: Unix, Windows.

`os.P_DETACH`

os.P_OVERLAY
Possible values for the *mode* parameter to the `spawn*` family of functions. These are less portable than those listed above. `P_DETACH` is similar to `P_NOWAIT`, but the new process is detached from the console of the calling process. If `P_OVERLAY` is used, the current process will be replaced; the `spawn*` function will not return.

Availability: Windows.

os.**startfile**(*path*[, *operation*])
Start a file with its associated application.

When *operation* is not specified or `'open'`, this acts like double-clicking the file in Windows Explorer, or giving the file name as an argument to the **start** command from the interactive command shell: the file is opened with whatever application (if any) its extension is associated.

When another *operation* is given, it must be a "command verb" that specifies what should be done with the file. Common verbs documented by Microsoft are `'print'` and `'edit'` (to be used on files) as well as `'explore'` and `'find'` (to be used on directories).

`startfile()` returns as soon as the associated application is launched. There is no option to wait for the application to close, and no way to retrieve the application's exit status. The *path* parameter is relative to the current directory. If you want to use an absolute path, make sure the first character is not a slash (`'/'`); the underlying Win32 `ShellExecute()` function doesn't work if it is. Use the `os.path.normpath()` function to ensure that the path is properly encoded for Win32.

To reduce interpreter startup overhead, the Win32 `ShellExecute()` function is not resolved until this function is first called. If the function cannot be resolved, `NotImplementedError` will be raised.

Availability: Windows.

os.**system**(*command*)
Execute the command (a string) in a subshell. This is implemented by calling the Standard C function `system()`, and has the same limitations. Changes to `sys.stdin`, etc. are not reflected in the environment of the executed command. If *command* generates any output, it will be sent to the interpreter standard output stream.

On Unix, the return value is the exit status of the process encoded in the format specified for `wait()`. Note that POSIX does not specify the meaning of the return value of the C `system()` function, so the return value of the Python function is system-dependent.

On Windows, the return value is that returned by the system shell after running *command*. The shell is given by the Windows environment variable `COMSPEC`: it is usually **cmd.exe**, which returns the exit status of the command run; on systems using a non-native shell, consult your shell documentation.

The `subprocess` module provides more powerful facilities for spawning new processes and retrieving their results; using that module is preferable to using this function. See the *Replacing Older Functions with the subprocess Module* section in the `subprocess` documentation for some helpful recipes.

Availability: Unix, Windows.

os.**times**()
Returns the current global process times. The return value is an object with five attributes:

- `user` - user time
- `system` - system time
- `children_user` - user time of all child processes
- `children_system` - system time of all child processes
- `elapsed` - elapsed real time since a fixed point in the past

For backwards compatibility, this object also behaves like a five-tuple containing `user`, `system`, `children_user`, `children_system`, and `elapsed` in that order.

See the Unix manual page *times(2)* or the corresponding Windows Platform API documentation. On Windows, only `user` and *system* are known; the other attributes are zero.

Availability: Unix, Windows.

Changed in version 3.3: Return type changed from a tuple to a tuple-like object with named attributes.

`os.wait()`

Wait for completion of a child process, and return a tuple containing its pid and exit status indication: a 16-bit number, whose low byte is the signal number that killed the process, and whose high byte is the exit status (if the signal number is zero); the high bit of the low byte is set if a core file was produced.

Availability: Unix.

`os.waitid(`*idtype*, *id*, *options*`)`

Wait for the completion of one or more child processes. *idtype* can be *P_PID*, *P_PGID* or *P_ALL*. *id* specifies the pid to wait on. *options* is constructed from the ORing of one or more of *WEXITED*, *WSTOPPED* or *WCONTINUED* and additionally may be ORed with *WNOHANG* or *WNOWAIT*. The return value is an object representing the data contained in the `siginfo_t` structure, namely: `si_pid`, `si_uid`, `si_signo`, `si_status`, `si_code` or `None` if *WNOHANG* is specified and there are no children in a waitable state.

Availability: Unix.

New in version 3.3.

`os.P_PID`
`os.P_PGID`
`os.P_ALL`

These are the possible values for *idtype* in *waitid()*. They affect how *id* is interpreted.

Availability: Unix.

New in version 3.3.

`os.WEXITED`
`os.WSTOPPED`
`os.WNOWAIT`

Flags that can be used in *options* in *waitid()* that specify what child signal to wait for.

Availability: Unix.

New in version 3.3.

`os.CLD_EXITED`
`os.CLD_DUMPED`
`os.CLD_TRAPPED`
`os.CLD_CONTINUED`

These are the possible values for `si_code` in the result returned by *waitid()*.

Availability: Unix.

New in version 3.3.

`os.waitpid(`*pid*, *options*`)`

The details of this function differ on Unix and Windows.

On Unix: Wait for completion of a child process given by process id *pid*, and return a tuple containing its process id and exit status indication (encoded as for *wait()*). The semantics of the call are affected by the value of the integer *options*, which should be `0` for normal operation.

If *pid* is greater than `0`, *waitpid()* requests status information for that specific process. If *pid* is `0`, the request is for the status of any child in the process group of the current process. If *pid* is `-1`, the request pertains to any child of the current process. If *pid* is less than `-1`, status is requested for any process in the process group `-pid` (the absolute value of *pid*).

An *OSError* is raised with the value of errno when the syscall returns -1.

On Windows: Wait for completion of a process given by process handle *pid*, and return a tuple containing *pid*, and its exit status shifted left by 8 bits (shifting makes cross-platform use of the function easier). A *pid* less than or equal to `0` has no special meaning on Windows, and raises an exception. The value of integer *options* has no effect. *pid* can refer to any process whose id is known, not necessarily a child process. The *spawn** functions called with *P_NOWAIT* return suitable process handles.

Changed in version 3.5: If the system call is interrupted and the signal handler does not raise an exception, the function now retries the system call instead of raising an *InterruptedError* exception (see PEP 475 for the rationale).

`os.wait3(`*options*`)`

Similar to *waitpid()*, except no process id argument is given and a 3-element tuple containing the child's process id, exit status indication, and resource usage information is returned. Refer to *resource.getrusage()* for details on resource usage information. The option argument is the same as that provided to *waitpid()* and *wait4()*.

Availability: Unix.

`os.wait4(`*pid, options*`)`

Similar to *waitpid()*, except a 3-element tuple, containing the child's process id, exit status indication, and resource usage information is returned. Refer to *resource.getrusage()* for details on resource usage information. The arguments to *wait4()* are the same as those provided to *waitpid()*.

Availability: Unix.

`os.WNOHANG`

The option for *waitpid()* to return immediately if no child process status is available immediately. The function returns `(0, 0)` in this case.

Availability: Unix.

`os.WCONTINUED`

This option causes child processes to be reported if they have been continued from a job control stop since their status was last reported.

Availability: some Unix systems.

`os.WUNTRACED`

This option causes child processes to be reported if they have been stopped but their current state has not been reported since they were stopped.

Availability: Unix.

The following functions take a process status code as returned by *system()*, *wait()*, or *waitpid()* as a parameter. They may be used to determine the disposition of a process.

`os.WCOREDUMP(`*status*`)`

Return `True` if a core dump was generated for the process, otherwise return `False`.

Availability: Unix.

`os.WIFCONTINUED(`*status*`)`

Return `True` if the process has been continued from a job control stop, otherwise return `False`.

Availability: Unix.

`os.WIFSTOPPED(`*status*`)`

Return `True` if the process has been stopped, otherwise return `False`.

Availability: Unix.

`os.WIFSIGNALED(status)`
Return `True` if the process exited due to a signal, otherwise return `False`.

Availability: Unix.

`os.WIFEXITED(status)`
Return `True` if the process exited using the *exit(2)* system call, otherwise return `False`.

Availability: Unix.

`os.WEXITSTATUS(status)`
If `WIFEXITED(status)` is true, return the integer parameter to the *exit(2)* system call. Otherwise, the return value is meaningless.

Availability: Unix.

`os.WSTOPSIG(status)`
Return the signal which caused the process to stop.

Availability: Unix.

`os.WTERMSIG(status)`
Return the signal which caused the process to exit.

Availability: Unix.

16.1.7 Interface to the scheduler

These functions control how a process is allocated CPU time by the operating system. They are only available on some Unix platforms. For more detailed information, consult your Unix manpages.

New in version 3.3.

The following scheduling policies are exposed if they are supported by the operating system.

`os.SCHED_OTHER`
The default scheduling policy.

`os.SCHED_BATCH`
Scheduling policy for CPU-intensive processes that tries to preserve interactivity on the rest of the computer.

`os.SCHED_IDLE`
Scheduling policy for extremely low priority background tasks.

`os.SCHED_SPORADIC`
Scheduling policy for sporadic server programs.

`os.SCHED_FIFO`
A First In First Out scheduling policy.

`os.SCHED_RR`
A round-robin scheduling policy.

`os.SCHED_RESET_ON_FORK`
This flag can be OR'ed with any other scheduling policy. When a process with this flag set forks, its child's scheduling policy and priority are reset to the default.

`class os.sched_param(sched_priority)`
This class represents tunable scheduling parameters used in `sched_setparam()`, `sched_setscheduler()`, and `sched_getparam()`. It is immutable.

At the moment, there is only one possible parameter:

sched_priority
The scheduling priority for a scheduling policy.

os.**sched_get_priority_min**(*policy*)
Get the minimum priority value for *policy*. *policy* is one of the scheduling policy constants above.

os.**sched_get_priority_max**(*policy*)
Get the maximum priority value for *policy*. *policy* is one of the scheduling policy constants above.

os.**sched_setscheduler**(*pid*, *policy*, *param*)
Set the scheduling policy for the process with PID *pid*. A *pid* of 0 means the calling process. *policy* is one of the scheduling policy constants above. *param* is a `sched_param` instance.

os.**sched_getscheduler**(*pid*)
Return the scheduling policy for the process with PID *pid*. A *pid* of 0 means the calling process. The result is one of the scheduling policy constants above.

os.**sched_setparam**(*pid*, *param*)
Set a scheduling parameters for the process with PID *pid*. A *pid* of 0 means the calling process. *param* is a `sched_param` instance.

os.**sched_getparam**(*pid*)
Return the scheduling parameters as a `sched_param` instance for the process with PID *pid*. A *pid* of 0 means the calling process.

os.**sched_rr_get_interval**(*pid*)
Return the round-robin quantum in seconds for the process with PID *pid*. A *pid* of 0 means the calling process.

os.**sched_yield**()
Voluntarily relinquish the CPU.

os.**sched_setaffinity**(*pid*, *mask*)
Restrict the process with PID *pid* (or the current process if zero) to a set of CPUs. *mask* is an iterable of integers representing the set of CPUs to which the process should be restricted.

os.**sched_getaffinity**(*pid*)
Return the set of CPUs the process with PID *pid* (or the current process if zero) is restricted to.

16.1.8 Miscellaneous System Information

os.**confstr**(*name*)
Return string-valued system configuration values. *name* specifies the configuration value to retrieve; it may be a string which is the name of a defined system value; these names are specified in a number of standards (POSIX, Unix 95, Unix 98, and others). Some platforms define additional names as well. The names known to the host operating system are given as the keys of the **confstr_names** dictionary. For configuration variables not included in that mapping, passing an integer for *name* is also accepted.

If the configuration value specified by *name* isn't defined, `None` is returned.

If *name* is a string and is not known, `ValueError` is raised. If a specific value for *name* is not supported by the host system, even if it is included in **confstr_names**, an `OSError` is raised with `errno.EINVAL` for the error number.

Availability: Unix.

os.**confstr_names**
Dictionary mapping names accepted by `confstr()` to the integer values defined for those names by the host operating system. This can be used to determine the set of names known to the system.

Availability: Unix.

os.**cpu_count**()
Return the number of CPUs in the system. Returns `None` if undetermined.

This number is not equivalent to the number of CPUs the current process can use. The number of usable CPUs can be obtained with `len(os.sched_getaffinity(0))`

New in version 3.4.

os.**getloadavg**()
Return the number of processes in the system run queue averaged over the last 1, 5, and 15 minutes or raises *OSError* if the load average was unobtainable.

Availability: Unix.

os.**sysconf**(*name*)
Return integer-valued system configuration values. If the configuration value specified by *name* isn't defined, `-1` is returned. The comments regarding the *name* parameter for *confstr()* apply here as well; the dictionary that provides information on the known names is given by `sysconf_names`.

Availability: Unix.

os.**sysconf_names**
Dictionary mapping names accepted by *sysconf()* to the integer values defined for those names by the host operating system. This can be used to determine the set of names known to the system.

Availability: Unix.

The following data values are used to support path manipulation operations. These are defined for all platforms.

Higher-level operations on pathnames are defined in the *os.path* module.

os.**curdir**
The constant string used by the operating system to refer to the current directory. This is `'.'` for Windows and POSIX. Also available via *os.path*.

os.**pardir**
The constant string used by the operating system to refer to the parent directory. This is `'..'` for Windows and POSIX. Also available via *os.path*.

os.**sep**
The character used by the operating system to separate pathname components. This is `'/'` for POSIX and `'\\'` for Windows. Note that knowing this is not sufficient to be able to parse or concatenate pathnames — use *os.path.split()* and *os.path.join()* — but it is occasionally useful. Also available via *os.path*.

os.**altsep**
An alternative character used by the operating system to separate pathname components, or `None` if only one separator character exists. This is set to `'/'` on Windows systems where `sep` is a backslash. Also available via *os.path*.

os.**extsep**
The character which separates the base filename from the extension; for example, the `'.'` in `os.py`. Also available via *os.path*.

os.**pathsep**
The character conventionally used by the operating system to separate search path components (as in `PATH`), such as `':'` for POSIX or `';'` for Windows. Also available via *os.path*.

os.**defpath**
The default search path used by *exec*p** and *spawn*p** if the environment doesn't have a `'PATH'` key. Also available via *os.path*.

os.linesep
The string used to separate (or, rather, terminate) lines on the current platform. This may be a single character, such as `'\n'` for POSIX, or multiple characters, for example, `'\r\n'` for Windows. Do not use *os.linesep* as a line terminator when writing files opened in text mode (the default); use a single `'\n'` instead, on all platforms.

os.devnull
The file path of the null device. For example: `'/dev/null'` for POSIX, `'nul'` for Windows. Also available via *os.path*.

os.RTLD_LAZY
os.RTLD_NOW
os.RTLD_GLOBAL
os.RTLD_LOCAL
os.RTLD_NODELETE
os.RTLD_NOLOAD
os.RTLD_DEEPBIND
Flags for use with the *setdlopenflags()* and *getdlopenflags()* functions. See the Unix manual page **dlopen(3)** for what the different flags mean.

New in version 3.3.

16.1.9 Random numbers

os.getrandom(*size*, *flags=0*)
Get up to *size* random bytes. The function can return less bytes than requested.

These bytes can be used to seed user-space random number generators or for cryptographic purposes.

`getrandom()` relies on entropy gathered from device drivers and other sources of environmental noise. Unnecessarily reading large quantities of data will have a negative impact on other users of the `/dev/random` and `/dev/urandom` devices.

The flags argument is a bit mask that can contain zero or more of the following values ORed together: *os.GRND_RANDOM* and *GRND_NONBLOCK*.

See also the Linux getrandom() manual page.

Availability: Linux 3.17 and newer.

New in version 3.6.

os.urandom(*size*)
Return a string of *size* random bytes suitable for cryptographic use.

This function returns random bytes from an OS-specific randomness source. The returned data should be unpredictable enough for cryptographic applications, though its exact quality depends on the OS implementation.

On Linux, if the `getrandom()` syscall is available, it is used in blocking mode: block until the system urandom entropy pool is initialized (128 bits of entropy are collected by the kernel). See the PEP 524 for the rationale. On Linux, the *getrandom()* function can be used to get random bytes in non-blocking mode (using the *GRND_NONBLOCK* flag) or to poll until the system urandom entropy pool is initialized.

On a Unix-like system, random bytes are read from the `/dev/urandom` device. If the `/dev/urandom` device is not available or not readable, the *NotImplementedError* exception is raised.

On Windows, it will use `CryptGenRandom()`.

See also:

The *secrets* module provides higher level functions. For an easy-to-use interface to the random number generator provided by your platform, please see *random.SystemRandom*.

Changed in version 3.6.0: On Linux, `getrandom()` is now used in blocking mode to increase the security.

Changed in version 3.5.2: On Linux, if the `getrandom()` syscall blocks (the urandom entropy pool is not initialized yet), fall back on reading `/dev/urandom`.

Changed in version 3.5: On Linux 3.17 and newer, the `getrandom()` syscall is now used when available. On OpenBSD 5.6 and newer, the C `getentropy()` function is now used. These functions avoid the usage of an internal file descriptor.

`os.GRND_NONBLOCK`
By default, when reading from `/dev/random`, *getrandom()* blocks if no random bytes are available, and when reading from `/dev/urandom`, it blocks if the entropy pool has not yet been initialized.

If the *GRND_NONBLOCK* flag is set, then *getrandom()* does not block in these cases, but instead immediately raises *BlockingIOError*.

New in version 3.6.

`os.GRND_RANDOM`
If this bit is set, then random bytes are drawn from the `/dev/random` pool instead of the `/dev/urandom` pool.

New in version 3.6.

16.2 io — Core tools for working with streams

Source code: Lib/io.py

16.2.1 Overview

The *io* module provides Python's main facilities for dealing with various types of I/O. There are three main types of I/O: *text I/O*, *binary I/O* and *raw I/O*. These are generic categories, and various backing stores can be used for each of them. A concrete object belonging to any of these categories is called a *file object*. Other common terms are *stream* and *file-like object*.

Independently of its category, each concrete stream object will also have various capabilities: it can be read-only, write-only, or read-write. It can also allow arbitrary random access (seeking forwards or backwards to any location), or only sequential access (for example in the case of a socket or pipe).

All streams are careful about the type of data you give to them. For example giving a *str* object to the `write()` method of a binary stream will raise a `TypeError`. So will giving a *bytes* object to the `write()` method of a text stream.

Changed in version 3.3: Operations that used to raise *IOError* now raise *OSError*, since *IOError* is now an alias of *OSError*.

Text I/O

Text I/O expects and produces *str* objects. This means that whenever the backing store is natively made of bytes (such as in the case of a file), encoding and decoding of data is made transparently as well as optional translation of platform-specific newline characters.

The easiest way to create a text stream is with *open()*, optionally specifying an encoding:

```
f = open("myfile.txt", "r", encoding="utf-8")
```

In-memory text streams are also available as *StringIO* objects:

```
f = io.StringIO("some initial text data")
```

The text stream API is described in detail in the documentation of *TextIOBase*.

Binary I/O

Binary I/O (also called *buffered I/O*) expects *bytes-like objects* and produces *bytes* objects. No encoding, decoding, or newline translation is performed. This category of streams can be used for all kinds of non-text data, and also when manual control over the handling of text data is desired.

The easiest way to create a binary stream is with *open()* with 'b' in the mode string:

```
f = open("myfile.jpg", "rb")
```

In-memory binary streams are also available as *BytesIO* objects:

```
f = io.BytesIO(b"some initial binary data: \x00\x01")
```

The binary stream API is described in detail in the docs of *BufferedIOBase*.

Other library modules may provide additional ways to create text or binary streams. See *socket.socket.makefile()* for example.

Raw I/O

Raw I/O (also called *unbuffered I/O*) is generally used as a low-level building-block for binary and text streams; it is rarely useful to directly manipulate a raw stream from user code. Nevertheless, you can create a raw stream by opening a file in binary mode with buffering disabled:

```
f = open("myfile.jpg", "rb", buffering=0)
```

The raw stream API is described in detail in the docs of *RawIOBase*.

16.2.2 High-level Module Interface

io.DEFAULT_BUFFER_SIZE
An int containing the default buffer size used by the module's buffered I/O classes. *open()* uses the file's blksize (as obtained by *os.stat()*) if possible.

io.open(*file, mode='r', buffering=-1, encoding=None, errors=None, newline=None, closefd=True, opener=None*)
This is an alias for the builtin *open()* function.

exception io.BlockingIOError
This is a compatibility alias for the builtin *BlockingIOError* exception.

exception io.UnsupportedOperation
An exception inheriting *OSError* and *ValueError* that is raised when an unsupported operation is called on a stream.

In-memory streams

It is also possible to use a *str* or *bytes-like object* as a file for both reading and writing. For strings *StringIO* can be used like a file opened in text mode. *BytesIO* can be used like a file opened in binary mode. Both provide full read-write capabilities with random access.

See also:

sys contains the standard IO streams: *sys.stdin*, *sys.stdout*, and *sys.stderr*.

16.2.3 Class hierarchy

The implementation of I/O streams is organized as a hierarchy of classes. First *abstract base classes* (ABCs), which are used to specify the various categories of streams, then concrete classes providing the standard stream implementations.

> **Note:** The abstract base classes also provide default implementations of some methods in order to help implementation of concrete stream classes. For example, *BufferedIOBase* provides unoptimized implementations of **readinto()** and *readline()*.

At the top of the I/O hierarchy is the abstract base class *IOBase*. It defines the basic interface to a stream. Note, however, that there is no separation between reading and writing to streams; implementations are allowed to raise *UnsupportedOperation* if they do not support a given operation.

The *RawIOBase* ABC extends *IOBase*. It deals with the reading and writing of bytes to a stream. *FileIO* subclasses *RawIOBase* to provide an interface to files in the machine's file system.

The *BufferedIOBase* ABC deals with buffering on a raw byte stream (*RawIOBase*). Its subclasses, *BufferedWriter*, *BufferedReader*, and *BufferedRWPair* buffer streams that are readable, writable, and both readable and writable. *BufferedRandom* provides a buffered interface to random access streams. Another *BufferedIOBase* subclass, *BytesIO*, is a stream of in-memory bytes.

The *TextIOBase* ABC, another subclass of *IOBase*, deals with streams whose bytes represent text, and handles encoding and decoding to and from strings. *TextIOWrapper*, which extends it, is a buffered text interface to a buffered raw stream (*BufferedIOBase*). Finally, *StringIO* is an in-memory stream for text.

Argument names are not part of the specification, and only the arguments of *open()* are intended to be used as keyword arguments.

The following table summarizes the ABCs provided by the *io* module:

ABC	Inherits	Stub Methods	Mixin Methods and Properties
IOBase		fileno, seek, and truncate	close, closed, __enter__, __exit__, flush, isatty, __iter__, __next__, readable, readline, readlines, seekable, tell, writable, and writelines
RawIOBase	*IOBase*	readinto and write	Inherited *IOBase* methods, read, and readall
BufferedIOBase	*IOBase*	detach, read, read1, and write	Inherited *IOBase* methods, readinto, and readinto1
TextIOBase	*IOBase*	detach, read, readline, and write	Inherited *IOBase* methods, encoding, errors, and newlines

I/O Base Classes

class io.IOBase

The abstract base class for all I/O classes, acting on streams of bytes. There is no public constructor.

This class provides empty abstract implementations for many methods that derived classes can override selectively; the default implementations represent a file that cannot be read, written or seeked.

Even though *IOBase* does not declare `read()`, `readinto()`, or `write()` because their signatures will vary, implementations and clients should consider those methods part of the interface. Also, implementations may raise a *ValueError* (or *UnsupportedOperation*) when operations they do not support are called.

The basic type used for binary data read from or written to a file is *bytes*. Other *bytes-like objects* are accepted as method arguments too. In some cases, such as *readinto()*, a writable object such as *bytearray* is required. Text I/O classes work with *str* data.

Note that calling any method (even inquiries) on a closed stream is undefined. Implementations may raise *ValueError* in this case.

IOBase (and its subclasses) supports the iterator protocol, meaning that an *IOBase* object can be iterated over yielding the lines in a stream. Lines are defined slightly differently depending on whether the stream is a binary stream (yielding bytes), or a text stream (yielding character strings). See *readline()* below.

IOBase is also a context manager and therefore supports the `with` statement. In this example, *file* is closed after the `with` statement's suite is finished—even if an exception occurs:

```
with open('spam.txt', 'w') as file:
    file.write('Spam and eggs!')
```

IOBase provides these data attributes and methods:

close()

Flush and close this stream. This method has no effect if the file is already closed. Once the file is closed, any operation on the file (e.g. reading or writing) will raise a *ValueError*.

As a convenience, it is allowed to call this method more than once; only the first call, however, will have an effect.

closed

`True` if the stream is closed.

fileno()

Return the underlying file descriptor (an integer) of the stream if it exists. An *OSError* is raised if the IO object does not use a file descriptor.

flush()

Flush the write buffers of the stream if applicable. This does nothing for read-only and non-blocking streams.

isatty()

Return `True` if the stream is interactive (i.e., connected to a terminal/tty device).

readable()

Return `True` if the stream can be read from. If `False`, `read()` will raise *OSError*.

readline(*size=-1*)

Read and return one line from the stream. If *size* is specified, at most *size* bytes will be read.

The line terminator is always `b'\n'` for binary files; for text files, the *newline* argument to *open()* can be used to select the line terminator(s) recognized.

readlines(*hint=-1*)
Read and return a list of lines from the stream. *hint* can be specified to control the number of lines read: no more lines will be read if the total size (in bytes/characters) of all lines so far exceeds *hint*.

Note that it's already possible to iterate on file objects using `for line in file: ...` without calling `file.readlines()`.

seek(*offset*[, *whence*])
Change the stream position to the given byte *offset*. *offset* is interpreted relative to the position indicated by *whence*. The default value for *whence* is `SEEK_SET`. Values for *whence* are:

- `SEEK_SET` or `0` – start of the stream (the default); *offset* should be zero or positive
- `SEEK_CUR` or `1` – current stream position; *offset* may be negative
- `SEEK_END` or `2` – end of the stream; *offset* is usually negative

Return the new absolute position.

New in version 3.1: The `SEEK_*` constants.

New in version 3.3: Some operating systems could support additional values, like `os.SEEK_HOLE` or `os.SEEK_DATA`. The valid values for a file could depend on it being open in text or binary mode.

seekable()
Return `True` if the stream supports random access. If `False`, `seek()`, `tell()` and `truncate()` will raise `OSError`.

tell()
Return the current stream position.

truncate(*size=None*)
Resize the stream to the given *size* in bytes (or the current position if *size* is not specified). The current stream position isn't changed. This resizing can extend or reduce the current file size. In case of extension, the contents of the new file area depend on the platform (on most systems, additional bytes are zero-filled). The new file size is returned.

Changed in version 3.5: Windows will now zero-fill files when extending.

writable()
Return `True` if the stream supports writing. If `False`, `write()` and `truncate()` will raise `OSError`.

writelines(*lines*)
Write a list of lines to the stream. Line separators are not added, so it is usual for each of the lines provided to have a line separator at the end.

__del__()
Prepare for object destruction. `IOBase` provides a default implementation of this method that calls the instance's `close()` method.

class io.**RawIOBase**
Base class for raw binary I/O. It inherits `IOBase`. There is no public constructor.

Raw binary I/O typically provides low-level access to an underlying OS device or API, and does not try to encapsulate it in high-level primitives (this is left to Buffered I/O and Text I/O, described later in this page).

In addition to the attributes and methods from `IOBase`, `RawIOBase` provides the following methods:

read(*size=-1*)
Read up to *size* bytes from the object and return them. As a convenience, if *size* is unspecified or -1, all bytes until EOF are returned. Otherwise, only one system call is ever made. Fewer than *size* bytes may be returned if the operating system call returns fewer than *size* bytes.

If 0 bytes are returned, and *size* was not 0, this indicates end of file. If the object is in non-blocking mode and no bytes are available, `None` is returned.

The default implementation defers to *readall()* and *readinto()*.

readall()

Read and return all the bytes from the stream until EOF, using multiple calls to the stream if necessary.

readinto(*b*)

Read bytes into a pre-allocated, writable *bytes-like object* *b*, and return the number of bytes read. If the object is in non-blocking mode and no bytes are available, `None` is returned.

write(*b*)

Write the given *bytes-like object*, *b*, to the underlying raw stream, and return the number of bytes written. This can be less than the length of *b* in bytes, depending on specifics of the underlying raw stream, and especially if it is in non-blocking mode. `None` is returned if the raw stream is set not to block and no single byte could be readily written to it. The caller may release or mutate *b* after this method returns, so the implementation should only access *b* during the method call.

class io.**BufferedIOBase**

Base class for binary streams that support some kind of buffering. It inherits *IOBase*. There is no public constructor.

The main difference with *RawIOBase* is that methods *read()*, *readinto()* and *write()* will try (respectively) to read as much input as requested or to consume all given output, at the expense of making perhaps more than one system call.

In addition, those methods can raise *BlockingIOError* if the underlying raw stream is in non-blocking mode and cannot take or give enough data; unlike their *RawIOBase* counterparts, they will never return `None`.

Besides, the *read()* method does not have a default implementation that defers to *readinto()*.

A typical *BufferedIOBase* implementation should not inherit from a *RawIOBase* implementation, but wrap one, like *BufferedWriter* and *BufferedReader* do.

BufferedIOBase provides or overrides these methods and attribute in addition to those from *IOBase*:

raw

The underlying raw stream (a *RawIOBase* instance) that *BufferedIOBase* deals with. This is not part of the *BufferedIOBase* API and may not exist on some implementations.

detach()

Separate the underlying raw stream from the buffer and return it.

After the raw stream has been detached, the buffer is in an unusable state.

Some buffers, like *BytesIO*, do not have the concept of a single raw stream to return from this method. They raise *UnsupportedOperation*.

New in version 3.1.

read(*size=-1*)

Read and return up to *size* bytes. If the argument is omitted, `None`, or negative, data is read and returned until EOF is reached. An empty *bytes* object is returned if the stream is already at EOF.

If the argument is positive, and the underlying raw stream is not interactive, multiple raw reads may be issued to satisfy the byte count (unless EOF is reached first). But for interactive raw streams, at most one raw read will be issued, and a short result does not imply that EOF is imminent.

A *BlockingIOError* is raised if the underlying raw stream is in non blocking-mode, and has no data available at the moment.

read1(*size=-1*)

Read and return up to *size* bytes, with at most one call to the underlying raw stream's *read()* (or *readinto()*) method. This can be useful if you are implementing your own buffering on top of a *BufferedIOBase* object.

readinto(*b*)

Read bytes into a pre-allocated, writable *bytes-like object* *b* and return the number of bytes read.

Like *read()*, multiple reads may be issued to the underlying raw stream, unless the latter is interactive.

A *BlockingIOError* is raised if the underlying raw stream is in non blocking-mode, and has no data available at the moment.

readinto1(*b*)

Read bytes into a pre-allocated, writable *bytes-like object* *b*, using at most one call to the underlying raw stream's *read()* (or *readinto()*) method. Return the number of bytes read.

A *BlockingIOError* is raised if the underlying raw stream is in non blocking-mode, and has no data available at the moment.

New in version 3.5.

write(*b*)

Write the given *bytes-like object*, *b*, and return the number of bytes written (always equal to the length of *b* in bytes, since if the write fails an *OSError* will be raised). Depending on the actual implementation, these bytes may be readily written to the underlying stream, or held in a buffer for performance and latency reasons.

When in non-blocking mode, a *BlockingIOError* is raised if the data needed to be written to the raw stream but it couldn't accept all the data without blocking.

The caller may release or mutate *b* after this method returns, so the implementation should only access *b* during the method call.

Raw File I/O

class io.**FileIO**(*name, mode='r', closefd=True, opener=None*)

FileIO represents an OS-level file containing bytes data. It implements the *RawIOBase* interface (and therefore the *IOBase* interface, too).

The *name* can be one of two things:

- a character string or *bytes* object representing the path to the file which will be opened. In this case closefd must be `True` (the default) otherwise an error will be raised.
- an integer representing the number of an existing OS-level file descriptor to which the resulting *FileIO* object will give access. When the FileIO object is closed this fd will be closed as well, unless *closefd* is set to `False`.

The *mode* can be `'r'`, `'w'`, `'x'` or `'a'` for reading (default), writing, exclusive creation or appending. The file will be created if it doesn't exist when opened for writing or appending; it will be truncated when opened for writing. *FileExistsError* will be raised if it already exists when opened for creating. Opening a file for creating implies writing, so this mode behaves in a similar way to `'w'`. Add a `'+'` to the mode to allow simultaneous reading and writing.

The `read()` (when called with a positive argument), `readinto()` and `write()` methods on this class will only make one system call.

A custom opener can be used by passing a callable as *opener*. The underlying file descriptor for the file object is then obtained by calling *opener* with (*name*, *flags*). *opener* must return an open file descriptor (passing `os.open` as *opener* results in functionality similar to passing `None`).

The newly created file is *non-inheritable*.

See the `open()` built-in function for examples on using the *opener* parameter.

Changed in version 3.3: The *opener* parameter was added. The `'x'` mode was added.

Changed in version 3.4: The file is now non-inheritable.

In addition to the attributes and methods from `IOBase` and `RawIOBase`, `FileIO` provides the following data attributes:

mode
The mode as given in the constructor.

name
The file name. This is the file descriptor of the file when no name is given in the constructor.

Buffered Streams

Buffered I/O streams provide a higher-level interface to an I/O device than raw I/O does.

class io.**BytesIO**([*initial_bytes*])
A stream implementation using an in-memory bytes buffer. It inherits `BufferedIOBase`. The buffer is discarded when the `close()` method is called.

The optional argument *initial_bytes* is a *bytes-like object* that contains initial data.

`BytesIO` provides or overrides these methods in addition to those from `BufferedIOBase` and `IOBase`:

getbuffer()
Return a readable and writable view over the contents of the buffer without copying them. Also, mutating the view will transparently update the contents of the buffer:

```
>>> b = io.BytesIO(b"abcdef")
>>> view = b.getbuffer()
>>> view[2:4] = b"56"
>>> b.getvalue()
b'ab56ef'
```

Note: As long as the view exists, the `BytesIO` object cannot be resized or closed.

New in version 3.2.

getvalue()
Return `bytes` containing the entire contents of the buffer.

read1()
In `BytesIO`, this is the same as `read()`.

readinto1()
In `BytesIO`, this is the same as `readinto()`.

New in version 3.5.

class io.**BufferedReader**(*raw*, *buffer_size=DEFAULT_BUFFER_SIZE*)
A buffer providing higher-level access to a readable, sequential `RawIOBase` object. It inherits `BufferedIOBase`. When reading data from this object, a larger amount of data may be requested

from the underlying raw stream, and kept in an internal buffer. The buffered data can then be returned directly on subsequent reads.

The constructor creates a `BufferedReader` for the given readable *raw* stream and *buffer_size*. If *buffer_size* is omitted, `DEFAULT_BUFFER_SIZE` is used.

`BufferedReader` provides or overrides these methods in addition to those from `BufferedIOBase` and `IOBase`:

peek([*size*])
Return bytes from the stream without advancing the position. At most one single read on the raw stream is done to satisfy the call. The number of bytes returned may be less or more than requested.

read([*size*])
Read and return *size* bytes, or if *size* is not given or negative, until EOF or if the read call would block in non-blocking mode.

read1(*size*)
Read and return up to *size* bytes with only one call on the raw stream. If at least one byte is buffered, only buffered bytes are returned. Otherwise, one raw stream read call is made.

class io.**BufferedWriter**(*raw*, *buffer_size=DEFAULT_BUFFER_SIZE*)
A buffer providing higher-level access to a writeable, sequential `RawIOBase` object. It inherits `BufferedIOBase`. When writing to this object, data is normally placed into an internal buffer. The buffer will be written out to the underlying `RawIOBase` object under various conditions, including:

- when the buffer gets too small for all pending data;
- when `flush()` is called;
- when a `seek()` is requested (for `BufferedRandom` objects);
- when the `BufferedWriter` object is closed or destroyed.

The constructor creates a `BufferedWriter` for the given writeable *raw* stream. If the *buffer_size* is not given, it defaults to `DEFAULT_BUFFER_SIZE`.

`BufferedWriter` provides or overrides these methods in addition to those from `BufferedIOBase` and `IOBase`:

flush()
Force bytes held in the buffer into the raw stream. A `BlockingIOError` should be raised if the raw stream blocks.

write(*b*)
Write the *bytes-like object*, *b*, and return the number of bytes written. When in non-blocking mode, a `BlockingIOError` is raised if the buffer needs to be written out but the raw stream blocks.

class io.**BufferedRandom**(*raw*, *buffer_size=DEFAULT_BUFFER_SIZE*)
A buffered interface to random access streams. It inherits `BufferedReader` and `BufferedWriter`, and further supports `seek()` and `tell()` functionality.

The constructor creates a reader and writer for a seekable raw stream, given in the first argument. If the *buffer_size* is omitted it defaults to `DEFAULT_BUFFER_SIZE`.

`BufferedRandom` is capable of anything `BufferedReader` or `BufferedWriter` can do.

class io.**BufferedRWPair**(*reader*, *writer*, *buffer_size=DEFAULT_BUFFER_SIZE*)
A buffered I/O object combining two unidirectional `RawIOBase` objects – one readable, the other writeable – into a single bidirectional endpoint. It inherits `BufferedIOBase`.

reader and *writer* are `RawIOBase` objects that are readable and writeable respectively. If the *buffer_size* is omitted it defaults to `DEFAULT_BUFFER_SIZE`.

BufferedRWPair implements all of *BufferedIOBase*'s methods except for *detach()*, which raises *UnsupportedOperation*.

> **Warning:** *BufferedRWPair* does not attempt to synchronize accesses to its underlying raw streams. You should not pass it the same object as reader and writer; use *BufferedRandom* instead.

Text I/O

class io.TextIOBase

Base class for text streams. This class provides a character and line based interface to stream I/O. There is no `readinto()` method because Python's character strings are immutable. It inherits *IOBase*. There is no public constructor.

TextIOBase provides or overrides these data attributes and methods in addition to those from *IOBase*:

encoding

The name of the encoding used to decode the stream's bytes into strings, and to encode strings into bytes.

errors

The error setting of the decoder or encoder.

newlines

A string, a tuple of strings, or `None`, indicating the newlines translated so far. Depending on the implementation and the initial constructor flags, this may not be available.

buffer

The underlying binary buffer (a *BufferedIOBase* instance) that *TextIOBase* deals with. This is not part of the *TextIOBase* API and may not exist in some implementations.

detach()

Separate the underlying binary buffer from the *TextIOBase* and return it.

After the underlying buffer has been detached, the *TextIOBase* is in an unusable state.

Some *TextIOBase* implementations, like *StringIO*, may not have the concept of an underlying buffer and calling this method will raise *UnsupportedOperation*.

New in version 3.1.

read(*size*)

Read and return at most *size* characters from the stream as a single *str*. If *size* is negative or `None`, reads until EOF.

readline(*size=-1*)

Read until newline or EOF and return a single `str`. If the stream is already at EOF, an empty string is returned.

If *size* is specified, at most *size* characters will be read.

seek(*offset*[, *whence*])

Change the stream position to the given *offset*. Behaviour depends on the *whence* parameter. The default value for *whence* is `SEEK_SET`.

- `SEEK_SET` or `0`: seek from the start of the stream (the default); *offset* must either be a number returned by *TextIOBase.tell()*, or zero. Any other *offset* value produces undefined behaviour.
- `SEEK_CUR` or `1`: "seek" to the current position; *offset* must be zero, which is a no-operation (all other values are unsupported).

- SEEK_END or 2: seek to the end of the stream; *offset* must be zero (all other values are unsupported).

Return the new absolute position as an opaque number.

New in version 3.1: The SEEK_* constants.

tell()

Return the current stream position as an opaque number. The number does not usually represent a number of bytes in the underlying binary storage.

write(*s*)

Write the string *s* to the stream and return the number of characters written.

class io.**TextIOWrapper**(*buffer*, *encoding=None*, *errors=None*, *newline=None*, *line_buffering=False*, *write_through=False*)

A buffered text stream over a *BufferedIOBase* binary stream. It inherits *TextIOBase*.

encoding gives the name of the encoding that the stream will be decoded or encoded with. It defaults to *locale.getpreferredencoding(False)*.

errors is an optional string that specifies how encoding and decoding errors are to be handled. Pass 'strict' to raise a *ValueError* exception if there is an encoding error (the default of None has the same effect), or pass 'ignore' to ignore errors. (Note that ignoring encoding errors can lead to data loss.) 'replace' causes a replacement marker (such as '?') to be inserted where there is malformed data. 'backslashreplace' causes malformed data to be replaced by a backslashed escape sequence. When writing, 'xmlcharrefreplace' (replace with the appropriate XML character reference) or 'namereplace' (replace with \N{...} escape sequences) can be used. Any other error handling name that has been registered with *codecs.register_error()* is also valid.

newline controls how line endings are handled. It can be None, '', '\n', '\r', and '\r\n'. It works as follows:

- When reading input from the stream, if *newline* is None, *universal newlines* mode is enabled. Lines in the input can end in '\n', '\r', or '\r\n', and these are translated into '\n' before being returned to the caller. If it is '', universal newlines mode is enabled, but line endings are returned to the caller untranslated. If it has any of the other legal values, input lines are only terminated by the given string, and the line ending is returned to the caller untranslated.
- When writing output to the stream, if *newline* is None, any '\n' characters written are translated to the system default line separator, *os.linesep*. If *newline* is '' or '\n', no translation takes place. If *newline* is any of the other legal values, any '\n' characters written are translated to the given string.

If *line_buffering* is True, flush() is implied when a call to write contains a newline character.

If *write_through* is True, calls to write() are guaranteed not to be buffered: any data written on the *TextIOWrapper* object is immediately handled to its underlying binary *buffer*.

Changed in version 3.3: The *write_through* argument has been added.

Changed in version 3.3: The default *encoding* is now locale.getpreferredencoding(False) instead of locale.getpreferredencoding(). Don't change temporary the locale encoding using *locale.setlocale()*, use the current locale encoding instead of the user preferred encoding.

TextIOWrapper provides one attribute in addition to those of *TextIOBase* and its parents:

line_buffering

Whether line buffering is enabled.

class io.**StringIO**(*initial_value=''*, *newline='\n'*)

An in-memory stream for text I/O. The text buffer is discarded when the *close()* method is called.

The initial value of the buffer can be set by providing *initial_value*. If newline translation is enabled, newlines will be encoded as if by *write()*. The stream is positioned at the start of the buffer.

The *newline* argument works like that of *TextIOWrapper*. The default is to consider only `\n` characters as ends of lines and to do no newline translation. If *newline* is set to `None`, newlines are written as `\n` on all platforms, but universal newline decoding is still performed when reading.

StringIO provides this method in addition to those from *TextIOBase* and its parents:

getvalue()
Return a `str` containing the entire contents of the buffer. Newlines are decoded as if by *read()*, although the stream position is not changed.

Example usage:

```
import io

output = io.StringIO()
output.write('First line.\n')
print('Second line.', file=output)

# Retrieve file contents -- this will be
# 'First line.\nSecond line.\n'
contents = output.getvalue()

# Close object and discard memory buffer --
# .getvalue() will now raise an exception.
output.close()
```

class io.IncrementalNewlineDecoder
A helper codec that decodes newlines for *universal newlines* mode. It inherits *codecs.IncrementalDecoder*.

16.2.4 Performance

This section discusses the performance of the provided concrete I/O implementations.

Binary I/O

By reading and writing only large chunks of data even when the user asks for a single byte, buffered I/O hides any inefficiency in calling and executing the operating system's unbuffered I/O routines. The gain depends on the OS and the kind of I/O which is performed. For example, on some modern OSes such as Linux, unbuffered disk I/O can be as fast as buffered I/O. The bottom line, however, is that buffered I/O offers predictable performance regardless of the platform and the backing device. Therefore, it is almost always preferable to use buffered I/O rather than unbuffered I/O for binary data.

Text I/O

Text I/O over a binary storage (such as a file) is significantly slower than binary I/O over the same storage, because it requires conversions between unicode and binary data using a character codec. This can become noticeable handling huge amounts of text data like large log files. Also, `TextIOWrapper.tell()` and `TextIOWrapper.seek()` are both quite slow due to the reconstruction algorithm used.

StringIO, however, is a native in-memory unicode container and will exhibit similar speed to *BytesIO*.

Multi-threading

FileIO objects are thread-safe to the extent that the operating system calls (such as `read(2)` under Unix) they wrap are thread-safe too.

Binary buffered objects (instances of *BufferedReader*, *BufferedWriter*, *BufferedRandom* and *BufferedRWPair*) protect their internal structures using a lock; it is therefore safe to call them from multiple threads at once.

TextIOWrapper objects are not thread-safe.

Reentrancy

Binary buffered objects (instances of *BufferedReader*, *BufferedWriter*, *BufferedRandom* and *BufferedRWPair*) are not reentrant. While reentrant calls will not happen in normal situations, they can arise from doing I/O in a *signal* handler. If a thread tries to re-enter a buffered object which it is already accessing, a *RuntimeError* is raised. Note this doesn't prohibit a different thread from entering the buffered object.

The above implicitly extends to text files, since the *open()* function will wrap a buffered object inside a *TextIOWrapper*. This includes standard streams and therefore affects the built-in function *print()* as well.

16.3 `time` — Time access and conversions

This module provides various time-related functions. For related functionality, see also the *datetime* and *calendar* modules.

Although this module is always available, not all functions are available on all platforms. Most of the functions defined in this module call platform C library functions with the same name. It may sometimes be helpful to consult the platform documentation, because the semantics of these functions varies among platforms.

An explanation of some terminology and conventions is in order.

- The *epoch* is the point where the time starts, and is platform dependent. For Unix, the epoch is January 1, 1970, 00:00:00 (UTC). To find out what the epoch is on a given platform, look at `time.gmtime(0)`.
- The term *seconds since the epoch* refers to the total number of elapsed seconds since the epoch, typically excluding leap seconds. Leap seconds are excluded from this total on all POSIX-compliant platforms.
- The functions in this module may not handle dates and times before the epoch or far in the future. The cut-off point in the future is determined by the C library; for 32-bit systems, it is typically in 2038.
- **Year 2000 (Y2K) issues**: Python depends on the platform's C library, which generally doesn't have year 2000 issues, since all dates and times are represented internally as seconds since the epoch. Function *strptime()* can parse 2-digit years when given `%y` format code. When 2-digit years are parsed, they are converted according to the POSIX and ISO C standards: values 69–99 are mapped to 1969–1999, and values 0–68 are mapped to 2000–2068.
- UTC is Coordinated Universal Time (formerly known as Greenwich Mean Time, or GMT). The acronym UTC is not a mistake but a compromise between English and French.
- DST is Daylight Saving Time, an adjustment of the timezone by (usually) one hour during part of the year. DST rules are magic (determined by local law) and can change from year to year. The C library has a table containing the local rules (often it is read from a system file for flexibility) and is the only source of True Wisdom in this respect.
- The precision of the various real-time functions may be less than suggested by the units in which their value or argument is expressed. E.g. on most Unix systems, the clock "ticks" only 50 or 100 times a second.

- On the other hand, the precision of *time()* and *sleep()* is better than their Unix equivalents: times are expressed as floating point numbers, *time()* returns the most accurate time available (using Unix `gettimeofday()` where available), and *sleep()* will accept a time with a nonzero fraction (Unix `select()` is used to implement this, where available).
- The time value as returned by *gmtime()*, *localtime()*, and *strptime()*, and accepted by *asctime()*, *mktime()* and *strftime()*, is a sequence of 9 integers. The return values of *gmtime()*, *localtime()*, and *strptime()* also offer attribute names for individual fields.

  See *struct_time* for a description of these objects.

  Changed in version 3.3: The *struct_time* type was extended to provide the `tm_gmtoff` and `tm_zone` attributes when platform supports corresponding `struct tm` members.

  Changed in version 3.6: The *struct_time* attributes `tm_gmtoff` and `tm_zone` are now available on all platforms.
- Use the following functions to convert between time representations:

From	To	Use
seconds since the epoch	*struct_time* in UTC	*gmtime()*
seconds since the epoch	*struct_time* in local time	*localtime()*
struct_time in UTC	seconds since the epoch	*calendar.timegm()*
struct_time in local time	seconds since the epoch	*mktime()*

16.3.1 Functions

`time.asctime([t])`

Convert a tuple or *struct_time* representing a time as returned by *gmtime()* or *localtime()* to a string of the following form: `'Sun Jun 20 23:21:05 1993'`. If *t* is not provided, the current time as returned by *localtime()* is used. Locale information is not used by *asctime()*.

Note: Unlike the C function of the same name, *asctime()* does not add a trailing newline.

`time.clock()`

On Unix, return the current processor time as a floating point number expressed in seconds. The precision, and in fact the very definition of the meaning of "processor time", depends on that of the C function of the same name.

On Windows, this function returns wall-clock seconds elapsed since the first call to this function, as a floating point number, based on the Win32 function `QueryPerformanceCounter()`. The resolution is typically better than one microsecond.

Deprecated since version 3.3: The behaviour of this function depends on the platform: use *perf_counter()* or *process_time()* instead, depending on your requirements, to have a well defined behaviour.

`time.clock_getres(clk_id)`

Return the resolution (precision) of the specified clock *clk_id*. Refer to *Clock ID Constants* for a list of accepted values for *clk_id*.

Availability: Unix.

New in version 3.3.

`time.clock_gettime(clk_id)`

Return the time of the specified clock *clk_id*. Refer to *Clock ID Constants* for a list of accepted values for *clk_id*.

Availability: Unix.

New in version 3.3.

`time.clock_settime(clk_id, time)`
Set the time of the specified clock *clk_id*. Currently, `CLOCK_REALTIME` is the only accepted value for *clk_id*.

Availability: Unix.

New in version 3.3.

`time.ctime([secs])`
Convert a time expressed in seconds since the epoch to a string representing local time. If *secs* is not provided or `None`, the current time as returned by `time()` is used. `ctime(secs)` is equivalent to `asctime(localtime(secs))`. Locale information is not used by `ctime()`.

`time.get_clock_info(name)`
Get information on the specified clock as a namespace object. Supported clock names and the corresponding functions to read their value are:

- `'clock'`: `time.clock()`
- `'monotonic'`: `time.monotonic()`
- `'perf_counter'`: `time.perf_counter()`
- `'process_time'`: `time.process_time()`
- `'time'`: `time.time()`

The result has the following attributes:

- *adjustable*: `True` if the clock can be changed automatically (e.g. by a NTP daemon) or manually by the system administrator, `False` otherwise
- *implementation*: The name of the underlying C function used to get the clock value. Refer to *Clock ID Constants* for possible values.
- *monotonic*: `True` if the clock cannot go backward, `False` otherwise
- *resolution*: The resolution of the clock in seconds (`float`)

New in version 3.3.

`time.gmtime([secs])`
Convert a time expressed in seconds since the epoch to a `struct_time` in UTC in which the dst flag is always zero. If *secs* is not provided or `None`, the current time as returned by `time()` is used. Fractions of a second are ignored. See above for a description of the `struct_time` object. See `calendar.timegm()` for the inverse of this function.

`time.localtime([secs])`
Like `gmtime()` but converts to local time. If *secs* is not provided or `None`, the current time as returned by `time()` is used. The dst flag is set to `1` when DST applies to the given time.

`time.mktime(t)`
This is the inverse function of `localtime()`. Its argument is the `struct_time` or full 9-tuple (since the dst flag is needed; use `-1` as the dst flag if it is unknown) which expresses the time in *local* time, not UTC. It returns a floating point number, for compatibility with `time()`. If the input value cannot be represented as a valid time, either `OverflowError` or `ValueError` will be raised (which depends on whether the invalid value is caught by Python or the underlying C libraries). The earliest date for which it can generate a time is platform-dependent.

`time.monotonic()`
Return the value (in fractional seconds) of a monotonic clock, i.e. a clock that cannot go backwards.

The clock is not affected by system clock updates. The reference point of the returned value is undefined, so that only the difference between the results of consecutive calls is valid.

On Windows versions older than Vista, *monotonic()* detects **GetTickCount()** integer overflow (32 bits, roll-over after 49.7 days). It increases an internal epoch (reference time) by 2^{32} each time that an overflow is detected. The epoch is stored in the process-local state and so the value of *monotonic()* may be different in two Python processes running for more than 49 days. On more recent versions of Windows and on other operating systems, *monotonic()* is system-wide.

New in version 3.3.

Changed in version 3.5: The function is now always available.

time.**perf_counter**()

Return the value (in fractional seconds) of a performance counter, i.e. a clock with the highest available resolution to measure a short duration. It does include time elapsed during sleep and is system-wide. The reference point of the returned value is undefined, so that only the difference between the results of consecutive calls is valid.

New in version 3.3.

time.**process_time**()

Return the value (in fractional seconds) of the sum of the system and user CPU time of the current process. It does not include time elapsed during sleep. It is process-wide by definition. The reference point of the returned value is undefined, so that only the difference between the results of consecutive calls is valid.

New in version 3.3.

time.**sleep**(*secs*)

Suspend execution of the calling thread for the given number of seconds. The argument may be a floating point number to indicate a more precise sleep time. The actual suspension time may be less than that requested because any caught signal will terminate the *sleep()* following execution of that signal's catching routine. Also, the suspension time may be longer than requested by an arbitrary amount because of the scheduling of other activity in the system.

Changed in version 3.5: The function now sleeps at least *secs* even if the sleep is interrupted by a signal, except if the signal handler raises an exception (see PEP 475 for the rationale).

time.**strftime**(*format*[, *t*])

Convert a tuple or *struct_time* representing a time as returned by *gmtime()* or *localtime()* to a string as specified by the *format* argument. If *t* is not provided, the current time as returned by *localtime()* is used. *format* must be a string. *ValueError* is raised if any field in *t* is outside of the allowed range.

0 is a legal argument for any position in the time tuple; if it is normally illegal the value is forced to a correct one.

The following directives can be embedded in the *format* string. They are shown without the optional field width and precision specification, and are replaced by the indicated characters in the *strftime()* result:

Directive	Meaning	Notes
%a	Locale's abbreviated weekday name.	
%A	Locale's full weekday name.	
%b	Locale's abbreviated month name.	
%B	Locale's full month name.	
%c	Locale's appropriate date and time representation.	
%d	Day of the month as a decimal number [01,31].	
%H	Hour (24-hour clock) as a decimal number [00,23].	
%I	Hour (12-hour clock) as a decimal number [01,12].	
%j	Day of the year as a decimal number [001,366].	
%m	Month as a decimal number [01,12].	
%M	Minute as a decimal number [00,59].	
%p	Locale's equivalent of either AM or PM.	(1)
%S	Second as a decimal number [00,61].	(2)
%U	Week number of the year (Sunday as the first day of the week) as a decimal number [00,53]. All days in a new year preceding the first Sunday are considered to be in week 0.	(3)
%w	Weekday as a decimal number [0(Sunday),6].	
%W	Week number of the year (Monday as the first day of the week) as a decimal number [00,53]. All days in a new year preceding the first Monday are considered to be in week 0.	(3)
%x	Locale's appropriate date representation.	
%X	Locale's appropriate time representation.	
%y	Year without century as a decimal number [00,99].	
%Y	Year with century as a decimal number.	
%z	Time zone offset indicating a positive or negative time difference from UTC/GMT of the form +HHMM or -HHMM, where H represents decimal hour digits and M represents decimal minute digits [-23:59, +23:59].	
%Z	Time zone name (no characters if no time zone exists).	
%%	A literal '%' character.	

Notes:

1. When used with the *strptime()* function, the %p directive only affects the output hour field if the %I directive is used to parse the hour.
2. The range really is 0 to 61; value 60 is valid in timestamps representing leap seconds and value 61 is supported for historical reasons.
3. When used with the *strptime()* function, %U and %W are only used in calculations when the day of the week and the year are specified.

Here is an example, a format for dates compatible with that specified in the RFC 2822 Internet email standard.[1]

```
>>> from time import gmtime, strftime
>>> strftime("%a, %d %b %Y %H:%M:%S +0000", gmtime())
'Thu, 28 Jun 2001 14:17:15 +0000'
```

[1] The use of %Z is now deprecated, but the %z escape that expands to the preferred hour/minute offset is not supported by all ANSI C libraries. Also, a strict reading of the original 1982 RFC 822 standard calls for a two-digit year (%y rather than %Y), but practice moved to 4-digit years long before the year 2000. After that, RFC 822 became obsolete and the 4-digit year has been first recommended by RFC 1123 and then mandated by RFC 2822.

Additional directives may be supported on certain platforms, but only the ones listed here have a meaning standardized by ANSI C. To see the full set of format codes supported on your platform, consult the ***strftime(3)*** documentation.

On some platforms, an optional field width and precision specification can immediately follow the initial `'%'` of a directive in the following order; this is also not portable. The field width is normally 2 except for `%j` where it is 3.

`time.strptime(`*string*[, *format*]`)`

Parse a string representing a time according to a format. The return value is a `struct_time` as returned by `gmtime()` or `localtime()`.

The *format* parameter uses the same directives as those used by `strftime()`; it defaults to `"%a %b %d %H:%M:%S %Y"` which matches the formatting returned by `ctime()`. If *string* cannot be parsed according to *format*, or if it has excess data after parsing, `ValueError` is raised. The default values used to fill in any missing data when more accurate values cannot be inferred are `(1900, 1, 1, 0, 0, 0, 0, 1, -1)`. Both *string* and *format* must be strings.

For example:

```
>>> import time
>>> time.strptime("30 Nov 00", "%d %b %y")
time.struct_time(tm_year=2000, tm_mon=11, tm_mday=30, tm_hour=0, tm_min=0,
                 tm_sec=0, tm_wday=3, tm_yday=335, tm_isdst=-1)
```

Support for the `%Z` directive is based on the values contained in `tzname` and whether `daylight` is true. Because of this, it is platform-specific except for recognizing UTC and GMT which are always known (and are considered to be non-daylight savings timezones).

Only the directives specified in the documentation are supported. Because `strftime()` is implemented per platform it can sometimes offer more directives than those listed. But `strptime()` is independent of any platform and thus does not necessarily support all directives available that are not documented as supported.

`class time.struct_time`

The type of the time value sequence returned by `gmtime()`, `localtime()`, and `strptime()`. It is an object with a *named tuple* interface: values can be accessed by index and by attribute name. The following values are present:

Index	Attribute	Values
0	`tm_year`	(for example, 1993)
1	`tm_mon`	range [1, 12]
2	`tm_mday`	range [1, 31]
3	`tm_hour`	range [0, 23]
4	`tm_min`	range [0, 59]
5	`tm_sec`	range [0, 61]; see **(2)** in `strftime()` description
6	`tm_wday`	range [0, 6], Monday is 0
7	`tm_yday`	range [1, 366]
8	`tm_isdst`	0, 1 or -1; see below
N/A	`tm_zone`	abbreviation of timezone name
N/A	`tm_gmtoff`	offset east of UTC in seconds

Note that unlike the C structure, the month value is a range of [1, 12], not [0, 11].

In calls to `mktime()`, `tm_isdst` may be set to 1 when daylight savings time is in effect, and 0 when it is not. A value of -1 indicates that this is not known, and will usually result in the correct state being filled in.

When a tuple with an incorrect length is passed to a function expecting a *struct_time*, or having elements of the wrong type, a *TypeError* is raised.

time.time()

Return the time in seconds since the epoch as a floating point number. The specific date of the epoch and the handling of leap seconds is platform dependent. On Windows and most Unix systems, the epoch is January 1, 1970, 00:00:00 (UTC) and leap seconds are not counted towards the time in seconds since the epoch. This is commonly referred to as Unix time. To find out what the epoch is on a given platform, look at `gmtime(0)`.

Note that even though the time is always returned as a floating point number, not all systems provide time with a better precision than 1 second. While this function normally returns non-decreasing values, it can return a lower value than a previous call if the system clock has been set back between the two calls.

The number returned by *time()* may be converted into a more common time format (i.e. year, month, day, hour, etc...) in UTC by passing it to *gmtime()* function or in local time by passing it to the *localtime()* function. In both cases a *struct_time* object is returned, from which the components of the calendar date may be accessed as attributes.

time.tzset()

Resets the time conversion rules used by the library routines. The environment variable `TZ` specifies how this is done.

Availability: Unix.

Note: Although in many cases, changing the `TZ` environment variable may affect the output of functions like *localtime()* without calling *tzset()*, this behavior should not be relied on.

The `TZ` environment variable should contain no whitespace.

The standard format of the `TZ` environment variable is (whitespace added for clarity):

```
std offset [dst [offset [,start[/time], end[/time]]]]
```

Where the components are:

std and dst Three or more alphanumerics giving the timezone abbreviations. These will be propagated into time.tzname

offset The offset has the form: ± `hh[:mm[:ss]]`. This indicates the value added the local time to arrive at UTC. If preceded by a '-', the timezone is east of the Prime Meridian; otherwise, it is west. If no offset follows dst, summer time is assumed to be one hour ahead of standard time.

start[/time], end[/time] Indicates when to change to and back from DST. The format of the start and end dates are one of the following:

Jn The Julian day *n* (1 <= *n* <= 365). Leap days are not counted, so in all years February 28 is day 59 and March 1 is day 60.

n The zero-based Julian day (0 <= *n* <= 365). Leap days are counted, and it is possible to refer to February 29.

Mm.n.d The *d*'th day (0 <= *d* <= 6) of week *n* of month *m* of the year (1 <= *n* <= 5, 1 <= *m* <= 12, where week 5 means "the last *d* day in month *m*" which may occur in either the fourth or the fifth week). Week 1 is the first week in which the *d*'th day occurs. Day zero is a Sunday.

`time` has the same format as `offset` except that no leading sign ('-' or '+') is allowed. The default, if time is not given, is 02:00:00.

```
>>> os.environ['TZ'] = 'EST+05EDT,M4.1.0,M10.5.0'
>>> time.tzset()
>>> time.strftime('%X %x %Z')
'02:07:36 05/08/03 EDT'
>>> os.environ['TZ'] = 'AEST-10AEDT-11,M10.5.0,M3.5.0'
>>> time.tzset()
>>> time.strftime('%X %x %Z')
'16:08:12 05/08/03 AEST'
```

On many Unix systems (including *BSD, Linux, Solaris, and Darwin), it is more convenient to use the system's zoneinfo (*tzfile(5)*) database to specify the timezone rules. To do this, set the `TZ` environment variable to the path of the required timezone datafile, relative to the root of the systems 'zoneinfo' timezone database, usually located at `/usr/share/zoneinfo`. For example, `'US/Eastern'`, `'Australia/Melbourne'`, `'Egypt'` or `'Europe/Amsterdam'`.

```
>>> os.environ['TZ'] = 'US/Eastern'
>>> time.tzset()
>>> time.tzname
('EST', 'EDT')
>>> os.environ['TZ'] = 'Egypt'
>>> time.tzset()
>>> time.tzname
('EET', 'EEST')
```

16.3.2 Clock ID Constants

These constants are used as parameters for *clock_getres()* and *clock_gettime()*.

`time.CLOCK_HIGHRES`
The Solaris OS has a `CLOCK_HIGHRES` timer that attempts to use an optimal hardware source, and may give close to nanosecond resolution. `CLOCK_HIGHRES` is the nonadjustable, high-resolution clock.

Availability: Solaris.

New in version 3.3.

`time.CLOCK_MONOTONIC`
Clock that cannot be set and represents monotonic time since some unspecified starting point.

Availability: Unix.

New in version 3.3.

`time.CLOCK_MONOTONIC_RAW`
Similar to *CLOCK_MONOTONIC*, but provides access to a raw hardware-based time that is not subject to NTP adjustments.

Availability: Linux 2.6.28 or later.

New in version 3.3.

`time.CLOCK_PROCESS_CPUTIME_ID`
High-resolution per-process timer from the CPU.

Availability: Unix.

New in version 3.3.

`time.CLOCK_THREAD_CPUTIME_ID`
Thread-specific CPU-time clock.

Availability: Unix.

New in version 3.3.

The following constant is the only parameter that can be sent to *clock_settime()*.

`time.CLOCK_REALTIME`
System-wide real-time clock. Setting this clock requires appropriate privileges.

Availability: Unix.

New in version 3.3.

16.3.3 Timezone Constants

`time.altzone`
The offset of the local DST timezone, in seconds west of UTC, if one is defined. This is negative if the local DST timezone is east of UTC (as in Western Europe, including the UK). Only use this if `daylight` is nonzero. See note below.

`time.daylight`
Nonzero if a DST timezone is defined. See note below.

`time.timezone`
The offset of the local (non-DST) timezone, in seconds west of UTC (negative in most of Western Europe, positive in the US, zero in the UK). See note below.

`time.tzname`
A tuple of two strings: the first is the name of the local non-DST timezone, the second is the name of the local DST timezone. If no DST timezone is defined, the second string should not be used. See note below.

Note: For the above Timezone constants (*altzone*, *daylight*, *timezone*, and *tzname*), the value is determined by the timezone rules in effect at module load time or the last time *tzset()* is called and may be incorrect for times in the past. It is recommended to use the `tm_gmtoff` and `tm_zone` results from *localtime()* to obtain timezone information.

See also:

Module `datetime` More object-oriented interface to dates and times.

Module `locale` Internationalization services. The locale setting affects the interpretation of many format specifiers in *strftime()* and *strptime()*.

Module `calendar` General calendar-related functions. *timegm()* is the inverse of *gmtime()* from this module.

16.4 `argparse` — Parser for command-line options, arguments and sub-commands

New in version 3.2.

Source code: Lib/argparse.py

Tutorial

This page contains the API reference information. For a more gentle introduction to Python command-line parsing, have a look at the argparse tutorial.

The *argparse* module makes it easy to write user-friendly command-line interfaces. The program defines what arguments it requires, and *argparse* will figure out how to parse those out of *sys.argv*. The *argparse* module also automatically generates help and usage messages and issues errors when users give the program invalid arguments.

16.4.1 Example

The following code is a Python program that takes a list of integers and produces either the sum or the max:

```
import argparse

parser = argparse.ArgumentParser(description='Process some integers.')
parser.add_argument('integers', metavar='N', type=int, nargs='+',
                    help='an integer for the accumulator')
parser.add_argument('--sum', dest='accumulate', action='store_const',
                    const=sum, default=max,
                    help='sum the integers (default: find the max)')

args = parser.parse_args()
print(args.accumulate(args.integers))
```

Assuming the Python code above is saved into a file called `prog.py`, it can be run at the command line and provides useful help messages:

```
$ python prog.py -h
usage: prog.py [-h] [--sum] N [N ...]

Process some integers.

positional arguments:
 N           an integer for the accumulator

optional arguments:
 -h, --help  show this help message and exit
 --sum       sum the integers (default: find the max)
```

When run with the appropriate arguments, it prints either the sum or the max of the command-line integers:

```
$ python prog.py 1 2 3 4
4

$ python prog.py 1 2 3 4 --sum
10
```

If invalid arguments are passed in, it will issue an error:

```
$ python prog.py a b c
usage: prog.py [-h] [--sum] N [N ...]
prog.py: error: argument N: invalid int value: 'a'
```

The following sections walk you through this example.

Creating a parser

The first step in using the *argparse* is creating an *ArgumentParser* object:

```
>>> parser = argparse.ArgumentParser(description='Process some integers.')
```

The *ArgumentParser* object will hold all the information necessary to parse the command line into Python data types.

Adding arguments

Filling an *ArgumentParser* with information about program arguments is done by making calls to the *add_argument()* method. Generally, these calls tell the *ArgumentParser* how to take the strings on the command line and turn them into objects. This information is stored and used when *parse_args()* is called. For example:

```
>>> parser.add_argument('integers', metavar='N', type=int, nargs='+',
...                     help='an integer for the accumulator')
>>> parser.add_argument('--sum', dest='accumulate', action='store_const',
...                     const=sum, default=max,
...                     help='sum the integers (default: find the max)')
```

Later, calling *parse_args()* will return an object with two attributes, `integers` and `accumulate`. The `integers` attribute will be a list of one or more ints, and the `accumulate` attribute will be either the *sum()* function, if `--sum` was specified at the command line, or the *max()* function if it was not.

Parsing arguments

ArgumentParser parses arguments through the *parse_args()* method. This will inspect the command line, convert each argument to the appropriate type and then invoke the appropriate action. In most cases, this means a simple *Namespace* object will be built up from attributes parsed out of the command line:

```
>>> parser.parse_args(['--sum', '7', '-1', '42'])
Namespace(accumulate=<built-in function sum>, integers=[7, -1, 42])
```

In a script, *parse_args()* will typically be called with no arguments, and the *ArgumentParser* will automatically determine the command-line arguments from *sys.argv*.

16.4.2 ArgumentParser objects

class argparse.ArgumentParser(*prog=None, usage=None, description=None, epilog=None, parents=[], formatter_class=argparse.HelpFormatter, prefix_chars='-', fromfile_prefix_chars=None, argument_default=None, conflict_handler='error', add_help=True, allow_abbrev=True*)

Create a new *ArgumentParser* object. All parameters should be passed as keyword arguments. Each parameter has its own more detailed description below, but in short they are:

- *prog* - The name of the program (default: `sys.argv[0]`)
- *usage* - The string describing the program usage (default: generated from arguments added to parser)
- *description* - Text to display before the argument help (default: none)
- *epilog* - Text to display after the argument help (default: none)

- *parents* - A list of `ArgumentParser` objects whose arguments should also be included
- *formatter_class* - A class for customizing the help output
- *prefix_chars* - The set of characters that prefix optional arguments (default: '-')
- *fromfile_prefix_chars* - The set of characters that prefix files from which additional arguments should be read (default: `None`)
- *argument_default* - The global default value for arguments (default: `None`)
- *conflict_handler* - The strategy for resolving conflicting optionals (usually unnecessary)
- *add_help* - Add a `-h/--help` option to the parser (default: `True`)
- *allow_abbrev* - Allows long options to be abbreviated if the abbreviation is unambiguous. (default: `True`)

Changed in version 3.5: *allow_abbrev* parameter was added.

The following sections describe how each of these are used.

prog

By default, `ArgumentParser` objects use `sys.argv[0]` to determine how to display the name of the program in help messages. This default is almost always desirable because it will make the help messages match how the program was invoked on the command line. For example, consider a file named `myprogram.py` with the following code:

```
import argparse
parser = argparse.ArgumentParser()
parser.add_argument('--foo', help='foo help')
args = parser.parse_args()
```

The help for this program will display `myprogram.py` as the program name (regardless of where the program was invoked from):

```
$ python myprogram.py --help
usage: myprogram.py [-h] [--foo FOO]

optional arguments:
 -h, --help  show this help message and exit
 --foo FOO   foo help
$ cd ..
$ python subdir/myprogram.py --help
usage: myprogram.py [-h] [--foo FOO]

optional arguments:
 -h, --help  show this help message and exit
 --foo FOO   foo help
```

To change this default behavior, another value can be supplied using the `prog=` argument to `ArgumentParser`:

```
>>> parser = argparse.ArgumentParser(prog='myprogram')
>>> parser.print_help()
usage: myprogram [-h]

optional arguments:
 -h, --help  show this help message and exit
```

Note that the program name, whether determined from `sys.argv[0]` or from the `prog=` argument, is available to help messages using the `%(prog)s` format specifier.

```
>>> parser = argparse.ArgumentParser(prog='myprogram')
>>> parser.add_argument('--foo', help='foo of the %(prog)s program')
>>> parser.print_help()
usage: myprogram [-h] [--foo FOO]

optional arguments:
 -h, --help  show this help message and exit
 --foo FOO   foo of the myprogram program
```

usage

By default, *ArgumentParser* calculates the usage message from the arguments it contains:

```
>>> parser = argparse.ArgumentParser(prog='PROG')
>>> parser.add_argument('--foo', nargs='?', help='foo help')
>>> parser.add_argument('bar', nargs='+', help='bar help')
>>> parser.print_help()
usage: PROG [-h] [--foo [FOO]] bar [bar ...]

positional arguments:
 bar          bar help

optional arguments:
 -h, --help   show this help message and exit
 --foo [FOO]  foo help
```

The default message can be overridden with the `usage=` keyword argument:

```
>>> parser = argparse.ArgumentParser(prog='PROG', usage='%(prog)s [options]')
>>> parser.add_argument('--foo', nargs='?', help='foo help')
>>> parser.add_argument('bar', nargs='+', help='bar help')
>>> parser.print_help()
usage: PROG [options]

positional arguments:
 bar          bar help

optional arguments:
 -h, --help   show this help message and exit
 --foo [FOO]  foo help
```

The `%(prog)s` format specifier is available to fill in the program name in your usage messages.

description

Most calls to the *ArgumentParser* constructor will use the `description=` keyword argument. This argument gives a brief description of what the program does and how it works. In help messages, the description is displayed between the command-line usage string and the help messages for the various arguments:

```
>>> parser = argparse.ArgumentParser(description='A foo that bars')
>>> parser.print_help()
usage: argparse.py [-h]
```

```
A foo that bars

optional arguments:
 -h, --help  show this help message and exit
```

By default, the description will be line-wrapped so that it fits within the given space. To change this behavior, see the *formatter_class* argument.

epilog

Some programs like to display additional description of the program after the description of the arguments. Such text can be specified using the **epilog=** argument to *ArgumentParser*:

```
>>> parser = argparse.ArgumentParser(
...     description='A foo that bars',
...     epilog="And that's how you'd foo a bar")
>>> parser.print_help()
usage: argparse.py [-h]

A foo that bars

optional arguments:
 -h, --help  show this help message and exit

And that's how you'd foo a bar
```

As with the *description* argument, the **epilog=** text is by default line-wrapped, but this behavior can be adjusted with the *formatter_class* argument to *ArgumentParser*.

parents

Sometimes, several parsers share a common set of arguments. Rather than repeating the definitions of these arguments, a single parser with all the shared arguments and passed to **parents=** argument to *ArgumentParser* can be used. The **parents=** argument takes a list of *ArgumentParser* objects, collects all the positional and optional actions from them, and adds these actions to the *ArgumentParser* object being constructed:

```
>>> parent_parser = argparse.ArgumentParser(add_help=False)
>>> parent_parser.add_argument('--parent', type=int)

>>> foo_parser = argparse.ArgumentParser(parents=[parent_parser])
>>> foo_parser.add_argument('foo')
>>> foo_parser.parse_args(['--parent', '2', 'XXX'])
Namespace(foo='XXX', parent=2)

>>> bar_parser = argparse.ArgumentParser(parents=[parent_parser])
>>> bar_parser.add_argument('--bar')
>>> bar_parser.parse_args(['--bar', 'YYY'])
Namespace(bar='YYY', parent=None)
```

Note that most parent parsers will specify **add_help=False**. Otherwise, the *ArgumentParser* will see two **-h/--help** options (one in the parent and one in the child) and raise an error.

Note: You must fully initialize the parsers before passing them via **parents=**. If you change the parent parsers after the child parser, those changes will not be reflected in the child.

---

formatter_class

ArgumentParser objects allow the help formatting to be customized by specifying an alternate formatting class. Currently, there are four such classes:

class argparse.RawDescriptionHelpFormatter
class argparse.RawTextHelpFormatter
class argparse.ArgumentDefaultsHelpFormatter
class argparse.MetavarTypeHelpFormatter

RawDescriptionHelpFormatter and *RawTextHelpFormatter* give more control over how textual descriptions are displayed. By default, *ArgumentParser* objects line-wrap the *description* and *epilog* texts in command-line help messages:

```
>>> parser = argparse.ArgumentParser(
...     prog='PROG',
...     description='''this description
...         was indented weird
...             but that is okay''',
...     epilog='''
...             likewise for this epilog whose whitespace will
...         be cleaned up and whose words will be wrapped
...         across a couple lines''')
>>> parser.print_help()
usage: PROG [-h]

this description was indented weird but that is okay

optional arguments:
 -h, --help  show this help message and exit

likewise for this epilog whose whitespace will be cleaned up and whose words
will be wrapped across a couple lines
```

Passing *RawDescriptionHelpFormatter* as **formatter_class=** indicates that *description* and *epilog* are already correctly formatted and should not be line-wrapped:

```
>>> parser = argparse.ArgumentParser(
...     prog='PROG',
...     formatter_class=argparse.RawDescriptionHelpFormatter,
...     description=textwrap.dedent('''\
...         Please do not mess up this text!
...         --------------------------------
...             I have indented it
...             exactly the way
...             I want it
...         '''))
>>> parser.print_help()
usage: PROG [-h]

Please do not mess up this text!
--------------------------------
   I have indented it
```

```
   exactly the way
   I want it

optional arguments:
 -h, --help  show this help message and exit
```

RawTextHelpFormatter maintains whitespace for all sorts of help text, including argument descriptions. However, multiple new lines are replaced with one. If you wish to preserve multiple blank lines, add spaces between the newlines.

ArgumentDefaultsHelpFormatter automatically adds information about default values to each of the argument help messages:

```
>>> parser = argparse.ArgumentParser(
...     prog='PROG',
...     formatter_class=argparse.ArgumentDefaultsHelpFormatter)
>>> parser.add_argument('--foo', type=int, default=42, help='FOO!')
>>> parser.add_argument('bar', nargs='*', default=[1, 2, 3], help='BAR!')
>>> parser.print_help()
usage: PROG [-h] [--foo FOO] [bar [bar ...]]

positional arguments:
 bar         BAR! (default: [1, 2, 3])

optional arguments:
 -h, --help  show this help message and exit
 --foo FOO   FOO! (default: 42)
```

MetavarTypeHelpFormatter uses the name of the *type* argument for each argument as the display name for its values (rather than using the *dest* as the regular formatter does):

```
>>> parser = argparse.ArgumentParser(
...     prog='PROG',
...     formatter_class=argparse.MetavarTypeHelpFormatter)
>>> parser.add_argument('--foo', type=int)
>>> parser.add_argument('bar', type=float)
>>> parser.print_help()
usage: PROG [-h] [--foo int] float

positional arguments:
  float

optional arguments:
  -h, --help  show this help message and exit
  --foo int
```

prefix_chars

Most command-line options will use `-` as the prefix, e.g. `-f/--foo`. Parsers that need to support different or additional prefix characters, e.g. for options like `+f` or `/foo`, may specify them using the `prefix_chars=` argument to the ArgumentParser constructor:

```
>>> parser = argparse.ArgumentParser(prog='PROG', prefix_chars='-+')
>>> parser.add_argument('+f')
>>> parser.add_argument('++bar')
>>> parser.parse_args('+f X ++bar Y'.split())
Namespace(bar='Y', f='X')
```

The `prefix_chars=` argument defaults to `'-'`. Supplying a set of characters that does not include `-` will cause `-f/--foo` options to be disallowed.

fromfile_prefix_chars

Sometimes, for example when dealing with a particularly long argument lists, it may make sense to keep the list of arguments in a file rather than typing it out at the command line. If the `fromfile_prefix_chars=` argument is given to the *ArgumentParser* constructor, then arguments that start with any of the specified characters will be treated as files, and will be replaced by the arguments they contain. For example:

```
>>> with open('args.txt', 'w') as fp:
...     fp.write('-f\nbar')
>>> parser = argparse.ArgumentParser(fromfile_prefix_chars='@')
>>> parser.add_argument('-f')
>>> parser.parse_args(['-f', 'foo', '@args.txt'])
Namespace(f='bar')
```

Arguments read from a file must by default be one per line (but see also *convert_arg_line_to_args()*) and are treated as if they were in the same place as the original file referencing argument on the command line. So in the example above, the expression `['-f', 'foo', '@args.txt']` is considered equivalent to the expression `['-f', 'foo', '-f', 'bar']`.

The `fromfile_prefix_chars=` argument defaults to `None`, meaning that arguments will never be treated as file references.

argument_default

Generally, argument defaults are specified either by passing a default to *add_argument()* or by calling the *set_defaults()* methods with a specific set of name-value pairs. Sometimes however, it may be useful to specify a single parser-wide default for arguments. This can be accomplished by passing the `argument_default=` keyword argument to *ArgumentParser*. For example, to globally suppress attribute creation on *parse_args()* calls, we supply `argument_default=SUPPRESS`:

```
>>> parser = argparse.ArgumentParser(argument_default=argparse.SUPPRESS)
>>> parser.add_argument('--foo')
>>> parser.add_argument('bar', nargs='?')
>>> parser.parse_args(['--foo', '1', 'BAR'])
Namespace(bar='BAR', foo='1')
>>> parser.parse_args([])
Namespace()
```

allow_abbrev

Normally, when you pass an argument list to the *parse_args()* method of an *ArgumentParser*, it *recognizes abbreviations* of long options.

This feature can be disabled by setting `allow_abbrev` to `False`:

```
>>> parser = argparse.ArgumentParser(prog='PROG', allow_abbrev=False)
>>> parser.add_argument('--foobar', action='store_true')
>>> parser.add_argument('--foonley', action='store_false')
>>> parser.parse_args(['--foon'])
usage: PROG [-h] [--foobar] [--foonley]
PROG: error: unrecognized arguments: --foon
```

New in version 3.5.

conflict_handler

ArgumentParser objects do not allow two actions with the same option string. By default, *ArgumentParser* objects raise an exception if an attempt is made to create an argument with an option string that is already in use:

```
>>> parser = argparse.ArgumentParser(prog='PROG')
>>> parser.add_argument('-f', '--foo', help='old foo help')
>>> parser.add_argument('--foo', help='new foo help')
Traceback (most recent call last):
 ..
ArgumentError: argument --foo: conflicting option string(s): --foo
```

Sometimes (e.g. when using *parents*) it may be useful to simply override any older arguments with the same option string. To get this behavior, the value `'resolve'` can be supplied to the `conflict_handler=` argument of *ArgumentParser*:

```
>>> parser = argparse.ArgumentParser(prog='PROG', conflict_handler='resolve')
>>> parser.add_argument('-f', '--foo', help='old foo help')
>>> parser.add_argument('--foo', help='new foo help')
>>> parser.print_help()
usage: PROG [-h] [-f FOO] [--foo FOO]

optional arguments:
 -h, --help  show this help message and exit
 -f FOO      old foo help
 --foo FOO   new foo help
```

Note that *ArgumentParser* objects only remove an action if all of its option strings are overridden. So, in the example above, the old `-f/--foo` action is retained as the `-f` action, because only the `--foo` option string was overridden.

add_help

By default, ArgumentParser objects add an option which simply displays the parser's help message. For example, consider a file named `myprogram.py` containing the following code:

```
import argparse
parser = argparse.ArgumentParser()
parser.add_argument('--foo', help='foo help')
args = parser.parse_args()
```

If `-h` or `--help` is supplied at the command line, the ArgumentParser help will be printed:

```
$ python myprogram.py --help
usage: myprogram.py [-h] [--foo FOO]

optional arguments:
 -h, --help  show this help message and exit
 --foo FOO   foo help
```

Occasionally, it may be useful to disable the addition of this help option. This can be achieved by passing `False` as the `add_help=` argument to *ArgumentParser*:

```
>>> parser = argparse.ArgumentParser(prog='PROG', add_help=False)
>>> parser.add_argument('--foo', help='foo help')
>>> parser.print_help()
usage: PROG [--foo FOO]

optional arguments:
 --foo FOO  foo help
```

The help option is typically `-h/--help`. The exception to this is if the `prefix_chars=` is specified and does not include `-`, in which case `-h` and `--help` are not valid options. In this case, the first character in `prefix_chars` is used to prefix the help options:

```
>>> parser = argparse.ArgumentParser(prog='PROG', prefix_chars='+/')
>>> parser.print_help()
usage: PROG [+h]

optional arguments:
  +h, ++help  show this help message and exit
```

16.4.3 The add_argument() method

`ArgumentParser.add_argument`(*name or flags...*[, *action*][, *nargs*][, *const*][, *default*][, *type*][, *choices*][, *required*][, *help*][, *metavar*][, *dest*])

Define how a single command-line argument should be parsed. Each parameter has its own more detailed description below, but in short they are:

- *name or flags* - Either a name or a list of option strings, e.g. `foo` or `-f, --foo`.
- *action* - The basic type of action to be taken when this argument is encountered at the command line.
- *nargs* - The number of command-line arguments that should be consumed.
- *const* - A constant value required by some *action* and *nargs* selections.
- *default* - The value produced if the argument is absent from the command line.
- *type* - The type to which the command-line argument should be converted.
- *choices* - A container of the allowable values for the argument.
- *required* - Whether or not the command-line option may be omitted (optionals only).
- *help* - A brief description of what the argument does.
- *metavar* - A name for the argument in usage messages.
- *dest* - The name of the attribute to be added to the object returned by *parse_args()*.

The following sections describe how each of these are used.

name or flags

The *add_argument()* method must know whether an optional argument, like `-f` or `--foo`, or a positional argument, like a list of filenames, is expected. The first arguments passed to *add_argument()* must therefore be either a series of flags, or a simple argument name. For example, an optional argument could be created like:

```
>>> parser.add_argument('-f', '--foo')
```

while a positional argument could be created like:

```
>>> parser.add_argument('bar')
```

When *parse_args()* is called, optional arguments will be identified by the - prefix, and the remaining arguments will be assumed to be positional:

```
>>> parser = argparse.ArgumentParser(prog='PROG')
>>> parser.add_argument('-f', '--foo')
>>> parser.add_argument('bar')
>>> parser.parse_args(['BAR'])
Namespace(bar='BAR', foo=None)
>>> parser.parse_args(['BAR', '--foo', 'FOO'])
Namespace(bar='BAR', foo='FOO')
>>> parser.parse_args(['--foo', 'FOO'])
usage: PROG [-h] [-f FOO] bar
PROG: error: too few arguments
```

action

ArgumentParser objects associate command-line arguments with actions. These actions can do just about anything with the command-line arguments associated with them, though most actions simply add an attribute to the object returned by *parse_args()*. The `action` keyword argument specifies how the command-line arguments should be handled. The supplied actions are:

- `'store'` - This just stores the argument's value. This is the default action. For example:

```
>>> parser = argparse.ArgumentParser()
>>> parser.add_argument('--foo')
>>> parser.parse_args('--foo 1'.split())
Namespace(foo='1')
```

- `'store_const'` - This stores the value specified by the *const* keyword argument. The `'store_const'` action is most commonly used with optional arguments that specify some sort of flag. For example:

```
>>> parser = argparse.ArgumentParser()
>>> parser.add_argument('--foo', action='store_const', const=42)
>>> parser.parse_args(['--foo'])
Namespace(foo=42)
```

- `'store_true'` and `'store_false'` - These are special cases of `'store_const'` used for storing the values `True` and `False` respectively. In addition, they create default values of `False` and `True` respectively. For example:

```
>>> parser = argparse.ArgumentParser()
>>> parser.add_argument('--foo', action='store_true')
>>> parser.add_argument('--bar', action='store_false')
>>> parser.add_argument('--baz', action='store_false')
>>> parser.parse_args('--foo --bar'.split())
Namespace(foo=True, bar=False, baz=True)
```

- `'append'` - This stores a list, and appends each argument value to the list. This is useful to allow an option to be specified multiple times. Example usage:

```
>>> parser = argparse.ArgumentParser()
>>> parser.add_argument('--foo', action='append')
```

```
>>> parser.parse_args('--foo 1 --foo 2'.split())
Namespace(foo=['1', '2'])
```

- `'append_const'` - This stores a list, and appends the value specified by the *const* keyword argument to the list. (Note that the *const* keyword argument defaults to `None`.) The `'append_const'` action is typically useful when multiple arguments need to store constants to the same list. For example:

```
>>> parser = argparse.ArgumentParser()
>>> parser.add_argument('--str', dest='types', action='append_const', const=str)
>>> parser.add_argument('--int', dest='types', action='append_const', const=int)
>>> parser.parse_args('--str --int'.split())
Namespace(types=[<class 'str'>, <class 'int'>])
```

- `'count'` - This counts the number of times a keyword argument occurs. For example, this is useful for increasing verbosity levels:

```
>>> parser = argparse.ArgumentParser()
>>> parser.add_argument('--verbose', '-v', action='count')
>>> parser.parse_args(['-vvv'])
Namespace(verbose=3)
```

- `'help'` - This prints a complete help message for all the options in the current parser and then exits. By default a help action is automatically added to the parser. See `ArgumentParser` for details of how the output is created.
- `'version'` - This expects a `version=` keyword argument in the `add_argument()` call, and prints version information and exits when invoked:

```
>>> import argparse
>>> parser = argparse.ArgumentParser(prog='PROG')
>>> parser.add_argument('--version', action='version', version='%(prog)s 2.0')
>>> parser.parse_args(['--version'])
PROG 2.0
```

You may also specify an arbitrary action by passing an Action subclass or other object that implements the same interface. The recommended way to do this is to extend `Action`, overriding the `__call__` method and optionally the `__init__` method.

An example of a custom action:

```
>>> class FooAction(argparse.Action):
...     def __init__(self, option_strings, dest, nargs=None, **kwargs):
...         if nargs is not None:
...             raise ValueError("nargs not allowed")
...         super(FooAction, self).__init__(option_strings, dest, **kwargs)
...     def __call__(self, parser, namespace, values, option_string=None):
...         print('%r %r %r' % (namespace, values, option_string))
...         setattr(namespace, self.dest, values)
...
>>> parser = argparse.ArgumentParser()
>>> parser.add_argument('--foo', action=FooAction)
>>> parser.add_argument('bar', action=FooAction)
>>> args = parser.parse_args('1 --foo 2'.split())
Namespace(bar=None, foo=None) '1' None
Namespace(bar='1', foo=None) '2' '--foo'
>>> args
Namespace(bar='1', foo='2')
```

For more details, see `Action`.

nargs

ArgumentParser objects usually associate a single command-line argument with a single action to be taken. The **nargs** keyword argument associates a different number of command-line arguments with a single action. The supported values are:

- N (an integer). N arguments from the command line will be gathered together into a list. For example:

```
>>> parser = argparse.ArgumentParser()
>>> parser.add_argument('--foo', nargs=2)
>>> parser.add_argument('bar', nargs=1)
>>> parser.parse_args('c --foo a b'.split())
Namespace(bar=['c'], foo=['a', 'b'])
```

  Note that **nargs=1** produces a list of one item. This is different from the default, in which the item is produced by itself.

- '?'. One argument will be consumed from the command line if possible, and produced as a single item. If no command-line argument is present, the value from *default* will be produced. Note that for optional arguments, there is an additional case - the option string is present but not followed by a command-line argument. In this case the value from *const* will be produced. Some examples to illustrate this:

```
>>> parser = argparse.ArgumentParser()
>>> parser.add_argument('--foo', nargs='?', const='c', default='d')
>>> parser.add_argument('bar', nargs='?', default='d')
>>> parser.parse_args(['XX', '--foo', 'YY'])
Namespace(bar='XX', foo='YY')
>>> parser.parse_args(['XX', '--foo'])
Namespace(bar='XX', foo='c')
>>> parser.parse_args([])
Namespace(bar='d', foo='d')
```

  One of the more common uses of **nargs='?'** is to allow optional input and output files:

```
>>> parser = argparse.ArgumentParser()
>>> parser.add_argument('infile', nargs='?', type=argparse.FileType('r'),
...                     default=sys.stdin)
>>> parser.add_argument('outfile', nargs='?', type=argparse.FileType('w'),
...                     default=sys.stdout)
>>> parser.parse_args(['input.txt', 'output.txt'])
Namespace(infile=<_io.TextIOWrapper name='input.txt' encoding='UTF-8'>,
          outfile=<_io.TextIOWrapper name='output.txt' encoding='UTF-8'>)
>>> parser.parse_args([])
Namespace(infile=<_io.TextIOWrapper name='<stdin>' encoding='UTF-8'>,
          outfile=<_io.TextIOWrapper name='<stdout>' encoding='UTF-8'>)
```

- '*'. All command-line arguments present are gathered into a list. Note that it generally doesn't make much sense to have more than one positional argument with **nargs='*'**, but multiple optional arguments with **nargs='*'** is possible. For example:

```
>>> parser = argparse.ArgumentParser()
>>> parser.add_argument('--foo', nargs='*')
>>> parser.add_argument('--bar', nargs='*')
>>> parser.add_argument('baz', nargs='*')
>>> parser.parse_args('a b --foo x y --bar 1 2'.split())
Namespace(bar=['1', '2'], baz=['a', 'b'], foo=['x', 'y'])
```

- `'+'`. Just like `'*'`, all command-line args present are gathered into a list. Additionally, an error message will be generated if there wasn't at least one command-line argument present. For example:

```
>>> parser = argparse.ArgumentParser(prog='PROG')
>>> parser.add_argument('foo', nargs='+')
>>> parser.parse_args(['a', 'b'])
Namespace(foo=['a', 'b'])
>>> parser.parse_args([])
usage: PROG [-h] foo [foo ...]
PROG: error: too few arguments
```

- `argparse.REMAINDER`. All the remaining command-line arguments are gathered into a list. This is commonly useful for command line utilities that dispatch to other command line utilities:

```
>>> parser = argparse.ArgumentParser(prog='PROG')
>>> parser.add_argument('--foo')
>>> parser.add_argument('command')
>>> parser.add_argument('args', nargs=argparse.REMAINDER)
>>> print(parser.parse_args('--foo B cmd --arg1 XX ZZ'.split()))
Namespace(args=['--arg1', 'XX', 'ZZ'], command='cmd', foo='B')
```

If the `nargs` keyword argument is not provided, the number of arguments consumed is determined by the *action*. Generally this means a single command-line argument will be consumed and a single item (not a list) will be produced.

const

The `const` argument of *add_argument()* is used to hold constant values that are not read from the command line but are required for the various *ArgumentParser* actions. The two most common uses of it are:

- When *add_argument()* is called with `action='store_const'` or `action='append_const'`. These actions add the `const` value to one of the attributes of the object returned by *parse_args()*. See the *action* description for examples.
- When *add_argument()* is called with option strings (like `-f` or `--foo`) and `nargs='?'`. This creates an optional argument that can be followed by zero or one command-line arguments. When parsing the command line, if the option string is encountered with no command-line argument following it, the value of `const` will be assumed instead. See the *nargs* description for examples.

With the `'store_const'` and `'append_const'` actions, the `const` keyword argument must be given. For other actions, it defaults to `None`.

default

All optional arguments and some positional arguments may be omitted at the command line. The `default` keyword argument of *add_argument()*, whose value defaults to `None`, specifies what value should be used if the command-line argument is not present. For optional arguments, the `default` value is used when the option string was not present at the command line:

```
>>> parser = argparse.ArgumentParser()
>>> parser.add_argument('--foo', default=42)
>>> parser.parse_args(['--foo', '2'])
Namespace(foo='2')
>>> parser.parse_args([])
Namespace(foo=42)
```

If the `default` value is a string, the parser parses the value as if it were a command-line argument. In particular, the parser applies any *type* conversion argument, if provided, before setting the attribute on the *Namespace* return value. Otherwise, the parser uses the value as is:

```
>>> parser = argparse.ArgumentParser()
>>> parser.add_argument('--length', default='10', type=int)
>>> parser.add_argument('--width', default=10.5, type=int)
>>> parser.parse_args()
Namespace(length=10, width=10.5)
```

For positional arguments with *nargs* equal to `?` or `*`, the `default` value is used when no command-line argument was present:

```
>>> parser = argparse.ArgumentParser()
>>> parser.add_argument('foo', nargs='?', default=42)
>>> parser.parse_args(['a'])
Namespace(foo='a')
>>> parser.parse_args([])
Namespace(foo=42)
```

Providing `default=argparse.SUPPRESS` causes no attribute to be added if the command-line argument was not present.:

```
>>> parser = argparse.ArgumentParser()
>>> parser.add_argument('--foo', default=argparse.SUPPRESS)
>>> parser.parse_args([])
Namespace()
>>> parser.parse_args(['--foo', '1'])
Namespace(foo='1')
```

type

By default, *ArgumentParser* objects read command-line arguments in as simple strings. However, quite often the command-line string should instead be interpreted as another type, like a *float* or *int*. The `type` keyword argument of *add_argument()* allows any necessary type-checking and type conversions to be performed. Common built-in types and functions can be used directly as the value of the `type` argument:

```
>>> parser = argparse.ArgumentParser()
>>> parser.add_argument('foo', type=int)
>>> parser.add_argument('bar', type=open)
>>> parser.parse_args('2 temp.txt'.split())
Namespace(bar=<_io.TextIOWrapper name='temp.txt' encoding='UTF-8'>, foo=2)
```

See the section on the *default* keyword argument for information on when the `type` argument is applied to default arguments.

To ease the use of various types of files, the argparse module provides the factory FileType which takes the `mode=`, `bufsize=`, `encoding=` and `errors=` arguments of the *open()* function. For example, `FileType('w')` can be used to create a writable file:

```
>>> parser = argparse.ArgumentParser()
>>> parser.add_argument('bar', type=argparse.FileType('w'))
>>> parser.parse_args(['out.txt'])
Namespace(bar=<_io.TextIOWrapper name='out.txt' encoding='UTF-8'>)
```

`type=` can take any callable that takes a single string argument and returns the converted value:

```
>>> def perfect_square(string):
...     value = int(string)
...     sqrt = math.sqrt(value)
...     if sqrt != int(sqrt):
...         msg = "%r is not a perfect square" % string
...         raise argparse.ArgumentTypeError(msg)
...     return value
...
>>> parser = argparse.ArgumentParser(prog='PROG')
>>> parser.add_argument('foo', type=perfect_square)
>>> parser.parse_args(['9'])
Namespace(foo=9)
>>> parser.parse_args(['7'])
usage: PROG [-h] foo
PROG: error: argument foo: '7' is not a perfect square
```

The *choices* keyword argument may be more convenient for type checkers that simply check against a range of values:

```
>>> parser = argparse.ArgumentParser(prog='PROG')
>>> parser.add_argument('foo', type=int, choices=range(5, 10))
>>> parser.parse_args(['7'])
Namespace(foo=7)
>>> parser.parse_args(['11'])
usage: PROG [-h] {5,6,7,8,9}
PROG: error: argument foo: invalid choice: 11 (choose from 5, 6, 7, 8, 9)
```

See the *choices* section for more details.

choices

Some command-line arguments should be selected from a restricted set of values. These can be handled by passing a container object as the *choices* keyword argument to `add_argument()`. When the command line is parsed, argument values will be checked, and an error message will be displayed if the argument was not one of the acceptable values:

```
>>> parser = argparse.ArgumentParser(prog='game.py')
>>> parser.add_argument('move', choices=['rock', 'paper', 'scissors'])
>>> parser.parse_args(['rock'])
Namespace(move='rock')
>>> parser.parse_args(['fire'])
usage: game.py [-h] {rock,paper,scissors}
game.py: error: argument move: invalid choice: 'fire' (choose from 'rock',
'paper', 'scissors')
```

Note that inclusion in the *choices* container is checked after any *type* conversions have been performed, so the type of the objects in the *choices* container should match the *type* specified:

```
>>> parser = argparse.ArgumentParser(prog='doors.py')
>>> parser.add_argument('door', type=int, choices=range(1, 4))
>>> print(parser.parse_args(['3']))
Namespace(door=3)
>>> parser.parse_args(['4'])
usage: doors.py [-h] {1,2,3}
doors.py: error: argument door: invalid choice: 4 (choose from 1, 2, 3)
```

Any object that supports the `in` operator can be passed as the *choices* value, so *dict* objects, *set* objects, custom containers, etc. are all supported.

required

In general, the *argparse* module assumes that flags like `-f` and `--bar` indicate *optional* arguments, which can always be omitted at the command line. To make an option *required*, `True` can be specified for the `required=` keyword argument to *add_argument()*:

```
>>> parser = argparse.ArgumentParser()
>>> parser.add_argument('--foo', required=True)
>>> parser.parse_args(['--foo', 'BAR'])
Namespace(foo='BAR')
>>> parser.parse_args([])
usage: argparse.py [-h] [--foo FOO]
argparse.py: error: option --foo is required
```

As the example shows, if an option is marked as `required`, *parse_args()* will report an error if that option is not present at the command line.

Note: Required options are generally considered bad form because users expect *options* to be *optional*, and thus they should be avoided when possible.

help

The `help` value is a string containing a brief description of the argument. When a user requests help (usually by using `-h` or `--help` at the command line), these `help` descriptions will be displayed with each argument:

```
>>> parser = argparse.ArgumentParser(prog='frobble')
>>> parser.add_argument('--foo', action='store_true',
...                     help='foo the bars before frobbling')
>>> parser.add_argument('bar', nargs='+',
...                     help='one of the bars to be frobbled')
>>> parser.parse_args(['-h'])
usage: frobble [-h] [--foo] bar [bar ...]

positional arguments:
 bar     one of the bars to be frobbled

optional arguments:
 -h, --help  show this help message and exit
 --foo   foo the bars before frobbling
```

The `help` strings can include various format specifiers to avoid repetition of things like the program name or the argument *default*. The available specifiers include the program name, `%(prog)s` and most keyword arguments to *add_argument()*, e.g. `%(default)s`, `%(type)s`, etc.:

```
>>> parser = argparse.ArgumentParser(prog='frobble')
>>> parser.add_argument('bar', nargs='?', type=int, default=42,
...                     help='the bar to %(prog)s (default: %(default)s)')
>>> parser.print_help()
usage: frobble [-h] [bar]

positional arguments:
```

```
bar     the bar to frobble (default: 42)

optional arguments:
 -h, --help  show this help message and exit
```

As the help string supports %-formatting, if you want a literal % to appear in the help string, you must escape it as %%.

argparse supports silencing the help entry for certain options, by setting the **help** value to **argparse.SUPPRESS**:

```
>>> parser = argparse.ArgumentParser(prog='frobble')
>>> parser.add_argument('--foo', help=argparse.SUPPRESS)
>>> parser.print_help()
usage: frobble [-h]

optional arguments:
  -h, --help  show this help message and exit
```

metavar

When *ArgumentParser* generates help messages, it needs some way to refer to each expected argument. By default, ArgumentParser objects use the *dest* value as the "name" of each object. By default, for positional argument actions, the *dest* value is used directly, and for optional argument actions, the *dest* value is uppercased. So, a single positional argument with `dest='bar'` will be referred to as `bar`. A single optional argument `--foo` that should be followed by a single command-line argument will be referred to as `FOO`. An example:

```
>>> parser = argparse.ArgumentParser()
>>> parser.add_argument('--foo')
>>> parser.add_argument('bar')
>>> parser.parse_args('X --foo Y'.split())
Namespace(bar='X', foo='Y')
>>> parser.print_help()
usage:  [-h] [--foo FOO] bar

positional arguments:
 bar

optional arguments:
 -h, --help  show this help message and exit
 --foo FOO
```

An alternative name can be specified with `metavar`:

```
>>> parser = argparse.ArgumentParser()
>>> parser.add_argument('--foo', metavar='YYY')
>>> parser.add_argument('bar', metavar='XXX')
>>> parser.parse_args('X --foo Y'.split())
Namespace(bar='X', foo='Y')
>>> parser.print_help()
usage:  [-h] [--foo YYY] XXX

positional arguments:
 XXX

optional arguments:
```

```
-h, --help  show this help message and exit
--foo YYY
```

Note that metavar only changes the *displayed* name - the name of the attribute on the *parse_args()* object is still determined by the *dest* value.

Different values of nargs may cause the metavar to be used multiple times. Providing a tuple to metavar specifies a different display for each of the arguments:

```
>>> parser = argparse.ArgumentParser(prog='PROG')
>>> parser.add_argument('-x', nargs=2)
>>> parser.add_argument('--foo', nargs=2, metavar=('bar', 'baz'))
>>> parser.print_help()
usage: PROG [-h] [-x X X] [--foo bar baz]

optional arguments:
 -h, --help     show this help message and exit
 -x X X
 --foo bar baz
```

dest

Most *ArgumentParser* actions add some value as an attribute of the object returned by *parse_args()*. The name of this attribute is determined by the dest keyword argument of *add_argument()*. For positional argument actions, dest is normally supplied as the first argument to *add_argument()*:

```
>>> parser = argparse.ArgumentParser()
>>> parser.add_argument('bar')
>>> parser.parse_args(['XXX'])
Namespace(bar='XXX')
```

For optional argument actions, the value of dest is normally inferred from the option strings. *ArgumentParser* generates the value of dest by taking the first long option string and stripping away the initial -- string. If no long option strings were supplied, dest will be derived from the first short option string by stripping the initial - character. Any internal - characters will be converted to _ characters to make sure the string is a valid attribute name. The examples below illustrate this behavior:

```
>>> parser = argparse.ArgumentParser()
>>> parser.add_argument('-f', '--foo-bar', '--foo')
>>> parser.add_argument('-x', '-y')
>>> parser.parse_args('-f 1 -x 2'.split())
Namespace(foo_bar='1', x='2')
>>> parser.parse_args('--foo 1 -y 2'.split())
Namespace(foo_bar='1', x='2')
```

dest allows a custom attribute name to be provided:

```
>>> parser = argparse.ArgumentParser()
>>> parser.add_argument('--foo', dest='bar')
>>> parser.parse_args('--foo XXX'.split())
Namespace(bar='XXX')
```

Action classes

Action classes implement the Action API, a callable which returns a callable which processes arguments from the command-line. Any object which follows this API may be passed as the action parameter to add_argument().

class argparse.Action(*option_strings, dest, nargs=None, const=None, default=None, type=None, choices=None, required=False, help=None, metavar=None*)

Action objects are used by an ArgumentParser to represent the information needed to parse a single argument from one or more strings from the command line. The Action class must accept the two positional arguments plus any keyword arguments passed to *ArgumentParser.add_argument()* except for the `action` itself.

Instances of Action (or return value of any callable to the `action` parameter) should have attributes "dest", "option_strings", "default", "type", "required", "help", etc. defined. The easiest way to ensure these attributes are defined is to call `Action.__init__`.

Action instances should be callable, so subclasses must override the `__call__` method, which should accept four parameters:

- `parser` - The ArgumentParser object which contains this action.
- `namespace` - The *Namespace* object that will be returned by *parse_args()*. Most actions add an attribute to this object using *setattr()*.
- `values` - The associated command-line arguments, with any type conversions applied. Type conversions are specified with the *type* keyword argument to *add_argument()*.
- `option_string` - The option string that was used to invoke this action. The `option_string` argument is optional, and will be absent if the action is associated with a positional argument.

The `__call__` method may perform arbitrary actions, but will typically set attributes on the `namespace` based on `dest` and `values`.

16.4.4 The parse_args() method

ArgumentParser.parse_args(*args=None, namespace=None*)

Convert argument strings to objects and assign them as attributes of the namespace. Return the populated namespace.

Previous calls to *add_argument()* determine exactly what objects are created and how they are assigned. See the documentation for *add_argument()* for details.

- *args* - List of strings to parse. The default is taken from *sys.argv*.
- *namespace* - An object to take the attributes. The default is a new empty *Namespace* object.

Option value syntax

The *parse_args()* method supports several ways of specifying the value of an option (if it takes one). In the simplest case, the option and its value are passed as two separate arguments:

```
>>> parser = argparse.ArgumentParser(prog='PROG')
>>> parser.add_argument('-x')
>>> parser.add_argument('--foo')
>>> parser.parse_args(['-x', 'X'])
Namespace(foo=None, x='X')
>>> parser.parse_args(['--foo', 'FOO'])
Namespace(foo='FOO', x=None)
```

For long options (options with names longer than a single character), the option and value can also be passed as a single command-line argument, using = to separate them:

```
>>> parser.parse_args(['--foo=FOO'])
Namespace(foo='FOO', x=None)
```

For short options (options only one character long), the option and its value can be concatenated:

```
>>> parser.parse_args(['-xX'])
Namespace(foo=None, x='X')
```

Several short options can be joined together, using only a single - prefix, as long as only the last option (or none of them) requires a value:

```
>>> parser = argparse.ArgumentParser(prog='PROG')
>>> parser.add_argument('-x', action='store_true')
>>> parser.add_argument('-y', action='store_true')
>>> parser.add_argument('-z')
>>> parser.parse_args(['-xyzZ'])
Namespace(x=True, y=True, z='Z')
```

Invalid arguments

While parsing the command line, *parse_args()* checks for a variety of errors, including ambiguous options, invalid types, invalid options, wrong number of positional arguments, etc. When it encounters such an error, it exits and prints the error along with a usage message:

```
>>> parser = argparse.ArgumentParser(prog='PROG')
>>> parser.add_argument('--foo', type=int)
>>> parser.add_argument('bar', nargs='?')

>>> # invalid type
>>> parser.parse_args(['--foo', 'spam'])
usage: PROG [-h] [--foo FOO] [bar]
PROG: error: argument --foo: invalid int value: 'spam'

>>> # invalid option
>>> parser.parse_args(['--bar'])
usage: PROG [-h] [--foo FOO] [bar]
PROG: error: no such option: --bar

>>> # wrong number of arguments
>>> parser.parse_args(['spam', 'badger'])
usage: PROG [-h] [--foo FOO] [bar]
PROG: error: extra arguments found: badger
```

Arguments containing -

The *parse_args()* method attempts to give errors whenever the user has clearly made a mistake, but some situations are inherently ambiguous. For example, the command-line argument -1 could either be an attempt to specify an option or an attempt to provide a positional argument. The *parse_args()* method is cautious here: positional arguments may only begin with - if they look like negative numbers and there are no options in the parser that look like negative numbers:

```
>>> parser = argparse.ArgumentParser(prog='PROG')
>>> parser.add_argument('-x')
>>> parser.add_argument('foo', nargs='?')

>>> # no negative number options, so -1 is a positional argument
>>> parser.parse_args(['-x', '-1'])
Namespace(foo=None, x='-1')
```

```
>>> # no negative number options, so -1 and -5 are positional arguments
>>> parser.parse_args(['-x', '-1', '-5'])
Namespace(foo='-5', x='-1')

>>> parser = argparse.ArgumentParser(prog='PROG')
>>> parser.add_argument('-1', dest='one')
>>> parser.add_argument('foo', nargs='?')

>>> # negative number options present, so -1 is an option
>>> parser.parse_args(['-1', 'X'])
Namespace(foo=None, one='X')

>>> # negative number options present, so -2 is an option
>>> parser.parse_args(['-2'])
usage: PROG [-h] [-1 ONE] [foo]
PROG: error: no such option: -2

>>> # negative number options present, so both -1s are options
>>> parser.parse_args(['-1', '-1'])
usage: PROG [-h] [-1 ONE] [foo]
PROG: error: argument -1: expected one argument
```

If you have positional arguments that must begin with - and don't look like negative numbers, you can insert the pseudo-argument `'--'` which tells *parse_args()* that everything after that is a positional argument:

```
>>> parser.parse_args(['--', '-f'])
Namespace(foo='-f', one=None)
```

Argument abbreviations (prefix matching)

The *parse_args()* method *by default* allows long options to be abbreviated to a prefix, if the abbreviation is unambiguous (the prefix matches a unique option):

```
>>> parser = argparse.ArgumentParser(prog='PROG')
>>> parser.add_argument('-bacon')
>>> parser.add_argument('-badger')
>>> parser.parse_args('-bac MMM'.split())
Namespace(bacon='MMM', badger=None)
>>> parser.parse_args('-bad WOOD'.split())
Namespace(bacon=None, badger='WOOD')
>>> parser.parse_args('-ba BA'.split())
usage: PROG [-h] [-bacon BACON] [-badger BADGER]
PROG: error: ambiguous option: -ba could match -badger, -bacon
```

An error is produced for arguments that could produce more than one options. This feature can be disabled by setting *allow_abbrev* to `False`.

Beyond `sys.argv`

Sometimes it may be useful to have an ArgumentParser parse arguments other than those of *sys.argv*. This can be accomplished by passing a list of strings to *parse_args()*. This is useful for testing at the interactive prompt:

```
>>> parser = argparse.ArgumentParser()
>>> parser.add_argument(
...     'integers', metavar='int', type=int, choices=range(10),
...     nargs='+', help='an integer in the range 0..9')
>>> parser.add_argument(
...     '--sum', dest='accumulate', action='store_const', const=sum,
...     default=max, help='sum the integers (default: find the max)')
>>> parser.parse_args(['1', '2', '3', '4'])
Namespace(accumulate=<built-in function max>, integers=[1, 2, 3, 4])
>>> parser.parse_args(['1', '2', '3', '4', '--sum'])
Namespace(accumulate=<built-in function sum>, integers=[1, 2, 3, 4])
```

The Namespace object

class argparse.Namespace

Simple class used by default by *parse_args()* to create an object holding attributes and return it.

This class is deliberately simple, just an *object* subclass with a readable string representation. If you prefer to have dict-like view of the attributes, you can use the standard Python idiom, *vars()*:

```
>>> parser = argparse.ArgumentParser()
>>> parser.add_argument('--foo')
>>> args = parser.parse_args(['--foo', 'BAR'])
>>> vars(args)
{'foo': 'BAR'}
```

It may also be useful to have an *ArgumentParser* assign attributes to an already existing object, rather than a new *Namespace* object. This can be achieved by specifying the **namespace=** keyword argument:

```
>>> class C:
...     pass
...
>>> c = C()
>>> parser = argparse.ArgumentParser()
>>> parser.add_argument('--foo')
>>> parser.parse_args(args=['--foo', 'BAR'], namespace=c)
>>> c.foo
'BAR'
```

16.4.5 Other utilities

Sub-commands

ArgumentParser.add_subparsers([*title*][, *description*][, *prog*][, *parser_class*][, *action*][, *option_string*][, *dest*][, *help*][, *metavar*])

Many programs split up their functionality into a number of sub-commands, for example, the svn program can invoke sub-commands like svn checkout, svn update, and svn commit. Splitting up functionality this way can be a particularly good idea when a program performs several different functions which require different kinds of command-line arguments. *ArgumentParser* supports the creation of such sub-commands with the *add_subparsers()* method. The *add_subparsers()* method is normally called with no arguments and returns a special action object. This object has a single method, add_parser(), which takes a command name and any *ArgumentParser* constructor arguments, and returns an *ArgumentParser* object that can be modified as usual.

Description of parameters:

- title - title for the sub-parser group in help output; by default "subcommands" if description is provided, otherwise uses title for positional arguments
- description - description for the sub-parser group in help output, by default `None`
- prog - usage information that will be displayed with sub-command help, by default the name of the program and any positional arguments before the subparser argument
- parser_class - class which will be used to create sub-parser instances, by default the class of the current parser (e.g. ArgumentParser)
- *action* - the basic type of action to be taken when this argument is encountered at the command line
- *dest* - name of the attribute under which sub-command name will be stored; by default `None` and no value is stored
- *help* - help for sub-parser group in help output, by default `None`
- *metavar* - string presenting available sub-commands in help; by default it is `None` and presents sub-commands in form {cmd1, cmd2, ..}

Some example usage:

```
>>> # create the top-level parser
>>> parser = argparse.ArgumentParser(prog='PROG')
>>> parser.add_argument('--foo', action='store_true', help='foo help')
>>> subparsers = parser.add_subparsers(help='sub-command help')
>>>
>>> # create the parser for the "a" command
>>> parser_a = subparsers.add_parser('a', help='a help')
>>> parser_a.add_argument('bar', type=int, help='bar help')
>>>
>>> # create the parser for the "b" command
>>> parser_b = subparsers.add_parser('b', help='b help')
>>> parser_b.add_argument('--baz', choices='XYZ', help='baz help')
>>>
>>> # parse some argument lists
>>> parser.parse_args(['a', '12'])
Namespace(bar=12, foo=False)
>>> parser.parse_args(['--foo', 'b', '--baz', 'Z'])
Namespace(baz='Z', foo=True)
```

Note that the object returned by *parse_args()* will only contain attributes for the main parser and the subparser that was selected by the command line (and not any other subparsers). So in the example above, when the `a` command is specified, only the `foo` and `bar` attributes are present, and when the `b` command is specified, only the `foo` and `baz` attributes are present.

Similarly, when a help message is requested from a subparser, only the help for that particular parser will be printed. The help message will not include parent parser or sibling parser messages. (A help message for each subparser command, however, can be given by supplying the `help=` argument to `add_parser()` as above.)

```
>>> parser.parse_args(['--help'])
usage: PROG [-h] [--foo] {a,b} ...

positional arguments:
  {a,b}   sub-command help
    a     a help
    b     b help
```

```
optional arguments:
  -h, --help  show this help message and exit
  --foo    foo help

>>> parser.parse_args(['a', '--help'])
usage: PROG a [-h] bar

positional arguments:
  bar      bar help

optional arguments:
  -h, --help  show this help message and exit

>>> parser.parse_args(['b', '--help'])
usage: PROG b [-h] [--baz {X,Y,Z}]

optional arguments:
  -h, --help     show this help message and exit
  --baz {X,Y,Z}  baz help
```

The *add_subparsers()* method also supports `title` and `description` keyword arguments. When either is present, the subparser's commands will appear in their own group in the help output. For example:

```
>>> parser = argparse.ArgumentParser()
>>> subparsers = parser.add_subparsers(title='subcommands',
...                                    description='valid subcommands',
...                                    help='additional help')
>>> subparsers.add_parser('foo')
>>> subparsers.add_parser('bar')
>>> parser.parse_args(['-h'])
usage:  [-h] {foo,bar} ...

optional arguments:
  -h, --help  show this help message and exit

subcommands:
  valid subcommands

  {foo,bar}   additional help
```

Furthermore, `add_parser` supports an additional `aliases` argument, which allows multiple strings to refer to the same subparser. This example, like `svn`, aliases `co` as a shorthand for `checkout`:

```
>>> parser = argparse.ArgumentParser()
>>> subparsers = parser.add_subparsers()
>>> checkout = subparsers.add_parser('checkout', aliases=['co'])
>>> checkout.add_argument('foo')
>>> parser.parse_args(['co', 'bar'])
Namespace(foo='bar')
```

One particularly effective way of handling sub-commands is to combine the use of the *add_subparsers()* method with calls to *set_defaults()* so that each subparser knows which Python function it should execute. For example:

```
>>> # sub-command functions
>>> def foo(args):
```

```
...     print(args.x * args.y)
...
>>> def bar(args):
...     print('((%s))' % args.z)
...
>>> # create the top-level parser
>>> parser = argparse.ArgumentParser()
>>> subparsers = parser.add_subparsers()
>>>
>>> # create the parser for the "foo" command
>>> parser_foo = subparsers.add_parser('foo')
>>> parser_foo.add_argument('-x', type=int, default=1)
>>> parser_foo.add_argument('y', type=float)
>>> parser_foo.set_defaults(func=foo)
>>>
>>> # create the parser for the "bar" command
>>> parser_bar = subparsers.add_parser('bar')
>>> parser_bar.add_argument('z')
>>> parser_bar.set_defaults(func=bar)
>>>
>>> # parse the args and call whatever function was selected
>>> args = parser.parse_args('foo 1 -x 2'.split())
>>> args.func(args)
2.0
>>>
>>> # parse the args and call whatever function was selected
>>> args = parser.parse_args('bar XYZYX'.split())
>>> args.func(args)
((XYZYX))
```

This way, you can let *parse_args()* do the job of calling the appropriate function after argument parsing is complete. Associating functions with actions like this is typically the easiest way to handle the different actions for each of your subparsers. However, if it is necessary to check the name of the subparser that was invoked, the `dest` keyword argument to the *add_subparsers()* call will work:

```
>>> parser = argparse.ArgumentParser()
>>> subparsers = parser.add_subparsers(dest='subparser_name')
>>> subparser1 = subparsers.add_parser('1')
>>> subparser1.add_argument('-x')
>>> subparser2 = subparsers.add_parser('2')
>>> subparser2.add_argument('y')
>>> parser.parse_args(['2', 'frobble'])
Namespace(subparser_name='2', y='frobble')
```

FileType objects

class `argparse.FileType`(*mode='r', bufsize=-1, encoding=None, errors=None*)

The *FileType* factory creates objects that can be passed to the type argument of *ArgumentParser.add_argument()*. Arguments that have *FileType* objects as their type will open command-line arguments as files with the requested modes, buffer sizes, encodings and error handling (see the *open()* function for more details):

```
>>> parser = argparse.ArgumentParser()
>>> parser.add_argument('--raw', type=argparse.FileType('wb', 0))
>>> parser.add_argument('out', type=argparse.FileType('w', encoding='UTF-8'))
>>> parser.parse_args(['--raw', 'raw.dat', 'file.txt'])
```

```
Namespace(out=<_io.TextIOWrapper name='file.txt' mode='w' encoding='UTF-8'>, raw=<_io.FileIO␣
↪name='raw.dat' mode='wb'>)
```

FileType objects understand the pseudo-argument `'-'` and automatically convert this into `sys.stdin` for readable *FileType* objects and `sys.stdout` for writable *FileType* objects:

```
>>> parser = argparse.ArgumentParser()
>>> parser.add_argument('infile', type=argparse.FileType('r'))
>>> parser.parse_args(['-'])
Namespace(infile=<_io.TextIOWrapper name='<stdin>' encoding='UTF-8'>)
```

New in version 3.4: The *encodings* and *errors* keyword arguments.

Argument groups

ArgumentParser.add_argument_group(*title=None*, *description=None*)

By default, *ArgumentParser* groups command-line arguments into "positional arguments" and "optional arguments" when displaying help messages. When there is a better conceptual grouping of arguments than this default one, appropriate groups can be created using the *add_argument_group()* method:

```
>>> parser = argparse.ArgumentParser(prog='PROG', add_help=False)
>>> group = parser.add_argument_group('group')
>>> group.add_argument('--foo', help='foo help')
>>> group.add_argument('bar', help='bar help')
>>> parser.print_help()
usage: PROG [--foo FOO] bar

group:
  bar    bar help
  --foo FOO  foo help
```

The *add_argument_group()* method returns an argument group object which has an *add_argument()* method just like a regular *ArgumentParser*. When an argument is added to the group, the parser treats it just like a normal argument, but displays the argument in a separate group for help messages. The *add_argument_group()* method accepts *title* and *description* arguments which can be used to customize this display:

```
>>> parser = argparse.ArgumentParser(prog='PROG', add_help=False)
>>> group1 = parser.add_argument_group('group1', 'group1 description')
>>> group1.add_argument('foo', help='foo help')
>>> group2 = parser.add_argument_group('group2', 'group2 description')
>>> group2.add_argument('--bar', help='bar help')
>>> parser.print_help()
usage: PROG [--bar BAR] foo

group1:
  group1 description

  foo    foo help

group2:
  group2 description

  --bar BAR  bar help
```

Note that any arguments not in your user-defined groups will end up back in the usual "positional arguments" and "optional arguments" sections.

Mutual exclusion

ArgumentParser.add_mutually_exclusive_group(*required=False*)

Create a mutually exclusive group. *argparse* will make sure that only one of the arguments in the mutually exclusive group was present on the command line:

```
>>> parser = argparse.ArgumentParser(prog='PROG')
>>> group = parser.add_mutually_exclusive_group()
>>> group.add_argument('--foo', action='store_true')
>>> group.add_argument('--bar', action='store_false')
>>> parser.parse_args(['--foo'])
Namespace(bar=True, foo=True)
>>> parser.parse_args(['--bar'])
Namespace(bar=False, foo=False)
>>> parser.parse_args(['--foo', '--bar'])
usage: PROG [-h] [--foo | --bar]
PROG: error: argument --bar: not allowed with argument --foo
```

The *add_mutually_exclusive_group()* method also accepts a *required* argument, to indicate that at least one of the mutually exclusive arguments is required:

```
>>> parser = argparse.ArgumentParser(prog='PROG')
>>> group = parser.add_mutually_exclusive_group(required=True)
>>> group.add_argument('--foo', action='store_true')
>>> group.add_argument('--bar', action='store_false')
>>> parser.parse_args([])
usage: PROG [-h] (--foo | --bar)
PROG: error: one of the arguments --foo --bar is required
```

Note that currently mutually exclusive argument groups do not support the *title* and *description* arguments of *add_argument_group()*.

Parser defaults

ArgumentParser.set_defaults(***kwargs*)

Most of the time, the attributes of the object returned by *parse_args()* will be fully determined by inspecting the command-line arguments and the argument actions. *set_defaults()* allows some additional attributes that are determined without any inspection of the command line to be added:

```
>>> parser = argparse.ArgumentParser()
>>> parser.add_argument('foo', type=int)
>>> parser.set_defaults(bar=42, baz='badger')
>>> parser.parse_args(['736'])
Namespace(bar=42, baz='badger', foo=736)
```

Note that parser-level defaults always override argument-level defaults:

```
>>> parser = argparse.ArgumentParser()
>>> parser.add_argument('--foo', default='bar')
>>> parser.set_defaults(foo='spam')
>>> parser.parse_args([])
Namespace(foo='spam')
```

Parser-level defaults can be particularly useful when working with multiple parsers. See the *add_subparsers()* method for an example of this type.

ArgumentParser.get_default(*dest*)
Get the default value for a namespace attribute, as set by either *add_argument()* or by *set_defaults()*:

```
>>> parser = argparse.ArgumentParser()
>>> parser.add_argument('--foo', default='badger')
>>> parser.get_default('foo')
'badger'
```

Printing help

In most typical applications, *parse_args()* will take care of formatting and printing any usage or error messages. However, several formatting methods are available:

ArgumentParser.print_usage(*file=None*)
Print a brief description of how the *ArgumentParser* should be invoked on the command line. If *file* is None, *sys.stdout* is assumed.

ArgumentParser.print_help(*file=None*)
Print a help message, including the program usage and information about the arguments registered with the *ArgumentParser*. If *file* is None, *sys.stdout* is assumed.

There are also variants of these methods that simply return a string instead of printing it:

ArgumentParser.format_usage()
Return a string containing a brief description of how the *ArgumentParser* should be invoked on the command line.

ArgumentParser.format_help()
Return a string containing a help message, including the program usage and information about the arguments registered with the *ArgumentParser*.

Partial parsing

ArgumentParser.parse_known_args(*args=None, namespace=None*)

Sometimes a script may only parse a few of the command-line arguments, passing the remaining arguments on to another script or program. In these cases, the *parse_known_args()* method can be useful. It works much like *parse_args()* except that it does not produce an error when extra arguments are present. Instead, it returns a two item tuple containing the populated namespace and the list of remaining argument strings.

```
>>> parser = argparse.ArgumentParser()
>>> parser.add_argument('--foo', action='store_true')
>>> parser.add_argument('bar')
>>> parser.parse_known_args(['--foo', '--badger', 'BAR', 'spam'])
(Namespace(bar='BAR', foo=True), ['--badger', 'spam'])
```

Warning: *Prefix matching* rules apply to parse_known_args(). The parser may consume an option even if it's just a prefix of one of its known options, instead of leaving it in the remaining arguments list.

Customizing file parsing

ArgumentParser.**convert_arg_line_to_args**(*arg_line*)

Arguments that are read from a file (see the *fromfile_prefix_chars* keyword argument to the *ArgumentParser* constructor) are read one argument per line. *convert_arg_line_to_args()* can be overridden for fancier reading.

This method takes a single argument *arg_line* which is a string read from the argument file. It returns a list of arguments parsed from this string. The method is called once per line read from the argument file, in order.

A useful override of this method is one that treats each space-separated word as an argument. The following example demonstrates how to do this:

```
class MyArgumentParser(argparse.ArgumentParser):
    def convert_arg_line_to_args(self, arg_line):
        return arg_line.split()
```

Exiting methods

ArgumentParser.**exit**(*status=0*, *message=None*)

This method terminates the program, exiting with the specified *status* and, if given, it prints a *message* before that.

ArgumentParser.**error**(*message*)

This method prints a usage message including the *message* to the standard error and terminates the program with a status code of 2.

16.4.6 Upgrading optparse code

Originally, the *argparse* module had attempted to maintain compatibility with *optparse*. However, *optparse* was difficult to extend transparently, particularly with the changes required to support the new `nargs=` specifiers and better usage messages. When most everything in *optparse* had either been copy-pasted over or monkey-patched, it no longer seemed practical to try to maintain the backwards compatibility.

The *argparse* module improves on the standard library *optparse* module in a number of ways including:

- Handling positional arguments.
- Supporting sub-commands.
- Allowing alternative option prefixes like `+` and `/`.
- Handling zero-or-more and one-or-more style arguments.
- Producing more informative usage messages.
- Providing a much simpler interface for custom `type` and `action`.

A partial upgrade path from *optparse* to *argparse*:

- Replace all *optparse.OptionParser.add_option()* calls with *ArgumentParser.add_argument()* calls.
- Replace `(options, args) = parser.parse_args()` with `args = parser.parse_args()` and add additional *ArgumentParser.add_argument()* calls for the positional arguments. Keep in mind that what was previously called `options`, now in the *argparse* context is called `args`.
- Replace *optparse.OptionParser.disable_interspersed_args()* by setting `nargs` of a positional argument to *argparse.REMAINDER*, or use *parse_known_args()* to collect unparsed argument strings in a separate list.

- Replace callback actions and the `callback_*` keyword arguments with `type` or `action` arguments.
- Replace string names for `type` keyword arguments with the corresponding type objects (e.g. int, float, complex, etc).
- Replace `optparse.Values` with *Namespace* and `optparse.OptionError` and `optparse.OptionValueError` with `ArgumentError`.
- Replace strings with implicit arguments such as `%default` or `%prog` with the standard Python syntax to use dictionaries to format strings, that is, `%(default)s` and `%(prog)s`.
- Replace the OptionParser constructor `version` argument with a call to `parser.add_argument('--version', action='version', version='<the version>')`.

16.5 getopt — C-style parser for command line options

Source code: Lib/getopt.py

Note: The *getopt* module is a parser for command line options whose API is designed to be familiar to users of the C `getopt()` function. Users who are unfamiliar with the C `getopt()` function or who would like to write less code and get better help and error messages should consider using the *argparse* module instead.

This module helps scripts to parse the command line arguments in `sys.argv`. It supports the same conventions as the Unix `getopt()` function (including the special meanings of arguments of the form '`-`' and '`--`'). Long options similar to those supported by GNU software may be used as well via an optional third argument.

This module provides two functions and an exception:

`getopt.getopt(`*args*, *shortopts*, *longopts=[]*`)`

Parses command line options and parameter list. *args* is the argument list to be parsed, without the leading reference to the running program. Typically, this means `sys.argv[1:]`. *shortopts* is the string of option letters that the script wants to recognize, with options that require an argument followed by a colon (`':'`; i.e., the same format that Unix `getopt()` uses).

Note: Unlike GNU `getopt()`, after a non-option argument, all further arguments are considered also non-options. This is similar to the way non-GNU Unix systems work.

longopts, if specified, must be a list of strings with the names of the long options which should be supported. The leading `'--'` characters should not be included in the option name. Long options which require an argument should be followed by an equal sign (`'='`). Optional arguments are not supported. To accept only long options, *shortopts* should be an empty string. Long options on the command line can be recognized so long as they provide a prefix of the option name that matches exactly one of the accepted options. For example, if *longopts* is `['foo', 'frob']`, the option `--fo` will match as `--foo`, but `--f` will not match uniquely, so *GetoptError* will be raised.

The return value consists of two elements: the first is a list of `(option, value)` pairs; the second is the list of program arguments left after the option list was stripped (this is a trailing slice of *args*). Each option-and-value pair returned has the option as its first element, prefixed with a hyphen for short options (e.g., `'-x'`) or two hyphens for long options (e.g., `'--long-option'`), and the option argument as its second element, or an empty string if the option has no argument. The options occur in the list in the same order in which they were found, thus allowing multiple occurrences. Long and short options may be mixed.

`getopt.gnu_getopt(args, shortopts, longopts=[])`
This function works like *getopt()*, except that GNU style scanning mode is used by default. This means that option and non-option arguments may be intermixed. The *getopt()* function stops processing options as soon as a non-option argument is encountered.

If the first character of the option string is `'+'`, or if the environment variable `POSIXLY_CORRECT` is set, then option processing stops as soon as a non-option argument is encountered.

exception `getopt.GetoptError`
This is raised when an unrecognized option is found in the argument list or when an option requiring an argument is given none. The argument to the exception is a string indicating the cause of the error. For long options, an argument given to an option which does not require one will also cause this exception to be raised. The attributes `msg` and `opt` give the error message and related option; if there is no specific option to which the exception relates, `opt` is an empty string.

exception `getopt.error`
Alias for *GetoptError*; for backward compatibility.

An example using only Unix style options:

```
>>> import getopt
>>> args = '-a -b -cfoo -d bar a1 a2'.split()
>>> args
['-a', '-b', '-cfoo', '-d', 'bar', 'a1', 'a2']
>>> optlist, args = getopt.getopt(args, 'abc:d:')
>>> optlist
[('-a', ''), ('-b', ''), ('-c', 'foo'), ('-d', 'bar')]
>>> args
['a1', 'a2']
```

Using long option names is equally easy:

```
>>> s = '--condition=foo --testing --output-file abc.def -x a1 a2'
>>> args = s.split()
>>> args
['--condition=foo', '--testing', '--output-file', 'abc.def', '-x', 'a1', 'a2']
>>> optlist, args = getopt.getopt(args, 'x', [
...     'condition=', 'output-file=', 'testing'])
>>> optlist
[('--condition', 'foo'), ('--testing', ''), ('--output-file', 'abc.def'), ('-x', '')]
>>> args
['a1', 'a2']
```

In a script, typical usage is something like this:

```
import getopt, sys

def main():
    try:
        opts, args = getopt.getopt(sys.argv[1:], "ho:v", ["help", "output="])
    except getopt.GetoptError as err:
        # print help information and exit:
        print(err)  # will print something like "option -a not recognized"
        usage()
        sys.exit(2)
    output = None
    verbose = False
    for o, a in opts:
        if o == "-v":
            verbose = True
```

```
        elif o in ("-h", "--help"):
            usage()
            sys.exit()
        elif o in ("-o", "--output"):
            output = a
        else:
            assert False, "unhandled option"
    # ...

if __name__ == "__main__":
    main()
```

Note that an equivalent command line interface could be produced with less code and more informative help and error messages by using the *argparse* module:

```
import argparse

if __name__ == '__main__':
    parser = argparse.ArgumentParser()
    parser.add_argument('-o', '--output')
    parser.add_argument('-v', dest='verbose', action='store_true')
    args = parser.parse_args()
    # ... do something with args.output ...
    # ... do something with args.verbose ..
```

See also:

Module *argparse* Alternative command line option and argument parsing library.

16.6 logging — Logging facility for Python

Source code: Lib/logging/__init__.py

Important

This page contains the API reference information. For tutorial information and discussion of more advanced topics, see

- Basic Tutorial
- Advanced Tutorial
- Logging Cookbook

This module defines functions and classes which implement a flexible event logging system for applications and libraries.

The key benefit of having the logging API provided by a standard library module is that all Python modules can participate in logging, so your application log can include your own messages integrated with messages from third-party modules.

The module provides a lot of functionality and flexibility. If you are unfamiliar with logging, the best way to get to grips with it is to see the tutorials (see the links on the right).

The basic classes defined by the module, together with their functions, are listed below.

- Loggers expose the interface that application code directly uses.
- Handlers send the log records (created by loggers) to the appropriate destination.
- Filters provide a finer grained facility for determining which log records to output.
- Formatters specify the layout of log records in the final output.

16.6.1 Logger Objects

Loggers have the following attributes and methods. Note that Loggers are never instantiated directly, but always through the module-level function `logging.getLogger(name)`. Multiple calls to *getLogger()* with the same name will always return a reference to the same Logger object.

The `name` is potentially a period-separated hierarchical value, like `foo.bar.baz` (though it could also be just plain `foo`, for example). Loggers that are further down in the hierarchical list are children of loggers higher up in the list. For example, given a logger with a name of `foo`, loggers with names of `foo.bar`, `foo.bar.baz`, and `foo.bam` are all descendants of `foo`. The logger name hierarchy is analogous to the Python package hierarchy, and identical to it if you organise your loggers on a per-module basis using the recommended construction `logging.getLogger(__name__)`. That's because in a module, `__name__` is the module's name in the Python package namespace.

class logging.Logger

propagate

If this attribute evaluates to true, events logged to this logger will be passed to the handlers of higher level (ancestor) loggers, in addition to any handlers attached to this logger. Messages are passed directly to the ancestor loggers' handlers - neither the level nor filters of the ancestor loggers in question are considered.

If this evaluates to false, logging messages are not passed to the handlers of ancestor loggers.

The constructor sets this attribute to `True`.

Note: If you attach a handler to a logger *and* one or more of its ancestors, it may emit the same record multiple times. In general, you should not need to attach a handler to more than one logger - if you just attach it to the appropriate logger which is highest in the logger hierarchy, then it will see all events logged by all descendant loggers, provided that their propagate setting is left set to `True`. A common scenario is to attach handlers only to the root logger, and to let propagation take care of the rest.

setLevel(*level*)

Sets the threshold for this logger to *level*. Logging messages which are less severe than *level* will be ignored; logging messages which have severity *level* or higher will be emitted by whichever handler or handlers service this logger, unless a handler's level has been set to a higher severity level than *level*.

When a logger is created, the level is set to `NOTSET` (which causes all messages to be processed when the logger is the root logger, or delegation to the parent when the logger is a non-root logger). Note that the root logger is created with level `WARNING`.

The term 'delegation to the parent' means that if a logger has a level of NOTSET, its chain of ancestor loggers is traversed until either an ancestor with a level other than NOTSET is found, or the root is reached.

If an ancestor is found with a level other than NOTSET, then that ancestor's level is treated as the effective level of the logger where the ancestor search began, and is used to determine how a logging event is handled.

If the root is reached, and it has a level of NOTSET, then all messages will be processed. Otherwise, the root's level will be used as the effective level.

See *Logging Levels* for a list of levels.

Changed in version 3.2: The *level* parameter now accepts a string representation of the level such as 'INFO' as an alternative to the integer constants such as `INFO`. Note, however, that levels are internally stored as integers, and methods such as e.g. `getEffectiveLevel()` and `isEnabledFor()` will return/expect to be passed integers.

isEnabledFor(*lvl*)
Indicates if a message of severity *lvl* would be processed by this logger. This method checks first the module-level level set by `logging.disable(lvl)` and then the logger's effective level as determined by `getEffectiveLevel()`.

getEffectiveLevel()
Indicates the effective level for this logger. If a value other than `NOTSET` has been set using `setLevel()`, it is returned. Otherwise, the hierarchy is traversed towards the root until a value other than `NOTSET` is found, and that value is returned. The value returned is an integer, typically one of `logging.DEBUG`, `logging.INFO` etc.

getChild(*suffix*)
Returns a logger which is a descendant to this logger, as determined by the suffix. Thus, `logging.getLogger('abc').getChild('def.ghi')` would return the same logger as would be returned by `logging.getLogger('abc.def.ghi')`. This is a convenience method, useful when the parent logger is named using e.g. `__name__` rather than a literal string.

New in version 3.2.

debug(*msg*, **args*, ***kwargs*)
Logs a message with level `DEBUG` on this logger. The *msg* is the message format string, and the *args* are the arguments which are merged into *msg* using the string formatting operator. (Note that this means that you can use keywords in the format string, together with a single dictionary argument.)

There are three keyword arguments in *kwargs* which are inspected: *exc_info*, *stack_info*, and *extra*.

If *exc_info* does not evaluate as false, it causes exception information to be added to the logging message. If an exception tuple (in the format returned by `sys.exc_info()`) or an exception instance is provided, it is used; otherwise, `sys.exc_info()` is called to get the exception information.

The second optional keyword argument is *stack_info*, which defaults to `False`. If true, stack information is added to the logging message, including the actual logging call. Note that this is not the same stack information as that displayed through specifying *exc_info*: The former is stack frames from the bottom of the stack up to the logging call in the current thread, whereas the latter is information about stack frames which have been unwound, following an exception, while searching for exception handlers.

You can specify *stack_info* independently of *exc_info*, e.g. to just show how you got to a certain point in your code, even when no exceptions were raised. The stack frames are printed following a header line which says:

```
Stack (most recent call last):
```

This mimics the `Traceback (most recent call last):` which is used when displaying exception frames.

The third keyword argument is *extra* which can be used to pass a dictionary which is used to populate the __dict__ of the LogRecord created for the logging event with user-defined attributes. These custom attributes can then be used as you like. For example, they could be incorporated into logged messages. For example:

```
FORMAT = '%(asctime)-15s %(clientip)s %(user)-8s %(message)s'
logging.basicConfig(format=FORMAT)
d = {'clientip': '192.168.0.1', 'user': 'fbloggs'}
logger = logging.getLogger('tcpserver')
logger.warning('Protocol problem: %s', 'connection reset', extra=d)
```

would print something like

```
2006-02-08 22:20:02,165 192.168.0.1 fbloggs  Protocol problem: connection reset
```

The keys in the dictionary passed in *extra* should not clash with the keys used by the logging system. (See the `Formatter` documentation for more information on which keys are used by the logging system.)

If you choose to use these attributes in logged messages, you need to exercise some care. In the above example, for instance, the `Formatter` has been set up with a format string which expects 'clientip' and 'user' in the attribute dictionary of the LogRecord. If these are missing, the message will not be logged because a string formatting exception will occur. So in this case, you always need to pass the *extra* dictionary with these keys.

While this might be annoying, this feature is intended for use in specialized circumstances, such as multi-threaded servers where the same code executes in many contexts, and interesting conditions which arise are dependent on this context (such as remote client IP address and authenticated user name, in the above example). In such circumstances, it is likely that specialized `Formatter`s would be used with particular `Handler`s.

New in version 3.2: The *stack_info* parameter was added.

Changed in version 3.5: The *exc_info* parameter can now accept exception instances.

info(*msg*, **args*, ***kwargs*)
Logs a message with level `INFO` on this logger. The arguments are interpreted as for `debug()`.

warning(*msg*, **args*, ***kwargs*)
Logs a message with level `WARNING` on this logger. The arguments are interpreted as for `debug()`.

Note: There is an obsolete method `warn` which is functionally identical to `warning`. As `warn` is deprecated, please do not use it - use `warning` instead.

error(*msg*, **args*, ***kwargs*)
Logs a message with level `ERROR` on this logger. The arguments are interpreted as for `debug()`.

critical(*msg*, **args*, ***kwargs*)
Logs a message with level `CRITICAL` on this logger. The arguments are interpreted as for `debug()`.

log(*lvl*, *msg*, **args*, ***kwargs*)
Logs a message with integer level *lvl* on this logger. The other arguments are interpreted as for `debug()`.

exception(*msg*, **args*, ***kwargs*)
Logs a message with level `ERROR` on this logger. The arguments are interpreted as for `debug()`. Exception info is added to the logging message. This method should only be called from an exception handler.

addFilter(*filter*)
Adds the specified filter *filter* to this logger.

`removeFilter(`*filter*`)`
Removes the specified filter *filter* from this logger.

`filter(`*record*`)`
Applies this logger's filters to the record and returns a true value if the record is to be processed. The filters are consulted in turn, until one of them returns a false value. If none of them return a false value, the record will be processed (passed to handlers). If one returns a false value, no further processing of the record occurs.

`addHandler(`*hdlr*`)`
Adds the specified handler *hdlr* to this logger.

`removeHandler(`*hdlr*`)`
Removes the specified handler *hdlr* from this logger.

`findCaller(`*stack_info=False*`)`
Finds the caller's source filename and line number. Returns the filename, line number, function name and stack information as a 4-element tuple. The stack information is returned as `None` unless *stack_info* is `True`.

`handle(`*record*`)`
Handles a record by passing it to all handlers associated with this logger and its ancestors (until a false value of *propagate* is found). This method is used for unpickled records received from a socket, as well as those created locally. Logger-level filtering is applied using `filter()`.

`makeRecord(`*name, lvl, fn, lno, msg, args, exc_info, func=None, extra=None, sinfo=None*`)`
This is a factory method which can be overridden in subclasses to create specialized `LogRecord` instances.

`hasHandlers()`
Checks to see if this logger has any handlers configured. This is done by looking for handlers in this logger and its parents in the logger hierarchy. Returns `True` if a handler was found, else `False`. The method stops searching up the hierarchy whenever a logger with the 'propagate' attribute set to false is found - that will be the last logger which is checked for the existence of handlers.

New in version 3.2.

Changed in version 3.7: Loggers can now be picked and unpickled.

16.6.2 Logging Levels

The numeric values of logging levels are given in the following table. These are primarily of interest if you want to define your own levels, and need them to have specific values relative to the predefined levels. If you define a level with the same numeric value, it overwrites the predefined value; the predefined name is lost.

Level	Numeric value
CRITICAL	50
ERROR	40
WARNING	30
INFO	20
DEBUG	10
NOTSET	0

16.6.3 Handler Objects

Handlers have the following attributes and methods. Note that *Handler* is never instantiated directly; this class acts as a base for more useful subclasses. However, the `__init__()` method in subclasses needs to call *Handler.__init__()*.

class logging.Handler

`__init__`(*level=NOTSET*)
Initializes the *Handler* instance by setting its level, setting the list of filters to the empty list and creating a lock (using *createLock()*) for serializing access to an I/O mechanism.

`createLock()`
Initializes a thread lock which can be used to serialize access to underlying I/O functionality which may not be threadsafe.

`acquire()`
Acquires the thread lock created with *createLock()*.

`release()`
Releases the thread lock acquired with *acquire()*.

`setLevel`(*level*)
Sets the threshold for this handler to *level*. Logging messages which are less severe than *level* will be ignored. When a handler is created, the level is set to `NOTSET` (which causes all messages to be processed).

See *Logging Levels* for a list of levels.

Changed in version 3.2: The *level* parameter now accepts a string representation of the level such as 'INFO' as an alternative to the integer constants such as `INFO`.

`setFormatter`(*fmt*)
Sets the *Formatter* for this handler to *fmt*.

`addFilter`(*filter*)
Adds the specified filter *filter* to this handler.

`removeFilter`(*filter*)
Removes the specified filter *filter* from this handler.

`filter`(*record*)
Applies this handler's filters to the record and returns a true value if the record is to be processed. The filters are consulted in turn, until one of them returns a false value. If none of them return a false value, the record will be emitted. If one returns a false value, the handler will not emit the record.

`flush()`
Ensure all logging output has been flushed. This version does nothing and is intended to be implemented by subclasses.

`close()`
Tidy up any resources used by the handler. This version does no output but removes the handler from an internal list of handlers which is closed when *shutdown()* is called. Subclasses should ensure that this gets called from overridden *close()* methods.

`handle`(*record*)
Conditionally emits the specified logging record, depending on filters which may have been added to the handler. Wraps the actual emission of the record with acquisition/release of the I/O thread lock.

handleError(*record*)
This method should be called from handlers when an exception is encountered during an *emit()* call. If the module-level attribute `raiseExceptions` is `False`, exceptions get silently ignored. This is what is mostly wanted for a logging system - most users will not care about errors in the logging system, they are more interested in application errors. You could, however, replace this with a custom handler if you wish. The specified record is the one which was being processed when the exception occurred. (The default value of `raiseExceptions` is `True`, as that is more useful during development).

format(*record*)
Do formatting for a record - if a formatter is set, use it. Otherwise, use the default formatter for the module.

emit(*record*)
Do whatever it takes to actually log the specified logging record. This version is intended to be implemented by subclasses and so raises a *NotImplementedError*.

For a list of handlers included as standard, see *logging.handlers*.

16.6.4 Formatter Objects

Formatter objects have the following attributes and methods. They are responsible for converting a *LogRecord* to (usually) a string which can be interpreted by either a human or an external system. The base *Formatter* allows a formatting string to be specified. If none is supplied, the default value of `'%(message)s'` is used, which just includes the message in the logging call. To have additional items of information in the formatted output (such as a timestamp), keep reading.

A Formatter can be initialized with a format string which makes use of knowledge of the *LogRecord* attributes - such as the default value mentioned above making use of the fact that the user's message and arguments are pre-formatted into a *LogRecord*'s *message* attribute. This format string contains standard Python %-style mapping keys. See section *printf-style String Formatting* for more information on string formatting.

The useful mapping keys in a *LogRecord* are given in the section on *LogRecord attributes*.

class logging.Formatter(*fmt=None*, *datefmt=None*, *style='%'*)
Returns a new instance of the *Formatter* class. The instance is initialized with a format string for the message as a whole, as well as a format string for the date/time portion of a message. If no *fmt* is specified, `'%(message)s'` is used. If no *datefmt* is specified, the ISO8601 date format is used.

The *style* parameter can be one of '%', '{' or '$' and determines how the format string will be merged with its data: using one of %-formatting, *str.format()* or *string.Template*. See formatting-styles for more information on using {- and $-formatting for log messages.

Changed in version 3.2: The *style* parameter was added.

format(*record*)
The record's attribute dictionary is used as the operand to a string formatting operation. Returns the resulting string. Before formatting the dictionary, a couple of preparatory steps are carried out. The *message* attribute of the record is computed using *msg* % *args*. If the formatting string contains `'(asctime)'`, *formatTime()* is called to format the event time. If there is exception information, it is formatted using *formatException()* and appended to the message. Note that the formatted exception information is cached in attribute *exc_text*. This is useful because the exception information can be pickled and sent across the wire, but you should be careful if you have more than one *Formatter* subclass which customizes the formatting of exception information. In this case, you will have to clear the cached value after a formatter has done its formatting, so that the next formatter to handle the event doesn't use the cached value but recalculates it afresh.

If stack information is available, it's appended after the exception information, using *formatStack()* to transform it if necessary.

formatTime(*record*, *datefmt=None*)

This method should be called from *format()* by a formatter which wants to make use of a formatted time. This method can be overridden in formatters to provide for any specific requirement, but the basic behavior is as follows: if *datefmt* (a string) is specified, it is used with *time.strftime()* to format the creation time of the record. Otherwise, the ISO8601 format is used. The resulting string is returned.

This function uses a user-configurable function to convert the creation time to a tuple. By default, *time.localtime()* is used; to change this for a particular formatter instance, set the `converter` attribute to a function with the same signature as *time.localtime()* or *time.gmtime()*. To change it for all formatters, for example if you want all logging times to be shown in GMT, set the `converter` attribute in the `Formatter` class.

Changed in version 3.3: Previously, the default ISO 8601 format was hard-coded as in this example: `2010-09-06 22:38:15,292` where the part before the comma is handled by a strptime format string (`'%Y-%m-%d %H:%M:%S'`), and the part after the comma is a millisecond value. Because strptime does not have a format placeholder for milliseconds, the millisecond value is appended using another format string, `'%s,%03d'` — and both of these format strings have been hardcoded into this method. With the change, these strings are defined as class-level attributes which can be overridden at the instance level when desired. The names of the attributes are `default_time_format` (for the strptime format string) and `default_msec_format` (for appending the millisecond value).

formatException(*exc_info*)

Formats the specified exception information (a standard exception tuple as returned by *sys.exc_info()*) as a string. This default implementation just uses *traceback.print_exception()*. The resulting string is returned.

formatStack(*stack_info*)

Formats the specified stack information (a string as returned by *traceback.print_stack()*, but with the last newline removed) as a string. This default implementation just returns the input value.

16.6.5 Filter Objects

`Filters` can be used by `Handlers` and `Loggers` for more sophisticated filtering than is provided by levels. The base filter class only allows events which are below a certain point in the logger hierarchy. For example, a filter initialized with 'A.B' will allow events logged by loggers 'A.B', 'A.B.C', 'A.B.C.D', 'A.B.D' etc. but not 'A.BB', 'B.A.B' etc. If initialized with the empty string, all events are passed.

class logging.Filter(*name=''*)

Returns an instance of the *Filter* class. If *name* is specified, it names a logger which, together with its children, will have its events allowed through the filter. If *name* is the empty string, allows every event.

filter(*record*)

Is the specified record to be logged? Returns zero for no, nonzero for yes. If deemed appropriate, the record may be modified in-place by this method.

Note that filters attached to handlers are consulted before an event is emitted by the handler, whereas filters attached to loggers are consulted whenever an event is logged (using *debug()*, *info()*, etc.), before sending an event to handlers. This means that events which have been generated by descendant loggers will not be filtered by a logger's filter setting, unless the filter has also been applied to those descendant loggers.

You don't actually need to subclass `Filter`: you can pass any instance which has a `filter` method with the same semantics.

Changed in version 3.2: You don't need to create specialized `Filter` classes, or use other classes with a `filter` method: you can use a function (or other callable) as a filter. The filtering logic will check to see if the filter object has a `filter` attribute: if it does, it's assumed to be a `Filter` and its *filter()* method is called. Otherwise, it's assumed to be a callable and called with the record as the single parameter. The returned value should conform to that returned by *filter()*.

Although filters are used primarily to filter records based on more sophisticated criteria than levels, they get to see every record which is processed by the handler or logger they're attached to: this can be useful if you want to do things like counting how many records were processed by a particular logger or handler, or adding, changing or removing attributes in the LogRecord being processed. Obviously changing the LogRecord needs to be done with some care, but it does allow the injection of contextual information into logs (see filters-contextual).

16.6.6 LogRecord Objects

LogRecord instances are created automatically by the *Logger* every time something is logged, and can be created manually via *makeLogRecord()* (for example, from a pickled event received over the wire).

class logging.LogRecord(*name, level, pathname, lineno, msg, args, exc_info, func=None, sinfo=None*)

Contains all the information pertinent to the event being logged.

The primary information is passed in `msg` and `args`, which are combined using `msg % args` to create the `message` field of the record.

Parameters

- **name** – The name of the logger used to log the event represented by this LogRecord. Note that this name will always have this value, even though it may be emitted by a handler attached to a different (ancestor) logger.
- **level** – The numeric level of the logging event (one of DEBUG, INFO etc.) Note that this is converted to *two* attributes of the LogRecord: `levelno` for the numeric value and `levelname` for the corresponding level name.
- **pathname** – The full pathname of the source file where the logging call was made.
- **lineno** – The line number in the source file where the logging call was made.
- **msg** – The event description message, possibly a format string with placeholders for variable data.
- **args** – Variable data to merge into the *msg* argument to obtain the event description.
- **exc_info** – An exception tuple with the current exception information, or `None` if no exception information is available.
- **func** – The name of the function or method from which the logging call was invoked.
- **sinfo** – A text string representing stack information from the base of the stack in the current thread, up to the logging call.

getMessage()

Returns the message for this *LogRecord* instance after merging any user-supplied arguments with the message. If the user-supplied message argument to the logging call is not a string, *str()* is called on it to convert it to a string. This allows use of user-defined classes as messages, whose `__str__` method can return the actual format string to be used.

Changed in version 3.2: The creation of a `LogRecord` has been made more configurable by providing a factory which is used to create the record. The factory can be set using *getLogRecordFactory()* and *setLogRecordFactory()* (see this for the factory's signature).

This functionality can be used to inject your own values into a LogRecord at creation time. You can use the following pattern:

```
old_factory = logging.getLogRecordFactory()

def record_factory(*args, **kwargs):
    record = old_factory(*args, **kwargs)
    record.custom_attribute = 0xdecafbad
    return record

logging.setLogRecordFactory(record_factory)
```

With this pattern, multiple factories could be chained, and as long as they don't overwrite each other's attributes or unintentionally overwrite the standard attributes listed above, there should be no surprises.

16.6.7 LogRecord attributes

The LogRecord has a number of attributes, most of which are derived from the parameters to the constructor. (Note that the names do not always correspond exactly between the LogRecord constructor parameters and the LogRecord attributes.) These attributes can be used to merge data from the record into the format string. The following table lists (in alphabetical order) the attribute names, their meanings and the corresponding placeholder in a %-style format string.

If you are using {}-formatting (*str.format()*), you can use **{attrname}** as the placeholder in the format string. If you are using $-formatting (*string.Template*), use the form **${attrname}**. In both cases, of course, replace **attrname** with the actual attribute name you want to use.

In the case of {}-formatting, you can specify formatting flags by placing them after the attribute name, separated from it with a colon. For example: a placeholder of **{msecs:03d}** would format a millisecond value of 4 as 004. Refer to the *str.format()* documentation for full details on the options available to you.

Attribute name	Format	Description
args	You shouldn't need to format this yourself.	The tuple of arguments merged into `msg` to produce `message`, or a dict whose values are used for the merge (when there is only one argument, and it is a dictionary).
asctime	`%(asctime)s`	Human-readable time when the *LogRecord* was created. By default this is of the form '2003-07-08 16:49:45,896' (the numbers after the comma are millisecond portion of the time).
created	`%(created)f`	Time when the *LogRecord* was created (as returned by *time.time()*).
exc_info	You shouldn't need to format this yourself.	Exception tuple (à la `sys.exc_info`) or, if no exception has occurred, `None`.
filename	`%(filename)s`	Filename portion of `pathname`.
funcName	`%(funcName)s`	Name of function containing the logging call.
levelname	`%(levelname)s`	Text logging level for the message (`'DEBUG'`, `'INFO'`, `'WARNING'`, `'ERROR'`, `'CRITICAL'`).
levelno	`%(levelno)s`	Numeric logging level for the message (`DEBUG`, `INFO`, `WARNING`, `ERROR`, `CRITICAL`).
lineno	`%(lineno)d`	Source line number where the logging call was issued (if available).
message	`%(message)s`	The logged message, computed as `msg % args`. This is set when *Formatter.format()* is invoked.
module	`%(module)s`	Module (name portion of `filename`).
msecs	`%(msecs)d`	Millisecond portion of the time when the *LogRecord* was created.
msg	You shouldn't need to format this yourself.	The format string passed in the original logging call. Merged with `args` to produce `message`, or an arbitrary object (see arbitrary-object-messages).
name	`%(name)s`	Name of the logger used to log the call.
pathname	`%(pathname)s`	Full pathname of the source file where the logging call was issued (if available).
process	`%(process)d`	Process ID (if available).
processName	`%(processName)s`	Process name (if available).
relativeCreated	`%(relativeCreated)d`	Time in milliseconds when the LogRecord was created, relative to the time the logging module was loaded.
stack_info	You shouldn't need to format this yourself.	Stack frame information (where available) from the bottom of the stack in the current thread, up to and including the stack frame of the logging call which resulted in the creation of this record.
thread	`%(thread)d`	Thread ID (if available).
threadName	`%(threadName)s`	Thread name (if available).

Changed in version 3.1: *processName* was added.

16.6.8 LoggerAdapter Objects

LoggerAdapter instances are used to conveniently pass contextual information into logging calls. For a usage example, see the section on adding contextual information to your logging output.

class logging.LoggerAdapter(*logger*, *extra*)
Returns an instance of *LoggerAdapter* initialized with an underlying *Logger* instance and a dict-like object.

process(*msg*, *kwargs*)
Modifies the message and/or keyword arguments passed to a logging call in order to insert contextual information. This implementation takes the object passed as *extra* to the constructor and adds it to *kwargs* using key 'extra'. The return value is a (*msg*, *kwargs*) tuple which has the (possibly modified) versions of the arguments passed in.

In addition to the above, *LoggerAdapter* supports the following methods of *Logger*: *debug()*, *info()*, *warning()*, *error()*, *exception()*, *critical()*, *log()*, *isEnabledFor()*, *getEffectiveLevel()*, *setLevel()* and *hasHandlers()*. These methods have the same signatures as their counterparts in *Logger*, so you can use the two types of instances interchangeably.

Changed in version 3.2: The *isEnabledFor()*, *getEffectiveLevel()*, *setLevel()* and *hasHandlers()* methods were added to *LoggerAdapter*. These methods delegate to the underlying logger.

16.6.9 Thread Safety

The logging module is intended to be thread-safe without any special work needing to be done by its clients. It achieves this though using threading locks; there is one lock to serialize access to the module's shared data, and each handler also creates a lock to serialize access to its underlying I/O.

If you are implementing asynchronous signal handlers using the *signal* module, you may not be able to use logging from within such handlers. This is because lock implementations in the *threading* module are not always re-entrant, and so cannot be invoked from such signal handlers.

16.6.10 Module-Level Functions

In addition to the classes described above, there are a number of module- level functions.

logging.getLogger(*name=None*)
Return a logger with the specified name or, if name is `None`, return a logger which is the root logger of the hierarchy. If specified, the name is typically a dot-separated hierarchical name like *'a'*, *'a.b'* or *'a.b.c.d'*. Choice of these names is entirely up to the developer who is using logging.

All calls to this function with a given name return the same logger instance. This means that logger instances never need to be passed between different parts of an application.

logging.getLoggerClass()
Return either the standard *Logger* class, or the last class passed to *setLoggerClass()*. This function may be called from within a new class definition, to ensure that installing a customized *Logger* class will not undo customizations already applied by other code. For example:

```
class MyLogger(logging.getLoggerClass()):
    # ... override behaviour here
```

logging.getLogRecordFactory()
Return a callable which is used to create a *LogRecord*.

New in version 3.2: This function has been provided, along with *setLogRecordFactory()*, to allow developers more control over how the *LogRecord* representing a logging event is constructed.

See *setLogRecordFactory()* for more information about the how the factory is called.

logging.debug(*msg*, **args*, ***kwargs*)

Logs a message with level DEBUG on the root logger. The *msg* is the message format string, and the *args* are the arguments which are merged into *msg* using the string formatting operator. (Note that this means that you can use keywords in the format string, together with a single dictionary argument.)

There are three keyword arguments in *kwargs* which are inspected: *exc_info* which, if it does not evaluate as false, causes exception information to be added to the logging message. If an exception tuple (in the format returned by *sys.exc_info()*) is provided, it is used; otherwise, *sys.exc_info()* is called to get the exception information.

The second optional keyword argument is *stack_info*, which defaults to False. If true, stack information is added to the logging message, including the actual logging call. Note that this is not the same stack information as that displayed through specifying *exc_info*: The former is stack frames from the bottom of the stack up to the logging call in the current thread, whereas the latter is information about stack frames which have been unwound, following an exception, while searching for exception handlers.

You can specify *stack_info* independently of *exc_info*, e.g. to just show how you got to a certain point in your code, even when no exceptions were raised. The stack frames are printed following a header line which says:

```
Stack (most recent call last):
```

This mimics the `Traceback (most recent call last):` which is used when displaying exception frames.

The third optional keyword argument is *extra* which can be used to pass a dictionary which is used to populate the __dict__ of the LogRecord created for the logging event with user-defined attributes. These custom attributes can then be used as you like. For example, they could be incorporated into logged messages. For example:

```
FORMAT = '%(asctime)-15s %(clientip)s %(user)-8s %(message)s'
logging.basicConfig(format=FORMAT)
d = {'clientip': '192.168.0.1', 'user': 'fbloggs'}
logging.warning('Protocol problem: %s', 'connection reset', extra=d)
```

would print something like:

```
2006-02-08 22:20:02,165 192.168.0.1 fbloggs  Protocol problem: connection reset
```

The keys in the dictionary passed in *extra* should not clash with the keys used by the logging system. (See the *Formatter* documentation for more information on which keys are used by the logging system.)

If you choose to use these attributes in logged messages, you need to exercise some care. In the above example, for instance, the *Formatter* has been set up with a format string which expects 'clientip' and 'user' in the attribute dictionary of the LogRecord. If these are missing, the message will not be logged because a string formatting exception will occur. So in this case, you always need to pass the *extra* dictionary with these keys.

While this might be annoying, this feature is intended for use in specialized circumstances, such as multi-threaded servers where the same code executes in many contexts, and interesting conditions which arise are dependent on this context (such as remote client IP address and authenticated user name, in the above example). In such circumstances, it is likely that specialized *Formatters* would be used with particular *Handlers*.

New in version 3.2: The *stack_info* parameter was added.

logging.info(*msg*, **args*, ***kwargs*)

Logs a message with level INFO on the root logger. The arguments are interpreted as for *debug()*.

`logging.warning(msg, *args, **kwargs)`
Logs a message with level `WARNING` on the root logger. The arguments are interpreted as for `debug()`.

Note: There is an obsolete function `warn` which is functionally identical to `warning`. As `warn` is deprecated, please do not use it - use `warning` instead.

`logging.error(msg, *args, **kwargs)`
Logs a message with level `ERROR` on the root logger. The arguments are interpreted as for `debug()`.

`logging.critical(msg, *args, **kwargs)`
Logs a message with level `CRITICAL` on the root logger. The arguments are interpreted as for `debug()`.

`logging.exception(msg, *args, **kwargs)`
Logs a message with level `ERROR` on the root logger. The arguments are interpreted as for `debug()`. Exception info is added to the logging message. This function should only be called from an exception handler.

`logging.log(level, msg, *args, **kwargs)`
Logs a message with level *level* on the root logger. The other arguments are interpreted as for `debug()`.

Note: The above module-level convenience functions, which delegate to the root logger, call `basicConfig()` to ensure that at least one handler is available. Because of this, they should *not* be used in threads, in versions of Python earlier than 2.7.1 and 3.2, unless at least one handler has been added to the root logger *before* the threads are started. In earlier versions of Python, due to a thread safety shortcoming in `basicConfig()`, this can (under rare circumstances) lead to handlers being added multiple times to the root logger, which can in turn lead to multiple messages for the same event.

`logging.disable(lvl=CRITICAL)`
Provides an overriding level *lvl* for all loggers which takes precedence over the logger's own level. When the need arises to temporarily throttle logging output down across the whole application, this function can be useful. Its effect is to disable all logging calls of severity *lvl* and below, so that if you call it with a value of INFO, then all INFO and DEBUG events would be discarded, whereas those of severity WARNING and above would be processed according to the logger's effective level. If `logging.disable(logging.NOTSET)` is called, it effectively removes this overriding level, so that logging output again depends on the effective levels of individual loggers.

Note that if you have defined any custom logging level higher than `CRITICAL` (this is not recommended), you won't be able to rely on the default value for the *lvl* parameter, but will have to explicitly supply a suitable value.

Changed in version 3.7: The *lvl* parameter was defaulted to level `CRITICAL`. See Issue #28524 for more information about this change.

`logging.addLevelName(lvl, levelName)`
Associates level *lvl* with text *levelName* in an internal dictionary, which is used to map numeric levels to a textual representation, for example when a `Formatter` formats a message. This function can also be used to define your own levels. The only constraints are that all levels used must be registered using this function, levels should be positive integers and they should increase in increasing order of severity.

Note: If you are thinking of defining your own levels, please see the section on custom-levels.

`logging.getLevelName(lvl)`
Returns the textual representation of logging level *lvl*. If the level is one of the predefined levels `CRITICAL`, `ERROR`, `WARNING`, `INFO` or `DEBUG` then you get the corresponding string. If you have associated

levels with names using `addLevelName()` then the name you have associated with *lvl* is returned. If a numeric value corresponding to one of the defined levels is passed in, the corresponding string representation is returned. Otherwise, the string 'Level %s' % lvl is returned.

Note: Levels are internally integers (as they need to be compared in the logging logic). This function is used to convert between an integer level and the level name displayed in the formatted log output by means of the `%(levelname)s` format specifier (see *LogRecord attributes*).

Changed in version 3.4: In Python versions earlier than 3.4, this function could also be passed a text level, and would return the corresponding numeric value of the level. This undocumented behaviour was considered a mistake, and was removed in Python 3.4, but reinstated in 3.4.2 due to retain backward compatibility.

`logging.`**`makeLogRecord`**`(`*attrdict*`)`
Creates and returns a new `LogRecord` instance whose attributes are defined by *attrdict*. This function is useful for taking a pickled `LogRecord` attribute dictionary, sent over a socket, and reconstituting it as a `LogRecord` instance at the receiving end.

`logging.`**`basicConfig`**`(`***kwargs*`)`
Does basic configuration for the logging system by creating a `StreamHandler` with a default `Formatter` and adding it to the root logger. The functions `debug()`, `info()`, `warning()`, `error()` and `critical()` will call `basicConfig()` automatically if no handlers are defined for the root logger.

This function does nothing if the root logger already has handlers configured for it.

Note: This function should be called from the main thread before other threads are started. In versions of Python prior to 2.7.1 and 3.2, if this function is called from multiple threads, it is possible (in rare circumstances) that a handler will be added to the root logger more than once, leading to unexpected results such as messages being duplicated in the log.

The following keyword arguments are supported.

Format	Description
`filename`	Specifies that a FileHandler be created, using the specified filename, rather than a StreamHandler.
`filemode`	Specifies the mode to open the file, if filename is specified (if filemode is unspecified, it defaults to 'a').
`format`	Use the specified format string for the handler.
`datefmt`	Use the specified date/time format.
`style`	If `format` is specified, use this style for the format string. One of '%', '{' or '$' for %-formatting, `str.format()` or `string.Template` respectively, and defaulting to '%' if not specified.
`level`	Set the root logger level to the specified level.
`stream`	Use the specified stream to initialize the StreamHandler. Note that this argument is incompatible with 'filename' - if both are present, a `ValueError` is raised.
`handlers`	If specified, this should be an iterable of already created handlers to add to the root logger. Any handlers which don't already have a formatter set will be assigned the default formatter created in this function. Note that this argument is incompatible with 'filename' or 'stream' - if both are present, a `ValueError` is raised.

Changed in version 3.2: The `style` argument was added.

Changed in version 3.3: The `handlers` argument was added. Additional checks were added to catch situations where incompatible arguments are specified (e.g. `handlers` together with `stream` or `filename`, or `stream` together with `filename`).

`logging.shutdown()`
Informs the logging system to perform an orderly shutdown by flushing and closing all handlers. This should be called at application exit and no further use of the logging system should be made after this call.

`logging.setLoggerClass(klass)`
Tells the logging system to use the class *klass* when instantiating a logger. The class should define `__init__()` such that only a name argument is required, and the `__init__()` should call `Logger.__init__()`. This function is typically called before any loggers are instantiated by applications which need to use custom logger behavior.

`logging.setLogRecordFactory(factory)`
Set a callable which is used to create a *LogRecord*.

Parameters `factory` – The factory callable to be used to instantiate a log record.

New in version 3.2: This function has been provided, along with *getLogRecordFactory()*, to allow developers more control over how the *LogRecord* representing a logging event is constructed.

The factory has the following signature:

`factory(name, level, fn, lno, msg, args, exc_info, func=None, sinfo=None, **kwargs)`

name The logger name.

level The logging level (numeric).

fn The full pathname of the file where the logging call was made.

lno The line number in the file where the logging call was made.

msg The logging message.

args The arguments for the logging message.

exc_info An exception tuple, or `None`.

func The name of the function or method which invoked the logging call.

sinfo A stack traceback such as is provided by *traceback.print_stack()*, showing the call hierarchy.

kwargs Additional keyword arguments.

16.6.11 Module-Level Attributes

`logging.lastResort`
A "handler of last resort" is available through this attribute. This is a *StreamHandler* writing to `sys.stderr` with a level of `WARNING`, and is used to handle logging events in the absence of any logging configuration. The end result is to just print the message to `sys.stderr`. This replaces the earlier error message saying that "no handlers could be found for logger XYZ". If you need the earlier behaviour for some reason, `lastResort` can be set to `None`.

New in version 3.2.

16.6.12 Integration with the warnings module

The *captureWarnings()* function can be used to integrate *logging* with the *warnings* module.

`logging.captureWarnings(capture)`

This function is used to turn the capture of warnings by logging on and off.

If *capture* is `True`, warnings issued by the *warnings* module will be redirected to the logging system. Specifically, a warning will be formatted using *warnings.formatwarning()* and the resulting string logged to a logger named `'py.warnings'` with a severity of `WARNING`.

If *capture* is `False`, the redirection of warnings to the logging system will stop, and warnings will be redirected to their original destinations (i.e. those in effect before `captureWarnings(True)` was called).

See also:

Module *logging.config* Configuration API for the logging module.

Module *logging.handlers* Useful handlers included with the logging module.

PEP 282 **- A Logging System** The proposal which described this feature for inclusion in the Python standard library.

Original Python logging package This is the original source for the *logging* package. The version of the package available from this site is suitable for use with Python 1.5.2, 2.1.x and 2.2.x, which do not include the *logging* package in the standard library.

16.7 logging.config — Logging configuration

Source code: Lib/logging/config.py

Important

This page contains only reference information. For tutorials, please see

- Basic Tutorial
- Advanced Tutorial
- Logging Cookbook

This section describes the API for configuring the logging module.

16.7.1 Configuration functions

The following functions configure the logging module. They are located in the *logging.config* module. Their use is optional — you can configure the logging module using these functions or by making calls to the main API (defined in *logging* itself) and defining handlers which are declared either in *logging* or *logging.handlers*.

`logging.config.dictConfig(config)`

Takes the logging configuration from a dictionary. The contents of this dictionary are described in *Configuration dictionary schema* below.

If an error is encountered during configuration, this function will raise a *ValueError*, *TypeError*, *AttributeError* or *ImportError* with a suitably descriptive message. The following is a (possibly incomplete) list of conditions which will raise an error:

- A `level` which is not a string or which is a string not corresponding to an actual logging level.

- A `propagate` value which is not a boolean.
- An id which does not have a corresponding destination.
- A non-existent handler id found during an incremental call.
- An invalid logger name.
- Inability to resolve to an internal or external object.

Parsing is performed by the `DictConfigurator` class, whose constructor is passed the dictionary used for configuration, and has a `configure()` method. The *logging.config* module has a callable attribute `dictConfigClass` which is initially set to `DictConfigurator`. You can replace the value of `dictConfigClass` with a suitable implementation of your own.

dictConfig() calls `dictConfigClass` passing the specified dictionary, and then calls the `configure()` method on the returned object to put the configuration into effect:

```
def dictConfig(config):
    dictConfigClass(config).configure()
```

For example, a subclass of `DictConfigurator` could call `DictConfigurator.__init__()` in its own `__init__()`, then set up custom prefixes which would be usable in the subsequent `configure()` call. `dictConfigClass` would be bound to this new subclass, and then *dictConfig()* could be called exactly as in the default, uncustomized state.

New in version 3.2.

`logging.config.fileConfig`(*fname, defaults=None, disable_existing_loggers=True*)

Reads the logging configuration from a *configparser*-format file. The format of the file should be as described in *Configuration file format*. This function can be called several times from an application, allowing an end user to select from various pre-canned configurations (if the developer provides a mechanism to present the choices and load the chosen configuration).

Parameters

- **fname** – A filename, or a file-like object, or an instance derived from *RawConfigParser*. If a `RawConfigParser`-derived instance is passed, it is used as is. Otherwise, a `Configparser` is instantiated, and the configuration read by it from the object passed in `fname`. If that has a *readline()* method, it is assumed to be a file-like object and read using *read_file()*; otherwise, it is assumed to be a filename and passed to *read()*.
- **defaults** – Defaults to be passed to the ConfigParser can be specified in this argument.
- **disable_existing_loggers** – If specified as `False`, loggers which exist when this call is made are left enabled. The default is `True` because this enables old behaviour in a backward-compatible way. This behaviour is to disable any existing loggers unless they or their ancestors are explicitly named in the logging configuration.

Changed in version 3.4: An instance of a subclass of *RawConfigParser* is now accepted as a value for `fname`. This facilitates:

- Use of a configuration file where logging configuration is just part of the overall application configuration.
- Use of a configuration read from a file, and then modified by the using application (e.g. based on command-line parameters or other aspects of the runtime environment) before being passed to `fileConfig`.

`logging.config.listen`(*port=DEFAULT_LOGGING_CONFIG_PORT, verify=None*)

Starts up a socket server on the specified port, and listens for new configurations. If no port is specified, the module's default `DEFAULT_LOGGING_CONFIG_PORT` is used. Logging configurations will be sent as a file suitable for processing by *dictConfig()* or *fileConfig()*. Returns a *Thread* instance on which you can call *start()* to start the server, and which you can *join()* when appropriate. To stop the server, call *stopListening()*.

The `verify` argument, if specified, should be a callable which should verify whether bytes received across the socket are valid and should be processed. This could be done by encrypting and/or signing what is sent across the socket, such that the `verify` callable can perform signature verification and/or decryption. The `verify` callable is called with a single argument - the bytes received across the socket - and should return the bytes to be processed, or `None` to indicate that the bytes should be discarded. The returned bytes could be the same as the passed in bytes (e.g. when only verification is done), or they could be completely different (perhaps if decryption were performed).

To send a configuration to the socket, read in the configuration file and send it to the socket as a sequence of bytes preceded by a four-byte length string packed in binary using `struct.pack('>L', n)`.

Note: Because portions of the configuration are passed through *eval()*, use of this function may open its users to a security risk. While the function only binds to a socket on `localhost`, and so does not accept connections from remote machines, there are scenarios where untrusted code could be run under the account of the process which calls *listen()*. Specifically, if the process calling *listen()* runs on a multi-user machine where users cannot trust each other, then a malicious user could arrange to run essentially arbitrary code in a victim user's process, simply by connecting to the victim's *listen()* socket and sending a configuration which runs whatever code the attacker wants to have executed in the victim's process. This is especially easy to do if the default port is used, but not hard even if a different port is used). To avoid the risk of this happening, use the `verify` argument to *listen()* to prevent unrecognised configurations from being applied.

Changed in version 3.4: The `verify` argument was added.

Note: If you want to send configurations to the listener which don't disable existing loggers, you will need to use a JSON format for the configuration, which will use *dictConfig()* for configuration. This method allows you to specify `disable_existing_loggers` as `False` in the configuration you send.

`logging.config.`**`stopListening`**`()`

Stops the listening server which was created with a call to *listen()*. This is typically called before calling `join()` on the return value from *listen()*.

16.7.2 Configuration dictionary schema

Describing a logging configuration requires listing the various objects to create and the connections between them; for example, you may create a handler named 'console' and then say that the logger named 'startup' will send its messages to the 'console' handler. These objects aren't limited to those provided by the *logging* module because you might write your own formatter or handler class. The parameters to these classes may also need to include external objects such as `sys.stderr`. The syntax for describing these objects and connections is defined in *Object connections* below.

Dictionary Schema Details

The dictionary passed to *dictConfig()* must contain the following keys:

- *version* - to be set to an integer value representing the schema version. The only valid value at present is 1, but having this key allows the schema to evolve while still preserving backwards compatibility.

All other keys are optional, but if present they will be interpreted as described below. In all cases below where a 'configuring dict' is mentioned, it will be checked for the special `'()'` key to see if a custom instantiation is required. If so, the mechanism described in *User-defined objects* below is used to create an instance; otherwise, the context is used to determine what to instantiate.

- *formatters* - the corresponding value will be a dict in which each key is a formatter id and each value is a dict describing how to configure the corresponding `Formatter` instance.

  The configuring dict is searched for keys `format` and `datefmt` (with defaults of `None`) and these are used to construct a `Formatter` instance.

- *filters* - the corresponding value will be a dict in which each key is a filter id and each value is a dict describing how to configure the corresponding Filter instance.

  The configuring dict is searched for the key `name` (defaulting to the empty string) and this is used to construct a `logging.Filter` instance.

- *handlers* - the corresponding value will be a dict in which each key is a handler id and each value is a dict describing how to configure the corresponding Handler instance.

  The configuring dict is searched for the following keys:

  - `class` (mandatory). This is the fully qualified name of the handler class.
  - `level` (optional). The level of the handler.
  - `formatter` (optional). The id of the formatter for this handler.
  - `filters` (optional). A list of ids of the filters for this handler.

  All *other* keys are passed through as keyword arguments to the handler's constructor. For example, given the snippet:

```
handlers:
  console:
    class : logging.StreamHandler
    formatter: brief
    level   : INFO
    filters: [allow_foo]
    stream  : ext://sys.stdout
  file:
    class : logging.handlers.RotatingFileHandler
    formatter: precise
    filename: logconfig.log
    maxBytes: 1024
    backupCount: 3
```

  the handler with id `console` is instantiated as a `logging.StreamHandler`, using `sys.stdout` as the underlying stream. The handler with id `file` is instantiated as a `logging.handlers.RotatingFileHandler` with the keyword arguments `filename='logconfig.log', maxBytes=1024, backupCount=3`.

- *loggers* - the corresponding value will be a dict in which each key is a logger name and each value is a dict describing how to configure the corresponding Logger instance.

  The configuring dict is searched for the following keys:

  - `level` (optional). The level of the logger.
  - `propagate` (optional). The propagation setting of the logger.
  - `filters` (optional). A list of ids of the filters for this logger.
  - `handlers` (optional). A list of ids of the handlers for this logger.

The specified loggers will be configured according to the level, propagation, filters and handlers specified.

- *root* - this will be the configuration for the root logger. Processing of the configuration will be as for any logger, except that the `propagate` setting will not be applicable.
- *incremental* - whether the configuration is to be interpreted as incremental to the existing configuration. This value defaults to `False`, which means that the specified configuration replaces the existing configuration with the same semantics as used by the existing *fileConfig()* API.

  If the specified value is `True`, the configuration is processed as described in the section on *Incremental Configuration*.
- *disable_existing_loggers* - whether any existing loggers are to be disabled. This setting mirrors the parameter of the same name in *fileConfig()*. If absent, this parameter defaults to `True`. This value is ignored if *incremental* is `True`.

Incremental Configuration

It is difficult to provide complete flexibility for incremental configuration. For example, because objects such as filters and formatters are anonymous, once a configuration is set up, it is not possible to refer to such anonymous objects when augmenting a configuration.

Furthermore, there is not a compelling case for arbitrarily altering the object graph of loggers, handlers, filters, formatters at run-time, once a configuration is set up; the verbosity of loggers and handlers can be controlled just by setting levels (and, in the case of loggers, propagation flags). Changing the object graph arbitrarily in a safe way is problematic in a multi-threaded environment; while not impossible, the benefits are not worth the complexity it adds to the implementation.

Thus, when the `incremental` key of a configuration dict is present and is `True`, the system will completely ignore any `formatters` and `filters` entries, and process only the `level` settings in the `handlers` entries, and the `level` and `propagate` settings in the `loggers` and `root` entries.

Using a value in the configuration dict lets configurations to be sent over the wire as pickled dicts to a socket listener. Thus, the logging verbosity of a long-running application can be altered over time with no need to stop and restart the application.

Object connections

The schema describes a set of logging objects - loggers, handlers, formatters, filters - which are connected to each other in an object graph. Thus, the schema needs to represent connections between the objects. For example, say that, once configured, a particular logger has attached to it a particular handler. For the purposes of this discussion, we can say that the logger represents the source, and the handler the destination, of a connection between the two. Of course in the configured objects this is represented by the logger holding a reference to the handler. In the configuration dict, this is done by giving each destination object an id which identifies it unambiguously, and then using the id in the source object's configuration to indicate that a connection exists between the source and the destination object with that id.

So, for example, consider the following YAML snippet:

```
formatters:
  brief:
    # configuration for formatter with id 'brief' goes here
  precise:
    # configuration for formatter with id 'precise' goes here
handlers:
  h1: #This is an id
   # configuration of handler with id 'h1' goes here
```

```
    formatter: brief
  h2: #This is another id
    # configuration of handler with id 'h2' goes here
    formatter: precise
loggers:
  foo.bar.baz:
    # other configuration for logger 'foo.bar.baz'
    handlers: [h1, h2]
```

(Note: YAML used here because it's a little more readable than the equivalent Python source form for the dictionary.)

The ids for loggers are the logger names which would be used programmatically to obtain a reference to those loggers, e.g. `foo.bar.baz`. The ids for Formatters and Filters can be any string value (such as `brief`, `precise` above) and they are transient, in that they are only meaningful for processing the configuration dictionary and used to determine connections between objects, and are not persisted anywhere when the configuration call is complete.

The above snippet indicates that logger named `foo.bar.baz` should have two handlers attached to it, which are described by the handler ids `h1` and `h2`. The formatter for `h1` is that described by id `brief`, and the formatter for `h2` is that described by id `precise`.

User-defined objects

The schema supports user-defined objects for handlers, filters and formatters. (Loggers do not need to have different types for different instances, so there is no support in this configuration schema for user-defined logger classes.)

Objects to be configured are described by dictionaries which detail their configuration. In some places, the logging system will be able to infer from the context how an object is to be instantiated, but when a user-defined object is to be instantiated, the system will not know how to do this. In order to provide complete flexibility for user-defined object instantiation, the user needs to provide a 'factory' - a callable which is called with a configuration dictionary and which returns the instantiated object. This is signalled by an absolute import path to the factory being made available under the special key `'()'`. Here's a concrete example:

```
formatters:
  brief:
    format: '%(message)s'
  default:
    format: '%(asctime)s %(levelname)-8s %(name)-15s %(message)s'
    datefmt: '%Y-%m-%d %H:%M:%S'
  custom:
      (): my.package.customFormatterFactory
      bar: baz
      spam: 99.9
      answer: 42
```

The above YAML snippet defines three formatters. The first, with id `brief`, is a standard *logging.Formatter* instance with the specified format string. The second, with id `default`, has a longer format and also defines the time format explicitly, and will result in a *logging.Formatter* initialized with those two format strings. Shown in Python source form, the `brief` and `default` formatters have configuration sub-dictionaries:

```
{
  'format' : '%(message)s'
}
```

and:

```
{
  'format' : '%(asctime)s %(levelname)-8s %(name)-15s %(message)s',
  'datefmt' : '%Y-%m-%d %H:%M:%S'
}
```

respectively, and as these dictionaries do not contain the special key `'()'`, the instantiation is inferred from the context: as a result, standard *logging.Formatter* instances are created. The configuration sub-dictionary for the third formatter, with id `custom`, is:

```
{
  '()' : 'my.package.customFormatterFactory',
  'bar' : 'baz',
  'spam' : 99.9,
  'answer' : 42
}
```

and this contains the special key `'()'`, which means that user-defined instantiation is wanted. In this case, the specified factory callable will be used. If it is an actual callable it will be used directly - otherwise, if you specify a string (as in the example) the actual callable will be located using normal import mechanisms. The callable will be called with the **remaining** items in the configuration sub-dictionary as keyword arguments. In the above example, the formatter with id `custom` will be assumed to be returned by the call:

```
my.package.customFormatterFactory(bar='baz', spam=99.9, answer=42)
```

The key `'()'` has been used as the special key because it is not a valid keyword parameter name, and so will not clash with the names of the keyword arguments used in the call. The `'()'` also serves as a mnemonic that the corresponding value is a callable.

Access to external objects

There are times where a configuration needs to refer to objects external to the configuration, for example `sys.stderr`. If the configuration dict is constructed using Python code, this is straightforward, but a problem arises when the configuration is provided via a text file (e.g. JSON, YAML). In a text file, there is no standard way to distinguish `sys.stderr` from the literal string `'sys.stderr'`. To facilitate this distinction, the configuration system looks for certain special prefixes in string values and treat them specially. For example, if the literal string `'ext://sys.stderr'` is provided as a value in the configuration, then the `ext://` will be stripped off and the remainder of the value processed using normal import mechanisms.

The handling of such prefixes is done in a way analogous to protocol handling: there is a generic mechanism to look for prefixes which match the regular expression `^(?P<prefix>[a-z]+)://(?P<suffix>.*)$` whereby, if the `prefix` is recognised, the `suffix` is processed in a prefix-dependent manner and the result of the processing replaces the string value. If the prefix is not recognised, then the string value will be left as-is.

Access to internal objects

As well as external objects, there is sometimes also a need to refer to objects in the configuration. This will be done implicitly by the configuration system for things that it knows about. For example, the string value `'DEBUG'` for a `level` in a logger or handler will automatically be converted to the value `logging.DEBUG`, and the `handlers`, `filters` and `formatter` entries will take an object id and resolve to the appropriate destination object.

However, a more generic mechanism is needed for user-defined objects which are not known to the *logging* module. For example, consider *logging.handlers.MemoryHandler*, which takes a `target` argument which is another handler to delegate to. Since the system already knows about this class, then in the configuration, the given `target` just needs to be the object id of the relevant target handler, and the system will resolve to the handler from the id. If, however, a user defines a `my.package.MyHandler` which has an `alternate` handler, the configuration system would not know that the `alternate` referred to a handler. To cater for this, a generic resolution system allows the user to specify:

```
handlers:
  file:
    # configuration of file handler goes here

  custom:
    (): my.package.MyHandler
    alternate: cfg://handlers.file
```

The literal string `'cfg://handlers.file'` will be resolved in an analogous way to strings with the `ext://` prefix, but looking in the configuration itself rather than the import namespace. The mechanism allows access by dot or by index, in a similar way to that provided by `str.format`. Thus, given the following snippet:

```
handlers:
  email:
    class: logging.handlers.SMTPHandler
    mailhost: localhost
    fromaddr: my_app@domain.tld
    toaddrs:
      - support_team@domain.tld
      - dev_team@domain.tld
    subject: Houston, we have a problem.
```

in the configuration, the string `'cfg://handlers'` would resolve to the dict with key `handlers`, the string `'cfg://handlers.email` would resolve to the dict with key `email` in the `handlers` dict, and so on. The string `'cfg://handlers.email.toaddrs[1]` would resolve to `'dev_team.domain.tld'` and the string `'cfg://handlers.email.toaddrs[0]'` would resolve to the value `'support_team@domain.tld'`. The `subject` value could be accessed using either `'cfg://handlers.email.subject'` or, equivalently, `'cfg://handlers.email[subject]'`. The latter form only needs to be used if the key contains spaces or non-alphanumeric characters. If an index value consists only of decimal digits, access will be attempted using the corresponding integer value, falling back to the string value if needed.

Given a string `cfg://handlers.myhandler.mykey.123`, this will resolve to `config_dict['handlers']['myhandler']['mykey']['123']`. If the string is specified as `cfg://handlers.myhandler.mykey[123]`, the system will attempt to retrieve the value from `config_dict['handlers']['myhandler']['mykey'][123]`, and fall back to `config_dict['handlers']['myhandler']['mykey']['123']` if that fails.

Import resolution and custom importers

Import resolution, by default, uses the builtin *`__import__()`* function to do its importing. You may want to replace this with your own importing mechanism: if so, you can replace the `importer` attribute of the `DictConfigurator` or its superclass, the `BaseConfigurator` class. However, you need to be careful because of the way functions are accessed from classes via descriptors. If you are using a Python callable to do your imports, and you want to define it at class level rather than instance level, you need to wrap it with *`staticmethod()`*. For example:

```
from importlib import import_module
from logging.config import BaseConfigurator

BaseConfigurator.importer = staticmethod(import_module)
```

You don't need to wrap with *staticmethod()* if you're setting the import callable on a configurator *instance*.

16.7.3 Configuration file format

The configuration file format understood by *fileConfig()* is based on *configparser* functionality. The file must contain sections called `[loggers]`, `[handlers]` and `[formatters]` which identify by name the entities of each type which are defined in the file. For each such entity, there is a separate section which identifies how that entity is configured. Thus, for a logger named `log01` in the `[loggers]` section, the relevant configuration details are held in a section `[logger_log01]`. Similarly, a handler called `hand01` in the `[handlers]` section will have its configuration held in a section called `[handler_hand01]`, while a formatter called `form01` in the `[formatters]` section will have its configuration specified in a section called `[formatter_form01]`. The root logger configuration must be specified in a section called `[logger_root]`.

Note: The *fileConfig()* API is older than the *dictConfig()* API and does not provide functionality to cover certain aspects of logging. For example, you cannot configure *Filter* objects, which provide for filtering of messages beyond simple integer levels, using *fileConfig()*. If you need to have instances of *Filter* in your logging configuration, you will need to use *dictConfig()*. Note that future enhancements to configuration functionality will be added to *dictConfig()*, so it's worth considering transitioning to this newer API when it's convenient to do so.

Examples of these sections in the file are given below.

```
[loggers]
keys=root,log02,log03,log04,log05,log06,log07

[handlers]
keys=hand01,hand02,hand03,hand04,hand05,hand06,hand07,hand08,hand09

[formatters]
keys=form01,form02,form03,form04,form05,form06,form07,form08,form09
```

The root logger must specify a level and a list of handlers. An example of a root logger section is given below.

```
[logger_root]
level=NOTSET
handlers=hand01
```

The `level` entry can be one of `DEBUG, INFO, WARNING, ERROR, CRITICAL` or `NOTSET`. For the root logger only, `NOTSET` means that all messages will be logged. Level values are *eval()*uated in the context of the `logging` package's namespace.

The `handlers` entry is a comma separated list of handler names, which must appear in the `[handlers]` section. These names must appear in the `[handlers]` section and have corresponding sections in the configuration file.

For loggers other than the root logger, some additional information is required. This is illustrated by the following example.

```
[logger_parser]
level=DEBUG
handlers=hand01
propagate=1
qualname=compiler.parser
```

The **level** and **handlers** entries are interpreted as for the root logger, except that if a non-root logger's level is specified as NOTSET, the system consults loggers higher up the hierarchy to determine the effective level of the logger. The **propagate** entry is set to 1 to indicate that messages must propagate to handlers higher up the logger hierarchy from this logger, or 0 to indicate that messages are **not** propagated to handlers up the hierarchy. The **qualname** entry is the hierarchical channel name of the logger, that is to say the name used by the application to get the logger.

Sections which specify handler configuration are exemplified by the following.

```
[handler_hand01]
class=StreamHandler
level=NOTSET
formatter=form01
args=(sys.stdout,)
```

The **class** entry indicates the handler's class (as determined by *eval()* in the logging package's namespace). The **level** is interpreted as for loggers, and NOTSET is taken to mean 'log everything'.

The **formatter** entry indicates the key name of the formatter for this handler. If blank, a default formatter (**logging._defaultFormatter**) is used. If a name is specified, it must appear in the **[formatters]** section and have a corresponding section in the configuration file.

The **args** entry, when *eval()*uated in the context of the logging package's namespace, is the list of arguments to the constructor for the handler class. Refer to the constructors for the relevant handlers, or to the examples below, to see how typical entries are constructed.

```
[handler_hand02]
class=FileHandler
level=DEBUG
formatter=form02
args=('python.log', 'w')

[handler_hand03]
class=handlers.SocketHandler
level=INFO
formatter=form03
args=('localhost', handlers.DEFAULT_TCP_LOGGING_PORT)

[handler_hand04]
class=handlers.DatagramHandler
level=WARN
formatter=form04
args=('localhost', handlers.DEFAULT_UDP_LOGGING_PORT)

[handler_hand05]
class=handlers.SysLogHandler
level=ERROR
formatter=form05
args=(('localhost', handlers.SYSLOG_UDP_PORT), handlers.SysLogHandler.LOG_USER)

[handler_hand06]
class=handlers.NTEventLogHandler
level=CRITICAL
formatter=form06
args=('Python Application', '', 'Application')

[handler_hand07]
class=handlers.SMTPHandler
level=WARN
```

```
formatter=form07
args=('localhost', 'from@abc', ['user1@abc', 'user2@xyz'], 'Logger Subject')

[handler_hand08]
class=handlers.MemoryHandler
level=NOTSET
formatter=form08
target=
args=(10, ERROR)

[handler_hand09]
class=handlers.HTTPHandler
level=NOTSET
formatter=form09
args=('localhost:9022', '/log', 'GET')
```

Sections which specify formatter configuration are typified by the following.

```
[formatter_form01]
format=F1 %(asctime)s %(levelname)s %(message)s
datefmt=
class=logging.Formatter
```

The `format` entry is the overall format string, and the `datefmt` entry is the `strftime()`-compatible date/time format string. If empty, the package substitutes ISO8601 format date/times, which is almost equivalent to specifying the date format string `'%Y-%m-%d %H:%M:%S'`. The ISO8601 format also specifies milliseconds, which are appended to the result of using the above format string, with a comma separator. An example time in ISO8601 format is `2003-01-23 00:29:50,411`.

The `class` entry is optional. It indicates the name of the formatter's class (as a dotted module and class name.) This option is useful for instantiating a *Formatter* subclass. Subclasses of *Formatter* can present exception tracebacks in an expanded or condensed format.

Note: Due to the use of *eval()* as described above, there are potential security risks which result from using the *listen()* to send and receive configurations via sockets. The risks are limited to where multiple users with no mutual trust run code on the same machine; see the *listen()* documentation for more information.

See also:

Module *logging* API reference for the logging module.

Module *logging.handlers* Useful handlers included with the logging module.

16.8 `logging.handlers` — Logging handlers

Source code: Lib/logging/handlers.py

Important

This page contains only reference information. For tutorials, please see

- Basic Tutorial
- Advanced Tutorial

- Logging Cookbook

The following useful handlers are provided in the package. Note that three of the handlers (*StreamHandler*, *FileHandler* and *NullHandler*) are actually defined in the *logging* module itself, but have been documented here along with the other handlers.

16.8.1 StreamHandler

The *StreamHandler* class, located in the core *logging* package, sends logging output to streams such as *sys.stdout*, *sys.stderr* or any file-like object (or, more precisely, any object which supports `write()` and `flush()` methods).

class logging.StreamHandler(*stream=None*)

Returns a new instance of the *StreamHandler* class. If *stream* is specified, the instance will use it for logging output; otherwise, *sys.stderr* will be used.

emit(*record*)

If a formatter is specified, it is used to format the record. The record is then written to the stream with a terminator. If exception information is present, it is formatted using *traceback.print_exception()* and appended to the stream.

flush()

Flushes the stream by calling its *flush()* method. Note that the `close()` method is inherited from *Handler* and so does no output, so an explicit *flush()* call may be needed at times.

Changed in version 3.2: The `StreamHandler` class now has a `terminator` attribute, default value `'\n'`, which is used as the terminator when writing a formatted record to a stream. If you don't want this newline termination, you can set the handler instance's `terminator` attribute to the empty string. In earlier versions, the terminator was hardcoded as `'\n'`.

16.8.2 FileHandler

The *FileHandler* class, located in the core *logging* package, sends logging output to a disk file. It inherits the output functionality from *StreamHandler*.

class logging.FileHandler(*filename, mode='a', encoding=None, delay=False*)

Returns a new instance of the *FileHandler* class. The specified file is opened and used as the stream for logging. If *mode* is not specified, `'a'` is used. If *encoding* is not `None`, it is used to open the file with that encoding. If *delay* is true, then file opening is deferred until the first call to *emit()*. By default, the file grows indefinitely.

Changed in version 3.6: As well as string values, *Path* objects are also accepted for the *filename* argument.

close()

Closes the file.

emit(*record*)

Outputs the record to the file.

16.8.3 NullHandler

New in version 3.1.

The *NullHandler* class, located in the core *logging* package, does not do any formatting or output. It is essentially a 'no-op' handler for use by library developers.

class logging.NullHandler

Returns a new instance of the *NullHandler* class.

emit(*record*)

This method does nothing.

handle(*record*)

This method does nothing.

createLock()

This method returns `None` for the lock, since there is no underlying I/O to which access needs to be serialized.

See library-config for more information on how to use *NullHandler*.

16.8.4 WatchedFileHandler

The *WatchedFileHandler* class, located in the *logging.handlers* module, is a `FileHandler` which watches the file it is logging to. If the file changes, it is closed and reopened using the file name.

A file change can happen because of usage of programs such as *newsyslog* and *logrotate* which perform log file rotation. This handler, intended for use under Unix/Linux, watches the file to see if it has changed since the last emit. (A file is deemed to have changed if its device or inode have changed.) If the file has changed, the old file stream is closed, and the file opened to get a new stream.

This handler is not appropriate for use under Windows, because under Windows open log files cannot be moved or renamed - logging opens the files with exclusive locks - and so there is no need for such a handler. Furthermore, *ST_INO* is not supported under Windows; *stat()* always returns zero for this value.

class logging.handlers.WatchedFileHandler(*filename, mode='a', encoding=None, delay=False*)

Returns a new instance of the *WatchedFileHandler* class. The specified file is opened and used as the stream for logging. If *mode* is not specified, `'a'` is used. If *encoding* is not `None`, it is used to open the file with that encoding. If *delay* is true, then file opening is deferred until the first call to *emit()*. By default, the file grows indefinitely.

Changed in version 3.6: As well as string values, *Path* objects are also accepted for the *filename* argument.

reopenIfNeeded()

Checks to see if the file has changed. If it has, the existing stream is flushed and closed and the file opened again, typically as a precursor to outputting the record to the file.

New in version 3.6.

emit(*record*)

Outputs the record to the file, but first calls *reopenIfNeeded()* to reopen the file if it has changed.

16.8.5 BaseRotatingHandler

The *BaseRotatingHandler* class, located in the *logging.handlers* module, is the base class for the rotating file handlers, *RotatingFileHandler* and *TimedRotatingFileHandler*. You should not need to instantiate this class, but it has attributes and methods you may need to override.

class logging.handlers.BaseRotatingHandler(*filename, mode, encoding=None, delay=False*)

The parameters are as for `FileHandler`. The attributes are:

namer
If this attribute is set to a callable, the *rotation_filename()* method delegates to this callable. The parameters passed to the callable are those passed to *rotation_filename()*.

Note: The namer function is called quite a few times during rollover, so it should be as simple and as fast as possible. It should also return the same output every time for a given input, otherwise the rollover behaviour may not work as expected.

New in version 3.3.

rotator
If this attribute is set to a callable, the *rotate()* method delegates to this callable. The parameters passed to the callable are those passed to *rotate()*.

New in version 3.3.

rotation_filename(*default_name*)
Modify the filename of a log file when rotating.

This is provided so that a custom filename can be provided.

The default implementation calls the 'namer' attribute of the handler, if it's callable, passing the default name to it. If the attribute isn't callable (the default is `None`), the name is returned unchanged.

Parameters **default_name** – The default name for the log file.

New in version 3.3.

rotate(*source*, *dest*)
When rotating, rotate the current log.

The default implementation calls the 'rotator' attribute of the handler, if it's callable, passing the source and dest arguments to it. If the attribute isn't callable (the default is `None`), the source is simply renamed to the destination.

Parameters

- **source** – The source filename. This is normally the base filename, e.g. 'test.log'.
- **dest** – The destination filename. This is normally what the source is rotated to, e.g. 'test.log.1'.

New in version 3.3.

The reason the attributes exist is to save you having to subclass - you can use the same callables for instances of *RotatingFileHandler* and *TimedRotatingFileHandler*. If either the namer or rotator callable raises an exception, this will be handled in the same way as any other exception during an `emit()` call, i.e. via the `handleError()` method of the handler.

If you need to make more significant changes to rotation processing, you can override the methods.

For an example, see cookbook-rotator-namer.

16.8.6 RotatingFileHandler

The *RotatingFileHandler* class, located in the *logging.handlers* module, supports rotation of disk log files.

class logging.handlers.RotatingFileHandler(*filename*, *mode='a'*, *maxBytes=0*, *backupCount=0*, *encoding=None*, *delay=False*)
Returns a new instance of the *RotatingFileHandler* class. The specified file is opened and used as

the stream for logging. If *mode* is not specified, 'a' is used. If *encoding* is not None, it is used to open the file with that encoding. If *delay* is true, then file opening is deferred until the first call to *emit()*. By default, the file grows indefinitely.

You can use the *maxBytes* and *backupCount* values to allow the file to *rollover* at a predetermined size. When the size is about to be exceeded, the file is closed and a new file is silently opened for output. Rollover occurs whenever the current log file is nearly *maxBytes* in length; but if either of *maxBytes* or *backupCount* is zero, rollover never occurs, so you generally want to set *backupCount* to at least 1, and have a non-zero *maxBytes*. When *backupCount* is non-zero, the system will save old log files by appending the extensions '.1', '.2' etc., to the filename. For example, with a *backupCount* of 5 and a base file name of `app.log`, you would get `app.log`, `app.log.1`, `app.log.2`, up to `app.log.5`. The file being written to is always `app.log`. When this file is filled, it is closed and renamed to `app.log.1`, and if files `app.log.1`, `app.log.2`, etc. exist, then they are renamed to `app.log.2`, `app.log.3` etc. respectively.

Changed in version 3.6: As well as string values, *Path* objects are also accepted for the *filename* argument.

doRollover()
Does a rollover, as described above.

emit(*record*)
Outputs the record to the file, catering for rollover as described previously.

16.8.7 TimedRotatingFileHandler

The *TimedRotatingFileHandler* class, located in the *logging.handlers* module, supports rotation of disk log files at certain timed intervals.

class logging.handlers.TimedRotatingFileHandler(*filename, when='h', interval=1, backupCount=0, encoding=None, delay=False, utc=False, atTime=None*)

Returns a new instance of the *TimedRotatingFileHandler* class. The specified file is opened and used as the stream for logging. On rotating it also sets the filename suffix. Rotating happens based on the product of *when* and *interval*.

You can use the *when* to specify the type of *interval*. The list of possible values is below. Note that they are not case sensitive.

Value	Type of interval	If/how *atTime* is used
'S'	Seconds	Ignored
'M'	Minutes	Ignored
'H'	Hours	Ignored
'D'	Days	Ignored
'W0'-'W6'	Weekday (0=Monday)	Used to compute initial rollover time
'midnight'	Roll over at midnight, if *atTime* not specified, else at time *atTime*	Used to compute initial rollover time

When using weekday-based rotation, specify 'W0' for Monday, 'W1' for Tuesday, and so on up to 'W6' for Sunday. In this case, the value passed for *interval* isn't used.

The system will save old log files by appending extensions to the filename. The extensions are date-and-time based, using the strftime format `%Y-%m-%d_%H-%M-%S` or a leading portion thereof, depending on the rollover interval.

When computing the next rollover time for the first time (when the handler is created), the last modification time of an existing log file, or else the current time, is used to compute when the next rotation will occur.

If the *utc* argument is true, times in UTC will be used; otherwise local time is used.

If *backupCount* is nonzero, at most *backupCount* files will be kept, and if more would be created when rollover occurs, the oldest one is deleted. The deletion logic uses the interval to determine which files to delete, so changing the interval may leave old files lying around.

If *delay* is true, then file opening is deferred until the first call to `emit()`.

If *atTime* is not `None`, it must be a `datetime.time` instance which specifies the time of day when rollover occurs, for the cases where rollover is set to happen "at midnight" or "on a particular weekday". Note that in these cases, the *atTime* value is effectively used to compute the *initial* rollover, and subsequent rollovers would be calculated via the normal interval calculation.

Note: Calculation of the initial rollover time is done when the handler is initialised. Calculation of subsequent rollover times is done only when rollover occurs, and rollover occurs only when emitting output. If this is not kept in mind, it might lead to some confusion. For example, if an interval of "every minute" is set, that does not mean you will always see log files with times (in the filename) separated by a minute; if, during application execution, logging output is generated more frequently than once a minute, *then* you can expect to see log files with times separated by a minute. If, on the other hand, logging messages are only output once every five minutes (say), then there will be gaps in the file times corresponding to the minutes where no output (and hence no rollover) occurred.

Changed in version 3.4: *atTime* parameter was added.

Changed in version 3.6: As well as string values, `Path` objects are also accepted for the *filename* argument.

doRollover()

Does a rollover, as described above.

emit(*record*)

Outputs the record to the file, catering for rollover as described above.

16.8.8 SocketHandler

The `SocketHandler` class, located in the `logging.handlers` module, sends logging output to a network socket. The base class uses a TCP socket.

class **logging.handlers.SocketHandler**(*host*, *port*)

Returns a new instance of the `SocketHandler` class intended to communicate with a remote machine whose address is given by *host* and *port*.

Changed in version 3.4: If `port` is specified as `None`, a Unix domain socket is created using the value in `host` - otherwise, a TCP socket is created.

close()

Closes the socket.

emit()

Pickles the record's attribute dictionary and writes it to the socket in binary format. If there is an error with the socket, silently drops the packet. If the connection was previously lost, re-establishes the connection. To unpickle the record at the receiving end into a `LogRecord`, use the `makeLogRecord()` function.

handleError()
Handles an error which has occurred during *emit()*. The most likely cause is a lost connection. Closes the socket so that we can retry on the next event.

makeSocket()
This is a factory method which allows subclasses to define the precise type of socket they want. The default implementation creates a TCP socket (*socket.SOCK_STREAM*).

makePickle(*record*)
Pickles the record's attribute dictionary in binary format with a length prefix, and returns it ready for transmission across the socket.

Note that pickles aren't completely secure. If you are concerned about security, you may want to override this method to implement a more secure mechanism. For example, you can sign pickles using HMAC and then verify them on the receiving end, or alternatively you can disable unpickling of global objects on the receiving end.

send(*packet*)
Send a pickled string *packet* to the socket. This function allows for partial sends which can happen when the network is busy.

createSocket()
Tries to create a socket; on failure, uses an exponential back-off algorithm. On initial failure, the handler will drop the message it was trying to send. When subsequent messages are handled by the same instance, it will not try connecting until some time has passed. The default parameters are such that the initial delay is one second, and if after that delay the connection still can't be made, the handler will double the delay each time up to a maximum of 30 seconds.

This behaviour is controlled by the following handler attributes:

- `retryStart` (initial delay, defaulting to 1.0 seconds).
- `retryFactor` (multiplier, defaulting to 2.0).
- `retryMax` (maximum delay, defaulting to 30.0 seconds).

This means that if the remote listener starts up *after* the handler has been used, you could lose messages (since the handler won't even attempt a connection until the delay has elapsed, but just silently drop messages during the delay period).

16.8.9 DatagramHandler

The *DatagramHandler* class, located in the *logging.handlers* module, inherits from *SocketHandler* to support sending logging messages over UDP sockets.

class logging.handlers.DatagramHandler(*host*, *port*)
Returns a new instance of the *DatagramHandler* class intended to communicate with a remote machine whose address is given by *host* and *port*.

Changed in version 3.4: If `port` is specified as `None`, a Unix domain socket is created using the value in `host` - otherwise, a TCP socket is created.

emit()
Pickles the record's attribute dictionary and writes it to the socket in binary format. If there is an error with the socket, silently drops the packet. To unpickle the record at the receiving end into a *LogRecord*, use the *makeLogRecord()* function.

makeSocket()
The factory method of *SocketHandler* is here overridden to create a UDP socket (*socket.SOCK_DGRAM*).

send(*s*)
Send a pickled string to a socket.

16.8.10 SysLogHandler

The `SysLogHandler` class, located in the `logging.handlers` module, supports sending logging messages to a remote or local Unix syslog.

class logging.handlers.SysLogHandler(*address=('localhost', SYSLOG_UDP_PORT), facility=LOG_USER, socktype=socket.SOCK_DGRAM*)
Returns a new instance of the `SysLogHandler` class intended to communicate with a remote Unix machine whose address is given by *address* in the form of a `(host, port)` tuple. If *address* is not specified, `('localhost', 514)` is used. The address is used to open a socket. An alternative to providing a `(host, port)` tuple is providing an address as a string, for example '/dev/log'. In this case, a Unix domain socket is used to send the message to the syslog. If *facility* is not specified, `LOG_USER` is used. The type of socket opened depends on the *socktype* argument, which defaults to `socket.SOCK_DGRAM` and thus opens a UDP socket. To open a TCP socket (for use with the newer syslog daemons such as rsyslog), specify a value of `socket.SOCK_STREAM`.

Note that if your server is not listening on UDP port 514, `SysLogHandler` may appear not to work. In that case, check what address you should be using for a domain socket - it's system dependent. For example, on Linux it's usually '/dev/log' but on OS/X it's '/var/run/syslog'. You'll need to check your platform and use the appropriate address (you may need to do this check at runtime if your application needs to run on several platforms). On Windows, you pretty much have to use the UDP option.

Changed in version 3.2: *socktype* was added.

close()
Closes the socket to the remote host.

emit(*record*)
The record is formatted, and then sent to the syslog server. If exception information is present, it is *not* sent to the server.

Changed in version 3.2.1: (See: bpo-12168.) In earlier versions, the message sent to the syslog daemons was always terminated with a NUL byte, because early versions of these daemons expected a NUL terminated message - even though it's not in the relevant specification (RFC 5424). More recent versions of these daemons don't expect the NUL byte but strip it off if it's there, and even more recent daemons (which adhere more closely to RFC 5424) pass the NUL byte on as part of the message.

To enable easier handling of syslog messages in the face of all these differing daemon behaviours, the appending of the NUL byte has been made configurable, through the use of a class-level attribute, `append_nul`. This defaults to `True` (preserving the existing behaviour) but can be set to `False` on a `SysLogHandler` instance in order for that instance to *not* append the NUL terminator.

Changed in version 3.3: (See: bpo-12419.) In earlier versions, there was no facility for an "ident" or "tag" prefix to identify the source of the message. This can now be specified using a class-level attribute, defaulting to `""` to preserve existing behaviour, but which can be overridden on a `SysLogHandler` instance in order for that instance to prepend the ident to every message handled. Note that the provided ident must be text, not bytes, and is prepended to the message exactly as is.

encodePriority(*facility, priority*)
Encodes the facility and priority into an integer. You can pass in strings or integers - if strings are passed, internal mapping dictionaries are used to convert them to integers.

The symbolic `LOG_` values are defined in *SysLogHandler* and mirror the values defined in the `sys/syslog.h` header file.

Priorities

Name (string)	Symbolic value
`alert`	LOG_ALERT
`crit` or `critical`	LOG_CRIT
`debug`	LOG_DEBUG
`emerg` or `panic`	LOG_EMERG
`err` or `error`	LOG_ERR
`info`	LOG_INFO
`notice`	LOG_NOTICE
`warn` or `warning`	LOG_WARNING

Facilities

Name (string)	Symbolic value
`auth`	LOG_AUTH
`authpriv`	LOG_AUTHPRIV
`cron`	LOG_CRON
`daemon`	LOG_DAEMON
`ftp`	LOG_FTP
`kern`	LOG_KERN
`lpr`	LOG_LPR
`mail`	LOG_MAIL
`news`	LOG_NEWS
`syslog`	LOG_SYSLOG
`user`	LOG_USER
`uucp`	LOG_UUCP
`local0`	LOG_LOCAL0
`local1`	LOG_LOCAL1
`local2`	LOG_LOCAL2
`local3`	LOG_LOCAL3
`local4`	LOG_LOCAL4
`local5`	LOG_LOCAL5
`local6`	LOG_LOCAL6
`local7`	LOG_LOCAL7

mapPriority(*levelname*)

Maps a logging level name to a syslog priority name. You may need to override this if you are using custom levels, or if the default algorithm is not suitable for your needs. The default algorithm maps `DEBUG`, `INFO`, `WARNING`, `ERROR` and `CRITICAL` to the equivalent syslog names, and all other level names to 'warning'.

16.8.11 NTEventLogHandler

The *NTEventLogHandler* class, located in the *logging.handlers* module, supports sending logging messages to a local Windows NT, Windows 2000 or Windows XP event log. Before you can use it, you need Mark Hammond's Win32 extensions for Python installed.

class `logging.handlers.`**NTEventLogHandler**(*appname*, *dllname=None*, *logtype='Application'*)

Returns a new instance of the *NTEventLogHandler* class. The *appname* is used to define the application name as it appears in the event log. An appropriate registry entry is created using this name. The *dllname* should give the fully qualified pathname of a .dll or .exe which contains message definitions to hold in the log (if not specified, `'win32service.pyd'` is used - this is installed with the Win32 extensions and contains some basic placeholder message definitions. Note that use of these placeholders will make your event logs big, as the entire message source is held in the log. If you want slimmer logs, you have to pass in the name of your own .dll or .exe which contains the message definitions you want to use in the event log). The *logtype* is one of `'Application'`, `'System'` or `'Security'`, and defaults to `'Application'`.

close()

At this point, you can remove the application name from the registry as a source of event log entries. However, if you do this, you will not be able to see the events as you intended in the Event Log Viewer - it needs to be able to access the registry to get the .dll name. The current version does not do this.

emit(*record*)

Determines the message ID, event category and event type, and then logs the message in the NT event log.

getEventCategory(*record*)

Returns the event category for the record. Override this if you want to specify your own categories. This version returns 0.

getEventType(*record*)

Returns the event type for the record. Override this if you want to specify your own types. This version does a mapping using the handler's typemap attribute, which is set up in `__init__()` to a dictionary which contains mappings for `DEBUG`, `INFO`, `WARNING`, `ERROR` and `CRITICAL`. If you are using your own levels, you will either need to override this method or place a suitable dictionary in the handler's *typemap* attribute.

getMessageID(*record*)

Returns the message ID for the record. If you are using your own messages, you could do this by having the *msg* passed to the logger being an ID rather than a format string. Then, in here, you could use a dictionary lookup to get the message ID. This version returns 1, which is the base message ID in `win32service.pyd`.

16.8.12 SMTPHandler

The `SMTPHandler` class, located in the `logging.handlers` module, supports sending logging messages to an email address via SMTP.

class logging.handlers.SMTPHandler(*mailhost*, *fromaddr*, *toaddrs*, *subject*, *credentials=None*, *secure=None*, *timeout=1.0*)

Returns a new instance of the `SMTPHandler` class. The instance is initialized with the from and to addresses and subject line of the email. The *toaddrs* should be a list of strings. To specify a non-standard SMTP port, use the (host, port) tuple format for the *mailhost* argument. If you use a string, the standard SMTP port is used. If your SMTP server requires authentication, you can specify a (username, password) tuple for the *credentials* argument.

To specify the use of a secure protocol (TLS), pass in a tuple to the *secure* argument. This will only be used when authentication credentials are supplied. The tuple should be either an empty tuple, or a single-value tuple with the name of a keyfile, or a 2-value tuple with the names of the keyfile and certificate file. (This tuple is passed to the `smtplib.SMTP.starttls()` method.)

A timeout can be specified for communication with the SMTP server using the *timeout* argument.

New in version 3.3: The *timeout* argument was added.

emit(*record*)
Formats the record and sends it to the specified addressees.

getSubject(*record*)
If you want to specify a subject line which is record-dependent, override this method.

16.8.13 MemoryHandler

The *MemoryHandler* class, located in the *logging.handlers* module, supports buffering of logging records in memory, periodically flushing them to a *target* handler. Flushing occurs whenever the buffer is full, or when an event of a certain severity or greater is seen.

MemoryHandler is a subclass of the more general *BufferingHandler*, which is an abstract class. This buffers logging records in memory. Whenever each record is added to the buffer, a check is made by calling **shouldFlush()** to see if the buffer should be flushed. If it should, then **flush()** is expected to do the flushing.

class logging.handlers.BufferingHandler(*capacity*)
Initializes the handler with a buffer of the specified capacity.

emit(*record*)
Appends the record to the buffer. If *shouldFlush()* returns true, calls *flush()* to process the buffer.

flush()
You can override this to implement custom flushing behavior. This version just zaps the buffer to empty.

shouldFlush(*record*)
Returns true if the buffer is up to capacity. This method can be overridden to implement custom flushing strategies.

class logging.handlers.MemoryHandler(*capacity, flushLevel=ERROR, target=None, flushOnClose=True*)
Returns a new instance of the *MemoryHandler* class. The instance is initialized with a buffer size of *capacity*. If *flushLevel* is not specified, `ERROR` is used. If no *target* is specified, the target will need to be set using *setTarget()* before this handler does anything useful. If *flushOnClose* is specified as `False`, then the buffer is *not* flushed when the handler is closed. If not specified or specified as `True`, the previous behaviour of flushing the buffer will occur when the handler is closed.

Changed in version 3.6: The *flushOnClose* parameter was added.

close()
Calls *flush()*, sets the target to `None` and clears the buffer.

flush()
For a *MemoryHandler*, flushing means just sending the buffered records to the target, if there is one. The buffer is also cleared when this happens. Override if you want different behavior.

setTarget(*target*)
Sets the target handler for this handler.

shouldFlush(*record*)
Checks for buffer full or a record at the *flushLevel* or higher.

16.8.14 HTTPHandler

The *HTTPHandler* class, located in the *logging.handlers* module, supports sending logging messages to a Web server, using either `GET` or `POST` semantics.

class logging.handlers.**HTTPHandler**(*host*, *url*, *method='GET'*, *secure=False*, *credentials=None*, *context=None*)

Returns a new instance of the *HTTPHandler* class. The *host* can be of the form `host:port`, should you need to use a specific port number. If no *method* is specified, `GET` is used. If *secure* is true, a HTTPS connection will be used. The *context* parameter may be set to a *ssl.SSLContext* instance to configure the SSL settings used for the HTTPS connection. If *credentials* is specified, it should be a 2-tuple consisting of userid and password, which will be placed in a HTTP 'Authorization' header using Basic authentication. If you specify credentials, you should also specify secure=True so that your userid and password are not passed in cleartext across the wire.

Changed in version 3.5: The *context* parameter was added.

mapLogRecord(*record*)

Provides a dictionary, based on `record`, which is to be URL-encoded and sent to the web server. The default implementation just returns `record.__dict__`. This method can be overridden if e.g. only a subset of *LogRecord* is to be sent to the web server, or if more specific customization of what's sent to the server is required.

emit(*record*)

Sends the record to the Web server as a URL-encoded dictionary. The *mapLogRecord()* method is used to convert the record to the dictionary to be sent.

Note: Since preparing a record for sending it to a Web server is not the same as a generic formatting operation, using *setFormatter()* to specify a *Formatter* for a *HTTPHandler* has no effect. Instead of calling *format()*, this handler calls *mapLogRecord()* and then *urllib.parse.urlencode()* to encode the dictionary in a form suitable for sending to a Web server.

16.8.15 QueueHandler

New in version 3.2.

The *QueueHandler* class, located in the *logging.handlers* module, supports sending logging messages to a queue, such as those implemented in the *queue* or *multiprocessing* modules.

Along with the *QueueListener* class, *QueueHandler* can be used to let handlers do their work on a separate thread from the one which does the logging. This is important in Web applications and also other service applications where threads servicing clients need to respond as quickly as possible, while any potentially slow operations (such as sending an email via *SMTPHandler*) are done on a separate thread.

class logging.handlers.**QueueHandler**(*queue*)

Returns a new instance of the *QueueHandler* class. The instance is initialized with the queue to send messages to. The queue can be any queue-like object; it's used as-is by the *enqueue()* method, which needs to know how to send messages to it.

emit(*record*)

Enqueues the result of preparing the LogRecord.

prepare(*record*)

Prepares a record for queuing. The object returned by this method is enqueued.

The base implementation formats the record to merge the message and arguments, and removes unpickleable items from the record in-place.

You might want to override this method if you want to convert the record to a dict or JSON string, or send a modified copy of the record while leaving the original intact.

enqueue(*record*)
Enqueues the record on the queue using `put_nowait()`; you may want to override this if you want to use blocking behaviour, or a timeout, or a customized queue implementation.

16.8.16 QueueListener

New in version 3.2.

The *QueueListener* class, located in the *logging.handlers* module, supports receiving logging messages from a queue, such as those implemented in the *queue* or *multiprocessing* modules. The messages are received from a queue in an internal thread and passed, on the same thread, to one or more handlers for processing. While *QueueListener* is not itself a handler, it is documented here because it works hand-in-hand with *QueueHandler*.

Along with the *QueueHandler* class, *QueueListener* can be used to let handlers do their work on a separate thread from the one which does the logging. This is important in Web applications and also other service applications where threads servicing clients need to respond as quickly as possible, while any potentially slow operations (such as sending an email via *SMTPHandler*) are done on a separate thread.

class logging.handlers.QueueListener(*queue*, **handlers*, *respect_handler_level=False*)
Returns a new instance of the *QueueListener* class. The instance is initialized with the queue to send messages to and a list of handlers which will handle entries placed on the queue. The queue can be any queue-like object; it's passed as-is to the *dequeue()* method, which needs to know how to get messages from it. If `respect_handler_level` is `True`, a handler's level is respected (compared with the level for the message) when deciding whether to pass messages to that handler; otherwise, the behaviour is as in previous Python versions - to always pass each message to each handler.

Changed in version 3.5: The `respect_handler_levels` argument was added.

dequeue(*block*)
Dequeues a record and return it, optionally blocking.

The base implementation uses `get()`. You may want to override this method if you want to use timeouts or work with custom queue implementations.

prepare(*record*)
Prepare a record for handling.

This implementation just returns the passed-in record. You may want to override this method if you need to do any custom marshalling or manipulation of the record before passing it to the handlers.

handle(*record*)
Handle a record.

This just loops through the handlers offering them the record to handle. The actual object passed to the handlers is that which is returned from *prepare()*.

start()
Starts the listener.

This starts up a background thread to monitor the queue for LogRecords to process.

stop()
Stops the listener.

This asks the thread to terminate, and then waits for it to do so. Note that if you don't call this before your application exits, there may be some records still left on the queue, which won't be processed.

enqueue_sentinel()
Writes a sentinel to the queue to tell the listener to quit. This implementation uses `put_nowait()`.

You may want to override this method if you want to use timeouts or work with custom queue implementations.

New in version 3.3.

See also:

Module *logging* API reference for the logging module.

Module *logging.config* Configuration API for the logging module.

16.9 getpass — Portable password input

Source code: Lib/getpass.py

The *getpass* module provides two functions:

`getpass.getpass(prompt='Password: ', stream=None)`
Prompt the user for a password without echoing. The user is prompted using the string *prompt*, which defaults to `'Password: '`. On Unix, the prompt is written to the file-like object *stream* using the replace error handler if needed. *stream* defaults to the controlling terminal (`/dev/tty`) or if that is unavailable to `sys.stderr` (this argument is ignored on Windows).

If echo free input is unavailable getpass() falls back to printing a warning message to *stream* and reading from `sys.stdin` and issuing a *GetPassWarning*.

Note: If you call getpass from within IDLE, the input may be done in the terminal you launched IDLE from rather than the idle window itself.

`exception getpass.GetPassWarning`
A *UserWarning* subclass issued when password input may be echoed.

`getpass.getuser()`
Return the "login name" of the user.

This function checks the environment variables `LOGNAME`, `USER`, `LNAME` and `USERNAME`, in order, and returns the value of the first one which is set to a non-empty string. If none are set, the login name from the password database is returned on systems which support the *pwd* module, otherwise, an exception is raised.

In general, this function should be preferred over *os.getlogin()*.

16.10 curses — Terminal handling for character-cell displays

The *curses* module provides an interface to the curses library, the de-facto standard for portable advanced terminal handling.

While curses is most widely used in the Unix environment, versions are available for Windows, DOS, and possibly other systems as well. This extension module is designed to match the API of ncurses, an open-source curses library hosted on Linux and the BSD variants of Unix.

Note: Whenever the documentation mentions a *character* it can be specified as an integer, a one-character Unicode string or a one-byte byte string.

Whenever the documentation mentions a *character string* it can be specified as a Unicode string or a byte string.

Note: Since version 5.4, the ncurses library decides how to interpret non-ASCII data using the `nl_langinfo` function. That means that you have to call `locale.setlocale()` in the application and encode Unicode strings using one of the system's available encodings. This example uses the system's default encoding:

```
import locale
locale.setlocale(locale.LC_ALL, '')
code = locale.getpreferredencoding()
```

Then use *code* as the encoding for `str.encode()` calls.

See also:

Module `curses.ascii` Utilities for working with ASCII characters, regardless of your locale settings.

Module `curses.panel` A panel stack extension that adds depth to curses windows.

Module `curses.textpad` Editable text widget for curses supporting **Emacs**-like bindings.

curses-howto Tutorial material on using curses with Python, by Andrew Kuchling and Eric Raymond.

The Tools/demo/ directory in the Python source distribution contains some example programs using the curses bindings provided by this module.

16.10.1 Functions

The module `curses` defines the following exception:

exception curses.error
Exception raised when a curses library function returns an error.

Note: Whenever *x* or *y* arguments to a function or a method are optional, they default to the current cursor location. Whenever *attr* is optional, it defaults to `A_NORMAL`.

The module `curses` defines the following functions:

`curses.baudrate()`
Return the output speed of the terminal in bits per second. On software terminal emulators it will have a fixed high value. Included for historical reasons; in former times, it was used to write output loops for time delays and occasionally to change interfaces depending on the line speed.

`curses.beep()`
Emit a short attention sound.

`curses.can_change_color()`
Return `True` or `False`, depending on whether the programmer can change the colors displayed by the terminal.

`curses.cbreak()`
Enter cbreak mode. In cbreak mode (sometimes called "rare" mode) normal tty line buffering is turned off and characters are available to be read one by one. However, unlike raw mode, special characters (interrupt, quit, suspend, and flow control) retain their effects on the tty driver and calling program. Calling first `raw()` then `cbreak()` leaves the terminal in cbreak mode.

curses.**color_content**(*color_number*)
Return the intensity of the red, green, and blue (RGB) components in the color *color_number*, which must be between 0 and COLORS. Return a 3-tuple, containing the R,G,B values for the given color, which will be between 0 (no component) and 1000 (maximum amount of component).

curses.**color_pair**(*color_number*)
Return the attribute value for displaying text in the specified color. This attribute value can be combined with A_STANDOUT, A_REVERSE, and the other A_* attributes. *pair_number()* is the counterpart to this function.

curses.**curs_set**(*visibility*)
Set the cursor state. *visibility* can be set to 0, 1, or 2, for invisible, normal, or very visible. If the terminal supports the visibility requested, return the previous cursor state; otherwise raise an exception. On many terminals, the "visible" mode is an underline cursor and the "very visible" mode is a block cursor.

curses.**def_prog_mode**()
Save the current terminal mode as the "program" mode, the mode when the running program is using curses. (Its counterpart is the "shell" mode, for when the program is not in curses.) Subsequent calls to *reset_prog_mode()* will restore this mode.

curses.**def_shell_mode**()
Save the current terminal mode as the "shell" mode, the mode when the running program is not using curses. (Its counterpart is the "program" mode, when the program is using curses capabilities.) Subsequent calls to *reset_shell_mode()* will restore this mode.

curses.**delay_output**(*ms*)
Insert an *ms* millisecond pause in output.

curses.**doupdate**()
Update the physical screen. The curses library keeps two data structures, one representing the current physical screen contents and a virtual screen representing the desired next state. The *doupdate()* ground updates the physical screen to match the virtual screen.

The virtual screen may be updated by a *noutrefresh()* call after write operations such as *addstr()* have been performed on a window. The normal *refresh()* call is simply **noutrefresh()** followed by **doupdate()**; if you have to update multiple windows, you can speed performance and perhaps reduce screen flicker by issuing **noutrefresh()** calls on all windows, followed by a single **doupdate()**.

curses.**echo**()
Enter echo mode. In echo mode, each character input is echoed to the screen as it is entered.

curses.**endwin**()
De-initialize the library, and return terminal to normal status.

curses.**erasechar**()
Return the user's current erase character as a one-byte bytes object. Under Unix operating systems this is a property of the controlling tty of the curses program, and is not set by the curses library itself.

curses.**filter**()
The *filter()* routine, if used, must be called before *initscr()* is called. The effect is that, during those calls, LINES is set to 1; the capabilities clear, cup, cud, cud1, cuu1, cuu, vpa are disabled; and the home string is set to the value of cr. The effect is that the cursor is confined to the current line, and so are screen updates. This may be used for enabling character-at-a-time line editing without touching the rest of the screen.

curses.**flash**()
Flash the screen. That is, change it to reverse-video and then change it back in a short interval. Some people prefer such as 'visible bell' to the audible attention signal produced by *beep()*.

curses.**flushinp**()

Flush all input buffers. This throws away any typeahead that has been typed by the user and has not yet been processed by the program.

curses.**getmouse**()

After *getch()* returns `KEY_MOUSE` to signal a mouse event, this method should be call to retrieve the queued mouse event, represented as a 5-tuple `(id, x, y, z, bstate)`. *id* is an ID value used to distinguish multiple devices, and *x*, *y*, *z* are the event's coordinates. (*z* is currently unused.) *bstate* is an integer value whose bits will be set to indicate the type of event, and will be the bitwise OR of one or more of the following constants, where *n* is the button number from 1 to 4: `BUTTONn_PRESSED`, `BUTTONn_RELEASED`, `BUTTONn_CLICKED`, `BUTTONn_DOUBLE_CLICKED`, `BUTTONn_TRIPLE_CLICKED`, `BUTTON_SHIFT`, `BUTTON_CTRL`, `BUTTON_ALT`.

curses.**getsyx**()

Return the current coordinates of the virtual screen cursor as a tuple `(y, x)`. If *leaveok* is currently `True`, then return `(-1, -1)`.

curses.**getwin**(*file*)

Read window related data stored in the file by an earlier `putwin()` call. The routine then creates and initializes a new window using that data, returning the new window object.

curses.**has_colors**()

Return `True` if the terminal can display colors; otherwise, return `False`.

curses.**has_ic**()

Return `True` if the terminal has insert- and delete-character capabilities. This function is included for historical reasons only, as all modern software terminal emulators have such capabilities.

curses.**has_il**()

Return `True` if the terminal has insert- and delete-line capabilities, or can simulate them using scrolling regions. This function is included for historical reasons only, as all modern software terminal emulators have such capabilities.

curses.**has_key**(*ch*)

Take a key value *ch*, and return `True` if the current terminal type recognizes a key with that value.

curses.**halfdelay**(*tenths*)

Used for half-delay mode, which is similar to cbreak mode in that characters typed by the user are immediately available to the program. However, after blocking for *tenths* tenths of seconds, raise an exception if nothing has been typed. The value of *tenths* must be a number between `1` and `255`. Use *nocbreak()* to leave half-delay mode.

curses.**init_color**(*color_number*, *r*, *g*, *b*)

Change the definition of a color, taking the number of the color to be changed followed by three RGB values (for the amounts of red, green, and blue components). The value of *color_number* must be between `0` and `COLORS`. Each of *r*, *g*, *b*, must be a value between `0` and `1000`. When *init_color()* is used, all occurrences of that color on the screen immediately change to the new definition. This function is a no-op on most terminals; it is active only if *can_change_color()* returns `True`.

curses.**init_pair**(*pair_number*, *fg*, *bg*)

Change the definition of a color-pair. It takes three arguments: the number of the color-pair to be changed, the foreground color number, and the background color number. The value of *pair_number* must be between `1` and `COLOR_PAIRS - 1` (the `0` color pair is wired to white on black and cannot be changed). The value of *fg* and *bg* arguments must be between `0` and `COLORS`. If the color-pair was previously initialized, the screen is refreshed and all occurrences of that color-pair are changed to the new definition.

curses.**initscr**()

Initialize the library. Return a *window* object which represents the whole screen.

Note: If there is an error opening the terminal, the underlying curses library may cause the interpreter to exit.

curses.**is_term_resized**(*nlines*, *ncols*)
Return `True` if *resize_term()* would modify the window structure, `False` otherwise.

curses.**isendwin**()
Return `True` if *endwin()* has been called (that is, the curses library has been deinitialized).

curses.**keyname**(*k*)
Return the name of the key numbered *k* as a bytes object. The name of a key generating printable ASCII character is the key's character. The name of a control-key combination is a two-byte bytes object consisting of a caret (`b'^'`) followed by the corresponding printable ASCII character. The name of an alt-key combination (128–255) is a bytes object consisting of the prefix `b'M-'` followed by the name of the corresponding ASCII character.

curses.**killchar**()
Return the user's current line kill character as a one-byte bytes object. Under Unix operating systems this is a property of the controlling tty of the curses program, and is not set by the curses library itself.

curses.**longname**()
Return a bytes object containing the terminfo long name field describing the current terminal. The maximum length of a verbose description is 128 characters. It is defined only after the call to *initscr()*.

curses.**meta**(*flag*)
If *flag* is `True`, allow 8-bit characters to be input. If *flag* is `False`, allow only 7-bit chars.

curses.**mouseinterval**(*interval*)
Set the maximum time in milliseconds that can elapse between press and release events in order for them to be recognized as a click, and return the previous interval value. The default value is 200 msec, or one fifth of a second.

curses.**mousemask**(*mousemask*)
Set the mouse events to be reported, and return a tuple `(availmask, oldmask)`. *availmask* indicates which of the specified mouse events can be reported; on complete failure it returns `0`. *oldmask* is the previous value of the given window's mouse event mask. If this function is never called, no mouse events are ever reported.

curses.**napms**(*ms*)
Sleep for *ms* milliseconds.

curses.**newpad**(*nlines*, *ncols*)
Create and return a pointer to a new pad data structure with the given number of lines and columns. Return a pad as a window object.

A pad is like a window, except that it is not restricted by the screen size, and is not necessarily associated with a particular part of the screen. Pads can be used when a large window is needed, and only a part of the window will be on the screen at one time. Automatic refreshes of pads (such as from scrolling or echoing of input) do not occur. The *refresh()* and *noutrefresh()* methods of a pad require 6 arguments to specify the part of the pad to be displayed and the location on the screen to be used for the display. The arguments are *pminrow*, *pmincol*, *sminrow*, *smincol*, *smaxrow*, *smaxcol*; the *p* arguments refer to the upper left corner of the pad region to be displayed and the *s* arguments define a clipping box on the screen within which the pad region is to be displayed.

curses.**newwin**(*nlines*, *ncols*)
curses.**newwin**(*nlines*, *ncols*, *begin_y*, *begin_x*)
Return a new *window*, whose left-upper corner is at `(begin_y, begin_x)`, and whose height/width is *nlines*/*ncols*.

By default, the window will extend from the specified position to the lower right corner of the screen.

`curses.nl()`
Enter newline mode. This mode translates the return key into newline on input, and translates newline into return and line-feed on output. Newline mode is initially on.

`curses.nocbreak()`
Leave cbreak mode. Return to normal "cooked" mode with line buffering.

`curses.noecho()`
Leave echo mode. Echoing of input characters is turned off.

`curses.nonl()`
Leave newline mode. Disable translation of return into newline on input, and disable low-level translation of newline into newline/return on output (but this does not change the behavior of `addch('\n')`, which always does the equivalent of return and line feed on the virtual screen). With translation off, curses can sometimes speed up vertical motion a little; also, it will be able to detect the return key on input.

`curses.noqiflush()`
When the `noqiflush()` routine is used, normal flush of input and output queues associated with the `INTR`, `QUIT` and `SUSP` characters will not be done. You may want to call `noqiflush()` in a signal handler if you want output to continue as though the interrupt had not occurred, after the handler exits.

`curses.noraw()`
Leave raw mode. Return to normal "cooked" mode with line buffering.

`curses.pair_content(`*pair_number*`)`
Return a tuple `(fg, bg)` containing the colors for the requested color pair. The value of *pair_number* must be between `1` and `COLOR_PAIRS - 1`.

`curses.pair_number(`*attr*`)`
Return the number of the color-pair set by the attribute value *attr*. `color_pair()` is the counterpart to this function.

`curses.putp(`*str*`)`
Equivalent to `tputs(str, 1, putchar)`; emit the value of a specified terminfo capability for the current terminal. Note that the output of `putp()` always goes to standard output.

`curses.qiflush(`[*flag*]`)`
If *flag* is `False`, the effect is the same as calling `noqiflush()`. If *flag* is `True`, or no argument is provided, the queues will be flushed when these control characters are read.

`curses.raw()`
Enter raw mode. In raw mode, normal line buffering and processing of interrupt, quit, suspend, and flow control keys are turned off; characters are presented to curses input functions one by one.

`curses.reset_prog_mode()`
Restore the terminal to "program" mode, as previously saved by `def_prog_mode()`.

`curses.reset_shell_mode()`
Restore the terminal to "shell" mode, as previously saved by `def_shell_mode()`.

`curses.resetty()`
Restore the state of the terminal modes to what it was at the last call to `savetty()`.

`curses.resize_term(`*nlines*, *ncols*`)`
Backend function used by `resizeterm()`, performing most of the work; when resizing the windows, `resize_term()` blank-fills the areas that are extended. The calling application should fill in these areas with appropriate data. The `resize_term()` function attempts to resize all windows. However,

due to the calling convention of pads, it is not possible to resize these without additional interaction with the application.

`curses.resizeterm(nlines, ncols)`
Resize the standard and current windows to the specified dimensions, and adjusts other bookkeeping data used by the curses library that record the window dimensions (in particular the SIGWINCH handler).

`curses.savetty()`
Save the current state of the terminal modes in a buffer, usable by `resetty()`.

`curses.setsyx(y, x)`
Set the virtual screen cursor to *y*, *x*. If *y* and *x* are both `-1`, then `leaveok` is set `True`.

`curses.setupterm(term=None, fd=-1)`
Initialize the terminal. *term* is a string giving the terminal name, or `None`; if omitted or `None`, the value of the `TERM` environment variable will be used. *fd* is the file descriptor to which any initialization sequences will be sent; if not supplied or `-1`, the file descriptor for `sys.stdout` will be used.

`curses.start_color()`
Must be called if the programmer wants to use colors, and before any other color manipulation routine is called. It is good practice to call this routine right after `initscr()`.

`start_color()` initializes eight basic colors (black, red, green, yellow, blue, magenta, cyan, and white), and two global variables in the `curses` module, `COLORS` and `COLOR_PAIRS`, containing the maximum number of colors and color-pairs the terminal can support. It also restores the colors on the terminal to the values they had when the terminal was just turned on.

`curses.termattrs()`
Return a logical OR of all video attributes supported by the terminal. This information is useful when a curses program needs complete control over the appearance of the screen.

`curses.termname()`
Return the value of the environment variable `TERM`, as a bytes object, truncated to 14 characters.

`curses.tigetflag(capname)`
Return the value of the Boolean capability corresponding to the terminfo capability name *capname* as an integer. Return the value `-1` if *capname* is not a Boolean capability, or `0` if it is canceled or absent from the terminal description.

`curses.tigetnum(capname)`
Return the value of the numeric capability corresponding to the terminfo capability name *capname* as an integer. Return the value `-2` if *capname* is not a numeric capability, or `-1` if it is canceled or absent from the terminal description.

`curses.tigetstr(capname)`
Return the value of the string capability corresponding to the terminfo capability name *capname* as a bytes object. Return `None` if *capname* is not a terminfo "string capability", or is canceled or absent from the terminal description.

`curses.tparm(str[, ...])`
Instantiate the bytes object *str* with the supplied parameters, where *str* should be a parameterized string obtained from the terminfo database. E.g. `tparm(tigetstr("cup"), 5, 3)` could result in `b'\033[6;4H'`, the exact result depending on terminal type.

`curses.typeahead(fd)`
Specify that the file descriptor *fd* be used for typeahead checking. If *fd* is `-1`, then no typeahead checking is done.

The curses library does "line-breakout optimization" by looking for typeahead periodically while updating the screen. If input is found, and it is coming from a tty, the current update is postponed until refresh or doupdate is called again, allowing faster response to commands typed in advance. This function allows specifying a different file descriptor for typeahead checking.

`curses.unctrl(ch)`
Return a bytes object which is a printable representation of the character *ch*. Control characters are represented as a caret followed by the character, for example as `b'^C'`. Printing characters are left as they are.

`curses.ungetch(ch)`
Push *ch* so the next *getch()* will return it.

Note: Only one *ch* can be pushed before `getch()` is called.

`curses.update_lines_cols()`
Update `LINES` and `COLS`. Useful for detecting manual screen resize.

New in version 3.5.

`curses.unget_wch(ch)`
Push *ch* so the next *get_wch()* will return it.

Note: Only one *ch* can be pushed before `get_wch()` is called.

New in version 3.3.

`curses.ungetmouse(id, x, y, z, bstate)`
Push a `KEY_MOUSE` event onto the input queue, associating the given state data with it.

`curses.use_env(flag)`
If used, this function should be called before *initscr()* or newterm are called. When *flag* is `False`, the values of lines and columns specified in the terminfo database will be used, even if environment variables `LINES` and `COLUMNS` (used by default) are set, or if curses is running in a window (in which case default behavior would be to use the window size if `LINES` and `COLUMNS` are not set).

`curses.use_default_colors()`
Allow use of default values for colors on terminals supporting this feature. Use this to support transparency in your application. The default color is assigned to the color number `-1`. After calling this function, `init_pair(x, curses.COLOR_RED, -1)` initializes, for instance, color pair *x* to a red foreground color on the default background.

`curses.wrapper(func, ...)`
Initialize curses and call another callable object, *func*, which should be the rest of your curses-using application. If the application raises an exception, this function will restore the terminal to a sane state before re-raising the exception and generating a traceback. The callable object *func* is then passed the main window 'stdscr' as its first argument, followed by any other arguments passed to `wrapper()`. Before calling *func*, `wrapper()` turns on cbreak mode, turns off echo, enables the terminal keypad, and initializes colors if the terminal has color support. On exit (whether normally or by exception) it restores cooked mode, turns on echo, and disables the terminal keypad.

16.10.2 Window Objects

Window objects, as returned by *initscr()* and *newwin()* above, have the following methods and attributes:

`window.addch(ch[, attr])`

`window.addch(y, x, ch[, attr])`
Paint character *ch* at `(y, x)` with attributes *attr*, overwriting any character previously painter at that location. By default, the character position and attributes are the current settings for the window object.

`window.addnstr(str, n[, attr])`
`window.addnstr(y, x, str, n[, attr])`
Paint at most *n* characters of the character string *str* at `(y, x)` with attributes *attr*, overwriting anything previously on the display.

`window.addstr(str[, attr])`
`window.addstr(y, x, str[, attr])`
Paint the character string *str* at `(y, x)` with attributes *attr*, overwriting anything previously on the display.

`window.attroff(attr)`
Remove attribute *attr* from the "background" set applied to all writes to the current window.

`window.attron(attr)`
Add attribute *attr* from the "background" set applied to all writes to the current window.

`window.attrset(attr)`
Set the "background" set of attributes to *attr*. This set is initially `0` (no attributes).

`window.bkgd(ch[, attr])`
Set the background property of the window to the character *ch*, with attributes *attr*. The change is then applied to every character position in that window:

- The attribute of every character in the window is changed to the new background attribute.
- Wherever the former background character appears, it is changed to the new background character.

`window.bkgdset(ch[, attr])`
Set the window's background. A window's background consists of a character and any combination of attributes. The attribute part of the background is combined (OR'ed) with all non-blank characters that are written into the window. Both the character and attribute parts of the background are combined with the blank characters. The background becomes a property of the character and moves with the character through any scrolling and insert/delete line/character operations.

`window.border([ls[, rs[, ts[, bs[, tl[, tr[, bl[, br]]]]]]]])`
Draw a border around the edges of the window. Each parameter specifies the character to use for a specific part of the border; see the table below for more details.

Note: A `0` value for any parameter will cause the default character to be used for that parameter. Keyword parameters can *not* be used. The defaults are listed in this table:

Parameter	Description	Default value
ls	Left side	`ACS_VLINE`
rs	Right side	`ACS_VLINE`
ts	Top	`ACS_HLINE`
bs	Bottom	`ACS_HLINE`
tl	Upper-left corner	`ACS_ULCORNER`
tr	Upper-right corner	`ACS_URCORNER`
bl	Bottom-left corner	`ACS_LLCORNER`
br	Bottom-right corner	`ACS_LRCORNER`

window.box([*vertch*, *horch*])
Similar to *border()*, but both *ls* and *rs* are *vertch* and both *ts* and *bs* are *horch*. The default corner characters are always used by this function.

window.chgat(*attr*)
window.chgat(*num*, *attr*)
window.chgat(*y*, *x*, *attr*)
window.chgat(*y*, *x*, *num*, *attr*)
Set the attributes of *num* characters at the current cursor position, or at position `(y, x)` if supplied. If *num* is not given or is `-1`, the attribute will be set on all the characters to the end of the line. This function moves cursor to position `(y, x)` if supplied. The changed line will be touched using the *touchline()* method so that the contents will be redisplayed by the next window refresh.

window.clear()
Like *erase()*, but also cause the whole window to be repainted upon next call to *refresh()*.

window.clearok(*flag*)
If *flag* is `True`, the next call to *refresh()* will clear the window completely.

window.clrtobot()
Erase from cursor to the end of the window: all lines below the cursor are deleted, and then the equivalent of *clrtoeol()* is performed.

window.clrtoeol()
Erase from cursor to the end of the line.

window.cursyncup()
Update the current cursor position of all the ancestors of the window to reflect the current cursor position of the window.

window.delch([*y*, *x*])
Delete any character at `(y, x)`.

window.deleteln()
Delete the line under the cursor. All following lines are moved up by one line.

window.derwin(*begin_y*, *begin_x*)
window.derwin(*nlines*, *ncols*, *begin_y*, *begin_x*)
An abbreviation for "derive window", *derwin()* is the same as calling *subwin()*, except that *begin_y* and *begin_x* are relative to the origin of the window, rather than relative to the entire screen. Return a window object for the derived window.

window.echochar(*ch*[, *attr*])
Add character *ch* with attribute *attr*, and immediately call *refresh()* on the window.

window.enclose(*y*, *x*)
Test whether the given pair of screen-relative character-cell coordinates are enclosed by the given window, returning `True` or `False`. It is useful for determining what subset of the screen windows enclose the location of a mouse event.

window.encoding
Encoding used to encode method arguments (Unicode strings and characters). The encoding attribute is inherited from the parent window when a subwindow is created, for example with *window.subwin()*. By default, the locale encoding is used (see *locale.getpreferredencoding()*).

New in version 3.3.

window.erase()
Clear the window.

window.getbegyx()
Return a tuple `(y, x)` of co-ordinates of upper-left corner.

window.**getbkgd**()
: Return the given window's current background character/attribute pair.

window.**getch**([*y*, *x*])
: Get a character. Note that the integer returned does *not* have to be in ASCII range: function keys, keypad keys and so on are represented by numbers higher than 255. In no-delay mode, return `-1` if there is no input, otherwise wait until a key is pressed.

window.**get_wch**([*y*, *x*])
: Get a wide character. Return a character for most keys, or an integer for function keys, keypad keys, and other special keys. In no-delay mode, raise an exception if there is no input.

  New in version 3.3.

window.**getkey**([*y*, *x*])
: Get a character, returning a string instead of an integer, as *getch()* does. Function keys, keypad keys and other special keys return a multibyte string containing the key name. In no-delay mode, raise an exception if there is no input.

window.**getmaxyx**()
: Return a tuple `(y, x)` of the height and width of the window.

window.**getparyx**()
: Return the beginning coordinates of this window relative to its parent window as a tuple `(y, x)`. Return `(-1, -1)` if this window has no parent.

window.**getstr**()
window.**getstr**(*n*)
window.**getstr**(*y*, *x*)
window.**getstr**(*y*, *x*, *n*)
: Read a bytes object from the user, with primitive line editing capacity.

window.**getyx**()
: Return a tuple `(y, x)` of current cursor position relative to the window's upper-left corner.

window.**hline**(*ch*, *n*)
window.**hline**(*y*, *x*, *ch*, *n*)
: Display a horizontal line starting at `(y, x)` with length *n* consisting of the character *ch*.

window.**idcok**(*flag*)
: If *flag* is `False`, curses no longer considers using the hardware insert/delete character feature of the terminal; if *flag* is `True`, use of character insertion and deletion is enabled. When curses is first initialized, use of character insert/delete is enabled by default.

window.**idlok**(*flag*)
: If *flag* is `True`, *curses* will try and use hardware line editing facilities. Otherwise, line insertion/deletion are disabled.

window.**immedok**(*flag*)
: If *flag* is `True`, any change in the window image automatically causes the window to be refreshed; you no longer have to call *refresh()* yourself. However, it may degrade performance considerably, due to repeated calls to wrefresh. This option is disabled by default.

window.**inch**([*y*, *x*])
: Return the character at the given position in the window. The bottom 8 bits are the character proper, and upper bits are the attributes.

window.**insch**(*ch*[, *attr*])
window.**insch**(*y*, *x*, *ch*[, *attr*])
: Paint character *ch* at `(y, x)` with attributes *attr*, moving the line from position *x* right by one character.

window.**insdelln**(*nlines*)
Insert *nlines* lines into the specified window above the current line. The *nlines* bottom lines are lost. For negative *nlines*, delete *nlines* lines starting with the one under the cursor, and move the remaining lines up. The bottom *nlines* lines are cleared. The current cursor position remains the same.

window.**insertln**()
Insert a blank line under the cursor. All following lines are moved down by one line.

window.**insnstr**(*str*, *n*[, *attr*])
window.**insnstr**(*y*, *x*, *str*, *n*[, *attr*])
Insert a character string (as many characters as will fit on the line) before the character under the cursor, up to *n* characters. If *n* is zero or negative, the entire string is inserted. All characters to the right of the cursor are shifted right, with the rightmost characters on the line being lost. The cursor position does not change (after moving to *y*, *x*, if specified).

window.**insstr**(*str*[, *attr*])
window.**insstr**(*y*, *x*, *str*[, *attr*])
Insert a character string (as many characters as will fit on the line) before the character under the cursor. All characters to the right of the cursor are shifted right, with the rightmost characters on the line being lost. The cursor position does not change (after moving to *y*, *x*, if specified).

window.**instr**([*n*])
window.**instr**(*y*, *x*[, *n*])
Return a bytes object of characters, extracted from the window starting at the current cursor position, or at *y*, *x* if specified. Attributes are stripped from the characters. If *n* is specified, `instr()` returns a string at most *n* characters long (exclusive of the trailing NUL).

window.**is_linetouched**(*line*)
Return `True` if the specified line was modified since the last call to `refresh()`; otherwise return `False`. Raise a `curses.error` exception if *line* is not valid for the given window.

window.**is_wintouched**()
Return `True` if the specified window was modified since the last call to `refresh()`; otherwise return `False`.

window.**keypad**(*flag*)
If *flag* is `True`, escape sequences generated by some keys (keypad, function keys) will be interpreted by `curses`. If *flag* is `False`, escape sequences will be left as is in the input stream.

window.**leaveok**(*flag*)
If *flag* is `True`, cursor is left where it is on update, instead of being at "cursor position." This reduces cursor movement where possible. If possible the cursor will be made invisible.

If *flag* is `False`, cursor will always be at "cursor position" after an update.

window.**move**(*new_y*, *new_x*)
Move cursor to `(new_y, new_x)`.

window.**mvderwin**(*y*, *x*)
Move the window inside its parent window. The screen-relative parameters of the window are not changed. This routine is used to display different parts of the parent window at the same physical position on the screen.

window.**mvwin**(*new_y*, *new_x*)
Move the window so its upper-left corner is at `(new_y, new_x)`.

window.**nodelay**(*flag*)
If *flag* is `True`, `getch()` will be non-blocking.

window.**notimeout**(*flag*)
If *flag* is `True`, escape sequences will not be timed out.

If *flag* is `False`, after a few milliseconds, an escape sequence will not be interpreted, and will be left in the input stream as is.

`window.noutrefresh()`
Mark for refresh but wait. This function updates the data structure representing the desired state of the window, but does not force an update of the physical screen. To accomplish that, call `doupdate()`.

`window.overlay(`*destwin*[, *sminrow*, *smincol*, *dminrow*, *dmincol*, *dmaxrow*, *dmaxcol*]`)`
Overlay the window on top of *destwin*. The windows need not be the same size, only the overlapping region is copied. This copy is non-destructive, which means that the current background character does not overwrite the old contents of *destwin*.

To get fine-grained control over the copied region, the second form of `overlay()` can be used. *sminrow* and *smincol* are the upper-left coordinates of the source window, and the other variables mark a rectangle in the destination window.

`window.overwrite(`*destwin*[, *sminrow*, *smincol*, *dminrow*, *dmincol*, *dmaxrow*, *dmaxcol*]`)`
Overwrite the window on top of *destwin*. The windows need not be the same size, in which case only the overlapping region is copied. This copy is destructive, which means that the current background character overwrites the old contents of *destwin*.

To get fine-grained control over the copied region, the second form of `overwrite()` can be used. *sminrow* and *smincol* are the upper-left coordinates of the source window, the other variables mark a rectangle in the destination window.

`window.putwin(`*file*`)`
Write all data associated with the window into the provided file object. This information can be later retrieved using the `getwin()` function.

`window.redrawln(`*beg*, *num*`)`
Indicate that the *num* screen lines, starting at line *beg*, are corrupted and should be completely redrawn on the next `refresh()` call.

`window.redrawwin()`
Touch the entire window, causing it to be completely redrawn on the next `refresh()` call.

`window.refresh(`[*pminrow*, *pmincol*, *sminrow*, *smincol*, *smaxrow*, *smaxcol*]`)`
Update the display immediately (sync actual screen with previous drawing/deleting methods).

The 6 optional arguments can only be specified when the window is a pad created with `newpad()`. The additional parameters are needed to indicate what part of the pad and screen are involved. *pminrow* and *pmincol* specify the upper left-hand corner of the rectangle to be displayed in the pad. *sminrow*, *smincol*, *smaxrow*, and *smaxcol* specify the edges of the rectangle to be displayed on the screen. The lower right-hand corner of the rectangle to be displayed in the pad is calculated from the screen coordinates, since the rectangles must be the same size. Both rectangles must be entirely contained within their respective structures. Negative values of *pminrow*, *pmincol*, *sminrow*, or *smincol* are treated as if they were zero.

`window.resize(`*nlines*, *ncols*`)`
Reallocate storage for a curses window to adjust its dimensions to the specified values. If either dimension is larger than the current values, the window's data is filled with blanks that have the current background rendition (as set by `bkgdset()`) merged into them.

`window.scroll(`[*lines=1*]`)`
Scroll the screen or scrolling region upward by *lines* lines.

`window.scrollok(`*flag*`)`
Control what happens when the cursor of a window is moved off the edge of the window or scrolling region, either as a result of a newline action on the bottom line, or typing the last character of the last line. If *flag* is `False`, the cursor is left on the bottom line. If *flag* is `True`, the window is scrolled up

one line. Note that in order to get the physical scrolling effect on the terminal, it is also necessary to call *idlok()*.

`window.setscrreg(top, bottom)`
Set the scrolling region from line *top* to line *bottom*. All scrolling actions will take place in this region.

`window.standend()`
Turn off the standout attribute. On some terminals this has the side effect of turning off all attributes.

`window.standout()`
Turn on attribute *A_STANDOUT*.

`window.subpad(begin_y, begin_x)`
`window.subpad(nlines, ncols, begin_y, begin_x)`
Return a sub-window, whose upper-left corner is at `(begin_y, begin_x)`, and whose width/height is *ncols/nlines*.

`window.subwin(begin_y, begin_x)`
`window.subwin(nlines, ncols, begin_y, begin_x)`
Return a sub-window, whose upper-left corner is at `(begin_y, begin_x)`, and whose width/height is *ncols/nlines*.

By default, the sub-window will extend from the specified position to the lower right corner of the window.

`window.syncdown()`
Touch each location in the window that has been touched in any of its ancestor windows. This routine is called by *refresh()*, so it should almost never be necessary to call it manually.

`window.syncok(flag)`
If *flag* is `True`, then *syncup()* is called automatically whenever there is a change in the window.

`window.syncup()`
Touch all locations in ancestors of the window that have been changed in the window.

`window.timeout(delay)`
Set blocking or non-blocking read behavior for the window. If *delay* is negative, blocking read is used (which will wait indefinitely for input). If *delay* is zero, then non-blocking read is used, and *getch()* will return `-1` if no input is waiting. If *delay* is positive, then *getch()* will block for *delay* milliseconds, and return `-1` if there is still no input at the end of that time.

`window.touchline(start, count[, changed])`
Pretend *count* lines have been changed, starting with line *start*. If *changed* is supplied, it specifies whether the affected lines are marked as having been changed (*changed*=`True`) or unchanged (*changed*=`False`).

`window.touchwin()`
Pretend the whole window has been changed, for purposes of drawing optimizations.

`window.untouchwin()`
Mark all lines in the window as unchanged since the last call to *refresh()*.

`window.vline(ch, n)`
`window.vline(y, x, ch, n)`
Display a vertical line starting at `(y, x)` with length *n* consisting of the character *ch*.

16.10.3 Constants

The *curses* module defines the following data members:

`curses.ERR`
Some curses routines that return an integer, such as `getch()`, return *ERR* upon failure.

`curses.OK`
Some curses routines that return an integer, such as *napms()*, return *OK* upon success.

`curses.version`
A bytes object representing the current version of the module. Also available as `__version__`.

Some constants are available to specify character cell attributes. The exact constants available are system dependent.

Attribute	Meaning
A_ALTCHARSET	Alternate character set mode
A_BLINK	Blink mode
A_BOLD	Bold mode
A_DIM	Dim mode
A_INVIS	Invisible or blank mode
A_NORMAL	Normal attribute
A_PROTECT	Protected mode
A_REVERSE	Reverse background and foreground colors
A_STANDOUT	Standout mode
A_UNDERLINE	Underline mode
A_HORIZONTAL	Horizontal highlight
A_LEFT	Left highlight
A_LOW	Low highlight
A_RIGHT	Right highlight
A_TOP	Top highlight
A_VERTICAL	Vertical highlight
A_CHARTEXT	Bit-mask to extract a character

Several constants are available to extract corresponding attributes returned by some methods.

Bit-mask	Meaning
A_ATTRIBUTES	Bit-mask to extract attributes
A_CHARTEXT	Bit-mask to extract a character
A_COLOR	Bit-mask to extract color-pair field information

Keys are referred to by integer constants with names starting with `KEY_`. The exact keycaps available are system dependent.

Key constant	Key
KEY_MIN	Minimum key value
KEY_BREAK	Break key (unreliable)
KEY_DOWN	Down-arrow
KEY_UP	Up-arrow
KEY_LEFT	Left-arrow
KEY_RIGHT	Right-arrow
KEY_HOME	Home key (upward+left arrow)
KEY_BACKSPACE	Backspace (unreliable)
KEY_F0	Function keys. Up to 64 function keys are supported.
KEY_Fn	Value of function key *n*
KEY_DL	Delete line
KEY_IL	Insert line
KEY_DC	Delete character

Continued on next page

Table 16.1 – continued from previous page

Key constant	Key
KEY_IC	Insert char or enter insert mode
KEY_EIC	Exit insert char mode
KEY_CLEAR	Clear screen
KEY_EOS	Clear to end of screen
KEY_EOL	Clear to end of line
KEY_SF	Scroll 1 line forward
KEY_SR	Scroll 1 line backward (reverse)
KEY_NPAGE	Next page
KEY_PPAGE	Previous page
KEY_STAB	Set tab
KEY_CTAB	Clear tab
KEY_CATAB	Clear all tabs
KEY_ENTER	Enter or send (unreliable)
KEY_SRESET	Soft (partial) reset (unreliable)
KEY_RESET	Reset or hard reset (unreliable)
KEY_PRINT	Print
KEY_LL	Home down or bottom (lower left)
KEY_A1	Upper left of keypad
KEY_A3	Upper right of keypad
KEY_B2	Center of keypad
KEY_C1	Lower left of keypad
KEY_C3	Lower right of keypad
KEY_BTAB	Back tab
KEY_BEG	Beg (beginning)
KEY_CANCEL	Cancel
KEY_CLOSE	Close
KEY_COMMAND	Cmd (command)
KEY_COPY	Copy
KEY_CREATE	Create
KEY_END	End
KEY_EXIT	Exit
KEY_FIND	Find
KEY_HELP	Help
KEY_MARK	Mark
KEY_MESSAGE	Message
KEY_MOVE	Move
KEY_NEXT	Next
KEY_OPEN	Open
KEY_OPTIONS	Options
KEY_PREVIOUS	Prev (previous)
KEY_REDO	Redo
KEY_REFERENCE	Ref (reference)
KEY_REFRESH	Refresh
KEY_REPLACE	Replace
KEY_RESTART	Restart
KEY_RESUME	Resume
KEY_SAVE	Save
KEY_SBEG	Shifted Beg (beginning)
KEY_SCANCEL	Shifted Cancel

Continued on next page

Table 16.1 – continued from previous page

Key constant	Key
KEY_SCOMMAND	Shifted Command
KEY_SCOPY	Shifted Copy
KEY_SCREATE	Shifted Create
KEY_SDC	Shifted Delete char
KEY_SDL	Shifted Delete line
KEY_SELECT	Select
KEY_SEND	Shifted End
KEY_SEOL	Shifted Clear line
KEY_SEXIT	Shifted Exit
KEY_SFIND	Shifted Find
KEY_SHELP	Shifted Help
KEY_SHOME	Shifted Home
KEY_SIC	Shifted Input
KEY_SLEFT	Shifted Left arrow
KEY_SMESSAGE	Shifted Message
KEY_SMOVE	Shifted Move
KEY_SNEXT	Shifted Next
KEY_SOPTIONS	Shifted Options
KEY_SPREVIOUS	Shifted Prev
KEY_SPRINT	Shifted Print
KEY_SREDO	Shifted Redo
KEY_SREPLACE	Shifted Replace
KEY_SRIGHT	Shifted Right arrow
KEY_SRSUME	Shifted Resume
KEY_SSAVE	Shifted Save
KEY_SSUSPEND	Shifted Suspend
KEY_SUNDO	Shifted Undo
KEY_SUSPEND	Suspend
KEY_UNDO	Undo
KEY_MOUSE	Mouse event has occurred
KEY_RESIZE	Terminal resize event
KEY_MAX	Maximum key value

On VT100s and their software emulations, such as X terminal emulators, there are normally at least four function keys (KEY_F1, KEY_F2, KEY_F3, KEY_F4) available, and the arrow keys mapped to KEY_UP, KEY_DOWN, KEY_LEFT and KEY_RIGHT in the obvious way. If your machine has a PC keyboard, it is safe to expect arrow keys and twelve function keys (older PC keyboards may have only ten function keys); also, the following keypad mappings are standard:

Keycap	Constant
Insert	KEY_IC
Delete	KEY_DC
Home	KEY_HOME
End	KEY_END
Page Up	KEY_PPAGE
Page Down	KEY_NPAGE

The following table lists characters from the alternate character set. These are inherited from the VT100 terminal, and will generally be available on software emulations such as X terminals. When there is no graphic available, curses falls back on a crude printable ASCII approximation.

Note: These are available only after *initscr()* has been called.

ACS code	Meaning
ACS_BBSS	alternate name for upper right corner
ACS_BLOCK	solid square block
ACS_BOARD	board of squares
ACS_BSBS	alternate name for horizontal line
ACS_BSSB	alternate name for upper left corner
ACS_BSSS	alternate name for top tee
ACS_BTEE	bottom tee
ACS_BULLET	bullet
ACS_CKBOARD	checker board (stipple)
ACS_DARROW	arrow pointing down
ACS_DEGREE	degree symbol
ACS_DIAMOND	diamond
ACS_GEQUAL	greater-than-or-equal-to
ACS_HLINE	horizontal line
ACS_LANTERN	lantern symbol
ACS_LARROW	left arrow
ACS_LEQUAL	less-than-or-equal-to
ACS_LLCORNER	lower left-hand corner
ACS_LRCORNER	lower right-hand corner
ACS_LTEE	left tee
ACS_NEQUAL	not-equal sign
ACS_PI	letter pi
ACS_PLMINUS	plus-or-minus sign
ACS_PLUS	big plus sign
ACS_RARROW	right arrow
ACS_RTEE	right tee
ACS_S1	scan line 1
ACS_S3	scan line 3
ACS_S7	scan line 7
ACS_S9	scan line 9
ACS_SBBS	alternate name for lower right corner
ACS_SBSB	alternate name for vertical line
ACS_SBSS	alternate name for right tee
ACS_SSBB	alternate name for lower left corner
ACS_SSBS	alternate name for bottom tee
ACS_SSSB	alternate name for left tee
ACS_SSSS	alternate name for crossover or big plus
ACS_STERLING	pound sterling
ACS_TTEE	top tee
ACS_UARROW	up arrow
ACS_ULCORNER	upper left corner
ACS_URCORNER	upper right corner
ACS_VLINE	vertical line

The following table lists the predefined colors:

Constant	Color
COLOR_BLACK	Black
COLOR_BLUE	Blue
COLOR_CYAN	Cyan (light greenish blue)
COLOR_GREEN	Green
COLOR_MAGENTA	Magenta (purplish red)
COLOR_RED	Red
COLOR_WHITE	White
COLOR_YELLOW	Yellow

16.11 curses.textpad — Text input widget for curses programs

The *curses.textpad* module provides a *Textbox* class that handles elementary text editing in a curses window, supporting a set of keybindings resembling those of Emacs (thus, also of Netscape Navigator, BBedit 6.x, FrameMaker, and many other programs). The module also provides a rectangle-drawing function useful for framing text boxes or for other purposes.

The module *curses.textpad* defines the following function:

curses.textpad.rectangle(*win*, *uly*, *ulx*, *lry*, *lrx*)

Draw a rectangle. The first argument must be a window object; the remaining arguments are coordinates relative to that window. The second and third arguments are the y and x coordinates of the upper left hand corner of the rectangle to be drawn; the fourth and fifth arguments are the y and x coordinates of the lower right hand corner. The rectangle will be drawn using VT100/IBM PC forms characters on terminals that make this possible (including xterm and most other software terminal emulators). Otherwise it will be drawn with ASCII dashes, vertical bars, and plus signs.

16.11.1 Textbox objects

You can instantiate a *Textbox* object as follows:

class curses.textpad.Textbox(*win*)

Return a textbox widget object. The *win* argument should be a curses *window* object in which the textbox is to be contained. The edit cursor of the textbox is initially located at the upper left hand corner of the containing window, with coordinates (0, 0). The instance's *stripspaces* flag is initially on.

Textbox objects have the following methods:

edit([*validator*])

This is the entry point you will normally use. It accepts editing keystrokes until one of the termination keystrokes is entered. If *validator* is supplied, it must be a function. It will be called for each keystroke entered with the keystroke as a parameter; command dispatch is done on the result. This method returns the window contents as a string; whether blanks in the window are included is affected by the *stripspaces* attribute.

do_command(*ch*)

Process a single command keystroke. Here are the supported special keystrokes:

Keystroke	Action
Control-A	Go to left edge of window.
Control-B	Cursor left, wrapping to previous line if appropriate.
Control-D	Delete character under cursor.
Control-E	Go to right edge (stripspaces off) or end of line (stripspaces on).
Control-F	Cursor right, wrapping to next line when appropriate.
Control-G	Terminate, returning the window contents.
Control-H	Delete character backward.
Control-J	Terminate if the window is 1 line, otherwise insert newline.
Control-K	If line is blank, delete it, otherwise clear to end of line.
Control-L	Refresh screen.
Control-N	Cursor down; move down one line.
Control-O	Insert a blank line at cursor location.
Control-P	Cursor up; move up one line.

Move operations do nothing if the cursor is at an edge where the movement is not possible. The following synonyms are supported where possible:

Constant	Keystroke
KEY_LEFT	Control-B
KEY_RIGHT	Control-F
KEY_UP	Control-P
KEY_DOWN	Control-N
KEY_BACKSPACE	Control-h

All other keystrokes are treated as a command to insert the given character and move right (with line wrapping).

gather()
Return the window contents as a string; whether blanks in the window are included is affected by the *stripspaces* member.

stripspaces
This attribute is a flag which controls the interpretation of blanks in the window. When it is on, trailing blanks on each line are ignored; any cursor motion that would land the cursor on a trailing blank goes to the end of that line instead, and trailing blanks are stripped when the window contents are gathered.

16.12 curses.ascii — Utilities for ASCII characters

The *curses.ascii* module supplies name constants for ASCII characters and functions to test membership in various ASCII character classes. The constants supplied are names for control characters as follows:

Name	Meaning
NUL	
SOH	Start of heading, console interrupt
STX	Start of text
ETX	End of text
EOT	End of transmission

Continued on next page

Table 16.3 – continued from previous page

Name	Meaning
ENQ	Enquiry, goes with ACK flow control
ACK	Acknowledgement
BEL	Bell
BS	Backspace
TAB	Tab
HT	Alias for TAB: "Horizontal tab"
LF	Line feed
NL	Alias for LF: "New line"
VT	Vertical tab
FF	Form feed
CR	Carriage return
SO	Shift-out, begin alternate character set
SI	Shift-in, resume default character set
DLE	Data-link escape
DC1	XON, for flow control
DC2	Device control 2, block-mode flow control
DC3	XOFF, for flow control
DC4	Device control 4
NAK	Negative acknowledgement
SYN	Synchronous idle
ETB	End transmission block
CAN	Cancel
EM	End of medium
SUB	Substitute
ESC	Escape
FS	File separator
GS	Group separator
RS	Record separator, block-mode terminator
US	Unit separator
SP	Space
DEL	Delete

Note that many of these have little practical significance in modern usage. The mnemonics derive from teleprinter conventions that predate digital computers.

The module supplies the following functions, patterned on those in the standard C library:

`curses.ascii.isalnum(c)`
: Checks for an ASCII alphanumeric character; it is equivalent to `isalpha(c) or isdigit(c)`.

`curses.ascii.isalpha(c)`
: Checks for an ASCII alphabetic character; it is equivalent to `isupper(c) or islower(c)`.

`curses.ascii.isascii(c)`
: Checks for a character value that fits in the 7-bit ASCII set.

`curses.ascii.isblank(c)`
: Checks for an ASCII whitespace character; space or horizontal tab.

`curses.ascii.iscntrl(c)`
: Checks for an ASCII control character (in the range 0x00 to 0x1f or 0x7f).

`curses.ascii.isdigit(c)`
: Checks for an ASCII decimal digit, `'0'` through `'9'`. This is equivalent to `c in string.digits`.

`curses.ascii.`**`isgraph`**`(c)`
Checks for ASCII any printable character except space.

`curses.ascii.`**`islower`**`(c)`
Checks for an ASCII lower-case character.

`curses.ascii.`**`isprint`**`(c)`
Checks for any ASCII printable character including space.

`curses.ascii.`**`ispunct`**`(c)`
Checks for any printable ASCII character which is not a space or an alphanumeric character.

`curses.ascii.`**`isspace`**`(c)`
Checks for ASCII white-space characters; space, line feed, carriage return, form feed, horizontal tab, vertical tab.

`curses.ascii.`**`isupper`**`(c)`
Checks for an ASCII uppercase letter.

`curses.ascii.`**`isxdigit`**`(c)`
Checks for an ASCII hexadecimal digit. This is equivalent to `c in string.hexdigits`.

`curses.ascii.`**`isctrl`**`(c)`
Checks for an ASCII control character (ordinal values 0 to 31).

`curses.ascii.`**`ismeta`**`(c)`
Checks for a non-ASCII character (ordinal values 0x80 and above).

These functions accept either integers or single-character strings; when the argument is a string, it is first converted using the built-in function *ord()*.

Note that all these functions check ordinal bit values derived from the character of the string you pass in; they do not actually know anything about the host machine's character encoding.

The following two functions take either a single-character string or integer byte value; they return a value of the same type.

`curses.ascii.`**`ascii`**`(c)`
Return the ASCII value corresponding to the low 7 bits of *c*.

`curses.ascii.`**`ctrl`**`(c)`
Return the control character corresponding to the given character (the character bit value is bitwise-anded with 0x1f).

`curses.ascii.`**`alt`**`(c)`
Return the 8-bit character corresponding to the given ASCII character (the character bit value is bitwise-ored with 0x80).

The following function takes either a single-character string or integer value; it returns a string.

`curses.ascii.`**`unctrl`**`(c)`
Return a string representation of the ASCII character *c*. If *c* is printable, this string is the character itself. If the character is a control character (0x00–0x1f) the string consists of a caret (`'^'`) followed by the corresponding uppercase letter. If the character is an ASCII delete (0x7f) the string is `'^?'`. If the character has its meta bit (0x80) set, the meta bit is stripped, the preceding rules applied, and `'!'` prepended to the result.

`curses.ascii.`**`controlnames`**
A 33-element string array that contains the ASCII mnemonics for the thirty-two ASCII control characters from 0 (NUL) to 0x1f (US), in order, plus the mnemonic `SP` for the space character.

16.13 `curses.panel` — A panel stack extension for curses

Panels are windows with the added feature of depth, so they can be stacked on top of each other, and only the visible portions of each window will be displayed. Panels can be added, moved up or down in the stack, and removed.

16.13.1 Functions

The module *curses.panel* defines the following functions:

`curses.panel.bottom_panel()`
Returns the bottom panel in the panel stack.

`curses.panel.new_panel(win)`
Returns a panel object, associating it with the given window *win*. Be aware that you need to keep the returned panel object referenced explicitly. If you don't, the panel object is garbage collected and removed from the panel stack.

`curses.panel.top_panel()`
Returns the top panel in the panel stack.

`curses.panel.update_panels()`
Updates the virtual screen after changes in the panel stack. This does not call *curses.doupdate()*, so you'll have to do this yourself.

16.13.2 Panel Objects

Panel objects, as returned by *new_panel()* above, are windows with a stacking order. There's always a window associated with a panel which determines the content, while the panel methods are responsible for the window's depth in the panel stack.

Panel objects have the following methods:

`Panel.above()`
Returns the panel above the current panel.

`Panel.below()`
Returns the panel below the current panel.

`Panel.bottom()`
Push the panel to the bottom of the stack.

`Panel.hidden()`
Returns `True` if the panel is hidden (not visible), `False` otherwise.

`Panel.hide()`
Hide the panel. This does not delete the object, it just makes the window on screen invisible.

`Panel.move(y, x)`
Move the panel to the screen coordinates `(y, x)`.

`Panel.replace(win)`
Change the window associated with the panel to the window *win*.

`Panel.set_userptr(obj)`
Set the panel's user pointer to *obj*. This is used to associate an arbitrary piece of data with the panel, and can be any Python object.

`Panel.show()`
Display the panel (which might have been hidden).

`Panel.top()`
Push panel to the top of the stack.

`Panel.userptr()`
Returns the user pointer for the panel. This might be any Python object.

`Panel.window()`
Returns the window object associated with the panel.

16.14 `platform` — Access to underlying platform's identifying data

Source code: Lib/platform.py

Note: Specific platforms listed alphabetically, with Linux included in the Unix section.

16.14.1 Cross Platform

`platform.architecture(`*executable=sys.executable, bits='', linkage=''*`)`
Queries the given executable (defaults to the Python interpreter binary) for various architecture information.

Returns a tuple `(bits, linkage)` which contain information about the bit architecture and the linkage format used for the executable. Both values are returned as strings.

Values that cannot be determined are returned as given by the parameter presets. If bits is given as `''`, the `sizeof(pointer)` (or `sizeof(long)` on Python version < 1.5.2) is used as indicator for the supported pointer size.

The function relies on the system's `file` command to do the actual work. This is available on most if not all Unix platforms and some non-Unix platforms and then only if the executable points to the Python interpreter. Reasonable defaults are used when the above needs are not met.

Note: On Mac OS X (and perhaps other platforms), executable files may be universal files containing multiple architectures.

To get at the "64-bitness" of the current interpreter, it is more reliable to query the *sys.maxsize* attribute:

```
is_64bits = sys.maxsize > 2**32
```

`platform.machine()`
Returns the machine type, e.g. `'i386'`. An empty string is returned if the value cannot be determined.

`platform.node()`
Returns the computer's network name (may not be fully qualified!). An empty string is returned if the value cannot be determined.

`platform.platform(`*aliased=0, terse=0*`)`
Returns a single string identifying the underlying platform with as much useful information as possible.

The output is intended to be *human readable* rather than machine parseable. It may look different on different platforms and this is intended.

If *aliased* is true, the function will use aliases for various platforms that report system names which differ from their common names, for example SunOS will be reported as Solaris. The `system_alias()` function is used to implement this.

Setting *terse* to true causes the function to return only the absolute minimum information needed to identify the platform.

`platform.processor()`
Returns the (real) processor name, e.g. `'amdk6'`.

An empty string is returned if the value cannot be determined. Note that many platforms do not provide this information or simply return the same value as for `machine()`. NetBSD does this.

`platform.python_build()`
Returns a tuple `(buildno, builddate)` stating the Python build number and date as strings.

`platform.python_compiler()`
Returns a string identifying the compiler used for compiling Python.

`platform.python_branch()`
Returns a string identifying the Python implementation SCM branch.

`platform.python_implementation()`
Returns a string identifying the Python implementation. Possible return values are: 'CPython', 'IronPython', 'Jython', 'PyPy'.

`platform.python_revision()`
Returns a string identifying the Python implementation SCM revision.

`platform.python_version()`
Returns the Python version as string `'major.minor.patchlevel'`.

Note that unlike the Python `sys.version`, the returned value will always include the patchlevel (it defaults to 0).

`platform.python_version_tuple()`
Returns the Python version as tuple `(major, minor, patchlevel)` of strings.

Note that unlike the Python `sys.version`, the returned value will always include the patchlevel (it defaults to `'0'`).

`platform.release()`
Returns the system's release, e.g. `'2.2.0'` or `'NT'` An empty string is returned if the value cannot be determined.

`platform.system()`
Returns the system/OS name, e.g. `'Linux'`, `'Windows'`, or `'Java'`. An empty string is returned if the value cannot be determined.

`platform.system_alias(system, release, version)`
Returns `(system, release, version)` aliased to common marketing names used for some systems. It also does some reordering of the information in some cases where it would otherwise cause confusion.

`platform.version()`
Returns the system's release version, e.g. `'#3 on degas'`. An empty string is returned if the value cannot be determined.

`platform.uname()`
Fairly portable uname interface. Returns a `namedtuple()` containing six attributes: `system`, `node`, `release`, `version`, `machine`, and `processor`.

Note that this adds a sixth attribute (*processor*) not present in the `os.uname()` result. Also, the attribute names are different for the first two attributes; `os.uname()` names them `sysname` and `nodename`.

Entries which cannot be determined are set to `''`.

Changed in version 3.3: Result changed from a tuple to a namedtuple.

16.14.2 Java Platform

`platform.java_ver(`*release='', vendor='', vminfo=('', '', ''), osinfo=('', '', '')*`)`
Version interface for Jython.

Returns a tuple `(release, vendor, vminfo, osinfo)` with *vminfo* being a tuple `(vm_name, vm_release, vm_vendor)` and *osinfo* being a tuple `(os_name, os_version, os_arch)`. Values which cannot be determined are set to the defaults given as parameters (which all default to `''`).

16.14.3 Windows Platform

`platform.win32_ver(`*release='', version='', csd='', ptype=''*`)`
Get additional version information from the Windows Registry and return a tuple `(release, version, csd, ptype)` referring to OS release, version number, CSD level (service pack) and OS type (multi/single processor).

As a hint: *ptype* is `'Uniprocessor Free'` on single processor NT machines and `'Multiprocessor Free'` on multi processor machines. The *'Free'* refers to the OS version being free of debugging code. It could also state *'Checked'* which means the OS version uses debugging code, i.e. code that checks arguments, ranges, etc.

Note: This function works best with Mark Hammond's `win32all` package installed, but also on Python 2.3 and later (support for this was added in Python 2.6). It obviously only runs on Win32 compatible platforms.

Win95/98 specific

`platform.popen(`*cmd, mode='r', bufsize=-1*`)`
Portable `popen()` interface. Find a working popen implementation preferring `win32pipe.popen()`. On Windows NT, `win32pipe.popen()` should work; on Windows 9x it hangs due to bugs in the MS C library.

Deprecated since version 3.3: This function is obsolete. Use the `subprocess` module. Check especially the *Replacing Older Functions with the subprocess Module* section.

16.14.4 Mac OS Platform

`platform.mac_ver(`*release='', versioninfo=('', '', ''), machine=''*`)`
Get Mac OS version information and return it as tuple `(release, versioninfo, machine)` with *versioninfo* being a tuple `(version, dev_stage, non_release_version)`.

Entries which cannot be determined are set to `''`. All tuple entries are strings.

16.14.5 Unix Platforms

`platform.dist`(*distname='', version='', id='', supported_dists=('SuSE', 'debian', 'redhat', 'mandrake', ...)*)

This is another name for *linux_distribution()*.

Deprecated since version 3.5, will be removed in version 3.7.

`platform.linux_distribution`(*distname='', version='', id='', supported_dists=('SuSE', 'debian', 'redhat', 'mandrake', ...), full_distribution_name=1*)

Tries to determine the name of the Linux OS distribution name.

`supported_dists` may be given to define the set of Linux distributions to look for. It defaults to a list of currently supported Linux distributions identified by their release file name.

If `full_distribution_name` is true (default), the full distribution read from the OS is returned. Otherwise the short name taken from `supported_dists` is used.

Returns a tuple `(distname,version,id)` which defaults to the args given as parameters. `id` is the item in parentheses after the version number. It is usually the version codename.

Deprecated since version 3.5, will be removed in version 3.7.

`platform.libc_ver`(*executable=sys.executable, lib='', version='', chunksize=2048*)

Tries to determine the libc version against which the file executable (defaults to the Python interpreter) is linked. Returns a tuple of strings `(lib, version)` which default to the given parameters in case the lookup fails.

Note that this function has intimate knowledge of how different libc versions add symbols to the executable is probably only usable for executables compiled using `gcc`.

The file is read and scanned in chunks of *chunksize* bytes.

16.15 errno — Standard errno system symbols

This module makes available standard `errno` system symbols. The value of each symbol is the corresponding integer value. The names and descriptions are borrowed from `linux/include/errno.h`, which should be pretty all-inclusive.

`errno.errorcode`

Dictionary providing a mapping from the errno value to the string name in the underlying system. For instance, `errno.errorcode[errno.EPERM]` maps to `'EPERM'`.

To translate a numeric error code to an error message, use *os.strerror()*.

Of the following list, symbols that are not used on the current platform are not defined by the module. The specific list of defined symbols is available as `errno.errorcode.keys()`. Symbols available can include:

`errno.EPERM`

Operation not permitted

`errno.ENOENT`

No such file or directory

`errno.ESRCH`

No such process

`errno.EINTR`

Interrupted system call.

See also:

This error is mapped to the exception *InterruptedError*.

`errno.EIO`
I/O error

`errno.ENXIO`
No such device or address

`errno.E2BIG`
Arg list too long

`errno.ENOEXEC`
Exec format error

`errno.EBADF`
Bad file number

`errno.ECHILD`
No child processes

`errno.EAGAIN`
Try again

`errno.ENOMEM`
Out of memory

`errno.EACCES`
Permission denied

`errno.EFAULT`
Bad address

`errno.ENOTBLK`
Block device required

`errno.EBUSY`
Device or resource busy

`errno.EEXIST`
File exists

`errno.EXDEV`
Cross-device link

`errno.ENODEV`
No such device

`errno.ENOTDIR`
Not a directory

`errno.EISDIR`
Is a directory

`errno.EINVAL`
Invalid argument

`errno.ENFILE`
File table overflow

`errno.EMFILE`
Too many open files

`errno.ENOTTY`
Not a typewriter

`errno.ETXTBSY`
Text file busy

errno.**EFBIG**
File too large

errno.**ENOSPC**
No space left on device

errno.**ESPIPE**
Illegal seek

errno.**EROFS**
Read-only file system

errno.**EMLINK**
Too many links

errno.**EPIPE**
Broken pipe

errno.**EDOM**
Math argument out of domain of func

errno.**ERANGE**
Math result not representable

errno.**EDEADLK**
Resource deadlock would occur

errno.**ENAMETOOLONG**
File name too long

errno.**ENOLCK**
No record locks available

errno.**ENOSYS**
Function not implemented

errno.**ENOTEMPTY**
Directory not empty

errno.**ELOOP**
Too many symbolic links encountered

errno.**EWOULDBLOCK**
Operation would block

errno.**ENOMSG**
No message of desired type

errno.**EIDRM**
Identifier removed

errno.**ECHRNG**
Channel number out of range

errno.**EL2NSYNC**
Level 2 not synchronized

errno.**EL3HLT**
Level 3 halted

errno.**EL3RST**
Level 3 reset

errno.**ELNRNG**
Link number out of range

errno.**EUNATCH**
Protocol driver not attached

errno.**ENOCSI**
No CSI structure available

errno.**EL2HLT**
Level 2 halted

errno.**EBADE**
Invalid exchange

errno.**EBADR**
Invalid request descriptor

errno.**EXFULL**
Exchange full

errno.**ENOANO**
No anode

errno.**EBADRQC**
Invalid request code

errno.**EBADSLT**
Invalid slot

errno.**EDEADLOCK**
File locking deadlock error

errno.**EBFONT**
Bad font file format

errno.**ENOSTR**
Device not a stream

errno.**ENODATA**
No data available

errno.**ETIME**
Timer expired

errno.**ENOSR**
Out of streams resources

errno.**ENONET**
Machine is not on the network

errno.**ENOPKG**
Package not installed

errno.**EREMOTE**
Object is remote

errno.**ENOLINK**
Link has been severed

errno.**EADV**
Advertise error

errno.**ESRMNT**
Srmount error

errno.**ECOMM**
Communication error on send

errno.**EPROTO**
Protocol error

errno.**EMULTIHOP**
Multihop attempted

errno.**EDOTDOT**
RFS specific error

errno.**EBADMSG**
Not a data message

errno.**EOVERFLOW**
Value too large for defined data type

errno.**ENOTUNIQ**
Name not unique on network

errno.**EBADFD**
File descriptor in bad state

errno.**EREMCHG**
Remote address changed

errno.**ELIBACC**
Can not access a needed shared library

errno.**ELIBBAD**
Accessing a corrupted shared library

errno.**ELIBSCN**
.lib section in a.out corrupted

errno.**ELIBMAX**
Attempting to link in too many shared libraries

errno.**ELIBEXEC**
Cannot exec a shared library directly

errno.**EILSEQ**
Illegal byte sequence

errno.**ERESTART**
Interrupted system call should be restarted

errno.**ESTRPIPE**
Streams pipe error

errno.**EUSERS**
Too many users

errno.**ENOTSOCK**
Socket operation on non-socket

errno.**EDESTADDRREQ**
Destination address required

errno.**EMSGSIZE**
Message too long

errno.**EPROTOTYPE**
Protocol wrong type for socket

errno.**ENOPROTOOPT**
Protocol not available

errno.EPROTONOSUPPORT
Protocol not supported

errno.ESOCKTNOSUPPORT
Socket type not supported

errno.EOPNOTSUPP
Operation not supported on transport endpoint

errno.EPFNOSUPPORT
Protocol family not supported

errno.EAFNOSUPPORT
Address family not supported by protocol

errno.EADDRINUSE
Address already in use

errno.EADDRNOTAVAIL
Cannot assign requested address

errno.ENETDOWN
Network is down

errno.ENETUNREACH
Network is unreachable

errno.ENETRESET
Network dropped connection because of reset

errno.ECONNABORTED
Software caused connection abort

errno.ECONNRESET
Connection reset by peer

errno.ENOBUFS
No buffer space available

errno.EISCONN
Transport endpoint is already connected

errno.ENOTCONN
Transport endpoint is not connected

errno.ESHUTDOWN
Cannot send after transport endpoint shutdown

errno.ETOOMANYREFS
Too many references: cannot splice

errno.ETIMEDOUT
Connection timed out

errno.ECONNREFUSED
Connection refused

errno.EHOSTDOWN
Host is down

errno.EHOSTUNREACH
No route to host

errno.EALREADY
Operation already in progress

errno.**EINPROGRESS**
Operation now in progress

errno.**ESTALE**
Stale NFS file handle

errno.**EUCLEAN**
Structure needs cleaning

errno.**ENOTNAM**
Not a XENIX named type file

errno.**ENAVAIL**
No XENIX semaphores available

errno.**EISNAM**
Is a named type file

errno.**EREMOTEIO**
Remote I/O error

errno.**EDQUOT**
Quota exceeded

16.16 ctypes — A foreign function library for Python

ctypes is a foreign function library for Python. It provides C compatible data types, and allows calling functions in DLLs or shared libraries. It can be used to wrap these libraries in pure Python.

16.16.1 ctypes tutorial

Note: The code samples in this tutorial use *doctest* to make sure that they actually work. Since some code samples behave differently under Linux, Windows, or Mac OS X, they contain doctest directives in comments.

Note: Some code samples reference the ctypes *c_int* type. On platforms where `sizeof(long) == sizeof(int)` it is an alias to *c_long*. So, you should not be confused if *c_long* is printed if you would expect *c_int* — they are actually the same type.

Loading dynamic link libraries

ctypes exports the *cdll*, and on Windows *windll* and *oledll* objects, for loading dynamic link libraries.

You load libraries by accessing them as attributes of these objects. *cdll* loads libraries which export functions using the standard `cdecl` calling convention, while *windll* libraries call functions using the `stdcall` calling convention. *oledll* also uses the `stdcall` calling convention, and assumes the functions return a Windows `HRESULT` error code. The error code is used to automatically raise an *OSError* exception when the function call fails.

Changed in version 3.3: Windows errors used to raise *WindowsError*, which is now an alias of *OSError*.

Here are some examples for Windows. Note that `msvcrt` is the MS standard C library containing most standard C functions, and uses the cdecl calling convention:

```
>>> from ctypes import *
>>> print(windll.kernel32)
<WinDLL 'kernel32', handle ... at ...>
>>> print(cdll.msvcrt)
<CDLL 'msvcrt', handle ... at ...>
>>> libc = cdll.msvcrt
>>>
```

Windows appends the usual `.dll` file suffix automatically.

Note: Accessing the standard C library through `cdll.msvcrt` will use an outdated version of the library that may be incompatible with the one being used by Python. Where possible, use native Python functionality, or else import and use the `msvcrt` module.

On Linux, it is required to specify the filename *including* the extension to load a library, so attribute access can not be used to load libraries. Either the `LoadLibrary()` method of the dll loaders should be used, or you should load the library by creating an instance of CDLL by calling the constructor:

```
>>> cdll.LoadLibrary("libc.so.6")
<CDLL 'libc.so.6', handle ... at ...>
>>> libc = CDLL("libc.so.6")
>>> libc
<CDLL 'libc.so.6', handle ... at ...>
>>>
```

Accessing functions from loaded dlls

Functions are accessed as attributes of dll objects:

```
>>> from ctypes import *
>>> libc.printf
<_FuncPtr object at 0x...>
>>> print(windll.kernel32.GetModuleHandleA)
<_FuncPtr object at 0x...>
>>> print(windll.kernel32.MyOwnFunction)
Traceback (most recent call last):
  File "<stdin>", line 1, in <module>
  File "ctypes.py", line 239, in __getattr__
    func = _StdcallFuncPtr(name, self)
AttributeError: function 'MyOwnFunction' not found
>>>
```

Note that win32 system dlls like `kernel32` and `user32` often export ANSI as well as UNICODE versions of a function. The UNICODE version is exported with an `W` appended to the name, while the ANSI version is exported with an `A` appended to the name. The win32 `GetModuleHandle` function, which returns a *module handle* for a given module name, has the following C prototype, and a macro is used to expose one of them as `GetModuleHandle` depending on whether UNICODE is defined or not:

```
/* ANSI version */
HMODULE GetModuleHandleA(LPCSTR lpModuleName);
/* UNICODE version */
HMODULE GetModuleHandleW(LPCWSTR lpModuleName);
```

windll does not try to select one of them by magic, you must access the version you need by specifying `GetModuleHandleA` or `GetModuleHandleW` explicitly, and then call it with bytes or string objects respectively.

Sometimes, dlls export functions with names which aren't valid Python identifiers, like "??2@YAPAXI@Z". In this case you have to use *getattr()* to retrieve the function:

```
>>> getattr(cdll.msvcrt, "??2@YAPAXI@Z")
<_FuncPtr object at 0x...>
>>>
```

On Windows, some dlls export functions not by name but by ordinal. These functions can be accessed by indexing the dll object with the ordinal number:

```
>>> cdll.kernel32[1]
<_FuncPtr object at 0x...>
>>> cdll.kernel32[0]
Traceback (most recent call last):
  File "<stdin>", line 1, in <module>
  File "ctypes.py", line 310, in __getitem__
    func = _StdcallFuncPtr(name, self)
AttributeError: function ordinal 0 not found
>>>
```

Calling functions

You can call these functions like any other Python callable. This example uses the `time()` function, which returns system time in seconds since the Unix epoch, and the `GetModuleHandleA()` function, which returns a win32 module handle.

This example calls both functions with a NULL pointer (`None` should be used as the NULL pointer):

```
>>> print(libc.time(None))
1150640792
>>> print(hex(windll.kernel32.GetModuleHandleA(None)))
0x1d000000
>>>
```

Note: *ctypes* may raise a *ValueError* after calling the function, if it detects that an invalid number of arguments were passed. This behavior should not be relied upon. It is deprecated in 3.6.2, and will be removed in 3.7.

ValueError is raised when you call an `stdcall` function with the `cdecl` calling convention, or vice versa:

```
>>> cdll.kernel32.GetModuleHandleA(None)
Traceback (most recent call last):
  File "<stdin>", line 1, in <module>
ValueError: Procedure probably called with not enough arguments (4 bytes missing)
>>>

>>> windll.msvcrt.printf(b"spam")
Traceback (most recent call last):
  File "<stdin>", line 1, in <module>
ValueError: Procedure probably called with too many arguments (4 bytes in excess)
>>>
```

To find out the correct calling convention you have to look into the C header file or the documentation for the function you want to call.

On Windows, *ctypes* uses win32 structured exception handling to prevent crashes from general protection faults when functions are called with invalid argument values:

```
>>> windll.kernel32.GetModuleHandleA(32)
Traceback (most recent call last):
  File "<stdin>", line 1, in <module>
OSError: exception: access violation reading 0x00000020
>>>
```

There are, however, enough ways to crash Python with *ctypes*, so you should be careful anyway. The *faulthandler* module can be helpful in debugging crashes (e.g. from segmentation faults produced by erroneous C library calls).

`None`, integers, bytes objects and (unicode) strings are the only native Python objects that can directly be used as parameters in these function calls. `None` is passed as a C `NULL` pointer, bytes objects and strings are passed as pointer to the memory block that contains their data (`char *` or `wchar_t *`). Python integers are passed as the platforms default C `int` type, their value is masked to fit into the C type.

Before we move on calling functions with other parameter types, we have to learn more about *ctypes* data types.

Fundamental data types

ctypes defines a number of primitive C compatible data types:

ctypes type	C type	Python type
c_bool	`_Bool`	bool (1)
c_char	`char`	1-character bytes object
c_wchar	`wchar_t`	1-character string
c_byte	`char`	int
c_ubyte	`unsigned char`	int
c_short	`short`	int
c_ushort	`unsigned short`	int
c_int	`int`	int
c_uint	`unsigned int`	int
c_long	`long`	int
c_ulong	`unsigned long`	int
c_longlong	`__int64` or `long long`	int
c_ulonglong	`unsigned __int64` or `unsigned long long`	int
c_size_t	`size_t`	int
c_ssize_t	`ssize_t` or `Py_ssize_t`	int
c_float	`float`	float
c_double	`double`	float
c_longdouble	`long double`	float
c_char_p	`char *` (NUL terminated)	bytes object or `None`
c_wchar_p	`wchar_t *` (NUL terminated)	string or `None`
c_void_p	`void *`	int or `None`

1. The constructor accepts any object with a truth value.

All these types can be created by calling them with an optional initializer of the correct type and value:

```
>>> c_int()
c_long(0)
>>> c_wchar_p("Hello, World")
c_wchar_p(140018365411392)
```

```
>>> c_ushort(-3)
c_ushort(65533)
>>>
```

Since these types are mutable, their value can also be changed afterwards:

```
>>> i = c_int(42)
>>> print(i)
c_long(42)
>>> print(i.value)
42
>>> i.value = -99
>>> print(i.value)
-99
>>>
```

Assigning a new value to instances of the pointer types *c_char_p*, *c_wchar_p*, and *c_void_p* changes the *memory location* they point to, *not the contents* of the memory block (of course not, because Python bytes objects are immutable):

```
>>> s = "Hello, World"
>>> c_s = c_wchar_p(s)
>>> print(c_s)
c_wchar_p(139966785747344)
>>> print(c_s.value)
Hello World
>>> c_s.value = "Hi, there"
>>> print(c_s)              # the memory location has changed
c_wchar_p(139966783348904)
>>> print(c_s.value)
Hi, there
>>> print(s)                # first object is unchanged
Hello, World
>>>
```

You should be careful, however, not to pass them to functions expecting pointers to mutable memory. If you need mutable memory blocks, ctypes has a *create_string_buffer()* function which creates these in various ways. The current memory block contents can be accessed (or changed) with the `raw` property; if you want to access it as NUL terminated string, use the `value` property:

```
>>> from ctypes import *
>>> p = create_string_buffer(3)           # create a 3 byte buffer, initialized to NUL bytes
>>> print(sizeof(p), repr(p.raw))
3 b'\x00\x00\x00'
>>> p = create_string_buffer(b"Hello")     # create a buffer containing a NUL terminated string
>>> print(sizeof(p), repr(p.raw))
6 b'Hello\x00'
>>> print(repr(p.value))
b'Hello'
>>> p = create_string_buffer(b"Hello", 10) # create a 10 byte buffer
>>> print(sizeof(p), repr(p.raw))
10 b'Hello\x00\x00\x00\x00\x00'
>>> p.value = b"Hi"
>>> print(sizeof(p), repr(p.raw))
10 b'Hi\x00lo\x00\x00\x00\x00\x00'
>>>
```

The *create_string_buffer()* function replaces the `c_buffer()` function (which is still available as an alias), as well as the `c_string()` function from earlier ctypes releases. To create a mutable memory block containing unicode characters of the C type `wchar_t` use the *create_unicode_buffer()* function.

Calling functions, continued

Note that printf prints to the real standard output channel, *not* to *sys.stdout*, so these examples will only work at the console prompt, not from within *IDLE* or *PythonWin*:

```
>>> printf = libc.printf
>>> printf(b"Hello, %s\n", b"World!")
Hello, World!
14
>>> printf(b"Hello, %S\n", "World!")
Hello, World!
14
>>> printf(b"%d bottles of beer\n", 42)
42 bottles of beer
19
>>> printf(b"%f bottles of beer\n", 42.5)
Traceback (most recent call last):
  File "<stdin>", line 1, in <module>
ArgumentError: argument 2: exceptions.TypeError: Don't know how to convert parameter 2
>>>
```

As has been mentioned before, all Python types except integers, strings, and bytes objects have to be wrapped in their corresponding *ctypes* type, so that they can be converted to the required C data type:

```
>>> printf(b"An int %d, a double %f\n", 1234, c_double(3.14))
An int 1234, a double 3.140000
31
>>>
```

Calling functions with your own custom data types

You can also customize *ctypes* argument conversion to allow instances of your own classes be used as function arguments. *ctypes* looks for an `_as_parameter_` attribute and uses this as the function argument. Of course, it must be one of integer, string, or bytes:

```
>>> class Bottles:
...     def __init__(self, number):
...         self._as_parameter_ = number
...
>>> bottles = Bottles(42)
>>> printf(b"%d bottles of beer\n", bottles)
42 bottles of beer
19
>>>
```

If you don't want to store the instance's data in the `_as_parameter_` instance variable, you could define a *property* which makes the attribute available on request.

Specifying the required argument types (function prototypes)

It is possible to specify the required argument types of functions exported from DLLs by setting the `argtypes` attribute.

argtypes must be a sequence of C data types (the printf function is probably not a good example here, because it takes a variable number and different types of parameters depending on the format string, on the other hand this is quite handy to experiment with this feature):

```
>>> printf.argtypes = [c_char_p, c_char_p, c_int, c_double]
>>> printf(b"String '%s', Int %d, Double %f\n", b"Hi", 10, 2.2)
String 'Hi', Int 10, Double 2.200000
37
>>>
```

Specifying a format protects against incompatible argument types (just as a prototype for a C function), and tries to convert the arguments to valid types:

```
>>> printf(b"%d %d %d", 1, 2, 3)
Traceback (most recent call last):
  File "<stdin>", line 1, in <module>
ArgumentError: argument 2: exceptions.TypeError: wrong type
>>> printf(b"%s %d %f\n", b"X", 2, 3)
X 2 3.000000
13
>>>
```

If you have defined your own classes which you pass to function calls, you have to implement a from_param() class method for them to be able to use them in the argtypes sequence. The from_param() class method receives the Python object passed to the function call, it should do a typecheck or whatever is needed to make sure this object is acceptable, and then return the object itself, its _as_parameter_ attribute, or whatever you want to pass as the C function argument in this case. Again, the result should be an integer, string, bytes, a *ctypes* instance, or an object with an _as_parameter_ attribute.

Return types

By default functions are assumed to return the C int type. Other return types can be specified by setting the restype attribute of the function object.

Here is a more advanced example, it uses the strchr function, which expects a string pointer and a char, and returns a pointer to a string:

```
>>> strchr = libc.strchr
>>> strchr(b"abcdef", ord("d"))
8059983
>>> strchr.restype = c_char_p    # c_char_p is a pointer to a string
>>> strchr(b"abcdef", ord("d"))
b'def'
>>> print(strchr(b"abcdef", ord("x")))
None
>>>
```

If you want to avoid the ord("x") calls above, you can set the argtypes attribute, and the second argument will be converted from a single character Python bytes object into a C char:

```
>>> strchr.restype = c_char_p
>>> strchr.argtypes = [c_char_p, c_char]
>>> strchr(b"abcdef", b"d")
'def'
>>> strchr(b"abcdef", b"def")
Traceback (most recent call last):
  File "<stdin>", line 1, in <module>
```

```
ArgumentError: argument 2: exceptions.TypeError: one character string expected
>>> print(strchr(b"abcdef", b"x"))
None
>>> strchr(b"abcdef", b"d")
'def'
>>>
```

You can also use a callable Python object (a function or a class for example) as the **restype** attribute, if the foreign function returns an integer. The callable will be called with the *integer* the C function returns, and the result of this call will be used as the result of your function call. This is useful to check for error return values and automatically raise an exception:

```
>>> GetModuleHandle = windll.kernel32.GetModuleHandleA
>>> def ValidHandle(value):
...     if value == 0:
...         raise WinError()
...     return value
...
>>>
>>> GetModuleHandle.restype = ValidHandle
>>> GetModuleHandle(None)
486539264
>>> GetModuleHandle("something silly")
Traceback (most recent call last):
  File "<stdin>", line 1, in <module>
  File "<stdin>", line 3, in ValidHandle
OSError: [Errno 126] The specified module could not be found.
>>>
```

`WinError` is a function which will call Windows `FormatMessage()` api to get the string representation of an error code, and *returns* an exception. `WinError` takes an optional error code parameter, if no one is used, it calls `GetLastError()` to retrieve it.

Please note that a much more powerful error checking mechanism is available through the `errcheck` attribute; see the reference manual for details.

Passing pointers (or: passing parameters by reference)

Sometimes a C api function expects a *pointer* to a data type as parameter, probably to write into the corresponding location, or if the data is too large to be passed by value. This is also known as *passing parameters by reference*.

`ctypes` exports the `byref()` function which is used to pass parameters by reference. The same effect can be achieved with the `pointer()` function, although `pointer()` does a lot more work since it constructs a real pointer object, so it is faster to use `byref()` if you don't need the pointer object in Python itself:

```
>>> i = c_int()
>>> f = c_float()
>>> s = create_string_buffer(b'\000' * 32)
>>> print(i.value, f.value, repr(s.value))
0 0.0 b''
>>> libc.sscanf(b"1 3.14 Hello", b"%d %f %s",
...             byref(i), byref(f), s)
3
>>> print(i.value, f.value, repr(s.value))
1 3.1400001049 b'Hello'
>>>
```

Structures and unions

Structures and unions must derive from the *Structure* and *Union* base classes which are defined in the *ctypes* module. Each subclass must define a **_fields_** attribute. **_fields_** must be a list of *2-tuples*, containing a *field name* and a *field type*.

The field type must be a *ctypes* type like *c_int*, or any other derived *ctypes* type: structure, union, array, pointer.

Here is a simple example of a POINT structure, which contains two integers named x and y, and also shows how to initialize a structure in the constructor:

```
>>> from ctypes import *
>>> class POINT(Structure):
...     _fields_ = [("x", c_int),
...                 ("y", c_int)]
...
>>> point = POINT(10, 20)
>>> print(point.x, point.y)
10 20
>>> point = POINT(y=5)
>>> print(point.x, point.y)
0 5
>>> POINT(1, 2, 3)
Traceback (most recent call last):
  File "<stdin>", line 1, in <module>
ValueError: too many initializers
>>>
```

You can, however, build much more complicated structures. A structure can itself contain other structures by using a structure as a field type.

Here is a RECT structure which contains two POINTs named *upperleft* and *lowerright*:

```
>>> class RECT(Structure):
...     _fields_ = [("upperleft", POINT),
...                 ("lowerright", POINT)]
...
>>> rc = RECT(point)
>>> print(rc.upperleft.x, rc.upperleft.y)
0 5
>>> print(rc.lowerright.x, rc.lowerright.y)
0 0
>>>
```

Nested structures can also be initialized in the constructor in several ways:

```
>>> r = RECT(POINT(1, 2), POINT(3, 4))
>>> r = RECT((1, 2), (3, 4))
```

Field *descriptors* can be retrieved from the *class*, they are useful for debugging because they can provide useful information:

```
>>> print(POINT.x)
<Field type=c_long, ofs=0, size=4>
>>> print(POINT.y)
<Field type=c_long, ofs=4, size=4>
>>>
```

> **Warning:** *ctypes* does not support passing unions or structures with bit-fields to functions by value. While this may work on 32-bit x86, it's not guaranteed by the library to work in the general case. Unions and structures with bit-fields should always be passed to functions by pointer.

Structure/union alignment and byte order

By default, Structure and Union fields are aligned in the same way the C compiler does it. It is possible to override this behavior be specifying a `_pack_` class attribute in the subclass definition. This must be set to a positive integer and specifies the maximum alignment for the fields. This is what `#pragma pack(n)` also does in MSVC.

ctypes uses the native byte order for Structures and Unions. To build structures with non-native byte order, you can use one of the *BigEndianStructure*, *LittleEndianStructure*, `BigEndianUnion`, and `LittleEndianUnion` base classes. These classes cannot contain pointer fields.

Bit fields in structures and unions

It is possible to create structures and unions containing bit fields. Bit fields are only possible for integer fields, the bit width is specified as the third item in the `_fields_` tuples:

```
>>> class Int(Structure):
...     _fields_ = [("first_16", c_int, 16),
...                 ("second_16", c_int, 16)]
...
>>> print(Int.first_16)
<Field type=c_long, ofs=0:0, bits=16>
>>> print(Int.second_16)
<Field type=c_long, ofs=0:16, bits=16>
>>>
```

Arrays

Arrays are sequences, containing a fixed number of instances of the same type.

The recommended way to create array types is by multiplying a data type with a positive integer:

```
TenPointsArrayType = POINT * 10
```

Here is an example of a somewhat artificial data type, a structure containing 4 POINTs among other stuff:

```
>>> from ctypes import *
>>> class POINT(Structure):
...     _fields_ = ("x", c_int), ("y", c_int)
...
>>> class MyStruct(Structure):
...     _fields_ = [("a", c_int),
...                 ("b", c_float),
...                 ("point_array", POINT * 4)]
>>>
>>> print(len(MyStruct().point_array))
4
>>>
```

Instances are created in the usual way, by calling the class:

```
arr = TenPointsArrayType()
for pt in arr:
    print(pt.x, pt.y)
```

The above code print a series of `0 0` lines, because the array contents is initialized to zeros.

Initializers of the correct type can also be specified:

```
>>> from ctypes import *
>>> TenIntegers = c_int * 10
>>> ii = TenIntegers(1, 2, 3, 4, 5, 6, 7, 8, 9, 10)
>>> print(ii)
<c_long_Array_10 object at 0x...>
>>> for i in ii: print(i, end=" ")
...
1 2 3 4 5 6 7 8 9 10
>>>
```

Pointers

Pointer instances are created by calling the *pointer()* function on a *ctypes* type:

```
>>> from ctypes import *
>>> i = c_int(42)
>>> pi = pointer(i)
>>>
```

Pointer instances have a *contents* attribute which returns the object to which the pointer points, the `i` object above:

```
>>> pi.contents
c_long(42)
>>>
```

Note that *ctypes* does not have OOR (original object return), it constructs a new, equivalent object each time you retrieve an attribute:

```
>>> pi.contents is i
False
>>> pi.contents is pi.contents
False
>>>
```

Assigning another *c_int* instance to the pointer's contents attribute would cause the pointer to point to the memory location where this is stored:

```
>>> i = c_int(99)
>>> pi.contents = i
>>> pi.contents
c_long(99)
>>>
```

Pointer instances can also be indexed with integers:

```
>>> pi[0]
99
>>>
```

Assigning to an integer index changes the pointed to value:

```
>>> print(i)
c_long(99)
>>> pi[0] = 22
>>> print(i)
c_long(22)
>>>
```

It is also possible to use indexes different from 0, but you must know what you're doing, just as in C: You can access or change arbitrary memory locations. Generally you only use this feature if you receive a pointer from a C function, and you *know* that the pointer actually points to an array instead of a single item.

Behind the scenes, the `pointer()` function does more than simply create pointer instances, it has to create pointer *types* first. This is done with the `POINTER()` function, which accepts any `ctypes` type, and returns a new type:

```
>>> PI = POINTER(c_int)
>>> PI
<class 'ctypes.LP_c_long'>
>>> PI(42)
Traceback (most recent call last):
  File "<stdin>", line 1, in <module>
TypeError: expected c_long instead of int
>>> PI(c_int(42))
<ctypes.LP_c_long object at 0x...>
>>>
```

Calling the pointer type without an argument creates a `NULL` pointer. `NULL` pointers have a `False` boolean value:

```
>>> null_ptr = POINTER(c_int)()
>>> print(bool(null_ptr))
False
>>>
```

`ctypes` checks for `NULL` when dereferencing pointers (but dereferencing invalid non-`NULL` pointers would crash Python):

```
>>> null_ptr[0]
Traceback (most recent call last):
    ....
ValueError: NULL pointer access
>>>

>>> null_ptr[0] = 1234
Traceback (most recent call last):
    ....
ValueError: NULL pointer access
>>>
```

Type conversions

Usually, ctypes does strict type checking. This means, if you have `POINTER(c_int)` in the `argtypes` list of a function or as the type of a member field in a structure definition, only instances of exactly the same type are accepted. There are some exceptions to this rule, where ctypes accepts other objects. For example, you can pass compatible array instances instead of pointer types. So, for `POINTER(c_int)`, ctypes accepts an array of c_int:

```
>>> class Bar(Structure):
...     _fields_ = [("count", c_int), ("values", POINTER(c_int))]
...
>>> bar = Bar()
>>> bar.values = (c_int * 3)(1, 2, 3)
>>> bar.count = 3
>>> for i in range(bar.count):
...     print(bar.values[i])
...
1
2
3
>>>
```

In addition, if a function argument is explicitly declared to be a pointer type (such as `POINTER(c_int)`) in `argtypes`, an object of the pointed type (`c_int` in this case) can be passed to the function. ctypes will apply the required *byref()* conversion in this case automatically.

To set a POINTER type field to `NULL`, you can assign `None`:

```
>>> bar.values = None
>>>
```

Sometimes you have instances of incompatible types. In C, you can cast one type into another type. *ctypes* provides a *cast()* function which can be used in the same way. The `Bar` structure defined above accepts `POINTER(c_int)` pointers or *c_int* arrays for its `values` field, but not instances of other types:

```
>>> bar.values = (c_byte * 4)()
Traceback (most recent call last):
  File "<stdin>", line 1, in <module>
TypeError: incompatible types, c_byte_Array_4 instance instead of LP_c_long instance
>>>
```

For these cases, the *cast()* function is handy.

The *cast()* function can be used to cast a ctypes instance into a pointer to a different ctypes data type. *cast()* takes two parameters, a ctypes object that is or can be converted to a pointer of some kind, and a ctypes pointer type. It returns an instance of the second argument, which references the same memory block as the first argument:

```
>>> a = (c_byte * 4)()
>>> cast(a, POINTER(c_int))
<ctypes.LP_c_long object at ...>
>>>
```

So, *cast()* can be used to assign to the `values` field of `Bar` the structure:

```
>>> bar = Bar()
>>> bar.values = cast((c_byte * 4)(), POINTER(c_int))
>>> print(bar.values[0])
0
>>>
```

Incomplete Types

Incomplete Types are structures, unions or arrays whose members are not yet specified. In C, they are specified by forward declarations, which are defined later:

```
struct cell; /* forward declaration */

struct cell {
    char *name;
    struct cell *next;
};
```

The straightforward translation into ctypes code would be this, but it does not work:

```
>>> class cell(Structure):
...     _fields_ = [("name", c_char_p),
...                 ("next", POINTER(cell))]
...
Traceback (most recent call last):
  File "<stdin>", line 1, in <module>
  File "<stdin>", line 2, in cell
NameError: name 'cell' is not defined
>>>
```

because the new `class cell` is not available in the class statement itself. In *ctypes*, we can define the `cell` class and set the `_fields_` attribute later, after the class statement:

```
>>> from ctypes import *
>>> class cell(Structure):
...     pass
...
>>> cell._fields_ = [("name", c_char_p),
...                  ("next", POINTER(cell))]
>>>
```

Lets try it. We create two instances of `cell`, and let them point to each other, and finally follow the pointer chain a few times:

```
>>> c1 = cell()
>>> c1.name = "foo"
>>> c2 = cell()
>>> c2.name = "bar"
>>> c1.next = pointer(c2)
>>> c2.next = pointer(c1)
>>> p = c1
>>> for i in range(8):
...     print(p.name, end=" ")
...     p = p.next[0]
...
foo bar foo bar foo bar foo bar
>>>
```

Callback functions

ctypes allows creating C callable function pointers from Python callables. These are sometimes called *callback functions*.

First, you must create a class for the callback function. The class knows the calling convention, the return type, and the number and types of arguments this function will receive.

The *CFUNCTYPE()* factory function creates types for callback functions using the `cdecl` calling convention. On Windows, the *WINFUNCTYPE()* factory function creates types for callback functions using the `stdcall` calling convention.

Both of these factory functions are called with the result type as first argument, and the callback functions expected argument types as the remaining arguments.

I will present an example here which uses the standard C library's `qsort()` function, that is used to sort items with the help of a callback function. `qsort()` will be used to sort an array of integers:

```
>>> IntArray5 = c_int * 5
>>> ia = IntArray5(5, 1, 7, 33, 99)
>>> qsort = libc.qsort
>>> qsort.restype = None
>>>
```

`qsort()` must be called with a pointer to the data to sort, the number of items in the data array, the size of one item, and a pointer to the comparison function, the callback. The callback will then be called with two pointers to items, and it must return a negative integer if the first item is smaller than the second, a zero if they are equal, and a positive integer otherwise.

So our callback function receives pointers to integers, and must return an integer. First we create the `type` for the callback function:

```
>>> CMPFUNC = CFUNCTYPE(c_int, POINTER(c_int), POINTER(c_int))
>>>
```

To get started, here is a simple callback that shows the values it gets passed:

```
>>> def py_cmp_func(a, b):
...     print("py_cmp_func", a[0], b[0])
...     return 0
...
>>> cmp_func = CMPFUNC(py_cmp_func)
>>>
```

The result:

```
>>> qsort(ia, len(ia), sizeof(c_int), cmp_func)
py_cmp_func 5 1
py_cmp_func 33 99
py_cmp_func 7 33
py_cmp_func 5 7
py_cmp_func 1 7
>>>
```

Now we can actually compare the two items and return a useful result:

```
>>> def py_cmp_func(a, b):
...     print("py_cmp_func", a[0], b[0])
...     return a[0] - b[0]
...
>>>
>>> qsort(ia, len(ia), sizeof(c_int), CMPFUNC(py_cmp_func))
py_cmp_func 5 1
py_cmp_func 33 99
py_cmp_func 7 33
```

```
py_cmp_func 1 7
py_cmp_func 5 7
>>>
```

As we can easily check, our array is sorted now:

```
>>> for i in ia: print(i, end=" ")
...
1 5 7 33 99
>>>
```

Note: Make sure you keep references to *CFUNCTYPE()* objects as long as they are used from C code. *ctypes* doesn't, and if you don't, they may be garbage collected, crashing your program when a callback is made.

Also, note that if the callback function is called in a thread created outside of Python's control (e.g. by the foreign code that calls the callback), ctypes creates a new dummy Python thread on every invocation. This behavior is correct for most purposes, but it means that values stored with *threading.local* will *not* survive across different callbacks, even when those calls are made from the same C thread.

Accessing values exported from dlls

Some shared libraries not only export functions, they also export variables. An example in the Python library itself is the `Py_OptimizeFlag`, an integer set to 0, 1, or 2, depending on the `-O` or `-OO` flag given on startup.

ctypes can access values like this with the `in_dll()` class methods of the type. *pythonapi* is a predefined symbol giving access to the Python C api:

```
>>> opt_flag = c_int.in_dll(pythonapi, "Py_OptimizeFlag")
>>> print(opt_flag)
c_long(0)
>>>
```

If the interpreter would have been started with `-O`, the sample would have printed `c_long(1)`, or `c_long(2)` if `-OO` would have been specified.

An extended example which also demonstrates the use of pointers accesses the `PyImport_FrozenModules` pointer exported by Python.

Quoting the docs for that value:

> This pointer is initialized to point to an array of `struct _frozen` records, terminated by one whose members are all *NULL* or zero. When a frozen module is imported, it is searched in this table. Third-party code could play tricks with this to provide a dynamically created collection of frozen modules.

So manipulating this pointer could even prove useful. To restrict the example size, we show only how this table can be read with *ctypes*:

```
>>> from ctypes import *
>>>
>>> class struct_frozen(Structure):
...     _fields_ = [("name", c_char_p),
...                 ("code", POINTER(c_ubyte)),
...                 ("size", c_int)]
...
>>>
```

We have defined the `struct _frozen` data type, so we can get the pointer to the table:

```
>>> FrozenTable = POINTER(struct_frozen)
>>> table = FrozenTable.in_dll(pythonapi, "PyImport_FrozenModules")
>>>
```

Since `table` is a `pointer` to the array of `struct_frozen` records, we can iterate over it, but we just have to make sure that our loop terminates, because pointers have no size. Sooner or later it would probably crash with an access violation or whatever, so it's better to break out of the loop when we hit the NULL entry:

```
>>> for item in table:
...     if item.name is None:
...         break
...     print(item.name.decode("ascii"), item.size)
...
_frozen_importlib 31764
_frozen_importlib_external 41499
__hello__ 161
__phello__ -161
__phello__.spam 161
>>>
```

The fact that standard Python has a frozen module and a frozen package (indicated by the negative size member) is not well known, it is only used for testing. Try it out with `import __hello__` for example.

Surprises

There are some edges in *ctypes* where you might expect something other than what actually happens.

Consider the following example:

```
>>> from ctypes import *
>>> class POINT(Structure):
...     _fields_ = ("x", c_int), ("y", c_int)
...
>>> class RECT(Structure):
...     _fields_ = ("a", POINT), ("b", POINT)
...
>>> p1 = POINT(1, 2)
>>> p2 = POINT(3, 4)
>>> rc = RECT(p1, p2)
>>> print(rc.a.x, rc.a.y, rc.b.x, rc.b.y)
1 2 3 4
>>> # now swap the two points
>>> rc.a, rc.b = rc.b, rc.a
>>> print(rc.a.x, rc.a.y, rc.b.x, rc.b.y)
3 4 3 4
>>>
```

Hm. We certainly expected the last statement to print `3 4 1 2`. What happened? Here are the steps of the `rc.a, rc.b = rc.b, rc.a` line above:

```
>>> temp0, temp1 = rc.b, rc.a
>>> rc.a = temp0
>>> rc.b = temp1
>>>
```

Note that temp0 and temp1 are objects still using the internal buffer of the rc object above. So executing rc.a = temp0 copies the buffer contents of temp0 into rc 's buffer. This, in turn, changes the contents of temp1. So, the last assignment rc.b = temp1, doesn't have the expected effect.

Keep in mind that retrieving sub-objects from Structure, Unions, and Arrays doesn't *copy* the sub-object, instead it retrieves a wrapper object accessing the root-object's underlying buffer.

Another example that may behave different from what one would expect is this:

```
>>> s = c_char_p()
>>> s.value = "abc def ghi"
>>> s.value
'abc def ghi'
>>> s.value is s.value
False
>>>
```

Why is it printing False? ctypes instances are objects containing a memory block plus some *descriptors* accessing the contents of the memory. Storing a Python object in the memory block does not store the object itself, instead the contents of the object is stored. Accessing the contents again constructs a new Python object each time!

Variable-sized data types

ctypes provides some support for variable-sized arrays and structures.

The *resize()* function can be used to resize the memory buffer of an existing ctypes object. The function takes the object as first argument, and the requested size in bytes as the second argument. The memory block cannot be made smaller than the natural memory block specified by the objects type, a *ValueError* is raised if this is tried:

```
>>> short_array = (c_short * 4)()
>>> print(sizeof(short_array))
8
>>> resize(short_array, 4)
Traceback (most recent call last):
    ...
ValueError: minimum size is 8
>>> resize(short_array, 32)
>>> sizeof(short_array)
32
>>> sizeof(type(short_array))
8
>>>
```

This is nice and fine, but how would one access the additional elements contained in this array? Since the type still only knows about 4 elements, we get errors accessing other elements:

```
>>> short_array[:]
[0, 0, 0, 0]
>>> short_array[7]
Traceback (most recent call last):
    ...
IndexError: invalid index
>>>
```

Another way to use variable-sized data types with *ctypes* is to use the dynamic nature of Python, and (re-)define the data type after the required size is already known, on a case by case basis.

16.16.2 ctypes reference

Finding shared libraries

When programming in a compiled language, shared libraries are accessed when compiling/linking a program, and when the program is run.

The purpose of the `find_library()` function is to locate a library in a way similar to what the compiler or runtime loader does (on platforms with several versions of a shared library the most recent should be loaded), while the ctypes library loaders act like when a program is run, and call the runtime loader directly.

The `ctypes.util` module provides a function which can help to determine the library to load.

`ctypes.util.find_library(`*name*`)`
Try to find a library and return a pathname. *name* is the library name without any prefix like *lib*, suffix like `.so`, `.dylib` or version number (this is the form used for the posix linker option `-l`). If no library can be found, returns `None`.

The exact functionality is system dependent.

On Linux, `find_library()` tries to run external programs (`/sbin/ldconfig`, `gcc`, `objdump` and `ld`) to find the library file. It returns the filename of the library file.

Changed in version 3.6: On Linux, the value of the environment variable `LD_LIBRARY_PATH` is used when searching for libraries, if a library cannot be found by any other means.

Here are some examples:

```
>>> from ctypes.util import find_library
>>> find_library("m")
'libm.so.6'
>>> find_library("c")
'libc.so.6'
>>> find_library("bz2")
'libbz2.so.1.0'
>>>
```

On OS X, `find_library()` tries several predefined naming schemes and paths to locate the library, and returns a full pathname if successful:

```
>>> from ctypes.util import find_library
>>> find_library("c")
'/usr/lib/libc.dylib'
>>> find_library("m")
'/usr/lib/libm.dylib'
>>> find_library("bz2")
'/usr/lib/libbz2.dylib'
>>> find_library("AGL")
'/System/Library/Frameworks/AGL.framework/AGL'
>>>
```

On Windows, `find_library()` searches along the system search path, and returns the full pathname, but since there is no predefined naming scheme a call like `find_library("c")` will fail and return `None`.

If wrapping a shared library with *ctypes*, it *may* be better to determine the shared library name at development time, and hardcode that into the wrapper module instead of using `find_library()` to locate the library at runtime.

Loading shared libraries

There are several ways to load shared libraries into the Python process. One way is to instantiate one of the following classes:

`class ctypes.CDLL(name, mode=DEFAULT_MODE, handle=None, use_errno=False, use_last_error=False)`
Instances of this class represent loaded shared libraries. Functions in these libraries use the standard C calling convention, and are assumed to return `int`.

`class ctypes.OleDLL(name, mode=DEFAULT_MODE, handle=None, use_errno=False, use_last_error=False)`
Windows only: Instances of this class represent loaded shared libraries, functions in these libraries use the `stdcall` calling convention, and are assumed to return the windows specific *HRESULT* code. *HRESULT* values contain information specifying whether the function call failed or succeeded, together with additional error code. If the return value signals a failure, an *OSError* is automatically raised.

Changed in version 3.3: *WindowsError* used to be raised.

`class ctypes.WinDLL(name, mode=DEFAULT_MODE, handle=None, use_errno=False, use_last_error=False)`
Windows only: Instances of this class represent loaded shared libraries, functions in these libraries use the `stdcall` calling convention, and are assumed to return `int` by default.

On Windows CE only the standard calling convention is used, for convenience the *WinDLL* and *OleDLL* use the standard calling convention on this platform.

The Python *global interpreter lock* is released before calling any function exported by these libraries, and reacquired afterwards.

`class ctypes.PyDLL(name, mode=DEFAULT_MODE, handle=None)`
Instances of this class behave like *CDLL* instances, except that the Python GIL is *not* released during the function call, and after the function execution the Python error flag is checked. If the error flag is set, a Python exception is raised.

Thus, this is only useful to call Python C api functions directly.

All these classes can be instantiated by calling them with at least one argument, the pathname of the shared library. If you have an existing handle to an already loaded shared library, it can be passed as the `handle` named parameter, otherwise the underlying platforms `dlopen` or `LoadLibrary` function is used to load the library into the process, and to get a handle to it.

The *mode* parameter can be used to specify how the library is loaded. For details, consult the ***dlopen(3)*** manpage. On Windows, *mode* is ignored. On posix systems, RTLD_NOW is always added, and is not configurable.

The *use_errno* parameter, when set to true, enables a ctypes mechanism that allows accessing the system *errno* error number in a safe way. *ctypes* maintains a thread-local copy of the systems *errno* variable; if you call foreign functions created with `use_errno=True` then the *errno* value before the function call is swapped with the ctypes private copy, the same happens immediately after the function call.

The function *ctypes.get_errno()* returns the value of the ctypes private copy, and the function *ctypes.set_errno()* changes the ctypes private copy to a new value and returns the former value.

The *use_last_error* parameter, when set to true, enables the same mechanism for the Windows error code which is managed by the *GetLastError()* and `SetLastError()` Windows API functions; *ctypes.get_last_error()* and *ctypes.set_last_error()* are used to request and change the ctypes private copy of the windows error code.

`ctypes.RTLD_GLOBAL`
Flag to use as *mode* parameter. On platforms where this flag is not available, it is defined as the integer zero.

`ctypes.RTLD_LOCAL`
Flag to use as *mode* parameter. On platforms where this is not available, it is the same as *RTLD_GLOBAL*.

`ctypes.DEFAULT_MODE`
The default mode which is used to load shared libraries. On OSX 10.3, this is *RTLD_GLOBAL*, otherwise it is the same as *RTLD_LOCAL*.

Instances of these classes have no public methods. Functions exported by the shared library can be accessed as attributes or by index. Please note that accessing the function through an attribute caches the result and therefore accessing it repeatedly returns the same object each time. On the other hand, accessing it through an index returns a new object each time:

```
>>> libc.time == libc.time
True
>>> libc['time'] == libc['time']
False
```

The following public attributes are available, their name starts with an underscore to not clash with exported function names:

`PyDLL._handle`
The system handle used to access the library.

`PyDLL._name`
The name of the library passed in the constructor.

Shared libraries can also be loaded by using one of the prefabricated objects, which are instances of the *LibraryLoader* class, either by calling the `LoadLibrary()` method, or by retrieving the library as attribute of the loader instance.

`class ctypes.LibraryLoader(`*dlltype*`)`
Class which loads shared libraries. *dlltype* should be one of the *CDLL*, *PyDLL*, *WinDLL*, or *OleDLL* types.

`__getattr__()` has special behavior: It allows loading a shared library by accessing it as attribute of a library loader instance. The result is cached, so repeated attribute accesses return the same library each time.

`LoadLibrary(`*name*`)`
Load a shared library into the process and return it. This method always returns a new instance of the library.

These prefabricated library loaders are available:

`ctypes.cdll`
Creates *CDLL* instances.

`ctypes.windll`
Windows only: Creates *WinDLL* instances.

`ctypes.oledll`
Windows only: Creates *OleDLL* instances.

`ctypes.pydll`
Creates *PyDLL* instances.

For accessing the C Python api directly, a ready-to-use Python shared library object is available:

`ctypes.pythonapi`
An instance of *PyDLL* that exposes Python C API functions as attributes. Note that all these functions are assumed to return C `int`, which is of course not always the truth, so you have to assign the correct `restype` attribute to use these functions.

Foreign functions

As explained in the previous section, foreign functions can be accessed as attributes of loaded shared libraries. The function objects created in this way by default accept any number of arguments, accept any ctypes data instances as arguments, and return the default result type specified by the library loader. They are instances of a private class:

class ctypes._FuncPtr
Base class for C callable foreign functions.

Instances of foreign functions are also C compatible data types; they represent C function pointers.

This behavior can be customized by assigning to special attributes of the foreign function object.

restype
Assign a ctypes type to specify the result type of the foreign function. Use `None` for `void`, a function not returning anything.

It is possible to assign a callable Python object that is not a ctypes type, in this case the function is assumed to return a C `int`, and the callable will be called with this integer, allowing further processing or error checking. Using this is deprecated, for more flexible post processing or error checking use a ctypes data type as *restype* and assign a callable to the *errcheck* attribute.

argtypes
Assign a tuple of ctypes types to specify the argument types that the function accepts. Functions using the `stdcall` calling convention can only be called with the same number of arguments as the length of this tuple; functions using the C calling convention accept additional, unspecified arguments as well.

When a foreign function is called, each actual argument is passed to the `from_param()` class method of the items in the *argtypes* tuple, this method allows adapting the actual argument to an object that the foreign function accepts. For example, a *c_char_p* item in the *argtypes* tuple will convert a string passed as argument into a bytes object using ctypes conversion rules.

New: It is now possible to put items in argtypes which are not ctypes types, but each item must have a `from_param()` method which returns a value usable as argument (integer, string, ctypes instance). This allows defining adapters that can adapt custom objects as function parameters.

errcheck
Assign a Python function or another callable to this attribute. The callable will be called with three or more arguments:

callable(*result, func, arguments*)
result is what the foreign function returns, as specified by the *restype* attribute.

func is the foreign function object itself, this allows reusing the same callable object to check or post process the results of several functions.

arguments is a tuple containing the parameters originally passed to the function call, this allows specializing the behavior on the arguments used.

The object that this function returns will be returned from the foreign function call, but it can also check the result value and raise an exception if the foreign function call failed.

exception ctypes.ArgumentError
This exception is raised when a foreign function call cannot convert one of the passed arguments.

Function prototypes

Foreign functions can also be created by instantiating function prototypes. Function prototypes are similar to function prototypes in C; they describe a function (return type, argument types, calling convention) without defining an implementation. The factory functions must be called with the desired result type and the argument types of the function.

`ctypes.CFUNCTYPE`(*restype*, **argtypes*, *use_errno=False*, *use_last_error=False*)
: The returned function prototype creates functions that use the standard C calling convention. The function will release the GIL during the call. If *use_errno* is set to true, the ctypes private copy of the system *errno* variable is exchanged with the real *errno* value before and after the call; *use_last_error* does the same for the Windows error code.

`ctypes.WINFUNCTYPE`(*restype*, **argtypes*, *use_errno=False*, *use_last_error=False*)
: Windows only: The returned function prototype creates functions that use the `stdcall` calling convention, except on Windows CE where *WINFUNCTYPE()* is the same as *CFUNCTYPE()*. The function will release the GIL during the call. *use_errno* and *use_last_error* have the same meaning as above.

`ctypes.PYFUNCTYPE`(*restype*, **argtypes*)
: The returned function prototype creates functions that use the Python calling convention. The function will *not* release the GIL during the call.

Function prototypes created by these factory functions can be instantiated in different ways, depending on the type and number of the parameters in the call:

`prototype`(*address*)
: Returns a foreign function at the specified address which must be an integer.

`prototype`(*callable*)
: Create a C callable function (a callback function) from a Python *callable*.

`prototype`(*func_spec*[, *paramflags*])
: Returns a foreign function exported by a shared library. *func_spec* must be a 2-tuple `(name_or_ordinal, library)`. The first item is the name of the exported function as string, or the ordinal of the exported function as small integer. The second item is the shared library instance.

`prototype`(*vtbl_index*, *name*[, *paramflags*[, *iid*]])
: Returns a foreign function that will call a COM method. *vtbl_index* is the index into the virtual function table, a small non-negative integer. *name* is name of the COM method. *iid* is an optional pointer to the interface identifier which is used in extended error reporting.

  COM methods use a special calling convention: They require a pointer to the COM interface as first argument, in addition to those parameters that are specified in the `argtypes` tuple.

The optional *paramflags* parameter creates foreign function wrappers with much more functionality than the features described above.

paramflags must be a tuple of the same length as `argtypes`.

Each item in this tuple contains further information about a parameter, it must be a tuple containing one, two, or three items.

The first item is an integer containing a combination of direction flags for the parameter:

1 Specifies an input parameter to the function.

2 Output parameter. The foreign function fills in a value.

4 Input parameter which defaults to the integer zero.

The optional second item is the parameter name as string. If this is specified, the foreign function can be called with named parameters.

The optional third item is the default value for this parameter.

This example demonstrates how to wrap the Windows `MessageBoxW` function so that it supports default parameters and named arguments. The C declaration from the windows header file is this:

```
WINUSERAPI int WINAPI
MessageBoxW(
    HWND hWnd,
    LPCWSTR lpText,
    LPCWSTR lpCaption,
    UINT uType);
```

Here is the wrapping with *ctypes*:

```
>>> from ctypes import c_int, WINFUNCTYPE, windll
>>> from ctypes.wintypes import HWND, LPCWSTR, UINT
>>> prototype = WINFUNCTYPE(c_int, HWND, LPCWSTR, LPCWSTR, UINT)
>>> paramflags = (1, "hwnd", 0), (1, "text", "Hi"), (1, "caption", "Hello from ctypes"), (1, "flags
→", 0)
>>> MessageBox = prototype(("MessageBoxW", windll.user32), paramflags)
```

The MessageBox foreign function can now be called in these ways:

```
>>> MessageBox()
>>> MessageBox(text="Spam, spam, spam")
>>> MessageBox(flags=2, text="foo bar")
```

A second example demonstrates output parameters. The win32 GetWindowRect function retrieves the dimensions of a specified window by copying them into RECT structure that the caller has to supply. Here is the C declaration:

```
WINUSERAPI BOOL WINAPI
GetWindowRect(
     HWND hWnd,
     LPRECT lpRect);
```

Here is the wrapping with *ctypes*:

```
>>> from ctypes import POINTER, WINFUNCTYPE, windll, WinError
>>> from ctypes.wintypes import BOOL, HWND, RECT
>>> prototype = WINFUNCTYPE(BOOL, HWND, POINTER(RECT))
>>> paramflags = (1, "hwnd"), (2, "lprect")
>>> GetWindowRect = prototype(("GetWindowRect", windll.user32), paramflags)
>>>
```

Functions with output parameters will automatically return the output parameter value if there is a single one, or a tuple containing the output parameter values when there are more than one, so the GetWindowRect function now returns a RECT instance, when called.

Output parameters can be combined with the errcheck protocol to do further output processing and error checking. The win32 GetWindowRect api function returns a BOOL to signal success or failure, so this function could do the error checking, and raises an exception when the api call failed:

```
>>> def errcheck(result, func, args):
...     if not result:
...         raise WinError()
...     return args
...
>>> GetWindowRect.errcheck = errcheck
>>>
```

If the errcheck function returns the argument tuple it receives unchanged, *ctypes* continues the normal processing it does on the output parameters. If you want to return a tuple of window coordinates instead of a RECT instance, you can retrieve the fields in the function and return them instead, the normal processing will no longer take place:

```
>>> def errcheck(result, func, args):
...     if not result:
...         raise WinError()
...     rc = args[1]
...     return rc.left, rc.top, rc.bottom, rc.right
...
>>> GetWindowRect.errcheck = errcheck
>>>
```

Utility functions

`ctypes.addressof(obj)`
: Returns the address of the memory buffer as integer. *obj* must be an instance of a ctypes type.

`ctypes.alignment(obj_or_type)`
: Returns the alignment requirements of a ctypes type. *obj_or_type* must be a ctypes type or instance.

`ctypes.byref(obj[, offset])`
: Returns a light-weight pointer to *obj*, which must be an instance of a ctypes type. *offset* defaults to zero, and must be an integer that will be added to the internal pointer value.

  `byref(obj, offset)` corresponds to this C code:

```
(((char *)&obj) + offset)
```

  The returned object can only be used as a foreign function call parameter. It behaves similar to `pointer(obj)`, but the construction is a lot faster.

`ctypes.cast(obj, type)`
: This function is similar to the cast operator in C. It returns a new instance of *type* which points to the same memory block as *obj*. *type* must be a pointer type, and *obj* must be an object that can be interpreted as a pointer.

`ctypes.create_string_buffer(init_or_size, size=None)`
: This function creates a mutable character buffer. The returned object is a ctypes array of `c_char`.

  init_or_size must be an integer which specifies the size of the array, or a bytes object which will be used to initialize the array items.

  If a bytes object is specified as first argument, the buffer is made one item larger than its length so that the last element in the array is a NUL termination character. An integer can be passed as second argument which allows specifying the size of the array if the length of the bytes should not be used.

`ctypes.create_unicode_buffer(init_or_size, size=None)`
: This function creates a mutable unicode character buffer. The returned object is a ctypes array of `c_wchar`.

  init_or_size must be an integer which specifies the size of the array, or a string which will be used to initialize the array items.

  If a string is specified as first argument, the buffer is made one item larger than the length of the string so that the last element in the array is a NUL termination character. An integer can be passed as second argument which allows specifying the size of the array if the length of the string should not be used.

`ctypes.DllCanUnloadNow()`
: Windows only: This function is a hook which allows implementing in-process COM servers with ctypes. It is called from the DllCanUnloadNow function that the _ctypes extension dll exports.

ctypes.**DllGetClassObject**()
Windows only: This function is a hook which allows implementing in-process COM servers with ctypes. It is called from the DllGetClassObject function that the `_ctypes` extension dll exports.

ctypes.util.**find_library**(*name*)
Try to find a library and return a pathname. *name* is the library name without any prefix like `lib`, suffix like `.so`, `.dylib` or version number (this is the form used for the posix linker option `-l`). If no library can be found, returns `None`.

The exact functionality is system dependent.

ctypes.util.**find_msvcrt**()
Windows only: return the filename of the VC runtime library used by Python, and by the extension modules. If the name of the library cannot be determined, `None` is returned.

If you need to free memory, for example, allocated by an extension module with a call to the `free(void *)`, it is important that you use the function in the same library that allocated the memory.

ctypes.**FormatError**([*code*])
Windows only: Returns a textual description of the error code *code*. If no error code is specified, the last error code is used by calling the Windows api function GetLastError.

ctypes.**GetLastError**()
Windows only: Returns the last error code set by Windows in the calling thread. This function calls the Windows *GetLastError()* function directly, it does not return the ctypes-private copy of the error code.

ctypes.**get_errno**()
Returns the current value of the ctypes-private copy of the system *errno* variable in the calling thread.

ctypes.**get_last_error**()
Windows only: returns the current value of the ctypes-private copy of the system `LastError` variable in the calling thread.

ctypes.**memmove**(*dst*, *src*, *count*)
Same as the standard C memmove library function: copies *count* bytes from *src* to *dst*. *dst* and *src* must be integers or ctypes instances that can be converted to pointers.

ctypes.**memset**(*dst*, *c*, *count*)
Same as the standard C memset library function: fills the memory block at address *dst* with *count* bytes of value *c*. *dst* must be an integer specifying an address, or a ctypes instance.

ctypes.**POINTER**(*type*)
This factory function creates and returns a new ctypes pointer type. Pointer types are cached and reused internally, so calling this function repeatedly is cheap. *type* must be a ctypes type.

ctypes.**pointer**(*obj*)
This function creates a new pointer instance, pointing to *obj*. The returned object is of the type `POINTER(type(obj))`.

Note: If you just want to pass a pointer to an object to a foreign function call, you should use `byref(obj)` which is much faster.

ctypes.**resize**(*obj*, *size*)
This function resizes the internal memory buffer of *obj*, which must be an instance of a ctypes type. It is not possible to make the buffer smaller than the native size of the objects type, as given by `sizeof(type(obj))`, but it is possible to enlarge the buffer.

ctypes.**set_errno**(*value*)
Set the current value of the ctypes-private copy of the system *errno* variable in the calling thread to *value* and return the previous value.

`ctypes.set_last_error(value)`
Windows only: set the current value of the ctypes-private copy of the system `LastError` variable in the calling thread to *value* and return the previous value.

`ctypes.sizeof(obj_or_type)`
Returns the size in bytes of a ctypes type or instance memory buffer. Does the same as the C `sizeof` operator.

`ctypes.string_at(address, size=-1)`
This function returns the C string starting at memory address *address* as a bytes object. If size is specified, it is used as size, otherwise the string is assumed to be zero-terminated.

`ctypes.WinError(code=None, descr=None)`
Windows only: this function is probably the worst-named thing in ctypes. It creates an instance of OSError. If *code* is not specified, `GetLastError` is called to determine the error code. If *descr* is not specified, `FormatError()` is called to get a textual description of the error.

Changed in version 3.3: An instance of `WindowsError` used to be created.

`ctypes.wstring_at(address, size=-1)`
This function returns the wide character string starting at memory address *address* as a string. If *size* is specified, it is used as the number of characters of the string, otherwise the string is assumed to be zero-terminated.

Data types

`class ctypes._CData`
This non-public class is the common base class of all ctypes data types. Among other things, all ctypes type instances contain a memory block that hold C compatible data; the address of the memory block is returned by the `addressof()` helper function. Another instance variable is exposed as `_objects`; this contains other Python objects that need to be kept alive in case the memory block contains pointers.

Common methods of ctypes data types, these are all class methods (to be exact, they are methods of the *metaclass*):

`from_buffer(source[, offset])`
This method returns a ctypes instance that shares the buffer of the *source* object. The *source* object must support the writeable buffer interface. The optional *offset* parameter specifies an offset into the source buffer in bytes; the default is zero. If the source buffer is not large enough a `ValueError` is raised.

`from_buffer_copy(source[, offset])`
This method creates a ctypes instance, copying the buffer from the *source* object buffer which must be readable. The optional *offset* parameter specifies an offset into the source buffer in bytes; the default is zero. If the source buffer is not large enough a `ValueError` is raised.

`from_address(address)`
This method returns a ctypes type instance using the memory specified by *address* which must be an integer.

`from_param(obj)`
This method adapts *obj* to a ctypes type. It is called with the actual object used in a foreign function call when the type is present in the foreign function's `argtypes` tuple; it must return an object that can be used as a function call parameter.

All ctypes data types have a default implementation of this classmethod that normally returns *obj* if that is an instance of the type. Some types accept other objects as well.

`in_dll(library, name)`

This method returns a ctypes type instance exported by a shared library. *name* is the name of the symbol that exports the data, *library* is the loaded shared library.

Common instance variables of ctypes data types:

`_b_base_`

Sometimes ctypes data instances do not own the memory block they contain, instead they share part of the memory block of a base object. The *_b_base_* read-only member is the root ctypes object that owns the memory block.

`_b_needsfree_`

This read-only variable is true when the ctypes data instance has allocated the memory block itself, false otherwise.

`_objects`

This member is either `None` or a dictionary containing Python objects that need to be kept alive so that the memory block contents is kept valid. This object is only exposed for debugging; never modify the contents of this dictionary.

Fundamental data types

`class ctypes._SimpleCData`

This non-public class is the base class of all fundamental ctypes data types. It is mentioned here because it contains the common attributes of the fundamental ctypes data types. *_SimpleCData* is a subclass of *_CData*, so it inherits their methods and attributes. ctypes data types that are not and do not contain pointers can now be pickled.

Instances have a single attribute:

`value`

This attribute contains the actual value of the instance. For integer and pointer types, it is an integer, for character types, it is a single character bytes object or string, for character pointer types it is a Python bytes object or string.

When the `value` attribute is retrieved from a ctypes instance, usually a new object is returned each time. *ctypes* does *not* implement original object return, always a new object is constructed. The same is true for all other ctypes object instances.

Fundamental data types, when returned as foreign function call results, or, for example, by retrieving structure field members or array items, are transparently converted to native Python types. In other words, if a foreign function has a `restype` of *c_char_p*, you will always receive a Python bytes object, *not* a *c_char_p* instance.

Subclasses of fundamental data types do *not* inherit this behavior. So, if a foreign functions `restype` is a subclass of *c_void_p*, you will receive an instance of this subclass from the function call. Of course, you can get the value of the pointer by accessing the `value` attribute.

These are the fundamental ctypes data types:

`class ctypes.c_byte`

Represents the C `signed char` datatype, and interprets the value as small integer. The constructor accepts an optional integer initializer; no overflow checking is done.

`class ctypes.c_char`

Represents the C `char` datatype, and interprets the value as a single character. The constructor accepts an optional string initializer, the length of the string must be exactly one character.

`class ctypes.c_char_p`

Represents the C `char *` datatype when it points to a zero-terminated string. For a general character pointer that may also point to binary data, `POINTER(c_char)` must be used. The constructor accepts an integer address, or a bytes object.

class ctypes.c_double
Represents the C `double` datatype. The constructor accepts an optional float initializer.

class ctypes.c_longdouble
Represents the C `long double` datatype. The constructor accepts an optional float initializer. On platforms where `sizeof(long double) == sizeof(double)` it is an alias to *c_double*.

class ctypes.c_float
Represents the C `float` datatype. The constructor accepts an optional float initializer.

class ctypes.c_int
Represents the C `signed int` datatype. The constructor accepts an optional integer initializer; no overflow checking is done. On platforms where `sizeof(int) == sizeof(long)` it is an alias to *c_long*.

class ctypes.c_int8
Represents the C 8-bit `signed int` datatype. Usually an alias for *c_byte*.

class ctypes.c_int16
Represents the C 16-bit `signed int` datatype. Usually an alias for *c_short*.

class ctypes.c_int32
Represents the C 32-bit `signed int` datatype. Usually an alias for *c_int*.

class ctypes.c_int64
Represents the C 64-bit `signed int` datatype. Usually an alias for *c_longlong*.

class ctypes.c_long
Represents the C `signed long` datatype. The constructor accepts an optional integer initializer; no overflow checking is done.

class ctypes.c_longlong
Represents the C `signed long long` datatype. The constructor accepts an optional integer initializer; no overflow checking is done.

class ctypes.c_short
Represents the C `signed short` datatype. The constructor accepts an optional integer initializer; no overflow checking is done.

class ctypes.c_size_t
Represents the C `size_t` datatype.

class ctypes.c_ssize_t
Represents the C `ssize_t` datatype.

New in version 3.2.

class ctypes.c_ubyte
Represents the C `unsigned char` datatype, it interprets the value as small integer. The constructor accepts an optional integer initializer; no overflow checking is done.

class ctypes.c_uint
Represents the C `unsigned int` datatype. The constructor accepts an optional integer initializer; no overflow checking is done. On platforms where `sizeof(int) == sizeof(long)` it is an alias for *c_ulong*.

class ctypes.c_uint8
Represents the C 8-bit `unsigned int` datatype. Usually an alias for *c_ubyte*.

class ctypes.c_uint16
Represents the C 16-bit `unsigned int` datatype. Usually an alias for *c_ushort*.

class ctypes.c_uint32
Represents the C 32-bit unsigned int datatype. Usually an alias for *c_uint*.

class ctypes.c_uint64
Represents the C 64-bit unsigned int datatype. Usually an alias for *c_ulonglong*.

class ctypes.c_ulong
Represents the C unsigned long datatype. The constructor accepts an optional integer initializer; no overflow checking is done.

class ctypes.c_ulonglong
Represents the C unsigned long long datatype. The constructor accepts an optional integer initializer; no overflow checking is done.

class ctypes.c_ushort
Represents the C unsigned short datatype. The constructor accepts an optional integer initializer; no overflow checking is done.

class ctypes.c_void_p
Represents the C void * type. The value is represented as integer. The constructor accepts an optional integer initializer.

class ctypes.c_wchar
Represents the C wchar_t datatype, and interprets the value as a single character unicode string. The constructor accepts an optional string initializer, the length of the string must be exactly one character.

class ctypes.c_wchar_p
Represents the C wchar_t * datatype, which must be a pointer to a zero-terminated wide character string. The constructor accepts an integer address, or a string.

class ctypes.c_bool
Represent the C bool datatype (more accurately, _Bool from C99). Its value can be True or False, and the constructor accepts any object that has a truth value.

class ctypes.HRESULT
Windows only: Represents a HRESULT value, which contains success or error information for a function or method call.

class ctypes.py_object
Represents the C PyObject * datatype. Calling this without an argument creates a NULL PyObject * pointer.

The ctypes.wintypes module provides quite some other Windows specific data types, for example HWND, WPARAM, or DWORD. Some useful structures like MSG or RECT are also defined.

Structured data types

class ctypes.**Union**(**args*, ***kw*)
Abstract base class for unions in native byte order.

class ctypes.**BigEndianStructure**(**args*, ***kw*)
Abstract base class for structures in *big endian* byte order.

class ctypes.**LittleEndianStructure**(**args*, ***kw*)
Abstract base class for structures in *little endian* byte order.

Structures with non-native byte order cannot contain pointer type fields, or any other data types containing pointer type fields.

class ctypes.**Structure**(**args*, ***kw*)
Abstract base class for structures in *native* byte order.

Concrete structure and union types must be created by subclassing one of these types, and at least define a *_fields_* class variable. *ctypes* will create descriptors which allow reading and writing the fields by direct attribute accesses. These are the

fields

A sequence defining the structure fields. The items must be 2-tuples or 3-tuples. The first item is the name of the field, the second item specifies the type of the field; it can be any ctypes data type.

For integer type fields like *c_int*, a third optional item can be given. It must be a small positive integer defining the bit width of the field.

Field names must be unique within one structure or union. This is not checked, only one field can be accessed when names are repeated.

It is possible to define the *_fields_* class variable *after* the class statement that defines the Structure subclass, this allows creating data types that directly or indirectly reference themselves:

```
class List(Structure):
    pass
List._fields_ = [("pnext", POINTER(List)),
                 ...
                ]
```

The *_fields_* class variable must, however, be defined before the type is first used (an instance is created, *sizeof()* is called on it, and so on). Later assignments to the *_fields_* class variable will raise an AttributeError.

It is possible to defined sub-subclasses of structure types, they inherit the fields of the base class plus the *_fields_* defined in the sub-subclass, if any.

pack

An optional small integer that allows overriding the alignment of structure fields in the instance. *_pack_* must already be defined when *_fields_* is assigned, otherwise it will have no effect.

anonymous

An optional sequence that lists the names of unnamed (anonymous) fields. *_anonymous_* must be already defined when *_fields_* is assigned, otherwise it will have no effect.

The fields listed in this variable must be structure or union type fields. *ctypes* will create descriptors in the structure type that allows accessing the nested fields directly, without the need to create the structure or union field.

Here is an example type (Windows):

```
class _U(Union):
    _fields_ = [("lptdesc", POINTER(TYPEDESC)),
                ("lpadesc", POINTER(ARRAYDESC)),
                ("hreftype", HREFTYPE)]

class TYPEDESC(Structure):
    _anonymous_ = ("u",)
    _fields_ = [("u", _U),
                ("vt", VARTYPE)]
```

The `TYPEDESC` structure describes a COM data type, the `vt` field specifies which one of the union fields is valid. Since the `u` field is defined as anonymous field, it is now possible to access the members directly off the TYPEDESC instance. `td.lptdesc` and `td.u.lptdesc` are equivalent, but the former is faster since it does not need to create a temporary union instance:

```
td = TYPEDESC()
td.vt = VT_PTR
td.lptdesc = POINTER(some_type)
td.u.lptdesc = POINTER(some_type)
```

It is possible to defined sub-subclasses of structures, they inherit the fields of the base class. If the subclass definition has a separate *_fields_* variable, the fields specified in this are appended to the fields of the base class.

Structure and union constructors accept both positional and keyword arguments. Positional arguments are used to initialize member fields in the same order as they are appear in *_fields_*. Keyword arguments in the constructor are interpreted as attribute assignments, so they will initialize *_fields_* with the same name, or create new attributes for names not present in *_fields_*.

Arrays and pointers

class ctypes.Array(args*)**

Abstract base class for arrays.

The recommended way to create concrete array types is by multiplying any *ctypes* data type with a positive integer. Alternatively, you can subclass this type and define *_length_* and *_type_* class variables. Array elements can be read and written using standard subscript and slice accesses; for slice reads, the resulting object is *not* itself an *Array*.

length

A positive integer specifying the number of elements in the array. Out-of-range subscripts result in an *IndexError*. Will be returned by *len()*.

type

Specifies the type of each element in the array.

Array subclass constructors accept positional arguments, used to initialize the elements in order.

class ctypes._Pointer

Private, abstract base class for pointers.

Concrete pointer types are created by calling *POINTER()* with the type that will be pointed to; this is done automatically by *pointer()*.

If a pointer points to an array, its elements can be read and written using standard subscript and slice accesses. Pointer objects have no size, so *len()* will raise *TypeError*. Negative subscripts will read from the memory *before* the pointer (as in C), and out-of-range subscripts will probably crash with an access violation (if you're lucky).

type

Specifies the type pointed to.

contents

Returns the object to which to pointer points. Assigning to this attribute changes the pointer to point to the assigned object.

CHAPTER

SEVENTEEN

CONCURRENT EXECUTION

The modules described in this chapter provide support for concurrent execution of code. The appropriate choice of tool will depend on the task to be executed (CPU bound vs IO bound) and preferred style of development (event driven cooperative multitasking vs preemptive multitasking). Here's an overview:

17.1 `threading` — Thread-based parallelism

Source code: Lib/threading.py

This module constructs higher-level threading interfaces on top of the lower level *_thread* module. See also the *queue* module.

The *dummy_threading* module is provided for situations where *threading* cannot be used because *_thread* is missing.

Note: While they are not listed below, the `camelCase` names used for some methods and functions in this module in the Python 2.x series are still supported by this module.

This module defines the following functions:

threading.active_count()
Return the number of *Thread* objects currently alive. The returned count is equal to the length of the list returned by *enumerate()*.

threading.current_thread()
Return the current *Thread* object, corresponding to the caller's thread of control. If the caller's thread of control was not created through the *threading* module, a dummy thread object with limited functionality is returned.

threading.get_ident()
Return the 'thread identifier' of the current thread. This is a nonzero integer. Its value has no direct meaning; it is intended as a magic cookie to be used e.g. to index a dictionary of thread-specific data. Thread identifiers may be recycled when a thread exits and another thread is created.

New in version 3.3.

threading.enumerate()
Return a list of all *Thread* objects currently alive. The list includes daemonic threads, dummy thread objects created by *current_thread()*, and the main thread. It excludes terminated threads and threads that have not yet been started.

threading.main_thread()
Return the main *Thread* object. In normal conditions, the main thread is the thread from which the Python interpreter was started.

New in version 3.4.

threading.settrace(*func*)
Set a trace function for all threads started from the *threading* module. The *func* will be passed to *sys.settrace()* for each thread, before its *run()* method is called.

threading.setprofile(*func*)
Set a profile function for all threads started from the *threading* module. The *func* will be passed to *sys.setprofile()* for each thread, before its *run()* method is called.

threading.stack_size([*size*])
Return the thread stack size used when creating new threads. The optional *size* argument specifies the stack size to be used for subsequently created threads, and must be 0 (use platform or configured default) or a positive integer value of at least 32,768 (32 KiB). If *size* is not specified, 0 is used. If changing the thread stack size is unsupported, a *RuntimeError* is raised. If the specified stack size is invalid, a *ValueError* is raised and the stack size is unmodified. 32 KiB is currently the minimum supported stack size value to guarantee sufficient stack space for the interpreter itself. Note that some platforms may have particular restrictions on values for the stack size, such as requiring a minimum stack size > 32 KiB or requiring allocation in multiples of the system memory page size - platform documentation should be referred to for more information (4 KiB pages are common; using multiples of 4096 for the stack size is the suggested approach in the absence of more specific information). Availability: Windows, systems with POSIX threads.

This module also defines the following constant:

threading.TIMEOUT_MAX
The maximum value allowed for the *timeout* parameter of blocking functions (*Lock.acquire()*, *RLock.acquire()*, *Condition.wait()*, etc.). Specifying a timeout greater than this value will raise an *OverflowError*.

New in version 3.2.

This module defines a number of classes, which are detailed in the sections below.

The design of this module is loosely based on Java's threading model. However, where Java makes locks and condition variables basic behavior of every object, they are separate objects in Python. Python's *Thread* class supports a subset of the behavior of Java's Thread class; currently, there are no priorities, no thread groups, and threads cannot be destroyed, stopped, suspended, resumed, or interrupted. The static methods of Java's Thread class, when implemented, are mapped to module-level functions.

All of the methods described below are executed atomically.

17.1.1 Thread-Local Data

Thread-local data is data whose values are thread specific. To manage thread-local data, just create an instance of *local* (or a subclass) and store attributes on it:

```
mydata = threading.local()
mydata.x = 1
```

The instance's values will be different for separate threads.

class threading.local
A class that represents thread-local data.

For more details and extensive examples, see the documentation string of the `_threading_local` module.

17.1.2 Thread Objects

The *Thread* class represents an activity that is run in a separate thread of control. There are two ways to specify the activity: by passing a callable object to the constructor, or by overriding the *run()* method in a subclass. No other methods (except for the constructor) should be overridden in a subclass. In other words, *only* override the `__init__()` and *run()* methods of this class.

Once a thread object is created, its activity must be started by calling the thread's *start()* method. This invokes the *run()* method in a separate thread of control.

Once the thread's activity is started, the thread is considered 'alive'. It stops being alive when its *run()* method terminates – either normally, or by raising an unhandled exception. The *is_alive()* method tests whether the thread is alive.

Other threads can call a thread's *join()* method. This blocks the calling thread until the thread whose *join()* method is called is terminated.

A thread has a name. The name can be passed to the constructor, and read or changed through the *name* attribute.

A thread can be flagged as a "daemon thread". The significance of this flag is that the entire Python program exits when only daemon threads are left. The initial value is inherited from the creating thread. The flag can be set through the *daemon* property or the *daemon* constructor argument.

Note: Daemon threads are abruptly stopped at shutdown. Their resources (such as open files, database transactions, etc.) may not be released properly. If you want your threads to stop gracefully, make them non-daemonic and use a suitable signalling mechanism such as an *Event*.

There is a "main thread" object; this corresponds to the initial thread of control in the Python program. It is not a daemon thread.

There is the possibility that "dummy thread objects" are created. These are thread objects corresponding to "alien threads", which are threads of control started outside the threading module, such as directly from C code. Dummy thread objects have limited functionality; they are always considered alive and daemonic, and cannot be *join()*ed. They are never deleted, since it is impossible to detect the termination of alien threads.

class threading.Thread(*group=None, target=None, name=None, args=(), kwargs={}, *, daemon=None*)

This constructor should always be called with keyword arguments. Arguments are:

group should be `None`; reserved for future extension when a `ThreadGroup` class is implemented.

target is the callable object to be invoked by the *run()* method. Defaults to `None`, meaning nothing is called.

name is the thread name. By default, a unique name is constructed of the form "Thread-*N*" where *N* is a small decimal number.

args is the argument tuple for the target invocation. Defaults to `()`.

kwargs is a dictionary of keyword arguments for the target invocation. Defaults to `{}`.

If not `None`, *daemon* explicitly sets whether the thread is daemonic. If `None` (the default), the daemonic property is inherited from the current thread.

If the subclass overrides the constructor, it must make sure to invoke the base class constructor (`Thread.__init__()`) before doing anything else to the thread.

Changed in version 3.3: Added the *daemon* argument.

start()

Start the thread's activity.

It must be called at most once per thread object. It arranges for the object's *run()* method to be invoked in a separate thread of control.

This method will raise a *RuntimeError* if called more than once on the same thread object.

run()
Method representing the thread's activity.

You may override this method in a subclass. The standard *run()* method invokes the callable object passed to the object's constructor as the *target* argument, if any, with sequential and keyword arguments taken from the *args* and *kwargs* arguments, respectively.

join(*timeout=None*)
Wait until the thread terminates. This blocks the calling thread until the thread whose *join()* method is called terminates – either normally or through an unhandled exception – or until the optional timeout occurs.

When the *timeout* argument is present and not None, it should be a floating point number specifying a timeout for the operation in seconds (or fractions thereof). As *join()* always returns None, you must call *is_alive()* after *join()* to decide whether a timeout happened – if the thread is still alive, the *join()* call timed out.

When the *timeout* argument is not present or None, the operation will block until the thread terminates.

A thread can be *join()*ed many times.

join() raises a *RuntimeError* if an attempt is made to join the current thread as that would cause a deadlock. It is also an error to *join()* a thread before it has been started and attempts to do so raise the same exception.

name
A string used for identification purposes only. It has no semantics. Multiple threads may be given the same name. The initial name is set by the constructor.

getName()
setName()
Old getter/setter API for *name*; use it directly as a property instead.

ident
The 'thread identifier' of this thread or None if the thread has not been started. This is a nonzero integer. See the *get_ident()* function. Thread identifiers may be recycled when a thread exits and another thread is created. The identifier is available even after the thread has exited.

is_alive()
Return whether the thread is alive.

This method returns True just before the *run()* method starts until just after the *run()* method terminates. The module function *enumerate()* returns a list of all alive threads.

daemon
A boolean value indicating whether this thread is a daemon thread (True) or not (False). This must be set before *start()* is called, otherwise *RuntimeError* is raised. Its initial value is inherited from the creating thread; the main thread is not a daemon thread and therefore all threads created in the main thread default to *daemon* = False.

The entire Python program exits when no alive non-daemon threads are left.

isDaemon()
setDaemon()
Old getter/setter API for *daemon*; use it directly as a property instead.

CPython implementation detail: In CPython, due to the *Global Interpreter Lock*, only one thread can execute Python code at once (even though certain performance-oriented libraries might overcome this limitation). If you want your application to make better use of the computational resources of multi-core machines, you are advised to use *multiprocessing* or *concurrent.futures.ProcessPoolExecutor*. However, threading is still an appropriate model if you want to run multiple I/O-bound tasks simultaneously.

17.1.3 Lock Objects

A primitive lock is a synchronization primitive that is not owned by a particular thread when locked. In Python, it is currently the lowest level synchronization primitive available, implemented directly by the *_thread* extension module.

A primitive lock is in one of two states, "locked" or "unlocked". It is created in the unlocked state. It has two basic methods, *acquire()* and *release()*. When the state is unlocked, *acquire()* changes the state to locked and returns immediately. When the state is locked, *acquire()* blocks until a call to *release()* in another thread changes it to unlocked, then the *acquire()* call resets it to locked and returns. The *release()* method should only be called in the locked state; it changes the state to unlocked and returns immediately. If an attempt is made to release an unlocked lock, a *RuntimeError* will be raised.

Locks also support the *context management protocol*.

When more than one thread is blocked in *acquire()* waiting for the state to turn to unlocked, only one thread proceeds when a *release()* call resets the state to unlocked; which one of the waiting threads proceeds is not defined, and may vary across implementations.

All methods are executed atomically.

class threading.Lock

The class implementing primitive lock objects. Once a thread has acquired a lock, subsequent attempts to acquire it block, until it is released; any thread may release it.

Note that `Lock` is actually a factory function which returns an instance of the most efficient version of the concrete Lock class that is supported by the platform.

acquire(*blocking=True, timeout=-1*)

Acquire a lock, blocking or non-blocking.

When invoked with the *blocking* argument set to `True` (the default), block until the lock is unlocked, then set it to locked and return `True`.

When invoked with the *blocking* argument set to `False`, do not block. If a call with *blocking* set to `True` would block, return `False` immediately; otherwise, set the lock to locked and return `True`.

When invoked with the floating-point *timeout* argument set to a positive value, block for at most the number of seconds specified by *timeout* and as long as the lock cannot be acquired. A *timeout* argument of `-1` specifies an unbounded wait. It is forbidden to specify a *timeout* when *blocking* is false.

The return value is `True` if the lock is acquired successfully, `False` if not (for example if the *timeout* expired).

Changed in version 3.2: The *timeout* parameter is new.

Changed in version 3.2: Lock acquires can now be interrupted by signals on POSIX.

release()

Release a lock. This can be called from any thread, not only the thread which has acquired the lock.

When the lock is locked, reset it to unlocked, and return. If any other threads are blocked waiting for the lock to become unlocked, allow exactly one of them to proceed.

When invoked on an unlocked lock, a *RuntimeError* is raised.

There is no return value.

17.1.4 RLock Objects

A reentrant lock is a synchronization primitive that may be acquired multiple times by the same thread. Internally, it uses the concepts of "owning thread" and "recursion level" in addition to the locked/unlocked state used by primitive locks. In the locked state, some thread owns the lock; in the unlocked state, no thread owns it.

To lock the lock, a thread calls its `acquire()` method; this returns once the thread owns the lock. To unlock the lock, a thread calls its `release()` method. `acquire()`/`release()` call pairs may be nested; only the final `release()` (the `release()` of the outermost pair) resets the lock to unlocked and allows another thread blocked in `acquire()` to proceed.

Reentrant locks also support the *context management protocol*.

class threading.RLock

This class implements reentrant lock objects. A reentrant lock must be released by the thread that acquired it. Once a thread has acquired a reentrant lock, the same thread may acquire it again without blocking; the thread must release it once for each time it has acquired it.

Note that `RLock` is actually a factory function which returns an instance of the most efficient version of the concrete RLock class that is supported by the platform.

acquire(*blocking=True*, *timeout=-1*)

Acquire a lock, blocking or non-blocking.

When invoked without arguments: if this thread already owns the lock, increment the recursion level by one, and return immediately. Otherwise, if another thread owns the lock, block until the lock is unlocked. Once the lock is unlocked (not owned by any thread), then grab ownership, set the recursion level to one, and return. If more than one thread is blocked waiting until the lock is unlocked, only one at a time will be able to grab ownership of the lock. There is no return value in this case.

When invoked with the *blocking* argument set to true, do the same thing as when called without arguments, and return true.

When invoked with the *blocking* argument set to false, do not block. If a call without an argument would block, return false immediately; otherwise, do the same thing as when called without arguments, and return true.

When invoked with the floating-point *timeout* argument set to a positive value, block for at most the number of seconds specified by *timeout* and as long as the lock cannot be acquired. Return true if the lock has been acquired, false if the timeout has elapsed.

Changed in version 3.2: The *timeout* parameter is new.

release()

Release a lock, decrementing the recursion level. If after the decrement it is zero, reset the lock to unlocked (not owned by any thread), and if any other threads are blocked waiting for the lock to become unlocked, allow exactly one of them to proceed. If after the decrement the recursion level is still nonzero, the lock remains locked and owned by the calling thread.

Only call this method when the calling thread owns the lock. A `RuntimeError` is raised if this method is called when the lock is unlocked.

There is no return value.

17.1.5 Condition Objects

A condition variable is always associated with some kind of lock; this can be passed in or one will be created by default. Passing one in is useful when several condition variables must share the same lock. The lock is part of the condition object: you don't have to track it separately.

A condition variable obeys the *context management protocol*: using the **with** statement acquires the associated lock for the duration of the enclosed block. The *acquire()* and *release()* methods also call the corresponding methods of the associated lock.

Other methods must be called with the associated lock held. The *wait()* method releases the lock, and then blocks until another thread awakens it by calling *notify()* or *notify_all()*. Once awakened, *wait()* re-acquires the lock and returns. It is also possible to specify a timeout.

The *notify()* method wakes up one of the threads waiting for the condition variable, if any are waiting. The *notify_all()* method wakes up all threads waiting for the condition variable.

Note: the *notify()* and *notify_all()* methods don't release the lock; this means that the thread or threads awakened will not return from their *wait()* call immediately, but only when the thread that called *notify()* or *notify_all()* finally relinquishes ownership of the lock.

The typical programming style using condition variables uses the lock to synchronize access to some shared state; threads that are interested in a particular change of state call *wait()* repeatedly until they see the desired state, while threads that modify the state call *notify()* or *notify_all()* when they change the state in such a way that it could possibly be a desired state for one of the waiters. For example, the following code is a generic producer-consumer situation with unlimited buffer capacity:

```
# Consume one item
with cv:
    while not an_item_is_available():
        cv.wait()
    get_an_available_item()

# Produce one item
with cv:
    make_an_item_available()
    cv.notify()
```

The **while** loop checking for the application's condition is necessary because *wait()* can return after an arbitrary long time, and the condition which prompted the *notify()* call may no longer hold true. This is inherent to multi-threaded programming. The *wait_for()* method can be used to automate the condition checking, and eases the computation of timeouts:

```
# Consume an item
with cv:
    cv.wait_for(an_item_is_available)
    get_an_available_item()
```

To choose between *notify()* and *notify_all()*, consider whether one state change can be interesting for only one or several waiting threads. E.g. in a typical producer-consumer situation, adding one item to the buffer only needs to wake up one consumer thread.

class threading.Condition(*lock=None*)

This class implements condition variable objects. A condition variable allows one or more threads to wait until they are notified by another thread.

If the *lock* argument is given and not `None`, it must be a *Lock* or *RLock* object, and it is used as the underlying lock. Otherwise, a new *RLock* object is created and used as the underlying lock.

Changed in version 3.3: changed from a factory function to a class.

acquire(**args*)

Acquire the underlying lock. This method calls the corresponding method on the underlying lock; the return value is whatever that method returns.

release()

Release the underlying lock. This method calls the corresponding method on the underlying lock;

there is no return value.

wait(*timeout=None*)
Wait until notified or until a timeout occurs. If the calling thread has not acquired the lock when this method is called, a *RuntimeError* is raised.

This method releases the underlying lock, and then blocks until it is awakened by a *notify()* or *notify_all()* call for the same condition variable in another thread, or until the optional timeout occurs. Once awakened or timed out, it re-acquires the lock and returns.

When the *timeout* argument is present and not `None`, it should be a floating point number specifying a timeout for the operation in seconds (or fractions thereof).

When the underlying lock is an *RLock*, it is not released using its *release()* method, since this may not actually unlock the lock when it was acquired multiple times recursively. Instead, an internal interface of the *RLock* class is used, which really unlocks it even when it has been recursively acquired several times. Another internal interface is then used to restore the recursion level when the lock is reacquired.

The return value is `True` unless a given *timeout* expired, in which case it is `False`.

Changed in version 3.2: Previously, the method always returned `None`.

wait_for(*predicate*, *timeout=None*)
Wait until a condition evaluates to true. *predicate* should be a callable which result will be interpreted as a boolean value. A *timeout* may be provided giving the maximum time to wait.

This utility method may call *wait()* repeatedly until the predicate is satisfied, or until a timeout occurs. The return value is the last return value of the predicate and will evaluate to `False` if the method timed out.

Ignoring the timeout feature, calling this method is roughly equivalent to writing:

```
while not predicate():
    cv.wait()
```

Therefore, the same rules apply as with *wait()*: The lock must be held when called and is re-acquired on return. The predicate is evaluated with the lock held.

New in version 3.2.

notify(*n=1*)
By default, wake up one thread waiting on this condition, if any. If the calling thread has not acquired the lock when this method is called, a *RuntimeError* is raised.

This method wakes up at most *n* of the threads waiting for the condition variable; it is a no-op if no threads are waiting.

The current implementation wakes up exactly *n* threads, if at least *n* threads are waiting. However, it's not safe to rely on this behavior. A future, optimized implementation may occasionally wake up more than *n* threads.

Note: an awakened thread does not actually return from its *wait()* call until it can reacquire the lock. Since *notify()* does not release the lock, its caller should.

notify_all()
Wake up all threads waiting on this condition. This method acts like *notify()*, but wakes up all waiting threads instead of one. If the calling thread has not acquired the lock when this method is called, a *RuntimeError* is raised.

17.1.6 Semaphore Objects

This is one of the oldest synchronization primitives in the history of computer science, invented by the early Dutch computer scientist Edsger W. Dijkstra (he used the names `P()` and `V()` instead of *acquire()* and *release()*).

A semaphore manages an internal counter which is decremented by each *acquire()* call and incremented by each *release()* call. The counter can never go below zero; when *acquire()* finds that it is zero, it blocks, waiting until some other thread calls *release()*.

Semaphores also support the *context management protocol*.

class threading.Semaphore(*value=1*)

This class implements semaphore objects. A semaphore manages an atomic counter representing the number of *release()* calls minus the number of *acquire()* calls, plus an initial value. The *acquire()* method blocks if necessary until it can return without making the counter negative. If not given, *value* defaults to 1.

The optional argument gives the initial *value* for the internal counter; it defaults to `1`. If the *value* given is less than 0, *ValueError* is raised.

Changed in version 3.3: changed from a factory function to a class.

acquire(*blocking=True, timeout=None*)

Acquire a semaphore.

When invoked without arguments:

- If the internal counter is larger than zero on entry, decrement it by one and return true immediately.
- If the internal counter is zero on entry, block until awoken by a call to *release()*. Once awoken (and the counter is greater than 0), decrement the counter by 1 and return true. Exactly one thread will be awoken by each call to *release()*. The order in which threads are awoken should not be relied on.

When invoked with *blocking* set to false, do not block. If a call without an argument would block, return false immediately; otherwise, do the same thing as when called without arguments, and return true.

When invoked with a *timeout* other than `None`, it will block for at most *timeout* seconds. If acquire does not complete successfully in that interval, return false. Return true otherwise.

Changed in version 3.2: The *timeout* parameter is new.

release()

Release a semaphore, incrementing the internal counter by one. When it was zero on entry and another thread is waiting for it to become larger than zero again, wake up that thread.

class threading.BoundedSemaphore(*value=1*)

Class implementing bounded semaphore objects. A bounded semaphore checks to make sure its current value doesn't exceed its initial value. If it does, *ValueError* is raised. In most situations semaphores are used to guard resources with limited capacity. If the semaphore is released too many times it's a sign of a bug. If not given, *value* defaults to 1.

Changed in version 3.3: changed from a factory function to a class.

`Semaphore` Example

Semaphores are often used to guard resources with limited capacity, for example, a database server. In any situation where the size of the resource is fixed, you should use a bounded semaphore. Before spawning any worker threads, your main thread would initialize the semaphore:

```
maxconnections = 5
# ...
pool_sema = BoundedSemaphore(value=maxconnections)
```

Once spawned, worker threads call the semaphore's acquire and release methods when they need to connect to the server:

```
with pool_sema:
    conn = connectdb()
    try:
        # ... use connection ...
    finally:
        conn.close()
```

The use of a bounded semaphore reduces the chance that a programming error which causes the semaphore to be released more than it's acquired will go undetected.

17.1.7 Event Objects

This is one of the simplest mechanisms for communication between threads: one thread signals an event and other threads wait for it.

An event object manages an internal flag that can be set to true with the *set()* method and reset to false with the *clear()* method. The *wait()* method blocks until the flag is true.

class threading.Event

Class implementing event objects. An event manages a flag that can be set to true with the *set()* method and reset to false with the *clear()* method. The *wait()* method blocks until the flag is true. The flag is initially false.

Changed in version 3.3: changed from a factory function to a class.

is_set()

Return true if and only if the internal flag is true.

set()

Set the internal flag to true. All threads waiting for it to become true are awakened. Threads that call *wait()* once the flag is true will not block at all.

clear()

Reset the internal flag to false. Subsequently, threads calling *wait()* will block until *set()* is called to set the internal flag to true again.

wait(*timeout=None*)

Block until the internal flag is true. If the internal flag is true on entry, return immediately. Otherwise, block until another thread calls *set()* to set the flag to true, or until the optional timeout occurs.

When the timeout argument is present and not `None`, it should be a floating point number specifying a timeout for the operation in seconds (or fractions thereof).

This method returns true if and only if the internal flag has been set to true, either before the wait call or after the wait starts, so it will always return `True` except if a timeout is given and the operation times out.

Changed in version 3.1: Previously, the method always returned `None`.

17.1.8 Timer Objects

This class represents an action that should be run only after a certain amount of time has passed — a timer. *Timer* is a subclass of *Thread* and as such also functions as an example of creating custom threads.

Timers are started, as with threads, by calling their **start()** method. The timer can be stopped (before its action has begun) by calling the *cancel()* method. The interval the timer will wait before executing its action may not be exactly the same as the interval specified by the user.

For example:

```
def hello():
    print("hello, world")

t = Timer(30.0, hello)
t.start()  # after 30 seconds, "hello, world" will be printed
```

class threading.Timer(*interval, function, args=None, kwargs=None*)

Create a timer that will run *function* with arguments *args* and keyword arguments *kwargs*, after *interval* seconds have passed. If *args* is `None` (the default) then an empty list will be used. If *kwargs* is `None` (the default) then an empty dict will be used.

Changed in version 3.3: changed from a factory function to a class.

cancel()

Stop the timer, and cancel the execution of the timer's action. This will only work if the timer is still in its waiting stage.

17.1.9 Barrier Objects

New in version 3.2.

This class provides a simple synchronization primitive for use by a fixed number of threads that need to wait for each other. Each of the threads tries to pass the barrier by calling the *wait()* method and will block until all of the threads have made their *wait()* calls. At this point, the threads are released simultaneously.

The barrier can be reused any number of times for the same number of threads.

As an example, here is a simple way to synchronize a client and server thread:

```
b = Barrier(2, timeout=5)

def server():
    start_server()
    b.wait()
    while True:
        connection = accept_connection()
        process_server_connection(connection)

def client():
    b.wait()
    while True:
        connection = make_connection()
        process_client_connection(connection)
```

class threading.Barrier(*parties, action=None, timeout=None*)

Create a barrier object for *parties* number of threads. An *action*, when provided, is a callable to be called by one of the threads when they are released. *timeout* is the default timeout value if none is specified for the *wait()* method.

wait(*timeout=None*)

Pass the barrier. When all the threads party to the barrier have called this function, they are all released simultaneously. If a *timeout* is provided, it is used in preference to any that was supplied to the class constructor.

The return value is an integer in the range 0 to *parties* – 1, different for each thread. This can be used to select a thread to do some special housekeeping, e.g.:

```
i = barrier.wait()
if i == 0:
    # Only one thread needs to print this
    print("passed the barrier")
```

If an *action* was provided to the constructor, one of the threads will have called it prior to being released. Should this call raise an error, the barrier is put into the broken state.

If the call times out, the barrier is put into the broken state.

This method may raise a *BrokenBarrierError* exception if the barrier is broken or reset while a thread is waiting.

reset()

Return the barrier to the default, empty state. Any threads waiting on it will receive the *BrokenBarrierError* exception.

Note that using this function may can require some external synchronization if there are other threads whose state is unknown. If a barrier is broken it may be better to just leave it and create a new one.

abort()

Put the barrier into a broken state. This causes any active or future calls to *wait()* to fail with the *BrokenBarrierError*. Use this for example if one of the needs to abort, to avoid deadlocking the application.

It may be preferable to simply create the barrier with a sensible *timeout* value to automatically guard against one of the threads going awry.

parties

The number of threads required to pass the barrier.

n_waiting

The number of threads currently waiting in the barrier.

broken

A boolean that is `True` if the barrier is in the broken state.

exception threading.BrokenBarrierError

This exception, a subclass of *RuntimeError*, is raised when the *Barrier* object is reset or broken.

17.1.10 Using locks, conditions, and semaphores in the `with` statement

All of the objects provided by this module that have `acquire()` and `release()` methods can be used as context managers for a `with` statement. The `acquire()` method will be called when the block is entered, and `release()` will be called when the block is exited. Hence, the following snippet:

```
with some_lock:
    # do something...
```

is equivalent to:

```
some_lock.acquire()
try:
    # do something...
finally:
    some_lock.release()
```

Currently, *Lock*, *RLock*, *Condition*, *Semaphore*, and *BoundedSemaphore* objects may be used as `with` statement context managers.

17.2 multiprocessing — Process-based parallelism

Source code: Lib/multiprocessing/

17.2.1 Introduction

multiprocessing is a package that supports spawning processes using an API similar to the *threading* module. The *multiprocessing* package offers both local and remote concurrency, effectively side-stepping the *Global Interpreter Lock* by using subprocesses instead of threads. Due to this, the *multiprocessing* module allows the programmer to fully leverage multiple processors on a given machine. It runs on both Unix and Windows.

The *multiprocessing* module also introduces APIs which do not have analogs in the *threading* module. A prime example of this is the *Pool* object which offers a convenient means of parallelizing the execution of a function across multiple input values, distributing the input data across processes (data parallelism). The following example demonstrates the common practice of defining such functions in a module so that child processes can successfully import that module. This basic example of data parallelism using *Pool*,

```
from multiprocessing import Pool

def f(x):
    return x*x

if __name__ == '__main__':
    with Pool(5) as p:
        print(p.map(f, [1, 2, 3]))
```

will print to standard output

```
[1, 4, 9]
```

The Process class

In *multiprocessing*, processes are spawned by creating a *Process* object and then calling its *start()* method. *Process* follows the API of *threading.Thread*. A trivial example of a multiprocess program is

```
from multiprocessing import Process

def f(name):
    print('hello', name)

if __name__ == '__main__':
```

```
    p = Process(target=f, args=('bob',))
    p.start()
    p.join()
```

To show the individual process IDs involved, here is an expanded example:

```
from multiprocessing import Process
import os

def info(title):
    print(title)
    print('module name:', __name__)
    print('parent process:', os.getppid())
    print('process id:', os.getpid())

def f(name):
    info('function f')
    print('hello', name)

if __name__ == '__main__':
    info('main line')
    p = Process(target=f, args=('bob',))
    p.start()
    p.join()
```

For an explanation of why the `if __name__ == '__main__'` part is necessary, see *Programming guidelines*.

Contexts and start methods

Depending on the platform, *multiprocessing* supports three ways to start a process. These *start methods* are

spawn The parent process starts a fresh python interpreter process. The child process will only inherit those resources necessary to run the process objects *run()* method. In particular, unnecessary file descriptors and handles from the parent process will not be inherited. Starting a process using this method is rather slow compared to using *fork* or *forkserver*.

Available on Unix and Windows. The default on Windows.

fork The parent process uses *os.fork()* to fork the Python interpreter. The child process, when it begins, is effectively identical to the parent process. All resources of the parent are inherited by the child process. Note that safely forking a multithreaded process is problematic.

Available on Unix only. The default on Unix.

forkserver When the program starts and selects the *forkserver* start method, a server process is started. From then on, whenever a new process is needed, the parent process connects to the server and requests that it fork a new process. The fork server process is single threaded so it is safe for it to use *os.fork()*. No unnecessary resources are inherited.

Available on Unix platforms which support passing file descriptors over Unix pipes.

Changed in version 3.4: *spawn* added on all unix platforms, and *forkserver* added for some unix platforms. Child processes no longer inherit all of the parents inheritable handles on Windows.

On Unix using the *spawn* or *forkserver* start methods will also start a *semaphore tracker* process which tracks the unlinked named semaphores created by processes of the program. When all processes have exited the semaphore tracker unlinks any remaining semaphores. Usually there should be none, but if a process was killed by a signal there may some "leaked" semaphores. (Unlinking the named semaphores is a serious matter since the system allows only a limited number, and they will not be automatically unlinked until the next reboot.)

To select a start method you use the *set_start_method()* in the `if __name__ == '__main__'` clause of the main module. For example:

```
import multiprocessing as mp

def foo(q):
    q.put('hello')

if __name__ == '__main__':
    mp.set_start_method('spawn')
    q = mp.Queue()
    p = mp.Process(target=foo, args=(q,))
    p.start()
    print(q.get())
    p.join()
```

set_start_method() should not be used more than once in the program.

Alternatively, you can use *get_context()* to obtain a context object. Context objects have the same API as the multiprocessing module, and allow one to use multiple start methods in the same program.

```
import multiprocessing as mp

def foo(q):
    q.put('hello')

if __name__ == '__main__':
    ctx = mp.get_context('spawn')
    q = ctx.Queue()
    p = ctx.Process(target=foo, args=(q,))
    p.start()
    print(q.get())
    p.join()
```

Note that objects related to one context may not be compatible with processes for a different context. In particular, locks created using the *fork* context cannot be passed to a processes started using the *spawn* or *forkserver* start methods.

A library which wants to use a particular start method should probably use *get_context()* to avoid interfering with the choice of the library user.

Exchanging objects between processes

multiprocessing supports two types of communication channel between processes:

Queues

The *Queue* class is a near clone of *queue.Queue*. For example:

```
from multiprocessing import Process, Queue

def f(q):
    q.put([42, None, 'hello'])

if __name__ == '__main__':
    q = Queue()
    p = Process(target=f, args=(q,))
```

```
    p.start()
    print(q.get())    # prints "[42, None, 'hello']"
    p.join()
```

Queues are thread and process safe.

Pipes

The *Pipe()* function returns a pair of connection objects connected by a pipe which by default is duplex (two-way). For example:

```
from multiprocessing import Process, Pipe

def f(conn):
    conn.send([42, None, 'hello'])
    conn.close()

if __name__ == '__main__':
    parent_conn, child_conn = Pipe()
    p = Process(target=f, args=(child_conn,))
    p.start()
    print(parent_conn.recv())   # prints "[42, None, 'hello']"
    p.join()
```

The two connection objects returned by *Pipe()* represent the two ends of the pipe. Each connection object has *send()* and *recv()* methods (among others). Note that data in a pipe may become corrupted if two processes (or threads) try to read from or write to the *same* end of the pipe at the same time. Of course there is no risk of corruption from processes using different ends of the pipe at the same time.

Synchronization between processes

multiprocessing contains equivalents of all the synchronization primitives from *threading*. For instance one can use a lock to ensure that only one process prints to standard output at a time:

```
from multiprocessing import Process, Lock

def f(l, i):
    l.acquire()
    try:
        print('hello world', i)
    finally:
        l.release()

if __name__ == '__main__':
    lock = Lock()

    for num in range(10):
        Process(target=f, args=(lock, num)).start()
```

Without using the lock output from the different processes is liable to get all mixed up.

Sharing state between processes

As mentioned above, when doing concurrent programming it is usually best to avoid using shared state as far as possible. This is particularly true when using multiple processes.

However, if you really do need to use some shared data then *multiprocessing* provides a couple of ways of doing so.

Shared memory

Data can be stored in a shared memory map using *Value* or *Array*. For example, the following code

```
from multiprocessing import Process, Value, Array

def f(n, a):
    n.value = 3.1415927
    for i in range(len(a)):
        a[i] = -a[i]

if __name__ == '__main__':
    num = Value('d', 0.0)
    arr = Array('i', range(10))

    p = Process(target=f, args=(num, arr))
    p.start()
    p.join()

    print(num.value)
    print(arr[:])
```

will print

```
3.1415927
[0, -1, -2, -3, -4, -5, -6, -7, -8, -9]
```

The `'d'` and `'i'` arguments used when creating `num` and `arr` are typecodes of the kind used by the *array* module: `'d'` indicates a double precision float and `'i'` indicates a signed integer. These shared objects will be process and thread-safe.

For more flexibility in using shared memory one can use the *multiprocessing.sharedctypes* module which supports the creation of arbitrary ctypes objects allocated from shared memory.

Server process

A manager object returned by `Manager()` controls a server process which holds Python objects and allows other processes to manipulate them using proxies.

A manager returned by `Manager()` will support types *list*, *dict*, *Namespace*, *Lock*, *RLock*, *Semaphore*, *BoundedSemaphore*, *Condition*, *Event*, *Barrier*, *Queue*, *Value* and *Array*. For example,

```
from multiprocessing import Process, Manager

def f(d, l):
    d[1] = '1'
    d['2'] = 2
    d[0.25] = None
    l.reverse()

if __name__ == '__main__':
    with Manager() as manager:
        d = manager.dict()
        l = manager.list(range(10))

        p = Process(target=f, args=(d, l))
```

```
        p.start()
        p.join()

        print(d)
        print(l)
```

will print

```
{0.25: None, 1: '1', '2': 2}
[9, 8, 7, 6, 5, 4, 3, 2, 1, 0]
```

Server process managers are more flexible than using shared memory objects because they can be made to support arbitrary object types. Also, a single manager can be shared by processes on different computers over a network. They are, however, slower than using shared memory.

Using a pool of workers

The *Pool* class represents a pool of worker processes. It has methods which allows tasks to be offloaded to the worker processes in a few different ways.

For example:

```
from multiprocessing import Pool, TimeoutError
import time
import os

def f(x):
    return x*x

if __name__ == '__main__':
    # start 4 worker processes
    with Pool(processes=4) as pool:

        # print "[0, 1, 4,..., 81]"
        print(pool.map(f, range(10)))

        # print same numbers in arbitrary order
        for i in pool.imap_unordered(f, range(10)):
            print(i)

        # evaluate "f(20)" asynchronously
        res = pool.apply_async(f, (20,))      # runs in *only* one process
        print(res.get(timeout=1))             # prints "400"

        # evaluate "os.getpid()" asynchronously
        res = pool.apply_async(os.getpid, ()) # runs in *only* one process
        print(res.get(timeout=1))             # prints the PID of that process

        # launching multiple evaluations asynchronously *may* use more processes
        multiple_results = [pool.apply_async(os.getpid, ()) for i in range(4)]
        print([res.get(timeout=1) for res in multiple_results])

        # make a single worker sleep for 10 secs
        res = pool.apply_async(time.sleep, (10,))
        try:
            print(res.get(timeout=1))
        except TimeoutError:
```

```
        print("We lacked patience and got a multiprocessing.TimeoutError")

    print("For the moment, the pool remains available for more work")

# exiting the 'with'-block has stopped the pool
print("Now the pool is closed and no longer available")
```

Note that the methods of a pool should only ever be used by the process which created it.

Note: Functionality within this package requires that the `__main__` module be importable by the children. This is covered in *Programming guidelines* however it is worth pointing out here. This means that some examples, such as the *multiprocessing.pool.Pool* examples will not work in the interactive interpreter. For example:

```
>>> from multiprocessing import Pool
>>> p = Pool(5)
>>> def f(x):
...     return x*x
...
>>> p.map(f, [1,2,3])
Process PoolWorker-1:
Process PoolWorker-2:
Process PoolWorker-3:
Traceback (most recent call last):
AttributeError: 'module' object has no attribute 'f'
AttributeError: 'module' object has no attribute 'f'
AttributeError: 'module' object has no attribute 'f'
```

(If you try this it will actually output three full tracebacks interleaved in a semi-random fashion, and then you may have to stop the master process somehow.)

17.2.2 Reference

The *multiprocessing* package mostly replicates the API of the *threading* module.

Process and exceptions

class multiprocessing.Process(*group=None, target=None, name=None, args=(), kwargs={}, *, daemon=None*)

Process objects represent activity that is run in a separate process. The *Process* class has equivalents of all the methods of *threading.Thread*.

The constructor should always be called with keyword arguments. *group* should always be `None`; it exists solely for compatibility with *threading.Thread*. *target* is the callable object to be invoked by the *run()* method. It defaults to `None`, meaning nothing is called. *name* is the process name (see *name* for more details). *args* is the argument tuple for the target invocation. *kwargs* is a dictionary of keyword arguments for the target invocation. If provided, the keyword-only *daemon* argument sets the process *daemon* flag to `True` or `False`. If `None` (the default), this flag will be inherited from the creating process.

By default, no arguments are passed to *target*.

If a subclass overrides the constructor, it must make sure it invokes the base class constructor (`Process.__init__()`) before doing anything else to the process.

Changed in version 3.3: Added the *daemon* argument.

run()
Method representing the process's activity.

You may override this method in a subclass. The standard *run()* method invokes the callable object passed to the object's constructor as the target argument, if any, with sequential and keyword arguments taken from the *args* and *kwargs* arguments, respectively.

start()
Start the process's activity.

This must be called at most once per process object. It arranges for the object's *run()* method to be invoked in a separate process.

join([*timeout*]**)**
If the optional argument *timeout* is `None` (the default), the method blocks until the process whose *join()* method is called terminates. If *timeout* is a positive number, it blocks at most *timeout* seconds. Note that the method returns `None` if its process terminates or if the method times out. Check the process's *exitcode* to determine if it terminated.

A process can be joined many times.

A process cannot join itself because this would cause a deadlock. It is an error to attempt to join a process before it has been started.

name
The process's name. The name is a string used for identification purposes only. It has no semantics. Multiple processes may be given the same name.

The initial name is set by the constructor. If no explicit name is provided to the constructor, a name of the form 'Process-N_1:N_2:...:N_k' is constructed, where each N_k is the N-th child of its parent.

is_alive()
Return whether the process is alive.

Roughly, a process object is alive from the moment the *start()* method returns until the child process terminates.

daemon
The process's daemon flag, a Boolean value. This must be set before *start()* is called.

The initial value is inherited from the creating process.

When a process exits, it attempts to terminate all of its daemonic child processes.

Note that a daemonic process is not allowed to create child processes. Otherwise a daemonic process would leave its children orphaned if it gets terminated when its parent process exits. Additionally, these are **not** Unix daemons or services, they are normal processes that will be terminated (and not joined) if non-daemonic processes have exited.

In addition to the *threading.Thread* API, *Process* objects also support the following attributes and methods:

pid
Return the process ID. Before the process is spawned, this will be `None`.

exitcode
The child's exit code. This will be `None` if the process has not yet terminated. A negative value *-N* indicates that the child was terminated by signal *N*.

authkey
The process's authentication key (a byte string).

When *multiprocessing* is initialized the main process is assigned a random string using *os.urandom()*.

When a *Process* object is created, it will inherit the authentication key of its parent process, although this may be changed by setting *authkey* to another byte string.

See *Authentication keys*.

sentinel

A numeric handle of a system object which will become "ready" when the process ends.

You can use this value if you want to wait on several events at once using *multiprocessing.connection.wait()*. Otherwise calling *join()* is simpler.

On Windows, this is an OS handle usable with the `WaitForSingleObject` and `WaitForMultipleObjects` family of API calls. On Unix, this is a file descriptor usable with primitives from the *select* module.

New in version 3.3.

terminate()

Terminate the process. On Unix this is done using the `SIGTERM` signal; on Windows `TerminateProcess()` is used. Note that exit handlers and finally clauses, etc., will not be executed.

Note that descendant processes of the process will *not* be terminated – they will simply become orphaned.

> **Warning:** If this method is used when the associated process is using a pipe or queue then the pipe or queue is liable to become corrupted and may become unusable by other process. Similarly, if the process has acquired a lock or semaphore etc. then terminating it is liable to cause other processes to deadlock.

Note that the *start()*, *join()*, *is_alive()*, *terminate()* and *exitcode* methods should only be called by the process that created the process object.

Example usage of some of the methods of *Process*:

```
>>> import multiprocessing, time, signal
>>> p = multiprocessing.Process(target=time.sleep, args=(1000,))
>>> print(p, p.is_alive())
<Process(Process-1, initial)> False
>>> p.start()
>>> print(p, p.is_alive())
<Process(Process-1, started)> True
>>> p.terminate()
>>> time.sleep(0.1)
>>> print(p, p.is_alive())
<Process(Process-1, stopped[SIGTERM])> False
>>> p.exitcode == -signal.SIGTERM
True
```

exception multiprocessing.ProcessError

The base class of all *multiprocessing* exceptions.

exception multiprocessing.BufferTooShort

Exception raised by *Connection.recv_bytes_into()* when the supplied buffer object is too small for the message read.

If `e` is an instance of *BufferTooShort* then `e.args[0]` will give the message as a byte string.

exception multiprocessing.AuthenticationError
Raised when there is an authentication error.

exception multiprocessing.TimeoutError
Raised by methods with a timeout when the timeout expires.

Pipes and Queues

When using multiple processes, one generally uses message passing for communication between processes and avoids having to use any synchronization primitives like locks.

For passing messages one can use `Pipe()` (for a connection between two processes) or a queue (which allows multiple producers and consumers).

The `Queue`, `SimpleQueue` and `JoinableQueue` types are multi-producer, multi-consumer FIFO queues modelled on the `queue.Queue` class in the standard library. They differ in that `Queue` lacks the `task_done()` and `join()` methods introduced into Python 2.5's `queue.Queue` class.

If you use `JoinableQueue` then you **must** call `JoinableQueue.task_done()` for each task removed from the queue or else the semaphore used to count the number of unfinished tasks may eventually overflow, raising an exception.

Note that one can also create a shared queue by using a manager object – see *Managers*.

Note: `multiprocessing` uses the usual `queue.Empty` and `queue.Full` exceptions to signal a timeout. They are not available in the `multiprocessing` namespace so you need to import them from `queue`.

Note: When an object is put on a queue, the object is pickled and a background thread later flushes the pickled data to an underlying pipe. This has some consequences which are a little surprising, but should not cause any practical difficulties – if they really bother you then you can instead use a queue created with a *manager*.

1. After putting an object on an empty queue there may be an infinitesimal delay before the queue's `empty()` method returns `False` and `get_nowait()` can return without raising `queue.Empty`.
2. If multiple processes are enqueuing objects, it is possible for the objects to be received at the other end out-of-order. However, objects enqueued by the same process will always be in the expected order with respect to each other.

Warning: If a process is killed using `Process.terminate()` or `os.kill()` while it is trying to use a `Queue`, then the data in the queue is likely to become corrupted. This may cause any other process to get an exception when it tries to use the queue later on.

Warning: As mentioned above, if a child process has put items on a queue (and it has not used `JoinableQueue.cancel_join_thread`), then that process will not terminate until all buffered items have been flushed to the pipe.

This means that if you try joining that process you may get a deadlock unless you are sure that all items which have been put on the queue have been consumed. Similarly, if the child process is non-daemonic then the parent process may hang on exit when it tries to join all its non-daemonic children.

Note that a queue created using a manager does not have this issue. See *Programming guidelines*.

For an example of the usage of queues for interprocess communication see *Examples*.

`multiprocessing.Pipe([duplex])`
Returns a pair `(conn1, conn2)` of *Connection* objects representing the ends of a pipe.

If *duplex* is `True` (the default) then the pipe is bidirectional. If *duplex* is `False` then the pipe is unidirectional: `conn1` can only be used for receiving messages and `conn2` can only be used for sending messages.

class `multiprocessing.Queue([maxsize])`
Returns a process shared queue implemented using a pipe and a few locks/semaphores. When a process first puts an item on the queue a feeder thread is started which transfers objects from a buffer into the pipe.

The usual *queue.Empty* and *queue.Full* exceptions from the standard library's *queue* module are raised to signal timeouts.

Queue implements all the methods of *queue.Queue* except for *task_done()* and *join()*.

`qsize()`
Return the approximate size of the queue. Because of multithreading/multiprocessing semantics, this number is not reliable.

Note that this may raise *NotImplementedError* on Unix platforms like Mac OS X where `sem_getvalue()` is not implemented.

`empty()`
Return `True` if the queue is empty, `False` otherwise. Because of multithreading/multiprocessing semantics, this is not reliable.

`full()`
Return `True` if the queue is full, `False` otherwise. Because of multithreading/multiprocessing semantics, this is not reliable.

`put(obj[, block[, timeout]])`
Put obj into the queue. If the optional argument *block* is `True` (the default) and *timeout* is `None` (the default), block if necessary until a free slot is available. If *timeout* is a positive number, it blocks at most *timeout* seconds and raises the *queue.Full* exception if no free slot was available within that time. Otherwise (*block* is `False`), put an item on the queue if a free slot is immediately available, else raise the *queue.Full* exception (*timeout* is ignored in that case).

`put_nowait(obj)`
Equivalent to `put(obj, False)`.

`get([block[, timeout]])`
Remove and return an item from the queue. If optional args *block* is `True` (the default) and *timeout* is `None` (the default), block if necessary until an item is available. If *timeout* is a positive number, it blocks at most *timeout* seconds and raises the *queue.Empty* exception if no item was available within that time. Otherwise (block is `False`), return an item if one is immediately available, else raise the *queue.Empty* exception (*timeout* is ignored in that case).

`get_nowait()`
Equivalent to `get(False)`.

multiprocessing.Queue has a few additional methods not found in *queue.Queue*. These methods are usually unnecessary for most code:

`close()`
Indicate that no more data will be put on this queue by the current process. The background thread will quit once it has flushed all buffered data to the pipe. This is called automatically when the queue is garbage collected.

join_thread()
Join the background thread. This can only be used after *close()* has been called. It blocks until the background thread exits, ensuring that all data in the buffer has been flushed to the pipe.

By default if a process is not the creator of the queue then on exit it will attempt to join the queue's background thread. The process can call *cancel_join_thread()* to make *join_thread()* do nothing.

cancel_join_thread()
Prevent *join_thread()* from blocking. In particular, this prevents the background thread from being joined automatically when the process exits – see *join_thread()*.

A better name for this method might be `allow_exit_without_flush()`. It is likely to cause enqueued data to lost, and you almost certainly will not need to use it. It is really only there if you need the current process to exit immediately without waiting to flush enqueued data to the underlying pipe, and you don't care about lost data.

Note: This class's functionality requires a functioning shared semaphore implementation on the host operating system. Without one, the functionality in this class will be disabled, and attempts to instantiate a *Queue* will result in an *ImportError*. See bpo-3770 for additional information. The same holds true for any of the specialized queue types listed below.

---

class multiprocessing.SimpleQueue
It is a simplified *Queue* type, very close to a locked *Pipe*.

empty()
Return `True` if the queue is empty, `False` otherwise.

get()
Remove and return an item from the queue.

put(*item*)
Put *item* into the queue.

class multiprocessing.JoinableQueue([*maxsize*])
JoinableQueue, a *Queue* subclass, is a queue which additionally has *task_done()* and *join()* methods.

task_done()
Indicate that a formerly enqueued task is complete. Used by queue consumers. For each *get()* used to fetch a task, a subsequent call to *task_done()* tells the queue that the processing on the task is complete.

If a *join()* is currently blocking, it will resume when all items have been processed (meaning that a *task_done()* call was received for every item that had been *put()* into the queue).

Raises a *ValueError* if called more times than there were items placed in the queue.

join()
Block until all items in the queue have been gotten and processed.

The count of unfinished tasks goes up whenever an item is added to the queue. The count goes down whenever a consumer calls *task_done()* to indicate that the item was retrieved and all work on it is complete. When the count of unfinished tasks drops to zero, *join()* unblocks.

Miscellaneous

multiprocessing.active_children()
Return list of all live children of the current process.

Calling this has the side effect of "joining" any processes which have already finished.

`multiprocessing.cpu_count()`
Return the number of CPUs in the system.

This number is not equivalent to the number of CPUs the current process can use. The number of usable CPUs can be obtained with `len(os.sched_getaffinity(0))`

May raise *NotImplementedError*.

See also:

os.cpu_count()

`multiprocessing.current_process()`
Return the *Process* object corresponding to the current process.

An analogue of *threading.current_thread()*.

`multiprocessing.freeze_support()`
Add support for when a program which uses *multiprocessing* has been frozen to produce a Windows executable. (Has been tested with **py2exe**, **PyInstaller** and **cx_Freeze**.)

One needs to call this function straight after the `if __name__ == '__main__'` line of the main module. For example:

```
from multiprocessing import Process, freeze_support

def f():
    print('hello world!')

if __name__ == '__main__':
    freeze_support()
    Process(target=f).start()
```

If the `freeze_support()` line is omitted then trying to run the frozen executable will raise *RuntimeError*.

Calling `freeze_support()` has no effect when invoked on any operating system other than Windows. In addition, if the module is being run normally by the Python interpreter on Windows (the program has not been frozen), then `freeze_support()` has no effect.

`multiprocessing.get_all_start_methods()`
Returns a list of the supported start methods, the first of which is the default. The possible start methods are `'fork'`, `'spawn'` and `'forkserver'`. On Windows only `'spawn'` is available. On Unix `'fork'` and `'spawn'` are always supported, with `'fork'` being the default.

New in version 3.4.

`multiprocessing.get_context(`*method=None*`)`
Return a context object which has the same attributes as the *multiprocessing* module.

If *method* is `None` then the default context is returned. Otherwise *method* should be `'fork'`, `'spawn'`, `'forkserver'`. *ValueError* is raised if the specified start method is not available.

New in version 3.4.

`multiprocessing.get_start_method(`*allow_none=False*`)`
Return the name of start method used for starting processes.

If the start method has not been fixed and *allow_none* is false, then the start method is fixed to the default and the name is returned. If the start method has not been fixed and *allow_none* is true then `None` is returned.

The return value can be `'fork'`, `'spawn'`, `'forkserver'` or `None`. `'fork'` is the default on Unix, while `'spawn'` is the default on Windows.

New in version 3.4.

multiprocessing.set_executable()
Sets the path of the Python interpreter to use when starting a child process. (By default *sys.executable* is used). Embedders will probably need to do some thing like

```
set_executable(os.path.join(sys.exec_prefix, 'pythonw.exe'))
```

before they can create child processes.

Changed in version 3.4: Now supported on Unix when the `'spawn'` start method is used.

multiprocessing.set_start_method(*method*)
Set the method which should be used to start child processes. *method* can be `'fork'`, `'spawn'` or `'forkserver'`.

Note that this should be called at most once, and it should be protected inside the `if __name__ == '__main__'` clause of the main module.

New in version 3.4.

Note: *multiprocessing* contains no analogues of *threading.active_count()*, *threading.enumerate()*, *threading.settrace()*, *threading.setprofile()*, *threading.Timer*, or *threading.local*.

Connection Objects

Connection objects allow the sending and receiving of picklable objects or strings. They can be thought of as message oriented connected sockets.

Connection objects are usually created using *Pipe()* – see also *Listeners and Clients*.

class multiprocessing.Connection

send(*obj*)
Send an object to the other end of the connection which should be read using *recv()*.

The object must be picklable. Very large pickles (approximately 32 MB+, though it depends on the OS) may raise a *ValueError* exception.

recv()
Return an object sent from the other end of the connection using *send()*. Blocks until there is something to receive. Raises *EOFError* if there is nothing left to receive and the other end was closed.

fileno()
Return the file descriptor or handle used by the connection.

close()
Close the connection.

This is called automatically when the connection is garbage collected.

poll([*timeout*])
Return whether there is any data available to be read.

If *timeout* is not specified then it will return immediately. If *timeout* is a number then this specifies the maximum time in seconds to block. If *timeout* is `None` then an infinite timeout is used.

Note that multiple connection objects may be polled at once by using *multiprocessing.connection.wait()*.

send_bytes(*buffer*[, *offset*[, *size*]])
Send byte data from a *bytes-like object* as a complete message.

If *offset* is given then data is read from that position in *buffer*. If *size* is given then that many bytes will be read from buffer. Very large buffers (approximately 32 MB+, though it depends on the OS) may raise a *ValueError* exception

recv_bytes([*maxlength*])
Return a complete message of byte data sent from the other end of the connection as a string. Blocks until there is something to receive. Raises *EOFError* if there is nothing left to receive and the other end has closed.

If *maxlength* is specified and the message is longer than *maxlength* then *OSError* is raised and the connection will no longer be readable.

Changed in version 3.3: This function used to raise *IOError*, which is now an alias of *OSError*.

recv_bytes_into(*buffer*[, *offset*])
Read into *buffer* a complete message of byte data sent from the other end of the connection and return the number of bytes in the message. Blocks until there is something to receive. Raises *EOFError* if there is nothing left to receive and the other end was closed.

buffer must be a writable *bytes-like object*. If *offset* is given then the message will be written into the buffer from that position. Offset must be a non-negative integer less than the length of *buffer* (in bytes).

If the buffer is too short then a *BufferTooShort* exception is raised and the complete message is available as `e.args[0]` where `e` is the exception instance.

Changed in version 3.3: Connection objects themselves can now be transferred between processes using *Connection.send()* and *Connection.recv()*.

New in version 3.3: Connection objects now support the context management protocol – see *Context Manager Types*. *__enter__()* returns the connection object, and *__exit__()* calls *close()*.

For example:

```
>>> from multiprocessing import Pipe
>>> a, b = Pipe()
>>> a.send([1, 'hello', None])
>>> b.recv()
[1, 'hello', None]
>>> b.send_bytes(b'thank you')
>>> a.recv_bytes()
b'thank you'
>>> import array
>>> arr1 = array.array('i', range(5))
>>> arr2 = array.array('i', [0] * 10)
>>> a.send_bytes(arr1)
>>> count = b.recv_bytes_into(arr2)
>>> assert count == len(arr1) * arr1.itemsize
>>> arr2
array('i', [0, 1, 2, 3, 4, 0, 0, 0, 0, 0])
```

> **Warning:** The *Connection.recv()* method automatically unpickles the data it receives, which can be a security risk unless you can trust the process which sent the message.

Therefore, unless the connection object was produced using *Pipe()* you should only use the *recv()* and *send()* methods after performing some sort of authentication. See *Authentication keys*.

Warning: If a process is killed while it is trying to read or write to a pipe then the data in the pipe is likely to become corrupted, because it may become impossible to be sure where the message boundaries lie.

Synchronization primitives

Generally synchronization primitives are not as necessary in a multiprocess program as they are in a multithreaded program. See the documentation for *threading* module.

Note that one can also create synchronization primitives by using a manager object – see *Managers*.

class multiprocessing.Barrier(*parties*[, *action*[, *timeout*]])
A barrier object: a clone of *threading.Barrier*.

New in version 3.3.

class multiprocessing.BoundedSemaphore([*value*])
A bounded semaphore object: a close analog of *threading.BoundedSemaphore*.

A solitary difference from its close analog exists: its `acquire` method's first argument is named *block*, as is consistent with *Lock.acquire()*.

Note: On Mac OS X, this is indistinguishable from *Semaphore* because `sem_getvalue()` is not implemented on that platform.

class multiprocessing.Condition([*lock*])
A condition variable: an alias for *threading.Condition*.

If *lock* is specified then it should be a *Lock* or *RLock* object from *multiprocessing*.

Changed in version 3.3: The *wait_for()* method was added.

class multiprocessing.Event
A clone of *threading.Event*.

class multiprocessing.Lock
A non-recursive lock object: a close analog of *threading.Lock*. Once a process or thread has acquired a lock, subsequent attempts to acquire it from any process or thread will block until it is released; any process or thread may release it. The concepts and behaviors of *threading.Lock* as it applies to threads are replicated here in *multiprocessing.Lock* as it applies to either processes or threads, except as noted.

Note that *Lock* is actually a factory function which returns an instance of `multiprocessing.synchronize.Lock` initialized with a default context.

Lock supports the *context manager* protocol and thus may be used in `with` statements.

acquire(*block=True*, *timeout=None*)
Acquire a lock, blocking or non-blocking.

With the *block* argument set to `True` (the default), the method call will block until the lock is in an unlocked state, then set it to locked and return `True`. Note that the name of this first argument differs from that in *threading.Lock.acquire()*.

With the *block* argument set to `False`, the method call does not block. If the lock is currently in a locked state, return `False`; otherwise set the lock to a locked state and return `True`.

When invoked with a positive, floating-point value for *timeout*, block for at most the number of seconds specified by *timeout* as long as the lock can not be acquired. Invocations with a negative value for *timeout* are equivalent to a *timeout* of zero. Invocations with a *timeout* value of `None` (the default) set the timeout period to infinite. Note that the treatment of negative or `None` values for *timeout* differs from the implemented behavior in `threading.Lock.acquire()`. The *timeout* argument has no practical implications if the *block* argument is set to `False` and is thus ignored. Returns `True` if the lock has been acquired or `False` if the timeout period has elapsed.

release()

Release a lock. This can be called from any process or thread, not only the process or thread which originally acquired the lock.

Behavior is the same as in `threading.Lock.release()` except that when invoked on an unlocked lock, a `ValueError` is raised.

class multiprocessing.RLock

A recursive lock object: a close analog of `threading.RLock`. A recursive lock must be released by the process or thread that acquired it. Once a process or thread has acquired a recursive lock, the same process or thread may acquire it again without blocking; that process or thread must release it once for each time it has been acquired.

Note that `RLock` is actually a factory function which returns an instance of `multiprocessing.synchronize.RLock` initialized with a default context.

`RLock` supports the *context manager* protocol and thus may be used in `with` statements.

acquire(*block=True*, *timeout=None*)

Acquire a lock, blocking or non-blocking.

When invoked with the *block* argument set to `True`, block until the lock is in an unlocked state (not owned by any process or thread) unless the lock is already owned by the current process or thread. The current process or thread then takes ownership of the lock (if it does not already have ownership) and the recursion level inside the lock increments by one, resulting in a return value of `True`. Note that there are several differences in this first argument's behavior compared to the implementation of `threading.RLock.acquire()`, starting with the name of the argument itself.

When invoked with the *block* argument set to `False`, do not block. If the lock has already been acquired (and thus is owned) by another process or thread, the current process or thread does not take ownership and the recursion level within the lock is not changed, resulting in a return value of `False`. If the lock is in an unlocked state, the current process or thread takes ownership and the recursion level is incremented, resulting in a return value of `True`.

Use and behaviors of the *timeout* argument are the same as in `Lock.acquire()`. Note that some of these behaviors of *timeout* differ from the implemented behaviors in `threading.RLock.acquire()`.

release()

Release a lock, decrementing the recursion level. If after the decrement the recursion level is zero, reset the lock to unlocked (not owned by any process or thread) and if any other processes or threads are blocked waiting for the lock to become unlocked, allow exactly one of them to proceed. If after the decrement the recursion level is still nonzero, the lock remains locked and owned by the calling process or thread.

Only call this method when the calling process or thread owns the lock. An `AssertionError` is raised if this method is called by a process or thread other than the owner or if the lock is in an unlocked (unowned) state. Note that the type of exception raised in this situation differs from the implemented behavior in `threading.RLock.release()`.

class multiprocessing.**Semaphore**([*value*])
A semaphore object: a close analog of *threading.Semaphore*.

A solitary difference from its close analog exists: its **acquire** method's first argument is named *block*, as is consistent with *Lock.acquire()*.

Note: On Mac OS X, `sem_timedwait` is unsupported, so calling `acquire()` with a timeout will emulate that function's behavior using a sleeping loop.

Note: If the SIGINT signal generated by `Ctrl-C` arrives while the main thread is blocked by a call to `BoundedSemaphore.acquire()`, *Lock.acquire()*, *RLock.acquire()*, `Semaphore.acquire()`, `Condition.acquire()` or `Condition.wait()` then the call will be immediately interrupted and *KeyboardInterrupt* will be raised.

This differs from the behaviour of *threading* where SIGINT will be ignored while the equivalent blocking calls are in progress.

Note: Some of this package's functionality requires a functioning shared semaphore implementation on the host operating system. Without one, the `multiprocessing.synchronize` module will be disabled, and attempts to import it will result in an *ImportError*. See bpo-3770 for additional information.

Shared ctypes Objects

It is possible to create shared objects using shared memory which can be inherited by child processes.

multiprocessing.**Value**(*typecode_or_type*, **args*, *lock=True*)
Return a *ctypes* object allocated from shared memory. By default the return value is actually a synchronized wrapper for the object. The object itself can be accessed via the *value* attribute of a *Value*.

typecode_or_type determines the type of the returned object: it is either a ctypes type or a one character typecode of the kind used by the *array* module. **args* is passed on to the constructor for the type.

If *lock* is `True` (the default) then a new recursive lock object is created to synchronize access to the value. If *lock* is a *Lock* or *RLock* object then that will be used to synchronize access to the value. If *lock* is `False` then access to the returned object will not be automatically protected by a lock, so it will not necessarily be "process-safe".

Operations like `+=` which involve a read and write are not atomic. So if, for instance, you want to atomically increment a shared value it is insufficient to just do

```
counter.value += 1
```

Assuming the associated lock is recursive (which it is by default) you can instead do

```
with counter.get_lock():
    counter.value += 1
```

Note that *lock* is a keyword-only argument.

multiprocessing.**Array**(*typecode_or_type*, *size_or_initializer*, ***, *lock=True*)
Return a ctypes array allocated from shared memory. By default the return value is actually a synchronized wrapper for the array.

typecode_or_type determines the type of the elements of the returned array: it is either a ctypes type or a one character typecode of the kind used by the `array` module. If *size_or_initializer* is an integer, then it determines the length of the array, and the array will be initially zeroed. Otherwise, *size_or_initializer* is a sequence which is used to initialize the array and whose length determines the length of the array.

If *lock* is `True` (the default) then a new lock object is created to synchronize access to the value. If *lock* is a `Lock` or `RLock` object then that will be used to synchronize access to the value. If *lock* is `False` then access to the returned object will not be automatically protected by a lock, so it will not necessarily be "process-safe".

Note that *lock* is a keyword only argument.

Note that an array of `ctypes.c_char` has *value* and *raw* attributes which allow one to use it to store and retrieve strings.

The `multiprocessing.sharedctypes` module

The `multiprocessing.sharedctypes` module provides functions for allocating `ctypes` objects from shared memory which can be inherited by child processes.

Note: Although it is possible to store a pointer in shared memory remember that this will refer to a location in the address space of a specific process. However, the pointer is quite likely to be invalid in the context of a second process and trying to dereference the pointer from the second process may cause a crash.

`multiprocessing.sharedctypes.`**`RawArray`**`(`*typecode_or_type, size_or_initializer*`)`

Return a ctypes array allocated from shared memory.

typecode_or_type determines the type of the elements of the returned array: it is either a ctypes type or a one character typecode of the kind used by the `array` module. If *size_or_initializer* is an integer then it determines the length of the array, and the array will be initially zeroed. Otherwise *size_or_initializer* is a sequence which is used to initialize the array and whose length determines the length of the array.

Note that setting and getting an element is potentially non-atomic – use `Array()` instead to make sure that access is automatically synchronized using a lock.

`multiprocessing.sharedctypes.`**`RawValue`**`(`*typecode_or_type, *args*`)`

Return a ctypes object allocated from shared memory.

typecode_or_type determines the type of the returned object: it is either a ctypes type or a one character typecode of the kind used by the `array` module. **args* is passed on to the constructor for the type.

Note that setting and getting the value is potentially non-atomic – use `Value()` instead to make sure that access is automatically synchronized using a lock.

Note that an array of `ctypes.c_char` has `value` and `raw` attributes which allow one to use it to store and retrieve strings – see documentation for `ctypes`.

`multiprocessing.sharedctypes.`**`Array`**`(`*typecode_or_type, size_or_initializer, *, lock=True*`)`

The same as `RawArray()` except that depending on the value of *lock* a process-safe synchronization wrapper may be returned instead of a raw ctypes array.

If *lock* is `True` (the default) then a new lock object is created to synchronize access to the value. If *lock* is a `Lock` or `RLock` object then that will be used to synchronize access to the value. If *lock* is `False` then access to the returned object will not be automatically protected by a lock, so it will not necessarily be "process-safe".

Note that *lock* is a keyword-only argument.

`multiprocessing.sharedctypes.Value(typecode_or_type, *args, lock=True)`

The same as `RawValue()` except that depending on the value of *lock* a process-safe synchronization wrapper may be returned instead of a raw ctypes object.

If *lock* is `True` (the default) then a new lock object is created to synchronize access to the value. If *lock* is a `Lock` or `RLock` object then that will be used to synchronize access to the value. If *lock* is `False` then access to the returned object will not be automatically protected by a lock, so it will not necessarily be "process-safe".

Note that *lock* is a keyword-only argument.

`multiprocessing.sharedctypes.copy(obj)`

Return a ctypes object allocated from shared memory which is a copy of the ctypes object *obj*.

`multiprocessing.sharedctypes.synchronized(obj[, lock])`

Return a process-safe wrapper object for a ctypes object which uses *lock* to synchronize access. If *lock* is `None` (the default) then a `multiprocessing.RLock` object is created automatically.

A synchronized wrapper will have two methods in addition to those of the object it wraps: `get_obj()` returns the wrapped object and `get_lock()` returns the lock object used for synchronization.

Note that accessing the ctypes object through the wrapper can be a lot slower than accessing the raw ctypes object.

Changed in version 3.5: Synchronized objects support the *context manager* protocol.

The table below compares the syntax for creating shared ctypes objects from shared memory with the normal ctypes syntax. (In the table `MyStruct` is some subclass of `ctypes.Structure`.)

ctypes	sharedctypes using type	sharedctypes using typecode
c_double(2.4)	RawValue(c_double, 2.4)	RawValue('d', 2.4)
MyStruct(4, 6)	RawValue(MyStruct, 4, 6)	
(c_short * 7)()	RawArray(c_short, 7)	RawArray('h', 7)
(c_int * 3)(9, 2, 8)	RawArray(c_int, (9, 2, 8))	RawArray('i', (9, 2, 8))

Below is an example where a number of ctypes objects are modified by a child process:

```
from multiprocessing import Process, Lock
from multiprocessing.sharedctypes import Value, Array
from ctypes import Structure, c_double

class Point(Structure):
    _fields_ = [('x', c_double), ('y', c_double)]

def modify(n, x, s, A):
    n.value **= 2
    x.value **= 2
    s.value = s.value.upper()
    for a in A:
        a.x **= 2
        a.y **= 2

if __name__ == '__main__':
    lock = Lock()

    n = Value('i', 7)
    x = Value(c_double, 1.0/3.0, lock=False)
    s = Array('c', b'hello world', lock=lock)
```

```
    A = Array(Point, [(1.875,-6.25), (-5.75,2.0), (2.375,9.5)], lock=lock)

    p = Process(target=modify, args=(n, x, s, A))
    p.start()
    p.join()

    print(n.value)
    print(x.value)
    print(s.value)
    print([(a.x, a.y) for a in A])
```

The results printed are

```
49
0.1111111111111111
HELLO WORLD
[(3.515625, 39.0625), (33.0625, 4.0), (5.640625, 90.25)]
```

Managers

Managers provide a way to create data which can be shared between different processes, including sharing over a network between processes running on different machines. A manager object controls a server process which manages *shared objects*. Other processes can access the shared objects by using proxies.

`multiprocessing.Manager()`
: Returns a started *SyncManager* object which can be used for sharing objects between processes. The returned manager object corresponds to a spawned child process and has methods which will create shared objects and return corresponding proxies.

Manager processes will be shutdown as soon as they are garbage collected or their parent process exits. The manager classes are defined in the *multiprocessing.managers* module:

class `multiprocessing.managers.BaseManager([address[, authkey]])`
: Create a BaseManager object.

Once created one should call *start()* or `get_server().serve_forever()` to ensure that the manager object refers to a started manager process.

address is the address on which the manager process listens for new connections. If *address* is `None` then an arbitrary one is chosen.

authkey is the authentication key which will be used to check the validity of incoming connections to the server process. If *authkey* is `None` then `current_process().authkey` is used. Otherwise *authkey* is used and it must be a byte string.

`start([initializer[, initargs]])`
: Start a subprocess to start the manager. If *initializer* is not `None` then the subprocess will call `initializer(*initargs)` when it starts.

`get_server()`
: Returns a `Server` object which represents the actual server under the control of the Manager. The `Server` object supports the `serve_forever()` method:

```
>>> from multiprocessing.managers import BaseManager
>>> manager = BaseManager(address=('', 50000), authkey=b'abc')
>>> server = manager.get_server()
>>> server.serve_forever()
```

`Server` additionally has an *address* attribute.

connect()

Connect a local manager object to a remote manager process:

```
>>> from multiprocessing.managers import BaseManager
>>> m = BaseManager(address=('127.0.0.1', 5000), authkey=b'abc')
>>> m.connect()
```

shutdown()

Stop the process used by the manager. This is only available if *start()* has been used to start the server process.

This can be called multiple times.

register(*typeid*[, *callable*[, *proxytype*[, *exposed*[, *method_to_typeid*[, *create_method*]]]]])

A classmethod which can be used for registering a type or callable with the manager class.

typeid is a "type identifier" which is used to identify a particular type of shared object. This must be a string.

callable is a callable used for creating objects for this type identifier. If a manager instance will be connected to the server using the *connect()* method, or if the *create_method* argument is `False` then this can be left as `None`.

proxytype is a subclass of *BaseProxy* which is used to create proxies for shared objects with this *typeid*. If `None` then a proxy class is created automatically.

exposed is used to specify a sequence of method names which proxies for this typeid should be allowed to access using *BaseProxy._callmethod()*. (If *exposed* is `None` then `proxytype._exposed_` is used instead if it exists.) In the case where no exposed list is specified, all "public methods" of the shared object will be accessible. (Here a "public method" means any attribute which has a `__call__()` method and whose name does not begin with `'_'`.)

method_to_typeid is a mapping used to specify the return type of those exposed methods which should return a proxy. It maps method names to typeid strings. (If *method_to_typeid* is `None` then `proxytype._method_to_typeid_` is used instead if it exists.) If a method's name is not a key of this mapping or if the mapping is `None` then the object returned by the method will be copied by value.

create_method determines whether a method should be created with name *typeid* which can be used to tell the server process to create a new shared object and return a proxy for it. By default it is `True`.

BaseManager instances also have one read-only property:

address

The address used by the manager.

Changed in version 3.3: Manager objects support the context management protocol – see *Context Manager Types*. *__enter__()* starts the server process (if it has not already started) and then returns the manager object. *__exit__()* calls *shutdown()*.

In previous versions *__enter__()* did not start the manager's server process if it was not already started.

class multiprocessing.managers.SyncManager

A subclass of *BaseManager* which can be used for the synchronization of processes. Objects of this type are returned by `multiprocessing.Manager()`.

Its methods create and return *Proxy Objects* for a number of commonly used data types to be synchronized across processes. This notably includes shared lists and dictionaries.

Barrier(*parties*[, *action*[, *timeout*]])

Create a shared *threading.Barrier* object and return a proxy for it.

New in version 3.3.

BoundedSemaphore([*value*])
Create a shared *threading.BoundedSemaphore* object and return a proxy for it.

Condition([*lock*])
Create a shared *threading.Condition* object and return a proxy for it.

If *lock* is supplied then it should be a proxy for a *threading.Lock* or *threading.RLock* object.

Changed in version 3.3: The *wait_for()* method was added.

Event()
Create a shared *threading.Event* object and return a proxy for it.

Lock()
Create a shared *threading.Lock* object and return a proxy for it.

Namespace()
Create a shared *Namespace* object and return a proxy for it.

Queue([*maxsize*])
Create a shared *queue.Queue* object and return a proxy for it.

RLock()
Create a shared *threading.RLock* object and return a proxy for it.

Semaphore([*value*])
Create a shared *threading.Semaphore* object and return a proxy for it.

Array(*typecode*, *sequence*)
Create an array and return a proxy for it.

Value(*typecode*, *value*)
Create an object with a writable `value` attribute and return a proxy for it.

dict()
dict(*mapping*)
dict(*sequence*)
Create a shared *dict* object and return a proxy for it.

list()
list(*sequence*)
Create a shared *list* object and return a proxy for it.

Changed in version 3.6: Shared objects are capable of being nested. For example, a shared container object such as a shared list can contain other shared objects which will all be managed and synchronized by the *SyncManager*.

class multiprocessing.managers.Namespace
A type that can register with *SyncManager*.

A namespace object has no public methods, but does have writable attributes. Its representation shows the values of its attributes.

However, when using a proxy for a namespace object, an attribute beginning with `'_'` will be an attribute of the proxy and not an attribute of the referent:

```
>>> manager = multiprocessing.Manager()
>>> Global = manager.Namespace()
>>> Global.x = 10
>>> Global.y = 'hello'
>>> Global._z = 12.3    # this is an attribute of the proxy
```

```
>>> print(Global)
Namespace(x=10, y='hello')
```

Customized managers

To create one's own manager, one creates a subclass of *BaseManager* and uses the *register()* classmethod to register new types or callables with the manager class. For example:

```
from multiprocessing.managers import BaseManager

class MathsClass:
    def add(self, x, y):
        return x + y
    def mul(self, x, y):
        return x * y

class MyManager(BaseManager):
    pass

MyManager.register('Maths', MathsClass)

if __name__ == '__main__':
    with MyManager() as manager:
        maths = manager.Maths()
        print(maths.add(4, 3))         # prints 7
        print(maths.mul(7, 8))         # prints 56
```

Using a remote manager

It is possible to run a manager server on one machine and have clients use it from other machines (assuming that the firewalls involved allow it).

Running the following commands creates a server for a single shared queue which remote clients can access:

```
>>> from multiprocessing.managers import BaseManager
>>> from queue import Queue
>>> queue = Queue()
>>> class QueueManager(BaseManager): pass
>>> QueueManager.register('get_queue', callable=lambda:queue)
>>> m = QueueManager(address=('', 50000), authkey=b'abracadabra')
>>> s = m.get_server()
>>> s.serve_forever()
```

One client can access the server as follows:

```
>>> from multiprocessing.managers import BaseManager
>>> class QueueManager(BaseManager): pass
>>> QueueManager.register('get_queue')
>>> m = QueueManager(address=('foo.bar.org', 50000), authkey=b'abracadabra')
>>> m.connect()
>>> queue = m.get_queue()
>>> queue.put('hello')
```

Another client can also use it:

```
>>> from multiprocessing.managers import BaseManager
>>> class QueueManager(BaseManager): pass
>>> QueueManager.register('get_queue')
>>> m = QueueManager(address=('foo.bar.org', 50000), authkey=b'abracadabra')
>>> m.connect()
>>> queue = m.get_queue()
>>> queue.get()
'hello'
```

Local processes can also access that queue, using the code from above on the client to access it remotely:

```
>>> from multiprocessing import Process, Queue
>>> from multiprocessing.managers import BaseManager
>>> class Worker(Process):
...     def __init__(self, q):
...         self.q = q
...         super(Worker, self).__init__()
...     def run(self):
...         self.q.put('local hello')
...
>>> queue = Queue()
>>> w = Worker(queue)
>>> w.start()
>>> class QueueManager(BaseManager): pass
...
>>> QueueManager.register('get_queue', callable=lambda: queue)
>>> m = QueueManager(address=('', 50000), authkey=b'abracadabra')
>>> s = m.get_server()
>>> s.serve_forever()
```

Proxy Objects

A proxy is an object which *refers* to a shared object which lives (presumably) in a different process. The shared object is said to be the *referent* of the proxy. Multiple proxy objects may have the same referent.

A proxy object has methods which invoke corresponding methods of its referent (although not every method of the referent will necessarily be available through the proxy). In this way, a proxy can be used just like its referent can:

```
>>> from multiprocessing import Manager
>>> manager = Manager()
>>> l = manager.list([i*i for i in range(10)])
>>> print(l)
[0, 1, 4, 9, 16, 25, 36, 49, 64, 81]
>>> print(repr(l))
<ListProxy object, typeid 'list' at 0x...>
>>> l[4]
16
>>> l[2:5]
[4, 9, 16]
```

Notice that applying *str()* to a proxy will return the representation of the referent, whereas applying *repr()* will return the representation of the proxy.

An important feature of proxy objects is that they are picklable so they can be passed between processes. As such, a referent can contain *Proxy Objects*. This permits nesting of these managed lists, dicts, and other *Proxy Objects*:

```
>>> a = manager.list()
>>> b = manager.list()
>>> a.append(b)         # referent of a now contains referent of b
>>> print(a, b)
[<ListProxy object, typeid 'list' at ...>] []
>>> b.append('hello')
>>> print(a[0], b)
['hello'] ['hello']
```

Similarly, dict and list proxies may be nested inside one another:

```
>>> l_outer = manager.list([ manager.dict() for i in range(2) ])
>>> d_first_inner = l_outer[0]
>>> d_first_inner['a'] = 1
>>> d_first_inner['b'] = 2
>>> l_outer[1]['c'] = 3
>>> l_outer[1]['z'] = 26
>>> print(l_outer[0])
{'a': 1, 'b': 2}
>>> print(l_outer[1])
{'c': 3, 'z': 26}
```

If standard (non-proxy) *list* or *dict* objects are contained in a referent, modifications to those mutable values will not be propagated through the manager because the proxy has no way of knowing when the values contained within are modified. However, storing a value in a container proxy (which triggers a `__setitem__` on the proxy object) does propagate through the manager and so to effectively modify such an item, one could re-assign the modified value to the container proxy:

```
# create a list proxy and append a mutable object (a dictionary)
lproxy = manager.list()
lproxy.append({})
# now mutate the dictionary
d = lproxy[0]
d['a'] = 1
d['b'] = 2
# at this point, the changes to d are not yet synced, but by
# updating the dictionary, the proxy is notified of the change
lproxy[0] = d
```

This approach is perhaps less convenient than employing nested *Proxy Objects* for most use cases but also demonstrates a level of control over the synchronization.

Note: The proxy types in *multiprocessing* do nothing to support comparisons by value. So, for instance, we have:

```
>>> manager.list([1,2,3]) == [1,2,3]
False
```

One should just use a copy of the referent instead when making comparisons.

class multiprocessing.managers.BaseProxy

Proxy objects are instances of subclasses of *BaseProxy*.

_callmethod(*methodname*[, *args*[, *kwds*]])

Call and return the result of a method of the proxy's referent.

If `proxy` is a proxy whose referent is `obj` then the expression

```
proxy._callmethod(methodname, args, kwds)
```

will evaluate the expression

```
getattr(obj, methodname)(*args, **kwds)
```

in the manager's process.

The returned value will be a copy of the result of the call or a proxy to a new shared object – see documentation for the *method_to_typeid* argument of `BaseManager.register()`.

If an exception is raised by the call, then is re-raised by `_callmethod()`. If some other exception is raised in the manager's process then this is converted into a `RemoteError` exception and is raised by `_callmethod()`.

Note in particular that an exception will be raised if *methodname* has not been *exposed*.

An example of the usage of `_callmethod()`:

```
>>> l = manager.list(range(10))
>>> l._callmethod('__len__')
10
>>> l._callmethod('__getitem__', (slice(2, 7),)) # equivalent to l[2:7]
[2, 3, 4, 5, 6]
>>> l._callmethod('__getitem__', (20,))          # equivalent to l[20]
Traceback (most recent call last):
...
IndexError: list index out of range
```

_getvalue()
Return a copy of the referent.

If the referent is unpicklable then this will raise an exception.

__repr__()
Return a representation of the proxy object.

__str__()
Return the representation of the referent.

Cleanup

A proxy object uses a weakref callback so that when it gets garbage collected it deregisters itself from the manager which owns its referent.

A shared object gets deleted from the manager process when there are no longer any proxies referring to it.

Process Pools

One can create a pool of processes which will carry out tasks submitted to it with the `Pool` class.

class multiprocessing.pool.Pool([*processes*[, *initializer*[, *initargs*[, *maxtasksperchild*[, *context*]]]]])

A process pool object which controls a pool of worker processes to which jobs can be submitted. It supports asynchronous results with timeouts and callbacks and has a parallel map implementation.

processes is the number of worker processes to use. If *processes* is `None` then the number returned by `os.cpu_count()` is used.

If *initializer* is not `None` then each worker process will call `initializer(*initargs)` when it starts.

maxtasksperchild is the number of tasks a worker process can complete before it will exit and be replaced with a fresh worker process, to enable unused resources to be freed. The default *maxtasksperchild* is `None`, which means worker processes will live as long as the pool.

context can be used to specify the context used for starting the worker processes. Usually a pool is created using the function `multiprocessing.Pool()` or the `Pool()` method of a context object. In both cases *context* is set appropriately.

Note that the methods of the pool object should only be called by the process which created the pool.

New in version 3.2: *maxtasksperchild*

New in version 3.4: *context*

Note: Worker processes within a `Pool` typically live for the complete duration of the Pool's work queue. A frequent pattern found in other systems (such as Apache, mod_wsgi, etc) to free resources held by workers is to allow a worker within a pool to complete only a set amount of work before being exiting, being cleaned up and a new process spawned to replace the old one. The *maxtasksperchild* argument to the `Pool` exposes this ability to the end user.

---

apply(*func*[, *args*[, *kwds*]])

Call *func* with arguments *args* and keyword arguments *kwds*. It blocks until the result is ready. Given this blocks, `apply_async()` is better suited for performing work in parallel. Additionally, *func* is only executed in one of the workers of the pool.

apply_async(*func*[, *args*[, *kwds*[, *callback*[, *error_callback*]]]])

A variant of the `apply()` method which returns a result object.

If *callback* is specified then it should be a callable which accepts a single argument. When the result becomes ready *callback* is applied to it, that is unless the call failed, in which case the *error_callback* is applied instead.

If *error_callback* is specified then it should be a callable which accepts a single argument. If the target function fails, then the *error_callback* is called with the exception instance.

Callbacks should complete immediately since otherwise the thread which handles the results will get blocked.

map(*func*, *iterable*[, *chunksize*])

A parallel equivalent of the `map()` built-in function (it supports only one *iterable* argument though). It blocks until the result is ready.

This method chops the iterable into a number of chunks which it submits to the process pool as separate tasks. The (approximate) size of these chunks can be specified by setting *chunksize* to a positive integer.

map_async(*func*, *iterable*[, *chunksize*[, *callback*[, *error_callback*]]])

A variant of the `map()` method which returns a result object.

If *callback* is specified then it should be a callable which accepts a single argument. When the result becomes ready *callback* is applied to it, that is unless the call failed, in which case the *error_callback* is applied instead.

If *error_callback* is specified then it should be a callable which accepts a single argument. If the target function fails, then the *error_callback* is called with the exception instance.

Callbacks should complete immediately since otherwise the thread which handles the results will get blocked.

imap(*func*, *iterable*[, *chunksize*])

A lazier version of `map()`.

The *chunksize* argument is the same as the one used by the map() method. For very long iterables using a large value for *chunksize* can make the job complete **much** faster than using the default value of 1.

Also if *chunksize* is 1 then the next() method of the iterator returned by the imap() method has an optional *timeout* parameter: next(timeout) will raise multiprocessing.TimeoutError if the result cannot be returned within *timeout* seconds.

imap_unordered(*func*, *iterable*[, *chunksize*])

The same as imap() except that the ordering of the results from the returned iterator should be considered arbitrary. (Only when there is only one worker process is the order guaranteed to be "correct".)

starmap(*func*, *iterable*[, *chunksize*])

Like map() except that the elements of the *iterable* are expected to be iterables that are unpacked as arguments.

Hence an *iterable* of [(1,2), (3, 4)] results in [func(1,2), func(3,4)].

New in version 3.3.

starmap_async(*func*, *iterable*[, *chunksize*[, *callback*[, *error_callback*]]])

A combination of starmap() and map_async() that iterates over *iterable* of iterables and calls *func* with the iterables unpacked. Returns a result object.

New in version 3.3.

close()

Prevents any more tasks from being submitted to the pool. Once all the tasks have been completed the worker processes will exit.

terminate()

Stops the worker processes immediately without completing outstanding work. When the pool object is garbage collected terminate() will be called immediately.

join()

Wait for the worker processes to exit. One must call close() or terminate() before using join().

New in version 3.3: Pool objects now support the context management protocol – see Context Manager Types. __enter__() returns the pool object, and __exit__() calls terminate().

class **multiprocessing.pool.AsyncResult**

The class of the result returned by Pool.apply_async() and Pool.map_async().

get([*timeout*])

Return the result when it arrives. If *timeout* is not None and the result does not arrive within *timeout* seconds then multiprocessing.TimeoutError is raised. If the remote call raised an exception then that exception will be reraised by get().

wait([*timeout*])

Wait until the result is available or until *timeout* seconds pass.

ready()

Return whether the call has completed.

successful()

Return whether the call completed without raising an exception. Will raise AssertionError if the result is not ready.

The following example demonstrates the use of a pool:

```
from multiprocessing import Pool
import time
```

```
def f(x):
    return x*x

if __name__ == '__main__':
    with Pool(processes=4) as pool:          # start 4 worker processes
        result = pool.apply_async(f, (10,)) # evaluate "f(10)" asynchronously in a single process
        print(result.get(timeout=1))        # prints "100" unless your computer is *very* slow

        print(pool.map(f, range(10)))       # prints "[0, 1, 4,..., 81]"

        it = pool.imap(f, range(10))
        print(next(it))                     # prints "0"
        print(next(it))                     # prints "1"
        print(it.next(timeout=1))           # prints "4" unless your computer is *very* slow

        result = pool.apply_async(time.sleep, (10,))
        print(result.get(timeout=1))        # raises multiprocessing.TimeoutError
```

Listeners and Clients

Usually message passing between processes is done using queues or by using `Connection` objects returned by `Pipe()`.

However, the `multiprocessing.connection` module allows some extra flexibility. It basically gives a high level message oriented API for dealing with sockets or Windows named pipes. It also has support for *digest authentication* using the `hmac` module, and for polling multiple connections at the same time.

`multiprocessing.connection.deliver_challenge`(*connection*, *authkey*)
Send a randomly generated message to the other end of the connection and wait for a reply.

If the reply matches the digest of the message using *authkey* as the key then a welcome message is sent to the other end of the connection. Otherwise `AuthenticationError` is raised.

`multiprocessing.connection.answer_challenge`(*connection*, *authkey*)
Receive a message, calculate the digest of the message using *authkey* as the key, and then send the digest back.

If a welcome message is not received, then `AuthenticationError` is raised.

`multiprocessing.connection.Client`(*address*[, *family*[, *authkey*]])
Attempt to set up a connection to the listener which is using address *address*, returning a `Connection`.

The type of the connection is determined by *family* argument, but this can generally be omitted since it can usually be inferred from the format of *address*. (See *Address Formats*)

If *authkey* is given and not None, it should be a byte string and will be used as the secret key for an HMAC-based authentication challenge. No authentication is done if *authkey* is None. `AuthenticationError` is raised if authentication fails. See *Authentication keys*.

class `multiprocessing.connection.Listener`([*address*[, *family*[, *backlog*[, *authkey*]]]])
A wrapper for a bound socket or Windows named pipe which is 'listening' for connections.

address is the address to be used by the bound socket or named pipe of the listener object.

Note: If an address of '0.0.0.0' is used, the address will not be a connectable end point on Windows. If you require a connectable end-point, you should use '127.0.0.1'.

family is the type of socket (or named pipe) to use. This can be one of the strings `'AF_INET'` (for a TCP socket), `'AF_UNIX'` (for a Unix domain socket) or `'AF_PIPE'` (for a Windows named pipe). Of these only the first is guaranteed to be available. If *family* is `None` then the family is inferred from the format of *address*. If *address* is also `None` then a default is chosen. This default is the family which is assumed to be the fastest available. See *Address Formats*. Note that if *family* is `'AF_UNIX'` and address is `None` then the socket will be created in a private temporary directory created using `tempfile.mkstemp()`.

If the listener object uses a socket then *backlog* (1 by default) is passed to the `listen()` method of the socket once it has been bound.

If *authkey* is given and not None, it should be a byte string and will be used as the secret key for an HMAC-based authentication challenge. No authentication is done if *authkey* is None. `AuthenticationError` is raised if authentication fails. See *Authentication keys*.

`accept()`
Accept a connection on the bound socket or named pipe of the listener object and return a `Connection` object. If authentication is attempted and fails, then `AuthenticationError` is raised.

`close()`
Close the bound socket or named pipe of the listener object. This is called automatically when the listener is garbage collected. However it is advisable to call it explicitly.

Listener objects have the following read-only properties:

`address`
The address which is being used by the Listener object.

`last_accepted`
The address from which the last accepted connection came. If this is unavailable then it is `None`.

New in version 3.3: Listener objects now support the context management protocol – see *Context Manager Types*. `__enter__()` returns the listener object, and `__exit__()` calls `close()`.

`multiprocessing.connection.wait(`*object_list*, *timeout=None*`)`
Wait till an object in *object_list* is ready. Returns the list of those objects in *object_list* which are ready. If *timeout* is a float then the call blocks for at most that many seconds. If *timeout* is `None` then it will block for an unlimited period. A negative timeout is equivalent to a zero timeout.

For both Unix and Windows, an object can appear in *object_list* if it is

- a readable `Connection` object;
- a connected and readable `socket.socket` object; or
- the `sentinel` attribute of a `Process` object.

A connection or socket object is ready when there is data available to be read from it, or the other end has been closed.

Unix: `wait(object_list, timeout)` almost equivalent `select.select(object_list, [], [], timeout)`. The difference is that, if `select.select()` is interrupted by a signal, it can raise `OSError` with an error number of `EINTR`, whereas `wait()` will not.

Windows: An item in *object_list* must either be an integer handle which is waitable (according to the definition used by the documentation of the Win32 function `WaitForMultipleObjects()`) or it can be an object with a `fileno()` method which returns a socket handle or pipe handle. (Note that pipe handles and socket handles are **not** waitable handles.)

New in version 3.3.

Examples

The following server code creates a listener which uses `'secret password'` as an authentication key. It then waits for a connection and sends some data to the client:

```
from multiprocessing.connection import Listener
from array import array

address = ('localhost', 6000)     # family is deduced to be 'AF_INET'

with Listener(address, authkey=b'secret password') as listener:
    with listener.accept() as conn:
        print('connection accepted from', listener.last_accepted)

        conn.send([2.25, None, 'junk', float])

        conn.send_bytes(b'hello')

        conn.send_bytes(array('i', [42, 1729]))
```

The following code connects to the server and receives some data from the server:

```
from multiprocessing.connection import Client
from array import array

address = ('localhost', 6000)

with Client(address, authkey=b'secret password') as conn:
    print(conn.recv())                  # => [2.25, None, 'junk', float]

    print(conn.recv_bytes())            # => 'hello'

    arr = array('i', [0, 0, 0, 0, 0])
    print(conn.recv_bytes_into(arr))    # => 8
    print(arr)                          # => array('i', [42, 1729, 0, 0, 0])
```

The following code uses `wait()` to wait for messages from multiple processes at once:

```
import time, random
from multiprocessing import Process, Pipe, current_process
from multiprocessing.connection import wait

def foo(w):
    for i in range(10):
        w.send((i, current_process().name))
    w.close()

if __name__ == '__main__':
    readers = []

    for i in range(4):
        r, w = Pipe(duplex=False)
        readers.append(r)
        p = Process(target=foo, args=(w,))
        p.start()
        # We close the writable end of the pipe now to be sure that
        # p is the only process which owns a handle for it.  This
        # ensures that when p closes its handle for the writable end,
        # wait() will promptly report the readable end as being ready.
        w.close()

    while readers:
        for r in wait(readers):
```

```
try:
    msg = r.recv()
except EOFError:
    readers.remove(r)
else:
    print(msg)
```

Address Formats

- An 'AF_INET' address is a tuple of the form (hostname, port) where *hostname* is a string and *port* is an integer.
- An 'AF_UNIX' address is a string representing a filename on the filesystem.
- **An 'AF_PIPE' address is a string of the form** r'\\.\pipe*PipeName*'. To use Client() to connect to a named pipe on a remote computer called *ServerName* one should use an address of the form r'*ServerName*\pipe*PipeName*' instead.

Note that any string beginning with two backslashes is assumed by default to be an 'AF_PIPE' address rather than an 'AF_UNIX' address.

Authentication keys

When one uses Connection.recv, the data received is automatically unpickled. Unfortunately unpickling data from an untrusted source is a security risk. Therefore Listener and Client() use the hmac module to provide digest authentication.

An authentication key is a byte string which can be thought of as a password: once a connection is established both ends will demand proof that the other knows the authentication key. (Demonstrating that both ends are using the same key does **not** involve sending the key over the connection.)

If authentication is requested but no authentication key is specified then the return value of current_process().authkey is used (see Process). This value will be automatically inherited by any Process object that the current process creates. This means that (by default) all processes of a multi-process program will share a single authentication key which can be used when setting up connections between themselves.

Suitable authentication keys can also be generated by using os.urandom().

Logging

Some support for logging is available. Note, however, that the logging package does not use process shared locks so it is possible (depending on the handler type) for messages from different processes to get mixed up.

multiprocessing.get_logger()
Returns the logger used by multiprocessing. If necessary, a new one will be created.

When first created the logger has level logging.NOTSET and no default handler. Messages sent to this logger will not by default propagate to the root logger.

Note that on Windows child processes will only inherit the level of the parent process's logger – any other customization of the logger will not be inherited.

multiprocessing.log_to_stderr()
This function performs a call to get_logger() but in addition to returning the logger created by

get_logger, it adds a handler which sends output to *sys.stderr* using format `'[%(levelname)s/%(processName)s] %(message)s'`.

Below is an example session with logging turned on:

```
>>> import multiprocessing, logging
>>> logger = multiprocessing.log_to_stderr()
>>> logger.setLevel(logging.INFO)
>>> logger.warning('doomed')
[WARNING/MainProcess] doomed
>>> m = multiprocessing.Manager()
[INFO/SyncManager-...] child process calling self.run()
[INFO/SyncManager-...] created temp directory /.../pymp-...
[INFO/SyncManager-...] manager serving at '/.../listener-...'
>>> del m
[INFO/MainProcess] sending shutdown message to manager
[INFO/SyncManager-...] manager exiting with exitcode 0
```

For a full table of logging levels, see the *logging* module.

The `multiprocessing.dummy` module

multiprocessing.dummy replicates the API of *multiprocessing* but is no more than a wrapper around the *threading* module.

17.2.3 Programming guidelines

There are certain guidelines and idioms which should be adhered to when using *multiprocessing*.

All start methods

The following applies to all start methods.

Avoid shared state

As far as possible one should try to avoid shifting large amounts of data between processes.

It is probably best to stick to using queues or pipes for communication between processes rather than using the lower level synchronization primitives.

Picklability

Ensure that the arguments to the methods of proxies are picklable.

Thread safety of proxies

Do not use a proxy object from more than one thread unless you protect it with a lock.

(There is never a problem with different processes using the *same* proxy.)

Joining zombie processes

On Unix when a process finishes but has not been joined it becomes a zombie. There should never be very many because each time a new process starts (or *active_children()* is called) all completed processes which have not yet been joined will be joined. Also calling a finished process's *Process.is_alive* will join the process. Even so it is probably good practice to explicitly join all the processes that you start.

Better to inherit than pickle/unpickle

When using the *spawn* or *forkserver* start methods many types from `multiprocessing` need to be picklable so that child processes can use them. However, one should generally avoid sending shared objects to other processes using pipes or queues. Instead you should arrange the program so that a process which needs access to a shared resource created elsewhere can inherit it from an ancestor process.

Avoid terminating processes

Using the `Process.terminate` method to stop a process is liable to cause any shared resources (such as locks, semaphores, pipes and queues) currently being used by the process to become broken or unavailable to other processes.

Therefore it is probably best to only consider using `Process.terminate` on processes which never use any shared resources.

Joining processes that use queues

Bear in mind that a process that has put items in a queue will wait before terminating until all the buffered items are fed by the "feeder" thread to the underlying pipe. (The child process can call the `Queue.cancel_join_thread` method of the queue to avoid this behaviour.)

This means that whenever you use a queue you need to make sure that all items which have been put on the queue will eventually be removed before the process is joined. Otherwise you cannot be sure that processes which have put items on the queue will terminate. Remember also that non-daemonic processes will be joined automatically.

An example which will deadlock is the following:

```
from multiprocessing import Process, Queue

def f(q):
    q.put('X' * 1000000)

if __name__ == '__main__':
    queue = Queue()
    p = Process(target=f, args=(queue,))
    p.start()
    p.join()                    # this deadlocks
    obj = queue.get()
```

A fix here would be to swap the last two lines (or simply remove the `p.join()` line).

Explicitly pass resources to child processes

On Unix using the *fork* start method, a child process can make use of a shared resource created in a parent process using a global resource. However, it is better to pass the object as an argument to the constructor for the child process.

Apart from making the code (potentially) compatible with Windows and the other start methods this also ensures that as long as the child process is still alive the object will not be garbage collected in the parent process. This might be important if some resource is freed when the object is garbage collected in the parent process.

So for instance

```
from multiprocessing import Process, Lock

def f():
    ... do something using "lock" ...

if __name__ == '__main__':
    lock = Lock()
```

```
    for i in range(10):
        Process(target=f).start()
```

should be rewritten as

```
from multiprocessing import Process, Lock

def f(l):
    ... do something using "l" ...

if __name__ == '__main__':
    lock = Lock()
    for i in range(10):
        Process(target=f, args=(lock,)).start()
```

Beware of replacing *sys.stdin* with a "file like object"

multiprocessing originally unconditionally called:

```
os.close(sys.stdin.fileno())
```

in the `multiprocessing.Process._bootstrap()` method — this resulted in issues with processes-in-processes. This has been changed to:

```
sys.stdin.close()
sys.stdin = open(os.open(os.devnull, os.O_RDONLY), closefd=False)
```

Which solves the fundamental issue of processes colliding with each other resulting in a bad file descriptor error, but introduces a potential danger to applications which replace *sys.stdin()* with a "file-like object" with output buffering. This danger is that if multiple processes call *close()* on this file-like object, it could result in the same data being flushed to the object multiple times, resulting in corruption.

If you write a file-like object and implement your own caching, you can make it fork-safe by storing the pid whenever you append to the cache, and discarding the cache when the pid changes. For example:

```
@property
def cache(self):
    pid = os.getpid()
    if pid != self._pid:
        self._pid = pid
        self._cache = []
    return self._cache
```

For more information, see bpo-5155, bpo-5313 and bpo-5331

The *spawn* and *forkserver* start methods

There are a few extra restriction which don't apply to the *fork* start method.

More picklability

Ensure that all arguments to `Process.__init__()` are picklable. Also, if you subclass *Process* then make sure that instances will be picklable when the *Process.start* method is called.

Global variables

Bear in mind that if code run in a child process tries to access a global variable, then the value it sees (if any) may not be the same as the value in the parent process at the time that *Process.start* was called.

However, global variables which are just module level constants cause no problems.

Safe importing of main module

Make sure that the main module can be safely imported by a new Python interpreter without causing unintended side effects (such a starting a new process).

For example, using the *spawn* or *forkserver* start method running the following module would fail with a *RuntimeError*:

```
from multiprocessing import Process

def foo():
    print('hello')

p = Process(target=foo)
p.start()
```

Instead one should protect the "entry point" of the program by using `if __name__ == '__main__':` as follows:

```
from multiprocessing import Process, freeze_support, set_start_method

def foo():
    print('hello')

if __name__ == '__main__':
    freeze_support()
    set_start_method('spawn')
    p = Process(target=foo)
    p.start()
```

(The `freeze_support()` line can be omitted if the program will be run normally instead of frozen.)

This allows the newly spawned Python interpreter to safely import the module and then run the module's `foo()` function.

Similar restrictions apply if a pool or manager is created in the main module.

17.2.4 Examples

Demonstration of how to create and use customized managers and proxies:

```
from multiprocessing import freeze_support
from multiprocessing.managers import BaseManager, BaseProxy
import operator

##

class Foo:
    def f(self):
        print('you called Foo.f()')
    def g(self):
        print('you called Foo.g()')
    def _h(self):
```

```
        print('you called Foo._h()')

# A simple generator function
def baz():
    for i in range(10):
        yield i*i

# Proxy type for generator objects
class GeneratorProxy(BaseProxy):
    _exposed_ = ['__next__']
    def __iter__(self):
        return self
    def __next__(self):
        return self._callmethod('__next__')

# Function to return the operator module
def get_operator_module():
    return operator

##

class MyManager(BaseManager):
    pass

# register the Foo class; make `f()` and `g()` accessible via proxy
MyManager.register('Foo1', Foo)

# register the Foo class; make `g()` and `_h()` accessible via proxy
MyManager.register('Foo2', Foo, exposed=('g', '_h'))

# register the generator function baz; use `GeneratorProxy` to make proxies
MyManager.register('baz', baz, proxytype=GeneratorProxy)

# register get_operator_module(); make public functions accessible via proxy
MyManager.register('operator', get_operator_module)

##

def test():
    manager = MyManager()
    manager.start()

    print('-' * 20)

    f1 = manager.Foo1()
    f1.f()
    f1.g()
    assert not hasattr(f1, '_h')
    assert sorted(f1._exposed_) == sorted(['f', 'g'])

    print('-' * 20)

    f2 = manager.Foo2()
    f2.g()
    f2._h()
    assert not hasattr(f2, 'f')
    assert sorted(f2._exposed_) == sorted(['g', '_h'])
```

```
    print('-' * 20)

    it = manager.baz()
    for i in it:
        print('<%d>' % i, end=' ')
    print()

    print('-' * 20)

    op = manager.operator()
    print('op.add(23, 45) =', op.add(23, 45))
    print('op.pow(2, 94) =', op.pow(2, 94))
    print('op._exposed_ =', op._exposed_)

##

if __name__ == '__main__':
    freeze_support()
    test()
```

Using *Pool*:

```
import multiprocessing
import time
import random
import sys

#
# Functions used by test code
#

def calculate(func, args):
    result = func(*args)
    return '%s says that %s%s = %s' % (
        multiprocessing.current_process().name,
        func.__name__, args, result
        )

def calculatestar(args):
    return calculate(*args)

def mul(a, b):
    time.sleep(0.5 * random.random())
    return a * b

def plus(a, b):
    time.sleep(0.5 * random.random())
    return a + b

def f(x):
    return 1.0 / (x - 5.0)

def pow3(x):
    return x ** 3

def noop(x):
    pass
```

```
#
# Test code
#

def test():
    PROCESSES = 4
    print('Creating pool with %d processes\n' % PROCESSES)

    with multiprocessing.Pool(PROCESSES) as pool:
        #
        # Tests
        #

        TASKS = [(mul, (i, 7)) for i in range(10)] + \
                [(plus, (i, 8)) for i in range(10)]

        results = [pool.apply_async(calculate, t) for t in TASKS]
        imap_it = pool.imap(calculatestar, TASKS)
        imap_unordered_it = pool.imap_unordered(calculatestar, TASKS)

        print('Ordered results using pool.apply_async():')
        for r in results:
            print('\t', r.get())
        print()

        print('Ordered results using pool.imap():')
        for x in imap_it:
            print('\t', x)
        print()

        print('Unordered results using pool.imap_unordered():')
        for x in imap_unordered_it:
            print('\t', x)
        print()

        print('Ordered results using pool.map() --- will block till complete:')
        for x in pool.map(calculatestar, TASKS):
            print('\t', x)
        print()

        #
        # Test error handling
        #

        print('Testing error handling:')

        try:
            print(pool.apply(f, (5,)))
        except ZeroDivisionError:
            print('\tGot ZeroDivisionError as expected from pool.apply()')
        else:
            raise AssertionError('expected ZeroDivisionError')

        try:
            print(pool.map(f, list(range(10))))
        except ZeroDivisionError:
            print('\tGot ZeroDivisionError as expected from pool.map()')
        else:
```

```
            raise AssertionError('expected ZeroDivisionError')

        try:
            print(list(pool.imap(f, list(range(10)))))
        except ZeroDivisionError:
            print('\tGot ZeroDivisionError as expected from list(pool.imap())')
        else:
            raise AssertionError('expected ZeroDivisionError')

        it = pool.imap(f, list(range(10)))
        for i in range(10):
            try:
                x = next(it)
            except ZeroDivisionError:
                if i == 5:
                    pass
            except StopIteration:
                break
            else:
                if i == 5:
                    raise AssertionError('expected ZeroDivisionError')

        assert i == 9
        print('\tGot ZeroDivisionError as expected from IMapIterator.next()')
        print()

        #
        # Testing timeouts
        #

        print('Testing ApplyResult.get() with timeout:', end=' ')
        res = pool.apply_async(calculate, TASKS[0])
        while 1:
            sys.stdout.flush()
            try:
                sys.stdout.write('\n\t%s' % res.get(0.02))
                break
            except multiprocessing.TimeoutError:
                sys.stdout.write('.')
        print()
        print()

        print('Testing IMapIterator.next() with timeout:', end=' ')
        it = pool.imap(calculatestar, TASKS)
        while 1:
            sys.stdout.flush()
            try:
                sys.stdout.write('\n\t%s' % it.next(0.02))
            except StopIteration:
                break
            except multiprocessing.TimeoutError:
                sys.stdout.write('.')
        print()
        print()


if __name__ == '__main__':
    multiprocessing.freeze_support()
```

```
    test()
```

An example showing how to use queues to feed tasks to a collection of worker processes and collect the results:

```
import time
import random

from multiprocessing import Process, Queue, current_process, freeze_support

#
# Function run by worker processes
#

def worker(input, output):
    for func, args in iter(input.get, 'STOP'):
        result = calculate(func, args)
        output.put(result)

#
# Function used to calculate result
#

def calculate(func, args):
    result = func(*args)
    return '%s says that %s%s = %s' % \
        (current_process().name, func.__name__, args, result)

#
# Functions referenced by tasks
#

def mul(a, b):
    time.sleep(0.5*random.random())
    return a * b

def plus(a, b):
    time.sleep(0.5*random.random())
    return a + b

#
#
#

def test():
    NUMBER_OF_PROCESSES = 4
    TASKS1 = [(mul, (i, 7)) for i in range(20)]
    TASKS2 = [(plus, (i, 8)) for i in range(10)]

    # Create queues
    task_queue = Queue()
    done_queue = Queue()

    # Submit tasks
    for task in TASKS1:
        task_queue.put(task)

    # Start worker processes
```

```
    for i in range(NUMBER_OF_PROCESSES):
        Process(target=worker, args=(task_queue, done_queue)).start()

    # Get and print results
    print('Unordered results:')
    for i in range(len(TASKS1)):
        print('\t', done_queue.get())

    # Add more tasks using `put()`
    for task in TASKS2:
        task_queue.put(task)

    # Get and print some more results
    for i in range(len(TASKS2)):
        print('\t', done_queue.get())

    # Tell child processes to stop
    for i in range(NUMBER_OF_PROCESSES):
        task_queue.put('STOP')


if __name__ == '__main__':
    freeze_support()
    test()
```

17.3 The concurrent package

Currently, there is only one module in this package:

- *concurrent.futures* – Launching parallel tasks

17.4 concurrent.futures — Launching parallel tasks

New in version 3.2.

Source code: Lib/concurrent/futures/thread.py and Lib/concurrent/futures/process.py

---

The *concurrent.futures* module provides a high-level interface for asynchronously executing callables.

The asynchronous execution can be performed with threads, using *ThreadPoolExecutor*, or separate processes, using *ProcessPoolExecutor*. Both implement the same interface, which is defined by the abstract *Executor* class.

17.4.1 Executor Objects

class concurrent.futures.Executor

An abstract class that provides methods to execute calls asynchronously. It should not be used directly, but through its concrete subclasses.

submit(*fn*, **args*, ***kwargs*)

Schedules the callable, *fn*, to be executed as `fn(*args **kwargs)` and returns a *Future* object representing the execution of the callable.

```
with ThreadPoolExecutor(max_workers=1) as executor:
    future = executor.submit(pow, 323, 1235)
    print(future.result())
```

map(*func*, **iterables*, *timeout=None*, *chunksize=1*)

Similar to *map(func, *iterables)* except:

- the *iterables* are collected immediately rather than lazily;
- *func* is executed asynchronously and several calls to *func* may be made concurrently.

The returned iterator raises a *concurrent.futures.TimeoutError* if *__next__()* is called and the result isn't available after *timeout* seconds from the original call to *Executor.map()*. *timeout* can be an int or a float. If *timeout* is not specified or None, there is no limit to the wait time.

If a *func* call raises an exception, then that exception will be raised when its value is retrieved from the iterator.

When using *ProcessPoolExecutor*, this method chops *iterables* into a number of chunks which it submits to the pool as separate tasks. The (approximate) size of these chunks can be specified by setting *chunksize* to a positive integer. For very long iterables, using a large value for *chunksize* can significantly improve performance compared to the default size of 1. With *ThreadPoolExecutor*, *chunksize* has no effect.

Changed in version 3.5: Added the *chunksize* argument.

shutdown(*wait=True*)

Signal the executor that it should free any resources that it is using when the currently pending futures are done executing. Calls to *Executor.submit()* and *Executor.map()* made after shutdown will raise *RuntimeError*.

If *wait* is True then this method will not return until all the pending futures are done executing and the resources associated with the executor have been freed. If *wait* is False then this method will return immediately and the resources associated with the executor will be freed when all pending futures are done executing. Regardless of the value of *wait*, the entire Python program will not exit until all pending futures are done executing.

You can avoid having to call this method explicitly if you use the with statement, which will shutdown the *Executor* (waiting as if *Executor.shutdown()* were called with *wait* set to True):

```
import shutil
with ThreadPoolExecutor(max_workers=4) as e:
    e.submit(shutil.copy, 'src1.txt', 'dest1.txt')
    e.submit(shutil.copy, 'src2.txt', 'dest2.txt')
    e.submit(shutil.copy, 'src3.txt', 'dest3.txt')
    e.submit(shutil.copy, 'src4.txt', 'dest4.txt')
```

17.4.2 ThreadPoolExecutor

ThreadPoolExecutor is an *Executor* subclass that uses a pool of threads to execute calls asynchronously.

Deadlocks can occur when the callable associated with a *Future* waits on the results of another *Future*. For example:

```
import time
def wait_on_b():
    time.sleep(5)
    print(b.result())  # b will never complete because it is waiting on a.
```

```
    return 5

def wait_on_a():
    time.sleep(5)
    print(a.result())  # a will never complete because it is waiting on b.
    return 6


executor = ThreadPoolExecutor(max_workers=2)
a = executor.submit(wait_on_b)
b = executor.submit(wait_on_a)
```

And:

```
def wait_on_future():
    f = executor.submit(pow, 5, 2)
    # This will never complete because there is only one worker thread and
    # it is executing this function.
    print(f.result())

executor = ThreadPoolExecutor(max_workers=1)
executor.submit(wait_on_future)
```

class `concurrent.futures.ThreadPoolExecutor`(*max_workers=None*, *thread_name_prefix=''*)

An *Executor* subclass that uses a pool of at most *max_workers* threads to execute calls asynchronously.

Changed in version 3.5: If *max_workers* is `None` or not given, it will default to the number of processors on the machine, multiplied by `5`, assuming that *ThreadPoolExecutor* is often used to overlap I/O instead of CPU work and the number of workers should be higher than the number of workers for *ProcessPoolExecutor*.

New in version 3.6: The *thread_name_prefix* argument was added to allow users to control the threading.Thread names for worker threads created by the pool for easier debugging.

ThreadPoolExecutor Example

```
import concurrent.futures
import urllib.request

URLS = ['http://www.foxnews.com/',
        'http://www.cnn.com/',
        'http://europe.wsj.com/',
        'http://www.bbc.co.uk/',
        'http://some-made-up-domain.com/']

# Retrieve a single page and report the URL and contents
def load_url(url, timeout):
    with urllib.request.urlopen(url, timeout=timeout) as conn:
        return conn.read()

# We can use a with statement to ensure threads are cleaned up promptly
with concurrent.futures.ThreadPoolExecutor(max_workers=5) as executor:
    # Start the load operations and mark each future with its URL
    future_to_url = {executor.submit(load_url, url, 60): url for url in URLS}
    for future in concurrent.futures.as_completed(future_to_url):
        url = future_to_url[future]
        try:
```

```
            data = future.result()
        except Exception as exc:
            print('%r generated an exception: %s' % (url, exc))
        else:
            print('%r page is %d bytes' % (url, len(data)))
```

17.4.3 ProcessPoolExecutor

The *ProcessPoolExecutor* class is an *Executor* subclass that uses a pool of processes to execute calls asynchronously. *ProcessPoolExecutor* uses the *multiprocessing* module, which allows it to side-step the *Global Interpreter Lock* but also means that only picklable objects can be executed and returned.

The `__main__` module must be importable by worker subprocesses. This means that *ProcessPoolExecutor* will not work in the interactive interpreter.

Calling *Executor* or *Future* methods from a callable submitted to a *ProcessPoolExecutor* will result in deadlock.

class concurrent.futures.ProcessPoolExecutor(*max_workers=None*)

An *Executor* subclass that executes calls asynchronously using a pool of at most *max_workers* processes. If *max_workers* is `None` or not given, it will default to the number of processors on the machine. If *max_workers* is lower or equal to `0`, then a *ValueError* will be raised.

Changed in version 3.3: When one of the worker processes terminates abruptly, a `BrokenProcessPool` error is now raised. Previously, behaviour was undefined but operations on the executor or its futures would often freeze or deadlock.

ProcessPoolExecutor Example

```
import concurrent.futures
import math

PRIMES = [
    112272535095293,
    112582705942171,
    112272535095293,
    115280095190773,
    115797848077099,
    1099726899285419]

def is_prime(n):
    if n % 2 == 0:
        return False

    sqrt_n = int(math.floor(math.sqrt(n)))
    for i in range(3, sqrt_n + 1, 2):
        if n % i == 0:
            return False
    return True

def main():
    with concurrent.futures.ProcessPoolExecutor() as executor:
        for number, prime in zip(PRIMES, executor.map(is_prime, PRIMES)):
            print('%d is prime: %s' % (number, prime))
```

```
if __name__ == '__main__':
    main()
```

17.4.4 Future Objects

The *Future* class encapsulates the asynchronous execution of a callable. *Future* instances are created by *Executor.submit()*.

class concurrent.futures.Future

Encapsulates the asynchronous execution of a callable. *Future* instances are created by *Executor.submit()* and should not be created directly except for testing.

cancel()

Attempt to cancel the call. If the call is currently being executed and cannot be cancelled then the method will return `False`, otherwise the call will be cancelled and the method will return `True`.

cancelled()

Return `True` if the call was successfully cancelled.

running()

Return `True` if the call is currently being executed and cannot be cancelled.

done()

Return `True` if the call was successfully cancelled or finished running.

result(*timeout=None*)

Return the value returned by the call. If the call hasn't yet completed then this method will wait up to *timeout* seconds. If the call hasn't completed in *timeout* seconds, then a *concurrent.futures.TimeoutError* will be raised. *timeout* can be an int or float. If *timeout* is not specified or `None`, there is no limit to the wait time.

If the future is cancelled before completing then *CancelledError* will be raised.

If the call raised, this method will raise the same exception.

exception(*timeout=None*)

Return the exception raised by the call. If the call hasn't yet completed then this method will wait up to *timeout* seconds. If the call hasn't completed in *timeout* seconds, then a *concurrent.futures.TimeoutError* will be raised. *timeout* can be an int or float. If *timeout* is not specified or `None`, there is no limit to the wait time.

If the future is cancelled before completing then *CancelledError* will be raised.

If the call completed without raising, `None` is returned.

add_done_callback(*fn*)

Attaches the callable *fn* to the future. *fn* will be called, with the future as its only argument, when the future is cancelled or finishes running.

Added callables are called in the order that they were added and are always called in a thread belonging to the process that added them. If the callable raises an *Exception* subclass, it will be logged and ignored. If the callable raises a *BaseException* subclass, the behavior is undefined.

If the future has already completed or been cancelled, *fn* will be called immediately.

The following *Future* methods are meant for use in unit tests and *Executor* implementations.

set_running_or_notify_cancel()

This method should only be called by *Executor* implementations before executing the work associated with the *Future* and by unit tests.

If the method returns `False` then the *Future* was cancelled, i.e. *Future.cancel()* was called and returned *True*. Any threads waiting on the *Future* completing (i.e. through *as_completed()* or *wait()*) will be woken up.

If the method returns `True` then the *Future* was not cancelled and has been put in the running state, i.e. calls to *Future.running()* will return *True*.

This method can only be called once and cannot be called after *Future.set_result()* or *Future.set_exception()* have been called.

set_result(*result*)
Sets the result of the work associated with the *Future* to *result*.

This method should only be used by *Executor* implementations and unit tests.

set_exception(*exception*)
Sets the result of the work associated with the *Future* to the *Exception* *exception*.

This method should only be used by *Executor* implementations and unit tests.

17.4.5 Module Functions

concurrent.futures.**wait**(*fs*, *timeout=None*, *return_when=ALL_COMPLETED*)
Wait for the *Future* instances (possibly created by different *Executor* instances) given by *fs* to complete. Returns a named 2-tuple of sets. The first set, named `done`, contains the futures that completed (finished or were cancelled) before the wait completed. The second set, named `not_done`, contains uncompleted futures.

timeout can be used to control the maximum number of seconds to wait before returning. *timeout* can be an int or float. If *timeout* is not specified or `None`, there is no limit to the wait time.

return_when indicates when this function should return. It must be one of the following constants:

Constant	Description
FIRST_COMPLETED	The function will return when any future finishes or is cancelled.
FIRST_EXCEPTION	The function will return when any future finishes by raising an exception. If no future raises an exception then it is equivalent to ALL_COMPLETED.
ALL_COMPLETED	The function will return when all futures finish or are cancelled.

concurrent.futures.**as_completed**(*fs*, *timeout=None*)
Returns an iterator over the *Future* instances (possibly created by different *Executor* instances) given by *fs* that yields futures as they complete (finished or were cancelled). Any futures given by *fs* that are duplicated will be returned once. Any futures that completed before *as_completed()* is called will be yielded first. The returned iterator raises a *concurrent.futures.TimeoutError* if *__next__()* is called and the result isn't available after *timeout* seconds from the original call to *as_completed()*. *timeout* can be an int or float. If *timeout* is not specified or `None`, there is no limit to the wait time.

See also:

PEP 3148 – **futures - execute computations asynchronously** The proposal which described this feature for inclusion in the Python standard library.

17.4.6 Exception classes

exception concurrent.futures.**CancelledError**
Raised when a future is cancelled.

exception concurrent.futures.**TimeoutError**
Raised when a future operation exceeds the given timeout.

exception concurrent.futures.process.BrokenProcessPool
Derived from *RuntimeError*, this exception class is raised when one of the workers of a `ProcessPoolExecutor` has terminated in a non-clean fashion (for example, if it was killed from the outside).

New in version 3.3.

17.5 subprocess — Subprocess management

Source code: Lib/subprocess.py

The *subprocess* module allows you to spawn new processes, connect to their input/output/error pipes, and obtain their return codes. This module intends to replace several older modules and functions:

```
os.system
os.spawn*
```

Information about how the *subprocess* module can be used to replace these modules and functions can be found in the following sections.

See also:

PEP 324 – PEP proposing the subprocess module

17.5.1 Using the subprocess Module

The recommended approach to invoking subprocesses is to use the *run()* function for all use cases it can handle. For more advanced use cases, the underlying *Popen* interface can be used directly.

The *run()* function was added in Python 3.5; if you need to retain compatibility with older versions, see the *Older high-level API* section.

subprocess.run(*args*, **, *stdin=None*, *input=None*, *stdout=None*, *stderr=None*, *shell=False*, *cwd=None*, *timeout=None*, *check=False*, *encoding=None*, *errors=None*)
Run the command described by *args*. Wait for command to complete, then return a *CompletedProcess* instance.

The arguments shown above are merely the most common ones, described below in *Frequently Used Arguments* (hence the use of keyword-only notation in the abbreviated signature). The full function signature is largely the same as that of the *Popen* constructor - apart from *timeout*, *input* and *check*, all the arguments to this function are passed through to that interface.

This does not capture stdout or stderr by default. To do so, pass *PIPE* for the *stdout* and/or *stderr* arguments.

The *timeout* argument is passed to *Popen.communicate()*. If the timeout expires, the child process will be killed and waited for. The *TimeoutExpired* exception will be re-raised after the child process has terminated.

The *input* argument is passed to *Popen.communicate()* and thus to the subprocess's stdin. If used it must be a byte sequence, or a string if *encoding* or *errors* is specified or *universal_newlines* is true. When used, the internal *Popen* object is automatically created with `stdin=PIPE`, and the *stdin* argument may not be used as well.

If *check* is true, and the process exits with a non-zero exit code, a *CalledProcessError* exception will be raised. Attributes of that exception hold the arguments, the exit code, and stdout and stderr if they were captured.

If *encoding* or *errors* are specified, or *universal_newlines* is true, file objects for stdin, stdout and stderr are opened in text mode using the specified *encoding* and *errors* or the *io.TextIOWrapper* default. Otherwise, file objects are opened in binary mode.

Examples:

```
>>> subprocess.run(["ls", "-l"])  # doesn't capture output
CompletedProcess(args=['ls', '-l'], returncode=0)

>>> subprocess.run("exit 1", shell=True, check=True)
Traceback (most recent call last):
  ...
subprocess.CalledProcessError: Command 'exit 1' returned non-zero exit status 1

>>> subprocess.run(["ls", "-l", "/dev/null"], stdout=subprocess.PIPE)
CompletedProcess(args=['ls', '-l', '/dev/null'], returncode=0,
stdout=b'crw-rw-rw- 1 root root 1, 3 Jan 23 16:23 /dev/null\n')
```

New in version 3.5.

Changed in version 3.6: Added *encoding* and *errors* parameters

class subprocess.CompletedProcess

The return value from *run()*, representing a process that has finished.

args

The arguments used to launch the process. This may be a list or a string.

returncode

Exit status of the child process. Typically, an exit status of 0 indicates that it ran successfully.

A negative value -N indicates that the child was terminated by signal N (POSIX only).

stdout

Captured stdout from the child process. A bytes sequence, or a string if *run()* was called with an encoding or errors. None if stdout was not captured.

If you ran the process with stderr=subprocess.STDOUT, stdout and stderr will be combined in this attribute, and *stderr* will be None.

stderr

Captured stderr from the child process. A bytes sequence, or a string if *run()* was called with an encoding or errors. None if stderr was not captured.

check_returncode()

If *returncode* is non-zero, raise a *CalledProcessError*.

New in version 3.5.

subprocess.DEVNULL

Special value that can be used as the *stdin*, *stdout* or *stderr* argument to *Popen* and indicates that the special file *os.devnull* will be used.

New in version 3.3.

subprocess.PIPE

Special value that can be used as the *stdin*, *stdout* or *stderr* argument to *Popen* and indicates that a pipe to the standard stream should be opened. Most useful with *Popen.communicate()*.

subprocess.STDOUT

Special value that can be used as the *stderr* argument to *Popen* and indicates that standard error should go into the same handle as standard output.

exception subprocess.SubprocessError
Base class for all other exceptions from this module.

New in version 3.3.

exception subprocess.TimeoutExpired
Subclass of *SubprocessError*, raised when a timeout expires while waiting for a child process.

cmd
Command that was used to spawn the child process.

timeout
Timeout in seconds.

output
Output of the child process if it was captured by *run()* or *check_output()*. Otherwise, None.

stdout
Alias for output, for symmetry with *stderr*.

stderr
Stderr output of the child process if it was captured by *run()*. Otherwise, None.

New in version 3.3.

Changed in version 3.5: *stdout* and *stderr* attributes added

exception subprocess.CalledProcessError
Subclass of *SubprocessError*, raised when a process run by *check_call()* or *check_output()* returns a non-zero exit status.

returncode
Exit status of the child process. If the process exited due to a signal, this will be the negative signal number.

cmd
Command that was used to spawn the child process.

output
Output of the child process if it was captured by *run()* or *check_output()*. Otherwise, None.

stdout
Alias for output, for symmetry with *stderr*.

stderr
Stderr output of the child process if it was captured by *run()*. Otherwise, None.

Changed in version 3.5: *stdout* and *stderr* attributes added

Frequently Used Arguments

To support a wide variety of use cases, the *Popen* constructor (and the convenience functions) accept a large number of optional arguments. For most typical use cases, many of these arguments can be safely left at their default values. The arguments that are most commonly needed are:

args is required for all calls and should be a string, or a sequence of program arguments. Providing a sequence of arguments is generally preferred, as it allows the module to take care of any required escaping and quoting of arguments (e.g. to permit spaces in file names). If passing a single string, either *shell* must be *True* (see below) or else the string must simply name the program to be executed without specifying any arguments.

stdin, *stdout* and *stderr* specify the executed program's standard input, standard output and standard error file handles, respectively. Valid values are *PIPE*, *DEVNULL*, an existing file descriptor (a positive integer), an existing file object, and None. *PIPE* indicates that a new pipe to the child should be created. *DEVNULL* indicates that the special file *os.devnull* will be used. With the default settings of None, no redirection will occur; the child's file handles will be inherited from the parent. Additionally, *stderr* can be *STDOUT*, which indicates that the stderr data from the child process should be captured into the same file handle as for *stdout*.

If *encoding* or *errors* are specified, or *universal_newlines* is true, the file objects *stdin*, *stdout* and *stderr* will be opened in text mode using the *encoding* and *errors* specified in the call or the defaults for *io.TextIOWrapper*.

For *stdin*, line ending characters '\n' in the input will be converted to the default line separator *os.linesep*. For *stdout* and *stderr*, all line endings in the output will be converted to '\n'. For more information see the documentation of the *io.TextIOWrapper* class when the *newline* argument to its constructor is None.

If text mode is not used, *stdin*, *stdout* and *stderr* will be opened as binary streams. No encoding or line ending conversion is performed.

New in version 3.6: Added *encoding* and *errors* parameters.

Note: The newlines attribute of the file objects *Popen.stdin*, *Popen.stdout* and *Popen.stderr* are not updated by the *Popen.communicate()* method.

If *shell* is True, the specified command will be executed through the shell. This can be useful if you are using Python primarily for the enhanced control flow it offers over most system shells and still want convenient access to other shell features such as shell pipes, filename wildcards, environment variable expansion, and expansion of ~ to a user's home directory. However, note that Python itself offers implementations of many shell-like features (in particular, *glob*, *fnmatch*, *os.walk()*, *os.path.expandvars()*, *os.path.expanduser()*, and *shutil*).

Changed in version 3.3: When *universal_newlines* is True, the class uses the encoding *locale.getpreferredencoding(False)* instead of locale.getpreferredencoding(). See the *io.TextIOWrapper* class for more information on this change.

Note: Read the *Security Considerations* section before using shell=True.

These options, along with all of the other options, are described in more detail in the *Popen* constructor documentation.

Popen Constructor

The underlying process creation and management in this module is handled by the *Popen* class. It offers a lot of flexibility so that developers are able to handle the less common cases not covered by the convenience functions.

class subprocess.Popen(*args, bufsize=-1, executable=None, stdin=None, stdout=None, stderr=None, preexec_fn=None, close_fds=True, shell=False, cwd=None, env=None, universal_newlines=False, startupinfo=None, creationflags=0, restore_signals=True, start_new_session=False, pass_fds=(), *, encoding=None, errors=None*)

Execute a child program in a new process. On POSIX, the class uses *os.execvp()*-like behavior to execute the child program. On Windows, the class uses the Windows CreateProcess() function. The arguments to *Popen* are as follows.

args should be a sequence of program arguments or else a single string. By default, the program to execute is the first item in *args* if *args* is a sequence. If *args* is a string, the interpretation is platform-dependent and described below. See the *shell* and *executable* arguments for additional differences from the default behavior. Unless otherwise stated, it is recommended to pass *args* as a sequence.

On POSIX, if *args* is a string, the string is interpreted as the name or path of the program to execute. However, this can only be done if not passing arguments to the program.

Note: *shlex.split()* can be useful when determining the correct tokenization for *args*, especially in complex cases:

```
>>> import shlex, subprocess
>>> command_line = input()
/bin/vikings -input eggs.txt -output "spam spam.txt" -cmd "echo '$MONEY'"
>>> args = shlex.split(command_line)
>>> print(args)
['/bin/vikings', '-input', 'eggs.txt', '-output', 'spam spam.txt', '-cmd', "echo '$MONEY'"]
>>> p = subprocess.Popen(args) # Success!
```

Note in particular that options (such as *-input*) and arguments (such as *eggs.txt*) that are separated by whitespace in the shell go in separate list elements, while arguments that need quoting or backslash escaping when used in the shell (such as filenames containing spaces or the *echo* command shown above) are single list elements.

On Windows, if *args* is a sequence, it will be converted to a string in a manner described in *Converting an argument sequence to a string on Windows*. This is because the underlying `CreateProcess()` operates on strings.

The *shell* argument (which defaults to `False`) specifies whether to use the shell as the program to execute. If *shell* is `True`, it is recommended to pass *args* as a string rather than as a sequence.

On POSIX with `shell=True`, the shell defaults to `/bin/sh`. If *args* is a string, the string specifies the command to execute through the shell. This means that the string must be formatted exactly as it would be when typed at the shell prompt. This includes, for example, quoting or backslash escaping filenames with spaces in them. If *args* is a sequence, the first item specifies the command string, and any additional items will be treated as additional arguments to the shell itself. That is to say, *Popen* does the equivalent of:

```
Popen(['/bin/sh', '-c', args[0], args[1], ...])
```

On Windows with `shell=True`, the `COMSPEC` environment variable specifies the default shell. The only time you need to specify `shell=True` on Windows is when the command you wish to execute is built into the shell (e.g. `dir` or `copy`). You do not need `shell=True` to run a batch file or console-based executable.

Note: Read the *Security Considerations* section before using `shell=True`

bufsize will be supplied as the corresponding argument to the *open()* function when creating the stdin/stdout/stderr pipe file objects:

- `0` means unbuffered (read and write are one system call and can return short)
- `1` means line buffered (only usable if `universal_newlines=True` i.e., in a text mode)
- any other positive value means use a buffer of approximately that size
- negative bufsize (the default) means the system default of io.DEFAULT_BUFFER_SIZE will be used.

Changed in version 3.3.1: *bufsize* now defaults to -1 to enable buffering by default to match the behavior that most code expects. In versions prior to Python 3.2.4 and 3.3.1 it incorrectly defaulted to `0` which was unbuffered and allowed short reads. This was unintentional and did not match the behavior of Python 2 as most code expected.

The *executable* argument specifies a replacement program to execute. It is very seldom needed. When `shell=False`, *executable* replaces the program to execute specified by *args*. However, the original *args* is still passed to the program. Most programs treat the program specified by *args* as the command name, which can then be different from the program actually executed. On POSIX, the *args* name becomes the display name for the executable in utilities such as **ps**. If `shell=True`, on POSIX the *executable* argument specifies a replacement shell for the default `/bin/sh`.

stdin, *stdout* and *stderr* specify the executed program's standard input, standard output and standard error file handles, respectively. Valid values are *PIPE*, *DEVNULL*, an existing file descriptor (a positive integer), an existing *file object*, and `None`. *PIPE* indicates that a new pipe to the child should be created. *DEVNULL* indicates that the special file `os.devnull` will be used. With the default settings of `None`, no redirection will occur; the child's file handles will be inherited from the parent. Additionally, *stderr* can be *STDOUT*, which indicates that the stderr data from the applications should be captured into the same file handle as for stdout.

If *preexec_fn* is set to a callable object, this object will be called in the child process just before the child is executed. (POSIX only)

Warning: The *preexec_fn* parameter is not safe to use in the presence of threads in your application. The child process could deadlock before exec is called. If you must use it, keep it trivial! Minimize the number of libraries you call into.

Note: If you need to modify the environment for the child use the *env* parameter rather than doing it in a *preexec_fn*. The *start_new_session* parameter can take the place of a previously common use of *preexec_fn* to call os.setsid() in the child.

If *close_fds* is true, all file descriptors except `0`, `1` and `2` will be closed before the child process is executed. (POSIX only). The default varies by platform: Always true on POSIX. On Windows it is true when *stdin*/*stdout*/*stderr* are `None`, false otherwise. On Windows, if *close_fds* is true then no handles will be inherited by the child process. Note that on Windows, you cannot set *close_fds* to true and also redirect the standard handles by setting *stdin*, *stdout* or *stderr*.

Changed in version 3.2: The default for *close_fds* was changed from `False` to what is described above.

pass_fds is an optional sequence of file descriptors to keep open between the parent and child. Providing any *pass_fds* forces *close_fds* to be `True`. (POSIX only)

New in version 3.2: The *pass_fds* parameter was added.

If *cwd* is not `None`, the function changes the working directory to *cwd* before executing the child. *cwd* can be a `str` and *path-like* object. In particular, the function looks for *executable* (or for the first item in *args*) relative to *cwd* if the executable path is a relative path.

Changed in version 3.6: *cwd* parameter accepts a *path-like object*.

If *restore_signals* is true (the default) all signals that Python has set to SIG_IGN are restored to SIG_DFL in the child process before the exec. Currently this includes the SIGPIPE, SIGXFZ and SIGXFSZ signals. (POSIX only)

Changed in version 3.2: *restore_signals* was added.

If *start_new_session* is true the setsid() system call will be made in the child process prior to the execution of the subprocess. (POSIX only)

Changed in version 3.2: *start_new_session* was added.

If *env* is not None, it must be a mapping that defines the environment variables for the new process; these are used instead of the default behavior of inheriting the current process' environment.

Note: If specified, *env* must provide any variables required for the program to execute. On Windows, in order to run a side-by-side assembly the specified *env* **must** include a valid SystemRoot.

If *encoding* or *errors* are specified, the file objects *stdin*, *stdout* and *stderr* are opened in text mode with the specified encoding and *errors*, as described above in *Frequently Used Arguments*. If *universal_newlines* is True, they are opened in text mode with default encoding. Otherwise, they are opened as binary streams.

New in version 3.6: *encoding* and *errors* were added.

If given, *startupinfo* will be a *STARTUPINFO* object, which is passed to the underlying CreateProcess function. *creationflags*, if given, can be *CREATE_NEW_CONSOLE* or *CREATE_NEW_PROCESS_GROUP*. (Windows only)

Popen objects are supported as context managers via the with statement: on exit, standard file descriptors are closed, and the process is waited for.

```
with Popen(["ifconfig"], stdout=PIPE) as proc:
    log.write(proc.stdout.read())
```

Changed in version 3.2: Added context manager support.

Changed in version 3.6: Popen destructor now emits a *ResourceWarning* warning if the child process is still running.

Exceptions

Exceptions raised in the child process, before the new program has started to execute, will be re-raised in the parent. Additionally, the exception object will have one extra attribute called child_traceback, which is a string containing traceback information from the child's point of view.

The most common exception raised is *OSError*. This occurs, for example, when trying to execute a non-existent file. Applications should prepare for *OSError* exceptions.

A *ValueError* will be raised if *Popen* is called with invalid arguments.

check_call() and *check_output()* will raise *CalledProcessError* if the called process returns a non-zero return code.

All of the functions and methods that accept a *timeout* parameter, such as *call()* and *Popen.communicate()* will raise *TimeoutExpired* if the timeout expires before the process exits.

Exceptions defined in this module all inherit from *SubprocessError*.

New in version 3.3: The *SubprocessError* base class was added.

17.5.2 Security Considerations

Unlike some other popen functions, this implementation will never implicitly call a system shell. This means that all characters, including shell metacharacters, can safely be passed to child processes. If the shell is invoked explicitly, via shell=True, it is the application's responsibility to ensure that all whitespace and metacharacters are quoted appropriately to avoid shell injection vulnerabilities.

When using `shell=True`, the *shlex.quote()* function can be used to properly escape whitespace and shell metacharacters in strings that are going to be used to construct shell commands.

17.5.3 Popen Objects

Instances of the *Popen* class have the following methods:

`Popen.poll()`
Check if child process has terminated. Set and return *returncode* attribute. Otherwise, returns `None`.

`Popen.wait(`*timeout=None*`)`
Wait for child process to terminate. Set and return *returncode* attribute.

If the process does not terminate after *timeout* seconds, raise a *TimeoutExpired* exception. It is safe to catch this exception and retry the wait.

Note: This will deadlock when using `stdout=PIPE` or `stderr=PIPE` and the child process generates enough output to a pipe such that it blocks waiting for the OS pipe buffer to accept more data. Use *Popen.communicate()* when using pipes to avoid that.

Note: The function is implemented using a busy loop (non-blocking call and short sleeps). Use the *asyncio* module for an asynchronous wait: see *asyncio.create_subprocess_exec*.

Changed in version 3.3: *timeout* was added.

Deprecated since version 3.4: Do not use the *endtime* parameter. It is was unintentionally exposed in 3.3 but was left undocumented as it was intended to be private for internal use. Use *timeout* instead.

`Popen.communicate(`*input=None*, *timeout=None*`)`
Interact with process: Send data to stdin. Read data from stdout and stderr, until end-of-file is reached. Wait for process to terminate. The optional *input* argument should be data to be sent to the child process, or `None`, if no data should be sent to the child. If streams were opened in text mode, *input* must be a string. Otherwise, it must be bytes.

communicate() returns a tuple `(stdout_data, stderr_data)`. The data will be strings if streams were opened in text mode; otherwise, bytes.

Note that if you want to send data to the process's stdin, you need to create the Popen object with `stdin=PIPE`. Similarly, to get anything other than `None` in the result tuple, you need to give `stdout=PIPE` and/or `stderr=PIPE` too.

If the process does not terminate after *timeout* seconds, a *TimeoutExpired* exception will be raised. Catching this exception and retrying communication will not lose any output.

The child process is not killed if the timeout expires, so in order to cleanup properly a well-behaved application should kill the child process and finish communication:

```
proc = subprocess.Popen(...)
try:
    outs, errs = proc.communicate(timeout=15)
except TimeoutExpired:
    proc.kill()
    outs, errs = proc.communicate()
```

Note: The data read is buffered in memory, so do not use this method if the data size is large or unlimited.

Changed in version 3.3: *timeout* was added.

`Popen.send_signal(signal)`
Sends the signal *signal* to the child.

Note: On Windows, SIGTERM is an alias for `terminate()`. CTRL_C_EVENT and CTRL_BREAK_EVENT can be sent to processes started with a *creationflags* parameter which includes *CREATE_NEW_PROCESS_GROUP*.

`Popen.terminate()`
Stop the child. On Posix OSs the method sends SIGTERM to the child. On Windows the Win32 API function `TerminateProcess()` is called to stop the child.

`Popen.kill()`
Kills the child. On Posix OSs the function sends SIGKILL to the child. On Windows `kill()` is an alias for `terminate()`.

The following attributes are also available:

`Popen.args`
The *args* argument as it was passed to `Popen` – a sequence of program arguments or else a single string.

New in version 3.3.

`Popen.stdin`
If the *stdin* argument was `PIPE`, this attribute is a writeable stream object as returned by `open()`. If the *encoding* or *errors* arguments were specified or the *universal_newlines* argument was `True`, the stream is a text stream, otherwise it is a byte stream. If the *stdin* argument was not `PIPE`, this attribute is `None`.

`Popen.stdout`
If the *stdout* argument was `PIPE`, this attribute is a readable stream object as returned by `open()`. Reading from the stream provides output from the child process. If the *encoding* or *errors* arguments were specified or the *universal_newlines* argument was `True`, the stream is a text stream, otherwise it is a byte stream. If the *stdout* argument was not `PIPE`, this attribute is `None`.

`Popen.stderr`
If the *stderr* argument was `PIPE`, this attribute is a readable stream object as returned by `open()`. Reading from the stream provides error output from the child process. If the *encoding* or *errors* arguments were specified or the *universal_newlines* argument was `True`, the stream is a text stream, otherwise it is a byte stream. If the *stderr* argument was not `PIPE`, this attribute is `None`.

Warning: Use `communicate()` rather than `.stdin.write`, `.stdout.read` or `.stderr.read` to avoid deadlocks due to any of the other OS pipe buffers filling up and blocking the child process.

`Popen.pid`
The process ID of the child process.

Note that if you set the *shell* argument to `True`, this is the process ID of the spawned shell.

`Popen.returncode`
The child return code, set by `poll()` and `wait()` (and indirectly by `communicate()`). A `None` value indicates that the process hasn't terminated yet.

A negative value -N indicates that the child was terminated by signal N (POSIX only).

17.5.4 Windows Popen Helpers

The *STARTUPINFO* class and following constants are only available on Windows.

class subprocess.STARTUPINFO
Partial support of the Windows STARTUPINFO structure is used for *Popen* creation.

dwFlags
A bit field that determines whether certain *STARTUPINFO* attributes are used when the process creates a window.

```
si = subprocess.STARTUPINFO()
si.dwFlags = subprocess.STARTF_USESTDHANDLES | subprocess.STARTF_USESHOWWINDOW
```

hStdInput
If *dwFlags* specifies *STARTF_USESTDHANDLES*, this attribute is the standard input handle for the process. If *STARTF_USESTDHANDLES* is not specified, the default for standard input is the keyboard buffer.

hStdOutput
If *dwFlags* specifies *STARTF_USESTDHANDLES*, this attribute is the standard output handle for the process. Otherwise, this attribute is ignored and the default for standard output is the console window's buffer.

hStdError
If *dwFlags* specifies *STARTF_USESTDHANDLES*, this attribute is the standard error handle for the process. Otherwise, this attribute is ignored and the default for standard error is the console window's buffer.

wShowWindow
If *dwFlags* specifies *STARTF_USESHOWWINDOW*, this attribute can be any of the values that can be specified in the nCmdShow parameter for the ShowWindow function, except for SW_SHOWDEFAULT. Otherwise, this attribute is ignored.

SW_HIDE is provided for this attribute. It is used when *Popen* is called with shell=True.

Constants

The *subprocess* module exposes the following constants.

subprocess.STD_INPUT_HANDLE
The standard input device. Initially, this is the console input buffer, CONIN$.

subprocess.STD_OUTPUT_HANDLE
The standard output device. Initially, this is the active console screen buffer, CONOUT$.

subprocess.STD_ERROR_HANDLE
The standard error device. Initially, this is the active console screen buffer, CONOUT$.

subprocess.SW_HIDE
Hides the window. Another window will be activated.

subprocess.STARTF_USESTDHANDLES
Specifies that the *STARTUPINFO.hStdInput*, *STARTUPINFO.hStdOutput*, and *STARTUPINFO.hStdError* attributes contain additional information.

subprocess.STARTF_USESHOWWINDOW
Specifies that the *STARTUPINFO.wShowWindow* attribute contains additional information.

subprocess.**CREATE_NEW_CONSOLE**

The new process has a new console, instead of inheriting its parent's console (the default).

subprocess.**CREATE_NEW_PROCESS_GROUP**

A *Popen* `creationflags` parameter to specify that a new process group will be created. This flag is necessary for using `os.kill()` on the subprocess.

This flag is ignored if *CREATE_NEW_CONSOLE* is specified.

17.5.5 Older high-level API

Prior to Python 3.5, these three functions comprised the high level API to subprocess. You can now use `run()` in many cases, but lots of existing code calls these functions.

subprocess.**call**(*args*, ***, *stdin=None*, *stdout=None*, *stderr=None*, *shell=False*, *cwd=None*, *timeout=None*)

Run the command described by *args*. Wait for command to complete, then return the `returncode` attribute.

This is equivalent to:

```
run(...).returncode
```

(except that the *input* and *check* parameters are not supported)

The arguments shown above are merely the most common ones. The full function signature is largely the same as that of the *Popen* constructor - this function passes all supplied arguments other than *timeout* directly through to that interface.

Note: Do not use `stdout=PIPE` or `stderr=PIPE` with this function. The child process will block if it generates enough output to a pipe to fill up the OS pipe buffer as the pipes are not being read from.

Changed in version 3.3: *timeout* was added.

subprocess.**check_call**(*args*, ***, *stdin=None*, *stdout=None*, *stderr=None*, *shell=False*, *cwd=None*, *timeout=None*)

Run command with arguments. Wait for command to complete. If the return code was zero then return, otherwise raise `CalledProcessError`. The `CalledProcessError` object will have the return code in the `returncode` attribute.

This is equivalent to:

```
run(..., check=True)
```

(except that the *input* parameter is not supported)

The arguments shown above are merely the most common ones. The full function signature is largely the same as that of the *Popen* constructor - this function passes all supplied arguments other than *timeout* directly through to that interface.

Note: Do not use `stdout=PIPE` or `stderr=PIPE` with this function. The child process will block if it generates enough output to a pipe to fill up the OS pipe buffer as the pipes are not being read from.

Changed in version 3.3: *timeout* was added.

subprocess.**check_output**(*args*, ***, *stdin=None*, *stderr=None*, *shell=False*, *cwd=None*, *encoding=None*, *errors=None*, *universal_newlines=False*, *timeout=None*)

Run command with arguments and return its output.

If the return code was non-zero it raises a *CalledProcessError*. The *CalledProcessError* object will have the return code in the *returncode* attribute and any output in the *output* attribute.

This is equivalent to:

```
run(..., check=True, stdout=PIPE).stdout
```

The arguments shown above are merely the most common ones. The full function signature is largely the same as that of *run()* - most arguments are passed directly through to that interface. However, explicitly passing `input=None` to inherit the parent's standard input file handle is not supported.

By default, this function will return the data as encoded bytes. The actual encoding of the output data may depend on the command being invoked, so the decoding to text will often need to be handled at the application level.

This behaviour may be overridden by setting *universal_newlines* to `True` as described above in *Frequently Used Arguments*.

To also capture standard error in the result, use `stderr=subprocess.STDOUT`:

```
>>> subprocess.check_output(
...     "ls non_existent_file; exit 0",
...     stderr=subprocess.STDOUT,
...     shell=True)
'ls: non_existent_file: No such file or directory\n'
```

New in version 3.1.

Changed in version 3.3: *timeout* was added.

Changed in version 3.4: Support for the *input* keyword argument was added.

17.5.6 Replacing Older Functions with the subprocess Module

In this section, "a becomes b" means that b can be used as a replacement for a.

Note: All "a" functions in this section fail (more or less) silently if the executed program cannot be found; the "b" replacements raise *OSError* instead.

In addition, the replacements using *check_output()* will fail with a *CalledProcessError* if the requested operation produces a non-zero return code. The output is still available as the *output* attribute of the raised exception.

In the following examples, we assume that the relevant functions have already been imported from the *subprocess* module.

Replacing /bin/sh shell backquote

```
output=`mycmd myarg`
```

becomes:

```
output = check_output(["mycmd", "myarg"])
```

Replacing shell pipeline

```
output=`dmesg | grep hda`
```

becomes:

```
p1 = Popen(["dmesg"], stdout=PIPE)
p2 = Popen(["grep", "hda"], stdin=p1.stdout, stdout=PIPE)
p1.stdout.close()  # Allow p1 to receive a SIGPIPE if p2 exits.
output = p2.communicate()[0]
```

The p1.stdout.close() call after starting the p2 is important in order for p1 to receive a SIGPIPE if p2 exits before p1.

Alternatively, for trusted input, the shell's own pipeline support may still be used directly:

```
output=`dmesg | grep hda`
```

becomes:

```
output=check_output("dmesg | grep hda", shell=True)
```

Replacing os.system()

```
sts = os.system("mycmd" + " myarg")
# becomes
sts = call("mycmd" + " myarg", shell=True)
```

Notes:

- Calling the program through the shell is usually not required.

A more realistic example would look like this:

```
try:
    retcode = call("mycmd" + " myarg", shell=True)
    if retcode < 0:
        print("Child was terminated by signal", -retcode, file=sys.stderr)
    else:
        print("Child returned", retcode, file=sys.stderr)
except OSError as e:
    print("Execution failed:", e, file=sys.stderr)
```

Replacing the os.spawn family

P_NOWAIT example:

```
pid = os.spawnlp(os.P_NOWAIT, "/bin/mycmd", "mycmd", "myarg")
==>
pid = Popen(["/bin/mycmd", "myarg"]).pid
```

P_WAIT example:

```
retcode = os.spawnlp(os.P_WAIT, "/bin/mycmd", "mycmd", "myarg")
==>
retcode = call(["/bin/mycmd", "myarg"])
```

Vector example:

```
os.spawnvp(os.P_NOWAIT, path, args)
==>
Popen([path] + args[1:])
```

Environment example:

```
os.spawnlpe(os.P_NOWAIT, "/bin/mycmd", "mycmd", "myarg", env)
==>
Popen(["/bin/mycmd", "myarg"], env={"PATH": "/usr/bin"})
```

Replacing os.popen(), os.popen2(), os.popen3()

```
(child_stdin, child_stdout) = os.popen2(cmd, mode, bufsize)
==>
p = Popen(cmd, shell=True, bufsize=bufsize,
          stdin=PIPE, stdout=PIPE, close_fds=True)
(child_stdin, child_stdout) = (p.stdin, p.stdout)
```

```
(child_stdin,
 child_stdout,
 child_stderr) = os.popen3(cmd, mode, bufsize)
==>
p = Popen(cmd, shell=True, bufsize=bufsize,
          stdin=PIPE, stdout=PIPE, stderr=PIPE, close_fds=True)
(child_stdin,
 child_stdout,
 child_stderr) = (p.stdin, p.stdout, p.stderr)
```

```
(child_stdin, child_stdout_and_stderr) = os.popen4(cmd, mode, bufsize)
==>
p = Popen(cmd, shell=True, bufsize=bufsize,
          stdin=PIPE, stdout=PIPE, stderr=STDOUT, close_fds=True)
(child_stdin, child_stdout_and_stderr) = (p.stdin, p.stdout)
```

Return code handling translates as follows:

```
pipe = os.popen(cmd, 'w')
...
rc = pipe.close()
if rc is not None and rc >> 8:
    print("There were some errors")
==>
process = Popen(cmd, stdin=PIPE)
...
process.stdin.close()
if process.wait() != 0:
    print("There were some errors")
```

Replacing functions from the popen2 module

Note: If the cmd argument to popen2 functions is a string, the command is executed through /bin/sh. If it is a list, the command is directly executed.

```
(child_stdout, child_stdin) = popen2.popen2("somestring", bufsize, mode)
==>
p = Popen("somestring", shell=True, bufsize=bufsize,
          stdin=PIPE, stdout=PIPE, close_fds=True)
(child_stdout, child_stdin) = (p.stdout, p.stdin)
```

```
(child_stdout, child_stdin) = popen2.popen2(["mycmd", "myarg"], bufsize, mode)
==>
p = Popen(["mycmd", "myarg"], bufsize=bufsize,
          stdin=PIPE, stdout=PIPE, close_fds=True)
(child_stdout, child_stdin) = (p.stdout, p.stdin)
```

`popen2.Popen3` and `popen2.Popen4` basically work as *subprocess.Popen*, except that:

- *Popen* raises an exception if the execution fails.
- the *capturestderr* argument is replaced with the *stderr* argument.
- `stdin=PIPE` and `stdout=PIPE` must be specified.
- popen2 closes all file descriptors by default, but you have to specify `close_fds=True` with *Popen* to guarantee this behavior on all platforms or past Python versions.

17.5.7 Legacy Shell Invocation Functions

This module also provides the following legacy functions from the 2.x `commands` module. These operations implicitly invoke the system shell and none of the guarantees described above regarding security and exception handling consistency are valid for these functions.

`subprocess.getstatusoutput(`*cmd*`)`

Return `(exitcode, output)` of executing *cmd* in a shell.

Execute the string *cmd* in a shell with `Popen.check_output()` and return a 2-tuple `(exitcode, output)`. The locale encoding is used; see the notes on *Frequently Used Arguments* for more details.

A trailing newline is stripped from the output. The exit code for the command can be interpreted as the return code of subprocess. Example:

```
>>> subprocess.getstatusoutput('ls /bin/ls')
(0, '/bin/ls')
>>> subprocess.getstatusoutput('cat /bin/junk')
(1, 'cat: /bin/junk: No such file or directory')
>>> subprocess.getstatusoutput('/bin/junk')
(127, 'sh: /bin/junk: not found')
>>> subprocess.getstatusoutput('/bin/kill $$')
(-15, '')
```

Availability: POSIX & Windows

Changed in version 3.3.4: Windows support was added.

The function now returns (exitcode, output) instead of (status, output) as it did in Python 3.3.3 and earlier. See `WEXITSTATUS()`.

`subprocess.getoutput(`*cmd*`)`

Return output (stdout and stderr) of executing *cmd* in a shell.

Like *getstatusoutput()*, except the exit status is ignored and the return value is a string containing the command's output. Example:

```
>>> subprocess.getoutput('ls /bin/ls')
'/bin/ls'
```

Availability: POSIX & Windows

Changed in version 3.3.4: Windows support added

17.5.8 Notes

Converting an argument sequence to a string on Windows

On Windows, an *args* sequence is converted to a string that can be parsed using the following rules (which correspond to the rules used by the MS C runtime):

1. Arguments are delimited by white space, which is either a space or a tab.
2. A string surrounded by double quotation marks is interpreted as a single argument, regardless of white space contained within. A quoted string can be embedded in an argument.
3. A double quotation mark preceded by a backslash is interpreted as a literal double quotation mark.
4. Backslashes are interpreted literally, unless they immediately precede a double quotation mark.
5. If backslashes immediately precede a double quotation mark, every pair of backslashes is interpreted as a literal backslash. If the number of backslashes is odd, the last backslash escapes the next double quotation mark as described in rule 3.

See also:

`shlex` Module which provides function to parse and escape command lines.

17.6 `sched` — Event scheduler

Source code: Lib/sched.py

The `sched` module defines a class which implements a general purpose event scheduler:

class sched.scheduler(*timefunc=time.monotonic, delayfunc=time.sleep*)

The `scheduler` class defines a generic interface to scheduling events. It needs two functions to actually deal with the "outside world" — *timefunc* should be callable without arguments, and return a number (the "time", in any units whatsoever). If time.monotonic is not available, the *timefunc* default is time.time instead. The *delayfunc* function should be callable with one argument, compatible with the output of *timefunc*, and should delay that many time units. *delayfunc* will also be called with the argument `0` after each event is run to allow other threads an opportunity to run in multi-threaded applications.

Changed in version 3.3: *timefunc* and *delayfunc* parameters are optional.

Changed in version 3.3: `scheduler` class can be safely used in multi-threaded environments.

Example:

```
>>> import sched, time
>>> s = sched.scheduler(time.time, time.sleep)
>>> def print_time(a='default'):
...     print("From print_time", time.time(), a)
...
>>> def print_some_times():
...     print(time.time())
...     s.enter(10, 1, print_time)
...     s.enter(5, 2, print_time, argument=('positional',))
...     s.enter(5, 1, print_time, kwargs={'a': 'keyword'})
...     s.run()
...     print(time.time())
...
>>> print_some_times()
930343690.257
From print_time 930343695.274 positional
From print_time 930343695.275 keyword
From print_time 930343700.273 default
930343700.276
```

17.6.1 Scheduler Objects

scheduler instances have the following methods and attributes:

`scheduler.enterabs`(*time, priority, action, argument=(), kwargs={}*)

Schedule a new event. The *time* argument should be a numeric type compatible with the return value of the *timefunc* function passed to the constructor. Events scheduled for the same *time* will be executed in the order of their *priority*. A lower number represents a higher priority.

Executing the event means executing `action(*argument, **kwargs)`. *argument* is a sequence holding the positional arguments for *action*. *kwargs* is a dictionary holding the keyword arguments for *action*.

Return value is an event which may be used for later cancellation of the event (see *cancel()*).

Changed in version 3.3: *argument* parameter is optional.

New in version 3.3: *kwargs* parameter was added.

`scheduler.enter`(*delay, priority, action, argument=(), kwargs={}*)

Schedule an event for *delay* more time units. Other than the relative time, the other arguments, the effect and the return value are the same as those for *enterabs()*.

Changed in version 3.3: *argument* parameter is optional.

New in version 3.3: *kwargs* parameter was added.

`scheduler.cancel`(*event*)

Remove the event from the queue. If *event* is not an event currently in the queue, this method will raise a *ValueError*.

`scheduler.empty()`

Return true if the event queue is empty.

`scheduler.run`(*blocking=True*)

Run all scheduled events. This method will wait (using the `delayfunc()` function passed to the constructor) for the next event, then execute it and so on until there are no more scheduled events.

If *blocking* is false executes the scheduled events due to expire soonest (if any) and then return the deadline of the next scheduled call in the scheduler (if any).

Either *action* or *delayfunc* can raise an exception. In either case, the scheduler will maintain a consistent state and propagate the exception. If an exception is raised by *action*, the event will not be attempted in future calls to `run()`.

If a sequence of events takes longer to run than the time available before the next event, the scheduler will simply fall behind. No events will be dropped; the calling code is responsible for canceling events which are no longer pertinent.

New in version 3.3: *blocking* parameter was added.

`scheduler.queue`
Read-only attribute returning a list of upcoming events in the order they will be run. Each event is shown as a *named tuple* with the following fields: time, priority, action, argument, kwargs.

17.7 queue — A synchronized queue class

Source code: Lib/queue.py

The `queue` module implements multi-producer, multi-consumer queues. It is especially useful in threaded programming when information must be exchanged safely between multiple threads. The `Queue` class in this module implements all the required locking semantics. It depends on the availability of thread support in Python; see the `threading` module.

The module implements three types of queue, which differ only in the order in which the entries are retrieved. In a FIFO queue, the first tasks added are the first retrieved. In a LIFO queue, the most recently added entry is the first retrieved (operating like a stack). With a priority queue, the entries are kept sorted (using the `heapq` module) and the lowest valued entry is retrieved first.

Internally, the module uses locks to temporarily block competing threads; however, it is not designed to handle reentrancy within a thread.

The `queue` module defines the following classes and exceptions:

`class queue.Queue(maxsize=0)`
Constructor for a FIFO queue. *maxsize* is an integer that sets the upperbound limit on the number of items that can be placed in the queue. Insertion will block once this size has been reached, until queue items are consumed. If *maxsize* is less than or equal to zero, the queue size is infinite.

`class queue.LifoQueue(maxsize=0)`
Constructor for a LIFO queue. *maxsize* is an integer that sets the upperbound limit on the number of items that can be placed in the queue. Insertion will block once this size has been reached, until queue items are consumed. If *maxsize* is less than or equal to zero, the queue size is infinite.

`class queue.PriorityQueue(maxsize=0)`
Constructor for a priority queue. *maxsize* is an integer that sets the upperbound limit on the number of items that can be placed in the queue. Insertion will block once this size has been reached, until queue items are consumed. If *maxsize* is less than or equal to zero, the queue size is infinite.

The lowest valued entries are retrieved first (the lowest valued entry is the one returned by `sorted(list(entries))[0]`). A typical pattern for entries is a tuple in the form: `(priority_number, data)`.

`exception queue.Empty`
Exception raised when non-blocking `get()` (or `get_nowait()`) is called on a `Queue` object which is empty.

`exception queue.Full`
Exception raised when non-blocking `put()` (or `put_nowait()`) is called on a `Queue` object which is full.

17.7.1 Queue Objects

Queue objects (*Queue*, *LifoQueue*, or *PriorityQueue*) provide the public methods described below.

Queue.qsize()
Return the approximate size of the queue. Note, qsize() > 0 doesn't guarantee that a subsequent get() will not block, nor will qsize() < maxsize guarantee that put() will not block.

Queue.empty()
Return `True` if the queue is empty, `False` otherwise. If empty() returns `True` it doesn't guarantee that a subsequent call to put() will not block. Similarly, if empty() returns `False` it doesn't guarantee that a subsequent call to get() will not block.

Queue.full()
Return `True` if the queue is full, `False` otherwise. If full() returns `True` it doesn't guarantee that a subsequent call to get() will not block. Similarly, if full() returns `False` it doesn't guarantee that a subsequent call to put() will not block.

Queue.put(*item*, *block=True*, *timeout=None*)
Put *item* into the queue. If optional args *block* is true and *timeout* is `None` (the default), block if necessary until a free slot is available. If *timeout* is a positive number, it blocks at most *timeout* seconds and raises the *Full* exception if no free slot was available within that time. Otherwise (*block* is false), put an item on the queue if a free slot is immediately available, else raise the *Full* exception (*timeout* is ignored in that case).

Queue.put_nowait(*item*)
Equivalent to `put(item, False)`.

Queue.get(*block=True*, *timeout=None*)
Remove and return an item from the queue. If optional args *block* is true and *timeout* is `None` (the default), block if necessary until an item is available. If *timeout* is a positive number, it blocks at most *timeout* seconds and raises the *Empty* exception if no item was available within that time. Otherwise (*block* is false), return an item if one is immediately available, else raise the *Empty* exception (*timeout* is ignored in that case).

Queue.get_nowait()
Equivalent to `get(False)`.

Two methods are offered to support tracking whether enqueued tasks have been fully processed by daemon consumer threads.

Queue.task_done()
Indicate that a formerly enqueued task is complete. Used by queue consumer threads. For each *get()* used to fetch a task, a subsequent call to *task_done()* tells the queue that the processing on the task is complete.

If a *join()* is currently blocking, it will resume when all items have been processed (meaning that a *task_done()* call was received for every item that had been *put()* into the queue).

Raises a *ValueError* if called more times than there were items placed in the queue.

Queue.join()
Blocks until all items in the queue have been gotten and processed.

The count of unfinished tasks goes up whenever an item is added to the queue. The count goes down whenever a consumer thread calls *task_done()* to indicate that the item was retrieved and all work on it is complete. When the count of unfinished tasks drops to zero, *join()* unblocks.

Example of how to wait for enqueued tasks to be completed:

```
def worker():
    while True:
```

```
        item = q.get()
        if item is None:
            break
        do_work(item)
        q.task_done()

q = queue.Queue()
threads = []
for i in range(num_worker_threads):
    t = threading.Thread(target=worker)
    t.start()
    threads.append(t)

for item in source():
    q.put(item)

# block until all tasks are done
q.join()

# stop workers
for i in range(num_worker_threads):
    q.put(None)
for t in threads:
    t.join()
```

See also:

Class *multiprocessing.Queue* A queue class for use in a multi-processing (rather than multi-threading) context.

collections.deque is an alternative implementation of unbounded queues with fast atomic *append()* and *popleft()* operations that do not require locking.

The following are support modules for some of the above services:

17.8 dummy_threading — Drop-in replacement for the threading module

Source code: Lib/dummy_threading.py

This module provides a duplicate interface to the *threading* module. It is meant to be imported when the *_thread* module is not provided on a platform.

Suggested usage is:

```
try:
    import threading
except ImportError:
    import dummy_threading as threading
```

Be careful to not use this module where deadlock might occur from a thread being created that blocks waiting for another thread to be created. This often occurs with blocking I/O.

17.9 _thread — Low-level threading API

This module provides low-level primitives for working with multiple threads (also called *light-weight processes* or *tasks*) — multiple threads of control sharing their global data space. For synchronization, simple locks (also called *mutexes* or *binary semaphores*) are provided. The `threading` module provides an easier to use and higher-level threading API built on top of this module.

The module is optional. It is supported on Windows, Linux, SGI IRIX, Solaris 2.x, as well as on systems that have a POSIX thread (a.k.a. "pthread") implementation. For systems lacking the `_thread` module, the `_dummy_thread` module is available. It duplicates this module's interface and can be used as a drop-in replacement.

It defines the following constants and functions:

exception _thread.error
: Raised on thread-specific errors.

  Changed in version 3.3: This is now a synonym of the built-in `RuntimeError`.

_thread.LockType
: This is the type of lock objects.

_thread.start_new_thread(*function*, *args*[, *kwargs*])
: Start a new thread and return its identifier. The thread executes the function *function* with the argument list *args* (which must be a tuple). The optional *kwargs* argument specifies a dictionary of keyword arguments. When the function returns, the thread silently exits. When the function terminates with an unhandled exception, a stack trace is printed and then the thread exits (but other threads continue to run).

_thread.interrupt_main()
: Raise a `KeyboardInterrupt` exception in the main thread. A subthread can use this function to interrupt the main thread.

_thread.exit()
: Raise the `SystemExit` exception. When not caught, this will cause the thread to exit silently.

_thread.allocate_lock()
: Return a new lock object. Methods of locks are described below. The lock is initially unlocked.

_thread.get_ident()
: Return the 'thread identifier' of the current thread. This is a nonzero integer. Its value has no direct meaning; it is intended as a magic cookie to be used e.g. to index a dictionary of thread-specific data. Thread identifiers may be recycled when a thread exits and another thread is created.

_thread.stack_size([*size*])
: Return the thread stack size used when creating new threads. The optional *size* argument specifies the stack size to be used for subsequently created threads, and must be 0 (use platform or configured default) or a positive integer value of at least 32,768 (32 KiB). If *size* is not specified, 0 is used. If changing the thread stack size is unsupported, a `RuntimeError` is raised. If the specified stack size is invalid, a `ValueError` is raised and the stack size is unmodified. 32 KiB is currently the minimum supported stack size value to guarantee sufficient stack space for the interpreter itself. Note that some platforms may have particular restrictions on values for the stack size, such as requiring a minimum stack size > 32 KiB or requiring allocation in multiples of the system memory page size - platform documentation should be referred to for more information (4 KiB pages are common; using multiples of 4096 for the stack size is the suggested approach in the absence of more specific information). Availability: Windows, systems with POSIX threads.

`_thread.TIMEOUT_MAX`

The maximum value allowed for the *timeout* parameter of `Lock.acquire()`. Specifying a timeout greater than this value will raise an *OverflowError*.

New in version 3.2.

Lock objects have the following methods:

`lock.acquire(waitflag=1, timeout=-1)`

Without any optional argument, this method acquires the lock unconditionally, if necessary waiting until it is released by another thread (only one thread at a time can acquire a lock — that's their reason for existence).

If the integer *waitflag* argument is present, the action depends on its value: if it is zero, the lock is only acquired if it can be acquired immediately without waiting, while if it is nonzero, the lock is acquired unconditionally as above.

If the floating-point *timeout* argument is present and positive, it specifies the maximum wait time in seconds before returning. A negative *timeout* argument specifies an unbounded wait. You cannot specify a *timeout* if *waitflag* is zero.

The return value is `True` if the lock is acquired successfully, `False` if not.

Changed in version 3.2: The *timeout* parameter is new.

Changed in version 3.2: Lock acquires can now be interrupted by signals on POSIX.

`lock.release()`

Releases the lock. The lock must have been acquired earlier, but not necessarily by the same thread.

`lock.locked()`

Return the status of the lock: `True` if it has been acquired by some thread, `False` if not.

In addition to these methods, lock objects can also be used via the `with` statement, e.g.:

```
import _thread

a_lock = _thread.allocate_lock()

with a_lock:
    print("a_lock is locked while this executes")
```

Caveats:

- Threads interact strangely with interrupts: the *KeyboardInterrupt* exception will be received by an arbitrary thread. (When the *signal* module is available, interrupts always go to the main thread.)
- Calling *sys.exit()* or raising the *SystemExit* exception is equivalent to calling *_thread.exit()*.
- It is not possible to interrupt the `acquire()` method on a lock — the *KeyboardInterrupt* exception will happen after the lock has been acquired.
- When the main thread exits, it is system defined whether the other threads survive. On most systems, they are killed without executing `try` ... `finally` clauses or executing object destructors.
- When the main thread exits, it does not do any of its usual cleanup (except that `try` ... `finally` clauses are honored), and the standard I/O files are not flushed.

17.10 `_dummy_thread` — Drop-in replacement for the `_thread` module

Source code: Lib/_dummy_thread.py

This module provides a duplicate interface to the *_thread* module. It is meant to be imported when the *_thread* module is not provided on a platform.

Suggested usage is:

```
try:
    import _thread
except ImportError:
    import _dummy_thread as _thread
```

Be careful to not use this module where deadlock might occur from a thread being created that blocks waiting for another thread to be created. This often occurs with blocking I/O.

CHAPTER

EIGHTEEN

INTERPROCESS COMMUNICATION AND NETWORKING

The modules described in this chapter provide mechanisms for different processes to communicate.

Some modules only work for two processes that are on the same machine, e.g. *signal* and *mmap*. Other modules support networking protocols that two or more processes can use to communicate across machines.

The list of modules described in this chapter is:

18.1 socket — Low-level networking interface

Source code: Lib/socket.py

This module provides access to the BSD *socket* interface. It is available on all modern Unix systems, Windows, MacOS, and probably additional platforms.

Note: Some behavior may be platform dependent, since calls are made to the operating system socket APIs.

The Python interface is a straightforward transliteration of the Unix system call and library interface for sockets to Python's object-oriented style: the *socket()* function returns a *socket object* whose methods implement the various socket system calls. Parameter types are somewhat higher-level than in the C interface: as with `read()` and `write()` operations on Python files, buffer allocation on receive operations is automatic, and buffer length is implicit on send operations.

See also:

Module *socketserver* Classes that simplify writing network servers.

Module *ssl* A TLS/SSL wrapper for socket objects.

18.1.1 Socket families

Depending on the system and the build options, various socket families are supported by this module.

The address format required by a particular socket object is automatically selected based on the address family specified when the socket object was created. Socket addresses are represented as follows:

- The address of an *AF_UNIX* socket bound to a file system node is represented as a string, using the file system encoding and the `'surrogateescape'` error handler (see PEP 383). An address in Linux's abstract namespace is returned as a *bytes-like object* with an initial null byte; note that sockets in this namespace can communicate with normal file system sockets, so programs intended to run on Linux may need to deal with both types of address. A string or bytes-like object can be used for either type of address when passing it as an argument.

Changed in version 3.3: Previously, *AF_UNIX* socket paths were assumed to use UTF-8 encoding.

Changed in version 3.5: Writable *bytes-like object* is now accepted.

- A pair `(host, port)` is used for the *AF_INET* address family, where *host* is a string representing either a hostname in Internet domain notation like `'daring.cwi.nl'` or an IPv4 address like `'100.50.200.5'`, and *port* is an integer.
- For *AF_INET6* address family, a four-tuple `(host, port, flowinfo, scopeid)` is used, where *flowinfo* and *scopeid* represent the `sin6_flowinfo` and `sin6_scope_id` members in `struct sockaddr_in6` in C. For `socket` module methods, *flowinfo* and *scopeid* can be omitted just for backward compatibility. Note, however, omission of *scopeid* can cause problems in manipulating scoped IPv6 addresses.
- `AF_NETLINK` sockets are represented as pairs `(pid, groups)`.
- Linux-only support for TIPC is available using the `AF_TIPC` address family. TIPC is an open, non-IP based networked protocol designed for use in clustered computer environments. Addresses are represented by a tuple, and the fields depend on the address type. The general tuple form is `(addr_type, v1, v2, v3 [, scope])`, where:
  - *addr_type* is one of `TIPC_ADDR_NAMESEQ`, `TIPC_ADDR_NAME`, or `TIPC_ADDR_ID`.
  - *scope* is one of `TIPC_ZONE_SCOPE`, `TIPC_CLUSTER_SCOPE`, and `TIPC_NODE_SCOPE`.
  - If *addr_type* is `TIPC_ADDR_NAME`, then *v1* is the server type, *v2* is the port identifier, and *v3* should be 0.

    If *addr_type* is `TIPC_ADDR_NAMESEQ`, then *v1* is the server type, *v2* is the lower port number, and *v3* is the upper port number.

    If *addr_type* is `TIPC_ADDR_ID`, then *v1* is the node, *v2* is the reference, and *v3* should be set to 0.
- A tuple `(interface, )` is used for the *AF_CAN* address family, where *interface* is a string representing a network interface name like `'can0'`. The network interface name `''` can be used to receive packets from all network interfaces of this family.
- A string or a tuple `(id, unit)` is used for the `SYSPROTO_CONTROL` protocol of the `PF_SYSTEM` family. The string is the name of a kernel control using a dynamically-assigned ID. The tuple can be used if ID and unit number of the kernel control are known or if a registered ID is used.

  New in version 3.3.
- `AF_BLUETOOTH` supports the following protocols and address formats:
  - `BTPROTO_L2CAP` accepts `(bdaddr, psm)` where `bdaddr` is the Bluetooth address as a string and `psm` is an integer.
  - `BTPROTO_RFCOMM` accepts `(bdaddr, channel)` where `bdaddr` is the Bluetooth address as a string and `channel` is an integer.
  - `BTPROTO_HCI` accepts `(device_id,)` where `device_id` is either an integer or a string with the Bluetooth address of the interface. (This depends on your OS; NetBSD and DragonFlyBSD expect a Bluetooth address while everything else expects an integer.)

    Changed in version 3.2: NetBSD and DragonFlyBSD support added.
  - `BTPROTO_SCO` accepts `bdaddr` where `bdaddr` is a `bytes` object containing the Bluetooth address in a string format. (ex. `b'12:23:34:45:56:67'`) This protocol is not supported under FreeBSD.
- *AF_ALG* is a Linux-only socket based interface to Kernel cryptography. An algorithm socket is configured with a tuple of two to four elements `(type, name [, feat [, mask]])`, where:
  - *type* is the algorithm type as string, e.g. `aead`, `hash`, `skcipher` or `rng`.
  - *name* is the algorithm name and operation mode as string, e.g. `sha256`, `hmac(sha256)`, `cbc(aes)` or `drbg_nopr_ctr_aes256`.

- *feat* and *mask* are unsigned 32bit integers.

  Availability Linux 2.6.38, some algorithm types require more recent Kernels.

  New in version 3.6.

- Certain other address families (`AF_PACKET`, *AF_CAN*) support specific representations.

For IPv4 addresses, two special forms are accepted instead of a host address: the empty string represents `INADDR_ANY`, and the string `'<broadcast>'` represents `INADDR_BROADCAST`. This behavior is not compatible with IPv6, therefore, you may want to avoid these if you intend to support IPv6 with your Python programs.

If you use a hostname in the *host* portion of IPv4/v6 socket address, the program may show a nondeterministic behavior, as Python uses the first address returned from the DNS resolution. The socket address will be resolved differently into an actual IPv4/v6 address, depending on the results from DNS resolution and/or the host configuration. For deterministic behavior use a numeric address in *host* portion.

All errors raise exceptions. The normal exceptions for invalid argument types and out-of-memory conditions can be raised; starting from Python 3.3, errors related to socket or address semantics raise *OSError* or one of its subclasses (they used to raise *socket.error*).

Non-blocking mode is supported through *setblocking()*. A generalization of this based on timeouts is supported through *settimeout()*.

18.1.2 Module contents

The module *socket* exports the following elements.

Exceptions

exception socket.error
A deprecated alias of *OSError*.

Changed in version 3.3: Following PEP 3151, this class was made an alias of *OSError*.

exception socket.herror
A subclass of *OSError*, this exception is raised for address-related errors, i.e. for functions that use *h_errno* in the POSIX C API, including *gethostbyname_ex()* and *gethostbyaddr()*. The accompanying value is a pair `(h_errno, string)` representing an error returned by a library call. *h_errno* is a numeric value, while *string* represents the description of *h_errno*, as returned by the `hstrerror()` C function.

Changed in version 3.3: This class was made a subclass of *OSError*.

exception socket.gaierror
A subclass of *OSError*, this exception is raised for address-related errors by *getaddrinfo()* and *getnameinfo()*. The accompanying value is a pair `(error, string)` representing an error returned by a library call. *string* represents the description of *error*, as returned by the `gai_strerror()` C function. The numeric *error* value will match one of the `EAI_*` constants defined in this module.

Changed in version 3.3: This class was made a subclass of *OSError*.

exception socket.timeout
A subclass of *OSError*, this exception is raised when a timeout occurs on a socket which has had timeouts enabled via a prior call to *settimeout()* (or implicitly through *setdefaulttimeout()*). The accompanying value is a string whose value is currently always "timed out".

Changed in version 3.3: This class was made a subclass of *OSError*.

Constants

The AF_* and SOCK_* constants are now `AddressFamily` and `SocketKind` *IntEnum* collections.

New in version 3.4.

`socket.AF_UNIX`
`socket.AF_INET`
`socket.AF_INET6`
These constants represent the address (and protocol) families, used for the first argument to `socket()`. If the `AF_UNIX` constant is not defined then this protocol is unsupported. More constants may be available depending on the system.

`socket.SOCK_STREAM`
`socket.SOCK_DGRAM`
`socket.SOCK_RAW`
`socket.SOCK_RDM`
`socket.SOCK_SEQPACKET`
These constants represent the socket types, used for the second argument to `socket()`. More constants may be available depending on the system. (Only `SOCK_STREAM` and `SOCK_DGRAM` appear to be generally useful.)

`socket.SOCK_CLOEXEC`
`socket.SOCK_NONBLOCK`
These two constants, if defined, can be combined with the socket types and allow you to set some flags atomically (thus avoiding possible race conditions and the need for separate calls).

See also:

Secure File Descriptor Handling for a more thorough explanation.

Availability: Linux >= 2.6.27.

New in version 3.2.

`SO_*`
`socket.SOMAXCONN`
`MSG_*`
`SOL_*`
`SCM_*`
`IPPROTO_*`
`IPPORT_*`
`INADDR_*`
`IP_*`
`IPV6_*`
`EAI_*`
`AI_*`
`NI_*`
`TCP_*`
Many constants of these forms, documented in the Unix documentation on sockets and/or the IP protocol, are also defined in the socket module. They are generally used in arguments to the `setsockopt()` and `getsockopt()` methods of socket objects. In most cases, only those symbols that are defined in the Unix header files are defined; for a few symbols, default values are provided.

Changed in version 3.6: `SO_DOMAIN`, `SO_PROTOCOL`, `SO_PEERSEC`, `SO_PASSSEC`, `TCP_USER_TIMEOUT`, `TCP_CONGESTION` were added.

`socket.AF_CAN`
`socket.PF_CAN`
`SOL_CAN_*`

CAN_*

Many constants of these forms, documented in the Linux documentation, are also defined in the socket module.

Availability: Linux >= 2.6.25.

New in version 3.3.

socket.**CAN_BCM**
CAN_BCM_*

CAN_BCM, in the CAN protocol family, is the broadcast manager (BCM) protocol. Broadcast manager constants, documented in the Linux documentation, are also defined in the socket module.

Availability: Linux >= 2.6.25.

New in version 3.4.

socket.**CAN_RAW_FD_FRAMES**

Enables CAN FD support in a CAN_RAW socket. This is disabled by default. This allows your application to send both CAN and CAN FD frames; however, you one must accept both CAN and CAN FD frames when reading from the socket.

This constant is documented in the Linux documentation.

Availability: Linux >= 3.6.

New in version 3.5.

socket.**AF_RDS**
socket.**PF_RDS**
socket.**SOL_RDS**
RDS_*

Many constants of these forms, documented in the Linux documentation, are also defined in the socket module.

Availability: Linux >= 2.6.30.

New in version 3.3.

socket.**SIO_RCVALL**
socket.**SIO_KEEPALIVE_VALS**
socket.**SIO_LOOPBACK_FAST_PATH**
RCVALL_*

Constants for Windows' WSAIoctl(). The constants are used as arguments to the *ioctl()* method of socket objects.

Changed in version 3.6: `SIO_LOOPBACK_FAST_PATH` was added.

TIPC_*

TIPC related constants, matching the ones exported by the C socket API. See the TIPC documentation for more information.

socket.**AF_ALG**
socket.**SOL_ALG**
ALG_*

Constants for Linux Kernel cryptography.

Availability: Linux >= 2.6.38.

New in version 3.6.

socket.**AF_LINK**

Availability: BSD, OSX.

New in version 3.4.

socket.**has_ipv6**
This constant contains a boolean value which indicates if IPv6 is supported on this platform.

socket.**BDADDR_ANY**
socket.**BDADDR_LOCAL**
These are string constants containing Bluetooth addresses with special meanings. For example, *BDADDR_ANY* can be used to indicate any address when specifying the binding socket with BTPROTO_RFCOMM.

socket.**HCI_FILTER**
socket.**HCI_TIME_STAMP**
socket.**HCI_DATA_DIR**
For use with BTPROTO_HCI. *HCI_FILTER* is not available for NetBSD or DragonFlyBSD. *HCI_TIME_STAMP* and *HCI_DATA_DIR* are not available for FreeBSD, NetBSD, or DragonFlyBSD.

Functions

Creating sockets

The following functions all create *socket objects*.

socket.**socket**(*family=AF_INET, type=SOCK_STREAM, proto=0, fileno=None*)
Create a new socket using the given address family, socket type and protocol number. The address family should be *AF_INET* (the default), *AF_INET6*, *AF_UNIX*, *AF_CAN* or *AF_RDS*. The socket type should be *SOCK_STREAM* (the default), *SOCK_DGRAM*, *SOCK_RAW* or perhaps one of the other SOCK_ constants. The protocol number is usually zero and may be omitted or in the case where the address family is *AF_CAN* the protocol should be one of CAN_RAW or *CAN_BCM*. If *fileno* is specified, the other arguments are ignored, causing the socket with the specified file descriptor to return. Unlike `socket.fromfd()`, *fileno* will return the same socket and not a duplicate. This may help close a detached socket using `socket.close()`.

The newly created socket is *non-inheritable*.

Changed in version 3.3: The AF_CAN family was added. The AF_RDS family was added.

Changed in version 3.4: The CAN_BCM protocol was added.

Changed in version 3.4: The returned socket is now non-inheritable.

socket.**socketpair**([*family*[, *type*[, *proto*]]])
Build a pair of connected socket objects using the given address family, socket type, and protocol number. Address family, socket type, and protocol number are as for the `socket()` function above. The default family is *AF_UNIX* if defined on the platform; otherwise, the default is *AF_INET*.

The newly created sockets are *non-inheritable*.

Changed in version 3.2: The returned socket objects now support the whole socket API, rather than a subset.

Changed in version 3.4: The returned sockets are now non-inheritable.

Changed in version 3.5: Windows support added.

socket.**create_connection**(*address*[, *timeout*[, *source_address*]])
Connect to a TCP service listening on the Internet *address* (a 2-tuple `(host, port)`), and return the socket object. This is a higher-level function than `socket.connect()`: if *host* is a non-numeric hostname, it will try to resolve it for both *AF_INET* and *AF_INET6*, and then try to connect to all possible addresses in turn until a connection succeeds. This makes it easy to write clients that are compatible to both IPv4 and IPv6.

Passing the optional *timeout* parameter will set the timeout on the socket instance before attempting to connect. If no *timeout* is supplied, the global default timeout setting returned by `getdefaulttimeout()` is used.

If supplied, *source_address* must be a 2-tuple `(host, port)` for the socket to bind to as its source address before connecting. If host or port are '' or 0 respectively the OS default behavior will be used.

Changed in version 3.2: *source_address* was added.

`socket.fromfd(fd, family, type, proto=0)`

Duplicate the file descriptor *fd* (an integer as returned by a file object's `fileno()` method) and build a socket object from the result. Address family, socket type and protocol number are as for the `socket()` function above. The file descriptor should refer to a socket, but this is not checked — subsequent operations on the object may fail if the file descriptor is invalid. This function is rarely needed, but can be used to get or set socket options on a socket passed to a program as standard input or output (such as a server started by the Unix inet daemon). The socket is assumed to be in blocking mode.

The newly created socket is *non-inheritable*.

Changed in version 3.4: The returned socket is now non-inheritable.

`socket.fromshare(data)`

Instantiate a socket from data obtained from the `socket.share()` method. The socket is assumed to be in blocking mode.

Availability: Windows.

New in version 3.3.

`socket.SocketType`

This is a Python type object that represents the socket object type. It is the same as `type(socket(...))`.

Other functions

The `socket` module also offers various network-related services:

`socket.getaddrinfo(host, port, family=0, type=0, proto=0, flags=0)`

Translate the *host/port* argument into a sequence of 5-tuples that contain all the necessary arguments for creating a socket connected to that service. *host* is a domain name, a string representation of an IPv4/v6 address or `None`. *port* is a string service name such as `'http'`, a numeric port number or `None`. By passing `None` as the value of *host* and *port*, you can pass `NULL` to the underlying C API.

The *family*, *type* and *proto* arguments can be optionally specified in order to narrow the list of addresses returned. Passing zero as a value for each of these arguments selects the full range of results. The *flags* argument can be one or several of the `AI_*` constants, and will influence how results are computed and returned. For example, `AI_NUMERICHOST` will disable domain name resolution and will raise an error if *host* is a domain name.

The function returns a list of 5-tuples with the following structure:

`(family, type, proto, canonname, sockaddr)`

In these tuples, *family*, *type*, *proto* are all integers and are meant to be passed to the `socket()` function. *canonname* will be a string representing the canonical name of the *host* if `AI_CANONNAME` is part of the *flags* argument; else *canonname* will be empty. *sockaddr* is a tuple describing a socket address, whose format depends on the returned *family* (a `(address, port)` 2-tuple for *AF_INET*, a `(address, port, flow info, scope id)` 4-tuple for *AF_INET6*), and is meant to be passed to the `socket.connect()` method.

The following example fetches address information for a hypothetical TCP connection to `example.org` on port 80 (results may differ on your system if IPv6 isn't enabled):

```
>>> socket.getaddrinfo("example.org", 80, proto=socket.IPPROTO_TCP)
[(<AddressFamily.AF_INET6: 10>, <SocketType.SOCK_STREAM: 1>,
 6, '', ('2606:2800:220:1:248:1893:25c8:1946', 80, 0, 0)),
 (<AddressFamily.AF_INET: 2>, <SocketType.SOCK_STREAM: 1>,
 6, '', ('93.184.216.34', 80))]
```

Changed in version 3.2: parameters can now be passed using keyword arguments.

`socket.`**`getfqdn`**`(`[*name*]`)`

Return a fully qualified domain name for *name*. If *name* is omitted or empty, it is interpreted as the local host. To find the fully qualified name, the hostname returned by *gethostbyaddr()* is checked, followed by aliases for the host, if available. The first name which includes a period is selected. In case no fully qualified domain name is available, the hostname as returned by *gethostname()* is returned.

`socket.`**`gethostbyname`**`(`*hostname*`)`

Translate a host name to IPv4 address format. The IPv4 address is returned as a string, such as `'100.50.200.5'`. If the host name is an IPv4 address itself it is returned unchanged. See *gethostbyname_ex()* for a more complete interface. *gethostbyname()* does not support IPv6 name resolution, and *getaddrinfo()* should be used instead for IPv4/v6 dual stack support.

`socket.`**`gethostbyname_ex`**`(`*hostname*`)`

Translate a host name to IPv4 address format, extended interface. Return a triple `(hostname, aliaslist, ipaddrlist)` where *hostname* is the primary host name responding to the given *ip_address*, *aliaslist* is a (possibly empty) list of alternative host names for the same address, and *ipaddrlist* is a list of IPv4 addresses for the same interface on the same host (often but not always a single address). *gethostbyname_ex()* does not support IPv6 name resolution, and *getaddrinfo()* should be used instead for IPv4/v6 dual stack support.

`socket.`**`gethostname`**`()`

Return a string containing the hostname of the machine where the Python interpreter is currently executing.

Note: *gethostname()* doesn't always return the fully qualified domain name; use *getfqdn()* for that.

`socket.`**`gethostbyaddr`**`(`*ip_address*`)`

Return a triple `(hostname, aliaslist, ipaddrlist)` where *hostname* is the primary host name responding to the given *ip_address*, *aliaslist* is a (possibly empty) list of alternative host names for the same address, and *ipaddrlist* is a list of IPv4/v6 addresses for the same interface on the same host (most likely containing only a single address). To find the fully qualified domain name, use the function *getfqdn()*. *gethostbyaddr()* supports both IPv4 and IPv6.

`socket.`**`getnameinfo`**`(`*sockaddr*, *flags*`)`

Translate a socket address *sockaddr* into a 2-tuple `(host, port)`. Depending on the settings of *flags*, the result can contain a fully-qualified domain name or numeric address representation in *host*. Similarly, *port* can contain a string port name or a numeric port number.

`socket.`**`getprotobyname`**`(`*protocolname*`)`

Translate an Internet protocol name (for example, `'icmp'`) to a constant suitable for passing as the (optional) third argument to the *socket()* function. This is usually only needed for sockets opened in "raw" mode (*SOCK_RAW*); for the normal socket modes, the correct protocol is chosen automatically if the protocol is omitted or zero.

`socket.`**`getservbyname`**`(`*servicename*[, *protocolname*]`)`

Translate an Internet service name and protocol name to a port number for that service. The optional protocol name, if given, should be `'tcp'` or `'udp'`, otherwise any protocol will match.

`socket.getservbyport(port[, protocolname])`
Translate an Internet port number and protocol name to a service name for that service. The optional protocol name, if given, should be `'tcp'` or `'udp'`, otherwise any protocol will match.

`socket.ntohl(x)`
Convert 32-bit positive integers from network to host byte order. On machines where the host byte order is the same as network byte order, this is a no-op; otherwise, it performs a 4-byte swap operation.

`socket.ntohs(x)`
Convert 16-bit positive integers from network to host byte order. On machines where the host byte order is the same as network byte order, this is a no-op; otherwise, it performs a 2-byte swap operation.

`socket.htonl(x)`
Convert 32-bit positive integers from host to network byte order. On machines where the host byte order is the same as network byte order, this is a no-op; otherwise, it performs a 4-byte swap operation.

`socket.htons(x)`
Convert 16-bit positive integers from host to network byte order. On machines where the host byte order is the same as network byte order, this is a no-op; otherwise, it performs a 2-byte swap operation.

`socket.inet_aton(ip_string)`
Convert an IPv4 address from dotted-quad string format (for example, '123.45.67.89') to 32-bit packed binary format, as a bytes object four characters in length. This is useful when conversing with a program that uses the standard C library and needs objects of type `struct in_addr`, which is the C type for the 32-bit packed binary this function returns.

`inet_aton()` also accepts strings with less than three dots; see the Unix manual page ***inet(3)*** for details.

If the IPv4 address string passed to this function is invalid, `OSError` will be raised. Note that exactly what is valid depends on the underlying C implementation of `inet_aton()`.

`inet_aton()` does not support IPv6, and `inet_pton()` should be used instead for IPv4/v6 dual stack support.

`socket.inet_ntoa(packed_ip)`
Convert a 32-bit packed IPv4 address (a *bytes-like object* four bytes in length) to its standard dotted-quad string representation (for example, '123.45.67.89'). This is useful when conversing with a program that uses the standard C library and needs objects of type `struct in_addr`, which is the C type for the 32-bit packed binary data this function takes as an argument.

If the byte sequence passed to this function is not exactly 4 bytes in length, `OSError` will be raised. `inet_ntoa()` does not support IPv6, and `inet_ntop()` should be used instead for IPv4/v6 dual stack support.

Changed in version 3.5: Writable *bytes-like object* is now accepted.

`socket.inet_pton(address_family, ip_string)`
Convert an IP address from its family-specific string format to a packed, binary format. `inet_pton()` is useful when a library or network protocol calls for an object of type `struct in_addr` (similar to `inet_aton()`) or `struct in6_addr`.

Supported values for *address_family* are currently `AF_INET` and `AF_INET6`. If the IP address string *ip_string* is invalid, `OSError` will be raised. Note that exactly what is valid depends on both the value of *address_family* and the underlying implementation of `inet_pton()`.

Availability: Unix (maybe not all platforms), Windows.

Changed in version 3.4: Windows support added

`socket.inet_ntop(address_family, packed_ip)`
Convert a packed IP address (a *bytes-like object* of some number of bytes) to its standard, family-specific string representation (for example, `'7.10.0.5'` or `'5aef:2b::8'`). `inet_ntop()` is useful

when a library or network protocol returns an object of type `struct in_addr` (similar to `inet_ntoa()`) or `struct in6_addr`.

Supported values for *address_family* are currently `AF_INET` and `AF_INET6`. If the bytes object *packed_ip* is not the correct length for the specified address family, `ValueError` will be raised. `OSError` is raised for errors from the call to `inet_ntop()`.

Availability: Unix (maybe not all platforms), Windows.

Changed in version 3.4: Windows support added

Changed in version 3.5: Writable *bytes-like object* is now accepted.

`socket.CMSG_LEN(`*length*`)`
Return the total length, without trailing padding, of an ancillary data item with associated data of the given *length*. This value can often be used as the buffer size for `recvmsg()` to receive a single item of ancillary data, but **RFC 3542** requires portable applications to use `CMSG_SPACE()` and thus include space for padding, even when the item will be the last in the buffer. Raises `OverflowError` if *length* is outside the permissible range of values.

Availability: most Unix platforms, possibly others.

New in version 3.3.

`socket.CMSG_SPACE(`*length*`)`
Return the buffer size needed for `recvmsg()` to receive an ancillary data item with associated data of the given *length*, along with any trailing padding. The buffer space needed to receive multiple items is the sum of the `CMSG_SPACE()` values for their associated data lengths. Raises `OverflowError` if *length* is outside the permissible range of values.

Note that some systems might support ancillary data without providing this function. Also note that setting the buffer size using the results of this function may not precisely limit the amount of ancillary data that can be received, since additional data may be able to fit into the padding area.

Availability: most Unix platforms, possibly others.

New in version 3.3.

`socket.getdefaulttimeout()`
Return the default timeout in seconds (float) for new socket objects. A value of `None` indicates that new socket objects have no timeout. When the socket module is first imported, the default is `None`.

`socket.setdefaulttimeout(`*timeout*`)`
Set the default timeout in seconds (float) for new socket objects. When the socket module is first imported, the default is `None`. See `settimeout()` for possible values and their respective meanings.

`socket.sethostname(`*name*`)`
Set the machine's hostname to *name*. This will raise an `OSError` if you don't have enough rights.

Availability: Unix.

New in version 3.3.

`socket.if_nameindex()`
Return a list of network interface information (index int, name string) tuples. `OSError` if the system call fails.

Availability: Unix.

New in version 3.3.

`socket.if_nametoindex(`*if_name*`)`
Return a network interface index number corresponding to an interface name. `OSError` if no interface with the given name exists.

Availability: Unix.

New in version 3.3.

`socket.if_indextoname(if_index)`
Return a network interface name corresponding to an interface index number. *OSError* if no interface with the given index exists.

Availability: Unix.

New in version 3.3.

18.1.3 Socket Objects

Socket objects have the following methods. Except for *makefile()*, these correspond to Unix system calls applicable to sockets.

Changed in version 3.2: Support for the *context manager* protocol was added. Exiting the context manager is equivalent to calling *close()*.

`socket.accept()`
Accept a connection. The socket must be bound to an address and listening for connections. The return value is a pair `(conn, address)` where *conn* is a *new* socket object usable to send and receive data on the connection, and *address* is the address bound to the socket on the other end of the connection.

The newly created socket is *non-inheritable*.

Changed in version 3.4: The socket is now non-inheritable.

Changed in version 3.5: If the system call is interrupted and the signal handler does not raise an exception, the method now retries the system call instead of raising an *InterruptedError* exception (see PEP 475 for the rationale).

`socket.bind(address)`
Bind the socket to *address*. The socket must not already be bound. (The format of *address* depends on the address family — see above.)

`socket.close()`
Mark the socket closed. The underlying system resource (e.g. a file descriptor) is also closed when all file objects from *makefile()* are closed. Once that happens, all future operations on the socket object will fail. The remote end will receive no more data (after queued data is flushed).

Sockets are automatically closed when they are garbage-collected, but it is recommended to *close()* them explicitly, or to use a `with` statement around them.

Changed in version 3.6: *OSError* is now raised if an error occurs when the underlying `close()` call is made.

Note: *close()* releases the resource associated with a connection but does not necessarily close the connection immediately. If you want to close the connection in a timely fashion, call *shutdown()* before *close()*.

`socket.connect(address)`
Connect to a remote socket at *address*. (The format of *address* depends on the address family — see above.)

If the connection is interrupted by a signal, the method waits until the connection completes, or raise a *socket.timeout* on timeout, if the signal handler doesn't raise an exception and the socket is blocking or has a timeout. For non-blocking sockets, the method raises an *InterruptedError* exception if the connection is interrupted by a signal (or the exception raised by the signal handler).

Changed in version 3.5: The method now waits until the connection completes instead of raising an *InterruptedError* exception if the connection is interrupted by a signal, the signal handler doesn't raise an exception and the socket is blocking or has a timeout (see the PEP 475 for the rationale).

`socket.connect_ex(address)`
Like `connect(address)`, but return an error indicator instead of raising an exception for errors returned by the C-level `connect()` call (other problems, such as "host not found," can still raise exceptions). The error indicator is `0` if the operation succeeded, otherwise the value of the `errno` variable. This is useful to support, for example, asynchronous connects.

`socket.detach()`
Put the socket object into closed state without actually closing the underlying file descriptor. The file descriptor is returned, and can be reused for other purposes.

New in version 3.2.

`socket.dup()`
Duplicate the socket.

The newly created socket is *non-inheritable*.

Changed in version 3.4: The socket is now non-inheritable.

`socket.fileno()`
Return the socket's file descriptor (a small integer), or -1 on failure. This is useful with `select.select()`.

Under Windows the small integer returned by this method cannot be used where a file descriptor can be used (such as `os.fdopen()`). Unix does not have this limitation.

`socket.get_inheritable()`
Get the *inheritable flag* of the socket's file descriptor or socket's handle: `True` if the socket can be inherited in child processes, `False` if it cannot.

New in version 3.4.

`socket.getpeername()`
Return the remote address to which the socket is connected. This is useful to find out the port number of a remote IPv4/v6 socket, for instance. (The format of the address returned depends on the address family — see above.) On some systems this function is not supported.

`socket.getsockname()`
Return the socket's own address. This is useful to find out the port number of an IPv4/v6 socket, for instance. (The format of the address returned depends on the address family — see above.)

`socket.getsockopt(level, optname[, buflen])`
Return the value of the given socket option (see the Unix man page *getsockopt(2)*). The needed symbolic constants (`SO_*` etc.) are defined in this module. If *buflen* is absent, an integer option is assumed and its integer value is returned by the function. If *buflen* is present, it specifies the maximum length of the buffer used to receive the option in, and this buffer is returned as a bytes object. It is up to the caller to decode the contents of the buffer (see the optional built-in module `struct` for a way to decode C structures encoded as byte strings).

`socket.gettimeout()`
Return the timeout in seconds (float) associated with socket operations, or `None` if no timeout is set. This reflects the last call to `setblocking()` or `settimeout()`.

`socket.ioctl(control, option)`

Platform Windows

The `ioctl()` method is a limited interface to the WSAIoctl system interface. Please refer to the Win32 documentation for more information.

On other platforms, the generic *fcntl.fcntl()* and *fcntl.ioctl()* functions may be used; they accept a socket object as their first argument.

Currently only the following control codes are supported: `SIO_RCVALL`, `SIO_KEEPALIVE_VALS`, and `SIO_LOOPBACK_FAST_PATH`.

Changed in version 3.6: `SIO_LOOPBACK_FAST_PATH` was added.

`socket.listen([backlog])`
Enable a server to accept connections. If *backlog* is specified, it must be at least 0 (if it is lower, it is set to 0); it specifies the number of unaccepted connections that the system will allow before refusing new connections. If not specified, a default reasonable value is chosen.

Changed in version 3.5: The *backlog* parameter is now optional.

`socket.makefile(mode='r', buffering=None, *, encoding=None, errors=None, newline=None)`
Return a *file object* associated with the socket. The exact returned type depends on the arguments given to *makefile()*. These arguments are interpreted the same way as by the built-in *open()* function, except the only supported *mode* values are `'r'` (default), `'w'` and `'b'`.

The socket must be in blocking mode; it can have a timeout, but the file object's internal buffer may end up in an inconsistent state if a timeout occurs.

Closing the file object returned by *makefile()* won't close the original socket unless all other file objects have been closed and *socket.close()* has been called on the socket object.

Note: On Windows, the file-like object created by *makefile()* cannot be used where a file object with a file descriptor is expected, such as the stream arguments of *subprocess.Popen()*.

`socket.recv(bufsize[, flags])`
Receive data from the socket. The return value is a bytes object representing the data received. The maximum amount of data to be received at once is specified by *bufsize*. See the Unix manual page *recv(2)* for the meaning of the optional argument *flags*; it defaults to zero.

Note: For best match with hardware and network realities, the value of *bufsize* should be a relatively small power of 2, for example, 4096.

Changed in version 3.5: If the system call is interrupted and the signal handler does not raise an exception, the method now retries the system call instead of raising an *InterruptedError* exception (see **PEP 475** for the rationale).

`socket.recvfrom(bufsize[, flags])`
Receive data from the socket. The return value is a pair `(bytes, address)` where *bytes* is a bytes object representing the data received and *address* is the address of the socket sending the data. See the Unix manual page *recv(2)* for the meaning of the optional argument *flags*; it defaults to zero. (The format of *address* depends on the address family — see above.)

Changed in version 3.5: If the system call is interrupted and the signal handler does not raise an exception, the method now retries the system call instead of raising an *InterruptedError* exception (see **PEP 475** for the rationale).

`socket.recvmsg(bufsize[, ancbufsize[, flags]])`
Receive normal data (up to *bufsize* bytes) and ancillary data from the socket. The *ancbufsize* argument sets the size in bytes of the internal buffer used to receive the ancillary data; it defaults to 0, meaning that no ancillary data will be received. Appropriate buffer sizes for ancillary data can be calculated using *CMSG_SPACE()* or *CMSG_LEN()*, and items which do not fit into the buffer might be truncated or discarded. The *flags* argument defaults to 0 and has the same meaning as for *recv()*.

The return value is a 4-tuple: (data, ancdata, msg_flags, address). The *data* item is a bytes object holding the non-ancillary data received. The *ancdata* item is a list of zero or more tuples (cmsg_level, cmsg_type, cmsg_data) representing the ancillary data (control messages) received: *cmsg_level* and *cmsg_type* are integers specifying the protocol level and protocol-specific type respectively, and *cmsg_data* is a bytes object holding the associated data. The *msg_flags* item is the bitwise OR of various flags indicating conditions on the received message; see your system documentation for details. If the receiving socket is unconnected, *address* is the address of the sending socket, if available; otherwise, its value is unspecified.

On some systems, *sendmsg()* and *recvmsg()* can be used to pass file descriptors between processes over an *AF_UNIX* socket. When this facility is used (it is often restricted to *SOCK_STREAM* sockets), *recvmsg()* will return, in its ancillary data, items of the form (socket.SOL_SOCKET, socket.SCM_RIGHTS, fds), where *fds* is a bytes object representing the new file descriptors as a binary array of the native C int type. If *recvmsg()* raises an exception after the system call returns, it will first attempt to close any file descriptors received via this mechanism.

Some systems do not indicate the truncated length of ancillary data items which have been only partially received. If an item appears to extend beyond the end of the buffer, *recvmsg()* will issue a *RuntimeWarning*, and will return the part of it which is inside the buffer provided it has not been truncated before the start of its associated data.

On systems which support the SCM_RIGHTS mechanism, the following function will receive up to *maxfds* file descriptors, returning the message data and a list containing the descriptors (while ignoring unexpected conditions such as unrelated control messages being received). See also *sendmsg()*.

```
import socket, array

def recv_fds(sock, msglen, maxfds):
    fds = array.array("i")   # Array of ints
    msg, ancdata, flags, addr = sock.recvmsg(msglen, socket.CMSG_LEN(maxfds * fds.itemsize))
    for cmsg_level, cmsg_type, cmsg_data in ancdata:
        if (cmsg_level == socket.SOL_SOCKET and cmsg_type == socket.SCM_RIGHTS):
            # Append data, ignoring any truncated integers at the end.
            fds.fromstring(cmsg_data[:len(cmsg_data) - (len(cmsg_data) % fds.itemsize)])
    return msg, list(fds)
```

Availability: most Unix platforms, possibly others.

New in version 3.3.

Changed in version 3.5: If the system call is interrupted and the signal handler does not raise an exception, the method now retries the system call instead of raising an *InterruptedError* exception (see PEP 475 for the rationale).

socket.**recvmsg_into**(*buffers*[, *ancbufsize*[, *flags*]])

Receive normal data and ancillary data from the socket, behaving as *recvmsg()* would, but scatter the non-ancillary data into a series of buffers instead of returning a new bytes object. The *buffers* argument must be an iterable of objects that export writable buffers (e.g. *bytearray* objects); these will be filled with successive chunks of the non-ancillary data until it has all been written or there are no more buffers. The operating system may set a limit (*sysconf()* value SC_IOV_MAX) on the number of buffers that can be used. The *ancbufsize* and *flags* arguments have the same meaning as for *recvmsg()*.

The return value is a 4-tuple: (nbytes, ancdata, msg_flags, address), where *nbytes* is the total number of bytes of non-ancillary data written into the buffers, and *ancdata*, *msg_flags* and *address* are the same as for *recvmsg()*.

Example:

```
>>> import socket
>>> s1, s2 = socket.socketpair()
>>> b1 = bytearray(b'----')
>>> b2 = bytearray(b'0123456789')
>>> b3 = bytearray(b'--------------')
>>> s1.send(b'Mary had a little lamb')
22
>>> s2.recvmsg_into([b1, memoryview(b2)[2:9], b3])
(22, [], 0, None)
>>> [b1, b2, b3]
[bytearray(b'Mary'), bytearray(b'01 had a 9'), bytearray(b'little lamb---')]
```

Availability: most Unix platforms, possibly others.

New in version 3.3.

`socket.recvfrom_into(`*buffer*[, *nbytes*[, *flags*]]`)`

Receive data from the socket, writing it into *buffer* instead of creating a new bytestring. The return value is a pair `(nbytes, address)` where *nbytes* is the number of bytes received and *address* is the address of the socket sending the data. See the Unix manual page *recv(2)* for the meaning of the optional argument *flags*; it defaults to zero. (The format of *address* depends on the address family — see above.)

`socket.recv_into(`*buffer*[, *nbytes*[, *flags*]]`)`

Receive up to *nbytes* bytes from the socket, storing the data into a buffer rather than creating a new bytestring. If *nbytes* is not specified (or 0), receive up to the size available in the given buffer. Returns the number of bytes received. See the Unix manual page *recv(2)* for the meaning of the optional argument *flags*; it defaults to zero.

`socket.send(`*bytes*[, *flags*]`)`

Send data to the socket. The socket must be connected to a remote socket. The optional *flags* argument has the same meaning as for `recv()` above. Returns the number of bytes sent. Applications are responsible for checking that all data has been sent; if only some of the data was transmitted, the application needs to attempt delivery of the remaining data. For further information on this topic, consult the socket-howto.

Changed in version 3.5: If the system call is interrupted and the signal handler does not raise an exception, the method now retries the system call instead of raising an `InterruptedError` exception (see PEP 475 for the rationale).

`socket.sendall(`*bytes*[, *flags*]`)`

Send data to the socket. The socket must be connected to a remote socket. The optional *flags* argument has the same meaning as for `recv()` above. Unlike `send()`, this method continues to send data from *bytes* until either all data has been sent or an error occurs. `None` is returned on success. On error, an exception is raised, and there is no way to determine how much data, if any, was successfully sent.

Changed in version 3.5: The socket timeout is no more reset each time data is sent successfully. The socket timeout is now the maximum total duration to send all data.

Changed in version 3.5: If the system call is interrupted and the signal handler does not raise an exception, the method now retries the system call instead of raising an `InterruptedError` exception (see PEP 475 for the rationale).

`socket.sendto(`*bytes*, *address*`)`
`socket.sendto(`*bytes*, *flags*, *address*`)`

Send data to the socket. The socket should not be connected to a remote socket, since the destination socket is specified by *address*. The optional *flags* argument has the same meaning as for `recv()` above. Return the number of bytes sent. (The format of *address* depends on the address family — see above.)

Changed in version 3.5: If the system call is interrupted and the signal handler does not raise an exception, the method now retries the system call instead of raising an *InterruptedError* exception (see **PEP 475** for the rationale).

socket.**sendmsg**(*buffers*[, *ancdata*[, *flags*[, *address*]]])

Send normal and ancillary data to the socket, gathering the non-ancillary data from a series of buffers and concatenating it into a single message. The *buffers* argument specifies the non-ancillary data as an iterable of *bytes-like objects* (e.g. `bytes` objects); the operating system may set a limit (`sysconf()` value `SC_IOV_MAX`) on the number of buffers that can be used. The *ancdata* argument specifies the ancillary data (control messages) as an iterable of zero or more tuples `(cmsg_level, cmsg_type, cmsg_data)`, where *cmsg_level* and *cmsg_type* are integers specifying the protocol level and protocol-specific type respectively, and *cmsg_data* is a bytes-like object holding the associated data. Note that some systems (in particular, systems without *CMSG_SPACE()*) might support sending only one control message per call. The *flags* argument defaults to 0 and has the same meaning as for `send()`. If *address* is supplied and not `None`, it sets a destination address for the message. The return value is the number of bytes of non-ancillary data sent.

The following function sends the list of file descriptors *fds* over an *AF_UNIX* socket, on systems which support the `SCM_RIGHTS` mechanism. See also `recvmsg()`.

```
import socket, array

def send_fds(sock, msg, fds):
    return sock.sendmsg([msg], [(socket.SOL_SOCKET, socket.SCM_RIGHTS, array.array("i",␣
↪fds))])
```

Availability: most Unix platforms, possibly others.

New in version 3.3.

Changed in version 3.5: If the system call is interrupted and the signal handler does not raise an exception, the method now retries the system call instead of raising an *InterruptedError* exception (see **PEP 475** for the rationale).

socket.**sendmsg_afalg**([*msg*], *, *op*[, *iv*[, *assoclen*[, *flags*]]])

Specialized version of `sendmsg()` for *AF_ALG* socket. Set mode, IV, AEAD associated data length and flags for *AF_ALG* socket.

Availability: Linux >= 2.6.38

New in version 3.6.

socket.**sendfile**(*file*, *offset=0*, *count=None*)

Send a file until EOF is reached by using high-performance `os.sendfile` and return the total number of bytes which were sent. *file* must be a regular file object opened in binary mode. If `os.sendfile` is not available (e.g. Windows) or *file* is not a regular file `send()` will be used instead. *offset* tells from where to start reading the file. If specified, *count* is the total number of bytes to transmit as opposed to sending the file until EOF is reached. File position is updated on return or also in case of error in which case `file.tell()` can be used to figure out the number of bytes which were sent. The socket must be of *SOCK_STREAM* type. Non-blocking sockets are not supported.

New in version 3.5.

socket.**set_inheritable**(*inheritable*)

Set the *inheritable flag* of the socket's file descriptor or socket's handle.

New in version 3.4.

socket.**setblocking**(*flag*)

Set blocking or non-blocking mode of the socket: if *flag* is false, the socket is set to non-blocking, else to blocking mode.

This method is a shorthand for certain *settimeout()* calls:

- `sock.setblocking(True)` is equivalent to `sock.settimeout(None)`
- `sock.setblocking(False)` is equivalent to `sock.settimeout(0.0)`

`socket.settimeout(value)`
Set a timeout on blocking socket operations. The *value* argument can be a nonnegative floating point number expressing seconds, or `None`. If a non-zero value is given, subsequent socket operations will raise a *timeout* exception if the timeout period *value* has elapsed before the operation has completed. If zero is given, the socket is put in non-blocking mode. If `None` is given, the socket is put in blocking mode.

For further information, please consult the *notes on socket timeouts*.

`socket.setsockopt(level, optname, value: int)`

`socket.setsockopt(level, optname, value: buffer)`

`socket.setsockopt(level, optname, None, optlen: int)`
Set the value of the given socket option (see the Unix manual page *setsockopt(2)*). The needed symbolic constants are defined in the *socket* module (`SO_*` etc.). The value can be an integer, `None` or a *bytes-like object* representing a buffer. In the later case it is up to the caller to ensure that the bytestring contains the proper bits (see the optional built-in module *struct* for a way to encode C structures as bytestrings). When value is set to `None`, optlen argument is required. It's equivalent to call setsockopt C function with optval=NULL and optlen=optlen.

Changed in version 3.5: Writable *bytes-like object* is now accepted.

Changed in version 3.6: setsockopt(level, optname, None, optlen: int) form added.

`socket.shutdown(how)`
Shut down one or both halves of the connection. If *how* is `SHUT_RD`, further receives are disallowed. If *how* is `SHUT_WR`, further sends are disallowed. If *how* is `SHUT_RDWR`, further sends and receives are disallowed.

`socket.share(process_id)`
Duplicate a socket and prepare it for sharing with a target process. The target process must be provided with *process_id*. The resulting bytes object can then be passed to the target process using some form of interprocess communication and the socket can be recreated there using *fromshare()*. Once this method has been called, it is safe to close the socket since the operating system has already duplicated it for the target process.

Availability: Windows.

New in version 3.3.

Note that there are no methods `read()` or `write()`; use *recv()* and *send()* without *flags* argument instead.

Socket objects also have these (read-only) attributes that correspond to the values given to the *socket* constructor.

`socket.family`
The socket family.

`socket.type`
The socket type.

`socket.proto`
The socket protocol.

18.1.4 Notes on socket timeouts

A socket object can be in one of three modes: blocking, non-blocking, or timeout. Sockets are by default always created in blocking mode, but this can be changed by calling `setdefaulttimeout()`.

- In *blocking mode*, operations block until complete or the system returns an error (such as connection timed out).
- In *non-blocking mode*, operations fail (with an error that is unfortunately system-dependent) if they cannot be completed immediately: functions from the `select` can be used to know when and whether a socket is available for reading or writing.
- In *timeout mode*, operations fail if they cannot be completed within the timeout specified for the socket (they raise a `timeout` exception) or if the system returns an error.

Note: At the operating system level, sockets in *timeout mode* are internally set in non-blocking mode. Also, the blocking and timeout modes are shared between file descriptors and socket objects that refer to the same network endpoint. This implementation detail can have visible consequences if e.g. you decide to use the `fileno()` of a socket.

Timeouts and the connect method

The `connect()` operation is also subject to the timeout setting, and in general it is recommended to call `settimeout()` before calling `connect()` or pass a timeout parameter to `create_connection()`. However, the system network stack may also return a connection timeout error of its own regardless of any Python socket timeout setting.

Timeouts and the accept method

If `getdefaulttimeout()` is not `None`, sockets returned by the `accept()` method inherit that timeout. Otherwise, the behaviour depends on settings of the listening socket:

- if the listening socket is in *blocking mode* or in *timeout mode*, the socket returned by `accept()` is in *blocking mode*;
- if the listening socket is in *non-blocking mode*, whether the socket returned by `accept()` is in blocking or non-blocking mode is operating system-dependent. If you want to ensure cross-platform behaviour, it is recommended you manually override this setting.

18.1.5 Example

Here are four minimal example programs using the TCP/IP protocol: a server that echoes all data that it receives back (servicing only one client), and a client using it. Note that a server must perform the sequence `socket()`, `bind()`, `listen()`, `accept()` (possibly repeating the `accept()` to service more than one client), while a client only needs the sequence `socket()`, `connect()`. Also note that the server does not `sendall()`/`recv()` on the socket it is listening on but on the new socket returned by `accept()`.

The first two examples support IPv4 only.

```
# Echo server program
import socket

HOST = ''                 # Symbolic name meaning all available interfaces
PORT = 50007              # Arbitrary non-privileged port
with socket.socket(socket.AF_INET, socket.SOCK_STREAM) as s:
```

```
    s.bind((HOST, PORT))
    s.listen(1)
    conn, addr = s.accept()
    with conn:
        print('Connected by', addr)
        while True:
            data = conn.recv(1024)
            if not data: break
            conn.sendall(data)
```

```
# Echo client program
import socket

HOST = 'daring.cwi.nl'    # The remote host
PORT = 50007              # The same port as used by the server
with socket.socket(socket.AF_INET, socket.SOCK_STREAM) as s:
    s.connect((HOST, PORT))
    s.sendall(b'Hello, world')
    data = s.recv(1024)
print('Received', repr(data))
```

The next two examples are identical to the above two, but support both IPv4 and IPv6. The server side will listen to the first address family available (it should listen to both instead). On most of IPv6-ready systems, IPv6 will take precedence and the server may not accept IPv4 traffic. The client side will try to connect to the all addresses returned as a result of the name resolution, and sends traffic to the first one connected successfully.

```
# Echo server program
import socket
import sys

HOST = None               # Symbolic name meaning all available interfaces
PORT = 50007              # Arbitrary non-privileged port
s = None
for res in socket.getaddrinfo(HOST, PORT, socket.AF_UNSPEC,
                              socket.SOCK_STREAM, 0, socket.AI_PASSIVE):
    af, socktype, proto, canonname, sa = res
    try:
        s = socket.socket(af, socktype, proto)
    except OSError as msg:
        s = None
        continue
    try:
        s.bind(sa)
        s.listen(1)
    except OSError as msg:
        s.close()
        s = None
        continue
    break
if s is None:
    print('could not open socket')
    sys.exit(1)
conn, addr = s.accept()
with conn:
    print('Connected by', addr)
    while True:
```

```
        data = conn.recv(1024)
        if not data: break
        conn.send(data)
```

```
# Echo client program
import socket
import sys

HOST = 'daring.cwi.nl'    # The remote host
PORT = 50007              # The same port as used by the server
s = None
for res in socket.getaddrinfo(HOST, PORT, socket.AF_UNSPEC, socket.SOCK_STREAM):
    af, socktype, proto, canonname, sa = res
    try:
        s = socket.socket(af, socktype, proto)
    except OSError as msg:
        s = None
        continue
    try:
        s.connect(sa)
    except OSError as msg:
        s.close()
        s = None
        continue
    break
if s is None:
    print('could not open socket')
    sys.exit(1)
with s:
    s.sendall(b'Hello, world')
    data = s.recv(1024)
print('Received', repr(data))
```

The next example shows how to write a very simple network sniffer with raw sockets on Windows. The example requires administrator privileges to modify the interface:

```
import socket

# the public network interface
HOST = socket.gethostbyname(socket.gethostname())

# create a raw socket and bind it to the public interface
s = socket.socket(socket.AF_INET, socket.SOCK_RAW, socket.IPPROTO_IP)
s.bind((HOST, 0))

# Include IP headers
s.setsockopt(socket.IPPROTO_IP, socket.IP_HDRINCL, 1)

# receive all packages
s.ioctl(socket.SIO_RCVALL, socket.RCVALL_ON)

# receive a package
print(s.recvfrom(65565))

# disabled promiscuous mode
s.ioctl(socket.SIO_RCVALL, socket.RCVALL_OFF)
```

The last example shows how to use the socket interface to communicate to a CAN network using the raw socket protocol. To use CAN with the broadcast manager protocol instead, open a socket with:

```
socket.socket(socket.AF_CAN, socket.SOCK_DGRAM, socket.CAN_BCM)
```

After binding (CAN_RAW) or connecting (*CAN_BCM*) the socket, you can use the *socket.send()*, and the *socket.recv()* operations (and their counterparts) on the socket object as usual.

This example might require special privileges:

```
import socket
import struct


# CAN frame packing/unpacking (see 'struct can_frame' in <linux/can.h>)

can_frame_fmt = "=IB3x8s"
can_frame_size = struct.calcsize(can_frame_fmt)

def build_can_frame(can_id, data):
    can_dlc = len(data)
    data = data.ljust(8, b'\x00')
    return struct.pack(can_frame_fmt, can_id, can_dlc, data)

def dissect_can_frame(frame):
    can_id, can_dlc, data = struct.unpack(can_frame_fmt, frame)
    return (can_id, can_dlc, data[:can_dlc])


# create a raw socket and bind it to the 'vcan0' interface
s = socket.socket(socket.AF_CAN, socket.SOCK_RAW, socket.CAN_RAW)
s.bind(('vcan0',))

while True:
    cf, addr = s.recvfrom(can_frame_size)

    print('Received: can_id=%x, can_dlc=%x, data=%s' % dissect_can_frame(cf))

    try:
        s.send(cf)
    except OSError:
        print('Error sending CAN frame')

    try:
        s.send(build_can_frame(0x01, b'\x01\x02\x03'))
    except OSError:
        print('Error sending CAN frame')
```

Running an example several times with too small delay between executions, could lead to this error:

```
OSError: [Errno 98] Address already in use
```

This is because the previous execution has left the socket in a TIME_WAIT state, and can't be immediately reused.

There is a *socket* flag to set, in order to prevent this, socket.SO_REUSEADDR:

```
s = socket.socket(socket.AF_INET, socket.SOCK_STREAM)
s.setsockopt(socket.SOL_SOCKET, socket.SO_REUSEADDR, 1)
s.bind((HOST, PORT))
```

the SO_REUSEADDR flag tells the kernel to reuse a local socket in TIME_WAIT state, without waiting for its natural timeout to expire.

See also:

For an introduction to socket programming (in C), see the following papers:

- *An Introductory 4.3BSD Interprocess Communication Tutorial*, by Stuart Sechrest
- *An Advanced 4.3BSD Interprocess Communication Tutorial*, by Samuel J. Leffler et al,

both in the UNIX Programmer's Manual, Supplementary Documents 1 (sections PS1:7 and PS1:8). The platform-specific reference material for the various socket-related system calls are also a valuable source of information on the details of socket semantics. For Unix, refer to the manual pages; for Windows, see the WinSock (or Winsock 2) specification. For IPv6-ready APIs, readers may want to refer to RFC 3493 titled Basic Socket Interface Extensions for IPv6.

18.2 ssl — TLS/SSL wrapper for socket objects

Source code: Lib/ssl.py

This module provides access to Transport Layer Security (often known as "Secure Sockets Layer") encryption and peer authentication facilities for network sockets, both client-side and server-side. This module uses the OpenSSL library. It is available on all modern Unix systems, Windows, Mac OS X, and probably additional platforms, as long as OpenSSL is installed on that platform.

Note: Some behavior may be platform dependent, since calls are made to the operating system socket APIs. The installed version of OpenSSL may also cause variations in behavior. For example, TLSv1.1 and TLSv1.2 come with openssl version 1.0.1.

Warning: Don't use this module without reading the *Security considerations*. Doing so may lead to a false sense of security, as the default settings of the ssl module are not necessarily appropriate for your application.

This section documents the objects and functions in the ssl module; for more general information about TLS, SSL, and certificates, the reader is referred to the documents in the "See Also" section at the bottom.

This module provides a class, `ssl.SSLSocket`, which is derived from the `socket.socket` type, and provides a socket-like wrapper that also encrypts and decrypts the data going over the socket with SSL. It supports additional methods such as `getpeercert()`, which retrieves the certificate of the other side of the connection, and `cipher()`,which retrieves the cipher being used for the secure connection.

For more sophisticated applications, the `ssl.SSLContext` class helps manage settings and certificates, which can then be inherited by SSL sockets created through the `SSLContext.wrap_socket()` method.

Changed in version 3.6: OpenSSL 0.9.8, 1.0.0 and 1.0.1 are deprecated and no longer supported. In the future the ssl module will require at least OpenSSL 1.0.2 or 1.1.0.

18.2.1 Functions, Constants, and Exceptions

exception ssl.SSLError

Raised to signal an error from the underlying SSL implementation (currently provided by the OpenSSL library). This signifies some problem in the higher-level encryption and authentication layer that's superimposed on the underlying network connection. This error is a subtype of *OSError*. The error code and message of *SSLError* instances are provided by the OpenSSL library.

Changed in version 3.3: *SSLError* used to be a subtype of *socket.error*.

library
A string mnemonic designating the OpenSSL submodule in which the error occurred, such as `SSL`, `PEM` or `X509`. The range of possible values depends on the OpenSSL version.

New in version 3.3.

reason
A string mnemonic designating the reason this error occurred, for example `CERTIFICATE_VERIFY_FAILED`. The range of possible values depends on the OpenSSL version.

New in version 3.3.

exception ssl.SSLZeroReturnError
A subclass of *SSLError* raised when trying to read or write and the SSL connection has been closed cleanly. Note that this doesn't mean that the underlying transport (read TCP) has been closed.

New in version 3.3.

exception ssl.SSLWantReadError
A subclass of *SSLError* raised by a *non-blocking SSL socket* when trying to read or write data, but more data needs to be received on the underlying TCP transport before the request can be fulfilled.

New in version 3.3.

exception ssl.SSLWantWriteError
A subclass of *SSLError* raised by a *non-blocking SSL socket* when trying to read or write data, but more data needs to be sent on the underlying TCP transport before the request can be fulfilled.

New in version 3.3.

exception ssl.SSLSyscallError
A subclass of *SSLError* raised when a system error was encountered while trying to fulfill an operation on a SSL socket. Unfortunately, there is no easy way to inspect the original errno number.

New in version 3.3.

exception ssl.SSLEOFError
A subclass of *SSLError* raised when the SSL connection has been terminated abruptly. Generally, you shouldn't try to reuse the underlying transport when this error is encountered.

New in version 3.3.

exception ssl.CertificateError
Raised to signal an error with a certificate (such as mismatching hostname). Certificate errors detected by OpenSSL, though, raise an *SSLError*.

Socket creation

The following function allows for standalone socket creation. Starting from Python 3.2, it can be more flexible to use *SSLContext.wrap_socket()* instead.

ssl.wrap_socket(*sock, keyfile=None, certfile=None, server_side=False, cert_reqs=CERT_NONE, ssl_version={see docs}, ca_certs=None, do_handshake_on_connect=True, suppress_ragged_eofs=True, ciphers=None*)
Takes an instance `sock` of *socket.socket*, and returns an instance of *ssl.SSLSocket*, a subtype of *socket.socket*, which wraps the underlying socket in an SSL context. `sock` must be a *SOCK_STREAM* socket; other socket types are unsupported.

For client-side sockets, the context construction is lazy; if the underlying socket isn't connected yet, the context construction will be performed after connect() is called on the socket. For server-side sockets, if the socket has no remote peer, it is assumed to be a listening socket, and the server-side SSL wrapping is automatically performed on client connections accepted via the accept() method. *wrap_socket()* may raise *SSLError*.

The keyfile and certfile parameters specify optional files which contain a certificate to be used to identify the local side of the connection. See the discussion of *Certificates* for more information on how the certificate is stored in the certfile.

The parameter server_side is a boolean which identifies whether server-side or client-side behavior is desired from this socket.

The parameter cert_reqs specifies whether a certificate is required from the other side of the connection, and whether it will be validated if provided. It must be one of the three values *CERT_NONE* (certificates ignored), *CERT_OPTIONAL* (not required, but validated if provided), or *CERT_REQUIRED* (required and validated). If the value of this parameter is not *CERT_NONE*, then the ca_certs parameter must point to a file of CA certificates.

The ca_certs file contains a set of concatenated "certification authority" certificates, which are used to validate certificates passed from the other end of the connection. See the discussion of *Certificates* for more information about how to arrange the certificates in this file.

The parameter ssl_version specifies which version of the SSL protocol to use. Typically, the server chooses a particular protocol version, and the client must adapt to the server's choice. Most of the versions are not interoperable with the other versions. If not specified, the default is *PROTOCOL_TLS*; it provides the most compatibility with other versions.

Here's a table showing which versions in a client (down the side) can connect to which versions in a server (along the top):

client / **server**	**SSLv2**	**SSLv3**	**TLS**[3]	**TLSv1**	**TLSv1.1**	**TLSv1.2**
SSLv2	yes	no	no[1]	no	no	no
SSLv3	no	yes	no[2]	no	no	no
TLS (SSLv23)[3]	no[1]	no[2]	yes	yes	yes	yes
TLSv1	no	no	yes	yes	no	no
TLSv1.1	no	no	yes	no	yes	no
TLSv1.2	no	no	yes	no	no	yes

Note: Which connections succeed will vary depending on the version of OpenSSL. For example, before OpenSSL 1.0.0, an SSLv23 client would always attempt SSLv2 connections.

The *ciphers* parameter sets the available ciphers for this SSL object. It should be a string in the OpenSSL cipher list format.

The parameter do_handshake_on_connect specifies whether to do the SSL handshake automatically after doing a socket.connect(), or whether the application program will call it explicitly, by invoking the *SSLSocket.do_handshake()* method. Calling *SSLSocket.do_handshake()* explicitly gives the program control over the blocking behavior of the socket I/O involved in the handshake.

The parameter suppress_ragged_eofs specifies how the SSLSocket.recv() method should signal unexpected EOF from the other end of the connection. If specified as *True* (the default), it returns a

[3] TLS 1.3 protocol will be available with *PROTOCOL_TLS* in OpenSSL >= 1.1.1. There is no dedicated PROTOCOL constant for just TLS 1.3.

[1] *SSLContext* disables SSLv2 with *OP_NO_SSLv2* by default.

[2] *SSLContext* disables SSLv3 with *OP_NO_SSLv3* by default.

normal EOF (an empty bytes object) in response to unexpected EOF errors raised from the underlying socket; if `False`, it will raise the exceptions back to the caller.

Changed in version 3.2: New optional argument *ciphers*.

Context creation

A convenience function helps create `SSLContext` objects for common purposes.

ssl.create_default_context(*purpose=Purpose.SERVER_AUTH, cafile=None, capath=None, cadata=None*)

Return a new `SSLContext` object with default settings for the given *purpose*. The settings are chosen by the `ssl` module, and usually represent a higher security level than when calling the `SSLContext` constructor directly.

cafile, *capath*, *cadata* represent optional CA certificates to trust for certificate verification, as in `SSLContext.load_verify_locations()`. If all three are `None`, this function can choose to trust the system's default CA certificates instead.

The settings are: `PROTOCOL_TLS`, `OP_NO_SSLv2`, and `OP_NO_SSLv3` with high encryption cipher suites without RC4 and without unauthenticated cipher suites. Passing `SERVER_AUTH` as *purpose* sets `verify_mode` to `CERT_REQUIRED` and either loads CA certificates (when at least one of *cafile*, *capath* or *cadata* is given) or uses `SSLContext.load_default_certs()` to load default CA certificates.

Note: The protocol, options, cipher and other settings may change to more restrictive values anytime without prior deprecation. The values represent a fair balance between compatibility and security.

If your application needs specific settings, you should create a `SSLContext` and apply the settings yourself.

Note: If you find that when certain older clients or servers attempt to connect with a `SSLContext` created by this function that they get an error stating "Protocol or cipher suite mismatch", it may be that they only support SSL3.0 which this function excludes using the `OP_NO_SSLv3`. SSL3.0 is widely considered to be completely broken. If you still wish to continue to use this function but still allow SSL 3.0 connections you can re-enable them using:

```
ctx = ssl.create_default_context(Purpose.CLIENT_AUTH)
ctx.options &= ~ssl.OP_NO_SSLv3
```

New in version 3.4.

Changed in version 3.4.4: RC4 was dropped from the default cipher string.

Changed in version 3.6: ChaCha20/Poly1305 was added to the default cipher string.

3DES was dropped from the default cipher string.

Changed in version 3.6.3: TLS 1.3 cipher suites TLS_AES_128_GCM_SHA256, TLS_AES_256_GCM_SHA384, and TLS_CHACHA20_POLY1305_SHA256 were added to the default cipher string.

Random generation

ssl.RAND_bytes(*num*)

Return *num* cryptographically strong pseudo-random bytes. Raises an `SSLError` if the PRNG has not been seeded with enough data or if the operation is not supported by the current RAND method.

RAND_status() can be used to check the status of the PRNG and *RAND_add()* can be used to seed the PRNG.

For almost all applications *os.urandom()* is preferable.

Read the Wikipedia article, Cryptographically secure pseudorandom number generator (CSPRNG), to get the requirements of a cryptographically generator.

New in version 3.3.

ssl.RAND_pseudo_bytes(*num*)

Return (bytes, is_cryptographic): bytes are *num* pseudo-random bytes, is_cryptographic is `True` if the bytes generated are cryptographically strong. Raises an *SSLError* if the operation is not supported by the current RAND method.

Generated pseudo-random byte sequences will be unique if they are of sufficient length, but are not necessarily unpredictable. They can be used for non-cryptographic purposes and for certain purposes in cryptographic protocols, but usually not for key generation etc.

For almost all applications *os.urandom()* is preferable.

New in version 3.3.

Deprecated since version 3.6: OpenSSL has deprecated *ssl.RAND_pseudo_bytes()*, use *ssl.RAND_bytes()* instead.

ssl.RAND_status()

Return `True` if the SSL pseudo-random number generator has been seeded with 'enough' randomness, and `False` otherwise. You can use *ssl.RAND_egd()* and *ssl.RAND_add()* to increase the randomness of the pseudo-random number generator.

ssl.RAND_egd(*path*)

If you are running an entropy-gathering daemon (EGD) somewhere, and *path* is the pathname of a socket connection open to it, this will read 256 bytes of randomness from the socket, and add it to the SSL pseudo-random number generator to increase the security of generated secret keys. This is typically only necessary on systems without better sources of randomness.

See http://egd.sourceforge.net/ or http://prngd.sourceforge.net/ for sources of entropy-gathering daemons.

Availability: not available with LibreSSL and OpenSSL > 1.1.0

ssl.RAND_add(*bytes*, *entropy*)

Mix the given *bytes* into the SSL pseudo-random number generator. The parameter *entropy* (a float) is a lower bound on the entropy contained in string (so you can always use `0.0`). See RFC 1750 for more information on sources of entropy.

Changed in version 3.5: Writable *bytes-like object* is now accepted.

Certificate handling

ssl.match_hostname(*cert*, *hostname*)

Verify that *cert* (in decoded format as returned by *SSLSocket.getpeercert()*) matches the given *hostname*. The rules applied are those for checking the identity of HTTPS servers as outlined in RFC 2818, RFC 5280 and RFC 6125. In addition to HTTPS, this function should be suitable for checking the identity of servers in various SSL-based protocols such as FTPS, IMAPS, POPS and others.

CertificateError is raised on failure. On success, the function returns nothing:

```
>>> cert = {'subject': ((('commonName', 'example.com'),),)}
>>> ssl.match_hostname(cert, "example.com")
>>> ssl.match_hostname(cert, "example.org")
```

```
Traceback (most recent call last):
  File "<stdin>", line 1, in <module>
  File "/home/py3k/Lib/ssl.py", line 130, in match_hostname
ssl.CertificateError: hostname 'example.org' doesn't match 'example.com'
```

New in version 3.2.

Changed in version 3.3.3: The function now follows RFC 6125, section 6.4.3 and does neither match multiple wildcards (e.g. `*.*.com` or `*a*.example.org`) nor a wildcard inside an internationalized domain names (IDN) fragment. IDN A-labels such as `www*.xn--pthon-kva.org` are still supported, but `x*.python.org` no longer matches `xn--tda.python.org`.

Changed in version 3.5: Matching of IP addresses, when present in the subjectAltName field of the certificate, is now supported.

`ssl.`**`cert_time_to_seconds`**`(`*cert_time*`)`

Return the time in seconds since the Epoch, given the `cert_time` string representing the "notBefore" or "notAfter" date from a certificate in `"%b %d %H:%M:%S %Y %Z"` strptime format (C locale).

Here's an example:

```
>>> import ssl
>>> timestamp = ssl.cert_time_to_seconds("Jan  5 09:34:43 2018 GMT")
>>> timestamp
1515144883
>>> from datetime import datetime
>>> print(datetime.utcfromtimestamp(timestamp))
2018-01-05 09:34:43
```

"notBefore" or "notAfter" dates must use GMT (RFC 5280).

Changed in version 3.5: Interpret the input time as a time in UTC as specified by 'GMT' timezone in the input string. Local timezone was used previously. Return an integer (no fractions of a second in the input format)

`ssl.`**`get_server_certificate`**`(`*addr, ssl_version=PROTOCOL_TLS, ca_certs=None*`)`

Given the address `addr` of an SSL-protected server, as a (*hostname*, *port-number*) pair, fetches the server's certificate, and returns it as a PEM-encoded string. If `ssl_version` is specified, uses that version of the SSL protocol to attempt to connect to the server. If `ca_certs` is specified, it should be a file containing a list of root certificates, the same format as used for the same parameter in *`wrap_socket()`*. The call will attempt to validate the server certificate against that set of root certificates, and will fail if the validation attempt fails.

Changed in version 3.3: This function is now IPv6-compatible.

Changed in version 3.5: The default *ssl_version* is changed from *`PROTOCOL_SSLv3`* to *`PROTOCOL_TLS`* for maximum compatibility with modern servers.

`ssl.`**`DER_cert_to_PEM_cert`**`(`*DER_cert_bytes*`)`

Given a certificate as a DER-encoded blob of bytes, returns a PEM-encoded string version of the same certificate.

`ssl.`**`PEM_cert_to_DER_cert`**`(`*PEM_cert_string*`)`

Given a certificate as an ASCII PEM string, returns a DER-encoded sequence of bytes for that same certificate.

`ssl.`**`get_default_verify_paths`**`()`

Returns a named tuple with paths to OpenSSL's default cafile and capath. The paths are the same as used by *`SSLContext.set_default_verify_paths()`*. The return value is a *named tuple* `DefaultVerifyPaths`:

- `cafile` - resolved path to cafile or `None` if the file doesn't exist,

- `capath` - resolved path to capath or `None` if the directory doesn't exist,
- `openssl_cafile_env` - OpenSSL's environment key that points to a cafile,
- `openssl_cafile` - hard coded path to a cafile,
- `openssl_capath_env` - OpenSSL's environment key that points to a capath,
- `openssl_capath` - hard coded path to a capath directory

Availability: LibreSSL ignores the environment vars `openssl_cafile_env` and `openssl_capath_env`

New in version 3.4.

`ssl.enum_certificates(store_name)`

Retrieve certificates from Windows' system cert store. *store_name* may be one of `CA`, `ROOT` or `MY`. Windows may provide additional cert stores, too.

The function returns a list of (cert_bytes, encoding_type, trust) tuples. The encoding_type specifies the encoding of cert_bytes. It is either `x509_asn` for X.509 ASN.1 data or `pkcs_7_asn` for PKCS#7 ASN.1 data. Trust specifies the purpose of the certificate as a set of OIDS or exactly `True` if the certificate is trustworthy for all purposes.

Example:

```
>>> ssl.enum_certificates("CA")
[(b'data...', 'x509_asn', {'1.3.6.1.5.5.7.3.1', '1.3.6.1.5.5.7.3.2'}),
 (b'data...', 'x509_asn', True)]
```

Availability: Windows.

New in version 3.4.

`ssl.enum_crls(store_name)`

Retrieve CRLs from Windows' system cert store. *store_name* may be one of `CA`, `ROOT` or `MY`. Windows may provide additional cert stores, too.

The function returns a list of (cert_bytes, encoding_type, trust) tuples. The encoding_type specifies the encoding of cert_bytes. It is either `x509_asn` for X.509 ASN.1 data or `pkcs_7_asn` for PKCS#7 ASN.1 data.

Availability: Windows.

New in version 3.4.

Constants

All constants are now *enum.IntEnum* or *enum.IntFlag* collections.

New in version 3.6.

`ssl.CERT_NONE`

Possible value for *SSLContext.verify_mode*, or the `cert_reqs` parameter to *wrap_socket()*. In this mode (the default), no certificates will be required from the other side of the socket connection. If a certificate is received from the other end, no attempt to validate it is made.

See the discussion of *Security considerations* below.

`ssl.CERT_OPTIONAL`

Possible value for *SSLContext.verify_mode*, or the `cert_reqs` parameter to *wrap_socket()*. In this mode no certificates will be required from the other side of the socket connection; but if they are provided, validation will be attempted and an *SSLError* will be raised on failure.

Use of this setting requires a valid set of CA certificates to be passed, either to *SSLContext.load_verify_locations()* or as a value of the `ca_certs` parameter to *wrap_socket()*.

`ssl.CERT_REQUIRED`

Possible value for *SSLContext.verify_mode*, or the **cert_reqs** parameter to *wrap_socket()*. In this mode, certificates are required from the other side of the socket connection; an *SSLError* will be raised if no certificate is provided, or if its validation fails.

Use of this setting requires a valid set of CA certificates to be passed, either to *SSLContext.load_verify_locations()* or as a value of the **ca_certs** parameter to *wrap_socket()*.

`class ssl.VerifyMode`

enum.IntEnum collection of CERT_* constants.

New in version 3.6.

`ssl.VERIFY_DEFAULT`

Possible value for *SSLContext.verify_flags*. In this mode, certificate revocation lists (CRLs) are not checked. By default OpenSSL does neither require nor verify CRLs.

New in version 3.4.

`ssl.VERIFY_CRL_CHECK_LEAF`

Possible value for *SSLContext.verify_flags*. In this mode, only the peer cert is check but non of the intermediate CA certificates. The mode requires a valid CRL that is signed by the peer cert's issuer (its direct ancestor CA). If no proper has been loaded *SSLContext.load_verify_locations*, validation will fail.

New in version 3.4.

`ssl.VERIFY_CRL_CHECK_CHAIN`

Possible value for *SSLContext.verify_flags*. In this mode, CRLs of all certificates in the peer cert chain are checked.

New in version 3.4.

`ssl.VERIFY_X509_STRICT`

Possible value for *SSLContext.verify_flags* to disable workarounds for broken X.509 certificates.

New in version 3.4.

`ssl.VERIFY_X509_TRUSTED_FIRST`

Possible value for *SSLContext.verify_flags*. It instructs OpenSSL to prefer trusted certificates when building the trust chain to validate a certificate. This flag is enabled by default.

New in version 3.4.4.

`class ssl.VerifyFlags`

enum.IntFlag collection of VERIFY_* constants.

New in version 3.6.

`ssl.PROTOCOL_TLS`

Selects the highest protocol version that both the client and server support. Despite the name, this option can select both "SSL" and "TLS" protocols.

New in version 3.6.

`ssl.PROTOCOL_TLS_CLIENT`

Auto-negotiate the highest protocol version like *PROTOCOL_TLS*, but only support client-side *SSLSocket* connections. The protocol enables *CERT_REQUIRED* and *check_hostname* by default.

New in version 3.6.

`ssl.PROTOCOL_TLS_SERVER`

Auto-negotiate the highest protocol version like *PROTOCOL_TLS*, but only support server-side *SSLSocket* connections.

New in version 3.6.

`ssl.PROTOCOL_SSLv23`
Alias for data:*PROTOCOL_TLS*.

Deprecated since version 3.6: Use *PROTOCOL_TLS* instead.

`ssl.PROTOCOL_SSLv2`
Selects SSL version 2 as the channel encryption protocol.

This protocol is not available if OpenSSL is compiled with the `OPENSSL_NO_SSL2` flag.

> **Warning:** SSL version 2 is insecure. Its use is highly discouraged.

Deprecated since version 3.6: OpenSSL has removed support for SSLv2.

`ssl.PROTOCOL_SSLv3`
Selects SSL version 3 as the channel encryption protocol.

This protocol is not be available if OpenSSL is compiled with the `OPENSSL_NO_SSLv3` flag.

> **Warning:** SSL version 3 is insecure. Its use is highly discouraged.

Deprecated since version 3.6: OpenSSL has deprecated all version specific protocols. Use the default protocol *PROTOCOL_TLS* with flags like *OP_NO_SSLv3* instead.

`ssl.PROTOCOL_TLSv1`
Selects TLS version 1.0 as the channel encryption protocol.

Deprecated since version 3.6: OpenSSL has deprecated all version specific protocols. Use the default protocol *PROTOCOL_TLS* with flags like *OP_NO_SSLv3* instead.

`ssl.PROTOCOL_TLSv1_1`
Selects TLS version 1.1 as the channel encryption protocol. Available only with openssl version 1.0.1+.

New in version 3.4.

Deprecated since version 3.6: OpenSSL has deprecated all version specific protocols. Use the default protocol *PROTOCOL_TLS* with flags like *OP_NO_SSLv3* instead.

`ssl.PROTOCOL_TLSv1_2`
Selects TLS version 1.2 as the channel encryption protocol. This is the most modern version, and probably the best choice for maximum protection, if both sides can speak it. Available only with openssl version 1.0.1+.

New in version 3.4.

Deprecated since version 3.6: OpenSSL has deprecated all version specific protocols. Use the default protocol *PROTOCOL_TLS* with flags like *OP_NO_SSLv3* instead.

`ssl.OP_ALL`
Enables workarounds for various bugs present in other SSL implementations. This option is set by default. It does not necessarily set the same flags as OpenSSL's `SSL_OP_ALL` constant.

New in version 3.2.

`ssl.OP_NO_SSLv2`
Prevents an SSLv2 connection. This option is only applicable in conjunction with *PROTOCOL_TLS*. It prevents the peers from choosing SSLv2 as the protocol version.

New in version 3.2.

Deprecated since version 3.6: SSLv2 is deprecated

`ssl.OP_NO_SSLv3`
Prevents an SSLv3 connection. This option is only applicable in conjunction with *PROTOCOL_TLS*. It prevents the peers from choosing SSLv3 as the protocol version.

New in version 3.2.

Deprecated since version 3.6: SSLv3 is deprecated

`ssl.OP_NO_TLSv1`
Prevents a TLSv1 connection. This option is only applicable in conjunction with *PROTOCOL_TLS*. It prevents the peers from choosing TLSv1 as the protocol version.

New in version 3.2.

`ssl.OP_NO_TLSv1_1`
Prevents a TLSv1.1 connection. This option is only applicable in conjunction with *PROTOCOL_TLS*. It prevents the peers from choosing TLSv1.1 as the protocol version. Available only with openssl version 1.0.1+.

New in version 3.4.

`ssl.OP_NO_TLSv1_2`
Prevents a TLSv1.2 connection. This option is only applicable in conjunction with *PROTOCOL_TLS*. It prevents the peers from choosing TLSv1.2 as the protocol version. Available only with openssl version 1.0.1+.

New in version 3.4.

`ssl.OP_NO_TLSv1_3`
Prevents a TLSv1.3 connection. This option is only applicable in conjunction with *PROTOCOL_TLS*. It prevents the peers from choosing TLSv1.3 as the protocol version. TLS 1.3 is available with OpenSSL 1.1.1 or later. When Python has been compiled against an older version of OpenSSL, the flag defaults to *0*.

New in version 3.6.3.

`ssl.OP_CIPHER_SERVER_PREFERENCE`
Use the server's cipher ordering preference, rather than the client's. This option has no effect on client sockets and SSLv2 server sockets.

New in version 3.3.

`ssl.OP_SINGLE_DH_USE`
Prevents re-use of the same DH key for distinct SSL sessions. This improves forward secrecy but requires more computational resources. This option only applies to server sockets.

New in version 3.3.

`ssl.OP_SINGLE_ECDH_USE`
Prevents re-use of the same ECDH key for distinct SSL sessions. This improves forward secrecy but requires more computational resources. This option only applies to server sockets.

New in version 3.3.

`ssl.OP_NO_COMPRESSION`
Disable compression on the SSL channel. This is useful if the application protocol supports its own compression scheme.

This option is only available with OpenSSL 1.0.0 and later.

New in version 3.3.

`class ssl.Options`
enum.IntFlag collection of OP_* constants.

ssl.**OP_NO_TICKET**
Prevent client side from requesting a session ticket.

New in version 3.6.

ssl.**HAS_ALPN**
Whether the OpenSSL library has built-in support for the *Application-Layer Protocol Negotiation* TLS extension as described in RFC 7301.

New in version 3.5.

ssl.**HAS_ECDH**
Whether the OpenSSL library has built-in support for Elliptic Curve-based Diffie-Hellman key exchange. This should be true unless the feature was explicitly disabled by the distributor.

New in version 3.3.

ssl.**HAS_SNI**
Whether the OpenSSL library has built-in support for the *Server Name Indication* extension (as defined in RFC 6066).

New in version 3.2.

ssl.**HAS_NPN**
Whether the OpenSSL library has built-in support for *Next Protocol Negotiation* as described in the NPN draft specification. When true, you can use the *SSLContext.set_npn_protocols()* method to advertise which protocols you want to support.

New in version 3.3.

ssl.**HAS_TLSv1_3**
Whether the OpenSSL library has built-in support for the TLS 1.3 protocol.

New in version 3.6.3.

ssl.**CHANNEL_BINDING_TYPES**
List of supported TLS channel binding types. Strings in this list can be used as arguments to *SSLSocket.get_channel_binding()*.

New in version 3.3.

ssl.**OPENSSL_VERSION**
The version string of the OpenSSL library loaded by the interpreter:

```
>>> ssl.OPENSSL_VERSION
'OpenSSL 1.0.2k  26 Jan 2017'
```

New in version 3.2.

ssl.**OPENSSL_VERSION_INFO**
A tuple of five integers representing version information about the OpenSSL library:

```
>>> ssl.OPENSSL_VERSION_INFO
(1, 0, 2, 11, 15)
```

New in version 3.2.

ssl.**OPENSSL_VERSION_NUMBER**
The raw version number of the OpenSSL library, as a single integer:

```
>>> ssl.OPENSSL_VERSION_NUMBER
268443839
>>> hex(ssl.OPENSSL_VERSION_NUMBER)
'0x100020bf'
```

New in version 3.2.

ssl.ALERT_DESCRIPTION_HANDSHAKE_FAILURE
ssl.ALERT_DESCRIPTION_INTERNAL_ERROR
ALERT_DESCRIPTION_*

Alert Descriptions from RFC 5246 and others. The IANA TLS Alert Registry contains this list and references to the RFCs where their meaning is defined.

Used as the return value of the callback function in *SSLContext.set_servername_callback()*.

New in version 3.4.

class ssl.AlertDescription

enum.IntEnum collection of ALERT_DESCRIPTION_* constants.

New in version 3.6.

Purpose.SERVER_AUTH

Option for *create_default_context()* and *SSLContext.load_default_certs()*. This value indicates that the context may be used to authenticate Web servers (therefore, it will be used to create client-side sockets).

New in version 3.4.

Purpose.CLIENT_AUTH

Option for *create_default_context()* and *SSLContext.load_default_certs()*. This value indicates that the context may be used to authenticate Web clients (therefore, it will be used to create server-side sockets).

New in version 3.4.

class ssl.SSLErrorNumber

enum.IntEnum collection of SSL_ERROR_* constants.

New in version 3.6.

18.2.2 SSL Sockets

class ssl.SSLSocket(*socket.socket*)

SSL sockets provide the following methods of *Socket Objects*:

- *accept()*
- *bind()*
- *close()*
- *connect()*
- *detach()*
- *fileno()*
- *getpeername()*, *getsockname()*
- *getsockopt()*, *setsockopt()*
- *gettimeout()*, *settimeout()*, *setblocking()*
- *listen()*
- *makefile()*
- *recv()*, *recv_into()* (but passing a non-zero `flags` argument is not allowed)
- *send()*, *sendall()* (with the same limitation)
- *sendfile()* (but *os.sendfile* will be used for plain-text sockets only, else *send()* will be used)

- *shutdown()*

However, since the SSL (and TLS) protocol has its own framing atop of TCP, the SSL sockets abstraction can, in certain respects, diverge from the specification of normal, OS-level sockets. See especially the *notes on non-blocking sockets*.

Usually, *SSLSocket* are not created directly, but using the *SSLContext.wrap_socket()* method.

Changed in version 3.5: The `sendfile()` method was added.

Changed in version 3.5: The `shutdown()` does not reset the socket timeout each time bytes are received or sent. The socket timeout is now to maximum total duration of the shutdown.

Deprecated since version 3.6: It is deprecated to create a *SSLSocket* instance directly, use *SSLContext.wrap_socket()* to wrap a socket.

SSL sockets also have the following additional methods and attributes:

`SSLSocket.`**`read`**`(`*len=1024*, *buffer=None*`)`

Read up to *len* bytes of data from the SSL socket and return the result as a `bytes` instance. If *buffer* is specified, then read into the buffer instead, and return the number of bytes read.

Raise *SSLWantReadError* or *SSLWantWriteError* if the socket is *non-blocking* and the read would block.

As at any time a re-negotiation is possible, a call to *read()* can also cause write operations.

Changed in version 3.5: The socket timeout is no more reset each time bytes are received or sent. The socket timeout is now to maximum total duration to read up to *len* bytes.

Deprecated since version 3.6: Use `recv()` instead of *read()*.

`SSLSocket.`**`write`**`(`*buf*`)`

Write *buf* to the SSL socket and return the number of bytes written. The *buf* argument must be an object supporting the buffer interface.

Raise *SSLWantReadError* or *SSLWantWriteError* if the socket is *non-blocking* and the write would block.

As at any time a re-negotiation is possible, a call to *write()* can also cause read operations.

Changed in version 3.5: The socket timeout is no more reset each time bytes are received or sent. The socket timeout is now to maximum total duration to write *buf*.

Deprecated since version 3.6: Use `send()` instead of *write()*.

Note: The *read()* and *write()* methods are the low-level methods that read and write unencrypted, application-level data and decrypt/encrypt it to encrypted, wire-level data. These methods require an active SSL connection, i.e. the handshake was completed and *SSLSocket.unwrap()* was not called.

Normally you should use the socket API methods like *recv()* and *send()* instead of these methods.

`SSLSocket.`**`do_handshake`**`()`

Perform the SSL setup handshake.

Changed in version 3.4: The handshake method also performs *match_hostname()* when the *check_hostname* attribute of the socket's *context* is true.

Changed in version 3.5: The socket timeout is no more reset each time bytes are received or sent. The socket timeout is now to maximum total duration of the handshake.

`SSLSocket.`**`getpeercert`**`(`*binary_form=False*`)`

If there is no certificate for the peer on the other end of the connection, return `None`. If the SSL handshake hasn't been done yet, raise *ValueError*.

If the `binary_form` parameter is *False*, and a certificate was received from the peer, this method returns a *dict* instance. If the certificate was not validated, the dict is empty. If the certificate was validated, it returns a dict with several keys, amongst them `subject` (the principal for which the certificate was issued) and `issuer` (the principal issuing the certificate). If a certificate contains an instance of the *Subject Alternative Name* extension (see RFC 3280), there will also be a `subjectAltName` key in the dictionary.

The `subject` and `issuer` fields are tuples containing the sequence of relative distinguished names (RDNs) given in the certificate's data structure for the respective fields, and each RDN is a sequence of name-value pairs. Here is a real-world example:

```
{'issuer': ((('countryName', 'IL'),),
            (('organizationName', 'StartCom Ltd.'),),
            (('organizationalUnitName',
              'Secure Digital Certificate Signing'),),
            (('commonName',
              'StartCom Class 2 Primary Intermediate Server CA'),)),
 'notAfter': 'Nov 22 08:15:19 2013 GMT',
 'notBefore': 'Nov 21 03:09:52 2011 GMT',
 'serialNumber': '95F0',
 'subject': ((('description', '571208-SLe257oHY9fVQ07Z'),),
             (('countryName', 'US'),),
             (('stateOrProvinceName', 'California'),),
             (('localityName', 'San Francisco'),),
             (('organizationName', 'Electronic Frontier Foundation, Inc.'),),
             (('commonName', '*.eff.org'),),
             (('emailAddress', 'hostmaster@eff.org'),)),
 'subjectAltName': (('DNS', '*.eff.org'), ('DNS', 'eff.org')),
 'version': 3}
```

Note: To validate a certificate for a particular service, you can use the *match_hostname()* function.

If the `binary_form` parameter is *True*, and a certificate was provided, this method returns the DER-encoded form of the entire certificate as a sequence of bytes, or *None* if the peer did not provide a certificate. Whether the peer provides a certificate depends on the SSL socket's role:

- for a client SSL socket, the server will always provide a certificate, regardless of whether validation was required;
- for a server SSL socket, the client will only provide a certificate when requested by the server; therefore *getpeercert()* will return *None* if you used *CERT_NONE* (rather than *CERT_OPTIONAL* or *CERT_REQUIRED*).

Changed in version 3.2: The returned dictionary includes additional items such as `issuer` and `notBefore`.

Changed in version 3.4: *ValueError* is raised when the handshake isn't done. The returned dictionary includes additional X509v3 extension items such as `crlDistributionPoints`, `caIssuers` and `OCSP` URIs.

`SSLSocket.cipher()`

Returns a three-value tuple containing the name of the cipher being used, the version of the SSL protocol that defines its use, and the number of secret bits being used. If no connection has been established, returns `None`.

`SSLSocket.shared_ciphers()`

Return the list of ciphers shared by the client during the handshake. Each entry of the returned list is a three-value tuple containing the name of the cipher, the version of the SSL protocol that defines its use, and the number of secret bits the cipher uses. *shared_ciphers()* returns `None` if no connection has been established or the socket is a client socket.

New in version 3.5.

`SSLSocket.compression()`
Return the compression algorithm being used as a string, or `None` if the connection isn't compressed.

If the higher-level protocol supports its own compression mechanism, you can use *OP_NO_COMPRESSION* to disable SSL-level compression.

New in version 3.3.

`SSLSocket.get_channel_binding(cb_type="tls-unique")`
Get channel binding data for current connection, as a bytes object. Returns `None` if not connected or the handshake has not been completed.

The *cb_type* parameter allow selection of the desired channel binding type. Valid channel binding types are listed in the *CHANNEL_BINDING_TYPES* list. Currently only the 'tls-unique' channel binding, defined by RFC 5929, is supported. *ValueError* will be raised if an unsupported channel binding type is requested.

New in version 3.3.

`SSLSocket.selected_alpn_protocol()`
Return the protocol that was selected during the TLS handshake. If *SSLContext.set_alpn_protocols()* was not called, if the other party does not support ALPN, if this socket does not support any of the client's proposed protocols, or if the handshake has not happened yet, `None` is returned.

New in version 3.5.

`SSLSocket.selected_npn_protocol()`
Return the higher-level protocol that was selected during the TLS/SSL handshake. If *SSLContext.set_npn_protocols()* was not called, or if the other party does not support NPN, or if the handshake has not yet happened, this will return `None`.

New in version 3.3.

`SSLSocket.unwrap()`
Performs the SSL shutdown handshake, which removes the TLS layer from the underlying socket, and returns the underlying socket object. This can be used to go from encrypted operation over a connection to unencrypted. The returned socket should always be used for further communication with the other side of the connection, rather than the original socket.

`SSLSocket.version()`
Return the actual SSL protocol version negotiated by the connection as a string, or `None` is no secure connection is established. As of this writing, possible return values include `"SSLv2"`, `"SSLv3"`, `"TLSv1"`, `"TLSv1.1"` and `"TLSv1.2"`. Recent OpenSSL versions may define more return values.

New in version 3.5.

`SSLSocket.pending()`
Returns the number of already decrypted bytes available for read, pending on the connection.

`SSLSocket.context`
The *SSLContext* object this SSL socket is tied to. If the SSL socket was created using the top-level *wrap_socket()* function (rather than *SSLContext.wrap_socket()*), this is a custom context object created for this SSL socket.

New in version 3.2.

`SSLSocket.server_side`
A boolean which is `True` for server-side sockets and `False` for client-side sockets.

New in version 3.2.

`SSLSocket.server_hostname`
Hostname of the server: *str* type, or None for server-side socket or if the hostname was not specified in the constructor.

New in version 3.2.

`SSLSocket.session`
The *SSLSession* for this SSL connection. The session is available for client and server side sockets after the TLS handshake has been performed. For client sockets the session can be set before *do_handshake()* has been called to reuse a session.

New in version 3.6.

`SSLSocket.session_reused`
New in version 3.6.

18.2.3 SSL Contexts

New in version 3.2.

An SSL context holds various data longer-lived than single SSL connections, such as SSL configuration options, certificate(s) and private key(s). It also manages a cache of SSL sessions for server-side sockets, in order to speed up repeated connections from the same clients.

`class ssl.SSLContext(protocol=PROTOCOL_TLS)`
Create a new SSL context. You may pass *protocol* which must be one of the PROTOCOL_* constants defined in this module. *PROTOCOL_TLS* is currently recommended for maximum interoperability and default value.

See also:

create_default_context() lets the *ssl* module choose security settings for a given purpose.

Changed in version 3.6: The context is created with secure default values. The options *OP_NO_COMPRESSION*, *OP_CIPHER_SERVER_PREFERENCE*, *OP_SINGLE_DH_USE*, *OP_SINGLE_ECDH_USE*, *OP_NO_SSLv2* (except for *PROTOCOL_SSLv2*), and *OP_NO_SSLv3* (except for *PROTOCOL_SSLv3*) are set by default. The initial cipher suite list contains only HIGH ciphers, no NULL ciphers and no MD5 ciphers (except for *PROTOCOL_SSLv2*).

SSLContext objects have the following methods and attributes:

`SSLContext.cert_store_stats()`
Get statistics about quantities of loaded X.509 certificates, count of X.509 certificates flagged as CA certificates and certificate revocation lists as dictionary.

Example for a context with one CA cert and one other cert:

```
>>> context.cert_store_stats()
{'crl': 0, 'x509_ca': 1, 'x509': 2}
```

New in version 3.4.

`SSLContext.load_cert_chain(certfile, keyfile=None, password=None)`
Load a private key and the corresponding certificate. The *certfile* string must be the path to a single file in PEM format containing the certificate as well as any number of CA certificates needed to establish the certificate's authenticity. The *keyfile* string, if present, must point to a file containing the private key in. Otherwise the private key will be taken from *certfile* as well. See the discussion of *Certificates* for more information on how the certificate is stored in the *certfile*.

The *password* argument may be a function to call to get the password for decrypting the private key. It will only be called if the private key is encrypted and a password is necessary. It will be called with no arguments, and it should return a string, bytes, or bytearray. If the return value is a string it will be encoded as UTF-8 before using it to decrypt the key. Alternatively a string, bytes, or bytearray value may be supplied directly as the *password* argument. It will be ignored if the private key is not encrypted and no password is needed.

If the *password* argument is not specified and a password is required, OpenSSL's built-in password prompting mechanism will be used to interactively prompt the user for a password.

An `SSLError` is raised if the private key doesn't match with the certificate.

Changed in version 3.3: New optional argument *password*.

`SSLContext.load_default_certs(purpose=Purpose.SERVER_AUTH)`

Load a set of default "certification authority" (CA) certificates from default locations. On Windows it loads CA certs from the `CA` and `ROOT` system stores. On other systems it calls `SSLContext.set_default_verify_paths()`. In the future the method may load CA certificates from other locations, too.

The *purpose* flag specifies what kind of CA certificates are loaded. The default settings `Purpose.SERVER_AUTH` loads certificates, that are flagged and trusted for TLS web server authentication (client side sockets). `Purpose.CLIENT_AUTH` loads CA certificates for client certificate verification on the server side.

New in version 3.4.

`SSLContext.load_verify_locations(cafile=None, capath=None, cadata=None)`

Load a set of "certification authority" (CA) certificates used to validate other peers' certificates when `verify_mode` is other than `CERT_NONE`. At least one of *cafile* or *capath* must be specified.

This method can also load certification revocation lists (CRLs) in PEM or DER format. In order to make use of CRLs, `SSLContext.verify_flags` must be configured properly.

The *cafile* string, if present, is the path to a file of concatenated CA certificates in PEM format. See the discussion of *Certificates* for more information about how to arrange the certificates in this file.

The *capath* string, if present, is the path to a directory containing several CA certificates in PEM format, following an OpenSSL specific layout.

The *cadata* object, if present, is either an ASCII string of one or more PEM-encoded certificates or a *bytes-like object* of DER-encoded certificates. Like with *capath* extra lines around PEM-encoded certificates are ignored but at least one certificate must be present.

Changed in version 3.4: New optional argument *cadata*

`SSLContext.get_ca_certs(binary_form=False)`

Get a list of loaded "certification authority" (CA) certificates. If the `binary_form` parameter is `False` each list entry is a dict like the output of `SSLSocket.getpeercert()`. Otherwise the method returns a list of DER-encoded certificates. The returned list does not contain certificates from *capath* unless a certificate was requested and loaded by a SSL connection.

Note: Certificates in a capath directory aren't loaded unless they have been used at least once.

New in version 3.4.

`SSLContext.get_ciphers()`

Get a list of enabled ciphers. The list is in order of cipher priority. See `SSLContext.set_ciphers()`.

Example:

```
>>> ctx = ssl.SSLContext(ssl.PROTOCOL_SSLv23)
>>> ctx.set_ciphers('ECDHE+AESGCM:!ECDSA')
>>> ctx.get_ciphers()  # OpenSSL 1.0.x
[{'alg_bits': 256,
  'description': 'ECDHE-RSA-AES256-GCM-SHA384 TLSv1.2 Kx=ECDH     Au=RSA  '
                 'Enc=AESGCM(256) Mac=AEAD',
  'id': 50380848,
  'name': 'ECDHE-RSA-AES256-GCM-SHA384',
  'protocol': 'TLSv1/SSLv3',
  'strength_bits': 256},
 {'alg_bits': 128,
  'description': 'ECDHE-RSA-AES128-GCM-SHA256 TLSv1.2 Kx=ECDH     Au=RSA  '
                 'Enc=AESGCM(128) Mac=AEAD',
  'id': 50380847,
  'name': 'ECDHE-RSA-AES128-GCM-SHA256',
  'protocol': 'TLSv1/SSLv3',
  'strength_bits': 128}]
```

On OpenSSL 1.1 and newer the cipher dict contains additional fields::

```
>>> ctx.get_ciphers()  # OpenSSL 1.1+
[{'aead': True,
  'alg_bits': 256,
  'auth': 'auth-rsa',
  'description': 'ECDHE-RSA-AES256-GCM-SHA384 TLSv1.2 Kx=ECDH     Au=RSA  '
                 'Enc=AESGCM(256) Mac=AEAD',
  'digest': None,
  'id': 50380848,
  'kea': 'kx-ecdhe',
  'name': 'ECDHE-RSA-AES256-GCM-SHA384',
  'protocol': 'TLSv1.2',
  'strength_bits': 256,
  'symmetric': 'aes-256-gcm'},
 {'aead': True,
  'alg_bits': 128,
  'auth': 'auth-rsa',
  'description': 'ECDHE-RSA-AES128-GCM-SHA256 TLSv1.2 Kx=ECDH     Au=RSA  '
                 'Enc=AESGCM(128) Mac=AEAD',
  'digest': None,
  'id': 50380847,
  'kea': 'kx-ecdhe',
  'name': 'ECDHE-RSA-AES128-GCM-SHA256',
  'protocol': 'TLSv1.2',
  'strength_bits': 128,
  'symmetric': 'aes-128-gcm'}]
```

Availability: OpenSSL 1.0.2+

New in version 3.6.

`SSLContext.`**`set_default_verify_paths`**`()`

Load a set of default "certification authority" (CA) certificates from a filesystem path defined when building the OpenSSL library. Unfortunately, there's no easy way to know whether this method succeeds: no error is returned if no certificates are to be found. When the OpenSSL library is provided as part of the operating system, though, it is likely to be configured properly.

`SSLContext.`**`set_ciphers`**`(`*ciphers*`)`

Set the available ciphers for sockets created with this context. It should be a string in the OpenSSL cipher list format. If no cipher can be selected (because compile-time options or other configuration forbids use of all the specified ciphers), an *SSLError* will be raised.

Note: when connected, the *SSLSocket.cipher()* method of SSL sockets will give the currently selected cipher.

SSLContext.**set_alpn_protocols**(*protocols*)
Specify which protocols the socket should advertise during the SSL/TLS handshake. It should be a list of ASCII strings, like `['http/1.1', 'spdy/2']`, ordered by preference. The selection of a protocol will happen during the handshake, and will play out according to RFC 7301. After a successful handshake, the *SSLSocket.selected_alpn_protocol()* method will return the agreed-upon protocol.

This method will raise *NotImplementedError* if *HAS_ALPN* is False.

OpenSSL 1.1.0 to 1.1.0e will abort the handshake and raise *SSLError* when both sides support ALPN but cannot agree on a protocol. 1.1.0f+ behaves like 1.0.2, *SSLSocket.selected_alpn_protocol()* returns None.

New in version 3.5.

SSLContext.**set_npn_protocols**(*protocols*)
Specify which protocols the socket should advertise during the SSL/TLS handshake. It should be a list of strings, like `['http/1.1', 'spdy/2']`, ordered by preference. The selection of a protocol will happen during the handshake, and will play out according to the NPN draft specification. After a successful handshake, the *SSLSocket.selected_npn_protocol()* method will return the agreed-upon protocol.

This method will raise *NotImplementedError* if *HAS_NPN* is False.

New in version 3.3.

SSLContext.**set_servername_callback**(*server_name_callback*)
Register a callback function that will be called after the TLS Client Hello handshake message has been received by the SSL/TLS server when the TLS client specifies a server name indication. The server name indication mechanism is specified in RFC 6066 section 3 - Server Name Indication.

Only one callback can be set per `SSLContext`. If *server_name_callback* is `None` then the callback is disabled. Calling this function a subsequent time will disable the previously registered callback.

The callback function, *server_name_callback*, will be called with three arguments; the first being the *ssl.SSLSocket*, the second is a string that represents the server name that the client is intending to communicate (or *None* if the TLS Client Hello does not contain a server name) and the third argument is the original *SSLContext*. The server name argument is the IDNA decoded server name.

A typical use of this callback is to change the *ssl.SSLSocket*'s *SSLSocket.context* attribute to a new object of type *SSLContext* representing a certificate chain that matches the server name.

Due to the early negotiation phase of the TLS connection, only limited methods and attributes are usable like *SSLSocket.selected_alpn_protocol()* and *SSLSocket.context*. *SSLSocket.getpeercert()*, *SSLSocket.getpeercert()*, *SSLSocket.cipher()* and `SSLSocket.compress()` methods require that the TLS connection has progressed beyond the TLS Client Hello and therefore will not contain return meaningful values nor can they be called safely.

The *server_name_callback* function must return `None` to allow the TLS negotiation to continue. If a TLS failure is required, a constant *ALERT_DESCRIPTION_** can be returned. Other return values will result in a TLS fatal error with *ALERT_DESCRIPTION_INTERNAL_ERROR*.

If there is an IDNA decoding error on the server name, the TLS connection will terminate with an *ALERT_DESCRIPTION_INTERNAL_ERROR* fatal TLS alert message to the client.

If an exception is raised from the *server_name_callback* function the TLS connection will terminate with a fatal TLS alert message `ALERT_DESCRIPTION_HANDSHAKE_FAILURE`.

This method will raise `NotImplementedError` if the OpenSSL library had OPENSSL_NO_TLSEXT defined when it was built.

New in version 3.4.

`SSLContext.load_dh_params`(*dhfile*)

Load the key generation parameters for Diffie-Helman (DH) key exchange. Using DH key exchange improves forward secrecy at the expense of computational resources (both on the server and on the client). The *dhfile* parameter should be the path to a file containing DH parameters in PEM format.

This setting doesn't apply to client sockets. You can also use the `OP_SINGLE_DH_USE` option to further improve security.

New in version 3.3.

`SSLContext.set_ecdh_curve`(*curve_name*)

Set the curve name for Elliptic Curve-based Diffie-Hellman (ECDH) key exchange. ECDH is significantly faster than regular DH while arguably as secure. The *curve_name* parameter should be a string describing a well-known elliptic curve, for example `prime256v1` for a widely supported curve.

This setting doesn't apply to client sockets. You can also use the `OP_SINGLE_ECDH_USE` option to further improve security.

This method is not available if `HAS_ECDH` is `False`.

New in version 3.3.

See also:

SSL/TLS & Perfect Forward Secrecy Vincent Bernat.

`SSLContext.wrap_socket`(*sock, server_side=False, do_handshake_on_connect=True, suppress_ragged_eofs=True, server_hostname=None, session=None*)

Wrap an existing Python socket *sock* and return an `SSLSocket` object. *sock* must be a `SOCK_STREAM` socket; other socket types are unsupported.

The returned SSL socket is tied to the context, its settings and certificates. The parameters *server_side*, *do_handshake_on_connect* and *suppress_ragged_eofs* have the same meaning as in the top-level `wrap_socket()` function.

On client connections, the optional parameter *server_hostname* specifies the hostname of the service which we are connecting to. This allows a single server to host multiple SSL-based services with distinct certificates, quite similarly to HTTP virtual hosts. Specifying *server_hostname* will raise a `ValueError` if *server_side* is true.

session, see `session`.

Changed in version 3.5: Always allow a server_hostname to be passed, even if OpenSSL does not have SNI.

Changed in version 3.6: *session* argument was added.

`SSLContext.wrap_bio`(*incoming, outgoing, server_side=False, server_hostname=None, session=None*)

Create a new `SSLObject` instance by wrapping the BIO objects *incoming* and *outgoing*. The SSL routines will read input data from the incoming BIO and write data to the outgoing BIO.

The *server_side*, *server_hostname* and *session* parameters have the same meaning as in `SSLContext.wrap_socket()`.

Changed in version 3.6: *session* argument was added.

`SSLContext.session_stats()`

Get statistics about the SSL sessions created or managed by this context. A dictionary is returned which maps the names of each piece of information to their numeric values. For example, here is the total number of hits and misses in the session cache since the context was created:

```
>>> stats = context.session_stats()
>>> stats['hits'], stats['misses']
(0, 0)
```

`SSLContext.check_hostname`

Whether to match the peer cert's hostname with *match_hostname()* in *SSLSocket.do_handshake()*. The context's *verify_mode* must be set to *CERT_OPTIONAL* or *CERT_REQUIRED*, and you must pass *server_hostname* to *wrap_socket()* in order to match the hostname.

Example:

```
import socket, ssl

context = ssl.SSLContext(ssl.PROTOCOL_TLSv1)
context.verify_mode = ssl.CERT_REQUIRED
context.check_hostname = True
context.load_default_certs()

s = socket.socket(socket.AF_INET, socket.SOCK_STREAM)
ssl_sock = context.wrap_socket(s, server_hostname='www.verisign.com')
ssl_sock.connect(('www.verisign.com', 443))
```

New in version 3.4.

Note: This features requires OpenSSL 0.9.8f or newer.

`SSLContext.options`

An integer representing the set of SSL options enabled on this context. The default value is *OP_ALL*, but you can specify other options such as *OP_NO_SSLv2* by ORing them together.

Note: With versions of OpenSSL older than 0.9.8m, it is only possible to set options, not to clear them. Attempting to clear an option (by resetting the corresponding bits) will raise a `ValueError`.

Changed in version 3.6: *SSLContext.options* returns *Options* flags:

```
>>> ssl.create_default_context().options
<Options.OP_ALL|OP_NO_SSLv3|OP_NO_SSLv2|OP_NO_COMPRESSION: 2197947391>
```

`SSLContext.protocol`

The protocol version chosen when constructing the context. This attribute is read-only.

`SSLContext.verify_flags`

The flags for certificate verification operations. You can set flags like *VERIFY_CRL_CHECK_LEAF* by ORing them together. By default OpenSSL does neither require nor verify certificate revocation lists (CRLs). Available only with openssl version 0.9.8+.

New in version 3.4.

Changed in version 3.6: *SSLContext.verify_flags* returns *VerifyFlags* flags:

```
>>> ssl.create_default_context().verify_flags
<VerifyFlags.VERIFY_X509_TRUSTED_FIRST: 32768>
```

`SSLContext.verify_mode`

Whether to try to verify other peers' certificates and how to behave if verification fails. This attribute must be one of *CERT_NONE*, *CERT_OPTIONAL* or *CERT_REQUIRED*.

Changed in version 3.6: *SSLContext.verify_mode* returns *VerifyMode* enum:

```
>>> ssl.create_default_context().verify_mode
<VerifyMode.CERT_REQUIRED: 2>
```

18.2.4 Certificates

Certificates in general are part of a public-key / private-key system. In this system, each *principal*, (which may be a machine, or a person, or an organization) is assigned a unique two-part encryption key. One part of the key is public, and is called the *public key*; the other part is kept secret, and is called the *private key*. The two parts are related, in that if you encrypt a message with one of the parts, you can decrypt it with the other part, and **only** with the other part.

A certificate contains information about two principals. It contains the name of a *subject*, and the subject's public key. It also contains a statement by a second principal, the *issuer*, that the subject is who he claims to be, and that this is indeed the subject's public key. The issuer's statement is signed with the issuer's private key, which only the issuer knows. However, anyone can verify the issuer's statement by finding the issuer's public key, decrypting the statement with it, and comparing it to the other information in the certificate. The certificate also contains information about the time period over which it is valid. This is expressed as two fields, called "notBefore" and "notAfter".

In the Python use of certificates, a client or server can use a certificate to prove who they are. The other side of a network connection can also be required to produce a certificate, and that certificate can be validated to the satisfaction of the client or server that requires such validation. The connection attempt can be set to raise an exception if the validation fails. Validation is done automatically, by the underlying OpenSSL framework; the application need not concern itself with its mechanics. But the application does usually need to provide sets of certificates to allow this process to take place.

Python uses files to contain certificates. They should be formatted as "PEM" (see RFC 1422), which is a base-64 encoded form wrapped with a header line and a footer line:

```
-----BEGIN CERTIFICATE-----
... (certificate in base64 PEM encoding) ...
-----END CERTIFICATE-----
```

Certificate chains

The Python files which contain certificates can contain a sequence of certificates, sometimes called a *certificate chain*. This chain should start with the specific certificate for the principal who "is" the client or server, and then the certificate for the issuer of that certificate, and then the certificate for the issuer of *that* certificate, and so on up the chain till you get to a certificate which is *self-signed*, that is, a certificate which has the same subject and issuer, sometimes called a *root certificate*. The certificates should just be concatenated together in the certificate file. For example, suppose we had a three certificate chain, from our server certificate to the certificate of the certification authority that signed our server certificate, to the root certificate of the agency which issued the certification authority's certificate:

```
-----BEGIN CERTIFICATE-----
... (certificate for your server)...
-----END CERTIFICATE-----
-----BEGIN CERTIFICATE-----
... (the certificate for the CA)...
```

```
-----END CERTIFICATE-----
-----BEGIN CERTIFICATE-----
... (the root certificate for the CA's issuer)...
-----END CERTIFICATE-----
```

CA certificates

If you are going to require validation of the other side of the connection's certificate, you need to provide a "CA certs" file, filled with the certificate chains for each issuer you are willing to trust. Again, this file just contains these chains concatenated together. For validation, Python will use the first chain it finds in the file which matches. The platform's certificates file can be used by calling *SSLContext.load_default_certs()*, this is done automatically with *create_default_context()*.

Combined key and certificate

Often the private key is stored in the same file as the certificate; in this case, only the `certfile` parameter to *SSLContext.load_cert_chain()* and *wrap_socket()* needs to be passed. If the private key is stored with the certificate, it should come before the first certificate in the certificate chain:

```
-----BEGIN RSA PRIVATE KEY-----
... (private key in base64 encoding) ...
-----END RSA PRIVATE KEY-----
-----BEGIN CERTIFICATE-----
... (certificate in base64 PEM encoding) ...
-----END CERTIFICATE-----
```

Self-signed certificates

If you are going to create a server that provides SSL-encrypted connection services, you will need to acquire a certificate for that service. There are many ways of acquiring appropriate certificates, such as buying one from a certification authority. Another common practice is to generate a self-signed certificate. The simplest way to do this is with the OpenSSL package, using something like the following:

```
% openssl req -new -x509 -days 365 -nodes -out cert.pem -keyout cert.pem
Generating a 1024 bit RSA private key
.......++++++
.............................++++++
writing new private key to 'cert.pem'
-----
You are about to be asked to enter information that will be incorporated
into your certificate request.
What you are about to enter is what is called a Distinguished Name or a DN.
There are quite a few fields but you can leave some blank
For some fields there will be a default value,
If you enter '.', the field will be left blank.
-----
Country Name (2 letter code) [AU]:US
State or Province Name (full name) [Some-State]:MyState
Locality Name (eg, city) []:Some City
Organization Name (eg, company) [Internet Widgits Pty Ltd]:My Organization, Inc.
Organizational Unit Name (eg, section) []:My Group
Common Name (eg, YOUR name) []:myserver.mygroup.myorganization.com
Email Address []:ops@myserver.mygroup.myorganization.com
%
```

The disadvantage of a self-signed certificate is that it is its own root certificate, and no one else will have it in their cache of known (and trusted) root certificates.

18.2.5 Examples

Testing for SSL support

To test for the presence of SSL support in a Python installation, user code should use the following idiom:

```
try:
    import ssl
except ImportError:
    pass
else:
    ...  # do something that requires SSL support
```

Client-side operation

This example creates a SSL context with the recommended security settings for client sockets, including automatic certificate verification:

```
>>> context = ssl.create_default_context()
```

If you prefer to tune security settings yourself, you might create a context from scratch (but beware that you might not get the settings right):

```
>>> context = ssl.SSLContext(ssl.PROTOCOL_TLS)
>>> context.verify_mode = ssl.CERT_REQUIRED
>>> context.check_hostname = True
>>> context.load_verify_locations("/etc/ssl/certs/ca-bundle.crt")
```

(this snippet assumes your operating system places a bundle of all CA certificates in `/etc/ssl/certs/ca-bundle.crt`; if not, you'll get an error and have to adjust the location)

When you use the context to connect to a server, *CERT_REQUIRED* validates the server certificate: it ensures that the server certificate was signed with one of the CA certificates, and checks the signature for correctness:

```
>>> conn = context.wrap_socket(socket.socket(socket.AF_INET),
...                            server_hostname="www.python.org")
>>> conn.connect(("www.python.org", 443))
```

You may then fetch the certificate:

```
>>> cert = conn.getpeercert()
```

Visual inspection shows that the certificate does identify the desired service (that is, the HTTPS host `www.python.org`):

```
>>> pprint.pprint(cert)
{'OCSP': ('http://ocsp.digicert.com',),
 'caIssuers': ('http://cacerts.digicert.com/DigiCertSHA2ExtendedValidationServerCA.crt',),
 'crlDistributionPoints': ('http://crl3.digicert.com/sha2-ev-server-g1.crl',
                           'http://crl4.digicert.com/sha2-ev-server-g1.crl'),
 'issuer': ((('countryName', 'US'),),
```

```
            (('organizationName', 'DigiCert Inc'),),
            (('organizationalUnitName', 'www.digicert.com'),),
            (('commonName', 'DigiCert SHA2 Extended Validation Server CA'),)),
 'notAfter': 'Sep  9 12:00:00 2016 GMT',
 'notBefore': 'Sep  5 00:00:00 2014 GMT',
 'serialNumber': '01BB6F00122B177F36CAB49CEA8B6B26',
 'subject': ((('businessCategory', 'Private Organization'),),
             (('1.3.6.1.4.1.311.60.2.1.3', 'US'),),
             (('1.3.6.1.4.1.311.60.2.1.2', 'Delaware'),),
             (('serialNumber', '3359300'),),
             (('streetAddress', '16 Allen Rd'),),
             (('postalCode', '03894-4801'),),
             (('countryName', 'US'),),
             (('stateOrProvinceName', 'NH'),),
             (('localityName', 'Wolfeboro,'),),
             (('organizationName', 'Python Software Foundation'),),
             (('commonName', 'www.python.org'),)),
 'subjectAltName': (('DNS', 'www.python.org'),
                    ('DNS', 'python.org'),
                    ('DNS', 'pypi.python.org'),
                    ('DNS', 'docs.python.org'),
                    ('DNS', 'testpypi.python.org'),
                    ('DNS', 'bugs.python.org'),
                    ('DNS', 'wiki.python.org'),
                    ('DNS', 'hg.python.org'),
                    ('DNS', 'mail.python.org'),
                    ('DNS', 'packaging.python.org'),
                    ('DNS', 'pythonhosted.org'),
                    ('DNS', 'www.pythonhosted.org'),
                    ('DNS', 'test.pythonhosted.org'),
                    ('DNS', 'us.pycon.org'),
                    ('DNS', 'id.python.org')),
 'version': 3}
```

Now the SSL channel is established and the certificate verified, you can proceed to talk with the server:

```
>>> conn.sendall(b"HEAD / HTTP/1.0\r\nHost: linuxfr.org\r\n\r\n")
>>> pprint.pprint(conn.recv(1024).split(b"\r\n"))
[b'HTTP/1.1 200 OK',
 b'Date: Sat, 18 Oct 2014 18:27:20 GMT',
 b'Server: nginx',
 b'Content-Type: text/html; charset=utf-8',
 b'X-Frame-Options: SAMEORIGIN',
 b'Content-Length: 45679',
 b'Accept-Ranges: bytes',
 b'Via: 1.1 varnish',
 b'Age: 2188',
 b'X-Served-By: cache-lcy1134-LCY',
 b'X-Cache: HIT',
 b'X-Cache-Hits: 11',
 b'Vary: Cookie',
 b'Strict-Transport-Security: max-age=63072000; includeSubDomains',
 b'Connection: close',
 b'',
 b'']
```

See the discussion of *Security considerations* below.

Server-side operation

For server operation, typically you'll need to have a server certificate, and private key, each in a file. You'll first create a context holding the key and the certificate, so that clients can check your authenticity. Then you'll open a socket, bind it to a port, call `listen()` on it, and start waiting for clients to connect:

```
import socket, ssl

context = ssl.create_default_context(ssl.Purpose.CLIENT_AUTH)
context.load_cert_chain(certfile="mycertfile", keyfile="mykeyfile")

bindsocket = socket.socket()
bindsocket.bind(('myaddr.mydomain.com', 10023))
bindsocket.listen(5)
```

When a client connects, you'll call `accept()` on the socket to get the new socket from the other end, and use the context's *SSLContext.wrap_socket()* method to create a server-side SSL socket for the connection:

```
while True:
    newsocket, fromaddr = bindsocket.accept()
    connstream = context.wrap_socket(newsocket, server_side=True)
    try:
        deal_with_client(connstream)
    finally:
        connstream.shutdown(socket.SHUT_RDWR)
        connstream.close()
```

Then you'll read data from the `connstream` and do something with it till you are finished with the client (or the client is finished with you):

```
def deal_with_client(connstream):
    data = connstream.recv(1024)
    # empty data means the client is finished with us
    while data:
        if not do_something(connstream, data):
            # we'll assume do_something returns False
            # when we're finished with client
            break
        data = connstream.recv(1024)
    # finished with client
```

And go back to listening for new client connections (of course, a real server would probably handle each client connection in a separate thread, or put the sockets in *non-blocking mode* and use an event loop).

18.2.6 Notes on non-blocking sockets

SSL sockets behave slightly different than regular sockets in non-blocking mode. When working with non-blocking sockets, there are thus several things you need to be aware of:

- Most *SSLSocket* methods will raise either *SSLWantWriteError* or *SSLWantReadError* instead of *BlockingIOError* if an I/O operation would block. *SSLWantReadError* will be raised if a read operation on the underlying socket is necessary, and *SSLWantWriteError* for a write operation on the underlying socket. Note that attempts to *write* to an SSL socket may require *reading* from the underlying socket first, and attempts to *read* from the SSL socket may require a prior *write* to the underlying socket.

  Changed in version 3.5: In earlier Python versions, the `SSLSocket.send()` method returned zero instead of raising *SSLWantWriteError* or *SSLWantReadError*.

- Calling *select()* tells you that the OS-level socket can be read from (or written to), but it does not imply that there is sufficient data at the upper SSL layer. For example, only part of an SSL frame might have arrived. Therefore, you must be ready to handle `SSLSocket.recv()` and `SSLSocket.send()` failures, and retry after another call to *select()*.
- Conversely, since the SSL layer has its own framing, a SSL socket may still have data available for reading without *select()* being aware of it. Therefore, you should first call `SSLSocket.recv()` to drain any potentially available data, and then only block on a *select()* call if still necessary.

  (of course, similar provisions apply when using other primitives such as *poll()*, or those in the *selectors* module)
- The SSL handshake itself will be non-blocking: the *SSLSocket.do_handshake()* method has to be retried until it returns successfully. Here is a synopsis using *select()* to wait for the socket's readiness:

```
while True:
    try:
        sock.do_handshake()
        break
    except ssl.SSLWantReadError:
        select.select([sock], [], [])
    except ssl.SSLWantWriteError:
        select.select([], [sock], [])
```

See also:

The *asyncio* module supports *non-blocking SSL sockets* and provides a higher level API. It polls for events using the *selectors* module and handles *SSLWantWriteError*, *SSLWantReadError* and *BlockingIOError* exceptions. It runs the SSL handshake asynchronously as well.

18.2.7 Memory BIO Support

New in version 3.5.

Ever since the SSL module was introduced in Python 2.6, the *SSLSocket* class has provided two related but distinct areas of functionality:

- SSL protocol handling
- Network IO

The network IO API is identical to that provided by *socket.socket*, from which *SSLSocket* also inherits. This allows an SSL socket to be used as a drop-in replacement for a regular socket, making it very easy to add SSL support to an existing application.

Combining SSL protocol handling and network IO usually works well, but there are some cases where it doesn't. An example is async IO frameworks that want to use a different IO multiplexing model than the "select/poll on a file descriptor" (readiness based) model that is assumed by *socket.socket* and by the internal OpenSSL socket IO routines. This is mostly relevant for platforms like Windows where this model is not efficient. For this purpose, a reduced scope variant of *SSLSocket* called *SSLObject* is provided.

class ssl.SSLObject

A reduced-scope variant of *SSLSocket* representing an SSL protocol instance that does not contain any network IO methods. This class is typically used by framework authors that want to implement asynchronous IO for SSL through memory buffers.

This class implements an interface on top of a low-level SSL object as implemented by OpenSSL. This object captures the state of an SSL connection but does not provide any network IO itself. IO needs to be performed through separate "BIO" objects which are OpenSSL's IO abstraction layer.

An *SSLObject* instance can be created using the *wrap_bio()* method. This method will create the *SSLObject* instance and bind it to a pair of BIOs. The *incoming* BIO is used to pass data from Python to the SSL protocol instance, while the *outgoing* BIO is used to pass data the other way around.

The following methods are available:

- *context*
- *server_side*
- *server_hostname*
- *session*
- *session_reused*
- *read()*
- *write()*
- *getpeercert()*
- *selected_npn_protocol()*
- *cipher()*
- *shared_ciphers()*
- *compression()*
- *pending()*
- *do_handshake()*
- *unwrap()*
- *get_channel_binding()*

When compared to *SSLSocket*, this object lacks the following features:

- Any form of network IO; `recv()` and `send()` read and write only to the underlying *MemoryBIO* buffers.
- There is no *do_handshake_on_connect* machinery. You must always manually call *do_handshake()* to start the handshake.
- There is no handling of *suppress_ragged_eofs*. All end-of-file conditions that are in violation of the protocol are reported via the *SSLEOFError* exception.
- The method *unwrap()* call does not return anything, unlike for an SSL socket where it returns the underlying socket.
- The *server_name_callback* callback passed to *SSLContext.set_servername_callback()* will get an *SSLObject* instance instead of a *SSLSocket* instance as its first parameter.

Some notes related to the use of *SSLObject*:

- All IO on an *SSLObject* is *non-blocking*. This means that for example *read()* will raise an *SSLWantReadError* if it needs more data than the incoming BIO has available.
- There is no module-level `wrap_bio()` call like there is for *wrap_socket()*. An *SSLObject* is always created via an *SSLContext*.

An SSLObject communicates with the outside world using memory buffers. The class *MemoryBIO* provides a memory buffer that can be used for this purpose. It wraps an OpenSSL memory BIO (Basic IO) object:

class ssl.MemoryBIO
A memory buffer that can be used to pass data between Python and an SSL protocol instance.

pending
Return the number of bytes currently in the memory buffer.

eof
A boolean indicating whether the memory BIO is current at the end-of-file position.

read(*n=-1*)
Read up to *n* bytes from the memory buffer. If *n* is not specified or negative, all bytes are returned.

write(*buf*)
Write the bytes from *buf* to the memory BIO. The *buf* argument must be an object supporting the buffer protocol.

The return value is the number of bytes written, which is always equal to the length of *buf*.

write_eof()
Write an EOF marker to the memory BIO. After this method has been called, it is illegal to call `write()`. The attribute `eof` will become true after all data currently in the buffer has been read.

18.2.8 SSL session

New in version 3.6.

class ssl.SSLSession
Session object used by `session`.

id

time

timeout

ticket_lifetime_hint

has_ticket

18.2.9 Security considerations

Best defaults

For **client use**, if you don't have any special requirements for your security policy, it is highly recommended that you use the `create_default_context()` function to create your SSL context. It will load the system's trusted CA certificates, enable certificate validation and hostname checking, and try to choose reasonably secure protocol and cipher settings.

For example, here is how you would use the `smtplib.SMTP` class to create a trusted, secure connection to a SMTP server:

```
>>> import ssl, smtplib
>>> smtp = smtplib.SMTP("mail.python.org", port=587)
>>> context = ssl.create_default_context()
>>> smtp.starttls(context=context)
(220, b'2.0.0 Ready to start TLS')
```

If a client certificate is needed for the connection, it can be added with `SSLContext.load_cert_chain()`.

By contrast, if you create the SSL context by calling the `SSLContext` constructor yourself, it will not have certificate validation nor hostname checking enabled by default. If you do so, please read the paragraphs below to achieve a good security level.

Manual settings

Verifying certificates

When calling the *SSLContext* constructor directly, *CERT_NONE* is the default. Since it does not authenticate the other peer, it can be insecure, especially in client mode where most of time you would like to ensure the authenticity of the server you're talking to. Therefore, when in client mode, it is highly recommended to use *CERT_REQUIRED*. However, it is in itself not sufficient; you also have to check that the server certificate, which can be obtained by calling *SSLSocket.getpeercert()*, matches the desired service. For many protocols and applications, the service can be identified by the hostname; in this case, the *match_hostname()* function can be used. This common check is automatically performed when *SSLContext.check_hostname* is enabled.

In server mode, if you want to authenticate your clients using the SSL layer (rather than using a higher-level authentication mechanism), you'll also have to specify *CERT_REQUIRED* and similarly check the client certificate.

Note: In client mode, *CERT_OPTIONAL* and *CERT_REQUIRED* are equivalent unless anonymous ciphers are enabled (they are disabled by default).

Protocol versions

SSL versions 2 and 3 are considered insecure and are therefore dangerous to use. If you want maximum compatibility between clients and servers, it is recommended to use *PROTOCOL_TLS_CLIENT* or *PROTOCOL_TLS_SERVER* as the protocol version. SSLv2 and SSLv3 are disabled by default.

```
>>> client_context = ssl.SSLContext(ssl.PROTOCOL_TLS_CLIENT)
>>> client_context.options |= ssl.OP_NO_TLSv1
>>> client_context.options |= ssl.OP_NO_TLSv1_1
```

The SSL context created above will only allow TLSv1.2 and later (if supported by your system) connections to a server. *PROTOCOL_TLS_CLIENT* implies certificate validation and hostname checks by default. You have to load certificates into the context.

Cipher selection

If you have advanced security requirements, fine-tuning of the ciphers enabled when negotiating a SSL session is possible through the *SSLContext.set_ciphers()* method. Starting from Python 3.2.3, the ssl module disables certain weak ciphers by default, but you may want to further restrict the cipher choice. Be sure to read OpenSSL's documentation about the cipher list format. If you want to check which ciphers are enabled by a given cipher list, use *SSLContext.get_ciphers()* or the `openssl ciphers` command on your system.

Multi-processing

If using this module as part of a multi-processed application (using, for example the *multiprocessing* or *concurrent.futures* modules), be aware that OpenSSL's internal random number generator does not properly handle forked processes. Applications must change the PRNG state of the parent process if they use any SSL feature with *os.fork()*. Any successful call of *RAND_add()*, *RAND_bytes()* or *RAND_pseudo_bytes()* is sufficient.

See also:

Class *socket.socket* Documentation of underlying *socket* class

SSL/TLS Strong Encryption: An Introduction Intro from the Apache webserver documentation

RFC 1422: Privacy Enhancement for Internet Electronic Mail: Part II: Certificate-Based Key Manageme
Steve Kent

RFC 4086: Randomness Requirements for Security Donald E., Jeffrey I. Schiller

RFC 5280: Internet X.509 Public Key Infrastructure Certificate and Certificate Revocation List (CRL) P
D. Cooper

RFC 5246: The Transport Layer Security (TLS) Protocol Version 1.2 T. Dierks et. al.

RFC 6066: Transport Layer Security (TLS) Extensions D. Eastlake

IANA TLS: Transport Layer Security (TLS) Parameters IANA

RFC 7525: Recommendations for Secure Use of Transport Layer Security (TLS) and Datagram Transport
IETF

Mozilla's Server Side TLS recommendations Mozilla

18.3 `select` — Waiting for I/O completion

This module provides access to the `select()` and `poll()` functions available in most operating systems, `devpoll()` available on Solaris and derivatives, `epoll()` available on Linux 2.5+ and `kqueue()` available on most BSD. Note that on Windows, it only works for sockets; on other operating systems, it also works for other file types (in particular, on Unix, it works on pipes). It cannot be used on regular files to determine whether a file has grown since it was last read.

Note: The `selectors` module allows high-level and efficient I/O multiplexing, built upon the `select` module primitives. Users are encouraged to use the `selectors` module instead, unless they want precise control over the OS-level primitives used.

The module defines the following:

exception select.error
A deprecated alias of `OSError`.

Changed in version 3.3: Following PEP 3151, this class was made an alias of `OSError`.

select.devpoll()
(Only supported on Solaris and derivatives.) Returns a `/dev/poll` polling object; see section */dev/poll Polling Objects* below for the methods supported by devpoll objects.

`devpoll()` objects are linked to the number of file descriptors allowed at the time of instantiation. If your program reduces this value, `devpoll()` will fail. If your program increases this value, `devpoll()` may return an incomplete list of active file descriptors.

The new file descriptor is *non-inheritable*.

New in version 3.3.

Changed in version 3.4: The new file descriptor is now non-inheritable.

select.epoll(*sizehint=-1, flags=0*)
(Only supported on Linux 2.5.44 and newer.) Return an edge polling object, which can be used as Edge or Level Triggered interface for I/O events. *sizehint* and *flags* are deprecated and completely ignored.

See the *Edge and Level Trigger Polling (epoll) Objects* section below for the methods supported by epolling objects.

`epoll` objects support the context management protocol: when used in a `with` statement, the new file descriptor is automatically closed at the end of the block.

The new file descriptor is *non-inheritable*.

Changed in version 3.3: Added the *flags* parameter.

Changed in version 3.4: Support for the `with` statement was added. The new file descriptor is now non-inheritable.

Deprecated since version 3.4: The *flags* parameter. `select.EPOLL_CLOEXEC` is used by default now. Use `os.set_inheritable()` to make the file descriptor inheritable.

`select.poll()`

(Not supported by all operating systems.) Returns a polling object, which supports registering and unregistering file descriptors, and then polling them for I/O events; see section *Polling Objects* below for the methods supported by polling objects.

`select.kqueue()`

(Only supported on BSD.) Returns a kernel queue object; see section *Kqueue Objects* below for the methods supported by kqueue objects.

The new file descriptor is *non-inheritable*.

Changed in version 3.4: The new file descriptor is now non-inheritable.

`select.kevent(`*ident, filter=KQ_FILTER_READ, flags=KQ_EV_ADD, fflags=0, data=0, udata=0*`)`

(Only supported on BSD.) Returns a kernel event object; see section *Kevent Objects* below for the methods supported by kevent objects.

`select.select(`*rlist, wlist, xlist*[, *timeout*]`)`

This is a straightforward interface to the Unix `select()` system call. The first three arguments are sequences of 'waitable objects': either integers representing file descriptors or objects with a parameterless method named `fileno()` returning such an integer:

- *rlist*: wait until ready for reading
- *wlist*: wait until ready for writing
- *xlist*: wait for an "exceptional condition" (see the manual page for what your system considers such a condition)

Empty sequences are allowed, but acceptance of three empty sequences is platform-dependent. (It is known to work on Unix but not on Windows.) The optional *timeout* argument specifies a time-out as a floating point number in seconds. When the *timeout* argument is omitted the function blocks until at least one file descriptor is ready. A time-out value of zero specifies a poll and never blocks.

The return value is a triple of lists of objects that are ready: subsets of the first three arguments. When the time-out is reached without a file descriptor becoming ready, three empty lists are returned.

Among the acceptable object types in the sequences are Python *file objects* (e.g. `sys.stdin`, or objects returned by `open()` or `os.popen()`), socket objects returned by `socket.socket()`. You may also define a *wrapper* class yourself, as long as it has an appropriate `fileno()` method (that really returns a file descriptor, not just a random integer).

Note: File objects on Windows are not acceptable, but sockets are. On Windows, the underlying `select()` function is provided by the WinSock library, and does not handle file descriptors that don't originate from WinSock.

Changed in version 3.5: The function is now retried with a recomputed timeout when interrupted by a signal, except if the signal handler raises an exception (see PEP 475 for the rationale), instead of raising *InterruptedError*.

`select.PIPE_BUF`
The minimum number of bytes which can be written without blocking to a pipe when the pipe has been reported as ready for writing by *select()*, *poll()* or another interface in this module. This doesn't apply to other kind of file-like objects such as sockets.

This value is guaranteed by POSIX to be at least 512. Availability: Unix.

New in version 3.2.

18.3.1 /dev/poll Polling Objects

Solaris and derivatives have `/dev/poll`. While `select()` is O(highest file descriptor) and `poll()` is O(number of file descriptors), `/dev/poll` is O(active file descriptors).

`/dev/poll` behaviour is very close to the standard `poll()` object.

`devpoll.close()`
Close the file descriptor of the polling object.

New in version 3.4.

`devpoll.closed`
`True` if the polling object is closed.

New in version 3.4.

`devpoll.fileno()`
Return the file descriptor number of the polling object.

New in version 3.4.

`devpoll.register(`*fd*[, *eventmask*]`)`
Register a file descriptor with the polling object. Future calls to the *poll()* method will then check whether the file descriptor has any pending I/O events. *fd* can be either an integer, or an object with a *fileno()* method that returns an integer. File objects implement `fileno()`, so they can also be used as the argument.

eventmask is an optional bitmask describing the type of events you want to check for. The constants are the same that with `poll()` object. The default value is a combination of the constants `POLLIN`, `POLLPRI`, and `POLLOUT`.

> **Warning:** Registering a file descriptor that's already registered is not an error, but the result is undefined. The appropriate action is to unregister or modify it first. This is an important difference compared with `poll()`.

`devpoll.modify(`*fd*[, *eventmask*]`)`
This method does an *unregister()* followed by a *register()*. It is (a bit) more efficient that doing the same explicitly.

`devpoll.unregister(`*fd*`)`
Remove a file descriptor being tracked by a polling object. Just like the *register()* method, *fd* can be an integer or an object with a *fileno()* method that returns an integer.

Attempting to remove a file descriptor that was never registered is safely ignored.

`devpoll.poll([timeout])`

Polls the set of registered file descriptors, and returns a possibly-empty list containing `(fd, event)` 2-tuples for the descriptors that have events or errors to report. *fd* is the file descriptor, and *event* is a bitmask with bits set for the reported events for that descriptor — `POLLIN` for waiting input, `POLLOUT` to indicate that the descriptor can be written to, and so forth. An empty list indicates that the call timed out and no file descriptors had any events to report. If *timeout* is given, it specifies the length of time in milliseconds which the system will wait for events before returning. If *timeout* is omitted, -1, or *None*, the call will block until there is an event for this poll object.

Changed in version 3.5: The function is now retried with a recomputed timeout when interrupted by a signal, except if the signal handler raises an exception (see PEP 475 for the rationale), instead of raising *InterruptedError*.

18.3.2 Edge and Level Trigger Polling (epoll) Objects

http://linux.die.net/man/4/epoll

eventmask

Constant	Meaning
EPOLLIN	Available for read
EPOLLOUT	Available for write
EPOLLPRI	Urgent data for read
EPOLLERR	Error condition happened on the assoc. fd
EPOLLHUP	Hang up happened on the assoc. fd
EPOLLET	Set Edge Trigger behavior, the default is Level Trigger behavior
EPOLLONESHOT	Set one-shot behavior. After one event is pulled out, the fd is internally disabled
EPOLLEXCLUSIVE	Wake only one epoll object when the associated fd has an event. The default (if this flag is not set) is to wake all epoll objects polling on a fd.
EPOLLRDHUP	Stream socket peer closed connection or shut down writing half of connection.
EPOLLRDNORM	Equivalent to `EPOLLIN`
EPOLLRDBAND	Priority data band can be read.
EPOLLWRNORM	Equivalent to `EPOLLOUT`
EPOLLWRBAND	Priority data may be written.
EPOLLMSG	Ignored.

`epoll.close()`

Close the control file descriptor of the epoll object.

`epoll.closed`

`True` if the epoll object is closed.

`epoll.fileno()`

Return the file descriptor number of the control fd.

`epoll.fromfd(fd)`

Create an epoll object from a given file descriptor.

`epoll.register(fd[, eventmask])`

Register a fd descriptor with the epoll object.

`epoll.modify(fd, eventmask)`

Modify a registered file descriptor.

`epoll.unregister(fd)`

Remove a registered file descriptor from the epoll object.

`epoll.poll(timeout=-1, maxevents=-1)`

Wait for events. timeout in seconds (float)

Changed in version 3.5: The function is now retried with a recomputed timeout when interrupted by a signal, except if the signal handler raises an exception (see PEP 475 for the rationale), instead of raising *InterruptedError*.

18.3.3 Polling Objects

The `poll()` system call, supported on most Unix systems, provides better scalability for network servers that service many, many clients at the same time. `poll()` scales better because the system call only requires listing the file descriptors of interest, while `select()` builds a bitmap, turns on bits for the fds of interest, and then afterward the whole bitmap has to be linearly scanned again. `select()` is O(highest file descriptor), while `poll()` is O(number of file descriptors).

`poll.register(fd[, eventmask])`

Register a file descriptor with the polling object. Future calls to the *poll()* method will then check whether the file descriptor has any pending I/O events. *fd* can be either an integer, or an object with a *fileno()* method that returns an integer. File objects implement `fileno()`, so they can also be used as the argument.

eventmask is an optional bitmask describing the type of events you want to check for, and can be a combination of the constants `POLLIN`, `POLLPRI`, and `POLLOUT`, described in the table below. If not specified, the default value used will check for all 3 types of events.

Constant	Meaning
POLLIN	There is data to read
POLLPRI	There is urgent data to read
POLLOUT	Ready for output: writing will not block
POLLERR	Error condition of some sort
POLLHUP	Hung up
POLLRDHUP	Stream socket peer closed connection, or shut down writing half of connection
POLLNVAL	Invalid request: descriptor not open

Registering a file descriptor that's already registered is not an error, and has the same effect as registering the descriptor exactly once.

`poll.modify(fd, eventmask)`

Modifies an already registered fd. This has the same effect as `register(fd, eventmask)`. Attempting to modify a file descriptor that was never registered causes an *OSError* exception with errno `ENOENT` to be raised.

`poll.unregister(fd)`

Remove a file descriptor being tracked by a polling object. Just like the *register()* method, *fd* can be an integer or an object with a *fileno()* method that returns an integer.

Attempting to remove a file descriptor that was never registered causes a *KeyError* exception to be raised.

`poll.poll([timeout])`

Polls the set of registered file descriptors, and returns a possibly-empty list containing `(fd, event)` 2-tuples for the descriptors that have events or errors to report. *fd* is the file descriptor, and *event* is a bitmask with bits set for the reported events for that descriptor — `POLLIN` for waiting input, `POLLOUT` to indicate that the descriptor can be written to, and so forth. An empty list indicates that the call timed out and no file descriptors had any events to report. If *timeout* is given, it specifies the length of time in milliseconds which the system will wait for events before returning. If *timeout* is omitted, negative, or *None*, the call will block until there is an event for this poll object.

Changed in version 3.5: The function is now retried with a recomputed timeout when interrupted by a signal, except if the signal handler raises an exception (see PEP 475 for the rationale), instead of raising *InterruptedError*.

18.3.4 Kqueue Objects

`kqueue.close()`
Close the control file descriptor of the kqueue object.

`kqueue.closed`
`True` if the kqueue object is closed.

`kqueue.fileno()`
Return the file descriptor number of the control fd.

`kqueue.fromfd(fd)`
Create a kqueue object from a given file descriptor.

`kqueue.control(changelist, max_events[, timeout=None])` → eventlist
Low level interface to kevent

- changelist must be an iterable of kevent object or `None`
- max_events must be 0 or a positive integer
- timeout in seconds (floats possible)

Changed in version 3.5: The function is now retried with a recomputed timeout when interrupted by a signal, except if the signal handler raises an exception (see PEP 475 for the rationale), instead of raising *InterruptedError*.

18.3.5 Kevent Objects

https://www.freebsd.org/cgi/man.cgi?query=kqueue&sektion=2

`kevent.ident`
Value used to identify the event. The interpretation depends on the filter but it's usually the file descriptor. In the constructor ident can either be an int or an object with a *fileno()* method. kevent stores the integer internally.

`kevent.filter`
Name of the kernel filter.

Constant	Meaning
KQ_FILTER_READ	Takes a descriptor and returns whenever there is data available to read
KQ_FILTER_WRITE	Takes a descriptor and returns whenever there is data available to write
KQ_FILTER_AIO	AIO requests
KQ_FILTER_VNODE	Returns when one or more of the requested events watched in *fflag* occurs
KQ_FILTER_PROC	Watch for events on a process id
KQ_FILTER_NETDEV	Watch for events on a network device [not available on Mac OS X]
KQ_FILTER_SIGNAL	Returns whenever the watched signal is delivered to the process
KQ_FILTER_TIMER	Establishes an arbitrary timer

`kevent.flags`
Filter action.

Constant	Meaning
KQ_EV_ADD	Adds or modifies an event
KQ_EV_DELETE	Removes an event from the queue
KQ_EV_ENABLE	Permitscontrol() to returns the event
KQ_EV_DISABLE	Disablesevent
KQ_EV_ONESHOT	Removes event after first occurrence
KQ_EV_CLEAR	Reset the state after an event is retrieved
KQ_EV_SYSFLAGS	internal event
KQ_EV_FLAG1	internal event
KQ_EV_EOF	Filter specific EOF condition
KQ_EV_ERROR	See return values

kevent.**fflags**

Filter specific flags.

KQ_FILTER_READ and KQ_FILTER_WRITE filter flags:

Constant	Meaning
KQ_NOTE_LOWAT	low water mark of a socket buffer

KQ_FILTER_VNODE filter flags:

Constant	Meaning
KQ_NOTE_DELETE	*unlink()* was called
KQ_NOTE_WRITE	a write occurred
KQ_NOTE_EXTEND	the file was extended
KQ_NOTE_ATTRIB	an attribute was changed
KQ_NOTE_LINK	the link count has changed
KQ_NOTE_RENAME	the file was renamed
KQ_NOTE_REVOKE	access to the file was revoked

KQ_FILTER_PROC filter flags:

Constant	Meaning
KQ_NOTE_EXIT	the process has exited
KQ_NOTE_FORK	the process has called *fork()*
KQ_NOTE_EXEC	the process has executed a new process
KQ_NOTE_PCTRLMASK	internal filter flag
KQ_NOTE_PDATAMASK	internal filter flag
KQ_NOTE_TRACK	follow a process across *fork()*
KQ_NOTE_CHILD	returned on the child process for *NOTE_TRACK*
KQ_NOTE_TRACKERR	unable to attach to a child

KQ_FILTER_NETDEV filter flags (not available on Mac OS X):

Constant	Meaning
KQ_NOTE_LINKUP	link is up
KQ_NOTE_LINKDOWN	link is down
KQ_NOTE_LINKINV	link state is invalid

kevent.**data**

Filter specific data.

kevent.udata
User defined value.

18.4 selectors — High-level I/O multiplexing

New in version 3.4.

Source code: Lib/selectors.py

18.4.1 Introduction

This module allows high-level and efficient I/O multiplexing, built upon the *select* module primitives. Users are encouraged to use this module instead, unless they want precise control over the OS-level primitives used.

It defines a *BaseSelector* abstract base class, along with several concrete implementations (*KqueueSelector*, *EpollSelector*...), that can be used to wait for I/O readiness notification on multiple file objects. In the following, "file object" refers to any object with a `fileno()` method, or a raw file descriptor. See *file object*.

DefaultSelector is an alias to the most efficient implementation available on the current platform: this should be the default choice for most users.

Note: The type of file objects supported depends on the platform: on Windows, sockets are supported, but not pipes, whereas on Unix, both are supported (some other types may be supported as well, such as fifos or special file devices).

See also:

select Low-level I/O multiplexing module.

18.4.2 Classes

Classes hierarchy:

```
BaseSelector
+-- SelectSelector
+-- PollSelector
+-- EpollSelector
+-- DevpollSelector
+-- KqueueSelector
```

In the following, *events* is a bitwise mask indicating which I/O events should be waited for on a given file object. It can be a combination of the modules constants below:

Constant	Meaning
EVENT_READ	Available for read
EVENT_WRITE	Available for write

class selectors.SelectorKey
A *SelectorKey* is a *namedtuple* used to associate a file object to its underlying file descriptor, selected event mask and attached data. It is returned by several *BaseSelector* methods.

fileobj
File object registered.

fd
Underlying file descriptor.

events
Events that must be waited for on this file object.

data
Optional opaque data associated to this file object: for example, this could be used to store a per-client session ID.

class selectors.BaseSelector
A *BaseSelector* is used to wait for I/O event readiness on multiple file objects. It supports file stream registration, unregistration, and a method to wait for I/O events on those streams, with an optional timeout. It's an abstract base class, so cannot be instantiated. Use *DefaultSelector* instead, or one of *SelectSelector*, *KqueueSelector* etc. if you want to specifically use an implementation, and your platform supports it. *BaseSelector* and its concrete implementations support the *context manager* protocol.

abstractmethod register(*fileobj, events, data=None*)
Register a file object for selection, monitoring it for I/O events.

fileobj is the file object to monitor. It may either be an integer file descriptor or an object with a `fileno()` method. *events* is a bitwise mask of events to monitor. *data* is an opaque object.

This returns a new *SelectorKey* instance, or raises a *ValueError* in case of invalid event mask or file descriptor, or *KeyError* if the file object is already registered.

abstractmethod unregister(*fileobj*)
Unregister a file object from selection, removing it from monitoring. A file object shall be unregistered prior to being closed.

fileobj must be a file object previously registered.

This returns the associated *SelectorKey* instance, or raises a *KeyError* if *fileobj* is not registered. It will raise *ValueError* if *fileobj* is invalid (e.g. it has no `fileno()` method or its `fileno()` method has an invalid return value).

modify(*fileobj, events, data=None*)
Change a registered file object's monitored events or attached data.

This is equivalent to `BaseSelector.unregister(fileobj)()` followed by `BaseSelector.register(fileobj, events, data)()`, except that it can be implemented more efficiently.

This returns a new *SelectorKey* instance, or raises a *ValueError* in case of invalid event mask or file descriptor, or *KeyError* if the file object is not registered.

abstractmethod select(*timeout=None*)
Wait until some registered file objects become ready, or the timeout expires.

If `timeout > 0`, this specifies the maximum wait time, in seconds. If `timeout <= 0`, the call won't block, and will report the currently ready file objects. If *timeout* is `None`, the call will block until a monitored file object becomes ready.

This returns a list of `(key, events)` tuples, one for each ready file object.

key is the *SelectorKey* instance corresponding to a ready file object. *events* is a bitmask of events ready on this file object.

Note: This method can return before any file object becomes ready or the timeout has elapsed if the current process receives a signal: in this case, an empty list will be returned.

Changed in version 3.5: The selector is now retried with a recomputed timeout when interrupted by a signal if the signal handler did not raise an exception (see PEP 475 for the rationale), instead of returning an empty list of events before the timeout.

`close()`
Close the selector.

This must be called to make sure that any underlying resource is freed. The selector shall not be used once it has been closed.

`get_key(`*fileobj*`)`
Return the key associated with a registered file object.

This returns the *SelectorKey* instance associated to this file object, or raises *KeyError* if the file object is not registered.

`abstractmethod get_map()`
Return a mapping of file objects to selector keys.

This returns a *Mapping* instance mapping registered file objects to their associated *SelectorKey* instance.

`class selectors.DefaultSelector`
The default selector class, using the most efficient implementation available on the current platform. This should be the default choice for most users.

`class selectors.SelectSelector`
select.select()-based selector.

`class selectors.PollSelector`
select.poll()-based selector.

`class selectors.EpollSelector`
select.epoll()-based selector.

`fileno()`
This returns the file descriptor used by the underlying *select.epoll()* object.

`class selectors.DevpollSelector`
select.devpoll()-based selector.

`fileno()`
This returns the file descriptor used by the underlying *select.devpoll()* object.

New in version 3.5.

`class selectors.KqueueSelector`
select.kqueue()-based selector.

`fileno()`
This returns the file descriptor used by the underlying *select.kqueue()* object.

18.4.3 Examples

Here is a simple echo server implementation:

```
import selectors
import socket

sel = selectors.DefaultSelector()
```

```
def accept(sock, mask):
    conn, addr = sock.accept()  # Should be ready
    print('accepted', conn, 'from', addr)
    conn.setblocking(False)
    sel.register(conn, selectors.EVENT_READ, read)

def read(conn, mask):
    data = conn.recv(1000)  # Should be ready
    if data:
        print('echoing', repr(data), 'to', conn)
        conn.send(data)  # Hope it won't block
    else:
        print('closing', conn)
        sel.unregister(conn)
        conn.close()

sock = socket.socket()
sock.bind(('localhost', 1234))
sock.listen(100)
sock.setblocking(False)
sel.register(sock, selectors.EVENT_READ, accept)

while True:
    events = sel.select()
    for key, mask in events:
        callback = key.data
        callback(key.fileobj, mask)
```

18.5 asyncio — Asynchronous I/O, event loop, coroutines and tasks

New in version 3.4.

Source code: Lib/asyncio/

This module provides infrastructure for writing single-threaded concurrent code using coroutines, multiplexing I/O access over sockets and other resources, running network clients and servers, and other related primitives. Here is a more detailed list of the package contents:

- a pluggable *event loop* with various system-specific implementations;
- *transport* and *protocol* abstractions (similar to those in Twisted);
- concrete support for TCP, UDP, SSL, subprocess pipes, delayed calls, and others (some may be system-dependent);
- a `Future` class that mimics the one in the `concurrent.futures` module, but adapted for use with the event loop;
- coroutines and tasks based on `yield from` (PEP 380), to help write concurrent code in a sequential fashion;
- cancellation support for `Future`s and coroutines;
- *synchronization primitives* for use between coroutines in a single thread, mimicking those in the `threading` module;

- an interface for passing work off to a threadpool, for times when you absolutely, positively have to use a library that makes blocking I/O calls.

Asynchronous programming is more complex than classical "sequential" programming: see the *Develop with asyncio* page which lists common traps and explains how to avoid them. *Enable the debug mode* during development to detect common issues.

Table of contents:

18.5.1 Base Event Loop

Source code: Lib/asyncio/events.py

The event loop is the central execution device provided by *asyncio*. It provides multiple facilities, including:

- Registering, executing and cancelling delayed calls (timeouts).
- Creating client and server *transports* for various kinds of communication.
- Launching subprocesses and the associated *transports* for communication with an external program.
- Delegating costly function calls to a pool of threads.

`class asyncio.BaseEventLoop`

This class is an implementation detail. It is a subclass of *AbstractEventLoop* and may be a base class of concrete event loop implementations found in *asyncio*. It should not be used directly; use *AbstractEventLoop* instead. `BaseEventLoop` should not be subclassed by third-party code; the internal interface is not stable.

`class asyncio.AbstractEventLoop`

Abstract base class of event loops.

This class is *not thread safe*.

Run an event loop

`AbstractEventLoop.run_forever()`

Run until *stop()* is called. If *stop()* is called before *run_forever()* is called, this polls the I/O selector once with a timeout of zero, runs all callbacks scheduled in response to I/O events (and those that were already scheduled), and then exits. If *stop()* is called while *run_forever()* is running, this will run the current batch of callbacks and then exit. Note that callbacks scheduled by callbacks will not run in that case; they will run the next time *run_forever()* is called.

Changed in version 3.5.1.

`AbstractEventLoop.run_until_complete(future)`

Run until the *Future* is done.

If the argument is a *coroutine object*, it is wrapped by *ensure_future()*.

Return the Future's result, or raise its exception.

`AbstractEventLoop.is_running()`

Returns running status of event loop.

`AbstractEventLoop.stop()`

Stop running the event loop.

This causes *run_forever()* to exit at the next suitable opportunity (see there for more details).

Changed in version 3.5.1.

`AbstractEventLoop.is_closed()`
Returns `True` if the event loop was closed.

New in version 3.4.2.

`AbstractEventLoop.close()`
Close the event loop. The loop must not be running. Pending callbacks will be lost.

This clears the queues and shuts down the executor, but does not wait for the executor to finish.

This is idempotent and irreversible. No other methods should be called after this one.

`coroutine AbstractEventLoop.shutdown_asyncgens()`
Schedule all currently open *asynchronous generator* objects to close with an `aclose()` call. After calling this method, the event loop will issue a warning whenever a new asynchronous generator is iterated. Should be used to finalize all scheduled asynchronous generators reliably. Example:

```
try:
    loop.run_forever()
finally:
    loop.run_until_complete(loop.shutdown_asyncgens())
    loop.close()
```

New in version 3.6.

Calls

Most *asyncio* functions don't accept keywords. If you want to pass keywords to your callback, use *functools.partial()*. For example, `loop.call_soon(functools.partial(print, "Hello", flush=True))` will call `print("Hello", flush=True)`.

Note: *functools.partial()* is better than `lambda` functions, because *asyncio* can inspect *functools.partial()* object to display parameters in debug mode, whereas `lambda` functions have a poor representation.

`AbstractEventLoop.call_soon(`*callback*, **args*`)`
Arrange for a callback to be called as soon as possible. The callback is called after *call_soon()* returns, when control returns to the event loop.

This operates as a FIFO queue, callbacks are called in the order in which they are registered. Each callback will be called exactly once.

Any positional arguments after the callback will be passed to the callback when it is called.

An instance of *asyncio.Handle* is returned, which can be used to cancel the callback.

Use functools.partial to pass keywords to the callback.

`AbstractEventLoop.call_soon_threadsafe(`*callback*, **args*`)`
Like *call_soon()*, but thread safe.

See the *concurrency and multithreading* section of the documentation.

Delayed calls

The event loop has its own internal clock for computing timeouts. Which clock is used depends on the (platform-specific) event loop implementation; ideally it is a monotonic clock. This will generally be a different clock than *time.time()*.

Note: Timeouts (relative *delay* or absolute *when*) should not exceed one day.

`AbstractEventLoop.call_later(`*delay, callback, *args*`)`

Arrange for the *callback* to be called after the given *delay* seconds (either an int or float).

An instance of *asyncio.Handle* is returned, which can be used to cancel the callback.

callback will be called exactly once per call to *call_later()*. If two callbacks are scheduled for exactly the same time, it is undefined which will be called first.

The optional positional *args* will be passed to the callback when it is called. If you want the callback to be called with some named arguments, use a closure or *functools.partial()*.

Use functools.partial to pass keywords to the callback.

`AbstractEventLoop.call_at(`*when, callback, *args*`)`

Arrange for the *callback* to be called at the given absolute timestamp *when* (an int or float), using the same time reference as *AbstractEventLoop.time()*.

This method's behavior is the same as *call_later()*.

An instance of *asyncio.Handle* is returned, which can be used to cancel the callback.

Use functools.partial to pass keywords to the callback.

`AbstractEventLoop.time()`

Return the current time, as a *float* value, according to the event loop's internal clock.

See also:

The *asyncio.sleep()* function.

Futures

`AbstractEventLoop.create_future()`

Create an *asyncio.Future* object attached to the loop.

This is a preferred way to create futures in asyncio, as event loop implementations can provide alternative implementations of the Future class (with better performance or instrumentation).

New in version 3.5.2.

Tasks

`AbstractEventLoop.create_task(`*coro*`)`

Schedule the execution of a *coroutine object*: wrap it in a future. Return a *Task* object.

Third-party event loops can use their own subclass of *Task* for interoperability. In this case, the result type is a subclass of *Task*.

This method was added in Python 3.4.2. Use the *async()* function to support also older Python versions.

New in version 3.4.2.

`AbstractEventLoop.set_task_factory(`*factory*`)`

Set a task factory that will be used by *AbstractEventLoop.create_task()*.

If *factory* is `None` the default task factory will be set.

If *factory* is a *callable*, it should have a signature matching `(loop, coro)`, where *loop* will be a reference to the active event loop, *coro* will be a coroutine object. The callable must return an *asyncio.Future* compatible object.

New in version 3.4.4.

`AbstractEventLoop.get_task_factory()`

Return a task factory, or `None` if the default one is in use.

New in version 3.4.4.

Creating connections

`coroutine AbstractEventLoop.create_connection(`*protocol_factory, host=None, port=None, *, ssl=None, family=0, proto=0, flags=0, sock=None, local_addr=None, server_hostname=None*`)`

Create a streaming transport connection to a given Internet *host* and *port*: socket family *AF_INET* or *AF_INET6* depending on *host* (or *family* if specified), socket type *SOCK_STREAM*. *protocol_factory* must be a callable returning a *protocol* instance.

This method is a *coroutine* which will try to establish the connection in the background. When successful, the coroutine returns a `(transport, protocol)` pair.

The chronological synopsis of the underlying operation is as follows:

1. The connection is established, and a *transport* is created to represent it.
2. *protocol_factory* is called without arguments and must return a *protocol* instance.
3. The protocol instance is tied to the transport, and its `connection_made()` method is called.
4. The coroutine returns successfully with the `(transport, protocol)` pair.

The created transport is an implementation-dependent bidirectional stream.

Note: *protocol_factory* can be any kind of callable, not necessarily a class. For example, if you want to use a pre-created protocol instance, you can pass `lambda: my_protocol`.

Options that change how the connection is created:

- *ssl*: if given and not false, a SSL/TLS transport is created (by default a plain TCP transport is created). If *ssl* is a `ssl.SSLContext` object, this context is used to create the transport; if *ssl* is `True`, a context with some unspecified default settings is used.

  See also:

  SSL/TLS security considerations

- *server_hostname*, is only for use together with *ssl*, and sets or overrides the hostname that the target server's certificate will be matched against. By default the value of the *host* argument is used. If *host* is empty, there is no default and you must pass a value for *server_hostname*. If *server_hostname* is an empty string, hostname matching is disabled (which is a serious security risk, allowing for man-in-the-middle-attacks).
- *family*, *proto*, *flags* are the optional address family, protocol and flags to be passed through to getaddrinfo() for *host* resolution. If given, these should all be integers from the corresponding `socket` module constants.
- *sock*, if given, should be an existing, already connected `socket.socket` object to be used by the transport. If *sock* is given, none of *host*, *port*, *family*, *proto*, *flags* and *local_addr* should be specified.
- *local_addr*, if given, is a `(local_host, local_port)` tuple used to bind the socket to locally. The *local_host* and *local_port* are looked up using getaddrinfo(), similarly to *host* and *port*.

Changed in version 3.5: On Windows with *ProactorEventLoop*, SSL/TLS is now supported.

See also:

The *open_connection()* function can be used to get a pair of (*StreamReader*, *StreamWriter*) instead of a protocol.

coroutine AbstractEventLoop.create_datagram_endpoint(*protocol_factory, local_addr=None, remote_addr=None, *, family=0, proto=0, flags=0, reuse_address=None, reuse_port=None, allow_broadcast=None, sock=None*)

Create datagram connection: socket family *AF_INET* or *AF_INET6* depending on *host* (or *family* if specified), socket type *SOCK_DGRAM*. *protocol_factory* must be a callable returning a *protocol* instance.

This method is a *coroutine* which will try to establish the connection in the background. When successful, the coroutine returns a `(transport, protocol)` pair.

Options changing how the connection is created:

- *local_addr*, if given, is a `(local_host, local_port)` tuple used to bind the socket to locally. The *local_host* and *local_port* are looked up using *getaddrinfo()*.
- *remote_addr*, if given, is a `(remote_host, remote_port)` tuple used to connect the socket to a remote address. The *remote_host* and *remote_port* are looked up using *getaddrinfo()*.
- *family*, *proto*, *flags* are the optional address family, protocol and flags to be passed through to *getaddrinfo()* for *host* resolution. If given, these should all be integers from the corresponding *socket* module constants.
- *reuse_address* tells the kernel to reuse a local socket in TIME_WAIT state, without waiting for its natural timeout to expire. If not specified will automatically be set to `True` on UNIX.
- *reuse_port* tells the kernel to allow this endpoint to be bound to the same port as other existing endpoints are bound to, so long as they all set this flag when being created. This option is not supported on Windows and some UNIX's. If the `SO_REUSEPORT` constant is not defined then this capability is unsupported.
- *allow_broadcast* tells the kernel to allow this endpoint to send messages to the broadcast address.
- *sock* can optionally be specified in order to use a preexisting, already connected, *socket.socket* object to be used by the transport. If specified, *local_addr* and *remote_addr* should be omitted (must be *None*).

On Windows with *ProactorEventLoop*, this method is not supported.

See *UDP echo client protocol* and *UDP echo server protocol* examples.

coroutine AbstractEventLoop.create_unix_connection(*protocol_factory, path, *, ssl=None, sock=None, server_hostname=None*)

Create UNIX connection: socket family *AF_UNIX*, socket type *SOCK_STREAM*. The *AF_UNIX* socket family is used to communicate between processes on the same machine efficiently.

This method is a *coroutine* which will try to establish the connection in the background. When successful, the coroutine returns a `(transport, protocol)` pair.

path is the name of a UNIX domain socket, and is required unless a *sock* parameter is specified. Abstract UNIX sockets, *str*, and *bytes* paths are supported.

See the *AbstractEventLoop.create_connection()* method for parameters.

Availability: UNIX.

Creating listening connections

coroutine AbstractEventLoop.create_server(*protocol_factory, host=None, port=None, *, family=socket.AF_UNSPEC, flags=socket.AI_PASSIVE, sock=None, backlog=100, ssl=None, reuse_address=None, reuse_port=None*)

Create a TCP server (socket type *SOCK_STREAM*) bound to *host* and *port*.

Return a *Server* object, its *sockets* attribute contains created sockets. Use the *Server.close()* method to stop the server: close listening sockets.

Parameters:

- The *host* parameter can be a string, in that case the TCP server is bound to *host* and *port*. The *host* parameter can also be a sequence of strings and in that case the TCP server is bound to all hosts of the sequence. If *host* is an empty string or `None`, all interfaces are assumed and a list of multiple sockets will be returned (most likely one for IPv4 and another one for IPv6).
- *family* can be set to either *socket.AF_INET* or *AF_INET6* to force the socket to use IPv4 or IPv6. If not set it will be determined from host (defaults to `socket.AF_UNSPEC`).
- *flags* is a bitmask for *getaddrinfo()*.
- *sock* can optionally be specified in order to use a preexisting socket object. If specified, *host* and *port* should be omitted (must be *None*).
- *backlog* is the maximum number of queued connections passed to *listen()* (defaults to 100).
- *ssl* can be set to an *SSLContext* to enable SSL over the accepted connections.
- *reuse_address* tells the kernel to reuse a local socket in TIME_WAIT state, without waiting for its natural timeout to expire. If not specified will automatically be set to `True` on UNIX.
- *reuse_port* tells the kernel to allow this endpoint to be bound to the same port as other existing endpoints are bound to, so long as they all set this flag when being created. This option is not supported on Windows.

This method is a *coroutine*.

Changed in version 3.5: On Windows with *ProactorEventLoop*, SSL/TLS is now supported.

See also:

The function *start_server()* creates a (*StreamReader*, *StreamWriter*) pair and calls back a function with this pair.

Changed in version 3.5.1: The *host* parameter can now be a sequence of strings.

coroutine AbstractEventLoop.create_unix_server(*protocol_factory, path=None, *, sock=None, backlog=100, ssl=None*)

Similar to *AbstractEventLoop.create_server()*, but specific to the socket family *AF_UNIX*.

This method is a *coroutine*.

Availability: UNIX.

coroutine BaseEventLoop.connect_accepted_socket(*protocol_factory, sock, *, ssl=None*)

Handle an accepted connection.

This is used by servers that accept connections outside of asyncio but that use asyncio to handle them.

Parameters:

- *sock* is a preexisting socket object returned from an `accept` call.
- *ssl* can be set to an *SSLContext* to enable SSL over the accepted connections.

This method is a *coroutine*. When completed, the coroutine returns a `(transport, protocol)` pair.

New in version 3.5.3.

Watch file descriptors

On Windows with `SelectorEventLoop`, only socket handles are supported (ex: pipe file descriptors are not supported).

On Windows with `ProactorEventLoop`, these methods are not supported.

`AbstractEventLoop.add_reader(fd, callback, *args)`
Start watching the file descriptor for read availability and then call the *callback* with specified arguments.

Use functools.partial to pass keywords to the callback.

`AbstractEventLoop.remove_reader(fd)`
Stop watching the file descriptor for read availability.

`AbstractEventLoop.add_writer(fd, callback, *args)`
Start watching the file descriptor for write availability and then call the *callback* with specified arguments.

Use functools.partial to pass keywords to the callback.

`AbstractEventLoop.remove_writer(fd)`
Stop watching the file descriptor for write availability.

The *watch a file descriptor for read events* example uses the low-level `AbstractEventLoop.add_reader()` method to register the file descriptor of a socket.

Low-level socket operations

`coroutine AbstractEventLoop.sock_recv(sock, nbytes)`
Receive data from the socket. Modeled after blocking `socket.socket.recv()` method.

The return value is a bytes object representing the data received. The maximum amount of data to be received at once is specified by *nbytes*.

With `SelectorEventLoop` event loop, the socket *sock* must be non-blocking.

This method is a *coroutine*.

`coroutine AbstractEventLoop.sock_sendall(sock, data)`
Send data to the socket. Modeled after blocking `socket.socket.sendall()` method.

The socket must be connected to a remote socket. This method continues to send data from *data* until either all data has been sent or an error occurs. `None` is returned on success. On error, an exception is raised, and there is no way to determine how much data, if any, was successfully processed by the receiving end of the connection.

With `SelectorEventLoop` event loop, the socket *sock* must be non-blocking.

This method is a *coroutine*.

`coroutine AbstractEventLoop.sock_connect(sock, address)`
Connect to a remote socket at *address*. Modeled after blocking `socket.socket.connect()` method.

With `SelectorEventLoop` event loop, the socket *sock* must be non-blocking.

This method is a *coroutine*.

Changed in version 3.5.2: `address` no longer needs to be resolved. `sock_connect` will try to check if the *address* is already resolved by calling `socket.inet_pton()`. If not, `AbstractEventLoop.getaddrinfo()` will be used to resolve the *address*.

See also:

`AbstractEventLoop.create_connection()` and `asyncio.open_connection()`.

coroutine AbstractEventLoop.sock_accept(*sock*)
Accept a connection. Modeled after blocking `socket.socket.accept()`.

The socket must be bound to an address and listening for connections. The return value is a pair `(conn, address)` where *conn* is a *new* socket object usable to send and receive data on the connection, and *address* is the address bound to the socket on the other end of the connection.

The socket *sock* must be non-blocking.

This method is a *coroutine*.

See also:

`AbstractEventLoop.create_server()` and `start_server()`.

Resolve host name

coroutine AbstractEventLoop.getaddrinfo(*host, port, *, family=0, type=0, proto=0, flags=0*)
This method is a *coroutine*, similar to `socket.getaddrinfo()` function but non-blocking.

coroutine AbstractEventLoop.getnameinfo(*sockaddr, flags=0*)
This method is a *coroutine*, similar to `socket.getnameinfo()` function but non-blocking.

Connect pipes

On Windows with `SelectorEventLoop`, these methods are not supported. Use `ProactorEventLoop` to support pipes on Windows.

coroutine AbstractEventLoop.connect_read_pipe(*protocol_factory, pipe*)
Register read pipe in eventloop.

protocol_factory should instantiate object with `Protocol` interface. *pipe* is a *file-like object*. Return pair `(transport, protocol)`, where *transport* supports the `ReadTransport` interface.

With `SelectorEventLoop` event loop, the *pipe* is set to non-blocking mode.

This method is a *coroutine*.

coroutine AbstractEventLoop.connect_write_pipe(*protocol_factory, pipe*)
Register write pipe in eventloop.

protocol_factory should instantiate object with `BaseProtocol` interface. *pipe* is *file-like object*. Return pair `(transport, protocol)`, where *transport* supports `WriteTransport` interface.

With `SelectorEventLoop` event loop, the *pipe* is set to non-blocking mode.

This method is a *coroutine*.

See also:

The `AbstractEventLoop.subprocess_exec()` and `AbstractEventLoop.subprocess_shell()` methods.

UNIX signals

Availability: UNIX only.

`AbstractEventLoop.add_signal_handler(signum, callback, *args)`
Add a handler for a signal.

Raise *ValueError* if the signal number is invalid or uncatchable. Raise *RuntimeError* if there is a problem setting up the handler.

Use functools.partial to pass keywords to the callback.

`AbstractEventLoop.remove_signal_handler(sig)`
Remove a handler for a signal.

Return `True` if a signal handler was removed, `False` if not.

See also:

The *signal* module.

Executor

Call a function in an *Executor* (pool of threads or pool of processes). By default, an event loop uses a thread pool executor (*ThreadPoolExecutor*).

`coroutine AbstractEventLoop.run_in_executor(executor, func, *args)`
Arrange for a *func* to be called in the specified executor.

The *executor* argument should be an *Executor* instance. The default executor is used if *executor* is `None`.

*Use functools.partial to pass keywords to the *func*.*

This method is a *coroutine*.

Changed in version 3.5.3: `BaseEventLoop.run_in_executor()` no longer configures the `max_workers` of the thread pool executor it creates, instead leaving it up to the thread pool executor (*ThreadPoolExecutor*) to set the default.

`AbstractEventLoop.set_default_executor(executor)`
Set the default executor used by *run_in_executor()*.

Error Handling API

Allows customizing how exceptions are handled in the event loop.

`AbstractEventLoop.set_exception_handler(handler)`
Set *handler* as the new event loop exception handler.

If *handler* is `None`, the default exception handler will be set.

If *handler* is a callable object, it should have a matching signature to `(loop, context)`, where `loop` will be a reference to the active event loop, `context` will be a `dict` object (see *call_exception_handler()* documentation for details about context).

`AbstractEventLoop.get_exception_handler()`
Return the exception handler, or `None` if the default one is in use.

New in version 3.5.2.

AbstractEventLoop.**default_exception_handler**(*context*)
Default exception handler.

This is called when an exception occurs and no exception handler is set, and can be called by a custom exception handler that wants to defer to the default behavior.

context parameter has the same meaning as in *call_exception_handler()*.

AbstractEventLoop.**call_exception_handler**(*context*)
Call the current event loop exception handler.

context is a `dict` object containing the following keys (new keys may be introduced later):

- 'message': Error message;
- 'exception' (optional): Exception object;
- 'future' (optional): *asyncio.Future* instance;
- 'handle' (optional): *asyncio.Handle* instance;
- 'protocol' (optional): *Protocol* instance;
- 'transport' (optional): *Transport* instance;
- 'socket' (optional): *socket.socket* instance.

Note: Note: this method should not be overloaded in subclassed event loops. For any custom exception handling, use *set_exception_handler()* method.

Debug mode

AbstractEventLoop.**get_debug**()
Get the debug mode (*bool*) of the event loop.

The default value is `True` if the environment variable `PYTHONASYNCIODEBUG` is set to a non-empty string, `False` otherwise.

New in version 3.4.2.

AbstractEventLoop.**set_debug**(*enabled: bool*)
Set the debug mode of the event loop.

New in version 3.4.2.

See also:

The *debug mode of asyncio*.

Server

class asyncio.**Server**
Server listening on sockets.

Object created by the *AbstractEventLoop.create_server()* method and the *start_server()* function. Don't instantiate the class directly.

close()
Stop serving: close listening sockets and set the *sockets* attribute to `None`.

The sockets that represent existing incoming client connections are left open.

The server is closed asynchronously, use the *wait_closed()* coroutine to wait until the server is closed.

coroutine wait_closed()
Wait until the *close()* method completes.

This method is a *coroutine*.

sockets
List of *socket.socket* objects the server is listening to, or None if the server is closed.

Handle

class asyncio.Handle
A callback wrapper object returned by *AbstractEventLoop.call_soon()*, *AbstractEventLoop.call_soon_threadsafe()*, *AbstractEventLoop.call_later()*, and *AbstractEventLoop.call_at()*.

cancel()
Cancel the call. If the callback is already canceled or executed, this method has no effect.

Event loop examples

Hello World with call_soon()

Example using the *AbstractEventLoop.call_soon()* method to schedule a callback. The callback displays "Hello World" and then stops the event loop:

```
import asyncio

def hello_world(loop):
    print('Hello World')
    loop.stop()

loop = asyncio.get_event_loop()

# Schedule a call to hello_world()
loop.call_soon(hello_world, loop)

# Blocking call interrupted by loop.stop()
loop.run_forever()
loop.close()
```

See also:

The *Hello World coroutine* example uses a *coroutine*.

Display the current date with call_later()

Example of callback displaying the current date every second. The callback uses the *AbstractEventLoop.call_later()* method to reschedule itself during 5 seconds, and then stops the event loop:

```
import asyncio
import datetime

def display_date(end_time, loop):
    print(datetime.datetime.now())
    if (loop.time() + 1.0) < end_time:
        loop.call_later(1, display_date, end_time, loop)
```

```
    else:
        loop.stop()

loop = asyncio.get_event_loop()

# Schedule the first call to display_date()
end_time = loop.time() + 5.0
loop.call_soon(display_date, end_time, loop)

# Blocking call interrupted by loop.stop()
loop.run_forever()
loop.close()
```

See also:

The *coroutine displaying the current date* example uses a *coroutine*.

Watch a file descriptor for read events

Wait until a file descriptor received some data using the `AbstractEventLoop.add_reader()` method and then close the event loop:

```
import asyncio
try:
    from socket import socketpair
except ImportError:
    from asyncio.windows_utils import socketpair

# Create a pair of connected file descriptors
rsock, wsock = socketpair()
loop = asyncio.get_event_loop()

def reader():
    data = rsock.recv(100)
    print("Received:", data.decode())
    # We are done: unregister the file descriptor
    loop.remove_reader(rsock)
    # Stop the event loop
    loop.stop()

# Register the file descriptor for read event
loop.add_reader(rsock, reader)

# Simulate the reception of data from the network
loop.call_soon(wsock.send, 'abc'.encode())

# Run the event loop
loop.run_forever()

# We are done, close sockets and the event loop
rsock.close()
wsock.close()
loop.close()
```

See also:

The *register an open socket to wait for data using a protocol* example uses a low-level protocol created by the `AbstractEventLoop.create_connection()` method.

The *register an open socket to wait for data using streams* example uses high-level streams created by the *open_connection()* function in a coroutine.

Set signal handlers for SIGINT and SIGTERM

Register handlers for signals SIGINT and SIGTERM using the *AbstractEventLoop.add_signal_handler()* method:

```
import asyncio
import functools
import os
import signal

def ask_exit(signame):
    print("got signal %s: exit" % signame)
    loop.stop()

loop = asyncio.get_event_loop()
for signame in ('SIGINT', 'SIGTERM'):
    loop.add_signal_handler(getattr(signal, signame),
                            functools.partial(ask_exit, signame))

print("Event loop running forever, press Ctrl+C to interrupt.")
print("pid %s: send SIGINT or SIGTERM to exit." % os.getpid())
try:
    loop.run_forever()
finally:
    loop.close()
```

This example only works on UNIX.

18.5.2 Event loops

Source code: Lib/asyncio/events.py

Event loop functions

The following functions are convenient shortcuts to accessing the methods of the global policy. Note that this provides access to the default policy, unless an alternative policy was set by calling *set_event_loop_policy()* earlier in the execution of the process.

asyncio.**get_event_loop**()
    Equivalent to calling get_event_loop_policy().get_event_loop().

asyncio.**set_event_loop**(*loop*)
    Equivalent to calling get_event_loop_policy().set_event_loop(loop).

asyncio.**new_event_loop**()
    Equivalent to calling get_event_loop_policy().new_event_loop().

Available event loops

asyncio currently provides two implementations of event loops: *SelectorEventLoop* and *ProactorEventLoop*.

class asyncio.SelectorEventLoop

Event loop based on the *selectors* module. Subclass of *AbstractEventLoop*.

Use the most efficient selector available on the platform.

On Windows, only sockets are supported (ex: pipes are not supported): see the MSDN documentation of select.

class asyncio.ProactorEventLoop

Proactor event loop for Windows using "I/O Completion Ports" aka IOCP. Subclass of *AbstractEventLoop*.

Availability: Windows.

See also:

MSDN documentation on I/O Completion Ports.

Example to use a *ProactorEventLoop* on Windows:

```
import asyncio, sys

if sys.platform == 'win32':
    loop = asyncio.ProactorEventLoop()
    asyncio.set_event_loop(loop)
```

Platform support

The *asyncio* module has been designed to be portable, but each platform still has subtle differences and may not support all *asyncio* features.

Windows

Common limits of Windows event loops:

- *create_unix_connection()* and *create_unix_server()* are not supported: the socket family *socket.AF_UNIX* is specific to UNIX
- *add_signal_handler()* and *remove_signal_handler()* are not supported
- `EventLoopPolicy.set_child_watcher()` is not supported. *ProactorEventLoop* supports subprocesses. It has only one implementation to watch child processes, there is no need to configure it.

SelectorEventLoop specific limits:

- *SelectSelector* is used which only supports sockets and is limited to 512 sockets.
- *add_reader()* and *add_writer()* only accept file descriptors of sockets
- Pipes are not supported (ex: *connect_read_pipe()*, *connect_write_pipe()*)
- *Subprocesses* are not supported (ex: *subprocess_exec()*, *subprocess_shell()*)

ProactorEventLoop specific limits:

- *create_datagram_endpoint()* (UDP) is not supported
- *add_reader()* and *add_writer()* are not supported

The resolution of the monotonic clock on Windows is usually around 15.6 msec. The best resolution is 0.5 msec. The resolution depends on the hardware (availability of HPET) and on the Windows configuration. See *asyncio delayed calls*.

Changed in version 3.5: *ProactorEventLoop* now supports SSL.

Mac OS X

Character devices like PTY are only well supported since Mavericks (Mac OS 10.9). They are not supported at all on Mac OS 10.5 and older.

On Mac OS 10.6, 10.7 and 10.8, the default event loop is *SelectorEventLoop* which uses *selectors.KqueueSelector*. *selectors.KqueueSelector* does not support character devices on these versions. The *SelectorEventLoop* can be used with *SelectSelector* or *PollSelector* to support character devices on these versions of Mac OS X. Example:

```
import asyncio
import selectors

selector = selectors.SelectSelector()
loop = asyncio.SelectorEventLoop(selector)
asyncio.set_event_loop(loop)
```

Event loop policies and the default policy

Event loop management is abstracted with a *policy* pattern, to provide maximal flexibility for custom platforms and frameworks. Throughout the execution of a process, a single global policy object manages the event loops available to the process based on the calling context. A policy is an object implementing the *AbstractEventLoopPolicy* interface.

For most users of *asyncio*, policies never have to be dealt with explicitly, since the default global policy is sufficient (see below).

The module-level functions *get_event_loop()* and *set_event_loop()* provide convenient access to event loops managed by the default policy.

Event loop policy interface

An event loop policy must implement the following interface:

class asyncio.AbstractEventLoopPolicy
Event loop policy.

get_event_loop()
Get the event loop for the current context.

Returns an event loop object implementing the *AbstractEventLoop* interface.

Raises an exception in case no event loop has been set for the current context and the current policy does not specify to create one. It must never return `None`.

set_event_loop(*loop*)
Set the event loop for the current context to *loop*.

new_event_loop()
Create and return a new event loop object according to this policy's rules.

If there's need to set this loop as the event loop for the current context, *set_event_loop()* must be called explicitly.

The default policy defines context as the current thread, and manages an event loop per thread that interacts with *asyncio*. If the current thread doesn't already have an event loop associated with it, the default policy's *get_event_loop()* method creates one when called from the main thread, but raises *RuntimeError* otherwise.

Access to the global loop policy

`asyncio.get_event_loop_policy()`
Get the current event loop policy.

`asyncio.set_event_loop_policy(policy)`
Set the current event loop policy. If *policy* is `None`, the default policy is restored.

Customizing the event loop policy

To implement a new event loop policy, it is recommended you subclass the concrete default event loop policy `DefaultEventLoopPolicy` and override the methods for which you want to change behavior, for example:

```
class MyEventLoopPolicy(asyncio.DefaultEventLoopPolicy):

    def get_event_loop(self):
        """Get the event loop.

        This may be None or an instance of EventLoop.
        """
        loop = super().get_event_loop()
        # Do something with loop ...
        return loop

asyncio.set_event_loop_policy(MyEventLoopPolicy())
```

18.5.3 Tasks and coroutines

Source code: Lib/asyncio/tasks.py

Source code: Lib/asyncio/coroutines.py

Coroutines

Coroutines used with *asyncio* may be implemented using the `async def` statement, or by using *generators*. The `async def` type of coroutine was added in Python 3.5, and is recommended if there is no need to support older Python versions.

Generator-based coroutines should be decorated with *@asyncio.coroutine*, although this is not strictly enforced. The decorator enables compatibility with `async def` coroutines, and also serves as documentation. Generator-based coroutines use the `yield from` syntax introduced in PEP 380, instead of the original `yield` syntax.

The word "coroutine", like the word "generator", is used for two different (though related) concepts:

- The function that defines a coroutine (a function definition using `async def` or decorated with `@asyncio.coroutine`). If disambiguation is needed we will call this a *coroutine function* (*iscoroutinefunction()* returns `True`).
- The object obtained by calling a coroutine function. This object represents a computation or an I/O operation (usually a combination) that will complete eventually. If disambiguation is needed we will call it a *coroutine object* (*iscoroutine()* returns `True`).

Things a coroutine can do:

- `result = await future` or `result = yield from future` – suspends the coroutine until the future is done, then returns the future's result, or raises an exception, which will be propagated. (If the future is cancelled, it will raise a CancelledError exception.) Note that tasks are futures, and everything said about futures also applies to tasks.

- result = await coroutine or result = yield from coroutine – wait for another coroutine to produce a result (or raise an exception, which will be propagated). The coroutine expression must be a *call* to another coroutine.
- return expression – produce a result to the coroutine that is waiting for this one using await or yield from.
- raise exception – raise an exception in the coroutine that is waiting for this one using await or yield from.

Calling a coroutine does not start its code running – the coroutine object returned by the call doesn't do anything until you schedule its execution. There are two basic ways to start it running: call await coroutine or yield from coroutine from another coroutine (assuming the other coroutine is already running!), or schedule its execution using the *ensure_future()* function or the *AbstractEventLoop.create_task()* method.

Coroutines (and tasks) can only run when the event loop is running.

@asyncio.coroutine

Decorator to mark generator-based coroutines. This enables the generator use yield from to call async def coroutines, and also enables the generator to be called by async def coroutines, for instance using an await expression.

There is no need to decorate async def coroutines themselves.

If the generator is not yielded from before it is destroyed, an error message is logged. See *Detect coroutines never scheduled*.

Note: In this documentation, some methods are documented as coroutines, even if they are plain Python functions returning a *Future*. This is intentional to have a freedom of tweaking the implementation of these functions in the future. If such a function is needed to be used in a callback-style code, wrap its result with *ensure_future()*.

Example: Hello World coroutine

Example of coroutine displaying "Hello World":

```
import asyncio

async def hello_world():
    print("Hello World!")

loop = asyncio.get_event_loop()
# Blocking call which returns when the hello_world() coroutine is done
loop.run_until_complete(hello_world())
loop.close()
```

See also:

The *Hello World with call_soon()* example uses the *AbstractEventLoop.call_soon()* method to schedule a callback.

Example: Coroutine displaying the current date

Example of coroutine displaying the current date every second during 5 seconds using the *sleep()* function:

```
import asyncio
import datetime

async def display_date(loop):
    end_time = loop.time() + 5.0
    while True:
        print(datetime.datetime.now())
        if (loop.time() + 1.0) >= end_time:
            break
        await asyncio.sleep(1)

loop = asyncio.get_event_loop()
# Blocking call which returns when the display_date() coroutine is done
loop.run_until_complete(display_date(loop))
loop.close()
```

See also:

The *display the current date with call_later()* example uses a callback with the *AbstractEventLoop.call_later()* method.

Example: Chain coroutines

Example chaining coroutines:

```
import asyncio

async def compute(x, y):
    print("Compute %s + %s ..." % (x, y))
    await asyncio.sleep(1.0)
    return x + y

async def print_sum(x, y):
    result = await compute(x, y)
    print("%s + %s = %s" % (x, y, result))

loop = asyncio.get_event_loop()
loop.run_until_complete(print_sum(1, 2))
loop.close()
```

`compute()` is chained to `print_sum()`: `print_sum()` coroutine waits until `compute()` is completed before returning its result.

Sequence diagram of the example:

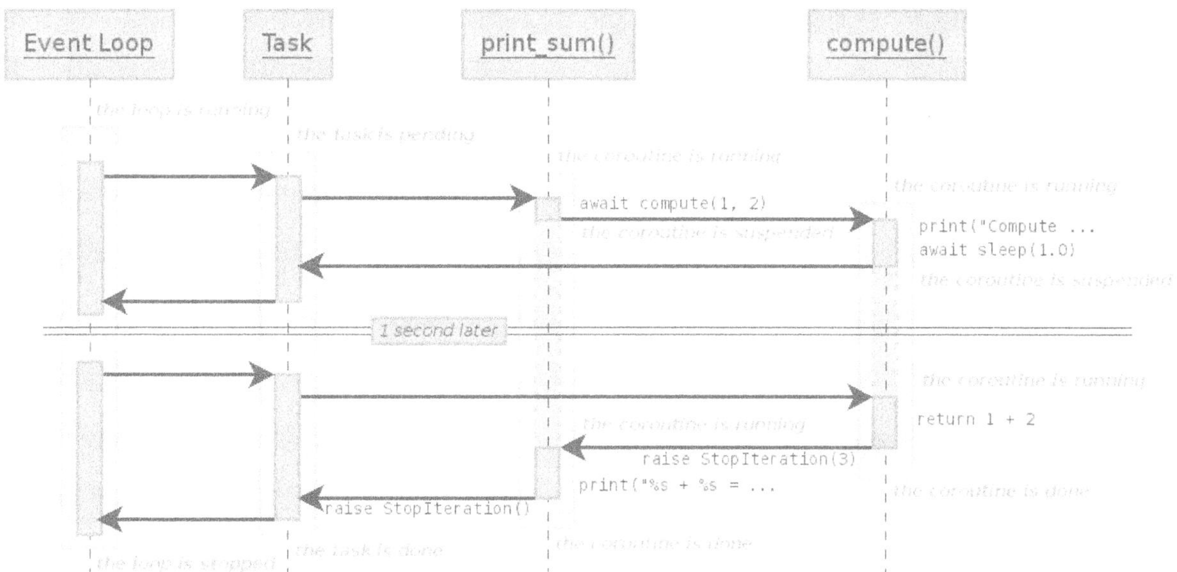

The "Task" is created by the *AbstractEventLoop.run_until_complete()* method when it gets a coroutine object instead of a task.

The diagram shows the control flow, it does not describe exactly how things work internally. For example, the sleep coroutine creates an internal future which uses *AbstractEventLoop.call_later()* to wake up the task in 1 second.

InvalidStateError

exception asyncio.InvalidStateError
The operation is not allowed in this state.

TimeoutError

exception asyncio.TimeoutError
The operation exceeded the given deadline.

Note: This exception is different from the builtin *TimeoutError* exception!

Future

class asyncio.Future(**, loop=None*)
This class is *almost* compatible with *concurrent.futures.Future*.

Differences:

- *result()* and *exception()* do not take a timeout argument and raise an exception when the future isn't done yet.
- Callbacks registered with *add_done_callback()* are always called via the event loop's *call_soon()*.
- This class is not compatible with the *wait()* and *as_completed()* functions in the *concurrent.futures* package.

This class is *not thread safe*.

cancel()
Cancel the future and schedule callbacks.

If the future is already done or cancelled, return `False`. Otherwise, change the future's state to cancelled, schedule the callbacks and return `True`.

cancelled()
Return `True` if the future was cancelled.

done()
Return `True` if the future is done.

Done means either that a result / exception are available, or that the future was cancelled.

result()
Return the result this future represents.

If the future has been cancelled, raises `CancelledError`. If the future's result isn't yet available, raises *InvalidStateError*. If the future is done and has an exception set, this exception is raised.

exception()
Return the exception that was set on this future.

The exception (or `None` if no exception was set) is returned only if the future is done. If the future has been cancelled, raises `CancelledError`. If the future isn't done yet, raises *InvalidStateError*.

add_done_callback(*fn*)
Add a callback to be run when the future becomes done.

The callback is called with a single argument - the future object. If the future is already done when this is called, the callback is scheduled with *call_soon()*.

Use functools.partial to pass parameters to the callback. For example, `fut.add_done_callback(functools.partial(print, "Future:", flush=True))` will call `print("Future:", fut, flush=True)`.

remove_done_callback(*fn*)
Remove all instances of a callback from the "call when done" list.

Returns the number of callbacks removed.

set_result(*result*)
Mark the future done and set its result.

If the future is already done when this method is called, raises *InvalidStateError*.

set_exception(*exception*)
Mark the future done and set an exception.

If the future is already done when this method is called, raises *InvalidStateError*.

Example: Future with run_until_complete()

Example combining a *Future* and a *coroutine function*:

```
import asyncio

async def slow_operation(future):
    await asyncio.sleep(1)
    future.set_result('Future is done!')
```

```
loop = asyncio.get_event_loop()
future = asyncio.Future()
asyncio.ensure_future(slow_operation(future))
loop.run_until_complete(future)
print(future.result())
loop.close()
```

The coroutine function is responsible for the computation (which takes 1 second) and it stores the result into the future. The *run_until_complete()* method waits for the completion of the future.

Note: The *run_until_complete()* method uses internally the *add_done_callback()* method to be notified when the future is done.

Example: Future with run_forever()

The previous example can be written differently using the *Future.add_done_callback()* method to describe explicitly the control flow:

```
import asyncio

async def slow_operation(future):
    await asyncio.sleep(1)
    future.set_result('Future is done!')

def got_result(future):
    print(future.result())
    loop.stop()

loop = asyncio.get_event_loop()
future = asyncio.Future()
asyncio.ensure_future(slow_operation(future))
future.add_done_callback(got_result)
try:
    loop.run_forever()
finally:
    loop.close()
```

In this example, the future is used to link `slow_operation()` to `got_result()`: when `slow_operation()` is done, `got_result()` is called with the result.

Task

class asyncio.Task(*coro*, *, *loop=None*)

Schedule the execution of a *coroutine*: wrap it in a future. A task is a subclass of *Future*.

A task is responsible for executing a coroutine object in an event loop. If the wrapped coroutine yields from a future, the task suspends the execution of the wrapped coroutine and waits for the completion of the future. When the future is done, the execution of the wrapped coroutine restarts with the result or the exception of the future.

Event loops use cooperative scheduling: an event loop only runs one task at a time. Other tasks may run in parallel if other event loops are running in different threads. While a task waits for the completion of a future, the event loop executes a new task.

The cancellation of a task is different from the cancelation of a future. Calling *cancel()* will throw a *CancelledError* to the wrapped coroutine. *cancelled()* only returns True if the wrapped coroutine did not catch the *CancelledError* exception, or raised a *CancelledError* exception.

If a pending task is destroyed, the execution of its wrapped *coroutine* did not complete. It is probably a bug and a warning is logged: see *Pending task destroyed*.

Don't directly create *Task* instances: use the *ensure_future()* function or the *AbstractEventLoop.create_task()* method.

This class is *not thread safe*.

classmethod all_tasks(*loop=None*)

Return a set of all tasks for an event loop.

By default all tasks for the current event loop are returned.

classmethod current_task(*loop=None*)

Return the currently running task in an event loop or None.

By default the current task for the current event loop is returned.

None is returned when called not in the context of a *Task*.

cancel()

Request that this task cancel itself.

This arranges for a *CancelledError* to be thrown into the wrapped coroutine on the next cycle through the event loop. The coroutine then has a chance to clean up or even deny the request using try/except/finally.

Unlike *Future.cancel()*, this does not guarantee that the task will be cancelled: the exception might be caught and acted upon, delaying cancellation of the task or preventing cancellation completely. The task may also return a value or raise a different exception.

Immediately after this method is called, *cancelled()* will not return True (unless the task was already cancelled). A task will be marked as cancelled when the wrapped coroutine terminates with a *CancelledError* exception (even if *cancel()* was not called).

get_stack(**, limit=None*)

Return the list of stack frames for this task's coroutine.

If the coroutine is not done, this returns the stack where it is suspended. If the coroutine has completed successfully or was cancelled, this returns an empty list. If the coroutine was terminated by an exception, this returns the list of traceback frames.

The frames are always ordered from oldest to newest.

The optional limit gives the maximum number of frames to return; by default all available frames are returned. Its meaning differs depending on whether a stack or a traceback is returned: the newest frames of a stack are returned, but the oldest frames of a traceback are returned. (This matches the behavior of the traceback module.)

For reasons beyond our control, only one stack frame is returned for a suspended coroutine.

print_stack(**, limit=None, file=None*)

Print the stack or traceback for this task's coroutine.

This produces output similar to that of the traceback module, for the frames retrieved by get_stack(). The limit argument is passed to get_stack(). The file argument is an I/O stream to which the output is written; by default output is written to sys.stderr.

Example: Parallel execution of tasks

Example executing 3 tasks (A, B, C) in parallel:

```
import asyncio

async def factorial(name, number):
    f = 1
    for i in range(2, number+1):
        print("Task %s: Compute factorial(%s)..." % (name, i))
        await asyncio.sleep(1)
        f *= i
    print("Task %s: factorial(%s) = %s" % (name, number, f))

loop = asyncio.get_event_loop()
loop.run_until_complete(asyncio.gather(
    factorial("A", 2),
    factorial("B", 3),
    factorial("C", 4),
))
loop.close()
```

Output:

```
Task A: Compute factorial(2)...
Task B: Compute factorial(2)...
Task C: Compute factorial(2)...
Task A: factorial(2) = 2
Task B: Compute factorial(3)...
Task C: Compute factorial(3)...
Task B: factorial(3) = 6
Task C: Compute factorial(4)...
Task C: factorial(4) = 24
```

A task is automatically scheduled for execution when it is created. The event loop stops when all tasks are done.

Task functions

Note: In the functions below, the optional *loop* argument allows explicitly setting the event loop object used by the underlying task or coroutine. If it's not provided, the default event loop is used.

`asyncio.as_completed`(*fs*, ***, *loop=None*, *timeout=None*)

Return an iterator whose values, when waited for, are *Future* instances.

Raises *asyncio.TimeoutError* if the timeout occurs before all Futures are done.

Example:

```
for f in as_completed(fs):
    result = yield from f  # The 'yield from' may raise
    # Use result
```

Note: The futures `f` are not necessarily members of fs.

asyncio.**ensure_future**(*coro_or_future*, *, *loop=None*)

Schedule the execution of a *coroutine object*: wrap it in a future. Return a *Task* object.

If the argument is a *Future*, it is returned directly.

New in version 3.4.4.

Changed in version 3.5.1: The function accepts any *awaitable* object.

See also:

The *AbstractEventLoop.create_task()* method.

asyncio.**async**(*coro_or_future*, *, *loop=None*)

A deprecated alias to *ensure_future()*.

Deprecated since version 3.4.4.

asyncio.**wrap_future**(*future*, *, *loop=None*)

Wrap a *concurrent.futures.Future* object in a *Future* object.

asyncio.**gather**(**coros_or_futures*, *loop=None*, *return_exceptions=False*)

Return a future aggregating results from the given coroutine objects or futures.

All futures must share the same event loop. If all the tasks are done successfully, the returned future's result is the list of results (in the order of the original sequence, not necessarily the order of results arrival). If *return_exceptions* is true, exceptions in the tasks are treated the same as successful results, and gathered in the result list; otherwise, the first raised exception will be immediately propagated to the returned future.

Cancellation: if the outer Future is cancelled, all children (that have not completed yet) are also cancelled. If any child is cancelled, this is treated as if it raised *CancelledError* – the outer Future is *not* cancelled in this case. (This is to prevent the cancellation of one child to cause other children to be cancelled.)

asyncio.**iscoroutine**(*obj*)

Return `True` if *obj* is a *coroutine object*, which may be based on a generator or an `async def` coroutine.

asyncio.**iscoroutinefunction**(*func*)

Return `True` if *func* is determined to be a *coroutine function*, which may be a decorated generator function or an `async def` function.

asyncio.**run_coroutine_threadsafe**(*coro*, *loop*)

Submit a *coroutine object* to a given event loop.

Return a *concurrent.futures.Future* to access the result.

This function is meant to be called from a different thread than the one where the event loop is running. Usage:

```
# Create a coroutine
coro = asyncio.sleep(1, result=3)
# Submit the coroutine to a given loop
future = asyncio.run_coroutine_threadsafe(coro, loop)
# Wait for the result with an optional timeout argument
assert future.result(timeout) == 3
```

If an exception is raised in the coroutine, the returned future will be notified. It can also be used to cancel the task in the event loop:

```
try:
    result = future.result(timeout)
except asyncio.TimeoutError:
    print('The coroutine took too long, cancelling the task...')
```

```
    future.cancel()
except Exception as exc:
    print('The coroutine raised an exception: {!r}'.format(exc))
else:
    print('The coroutine returned: {!r}'.format(result))
```

See the *concurrency and multithreading* section of the documentation.

Note: Unlike other functions from the module, *run_coroutine_threadsafe()* requires the *loop* argument to be passed explicitly.

New in version 3.5.1.

coroutine asyncio.sleep(*delay*, *result=None*, ***, *loop=None*)

Create a *coroutine* that completes after a given time (in seconds). If *result* is provided, it is produced to the caller when the coroutine completes.

The resolution of the sleep depends on the *granularity of the event loop*.

This function is a *coroutine*.

asyncio.shield(*arg*, ***, *loop=None*)

Wait for a future, shielding it from cancellation.

The statement:

```
res = yield from shield(something())
```

is exactly equivalent to the statement:

```
res = yield from something()
```

except that if the coroutine containing it is cancelled, the task running in `something()` is not cancelled. From the point of view of `something()`, the cancellation did not happen. But its caller is still cancelled, so the yield-from expression still raises *CancelledError*. Note: If `something()` is cancelled by other means this will still cancel `shield()`.

If you want to completely ignore cancellation (not recommended) you can combine `shield()` with a try/except clause, as follows:

```
try:
    res = yield from shield(something())
except CancelledError:
    res = None
```

coroutine asyncio.wait(*futures*, ***, *loop=None*, *timeout=None*, *return_when=ALL_COMPLETED*)

Wait for the Futures and coroutine objects given by the sequence *futures* to complete. Coroutines will be wrapped in Tasks. Returns two sets of *Future*: (done, pending).

The sequence *futures* must not be empty.

timeout can be used to control the maximum number of seconds to wait before returning. *timeout* can be an int or float. If *timeout* is not specified or `None`, there is no limit to the wait time.

return_when indicates when this function should return. It must be one of the following constants of the *concurrent.futures* module:

Constant	Description
FIRST_COMPLETED	The function will return when any future finishes or is cancelled.
FIRST_EXCEPTION	The function will return when any future finishes by raising an exception. If no future raises an exception then it is equivalent to ALL_COMPLETED.
ALL_COMPLETED	The function will return when all futures finish or are cancelled.

This function is a *coroutine*.

Usage:

```
done, pending = yield from asyncio.wait(fs)
```

Note: This does not raise *asyncio.TimeoutError*! Futures that aren't done when the timeout occurs are returned in the second set.

coroutine asyncio.wait_for(*fut*, *timeout*, ***, *loop=None*)

Wait for the single *Future* or *coroutine object* to complete with timeout. If *timeout* is None, block until the future completes.

Coroutine will be wrapped in *Task*.

Returns result of the Future or coroutine. When a timeout occurs, it cancels the task and raises *asyncio.TimeoutError*. To avoid the task cancellation, wrap it in *shield()*.

If the wait is cancelled, the future *fut* is also cancelled.

This function is a *coroutine*, usage:

```
result = yield from asyncio.wait_for(fut, 60.0)
```

Changed in version 3.4.3: If the wait is cancelled, the future *fut* is now also cancelled.

18.5.4 Transports and protocols (callback based API)

Source code: Lib/asyncio/transports.py

Source code: Lib/asyncio/protocols.py

Transports

Transports are classes provided by *asyncio* in order to abstract various kinds of communication channels. You generally won't instantiate a transport yourself; instead, you will call an *AbstractEventLoop* method which will create the transport and try to initiate the underlying communication channel, calling you back when it succeeds.

Once the communication channel is established, a transport is always paired with a *protocol* instance. The protocol can then call the transport's methods for various purposes.

asyncio currently implements transports for TCP, UDP, SSL, and subprocess pipes. The methods available on a transport depend on the transport's kind.

The transport classes are *not thread safe*.

Changed in version 3.6: The socket option TCP_NODELAY is now set by default.

BaseTransport

class asyncio.BaseTransport
Base class for transports.

close()
Close the transport. If the transport has a buffer for outgoing data, buffered data will be flushed asynchronously. No more data will be received. After all buffered data is flushed, the protocol's `connection_lost()` method will be called with *None* as its argument.

is_closing()
Return `True` if the transport is closing or is closed.

New in version 3.5.1.

get_extra_info(*name*, *default=None*)
Return optional transport information. *name* is a string representing the piece of transport-specific information to get, *default* is the value to return if the information doesn't exist.

This method allows transport implementations to easily expose channel-specific information.

- socket:
  - `'peername'`: the remote address to which the socket is connected, result of *socket.socket.getpeername()* (`None` on error)
  - `'socket'`: *socket.socket* instance
  - `'sockname'`: the socket's own address, result of *socket.socket.getsockname()*
- SSL socket:
  - `'compression'`: the compression algorithm being used as a string, or `None` if the connection isn't compressed; result of *ssl.SSLSocket.compression()*
  - `'cipher'`: a three-value tuple containing the name of the cipher being used, the version of the SSL protocol that defines its use, and the number of secret bits being used; result of *ssl.SSLSocket.cipher()*
  - `'peercert'`: peer certificate; result of *ssl.SSLSocket.getpeercert()*
  - `'sslcontext'`: *ssl.SSLContext* instance
  - `'ssl_object'`: *ssl.SSLObject* or *ssl.SSLSocket* instance
- pipe:
  - `'pipe'`: pipe object
- subprocess:
  - `'subprocess'`: *subprocess.Popen* instance

set_protocol(*protocol*)
Set a new protocol. Switching protocol should only be done when both protocols are documented to support the switch.

New in version 3.5.3.

get_protocol()
Return the current protocol.

New in version 3.5.3.

Changed in version 3.5.1: `'ssl_object'` info was added to SSL sockets.

ReadTransport

class asyncio.**ReadTransport**
Interface for read-only transports.

pause_reading()
Pause the receiving end of the transport. No data will be passed to the protocol's `data_received()` method until *resume_reading()* is called.

resume_reading()
Resume the receiving end. The protocol's `data_received()` method will be called once again if some data is available for reading.

WriteTransport

class asyncio.**WriteTransport**
Interface for write-only transports.

abort()
Close the transport immediately, without waiting for pending operations to complete. Buffered data will be lost. No more data will be received. The protocol's `connection_lost()` method will eventually be called with *None* as its argument.

can_write_eof()
Return *True* if the transport supports *write_eof()*, *False* if not.

get_write_buffer_size()
Return the current size of the output buffer used by the transport.

get_write_buffer_limits()
Get the *high*- and *low*-water limits for write flow control. Return a tuple `(low, high)` where *low* and *high* are positive number of bytes.

Use *set_write_buffer_limits()* to set the limits.

New in version 3.4.2.

set_write_buffer_limits(*high=None*, *low=None*)
Set the *high*- and *low*-water limits for write flow control.

These two values (measured in number of bytes) control when the protocol's `pause_writing()` and `resume_writing()` methods are called. If specified, the low-water limit must be less than or equal to the high-water limit. Neither *high* nor *low* can be negative.

`pause_writing()` is called when the buffer size becomes greater than or equal to the *high* value. If writing has been paused, `resume_writing()` is called when the buffer size becomes less than or equal to the *low* value.

The defaults are implementation-specific. If only the high-water limit is given, the low-water limit defaults to an implementation-specific value less than or equal to the high-water limit. Setting *high* to zero forces *low* to zero as well, and causes `pause_writing()` to be called whenever the buffer becomes non-empty. Setting *low* to zero causes `resume_writing()` to be called only once the buffer is empty. Use of zero for either limit is generally sub-optimal as it reduces opportunities for doing I/O and computation concurrently.

Use *get_write_buffer_limits()* to get the limits.

write(*data*)
Write some *data* bytes to the transport.

This method does not block; it buffers the data and arranges for it to be sent out asynchronously.

writelines(*list_of_data*)
Write a list (or any iterable) of data bytes to the transport. This is functionally equivalent to calling *write()* on each element yielded by the iterable, but may be implemented more efficiently.

write_eof()
Close the write end of the transport after flushing buffered data. Data may still be received.

This method can raise *NotImplementedError* if the transport (e.g. SSL) doesn't support half-closes.

DatagramTransport

DatagramTransport.**sendto**(*data*, *addr=None*)
Send the *data* bytes to the remote peer given by *addr* (a transport-dependent target address). If *addr* is *None*, the data is sent to the target address given on transport creation.

This method does not block; it buffers the data and arranges for it to be sent out asynchronously.

DatagramTransport.**abort**()
Close the transport immediately, without waiting for pending operations to complete. Buffered data will be lost. No more data will be received. The protocol's `connection_lost()` method will eventually be called with *None* as its argument.

BaseSubprocessTransport

class asyncio.**BaseSubprocessTransport**

get_pid()
Return the subprocess process id as an integer.

get_pipe_transport(*fd*)
Return the transport for the communication pipe corresponding to the integer file descriptor *fd*:

- `0`: readable streaming transport of the standard input (*stdin*), or *None* if the subprocess was not created with `stdin=PIPE`
- `1`: writable streaming transport of the standard output (*stdout*), or *None* if the subprocess was not created with `stdout=PIPE`
- `2`: writable streaming transport of the standard error (*stderr*), or *None* if the subprocess was not created with `stderr=PIPE`
- other *fd*: *None*

get_returncode()
Return the subprocess returncode as an integer or *None* if it hasn't returned, similarly to the *subprocess.Popen.returncode* attribute.

kill()
Kill the subprocess, as in *subprocess.Popen.kill()*.

On POSIX systems, the function sends SIGKILL to the subprocess. On Windows, this method is an alias for *terminate()*.

send_signal(*signal*)
Send the *signal* number to the subprocess, as in *subprocess.Popen.send_signal()*.

terminate()
Ask the subprocess to stop, as in *subprocess.Popen.terminate()*. This method is an alias for the *close()* method.

On POSIX systems, this method sends SIGTERM to the subprocess. On Windows, the Windows API function TerminateProcess() is called to stop the subprocess.

`close()`
Ask the subprocess to stop by calling the *terminate()* method if the subprocess hasn't returned yet, and close transports of all pipes (*stdin*, *stdout* and *stderr*).

Protocols

asyncio provides base classes that you can subclass to implement your network protocols. Those classes are used in conjunction with *transports* (see below): the protocol parses incoming data and asks for the writing of outgoing data, while the transport is responsible for the actual I/O and buffering.

When subclassing a protocol class, it is recommended you override certain methods. Those methods are callbacks: they will be called by the transport on certain events (for example when some data is received); you shouldn't call them yourself, unless you are implementing a transport.

Note: All callbacks have default implementations, which are empty. Therefore, you only need to implement the callbacks for the events in which you are interested.

Protocol classes

`class asyncio.Protocol`
The base class for implementing streaming protocols (for use with e.g. TCP and SSL transports).

`class asyncio.DatagramProtocol`
The base class for implementing datagram protocols (for use with e.g. UDP transports).

`class asyncio.SubprocessProtocol`
The base class for implementing protocols communicating with child processes (through a set of unidirectional pipes).

Connection callbacks

These callbacks may be called on *Protocol*, *DatagramProtocol* and *SubprocessProtocol* instances:

`BaseProtocol.connection_made(`*transport*`)`
Called when a connection is made.

The *transport* argument is the transport representing the connection. You are responsible for storing it somewhere (e.g. as an attribute) if you need to.

`BaseProtocol.connection_lost(`*exc*`)`
Called when the connection is lost or closed.

The argument is either an exception object or *None*. The latter means a regular EOF is received, or the connection was aborted or closed by this side of the connection.

connection_made() and *connection_lost()* are called exactly once per successful connection. All other callbacks will be called between those two methods, which allows for easier resource management in your protocol implementation.

The following callbacks may be called only on *SubprocessProtocol* instances:

`SubprocessProtocol.pipe_data_received(`*fd*, *data*`)`
Called when the child process writes data into its stdout or stderr pipe. *fd* is the integer file descriptor of the pipe. *data* is a non-empty bytes object containing the data.

`SubprocessProtocol.`**`pipe_connection_lost`**`(`*fd*, *exc*`)`
Called when one of the pipes communicating with the child process is closed. *fd* is the integer file descriptor that was closed.

`SubprocessProtocol.`**`process_exited`**`()`
Called when the child process has exited.

Streaming protocols

The following callbacks are called on *Protocol* instances:

`Protocol.`**`data_received`**`(`*data*`)`
Called when some data is received. *data* is a non-empty bytes object containing the incoming data.

Note: Whether the data is buffered, chunked or reassembled depends on the transport. In general, you shouldn't rely on specific semantics and instead make your parsing generic and flexible enough. However, data is always received in the correct order.

`Protocol.`**`eof_received`**`()`
Called when the other end signals it won't send any more data (for example by calling `write_eof()`, if the other end also uses asyncio).

This method may return a false value (including `None`), in which case the transport will close itself. Conversely, if this method returns a true value, closing the transport is up to the protocol. Since the default implementation returns `None`, it implicitly closes the connection.

Note: Some transports such as SSL don't support half-closed connections, in which case returning true from this method will not prevent closing the connection.

`data_received()` can be called an arbitrary number of times during a connection. However, `eof_received()` is called at most once and, if called, `data_received()` won't be called after it.

State machine:

start -> *connection_made()* [-> *data_received()* *] [-> *eof_received()* ?] -> *connection_lost()* -> end

Datagram protocols

The following callbacks are called on *DatagramProtocol* instances.

`DatagramProtocol.`**`datagram_received`**`(`*data*, *addr*`)`
Called when a datagram is received. *data* is a bytes object containing the incoming data. *addr* is the address of the peer sending the data; the exact format depends on the transport.

`DatagramProtocol.`**`error_received`**`(`*exc*`)`
Called when a previous send or receive operation raises an *OSError*. *exc* is the *OSError* instance.

This method is called in rare conditions, when the transport (e.g. UDP) detects that a datagram couldn't be delivered to its recipient. In many conditions though, undeliverable datagrams will be silently dropped.

Flow control callbacks

These callbacks may be called on *Protocol*, *DatagramProtocol* and *SubprocessProtocol* instances:

`BaseProtocol.pause_writing()`
Called when the transport's buffer goes over the high-water mark.

`BaseProtocol.resume_writing()`
Called when the transport's buffer drains below the low-water mark.

`pause_writing()` and `resume_writing()` calls are paired – `pause_writing()` is called once when the buffer goes strictly over the high-water mark (even if subsequent writes increases the buffer size even more), and eventually `resume_writing()` is called once when the buffer size reaches the low-water mark.

Note: If the buffer size equals the high-water mark, `pause_writing()` is not called – it must go strictly over. Conversely, `resume_writing()` is called when the buffer size is equal or lower than the low-water mark. These end conditions are important to ensure that things go as expected when either mark is zero.

Note: On BSD systems (OS X, FreeBSD, etc.) flow control is not supported for *DatagramProtocol*, because send failures caused by writing too many packets cannot be detected easily. The socket always appears 'ready' and excess packets are dropped; an *OSError* with errno set to *errno.ENOBUFS* may or may not be raised; if it is raised, it will be reported to *DatagramProtocol.error_received()* but otherwise ignored.

Coroutines and protocols

Coroutines can be scheduled in a protocol method using *ensure_future()*, but there is no guarantee made about the execution order. Protocols are not aware of coroutines created in protocol methods and so will not wait for them.

To have a reliable execution order, use *stream objects* in a coroutine with `yield from`. For example, the *StreamWriter.drain()* coroutine can be used to wait until the write buffer is flushed.

Protocol examples

TCP echo client protocol

TCP echo client using the *AbstractEventLoop.create_connection()* method, send data and wait until the connection is closed:

```
import asyncio

class EchoClientProtocol(asyncio.Protocol):
    def __init__(self, message, loop):
        self.message = message
        self.loop = loop

    def connection_made(self, transport):
        transport.write(self.message.encode())
        print('Data sent: {!r}'.format(self.message))

    def data_received(self, data):
        print('Data received: {!r}'.format(data.decode()))
```

```
    def connection_lost(self, exc):
        print('The server closed the connection')
        print('Stop the event loop')
        self.loop.stop()

loop = asyncio.get_event_loop()
message = 'Hello World!'
coro = loop.create_connection(lambda: EchoClientProtocol(message, loop),
                              '127.0.0.1', 8888)
loop.run_until_complete(coro)
loop.run_forever()
loop.close()
```

The event loop is running twice. The *run_until_complete()* method is preferred in this short example to raise an exception if the server is not listening, instead of having to write a short coroutine to handle the exception and stop the running loop. At *run_until_complete()* exit, the loop is no longer running, so there is no need to stop the loop in case of an error.

See also:

The *TCP echo client using streams* example uses the *asyncio.open_connection()* function.

TCP echo server protocol

TCP echo server using the *AbstractEventLoop.create_server()* method, send back received data and close the connection:

```
import asyncio

class EchoServerClientProtocol(asyncio.Protocol):
    def connection_made(self, transport):
        peername = transport.get_extra_info('peername')
        print('Connection from {}'.format(peername))
        self.transport = transport

    def data_received(self, data):
        message = data.decode()
        print('Data received: {!r}'.format(message))

        print('Send: {!r}'.format(message))
        self.transport.write(data)

        print('Close the client socket')
        self.transport.close()

loop = asyncio.get_event_loop()
# Each client connection will create a new protocol instance
coro = loop.create_server(EchoServerClientProtocol, '127.0.0.1', 8888)
server = loop.run_until_complete(coro)

# Serve requests until Ctrl+C is pressed
print('Serving on {}'.format(server.sockets[0].getsockname()))
try:
    loop.run_forever()
except KeyboardInterrupt:
    pass
```

```
# Close the server
server.close()
loop.run_until_complete(server.wait_closed())
loop.close()
```

`Transport.close()` can be called immediately after *WriteTransport.write()* even if data are not sent yet on the socket: both methods are asynchronous. **yield from** is not needed because these transport methods are not coroutines.

See also:

The *TCP echo server using streams* example uses the *asyncio.start_server()* function.

UDP echo client protocol

UDP echo client using the *AbstractEventLoop.create_datagram_endpoint()* method, send data and close the transport when we received the answer:

```
import asyncio

class EchoClientProtocol:
    def __init__(self, message, loop):
        self.message = message
        self.loop = loop
        self.transport = None

    def connection_made(self, transport):
        self.transport = transport
        print('Send:', self.message)
        self.transport.sendto(self.message.encode())

    def datagram_received(self, data, addr):
        print("Received:", data.decode())

        print("Close the socket")
        self.transport.close()

    def error_received(self, exc):
        print('Error received:', exc)

    def connection_lost(self, exc):
        print("Socket closed, stop the event loop")
        loop = asyncio.get_event_loop()
        loop.stop()

loop = asyncio.get_event_loop()
message = "Hello World!"
connect = loop.create_datagram_endpoint(
    lambda: EchoClientProtocol(message, loop),
    remote_addr=('127.0.0.1', 9999))
transport, protocol = loop.run_until_complete(connect)
loop.run_forever()
transport.close()
loop.close()
```

UDP echo server protocol

UDP echo server using the *AbstractEventLoop.create_datagram_endpoint()* method, send back received data:

```
import asyncio

class EchoServerProtocol:
    def connection_made(self, transport):
        self.transport = transport

    def datagram_received(self, data, addr):
        message = data.decode()
        print('Received %r from %s' % (message, addr))
        print('Send %r to %s' % (message, addr))
        self.transport.sendto(data, addr)

loop = asyncio.get_event_loop()
print("Starting UDP server")
# One protocol instance will be created to serve all client requests
listen = loop.create_datagram_endpoint(
    EchoServerProtocol, local_addr=('127.0.0.1', 9999))
transport, protocol = loop.run_until_complete(listen)

try:
    loop.run_forever()
except KeyboardInterrupt:
    pass

transport.close()
loop.close()
```

Register an open socket to wait for data using a protocol

Wait until a socket receives data using the *AbstractEventLoop.create_connection()* method with a protocol, and then close the event loop

```
import asyncio
try:
    from socket import socketpair
except ImportError:
    from asyncio.windows_utils import socketpair

# Create a pair of connected sockets
rsock, wsock = socketpair()
loop = asyncio.get_event_loop()

class MyProtocol(asyncio.Protocol):
    transport = None

    def connection_made(self, transport):
        self.transport = transport

    def data_received(self, data):
        print("Received:", data.decode())
```

```
        # We are done: close the transport (it will call connection_lost())
        self.transport.close()

    def connection_lost(self, exc):
        # The socket has been closed, stop the event loop
        loop.stop()

# Register the socket to wait for data
connect_coro = loop.create_connection(MyProtocol, sock=rsock)
transport, protocol = loop.run_until_complete(connect_coro)

# Simulate the reception of data from the network
loop.call_soon(wsock.send, 'abc'.encode())

# Run the event loop
loop.run_forever()

# We are done, close sockets and the event loop
rsock.close()
wsock.close()
loop.close()
```

See also:

The *watch a file descriptor for read events* example uses the low-level `AbstractEventLoop.add_reader()` method to register the file descriptor of a socket.

The *register an open socket to wait for data using streams* example uses high-level streams created by the `open_connection()` function in a coroutine.

18.5.5 Streams (coroutine based API)

Source code: Lib/asyncio/streams.py

Stream functions

Note: The top-level functions in this module are meant as convenience wrappers only; there's really nothing special there, and if they don't do exactly what you want, feel free to copy their code.

coroutine asyncio.open_connection(*host=None*, *port=None*, ***, *loop=None*, *limit=None*, ***kwds*)

A wrapper for `create_connection()` returning a (reader, writer) pair.

The reader returned is a `StreamReader` instance; the writer is a `StreamWriter` instance.

The arguments are all the usual arguments to `AbstractEventLoop.create_connection()` except *protocol_factory*; most common are positional host and port, with various optional keyword arguments following.

Additional optional keyword arguments are *loop* (to set the event loop instance to use) and *limit* (to set the buffer limit passed to the `StreamReader`).

This function is a *coroutine*.

coroutine asyncio.start_server(*client_connected_cb*, *host=None*, *port=None*, ***, *loop=None*, *limit=None*, ***kwds*)

Start a socket server, with a callback for each client connected. The return value is the same as `create_server()`.

The *client_connected_cb* parameter is called with two parameters: *client_reader*, *client_writer*. *client_reader* is a `StreamReader` object, while *client_writer* is a `StreamWriter` object. The *client_connected_cb* parameter can either be a plain callback function or a *coroutine function*; if it is a coroutine function, it will be automatically converted into a `Task`.

The rest of the arguments are all the usual arguments to `create_server()` except *protocol_factory*; most common are positional *host* and *port*, with various optional keyword arguments following.

Additional optional keyword arguments are *loop* (to set the event loop instance to use) and *limit* (to set the buffer limit passed to the `StreamReader`).

This function is a *coroutine*.

coroutine asyncio.open_unix_connection(*path=None*, ***, *loop=None*, *limit=None*, ***kwds*)

A wrapper for `create_unix_connection()` returning a (reader, writer) pair.

See `open_connection()` for information about return value and other details.

This function is a *coroutine*.

Availability: UNIX.

coroutine asyncio.start_unix_server(*client_connected_cb*, *path=None*, ***, *loop=None*, *limit=None*, ***kwds*)

Start a UNIX Domain Socket server, with a callback for each client connected.

See `start_server()` for information about return value and other details.

This function is a *coroutine*.

Availability: UNIX.

StreamReader

class asyncio.StreamReader(*limit=None*, *loop=None*)

This class is *not thread safe*.

exception()

Get the exception.

feed_eof()

Acknowledge the EOF.

feed_data(*data*)

Feed *data* bytes in the internal buffer. Any operations waiting for the data will be resumed.

set_exception(*exc*)

Set the exception.

set_transport(*transport*)

Set the transport.

coroutine read(*n=-1*)

Read up to *n* bytes. If *n* is not provided, or set to `-1`, read until EOF and return all read bytes.

If the EOF was received and the internal buffer is empty, return an empty `bytes` object.

This method is a *coroutine*.

coroutine readline()

Read one line, where "line" is a sequence of bytes ending with `\n`.

If EOF is received, and `\n` was not found, the method will return the partial read bytes.

If the EOF was received and the internal buffer is empty, return an empty `bytes` object.

This method is a *coroutine*.

coroutine readexactly(*n*)

Read exactly *n* bytes. Raise an *IncompleteReadError* if the end of the stream is reached before *n* can be read, the *IncompleteReadError.partial* attribute of the exception contains the partial read bytes.

This method is a *coroutine*.

coroutine readuntil(*separator=b'\n'*)

Read data from the stream until `separator` is found.

On success, the data and separator will be removed from the internal buffer (consumed). Returned data will include the separator at the end.

Configured stream limit is used to check result. Limit sets the maximal length of data that can be returned, not counting the separator.

If an EOF occurs and the complete separator is still not found, an *IncompleteReadError* exception will be raised, and the internal buffer will be reset. The *IncompleteReadError.partial* attribute may contain the separator partially.

If the data cannot be read because of over limit, a *LimitOverrunError* exception will be raised, and the data will be left in the internal buffer, so it can be read again.

New in version 3.5.2.

at_eof()

Return `True` if the buffer is empty and *feed_eof()* was called.

StreamWriter

class asyncio.StreamWriter(*transport, protocol, reader, loop*)

Wraps a Transport.

This exposes *write()*, *writelines()*, *can_write_eof()*, *write_eof()*, *get_extra_info()* and *close()*. It adds *drain()* which returns an optional *Future* on which you can wait for flow control. It also adds a transport attribute which references the `Transport` directly.

This class is *not thread safe*.

transport

Transport.

can_write_eof()

Return *True* if the transport supports *write_eof()*, *False* if not. See *WriteTransport.can_write_eof()*.

close()

Close the transport: see *BaseTransport.close()*.

coroutine drain()

Let the write buffer of the underlying transport a chance to be flushed.

The intended use is to write:

```
w.write(data)
yield from w.drain()
```

When the size of the transport buffer reaches the high-water limit (the protocol is paused), block until the size of the buffer is drained down to the low-water limit and the protocol is resumed. When there is nothing to wait for, the yield-from continues immediately.

Yielding from `drain()` gives the opportunity for the loop to schedule the write operation and flush the buffer. It should especially be used when a possibly large amount of data is written to the transport, and the coroutine does not yield-from between calls to `write()`.

This method is a *coroutine*.

get_extra_info(*name*, *default=None*)
Return optional transport information: see `BaseTransport.get_extra_info()`.

write(*data*)
Write some *data* bytes to the transport: see `WriteTransport.write()`.

writelines(*data*)
Write a list (or any iterable) of data bytes to the transport: see `WriteTransport.writelines()`.

write_eof()
Close the write end of the transport after flushing buffered data: see `WriteTransport.write_eof()`.

StreamReaderProtocol

class asyncio.**StreamReaderProtocol**(*stream_reader*, *client_connected_cb=None*, *loop=None*)
Trivial helper class to adapt between `Protocol` and `StreamReader`. Subclass of `Protocol`.

stream_reader is a `StreamReader` instance, *client_connected_cb* is an optional function called with (stream_reader, stream_writer) when a connection is made, *loop* is the event loop instance to use.

(This is a helper class instead of making `StreamReader` itself a `Protocol` subclass, because the `StreamReader` has other potential uses, and to prevent the user of the `StreamReader` from accidentally calling inappropriate methods of the protocol.)

IncompleteReadError

exception asyncio.**IncompleteReadError**

Incomplete read error, subclass of `EOFError`.

expected
Total number of expected bytes (`int`).

partial
Read bytes string before the end of stream was reached (`bytes`).

LimitOverrunError

exception asyncio.**LimitOverrunError**
Reached the buffer limit while looking for a separator.

consumed
Total number of to be consumed bytes.

Stream examples

TCP echo client using streams

TCP echo client using the `asyncio.open_connection()` function:

```
import asyncio

@asyncio.coroutine
def tcp_echo_client(message, loop):
    reader, writer = yield from asyncio.open_connection('127.0.0.1', 8888,
                                                        loop=loop)

    print('Send: %r' % message)
    writer.write(message.encode())

    data = yield from reader.read(100)
    print('Received: %r' % data.decode())

    print('Close the socket')
    writer.close()

message = 'Hello World!'
loop = asyncio.get_event_loop()
loop.run_until_complete(tcp_echo_client(message, loop))
loop.close()
```

See also:

The *TCP echo client protocol* example uses the *AbstractEventLoop.create_connection()* method.

TCP echo server using streams

TCP echo server using the *asyncio.start_server()* function:

```
import asyncio

@asyncio.coroutine
def handle_echo(reader, writer):
    data = yield from reader.read(100)
    message = data.decode()
    addr = writer.get_extra_info('peername')
    print("Received %r from %r" % (message, addr))

    print("Send: %r" % message)
    writer.write(data)
    yield from writer.drain()

    print("Close the client socket")
    writer.close()

loop = asyncio.get_event_loop()
coro = asyncio.start_server(handle_echo, '127.0.0.1', 8888, loop=loop)
server = loop.run_until_complete(coro)

# Serve requests until Ctrl+C is pressed
print('Serving on {}'.format(server.sockets[0].getsockname()))
try:
    loop.run_forever()
except KeyboardInterrupt:
    pass

# Close the server
```

```
server.close()
loop.run_until_complete(server.wait_closed())
loop.close()
```

See also:

The *TCP echo server protocol* example uses the `AbstractEventLoop.create_server()` method.

Get HTTP headers

Simple example querying HTTP headers of the URL passed on the command line:

```
import asyncio
import urllib.parse
import sys

@asyncio.coroutine
def print_http_headers(url):
    url = urllib.parse.urlsplit(url)
    if url.scheme == 'https':
        connect = asyncio.open_connection(url.hostname, 443, ssl=True)
    else:
        connect = asyncio.open_connection(url.hostname, 80)
    reader, writer = yield from connect
    query = ('HEAD {path} HTTP/1.0\r\n'
             'Host: {hostname}\r\n'
             '\r\n').format(path=url.path or '/', hostname=url.hostname)
    writer.write(query.encode('latin-1'))
    while True:
        line = yield from reader.readline()
        if not line:
            break
        line = line.decode('latin1').rstrip()
        if line:
            print('HTTP header> %s' % line)

    # Ignore the body, close the socket
    writer.close()

url = sys.argv[1]
loop = asyncio.get_event_loop()
task = asyncio.ensure_future(print_http_headers(url))
loop.run_until_complete(task)
loop.close()
```

Usage:

```
python example.py http://example.com/path/page.html
```

or with HTTPS:

```
python example.py https://example.com/path/page.html
```

Register an open socket to wait for data using streams

Coroutine waiting until a socket receives data using the `open_connection()` function:

```
import asyncio
try:
    from socket import socketpair
except ImportError:
    from asyncio.windows_utils import socketpair

@asyncio.coroutine
def wait_for_data(loop):
    # Create a pair of connected sockets
    rsock, wsock = socketpair()

    # Register the open socket to wait for data
    reader, writer = yield from asyncio.open_connection(sock=rsock, loop=loop)

    # Simulate the reception of data from the network
    loop.call_soon(wsock.send, 'abc'.encode())

    # Wait for data
    data = yield from reader.read(100)

    # Got data, we are done: close the socket
    print("Received:", data.decode())
    writer.close()

    # Close the second socket
    wsock.close()

loop = asyncio.get_event_loop()
loop.run_until_complete(wait_for_data(loop))
loop.close()
```

See also:

The *register an open socket to wait for data using a protocol* example uses a low-level protocol created by the *AbstractEventLoop.create_connection()* method.

The *watch a file descriptor for read events* example uses the low-level *AbstractEventLoop.add_reader()* method to register the file descriptor of a socket.

18.5.6 Subprocess

Source code: Lib/asyncio/subprocess.py

Windows event loop

On Windows, the default event loop is *SelectorEventLoop* which does not support subprocesses. *ProactorEventLoop* should be used instead. Example to use it on Windows:

```
import asyncio, sys

if sys.platform == 'win32':
    loop = asyncio.ProactorEventLoop()
    asyncio.set_event_loop(loop)
```

See also:

Available event loops and *Platform support*.

Create a subprocess: high-level API using Process

coroutine asyncio.create_subprocess_exec(**args, stdin=None, stdout=None, stderr=None, loop=None, limit=None, **kwds*)

Create a subprocess.

The *limit* parameter sets the buffer limit passed to the *StreamReader*. See *AbstractEventLoop.subprocess_exec()* for other parameters.

Return a *Process* instance.

This function is a *coroutine*.

coroutine asyncio.create_subprocess_shell(*cmd, stdin=None, stdout=None, stderr=None, loop=None, limit=None, **kwds*)

Run the shell command *cmd*.

The *limit* parameter sets the buffer limit passed to the *StreamReader*. See *AbstractEventLoop.subprocess_shell()* for other parameters.

Return a *Process* instance.

It is the application's responsibility to ensure that all whitespace and metacharacters are quoted appropriately to avoid shell injection vulnerabilities. The *shlex.quote()* function can be used to properly escape whitespace and shell metacharacters in strings that are going to be used to construct shell commands.

This function is a *coroutine*.

Use the *AbstractEventLoop.connect_read_pipe()* and *AbstractEventLoop.connect_write_pipe()* methods to connect pipes.

Create a subprocess: low-level API using subprocess.Popen

Run subprocesses asynchronously using the *subprocess* module.

coroutine AbstractEventLoop.subprocess_exec(*protocol_factory, *args, stdin=subprocess.PIPE, stdout=subprocess.PIPE, stderr=subprocess.PIPE, **kwargs*)

Create a subprocess from one or more string arguments (character strings or bytes strings encoded to the *filesystem encoding*), where the first string specifies the program to execute, and the remaining strings specify the program's arguments. (Thus, together the string arguments form the `sys.argv` value of the program, assuming it is a Python script.) This is similar to the standard library *subprocess.Popen* class called with shell=False and the list of strings passed as the first argument; however, where *Popen* takes a single argument which is list of strings, *subprocess_exec()* takes multiple string arguments.

The *protocol_factory* must instantiate a subclass of the *asyncio.SubprocessProtocol* class.

Other parameters:

- *stdin*: Either a file-like object representing the pipe to be connected to the subprocess's standard input stream using *connect_write_pipe()*, or the constant *subprocess.PIPE* (the default). By default a new pipe will be created and connected.
- *stdout*: Either a file-like object representing the pipe to be connected to the subprocess's standard output stream using *connect_read_pipe()*, or the constant *subprocess.PIPE* (the default). By default a new pipe will be created and connected.
- *stderr*: Either a file-like object representing the pipe to be connected to the subprocess's standard error stream using *connect_read_pipe()*, or one of the constants *subprocess.PIPE* (the default) or *subprocess.STDOUT*. By default a new pipe will be created and connected. When *subprocess.STDOUT* is specified, the subprocess's standard error stream will be connected to the same pipe as the standard output stream.

- All other keyword arguments are passed to *subprocess.Popen* without interpretation, except for *bufsize*, *universal_newlines* and *shell*, which should not be specified at all.

Returns a pair of `(transport, protocol)`, where *transport* is an instance of *BaseSubprocessTransport*.

This method is a *coroutine*.

See the constructor of the *subprocess.Popen* class for parameters.

coroutine AbstractEventLoop.subprocess_shell(*protocol_factory, cmd, *, stdin=subprocess.PIPE, stdout=subprocess.PIPE, stderr=subprocess.PIPE, **kwargs*)

Create a subprocess from *cmd*, which is a character string or a bytes string encoded to the *filesystem encoding*, using the platform's "shell" syntax. This is similar to the standard library *subprocess.Popen* class called with `shell=True`.

The *protocol_factory* must instantiate a subclass of the *asyncio.SubprocessProtocol* class.

See *subprocess_exec()* for more details about the remaining arguments.

Returns a pair of `(transport, protocol)`, where *transport* is an instance of *BaseSubprocessTransport*.

It is the application's responsibility to ensure that all whitespace and metacharacters are quoted appropriately to avoid shell injection vulnerabilities. The *shlex.quote()* function can be used to properly escape whitespace and shell metacharacters in strings that are going to be used to construct shell commands.

This method is a *coroutine*.

See also:

The *AbstractEventLoop.connect_read_pipe()* and *AbstractEventLoop.connect_write_pipe()* methods.

Constants

`asyncio.subprocess.PIPE`

Special value that can be used as the *stdin*, *stdout* or *stderr* argument to *create_subprocess_shell()* and *create_subprocess_exec()* and indicates that a pipe to the standard stream should be opened.

`asyncio.subprocess.STDOUT`

Special value that can be used as the *stderr* argument to *create_subprocess_shell()* and *create_subprocess_exec()* and indicates that standard error should go into the same handle as standard output.

`asyncio.subprocess.DEVNULL`

Special value that can be used as the *stdin*, *stdout* or *stderr* argument to *create_subprocess_shell()* and *create_subprocess_exec()* and indicates that the special file *os.devnull* will be used.

Process

`class asyncio.subprocess.Process`

A subprocess created by the *create_subprocess_exec()* or the *create_subprocess_shell()* function.

The API of the *Process* class was designed to be close to the API of the *subprocess.Popen* class, but there are some differences:

- There is no explicit *poll()* method

- The *communicate()* and *wait()* methods don't take a *timeout* parameter: use the *wait_for()* function
- The *universal_newlines* parameter is not supported (only bytes strings are supported)
- The *wait()* method of the *Process* class is asynchronous whereas the *wait()* method of the *Popen* class is implemented as a busy loop.

This class is *not thread safe*. See also the *Subprocess and threads* section.

coroutine wait()

Wait for child process to terminate. Set and return *returncode* attribute.

This method is a *coroutine*.

Note: This will deadlock when using `stdout=PIPE` or `stderr=PIPE` and the child process generates enough output to a pipe such that it blocks waiting for the OS pipe buffer to accept more data. Use the *communicate()* method when using pipes to avoid that.

coroutine communicate(*input=None*)

Interact with process: Send data to stdin. Read data from stdout and stderr, until end-of-file is reached. Wait for process to terminate. The optional *input* argument should be data to be sent to the child process, or `None`, if no data should be sent to the child. The type of *input* must be bytes.

communicate() returns a tuple `(stdout_data, stderr_data)`.

If a *BrokenPipeError* or *ConnectionResetError* exception is raised when writing *input* into stdin, the exception is ignored. It occurs when the process exits before all data are written into stdin.

Note that if you want to send data to the process's stdin, you need to create the Process object with `stdin=PIPE`. Similarly, to get anything other than `None` in the result tuple, you need to give `stdout=PIPE` and/or `stderr=PIPE` too.

This method is a *coroutine*.

Note: The data read is buffered in memory, so do not use this method if the data size is large or unlimited.

Changed in version 3.4.2: The method now ignores *BrokenPipeError* and *ConnectionResetError*.

send_signal(*signal*)

Sends the signal *signal* to the child process.

Note: On Windows, `SIGTERM` is an alias for *terminate()*. `CTRL_C_EVENT` and `CTRL_BREAK_EVENT` can be sent to processes started with a *creationflags* parameter which includes `CREATE_NEW_PROCESS_GROUP`.

terminate()

Stop the child. On Posix OSs the method sends `signal.SIGTERM` to the child. On Windows the Win32 API function `TerminateProcess()` is called to stop the child.

kill()

Kills the child. On Posix OSs the function sends `SIGKILL` to the child. On Windows *kill()* is an alias for *terminate()*.

stdin
Standard input stream (*StreamWriter*), None if the process was created with stdin=None.

stdout
Standard output stream (*StreamReader*), None if the process was created with stdout=None.

stderr
Standard error stream (*StreamReader*), None if the process was created with stderr=None.

> **Warning:** Use the *communicate()* method rather than *.stdin.write*, *.stdout.read* or *.stderr.read* to avoid deadlocks due to streams pausing reading or writing and blocking the child process.

pid
The identifier of the process.

Note that for processes created by the *create_subprocess_shell()* function, this attribute is the process identifier of the spawned shell.

returncode
Return code of the process when it exited. A None value indicates that the process has not terminated yet.

A negative value -N indicates that the child was terminated by signal N (Unix only).

Subprocess and threads

asyncio supports running subprocesses from different threads, but there are limits:

- An event loop must run in the main thread
- The child watcher must be instantiated in the main thread, before executing subprocesses from other threads. Call the get_child_watcher() function in the main thread to instantiate the child watcher.

The *asyncio.subprocess.Process* class is not thread safe.

See also:

The *Concurrency and multithreading in asyncio* section.

Subprocess examples

Subprocess using transport and protocol

Example of a subprocess protocol using to get the output of a subprocess and to wait for the subprocess exit. The subprocess is created by the *AbstractEventLoop.subprocess_exec()* method:

```
import asyncio
import sys

class DateProtocol(asyncio.SubprocessProtocol):
    def __init__(self, exit_future):
        self.exit_future = exit_future
        self.output = bytearray()

    def pipe_data_received(self, fd, data):
        self.output.extend(data)
```

```
    def process_exited(self):
        self.exit_future.set_result(True)

@asyncio.coroutine
def get_date(loop):
    code = 'import datetime; print(datetime.datetime.now())'
    exit_future = asyncio.Future(loop=loop)

    # Create the subprocess controlled by the protocol DateProtocol,
    # redirect the standard output into a pipe
    create = loop.subprocess_exec(lambda: DateProtocol(exit_future),
                                  sys.executable, '-c', code,
                                  stdin=None, stderr=None)
    transport, protocol = yield from create

    # Wait for the subprocess exit using the process_exited() method
    # of the protocol
    yield from exit_future

    # Close the stdout pipe
    transport.close()

    # Read the output which was collected by the pipe_data_received()
    # method of the protocol
    data = bytes(protocol.output)
    return data.decode('ascii').rstrip()

if sys.platform == "win32":
    loop = asyncio.ProactorEventLoop()
    asyncio.set_event_loop(loop)
else:
    loop = asyncio.get_event_loop()

date = loop.run_until_complete(get_date(loop))
print("Current date: %s" % date)
loop.close()
```

Subprocess using streams

Example using the *Process* class to control the subprocess and the *StreamReader* class to read from the standard output. The subprocess is created by the *create_subprocess_exec()* function:

```
import asyncio.subprocess
import sys

@asyncio.coroutine
def get_date():
    code = 'import datetime; print(datetime.datetime.now())'

    # Create the subprocess, redirect the standard output into a pipe
    create = asyncio.create_subprocess_exec(sys.executable, '-c', code,
                                            stdout=asyncio.subprocess.PIPE)
    proc = yield from create

    # Read one line of output
    data = yield from proc.stdout.readline()
```

```
    line = data.decode('ascii').rstrip()

    # Wait for the subprocess exit
    yield from proc.wait()
    return line

if sys.platform == "win32":
    loop = asyncio.ProactorEventLoop()
    asyncio.set_event_loop(loop)
else:
    loop = asyncio.get_event_loop()

date = loop.run_until_complete(get_date())
print("Current date: %s" % date)
loop.close()
```

18.5.7 Synchronization primitives

Source code: Lib/asyncio/locks.py

Locks:

- *Lock*
- *Event*
- *Condition*

Semaphores:

- *Semaphore*
- *BoundedSemaphore*

asyncio lock API was designed to be close to classes of the *threading* module (*Lock*, *Event*, *Condition*, *Semaphore*, *BoundedSemaphore*), but it has no *timeout* parameter. The *asyncio.wait_for()* function can be used to cancel a task after a timeout.

Locks

Lock

class asyncio.Lock(*, *loop=None*)

Primitive lock objects.

A primitive lock is a synchronization primitive that is not owned by a particular coroutine when locked. A primitive lock is in one of two states, 'locked' or 'unlocked'.

It is created in the unlocked state. It has two basic methods, *acquire()* and *release()*. When the state is unlocked, acquire() changes the state to locked and returns immediately. When the state is locked, acquire() blocks until a call to release() in another coroutine changes it to unlocked, then the acquire() call resets it to locked and returns. The release() method should only be called in the locked state; it changes the state to unlocked and returns immediately. If an attempt is made to release an unlocked lock, a *RuntimeError* will be raised.

When more than one coroutine is blocked in acquire() waiting for the state to turn to unlocked, only one coroutine proceeds when a release() call resets the state to unlocked; first coroutine which is blocked in acquire() is being processed.

acquire() is a coroutine and should be called with `yield from`.

Locks also support the context management protocol. `(yield from lock)` should be used as the context manager expression.

This class is *not thread safe*.

Usage:

```
lock = Lock()
...
yield from lock
try:
    ...
finally:
    lock.release()
```

Context manager usage:

```
lock = Lock()
...
with (yield from lock):
    ...
```

Lock objects can be tested for locking state:

```
if not lock.locked():
    yield from lock
else:
    # lock is acquired
    ...
```

locked()
Return `True` if the lock is acquired.

coroutine acquire()
Acquire a lock.

This method blocks until the lock is unlocked, then sets it to locked and returns `True`.

This method is a *coroutine*.

release()
Release a lock.

When the lock is locked, reset it to unlocked, and return. If any other coroutines are blocked waiting for the lock to become unlocked, allow exactly one of them to proceed.

When invoked on an unlocked lock, a `RuntimeError` is raised.

There is no return value.

Event

class asyncio.Event(*, *loop=None*)
An Event implementation, asynchronous equivalent to `threading.Event`.

Class implementing event objects. An event manages a flag that can be set to true with the `set()` method and reset to false with the `clear()` method. The `wait()` method blocks until the flag is true. The flag is initially false.

This class is *not thread safe*.

clear()
Reset the internal flag to false. Subsequently, coroutines calling *wait()* will block until *set()* is called to set the internal flag to true again.

is_set()
Return `True` if and only if the internal flag is true.

set()
Set the internal flag to true. All coroutines waiting for it to become true are awakened. Coroutine that call *wait()* once the flag is true will not block at all.

coroutine wait()
Block until the internal flag is true.

If the internal flag is true on entry, return `True` immediately. Otherwise, block until another coroutine calls *set()* to set the flag to true, then return `True`.

This method is a *coroutine*.

Condition

class asyncio.Condition(*lock=None*, *, *loop=None*)
A Condition implementation, asynchronous equivalent to *threading.Condition*.

This class implements condition variable objects. A condition variable allows one or more coroutines to wait until they are notified by another coroutine.

If the *lock* argument is given and not `None`, it must be a *Lock* object, and it is used as the underlying lock. Otherwise, a new *Lock* object is created and used as the underlying lock.

This class is *not thread safe*.

coroutine acquire()
Acquire the underlying lock.

This method blocks until the lock is unlocked, then sets it to locked and returns `True`.

This method is a *coroutine*.

notify(*n=1*)
By default, wake up one coroutine waiting on this condition, if any. If the calling coroutine has not acquired the lock when this method is called, a *RuntimeError* is raised.

This method wakes up at most *n* of the coroutines waiting for the condition variable; it is a no-op if no coroutines are waiting.

Note: An awakened coroutine does not actually return from its *wait()* call until it can reacquire the lock. Since *notify()* does not release the lock, its caller should.

locked()
Return `True` if the underlying lock is acquired.

notify_all()
Wake up all coroutines waiting on this condition. This method acts like *notify()*, but wakes up all waiting coroutines instead of one. If the calling coroutine has not acquired the lock when this method is called, a *RuntimeError* is raised.

release()
Release the underlying lock.

When the lock is locked, reset it to unlocked, and return. If any other coroutines are blocked waiting for the lock to become unlocked, allow exactly one of them to proceed.

When invoked on an unlocked lock, a *RuntimeError* is raised.

There is no return value.

coroutine wait()
Wait until notified.

If the calling coroutine has not acquired the lock when this method is called, a *RuntimeError* is raised.

This method releases the underlying lock, and then blocks until it is awakened by a *notify()* or *notify_all()* call for the same condition variable in another coroutine. Once awakened, it re-acquires the lock and returns True.

This method is a *coroutine*.

coroutine wait_for(*predicate*)
Wait until a predicate becomes true.

The predicate should be a callable which result will be interpreted as a boolean value. The final predicate value is the return value.

This method is a *coroutine*.

Semaphores

Semaphore

class asyncio.Semaphore(*value=1*, *, *loop=None*)
A Semaphore implementation.

A semaphore manages an internal counter which is decremented by each *acquire()* call and incremented by each *release()* call. The counter can never go below zero; when *acquire()* finds that it is zero, it blocks, waiting until some other coroutine calls *release()*.

Semaphores also support the context management protocol.

The optional argument gives the initial value for the internal counter; it defaults to 1. If the value given is less than 0, *ValueError* is raised.

This class is *not thread safe*.

coroutine acquire()
Acquire a semaphore.

If the internal counter is larger than zero on entry, decrement it by one and return True immediately. If it is zero on entry, block, waiting until some other coroutine has called *release()* to make it larger than 0, and then return True.

This method is a *coroutine*.

locked()
Returns True if semaphore can not be acquired immediately.

release()
Release a semaphore, incrementing the internal counter by one. When it was zero on entry and another coroutine is waiting for it to become larger than zero again, wake up that coroutine.

BoundedSemaphore

class asyncio.BoundedSemaphore(*value=1*, *, *loop=None*)
A bounded semaphore implementation. Inherit from *Semaphore*.

This raises *ValueError* in *release()* if it would increase the value above the initial value.

18.5.8 Queues

Source code: Lib/asyncio/queues.py

Queues:

- *Queue*
- *PriorityQueue*
- *LifoQueue*

asyncio queue API was designed to be close to classes of the *queue* module (*Queue*, *PriorityQueue*, *LifoQueue*), but it has no *timeout* parameter. The *asyncio.wait_for()* function can be used to cancel a task after a timeout.

Queue

`class asyncio.Queue(maxsize=0, *, loop=None)`

A queue, useful for coordinating producer and consumer coroutines.

If *maxsize* is less than or equal to zero, the queue size is infinite. If it is an integer greater than `0`, then `yield from put()` will block when the queue reaches *maxsize*, until an item is removed by *get()*.

Unlike the standard library *queue*, you can reliably know this Queue's size with *qsize()*, since your single-threaded asyncio application won't be interrupted between calling *qsize()* and doing an operation on the Queue.

This class is *not thread safe*.

Changed in version 3.4.4: New *join()* and *task_done()* methods.

`empty()`

Return `True` if the queue is empty, `False` otherwise.

`full()`

Return `True` if there are *maxsize* items in the queue.

Note: If the Queue was initialized with `maxsize=0` (the default), then *full()* is never `True`.

`coroutine get()`

Remove and return an item from the queue. If queue is empty, wait until an item is available.

This method is a *coroutine*.

See also:

The *empty()* method.

`get_nowait()`

Remove and return an item from the queue.

Return an item if one is immediately available, else raise *QueueEmpty*.

`coroutine join()`

Block until all items in the queue have been gotten and processed.

The count of unfinished tasks goes up whenever an item is added to the queue. The count goes down whenever a consumer thread calls *task_done()* to indicate that the item was retrieved and all work on it is complete. When the count of unfinished tasks drops to zero, *join()* unblocks.

This method is a *coroutine*.

New in version 3.4.4.

coroutine put(*item*)
Put an item into the queue. If the queue is full, wait until a free slot is available before adding item.

This method is a *coroutine*.

See also:

The *full()* method.

put_nowait(*item*)
Put an item into the queue without blocking.

If no free slot is immediately available, raise *QueueFull*.

qsize()
Number of items in the queue.

task_done()
Indicate that a formerly enqueued task is complete.

Used by queue consumers. For each *get()* used to fetch a task, a subsequent call to *task_done()* tells the queue that the processing on the task is complete.

If a *join()* is currently blocking, it will resume when all items have been processed (meaning that a *task_done()* call was received for every item that had been *put()* into the queue).

Raises *ValueError* if called more times than there were items placed in the queue.

New in version 3.4.4.

maxsize
Number of items allowed in the queue.

PriorityQueue

class asyncio.PriorityQueue
A subclass of *Queue*; retrieves entries in priority order (lowest first).

Entries are typically tuples of the form: (priority number, data).

LifoQueue

class asyncio.LifoQueue
A subclass of *Queue* that retrieves most recently added entries first.

Exceptions

exception asyncio.QueueEmpty
Exception raised when the *get_nowait()* method is called on a *Queue* object which is empty.

exception asyncio.QueueFull
Exception raised when the *put_nowait()* method is called on a *Queue* object which is full.

18.5.9 Develop with asyncio

Asynchronous programming is different than classical "sequential" programming. This page lists common traps and explains how to avoid them.

Debug mode of asyncio

The implementation of *asyncio* has been written for performance. In order to ease the development of asynchronous code, you may wish to enable *debug mode*.

To enable all debug checks for an application:

- Enable the asyncio debug mode globally by setting the environment variable `PYTHONASYNCIODEBUG` to `1`, or by calling *AbstractEventLoop.set_debug()*.
- Set the log level of the *asyncio logger* to `logging.DEBUG`. For example, call `logging.basicConfig(level=logging.DEBUG)` at startup.
- Configure the *warnings* module to display *ResourceWarning* warnings. For example, use the `-Wdefault` command line option of Python to display them.

Examples debug checks:

- Log *coroutines defined but never "yielded from"*
- *call_soon()* and *call_at()* methods raise an exception if they are called from the wrong thread.
- Log the execution time of the selector
- Log callbacks taking more than 100 ms to be executed. The `AbstractEventLoop.slow_callback_duration` attribute is the minimum duration in seconds of "slow" callbacks.
- *ResourceWarning* warnings are emitted when transports and event loops are *not closed explicitly*.

See also:

The *AbstractEventLoop.set_debug()* method and the *asyncio logger*.

Cancellation

Cancellation of tasks is not common in classic programming. In asynchronous programming, not only is it something common, but you have to prepare your code to handle it.

Futures and tasks can be cancelled explicitly with their *Future.cancel()* method. The *wait_for()* function cancels the waited task when the timeout occurs. There are many other cases where a task can be cancelled indirectly.

Don't call *set_result()* or *set_exception()* method of *Future* if the future is cancelled: it would fail with an exception. For example, write:

```
if not fut.cancelled():
    fut.set_result('done')
```

Don't schedule directly a call to the *set_result()* or the *set_exception()* method of a future with *AbstractEventLoop.call_soon()*: the future can be cancelled before its method is called.

If you wait for a future, you should check early if the future was cancelled to avoid useless operations. Example:

```
@coroutine
def slow_operation(fut):
    if fut.cancelled():
```

```
        return
    # ... slow computation ...
    yield from fut
    # ...
```

The *shield()* function can also be used to ignore cancellation.

Concurrency and multithreading

An event loop runs in a thread and executes all callbacks and tasks in the same thread. While a task is running in the event loop, no other task is running in the same thread. But when the task uses `yield from`, the task is suspended and the event loop executes the next task.

To schedule a callback from a different thread, the *AbstractEventLoop.call_soon_threadsafe()* method should be used. Example:

```
loop.call_soon_threadsafe(callback, *args)
```

Most asyncio objects are not thread safe. You should only worry if you access objects outside the event loop. For example, to cancel a future, don't call directly its *Future.cancel()* method, but:

```
loop.call_soon_threadsafe(fut.cancel)
```

To handle signals and to execute subprocesses, the event loop must be run in the main thread.

To schedule a coroutine object from a different thread, the *run_coroutine_threadsafe()* function should be used. It returns a *concurrent.futures.Future* to access the result:

```
future = asyncio.run_coroutine_threadsafe(coro_func(), loop)
result = future.result(timeout)  # Wait for the result with a timeout
```

The *AbstractEventLoop.run_in_executor()* method can be used with a thread pool executor to execute a callback in different thread to not block the thread of the event loop.

See also:

The *Synchronization primitives* section describes ways to synchronize tasks.

The *Subprocess and threads* section lists asyncio limitations to run subprocesses from different threads.

Handle blocking functions correctly

Blocking functions should not be called directly. For example, if a function blocks for 1 second, other tasks are delayed by 1 second which can have an important impact on reactivity.

For networking and subprocesses, the *asyncio* module provides high-level APIs like *protocols*.

An executor can be used to run a task in a different thread or even in a different process, to not block the thread of the event loop. See the *AbstractEventLoop.run_in_executor()* method.

See also:

The *Delayed calls* section details how the event loop handles time.

Logging

The *asyncio* module logs information with the *logging* module in the logger `'asyncio'`.

The default log level for the *asyncio* module is `logging.INFO`. For those not wanting such verbosity from *asyncio* the log level can be changed. For example, to change the level to `logging.WARNING`:

```
logging.getLogger('asyncio').setLevel(logging.WARNING)
```

Detect coroutine objects never scheduled

When a coroutine function is called and its result is not passed to *ensure_future()* or to the *AbstractEventLoop.create_task()* method, the execution of the coroutine object will never be scheduled which is probably a bug. *Enable the debug mode of asyncio* to *log a warning* to detect it.

Example with the bug:

```
import asyncio

@asyncio.coroutine
def test():
    print("never scheduled")

test()
```

Output in debug mode:

```
Coroutine test() at test.py:3 was never yielded from
Coroutine object created at (most recent call last):
  File "test.py", line 7, in <module>
    test()
```

The fix is to call the *ensure_future()* function or the *AbstractEventLoop.create_task()* method with the coroutine object.

See also:

Pending task destroyed.

Detect exceptions never consumed

Python usually calls *sys.excepthook()* on unhandled exceptions. If *Future.set_exception()* is called, but the exception is never consumed, *sys.excepthook()* is not called. Instead, *a log is emitted* when the future is deleted by the garbage collector, with the traceback where the exception was raised.

Example of unhandled exception:

```
import asyncio

@asyncio.coroutine
def bug():
    raise Exception("not consumed")

loop = asyncio.get_event_loop()
asyncio.ensure_future(bug())
loop.run_forever()
loop.close()
```

Output:

```
Task exception was never retrieved
future: <Task finished coro=<coro() done, defined at asyncio/coroutines.py:139>␣
↪exception=Exception('not consumed',)>
Traceback (most recent call last):
  File "asyncio/tasks.py", line 237, in _step
    result = next(coro)
  File "asyncio/coroutines.py", line 141, in coro
    res = func(*args, **kw)
  File "test.py", line 5, in bug
    raise Exception("not consumed")
Exception: not consumed
```

Enable the debug mode of asyncio to get the traceback where the task was created. Output in debug mode:

```
Task exception was never retrieved
future: <Task finished coro=<bug() done, defined at test.py:3> exception=Exception('not consumed',
↪) created at test.py:8>
source_traceback: Object created at (most recent call last):
  File "test.py", line 8, in <module>
    asyncio.ensure_future(bug())
Traceback (most recent call last):
  File "asyncio/tasks.py", line 237, in _step
    result = next(coro)
  File "asyncio/coroutines.py", line 79, in __next__
    return next(self.gen)
  File "asyncio/coroutines.py", line 141, in coro
    res = func(*args, **kw)
  File "test.py", line 5, in bug
    raise Exception("not consumed")
Exception: not consumed
```

There are different options to fix this issue. The first option is to chain the coroutine in another coroutine and use classic try/except:

```
@asyncio.coroutine
def handle_exception():
    try:
        yield from bug()
    except Exception:
        print("exception consumed")

loop = asyncio.get_event_loop()
asyncio.ensure_future(handle_exception())
loop.run_forever()
loop.close()
```

Another option is to use the *AbstractEventLoop.run_until_complete()* function:

```
task = asyncio.ensure_future(bug())
try:
    loop.run_until_complete(task)
except Exception:
    print("exception consumed")
```

See also:

The *Future.exception()* method.

Chain coroutines correctly

When a coroutine function calls other coroutine functions and tasks, they should be chained explicitly with `yield from`. Otherwise, the execution is not guaranteed to be sequential.

Example with different bugs using *asyncio.sleep()* to simulate slow operations:

```
import asyncio

@asyncio.coroutine
def create():
    yield from asyncio.sleep(3.0)
    print("(1) create file")

@asyncio.coroutine
def write():
    yield from asyncio.sleep(1.0)
    print("(2) write into file")

@asyncio.coroutine
def close():
    print("(3) close file")

@asyncio.coroutine
def test():
    asyncio.ensure_future(create())
    asyncio.ensure_future(write())
    asyncio.ensure_future(close())
    yield from asyncio.sleep(2.0)
    loop.stop()

loop = asyncio.get_event_loop()
asyncio.ensure_future(test())
loop.run_forever()
print("Pending tasks at exit: %s" % asyncio.Task.all_tasks(loop))
loop.close()
```

Expected output:

```
(1) create file
(2) write into file
(3) close file
Pending tasks at exit: set()
```

Actual output:

```
(3) close file
(2) write into file
Pending tasks at exit: {<Task pending create() at test.py:7 wait_for=<Future pending cb=[Task._
↪wakeup()]>>}
Task was destroyed but it is pending!
task: <Task pending create() done at test.py:5 wait_for=<Future pending cb=[Task._wakeup()]>>
```

The loop stopped before the `create()` finished, `close()` has been called before `write()`, whereas coroutine functions were called in this order: `create()`, `write()`, `close()`.

To fix the example, tasks must be marked with `yield from`:

```
@asyncio.coroutine
def test():
    yield from asyncio.ensure_future(create())
    yield from asyncio.ensure_future(write())
    yield from asyncio.ensure_future(close())
    yield from asyncio.sleep(2.0)
    loop.stop()
```

Or without `asyncio.ensure_future()`:

```
@asyncio.coroutine
def test():
    yield from create()
    yield from write()
    yield from close()
    yield from asyncio.sleep(2.0)
    loop.stop()
```

Pending task destroyed

If a pending task is destroyed, the execution of its wrapped *coroutine* did not complete. It is probably a bug and so a warning is logged.

Example of log:

```
Task was destroyed but it is pending!
task: <Task pending coro=<kill_me() done, defined at test.py:5> wait_for=<Future pending cb=[Task._
↪wakeup()]>>
```

Enable the debug mode of asyncio to get the traceback where the task was created. Example of log in debug mode:

```
Task was destroyed but it is pending!
source_traceback: Object created at (most recent call last):
  File "test.py", line 15, in <module>
    task = asyncio.ensure_future(coro, loop=loop)
task: <Task pending coro=<kill_me() done, defined at test.py:5> wait_for=<Future pending cb=[Task._
↪wakeup()] created at test.py:7> created at test.py:15>
```

See also:

Detect coroutine objects never scheduled.

Close transports and event loops

When a transport is no more needed, call its `close()` method to release resources. Event loops must also be closed explicitly.

If a transport or an event loop is not closed explicitly, a *ResourceWarning* warning will be emitted in its destructor. By default, *ResourceWarning* warnings are ignored. The *Debug mode of asyncio* section explains how to display them.

See also:

The *asyncio* module was designed in PEP 3156. For a motivational primer on transports and protocols, see PEP 3153.

18.6 asyncore — Asynchronous socket handler

Source code: Lib/asyncore.py

Deprecated since version 3.6: Please use *asyncio* instead.

Note: This module exists for backwards compatibility only. For new code we recommend using *asyncio*.

This module provides the basic infrastructure for writing asynchronous socket service clients and servers.

There are only two ways to have a program on a single processor do "more than one thing at a time." Multi-threaded programming is the simplest and most popular way to do it, but there is another very different technique, that lets you have nearly all the advantages of multi-threading, without actually using multiple threads. It's really only practical if your program is largely I/O bound. If your program is processor bound, then pre-emptive scheduled threads are probably what you really need. Network servers are rarely processor bound, however.

If your operating system supports the `select()` system call in its I/O library (and nearly all do), then you can use it to juggle multiple communication channels at once; doing other work while your I/O is taking place in the "background." Although this strategy can seem strange and complex, especially at first, it is in many ways easier to understand and control than multi-threaded programming. The *asyncore* module solves many of the difficult problems for you, making the task of building sophisticated high-performance network servers and clients a snap. For "conversational" applications and protocols the companion *asynchat* module is invaluable.

The basic idea behind both modules is to create one or more network *channels*, instances of class *asyncore.dispatcher* and *asynchat.async_chat*. Creating the channels adds them to a global map, used by the *loop()* function if you do not provide it with your own *map*.

Once the initial channel(s) is(are) created, calling the *loop()* function activates channel service, which continues until the last channel (including any that have been added to the map during asynchronous service) is closed.

`asyncore.loop([timeout[, use_poll[, map[, count]]]])`

Enter a polling loop that terminates after count passes or all open channels have been closed. All arguments are optional. The *count* parameter defaults to `None`, resulting in the loop terminating only when all channels have been closed. The *timeout* argument sets the timeout parameter for the appropriate *select()* or *poll()* call, measured in seconds; the default is 30 seconds. The *use_poll* parameter, if true, indicates that *poll()* should be used in preference to *select()* (the default is `False`).

The *map* parameter is a dictionary whose items are the channels to watch. As channels are closed they are deleted from their map. If *map* is omitted, a global map is used. Channels (instances of *asyncore.dispatcher*, *asynchat.async_chat* and subclasses thereof) can freely be mixed in the map.

`class asyncore.dispatcher`

The *dispatcher* class is a thin wrapper around a low-level socket object. To make it more useful, it has a few methods for event-handling which are called from the asynchronous loop. Otherwise, it can be treated as a normal non-blocking socket object.

The firing of low-level events at certain times or in certain connection states tells the asynchronous loop that certain higher-level events have taken place. For example, if we have asked for a socket to connect to another host, we know that the connection has been made when the socket becomes writable for the first time (at this point you know that you may write to it with the expectation of success). The implied higher-level events are:

Event	Description
`handle_connect()`	Implied by the first read or write event
`handle_close()`	Implied by a read event with no data available
`handle_accepted()`	Implied by a read event on a listening socket

During asynchronous processing, each mapped channel's *readable()* and *writable()* methods are used to determine whether the channel's socket should be added to the list of channels `select()`ed or `poll()`ed for read and write events.

Thus, the set of channel events is larger than the basic socket events. The full set of methods that can be overridden in your subclass follows:

handle_read()
Called when the asynchronous loop detects that a `read()` call on the channel's socket will succeed.

handle_write()
Called when the asynchronous loop detects that a writable socket can be written. Often this method will implement the necessary buffering for performance. For example:

```
def handle_write(self):
    sent = self.send(self.buffer)
    self.buffer = self.buffer[sent:]
```

handle_expt()
Called when there is out of band (OOB) data for a socket connection. This will almost never happen, as OOB is tenuously supported and rarely used.

handle_connect()
Called when the active opener's socket actually makes a connection. Might send a "welcome" banner, or initiate a protocol negotiation with the remote endpoint, for example.

handle_close()
Called when the socket is closed.

handle_error()
Called when an exception is raised and not otherwise handled. The default version prints a condensed traceback.

handle_accept()
Called on listening channels (passive openers) when a connection can be established with a new remote endpoint that has issued a *connect()* call for the local endpoint. Deprecated in version 3.2; use *handle_accepted()* instead.

Deprecated since version 3.2.

handle_accepted(*sock*, *addr*)
Called on listening channels (passive openers) when a connection has been established with a new remote endpoint that has issued a *connect()* call for the local endpoint. *sock* is a *new* socket object usable to send and receive data on the connection, and *addr* is the address bound to the socket on the other end of the connection.

New in version 3.2.

readable()
Called each time around the asynchronous loop to determine whether a channel's socket should be added to the list on which read events can occur. The default method simply returns `True`, indicating that by default, all channels will be interested in read events.

writable()
Called each time around the asynchronous loop to determine whether a channel's socket should

be added to the list on which write events can occur. The default method simply returns `True`, indicating that by default, all channels will be interested in write events.

In addition, each channel delegates or extends many of the socket methods. Most of these are nearly identical to their socket partners.

create_socket(*family=socket.AF_INET, type=socket.SOCK_STREAM*)
This is identical to the creation of a normal socket, and will use the same options for creation. Refer to the *socket* documentation for information on creating sockets.

Changed in version 3.3: *family* and *type* arguments can be omitted.

connect(*address*)
As with the normal socket object, *address* is a tuple with the first element the host to connect to, and the second the port number.

send(*data*)
Send *data* to the remote end-point of the socket.

recv(*buffer_size*)
Read at most *buffer_size* bytes from the socket's remote end-point. An empty bytes object implies that the channel has been closed from the other end.

Note that *recv()* may raise *BlockingIOError* , even though *select.select()* or *select.poll()* has reported the socket ready for reading.

listen(*backlog*)
Listen for connections made to the socket. The *backlog* argument specifies the maximum number of queued connections and should be at least 1; the maximum value is system-dependent (usually 5).

bind(*address*)
Bind the socket to *address*. The socket must not already be bound. (The format of *address* depends on the address family — refer to the *socket* documentation for more information.) To mark the socket as re-usable (setting the `SO_REUSEADDR` option), call the *dispatcher* object's `set_reuse_addr()` method.

accept()
Accept a connection. The socket must be bound to an address and listening for connections. The return value can be either `None` or a pair `(conn, address)` where *conn* is a *new* socket object usable to send and receive data on the connection, and *address* is the address bound to the socket on the other end of the connection. When `None` is returned it means the connection didn't take place, in which case the server should just ignore this event and keep listening for further incoming connections.

close()
Close the socket. All future operations on the socket object will fail. The remote end-point will receive no more data (after queued data is flushed). Sockets are automatically closed when they are garbage-collected.

class asyncore.dispatcher_with_send
A *dispatcher* subclass which adds simple buffered output capability, useful for simple clients. For more sophisticated usage use *asynchat.async_chat*.

class asyncore.file_dispatcher
A file_dispatcher takes a file descriptor or *file object* along with an optional map argument and wraps it for use with the `poll()` or `loop()` functions. If provided a file object or anything with a `fileno()` method, that method will be called and passed to the *file_wrapper* constructor. Availability: UNIX.

class asyncore.file_wrapper
A file_wrapper takes an integer file descriptor and calls *os.dup()* to duplicate the handle so that

the original handle may be closed independently of the file_wrapper. This class implements sufficient methods to emulate a socket for use by the *file_dispatcher* class. Availability: UNIX.

18.6.1 asyncore Example basic HTTP client

Here is a very basic HTTP client that uses the *dispatcher* class to implement its socket handling:

```
import asyncore

class HTTPClient(asyncore.dispatcher):

    def __init__(self, host, path):
        asyncore.dispatcher.__init__(self)
        self.create_socket()
        self.connect( (host, 80) )
        self.buffer = bytes('GET %s HTTP/1.0\r\nHost: %s\r\n\r\n' %
                            (path, host), 'ascii')

    def handle_connect(self):
        pass

    def handle_close(self):
        self.close()

    def handle_read(self):
        print(self.recv(8192))

    def writable(self):
        return (len(self.buffer) > 0)

    def handle_write(self):
        sent = self.send(self.buffer)
        self.buffer = self.buffer[sent:]


client = HTTPClient('www.python.org', '/')
asyncore.loop()
```

18.6.2 asyncore Example basic echo server

Here is a basic echo server that uses the *dispatcher* class to accept connections and dispatches the incoming connections to a handler:

```
import asyncore

class EchoHandler(asyncore.dispatcher_with_send):

    def handle_read(self):
        data = self.recv(8192)
        if data:
            self.send(data)

class EchoServer(asyncore.dispatcher):

    def __init__(self, host, port):
        asyncore.dispatcher.__init__(self)
```

```
        self.create_socket()
        self.set_reuse_addr()
        self.bind((host, port))
        self.listen(5)

    def handle_accepted(self, sock, addr):
        print('Incoming connection from %s' % repr(addr))
        handler = EchoHandler(sock)

server = EchoServer('localhost', 8080)
asyncore.loop()
```

18.7 asynchat — Asynchronous socket command/response handler

Source code: Lib/asynchat.py

Deprecated since version 3.6: Please use *asyncio* instead.

Note: This module exists for backwards compatibility only. For new code we recommend using *asyncio*.

This module builds on the *asyncore* infrastructure, simplifying asynchronous clients and servers and making it easier to handle protocols whose elements are terminated by arbitrary strings, or are of variable length. *asynchat* defines the abstract class *async_chat* that you subclass, providing implementations of the `collect_incoming_data()` and `found_terminator()` methods. It uses the same asynchronous loop as *asyncore*, and the two types of channel, *asyncore.dispatcher* and *asynchat.async_chat*, can freely be mixed in the channel map. Typically an *asyncore.dispatcher* server channel generates new *asynchat.async_chat* channel objects as it receives incoming connection requests.

class asynchat.async_chat

This class is an abstract subclass of *asyncore.dispatcher*. To make practical use of the code you must subclass *async_chat*, providing meaningful *collect_incoming_data()* and *found_terminator()* methods. The *asyncore.dispatcher* methods can be used, although not all make sense in a message/response context.

Like *asyncore.dispatcher*, *async_chat* defines a set of events that are generated by an analysis of socket conditions after a `select()` call. Once the polling loop has been started the *async_chat* object's methods are called by the event-processing framework with no action on the part of the programmer.

Two class attributes can be modified, to improve performance, or possibly even to conserve memory.

ac_in_buffer_size

The asynchronous input buffer size (default 4096).

ac_out_buffer_size

The asynchronous output buffer size (default 4096).

Unlike *asyncore.dispatcher*, *async_chat* allows you to define a FIFO queue of *producers*. A producer need have only one method, `more()`, which should return data to be transmitted on the channel. The producer indicates exhaustion (*i.e.* that it contains no more data) by having its `more()` method return the empty bytes object. At this point the *async_chat* object removes the producer from the queue and starts using the next producer, if any. When the producer queue is empty the `handle_write()` method does nothing. You use the channel object's *set_terminator()* method to describe how to recognize the end of, or an important breakpoint in, an incoming transmission from the remote endpoint.

To build a functioning *async_chat* subclass your input methods *collect_incoming_data()* and *found_terminator()* must handle the data that the channel receives asynchronously. The methods are described below.

async_chat.close_when_done()
Pushes a `None` on to the producer queue. When this producer is popped off the queue it causes the channel to be closed.

async_chat.collect_incoming_data(*data*)
Called with *data* holding an arbitrary amount of received data. The default method, which must be overridden, raises a *NotImplementedError* exception.

async_chat.discard_buffers()
In emergencies this method will discard any data held in the input and/or output buffers and the producer queue.

async_chat.found_terminator()
Called when the incoming data stream matches the termination condition set by *set_terminator()*. The default method, which must be overridden, raises a *NotImplementedError* exception. The buffered input data should be available via an instance attribute.

async_chat.get_terminator()
Returns the current terminator for the channel.

async_chat.push(*data*)
Pushes data on to the channel's queue to ensure its transmission. This is all you need to do to have the channel write the data out to the network, although it is possible to use your own producers in more complex schemes to implement encryption and chunking, for example.

async_chat.push_with_producer(*producer*)
Takes a producer object and adds it to the producer queue associated with the channel. When all currently-pushed producers have been exhausted the channel will consume this producer's data by calling its `more()` method and send the data to the remote endpoint.

async_chat.set_terminator(*term*)
Sets the terminating condition to be recognized on the channel. `term` may be any of three types of value, corresponding to three different ways to handle incoming protocol data.

term	Description
string	Will call *found_terminator()* when the string is found in the input stream
integer	Will call *found_terminator()* when the indicated number of characters have been received
`None`	The channel continues to collect data forever

Note that any data following the terminator will be available for reading by the channel after *found_terminator()* is called.

18.7.1 asynchat Example

The following partial example shows how HTTP requests can be read with *async_chat*. A web server might create an `http_request_handler` object for each incoming client connection. Notice that initially the channel terminator is set to match the blank line at the end of the HTTP headers, and a flag indicates that the headers are being read.

Once the headers have been read, if the request is of type POST (indicating that further data are present in the input stream) then the `Content-Length:` header is used to set a numeric terminator to read the right amount of data from the channel.

The **handle_request()** method is called once all relevant input has been marshalled, after setting the channel terminator to None to ensure that any extraneous data sent by the web client are ignored.

```
import asynchat

class http_request_handler(asynchat.async_chat):

    def __init__(self, sock, addr, sessions, log):
        asynchat.async_chat.__init__(self, sock=sock)
        self.addr = addr
        self.sessions = sessions
        self.ibuffer = []
        self.obuffer = b""
        self.set_terminator(b"\r\n\r\n")
        self.reading_headers = True
        self.handling = False
        self.cgi_data = None
        self.log = log

    def collect_incoming_data(self, data):
        """Buffer the data"""
        self.ibuffer.append(data)

    def found_terminator(self):
        if self.reading_headers:
            self.reading_headers = False
            self.parse_headers(b"".join(self.ibuffer))
            self.ibuffer = []
            if self.op.upper() == b"POST":
                clen = self.headers.getheader("content-length")
                self.set_terminator(int(clen))
            else:
                self.handling = True
                self.set_terminator(None)
                self.handle_request()
        elif not self.handling:
            self.set_terminator(None)  # browsers sometimes over-send
            self.cgi_data = parse(self.headers, b"".join(self.ibuffer))
            self.handling = True
            self.ibuffer = []
            self.handle_request()
```

18.8 signal — Set handlers for asynchronous events

This module provides mechanisms to use signal handlers in Python.

18.8.1 General rules

The *signal.signal()* function allows defining custom handlers to be executed when a signal is received. A small number of default handlers are installed: SIGPIPE is ignored (so write errors on pipes and sockets can be reported as ordinary Python exceptions) and SIGINT is translated into a *KeyboardInterrupt* exception.

A handler for a particular signal, once set, remains installed until it is explicitly reset (Python emulates the BSD style interface regardless of the underlying implementation), with the exception of the handler for SIGCHLD, which follows the underlying implementation.

Execution of Python signal handlers

A Python signal handler does not get executed inside the low-level (C) signal handler. Instead, the low-level signal handler sets a flag which tells the *virtual machine* to execute the corresponding Python signal handler at a later point(for example at the next *bytecode* instruction). This has consequences:

- It makes little sense to catch synchronous errors like SIGFPE or SIGSEGV that are caused by an invalid operation in C code. Python will return from the signal handler to the C code, which is likely to raise the same signal again, causing Python to apparently hang. From Python 3.3 onwards, you can use the *faulthandler* module to report on synchronous errors.
- A long-running calculation implemented purely in C (such as regular expression matching on a large body of text) may run uninterrupted for an arbitrary amount of time, regardless of any signals received. The Python signal handlers will be called when the calculation finishes.

Signals and threads

Python signal handlers are always executed in the main Python thread, even if the signal was received in another thread. This means that signals can't be used as a means of inter-thread communication. You can use the synchronization primitives from the *threading* module instead.

Besides, only the main thread is allowed to set a new signal handler.

18.8.2 Module contents

Changed in version 3.5: signal (SIG*), handler (*SIG_DFL*, *SIG_IGN*) and sigmask (*SIG_BLOCK*, *SIG_UNBLOCK*, *SIG_SETMASK*) related constants listed below were turned into *enums*. *getsignal()*, *pthread_sigmask()*, *sigpending()* and *sigwait()* functions return human-readable *enums*.

The variables defined in the *signal* module are:

`signal.SIG_DFL`
: This is one of two standard signal handling options; it will simply perform the default function for the signal. For example, on most systems the default action for SIGQUIT is to dump core and exit, while the default action for SIGCHLD is to simply ignore it.

`signal.SIG_IGN`
: This is another standard signal handler, which will simply ignore the given signal.

`SIG*`
: All the signal numbers are defined symbolically. For example, the hangup signal is defined as signal.SIGHUP; the variable names are identical to the names used in C programs, as found in <signal.h>. The Unix man page for 'signal()' lists the existing signals (on some systems this is *signal(2)*, on others the list is in *signal(7)*). Note that not all systems define the same set of signal names; only those names defined by the system are defined by this module.

`signal.CTRL_C_EVENT`
: The signal corresponding to the Ctrl+C keystroke event. This signal can only be used with *os.kill()*.

  Availability: Windows.

  New in version 3.2.

signal.CTRL_BREAK_EVENT
The signal corresponding to the `Ctrl+Break` keystroke event. This signal can only be used with *os.kill()*.

Availability: Windows.

New in version 3.2.

signal.NSIG
One more than the number of the highest signal number.

signal.ITIMER_REAL
Decrements interval timer in real time, and delivers `SIGALRM` upon expiration.

signal.ITIMER_VIRTUAL
Decrements interval timer only when the process is executing, and delivers SIGVTALRM upon expiration.

signal.ITIMER_PROF
Decrements interval timer both when the process executes and when the system is executing on behalf of the process. Coupled with ITIMER_VIRTUAL, this timer is usually used to profile the time spent by the application in user and kernel space. SIGPROF is delivered upon expiration.

signal.SIG_BLOCK
A possible value for the *how* parameter to *pthread_sigmask()* indicating that signals are to be blocked.

New in version 3.3.

signal.SIG_UNBLOCK
A possible value for the *how* parameter to *pthread_sigmask()* indicating that signals are to be unblocked.

New in version 3.3.

signal.SIG_SETMASK
A possible value for the *how* parameter to *pthread_sigmask()* indicating that the signal mask is to be replaced.

New in version 3.3.

The *signal* module defines one exception:

exception signal.ItimerError
Raised to signal an error from the underlying *setitimer()* or *getitimer()* implementation. Expect this error if an invalid interval timer or a negative time is passed to *setitimer()*. This error is a subtype of *OSError*.

New in version 3.3: This error used to be a subtype of *IOError*, which is now an alias of *OSError*.

The *signal* module defines the following functions:

signal.alarm(*time*)
If *time* is non-zero, this function requests that a `SIGALRM` signal be sent to the process in *time* seconds. Any previously scheduled alarm is canceled (only one alarm can be scheduled at any time). The returned value is then the number of seconds before any previously set alarm was to have been delivered. If *time* is zero, no alarm is scheduled, and any scheduled alarm is canceled. If the return value is zero, no alarm is currently scheduled. (See the Unix man page ***alarm(2)***.) Availability: Unix.

signal.getsignal(*signalnum*)
Return the current signal handler for the signal *signalnum*. The returned value may be a callable Python object, or one of the special values *signal.SIG_IGN*, *signal.SIG_DFL* or *None*. Here, *signal.SIG_IGN* means that the signal was previously ignored, *signal.SIG_DFL* means that the default way of handling the signal was previously in use, and `None` means that the previous signal handler was not installed from Python.

signal.pause()
Cause the process to sleep until a signal is received; the appropriate handler will then be called. Returns nothing. Not on Windows. (See the Unix man page *signal(2)*.)

See also *sigwait()*, *sigwaitinfo()*, *sigtimedwait()* and *sigpending()*.

signal.pthread_kill(*thread_id*, *signalnum*)
Send the signal *signalnum* to the thread *thread_id*, another thread in the same process as the caller. The target thread can be executing any code (Python or not). However, if the target thread is executing the Python interpreter, the Python signal handlers will be *executed by the main thread*. Therefore, the only point of sending a signal to a particular Python thread would be to force a running system call to fail with *InterruptedError*.

Use *threading.get_ident()* or the *ident* attribute of *threading.Thread* objects to get a suitable value for *thread_id*.

If *signalnum* is 0, then no signal is sent, but error checking is still performed; this can be used to check if the target thread is still running.

Availability: Unix (see the man page *pthread_kill(3)* for further information).

See also *os.kill()*.

New in version 3.3.

signal.pthread_sigmask(*how*, *mask*)
Fetch and/or change the signal mask of the calling thread. The signal mask is the set of signals whose delivery is currently blocked for the caller. Return the old signal mask as a set of signals.

The behavior of the call is dependent on the value of *how*, as follows.

- *SIG_BLOCK*: The set of blocked signals is the union of the current set and the *mask* argument.
- *SIG_UNBLOCK*: The signals in *mask* are removed from the current set of blocked signals. It is permissible to attempt to unblock a signal which is not blocked.
- *SIG_SETMASK*: The set of blocked signals is set to the *mask* argument.

mask is a set of signal numbers (e.g. {`signal.SIGINT`, `signal.SIGTERM`}). Use `range(1, signal.NSIG)` for a full mask including all signals.

For example, `signal.pthread_sigmask(signal.SIG_BLOCK, [])` reads the signal mask of the calling thread.

Availability: Unix. See the man page *sigprocmask(3)* and *pthread_sigmask(3)* for further information.

See also *pause()*, *sigpending()* and *sigwait()*.

New in version 3.3.

signal.setitimer(*which*, *seconds*[, *interval*])
Sets given interval timer (one of *signal.ITIMER_REAL*, *signal.ITIMER_VIRTUAL* or *signal.ITIMER_PROF*) specified by *which* to fire after *seconds* (float is accepted, different from *alarm()*) and after that every *interval* seconds. The interval timer specified by *which* can be cleared by setting seconds to zero.

When an interval timer fires, a signal is sent to the process. The signal sent is dependent on the timer being used; *signal.ITIMER_REAL* will deliver `SIGALRM`, *signal.ITIMER_VIRTUAL* sends `SIGVTALRM`, and *signal.ITIMER_PROF* will deliver `SIGPROF`.

The old values are returned as a tuple: (delay, interval).

Attempting to pass an invalid interval timer will cause an *ItimerError*. Availability: Unix.

signal.getitimer(*which*)
Returns current value of a given interval timer specified by *which*. Availability: Unix.

`signal.set_wakeup_fd(fd)`

Set the wakeup file descriptor to *fd*. When a signal is received, the signal number is written as a single byte into the fd. This can be used by a library to wakeup a poll or select call, allowing the signal to be fully processed.

The old wakeup fd is returned (or -1 if file descriptor wakeup was not enabled). If *fd* is -1, file descriptor wakeup is disabled. If not -1, *fd* must be non-blocking. It is up to the library to remove any bytes from *fd* before calling poll or select again.

Use for example `struct.unpack('%uB' % len(data), data)` to decode the signal numbers list.

When threads are enabled, this function can only be called from the main thread; attempting to call it from other threads will cause a *ValueError* exception to be raised.

Changed in version 3.5: On Windows, the function now also supports socket handles.

`signal.siginterrupt(signalnum, flag)`

Change system call restart behaviour: if *flag* is *False*, system calls will be restarted when interrupted by signal *signalnum*, otherwise system calls will be interrupted. Returns nothing. Availability: Unix (see the man page ***siginterrupt(3)*** for further information).

Note that installing a signal handler with *signal()* will reset the restart behaviour to interruptible by implicitly calling `siginterrupt()` with a true *flag* value for the given signal.

`signal.signal(signalnum, handler)`

Set the handler for signal *signalnum* to the function *handler*. *handler* can be a callable Python object taking two arguments (see below), or one of the special values *signal.SIG_IGN* or *signal.SIG_DFL*. The previous signal handler will be returned (see the description of *getsignal()* above). (See the Unix man page ***signal(2)***.)

When threads are enabled, this function can only be called from the main thread; attempting to call it from other threads will cause a *ValueError* exception to be raised.

The *handler* is called with two arguments: the signal number and the current stack frame (`None` or a frame object; for a description of frame objects, see the description in the type hierarchy or see the attribute descriptions in the *inspect* module).

On Windows, *signal()* can only be called with `SIGABRT`, `SIGFPE`, `SIGILL`, `SIGINT`, `SIGSEGV`, `SIGTERM`, or `SIGBREAK`. A *ValueError* will be raised in any other case. Note that not all systems define the same set of signal names; an *AttributeError* will be raised if a signal name is not defined as `SIG*` module level constant.

`signal.sigpending()`

Examine the set of signals that are pending for delivery to the calling thread (i.e., the signals which have been raised while blocked). Return the set of the pending signals.

Availability: Unix (see the man page ***sigpending(2)*** for further information).

See also *pause()*, *pthread_sigmask()* and *sigwait()*.

New in version 3.3.

`signal.sigwait(sigset)`

Suspend execution of the calling thread until the delivery of one of the signals specified in the signal set *sigset*. The function accepts the signal (removes it from the pending list of signals), and returns the signal number.

Availability: Unix (see the man page ***sigwait(3)*** for further information).

See also *pause()*, *pthread_sigmask()*, *sigpending()*, *sigwaitinfo()* and *sigtimedwait()*.

New in version 3.3.

`signal.sigwaitinfo(sigset)`

Suspend execution of the calling thread until the delivery of one of the signals specified in the signal set *sigset*. The function accepts the signal and removes it from the pending list of signals. If one of the signals in *sigset* is already pending for the calling thread, the function will return immediately with information about that signal. The signal handler is not called for the delivered signal. The function raises an *InterruptedError* if it is interrupted by a signal that is not in *sigset*.

The return value is an object representing the data contained in the **siginfo_t** structure, namely: **si_signo**, **si_code**, **si_errno**, **si_pid**, **si_uid**, **si_status**, **si_band**.

Availability: Unix (see the man page ***sigwaitinfo(2)*** for further information).

See also *pause()*, *sigwait()* and *sigtimedwait()*.

New in version 3.3.

Changed in version 3.5: The function is now retried if interrupted by a signal not in *sigset* and the signal handler does not raise an exception (see PEP 475 for the rationale).

signal.sigtimedwait(*sigset*, *timeout*)

Like *sigwaitinfo()*, but takes an additional *timeout* argument specifying a timeout. If *timeout* is specified as 0, a poll is performed. Returns *None* if a timeout occurs.

Availability: Unix (see the man page ***sigtimedwait(2)*** for further information).

See also *pause()*, *sigwait()* and *sigwaitinfo()*.

New in version 3.3.

Changed in version 3.5: The function is now retried with the recomputed *timeout* if interrupted by a signal not in *sigset* and the signal handler does not raise an exception (see PEP 475 for the rationale).

18.8.3 Example

Here is a minimal example program. It uses the *alarm()* function to limit the time spent waiting to open a file; this is useful if the file is for a serial device that may not be turned on, which would normally cause the *os.open()* to hang indefinitely. The solution is to set a 5-second alarm before opening the file; if the operation takes too long, the alarm signal will be sent, and the handler raises an exception.

```
import signal, os

def handler(signum, frame):
    print('Signal handler called with signal', signum)
    raise OSError("Couldn't open device!")

# Set the signal handler and a 5-second alarm
signal.signal(signal.SIGALRM, handler)
signal.alarm(5)

# This open() may hang indefinitely
fd = os.open('/dev/ttyS0', os.O_RDWR)

signal.alarm(0)          # Disable the alarm
```

18.9 mmap — Memory-mapped file support

Memory-mapped file objects behave like both *bytearray* and like *file objects*. You can use mmap objects in most places where *bytearray* are expected; for example, you can use the *re* module to search through a memory-mapped file. You can also change a single byte by doing `obj[index] = 97`, or change a subsequence by assigning to a slice: `obj[i1:i2] = b'...'`. You can also read and write data starting at the current file position, and `seek()` through the file to different positions.

A memory-mapped file is created by the *mmap* constructor, which is different on Unix and on Windows. In either case you must provide a file descriptor for a file opened for update. If you wish to map an existing Python file object, use its `fileno()` method to obtain the correct value for the *fileno* parameter. Otherwise, you can open the file using the *os.open()* function, which returns a file descriptor directly (the file still needs to be closed when done).

Note: If you want to create a memory-mapping for a writable, buffered file, you should *flush()* the file first. This is necessary to ensure that local modifications to the buffers are actually available to the mapping.

For both the Unix and Windows versions of the constructor, *access* may be specified as an optional keyword parameter. *access* accepts one of three values: `ACCESS_READ`, `ACCESS_WRITE`, or `ACCESS_COPY` to specify read-only, write-through or copy-on-write memory respectively. *access* can be used on both Unix and Windows. If *access* is not specified, Windows mmap returns a write-through mapping. The initial memory values for all three access types are taken from the specified file. Assignment to an `ACCESS_READ` memory map raises a *TypeError* exception. Assignment to an `ACCESS_WRITE` memory map affects both memory and the underlying file. Assignment to an `ACCESS_COPY` memory map affects memory but does not update the underlying file.

To map anonymous memory, -1 should be passed as the fileno along with the length.

class mmap.mmap(*fileno, length, tagname=None, access=ACCESS_DEFAULT*[, *offset*])

(**Windows version**) Maps *length* bytes from the file specified by the file handle *fileno*, and creates a mmap object. If *length* is larger than the current size of the file, the file is extended to contain *length* bytes. If *length* is `0`, the maximum length of the map is the current size of the file, except that if the file is empty Windows raises an exception (you cannot create an empty mapping on Windows).

tagname, if specified and not `None`, is a string giving a tag name for the mapping. Windows allows you to have many different mappings against the same file. If you specify the name of an existing tag, that tag is opened, otherwise a new tag of this name is created. If this parameter is omitted or `None`, the mapping is created without a name. Avoiding the use of the tag parameter will assist in keeping your code portable between Unix and Windows.

offset may be specified as a non-negative integer offset. mmap references will be relative to the offset from the beginning of the file. *offset* defaults to 0. *offset* must be a multiple of the ALLOCATIONGRANULARITY.

class mmap.mmap(*fileno, length, flags=MAP_SHARED, prot=PROT_WRITE|PROT_READ, access=ACCESS_DEFAULT*[, *offset*])

(**Unix version**) Maps *length* bytes from the file specified by the file descriptor *fileno*, and returns a mmap object. If *length* is `0`, the maximum length of the map will be the current size of the file when *mmap* is called.

flags specifies the nature of the mapping. `MAP_PRIVATE` creates a private copy-on-write mapping, so changes to the contents of the mmap object will be private to this process, and `MAP_SHARED` creates a mapping that's shared with all other processes mapping the same areas of the file. The default value is `MAP_SHARED`.

prot, if specified, gives the desired memory protection; the two most useful values are `PROT_READ` and `PROT_WRITE`, to specify that the pages may be read or written. *prot* defaults to `PROT_READ | PROT_WRITE`.

access may be specified in lieu of *flags* and *prot* as an optional keyword parameter. It is an error to specify both *flags*, *prot* and *access*. See the description of *access* above for information on how to use this parameter.

offset may be specified as a non-negative integer offset. mmap references will be relative to the offset from the beginning of the file. *offset* defaults to 0. *offset* must be a multiple of the PAGESIZE or ALLOCATIONGRANULARITY.

To ensure validity of the created memory mapping the file specified by the descriptor *fileno* is internally automatically synchronized with physical backing store on Mac OS X and OpenVMS.

This example shows a simple way of using *mmap*:

```
import mmap

# write a simple example file
with open("hello.txt", "wb") as f:
    f.write(b"Hello Python!\n")

with open("hello.txt", "r+b") as f:
    # memory-map the file, size 0 means whole file
    mm = mmap.mmap(f.fileno(), 0)
    # read content via standard file methods
    print(mm.readline())  # prints b"Hello Python!\n"
    # read content via slice notation
    print(mm[:5])  # prints b"Hello"
    # update content using slice notation;
    # note that new content must have same size
    mm[6:] = b" world!\n"
    # ... and read again using standard file methods
    mm.seek(0)
    print(mm.readline())  # prints b"Hello  world!\n"
    # close the map
    mm.close()
```

mmap can also be used as a context manager in a `with` statement.:

```
import mmap

with mmap.mmap(-1, 13) as mm:
    mm.write(b"Hello world!")
```

New in version 3.2: Context manager support.

The next example demonstrates how to create an anonymous map and exchange data between the parent and child processes:

```
import mmap
import os

mm = mmap.mmap(-1, 13)
mm.write(b"Hello world!")

pid = os.fork()

if pid == 0:  # In a child process
    mm.seek(0)
    print(mm.readline())

    mm.close()
```

Memory-mapped file objects support the following methods:

`close()`

Closes the mmap. Subsequent calls to other methods of the object will result in a ValueError exception being raised. This will not close the open file.

closed

`True` if the file is closed.

New in version 3.2.

find(*sub*[, *start*[, *end*]])

Returns the lowest index in the object where the subsequence *sub* is found, such that *sub* is contained in the range [*start*, *end*]. Optional arguments *start* and *end* are interpreted as in slice notation. Returns `-1` on failure.

Changed in version 3.5: Writable *bytes-like object* is now accepted.

flush([*offset*[, *size*]])

Flushes changes made to the in-memory copy of a file back to disk. Without use of this call there is no guarantee that changes are written back before the object is destroyed. If *offset* and *size* are specified, only changes to the given range of bytes will be flushed to disk; otherwise, the whole extent of the mapping is flushed.

(Windows version) A nonzero value returned indicates success; zero indicates failure.

(Unix version) A zero value is returned to indicate success. An exception is raised when the call failed.

move(*dest*, *src*, *count*)

Copy the *count* bytes starting at offset *src* to the destination index *dest*. If the mmap was created with `ACCESS_READ`, then calls to move will raise a `TypeError` exception.

read([*n*])

Return a `bytes` containing up to *n* bytes starting from the current file position. If the argument is omitted, `None` or negative, return all bytes from the current file position to the end of the mapping. The file position is updated to point after the bytes that were returned.

Changed in version 3.3: Argument can be omitted or `None`.

read_byte()

Returns a byte at the current file position as an integer, and advances the file position by 1.

readline()

Returns a single line, starting at the current file position and up to the next newline.

resize(*newsize*)

Resizes the map and the underlying file, if any. If the mmap was created with `ACCESS_READ` or `ACCESS_COPY`, resizing the map will raise a `TypeError` exception.

rfind(*sub*[, *start*[, *end*]])

Returns the highest index in the object where the subsequence *sub* is found, such that *sub* is contained in the range [*start*, *end*]. Optional arguments *start* and *end* are interpreted as in slice notation. Returns `-1` on failure.

Changed in version 3.5: Writable *bytes-like object* is now accepted.

seek(*pos*[, *whence*])

Set the file's current position. *whence* argument is optional and defaults to `os.SEEK_SET` or `0` (absolute file positioning); other values are `os.SEEK_CUR` or `1` (seek relative to the current position) and `os.SEEK_END` or `2` (seek relative to the file's end).

size()

Return the length of the file, which can be larger than the size of the memory-mapped area.

tell()

Returns the current position of the file pointer.

write(*bytes*)

Write the bytes in *bytes* into memory at the current position of the file pointer and return the number of bytes written (never less than `len(bytes)`, since if the write fails, a *ValueError* will be raised). The file position is updated to point after the bytes that were written. If the mmap was created with `ACCESS_READ`, then writing to it will raise a *TypeError* exception.

Changed in version 3.5: Writable *bytes-like object* is now accepted.

Changed in version 3.6: The number of bytes written is now returned.

write_byte(*byte*)

Write the integer *byte* into memory at the current position of the file pointer; the file position is advanced by `1`. If the mmap was created with `ACCESS_READ`, then writing to it will raise a *TypeError* exception.

APPENDIX

A

GLOSSARY

>>> The default Python prompt of the interactive shell. Often seen for code examples which can be executed interactively in the interpreter.

... The default Python prompt of the interactive shell when entering code for an indented code block or within a pair of matching left and right delimiters (parentheses, square brackets or curly braces).

2to3 A tool that tries to convert Python 2.x code to Python 3.x code by handling most of the incompatibilities which can be detected by parsing the source and traversing the parse tree.

2to3 is available in the standard library as *lib2to3*; a standalone entry point is provided as `Tools/scripts/2to3`. See *2to3 - Automated Python 2 to 3 code translation*.

abstract base class Abstract base classes complement *duck-typing* by providing a way to define interfaces when other techniques like *hasattr()* would be clumsy or subtly wrong (for example with magic methods). ABCs introduce virtual subclasses, which are classes that don't inherit from a class but are still recognized by *isinstance()* and *issubclass()*; see the *abc* module documentation. Python comes with many built-in ABCs for data structures (in the *collections.abc* module), numbers (in the *numbers* module), streams (in the *io* module), import finders and loaders (in the *importlib.abc* module). You can create your own ABCs with the *abc* module.

argument A value passed to a *function* (or *method*) when calling the function. There are two kinds of argument:

- *keyword argument*: an argument preceded by an identifier (e.g. `name=`) in a function call or passed as a value in a dictionary preceded by `**`. For example, `3` and `5` are both keyword arguments in the following calls to *complex()*:

```
complex(real=3, imag=5)
complex(**{'real': 3, 'imag': 5})
```

- *positional argument*: an argument that is not a keyword argument. Positional arguments can appear at the beginning of an argument list and/or be passed as elements of an *iterable* preceded by `*`. For example, `3` and `5` are both positional arguments in the following calls:

```
complex(3, 5)
complex(*(3, 5))
```

Arguments are assigned to the named local variables in a function body. See the calls section for the rules governing this assignment. Syntactically, any expression can be used to represent an argument; the evaluated value is assigned to the local variable.

See also the *parameter* glossary entry, the FAQ question on the difference between arguments and parameters, and PEP 362.

asynchronous context manager An object which controls the environment seen in an `async with` statement by defining `__aenter__()` and `__aexit__()` methods. Introduced by PEP 492.

asynchronous generator A function which returns an *asynchronous generator iterator*. It looks like a coroutine function defined with `async def` except that it contains `yield` expressions for producing a series of values usable in an `async for` loop.

Usually refers to a asynchronous generator function, but may refer to an *asynchronous generator iterator* in some contexts. In cases where the intended meaning isn't clear, using the full terms avoids ambiguity.

An asynchronous generator function may contain `await` expressions as well as `async for`, and `async with` statements.

asynchronous generator iterator An object created by a *asynchronous generator* function.

This is an *asynchronous iterator* which when called using the `__anext__()` method returns an awaitable object which will execute that the body of the asynchronous generator function until the next `yield` expression.

Each `yield` temporarily suspends processing, remembering the location execution state (including local variables and pending try-statements). When the *asynchronous generator iterator* effectively resumes with another awaitable returned by `__anext__()`, it picks-up where it left-off. See PEP 492 and PEP 525.

asynchronous iterable An object, that can be used in an `async for` statement. Must return an *asynchronous iterator* from its `__aiter__()` method. Introduced by PEP 492.

asynchronous iterator An object that implements `__aiter__()` and `__anext__()` methods. `__anext__` must return an *awaitable* object. `async for` resolves awaitable returned from asynchronous iterator's `__anext__()` method until it raises `StopAsyncIteration` exception. Introduced by PEP 492.

attribute A value associated with an object which is referenced by name using dotted expressions. For example, if an object *o* has an attribute *a* it would be referenced as *o.a*.

awaitable An object that can be used in an `await` expression. Can be a *coroutine* or an object with an `__await__()` method. See also PEP 492.

BDFL Benevolent Dictator For Life, a.k.a. Guido van Rossum, Python's creator.

binary file A *file object* able to read and write *bytes-like objects*. Examples of binary files are files opened in binary mode (`'rb'`, `'wb'` or `'rb+'`), `sys.stdin.buffer`, `sys.stdout.buffer`, and instances of `io.BytesIO` and `gzip.GzipFile`.

See also:

A *text file* reads and writes `str` objects.

bytes-like object An object that supports the bufferobjects and can export a C-*contiguous* buffer. This includes all `bytes`, `bytearray`, and `array.array` objects, as well as many common `memoryview` objects. Bytes-like objects can be used for various operations that work with binary data; these include compression, saving to a binary file, and sending over a socket.

Some operations need the binary data to be mutable. The documentation often refers to these as "read-write bytes-like objects". Example mutable buffer objects include `bytearray` and a `memoryview` of a `bytearray`. Other operations require the binary data to be stored in immutable objects ("read-only bytes-like objects"); examples of these include `bytes` and a `memoryview` of a `bytes` object.

bytecode Python source code is compiled into bytecode, the internal representation of a Python program in the CPython interpreter. The bytecode is also cached in `.pyc` files so that executing the same file is faster the second time (recompilation from source to bytecode can be avoided). This "intermediate language" is said to run on a *virtual machine* that executes the machine code corresponding to each bytecode. Do note that bytecodes are not expected to work between different Python virtual machines, nor to be stable between Python releases.

A list of bytecode instructions can be found in the documentation for *the dis module*.

class A template for creating user-defined objects. Class definitions normally contain method definitions which operate on instances of the class.

coercion The implicit conversion of an instance of one type to another during an operation which involves two arguments of the same type. For example, `int(3.15)` converts the floating point number to the integer `3`, but in `3+4.5`, each argument is of a different type (one int, one float), and both must be converted to the same type before they can be added or it will raise a `TypeError`. Without coercion, all arguments of even compatible types would have to be normalized to the same value by the programmer, e.g., `float(3)+4.5` rather than just `3+4.5`.

complex number An extension of the familiar real number system in which all numbers are expressed as a sum of a real part and an imaginary part. Imaginary numbers are real multiples of the imaginary unit (the square root of `-1`), often written `i` in mathematics or `j` in engineering. Python has built-in support for complex numbers, which are written with this latter notation; the imaginary part is written with a `j` suffix, e.g., `3+1j`. To get access to complex equivalents of the *math* module, use *cmath*. Use of complex numbers is a fairly advanced mathematical feature. If you're not aware of a need for them, it's almost certain you can safely ignore them.

context manager An object which controls the environment seen in a `with` statement by defining `__enter__()` and `__exit__()` methods. See PEP 343.

contiguous A buffer is considered contiguous exactly if it is either *C-contiguous* or *Fortran contiguous*. Zero-dimensional buffers are C and Fortran contiguous. In one-dimensional arrays, the items must be laid out in memory next to each other, in order of increasing indexes starting from zero. In multidimensional C-contiguous arrays, the last index varies the fastest when visiting items in order of memory address. However, in Fortran contiguous arrays, the first index varies the fastest.

coroutine Coroutines is a more generalized form of subroutines. Subroutines are entered at one point and exited at another point. Coroutines can be entered, exited, and resumed at many different points. They can be implemented with the `async def` statement. See also PEP 492.

coroutine function A function which returns a *coroutine* object. A coroutine function may be defined with the `async def` statement, and may contain `await`, `async for`, and `async with` keywords. These were introduced by PEP 492.

CPython The canonical implementation of the Python programming language, as distributed on python.org. The term "CPython" is used when necessary to distinguish this implementation from others such as Jython or IronPython.

decorator A function returning another function, usually applied as a function transformation using the `@wrapper` syntax. Common examples for decorators are *classmethod()* and *staticmethod()*.

The decorator syntax is merely syntactic sugar, the following two function definitions are semantically equivalent:

```
def f(...):
    ...
f = staticmethod(f)

@staticmethod
def f(...):
    ...
```

The same concept exists for classes, but is less commonly used there. See the documentation for function definitions and class definitions for more about decorators.

descriptor Any object which defines the methods `__get__()`, `__set__()`, or `__delete__()`. When a class attribute is a descriptor, its special binding behavior is triggered upon attribute lookup. Normally, using *a.b* to get, set or delete an attribute looks up the object named *b* in the class dictionary for *a*, but if *b* is a descriptor, the respective descriptor method gets called. Understanding descriptors is a key to a deep understanding of Python because they are the basis for many features including functions, methods, properties, class methods, static methods, and reference to super classes.

For more information about descriptors' methods, see descriptors.

dictionary An associative array, where arbitrary keys are mapped to values. The keys can be any object with `__hash__()` and `__eq__()` methods. Called a hash in Perl.

dictionary view The objects returned from *dict.keys()*, *dict.values()*, and *dict.items()* are called dictionary views. They provide a dynamic view on the dictionary's entries, which means that when the dictionary changes, the view reflects these changes. To force the dictionary view to become a full list use `list(dictview)`. See *Dictionary view objects*.

docstring A string literal which appears as the first expression in a class, function or module. While ignored when the suite is executed, it is recognized by the compiler and put into the `__doc__` attribute of the enclosing class, function or module. Since it is available via introspection, it is the canonical place for documentation of the object.

duck-typing A programming style which does not look at an object's type to determine if it has the right interface; instead, the method or attribute is simply called or used ("If it looks like a duck and quacks like a duck, it must be a duck.") By emphasizing interfaces rather than specific types, well-designed code improves its flexibility by allowing polymorphic substitution. Duck-typing avoids tests using *type()* or *isinstance()*. (Note, however, that duck-typing can be complemented with *abstract base classes*.) Instead, it typically employs *hasattr()* tests or *EAFP* programming.

EAFP Easier to ask for forgiveness than permission. This common Python coding style assumes the existence of valid keys or attributes and catches exceptions if the assumption proves false. This clean and fast style is characterized by the presence of many `try` and `except` statements. The technique contrasts with the *LBYL* style common to many other languages such as C.

expression A piece of syntax which can be evaluated to some value. In other words, an expression is an accumulation of expression elements like literals, names, attribute access, operators or function calls which all return a value. In contrast to many other languages, not all language constructs are expressions. There are also *statement*s which cannot be used as expressions, such as `if`. Assignments are also statements, not expressions.

extension module A module written in C or C++, using Python's C API to interact with the core and with user code.

f-string String literals prefixed with `'f'` or `'F'` are commonly called "f-strings" which is short for formatted string literals. See also PEP 498.

file object An object exposing a file-oriented API (with methods such as `read()` or `write()`) to an underlying resource. Depending on the way it was created, a file object can mediate access to a real on-disk file or to another type of storage or communication device (for example standard input/output, in-memory buffers, sockets, pipes, etc.). File objects are also called *file-like objects* or *streams*.

There are actually three categories of file objects: raw *binary files*, buffered *binary files* and *text files*. Their interfaces are defined in the *io* module. The canonical way to create a file object is by using the *open()* function.

file-like object A synonym for *file object*.

finder An object that tries to find the *loader* for a module that is being imported.

Since Python 3.3, there are two types of finder: *meta path finders* for use with *sys.meta_path*, and *path entry finders* for use with *sys.path_hooks*.

See PEP 302, PEP 420 and PEP 451 for much more detail.

floor division Mathematical division that rounds down to nearest integer. The floor division operator is `//`. For example, the expression `11 // 4` evaluates to `2` in contrast to the `2.75` returned by float true division. Note that `(-11) // 4` is `-3` because that is `-2.75` rounded *downward*. See PEP 238.

function A series of statements which returns some value to a caller. It can also be passed zero or more *arguments* which may be used in the execution of the body. See also *parameter*, *method*, and the function section.

function annotation An arbitrary metadata value associated with a function parameter or return value. Its syntax is explained in section function. Annotations may be accessed via the `__annotations__` special attribute of a function object.

Python itself does not assign any particular meaning to function annotations. They are intended to be interpreted by third-party libraries or tools. See PEP 3107, which describes some of their potential uses.

__future__ A pseudo-module which programmers can use to enable new language features which are not compatible with the current interpreter.

By importing the *__future__* module and evaluating its variables, you can see when a new feature was first added to the language and when it becomes the default:

```
>>> import __future__
>>> __future__.division
_Feature((2, 2, 0, 'alpha', 2), (3, 0, 0, 'alpha', 0), 8192)
```

garbage collection The process of freeing memory when it is not used anymore. Python performs garbage collection via reference counting and a cyclic garbage collector that is able to detect and break reference cycles. The garbage collector can be controlled using the *gc* module.

generator A function which returns a *generator iterator*. It looks like a normal function except that it contains `yield` expressions for producing a series of values usable in a for-loop or that can be retrieved one at a time with the *next()* function.

Usually refers to a generator function, but may refer to a *generator iterator* in some contexts. In cases where the intended meaning isn't clear, using the full terms avoids ambiguity.

generator iterator An object created by a *generator* function.

Each `yield` temporarily suspends processing, remembering the location execution state (including local variables and pending try-statements). When the *generator iterator* resumes, it picks-up where it left-off (in contrast to functions which start fresh on every invocation).

generator expression An expression that returns an iterator. It looks like a normal expression followed by a `for` expression defining a loop variable, range, and an optional `if` expression. The combined expression generates values for an enclosing function:

```
>>> sum(i*i for i in range(10))         # sum of squares 0, 1, 4, ... 81
285
```

generic function A function composed of multiple functions implementing the same operation for different types. Which implementation should be used during a call is determined by the dispatch algorithm.

See also the *single dispatch* glossary entry, the *functools.singledispatch()* decorator, and PEP 443.

GIL See *global interpreter lock*.

global interpreter lock The mechanism used by the *CPython* interpreter to assure that only one thread executes Python *bytecode* at a time. This simplifies the CPython implementation by making the object model (including critical built-in types such as *dict*) implicitly safe against concurrent access. Locking the entire interpreter makes it easier for the interpreter to be multi-threaded, at the expense of much of the parallelism afforded by multi-processor machines.

However, some extension modules, either standard or third-party, are designed so as to release the GIL when doing computationally-intensive tasks such as compression or hashing. Also, the GIL is always released when doing I/O.

Past efforts to create a "free-threaded" interpreter (one which locks shared data at a much finer granularity) have not been successful because performance suffered in the common single-processor case. It is believed that overcoming this performance issue would make the implementation much more complicated and therefore costlier to maintain.

hashable An object is *hashable* if it has a hash value which never changes during its lifetime (it needs a `__hash__()` method), and can be compared to other objects (it needs an `__eq__()` method). Hashable objects which compare equal must have the same hash value.

Hashability makes an object usable as a dictionary key and a set member, because these data structures use the hash value internally.

All of Python's immutable built-in objects are hashable; mutable containers (such as lists or dictionaries) are not. Objects which are instances of user-defined classes are hashable by default. They all compare unequal (except with themselves), and their hash value is derived from their *id()*.

IDLE An Integrated Development Environment for Python. IDLE is a basic editor and interpreter environment which ships with the standard distribution of Python.

immutable An object with a fixed value. Immutable objects include numbers, strings and tuples. Such an object cannot be altered. A new object has to be created if a different value has to be stored. They play an important role in places where a constant hash value is needed, for example as a key in a dictionary.

import path A list of locations (or *path entries*) that are searched by the *path based finder* for modules to import. During import, this list of locations usually comes from *sys.path*, but for subpackages it may also come from the parent package's `__path__` attribute.

importing The process by which Python code in one module is made available to Python code in another module.

importer An object that both finds and loads a module; both a *finder* and *loader* object.

interactive Python has an interactive interpreter which means you can enter statements and expressions at the interpreter prompt, immediately execute them and see their results. Just launch `python` with no arguments (possibly by selecting it from your computer's main menu). It is a very powerful way to test out new ideas or inspect modules and packages (remember `help(x)`).

interpreted Python is an interpreted language, as opposed to a compiled one, though the distinction can be blurry because of the presence of the bytecode compiler. This means that source files can be run directly without explicitly creating an executable which is then run. Interpreted languages typically have a shorter development/debug cycle than compiled ones, though their programs generally also run more slowly. See also *interactive*.

interpreter shutdown When asked to shut down, the Python interpreter enters a special phase where it gradually releases all allocated resources, such as modules and various critical internal structures. It also makes several calls to the *garbage collector*. This can trigger the execution of code in user-defined destructors or weakref callbacks. Code executed during the shutdown phase can encounter various exceptions as the resources it relies on may not function anymore (common examples are library modules or the warnings machinery).

The main reason for interpreter shutdown is that the `__main__` module or the script being run has finished executing.

iterable An object capable of returning its members one at a time. Examples of iterables include all sequence types (such as *list*, *str*, and *tuple*) and some non-sequence types like *dict*, *file objects*, and objects of any classes you define with an `__iter__()` method or with a `__getitem__()` method that implements *Sequence* semantics.

Iterables can be used in a `for` loop and in many other places where a sequence is needed (*zip()*, *map()*, ...). When an iterable object is passed as an argument to the built-in function *iter()*, it returns an iterator for the object. This iterator is good for one pass over the set of values. When using iterables, it is usually not necessary to call *iter()* or deal with iterator objects yourself. The `for` statement does that automatically for you, creating a temporary unnamed variable to hold the iterator for the duration of the loop. See also *iterator*, *sequence*, and *generator*.

iterator An object representing a stream of data. Repeated calls to the iterator's *__next__()* method (or passing it to the built-in function *next()*) return successive items in the stream. When no more data are available a *StopIteration* exception is raised instead. At this point, the iterator object is exhausted and any further calls to its `__next__()` method just raise *StopIteration* again. Iterators are required to have an `__iter__()` method that returns the iterator object itself so every iterator is also iterable and may be used in most places where other iterables are accepted. One notable exception is code which attempts multiple iteration passes. A container object (such as a *list*) produces a fresh new iterator each time you pass it to the *iter()* function or use it in a `for` loop. Attempting this with an iterator will just return the same exhausted iterator object used in the previous iteration pass, making it appear like an empty container.

More information can be found in *Iterator Types*.

key function A key function or collation function is a callable that returns a value used for sorting or ordering. For example, *locale.strxfrm()* is used to produce a sort key that is aware of locale specific sort conventions.

A number of tools in Python accept key functions to control how elements are ordered or grouped. They include *min()*, *max()*, *sorted()*, *list.sort()*, *heapq.merge()*, *heapq.nsmallest()*, *heapq.nlargest()*, and *itertools.groupby()*.

There are several ways to create a key function. For example. the *str.lower()* method can serve as a key function for case insensitive sorts. Alternatively, a key function can be built from a `lambda` expression such as `lambda r: (r[0], r[2])`. Also, the *operator* module provides three key function constructors: *attrgetter()*, *itemgetter()*, and *methodcaller()*. See the Sorting HOW TO for examples of how to create and use key functions.

keyword argument See *argument*.

lambda An anonymous inline function consisting of a single *expression* which is evaluated when the function is called. The syntax to create a lambda function is `lambda [arguments]: expression`

LBYL Look before you leap. This coding style explicitly tests for pre-conditions before making calls or lookups. This style contrasts with the *EAFP* approach and is characterized by the presence of many `if` statements.

In a multi-threaded environment, the LBYL approach can risk introducing a race condition between "the looking" and "the leaping". For example, the code, `if key in mapping: return mapping[key]` can fail if another thread removes *key* from *mapping* after the test, but before the lookup. This issue can be solved with locks or by using the EAFP approach.

list A built-in Python *sequence*. Despite its name it is more akin to an array in other languages than to a linked list since access to elements are O(1).

list comprehension A compact way to process all or part of the elements in a sequence and return a list with the results. `result = ['{:#04x}'.format(x) for x in range(256) if x % 2 == 0]` generates a list of strings containing even hex numbers (0x..) in the range from 0 to 255. The `if` clause is optional. If omitted, all elements in `range(256)` are processed.

loader An object that loads a module. It must define a method named `load_module()`. A loader is typically returned by a *finder*. See **PEP 302** for details and *importlib.abc.Loader* for an *abstract base class*.

mapping A container object that supports arbitrary key lookups and implements the methods specified in the *Mapping* or *MutableMapping* *abstract base classes*. Examples include *dict*, *collections.defaultdict*, *collections.OrderedDict* and *collections.Counter*.

meta path finder A *finder* returned by a search of *sys.meta_path*. Meta path finders are related to, but different from *path entry finders*.

See *importlib.abc.MetaPathFinder* for the methods that meta path finders implement.

metaclass The class of a class. Class definitions create a class name, a class dictionary, and a list of base classes. The metaclass is responsible for taking those three arguments and creating the class. Most object oriented programming languages provide a default implementation. What makes Python special is that it is possible to create custom metaclasses. Most users never need this tool, but when the need arises, metaclasses can provide powerful, elegant solutions. They have been used for logging attribute access, adding thread-safety, tracking object creation, implementing singletons, and many other tasks.

More information can be found in metaclasses.

method A function which is defined inside a class body. If called as an attribute of an instance of that class, the method will get the instance object as its first *argument* (which is usually called `self`). See *function* and *nested scope*.

method resolution order Method Resolution Order is the order in which base classes are searched for a member during lookup. See The Python 2.3 Method Resolution Order for details of the algorithm used by the Python interpreter since the 2.3 release.

module An object that serves as an organizational unit of Python code. Modules have a namespace containing arbitrary Python objects. Modules are loaded into Python by the process of *importing*.

See also *package*.

module spec A namespace containing the import-related information used to load a module. An instance of *importlib.machinery.ModuleSpec*.

MRO See *method resolution order*.

mutable Mutable objects can change their value but keep their *id()*. See also *immutable*.

named tuple Any tuple-like class whose indexable elements are also accessible using named attributes (for example, *time.localtime()* returns a tuple-like object where the *year* is accessible either with an index such as `t[0]` or with a named attribute like `t.tm_year`).

A named tuple can be a built-in type such as *time.struct_time*, or it can be created with a regular class definition. A full featured named tuple can also be created with the factory function *collections.namedtuple()*. The latter approach automatically provides extra features such as a self-documenting representation like `Employee(name='jones', title='programmer')`.

namespace The place where a variable is stored. Namespaces are implemented as dictionaries. There are the local, global and built-in namespaces as well as nested namespaces in objects (in methods). Namespaces support modularity by preventing naming conflicts. For instance, the functions *builtins.open* and *os.open()* are distinguished by their namespaces. Namespaces also aid readability and maintainability by making it clear which module implements a function. For instance, writing *random.seed()* or *itertools.islice()* makes it clear that those functions are implemented by the *random* and *itertools* modules, respectively.

namespace package A PEP 420 *package* which serves only as a container for subpackages. Namespace packages may have no physical representation, and specifically are not like a *regular package* because they have no `__init__.py` file.

See also *module*.

nested scope The ability to refer to a variable in an enclosing definition. For instance, a function defined inside another function can refer to variables in the outer function. Note that nested scopes by default work only for reference and not for assignment. Local variables both read and write in the innermost scope. Likewise, global variables read and write to the global namespace. The `nonlocal` allows writing to outer scopes.

new-style class Old name for the flavor of classes now used for all class objects. In earlier Python versions, only new-style classes could use Python's newer, versatile features like `__slots__`, descriptors, properties, `__getattribute__()`, class methods, and static methods.

object Any data with state (attributes or value) and defined behavior (methods). Also the ultimate base class of any *new-style class*.

package A Python *module* which can contain submodules or recursively, subpackages. Technically, a package is a Python module with an `__path__` attribute.

See also *regular package* and *namespace package*.

parameter A named entity in a *function* (or method) definition that specifies an *argument* (or in some cases, arguments) that the function can accept. There are five kinds of parameter:

- *positional-or-keyword*: specifies an argument that can be passed either *positionally* or as a *keyword argument*. This is the default kind of parameter, for example *foo* and *bar* in the following:

```
def func(foo, bar=None): ...
```

- *positional-only*: specifies an argument that can be supplied only by position. Python has no syntax for defining positional-only parameters. However, some built-in functions have positional-only parameters (e.g. `abs()`).
- *keyword-only*: specifies an argument that can be supplied only by keyword. Keyword-only parameters can be defined by including a single var-positional parameter or bare `*` in the parameter list of the function definition before them, for example *kw_only1* and *kw_only2* in the following:

```
def func(arg, *, kw_only1, kw_only2): ...
```

- *var-positional*: specifies that an arbitrary sequence of positional arguments can be provided (in addition to any positional arguments already accepted by other parameters). Such a parameter can be defined by prepending the parameter name with `*`, for example *args* in the following:

```
def func(*args, **kwargs): ...
```

- *var-keyword*: specifies that arbitrarily many keyword arguments can be provided (in addition to any keyword arguments already accepted by other parameters). Such a parameter can be defined by prepending the parameter name with `**`, for example *kwargs* in the example above.

Parameters can specify both optional and required arguments, as well as default values for some optional arguments.

See also the *argument* glossary entry, the FAQ question on the difference between arguments and parameters, the `inspect.Parameter` class, the function section, and PEP 362.

path entry A single location on the *import path* which the *path based finder* consults to find modules for importing.

path entry finder A *finder* returned by a callable on `sys.path_hooks` (i.e. a *path entry hook*) which knows how to locate modules given a *path entry*.

See `importlib.abc.PathEntryFinder` for the methods that path entry finders implement.

path entry hook A callable on the `sys.path_hook` list which returns a *path entry finder* if it knows how to find modules on a specific *path entry*.

path based finder One of the default *meta path finders* which searches an *import path* for modules.

path-like object An object representing a file system path. A path-like object is either a `str` or `bytes` object representing a path, or an object implementing the `os.PathLike` protocol. An object that supports the `os.PathLike` protocol can be converted to a `str` or `bytes` file system path by calling the *os.fspath()* function; *os.fsdecode()* and *os.fsencode()* can be used to guarantee a *str* or *bytes* result instead, respectively. Introduced by PEP 519.

portion A set of files in a single directory (possibly stored in a zip file) that contribute to a namespace package, as defined in PEP 420.

positional argument See *argument*.

provisional API A provisional API is one which has been deliberately excluded from the standard library's backwards compatibility guarantees. While major changes to such interfaces are not expected, as long as they are marked provisional, backwards incompatible changes (up to and including removal of the interface) may occur if deemed necessary by core developers. Such changes will not be made gratuitously – they will occur only if serious fundamental flaws are uncovered that were missed prior to the inclusion of the API.

Even for provisional APIs, backwards incompatible changes are seen as a "solution of last resort" - every attempt will still be made to find a backwards compatible resolution to any identified problems.

This process allows the standard library to continue to evolve over time, without locking in problematic design errors for extended periods of time. See PEP 411 for more details.

provisional package See *provisional API*.

Python 3000 Nickname for the Python 3.x release line (coined long ago when the release of version 3 was something in the distant future.) This is also abbreviated "Py3k".

Pythonic An idea or piece of code which closely follows the most common idioms of the Python language, rather than implementing code using concepts common to other languages. For example, a common idiom in Python is to loop over all elements of an iterable using a `for` statement. Many other languages don't have this type of construct, so people unfamiliar with Python sometimes use a numerical counter instead:

```
for i in range(len(food)):
    print(food[i])
```

As opposed to the cleaner, Pythonic method:

```
for piece in food:
    print(piece)
```

qualified name A dotted name showing the "path" from a module's global scope to a class, function or method defined in that module, as defined in PEP 3155. For top-level functions and classes, the qualified name is the same as the object's name:

```
>>> class C:
...     class D:
...         def meth(self):
...             pass
...
>>> C.__qualname__
'C'
>>> C.D.__qualname__
'C.D'
>>> C.D.meth.__qualname__
'C.D.meth'
```

When used to refer to modules, the *fully qualified name* means the entire dotted path to the module, including any parent packages, e.g. `email.mime.text`:

```
>>> import email.mime.text
>>> email.mime.text.__name__
'email.mime.text'
```

reference count The number of references to an object. When the reference count of an object drops to zero, it is deallocated. Reference counting is generally not visible to Python code, but it is a key element of the *CPython* implementation. The *sys* module defines a *getrefcount()* function that programmers can call to return the reference count for a particular object.

regular package A traditional *package*, such as a directory containing an `__init__.py` file.

See also *namespace package*.

__slots__ A declaration inside a class that saves memory by pre-declaring space for instance attributes and eliminating instance dictionaries. Though popular, the technique is somewhat tricky to get right and is best reserved for rare cases where there are large numbers of instances in a memory-critical application.

sequence An *iterable* which supports efficient element access using integer indices via the `__getitem__()` special method and defines a `__len__()` method that returns the length of the sequence. Some built-in sequence types are *list*, *str*, *tuple*, and *bytes*. Note that *dict* also supports `__getitem__()` and `__len__()`, but is considered a mapping rather than a sequence because the lookups use arbitrary *immutable* keys rather than integers.

The *collections.abc.Sequence* abstract base class defines a much richer interface that goes beyond just `__getitem__()` and `__len__()`, adding `count()`, `index()`, `__contains__()`, and `__reversed__()`. Types that implement this expanded interface can be registered explicitly using `register()`.

single dispatch A form of *generic function* dispatch where the implementation is chosen based on the type of a single argument.

slice An object usually containing a portion of a *sequence*. A slice is created using the subscript notation, `[]` with colons between numbers when several are given, such as in `variable_name[1:3:5]`. The bracket (subscript) notation uses *slice* objects internally.

special method A method that is called implicitly by Python to execute a certain operation on a type, such as addition. Such methods have names starting and ending with double underscores. Special methods are documented in specialnames.

statement A statement is part of a suite (a "block" of code). A statement is either an *expression* or one of several constructs with a keyword, such as `if`, `while` or `for`.

struct sequence A tuple with named elements. Struct sequences expose an interface similar to *named tuple* in that elements can either be accessed either by index or as an attribute. However, they do not have any of the named tuple methods like *_make()* or *_asdict()*. Examples of struct sequences include *sys.float_info* and the return value of *os.stat()*.

text encoding A codec which encodes Unicode strings to bytes.

text file A *file object* able to read and write *str* objects. Often, a text file actually accesses a byte-oriented datastream and handles the *text encoding* automatically. Examples of text files are files opened in text mode (`'r'` or `'w'`), *sys.stdin*, *sys.stdout*, and instances of *io.StringIO*.

See also:

A *binary file* reads and write *bytes* objects.

triple-quoted string A string which is bound by three instances of either a quotation mark (") or an apostrophe ('). While they don't provide any functionality not available with single-quoted strings, they are useful for a number of reasons. They allow you to include unescaped single and double quotes within a string and they can span multiple lines without the use of the continuation character, making them especially useful when writing docstrings.

type The type of a Python object determines what kind of object it is; every object has a type. An object's type is accessible as its *__class__* attribute or can be retrieved with `type(obj)`.

universal newlines A manner of interpreting text streams in which all of the following are recognized as ending a line: the Unix end-of-line convention `'\n'`, the Windows convention `'\r\n'`, and the old Macintosh convention `'\r'`. See PEP 278 and PEP 3116, as well as *bytes.splitlines()* for an additional use.

variable annotation A type metadata value associated with a module global variable or a class attribute. Its syntax is explained in section annassign. Annotations are stored in the `__annotations__` special attribute of a class or module object and can be accessed using *typing.get_type_hints()*.

Python itself does not assign any particular meaning to variable annotations. They are intended to be interpreted by third-party libraries or type checking tools. See PEP 526, PEP 484 which describe some of their potential uses.

virtual environment A cooperatively isolated runtime environment that allows Python users and applications to install and upgrade Python distribution packages without interfering with the behaviour of other Python applications running on the same system.

See also *venv*.

virtual machine A computer defined entirely in software. Python's virtual machine executes the *bytecode* emitted by the bytecode compiler.

Zen of Python Listing of Python design principles and philosophies that are helpful in understanding and using the language. The listing can be found by typing "`import this`" at the interactive prompt.

BIBLIOGRAPHY

[C99] ISO/IEC 9899:1999. "Programming languages – C." A public draft of this standard is available at http://www.open-std.org/jtc1/sc22/wg14/www/docs/n1256.pdf.

APPENDIX

B

ABOUT THESE DOCUMENTS

These documents are generated from reStructuredText sources by Sphinx, a document processor specifically written for the Python documentation.

Development of the documentation and its toolchain is an entirely volunteer effort, just like Python itself. If you want to contribute, please take a look at the reporting-bugs page for information on how to do so. New volunteers are always welcome!

Many thanks go to:

- Fred L. Drake, Jr., the creator of the original Python documentation toolset and writer of much of the content;
- the Docutils project for creating reStructuredText and the Docutils suite;
- Fredrik Lundh for his Alternative Python Reference project from which Sphinx got many good ideas.

B.1 Contributors to the Python Documentation

Many people have contributed to the Python language, the Python standard library, and the Python documentation. See Misc/ACKS in the Python source distribution for a partial list of contributors.

It is only with the input and contributions of the Python community that Python has such wonderful documentation – Thank You!

APPENDIX

C

HISTORY AND LICENSE

C.1 History of the software

Python was created in the early 1990s by Guido van Rossum at Stichting Mathematisch Centrum (CWI, see https://www.cwi.nl/) in the Netherlands as a successor of a language called ABC. Guido remains Python's principal author, although it includes many contributions from others.

In 1995, Guido continued his work on Python at the Corporation for National Research Initiatives (CNRI, see https://www.cnri.reston.va.us/) in Reston, Virginia where he released several versions of the software.

In May 2000, Guido and the Python core development team moved to BeOpen.com to form the BeOpen PythonLabs team. In October of the same year, the PythonLabs team moved to Digital Creations (now Zope Corporation; see http://www.zope.com/). In 2001, the Python Software Foundation (PSF, see https://www.python.org/psf/) was formed, a non-profit organization created specifically to own Python-related Intellectual Property. Zope Corporation is a sponsoring member of the PSF.

All Python releases are Open Source (see https://opensource.org/ for the Open Source Definition). Historically, most, but not all, Python releases have also been GPL-compatible; the table below summarizes the various releases.

Release	Derived from	Year	Owner	GPL compatible?
0.9.0 thru 1.2	n/a	1991-1995	CWI	yes
1.3 thru 1.5.2	1.2	1995-1999	CNRI	yes
1.6	1.5.2	2000	CNRI	no
2.0	1.6	2000	BeOpen.com	no
1.6.1	1.6	2001	CNRI	no
2.1	2.0+1.6.1	2001	PSF	no
2.0.1	2.0+1.6.1	2001	PSF	yes
2.1.1	2.1+2.0.1	2001	PSF	yes
2.1.2	2.1.1	2002	PSF	yes
2.1.3	2.1.2	2002	PSF	yes
2.2 and above	2.1.1	2001-now	PSF	yes

Note: GPL-compatible doesn't mean that we're distributing Python under the GPL. All Python licenses, unlike the GPL, let you distribute a modified version without making your changes open source. The GPL-compatible licenses make it possible to combine Python with other software that is released under the GPL; the others don't.

Thanks to the many outside volunteers who have worked under Guido's direction to make these releases possible.

C.2 Terms and conditions for accessing or otherwise using Python

C.2.1 PSF LICENSE AGREEMENT FOR PYTHON 3.6.4

```
1. This LICENSE AGREEMENT is between the Python Software Foundation ("PSF"), and
   the Individual or Organization ("Licensee") accessing and otherwise using Python
   3.6.4 software in source or binary form and its associated documentation.

2. Subject to the terms and conditions of this License Agreement, PSF hereby
   grants Licensee a nonexclusive, royalty-free, world-wide license to reproduce,
   analyze, test, perform and/or display publicly, prepare derivative works,
   distribute, and otherwise use Python 3.6.4 alone or in any derivative
   version, provided, however, that PSF's License Agreement and PSF's notice of
   copyright, i.e., "Copyright © 2001-2018 Python Software Foundation; All Rights
   Reserved" are retained in Python 3.6.4 alone or in any derivative version
   prepared by Licensee.

3. In the event Licensee prepares a derivative work that is based on or
   incorporates Python 3.6.4 or any part thereof, and wants to make the
   derivative work available to others as provided herein, then Licensee hereby
   agrees to include in any such work a brief summary of the changes made to Python
   3.6.4.

4. PSF is making Python 3.6.4 available to Licensee on an "AS IS" basis.
   PSF MAKES NO REPRESENTATIONS OR WARRANTIES, EXPRESS OR IMPLIED.  BY WAY OF
   EXAMPLE, BUT NOT LIMITATION, PSF MAKES NO AND DISCLAIMS ANY REPRESENTATION OR
   WARRANTY OF MERCHANTABILITY OR FITNESS FOR ANY PARTICULAR PURPOSE OR THAT THE
   USE OF PYTHON 3.6.4 WILL NOT INFRINGE ANY THIRD PARTY RIGHTS.

5. PSF SHALL NOT BE LIABLE TO LICENSEE OR ANY OTHER USERS OF PYTHON 3.6.4
   FOR ANY INCIDENTAL, SPECIAL, OR CONSEQUENTIAL DAMAGES OR LOSS AS A RESULT OF
   MODIFYING, DISTRIBUTING, OR OTHERWISE USING PYTHON 3.6.4, OR ANY DERIVATIVE
   THEREOF, EVEN IF ADVISED OF THE POSSIBILITY THEREOF.

6. This License Agreement will automatically terminate upon a material breach of
   its terms and conditions.

7. Nothing in this License Agreement shall be deemed to create any relationship
   of agency, partnership, or joint venture between PSF and Licensee.  This License
   Agreement does not grant permission to use PSF trademarks or trade name in a
   trademark sense to endorse or promote products or services of Licensee, or any
   third party.

8. By copying, installing or otherwise using Python 3.6.4, Licensee agrees
   to be bound by the terms and conditions of this License Agreement.
```

C.2.2 BEOPEN.COM LICENSE AGREEMENT FOR PYTHON 2.0

BEOPEN PYTHON OPEN SOURCE LICENSE AGREEMENT VERSION 1

```
1. This LICENSE AGREEMENT is between BeOpen.com ("BeOpen"), having an office at
   160 Saratoga Avenue, Santa Clara, CA 95051, and the Individual or Organization
   ("Licensee") accessing and otherwise using this software in source or binary
```

```
   form and its associated documentation ("the Software").

2. Subject to the terms and conditions of this BeOpen Python License Agreement,
   BeOpen hereby grants Licensee a non-exclusive, royalty-free, world-wide license
   to reproduce, analyze, test, perform and/or display publicly, prepare derivative
   works, distribute, and otherwise use the Software alone or in any derivative
   version, provided, however, that the BeOpen Python License is retained in the
   Software, alone or in any derivative version prepared by Licensee.

3. BeOpen is making the Software available to Licensee on an "AS IS" basis.
   BEOPEN MAKES NO REPRESENTATIONS OR WARRANTIES, EXPRESS OR IMPLIED.  BY WAY OF
   EXAMPLE, BUT NOT LIMITATION, BEOPEN MAKES NO AND DISCLAIMS ANY REPRESENTATION OR
   WARRANTY OF MERCHANTABILITY OR FITNESS FOR ANY PARTICULAR PURPOSE OR THAT THE
   USE OF THE SOFTWARE WILL NOT INFRINGE ANY THIRD PARTY RIGHTS.

4. BEOPEN SHALL NOT BE LIABLE TO LICENSEE OR ANY OTHER USERS OF THE SOFTWARE FOR
   ANY INCIDENTAL, SPECIAL, OR CONSEQUENTIAL DAMAGES OR LOSS AS A RESULT OF USING,
   MODIFYING OR DISTRIBUTING THE SOFTWARE, OR ANY DERIVATIVE THEREOF, EVEN IF
   ADVISED OF THE POSSIBILITY THEREOF.

5. This License Agreement will automatically terminate upon a material breach of
   its terms and conditions.

6. This License Agreement shall be governed by and interpreted in all respects
   by the law of the State of California, excluding conflict of law provisions.
   Nothing in this License Agreement shall be deemed to create any relationship of
   agency, partnership, or joint venture between BeOpen and Licensee.  This License
   Agreement does not grant permission to use BeOpen trademarks or trade names in a
   trademark sense to endorse or promote products or services of Licensee, or any
   third party.  As an exception, the "BeOpen Python" logos available at
   http://www.pythonlabs.com/logos.html may be used according to the permissions
   granted on that web page.

7. By copying, installing or otherwise using the software, Licensee agrees to be
   bound by the terms and conditions of this License Agreement.
```

C.2.3 CNRI LICENSE AGREEMENT FOR PYTHON 1.6.1

```
1. This LICENSE AGREEMENT is between the Corporation for National Research
   Initiatives, having an office at 1895 Preston White Drive, Reston, VA 20191
   ("CNRI"), and the Individual or Organization ("Licensee") accessing and
   otherwise using Python 1.6.1 software in source or binary form and its
   associated documentation.

2. Subject to the terms and conditions of this License Agreement, CNRI hereby
   grants Licensee a nonexclusive, royalty-free, world-wide license to reproduce,
   analyze, test, perform and/or display publicly, prepare derivative works,
   distribute, and otherwise use Python 1.6.1 alone or in any derivative version,
   provided, however, that CNRI's License Agreement and CNRI's notice of copyright,
   i.e., "Copyright © 1995-2001 Corporation for National Research Initiatives; All
   Rights Reserved" are retained in Python 1.6.1 alone or in any derivative version
   prepared by Licensee.  Alternately, in lieu of CNRI's License Agreement,
   Licensee may substitute the following text (omitting the quotes): "Python 1.6.1
   is made available subject to the terms and conditions in CNRI's License
   Agreement.  This Agreement together with Python 1.6.1 may be located on the
   Internet using the following unique, persistent identifier (known as a handle):
```

```
   1895.22/1013.  This Agreement may also be obtained from a proxy server on the
   Internet using the following URL: http://hdl.handle.net/1895.22/1013."

3. In the event Licensee prepares a derivative work that is based on or
   incorporates Python 1.6.1 or any part thereof, and wants to make the derivative
   work available to others as provided herein, then Licensee hereby agrees to
   include in any such work a brief summary of the changes made to Python 1.6.1.

4. CNRI is making Python 1.6.1 available to Licensee on an "AS IS" basis.  CNRI
   MAKES NO REPRESENTATIONS OR WARRANTIES, EXPRESS OR IMPLIED.  BY WAY OF EXAMPLE,
   BUT NOT LIMITATION, CNRI MAKES NO AND DISCLAIMS ANY REPRESENTATION OR WARRANTY
   OF MERCHANTABILITY OR FITNESS FOR ANY PARTICULAR PURPOSE OR THAT THE USE OF
   PYTHON 1.6.1 WILL NOT INFRINGE ANY THIRD PARTY RIGHTS.

5. CNRI SHALL NOT BE LIABLE TO LICENSEE OR ANY OTHER USERS OF PYTHON 1.6.1 FOR
   ANY INCIDENTAL, SPECIAL, OR CONSEQUENTIAL DAMAGES OR LOSS AS A RESULT OF
   MODIFYING, DISTRIBUTING, OR OTHERWISE USING PYTHON 1.6.1, OR ANY DERIVATIVE
   THEREOF, EVEN IF ADVISED OF THE POSSIBILITY THEREOF.

6. This License Agreement will automatically terminate upon a material breach of
   its terms and conditions.

7. This License Agreement shall be governed by the federal intellectual property
   law of the United States, including without limitation the federal copyright
   law, and, to the extent such U.S. federal law does not apply, by the law of the
   Commonwealth of Virginia, excluding Virginia's conflict of law provisions.
   Notwithstanding the foregoing, with regard to derivative works based on Python
   1.6.1 that incorporate non-separable material that was previously distributed
   under the GNU General Public License (GPL), the law of the Commonwealth of
   Virginia shall govern this License Agreement only as to issues arising under or
   with respect to Paragraphs 4, 5, and 7 of this License Agreement.  Nothing in
   this License Agreement shall be deemed to create any relationship of agency,
   partnership, or joint venture between CNRI and Licensee.  This License Agreement
   does not grant permission to use CNRI trademarks or trade name in a trademark
   sense to endorse or promote products or services of Licensee, or any third
   party.

8. By clicking on the "ACCEPT" button where indicated, or by copying, installing
   or otherwise using Python 1.6.1, Licensee agrees to be bound by the terms and
   conditions of this License Agreement.
```

C.2.4 CWI LICENSE AGREEMENT FOR PYTHON 0.9.0 THROUGH 1.2

```
Copyright © 1991 - 1995, Stichting Mathematisch Centrum Amsterdam, The
Netherlands.  All rights reserved.

Permission to use, copy, modify, and distribute this software and its
documentation for any purpose and without fee is hereby granted, provided that
the above copyright notice appear in all copies and that both that copyright
notice and this permission notice appear in supporting documentation, and that
the name of Stichting Mathematisch Centrum or CWI not be used in advertising or
publicity pertaining to distribution of the software without specific, written
prior permission.

STICHTING MATHEMATISCH CENTRUM DISCLAIMS ALL WARRANTIES WITH REGARD TO THIS
SOFTWARE, INCLUDING ALL IMPLIED WARRANTIES OF MERCHANTABILITY AND FITNESS, IN NO
```

```
EVENT SHALL STICHTING MATHEMATISCH CENTRUM BE LIABLE FOR ANY SPECIAL, INDIRECT
OR CONSEQUENTIAL DAMAGES OR ANY DAMAGES WHATSOEVER RESULTING FROM LOSS OF USE,
DATA OR PROFITS, WHETHER IN AN ACTION OF CONTRACT, NEGLIGENCE OR OTHER TORTIOUS
ACTION, ARISING OUT OF OR IN CONNECTION WITH THE USE OR PERFORMANCE OF THIS
SOFTWARE.
```

C.3 Licenses and Acknowledgements for Incorporated Software

This section is an incomplete, but growing list of licenses and acknowledgements for third-party software incorporated in the Python distribution.

C.3.1 Mersenne Twister

The `_random` module includes code based on a download from http://www.math.sci.hiroshima-u.ac.jp/~m-mat/MT/MT2002/emt19937ar.html. The following are the verbatim comments from the original code:

```
A C-program for MT19937, with initialization improved 2002/1/26.
Coded by Takuji Nishimura and Makoto Matsumoto.

Before using, initialize the state by using init_genrand(seed)
or init_by_array(init_key, key_length).

Copyright (C) 1997 - 2002, Makoto Matsumoto and Takuji Nishimura,
All rights reserved.

Redistribution and use in source and binary forms, with or without
modification, are permitted provided that the following conditions
are met:

 1. Redistributions of source code must retain the above copyright
    notice, this list of conditions and the following disclaimer.

 2. Redistributions in binary form must reproduce the above copyright
    notice, this list of conditions and the following disclaimer in the
    documentation and/or other materials provided with the distribution.

 3. The names of its contributors may not be used to endorse or promote
    products derived from this software without specific prior written
    permission.

THIS SOFTWARE IS PROVIDED BY THE COPYRIGHT HOLDERS AND CONTRIBUTORS
"AS IS" AND ANY EXPRESS OR IMPLIED WARRANTIES, INCLUDING, BUT NOT
LIMITED TO, THE IMPLIED WARRANTIES OF MERCHANTABILITY AND FITNESS FOR
A PARTICULAR PURPOSE ARE DISCLAIMED.  IN NO EVENT SHALL THE COPYRIGHT OWNER OR
CONTRIBUTORS BE LIABLE FOR ANY DIRECT, INDIRECT, INCIDENTAL, SPECIAL,
EXEMPLARY, OR CONSEQUENTIAL DAMAGES (INCLUDING, BUT NOT LIMITED TO,
PROCUREMENT OF SUBSTITUTE GOODS OR SERVICES; LOSS OF USE, DATA, OR
PROFITS; OR BUSINESS INTERRUPTION) HOWEVER CAUSED AND ON ANY THEORY OF
LIABILITY, WHETHER IN CONTRACT, STRICT LIABILITY, OR TORT (INCLUDING
NEGLIGENCE OR OTHERWISE) ARISING IN ANY WAY OUT OF THE USE OF THIS
SOFTWARE, EVEN IF ADVISED OF THE POSSIBILITY OF SUCH DAMAGE.


Any feedback is very welcome.
```

```
http://www.math.sci.hiroshima-u.ac.jp/~m-mat/MT/emt.html
email: m-mat @ math.sci.hiroshima-u.ac.jp (remove space)
```

C.3.2 Sockets

The *socket* module uses the functions, `getaddrinfo()`, and `getnameinfo()`, which are coded in separate source files from the WIDE Project, http://www.wide.ad.jp/.

C.3.3 Floating point exception control

The source for the *fpectl* module includes the following notice:

```
|                             DISCLAIMER                            |
|                                                                   |
|   This  software was prepared as an account of work sponsored by an  |
|   agency of the United States Government. Neither the United States  |
|   Government  nor the University of California nor any of their em-  |
|   ployees, makes any warranty, express or implied, or  assumes  any  |
|   liability  or  responsibility  for the accuracy, completeness, or  |
|   usefulness of any information,  apparatus,  product,  or  process  |
|   disclosed,   or  represents  that  its  use  would  not  infringe  |
|   privately-owned rights. Reference herein to any specific  commer-  |
|   cial  products,  process,  or  service  by trade name, trademark,  |
|   manufacturer, or otherwise, does not  necessarily  constitute  or  |
|   imply  its endorsement, recommendation, or favoring by the United  |
|   States Government or the University of California. The views  and  |
|   opinions  of authors expressed herein do not necessarily state or  |
|   reflect those of the United States Government or  the  University  |
|   of  California,  and shall not be used for advertising or product  |
 \  endorsement purposes.                                            /
  ---------------------------------------------------------------------
```

C.3.4 Asynchronous socket services

The *asynchat* and *asyncore* modules contain the following notice:

```
Copyright 1996 by Sam Rushing

                        All Rights Reserved

Permission to use, copy, modify, and distribute this software and
its documentation for any purpose and without fee is hereby
granted, provided that the above copyright notice appear in all
copies and that both that copyright notice and this permission
notice appear in supporting documentation, and that the name of Sam
Rushing not be used in advertising or publicity pertaining to
distribution of the software without specific, written prior
permission.

SAM RUSHING DISCLAIMS ALL WARRANTIES WITH REGARD TO THIS SOFTWARE,
INCLUDING ALL IMPLIED WARRANTIES OF MERCHANTABILITY AND FITNESS, IN
NO EVENT SHALL SAM RUSHING BE LIABLE FOR ANY SPECIAL, INDIRECT OR
CONSEQUENTIAL DAMAGES OR ANY DAMAGES WHATSOEVER RESULTING FROM LOSS
OF USE, DATA OR PROFITS, WHETHER IN AN ACTION OF CONTRACT,
NEGLIGENCE OR OTHER TORTIOUS ACTION, ARISING OUT OF OR IN
CONNECTION WITH THE USE OR PERFORMANCE OF THIS SOFTWARE.
```

C.3.5 Cookie management

The *http.cookies* module contains the following notice:

```
Copyright 2000 by Timothy O'Malley <timo@alum.mit.edu>

               All Rights Reserved

Permission to use, copy, modify, and distribute this software
and its documentation for any purpose and without fee is hereby
```

```
granted, provided that the above copyright notice appear in all
copies and that both that copyright notice and this permission
notice appear in supporting documentation, and that the name of
Timothy O'Malley  not be used in advertising or publicity
pertaining to distribution of the software without specific, written
prior permission.

Timothy O'Malley DISCLAIMS ALL WARRANTIES WITH REGARD TO THIS
SOFTWARE, INCLUDING ALL IMPLIED WARRANTIES OF MERCHANTABILITY
AND FITNESS, IN NO EVENT SHALL Timothy O'Malley BE LIABLE FOR
ANY SPECIAL, INDIRECT OR CONSEQUENTIAL DAMAGES OR ANY DAMAGES
WHATSOEVER RESULTING FROM LOSS OF USE, DATA OR PROFITS,
WHETHER IN AN ACTION OF CONTRACT, NEGLIGENCE OR OTHER TORTIOUS
ACTION, ARISING OUT OF OR IN CONNECTION WITH THE USE OR
PERFORMANCE OF THIS SOFTWARE.
```

C.3.6 Execution tracing

The *trace* module contains the following notice:

```
portions copyright 2001, Autonomous Zones Industries, Inc., all rights...
err...  reserved and offered to the public under the terms of the
Python 2.2 license.
Author: Zooko O'Whielacronx
http://zooko.com/
mailto:zooko@zooko.com

Copyright 2000, Mojam Media, Inc., all rights reserved.
Author: Skip Montanaro

Copyright 1999, Bioreason, Inc., all rights reserved.
Author: Andrew Dalke

Copyright 1995-1997, Automatrix, Inc., all rights reserved.
Author: Skip Montanaro

Copyright 1991-1995, Stichting Mathematisch Centrum, all rights reserved.


Permission to use, copy, modify, and distribute this Python software and
its associated documentation for any purpose without fee is hereby
granted, provided that the above copyright notice appears in all copies,
and that both that copyright notice and this permission notice appear in
supporting documentation, and that the name of neither Automatrix,
Bioreason or Mojam Media be used in advertising or publicity pertaining to
distribution of the software without specific, written prior permission.
```

C.3.7 UUencode and UUdecode functions

The *uu* module contains the following notice:

```
Copyright 1994 by Lance Ellinghouse
Cathedral City, California Republic, United States of America.
                       All Rights Reserved
Permission to use, copy, modify, and distribute this software and its
```

C.3.8 XML Remote Procedure Calls

The *xmlrpc.client* module contains the following notice:

C.3.9 test_epoll

The `test_epoll` module contains the following notice:

C.3.10 Select kqueue

The *select* module contains the following notice for the kqueue interface:

C.3.11 SipHash24

The file `Python/pyhash.c` contains Marek Majkowski' implementation of Dan Bernstein's SipHash24 algorithm. The contains the following note:

```
<MIT License>
Copyright (c) 2013  Marek Majkowski <marek@popcount.org>

Permission is hereby granted, free of charge, to any person obtaining a copy
of this software and associated documentation files (the "Software"), to deal
in the Software without restriction, including without limitation the rights
to use, copy, modify, merge, publish, distribute, sublicense, and/or sell
copies of the Software, and to permit persons to whom the Software is
furnished to do so, subject to the following conditions:

The above copyright notice and this permission notice shall be included in
all copies or substantial portions of the Software.
</MIT License>

Original location:
   https://github.com/majek/csiphash/

Solution inspired by code from:
   Samuel Neves (supercop/crypto_auth/siphash24/little)
   djb (supercop/crypto_auth/siphash24/little2)
   Jean-Philippe Aumasson (https://131002.net/siphash/siphash24.c)
```

C.3.12 strtod and dtoa

The file `Python/dtoa.c`, which supplies C functions dtoa and strtod for conversion of C doubles to and from strings, is derived from the file of the same name by David M. Gay, currently available from http://www.netlib.org/fp/. The original file, as retrieved on March 16, 2009, contains the following copyright and licensing notice:

```
/****************************************************************
 *
 * The author of this software is David M. Gay.
 *
 * Copyright (c) 1991, 2000, 2001 by Lucent Technologies.
 *
 * Permission to use, copy, modify, and distribute this software for any
 * purpose without fee is hereby granted, provided that this entire notice
 * is included in all copies of any software which is or includes a copy
 * or modification of this software and in all copies of the supporting
 * documentation for such software.
 *
 * THIS SOFTWARE IS BEING PROVIDED "AS IS", WITHOUT ANY EXPRESS OR IMPLIED
 * WARRANTY.  IN PARTICULAR, NEITHER THE AUTHOR NOR LUCENT MAKES ANY
 * REPRESENTATION OR WARRANTY OF ANY KIND CONCERNING THE MERCHANTABILITY
 * OF THIS SOFTWARE OR ITS FITNESS FOR ANY PARTICULAR PURPOSE.
 *
 ***************************************************************/
```

C.3.13 OpenSSL

The modules *hashlib*, *posix*, *ssl*, *crypt* use the OpenSSL library for added performance if made available by the operating system. Additionally, the Windows and Mac OS X installers for Python may include a copy of the OpenSSL libraries, so we include a copy of the OpenSSL license here:

```
LICENSE ISSUES
==============

The OpenSSL toolkit stays under a dual license, i.e. both the conditions of
the OpenSSL License and the original SSLeay license apply to the toolkit.
See below for the actual license texts. Actually both licenses are BSD-style
Open Source licenses. In case of any license issues related to OpenSSL
please contact openssl-core@openssl.org.

OpenSSL License
---------------

  /* ====================================================================
   * Copyright (c) 1998-2008 The OpenSSL Project.  All rights reserved.
   *
   * Redistribution and use in source and binary forms, with or without
   * modification, are permitted provided that the following conditions
   * are met:
   *
   * 1. Redistributions of source code must retain the above copyright
   *    notice, this list of conditions and the following disclaimer.
   *
   * 2. Redistributions in binary form must reproduce the above copyright
   *    notice, this list of conditions and the following disclaimer in
   *    the documentation and/or other materials provided with the
   *    distribution.
   *
   * 3. All advertising materials mentioning features or use of this
   *    software must display the following acknowledgment:
   *    "This product includes software developed by the OpenSSL Project
   *    for use in the OpenSSL Toolkit. (http://www.openssl.org/)"
   *
   * 4. The names "OpenSSL Toolkit" and "OpenSSL Project" must not be used to
   *    endorse or promote products derived from this software without
   *    prior written permission. For written permission, please contact
   *    openssl-core@openssl.org.
   *
   * 5. Products derived from this software may not be called "OpenSSL"
   *    nor may "OpenSSL" appear in their names without prior written
   *    permission of the OpenSSL Project.
   *
   * 6. Redistributions of any form whatsoever must retain the following
   *    acknowledgment:
   *    "This product includes software developed by the OpenSSL Project
   *    for use in the OpenSSL Toolkit (http://www.openssl.org/)"
   *
   * THIS SOFTWARE IS PROVIDED BY THE OpenSSL PROJECT ``AS IS'' AND ANY
   * EXPRESSED OR IMPLIED WARRANTIES, INCLUDING, BUT NOT LIMITED TO, THE
   * IMPLIED WARRANTIES OF MERCHANTABILITY AND FITNESS FOR A PARTICULAR
   * PURPOSE ARE DISCLAIMED.  IN NO EVENT SHALL THE OpenSSL PROJECT OR
   * ITS CONTRIBUTORS BE LIABLE FOR ANY DIRECT, INDIRECT, INCIDENTAL,
   * SPECIAL, EXEMPLARY, OR CONSEQUENTIAL DAMAGES (INCLUDING, BUT
   * NOT LIMITED TO, PROCUREMENT OF SUBSTITUTE GOODS OR SERVICES;
   * LOSS OF USE, DATA, OR PROFITS; OR BUSINESS INTERRUPTION)
   * HOWEVER CAUSED AND ON ANY THEORY OF LIABILITY, WHETHER IN CONTRACT,
   * STRICT LIABILITY, OR TORT (INCLUDING NEGLIGENCE OR OTHERWISE)
   * ARISING IN ANY WAY OUT OF THE USE OF THIS SOFTWARE, EVEN IF ADVISED
   * OF THE POSSIBILITY OF SUCH DAMAGE.
```

```
 * ====================================================================
 *
 * This product includes cryptographic software written by Eric Young
 * (eay@cryptsoft.com).  This product includes software written by Tim
 * Hudson (tjh@cryptsoft.com).
 *
 */

Original SSLeay License
-----------------------

/* Copyright (C) 1995-1998 Eric Young (eay@cryptsoft.com)
 * All rights reserved.
 *
 * This package is an SSL implementation written
 * by Eric Young (eay@cryptsoft.com).
 * The implementation was written so as to conform with Netscapes SSL.
 *
 * This library is free for commercial and non-commercial use as long as
 * the following conditions are aheared to.  The following conditions
 * apply to all code found in this distribution, be it the RC4, RSA,
 * lhash, DES, etc., code; not just the SSL code.  The SSL documentation
 * included with this distribution is covered by the same copyright terms
 * except that the holder is Tim Hudson (tjh@cryptsoft.com).
 *
 * Copyright remains Eric Young's, and as such any Copyright notices in
 * the code are not to be removed.
 * If this package is used in a product, Eric Young should be given attribution
 * as the author of the parts of the library used.
 * This can be in the form of a textual message at program startup or
 * in documentation (online or textual) provided with the package.
 *
 * Redistribution and use in source and binary forms, with or without
 * modification, are permitted provided that the following conditions
 * are met:
 * 1. Redistributions of source code must retain the copyright
 *    notice, this list of conditions and the following disclaimer.
 * 2. Redistributions in binary form must reproduce the above copyright
 *    notice, this list of conditions and the following disclaimer in the
 *    documentation and/or other materials provided with the distribution.
 * 3. All advertising materials mentioning features or use of this software
 *    must display the following acknowledgement:
 *    "This product includes cryptographic software written by
 *     Eric Young (eay@cryptsoft.com)"
 *    The word 'cryptographic' can be left out if the rouines from the library
 *    being used are not cryptographic related :-).
 * 4. If you include any Windows specific code (or a derivative thereof) from
 *    the apps directory (application code) you must include an acknowledgement:
 *    "This product includes software written by Tim Hudson (tjh@cryptsoft.com)"
 *
 * THIS SOFTWARE IS PROVIDED BY ERIC YOUNG ``AS IS'' AND
 * ANY EXPRESS OR IMPLIED WARRANTIES, INCLUDING, BUT NOT LIMITED TO, THE
 * IMPLIED WARRANTIES OF MERCHANTABILITY AND FITNESS FOR A PARTICULAR PURPOSE
 * ARE DISCLAIMED.  IN NO EVENT SHALL THE AUTHOR OR CONTRIBUTORS BE LIABLE
 * FOR ANY DIRECT, INDIRECT, INCIDENTAL, SPECIAL, EXEMPLARY, OR CONSEQUENTIAL
 * DAMAGES (INCLUDING, BUT NOT LIMITED TO, PROCUREMENT OF SUBSTITUTE GOODS
 * OR SERVICES; LOSS OF USE, DATA, OR PROFITS; OR BUSINESS INTERRUPTION)
 * HOWEVER CAUSED AND ON ANY THEORY OF LIABILITY, WHETHER IN CONTRACT, STRICT
```

```
 * LIABILITY, OR TORT (INCLUDING NEGLIGENCE OR OTHERWISE) ARISING IN ANY WAY
 * OUT OF THE USE OF THIS SOFTWARE, EVEN IF ADVISED OF THE POSSIBILITY OF
 * SUCH DAMAGE.
 *
 * The licence and distribution terms for any publically available version or
 * derivative of this code cannot be changed.  i.e. this code cannot simply be
 * copied and put under another distribution licence
 * [including the GNU Public Licence.]
 */
```

C.3.14 expat

The pyexpat extension is built using an included copy of the expat sources unless the build is configured --with-system-expat:

```
Copyright (c) 1998, 1999, 2000 Thai Open Source Software Center Ltd
                               and Clark Cooper

Permission is hereby granted, free of charge, to any person obtaining
a copy of this software and associated documentation files (the
"Software"), to deal in the Software without restriction, including
without limitation the rights to use, copy, modify, merge, publish,
distribute, sublicense, and/or sell copies of the Software, and to
permit persons to whom the Software is furnished to do so, subject to
the following conditions:

The above copyright notice and this permission notice shall be included
in all copies or substantial portions of the Software.

THE SOFTWARE IS PROVIDED "AS IS", WITHOUT WARRANTY OF ANY KIND,
EXPRESS OR IMPLIED, INCLUDING BUT NOT LIMITED TO THE WARRANTIES OF
MERCHANTABILITY, FITNESS FOR A PARTICULAR PURPOSE AND NONINFRINGEMENT.
IN NO EVENT SHALL THE AUTHORS OR COPYRIGHT HOLDERS BE LIABLE FOR ANY
CLAIM, DAMAGES OR OTHER LIABILITY, WHETHER IN AN ACTION OF CONTRACT,
TORT OR OTHERWISE, ARISING FROM, OUT OF OR IN CONNECTION WITH THE
SOFTWARE OR THE USE OR OTHER DEALINGS IN THE SOFTWARE.
```

C.3.15 libffi

The _ctypes extension is built using an included copy of the libffi sources unless the build is configured --with-system-libffi:

```
Copyright (c) 1996-2008  Red Hat, Inc and others.

Permission is hereby granted, free of charge, to any person obtaining
a copy of this software and associated documentation files (the
``Software''), to deal in the Software without restriction, including
without limitation the rights to use, copy, modify, merge, publish,
distribute, sublicense, and/or sell copies of the Software, and to
permit persons to whom the Software is furnished to do so, subject to
the following conditions:

The above copyright notice and this permission notice shall be included
in all copies or substantial portions of the Software.
```

```
THE SOFTWARE IS PROVIDED ``AS IS'', WITHOUT WARRANTY OF ANY KIND,
EXPRESS OR IMPLIED, INCLUDING BUT NOT LIMITED TO THE WARRANTIES OF
MERCHANTABILITY, FITNESS FOR A PARTICULAR PURPOSE AND
NONINFRINGEMENT.  IN NO EVENT SHALL THE AUTHORS OR COPYRIGHT
HOLDERS BE LIABLE FOR ANY CLAIM, DAMAGES OR OTHER LIABILITY,
WHETHER IN AN ACTION OF CONTRACT, TORT OR OTHERWISE, ARISING FROM,
OUT OF OR IN CONNECTION WITH THE SOFTWARE OR THE USE OR OTHER
DEALINGS IN THE SOFTWARE.
```

C.3.16 zlib

The *zlib* extension is built using an included copy of the zlib sources if the zlib version found on the system is too old to be used for the build:

```
Copyright (C) 1995-2011 Jean-loup Gailly and Mark Adler

This software is provided 'as-is', without any express or implied
warranty.  In no event will the authors be held liable for any damages
arising from the use of this software.

Permission is granted to anyone to use this software for any purpose,
including commercial applications, and to alter it and redistribute it
freely, subject to the following restrictions:

1. The origin of this software must not be misrepresented; you must not
   claim that you wrote the original software. If you use this software
   in a product, an acknowledgment in the product documentation would be
   appreciated but is not required.

2. Altered source versions must be plainly marked as such, and must not be
   misrepresented as being the original software.

3. This notice may not be removed or altered from any source distribution.

Jean-loup Gailly        Mark Adler
jloup@gzip.org          madler@alumni.caltech.edu
```

C.3.17 cfuhash

The implementation of the hash table used by the *tracemalloc* is based on the cfuhash project:

```
Copyright (c) 2005 Don Owens
All rights reserved.

This code is released under the BSD license:

Redistribution and use in source and binary forms, with or without
modification, are permitted provided that the following conditions
are met:

  * Redistributions of source code must retain the above copyright
    notice, this list of conditions and the following disclaimer.

  * Redistributions in binary form must reproduce the above
    copyright notice, this list of conditions and the following
```

```
    disclaimer in the documentation and/or other materials provided
    with the distribution.

  * Neither the name of the author nor the names of its
    contributors may be used to endorse or promote products derived
    from this software without specific prior written permission.

THIS SOFTWARE IS PROVIDED BY THE COPYRIGHT HOLDERS AND CONTRIBUTORS
"AS IS" AND ANY EXPRESS OR IMPLIED WARRANTIES, INCLUDING, BUT NOT
LIMITED TO, THE IMPLIED WARRANTIES OF MERCHANTABILITY AND FITNESS
FOR A PARTICULAR PURPOSE ARE DISCLAIMED. IN NO EVENT SHALL THE
COPYRIGHT OWNER OR CONTRIBUTORS BE LIABLE FOR ANY DIRECT, INDIRECT,
INCIDENTAL, SPECIAL, EXEMPLARY, OR CONSEQUENTIAL DAMAGES
(INCLUDING, BUT NOT LIMITED TO, PROCUREMENT OF SUBSTITUTE GOODS OR
SERVICES; LOSS OF USE, DATA, OR PROFITS; OR BUSINESS INTERRUPTION)
HOWEVER CAUSED AND ON ANY THEORY OF LIABILITY, WHETHER IN CONTRACT,
STRICT LIABILITY, OR TORT (INCLUDING NEGLIGENCE OR OTHERWISE)
ARISING IN ANY WAY OUT OF THE USE OF THIS SOFTWARE, EVEN IF ADVISED
OF THE POSSIBILITY OF SUCH DAMAGE.
```

C.3.18 libmpdec

The `_decimal` module is built using an included copy of the libmpdec library unless the build is configured `--with-system-libmpdec`:

```
Copyright (c) 2008-2016 Stefan Krah. All rights reserved.

Redistribution and use in source and binary forms, with or without
modification, are permitted provided that the following conditions
are met:

1. Redistributions of source code must retain the above copyright
   notice, this list of conditions and the following disclaimer.

2. Redistributions in binary form must reproduce the above copyright
   notice, this list of conditions and the following disclaimer in the
   documentation and/or other materials provided with the distribution.

THIS SOFTWARE IS PROVIDED BY THE AUTHOR AND CONTRIBUTORS "AS IS" AND
ANY EXPRESS OR IMPLIED WARRANTIES, INCLUDING, BUT NOT LIMITED TO, THE
IMPLIED WARRANTIES OF MERCHANTABILITY AND FITNESS FOR A PARTICULAR PURPOSE
ARE DISCLAIMED.  IN NO EVENT SHALL THE AUTHOR OR CONTRIBUTORS BE LIABLE
FOR ANY DIRECT, INDIRECT, INCIDENTAL, SPECIAL, EXEMPLARY, OR CONSEQUENTIAL
DAMAGES (INCLUDING, BUT NOT LIMITED TO, PROCUREMENT OF SUBSTITUTE GOODS
OR SERVICES; LOSS OF USE, DATA, OR PROFITS; OR BUSINESS INTERRUPTION)
HOWEVER CAUSED AND ON ANY THEORY OF LIABILITY, WHETHER IN CONTRACT, STRICT
LIABILITY, OR TORT (INCLUDING NEGLIGENCE OR OTHERWISE) ARISING IN ANY WAY
OUT OF THE USE OF THIS SOFTWARE, EVEN IF ADVISED OF THE POSSIBILITY OF
SUCH DAMAGE.
```

APPENDIX

D

COPYRIGHT

Python and this documentation is:

See *History and License* for complete license and permissions information.

PYTHON MODULE INDEX

INDEX

Symbols

A

B

C

D

E

F

G

H

I

J

K

L

M

N

P

Q

R

S

T

U

V

W

X

Y

Z

www.ingramcontent.com/pod-product-compliance
Lightning Source LLC
Chambersburg PA
CBHW082116070326
40690CB00049B/2701
9781680921588